The Wiley Handbook of Obsessive Compulsive Disorders

The Wiley Handbook of Obsessive Compulsive Disorders

Volume I

Edited by

**Jonathan S. Abramowitz,
Dean McKay, and Eric A. Storch**

WILEY Blackwell

Registered Offices
John Wiley & Sons, Inc., 111 River Street, Hoboken, NJ 07030, USA
John Wiley & Sons Ltd, The Atrium, Southern Gate, Chichester, West Sussex, PO19 8SQ, UK

Editorial Office
The Atrium, Southern Gate, Chichester, West Sussex, PO19 8SQ, UK
For details of our global editorial offices, customer services, and more information about Wiley products visit us at www.wiley.com.

Library of Congress Cataloging-in-Publication Data

Names: Abramowitz, Jonathan S., editor. | McKay, Dean, 1966– editor. |
    Storch, Eric A., editor.
Title: The Wiley handbook of obsessive compulsive disorders /edited by
    Jonathan S. Abramowitz, Dean McKay, Eric A. Storch.
Description: Chichester, UK; Hoboken, NJ : John Wiley & Sons, 2017. |
    Includes bibliographical references and index.
Identifiers: LCCN 2016055381 (print) | LCCN 2017001685 (ebook) |
    ISBN 9781118889640 (cloth : alk. paper) | ISBN 9781118890257 (Adobe PDF) |
    ISBN 9781118890264 (ePub)
Subjects: LCSH: Obsessive-compulsive disorder–Handbooks, manuals, etc.
Classification: LCC RC533 .W47 2017 (print) | LCC RC533 (ebook) | DDC 616.85/227–dc23
LC record available at https://lccn.loc.gov/2016055381

Cover Image: © shotsstudio/Gettyimages
Cover Design: Wiley

Set in 10/12pt Galliard by SPi Global, Pondicherry, India

Printed in Singapore by C.O.S. Printers Pte Ltd

10 9 8 7 6 5 4 3 2 1

Contents

List of Contributors

Jonathan S. Abramowitz, Department of Psychology, University of North Carolina, Chapel Hill, North Carolina, United States

Gillian M. Alcolado, Department of Psychology, Concordia University, Quebec, Canada

Pino Alonso, Department of Psychiatry, University of Barcelona, Barcelona, Spain

Erik Andersson, Karolinska Institutet, Solna, Sweden

Elysse A. Arnold, Department of Psychology, University of South Florida, Tampa, Florida

Catherine R. Ayers, VA San Diego Healthcare System, University of California, San Diego, United States

Amanda M. Balki, Division of Medical Psychology, Department of Psychiatry and Department of Clinical and Health Psychology, University of Florida, Florida, United States

Kristen Benito, Alpert Medical School of Brown University, Rhode Island, United States

Sophie Bennett, Institute of Child Health, University College London, United Kingdom

Noah C. Berman, Massachusetts General Hospital, Boston, United States

Jennifer M. Birnkrant, Department of Psychological Sciences, Case Western Reserve University, Cleveland, Ohio, United States

Shannon M. Blakey, University of North Carolina at Chapel Hill, North Carolina, United States

Ellen J. Bluett, Utah State University, Logan, United States

Sean Carp, Department of Psychology, Fordham University, New York, United States

L. K. Chapman, Department of Psychological and Brain Sciences, University of Louisville, Louisville, United States

Tommy Chou, Department of Psychology, Florida International University, Miami, Florida, United States

David A. Clark, Department of Psychology, University of New Brunswick, New Brunswick, Canada

Ann Clawson, Department of Psychology, Brigham Young University, Provo, Utah

Jonathan S. Comer, Department of Psychology, Florida International University, Miami, Florida, United States

Anna E. Coughtrey, School of Psychology and Clinical Languages Sciences, University of Reading, Berkshire, United Kingdom

Lorena Fernández de la Cruz, Department of Clinical Neuroscience, Karolinska Institutet, Stockholm, Sweden

Danny Derby, Cognetica – The Israeli Center for Cognitive Behavioral Therapy, Boston, MA, United States

Mariah DeSerisy, Department of Psychology, Florida International University, Miami, Florida, United States

Jessie Destro, School of Psychology, University of Queensland, Brisbane, Australia

Guy Doron, Interdisciplinary Center (IDC) Herzliya, Herzliya, Israel

Mary E. Dozier, VA San Diego Healthcare System, San Diego State University/ University of California

Lara J. Farrell, School of Applied Psychology and Behavioural Basis of Health, Griffith University, Nathan, Australia

Sarah M. Fayad, Department of Psychiatry, University of Florida, Florida, United States

Peter Fisher, University of Liverpool, Liverpool, United Kingdom

Cindi Flores, Division of Medical Psychology, Department of Psychiatry, University of Florida, Florida, United States

Hannah Frank, Alpert Medical School of Brown University, Rhode Island, United States

Jennifer B. Freeman, Department of Psychiatry and Human Development, Brown University, Rhode Island, United States

Miquel A. Fullana, Institute of Neuropsychiatry and Addictions, Department of Psychiatry, Universitat Autònoma de Barcelona, Barcelona, Spain

Abbe M. Garcia, Department of Psychiatry and Human Development, Brown University, Rhode Island, United States

Gary R. Geffken, Division of Medical Psychology, Department of Psychiatry and Department of Clinical and Health Psychology, University of Florida, Archer Rd Gainesville, United States

Jon E. Grant, Department of Psychiatry & Behavioral Neuroscience, University of Chicago, Chicago, United States

Andrew G. Guzick, Division of Medical Psychology, Department of Psychiatry and Department of Clinical and Health Psychology, University of Florida, Archer Rd Gainesville, United States

Anyaliese D. Hancock-Smith, Division of Medical Psychology, Department of Psychiatry, University of Florida, Florida, United States

Jennifer Herren, Alpert Medical School of Brown University, Rhode Island, United States

Catherine A. Hilchey, University of New Brunswick, New Brunswick, Canada

Jonathan D. Huppert, The Hebrew University of Jerusalem, Israel

Tord Ivarsson, Center for Child and Adolescent Mental Health, Eastern and Southern Norway, Oslo, Norway

Amy M. Jacobsen, Kansas City Center for Anxiety Treatment, University of Missouri-Kansas City, Kansas, United States

Ryan J. Jacoby, University of North Carolina at Chapel Hill, North Carolina, United States

Sophie C. James, School of Applied Psychology and Behavioural Basis of Health, Griffith University, Nathan, Australia

Carly Johnco, Department of Pediatrics, University of South Florida, Florida, United States

Georgina Krebs, Maudsley NHS Foundation Trust, London, United Kingdom

Caleb W. Lack, University of Central Oklahoma, Oklahoma, United States

Michael J. Larson, Department of Psychology and Neuroscience Center, Brigham Young University, Provo, Utah

Eric B. Lee, Utah State University, Logan, United States

Eric W. Leppink, Department of Psychiatry & Behavioral Neuroscience, University of Chicago, Chicago, United States

Adam B. Lewin, Department of Pediatrics, Rothman Center for Neuropsychiatry, University of South Florida, United States

Adrian S. Loh, Singapore Armed Forces Medical Corps, National University of Singapore, and Institute of Mental Health, Singapore

Clara López-Sola, Bellvitge Biomedical Research Institute-IDIBELL, Department of Psychiatry, Barcelona, Spain

David Mataix-Cols, Karolinska Institutet, Solna, Sweden

Dean McKay, Department of Psychology, Fordham University, Bronx, New York, United States

Joseph P. H. McNamara, Division of Medical Psychology, Department of Psychiatry, University of Florida, Florida, United States

Greg Muller, Division of Medical Psychology, Department of Psychiatry, University of Florida, Florida, United States

Samuel Myers, Israel Center for the Treatment of Psychotrauma, Jerusalem, Israel

Rachael L. Neal, Department of Psychology, Concordia University, Quebec, Canada

Brian Olsen, Division of Medical Psychology, Department of Psychiatry, University of Florida, Florida, United States

Jennifer Park, Massachusetts General Hospital, Boston, Massachusetts, United States

Tara S. Peris, Division of Child and Adolescent Psychiatry, University of California, Los Angeles, California, United States

Amy Przeworski, Department of Psychological Sciences, Case Western Reserve University, Cleveland, Ohio, United States

Adam. S. Radomsky, Department of Psychology, Concordia University, Quebec, Canada

Adam M. Reid, Division of Medical Psychology, Department of Psychiatry and Department of Clinical and Health Psychology, University of Florida, Florida, United States

Lillian Reuman, University of North Carolina at Chapel Hill, North Carolina, United States

Brittany M. Riggin, University of Central Oklahoma, Oklahoma, United States

Michelle Rozenman, Division of Child and Adolescent Psychiatry, University of California, Los Angeles, California, United States

Christian Rück, Karolinska Institutet, Solna, Sweden

Rachel Schwartz, Massachusetts General Hospital, Boston, Massachusetts, United States

Robert R. Selles, Department of Psychology, University of South Florida, Tampa, Florida, United States

Roz Shafran, Institute of Child Health, University College London, United Kingdom

Jedidiah Siev, Nova Southeastern University, Florida, United States

J. V. Simms, Department of Psychological and Brain Sciences, University of Louisville, Louisville, United States

Michael Simons, RWTH Aachen University, Aachen, Germany

Gudmundur Skarphedinsson, Center for Child and Adolescent Mental Health, Eastern and Southern Norway, Oslo, Norway

Ashley J. Smith, Kansas City Center for Anxiety Treatment, University of Missouri-Kansas City, Kansas, United States

Brooke M. Smith, Utah State University, Logan, United States

Stian Solem, Department of Psychology, Norwegian University of Science and Technology, Trondheim, Norway

Elyse Stewart, Alpert Medical School of Brown University, Rhode Island, United States

S. Evelyn Stewart, Department of Pediatrics, University of British Columbia, Vancouver, British Columbia, Canada

Eric A. Storch, Department of Pediatrics, University of South Florida, Tampa, Florida, United States

Steven Taylor, Department of Psychiatry, University of British Columbia, British Columbia, Canada

G. Tellawi, Department of Psychological & Brain Sciences, University of Louisville, Louisville, Kentucky

Cynthia Turner, School of Psychology, University of Queensland, Brisbane, Australia

Michael P. Twohig, Utah State University, Logan, United States

Robert Valderhaug, Regional Center for Child and Youth Mental Health and Child Welfare, Norwegian University of Science and Technology, Trondheim, Norway

Patrick A. Vogel, Department of Psychology, Norwegian University of Science and Technology, Trondheim, Norway

Allison Vreeland, Division of Child and Adolescent Psychiatry, University of California, Los Angeles, California, United States

Herbert E. Ward, Department of Psychiatry, University of Florida, Florida, United States

Bernhard Weidle, Regional Center for Child and Youth Mental Health and Child Welfare, Norwegian University of Science and Technology, Trondheim, Norway

Adrian Wells, University of Manchester, Manchester, United Kingdom

Maureen L. Whittal, Vancouver CBT Centre, Vancouver, British Columbia, Canada

M. T. Williams, Department of Psychological Sciences, University of Connecticut, Storrs, Connecticut, United States

Kevin D. Wu, Department of Psychology, Northern Illinois University, United States

Monica S. Wu, Department of Pediatrics, Rothman Center for Neuropsychiatry, University of South Florida, United States

Morag Yule, Department of Psychology, University of British Columbia, Vancouver, British Columbia, Canada

Melanie J. Zimmer-Gembeck, School of Applied Psychology and Behavioural Basis of Health, Griffith University, Nathan, Australia

Shelby E. Zuckerman, Nova Southeastern University, Florida, United States

Obsessive-Compulsive and Related Disorders

Where Have We Been?

Dean McKay, Jonathan S. Abramowitz, and Eric A. Storch

Obsessive compulsive disorder (OCD) was once considered a very rare and untreatable condition (Kringlen, 1965). However, in the past fifty years changes in how the condition is defined and understood has led to the identification of a broad swath of symptoms and associated features that suggest the disorder is fairly common, afflicting up to approximately 1.2%–3% of the population (i.e., Ruscio, Stein, Chiu, & Kessler, 2010; Yuki, Meinlschmidt, Gloster, & Lieb, 2012). Further, research has shown that those with OCD have high rates of disability and occupational and social role dysfunction (Markarian et al., 2010). When the prevalence and functional impairment are considered together with the anxiety and distress that individuals with this condition experience, one recognizes that OCD represents a significant public health concern.

Given the frequency of OCD in the general population, the need to develop effective interventions became clear. At the present time, practice guidelines for OCD treatment emphasize two broad approaches: cognitive-behavior therapy (CBT), particularly exposure with response prevention (ERP); and/or cognitive interventions aimed at specific obsessional belief structures, or serotonin reuptake inhibitor (SRI) medications. Treatment employing CBT is presently associated with large effect sizes (McKay et al., 2015) for both ERP and cognitive therapy tailored to the condition. Relative to psychotherapeutic interventions, SRI medications have somewhat lower effect sizes for symptom relief (Fineberg et al., 2015). These two treatment approaches, broadly speaking, have improved the lives of countless OCD sufferers.

Unfortunately, however, the outlook is not necessarily so rosy for all people with OCD. First, a significant minority fail to respond to the available treatments, with estimates of non-response as high as 30%. Research has suggested that factors that contribute to non-response include high levels of scrupulosity; overvalued ideas regarding the accuracy of obsessions and/or necessity of compulsions; comorbid psychopathology, such as depression or trauma; emotional states other than anxiety as motivator of avoidance; and noncompliance with the demands of treatment. Second, there are additional factors that can contribute to poor outcome that include poor delivery or implementation of CBT, erroneous functional assessment of primary

The Wiley Handbook of Obsessive Compulsive Disorders, Volume I, First Edition.
Edited by Jonathan S. Abramowitz, Dean McKay, and Eric A. Storch.
© 2017 John Wiley & Sons Ltd. Published 2017 by John Wiley & Sons Ltd.

symptoms, and inadequate attention to cultural factors (reviewed in McKay, Arocho, & Brand, 2014). Third, it has also been shown that some specific symptoms of the condition respond better to treatment than others (i.e., checking versus symmetry/ ordering; Abramowitz, Franklin, Schwartz, & Furr, 2003). These are significant issues to reckon with in the delivery of care for OCD.

The aim of Volume 1 of this two-volume set is to provide practitioners and researchers with a comprehensive resource for conceptualizing, assessing, and treating the full range of obsessive-compulsive symptoms. While the DSM-5 definition of OCD captures a broad array of symptoms, clinicians and researchers have observed that patients with specific types of symptoms are differentially responsive to available treatments. This differential treatment response has led researchers and clinicians to propose that clinically important subtypes of OCD exist. In turn, these proposals have prompted the development of theoretical mini-models for various presentations of the condition (e.g., contamination, scrupulosity), each with their own assessment and treatment implications. Given the impressive heterogeneity of the disorder, and the need to understand specific symptom subtypes in the unique manner of their manifestation, it is our expectation that the chapters in Volume 1 will be an invaluable resource for providing effective care to the full range of OCD sufferers.

Once it is appreciated how obsessional experiences manifest, it is tempting to examine other forms of psychopathology to determine what, if any, characteristics might resemble OCD. For more than two decades, efforts to conceptualize a range of psychopathology as part of a putative obsessive-compulsive spectrum have been underway (i.e., Hollander, 1993). The list of candidate disorders for this spectrum has varied, with some writing suggesting a large proportion of DSM-defined disorders fitting in the category, to narrower conceptualizations with a much more conservative set of so-called "spectrum" conditions (Hollander, Braun, & Simeon, 2008; Storch, Abramowitz, & Goodman, 2008).

The theoretical, conceptual, and clinical justifications for including or excluding certain conditions from the obsessive-compulsive spectrum has varied, with some taking a pragmatic model approach via commonalities in phenomenology and response to comparable treatments (i.e., Fineberg, Saxena, Zohar, & Craig, 2011) to a more theory-driven model premised on a breakdown in behavioral inhibition (Hollander & Rosen, 2000). The former approach derives from several sources. First, individuals with a range of other psychopathology report intrusive images and seemingly "compulsive" behavior germane to their diagnosis. Therefore, an individual with hoarding could be said to have "obsessions" regarding opportunities to gather new material goods that would interfere with her or his cognitive processing of other information. Similarly, someone with body dysmorphic disorder (BDD) "compulsively" checks their appearance to reduce distress. Second, individuals with some other forms of psychopathology respond to treatments that are effective for OCD. Research suggests that SRI medication can be helpful in alleviating body image concerns associated with BDD (Phillips, 2004). Third, it has been suggested that putative obsessive-compulsive spectrum disorders share clinical and demographic characteristics, such as family history, comorbidity, and course of illness. The impetus from this pragmatic perspective provides an intuitive rationale for a spectrum of obsessive-compulsive disorders, since this conceptualization could serve to streamline the way in which clinicians develop treatments for a much larger range of clientele. Notably, others have questioned this approach on the basis of its conceptual foundation and lack of definitive data (e.g., Abramowitz & Jacoby, 2015; Storch et al., 2008).

The latter approach, a breakdown in behavioral inhibition, derives from a brain-based model of executive functioning related to control over actions. A theory-derived model would also have wide appeal, since it would permit researchers and clinicians to conceptualize a wide range of conditions within a single theoretical model, and again have the net effect of streamlining treatment. Advocates for this approach, now referred to as the obsessive-compulsive related disorders (OCRDs), cite these factors in support of the recent addition of this category to the Diagnostic and Statistical Manual (DSM-5; American Psychiatric Association, 2013). Given the degree that there are disorders conceptualized in this manner, a journal has been launched devoted entirely to this category of disorders (*Journal of Obsessive-Compulsive and Related Disorders*). While the research on shared and unique features that other psychopathology may have with OCD continues, the conditions that are formally part of this category in the DSM-5 are as follows: OCD, Hoarding, Excoriation Disorder, Trichotillomania, and Body Dysmorphic Disorder. While there have been a number of virtues raised regarding this model, there have also been a number of critiques that range from limited support for the conceptualization in the empirical research (Abramowitz et al., 2009; McKay, Abramowitz, & Taylor, 2008) to faulty conceptualization of the research itself (McKay & Neziroglu, 2009).

In light of the heterogeneity of OCD, it should not come as a surprise that the disorders that form the OCRD are likewise complex and varied. In conceptualizing and developing this two-volume set, we determined that readers would be best served by chapters that cover not only the disorders that form the newly developed OCRD class of conditions in DSM-5, but a wider range of conditions that have, at one point or another, been characterized in the research as a possible member of this category. Accordingly, this includes health anxiety (and formerly Hypochondriasis) as well as Tourette Syndrome. It also led to the identification of problems commonly associated with OCD that may also play a role in putative related disorders. To cite one example, sensory intolerance is a problem that has been gaining increased recognition among practitioners and researchers. It is also a problem observed in some conditions associated with OCD, such as Tourette Syndrome.

As a result of this broad-reaching categorization for the OCRD, the chapters in Volume 2 cover a diverse array of conditions, associated treatments, and interventions for ancillary problems observed in OCD as well as the OCRD, such as the aforementioned sensory intolerance, problems in incompleteness and harm avoidance, and remote treatment delivery. It is hoped that readers will come away with a sense of optimism that the treatment needs of a very large segment of sufferers can be addressed with the range of material available in these two volumes. It is likewise the wish of the editors that these texts will further stimulate discussion and scholarship about the nature and treatment of these conditions.

References

Abramowitz, J., Franklin, M., Schwartz, S., & Furr, J. (2003). Symptom presentation and outcome of cognitive-behavior therapy for obsessive-compulsive disorder. *Journal of Consulting and Clinical Psychology*, *71*, 1049–1057.

Abramowitz, J. S., & Jacoby, R. J. (2015). Obsessive-compulsive related disorders: A critical review of the new diagnostic class. *Annual Review of Clinical Psychology*, *11*, 165–186.

Abramowitz, J. S., Storch, E. A., McKay, D., Taylor, S., & Asmundson, G. J. G. (2009). The obsessive-compulsive spectrum: A critical review. In D. McKay, J. S. Abramowitz, S. Taylor, & G. J. G. Asmundson (Eds.), *Current perspectives on anxiety disorders: Implications for DSM-V and beyond* (pp. 329–352). New York: Springer.

American Psychiatric Association (2013). *Diagnostic and statistical manual of mental disorders* (5th ed.). Washington, DC: Author.

Fineberg, N. A., Regunandanan, S., Simpson, H. B., Phillips, K. A., Richter, M. A., Matthews, K., Stein, D. J., Sareen, J., Brown, A., & Sookman, D. (2015). Obsessive-compulsive disorder (OCD): Practical strategies for pharmacological and somatic treatment in adults. *Psychiatry Research, 227*, 114–125.

Fineberg, N. A., Saxena, S., Zohar, J., & Craig, K. J. (2011). Obsessive-compulsive disorder: Boundary issues. In E. Hollander, J. Zohar, P. J. Sirovatka, & D. A. Regier (Eds.), *Obsessive-compulsive spectrum disorders: Refining the research agenda for DSM-V* (pp. 1–32). Washington, DC: American Psychiatric Association

Hollander, E. (1993). *Obsessive Compulsive Related Disorders*. Washington, DC: American Psychiatric Press.

Hollander, E., Braun, A., & Simeon, D. (2008). Should OCD leave the anxiety disorders in DSM-V? The case for obsessive compulsive-related disorders. *Depression and Anxiety, 25*, 317–329.

Hollander, E., & Rosen, J. (2000). Obsessive-compulsive spectrum disorders: A review. In M. Maj, N. Sartorius, A. Okasha, & J. Zohar (Eds.), *Obsessive-compulsive disorder* (pp. 203–224). Chichester: Wiley.

Kringlen, E. (1965). Obsessional neurotics: Long-term outcome. *British Journal of Psychiatry, 111*, 709–722.

Markarian, Y., Larson, M. J., Aldea, M. A., Baldwin, S. A., Good, D., Berkeljon, A., Murphy, T. K., Storch, E. A., & McKay, D. (2010). Multiple pathways to functional impairment in obsessive compulsive disorder. *Clinical Psychology Review, 30*, 78–88.

McKay, D., Abramowitz, J. S., & Taylor, S. (2008). How should we conceptualize the Obsessive-Compulsive Spectrum? In J. S. Abramowitz, D. McKay, & S. Taylor (Eds.), *Obsessive-Compulsive Disorder: Subtypes and spectrum conditions* (pp. 287–300). Oxford: Elsevier.

McKay, D., Arocho, J., & Brand, J. (2014). Cognitive-behavior therapy for anxiety disorders: When intervention fails. In P. M. G. Emmelkamp & T. Ehring (Eds.), *International Handbook of Anxiety Disorders* (Vol. II) (pp. 1197–1214). Chichester: Wiley.

McKay, D., & Neziroglu, F. (2009). Methodological issues in the obsessive-compulsive spectrum. *Psychiatry Research, 170*, 61–65.

McKay, D., Sookman, D., Neziroglu, F., Wilhelm, S., Stein, D., Kyrios, M., Mathews, K., & Veale, D. (2015). Efficacy of cognitive-behavior therapy for obsessive-compulsive disorder. *Psychiatry Research, 225*, 236–246.

Phillips, K. A. (2004). Treating body dysmorphic disorder using medication. *Psychiatric Annals, 34*, 945–953.

Ruscio, A. M., Stein, D. J., Chiu, W. T., & Kessler, R.C. (2010). The epidemiology of obsessive-compulsive disorder in the National Comorbidity Survey. *Molecular Psychiatry, 15*, 53–63.

Storch, E. A., Abramowitz, J., and Goodman, W. K. (2008). Where does obsessive-compulsive disorder belong in DSM-V? *Depression and Anxiety, 25*, 336–347.

Yuki, A., Meinlschmidt, G., Gloster, A. T., & Lieb, R. (2012). Obsessive compulsive disorder in the community: 12-month prevalence, comorbidity and impairment. *Social Psychiatry and Psychiatric Epidemiology, 47*, 339–349.

1

Description and Prevalence of OCD in Children and Adolescents

Sophie C. James, Lara J. Farrell, and Melanie J. Zimmer-Gembeck

Early case descriptions of children and adolescents with symptoms of what we now know as obsessive-compulsive disorder (OCD) were believed to be extremely rare, with little knowledge of prevalence, course, and effective treatment. The first description of childhood OCD is thought to have been described by Pierre Janet in 1903, when he presented the cases of two children aged 5 and 11 years. When describing the 5-year-old, Janet (1903) penned "no reassuring satisfies: the patient must be forever verifying his honesty, cleanliness, sanity, perceptions, and what he did last." In another early description of OCD, Kanner (1962) described children with "constricted" premorbid personalities, having been raised with an "overdose of parental perfectionism."

The changing landscape of definitions and knowledge of OCD is most evident in the evolution of diagnostic criteria, with revisions to criterion reflecting advancement in science and knowledge about this condition. The release of the *Diagnostic and Statistics Manual,* third edition (DSM-III) (American Psychiatric Association [APA], 1980) was a significant shift that saw diagnostic criteria for mental disorders described in more categorical terms, which attempted to remove all evidence of earlier psychodynamic explanations for disorders and, instead, reframed diagnostic categories according to symptom clusters or patterns (Clegg, 2012). It was after the release of the DSM-III with clear categorical descriptions of OCD, that research particularly focused on children and adolescents came to the forefront. The DSM-III was not long followed by the release of the DSM-III-R (APA, 1987), with the updated version being a reflection of the most current knowledge derived from evidence-based research. In the case of OCD, the DSM-III stated the disorder was rare in the general population; this was updated in the revised edition to reflect the recent community studies examining prevalence, suggesting mild forms of the disorder may be relatively common. Evolving knowledge from clinical trials (e.g., POTS, 2004), as well as neurobiological and genetic research (see Pauls, Abramovitch, Rauch, & Geller, 2014), has informed the most current description of the disorder in the latest revision of the

The Wiley Handbook of Obsessive Compulsive Disorders, Volume I, First Edition.
Edited by Jonathan S. Abramowitz, Dean McKay, and Eric A. Storch.
© 2017 John Wiley & Sons Ltd. Published 2017 by John Wiley & Sons Ltd.

DSM (APA, 2013). In the DSM-5, OCD is characterized by the presence of obsessions, defined as "recurrent and persistent thoughts, urges, or images that are experienced, at some time during the disturbance, as intrusive and unwanted, and that in most individuals cause marked anxiety or distress"; and/or compulsions, defined as "repetitive behaviors or mental acts that the individual feels driven to perform in response to an obsession or according to rules that must be applied rigidly" (APA, 2013: 237).

With the recent release of the DSM-5, it is timely to review the description and prevalence of this disorder, investigating the changes to diagnostic criteria, as well as subtypes and specifiers, that have improved diagnostic validity and clinical utility. OCD is considered a prominent mental health condition affecting children and adolescents, as well as adults. This chapter presents a description of OCD in children and adolescence, highlighting advances in knowledge of OCD in recent decades and the implications this has had on the structure of diagnosis, symptomology, comorbidities, prevalence, and course.

Diagnosis

There are two predominant diagnostic manuals used for describing psychiatric conditions, the International Classification of Diseases (ICD) and the Diagnostic and Statistics Manual (DSM). The ICD is a core function of the World Health Organization (WHO), a global health agency of the United Nations, and represents an international manual that defines diseases, disorders, injuries, and other related health conditions. The current version, the ICD-10, was endorsed in 1990 and is currently under review with the eleventh version, ICD-11, expected to be released in 2015.

The DSM, now in its fifth revision, is the standard classification of mental disorders used in the United States, and contains a listing of diagnostic criteria for every psychiatric disorder recognized by the US healthcare system. Both the ICD-10 and DSM-5 give diagnostic criteria for OCD, which differ slightly (see Table 1.1).

An important shift in classification of OCD occurred in the DSM-5 revision (APA, 2013), whereby OCD was removed from the anxiety disorders section and placed in the newly established Obsessive-Compulsive and Related Disorders (OCRD) category. The newly created category consists of OCD and other related disorders, including body dysmorphic disorder (BDD), trichotillomania (hair-pulling disorder), hoarding disorder, excoriation (skin-picking), substance/medication-induced obsessive-compulsive and related disorder, obsessive-compulsive and related disorder due to another medical condition, other specified obsessive-compulsive and related disorder, and unspecified obsessive-compulsive and related disorder. This grouping does not imply that people with obsessive-compulsive disorder are non-anxious; but rather reflects research findings that the disorder has more similarity to other obsessive-compulsive-related disorders than to anxiety disorders (Abramowitz, Taylor, & McKay, 2009). The cluster of disorders comprising the OCRD chapter share core features such as an obsessive preoccupation and repetitive behaviors. Further, the OCRDs also overlap in their phenomenology, comorbidity, neurotransmitter/peptide systems, neurocircuitry, family history and genetic factors, and treatment response (Hollender, Braun, & Simeon, 2008).

Table 1.1 Diagnostic criteria for Obsessive-Compulsive Disorder based on ICD-10 and DSM-5

Criteria	ICD-10	DSM-5
Symptoms	Either obsessions or compulsions (or both)	Presence of obsessions, compulsions, or both
Definition of symptoms	Obsessions (thoughts, ideas, or images) and compulsions (acts) share the following features, all of which must be present: • acknowledged as originating in the mind of the patient; • they are repetitive and unpleasant, and at least one obsession or compulsion must be present that is acknowledged as excessive or unreasonable; • the subject tries to resist them and at least one obsession or compulsion must be present that is unsuccessfully resisted; • carrying out the obsessive thought or compulsive act is not pleasurable.	Obsessions are recurrent and persistent thoughts, urges, or images that are experienced, at some time during the disturbance, as intrusive and unwanted, and that in most individuals cause marked anxiety or distress. Compulsions are repetitive behaviors (e.g., hand-washing, ordering, checking) or mental acts (e.g., praying, counting, repeating words silently) that the individual feels driven to perform in response to an obsession or according to rules that must be applied rigidly.
Duration	Present on most days for a period of at least two weeks.	The obsessions or compulsions are time-consuming (e.g., take more than 1 hour/day).
Impact on functioning	The obsessions or compulsions cause distress or interfere with the subject's social or individual functioning, usually by wasting time.	Symptoms cause clinically significant distress or impairment in social, occupational, or other important areas of functioning.
Exclusionary criteria	Not due to other mental disorders.	Symptoms are not attributable to the physiological effects of a substance (e.g., a drug of abuse, a medication) or another medical condition. The disturbance is not better explained by the symptoms of another mental disorder.
Specifiers	• Predominantly obsessional thoughts and ruminations. • Predominantly compulsive acts. • Mixed obsessional thoughts and acts. • Other obsessive-compulsive disorders. • Obsessive-compulsive disorder, unspecified.	Insight specifier: • with good or fair insight; • with poor insight; • with absent insight/delusional beliefs; Tic subtype specifier: • the individual has a current or past history of a tic disorder.

As it is widely accepted that these disorders are often under-recognized, undertreated, and understudied, the DSM-5 approach to categorizing OCRDs may help clinicians better identify and treat individuals suffering from these disorders (Hollender et al., 2008). Moreover, given the high degree of comorbidity observed between the OCRDs, clinicians should routinely assess children and adolescents for these related disorders if one or more conditions from this cluster has already been diagnosed (Van Ameringen, Patterson, & Simpson, 2014). While these disorders share similarities that conceptually guided the decision to group them together, there are also important differences among them that distinguish distinct diagnoses and call for unique approaches to cognitive-behavior therapy (CBT).

The revision of the "insight" criterion in the DSM-5 reflects the substantial advancement in research of the disorder since the publication of the DSM-IV-TR (APA, 2000). The DSM-IV-TR criteria requiring that individuals realize that their obsessions and compulsions are unreasonable or excessive has been removed in the DSM-5, and the specifier *with poor insight* added allowing for a more dimensional approach to record insight: w*ith good or fair insight*, *with poor insight*, or *with absent insight/delusional beliefs.* This is a reflection of empirical evidence that insight falls on a continuum, with many individuals not recognizing the excessive and unreasonable nature of their obsessive or compulsive symptoms (Storch et al., 2014). It is known that children tend to have less insight regarding their illness than their adult counterparts (Foa & Kozak, 1995), which has implications for assessment, treatment provision, and treatment outcome (Storch et al., 2014). Storch and colleagues explain that youth with poor insight may not recognize their symptoms as problematic and therefore often resist engaging in the treatment process due to limited motivation or disruptiveness contributing to negative treatment outcomes. Moreover, insight has been associated with a number of clinical characteristics, including symptom severity, preponderance of compulsions, illness chronicity, limited patient resistance against and presumably control of symptoms, early symptom onset, and a positive family history of OCD (Storch et al., 2014).

The DSM-5 also introduces an additional specifier if the condition is tic-related, whereby the individual has a current or past history of a tic disorder. Epidemiological research has reported a high comorbidity between OCD and Tourette's Syndrome/tic disorders, estimated to be between 26% and 59% (Eichstedt & Arnold, 2001). A tic is described by the DSM-5 (2013) as a sudden, rapid, recurrent, nonrhythmic motor movement or vocalization. Compared with patients with OCD alone, patients with comorbid tics usually present with an earlier age of onset and are more frequently males, suggesting there are phenotypic differences in OCD patients with Tourette's Syndrome/tic disorders (Diniz et al., 2006; Leckman et al., 1994a; Leonard et al., 1992). Moreover, tic-related OCD presentations are likely to be accompanied by presence of antecedent sensory phenomena (Leckman et al., 1994b; Miguel et al., 2006; Prado et al., 2008). Leckman and colleagues (2010) describe sensory phenomena, including localized tactile and muscle–skeletal sensations; "just-right" perceptions associated with visual, tactile, or auditory stimuli; feelings of "incompleteness"; and an "urge." Of clinical importance, a poorer treatment response with selective serotonin re-uptake inhibitor (SSRI) monotherapy in children and adolescents with OCD and comorbid tics (versus those without tics) was reported in a prospective study of children (March et al., 2007). Consistent with Geller and colleagues (2003a), the use of an SSRI was superior to placebo only in patients without tics (March et al.,

2007). Therefore, March and colleagues recommended that children and adolescents with OCD, as well as a comorbid tic disorder, should begin treatment with CBT alone or the combination of CBT plus an SSRI.

Symptomology

OCD in childhood and adolescence is a heterogeneous condition; with most children and youth presenting with a wide constellation of obsessional concerns and compulsive behaviors. Due to symptoms varying widely from patient to patient, the diagnostic manuals, namely, the International Classification of Diseases (ICD) (World Health Organization, 1992) and the DSM (APA, 2013), give general definitions of obsessions and compulsions that may be present in conjunction with, or in the absence of, the other symptoms. Childhood OCD can be episodic in presentation and is frequently reactive to stress, whereby children and adolescents experience acute symptom exacerbations during times of psychosocial challenge, such as the start of school year or moving to a new home (Piacentini & Bergman, 2000; Swedo, Rapoport, Leonard, Lenane, & Cheslow, 1989).

OCD is indeed a complex and debilitating disorder, with most young people endorsing numerous symptoms at any one point in time (Geller & March, 2012). Symptoms in children and adolescents may comprise compulsive washing, checking, repeating, counting, ordering, hoarding, magical thinking or rituals involving other people, as well as obsessions regarding contamination, aggressive thoughts, hoarding, somatic, religious, superstitious and sexual beliefs (Scahill, Riddle, & McSwiggin-Hardin, 1997). In children and youth, OCD presents in widely diverse forms as can be seen from case illustrations in Table 1.2, which describes a variety of cases included in our current clinical trials at Griffith University.

Recently, research has begun to investigate if differences exist in symptomology seen in younger versus older children. In a recent clinical study, Selles, Storch, and Lewin (2014) investigated the presentation of obsessive-compulsive symptoms in younger children aged 3–9 years old versus older children aged 10–18 years. The younger group were described as having less resistance and control of compulsions, and exhibited significantly poorer insight, increased incidence of hoarding compulsions, higher rates of comorbid attention deficit/hyperactivity disorder, disruptive behavior, and parent-rated anxiety. Older youth demonstrated stronger intensity of obsessive and compulsive symptoms, exhibited increased occurrence of comorbid depression, and an increased occurrence of sexual, magical thinking, and somatic obsessions, as well as, checking, counting and magical thinking compulsions.

Researchers and clinicians have hypothesized that patients with specific types of symptoms and comorbid presentations may represent different subtypes of the disorder, associated with diverse etiologies and response to treatments. The heterogeneous array of symptoms observed in OCD, coupled with the disparity in response to treatment, has prompted the development of methods for identifying subtypes of OCD to allow for systematic evaluation of possible differences in treatment response or disorder etiology associated with these different subtypes (McKay et al., 2004). In the adult literature, researchers have looked to the Yale–Brown Obsessive Compulsive Scale (Y-BOCS) (Goodman et al., 1989) due to the comprehensive checklist of over

Table 1.2 Case illustrations of children and adolescents with Obsessive-Compulsive Disorder

Name	CY-BOCS score	Primary obsession	Primary compulsion/avoidance	Other OC symptoms	Diagnostic profile (ADIS-IV-P CSR rating)
Grace 15 yr	32	Aggressive/sexual: fear that she is a pedophile and will make sexual advances toward young children.	Would avoid parks, playgrounds, the beach, school play time, so that she would not come into contact with young children.	• Contamination fears • Just right: school work	OCD (6) Specific phobia of spiders (4) GAD (4)
Zoe 12 yr	30	Not just right: fear of not being good enough, failing, being "wrong."	Repeating compulsions: will rip out pages from books if they are not perfect. Slowness with handwriting. Will rub out school work and re-write.	• Checking • Hoarding	OCD (5) BDD (4) GAD (4) Specific phobia vomiting (4)
Liam 16 yr	38	Contamination: fear of contracting AIDS or illness through bodily fluids and spreading contamination to his family.	Washing and cleaning: clean toilet and bathroom for up to 8 hours day. Excessive use of chemical cleaning products and hand-washing.	• Checking • Magical beliefs • Rituals involving others • Hoarding	OCD (7) ODD (4)
Ryan 10 yr	27	Aggressive/harm: fears taps will leak and flood the house, as well as power points and light switches will cause a fire.	Checks the taps, light switches, and power points are turned off up to 30 times/day	• Arranging/symmetry • Rituals involving others • Doubting	OCD (5) Social phobia (5) GAD (4) Specific phobias: high places (4), planes (4), and elevators (4)

Note: CY-BOCS = Children's Yale–Brown Obsessive Compulsive Scale (Scahill et al., 1997); Primary obsessions/compulsions defined as those OC symptoms causing highest level of functional impairment; CY-BOCS score range = 0–7 subclinical, 8–15 mild, 16–23 moderate, 24–31 severe, 32–40 Extreme; ADIS-IV-P = Anxiety Disorders Interview Schedule for DSM-IV: Parent Version (Silverman & Albano, 1996); CSR = Clinician Severity Rating; based on clinician judgment, scored 0–8, with a score of 4 indicating a clinically significant diagnosis; GAD = Generalized Anxiety Disorder; BDD = Body Dysmorphic Disorder; ODD = Oppositional Defiant Disorder.

60 specific OCD symptoms organized into obsession and compulsion categories. Researchers have applied factor analysis to subtype symptom representations.

Adult studies have generally supported a four-factor model to explain OCD symptom clusters. For example, Albert and colleagues (2010) conducted a factor analysis on a sample of 329 adults (mean Y-BOCS score of 24.9) and yielded a four-factor solution accounting for 58% of the variance of the Y-BOCS data. The factors included (a) symmetry, (b) forbidden thoughts, (c) cleaning, and (d) hoarding, which are representative of the international literature (see Bloch, Landeros-Weisenberger, Rosario, Pittenger, & Leckman, 2008; Cullen et al., 2007; Leckman et al., 1997). This four-factor model has also been replicated in a small number of studies involving children using the Children's Yale–Brown Obsessive Compulsive Scale (CY-BOCS) (Scahill et al., 1997; see Delorme et al., 2006; Mataix-Cols, Nakatani, Micali, & Heyman, 2008; McKay et al., 2006; Stewart et al., 2007). Bloch and colleagues conducted a meta-analysis of child studies investigating the factor structure of the CY-BOCS. On the basis of four studies involving 679 participants, the authors reported the four-factor structure explained 81.7% of the heterogeneity in the clinical symptoms of childhood OCD. Symmetry obsessions and checking, repeating, ordering, and counting compulsions loaded highly on factor 1 (symmetry, 28.7%). Cleaning, contamination, and somatic obsessions loaded highly on factor 2 (cleaning, 19.9%). Hoarding obsessions and compulsions loaded highly on factor 3 (hoarding, 16.7%). Aggressive, sexual, and religious obsessions loaded highly on factor 4 (forbidden thoughts, 16.4%). When comparing the factor structure between adults and children, Bloch and colleagues reported that they were identical with the exception of two minor differences. The first of these differences, checking compulsions, loaded highest on the forbidden thoughts factor in adults and on the symmetry factor in children; and, second, the somatic obsessions loaded highest on the forbidden thoughts factor in adults and on the cleaning factor in children.

While the few child studies conducted to date have consistently supported a four-factor model, there is some variability across studies at an item level within each of the factors. The variability observed among symptoms within the factors possibly reflects a combination of the differences between samples and ambiguity of some CY-BOCS items used in assessing OCD symptomology (Stewart et al., 2007). Of particular consideration, in each of the CY-BOCS factor studies, several symptom domains items were associated with more than one factor. This suggests the possibility that in childhood, symptom dimensions are less well developed and discrete dimensions of symptoms in OCD is not evident until later in development, or only after the symptoms have been present for a longer period of time (McKay et al., 2006). These findings are consistent with both research and clinical observations of OCD during childhood and adolescence, whereby young people frequently present with a wide and diverse constellation of symptoms that frequently change over time.

Leckman, Bloch, and King (2009) proposed distinct subtypes within pediatric OCD offering potentially useful categorical distinctions that better capture the heterogeneity of the disorder. Subtypes included tic-related OCD, familial non-tic-related early onset OCD, and pediatric autoimmune neuropsychiatric disorders associated with streptococcal (PANDAS) infections. Tic-related OCD was defined as when tics are observed either in the proband or in one or more first-degree family members. This subtype generally shows a male predominance, as well as symptoms that correspond to symmetry, forbidden thoughts, and hoarding dimensions (Leckman et al., 2009). In the case of familial OCD, higher than expected rates of anxiety and affective disorders are seen in early-onset cases and their first-degree family members. Moreover, children are likely to suffer with obsessional concerns about the safety of family members as well as contamination and compulsive washing compulsions. Finally, some susceptible individuals develop OC symptoms as a result of post-infectious autoimmune processes (Leckman et al., 2009). In recent times, an increase in evidence has pointed to immune-related causation in a minority of cases of childhood-onset OCD, most likely due to a Group A streptococcus (GAS) infection (Murphy et al., 2004). Despite interest and evidence for PANDAS, there are issues that preclude this as a formal OCD subtype in diagnostic terms due to concerns over reliability of the diagnosis, testing procedures, the use of antibiotics in treatment, and it seems that PANDAS can lead to a broader spectrum of developmental disorders in addition to just OCD (Thomsen, 2013).

In a novel study, Storch and colleagues (2008a) examined the extent to which symptom dimensions among youth with OCD were associated with CBT response in a sample of 92 children and adolescents aged 7–19 years, diagnosed with OCD. Symptom subtypes included symmetry/ordering, contamination/cleaning, sexual/religious obsessions, aggressive/checking, and hoarding symptoms. The majority of participants (76%) were rated as much improved or very much improved after 14 CBT sessions, supporting the guidelines that CBT should be recommended as the first-line treatment for youth with OCD, regardless of presenting symptoms (Geller & March, 2012). Overall, there was no difference in the response to CBT across pediatric OCD subtypes. However, participants with aggressive/checking symptoms at baseline showed a trend toward being more likely to respond to treatment than those who endorsed only nonaggressive/checking ($p=0.06$). The authors hypothesized the reason patients with checking rituals and harm obsessions had a better response to CBT is the length of time between the onset of the obsession and the feared consequence is typically quite short. Drawing from operant conditioning theory, these symptoms may be more acquiescent to extinction with exposure and response prevention due to the close temporal connection between behavior (e.g., exposure) and punishment (e.g., feared consequence) (Storch et al., 2008a). Further understanding of treatment response profiles for specific presentations of OCD in youth may help to inform efforts to individualize treatment approaches based on symptom and subtype presentations, which may translate to improved treatment out-comes. However, beyond the psychopathology of dimensions and subtypes, there is ample evidence to suggest that to be effective, cognitive-behavioral treatment proce-dures indeed should be adjusted to each individual in order to address the specific symptom manifestations in OCD (McKay et al., 2004).

Comorbidity

It is widely understood that comorbid conditions are frequent in OCD, with the addition of the DSM specifier for tic-related OCD highlighting the important role comorbidity plays in understanding the nature of the unique presentation and the likely heterogeneity of treatment response. Comorbidity is indeed a serious consideration in pediatric OCD and has been reported to be as high as 86% in a recent clinical sample (Farrell, Waters, Milliner, & Ollendick, 2012), with as many as 50–60% of youth experiencing two or more other mental disorders during their lifetime (Rasmussen & Eisen, 1990). Comorbid conditions heavily contribute to the debilitating nature of this disorder, the complexity in treating OCD patients, and why it is so often described as a complex psychiatric disorder (Farrell et al., 2012; Geller et al., 2003b; Masi et al., 2006; Sukhodolsky et al., 2005). The most common comorbid conditions of pediatric OCD include anxiety disorders, depression, tics and Tourette's Syndrome, attention deficit/hyperactivity disorders (ADHD), disruptive behavioral disorders, and pervasive developmental disorders (PDD) (Farrell et al., 2012). The frequency of these common comorbid disorders based on a selection of studies that have specifically investigated comorbidity in children and adolescents is presented in Table 1.3.

Certain comorbid disorders associated with OCD in youth (e.g., disruptive behavioral disorders, depression, attention deficit disorder) impact heavily upon the severity of a child's OCD, and have a negative effect on children's psychosocial functioning, and also response to treatment (Storch et al., 2008b; Storch, Lewin, DeNadai, & Murphy, 2010). Storch and colleagues (2008b) examined the impact of comorbidity in CBT response in a sample of youth with a primary diagnosis of OCD. In this study, it was found that having one or more comorbid conditions was associated with a poorer response to CBT outcome, and that the combined number of comorbid conditions was negatively related to outcome. Similar findings were found by Farrell and colleagues (2012) in a study of the effectiveness of group CBT for children and adolescents who presented with OCD and complex comorbid conditions. Comorbidity was not associated with poorer treatment outcomes at post-assessment; however, at 6-month follow-up outcomes were poorer for youth with multiple comorbid conditions and for those with attention deficit/hyperactivity disorder. Taken together, research indicates the presence of a comorbid externalizing disorder (i.e., attention deficit/hyperactivity disorder, oppositional defiant disorder (ODD), and conduct disorder) is associated with poorer treatment response and lower treatment remission rates (Garcia et al., 2010; Ginsburg, Newman Kingery, Drake, & Grados, 2008; Storch et al., 2008b).

Prevalence

Less than three decades ago, OCD was thought to be a rare condition in children, with limited literature available describing childhood OCD prevalence from retrospective reviews of child psychiatric samples (Flament et al., 1988). One of the first studies of reported prevalence found six cases of obsessive compulsive neurosis in a sample of more than 3,000 children admitted to a hospital or children's treatment facility, giving an estimated prevalence of 0.2% (Berman, 1942). In an early adult sample, Skoog (1965) described "obsessive neurosis" symptoms starting before the age of 19 in 15% of patients, recognizing OC symptoms as starting earlier than most other psychiatric problems of adulthood.

Judd (1965) conducted a chart audit to investigate the descriptive characteristics of obsessive compulsive neurosis in children aged 12 years or under. A total of 405 children from the child psychiatry service of UCLA Neuropsychiatric Institute were evaluated,

Table 1.3 Summary of OCD comorbidity among children and adolescents across a sample of studies

Author	Study design	n	Assessment tool	Social phobia	SAD	GAD	Phobia	Depression (%) (n)	Tics/ Tourette's	ADHD	Disruptive behavioral
Farrell et al. (2012)	Evaluated the effectiveness of group CBT on treatment outcomes: open trial	43	ADIS-IV-P	18.6 (8)	9.3 (4)	37.2 (16)	25.6 (11)	11.6 (5)	39.5 (17)	18.6 (8)	2.3 (1)
Ivarsson Melin, & Wallin (2008)	Investigated the presence of diagnostic heterogeneity in OCD. Within groups: age and gender	113	K-SADS-PL	7.1 (8)	4.4 (5)		24.8 (28)	24.8 (28)	27.4 (31)	17.7 (20)	8.8 (10)
Flament et al. (1990)	Prospective follow-up study (2–7yr), OCD vs normal controls	27	DICA	7.4 (2)			3.7 (1)	22.6 (6)			11.1 (3)
Thomsen (1994)	Study of phenomenology and family functioning: OCD vs psychiatric control group	20	Child Assessment Schedule				20.0 (4)	40.0 (8)	50.0 (10)	30.0 (6)	10.0 (2)
Geller et al. (2001a)	Evaluation of chronological age and age at onset: children, adolescents with childhood onset, adolescents with adolescent onset	101	K-SADS-E	13.9 (14)	43.6 (44)		27.7 (28)	51.5 (52)	15.8 (16)	42.6 (43)	56.4 (57)
Storch et al. (2008)	Impact of severity and impairment on comorbidity with clinical sample	75	ADIS-IV-P	14.7 (11)		30.7 (23)		16.0 (12)		21.3 (16)	12.0 (9)
Geller et al. (2003a)	Impact of comorbidity on treatment response to Paroxetine: randomized control trial	335	K-SADS-PL		10.1 (34)	20.0 (67)	16.1 (54)	14.4 (48)	15.2 (51)	18.8 (63)	8.4 (28)
Masi et al. (2010)	The impact of gender, age at onset, phenotype and comorbidity with clinical sample: descriptive analyses	257	K-SADS-PL	38.1 (98)	28.4 (73)	39.3 (101)	18.3 (47)	27.2 (70)	31.6 (81)	17.1 (44)	31.9 (82)

Note: SAD = Separation Anxiety Disorder; GAD = Generalized Anxiety Disorder; ADHD = Attention Deficit/Hyperactivity Disorder; ADIS-IV-P = Anxiety Disorders Interview Schedule for DSM-IV: Parent Version (Silverman & Albano, 1996); K-SADS-PL = Kiddie Schedule for Affective Disorders and Schizophrenia for School-Age Children Present and Lifetime (Kaufman et al., 1997); DICA = Diagnostic Interview for Children and Adolescents (Herjanic & Campbell, 1977; Welner, Reich, Herjanic, Jung, & Amado, 1987); K-SADS-E = Kiddie-Schedule for Affective Disorders and Schizophrenia-Epidemiological Version (Orvaschel & Puig-Antich, 1994).

of whom 34 were described as having obsessive compulsive symptoms. Out of these, five children met criteria of what was described as obsessive compulsive neurosis, a point prevalence of 1.2%. Criteria for this review included well-defined obsessive compulsive symptoms; the symptoms had to be the most prominent evidence of psychopathology in the patient's clinical picture and had to impair the child's functioning.

These early clinical studies provided the foundation for child and adolescent OCD being recognized as a serious and relatively prevalent mental health condition. However, they are also reflective of an ascertainment bias as these studies were often carried out in predominately Caucasian areas on children and adolescents who have been referred for care, from middle- and upper-class families (Valleni-Basile et al., 1994). Indeed, prevalence estimates in OCD clinical samples often yield lower results as they can be biased toward more severe cases, and individuals with OCD are frequently secretive about their symptoms and wait until serious social interference occurs before seeking treatment (Zohar et al., 1992). Epidemiological research using large community samples have been able to overcome many of these limitations and provide more reliable estimates of the prevalence of mental health conditions in the general community.

In the 1980s, the National Institute of Mental Health (NIMH) published a longitudinal study of OCD in a community sample of 5,596 adolescents in 9th through 12th grades, across eight schools, assessed against specific criteria outlined in the DSM-III (APA, 1980). A point prevalence rate of 1%, and an estimated a lifetime prevalence rate of 1.9% was reported. The mean age of onset was found to be 12.8 years, with a male predominance. The most common obsessions concerned contamination or harm, and the most common compulsions were washing/cleaning, checking and straightening, with 70% of cases having multiple obsessions/compulsions. The prevalence estimate was hypothesized to be under estimating the true figure with the authors suggesting the most severe cases would not be attending school (Flament, 1988). This was the first study to suggest OCD was not a rare condition, but rather the disorder went largely unrecognized by health care professionals.

Valleni-Basile and colleagues (1994) investigated the prevalence of OCD in a community sample between 1986 and 1988. The sample consisted of more than 3,000 adolescents enrolled across four public middle schools. The reported prevalence rate was 3% and the prevalence of subclinical OCD was 19%. Prevalence for males and females was similar for the OCD group. The most commonly reported compulsions were arranging, counting, collecting, and washing. The nature of obsessions was not collected in this study based on the nature of the assessment interview (i.e., Schedule for Affective Disorders and Schizophrenia for School-Age Children; Chambers et al., 1985), which recorded only the presence of obsessions.

In a sample of 562 older adolescents (aged 16 and 17 years), who underwent mandatory screening for entry into the Israel Defense Force, Zohar and colleagues (1992) examined the prevalence of mental health problems, social functioning, and cognitive performance, using a structured interview schedule based on DSM-III-R (APA, 1987) criteria, which consisted of items from the Y-BOCS (Goodman et al., 1989) to screen for OCD. The induction centers screen over 95% of a complete national cohort of 16–17-year-old adolescents. Further, institutionalized individuals are able to be captured as they are assessed using their medical records. OCD caseness was present in 3.56% of the sample and an additional 1.25% of the sample were identified as exhibiting OC symptomology. There was no significant sex differences found in the prevalence of the disorder.

A British Child Mental Health Survey of more than 10,000 young people aged 5–15 years was reported on by Heyman and colleagues (2001, 2003). The estimated point prevalence of OCD for the entire sample was 0.25% (95% CI 0.14–0.35). This study in particular captured younger prepubertal children, differing from many other studies which have largely only captured adolescents. Prevalence rates differed across age bands, with the incidence of OCD rising exponentially with increasing age: 5–7 years, 0.026% (95% CI 0.00–0.08); 8–10 years, 0.14% (95% CI 0.002–0.28); 11–12 years, 0.21% (95% CI 0.004–0.41); 13–15 years, 0.63% (95% CI 0.30–0.95). There was an equal distribution of gender across the sample. Among the children identified with OCD, almost 90% of cases had been undetected and untreated. This study had limitations in that lay interviewers were used and children under 11 years were not interviewed. A diagnosis was made by computer algorithm based on interview data and teacher reports.

Clinical characteristics of OCD were investigated by reviewing 11 childhood OCD clinic-based studies involving 419 children diagnosed with OCD. Geller and colleagues (1998b) found the average age of onset ranges between 7.5 and 12.5 years, with a mean of 10.3 years. Geller and colleagues also found a consensus in the literature for a male predominance in childhood OCD, with a 3:2 male–female ratio. Rapoport (1989) found that in an early onset of the disorder a male predominance was present; however, the male to female ratio becomes more equal with age and by late adolescence the ratio is even.

While these estimates suggest that OCD is indeed a relatively prevalent condition, the reality is that they are probably an underrepresentation of the real numbers of children and youth who suffer in silence. Children and adolescents with OCD are susceptible to underdiagnosis and undertreatment due to: (a) factors inherent to the disorder, such as secretiveness and lack of insight; (b) health care provider factors, such as incorrect diagnosis and either lack of familiarity with or unwillingness to use proven treatments; and (c) general factors, such as lack of access to treatment resources (Moore, Mariaskin, March, & Franklin, 2007). The disorder appears to have a similar prevalence to adults with the disorder, suggesting that not all cases of childhood OCD persist into adulthood as a cumulative prevalence of the disorder would be observed with new cases adding to the population over time (Geller, 1998a). However, unlike some other emotional disorders of childhood and adolescence, OCD appears to be persistent, with only a minority of sufferers recovering fully without treatment (Wilmshurst, 2005). Even with optimal treatment, an average of 50% of affected individuals continue to meet the diagnosis of OCD (Geller et al., 1998b).

Course

A meta-analysis and qualitative review of the long-term outcomes of child and adolescent onset OCD based on 16 studies with a total of 521 youth demonstrated that rates of persistence of OCD in childhood-onset cases are lower than previously believed (Stewart et al., 2004). Across follow-up periods ranging from 1 to 15.6 years, OCD was persistent in a mean of 60% of the pooled samples, indicating an overall remission rate (not meeting criteria for full or subthreshold OCD) of 40%. The implication that a substantial proportion of children with OCD remit over time is in opposition with early studies that suggested OCD in youth is usually a chronic and debilitating disorder (Flament et al., 1988; Hollingsworth, Tanguay, Grossman, & Pabst, 1980), an idea that has become established as "clinical lore" (Stewart et al., 2004). This is further evidenced in the DSM-IV-TR (2000), which stated that the course of OCD is chronic for the majority of individuals. This description has been changed slightly in the DSM-5 (2013) to say the course is usually chronic. With approximately one-third to one-half of adults with OCD developing their condition in childhood (Pauls, Alsobrook, Goodman, Rasmussen, & Leckman, 1995; Rasmussen & Eisen, 1990), the equal prevalence seen in young people and adults indicates that a proportion of youth with OCD may become subsyndromal over time (Stewart et al., 2004).

Stewart and colleagues (2004) found three independent variables to be associated with a significant increased rate of persistence of the disorder in childhood, including in-patient status (an indicator or severity), longer duration of illness at baseline, and an earlier age at onset. In contrast, gender, age at assessment, and length of follow-up were not reported as predictors of remission or persistence (Stewart et al., 2004). Several studies have indicated comorbidities also have implications in the course of OCD, with the presence of a tic or mood disorder being associated with increased OCD severity (Leonard et al., 1993; Wewetzer et al., 2001), and poorer treatment outcomes at follow up for youth with multiple comorbid conditions and for those with attention deficit/hyperactivity disorder (Farrell et al., 2012). These findings are in agreement with reports of treatment resistance in comorbid youth with OCD (Geller et al., 2003a).

Summary

Obsessive-compulsive disorder, characterized by the presence of obsessions and/or compulsions, is a serious mental health condition for children and adolescents. Knowledge of the disorder has advanced exponentially over the past 30 years with advancements made in prevalence estimates, diagnosis, presentation, treatment, and phenomenology. These advancements are evident in the changing description and clarity that has come with the classification of OCD in the recently revised DSM, being placed in the newly created OCRD chapter.

Children and adolescents often present with a wide variation of symptoms and these frequently transform over time. Advancements in recognition of differing symptom dimensions, as well as subtypes of OCD, have been seen especially in the child and adolescent literature. Research into the different content of obsessions and compulsions seen in younger versus older youth, as well as treatment response in dimensions of the disorder can help clinicians to accurately assess their patient's OC symptoms and improve their approach to delivering treatment. OCD observed in children and adolescence is marked by three distinct subtypes that are unique to this population – tic-related, familial, and PANDAS – which may be useful for categorizing the disorder, as well as determining treatment approaches and predicting response.

The much anticipated DSM-5 has seen one of the biggest changes to the classification of OCD in many years. The newly created OCRD chapter is a reflection of empirical research recognizing the underlying obsessive-compulsive element that underscores OCD, BDD, trichotillomania, and hoarding disorder. The logical grouping of these disorders in the ORCD chapter acknowledges the often comorbid nature of these disorders, highlighting to clinicians and researchers alike the importance of screening for comorbid disorders when a client presents with one of the OCRD diagnoses.

Increased accuracy of prevalence estimates began in the 1980s, which saw the beginnings of the first community samples to estimate the true prevalence of OCD in children and adolescence. It was at this time that the relatively prevalent nature of the disorder was beginning to be acknowledged, coupled with the increased understanding of the secrecy that often led to underdiagnosis and undertreatment for young sufferers. Large community estimates over recent decades have estimated the prevalence of OCD to be somewhere close to 3%. Research on the long-term outcomes of child and adolescent onset of OCD indicate mixed prognosis, with some youth becoming subsyndromal over time, whereas others having a long-term persistent battle with this debilitating disorder. Rapidly advancing scientific knowledge about the diverse etiologies, symptom dimensions, subtypes, and comorbidity profiles among children and youth with OCD has guided recent changes to the diagnostics formulation of the disorder, and has provided preliminary evidence to inform more individualized approaches to evidence-based treatment. While there remains much to be learnt, the future for pediatric OCD research is looking bright.

References

Abramowitz, J. S., Taylor, S., & McKay, D. (2009). Obsessive-compulsive disorder. *Lancet*, *374*, 491–499.

Albert, U., Bogetto, F., Maina, G., Saracco, P., Brunatto, C., & Mataix-Cols, D. (2010). Family accommodation in obsessive-compulsive disorder: Relation to symptom dimensions, clinical and family characteristics. *Psychiatry Research*, *179*, 204–211. doi: 10.1016/j.psychres.2009.06.008.

American Psychiatric Association. (1980). *Diagnostic and statistical manual of mental disorders* (3rd ed.). Washington, DC: Author.

American Psychiatric Association. (1987). *Diagnostic and statistical manual of mental disorders* (3rd ed., rev.). Washington, DC: Author.

American Psychiatric Association. (2000). *Diagnostic and statistical manual of mental disorders* (4th ed., text rev.). Washington, DC: Author.

American Psychiatric Association. (2013). *Diagnostic and statistical manual of mental disorders* (5th ed.). Arlington, VA: American Psychiatric Publishing.

Berman, L. (1942). The obsessive-compulsive neurosis in children. *Journal of Nervous and Mental Disease*, *85*, 26–39.

Bloch, M. H., Landeros-Weisenberger, A., Rosário, M. C., Pittenger, C., & Leckman, J. F. (2008). Meta-analysis of the symptom structure of obsessive-compulsive disorder. *American Journal of Psychiatry*, *165*, 1532–1542.

Chambers, W. J., Puig-Antich, J., Hirsch, M., Paez, P., Ambrosini, P. J., Tabrizi, M. A., & Davies. M. (1985). The assessment of affective disorders in children and adolescents by semi-structured interview: Test–retest reliability of the schedule of affective disorders and schizophrenia for school-age children, present episode version. *Archives of General Psychiatry*, *42*, 696–702. doi: 10.1001/archpsyc.1985.01790300064008.

Clegg, J. W. (2012). Teaching about mental health and illness through the history of the DSM. *History of Psychology, 15*, 364–370. doi: 10.1037/a0027249.

Cullen, B., Brown, C. H., Riddle, M. A., Grados, M., Bienvenu, O. J., Hoehn-Saric, R., … Nestadt, G. (2007). Factor analysis of the Yale–Brown Obsessive Compulsive scale in a family study of obsessive-compulsive disorder. *Depression and Anxiety, 24*, 130–138. doi: 10.1002/da.20204.

Delorme, R., Bille, A., Betancur, C., Mathieu1, F., Chabane, N., Mouren-Simeoni, M. C., & Leboyer, M. (2006). Exploratory analysis of obsessive compulsive symptom dimensions in children and adolescents: A prospective follow-up study. *BioMed Central Psychiatry, 6*, 1–10. doi:10.1186/1471-244X-6-1.

Diniz, J. B., Rosario-Campos, M. C., Hounie, A. G., Curi, M., Shavitt, R. G., Lopes, A. C., & Miguel, E. C. (2006). Chronic tics and Tourette syndrome in patients with obsessive-compulsive disorder. *Journal of Psychiatric Research, 40*, 487–493.

Eichstedt, J. S., & Arnold S. L. (2001). Childhood-onset obsessive compulsive disorder: A tic-related subtype of OCD? *Clinical Psychology Review, 21*, 137–158.

Farrell, L. J., Waters, A. M., Milliner, E., & Ollendick, T. H. (2012). Impact of comorbidity on group cognitive-behavioural treatment response in pediatric OCD. *Psychiatry Research, 99*, 115–123. doi: 10.1016/j.psychres.2012.04.035.

Flament, M. F., Koby, E., Rapport, J. L., Berg, J., Zahn, T., Cox, C., … Lenane, M. (1990). Obsessive-compulsive disorder: A prospective follow-up study. *Journal of Child Psychology and Psychiatry, 31*, 363–380. doi: 10.1111/j.1469-7610.1990.tb01575.x.

Flament, M. F., Whitaker, A., Rapoport, J. L., Davies, M., Zaremba Berg, C., Kalikow, K., … Shaffer, D. (1988). Obsessive compulsive disorder in adolescence: An epidemiological study. *Journal of the American Academy of Child and Adolescent Psychiatry, 27*, 764–771. doi: 10.1097/00004583-198811000-00018.

Foa, E. B., & Kozak, M. J. (1995). DSM-IV field trial: Obsessive-compulsive disorder. *American Journal of Psychiatry, 152*, 90–96.

Garcia, A. M., Sapyta, J. J., Moore, P. S., Freeman, J. B., Franklin, M. E., March, J. S., & Foa, E. B. (2010). Predictors and moderators of treatment outcome in the Pediatric Obsessive Compulsive Treatment Study (POTS I). *Journal of the American Academy of Child and Adolescent Psychiatry, 49*, 1024–1033.

Geller, D. A., Biederman, J., Faraone, S., Agranat, A., Cradlock, K., Hagermoser, L., … Coffey, B. J. (2001a). Developmental aspects of obsessive-compulsive disorder: Findings in children, adolescents and adults. *Journal of Nervous and Mental Disease, 189*, 471–477.

Geller, D. A., Biederman, J., Jones, J., Park, K., Schwartz, S., Shapiro, S., & Coffey, B. (1998a). Is juvenile obsessive-compulsive disorder a developmental subtype of the disorder? A review of the pediatric literature. *Journal of the American Academy of Child and Adolescent Psychiatry, 37*, 420–427.

Geller, D. A., Biederman, J., Jones, Shapiro, S., Schwartz, S., & Park, K. (1998b). Obsessive-compulsive disorder in children and adolescents: A review. *Harvard Review of Psychiatry, 5*, 260–273.

Geller, D. A., Biederman, J., Stewart, S. E., Mullin, B., Farrell, C., Wagner, K. D., … Carpenter, D. (2003a). Impact of comorbidity on treatment response to paroxetine in pediatric obsessive compulsive disorder: Is the use of exclusion criteria empirically supported in randomized clinical trials? *Journal of Child and Adolescent Psychopharmacology, 13*, 19–29. doi:10.1089/104454603322126313.

Geller, D. A., Coffey, B., Faraone, S., Hagermoser, L., Zaman, N., Farrell, C. L., … Biederman, J. (2003b). Does comorbid attention-deficit hyperactivity disorder impact the clinical expression of pediatric obsessive compulsive disorder? *CNS Spectrums, 8*, 259–264.

Geller, D. A., & March, J. (2012). Practice parameter for the assessment and treatment of children and adolescents with obsessive-compulsive disorder. *Journal of the American Academy of Child and Adolescent Psychiatry, 51*, 98–113. doi: 10.1016/j.jaac.2011.09.019.

Ginsburg, G. S., Newman Kingery, J., Drake, K. L., & Grados, M. A. (2008). Predictors of treatment response in pediatric obsessive-compulsive disorder. *Journal of the American Academy of Child and Adolescent Psychiatry*, *47*, 868–878. doi: 10.1097/CHI.0b013e3181799ebd.

Goodman, W. K., Price, L. H., Rasmussen, S. A., Mazure, C., Delgado, P., Heninger, G. R., & Charney, D. S. (1989). The Yale–Brown Obsessive-Compulsive Scale: Development, use, reliability, and validity. *Archives of General Psychiatry*, *46*, 1006–1016.

Herjanic, B., & Campbell, J. W. (1977). Differentiating psychiatrically disturbed children on the basis of a structured interview. *Journal of Abnormal Child Psychology*, *5*, 127–135.

Heyman, I., Fombonne, E., Simmons, H., Ford, T., Meltzer, H., & Goodman, R. (2001). Prevalence of obsessive-compulsive disorder in the British nationwide survey of child mental health. *British Journal of Psychiatry*, *179*, 324–329. doi: 10.1192/bjp.179.4.324.

Heyman, I., Fombonne, E., Simmons, H., Ford, T., Meltzer, H., & Goodman, R. (2003). Prevalence of obsessive-compulsive disorder in the British nationwide survey of child mental health. *International Review of Psychiatry*, *15*, 178–184. doi: 10.1080/0954026021000046146.

Hollander, E., Braun, A., & Simeon, D. (2008). Should OCD leave the anxiety disorders in DSM-V? The case for obsessive-compulsive-related disorders. *Depression and Anxiety*, *25*, 317–329. doi: 10.1002/da.20500.

Hollingsworth, C., Tanguay, E., Grossman, L., & Pabst, P. (1980). Long-term outcome of obsessive-compulsive disorder in childhood. *Journal of the American Academy of Child Psychiatry*, *19*, 134–144. doi: 10.1016/S0002-7138(09)60658-0.

Ivarsson, T., Melin, K., & Wallin, L. (2008). Categorical and dimensional aspects of comorbidity in obsessive-compulsive disorder (OCD). *European Journal of Child and Adolescent Psychiatry*, *17*, 20–31. doi: 10.1007/s00787-007-0626-z.

Janet, P. (1903). *Les obsessions et al psychasthenie* (Vol. *1*). Paris: Felix Alcan.

Judd, L. L. (1965). Obsessive compulsive neurosis in children. *Archives of General Psychiatry*, *12*, 136–143.

Kanner, L. (1962). *Child psychiatry* (3rd ed.). Springfield, IL: Charles C. Thomas.

Kaufman, J., Birmaher, B., Brent, D. A., Rao, U., Flynn, C., Moreci, P., ... Ryan, N. (1997). Schedule for Affective Disorders and Schizophrenia for School-Age Children-Present and Lifetime Version (K-SADS-PL): Initial reliability and validity data. *Journal of the American Academy of Child and Adolescent Psychiatry*, *36*, 980–988. doi: 10.1097/00004583-199707000-00021.

Leckman, J. F., Bloch, M. H., & King, R. A. (2009). Symptom dimensions and subtypes of obsessive-compulsive disorder: A developmental perspective. *Dialogues in Clinical Neuroscience*, *11*, 21–33.

Leckman, J. F., Grice, D. E., Boardman, J., Zhang, H., Vitale, A., Bondi, C., ... Pauls, D. L. (1997). Symptoms of obsessive-compulsive disorder. *American Journal of Psychiatry*, *154*, 911–917.

Leckman, J. F., Grice, D. E., Barr, L. C., de Vries, A. L. C., Martin, C., Cohen, D. J., ... Rasmussen, S. A. (1994a). Tic-related vs. non-tic-related obsessive compulsive disorder. *Anxiety*, *1*, 208–215. doi: 10.1002/anxi.3070010504.

Leckman, J. F., Denys, D., Simpson, H. B., Mataix-Cols, D., Hollander, E., Saxena, S., ... Stein, D. J. (2010). Obsessive-compulsive disorder: A review of the diagnostic criteria and possible subtypes and dimensional specifiers for DSM-V. *Depression and Anxiety*, *27*, 507–527. doi: 10.1002/da.20669.

Leckman, J. F., Walker, D. E., Goodman, W. K., Pauls, D. L., & Cohen, D. J. (1994b). "Just right" perceptions associated with compulsive behaviors in Tourette's syndrome. *American Journal of Psychiatry*, *151*, 675–680.

Leonard, H. L., Lenane, M. C., Swedo, S. E., Rettew, D. C., Gershon, E. S., & Rapoport, J. L. (1992). Tics and Tourette's disorder: A 2- to 7-year follow-up of 54 obsessive-compulsive children. *American Journal of Psychiatry, 149*, 1244–1251.

Leonard, H. L., Swedo, S. E., Lenane, M. C., Rettew, D. C., Hamburger, S. D., Bartko, J. J., & Rapoport, J. L. (1993). A 2- to 7-year follow-up study of 54 obsessive-compulsive children and adolescents. *Archives of General Psychiatry, 50*, 429–439.

March J. S., Franklin, M. E., Leonard, H., Garcia, A., Moore, P., Freeman, J., & Foa, E. (2007). Tics moderate treatment outcome with sertraline but not cognitive-behavior therapy in pediatric obsessive-compulsive disorder. *Biological Psychiatry, 61*, 344–347. doi:10.1016/j.biopsych.2006.09.035.

Masi, G., Millepiedi, S., Mucci, M., Bertini, N., Pfanner, C., & Arcangeli, F. (2006). Comorbidity of obsessive compulsive disorder and attention deficit hyper-activity disorder in referred children and adolescents. *Comprehensive Psychiatry, 46*, 42–47.

Masi, G., Millepiedi, S., Perugi, G., Pfanner, C., Berloffa, S., Pari, C., … Akiskal, H. S. (2010). A naturalistic exploratory study of the impact of demographic, phenotypic and comorbid features in pediatric obsessive-compulsive disorder. *Psychopathology, 43*, 69–78. doi:10.1159/000274175.

Mataix-Cols, D., Nakatani, E., Micali, N., & Heyman, I. (2008). Structure of obsessive-compulsive symptoms in pediatric OCD. *Journal of the American Academy of Child and Adolescent Psychiatry, 47*, 773–778. doi: 10.1097/CHI.0b013e31816b73c0.

McKay, D., Abramowitz, J. S., Calamari, J. E., Kyrios, M., Radomsky, A., Sookman, D., … Wilhelm, S. (2004). A critical evaluation of obsessive-compulsive disorder subtypes: Symptoms versus mechanisms. *Clinical Psychology Review, 24*, 283–313. doi: 10.1016/j.cpr.2004.04.003.

McKay, D., Piacentini, J., Greisberg, S., Graae, F., Jaffer, M., & Miller, J. (2006). The structure of childhood obsessions and compulsions: Dimensions in an outpatient sample. *Behavior Research and Therapy, 44*, 137–146. doi: 10.1016/j.brat.2005.02.001.

Miguel E. C., do Rosário, M. C., Prado, H. S., do Valle, R., Rauch, S. L., Coffey, B. J., … Leckman, J. F. (2006). Sensory phenomena in obsessive-compulsive disorder and Tourette's disorder. *Journal of Clinical Psychiatry, 61*, 150–156.

Moore, P. S., Mariaskin, A., March, J., & Franklin, M. E. (2007). Obsessive-compulsive disorder in children and adolescents: Diagnosis, comorbidity, and developmental factors. In E. A. Storch, G. G. Geffken, & T. K. Murphy (Eds.), *Handbook of child and adolescent obsessive-compulsive disorder* (pp. 17–45). Mahwah, NJ: Lawrence Erlbaum.

Murphy, T., Sajid, M., Soto, O., Shapira, N., Edge, P., Yang, M., … Goodman, W. K. (2004). Detecting pediatric autoimmune neuropsychiatric disorders associated with streptococcus in children with obsessive-compulsive disorder and tics. *Biological Psychiatry, 55*, 61–68. doi:10.1016/s0006-3223(03)00704-2.

Orvaschel, H., & Puig-Antich, J. (1994). *Schedule for Affective Disorder and Schizophrenia for School-age Children, Epidemiologic version*. Fort Lauderdale, FL: Nova University, Center for Psychological Study.

Pauls, D., Alsobrook, J,. II, Goodman, W., Rasmussen, S., & Leckman, J. (1995). A family study of obsessive-compulsive disorder. *American Journal of Psychiatry, 152*, 76–84

Pauls, D. L., Abramovitch, A., Rauch, S. L., & Geller, D. A. (2014). Obsessive-compulsive disorder: An integrative genetic and neurobiological perspective. *Nature Reviews Neuroscience, 15*, 410–424. doi: 10.1038/nrn3746.

Piacentini, J., & Bergman, R. L. (2000). Obsessive-compulsive disorder in children. *Psychiatric Clinics, 23*(3), 519–533. doi: 10.1016/S0193-953X(05)70178-7.

Prado H. S., Rosário, M. C., Lee, J., Hounie, A. G., Shavitt, R. G., & Miguel, E. C. (2008). Sensory phenomena in obsessive-compulsive disorder and tic disorders: A review of the literature. *CNS Spectrums, 13*, 425–432.

Rapoport, J. L. (1989). *Obsessive-compulsive disorder in children and adolescents*. Washington, DC: American Psychiatric Press.

Rasmussen, S. A., & Eisen, J. L., (1990). Epidemiology of obsessive compulsive disorder. *Journal of Clinical Psychiatry, 51* (suppl. 10/3, discussion 14).

Scahill, L., Riddle, M. A., & McSwiggin-Hardin, M. (1997). Children's Yale–Brown obsessive-compulsive scale: Reliability and validity. *Journal of the American Academy of Child and Adolescent Psychiatry, 36,* 844–852.

Selles, R. R., Storch, E. A., & Lewin, A. B. (2014). Variations in symptom prevalence and clinical correlates in younger versus older youth with obsessive-compulsive disorder. *Child Psychiatry & Human Development.* doi: 10.1007/s10578-014-0435-9.

Silverman, W. K., & Albano, A. M. (1996). *The anxiety disorders interview schedule for DSM-IV. Child and parent versions.* Oxford: Oxford University Press.

Skoog, G. (1965). Onset of anancastic conditions. *Acta Psychiatrica Scandinavica, 14,* 1–84.

Stewart, S. E., Geller, D. A., Jenike, M., Pauls, D., Shaw, D., Mullin, B., & Faraone, S. V. (2004). Long-term outcome of pediatric obsessive-compulsive disorder: A meta-analysis and qualitative review of the literature. *Acta Psychiatrica Scandinavica, 110,* 4–13.

Stewart, S. E., Rosario, M. C., Brown, T. A., Carter, A. S., Leckman, J. F., Sukhodolsky, D., … Pauls, D. L. (2007). Principal components analysis of obsessive-compulsive disorder symptoms in children and adolescents. *Biological Psychiatry, 61,* 285–291. doi: 10.1016/j.biopsych.2006.08.040.

Storch, E. A., De Nadai, A. S., Jacob, M. L., Lewin, A. B., Muroff, J., Eisen, J., … Murphy, T. K. (2014). Phenomenology and correlates of insight in pediatric obsessive-compulsive disorder. *Comprehensive Psychiatry, 55,* 613–620. doi: 10.1016/j.comppsych.2013.09.014.

Storch, E. A., Larson, M. J., Merlo, L. J., Keeley, M. L., Jacob, M. L., Geffken, G. R., … Goodman, W. K. (2008). Comorbidity of pediatric obsessive-compulsive disorder and anxiety disorders: Impact on symptom severity and impairment. *Journal of Psychopathology and Behavioral Assessment, 30,* 111–120. doi: 10.1007/s10862-007-9057-x.

Storch, E. A., Lewin, A. B., DeNadai, A. S., & Murphy, T. K., (2010). Defining treatment response and remission in obsessive-compulsive disorder: A signal detection analysis of the Children's Yale–Brown Obsessive Compulsive Scale. *Journal of American Academy of Child and Adolescent Psychiatry, 49,* 708–717. doi: 10.1016/j.jaac.2010.04.005.

Storch, E. A., Merlo, L. J., Larson, M. J., Bloss, C. S., Geffken, G. R., Jacob, M. L., … Goodman, W. K. (2008a). Symptom dimensions and cognitive-behavioral therapy outcome for pediatric obsessive-compulsive disorder. *Acta Psychiatrica Scandinavica, 117,* 67–75. doi: 10.1111/j.1600-0447.2007.01113.x.

Storch, E. A., Merlo, L. J., Larson, M. J., Geffken, G. R., Lehmkuhl, H. D., Jacob, M. L., … Goodman, W. K. (2008b). Impact of comorbidity on cognitive behavioral therapy response in pediatric obsessive-compulsive disorder. *Journal of American Academy of Child and Adolescent Psychiatry, 47,* 583–590. doi: 10.1097/CHI.0b013e31816774b1.

Sukhodolsky, D. G., do Rosário-Campos, M. C., Scahill, L., Katsovich, L., Pauls, D. L., Peterson, B. S., … Leckman, J. F. (2005). Adaptive emotional and family functioning of children with obsessive compulsive disorder and comorbid attention deficit hyperactivity disorder. *American Journal of Psychiatry, 162,* 1125–1132. doi: 10.1176/appi.ajp.162.6.1125.

Swedo, S. E., Rapoport, J. L., Leonard, H., Lenane, M., & Cheslow, D. (1989). Obsessive compulsive disorder in children and adolescents: Clinical phenomenology of 70 consecutive cases. *Archives of General Psychiatry, 46,* 335–341.

The Pediatric OCD Treatment Study (POTS) Team. (2004). Cognitive-behavior therapy, sertraline, and their combination for children and adolescents with obsessive-compulsive disorder: The pediatric OCD treatment study (POTS) randomized controlled trial. *Journal of the American Medical Association, 292,* 1969–1976. doi: 10.1001/jama.292.16.1969.

Thomsen, P. H. (1994). Obsessive-compulsive disorder in children and adolescence: A study of phenomenology and family functioning in 20 consecutive Danish cases. *European Child and Adolescent Psychiatry, 3,* 29–36.

Thomsen, P. H. (2013). Obsessive-compulsive disorders. *European Child and Adolescent Psychiatry, 22,* 23–28. doi: 10.1007/s00787-012-0357-7.

Valleni-Basile, L. A., Garrison, C. Z., Jackson, K. L., Waller, J. L., McKeown, R. E., Addy, C. L., & Cuffe, S. P. (1994). Frequency of obsessive-compulsive disorder in a community sample of young adolescents. *Journal of the American Academy of Child and Adolescent Psychiatry*, *33*, 782–791. doi: 10.1097/00004583-199407000-00002.

Van Ameringen, M., Patterson, B., & Simpson, W. (2014). DSM-5 obsessive-compulsive and related disorders: Clinical implications of new criteria. *Depression and Anxiety*, *31*, 487–493. doi: 10.1002/da.22259.

Wewetzer C, Jans T, Muller B, Neudörfl, A., Bücherl, U., Remschmidt, H., ... Herpertz-Dahlmann, B. (2001). Long-term outcome and prognosis of obsessive-compulsive disorder with onset in childhood or adolescence. *European Child and Adolescent Psychiatry*, *10*, 37–46.

Welner, Z., Reich, W., Herjanic, B., Jung, K., & Amado, H. (1987). Reliability, validity and parent–child agreement studies of the diagnostic interview for children and adolescents (DICA). *Journal of the American Academy of Child and Adolescent Psychiatry*, *26*, 649–653.

Wilmshurst, L. (2005). *Essentials of child osychopathology*. Hoboken, NJ: Wiley.

World Health Organization. (1992). *International statistical classification of diseases and related health problems*. 10th Revision (ICD-10). Geneva: World Health Organization.

Zohar, A. H., Ratzoni, G., Pauls, D. L., Apter, A., Bleich, A., Kron, S., ... Cohen, D. J. (1992). An epidemiological study of obsessive-compulsive disorder and related disorders in Israeli adolescents. *Journal of the American Academy of Child and Adolescent Psychiatry*, *31*, 1057–1061.

2

Diagnostic Description and Prevalence

Andrew G. Guzick, Adam M. Reid, Amanda M. Balki, Cindi Flores, Anyaliese D. Hancock-Smith, Brian Olsen, Greg Muller, Gary R. Geffken, and Joseph P. H. McNamara

Symptom Presentation

Obsessive-Compulsive Disorder (OCD) is a psychiatric condition in which an individual engages in repetitive behaviors or mental acts (compulsions) in response to intrusive, distressing thoughts, impulses, or urges (obsessions). While this broad definition officially conceptualizes the disorder (American Psychiatric Association [APA], 2013a), adults with OCD consistently have a heterogeneous clinical presentation (Mataix-Cols, Rosário-Campos, & Leckman, 2005). These significant variations ensure that clinicians treating OCD their entire career will not see the exact same symptom profile twice. This phenomenon is exemplified by assessment measures that include 67 different potential obsessions and compulsions, which even themselves may present with a great deal of diversity (Goodman et al., 1989). Furthermore, the profile of symptoms that an individual endorses at one time in life might vary from the symptoms they report months to years later, as symptoms naturally wax and wane, and might change topographically, based on various environmental triggers (Rufer, Grothusen, Mass, Peter, & Hand, 2005).

Despite this heterogeneity, formal nosology in diagnostic manuals conceptualizes that all obsessive-compulsive symptoms be classified as an expression of one disorder (APA, 2013a). Although there is potential weakness in defining OCD so broadly (Brown & Barlow, 2005; 2009), this categorical classification does have some clinical advantages, mostly in facilitating communication between clinicians, and also has support from the scientific literature. For example, these obsessive-compulsive symptoms consistently fit into "bins" that often present together, have thematic similarities, and are more appropriately conceptualized as dimensions of one disorder than multiple distinct disorders (Mataix-Cols et al., 2005). A number of studies suggest four symptom domains, including (a) contamination obsessions and compulsions, (b) repugnant obsessions with mental and checking compulsions,

The Wiley Handbook of Obsessive Compulsive Disorders, Volume I, First Edition.
Edited by Jonathan S. Abramowitz, Dean McKay, and Eric A. Storch.
© 2017 John Wiley & Sons Ltd. Published 2017 by John Wiley & Sons Ltd.

(c) obsessions about responsibility for causing disasters and checking or reassurance-seeking compulsions, and (d) symmetry obsessions and compulsions (e.g., Abramowitz et al., 2010; Bloch, Landeros-Weisenberger, Rosário, Pittenger, & Leckman, 2008).

Cultural Differences

Cultural variations in adult OCD do exist and should be considered in the conceptualization and treatment of OCD. Some aspects of adult obsessive-compulsive symptoms appear to be somewhat homogeneous across cultures, such as a higher prevalence in females, early-life onset, and presentation of multiple obsessions and compulsions (Clark & Inozu, 2014; Fontenelle, Mendlowicz, Marques, & Versiani, 2004). However, culture does seem to influence the frequency and distribution of symptom dimensions (Fontenelle et al., 2004; Yorulmaz, Gencöz, & Woody, 2009), the compulsive behavior triggered by certain types of obsessions (Wheaton, Berman, Fabricant, & Abramowitz, 2013), as well as the content of obsessions experienced (Clark & Inozu, 2014). Religion also appears to impact the expression of OCD in diverse ways, with religious identification being related to insight, symptom domain, and cognitive distortions associated with religious obsessions (Siev, Chambless, & Huppert, 2010; Inozu, Karanci, & Clark, 2012).

Symptom presentation can vary by geographic location as well. For example, aggressive obsessions are more common in Brazil, while religious obsessions are more common in the Middle East, and contamination is more common in Western countries (Fontenelle et al., 2004). Evidence also suggests that individuals suffering with OCD in Indian cultures report less comorbidity with OCD spectrum disorders than do OCD sufferers in most other cultures (Cherian et al., 2014). Thought control strategies used in response to obsessional thoughts may also vary, with thought suppression and worry being more common in some cultures (e.g., Turkey) while self-punishment is more common in others (e.g. Canada; Yorulmaz et al., 2009).

In general, research on cultural influences in adult OCD is preliminary and relies on cross-cultural comparisons rather than in-depth assessment of presenting symptoms within the cultural context. Thus, little is known about the mechanisms underlying the differences that have been identified. Some of the most pressing cultural questions remain unclear, such as the universality of maintaining mechanisms of obsessive-compulsive symptomology (e.g., Moulding et al., 2014; Nota et al., 2014).

Diagnostic Changes in DSM 5

In the *Diagnostic and Statistical Manual*, Fourth Edition, Text Revision (DSM-IV-TR), OCD was classified as an anxiety disorder (APA, 2000). In the DSM-5, OCD was re-classified in a separate category called Obsessive Compulsive and Related Disorders (OCRDs), which includes the following conditions: OCD, body dysmorphic disorder (BDD), hoarding disorder, trichotillomania (hair-pulling), excoriation (skin-picking) disorder, substance/medication-induced OCRDs, OCRDs due to another medical condition, and other specified OCRDs and unspecified OCRDs (APA, 2013b).

This change reflects emerging evidence regarding the phenomenology of OCRDs. While OC symptoms produce significant amounts of anxiety and distress to an individual, some findings suggest OC symptoms differ significantly in structure from the other anxiety disorders that OCD was grouped with in the DSM-IV-TR, as no other anxiety disorder is characterized by the inability to resist repetitive impulses and urges (Hollander, Braun, & Simeon, 2008). In addition, several other conditions that share seemingly similar features were not included in the domain of anxiety disorders (Phillips et al., 2010). Therefore, the OCD was removed from the classification of anxiety disorders and sections were added on related conditions to create a separate chapter (Hollander et al., 2008). Importantly, not all authors agree on the basis for this change in DSM-5 (Abramowitz & Jacoby, 2015; Storch, Abramowitz, & Goodman, 2008).

OCD diagnostic criteria changes. The description of obsessions within the DSM-5 has a few semantic deviations from the DSM-IV-TR. Obsessions are defined as "recurrent and persistent thoughts, urges, or images that are experienced, at some time during the disturbance, as intrusive and unwanted, and that in most individuals cause marked anxiety or distress" (APA, 2013b). The main wording changes from the DSM-IV-TR (APA, 2000) include the change from obsessions being "inappropriate" to "unwanted" and "causes anxiety" to "in most individuals cause marked anxiety or distress."

The DSM-5 also introduces changes to the criteria for insight into the disorder. Previously, a key criterion was recognition that obsessive-compulsive symptoms were products of an individual's own mind and that they were excessive or unreasonable. In the DSM-5, the diagnosis allows for a spectrum of insight to include multiple categories, including good or fair insight, poor insight, or absent insight/delusional beliefs. Additionally, the criterion that "the thoughts, impulses, or images are not simply excessive worries about real-life problems" was eliminated.

In addition to the insight specifier, the DSM-5 added a specifier to include a tic-related OCD diagnosis (APA, 2013a). Important differences in clinical presentation exist in both children and adults with tic related diagnoses, such as more obsessions/compulsions regarding symmetry and arranging (Leckman et al., 1997), and the experience of sensory phenomena such as tactile and musculoskeletal perceptions of something being "not just right" and the presence of sensory tics (Prado et al., 2008). A skilled clinician must be aware of these nuances in presentation, as up to 26.2% of people with OCD are estimated to have comorbid tics (Nestadt et al., 2009). Despite these differences, studies have not found tics to influence OCD symptom severity (e.g., Diniz et al., 2006).

Obsessive-compulsive related disorders. The DSM-5 classifies hoarding disorder as a distinct diagnosis for the first time. This change reflects recent research indicating that hoarding behavior tends to present as being independent from OCPD, OCD, and other psychiatric conditions (Mataix-Cols et al., 2010).

The diagnostic criteria remain largely unchanged for BDD, trichotillomania, and substance/medication-induced OCRDs, although a thorough discussion of these related disorders is beyond the scope of this chapter. Excoriation disorder is a newly added condition and was included in the DSM-5 due to substantial research indicating high prevalence rates (2–4% of the population), possible medical complications (e.g., infections, skin lesions, and scarring), and treatment approaches. As with all of the sections in the DSM-5, the OCRDs include an "other specified" and "unspecified" diagnosis, which allows clinicians to make appropriate diagnosis for symptoms that are similar to an OCRD that cause clinically significant distress or impairment in a major life activity and do not precisely fit any of the specific OCRDs (e.g., cheek chewing, obsessional jealousy) (APA, 2013b).

Symptom Presentation Summary

OCD is characterized by distressing cognitions and behaviors in which specific obsessions and compulsions as well as distorted patterns of thinking cause significant amounts of distress. Although the trends in presentation may vary across cultures, research has provided an excellent framework to describe intrusive thoughts and repetitive behaviors exhibited in OCD, with clinically useful dimensions emerging. Specifically, people with OCD experience obsessions and compulsions related to contamination, responsibility for harm, repugnance, and symmetry. Besides OCD's new classification in the DSM-5, the most salient changes in the new DSM include broadening the insight specifier, including a tic specifier regarding whether the individual has current or past history of a tic disorder, and introducing hoarding disorder as a separate diagnosis, as opposed to a symptom dimension of OCD.

Prevalence and Comorbidity

In total, the lifetime prevalence of OCD is estimated to be between 1% and 3%; this prevalence rate has been demonstrated consistently across numerous countries and cultures (Kessler, Petukhova, Sampson, Zaslavsky, & Wittchen, 2012; Ruscio, Stein, Chiu, & Kessler, 2010; Subramaniam, Abdin, Vaingankar, & Chong, 2012). The first manifestations of OCD often appear between ages 8 and 11, with an increase in OCD diagnoses during puberty and again in early adulthood (Farrell, Barrett, & Piacentini, 2006; Zohar, 1999). During childhood, OCD disproportionately impacts males with a 2:1 male predominance (Farrell et al., 2006; Zohar, 1999). By early adulthood, the gender distribution is more equal, with some researchers suggesting a female predominance, although this could be due to women sometimes developing OCD at an older age (Castle, Deale, & Marks, 1995; Kessler et al., 2012). Research suggests any slight gender imbalance diminishes by age 65 (Kessler et al., 2012).

Psychological Comorbidities

Individuals who have OCD are at risk for a variety of other psychological issues; it has been estimated that 62–92% of people with OCD have at least one psychiatric comorbidity (Torres et al., 2006; LaSalle et al., 2004). This is especially concerning when considering the especially poor prognosis of individuals with adult OCD and psychological comorbidity, in terms of both OCD symptom severity and treatment outcome (Steketee, Henninger, & Pollard, 2000; Poyurovsky & Koran, 2005). See Table 2.1 for a summary of OCD comorbidities and their impact on OCD symptom severity and presentation.

Table 2.1 Psychological comorbidities

Diagnosis	Lifetime prevalence estimate	Impact on OCD severity	Impact on OCD presentation
Anxiety disorders	Up to 75% (Horwath & Weissman, 2000).	Does not influence symptom severity (Miyazaki, Yoshino, & Nomura, 2011).	Does not influence treatment outcome, except for PTSD, which has been shown to attenuate treatment outcome for OCD (Gershuny et al., 2002). There is also potential for different presentation. For example, individuals with OCD and GAD are more likely to have higher rates of indecisiveness as well as greater struggles with overestimation of responsibility (Abramowitz & Foa, 1998).
Bipolar disorder	6–10% (Amerio, Odone, Liapis, & Ghaemi, 2014).	Increased symptom severity (Quarantini et al., 2011; Timpano, Rubenstein, & Murphy, 2012).	More obsessions (Timpano et al., 2012), more symmetry symptoms (Hasler et al., 2005).
Body dysmorphic disorder	Up to 12% (Simeon, Hollander, Stein, Cohen, & Aronowitz, 1995).	Slightly increased symptom severity (Phillips et al., 2007).	More frequent hoarding and depressive symptoms (Phillips, Gunderson, Mallya, McElroy, & Carter, 1998).
Eating disorders	3–17% for Anorexia Nervosa (Halmi et al., 2003); 3–10% for Bulimia Nervosa (Matsunaga et al., 1999).	Limited research.	More frequent contamination symptoms (Hasler et al., 2005).
Excoriation	Up to 16.3% (Lovato et al., 2012).	Does not influence symptom severity (Lovato et al., 2012).	More obsessions, more frequent hoarding symptoms (Lovato et al., 2012).

Hoarding disorder	18–40% (Mataix-Cols et al., 2010).	Does not influence symptom severity (Petrusa et al., 2008).	Increased symmetry symptoms (Petrusa et al., 2008).
Major depressive disorder	63% (Ruscio et al., 2010).	Increased OCD symptom severity (Quarantini et al., 2011; Timpano et al., 2012).	More compulsions (Timpano et al., 2012), more repugnant obsessions.
Obsessive-Compulsive Personality disorder	23–36% (Coles, Pinto, Mancebo, Rasmussen, & Eisen, 2008; Garyfallos et al., 2010).	Does not influence symptom severity (Coles et al., 2008; Garyfallos et al., 2010).	Increased perfectionism and preoccupation with morality; increased symmetry, hoarding, and checking symptoms (Coles et al., 2008; Garyfallos et al., 2010).
Substance abuse/ dependence	Up to 20% for alcohol abuse, up to 14% for other substance abuse (Torres et al., 2006).	Limited research.	More frequent aggressive and symmetry symptoms (Hasler et al., 2005).
Tic disorder	Up to 26% (Nestadt et al., 2009).	Does not influence symptom severity: see *Tic specifier* section.	Different symptoms presentation: see *Tic specifier* section.
Trichotillo-mania	5% (Lovato et al., 2012).	Does not influence symptom severity (Lovato et al., 2012).	More obsessions, more frequent hoarding symptoms (Lovato et al., 2012).

Areas in need of special consideration. In addition to the most commonly comorbid conditions described above, OCD's relationship with Autism Spectrum Disorder (ASD) and suicidal ideation are areas that require special attention and consideration. Specifically, OCD can have significant, distressing symptoms that overlap with these conditions that can render standard comorbidity rates ineffective at describing symptom areas.

Individuals with OCD alone may also exhibit obsessive thoughts and compulsive behaviors similar to those seen in individuals with ASD (Anholt et al., 2010; Ivarsson & Melin, 2008). People with OCD may also experience social skills deficits and executive functioning skills comparable to those exhibited by individuals with ASD (Anholt et al., 2010). Because of these overlapping symptoms, it can sometimes be difficult to differentiate between the two disorders, but nuances do exist. For instance, the content of obsessions and compulsions are different, with adults with OCD experiencing ego dystonic obsessional thoughts, while adults with ASD experiencing ego syntonic perseverative thoughts. For instance, while an individual with OCD may spend hours arranging furniture in response to distressing thoughts about the room being "not right," an adult with ASD may spend hours arranging objects that they take particular interest in, like a collection of special interest books. Adults with OCD may clean, count, and check more often, while adults with ASD may engage in more hoarding, ordering, and self-mutilating behaviors that are not necessarily related to their perseverative thoughts (Goodman, Naylor, & Volkmar, 1995). Thus, the link between obsession and compulsion that typifies OCD is not necessarily present in ASD.

It is somewhat common for individuals with OCD to experience suicidal ideation, but evidence regarding actual suicide attempts is mixed due to discrepancies between suicide attempts and self-harm obsessions/compulsions (Alonso et al., 2010; Balci & Sevincok, 2010; Hollander, Kwon, Stein, & Broatch, 1996). However, individuals with OCD and comorbid Major Depressive Disorder (MDD) or bipolar disorder (BPD) are at greater risk for having attempted suicide at least once in their lifetime (Alonso et al., 2010; Balci & Sevincok, 2010). In addition, other studies have suggested that suicide attempts made by individuals with comorbid OCD and an affective disorder tend to be more serious than attempts made by individuals singly affected by either OCD or an affective disorder (Alonso et al., 2010).

Summary of Prevalence and Comorbidity

Impacting 1–3% of the population, OCD has significant influence on an individual. Many are also diagnosed with another psychological disorder, possibly leading to an exacerbation of their OCD symptoms, and a host of other difficulties stemming from the comorbid disorder, or an interaction among disorders. Clinically, it is especially important to be aware of these comorbidities, as some conditions (e.g., bipolar disorder, Obsessive-Compulsive Personality Disorder) can mask or alter the presentation of OCD symptoms. Given these concerns, research regarding clinical outcomes and symptom etiology is still needed to clarify inconsistent findings (e.g., suicidal behaviors in individuals with OCD) and to build on other limitations in this area.

Risk Factors for the Development of OCD

Environmental Risk Factors

Twin studies have found that approximately 50% of individual variation in OCD symptoms is due to nongenetic, environmental factors (Samuels, 2009). There are shared as well as unique factors regarding childhood and adult OCD. For instance, pregnancy and substance use have only been identified as risk factors for the development of adulthood OCD (Regier et al., 1990; Russell, Fawcett, & Mazmanian, 2013), while a behaviorally inhibited temperament during childhood and traumatic life events have been identified as risk factors for the development of OCD in both childhood and adulthood (Coles, Schofield, & Pietrefesa, 2006; Gershuny et al., 2008; Lafleur et al., 2011). Risk factors for adult OCD include pregnancy, stressful/traumatic life events, and substance abuse (Grisham et al., 2011; Russell et al., 2013). As noted, other variables like religion and comorbid tics may serve as risk factors for certain OCD symptom presentations, as more religious adults may be at greater risk for lower insight and obsessions related to sinning and morality, while adults with comorbid tics are more likely to have more "just not right" intrusive thoughts (Prado et al., 2008; Siev et al., 2010; Inozu et al., 2012).

Substance abuse. A study using Epidemiological Catchment Area (ECA) Program data examined the extent to which OCD would be present among young adults who actively used illicit drugs. Results indicated that individuals engaging in polysubstance abuse are 7.2 times more likely than individuals who do not abuse illicit drugs to develop OCD (Regier et al., 1990). Similarly, Douglass and colleagues (1995) showed that 18-year-olds diagnosed with OCD were significantly more likely to report using psychoactive substances at age 15 than a group of adults who did not abuse substances. Those who used psychoactive substances at 15 were also more likely to develop OCD than a group of adults who were depressed and anxious but did not use psychoactive substances. Additionally, research suggests that the temporal stability of the diagnosis of OCD is higher when alcohol abuse/dependence and OCD coexist in the initial assessment (Nelson & Rice, 1997). As such, proper assessment of substance use is essential in OCD treatment. Importantly, these studies are merely correlational, meaning that the association between OCD and substance use is not necessarily a causal one. There is no evidence that substance abuse leads to OCD or vice versa – merely that one is associated with the other.

Pregnancy. Previous research has shown that all stages of pregnancy (i.e., prenatal, perinatal, and postnatal/postpartum) serve as risk factors for the development of OCD (Russell et al., 2013; Santangelo et al., 1994). Current prevalence rates for OCD during pregnancy range between .3% and 29% and between 1.7% and 9% for the postpartum period. Pregnancy and childbirth have been supported as risk factors for the development of OCD with up to 40% of women diagnosed with OCD reporting symptom onset during the perinatal period (Abramowitz, Schwartz, Moore, & Luenzmann, 2003; Forray, Focseneanu, Pittman, McDougle, & Epperson, 2010) and up to 30% of women report symptom onset during the postpartum period (Labad et al., 2005). Complications of pregnancy and delivery, namely edema and prolonged labor, also serve as risk factors (Vasconcelos et al., 2007).

Trauma and stressful life events. Research has shown a link between stressful and traumatic life events and OCD. In fact, up to 82% of treatment-seeking OCD patients may have experienced at least one trauma during their lives. In that same sample, 39.4% met criteria for comorbid PTSD. The most common types of trauma experienced by OCD patients in this study were related to witnessing violence or life-threatening accidents, both occurring in over 40% of the sample, followed by physical abuse in childhood or adulthood, sexual abuse in childhood, and experiencing a natural disaster, all occurring in more than 20% of the sample (Gershuny et al., 2008). Additionally, general childhood trauma, specifically emotional neglect, was found to occur much higher in women with OCD compared with controls (Lochner et al., 2002). Again, this evidence is merely correlational – despite the history of trauma among many OCD patients, one cannot conclude from the available research that trauma leads to OCD (or vice versa).

Genetic Risk Factors

Research regarding heritability of OCD, specifically twin studies, has shown an increased prevalence of OCD among relatives, and that etiological bases for OCD include genetically mediated phenotypes (Fontenelle & Hasler, 2008; Stewart & Pauls, 2010).

Family history. During the last 30 years, several family studies of patients with OCD have been carried out, with most findings showing a familial aggregation of OCD (Fontenelle & Hasler, 2008). Although the estimates of heritability and familial aggregation have varied across studies, the evidence of existence for such heritability has been consistently empirically supported (Fontenelle & Hasler, 2008; Grados, Walkup, & Walford, 2003). Prevalence of OCD among first-degree relatives of patients with OCD ranged from 1% to 11.7%; while healthy controls varied from 0% to 2.7% (Black, Noyes, Goldstein, & Blum, 1992; Fyer, Lipsitz, Mannuzza, Aronowitz, & Chapman, 2005; Lipsitz et al., 2005; McKeon & Murray, 1987; Nestadt et al., 2000). In more recent research, relatives of adults with OCD were approximately two to six times more likely to develop OCD than controls (Fyer et al., 2005; Lipsitz et al., 2005; Nestadt et al., 2000; Stewart & Pauls, 2010). Twin studies have shown that the concordance rate differences between monozygotic and dizygotic twins serve as an estimate of OCD heritability. A meta-analysis of OCD twin studies and found heritability estimates ranging between 27% and 47% in adults (van Grootheest, Cath, Beekman, & Boomsma, 2005). Interestingly, family history of tics may also predict OCD. Research has revealed that among people with OCD, 6.2% had first-degree relatives with tics compared with 1.7% in controls (Grados et al., 2001).

Genomics. Research conducted to identify potential genes involved in the heritability of OCD, include molecular genetic studies that ascertain regions in the genome that may contain vulnerability genes (Stewart & Pauls, 2010). Results of these studies have yielded genomic regions of interests, but no genomic-wide significant findings (Hanna et al., 2002; Hanna et al., 2007; Shugart et al., 2006). Over the past decade, more than 80 candidate gene studies examining positional candidates or functional candidates in the development and heritability of OCD were conducted (Pauls, 2010; Stewart & Pauls, 2010). Specifically, those genes with serotonin, dopamine, and glutamate pathways, as well as those involved in white matter formation were the focus of the candidate studies. The glutamate transporter gene, SLC1A1 is the only gene that has been consistently identified as a part of the OCD gene across OCD samples

(Stewart & Pauls, 2010). It should be noted that results identifying this gene; however, have not been observed at genome-wide significance levels and as such, future research is necessary.

Summary of Risk Factors for the Development of OCD

Although certain genetic predispositions exist that leave an individual more susceptible to developing OCD, the disorder sometimes develops without clear environmental triggers. Beyond specific causes like pregnancy or trauma that have been linked to the development of OCD, more mundane events may elicit OCD symptoms as well. For instance, contamination obsessions about germs may occur after observing organisms under a microscope in a science class.

Impairment and Quality of Life in OCD

A quintessential feature of OCD is its impairment in daily life. A recent epidemiological study reported that people with chronic OCD experience obsessions for an average of 5.9 hours per day and compulsions for an average of 4.6 hours (Ruscio et al., 2010). With so much of the day taken up by the intrusive symptoms of OCD, it is no wonder that the World Health Organization (WHO) ranks OCD as the tenth most disabling medical condition (Murray & Lopez, 1996). Research has also shown that OCD may be at least as impairing, if not more impairing, than MDD, schizophrenia, and PTSD (Olatunji, Cisler, & Tolin, 2007; Stengler-Wenzke, Kroll, Riedel-Heller, Matschinger, & Angermeyer, 2007). Thus, a full understanding of OCD must examine how impairing the disorder is and how detrimental it is to quality of life (QOL).[1]

Predictors of Impairment

Depression/comorbidity. The WHO considers MDD to be the most disabling medical or mental condition (Murray & Lopez, 1996), so when considering its high comorbidity with OCD, estimated to be as much as 67.2% (Pinto et al., 2006), it is no surprise that depression severity has emerged in many studies as the single most prominent predictor of impairment and lower QOL among people with OCD (e.g., Jacoby, Leonard, Riemann, & Abramowitz, 2014; Rodriguez-Salgado et al., 2006). It is also worth noting that when hoarding was classified as a dimension of OCD, it was consistently reported that presentation of hoarding symptoms was associated with elevated impairment (Fontenelle et al., 2010; Petrusa et al., 2008). While comorbid depression and hoarding are particularly crucial to QOL and impairment in OCD,

[1] While QOL has been defined in the literature as an "individuals' perception of their position in life in the context of the culture and value systems in which they live and in relation to their goals, expectations, standards and concerns" (WHOQOL Group, 1995), functional impairment is defined as more objective measures of daily impairment in occupational, social, or other areas of functioning (APA, 2013a). When taken together, both constructs are important to consider when evaluating how a disorder impacts a person's life. Researchers have attempted to differentiate the two with a number of self-report measures. When referring to QOL or impairment in the following section, each concept will be referenced to consistently with how the authors defined each variable in their respective studies.

any psychiatric comorbidity leaves an individual with OCD more vulnerable to functional impairment in social, occupational, and family life domains, as well as poorer QOL (Huppert, Simpson, Nissenson, Liebowitz, & Foa, 2009).

Symptom severity. Symptom severity is a prominent predictor of OCD-related impairment and an independent influence on certain areas of impairment. For example, OCD symptom severity has been shown to be responsible for occupational, social, and family life disability, even after controlling for depression (Huppert et al., 2009). There is contention among researchers as to whether obsessions or compulsions carry more influence over impairment. While obsessions like worrying that an individual will cause horrendous harm to close family members causes chronic and debilitating anxiety, compulsions like repeated checking or constant praying inhibit a person from doing even simple tasks efficiently. Clearly, both are crucial factors to understanding OCD-related disability and researchers have found support for both being crucial to QOL and overall functioning (Eisen et al., 2006; Huppert et al., 2009; Masellis, Rector, & Richter, 2003; Moritz et al, 2005; Stengler-Wenzke et al., 2007).

Symptom dimension. Evidence suggests that impairment is associated with symptom dimensions of OCD, although this research is only in its preliminary stages. It appears that individuals with contamination symptoms experience the greatest difficulty with functioning in their daily lives (e.g., Huppert et al., 2009, Jacoby et al., 2014; Moritz et al., 2005). Additionally, patients with checking compulsions, as compared with those without checking compulsions, may experience lower QOL in the domains of mental health and role limitation (Moritz et al., 2005). Still, not all studies have found significant differences between dimensions (e.g., Fontenelle et al., 2010); thus, more research is needed to clarify these potential relationships. Whether OCD symptom severity, presentation, or comorbidity are the most profound predictors of impairment is not entirely clear, but overall, the literature suggests that it is important to consider all these factors when evaluating how much OCD affects a person's daily life.

Areas of Impairment

Occupational functioning. One of the most significant areas in which OCD causes impairment is in an individual's work life. Previous studies have observed 22–38% unemployment rates among those with OCD, compared with 6–8% of the general population at the time of writing (Eisen et al., 2006; Koran, Thienemann, & Davenport, 1996; Mancebo et al., 2008). One study found that while 34% of their sample reported inability to work due to psychopathology, only 14% reported receiving disability payments because of OCD, raising questions about financial stability of those with OCD (Eisen et al., 2006). Even worse, unemployment may serve as a risk factor for OCD and may exacerbate OCD symptoms (Fontenelle & Hasler, 2008). Thus, a vicious cycle is initiated when a person with OCD is out of work: worsening symptoms make it more difficult to regain employment, while OCD may have prevented an individual from being able to hold onto work in the first place.

Social functioning. Another way OCD interferes with day-to-day functioning is its impact on social life. Many patients suffer in the process of trying to simultaneously maintain a social life and manage the chronic distress that comes from living with OCD. People with OCD avoid places and situations that may exacerbate or trigger their symptoms, which often come at the cost of engaging in social activities. As noted above, numerous studies have indicated that people with OCD suffer tremendously socially compared with the general population, or even with other mental disorders (e.g., Albert, Maina, Bogetto, Chiarle, & Mataix-Cols, 2010; Huppert et al., 2009). Previous research indicates fewer friendships, more difficulty maintaining friendships, and feelings of being left out relative to the general population (Hollander et al., 1996; Moritz, 2008).

Family functioning. OCD not only affects the quality of life of the sufferer, but everyone around him or her as well. Families often alter their routines, activities, and general way of life to accommodate their family member's disorder (Calvocoressi et al., 1995). This accommodation represents an especially significant issue when considering the disproportionate number of adults with OCD who live with their parents (25% of treatment-seeking adults in one study) (Steketee, Grayson, & Foa, 1985), as caregivers are often needed to help their loved ones cope with OCD. Thus, family members of those with OCD face tremendous burdens, and have been shown to have significantly lower QOL compared with the general population (Stengler-Wenzke et al., 2007).

Patients with OCD also often have trouble finding or maintaining a partner, as approximately 36–58% of adults with OCD are unmarried (Eisen et al, 2006; Rodriguez-Salgado et al., 2006). Even when people with OCD do get married, their marriages often suffer because of their disorder and because of substantial symptom accommodation. Moritz (2008) found that 59.1% of people with OCD endorse tensions in their partnerships, and that 58.1% have sexual problems due to OCD. This latter issue is not surprising when considering the prevalence of sexual obsessions reported in people with OCD, which represents an area of conflict unique to romantic partnerships.

Cognitive functioning. Impairment from OCD extends beyond psychosocial boundaries, and includes cognitive domains as well. Some work has found that memory in those with OCD does not differ from that of healthy controls (e.g., Moritz, Ruhe, Jelinek, & Naber, 2009; Tekcan, Topçuoğlu, & Kaya, 2007), while other studies find that people with OCD do have memory impairment (e.g., Cha et al., 2008; Muller & Roberts, 2005). Similarly, the literature yielded inconsistent results regarding executive functioning deficits, with some work reporting comparable findings (e.g., Abramovitch, Dar, Schweiger, & Hermesh, 2011; Henry, 2006), and other work indicating inferior executive functioning (e.g., Krishna et al., 2011). To resolve this discrepancy, a large meta-analysis of neuropsychological functioning in people with OCD was conducted which found medium to large effect sizes that equated to minimal and clinically nonsignificant neuropsychological deficits among people with OCD (Abramovitch, Abramowitz, & Mittelman, 2013). So, while differences in cognition were present across domains, including attention, executive functioning, memory, visual spatial abilities, processing speed, and working memory, this discrepancy may not indicate a noticeable clinical difference.

Not only does cognitive dysfunction independently contribute to impairment, these deficits may also influence other areas of functioning. Recent research suggests OCD-specific cognitions may influence disability. Kugler and colleagues (2013) found that interference due to symptoms partially mediates the relationship between symptom severity and areas of life impairment, such as emotional health, social functioning, and general health QOL. Increased resistance *against* symptoms mediated the relationship between symptom severity and social functioning. Similarly, Storch, Abramowitz, and Keeley (2009) found that misinterpretation of obsessive thoughts and lower resistance to both obsessions and compulsions is associated with greater functional disability. These studies demonstrated that how an individual confronts and thinks about their symptoms will influence how much the disorder influences QOL and general functioning.

Summary of Impairment and Quality of Life in OCD

Beyond obsessive-compulsive-specific symptoms, how OCD affects a person's life is critical to understanding the disorder. Areas of life that are most impaired, and appropriately targeted in the scientific literature, include social, occupational, family, and cognitive impairments. A variety of factors lead to these deficits beyond symptom severity, including depression severity, symptom presentation, and other life circumstances, and must all be considered when evaluating how well an individual with OCD is doing on a daily basis.

Conclusion

The goal of this chapter is to provide a holistic representation of OCD dimensions and symptomology. With the advent of DSM-5's publication, OCD's classification as an anxiety disorder was changed into its own unique class of disorders, Obsessive-Compulsive and Related Disorders. A shift to a spectrum based approach for assessing patient insight and a tic specifier for OCD diagnosis was included as well. Notably, hoarding is now a distinct disorder.

As with most mental illness, a composite approach for assessing risk factors for OCD onset is needed. Environmental factors have been shown to account for half of individual variation in OCD symptomology. Most explicitly, traumatic life experiences and polysubstance abuse are substantially correlated with the presence of OCD. Additionally, innate risk factors like pregnancy, genetics, and a family history of the disorder are also notable.

Future research is needed to explore cultural differences in OCD symptomology. Research is also needed to assess the interplay between symptom presentation and impairment to improve clinical interventions. OCD's impact on individual quality of life cannot be understated. The WHO ranks OCD as one of the ten most debilitating illnesses. OCD results in a wholesale impairment of a person's life, ranging from cognitive functioning to social and occupational affairs. Comorbidities can have a significant impact on OCD symptom intensity, with greater than 50% of OCD cases bearing a comorbid disorder of some kind. Providing treatments that result in optimal clinical outcomes is essential.

References

Abramovitch, A., Abramowitz, J. S., & Mittelman, A. (2013). The neuropsychology of adult obsessive-compulsive disorder: A meta-analysis. *Clinical Psychology Review, 33*(8), 1163–1171.

Abramovitch, A., Dar, R., Schweiger, A., & Hermesh, H. (2011). Neuropsychological impairments and their association with obsessive-compulsive symptom severity in obsessive-compulsive disorder. *Archives of Clinical Neuropsychology, 26*(4), 364–376.

Abramowitz, J. S., Deacon, B., Olatunji, B., Wheaton, M. G., Berman, N., Losardo, D., Timpano, K., ... Hale, L. (2010). Assessment of obsessive-compulsive symptom dimensions: Development and evaluation of the Dimensional Obsessive-Compulsive Scale. *Psychological Assessment, 22,* 180–198.

Abramowitz, J. S., & Foa, E. B. (1998). Worries and obsessions in individuals with obsessive-compulsive disorder with and without comorbid generalized anxiety disorder. *Behaviour Research and Therapy, 36*(7), 695–700.

Abramowitz, J. S., & Jacoby, R. J. (2015). Obsessive-compulsive and related disorders: A critical review of the new diagnostic class. *Annual review of Clinical Psychology, 11,* 165–186.

Abramowitz, J. S., Schwartz, S. A., Moore, K. M., & Luenzmann, K. R. (2003). Obsessive-compulsive symptoms in pregnancy and the puerperium: A review of the literature. *Journal of Anxiety Disorders, 17*(4), 461–478.

Albert, U., Maina, G., Bogetto, F., Chiarle, A., & Mataix-Cols, D. (2010). Clinical predictors of health-related quality of life in obsessive-compulsive disorder. *Comprehensive Psychiatry, 51*(2), 193–200.

Alonso, P., Segalas, C., Real, E., Pertusa, A., Labad, J., Jiménez-Murcia, S., ... & Menchón, J. M. (2010). Suicide in patients treated for obsessive-compulsive disorder: A prospective follow-up study. *Journal of Affective Disorders, 124*(3), 300–308.

American Psychiatric Association. (2000). *Diagnostic and Statistical Manual of Mental Disorders* (4th ed., text rev.). Arlington, VA: American Psychiatric Publishing.

American Psychiatric Association. (2013a). *Diagnostic and Statistical Manual of Mental Disorders* (5th ed.). Arlington, VA: American Psychiatric Publishing.

American Psychiatric Association. (2013b). Highlights of Changes from DSM-IV-TR to DSM-5. Retrieved from http://www.dsm5.org/Documents/changes%20from%20dsm-iv-tr%20to%20dsm-5.pdf.

Amerio, A., Odone, A., Liapis, C. C., & Ghaemi, S. N. (2014). Diagnostic validity of comorbid bipolar disorder and obsessive–compulsive disorder: A systematic review. *Acta Psychiatrica Scandinavica, 129*(5), 343–358.

Anholt, G. E., Cath, D. C., van Oppen, P., Eikelenboom, M., Smit, J. H., van Megen, H., & van Balkom, A. J. (2010). Autism and ADHD symptoms in patients with OCD: Are they associated with specific OC symptom dimensions or OC symptom severity? *Journal of Autism and Developmental Disorders, 40*(5), 580–589.

Balci, V., & Sevincok, L. (2010). Suicidal ideation in patients with obsessive-compulsive disorder. *Psychiatry Research, 175*(1), 104–108.

Black, D. W., Noyes, Jr., R., Goldstein, R. B., & Blum, N. (1992). A family study of obsessive-compulsive disorder. *Archives of General Psychiatry, 49*(5), 362.

Bloch, M., Landeros-Weisenberger, A., Rosário, M., Pittenger, C., & Leckman, J. (2008). Meta-analysis of the symptom structure of obsessive-compulsive disorder. *American Journal of Psychiatry, 165*(12), 1532–1542.

Brown, T. A., & Barlow, D. H. (2005). Dimensional versus categorical classification of mental disorders in the fifth edition of the Diagnostic and Statistical Manual of Mental Disorders and beyond: Comment on the special section. *Journal of Abnormal Psychology, 114*(4), 551.

Brown, T. A., & Barlow, D. H. (2009). A proposal for a dimensional classification system based on the shared features of the DSM-IV anxiety and mood disorders: Implications for assessment and treatment. *Psychological Assessment, 21*(3), 256.

Castle, D. J., Deale, A., & Marks, I. M. (1995). Gender differences in obsessive compulsive disorder. *Australian and New Zealand Journal of Psychiatry, 29*(1), 114–117.

Calvocoressi, L., Lewis, B., Harris, M., Trufan, S. J., Goodman, W. K., McDougle, C. J., & Price, L. H. (1995). Family accommodation in obsessive-compulsive disorder. *American Journal of Psychiatry, 152*(3), 441–443.

Cha, K. R., Koo, M. S., Kim, C. H., Kim, J. W., Oh, W. J., Suh, H. S., & Lee, H. S. (2008). Nonverbal memory dysfunction in obsessive-compulsive disorder patients with checking compulsions. *Depression and Anxiety, 25*(11), E115–E120.

Cherian, A. V., Narayanaswamy, J. C., Viswanath, B., Guru, N., George, C. M., Bada Math, S., ... & Janardhan Reddy, Y. C. (2014). Gender differences in obsessive-compulsive disorder: Findings from a large Indian sample. *Asian Journal of Psychiatry, 9*, 17–21.

Clark, D. A., & Inozu, M. (2014). Unwanted intrusive thoughts: Cultural, contextual, covariational, and characterological determinants of diversity. *Journal of Obsessive-Compulsive and Related Disorders, 3*(2), 195–204.

Coles, M. E., Pinto, A., Mancebo, M. C., Rasmussen, S. A., & Eisen, J. L. (2008). OCD with comorbid OCPD: A subtype of OCD? *Journal of Psychiatric Research, 42*(4), 289–296.

Coles, M. E., Schofield, C. A., & Pietrefesa, A. S. (2006). Behavioral inhibition and obsessive-compulsive disorder. *Journal of anxiety disorders, 20*(8), 1118–1132.

Diniz, J. B., Rosário-Campos, M. C., Hounie, A. G., Curi, M., Shavitt, R. G., Lopes, A. C., & Miguel, E. C. (2006). Chronic tics and Tourette syndrome in patients with obsessive-compulsive disorder. *Journal of Psychiatric Research, 40*(6), 487–493.

Douglass, H. M., Moffitt, T. E., Dar, R., McGee, R. O. B., & Silva, P. (1995). Obsessive-compulsive disorder in a birth cohort of 18-year-olds: Prevalence and predictors. *Journal of the American Academy of Child & Adolescent Psychiatry, 34*(11), 1424–1431.

Eisen, J. L., Mancebo, M. A., Pinto, A., Coles, M. E., Pagano, M. E., Stout, R., & Rasmussen, S. A. (2006). Impact of obsessive-compulsive disorder on quality of life. *Comprehensive Psychiatry, 47*(4), 270–275.

Farrell, L., Barrett, P., & Piacentini, J. (2006). Obsessive-compulsive disorder across the developmental trajectory: Clinical correlates in children, adolescents and adults. *Behaviour Change, 23*(02), 103–120.

Fontenelle, I. S., Fontenelle, L. F., Borges, M. C., Prazeres, A. M., Rangé, B. P., Mendlowicz, M. V., & Versiani, M. (2010). Quality of life and symptom dimensions of patients with obsessive-compulsive disorder. *Psychiatry Research, 179*(2), 198–203.

Fontenelle, L. F., & Hasler, G. (2008). The analytical epidemiology of obsessive-compulsive disorder: Risk factors and correlates. *Progress in Neuro-Psychopharmacology and Biological Psychiatry, 32*(1), 1–15.

Fontenelle, L. F., Mendlowicz, M. V., Marques, C., & Versiani, M. (2004). Trans-cultural aspects of obsessive-compulsive disorder: A description of a Brazilian sample and a systematic review of international clinical studies. *Journal of Psychiatric Research, 38*(4), 403–411.

Forray, A., Focseneanu, M., Pittman, B., McDougle, C. J., & Epperson, C. N. (2010). Onset and exacerbation of obsessive-compulsive disorder in pregnancy and the postpartum period. *Journal of Clinical Psychiatry, 71*(8), 1061–1068.

Fyer, A. J., Lipsitz, J. D., Mannuzza, S., Aronowitz, B., & Chapman, T. F. (2005). A direct interview family study of obsessive-compulsive disorder. I. *Psychological Medicine, 35*(11), 1611–1622.

Garyfallos, G., Katsigiannopoulos, K., Adamopoulou, A., Papazisis, G., Karastergiou, A., & Bozikas, V. P. (2010). Comorbidity of obsessive-compulsive disorder with obsessive–compulsive personality disorder: Does it imply a specific subtype of obsessive-compulsive disorder? *Psychiatry Research, 177*(1), 156–160.

Gershuny, B. S., Baer, L., Jenike, M. A., Minichiello, W. E., & Wilhelm, S. (2002). Comorbid posttraumatic stress disorder: impact on treatment outcome for obsessive-compulsive disorder. *American Journal of Psychiatry, 159*(5), 852–854.

Gershuny, B. S., Baer, L., Parker, H., Gentes, E. L., Infield, A. L., & Jenike, M. A. (2008). Trauma and posttraumatic stress disorder in treatment-resistant obsessive-compulsive disorder. *Depression and Anxiety, 25*(1), 69–71.

Goodman, W. K., Naylor, S. T., & Volkmar, F. R. (1995). A case-controlled study of repetitive thoughts and behavior in adults with autistic disorder and obsessive-compulsive disorder. *American Journal of Psychiatry, 152*, 5.

Goodman, W. K., Price, L. H., Rasmussen, S. A., Mazure, C., Fleischmann, R. L., Hill, C. L., … & Charney, D. S. (1989). The Yale–Brown obsessive compulsive scale: I. Development, use, and reliability. *Archives of General Psychiatry, 46*(11), 1006–1011.

Grados, M. A., Riddle, M. A., Samuels, J. F., Liang, K. Y., Hoehn-Saric, R., Bienvenu, O. J., … & Nestadt, G. (2001). The familial phenotype of obsessive-compulsive disorder in relation to tic disorders: The Hopkins OCD family study. *Biological Psychiatry, 50*(8), 559–565.

Grados, M. A., Walkup, J., & Walford, S. (2003). Genetics of obsessive-compulsive disorders: New findings and challenges. *Brain and Development, 25*, S55–S61.

Grisham, J. R., Fullana, M. A., Mataix-Cols, D., Moffitt, T. E., Caspi, A., & Poulton, R. (2011). Risk factors prospectively associated with adult obsessive-compulsive symptom dimensions and obsessive-compulsive disorder. *Psychological Medicine, 41*(12), 2495–2506.

Halmi, K. A., Sunday, S. R., Klump, K. L., Strober, M., Leckman, J. F., Fichter, M., … & Kaye, W. H. (2003). Obsessions and compulsions in anorexia nervosa subtypes. *International Journal of Eating Disorders, 33*(3), 308–319.

Hanna, G. L., Veenstra-VanderWeele, J., Cox, N. J., Boehnke, M., Himle, J. A., Curtis, G. C., … & Cook, E. H. (2002). Genome-wide linkage analysis of families with obsessive-compulsive disorder ascertained through pediatric probands. *American Journal of Medical Genetics, 114*(5), 541–552.

Hanna, G. L., Veenstra-VanderWeele, J., Cox, N. J., Van Etten, M., Fischer, D. J., Himle, J. A., … & Cook, Jr., E. H. (2007). Evidence for a susceptibility locus on chromosome 10p15 in early-onset obsessive-compulsive disorder. *Biological Psychiatry, 62*(8), 856–862.

Hasler, G., LaSalle-Ricci, V. H., Ronquillo, J. G., Crawley, S. A., Cochran, L. W., Kazuba, D., … & Murphy, D. L. (2005). Obsessive-compulsive disorder symptom dimensions show specific relationships to psychiatric comorbidity. *Psychiatry Research, 135*(2), 121–132.

Henry, J. (2006). A meta-analytic review of Wisconsin Card Sorting Test and verbal fluency performance in obsessive-compulsive disorder. *Cognitive Neuropsychiatry, 11*(2), 156–176.

Hollander, E., Braun, A., & Simeon, D. (2008). Should OCD leave the anxiety disorders in DSM-V? The case for obsessive compulsive-related disorders. *Depression and Anxiety, 25*(4), 317–329.

Hollander, E., Kwon, J. H., Stein, D. J., & Broatch, J. (1996). Obsessive-compulsive and spectrum disorders: Overview and quality of life issues. *Journal of Clinical Psychiatry, 57*, Suppl 8, 3–6.

Horwath, E., & Weissman, M. M. (2000). The epidemiology and cross-national presentation of obsessive-compulsive disorder. *Psychiatric Clinics of North America, 23*(3), 493–507.

Huppert, J. D., Simpson, H. B., Nissenson, K. J., Liebowitz, M. R., & Foa, E. B. (2009). Quality of life and functional impairment in obsessive-compulsive disorder: A comparison of patients with and without comorbidity, patients in remission, and healthy controls. *Depression and Anxiety, 26*(1), 39–45.

Inozu, M., Karanci, A. N., & Clark, D. A. (2012). Why are religious individuals more obsessional? The role of mental control beliefs and guilt in Muslims and Christians. *Journal of Behavior Therapy and Experimental Psychiatry, 43*(3), 959–966.

Ivarsson, T., & Melin, K. (2008). Autism spectrum traits in children and adolescents with obsessive-compulsive disorder (OCD). *Journal of Anxiety Disorders, 22*(6), 969–978.

Jacoby, R. J., Leonard, R. C., Riemann, B. C., & Abramowitz, J. S. (2014). Predictors of quality of life and functional impairment in obsessive-compulsive Disorder. *Comprehensive Psychiatry, 55*(5), 1195–1202.

Kessler, R. C., Petukhova, M., Sampson, N. A., Zaslavsky, A. M., & Wittchen, H. U. (2012). Twelve-month and lifetime prevalence and lifetime morbid risk of anxiety and mood disorders in the United States. *International Journal of Methods in Psychiatric Research, 21*(3), 169–184.

Koran, L. M., Thienemann, M. L., & Davenport, R. (1996). Quality of life for patients with obsessive-compulsive disorder. *American Journal of Psychiatry, 153*(6), 784–788.

Krishna, R., Udupa, S., George, C. M., Kumar, K. J., Viswanath, B., Kandavel, T., ... & Reddy, Y. C. (2011). Neuropsychological performance in OCD: A study in medication-naïve patients. *Progress in Neuro-Psychopharmacology and Biological Psychiatry, 35*(8), 1969–1976.

Kugler, B. B., Lewin, A. B., Phares, V., Geffken, G. R., Murphy, T. K., & Storch, E. A. (2013). Quality of life in obsessive-compulsive disorder: The role of mediating variables. *Psychiatry Research, 206*(1), 43–49.

Labad, J., Menchón, J. M., Alonso, P., Segalàs, C., Jimenez, S., & Vallejo, J. (2005). Female reproductive cycle and obsessive-compulsive disorder. *Journal of Clinical Psychiatry, 66*(4), 428–35.

Lafleur, D. L., Petty, C., Mancuso, E., McCarthy, K., Biederman, J., Faro, A., ... & Geller, D. A. (2011). Traumatic events and obsessive compulsive disorder in children and adolescents: Is there a link? *Journal of Anxiety Disorders, 25*(4), 513–519.

LaSalle, V. H., Cromer, K. R., Nelson, K. N., Kazuba, D., Justement, L., & Murphy, D. L. (2004). Diagnostic interview assessed neuropsychiatric disorder comorbidity in 334 individuals with obsessive-compulsive disorder. *Depression and Anxiety, 19*(3), 163–173.

Leckman, J. F., Grice, D. E. Boardman, J., Zhang, H., Vitale, A., Bondi, C., Alsobrook, J., ... Pauls, D. L. (1997). *American Journal of Psychiatry, 154,* 911–917.

Lipsitz, J. D., Mannuzza, S., Chapman, T. F., Foa, E. B., Franklin, M. E., Goodwin, R. D., & Fyer, A. J. (2005). A direct interview family study of obsessive-compulsive disorder. II. Contribution of proband informant information. *Psychological Medicine, 35*(11), 1623–1632.

Lochner, C., du Toit, P. L., Zungu-Dirwayi, N., Marais, A., van Kradenburg, J., Seedat, S., ... & Stein, D. J. (2002). Childhood trauma in obsessive-compulsive disorder, trichotillomania, and controls. *Depression and Anxiety, 15*(2), 66–68.

Lovato, L., Ferrão, Y. A., Stein, D. J., Shavitt, R. G., Fontenelle, L. F., Vivan, A., ... & Cordioli, A. V. (2012). Skin picking and trichotillomania in adults with obsessive-compulsive disorder. *Comprehensive Psychiatry, 53*(5), 562–568.

Mancebo, M. C., Greenberg, B., Grant, J. E., Pinto, A., Eisen, J. L., Dyck, I., & Rasmussen, S. A. (2008). Correlates of occupational disability in a clinical sample of obsessive-compulsive disorder. *Comprehensive Psychiatry, 49*(1), 43–50.

Masellis, M., Rector, N. A., & Richter, M. A. (2003). Quality of life in OCD: Differential impact of obsessions, compulsions, and depression comorbidity. *Canadian Journal of Psychiatry, 48*(2), 72–77.

Mataix-Cols, D., do Rosário-Campos, M. C., & Leckman, J. F. (2005). A multidimensional model of obsessive-compulsive disorder. *American Journal of Psychiatry, 162*(2), 228–238.

Mataix-Cols, D., Frost, R. O., Pertusa, A., Clark, L. A., Saxena, S., Leckman, J. F., ... & Wilhelm, S. (2010). Hoarding disorder: A new diagnosis for DSM-V? *Depression and Anxiety, 27*(6), 556–572.

Matsunaga, H., Kiriike, N., Miyata, A., Iwasaki, Y., Matsui, T., Fujimoto, K., ... & Kaye, W. H. (1999). Prevalence and symptomatology of comorbid obsessive-compulsive disorder among bulimic patients. *Psychiatry and Clinical Neurosciences, 53*(6), 661–666.

McKeon, P., & Murray, R. (1987). Familial aspects of obsessive-compulsive neurosis. *British Journal of Psychiatry, 151*(4), 528–534.

Miyazaki, M., Yoshino, A., & Nomura, S. (2011). Relationships between anxiety severity, diagnosis of multiple anxiety disorders, and comorbid major depressive disorder. *Asian Journal of Psychiatry, 4*(4), 293–296.

Moritz, S. (2008). A review on quality of life and depression in obsessive-compulsive disorder. *CNS Spectrum, 13*(14), 16–22.

Moritz, S., Rufer, M., Fricke, S., Karow, A., Morfeld, M., Jelinek, L., & Jacobsen, D. (2005). Quality of life in obsessive-compulsive disorder before and after treatment. *Comprehensive Psychiatry, 46*(6), 453–459.

Moritz, S., Ruhe, C., Jelinek, L., & Naber, D. (2009). No deficits in nonverbal memory, metamemory and internal as well as external source memory in obsessive-compulsive disorder (OCD). *Behaviour Research and Therapy*, *47*(4), 308–315.

Moulding, R., Coles, M. E., Abramowitz, J. S., Alcolado, G. M., Alonso, P., Belloch, A., ... & Wong, W. (2014). Part 2. They scare because we care: The relationship between obsessive intrusive thoughts and appraisals and control strategies across 15 cities. *Journal of Obsessive-Compulsive and Related Disorders*, *3*(3), 280–291.

Muller, J., & Roberts, J. E. (2005). Memory and attention in obsessive-compulsive disorder: A review. *Journal of Anxiety Disorders*, *19*(1), 1–28.

Murray, C. J., & Lopez, A. D. (1996). *Global burden of disease* (Vol. *1*). Boston, MA: Harvard University Press.

Nelson, E., & Rice, J. (1997). Stability of diagnosis of obsessive-compulsive disorder in the Epidemiologic Catchment Area study. *American Journal of Psychiatry*, *154*(6), 826–831.

Nestadt, G., Di, C. Z., Riddle, M. A., Grados, M. A., Greenberg, B. D., Fyer, A. J., ... & Roche, K. B. (2009). Obsessive-compulsive disorder: Subclassification based on co-morbidity. *Psychological Medicine*, *39*(9), 1491–1501.

Nestadt, G., Samuels, J., Riddle, M., Bienvenu, O. J., Liang, K. Y., LaBuda, M., ... & Hoehn-Saric, R. (2000). A family study of obsessive-compulsive disorder. *Archives of General Psychiatry*, *57*(4), 358–363.

Nota, J. A., Blakey, S. M., George-Denn, D. A., Jacoby, R. J., Schubert, J. R., Abramowitz, J. S., & Coles, M. E. (2014). The experience of OCD-related intrusive thoughts in African and European Americans: Testing the generalizability of cognitive models of obsessive compulsive disorder. *Journal of Obsessive-Compulsive and Related Disorders*, *3*(2), 115–123.

Obsessive Compulsive Cognitions Working Group. (1997). Cognitive assessment of obsessive-compulsive disorder. *Behaviour Research and Therapy*, *35*(7), 667–681.

Olatunji, B. O., Cisler, J. M., & Tolin, D. F. (2007). Quality of life in the anxiety disorders: a meta-analytic review. *Clinical Psychology Review*, *27*(5), 572–581.

Pauls, D. L. (2010). The genetics of obsessive-compulsive disorder: A review. *Dialogues in Clinical Neuroscience*, *12*(2), 149.

Petrusa, A., Fullana, M., Singh, S., Alonso, P., Menchón, J., & Mataix-Cols, D. (2008). Compulsive hoarding: OCD symptom, distinct clinical syndrome, or both? *American Journal of Psychiatry*, *165*(10), 1289–1298.

Phillips, K. A., Gunderson, C. G., Mallya, G., McElroy, S. L., & Carter, W. (1998). A comparison study of body dysmorphic disorder and obsessive-compulsive disorder. *Journal of Clinical Psychiatry*, *59*(11), 568–575.

Phillips, K. A., Pinto, A., Menard, W., Eisen, J. L., Mancebo, M., & Rasmussen, S. A. (2007). Obsessive-compulsive disorder versus body dysmorphic disorder: A comparison study of two possibly related disorders. *Depression and Anxiety*, *24*(6), 399–409.

Phillips, K. A., Stein, D. J., Rauch, S. L., Hollander, E., Fallon, B. A., Barsky, A., ... & Leckman, J. (2010). Should an obsessive-compulsive spectrum grouping of disorders be included in DSM-V? *Depression and Anxiety*, *27*(6), 528–555.

Pinto, A., Mancebo, M. C., Eisen, J. L., Pagano, M. E., & Rasmussen, S. A. (2006). The Brown Longitudinal Obsessive Compulsive Study: Clinical features and symptoms of the sample at intake. *Journal of Clinical Psychiatry*, *67*(5), 703–711.

Poyurovsky, M., & Koran, L. M. (2005). Obsessive-compulsive disorder (OCD) with schizotypy vs. schizophrenia with OCD: diagnostic dilemmas and therapeutic implications. *Journal of Psychiatric Research*, *39*(4), 399–408.

Prado, H. D. S., Rosário, M. C., Lee, J., Hounie, A. G., Shavitt, R. G., & Miguel, E. C. (2008). Sensory phenomena in obsessive-compulsive disorder and tic disorders: A review of the literature. *CNS Spectrums*, *13*(5), 425–432.

Quarantini, L. C., Torres, A. R., Sampaio, A. S., Fossaluza, V., Mathis, M. A. D., do Rosário, M. C., ... & Koenen, K. C. (2011). Comorbid major depression in obsessive-compulsive disorder patients. *Comprehensive Psychiatry*, *52*(4), 386–393.

Regier, D. A., Farmer, M. D., Rae, D. S., Ocke, B. A., Keith, S. J., Judd, L. L., & Goodwin, F. K. (1990). Comorbidity of mental disorders with alcohol and other drug abuse: Results from the Epidemiological Catchment Area Study. *Journal of the American Medical Association, 264*(19), 2511–2518.

Rodriguez-Salgado, B., Dolengevich-Segal, H., Arrojo-Romero, M., Castelli-Candia, P., Navio-Acosta, M., Perez-Rodriguez, M., Saiz-Ruiz, J., & Baca-Garcia, E. (2006). Perceived quality of life in obsessive-compulsive disorder: Related factors. *BMC Psychiatry, 6*(1), 20.

Rufer, M., Grothusen, A., Mass, R., Peter, H., & Hand, I. (2005). Temporal stability of symptom dimensions in adult patients with obsessive-compulsive disorder. *Journal of Affective Disorders, 88*(1), 99–102.

Ruscio, A. M., Stein, D. J., Chiu, W. T., & Kessler, R. C. (2010). The epidemiology of obsessive-compulsive disorder in the National Comorbidity Survey Replication. *Molecular Psychiatry, 15*(1), 53–63.

Russell, E. J., Fawcett, J. M., & Mazmanian, D. (2013). Risk of obsessive-compulsive disorder in pregnant and postpartum women: A meta-analysis. *Journal of Clinical Psychiatry, 74*(4), 377–385.

Samuels, J. F. (2009). Recent advances in the genetics of obsessive-compulsive disorder. *Current Psychiatry Reports, 11*(4), 277–282.

Santangelo, S. L., Pauls, D. L., Goldstein, J. M., Faraone, S. V., Tsuang, M. T., & Leckman, J. F. (1994). Tourette's syndrome: What are the influences of gender and comorbid obsessive-compulsive disorder? *Journal of the American Academy of Child & Adolescent Psychiatry, 33*(6), 795–804.

Shugart, Y. Y., Samuels, J., Willour, V. L., Grados, M. A., Greenberg, B. D., Knowles, J. A., ... & Nestadt, G. (2006). Genomewide linkage scan for obsessive-compulsive disorder: Evidence for susceptibility loci on chromosomes 3q, 7p, 1q, 15q, and 6q. *Molecular Psychiatry, 11*(8), 763–770.

Siev, J., Chambless, D. L., & Huppert, J. D. (2010). Moral thought–action fusion and OCD symptoms: The moderating role of religious affiliation. *Journal of Anxiety Disorders, 24*(3), 309–312.

Simeon, D., Hollander, E., Stein, D. J., Cohen, L., & Aronowitz, B. (1995). Body dysmorphic disorder in the DSM-IV field trial for obsessive-compulsive disorder. *American Journal of Psychiatry, 152*(8), 1207–1209.

Steketee, G. S., Grayson, J. B., & Foa, E. B. (1985). Obsessive-compulsive disorder: Differences between washers and checkers. *Behaviour Research and Therapy, 23*(2), 197–201.

Steketee, G., Henninger, N. J., & Pollard, C. A. (2000). Predicting treatment outcomes for obsessive-compulsive disorder: Effects of comorbidity. In W. K. Goodman, M. V. Rudorfer, & J. D. Maser (Eds.), *Obsessive-Compulsive Disorder: Contemporary issues in treatment* (pp. 257–276). Mahwah, NJ: Lawrence Erlbaum.

Stengler-Wenzke, K., Kroll, M., Riedel-Heller, S., Matschinger, H., & Angermeyer, M. C. (2007). Quality of life in obsessive-compulsive disorder: The different impact of obsessions and compulsions. *Psychopathology, 40*(5), 282–289.

Stewart, S. E., & Pauls, D. L. (2010). The genetics of obsessive-compulsive disorder. *FOCUS: The Journal of Lifelong Learning in Psychiatry, 8*(3), 350–357.

Storch, E. A., Abramowitz, J. S., & Goodman, W. K. (2008). Does obsessive-compulsive disorder belong among the anxiety disorders in DSM-V? *Depression and Anxiety, 25,* 326–347.

Storch, E. A., Abramowitz, J. S., Keeley, M. (2009). Correlates and mediators of functional disability in obsessive-compulsive disorder. *Depression and Anxiety, 26*(9), 806–813.

Subramaniam, M., Abdin, E., Vaingankar, J. A., & Chong, S. A. (2012). Obsessive-compulsive disorder: Prevalence, correlates, help-seeking and quality of life in a multiracial Asian population. *Social Psychiatry and Psychiatric Epidemiology, 47*(12), 2035–2043.

Tekcan, A. İ., Topçuoğlu, V., & Kaya, B. (2007). Memory and metamemory for semantic information in obsessive-compulsive disorder. *Behaviour Research and Therapy, 45*(9), 2164–2172.

Timpano, K. R., Rubenstein, L. M., & Murphy, D. L. (2012). Phenomenological features and clinical impact of affective disorders in OCD: A focus on the bipolar disorder and OCD connection. *Depression and Anxiety, 29*(3), 226–233.

Torres, A., Prince, M., Bebbington, P., Bhugra, D., Brugha, T., Farrell, M., ... & Singleton, N. (2006). Obsessive-compulsive disorder: Prevalence, comorbidity, impact, and help-seeking in the British National Psychiatric Morbidity Survey of 2000. *American Journal of Psychiatry, 163*(11), 1978–1985.

van Grootheest, D. S., Cath, D. C., Beekman, A. T., & Boomsma, D. I. (2005). Twin studies on obsessive-compulsive disorder: A review. *Twin Research and Human Genetics, 8*(05), 450–458.

Vasconcelos, M. S., Sampaio, A. S., Hounie, A. G., Akkerman, F., Curi, M., Lopes, A. C., & Miguel, E. C. (2007). Prenatal, perinatal, and postnatal risk factors in obsessive-compulsive disorder. *Biological Psychiatry, 61*(3), 301–307.

Wheaton, M. G., Berman, N. C., Fabricant, L. E., & Abramowitz, J. S. (2013). Differences in obsessive-compulsive symptoms and obsessive beliefs: A comparison between African Americans, Latino Americans, and European Americans. *Cognitive Behavior Therapy, 42*(1), 9–20.

Yorulmaz, O., Gençöz, T., & Woody, S. (2009). OCD cognitions and symptoms in different religious contexts. *Journal of Anxiety Disorders, 23*(3), 401–406.

Zohar, A. H. (1999). The epidemiology of obsessive-compulsive disorder in children and adolescents. *Child and Adolescent Psychiatric Clinics of North America, 8*, 445–460.

3

Description and Prevalence of OCD in the Elderly

Mary E. Dozier and Catherine R. Ayers

Obsessive-compulsive disorder (OCD) is characterized by recurrent unwanted thoughts (i.e., obsessions) and consequent repetitive behaviors (i.e., compulsions) (American Psychiatric Association, 2013). Compulsions can be physical, such as checking behaviors, or mental, such as silent counting. The compulsions are performed to reduce the anxiety generated by the obsessions, whereas the compulsions are typically either excessive in nature (e.g., checking the locks on the same door three times) or not causally related to the obsession (e.g., thinking of the number four in response to "sinful" thoughts) (American Psychiatric Association, 2013). In older adults, individuals may have suffered from symptoms for many decades or experience a sudden onset late in life. The causes and prevalence of chronic and late-onset OCD may be different in older adults, as well as intervention strategies. Unfortunately, little research has been empirically examined with respect to the treatment of late-life OCD and so any synopsis of OCD in the elderly must rely on case studies, understanding of OCD in midlife, and typical accommodations for working with older adults with mental illness.

Prevalence of OCD in the Elderly

A common problem among clinicians is the overestimation of base rates due to clinician specialization. For example, a clinician who specializes in OCD may disproportionately assume that patients presenting with similar symptoms may have OCD when other explanatory factors may better account for the presenting problems. This may be particularly relevant for older adults as prevalence estimates are relatively low compared with other mental health disorders (Flint, 1994; Kessler et al., 2005). Lifetime prevalence rates for OCD are estimated to range up to 2.3% for individuals aged 33–44 years, but the prevalence rate of OCD in older adults is considerably lower, with only 0.7% of adults ages 60 and over estimated to meet DSM-IV criteria for OCD (Kessler et al., 2005). Clinicians need to be aware of the actual base rates of late-life OCD in order to prevent misdiagnosis.

The Wiley Handbook of Obsessive Compulsive Disorders, Volume I, First Edition.
Edited by Jonathan S. Abramowitz, Dean McKay, and Eric A. Storch.
© 2017 John Wiley & Sons Ltd. Published 2017 by John Wiley & Sons Ltd.

Other studies of the prevalence rates of OCD across the lifespan have found higher levels of prevalence in older adults than was reported by Kessler and colleagues (2005), with multiple studies reporting prevalence rates of OCD in up to 1.5% of community-dwelling older adults (aged 65+) (Blazer, George, & Hughes, 1991; Kolada, Bland, & Newman, 1994; Grenier, Préville, Boyer, & O'Conner, 2009). However, such estimates are still much lower than estimates of the prevalence of mood and anxiety disorders in late life, including major depressive disorder (10.6%) and generalized anxiety disorder (3.6%) (Kessler et al., 2005). The projected lifetime prevalence of OCD (1.9%) is also considerably lower than for major depressive disorder (23.2%) or generalized anxiety disorder (8.3%), with agoraphobia without panic being the only DSM-IV diagnosis to have a lower lifetime risk (1.6%) (Kessler et al., 2005).

The prevalence of OCD in older adults may also depend on the living situation of the individual. Flint (1994) reported drastically larger estimates of the prevalence of OCD for older adults living in institutions (3.5%). This would suggest that clinicians working in nursing homes or other assisted living facilities should be aware of any biases toward *under*estimating the base rates of OCD in their population as the prevalence of late-life OCD in such institutions may be higher than the incidence in community-dwelling middle-aged adults. Although there has been little investigation of the characterization of OCD in institutionalized older adults, possible reasons for the increased prevalence of late-life OCD in nursing homes and assisted living facilities include the interaction of impairment due to normal aging and the impairment caused by OCD symptoms, which could result in an increased need for assistance with both instrumental activities of daily living (e.g., cooking, driving, managing medications) as well as activities of daily living (e.g., bathing, dressing, eating).

The estimates of prevalence of OCD in late life do not include individuals who may experience significant impairment as a result of OCD-related symptoms but do not meet DSM criteria for diagnosis. There is some evidence that older adults report increased anxiety symptoms despite the lower prevalence of anxiety diagnoses (Himmelfaub & Murrell, 1984), and such a phenomenon may also be true for older adults with obsessive-compulsive and related disorders. Older adults may also be less likely than younger adults to endorse their true levels of symptom severity and may underreport their impairment (Gurian & Minor, 1991). There is also evidence to suggest that older adults may be less capable of identifying mental health symptoms (Wetherell et al., 2009).

Finally, it should be noted that these estimates were not made using criteria from the current edition of the *Diagnostic and Statistical Manual of Mental Health Disorders* (DSM-5) (American Psychiatric Association, 2013). Unlike the DSM-IV-TR, the DSM-5 does not require that individuals acknowledge that their obsessions emerged from within themselves and not as a result of external causes (American Psychiatric Association, 2000; 2013). In the DSM-IV-TR, patients were required to have acknowledged that that the obsessions or compulsions were "excessive or unreasonable" at some point in the course of their symptoms, even if they had poor insight during the current episode. Because the criteria for OCD has been made less stringent, it is also possible that the base rates of OCD in older adults may now increase, as well as the base rates of OCD comorbidity with psychotic disorders such as schizophrenia. Clinicians who frequently encounter patients potentially meeting the criteria for late-life OCD should stay abreast of emerging publications about the prevalence of OCD diagnoses using the DSM-5 criteria – with and without comorbid psychotic disorders – in order to prevent their own biases from unduly influencing their diagnoses in older adults.

Late-Onset OCD

While the majority of older adults have a chronic course of OCD (Fineberg et al., 2013), it is possible for OCD to develop later in life. Late onset of OCD is typically defined as onset at or after the age of 40 (Frydman et al., 2014). Estimates of the prevalence of late-onset OCD vary widely. Frydman and colleagues (2014) estimated that 8.6% of cases of older adults with OCD had onset at or after the age of 40, while Weiss and Jenike (2000) speculated that onset after the age of 50 would have a much lower prevalence. In contrast, Grenier and colleagues (2009) reported onset of OCD symptoms after the age of 60 in 17.6% of community-dwelling older adults. Unfortunately, there is a dearth of data on the prevalence and presentation of the onset in the later decades of older adulthood (e.g., 70s and 80s), although there is some anecdotal evidence to suggest that within the OCD patient population the prevalence of onset after age 50 may be as low as .5% (Weiss & Jenike, 2000). The varying estimates of late-onset OCD may be do to different sampling methodologies as well as sample populations, and ultimately illustrate the need for further research into late-onset OCD, and, in particular, late-onset OCD in older adults.

Despite the lack of evidence of the patient characteristics that might predispose individuals to develop late-onset OCD, several predictive factors have some come to light. A major predictor of late-onset OCD is gender: women have a much higher incident of late-onset OCD than do men (Frydman et al., 2014). Other predictors of late-onset OCD include ten or more years of subclinical obsessive-compulsive symptoms (such as mild obsessions or compulsions), diagnosis of PTSD after age 40, and recent pregnancy (in females) or recent pregnancy of significant other (in males) (Frydman et al., 2014). These predictors are not necessarily present in all cases of late-onset OCD, but clinicians can benefit from consideration of such factors in determining their differential diagnosis.

Individuals with late-onset OCD may present with impaired memory deficits beyond what is expected due to normal aging; however, there is also some evidence that late-onset OCD is not associated with greater impairment in executive functioning (Hwang et al., 2007). A case study of four older adults with late-onset OCD reported that the individuals had impairments in neuropsychological tasks requiring verbal fluency and visuo-spatial skills, but no global intellectual impairment (Philpot & Banerjee, 1998). An additional case study of five older adults (aged 56–75) with late-onset OCD suggested that symptoms were most likely associated with the onset of specific cerebral lesions (Weiss & Jenike, 2000). The authors found the association to be particularly compelling since the five patients profiled in their article were the only examples of onset of OCD in late life they could identify out of a sample of OCD patients numbering over 1,000 (Weiss & Jenike, 2000), suggesting that, although not an ideal sample size, the five cases described might still be representative of late-onset cases of OCD. Neuroimaging case studies suggest that late-onset OCD may be linked specifically to a lack of serotonin, most likely caused by cerebral lesions in the caudate nuclei of the basal ganglia (Cottraux & Gerard, 1998). Unfortunately, case studies do not provide firm evidence, especially since there are also cases in which older adults developed OCD in late life without any cerebral abnormalities (Bhattacharyya & Khanna, 2004).

There may also be a more cognition-driven reason for late-onset OCD. Some evidence suggests that older adults' increased concern with their own cognitive declines may serve as a partial mediator of their OCD symptoms and possibly also the onset of OCD in late life (Teachman, 2007). Older adults with predispositions toward developing OCD may not have encountered a worry area intense enough to trigger clinical levels of OCD symptoms until they developed obsessions with the possibility of cognitive declines in older adulthood. Thus, as they become increasingly preoccupied with their imminent cognitive declines, older adults who may have exhibited subclinical levels of OCD symptoms for decades may appear to suddenly meet DSM-5 criteria for OCD. Clinicians working with older adults who exhibit subclinical OCD symptoms should query their patients for possible excessive concern about cognitive decline, which may be a warning sign of increasing OCD symptom severity and late-onset OCD. Other worry areas specific to older adults, such as financial problems or failing health, may also serve in a similar mediatory capacity to elicit clinical levels of OCD symptoms and should likewise be evaluated by clinicians working with samples vulnerable to the development of late-onset OCD.

Presentation in Late Life

The presentation of OCD in older adults may be different than in younger cohorts and there is some evidence that certain symptom dimensions are more prevalent in older adults. While certain symptom dimensions that are more frequent in older adults with OCD are consistent with fear associated with the aging process, such as fear of forgetting (Grant et al., 2007; Jenike, 1991), others may be more due to a cohort effect, such as fear of having sinned (Fallon et al., 1990; Kohn, Westlake, Rasmussen, Marsland, & Norman, 1997). The increased frequency of fear of having sinned may be the result of an older generation that also has a higher degree of religious adherence than the comparative younger cohort.

On the other hand, many symptom dimensions are more prevalent in younger or middle-aged adults, such as need to know, counting, or symmetry (Kohn et al., 1997), and contamination-related symptom dimensions appear in equal frequencies across the lifespan (Calamari, Faber, Hitsman, & Poppe, 1994; Kohn et al., 1997). Based on a large Canadian study of community-dwelling older adults with OCD, the most common OCD symptom dimensions in older adults include washing (22%), ordering (22%), checking (17%), and counting (15%) (Grenier et al., 2009).

Unfortunately, there is little evidence as to the specific reasons that any particular symptom dimensions might be more or less common in older adults. Longitudinal studies of obsessions and compulsions in adults with OCD are needed to know how the prevalence of symptom dimensions truly wax and wane with age. Meanwhile, clinicians should be aware of the different ways in which older adults may present with OCD symptoms. Knowledge of the differential rates with which the various symptom dimensions of OCD are present in older adults can be especially informative when deciding which probing question will be most fruitful to ask of a particular patient. There is little empirical research about the presentation in samples that go undiagnosed or misdiagnosed until late adulthood. It is possible that certain symptom dimensions of OCD are more likely to go undetected by a mental health care provider for longer, such as mental compulsions (e.g., counting within one's head).

Assessment

Proper assessment of a patient is a critical component of any treatment intervention, and the treatment of late-life OCD is no exception. One of the more important components of assessing older adults with potential OCD is to rule out other possible diagnoses, including psychotic disorders and any medical conditions that may mimic the symptoms of OCD. This includes medical conditions that are more prevalent in older adults, such as cerebrovascular lesions, which have been found to present with symptoms similar to OCD (Simpson & Baldwin, 1995). Thus, it is important for clinicians working with older adults reporting OCD-type symptoms to consult with medical providers on potential other explanations of symptoms. Although mental health workers operating in a hospital or another institutionalized setting have access to patient medical records, clinicians in private practice will need to be more proactive in acquiring the necessary information to form a differential diagnosis. This will involve a thorough discussion with the older adult (and possible his or her care-taker or family members) about the necessity of communication between mental and medical health care providers in order to obtain a release of information.

With respect to assessment administration, older adults may have age-related sensory failing which could impair their ability to participate in the typical assessment process. One such problem is an increased thickness of the eye lens with age, causing older adults to have increased vulnerability to glare-related vision problems and thus, a decreased ability to process information through mediums that are prone to glare, such as computer screens. Clinicians should consult with older patients about their visual capabilities when deciding whether or not to employ technology into their assessment routine.

The utilization of eyeglasses, large print, and visual cues should be employed as needed. Older adults also have decreased ability to focus on objects up close; clinicians should be wary that typical font sizes might be too small for many older adults. The best practice is to inquire if the patient usually wears corrective lenses and if they would prefer to have the questionnaires in a larger font size. Older adults may be sensitive about their failing abilities, and so such choices should always be given in a neutral manner so as to increase the likelihood of the individual receiving the properly sized font for their visual acuity. Clinicians who mainly work with older adults may want to print all of their assessments in a larger font in order to prevent the risk of administering a questionnaire (or other treatment materials, such as handouts or manual pages) that is printed too small for the patient to read.

Older adults may also suffer from hearing problems that can decrease the validity of assessments that rely on an auditory administration, such as neuropsychological batteries or verbal clinician administered measures. Clinicians may want to interview the patient, and, if possible, a care-taker or relative, before compiling a neuropsychological battery so that the patient's sensory strengths and weaknesses can be considered when deciding on tests that may access the same cognitive profiles using different sensory modalities.

An additional consideration is the diminished ability of older adults to sit for a lengthy assessment. In addition to an increased occurrence of physical ailments limiting the time they are able to remain seated (e.g., restless leg syndrome, urinary incontinence), older adults are also more likely to have problems with attention and may not be able to perform as adequately on neuropsychological assessments that last for multiple hours as their younger counterparts. Clinicians should be weary of such limitations and provide for multiple breaks within the testing process and possibly plan either a shorter battery of tests or else schedule multiple sessions in which to accomplish the testing. For example, instead of administering the widely used Yale–Brown Obsessive Compulsive Scale symptom checklist interview (Y-BOCS) (Goodman et al., 1989), which is a 64-item clinician-administered measure, clinicians may want to consider using the Obsessive-Compulsive Inventory (OCI) (Foa, Kozak, Salkovskis, Coles, & Amir, 1998), a 42-item self-report instrument. A revised version of the OCI with only 18 items is also available (Foa et al., 2002).

Finally, older adults are likely to have age-related memory impairment that could hinder their recall of relevant signs and symptoms. Clinicians should employ patients' family and care-takers as corroborators for any reported symptoms. Older adults with OCD may also receive additional benefit from keeping a journal of the occurrences of their obsessions and compulsions so that the clinician can get a more thorough understanding of the frequency and degree of their symptoms, as well as any associated impairments.

Psychotropic Interventions

Older adults are more likely to discuss mental health related symptoms with their primary care provider (Wang et al., 2005), resulting in the frequent use of medication as the first course of treatment for many mental health disorders in older adults, and OCD is no exception. In addition to ease of administration, medication has the added benefit in older adults of not requiring any physical or cognitive exertion on the part of the patient. Unfortunately, the majority of research on the efficacy of psychotropic interventions for OCD has been limited to midlife individuals (see Romanelli, Wu, Gamba, Mojtabai, & Segal, 2014, for a review of OCD treatment outcome literature). There is some evidence for the efficacy of fluoxetine and clomipramine in older adults with OCD (e.g., Austin, Zealberg, & Lydiard, 1991), but most evidence is limited to case reports and to date there have been no published randomized controlled trials comparing different psychotropic interventions for OCD in late life.

The success of selective serotonin reuptake inhibitors (SSRIs), such as fluoxetine, and tricyclic antidepressants (TCA), such as clomipramine, in treating OCD in older adults, no matter the scope of the investigations studying the effects of the antidepressants, may add weight to the theory that serotonergic imbalances in the cerebral cortex may lead to the development of OCD (Cottraux & Gerard, 1998; Philpot & Banerjee, 1998). Further research is needed to investigate the exact mechanisms of action with which SSRIs and TCAs mitigate the symptoms of OCD; however, clinicians looking for a psychotropic intervention for late-life OCD should consider these antidepressants to be the treatment of choice. Clinicians considering the prescription of these drugs to older adults with OCD are also advised to carefully discuss the current evidence for the use of these drugs, as well as the side effects and potential drug interactions, with both their patient as well as the patient's care taker or family, when appropriate.

Tricyclic antidepressants, more so than SSRIs, have been found to have an increased rate of adverse effects in older adults, including blurred vision, fatigue, and sexual dysfunction (Jenike, 1991). The adverse effects seen in older adults taking TCAs may be even further magnified by the presence of such symptoms as a result of old age. Late-life patients who present with poor vision or sexual dysfunction initially may be worse candidates for TCAs than older adults with otherwise intact functioning at before taking any prescription medications. Another factor inherit to older adulthood that may decrease the benefits of psychotropic interventions for OCD in late life include increased medical comorbidities, such as cardiovascular disease or arthritis, that also increase the number of medications a patient is take, and thus increase their risk for a possible pharmacological interaction (Markovitz, 1993; Stoudemire & Moran, 1993). Finally, older adults may be at increased risk of pharmacological complications due to age-related in the metabolism of psychotropic medications (Carmin, Pollard, & Gillock, 1999a).

Empirically-based Psychotherapeutic Interventions

Although medication may seem like a simple solution to late-life OCD, the large number of possible adverse effects of medications in older adults, including bone loss in women as a result of long-term use of SSRIs (Diem et al., 2007), requires vigilance and monitoring on the part of the prescribing physician (see Steinman, Handler, Gurwitz, Schiff, & Covinsky, 2011, for a discussion of the importance of medication monitoring). Such monitoring may be beyond the scope of practice of many prescribing clinicians and older adults may be weary of the addition of another medication if they are already prescribed multiple drugs for age-related physical ailments (Wetherell et al., 2004). In contrast, cognitive-behavioral-based interventions are designed to involve a treatment program that lasts for a finite amount of time (typically 6–20 sessions), but provides long-ranging effects (Veale, 2007).

The most commonly recommended form of evidence-based treatment for OCD is exposure and response prevention (ERP), a version of cognitive-behavioral treatment (CBT) interventions based on learning theory (March, Frances, Carpenter, & Kahn, 1997). The effectiveness of CBT in treating late-life anxiety disorders is well documented (e.g., Barrowclough et al., 2001; Stanley et al., 2003), although some evidence suggests that it may not be as effective for older adults as for younger individuals (e.g., Wolitzky-Taylor, Castriotta, Lenze, Stanley, & Craske, 2010). Although not yet tested in older adults with OCD, there is some evidence to suggest that CBT may be an effective treatment for anxiety disorders even in older adults also suffering from dementia (Stanley et al., 2013). Finally, there has been little investigation of CBT compared with other active treatment interventions for anxiety disorders in late life. Although the DSM-5 categorized OCD as distinct from anxiety disorders, expert consensus on this decision was mixed (Mataix-Cols, Pertusa, & Leckman, 2007) and patients with OCD and anxiety disorders have similar response rates to CBT (DiMauro, Domingues, Fernandex, & Tolin, 2013).

There is increasing evidence suggesting that ERP-based interventions for OCD may be more effective than SSRIs, although the specific methodological techniques employed by the clinician can create wide variability in the level of effectiveness of the intervention (Kobak, Greist, Jefferson, Katzelnick, & Henk, 1998). Further, may patients, especially rural older adults, may not have access to a mental health professional properly trained in the techniques of ERP. An increasingly common solution to increasing mental health access to rural older adults is the use of video-conferencing, although clinicians must consider the level of technological prowess of the individual in question before considering such a solution (Richardson, Frueh, Grubaugh, Egede, & Elhai, 2009).

There has been little rigorous investigation of the efficacy of ERP for older adults with OCD, although there is growing anecdotal evidence of the effectiveness and acceptability of ERP for late-life OCD provided through numerous case studies and single case designs (Bajulaiye & Addonizio, 1992; Calamari et al., 1994; Hirsh et al., 2006; Junginger & Ditto, 1984; Price & Salsman, 2010; Rowan, Holburn, Walker, & Siddique, 1984; Turner, Hersen, Bellack, & Wells, 1979). The most promising investigation to date was a comparison of 11 older and 11 younger inpatients being treated for OCD, which found nearly equivalent rates of improvement in both the younger (63% classified as treatment responders) and older (72% classified as treatment responders) inpatients (Carmin, Pollard, & Ownby, 1998). While larger investigations of the effectiveness of ERP for late-life OCD are needed, the current evidence suggests that clinicians seeking to treat older adults with OCD will achieve the best results in their patients through the employment of ERP-based treatment interventions, although some modification may be needed for older adults (Carmin, Pollard, & Ownby, 1999b).

The ERP treatment intervention for OCD has the same mechanistic targets across the lifespan. Because anxiety is the lynchpin that connects the obsessions with the compulsions, the primary goal of ERP is to decrease the anxiety felt in response to obsessions (Kozak & Foa, 1997), which can be done through exposure training to the thoughts. The next step is to practice the exposure in a more realistic setting, such as in the home, with the clinician and/or the patient's care-taker. As with all evidence-based interventions, it is important to track the progress of the patient in an objective manner. One such method for tracking distress levels during exposure exercises is to use ratings of subjective units of distress, or SUDS. Patients are instructed to rate their levels of anxiety from 0 to 100, where a score of 100 is the highest level of anxiety that the patient can imagine. In the case of older adults, who may find 100 points to be too confusing of a range to contemplate, the scale can be adjusted to range from 0 to 10, where a score of 10 is the highest possible level of distress. Patients should be instructed to rate their SUDS levels periodically during every exposure exercise, enabling both the patient and the clinician to see how their distress levels increase over the course of a session as well as over the course of the treatment.

Also critical to the elimination of learned fear responses in OCD is helping the patient to learn how to prevent acting out their compulsions (Kozak & Foa, 1997). For a typical OCD patient with a contamination fear, this may involve instructing them not to wash – under any circumstances – for 10–14 days. However, when working with an older adult, it is important for the clinician to talk to the patient's medical doctor and care takers to ensure that there would not be any adverse health consequences from a prolonged period of personal hygiene abstinence and possibly creating modified version of the intervention exercise, such as reduced washing or washing only under the supervision of a care-taker or family member. There are also contextual issues that need to be considered when working with older adults with contamination fears. If the patient lives in a nursing home or assisted living facility, the clinician may also need to coordinate with the staff at the facility to underscore the importance of the personal hygiene abstinence and to prevent them from inadvertently attempting to intervene.

Finally, ERP targets the obsessive thoughts that lead to the heightened anxiety and subsequent compulsions (Wilhelm & Steketee, 2006). An ERP-based intervention might involve cognitive-restructuring techniques aimed at the obsession, such as having the patient rate the likelihood of their fear coming true (e.g., "How likely is it that you will get sick from being in the same room as a dog?"). Older adults may struggle with the more complex parts of cognitive restructuring it is important to design the treatment intervention to the particular strengths and weaknesses of the individual client. This may involve a simplification of cognitive restructuring technique and using additional sessions to teach the skills to the patient.

Treatment Considerations

Despite evidence that up to a fifth of older adults with OCD may have serious chronic medical health problems and up to a third may have difficulties with social functioning (Grenier et al., 2009), only 10% of older adults suffering from OCD symptoms are estimated to seek treatment for their symptoms in a given year (Préville et al., 2008), possibly due to low insight into the severity of the symptoms or a lack of knowledge about available resources in the community. One way to increase the frequency with which older adults seek treatment is to educate medical care professionals. Mental health care providers desiring to work with the late-life OCD population should put effort into educating other disciplines on possible warning signs of late-life OCD in their patients.

Once patients have been appropriately identified, assessed, and entered into treatment, there may be numerous age-related confounds to psychotherapy. Cognitive ability declines with age, and over 22% of all adults over the age of 71 may suffer from cognitive impairment without dementia (Plassman et al., 2008), which can decrease the efficacy of the cognitive portions of CBT interventions such as ERP. Clinicians should also consider the ramifications of age-related physical impairment, including declining vision and hearing as well as declining maneuverability (Carmin et al., 1999b). Carmin and colleagues (1999b) provide an in-depth discussion of how standard ERP interventions for OCD can be adjusted to accommodate the unique needs of older adults, including the need to be flexible in response to fluctuations in health status, increased time devoted to motivational interviewing to address cohort-related resistance to treatment, and the inclusion of care-takers and family members. Finally, the clinician may need to take a more active role in relapse prevention when treating older adults with OCD, such as scheduling maintenance visits ahead of time instead of waiting for patients to re-initiate treatment (Carmin et al., 1999b).

Summary

Obsessive-compulsive disorder is a chronic mental health condition that may be further confounded by factors unique to old age. When assessing or treating older adults for OCD, clinicians should the possible ramifications of age in the presentation OCD symptoms and in the efficacy of treatment interventions for OCD. Unfortunately, much is still unknown about which treatment interventions may prove most efficacious for older adults with OCD.

References

American Psychiatric Association. (2000). *Diagnostic and Statistical Manual of Mental Disorders* (4th ed., rev. text). Washington, DC: American Psychiatric Publishing.

American Psychiatric Association. (2013). *Diagnostic and Statistical Manual of Mental Health Disorders (DSM-5)* (5th ed.). Washington, DC: American Psychiatric Publishing.

Austin, L. S., Zealberg, J. J., & Lydiard, R. B. (1991). Three cases of pharmacotherapy of obsessive-compulsive disorder in the elderly. *Journal of Nervous and Mental Disease, 179*, 634–635.

Bajulaiye, R., & Addonizio, G. (1993). Obsessive-compulsive disorder arising in a 75-year-old woman. *International Journal of Geriatric Psychiatry, 7*, 139–142.

Barrowclough, C., King, P., Colville, J., Russell, E., Burns, A., & Tarrier, N. (2001). A randomized trial of the effectiveness of cognitive-behavioral therapy and supportive counseling for anxiety symptoms in older adults. *Journal of Consulting & Clinical Psychology, 69*, 756–762.

Bhattacharyya, S., & Khanna, S. (2004). Late onset OCD. *Australian and New Zealand Journal of Psychiatry, 38*, 477–478.

Blazer, D., George, L. K., & Hughes, D. (1991). The epidemiology of anxiety disorders: An age comparison. In C. Salzman & B. D. Liebowitz (Eds.), *Anxiety in the elderly: Treatment and research* (pp. 17–30). New York: Springer.

Calamari, J. E., Faber, S. D., Hitsman, B. L., & Poppe, C. J. (1994). Treatment of obsessive-compulsive disorder in the elderly: A review and case example. *Journal of Behavior Therapy and Experimental Psychiatry, 25*, 95–104.

Carmin, C. N., Pollard, C. A., & Ownby, R. L. (1998). Obsessive-compulsive disorder: Cognitive behavioral treatment of older versus younger adults. *Clinical Gerontologist, 19*, 77–81.

Carmin, C. N., Pollard, C. A., & Gillock, K.L. (1999a). Assessment of anxiety disorders in the elderly. In P. Lichtenberg (Ed.), *Handbook of Assessment in Clinical Gerontology*. New York: Wiley.

Carmin, C. N., Pollard, C. A., & Ownby, R. L. (1999b). Cognitive behavioral treatment of older adults with obsessive-compulsive disorder. *Cognitive and Behavioral Practice, 6*, 110–119.

Cottraux, J., & Gerard, D. (1998). Neuroimaging and neuroanatomical issues in obsessive-compulsive disorder. In: R. P. Swinson, M. M. Antony, S. Rachman, & M. A. Richter (Eds.). *Obsessive-compulsive disorder: Theory, research, and treatment* (pp. 154–180). New York: Guilford Press.

Diem, S. J., Blackwell, T. L., Stone, K. L., Yaffe, K., Haney, E. M., Bliziotes, M. M., & Ensrud, K. E. (2007). Use of antidepressants and rates of hip bone loss in older women: The study of osteoporotic fractures. *Archives of Internal Medicine, 167*, 1240–1245.

DiMauro, J., Domingues, J., Fernandez, G., & Tolin, D. F. (2013). Long-term effectiveness of CBT for anxiety disorders in an adults outpatient clinic sample: A follow-up study. *Behaviour Research and Therapy, 51*, 82–86.

Fallon, B. A., Liebowitz, M. R., Hollander, E., Schneier, F. R., Campeas, R. B., Fairbanks, J., Papp, L. A., Hatterer, J. A., & Sandberg, D. (1990). The pharmacotherapy of moral or religious scrupulosity. *Journal of Clinical Psychiatry, 51*, 517–521.

Fineberg, N. A., Hengartner, M. P., Bergbaum, C., Gale, T., Rossler, W., & Angst, J. (2013). Remission of obsessive-compulsive disorders and syndromes; evidence from a prospective community cohort study over 30 years. *International Journal of Psychiatry in Clinical Practice, 17*(3), 179–197.

Flint, A. J. (1994). Epidemiology and comorbidity of anxiety disorders in the elderly. *American Journal of Psychiatry, 151*, 640–649.

Foa, E. B., Huppert, J. D., Leiberg, S., Langner, R., Kichic, R., Hajcak, G., & Salkovskis, P. M. (2002). The Obsessive-Compulsive Inventory: Development and validation of a short version. *Psychological Assessment, 14*, 485–496.

Foa, E. B., Kozak, M. J., Salkovskis, P. M., Coles, M. E., & Amir, N. (1998). The validation of a new obsessive-compulsive disorder scale: The Obsessive-Compulsive Inventory. *Psychological Assessment, 10,* 206–214.

Frydman, I., do Brasil, P. E., Torres, A. R., Shavitt, R. G., Ferrao, Y. A., Rosario, M. C., Miguel, E. C., & Fontenelle, L. F. (2014). Late-onset obsessive-compulsive disorder: Risk factors and correlates. *Journal of Psychiatric Research, 49,* 68–74.

Goodman, W. K., Price, L. H., Rasmussen, S. A., Mazure, C., Fleischmann, R. L., Hill, C. L., Heninger, G. R., & Charney, D. S. (1989). The Yale–Brown Obsessive Compulsive Scale I. Development, use, and reliability. *Archives of General Psychiatry, 46,* 1006–1011.

Grant, J. E., Mancebo, M. C., Pinto, A., Williams, K. A., Eisen, J. L., & Rasmussen, S. A. (2007). Late-onset obsessive compulsive disorder: Clinical characteristics and psychiatric comorbidity. *Psychiatry Research, 152,* 21–27.

Grenier, S., Préville, M., Boyer, R., & O'Conner, K. (2009). Prevalence and correlates of obsessive-compulsive disorder among older adults living in the community. *Journal of Anxiety Disorders, 23,* 858–865.

Gurian, B. S. & Minor, J. H. (1991). Anxiety in the elderly: Treatment and research. In C. Salzman & B. D. Lebowitz (Eds.), *Clinical presentation of anxiety in the elderly* (pp. 31–44). New York: Springer.

Himmelfaub, S., & Murrell, S.A. (1984). The prevalence and correlates of anxiety symptoms in older adults. *Journal of Psychology, 116,* 159–167.

Hirsh, A., O'Brien, K., Geffken, G. R., Adkins, J., Goodman, W. K., & Storch, E. A. (2006). Cognitive-behavioral treatment for obsessive-compulsive disorder in an elderly male with concurrent medical constraints. *American Journal of Geriatric Psychiatry, 14,* 380–381.

Hwang, S. H., Kwon, J. S., Shin, Y. W., Lee, K. J., Kim, Y. Y., & Kim, M. S. (2007). Neuropsychological profiles of patients with obsessive-compulsive disorder: Early onset versus late onset. *Journal of the International Neuropsychological Society, 13,* 30–37.

Jenike, J. A. (1991). Geriatric obsessive compulsive disorder. *Geriatric Psychiatry and Neurology, 4,* 34–39.

Junginger, J., & Ditto, B. (1984). Multitreatment of obsessive-compulsive checking in a geriatric patient. *Behavior Modification, 8,* 379–390.

Kessler, R. C., Berglund, P., Demler, O., Jin, R., Merikangas, K. R., & Walters, E. E. (2005). Lifetime prevalence and age-of-onset distributions of *DSM-IV* Disorders in the National Comorbidity Survey Replication. *Archives of General Psychiatry, 62,* 593–602.

Kobak, K. A., Greist, J. H., Jefferson, J. W., Katzelnick, D. J., & Henk, H. J. (1998). Behavioral versus pharmacological treatments of obsessive-compulsive disorder: A meta-analysis *Psychopharmacology, 136,* 205–216.

Kohn, R., Westlake, R. J., Rasmussen, S. A., Marsland, R. T., & Norman, W. H. (1997). Clinical features of Obsessive-Compulsive Disorder in elderly patients. *American Journal of Geriatric Psychiatry, 5,* 211–215.

Kolada, J. L., Bland, R. C., & Newman, S. C. (1994). Obsessive-compulsive disorder. *Acta Psychiatrica Scandinavia, 376,* 24–35.

Kozak, M., & Foa, E. (1997). *Mastery of obsessive-compulsive disorder: A cognitive-behavioral approach.* San Antonio, TX: Psychological Corporation.

March, J., Frances, A., Carpenter, D., & Kahn, D. (1997). The Expert Consensus Guideline Series: Treatment of obsessive-compulsive disorder. *Journal of Clinical Psychiatry, 58* (Suppl. 4).

Markovitz, P. J. (1993). Treatment of anxiety in the elderly. *Journal of Clinical Psychiatry, 54,* 64–68.

Mataix-Cols, D., Pertusa, A., & Leckman, J. F. (2007). Issues for DSM-V: How should obsessive-compulsive and related disorders be classified? *American Journal of Psychiatry, 164*(9), 1313–1314. doi: 10.1176/appi.ajp.2007.07040568.

Philpot, M. P., & Banerjee, S. (1998). Obsessive-compulsive disorder in the elderly. *Behavioural Neurology, 11,* 117–121.

Plassman, B. L., Langa, K. M., Fisher, G. G., Herringa, S. G., Weir, D. R., Ofstedal, M. B., Burke, J. R., ... Wallace, R. B. (2008). Prevalence of cognitive impairment without dementia in the United States. *Annals of Internal Medicine, 148*, 427–434.

Préville, M., Boyer, R., Grenier, S., Dubé, M., Voyer, P., Punti, R., Baril, M. C., ... Brassard, J. (2008). The epidemiology of psychiatric disorders in the Quebec older adult population. *Canadian Journal of Psychiatry, 53*, 822–832.

Price, M. C., & Salsman, N. L. (2010). Exposure and response prevention for the treatment of late-onset obsessive-compulsive disorder in an 82-year-old man. *Clinical Case Studies, 9*, 426–441.

Richardson, L. K., Frueh, B. C., Grubaugh, A. L., Egede, L., & Elhai, J. D. (2009). Current directions in videoconferencing tele-mental health research. *Clinical Psychology: Science and Practice, 16*, 323–338.

Romanelli, R. J., Wu, F. M., Gamba, R., Mojtabai, R., & Segal, J. B. (2014). Behavioral therapy and serotonin reuptake inhibitor pharmacotherapy in the treatment of obsessive-compulsive disorder: A systematic review and meta-analysis of head-to-head randomized controlled trials. *Depress Anxiety.* doi: 10.1002/da.22232.

Rowan, V. C., Holburn, S. W., Walker, J. R., & Siddique, A. (1984). A rapid multi-component treatment for an obsessive-compulsive disorder. *Journal of Behavior Therapy and Experimental Psychiatry, 15*, 347–352.

Simpson, S., & Baldwin, B. (1995). Neuropsychiatry and SPECT of an acute obsessive compulsive syndrome patient. *British Journal of Psychiatry, 166*, 390–392.

Stanley, M. A., Beck, J. G., Novy, D. M., Averill, P. M., Swann, A. C. Diefenbach, G. J., & Hopko, D. R. (2003). Cognitive-behavioral treatment of late-life generalized anxiety disorder. *Journal of Consulting & Clinical Psychology, 71*, 309–319.

Stanley, M. S., Calleo, J., Bush, A. L., Wilson, N., Snow, A. L., Krawu-Schuman, C., Paukert, A. L., ... & Kunik, M. E. (2013). The peaceful mind program: A pilot test of a cognitive-behavioral therapy-based intervention for anxious patients with dementia. *American Journal of Geriatric Psychiatry, 21*, 696–708.

Steinman, M. A., Handler, S. M., Gurwitz, J. H., Schiff, G. D., & Covinsky, K. E. (2011). Beyond the prescription: Medication monitoring and adverse drug events in older adults. *Journal of the American Geriatrics Society, 59*, 1513–1520.

Stoudemire, A., & Moran, M. G., (1993). Psychopharmacologic treatment of anxiety in the medically ill elderly patient: Special considerations. *Journal of Clinical Psychiatry, 54*, 27–33.

Teachman, B. A. (2007). Linking obsessional beliefs to OCD symptoms in older and younger adults. *Behaviour Research and Therapy, 45*, 1671–1681.

Turner, S. M., Hersen, M., Bellack, A. S., & Wells, K. C. (1979). Behavioral treatment of obsessive compulsive neurosis. *Behavior Research and Therapy, 17*, 95–106.

Veale, D. (2007). Cognitive-behavioural therapy for obsessive-compulsive disorder. *Advances in Psychiatric Treatment, 13*, 438–446.

Wang, P. S., Lane, M., Olfson, M., Pincus, H. A., Wells, K. B., & Kessler, R. C. (2005). Twelve-month use of mental health services in the United States. *Archives of General Psychiatry, 62*, 629–640.

Weiss, A. P., & Jenike, M. A. (2000). Late-onset obsessive-compulsive disorder: A case series. *Journal of Neuropsychiatry and Clinical Neurosciences, 12*, 265–268.

Wetherell, J. L., Kaplan, R. M., Kallenberg, G., Dresselhaus, T. R., Sieber, W. J., & Lang, A. J. (2004). Mental health treatment preferences of older and younger primary care patients. *International Journal of Psychiatry in Medicine, 34*, 219–233.

Wetherell, J. L., Petkus, A. J., McChesney, K., Stein, M. B., Judd, P. H., Rockwell, E., Sewell, D. D., & Patterson, T. L. (2009). Older adults are less accurate than younger adults at identifying symptoms of anxiety and depression. *Journal of Nervous and Mental Disorders, 197*, 623–626.

Wilhelm, S., & Steketee, S. (2006). *Cognitive therapy for obsessive-compulsive disorder: A guide for professionals.* Oakland, CA: New Harbinger.

Wolitzky-Taylor, K. B., Castriotta, N., Lenze, E. J., Stanley, M. A., & Craske, M. G. (2010). Anxiety disorders in older adults: a comprehensive review. *Depression and Anxiety, 7*, 190–211.

4

Cross-Cultural Phenomenology of Obsessive-Compulsive Disorder

M. T. Williams, L. K. Chapman, J. V. Simms, and G. Tellawi

Introduction

Obsessive-compulsive disorder (OCD) is a debilitating mental disorder, involving distressing obsessions and repetitive compulsions. Obsessions are intrusive, unwanted thoughts, images, or impulses that increase anxiety, whereas compulsions are repetitive behaviors or mental acts used to decrease anxiety. OCD appears in every culture, with the earliest reports dating back to the first half of the second millennium BC, described in ancient Babylonian texts. Although they had little knowledge of the brain or psychological functions, Babylonian physicians carefully recorded the abnormal behaviors that we now recognize as OCD. One such text states that the sufferer, "does not know why he has a morbid fear of beds, chairs, tables, lighted stoves, lamps, etc., of leaving or entering a city, city gate, or house, or of a street, temple, or road" (Reynolds & Wilson, 2011).

We do not know how many people suffered from OCD in ancient times, but in the contemporary United States, the National Comorbidity Survey Replication (NCS-R) found that approximately 1.6% of the population met criteria for OCD within their lifetime (Kessler et al., 2005a), with 1% of the sample meeting criteria within the last year (Kessler, Chiu, Demler, Merikangas, & Walters, 2005b). The prevalence of OCD appears to be roughly consistent across US ethnic groups, with African and Caribbean Americans having shown an OCD lifetime prevalence of 1.6% (Himle, et al., 2008). Epidemiologic studies conducted in other countries find similar rates cross-nationally (Weismann et al., 1994), ranging from 0.3% in Brazil to 2.7% in Hungary. Based on the current world population (US Census Bureau, 2014), it can be estimated that over 114 million people are afflicted worldwide with OCD.

Although many with OCD worry about cleanliness, symmetry, arranging, and perfectionism, OCD is a complex disorder that can manifest itself in a variety of symptom dimensions, including unacceptable or taboo thoughts and ruminations about morality (e.g., Bloch, Landeros-Weisenberger, Rosário, Pittenge, & Leckman, 2008; Williams, Mugno, Franklin, & Faber, 2013). Given the cultural relativity of what constitutes taboo and even morality, it is important that cultural differences be taken

The Wiley Handbook of Obsessive Compulsive Disorders, Volume I, First Edition.
Edited by Jonathan S. Abramowitz, Dean McKay, and Eric A. Storch.
© 2017 John Wiley & Sons Ltd. Published 2017 by John Wiley & Sons Ltd.

into account when considering diverse populations (Chapman, DeLapp, & Williams, 2014). Culture can have profound effects on the manifestation of psychopathology, particularly with a disorder as multi-faceted as OCD.

This chapter presents a survey of the cross-cultural manifestations of OCD world-wide, based on a comprehensive review of the psychological literature. We include an examination of differences found based on factors such as culture, ethnoracial minority status, geographical region, and religion.

OCD in Non-Hispanic Whites/European Americans & Western Cultures

An examination of OCD in the US by the National Comorbidity Survey Replication (NCS-R) (Ruscio, Stein, Chiu, & Kessler, 2010), found a wide range of symptoms, illustrated in Table 4.1. These symptom categories were not empirically derived, but instead are indicative of those symptoms most often reported by individuals diag-nosed with OCD. It should be noted that the findings of the NCS-R may be influ-enced by several study limitations, including a small sample size ($N=73$).

Many additional studies have examined symptom profiles in clinical samples. The DSM-IV Field Trial of OCD, a large treatment-seeking sample ($N=431$) (Foa et al., 1995), yielded symptom distributions different from those of the NCS-R. There were differences in Checking, with 79.3% reporting the symptom in the NCS-R, and only 28.2% in the DSM-IV Field Trial. Additionally, Ordering was reported by only 5.7% of the DSM-IV Field Trial participants, while it was ten times as prevalent in the NCS-R, at 57%. While the NCS-R sampled from the community, the DSM-IV Field Trial included clinical participants, and this may account for some of the differences, as well as differences in study methodology.

One of the most common means of understanding symptom dimensions in OCD is with the use of the Yale–Brown Obsessive Compulsive Symptom Checklist (YBOCS-SC) because it assesses the majority of obsessions and compulsions seen clinically in Western samples (Goodman et al., 1989). Since its development, many studies have attempted to create an empirically-based classification system that corresponds to the

Table 4.1 Distribution of OCD Symptoms in the NCS-R

	OCD cases reporting each symptom (%)
Checking	79.3
Hoarding	62.3
Ordering	57.0
Moral	43.0
Sexual/religious	30.2
Contamination	25.7
Harming	24.2
Illness	14.3
Other	19.0

Note: Totals exceed 100% given that each participant was allowed to choose multiple obsessions and compulsions.

symptoms listed in the YBOCS-SC. Baer (1994) conducted the first principal components analysis (PCA) of 13 major YBOCS-SC symptom categories. This resulted in
three factors: symmetry/hoarding, contamination/cleaning, and pure obsessions.
Pure obsessions were those with religious, aggressive, and/or sexual themes, and had
no identifiable compulsions. Bloch and colleagues (2008) conducted a meta-analysis
of 21 studies involving 5,124 participants, and did not find that symptom dimensions
varied greatly cross-culturally, however, 76% of the studies were from Western nations,
limiting generalizability. More recent studies have included other compulsions, such
as mental compulsions and reassurance, and tend to find five distinct dimensions: con-
tamination/cleaning, hoarding, symmetry/ordering, taboo thoughts/mental compulsions, and doubt/checking (Abramowitz, Franklin, Schwartz, & Furr, 2003; Pinto
et al., 2007; Williams et al., 2011). The hoarding dimension has since been classified
as a separate disorder (Hoarding Disorder; DSM-5, 2013).

In Western cultures, OCD is viewed as mental disorder caused largely by biological
factors (Coles & Coleman, 2010). Aggressive, religious, or sexual symptoms are not
as easily recognized as are symptoms related to washing, checking, and symmetry.
These obsessive themes are known as "taboo obsessions" and were previously thought
to be "pure obsessions," meaning they were not associated with the presence of any
compulsions, making them more difficult to identify (Pinto et al., 2007). However,
the concept of the pure obsessional was later refuted (Leonard & Riemann, 2012;
Williams et al., 2011). One type of taboo obsessions that may be culture-bound are
known as sexual orientation obsessions in OCD (SO-OCD), occurring in approximately 10% of US patients (Williams & Farris, 2011). SO-OCD centers around the
fear that one is going through an undesired change in their sexual orientation or
gender identity (Williams & Ching, 2016; Williams, Slimowicz, Tellawi, & Wetterneck,
2014). This has mainly been observed in Western cultures, and has not been reported
in the literature outside of the United States. This may be due to the societal tension
around non-heterosexual orientations in the United States. In some Eastern cultures,
homosexuality and transsexuality are embraced socially as a common form of life-
style/expression. In some cultures, there is evidence of sexual practices between people of the same sex (which would be considered by Westerners as "homosexual")
being seen as acceptable, and separate from one's sexuality (i.e., male coming of age
rituals in Papa New Guinea) (Knauft, 2010).

Additionally, taboo obsessions are more stigmatized (Cathey & Wetterneck, 2013),
which can lead to delays in treatment-seeking or hiding symptoms due to shame (Simonds
& Thorpe, 2003). As a result, this symptom presentation is likely underrepresented in
treatment-seeking populations. However, individuals with these symptoms may be more
motivated to seek treatment due to the high-levels of distress caused by such thoughts
(e.g., Williams, Wetterneck, Tellawi, & Duque, 2015). Additional research is needed to
determine the effect of these issues on help-seeking behaviors.

OCD in African Americans

Until recent years, research on OCD in African Americans and other ethnic and racial
minorities has been scarce (Williams, Powers, Yun, & Foa, 2010). One of the first studies
on African Americans with OCD (Lewis-Hall, 1991) was a naturalistic study examining
treatment-seeking adults in an urban clinic. The researchers observed differences in

treatment patterns, as only 2% of clinic patients with OCD were Black. Williams and colleagues (2012a) examined barriers to treatment among African Americans and European Americans. Barriers found to be unique to African Americans included fears about discrimination by treatment providers and not knowing where to go for help. Barriers to treatment were grouped into seven categories: treatment price, stigma/judgment, fear of forced change, lack of need for treatment, fears about therapy, doubts about the effectiveness of treatment, and being too busy for treatment.

The National Survey of American Life (NSAL) (Heeringa et al., 2004), the largest study of mental health disorders in US racial and ethnic minorities, examined three nationally representative samples: African Americans, blacks of Caribbean descent, and Non-Hispanic whites. Himle and colleagues (2008) found that 1.63% of African Americans and Caribbean black populations met diagnostic criteria for OCD, with both samples experiencing high rates for at least one other lifetime psychiatric disorder, 93.2% and 95.6%, respectively. This was consistent with previous research, as comorbidity is the norm for OCD (Ruscio et al., 2010; Saleem & Mahmood, 2009).

Williams, Proetto, Casiano, and Franklin (2012d) conducted the largest study of African Americans with OCD to date. They identified six discrete symptom dimensions, including contamination/washing, hoarding, sexual/reassurance, aggression/mental compulsions, symmetry/perfectionism, and doubt/checking. While these factors were similar to those found in primarily non-Hispanic white samples, African Americans with OCD experienced contamination symptoms at twice the rate of European Americans (Williams, Elstein, Bucker, Abelson, & Himle, 2012); findings from the NSAL study were similar, also noting increased contamination concerns among African Americans. Higher levels of obsessions and compulsions related to themes of cleanliness may hold cultural relevance for African Americans, as they have historically experienced segregation due to European Americans' fears of contamination through close contact or sharing items (i.e., drinking fountains, swimming pools, etc.). Additionally, research shows that when primed with culturally salient stereotypical images (i.e., Jim Crow law images), African American participants are likely to experience increased disgust sensitivity (Olatunji, Tomarken, & Zhao, 2014). Individuals with a lower socioeconomic status (SES) report greater concerns about contamination (Williams, Elstein, Bucker, Abelson, & Himle, 2012), which is consistent with the hypothesis that individuals with a lower SES may be more exposed to contaminants, leading to greater contamination concerns and cleaning behaviors (Williams, Abramowitz, & Olatunji, 2012b; Williams & Turkheimer, 2007).

Cultural differences were also found with regard to animal concerns, which is consistent with findings in nonclinical samples (Wheaton, Berman, Fabricant, & Abramowitz, 2013; Williams, Abramowitz, & Olatujni, 2012; Williams & Turkheimer, 2007). This increased level of animal concerns may be a result of historic events, such as dogs being used to hunt for slaves or attack civil rights protesters (Williams et al., 2012).

OCD in Western Christian Samples

Abramowitz, Deacon, Woods, and Tolin (2004) administered self-report measures to better understand the relationship between Protestant religiosity and OCD symptoms, such as washing, checking, and the importance of controlling one's thoughts. Participants were divided into three groups based on level of religiosity. Individuals high in religiosity reported more obsessive symptoms and compulsive washing, as well as more importance on their thoughts and the need to control them. The researchers referenced the Bible, in which Christ asserts that the thought of committing a sinful act is equal to committing it, as a way to explain the importance of control of thoughts in highly religious participants. Similar results were found in a sample of college students, with Christian students reporting higher levels of thought–action fusion (TAF), a symptom that highlights the importance of thoughts and controlling them (Shafran, Thordarson, & Rachman, 1996; Williams, Lau, & Grisham, 2013).

Sica, Novara, and Sanavio (2002) found similar results in Catholic Italian nuns and friars. Participants who reported high or medium levels of religiosity also reported high levels of obsessions related to the importance of thought control. The researchers attributed these findings to Catholic precepts, such as the notion that thoughts and behaviors are equal, as well as teachings about purity and perfectionism.

Overall, the research in Christian samples indicates differences in the importance of thought control and the notion that thoughts and actions are interchangeable. These beliefs may facilitate distress in Christians with OCD as they find they are unable to control their obsessions.

OCD in Jewish Communities

When obsessions in OCD focus on moral or religious issues, they are known as scrupulosity (Huppert, Siev, & Kushner, 2007). As Judaism is oriented around traditions and focuses on rituals and laws fundamental to Jewish life, many Jewish OCD sufferers experience scrupulosity (Huppert & Siev, 2010), although scrupulous obsessions may be experienced by individuals of other religions or even by people with no religion at all. Huppert and colleagues (2007) reported that when treating Jewish patients who suffer from scrupulosity, it may be difficult to distinguish between religious rituals and compulsive behaviors. Compulsions related to scrupulosity in Jewish individuals often include washing, prayer, and consultation with religious leaders (Huppert et al., 2007). Hand washing may be a particularly prominent compulsion because Jewish customs specify a detailed hand washing ritual in order to remove impurities (Huppert et al., 2007). However, religious rituals, if found outside the religious context or if extreme in nature, could be indicative of scrupulosity rather than religious devotion.

Rosmarin, Pirutinsky, and Siev (2010) studied attitudes of Orthodox and non-Orthodox Jews in the US toward OCD symptoms by giving participants descriptions of either religious (scrupulous) or nonreligious OCD symptoms. When confronted with descriptions of religious behaviors, such as excessive prayer, repeated crossings, and sky-gazing toward God, Orthodox participants were more likely to recognize the scrupulosity as OCD and recommend treatment than non-Orthodox participants, which was in direct opposition to the researchers' hypothesis. One potential reason for the discrepancy was that Orthodox participants had a more detailed understanding of normal religious practices due to a more "strict adherence to religious law" and could therefore identify behaviors outside the norm. Another reason was that non-Orthodox Jews may not have wanted to identify excessive religious behaviors as OCD for fear of offending other religious individuals (Rosmarin et al., 2010).

OCD in Middle Eastern Islamic Cultures

Several studies have been conducted examining the cultural components of OCD and its presentation in Islamic Middle Eastern countries. Mahgoub and Abdel-Hafiez (1991) examined a conservative Muslim sample in Saudi Arabia and found strong religious themes in their OCD symptomatology, including obsessions related to prayers and washing (50%), contamination (41%), and faith (34%). These obsessive themes may stem from a religious practice called *al-woodo*, in which the body must be systematically cleaned before prayer. The researchers noted that the need to frequently and meticulously perform these preparation rituals, may be a reason for the prevalence of repeating, washing, and checking compulsions in this sample. Religious obsessions related to contamination and purity, as well as compulsions involving washing, have been observed in many studies (Al-Salaim & Loewenthal, 2011; Okasha, Saad, Khalil, & Dawla, 1994; Saleem & Mahmood, 2009; Shooka, Al-Haddad, & Raees, 1998; Yorulmaz & Işık, 2011).

Yorulmaz and Işık (2011) noted that Islamic participants of Turkish descent experienced TAF, which is also noted in Western cultures (Abramowitz et al., 2004). The researchers concluded that this was due to similarities between certain beliefs in Islam and characteristics of OCD. While all participants in Yorulmaz and Işik (2011) reported an Islamic affiliation, the differences in symptom presentation are culturally significant because they exist between participants of reportedly equivalent ethnic descent. Those who had lived in Turkey from birth reported more severe symptoms, specifically in contamination/cleaning, when compared with Bulgarian-born Turkish participants and Turkish remigrates. The authors noted that Islam is more rigorous in Turkey, and could explain the more severe symptomatology for Turkish-born participants.

Okasha and colleagues (1994) found that most of their Egyptian sample were rated on the Y-BOCS as having moderate to severe symptom presentation, which the researchers took as indicative of Egyptian patients' high tolerance for psychiatric difficulties before seeking help. They also reported that mental health professionals are often a last option for participants, who instead tend to seek help from informal social networks of native healers, friends, elderly family members, and religious people (Okasha et al., 1994), as they may be less likely to manipulate or harm a patient (Al-Solaim & Loewenthal, 2011). This help-seeking pattern is parallel to that seen in African American communities (Hatch, Friedman, & Paradis, 1996), and suggests a preference for culturally and religiously relevant assistance with issues concerning psychological disorders.

Ghassenzadeh and colleagues (2002), found obsessive doubts and indecisiveness as the most frequent symptom, as well as washing compulsions. They also found that males most often reported blasphemous thoughts and ordering compulsions, while females reported greater concerns about impurity and contamination, and washing compulsions, which has been seen in other studies (Shooka et al., 1998) and other cultures (Jaisoorya, Reddy, Srinath, & Thennarasu, 2009; Labad et al., 2008). As 70% of the female participants were housewives, the authors concluded that this could affect the content of obsessions as cleaning would be a part of daily chores.

In a Pakistani sample, Saleem and Mahmood (2009) described "Napak," which is a "mix of unpleasant feelings of contamination with strong religious connotations of dirtiness and unholiness" in Islam. Two-thirds of participants added Napak to the questionnaire as an item within the category of contamination. If a Muslim is in the state of Napak, he cannot participate in religious rituals until he has cleaned himself systematically. Al-Solaim and Loewenthal (2011) also found that some participants believed that OCD was caused by an "evil eye," described as being an illness caused by social conflict or the envy of another individual.

Inozu, Clark, and Karanci (2012) compared the OCD symptomatology of a Canadian sample to a Turkish sample. They found that the predominantly Islamic Turkish sample scored significantly higher on the PIOS (a measure of scrupulosity) fear of God items than their Christian Canadian counterparts. These findings were attributed to a greater fear of God's punishment in Islamic cultures, as fear is a prized attribute in Muslim worship.

An emphasis on cleanliness, purity, and religion is normative in Islamic cultures. However, when rituals surrounding these beliefs are committed in excess, and the beliefs become obsessive, they can then become culturally significant aspects of OCD symptomatology. Adherents of other religious traditions that emphasize cleaning may also combine religion and cleanliness (i.e., Orthodox Jews), but this presentation may be particularly prevalent among Muslims with OCD due to the many cleaning rituals required in Islam.

OCD in India

The extent research in India has found typical OCD obsessions to be contamination, aggression, symmetry, sexual, religious and pathological doubt. One such study by Girishchandra and Khanna (2001) found that the most commonly reported symptoms in a sample of 202 Indian participants were doubts about having performed daily activities (64.9%) and contamination concerns about dirt and germs (50%). In a comprehensive review of the Indian literature Reddy, Jaideep, Khanna, and Srinath (2005) observed that contamination concerns and pathological doubt were highly prevalent. Reddy and colleagues found the lifetime prevalence rate of OCD to be approximately 0.6% in India, which is relatively low compared to the lifetime prevalence in other countries. Girishchandra and Sumant (2001) also noted a disproportionate number of males in the study compared to females, a ratio of over 2:1.

Jaisoorya and colleagues (2009) found male participants had a tendency to report sexual and symmetry obsessions coupled with checking and bizarre compulsions, while dirt, contamination, and cleaning related symptoms were reported more often by females (e.g., Labad et al., 2008). Similar findings were observed by Cherian and colleagues (2013), who observed that men exhibited a slightly earlier onset and a greater tendency to have comorbid Social Anxiety Disorder. They reported higher frequencies of sexual, religious obsessions, pathological doubt, and checking and repeating compulsions. Whereas women were more likely to be married, have comorbid depression, risk for suicide, and report a higher frequency for fear of contamination (Cherian et al., 2013). To explain the higher frequency of symptoms surrounding dirt, contamination, and cleaning, the authors commented that women were more often subjected to unclean conditions and could be more concerned with contamination. In Western samples, it has been suggested, as an explanation for females reporting higher levels of contamination concerns, that biological make-up and brain chemistry, specifically greater numbers of steroid hormone receptors the female brain may be causing a sexual dimorphism (Labad et al., 2008). The authors also mentioned that environmental differences could mediate the differences found (i.e., females being socialized to do a greater share of the domestic work).

In a study by Jaisoorya and colleagues, the majority of participants were men, which was also noted in Girishchandra and Sumant (2001). Although there has been little to no difference in help-seeking between men and women with OCD in Western samples historically, the difference between male and female participation in Indian samples presents a disparity in the literature (Goodwin, Koenen, Hellman, Guardino, & Struening, 2002; Torres et al., 2007). In the Indian sample, the authors commented that a possible explanation for this was the difference in access to health care, resulting from differing male versus female social status in India, where the males hold dominance within the social hierarchy. Despite the differences found in symptom presentation, it was found in a large clinical sample that "good insight" and a grounded understanding of the motivations behind thoughts and behaviors was correlated with a lower severity of OCD (Cherian et al., 2012).

In a study by Chowdhury, Mukherjee, Ghosh, and Chowdhury (2003), the culture-bound disorder termed "puppy pregnancy" was described as fears of being pregnant with a canine embryo after having been bitten by a dog, and this condition is ironically more common among men than women. Puppy pregnancy has been primarily found in reported in rural parts of India, and symptoms are comparable to OCD. Puppy pregnancy includes a fear of internal contamination (from the puppy fetus), disability (impotence due to damage to internal sexual organs), and death. One case reported excessive checking after having observed a dog licking milk cans and being bitten by the same dog. The subject was fearful that he was being chased by a dog, and would check all milk cans, worried that they had been licked by a dog. The authors also noted obsessive thoughts involving fear of dog bites and behavioral avoidance.

In general, however, research to date has found few differences in symptom dimensions in India from those found in Western studies. Bloch et al. (2008) noted some differences in symptom presentation for Indian participants when compared with studies of white and non-white samples. In Indian studies, the five-factor model of symptoms included a need to touch, tap, and rub, which could be associated with cultural traditions involving touching (i.e., touching the feet of elders as a sign of respect). When seeking treatment, it has been found that, although many psychotic disorders are believed by the lay public to be supernatural in nature, OCD and related disorders are believed to be a result of excessive worry and thinking. Despite this non-spiritual rationale, many in the Indian subcontinent with OCD prefer religious remedies, as many indigenous beliefs are at odds with the Western biomedical model for treating mental disorders (Chakraborty, Das, Dan, Bandyopadhyay, & Chatterjee, 2013; Grover et al., 2014).

OCD in Indonesia

In Bali, a primarily Hindu province, Lemelson (2003) conducted a study of 19 patients suffering from OCD, to understand the degree to which Balinese culture affected the illness experience. The most reported obsession was the need to know, which manifested as the necessity of knowing the identities of passers-by. Lemelson also found obsessions surrounding themes of magic, witchcraft, and spirits, which are all religious themes entwined in the Balinese culture.

As a caveat, it is important to note that other than in Bali, where Hindu has an emphasis on magic, witchcraft, and ancestor worship, the main religious affiliation of Indonesia is Islam. Therefore the phenomenology of OCD in other parts of Indonesia may be more similar to findings in other Islamic cultures. More research is required to validate this notion.

In relation to treatment, recently a study was conducted in Indonesia that supported the use of exposure response prevention (ERP) using the Trans-theoretical Model (TTM) to reduce the symptoms of OCD, as measured by the Y-BOCS total score (Rohayati & Fakrurrozi, 2013). These findings support the use of Western therapeutic techniques to treat OCD in Indonesia.

OCD in East Asia

Matsunaga and colleagues (2008) noted the most common obsessions in a Japanese sample as fear of contamination (48%), followed by obsessions with symmetry or exactness (42%) and aggression (36%). The most common compulsions reported were checking and washing (47%), and repeating rituals (31%). The study's focus was more psychobiological than cultural, and the authors described "transcultural stability" in the symptom presentation of OCD. However, the researchers only compared results with Western countries and did not evaluate differences with respect to other cultures.

In the first study of its kind from Taiwan, Juang and Liu (2001) found the most commonly reported obsessions to be fears of contamination (37%), pathological doubt (34%), and a need for symmetry (19%). The most commonly reported compulsions consisted of checking, washing, and orderliness/precision.

Kim, Lee, and Kim (2005) determined symptom dimensions, based on a factor analysis of the Y-BOCS-SC checklist in a study of Koreans. The factors identified included hoarding/repeating, contamination/cleaning, aggressive/sexual, and religious/somatic, with the latter two dimensions described as "pure obsessional" due to a lack of identified corresponding compulsions. Most Western studies group these two in to a single factor: unacceptable/taboo thoughts (Bloch et al., 2008). Also grouped together in the study was hoarding with repeating and counting compulsions, a combination not usually seen in Western samples. Moreover, the Korean sample differed from other studies originating in Asia by not including an obsession with symmetry. Other studies originating in Asia have shown symmetry obsessions to be among those most highly reported (Li, Marques, Hinton, Wang, & Xiao, 2009; Matsunaga et al., 2008).

The first OCD symptomology study to originate in mainland China, Li and colleagues (2009) assessed 139 patients with OCD in an attempt to determine if the symptom dimensions documented in other studies (unacceptable/taboo thoughts, symmetry/ordering, contamination/cleaning, and hoarding) were applicable in this particular culture. The most common symptoms reported were obsessions with symmetry (67.6%) and contamination (43.2%), followed by aggression (31.7%). A cultural propensity toward harmonious interpersonal relationships due to the presence of Confucianism and its precepts in China were cited as a possible explanation for fewer reports of aggression (Li et al., 2009). Albeit, the contrarian nature of OCD could be an explanation for aggression being the third most prevalent symptom in this sample.

Additional investigation in China found that caregiver burden was a source of significant OCD related stress in the home. A study by Siu, Lam, and Chan (2011) discovered that in a Chinese sample of 77 families, 76 reported significant objective and subjective caregiver distress as a result of financial burden, disruption of activities by OCD patient's demands, accommodating patients, participating in rituals, and personal feelings of distress. In one case, the cleanliness rituals of one patient contributed to a significant proportion of the family's overwhelming water bill. The aforementioned study indicated that female caregivers of single patients, primarily mothers, suffered most from subjective distress and may be in the most need of help.

A disproportionate ratio of males to females was noted in the study (almost 2:1). It was unclear whether this could have possibly been mediated by cultural norms, similar to some Indian samples, regarding help-seeking behavior in women as the authors noted that the males of the sample seemed more willing to participate (Girishchandra & Sumant, 2001; Jaisoorya et al., 2009). Contrarily, a study conducted in Singapore with a multiethnic community sample, mostly comprised of Chinese (76.9%), Malay (12.3%), and Indian (8.3%) participants, was slightly majority female. The authors noted that women with anxiety and related disorders reported more cognitive and social disability than their male counterparts (Subramaniam, Abdin, Vaingankar, & Chong, 2013). The authors suggest that in order to accommodate this need, mental health care providers should adhere to some cultural needs (i.e., evening and weekend clinic hours, and a stronger focus on treating the cognitive and social symptoms).

In another study by Subramaniam, Abdin, Vaingankar, and Chong (2012), the authors conducted one of the first investigations into the impact and prevalence of OCD in Singapore. Their large national sample consisted of equal parts Chinese, Malays, and Indians, reported a lifetime prevalence of OCD as 3.0%, with age being the largest demographic contributor. OCD was most common in those between the ages of 35–49, and although there were no gender or ethnic differences associated with OCD, marital status was significantly associated with OCD (i.e., separated or divorced participants having a higher rate of onset). Participants with lifetime OCD were found to have a greater likelihood for comorbid GAD, bipolar disorder, dysthymia, and MDD, as well as physical ailments like chronic pain and hypertension. Those with lifetime OCD who sought treatment was 10.2%, with an average of nine years between onset and seeking treatment.

In Eastern cultures there is an innate cultural emphasis on conformity, collectivism and harmony, often instilled from an early age (Li et al., 2009). The emphasis on symmetry in OCD may reflect these tenets to some degree. Nonetheless, there are some differences in symptoms between Chinese and Japanese with OCD, as reported by Liu, Cui, and Fang (2008). After studying two groups of OCD patients, the authors concluded that aggressive and contamination obsessions were more common in Japanese OCD patients, while religious and symmetry/exactness obsessions are more common among Chinese. Likewise, Japanese OCD patients were more likely to have cleaning/washing and ordering/arranging compulsions, while Chinese were more likely to have checking compulsions. These differences could be reflective of the greater emphasis on symmetry in Chinese culture than Japanese culture (Kim et al., 2005; Li et al., 2009).

One culture-bound disorder that is seen in Asian cultures is Taijin Kyofusho (TKS), which is referred to as an interpersonal fear disorder (Vriends, Pfaltz, Novianti, & Hadiyono, 2013). Although often considered a form of social anxiety disorder, there are several variants of TKS, including fear of offending others due to a physical defect or offensive facial expression, fears of blushing, fears of having a physical deformity, and the fear of one's own glance (Vriends et al., 2013). Another fear is that of having a foul body odor, which in the West is referred to as olfactory reference syndrome (Feusner, Phillips, & Stein, 2010), which, when paired with the cognitive preoccupations and repetitive behaviors, may be a form of OCD. For example, one study found that individuals with olfactory reference syndrome beliefs were preoccupied with the scent of various body parts, and almost the whole sample engaged in repetitive behaviors, similar to compulsions, such as excessive showering (Phillips & Menard, 2011).

Another culture bound disorder primarily observed in southeast Asian cultures is Koro. This disorder is described as the phenomenon where sexual organs (penis in males and nipples/breasts in women) retract back into the body, disappearing and potentially causing death (Roy et al., 2011). Although this condition has been noted as occurring within female samples, the majority of cases observed have been male (Davis, Steever, Terwillinger, & Williams, 2012). Similar to obsessions seen often in OCD, the Koro anxieties prompt significant anxiety and impairment in those suffering. Additionally, common reactions to symptoms that are reminiscent of compulsions are tugging and pulling on genitals to delay or halt the retraction process (Davis et al., 2012). More research is needed on the cause(s) of initial symptom manifestation, but in two cases studies the authors noted each Koro sufferer began to experience symptoms after being warned about an outbreak via social networking (i.e., a phone call and local news reports). In the case studies each Koro sufferer was checked by a physician for sexual organ abnormalities but none were found (Roy et al., 2011). Although predominantly found in Southeast Asia, isolated cases have been reported in the West. This indicates that Koro may not be simply a culture bound syndrome but an OCD-related phenomenon with more universal constructs (Davis et al., 2012).

OCD in Africa

Although much of the OCD related research in the continent of Africa has focused on comorbid obsessive-compulsive symptoms with trauma and psychotic disorders, there are some noteworthy OCD findings. A study conducted in Kenya found that 12.2% of psychiatric in-patients at a residential treatment facility met criteria for OCD, with over 60% of those being male. Comorbidity of anxiety, depression and other psychiatric disorders varied, with 17.8% of those with OCD also meeting criteria for schizophrenia. The symptomology of those with OCD was recurrent and persistent thoughts (14.3%), attempts to suppress thoughts (15.5%), impulses recognized as from one's own mind (11.9%), compulsions of washing hands, counting, and checking (13.1%), distress prevention behavior (9.6%), excessive thoughts (13.1%), and caused distress/time consuming (11.9%) (Ndetei et al., 2008). The study authors postulated that the Kenyan patients had difficulty distinguishing between OC and psychotic symptomology. Kenyans tend to believe that OCD is caused by witchcraft, and therefore patients consult traditional healers, with no results. They may consult one healer after another, while symptoms continue to worsen (Karume & Osiemo, 2014).

One rare glimpse into the phenomenology of OCD in Africa comes from a report that originates from the Republic of Benin, a west African country bordered by Nigeria. The authors provide a case series of OCD symptoms in five young males (Bertschy & Ahyi, 1991). The symptoms observed in the five cases included rituals of counting and checking, behavior obsessions, compulsive urges to act out embarrassing behavior, doubt obsessions and contamination rituals (Bertschy & Ahyi, 1991). The counting and checking behaviors were evident in a series of daily rituals that lasted for several months where the young man felt compelled to spend hours recounting all of the people he had associated with in his life. In the second case, the patient ruminated about smiling at inappropriate times and his religious convictions. Contamination rituals were also observed in two cases. One young man would refuse to use utensils if they did not meet his standard of cleanliness and would also not eat the section of food that had been touched by his hands, which was noted as deviating from the cultural standard in that region. The other case that exhibited contamination rituals was evidenced by a phobic reaction to dirt and excrement that resulted in nausea and vomiting from remembering such triggers (Bertschy & Ahyi, 1991). In three of the five cases, comorbid depressive episodes were documented, along with an additional case noting previous affective psychotic episodes. The authors conclude that despite cultural differences, OCD symptoms are generally similar to those seen in the West (Bertschy & Ahyi, 1991).

Another study conducted with an Afrikaner founder population (descendants of mostly White Dutch settlers in South Africa in the seventeenth and eighteenth centuries) found that among those with schizophrenia or schizoaffective disorder, 13.2% had OCD or OC symptoms. The most prevalent obsession was contamination, followed by religious obsessions, pathological doubt and sexual obsessions. Compulsions reported were checking behaviors, repetitive rituals, washing and counting (Seedat, Roos, Pretorius, Karayiorgou, & Nel, 2007). More research is needed to determine the OCD symptom dimensions separate from comorbid schizophrenia and schizoaffective disorder.

In post-conflict South Sudan, Ayazi, Lien, Eide, Swartz, and Hauff (2014) sought to find the association between exposure to traumatic events and the onset of anxiety disorders. In their community sample of 1,200 participants it was found that 12.7% had OCD. OCD was found to potentially be associated with exposure to traumatic events, although much higher prevalence rates were observed in other disorders (i.e., panic disorder, generalized anxiety disorder and post-traumatic stress disorder).

Unfortunately, on the African continent, many countries have no documented information on OCD (Karume & Osiemo, 2014), and thus more research is needed to identify the most prevalent specific obsessive-compulsive symptom dimensions.

OCD in Hispanic and South American Samples

To date there have been few studies conducted that address OCD in Hispanic and South American populations. Studies that have compared prevalence rates of OCD between Latino and European American populations in the US have yielded inconsistent findings. Studies of OCD in Latin America note a lifetime prevalence rate of 1.4% in Mexico City, 1.2% in Chile and 3.2% in Puerto Rico (Canino et al., 1987; Caraveo-Anduaga & Bermúdez, 2004; Vicente et al., 2006).

Although there have been few studies of symptom dimensions in Hispanic Americans, one study did note greater contamination concerns in a non-clinical sample (Williams, Turkheimer, Schmidt, & Oltmanns, 2005). In a study conducted in Costa Rica, participants reported lower levels of symptom severity, including lower levels of functional impairment and less perceived distress, when compared to their

US counterparts (Chavira et al., 2008). Culturally relevant explanations cited for the differences were a possible lack of psychosocial stressors in the Costa Rican sample, as the participants were from a primarily agrarian region of the country and lower levels of perceived stress possibly reflected the ability of the participants to "accommodate" their symptoms (i.e., avoiding driving due to the fear of harming others and this was easily avoided due to the ease of access in Costa Rican society) (Chavira, et al., 2008).

A study in Rio de Janeiro outlined differences with respect to content of obsessions, as the most commonly reported obsessions included the theme of aggression, (69.7%), followed by contamination (53.5%) (Fontenelle, Mendlowicz, Marques, & Versiani, 2004). This differs from findings in many other cultures, where issues of contamination seem to overshadow others in the spectrum of OCD manifestations (i.e., Matsunaga et al., 2008). Possible reasons for the findings of their study were the climbing rates of mortality and morbidity resulting from violent causes, therefore that population has likely prioritized avoiding violence. It is important to note that this study is from a single city in Brazil and reflects the urban culture of the participants.

In a Mexican study by Nicolini and colleagues (1997), contamination obsessions were the most common (58%), followed by sexual (31%), and aggressive obsessions (13%). The proportion of men to women in the study was disproportionate, with only 37% of the sample being men. The authors considered it a cultural phenomenon in which Mexican men have the tendency to deny having a mental illness. Men in the study were also found to have a slightly earlier onset of the disorder than women, with men's onset at 19.5 years and women's at 22 years.

In another Mexican study, a clinical sample and control were assessed for personality traits that correlate with the severity of OCD. Their findings supported previous research that found OCD patients to have higher levels of harm avoidance and lower levels of self-directedness and cooperativeness. Low self-directedness was found to correlate with increasing severity of OCD symptoms and comorbidity with Major Depressive Disorder (Cruz-Fuentes, Blas, Gonzalez, Camarena, & Nicolini, 2004).

Discussion

Although OCD is due in part to biological predisposition, culture plays an important role in shaping the phenomenology of the disorder. Obsessional content stems from that which is culturally relevant to the sufferer, resulting in large differences in the expression of symptoms.

Religious Differences

The presence of religious rituals in OCD symptomology is generally an indicator that faith is practiced in excess of cultural norms. In Christian samples the most often reported symptoms were obsessions with contamination and thought control, whereas the Catholic subgroup had an emphasis on perfectionism. The Jewish subgroup had obsessions of a religious nature (Huppert et al., 2007), and themes of morality and divine retribution. There were differences in symptom recognition and help-seeking behaviors between devout Orthodox Jews and their less observant counterparts. In Middle Eastern cultures we see high Islamic affiliation and symptom dimensions that reflect this, and obsessions in the Islamic subgroup centered on purity and religious themes (e.g., Okasha et al., 1994). The obsession with physical cleanliness in the symptomology of highly religious cultures seems to be a manifestation of the emphasis on spiritual purity within the society. OCD in Near Eastern countries tends to also reflect religious beliefs, as well as familial and societal values (e.g., kissing the feet of respected elders).

Research has noted that religious themed-OCD may be more resistant to treatments (e.g., Williams et al., 2014), and given how many experience these types of symptoms this has important implications for OCD sufferers worldwide. It may be difficult for a patient and/or clinician to distinguish between acceptable religious/moral thoughts or behavior versus excessive symptoms driven by OCD. Thus, cultural competence on the part of the therapists and a good understanding of a patient's belief system is essential (Chapman et al., 2014).

Regional Differences

Four or five factor models with the symptom dimensions contamination/cleaning, hoarding, symmetry/ordering, taboo thoughts/mental compulsions, and doubt/checking are commonplace in Western samples (Abramowitz et al., 2003; Bloch et al., 2008). However, the cultural diversity within Western samples has historically been scant (Williams et al., 2010). Research in Hispanic and Latin American samples has shown contamination and aggression to be among the most common symptom presentations. Indian samples emphasized themes concerning contamination and pathological doubt, with greater gender differences in symptom dimensions. In East Asian samples, symptom dimensions of contamination and symmetry were most prominent, with cultural differences between Japan and China noted (i.e., greater need of symmetry in China and contamination and aggression in Japan) (Liu et al., 2008). The findings suggest that there are elements of symptom dimension that generalize to certain regions and religious groups across the world.

Similarities in Symptoms

OCD sufferers around the world display cross-cultural similarities as well. The majority of the cultures studied include contamination fears as a primary dimension (e.g., Nicolini et al., 1997; Okasha et al., 1994; Reddy et al., 2005). This fear often results in hand-washing compulsions, seen in many cultures (Jaisoorya et al., 2009; Kim et al., 2005; Okasha et al., 1994; Williams, Elstein, Buckner, Abelson, & Himle, 2012c). Matsunaga et al. (2008) implicate biology as a decisive component in symptom presentation and highlight similarities across cultures. Symptom dimensions, like contamination, which are present cross-culturally, support this hypothesis. Additionally, Kim et al. (2005) found differences between the two genotypic groups with respect to religious/somatic obsessions, which provides additional evidence for a biological basis for symptom dimensions.

Conclusions

It is undeniable that cultural context is important in the diagnosis and treatment of OCD. Cross-cultural research in OCD is ongoing, and new findings will help to establish the degree to which cultural beliefs can exacerbate, ameliorate, or alter the symptom presentation and experience of OCD for those diagnosed. There is a paucity of research in certain regions and cultures that should be addressed, including African samples other than the highly Muslim Saharan region and White South Africa (e.g., Stein et al., 2008), Hispanic Americans, and ethnoracial minority groups in general. The implications of cross-cultural differences are pivotal in the development of empirically supported treatments for individuals of various cultural backgrounds, as well as for determining the applicability of contemporary literature to diverse cultural groups.

References

Abramowitz, J. S., Franklin, M. E., Schwartz, S. A., & Furr, J. M. (2003). Symptom presentation and outcome of cognitive-behavior therapy for obsessive-compulsive disorder. *Journal of Consulting and Clinical Psychology, 71*, 1049–1057.

Abramowitz, J. S., Deacon, B. J., Woods, C. M., & Tolin, D. F. (2004). Association between protestant religiosity and obsessive-compulsive symptoms and cognitions. *Depression and Anxiety, 20*(2), 70–76. doi:10.1002/da.20021.

Al-Solaim, L., & Loewenthal, K. (2011). Religion and obsessive-compulsive disorder (OCD) among young Muslim women in Saudi Arabia. *Mental Health, Religion & Culture, 14*(2), 169–182.

American Psychiatric Association. (2013). *Diagnostic and Statistical Manual of Mental Disorders* (5th ed.). Arlington, VA: American Psychiatric Publishing.

Ayazi, T., Lien, L., Eide, A., Swartz, L., & Hauff, E. (2014). Association between exposure to traumatic events and anxiety disorders in a post-conflict setting: A cross-sectional community study in South Sudan. *BMC Psychiatry, 14*(6), 1–10.

Baer, L. (1994). Factor analysis of symptom subtypes of obsessive compulsive disorder and their relation to personality and tic disorders. *Journal of Clinical Psychiatry, 55*(3, Suppl), 18–23.

Bertschy, G., & Ahyi, R. G. (1991). Obsessive-compulsive disorders in Benin: Five case reports. *Psychopathology, 24*, 398–401.

Bloch M. H., Landeros-Weisenberger, A., Rosário, M. C., Pittenge, C., & Leckman, J. F. (2008). Meta-analysis of the symptom structure of obsessive-compulsive disorder. *American Journal of Psychiatry, 165*, 1532–1542. doi:10.1176/appi.ajp.2008.08020320

Canino, G. J., Bird, H. R., Shrout, P. E., Rubio-Stipec, M., Bravo, M., Martinez, R., … Guevara, L. M. (1987). The prevalence of specific psychiatric disorders in Puerto Rico. *Archives of General Psychiatry, 44*(8), 727–735.

Caraveo-Anduaga, J. J., & Bermúdez, E. (2004). The epidemiology of obsessive-compulsive disorder in Mexico City. *Salud Mental, 27*(2), 1–6.

Cathey, A. J., & Wetterneck, C. T. (2013). Stigma and disclosure of intrusive thoughts about sexual themes. *Journal of Obsessive-Compulsive and Related Disorders, 2*, 439–443.

Chakraborty, K., Das, G., Dan, A., Bandyopadhyay, G., & Chatterjee, M. (2013). Perceptions about the cause of psychiatric disorders and subsequent help seeking patterns among psychiatric outpatients in a tertiary care centre in eastern India. *German Journal of Psychiatry, 16*, 7–15.

Chapman, L. K., DeLapp, R., & Williams, M. T. (2014). Impact of race, ethnicity, and culture on the expression and assessment of psychopathology. In D. C. Beidel, B. C. Frueh, & M. Hersen (Eds.), *Adult Psychopathology and Diagnosis* (7th ed.). Chichester: Wiley.

Chavira, D. A., Garrido, H., Bagnarello, M., Azzam, A., Reus, V. I., & Mathews, C. A. (2008). A comparative study of obsessive-compulsive disorder in Costa Rica and the United States. *Depression and Anxiety, 25*(7), 609–619. doi:10.1002/da.20357.

Cherian, A. V., Narayanaswamy, J. C., Srinivasaraju, R., Viswanath, B., Math, S. B., Kandavel, T., & Reddy, Y.C. J. (2012). Does insight have specific correlation with symptom dimensions in OCD? *Journal of Affective Disorders, 138*, 352–359.

Cherian, A. V., Narayanaswamy, J. C., Viswanath, B., Guru, N., George, C. M., Math, S. B., Kandavel, T., & Reddy, Y.C. J. (2013). Gender differences in obsessive-compulsive disorder: Findings from a large Indian sample. *Asian Journal of Psychiatry, 9*, 17–21.

Chowdhury, A. N., Mukherjee, H., Ghosh, K., & Chowdhury, S. (2003). Puppy pregnancy in humans: A culture-bound disorder in rural West Bengal, India. *International Journal of Social Psychiatry, 49*(1), 35–42.

Coles, M. E., & Coleman, S. L. (2010). Barriers to treatment seeking for anxiety disorders: Initial data on the role of mental health literacy. *Depression and Anxiety, 27*, 63–71. doi: 10.1002/da.20620.

Cruz-Fuentes, C., Blas, C., Gonzalez, L., Camarena, B., & Nicolini, H. (2004). Severity of obsessive-compulsive symptoms is related to self-directedness character trait in obsessive-compulsive disorder. *CNS Spectrums, 9*(8), 607–612.

Davis, D. M., Steever, A. M., Terwillinger, J. M., & Williams, M. T. (2012). The relationship between the culture-bound syndrome koro and obsessive-compulsive disorder. In G. R. Hayes & M. H. Bryant (Eds.), *Psychology of Culture* (pp. 213–221). New York: Nova Science Publishers.

Feusner, J. D., Phillips, K. A., & Stein, D. J. (2010). Olfactory reference syndrome: Issues for DSM-V. *Depression and Anxiety, 27*, 592–599.

Foa, E. B., Kozak, M. J., Goodman, W. K., Hollander, E., Jenike, M. A., & Rasmussen, S. A. (1995). DSM-IV field trial: Obsessive-compulsive disorder. *American Journal of Psychiatry, 152*(1), 90–96.

Fontenelle, L. F., Mendlowicz, M. V., Marques, C., & Versiani, M. (2004). Trans-cultural aspects of obsessive-compulsive disorder: A description of a Brazilian sample and a systematic review of international clinical studies. *Journal of Psychiatric Research, 38*(4), 403–411. doi: 10.1016/j.jpsychires.2003.12.004.

Ghassenzadeh, H., Moitabia, R., Khamseh, A., Ebrahimkhani, N., Issazadegan, A-A., & Saif-Nobakht, Z. (2002). Symptoms of obsessive-compulsive disorder in a sample of Iranian patients. *International Journal of Social Psychiatry, 48*(1), 20–28. doi: 10.1177/002076402128783055.

Goodman, W. K., Price, L. H., Rasmussen, S. A., Mazure, C., Fleischmann, R. L., Hill, C. L., & Charney, D. S. (1989). The Yale–Brown Obsessive Compulsive Scale. Part I. Development, use and reliability. *Archives of General Psychiatry, 46*(11), 1006–1011.

Goodwin, R., Koenen, K. C., Hellman, F., Guardino, M., & Struening, E. (2002). Help seeking and access to mental health treatment for obsessive-compulsive disorder. *Acta Psychiatrica Scandinavica, 106*(2), 143–149

Girishchandra, B. G., & Sumant, K. (2001). Phenomenology of obsessive-compulsive disorder: A factor analytic approach. *Indian Journal of Psychiatry, 43*(4), 306–316.

Grover, S., Patra, B. N., Aggarwal, M., Avasthi, A., Chakrabarti, S., & Malhotra, S. (2014). Relationship of supernatural beliefs and first treatment contact in patients with obsessive compulsive disorder: An exploratory study from India. *International Journal of Social Psychiatry*, doi: 10.1177/0020764014527266.

Hatch, M. L., Friedman, S., & Paradis, C. M. (1996). Behavioral treatment of obsessive-compulsive disorder in African Americans. *Cognitive and Behavioral Practice, 3*(2), 303–315.

Heeringa, S. G., Wagner, J., Torres, M., Duan, N., Adams, T., & Berglund, P. (2004). Sample designs and sampling methods for the Collaborative Psychiatric Epidemiology Studies (CPES). *International Journal of Methods in Psychiatric Research, 13*(4), 221–240.

Himle, J. A., Muroff, J. R., Taylor, R. J., Baser, R. E., Abelson, J. M., Hanna, G. L., & Jackson, J. S. (2008). Obsessive-compulsive disorder among African Americans and blacks of Caribbean descent: Results from the national survey of American life. *Depression and Anxiety, 25*, 993–1005.

Huppert, J. D., & Siev, J. (2010). Treating scrupulosity in religious individuals using cognitive-behavioral therapy. *Cognitive and Behavioral Practice, 17*, 382–392.

Huppert, J. D., Siev, J., & Kushner, E. S. (2007). When religion and obsessive-compulsive disorder collide: Treating scrupulosity in Ultra-Orthodox Jews. *Journal of Clinical Psychology, 63*(10), 925–941.

Inozu, M., Clark, D. A., & Karanci, A. N. (2012). Scrupulosity in Islam: A comparison of highly religious Turkish and Canadian samples. *Behavior Therapy, 43*, 190–202.

Jaisoorya, T. S., Reddy, Y., Srinath, S. S., & Thennarasu, K. K. (2009). Sex differences in Indian patients with obsessive-compulsive disorder. *Comprehensive Psychiatry, 50*(1), 70–75.

Juang, Y., & Liu, C. (2001). Phenomenology of obsessive-compulsive disorder in Taiwan. *Psychiatry And Clinical Neurosciences, 55*(6), 623–627

Karume, M. K., & Osiemo, I. K. (2014). Obsessive-compulsive disorder: Meta analysis. *Prime Journal of Business Administration and Management (BAM), 4*(6), 1507–1511.

Kessler, R. C., Berglund, P., Demler, O., Jin, R., Merikangas, K. R., & Walters, E. E. (2005a). Lifetime prevalence and age-of-onset distributions of DSM-IV disorders in the National Comorbidity Survey Replication. *Archives of General Psychiatry, 62*(6), 593–602. doi: 10.1001/archpsyc.62.6.593.

Kessler, R. C., Chiu, W. T., Demler, O., Merikangas, K. R., & Walters, E. E. (2005b). Prevalence, severity, and comorbidity of 12-month DSM-IV disorders in the National Comorbidity Survey Replication. *Archives of General Psychiatry, 62*(6), 617–627. doi: 10.1001/archpsyc.62.6.617.

Kim, S. J., Lee, H. S., & Kim, C. H. (2005). Obsessive-compulsive disorder, factor analyzed symptom dimensions and serotonin transporter polymorphism. *Neuropsychobiology, 52,* 176–182. doi: 10.1159/000088860.

Knauft, B. (2010). Spirits, sex, and celebration. In Ryan, M. (Ed.), *The Gebusi: Lives transformed in a rainforest world* (pp. 66–77). New York: McGraw Hill.

Labad, J., Mencho, J., Alonso, P., Segalas, C., Jimenez, S., Jaurrieta, N., & ... Vallejo, J. (2008). Gender differences in obsessive-compulsive symptom dimensions. *Depression and Anxiety, 25*(10), 832–838. doi: 10.1002/da.20332.

Lemelson, R. (2003). Obsessive-compulsive disorder in Bali: The cultural shaping of a neuropsychiatric disorder. *Transcultural Psychiatry, 40*(3), 377–408. doi: 10.1177/13634615030403004.

Leonard, R. C., & Riemann, B. C. (2012). The co-occurrence of obsessions and compulsions in OCD. *Journal of Obsessive-Compulsive and Related Disorders, 1,* 211–215.

Lewis-Hall, F. (1991). OCD said to be under-diagnosed in minority populations. *OCD Newsletter, 5,* 1–3.

Li, Y., Marques, L., Hinton, D. E., Wang, Y., & Xiao, Z. (2009). Symptom dimensions in Chinese patients with obsessive-compulsive disorder. *CNS Neuroscience and Therapeutics, 15*(3), 276–282. doi: 10.1111/j.1755-5949.2009.00099.x.

Liu, J., Cui, Y., & Fang, M. (2008). Trans-cultural comparative research on symptoms of neuroses in China and Japan. *Chinese Mental Health Journal, 22*(1), 1–4.

Mahgoub, O. M., & Abdel-Hafiez, H. B. (1991). Pattern of obsessive-compulsive disorder in eastern Saudi Arabia. *British Journal of Psychiatry, 158,* 840–842.

Matsunaga, H., Maebayashi, K., Hayashida, K., Okino, K., Matsui, T., Iketani, T., & Stein, D. J. (2008). Symptom structure in Japanese patients with obsessive-compulsive disorder. *American Journal of Psychiatry, 165*(2), 251–253.

Ndetei, D. M., Pizzo, M., Ongecha, F. A., Khasakhala, L. I., Maru, H., Mutiso, V., & Kokonya, D. A. (2008). Obsessive-compulsive (OC) symptoms in psychiatric in-patients at Mathari hospital, Kenya. *African Journal of Psychiatry, 11,* 182–186.

Nicolini, H., Benilde, O., Giuffra, L., Paez, F., Mejia, J., Sanchez de Carmona, M., Sidenberg, D., & Ramon de la Fuente, J. (1997). Age of onset, gender and severity in obsessive-compulsive disorder: A study on a Mexican population. *Salud Mental, 20*(3), 1–4.

Okasha, A. A., Saad, A. A., Khalil, A. H., & Dawla, A. (1994). Phenomenology of obsessive-compulsive disorder: A transcultural study. *Comprehensive Psychiatry, 35*(3), 191–197.

Olatunji, B. O., Tomarken, A., & Zhao, M. (2014). Effects of exposure to stereotype cues on contamination aversion and avoidance in African Americans. *Journal of Social and Clinical Psychology, 33*(3), 229–249.

Phillips, K. A., & Menard, W. (2011). Olfactory reference syndrome: Demographic and clinical features of imagined body odor. *General Hospital Psychiatry, 33,* 398–406.

Pinto, A., Eisen, J. L., Mancebo, M. C., Greenberg, B. D., Stout, R. L., & Rasmussen, S. A. (2007). Taboo thoughts and doubt/checking: A refinement of the factor structure for obsessive-compulsive disorder symptoms. *Psychiatry Research, 151*(3), 255–258.

Reddy, Y. C., Janardhan, Jaideep T., Khanna, S., & Srinath, S. (2005). Obsessive-Compulsive Disorder research in India: A review. In B. E. Ling (Ed.), *Obsessive compulsive disorder research* (pp. 93–120). New York: Nova Biomedical.

Reynolds, E. H., & Wilson, J. V. K. (2014). Obsessive compulsive disorder and psychopathic behavior in Babylon. *Journal of Neurology, Neurosurgery & Psychiatry, 83,* 199–201.

Rohayati, D., & Fakrurrozi, M. (2013). Efektifit as ERP dengan menggunakan tim untuk mengurangi gejala OCD (Effectiveness of using ERP team to reduce OCD symptoms). *Proceeding PESAT (Psikologi, Ekonomi, Sastra, Arsitektur & Teknik Sipil), 5,* 99–107.

Rosmarin, D. H., Pirutinsky, S., & Siev, J. (2010). Recognition of scrupulosity and non-religious OCD by Orthodox and non-Orthodox Jews. *Journal of Social and Clinical Psychology, 29*(8), 930–944. doi: 10.1521/jscp.2010.29.8.930.

Roy, D., Hazarika, S., Bhattacharya, A., Das, S., Nath, K., & Saddichha, S. (2011). Koro: Culture bound or mass hysteria? *Australian & New Zealand Journal of Psychiatry, 45*(8), 683.

Ruscio, A. M., Stein, D. J., Chiu, W. T., & Kessler, R. C. (2010). The epidemiology of obsessive- compulsive disorder in the National Comorbidity Survey Replication. *Molecular Psychiatry, 15,* 53–63.

Saleem, S., & Mahmood, Z. (2009). OCD in a cultural context: A phenomenological approach. *Pakistan Journal of Psychological Research, 24*(1/2), 27–42.

Seedat, F., Roos, J. L., Pretorius, H. W., Karayiorgou, M., & Nel, B. (2007). Prevalence and clinical characteristics of obsessive-compulsive disorder and obsessive compulsive symptoms in Afrikaner schizophrenia and schizoaffective disorder patients. *African Journal of Psychiatry, 10,* 219–224.

Shafran, R., Thordarson, D. S., & Rachman, S. (1996). Thought-action fusion in obsessive-compulsive disorder, *Journal of Anxiety Disorders, 10,* 379–391

Simonds, L. M., & Thorpe, S. J. (2003). Attitudes toward obsessive-compulsive disorders: An experimental investigation. *Social Psychiatry & Psychiatric Epidemiology, 38,* 331–336.

Shooka, A. A., Al-Haddad, M. K., & Raees, A. A. (1998). OCD in Bahrain: A phenomenological profile. *International Journal of Social Psychiatry, 44*(2), 147–154.

Sica, C., Novara, C., & Sanavio, E. (2002). Religiousness and obsessive-compulsive cognitions and symptoms in an Italian population. *Behaviour Research and Therapy, 40*(7), 813–823. doi: 10.1016/S0005-7967(01)00120-6.

Siu, B. W.M., Lam, C., & Chan, W. (2012). Pattern and determinants of burden in Chinese families of adults with obsessive-compulsive disorder. *Journal of Anxiety Disorders, 26,* 252–257.

Stein, D. J., Carey, P. D., Lochner, C., Seedat, S., Fineberg, N., & Andersen, E. W. (2008). Escitalopram in obsessive-compulsive disorder: response of symptom dimensions to pharmacotherapy. *CNS Spectrums, 13*(6), 492–498.

Subramaniam, M., Abdin, E., Vaingankar, J. A., & Chong, S. A. (2012). Obsessive-compulsive disorder: Prevalence, correlates, help-seeking and quality of life in a multiracial Asian population. *Social Psychiatry and Psychiatric Epidemiology, 47,* 2035–2043.

Subramaniam, M., Abdin, E., Vaingankar, J. A., & Chong, S. A. (2013). Gender differences in disability in a multiethnic Asian population: The Singapore mental health study. *Comprehensive Psychiatry, 54,* 381–387.

Torres, A. R., Prince, M. J., Bebbington, P. E., Bhugra, D. K., Brugha, T. S., Farrell, M., Jenkins, R., … Singleton, N. (2007). Treatment seeking by individuals with obsessive-compulsive disorder from the British Psychiatric Morbidity Survey of 2000. *Psychiatric Services, 58,* 977–982.

US Census Bureau. (2014). Population Clock. Retrieved from http://www.census.gov/population/popclockworld.html, last accessed June 29, 2014.

Vicente, B., Kohn, R., Rioseco, P., Saldivia, S., Levav, I., & Torres, S. (2006). Lifetime and 12-month prevalence of DSM-III-R disorders in the Chile psychiatric prevalence study. *American Journal of Psychiatry, 163,* 1362–1370.

Vriends, N. N., Pfaltz, M. C., Novianti, P. P., & Hadiyono, J. J. (2013). Taijin kyofusho and social anxiety and their clinical relevance in Indonesia and Switzerland. *Frontiers in Psychology, 4,* 1–9.

Weismann, M. M., Bland, R. C., Canino, G. J., Greenwald, S., Hwu, H. G., Chung, C., ... Yeh, E. K. (1994). The cross national epidemiology of obsessive compulsive disorder: The Cross National Collaborative Group. *Journal of Clinical Psychiatry*, 55(3 Suppl.), 5–10.

Wheaton, M. G., Berman, N. C., Fabricant, L. E., & Abramowitz, J. S. (2013). Differences in obsessive-compulsive symptoms and obsessive beliefs: A comparison between African Americans, Asian Americans, Latino Americans, and European Americans. *Cognitive Behaviour Therapy*, 42(1), 9–20

Williams, A. D., Lau, G., & Grisham, J. R. (2013). Thought–action fusion as a mediator of religiosity and obsessive-compulsive symptoms. *Journal of Behavior Therapy and Experimental Psychiatry*, 44, 207–212.

Williams, M. T., & Ching, T. H. W. (2016). Transgender anxiety, cultural issues, and cannabis in obsessive-compulsive disorder. *Endocrine Practice*, 2(3). doi: 10.4158/ep161356.co.

Williams, M. T., Slimowicz, J., Tellawi, G., & Wetterneck, C. (2014). Sexual orientation symptoms in obsessive compulsive disorder: Assessment and treatment with cognitive behavioral therapy. *Directions in Psychiatry*, 34(1), 37–50.

Williams, M. T., Domanico, J., Marques, L., Leblanc, N. J., & Turkheimer. (2012a). Barriers to treatment among African Americans with obsessive-compulsive disorder. *Journal of Anxiety Disorders*, 26, 555–563.

Williams, M. T., Abramowitz, J. S., & Olatunji, B. O. (2012b).The relationship between contamination cognitions, anxiety, and disgust in two ethnic groups. *Journal of Behavior Therapy and Experimental Psychiatry*, 43, 632–637, doi: 10.1016/j.jbtep.2011.09.003.

Williams, M. T., Elstein, J., Buckner, E., Abelson, J., & Himle, J. (2012c). Symptom dimensions in two samples of African Americans with obsessive-compulsive disorder. *Journal of Obsessive-Compulsive & Related Disorders*, 1(3), 145–152.

Williams, M. T., & Farris, S. G. (2011). Sexual orientation obsessions in obsessive-compulsive disorder: Prevalence and correlates. *Psychiatry Research*, 187, 156–159.

Williams, M. T., Farris, S. G., Turkheimer, E., Pinto, A., Ozanick, K., Franklin, M. E., Simpson, H. B., Liebowitz, M., & Foa, E. B. (2011). The myth of the pure obsessional type in obsessive-compulsive disorder. *Depression & Anxiety*, 28 (6), 495–500.

Williams, M. T., Mugno, B., Franklin, M. E., & Faber, S. (2013). Symptom dimensions in obsessive-compulsive disorder: phenomenology and treatment with exposure and ritual prevention. *Psychopathology*, 46, 365–376.

Williams, M., Powers, M., Yun, Y. G., & Foa, E. B. (2010). Minority representation in randomized controlled trials for obsessive-compulsive disorder. *Journal of Anxiety Disorders*, 24, 171–177.

Williams, M. T., Proetto, D., Casiano, D., & Franklin, M. E. (2012d). Recruitment of a hidden population: African Americans with obsessive-compulsive disorder. *Contemporary Clinical Trials*. doi:10.1016/j.cct.2011.09.001.

Williams, M. T., & Turkheimer, E. (2007). Identification and explanation of racial differences on contamination measures. *Behavior Research and Therapy*, 45(12), 3041–3050. doi: 10.1016/j.brat.2007.08.013.

Williams, M. T., Turkheimer, E., Schmidt, K., & Oltmanns, T. (2005). Ethnic identification biases responses to the Padua Inventory for obsessive-compulsive disorder. *Assessment*, 12(2), 174–185.

Williams, M. T., Wetterneck, C., Tellawi, G., & Duque, G. (2015). Domains of distress among people with sexual orientation obsessions. *Archives of Sexual Behavior*, 14(3), 783–789. doi: 10.1007/s10508-014-0421-0.

Yorulmaz, O., & Işık, B. (2011). Cultural context, obsessive-compulsive disorder symptoms, and cognitions: A preliminary study of three Turkish samples living in different countries. *International Journal of Psychology*, 46(2), 136–143.

5

Diagnostic Assessment and Measures of Symptom Severity for OCD in Adults

Kevin D. Wu

Effective assessment is requisite to quality treatment in all areas of clinical psychology, but obsessive-compulsive disorder (OCD) presents particular challenges. The aim of this chapter is to consider fundamental issues in adult OCD symptom assessment and provide an overview of common instruments so that readers will gain a sense of the challenges they are likely to face, thus preparing them for practical decision-making.

Overview

Fundamentally, OCD is the experience of intrusive and upsetting thoughts, to which people respond with rigid, repetitive, and excessive compensatory behaviors. Therefore, OCD assessment is about determining whether people have these experiences, and whether symptoms are severe enough to warrant a diagnosis, are better accounted for by another condition, and later, are responsive to treatment. Although its original cause is unknown, clinically severe OCD is fully defined by these distressing thoughts and difficult-to-control behaviors; no genetic or biological variable is necessary for, or pathognomonic of, its diagnosis. The question of whether the cause includes biological components is at this time outside the conversation of clinical assessment. Although this conflicts with references in the literature to OCD as a *brain disease* or a *neurological condition*, it reflects the state of the science: the only instruments currently available for clinical OCD assessment are client-, clinician-, or other-reports of subjective symptom experience and behavioral responses.

The Wiley Handbook of Obsessive Compulsive Disorders, Volume I, First Edition.
Edited by Jonathan S. Abramowitz, Dean McKay, and Eric A. Storch.
© 2017 John Wiley & Sons Ltd. Published 2017 by John Wiley & Sons Ltd.

The Challenges of OCD

Heterogeneity

The above description of OCD allows for a very broad range of *kinds* of intrusive thoughts, and therefore Challenge No. 1: symptom heterogeneity. For many years, OCD measurement has had a relative focus on specific content, rather than obsessions/compulsions in general. This is for several reasons, including differential diagnosis (e.g., distinction from *worry* in generalized anxiety) and attempts to identify homogeneous subgroups (e.g., *checkers* vs. *washers*). Many instruments, particularly questionnaires, target specific themes such as *sexual* or *contamination* obsessions, and *checking* or *washing* compulsions. This has permitted examination of subgroups and the study of unique associations regarding specific themes (e.g., relations between checking and the cognitive vulnerability intolerance of uncertainty). Although the field has converged on a finite list of broad OCD themes (Abramowitz et al., 2010), there is no universal list of specific content at the level of idiosyncratic thoughts and behaviors. Truly, the content is limitless. As a result, several OCD symptom measures have been developed over the years and they are not interchangeable (however, convergence is notable) (Wu & Carter, 2008). Beyond what may be considered "classic" OCD symptoms such as checking and washing, some measures include relatively unique content. For example, a version of the Padua Inventory (PI-WSUR) (Burns, Keortge, Formea, & Sternberger, 1996) includes measurement of impulses to harm another person. The Vancouver Obsessional Compulsive Inventory (VOCI) (Thordarson et al., 2004) assesses "just right" symptoms not found on most other measures. In this sense, it is difficult to consider an instrument *comprehensive* in terms of item-level content, and measurement idiosyncrasies can complicate matters (e.g., generalizability of research findings). Table 5.1 summarizes the content included in the most common OCD symptom measures.

Beyond cross-instrument challenges, a consequence of heterogeneity involves the use of total versus subscale scores. For relatively homogeneous constructs, clinical instruments tend to provide total scores. An example is depression assessment, which often relies on a sum total of measures such as the Beck Depression Inventory (BDI) (Beck, Steer, & Brown, 1996). Although some data support multifactor structures, use of a BDI total score is common practice. Comparisons are made to normative data, and cut-scores (reflecting varying degrees of severity for different purposes, such as screening vs. treatment response) can inform the relevant clinical question. In OCD assessment, content heterogeneity poses a risk to such an approach because an individual need not struggle with more than one type of symptom theme to qualify for a diagnosis. For example, an individual who endorses only inappropriate sexual obsessions may present with sufficient distress/impairment owing to these symptoms to meet the formal criteria for OCD; there is no requirement to endorse any of the other content on a given instrument. As such, reliance on a total score that spans multiple content domains risks underestimation of the severity of an individual's struggles with OCD. This is particularly true when working with a client who has a narrow symptom presentation, such as only one theme of intrusive thought. Endorsement of severe symptoms on only one subscale may not generate as high of a total score as mild/moderate endorsement of many subscales. Summerfeldt (2001) referred to this situation as confounding "variety with severity" and may be analogous to whether

Table 5.1 Snapshot of OCD symptom and related assessment instruments

Interviews	Length	Scales	Clinical application	Notes
SCID First et al. (2002)	90 min	DSM-IV Disorders	Diagnosis	Clinical/research versions; multiple translations; SCID-5 (forthcoming)
ADIS-IV DiNardo et al. (1994)	90 min	DSM-IV Anxiety + other domains	Diagnosis	Also provides dimensional assessment; ADIS-5
MINI Sheehan et al. (1998)	15–20 min	19 DSM-IV Disorders, including OCD	Screening	Multiple translations; MINI 7.0 for DSM-5
YBOCS Goodman et al. (1989)	40 min	Severity Total Obsessions Compulsions Investigational Items (e.g., insight)	Symptom content; Severity/Tx response	Not for screening/diagnosis; Self-report versions
DYBOCS Rosario-Campos et al. 2006	40 min	Harm Obsessions Sex/Religious Obsessions Symmetry/Counting Contamination Hoarding Miscellaneous	Symptom content; Severity/Tx response	Multiple translations

Note: SCID = Structured Clinical Interview for DSM-IV; ADIS-IV = Anxiety Disorders Interview Schedule for DSM-IV; MINI = Mini International Neuropsychiatric Interview; (D)YBOCS = (Dimensional) Yale–Brown Obsessive-Compulsive Scale.

(*Continued*)

Table 5.1 (Continued)

Questionnaires	Length	Scales	Clinical application	Notes
PI-WSUR Burns et al. (1996)	39 items	OCD Total Harm Obsessions Harm Impulses Checking Contamination Dressing/grooming	Screening	Revised to remove items targeting worry content; multiple translations
OCI-R Foa et al. (2002)	18 items	OCD Total Checking Washing Ordering Obsessing Neutralizing Hoarding	Screening	Revised from seven-scale, 42-item version; multiple translations
VOCI Thordarson et al. (2004)	55 items	OCD Total Checking Contamination Obsessions "Just Right" Indecisiveness Hoarding	Screening	Revised MOCI by expanding range of content; French translation

Note: PI-WSUR = Padua Inventory–Washington State University Revision; OCI-R = Obsessive-Compulsive Inventory – Revised; VOCI = Vancouver Obsessive-Compulsive Inventory; MOCI = Maudsley Obsessive-Compulsive Inventory.

Table 5.1 (Continued)

Questionnaires	Length	Scales	Clinical application	Notes
SCOPI Watson & Wu (2005)	47 items	OCD Total Checking Cleanliness Rituals Pathological impulses Hoarding	Screening	OCD total includes first 3 subscales
CBOCI Clark et al. (2005)	25 items	OCD Total Obsessions Compulsions	Screening; severity	Modeled after the BDI
FOCI Storch et al. (2007)	20 items	Symptom checklist total Symptom severity total	Symptom content; Severity/Tx response	Checklist items derived from YBOCS Symptom Checklist
DOCS Abramowitz et al. (2010)	20 items	OCD Total Contamination Responsibility for harm Unacceptable thoughts Symmetry	Screening; Severity/ Tx response	Multiple translations
SI-R Frost et al. (2004)	23 items	Hoarding Total Discarding Clutter Acquisition	Screening; Severity/Tx response	Assesses distress/impairment owing to each dimension; Multiple translations

Note. SCOPI = Schedule of Compulsions, Obsessions, and Pathological Impulses; CBOCI = Clark–Beck Obsessive-Compulsive Inventory; FOCI = Florida Obsessive-Compulsive Inventory; DOCS = Dimensional Obsessive-Compulsive Scale; SI-R = Saving Inventory-Revised.

(*Continued*)

Table 5.1 (Continued)

Related Variables	Length	Scales	Notes
OBQ-44 OCCWG (2005)	44 items	Obsessive beliefs total; Responsibility/threat estimation Importance/control of thoughts Perfectionism/certainty	Revised from 6-scale, 87-item version; Multiple translations
III OCCWG (2005)	31 items	Total score: appraisals of intrusive thought	Multiple translations
RAS Salkovskis et al. (2000)	26 items	Beliefs about responsibility	Sometimes referred to as the "R-Scale"
IUS-12 Carleton et al. (2007)	12 items	Intolerance of uncertainty	27-item English version; multiple translations of original French version
TAFS Shafran et al. (1996)	19 items	Thought–action fusion (TAF) total TAF likelihood TAF morality	Likelihood content breaks into "self" and "other" in some samples
BABS Eisen et al. (1998)	7 items	Multiple aspects of insight	Clinician-administered
OVIS Neziroglu et al. (1999)	11 items	Multiple Aspects of Insight	Can assess insight for up to three beliefs

Note: OBQ = Obsessive Beliefs Questionnaire; OCCWG = Obsessive-Compulsive Cognitions Working Group; III = Interpretation of Intrusions Inventory; RAS = Responsibility Attitude Scale; IUS = Intolerance of Uncertainty Scale; TAFS = Thought–Action Fusion Scale; BABS = Brown Assessment of Beliefs Scale; OVIS = Overvalued Ideas Scale.

seven scores of "3" on the BDI are equivalent to 21 scores of "1." Both total 21, but reflect different clinical presentations. Clinically, strict reliance on OCD total scores is not recommended; the importance/severity of individual scale scores should be evaluated.

Relevant then is the DSM-5 designation of Hoarding Disorder as distinct from OCD. When total scores are used, cut-offs that include hoarding content need to be revised. That is, with hoarding no longer considered "core" OCD content, hoarding items add non-specific variance. To the extent that total scores are used, empirically-based cut-offs that incorporate hoarding items must be updated by removing those items from total score calculations.

Conversely, whereas many OCD instruments target specific content, there are others that focus more generally on symptom *severity*. For example, some structured interviews (e.g., Mini International Neuropsychiatric Interview [MINI]) (Sheehan et al., 1998) and screening measures (e.g., Florida Obsessive-Compulsive Inventory) (Storch et al., 2007) provide relatively few examples of such content toward the primary goal of quickly determining severity/impairment. Thus, an important question is whether the user needs the instrument to help identify specific content through a lengthy listing of possible symptoms, or more focally to determine symptom severity irrespective of content. Some measures combine these goals. The Yale–Brown Obsessive-Compulsive Scale (YBO-CS) (Goodman et al., 1989) is an interview that first determines what symptom content is bothering an individual with OCD (e.g., *I have forbidden or perverse sexual thoughts, images, or impulses*) using a long list of examples. Then, severity is assessed for endorsed items via (1) amount of time occupied, (2) functional interference, (3) distress, (4) degree of resistance, and (5) success at resistance. Thus, it does not matter which checklist items were endorsed, only how severe the obsessions and compulsions have been. The Dimensional Obsessive-Compulsive Scale (DOCS) (Abramowitz et al., 2010) is a questionnaire that focuses on severity, within the context of four specific symptom domains. It includes five aspects of severity for each of the four domains and therefore is less susceptible to the total score issue raised previously. Like the YBOCS, if symptoms relate to only one theme, impairment specific to that theme may be assessed.

In sum, OCD symptom heterogeneity complicates assessment in multiple ways, including posing dangers to the use of simple total scores. A key consideration is whether a test user aims to determine the specific content of symptoms, their severity, or both. Tests vary as to content and major purpose.

Dimensionality

The prevailing view is that OCD symptoms exist on a continuum rather than as categorically distinct phenomena (Olatunji et al., 2008). The majority of the general population experiences intrusive thoughts (80%) (Rachman & DeSilva, 1978), including during stressful life events (e.g., first child birth) (Abramowitz et al., 2006), and nonclinical samples can be manipulated to become distressed by OCD-relevant thoughts and associated safety behaviors (e.g., regarding contamination fears) (Deacon & Maack, 2008). Therefore, the actual assessment goal usually is not to determine *whether* an individual experiences intrusions, but rather *to what degree*. This gives rise to Challenge No. 2: dimensionality. The debate as to the categorical or dimensional nature of mental illness is beyond the reach of this chapter, but its relevance to OCD symptom assessment is obvious. Studies of nonclinical samples routinely confirm that people who do not suffer from OCD provide non-zero scores on virtually all OCD symptom measures; a review of any of the validation studies for the Table 5.1 questionnaires will confirm this. Like depression or general anxiety, nearly everyone endorses the experience of unwanted thoughts – the task is to identify those for whom the experience is a clinical problem with an OCD presentation. One way to consider this challenge is to examine score distributions. Figure 5.1 reflects scores for clinical and student groups on the core OCD scales of the Schedule of Compulsions, Obsessions, and Pathological Impulses (SCOPI) (Watson & Wu, 2005). The group means and shapes of the distributions are different, but the distributions are notably overlapping. Similar to Olatunji and colleagues, there is no obvious or discrete break to support taxonicity. As such, the process of distinguishing clinical symptoms from sub- or nonclinical experiences requires further information, including symptom frequency, duration, number, content, appraisal of and reactions to thoughts, distress, and functional impairment.

As a practical consequence, OCD symptom measures must either (a) be developed for tailored purposes or for use in specific populations (e.g., diagnosed samples), or (b) account for a wide range of severity, spanning from passing intrusive thoughts that cause no/minimal distress to florid symptoms that constitute the most severe forms of clinical OCD. Without such range, users run the risk of hitting floor or ceiling effects. This is a notable challenge because it affects the way questions are framed. For example, a screening instrument aims to be inclusive; that is, targeting a relatively low "level" so that more individuals may endorse the items. This increases the risk of false positives in terms of formal OCD, but serves the major purpose of screening and minimizing the rate of false negatives. Note that most instruments use multiple-point (rather than dichotomous) response scales, allowing for the report of different degrees of experience or distress. The revised Obsessive-Compulsive Inventory (OCI-R) (Foa et al., 2002) is a common screener, and contains items such as *I check things more often than necessary* and *I collect things I don't need*. Such statements resonate with most

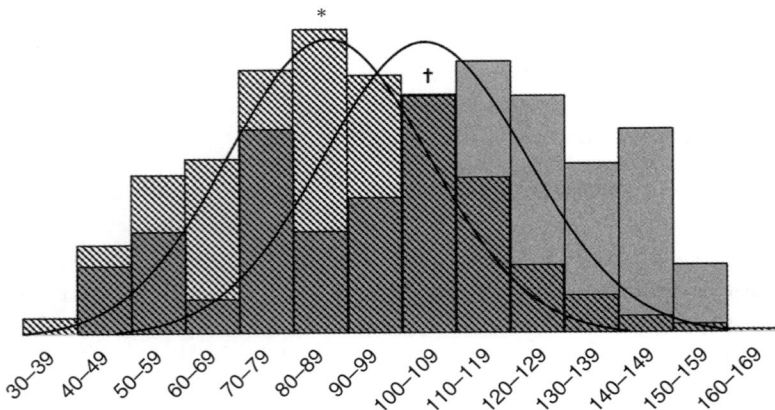

Figure 5.1 SCOPI OCD total score distributions in student and clinical samples
Note: $N = 656$ students; 53 individuals with DSM-IV OCD. Height of bars reflect proportion within each sample. Unpublished data (Wu, 2014). Key: *$M_{Students} = 87.1$ (23.7), hatched bars; †$M_{OCD} = 107.7$ (28.3), solid colored bars.

people, leading to non-zero endorsement on its five-point response scale (*not at all – a little – moderately – a lot – extremely*) in most samples.

Conversely, a diagnostic instrument must be more discriminating: a majority of the general population may endorse intrusions, but the 12-month prevalence of OCD is under 2% (American Psychiatric Association [APA], 2013) and false-positive errors are a serious threat. As such, the context provided for, and the wording of the questions themselves, must be written at a much higher level. An example is the Anxiety Disorders Interview Schedule (ADIS) (DiNardo, Brown, & Barlow, 1994). The OCD module contains a series of yes/no questions that address whether respondents are bothered by their thoughts, whether they recur in a nonsensical or inappropriate way, or are difficult to stop. This approach allows the clinician to consider whether intrusive thoughts are clinically meaningful versus normative; a *yes* is assigned only if a respondent endorses intrusive thoughts accompanied by requisite distress/impairment. Of note, such two-part information can be difficult to ascertain using a questionnaire-only method (e.g., items risk being double-barreled); multipoint response scales allow for reporting a range of severity, but single items may not clearly distinguish *does this happen?* from *does it substantially bother you?* The interview approach also allows for explicit consideration of whether symptoms are better accounted for by another disorder, thus facilitating differential diagnosis. For example, are intrusive thoughts related to the uncontrollable worry typical of generalized anxiety? Are they better explained as rumination within depression? Formal diagnostic instruments thus tend to cover a broader psychological space than instruments whose purpose is to assess only OCD symptoms (e.g., typically, specialized questionnaires).

A third level of symptom assessment involves instruments used for tracking treatment progress. Such measures need not determine whether sufficient symptoms are present to warrant a diagnosis or whether OCD-like symptoms are better accounted for by another problem – presumably, these issues already have been addressed. Instead, the goal is to assess whether previously reported symptoms maintain their intensity over time or during/after treatment – that is, estimation of stability vs. change. An example is the YBOCS: already described, this is the gold standard for assessing symptom severity in individuals with an established diagnosis of OCD. It has been used in many outcome studies because it is sensitive to treatment effects. Conversely, the YBOCS was not developed to screen for OCD or to measure symptoms in individuals who do not have a confirmed OCD diagnosis. For the same reasons it works well with individuals who struggle with clinical OCD, it is not indicated or recommended for use in broader groups. A review of its instructions and item wording reveals that it would be difficult for individuals who do not struggle with OCD to answer it validly. Doing so would be akin to asking people *How much do your obsessions interfere with your functioning?* when their genuine response would be *I don't have obsessions.* A response of "none" is not equivalent to that of a person who endorses obsessions but when asked about impairment, indicates "none."

In sum, intrusive thoughts are nearly ubiquitous and OCD symptoms are dimensional with respect to frequency and distress. Instruments typically are developed with a primary purpose in mind, and different instruments are better-suited for different purposes. Test users must identify a specific objective, and then choose from among the available instruments. Table 5.1 includes information as to which instruments are well-suited/supported for different goals.

Insight/Data Source

A classic OCD presentation involves a fear of contamination and associated washing behaviors that are rigid or excessive or both. With such a presentation, overt compulsions are relatively easy to observe. In contrast, obsession-only presentations and covert neutralization pose bigger obstacles. This gives rise to Challenge No. 3: insight and the private nature of OCD. Client report is the most common and most critical source of information; thus, insight as to whether experienced thoughts/behaviors are unreasonable or excessive is key. Traditionally, insight into one's own symptoms was a required feature of OCD that distinguished it from psychosis. However, intact insight has been de-emphasized; in DSM-5, it constitutes a specifier that may range from *good or fair insight* to *absent insight/delusional beliefs*. This can complicate OCD symptom assessment, particularly when individuals see what the clinician identifies as a *symptom* to be a perfectly reasonable belief. This can become very difficult when symptoms incorporate religious beliefs, for example. In some circumstances, the addition of a second data source may be of value. For example, individuals who once had clear insight as to the impact of their symptoms may have learned to accommodate compulsions so thoroughly that they cannot evaluate their excess in absolute terms. Similarly, compensatory behaviors (e.g., compulsive praying) may be thought of as *style* rather than recognized as *symptoms*. Regarding degree, if a person has at some point spent 6–8 hours per day washing, then currently spending "only" 3–4 hours may not be thought of – or reported as – *excessive*. As such, qualitative questions alone may be insufficient; quantitative estimates of symptom experience (e.g., time spent per day) should be considered. Some instruments allow for ratings of both current and past episodes, prompting the respondent to contrast different periods of time and functioning. Attention to symptom duration and change is especially important in OCD because the time between symptom onset and treatment-seeking is often many years. In some cases, expert evaluation via interview may be sufficient; if not, significant others such as parents and spouses may be sought. In fact, it can be especially helpful to obtain participation from family members of an OCD sufferer, due to the excessive reassurance-seeking that is so common in this problem. Family members often are brought directly into symptom experience via participation in rituals. In those instances, family members can be a strong source of clinical information.

Of course, family and friends have limited access to the private, inner experience of individuals with OCD – a situation which brings its own challenges. In the personality domain, consideration is given to *trait visibility* (Watson, Hubbard, & Wiese, 2000). Within the literature on accurately rating other people's personality traits, an issue is that those with clear behavioral markers simply are easier to see. Take extraversion, which spans a number of facet-level characteristics, such as warmth and gregariousness. A relatively gregarious person would by definition display directly observable behaviors relevant to being in social situations and engaging other people. Conversely, a trait such as entitlement may be more challenging to observe directly – in part, because there is a disincentive to overtly display relevant behaviors: to declare *I believe myself to be better than other people* holds negative social consequences. Similarly, mental compulsions such as silent counting or visual replacement of "bad" images with "good" images may be impossible to observe, especially if efforts are made to conceal them. In either scenario, the utility of other-reports may be limited.

Another issue to consider with respect to self- versus other-reports is the challenge of resolving imperfect agreement. Inter-rater reliability tends to be interpreted either by focusing on the magnitude of correlation between two reports or using a "gold standard" approach in which one rating is operationalized as correct and the second is evaluated on the basis of how closely it matches the first. When it comes to identifying and measuring OCD symptoms, the default standard is the symptom sufferer; as noted, reports made by significant others are imperfect proxies. However, the possibility of poor insight or symptom minimization is real. In such instances, the other-report may facilitate a dialogue as to how other people observe symptoms, or to raise client awareness of others' estimation of their functioning level. This situation may best be approached by integration of the available information without precisely specifying which report is more accurate; each reporter's input can offer unique insight and combine to provide a fuller symptom picture. When there is marked discrepancy, on the other hand, the clinician likely will need to address the issue with both parties directly, considering questions such as insight and motivation to report, without alienating either the client or the family member.

Overall then, insight as to the extent of pathology and concerns about reporting accuracy should be considered in the clinical context. A few measures for assessing OCD-related insight are listed in Table 5.1. Clinician-administered instruments which reduce reliance on client insight and the use of other-reports may be incorporated when feasible. Of course – and this always has been true with respect to the self-other agreement literature – the clinician must be prepared to address situations of weak overlap in reporting.

Formats

There are three major formats for collecting data: Interviews, questionnaires, and behavioral tasks. Each has a different use and will be considered, with examples.

Omnibus Interviews

Three major DSM diagnostic interviews include OCD modules and frequently are cited in the OCD assessment literature: the Structured Clinical Interview for DSM-IV (SCID) (First et al., 2002), ADIS, and MINI. Structured interviews allow for detailed assessment of multiple aspects of psychological functioning. Typically, they require substantial training for standardized administration, which offers improved reliability over unstructured interviews, but also the opportunity for interviewers to gather follow-up information for the most relevant domains. Interviewers control the context of the questioning and can clarify confusion or misunderstanding. Interviews rely less on client insight, although responses still contain a self-report element. Most interviews provide structured scoring systems that result in dichotomous diagnoses, including consideration of differential diagnosis. For example, all will result in a categorical yes/no OCD diagnosis and most have components that aim to distinguish types of symptoms (e.g., *obsessions* from *worry* from *rumination*). Differential diagnosis is particularly important in that OCD frequently is comorbid with other disorders, including conditions with symptomatology similarly focused on intrusive thought or repetitive behavior. The SCID, ADIS, and MINI all have been studied extensively and cover a wide range of DSM diagnoses. They target a fair amount of overlapping content, however, each has unique features that users may consider when selecting the most appropriate one to use. For example, the SCID-I covers all of the major DSM-IV categories; the ADIS allows for substantial detail for all of the DSM-IV Anxiety Disorders, plus other domains including mood disorders and substance use; the MINI offers an efficient screening for 19 DSM-IV disorders, including OCD. The ADIS recently was updated as the Anxiety and Related Disorders Interview Schedule for DSM-5 (Brown & Barlow, 2014); the SCID-5 (First, Williams, Karg, & Spitzer, 2015) was also updated to reflect DSM-5 diagnostic criteria; the MINI recently was updated as the MINI 7.0 for DSM-5. All three have been translated into multiple languages.

Disadvantages to structured interviews include the substantial investment required to administer them. Beyond the required training of interviewers, which can be extensive, the interviews themselves are time-consuming at roughly 90 minutes for the SCID and ADIS. The MINI offers a shorter time investment at roughly 15–20 minutes, but consequently provides less detail. Of note, a review of the empirical literature reflects that many researchers choose to administer only portions of these instruments for targeting a single or subset of DSM disorders. This practice reduces time cost, but also eliminates two of the major advantages of using these instruments, namely, broad assessment of functioning and differential diagnosis. The reader may find interesting a further consideration of the advantages and disadvantages of interviews from the perspective of the personality disorders literature (Segal & Coolidge, 2007). Overall, when the goal is to determine OCD diagnostic status according to formal DSM criteria, these structured interviews should be strongly considered.

Stand-alone OCD Interviews

Already introduced, the YBOCS interview has been shown reliable and valid for assessing symptom severity in individuals diagnosed with OCD. Thus, its primary application is immediately different from the interviews summarized above. It remains one of the most widely used instruments in this domain and for this purpose. A revision – the Dimensional YBOCS (Rosário-Campos et al., 2006) – was developed "for use by expert raters capable of properly assessing the dimension-specific OC symptom severity" (p. 496). This version includes a self-report module covering six content dimensions and clinician-administered modules for determining severity. Both YBOCS versions require approximately 40 minutes to administer. Benefits and limitations of the YBOCS parallel those for the omnibus interviews: the expertise of the administering clinician is valuable, but the time needed both to train the clinician and administer each interview is non-trivial compared to questionnaires.

Questionnaires

Questionnaires offer an efficient means of assessment, and there are several designed to assess OCD symptoms. More than the interviews, these questionnaires reflect the substantial variability in content highlighted previously, and this is the major difference among the questionnaires included in Table 5.1. A second consideration is instrument length: very brief measures such as the 18-item OCI-R are used widely in research settings. A drawback to this brevity is that the range of content clearly is narrower than what is covered within the longer instruments, and reliability can be lower (e.g., the OCI-R Neutralizing subscale has shown coefficient alphas as low as .34 in a non-clinical sample; Foa et al., 2002). Another difference is how severity is determined, consistent with the previous consideration of *variety versus severity*. As noted, the DOCS provides scores on the four most common content areas, as well as indices of severity stemming from each area. In this way, it may prove useful for combining two benefits: efficient self-report and severity assessment by content. However, and again not specific to OCD, questionnaires are vulnerable to symptom over-reporting and should not be used as the sole basis for clinical diagnosis. Indeed, none of the questionnaires available for the assessment of OCD include validity indices to provide information about whether a respondent has been consistent, tried to give socially desirable responses, or tried to minimize or exaggerate his or her symptoms. When there is reason to question insight or motivation, questionnaires should be followed by clinician-based assessment of such concerns. A final issue is that some of these instruments have been revised, in some cases, multiple times or to improve specific aspects of the older version (e.g., factor structure, discriminant validity). For example, there are at least four published versions of the Padua Inventory, most still in use in the OCD research literature (Overduin & Furnham, 2012). As such, it can be a challenge to sort through these options to decide which one is best or whether one version is markedly different from the others with respect to the specific objective for which it is needed. Consider the following: When strong psychometric performance is essential to a given objective, properties such as factor structure, internal consistency, and other scale-level properties take center stage. Conversely, if the objective is to identify a client's primary OCD symptoms from among the infinite list of possible content, the adequacy of an instrument's factor structure is not as critical as its content coverage. When trying to determine whether exposures have been effective, sensitivity to treatment effects is more important than demonstrated long-term retest reliability; reliability still is important, but an instrument that offers trait-like stability would be less useful as a treatment outcome measure. The shorter instruments provide relatively narrow coverage of symptom content; for screening purposes in time-sensitive situations, the shorter instruments serve an important role.

Overall, questionnaires are efficient and valuable in the diagnosis and conceptualization process, but generally should not be used as the only evidence of diagnostic standing. They serve as excellent screening tools, help to identify the content of OCD symptoms, and can be part of a broader clinical assessment process of determining symptom experience and severity over time.

Behavioral Measures

Behavioral avoidance (approach) tasks (BATs) are less susceptible to the limitations of self-report because they rely on objective *in vivo* observation of the individual's responses to specific stimuli. Such tasks have an important place in cognitive-behavioral interventions for OCD (e.g., exposure and response prevention) as they allow for individuals to confront their fears through behavioral experiments (see Morrison & Westbrook, 2004). Since BATs can be developed to match unique client symptoms, they do not represent a specific, static instrument per se. For example, Steketee,

Chambless, Tran, Worden, and Gillis (1996) developed and psychometrically tested a series of multi-step/multi-task BATs for individuals diagnosed with OCD. Tailored to specific symptoms, the BATs were designed to assess both overt behavioral responses (e.g., willingness to engage stimuli reflecting a range of idiosyncratic fear values across steps, operationalized as percentage of steps completed) and self-reported distress experienced upon exposure to stimuli. The order, number, and type of steps for each task provide an increasing level of discomfort as the BAT progresses. Steketee and colleagues reported good convergent validity with pretreatment OC symptoms, discriminant validity against depression symptoms, and treatment sensitivity as measured by pre- to post-effect sizes.

Another type of behavioral assessment involves computer-administered tasks (e.g., Rotge et al., 2008, whose challenge task examines checking behavior; Kuckertz, Amir Tobin, &, Najmi, 2013, whose Word Sentence Association Test examines interpretation bias). Taylor (1995) provided consideration of additional means of behavioral assessment, including direct observation (e.g., recording at-home behavior, time sampling behavior on hospital units) and diary methods. Whereas behavioral methods have been less studied from a psychometric perspective – with stimuli relatively unique to client fears – real-time behavioral sampling has gained in popularity due to technology advances and likely represents a major emphasis going forward, both for research and clinical purposes (Mehl & Conner, 2012).

Measurement of Related/Ancillary Constructs

Related Conditions

DSM-5 introduced the category of *Obsessive-Compulsive and Related Disorders*, removing OCD from its prior home among the *Anxiety Disorders*. Whereas anxiety remains an important aspect of the condition, its categorization reflects the view that conditions such as Body Dysmorphic Disorder and Hair-Pulling Disorder share similarities with OCD, and was intended in part to increase clinical utility. In fact, DSM-5 explicitly encourages clinicians "to screen for these conditions in individuals who present with one of them and be aware of overlaps between these conditions" (APA, 2013: 235). As such, truly comprehensive OCD assessment may include symptom dimensions believed to be shared among the disorders of this category, and also other conditions that commonly co-occur with OCD. In particular, OCD diagnostic assessment typically should address the other Obsessive-Compulsive and Related Disorders, the Anxiety Disorders, and major depression. Regarding depression, Richter, Cox, and Direnfeld (1994) suggested that "a measure of depression should always be included in OCD studies" (p. 143) due to strong correlations and high rates of co-occurrence.

A condition that warrants specific mention is Obsessive-Compulsive Personality Disorder (OCPD). Despite the similarity in names, there are key differences between OCD and OCPD, yet the literature as to the nature of their association is not definitive. The extant literature suggests that there is no special association between the two conditions, but interest in the possibility remains and some data support an opposing view. A practical recommendation is that a thorough assessment of OCD might include an evaluation of personality functioning – one not limited to only OCPD.

Assessment of an individual's standing with regard to all of the recognized personality disorders, as well as a broad range of personality traits, is likely to be most useful for individual treatment planning purposes and is consistent with contemporary views of personality assessment (APA, 2013; Wu, 2013).

Obsessive-Compulsive Cognitions

Cognitive-behavioral formulations (e.g., Salkovskis, 1985) have been useful for understanding and treating OCD. These models hold that intrusive thoughts are stimuli, to which individuals respond in the context of their personal beliefs – "obsessive" beliefs include, for example, feeling overly responsible for preventing harm and the belief that intrusive negative thoughts are highly personally significant. Such beliefs lead to a negative appraisal of normally occurring intrusive thoughts and subsequent distress over having had them (or their potential consequences). Moreover, the negative appraisal leads to compensatory behaviors that temporarily relieve the distress (e.g., compulsive rituals and avoidance). Within such models, beliefs play a critical role in an individual's appraisal of a cognitive experience. In fact, Grayson (2010) indicated that addressing a client's beliefs about *intolerance of uncertainty* is a critical early step in OCD treatment. Accordingly, measuring these cognitive variables will serve a useful role. The most common measure of these beliefs is the Obsessive Beliefs Questionnaire (Obsessive Compulsive Cognitions Working Group, 2005), which was developed to include all of the major belief domains identified in the published OCD literature. The OBQ and a few other measures of OCD-related beliefs are included in Table 5.1.

Issues of Diversity, Sex, and Culture

Psychological assessment in minority groups, broadly construed, presents challenges (Okazaki & Sue, 1995), but instrument testing and validation need to include broad groups of people. Hardly unique to OCD, a basic challenge facing psychopathology is to determine whether (a) the disorder is manifested similarly in diverse groups of people, and (b) a given instrument equivalently measures the relevant experience. These are related, but distinct issues, and they can be a challenge to address separately. That is, if data from one instrument suggest between-group differences, is the appropriate conclusion that the instrument does not perform equivalently across the groups, or that it is (validly) reflecting actual differences in how the construct is expressed in those groups? An example from the depression literature is illustrative: Chinese samples have been shown to express depression via somatic symptoms, whereas Euro-Canadians show more psychological symptoms (Ryder et al., 2008). Thus, so as not to over- or underestimate client symptom severity, multiple sets of normative data may be needed for interpreting scores on an instrument used in broad samples. This is common practice in the neuropsychological assessment field, in which quite narrow reference groups are identified for normative comparison (e.g., right-handed men of a certain age and educational attainment). Note that this example is for illustrative purposes; the state of the current OCD literature does not warrant such fine-grained specificity.

In OCD, there is a relatively small literature that addresses cultural issues, including instrument translations (see Table 5.1) (Overduin & Furnham, 2012). A few studies have compared racial groups on issues such as factor structure and mean-level scores. Williams and Turkheimer (2007) found that higher black endorsement of contamination items (a finding reported in other studies) did not reflect greater psychopathology than for white respondents, but instead reflected attitudes toward cleanliness. Washington, Norton, and Temple (2008) studied four racial groups and found that Asians scored the highest overall, and also on contamination/washing scores. This work offers a useful start to cultural examinations of OCD symptom presentation; additional work must be as inclusive as possible and investigate variables beyond race. At this point, such work is exploratory in that there seems to be little evidence on which to make a priori hypotheses as to group-based differences in clinical settings. An exception may be that elevated OCD scores in some racial minority groups may not reflect elevated distress/impairment.

With respect to possible sex-based differences, men appear to have an earlier age of symptom onset than women (APA, 2013); and different patterns of comorbidity have been reported (e.g., men more frequently present with tic disorders [APA, 2013]; women more frequently present with eating disorders [Bogetto, Venturello, Maina, & Ravizza, 1999]). Overall, however, relatively few sex-based differences have been reported – most data are organized by clinical status collapsed across sex – and contemporary normative data and cut-off scores tend to be unisex. Similar to the state of the science with respect to racial/cultural considerations, it generally is true that unless the major focus of a given study is sex, these issues are not reported in the bulk of the OCD assessment literature. Increased attention to the possibility of such differences is warranted, for example, to determine whether different critical values should be used for the different sexes to maximize assessment effectiveness.

Perhaps related to increased awareness of its prevalence, OCD has gained in popularity in the media – a culture of its own in some respects. Books, television programs, and feature-length films address the subject in one way or another, such as by relaying personal struggles with the condition. Noted experts even have been involved in raising awareness through such media (e.g., David Tolin's television program "The OCD Project"). Along with the efforts of organizations such as the International Obsessive-Compulsive Disorder Foundation, the common view of the condition may be beginning to change toward increased understanding. Nevertheless, the stigma associated with diagnosis of any form of mental illness has not been eliminated, and therefore assessment endeavors still must contend with a client's potential reluctance to disclose due to shame or embarrassment – which goes beyond the issues of insight and motivation noted previously. This is a particular concern in OCD symptom assessment, in which clients often express feeling ashamed of their symptoms. An initial step in the assessment process may be motivational interviewing: the goal is to help individuals to express their struggles openly, in a setting that allows them to overcome any hesitation to disclose. Success in that realm will only increase the likelihood of successful treatment and indeed may be a substantial initial asset.

Previous Reviews

In terms of highlighting additional resources on this subject, several helpful reviews are available. Rather than repeat those efforts here, the reader is encouraged to access them for fine-grained considerations, such as vetting specific psychometric properties of single instruments for use in a given setting, as well as case examples of assessment situations. These include Antony (2001), Grabill et al. (2008), Taylor, Abramowitz, and McKay (2010), and Overduin and Furnham (2012). Each offers a certain emphasis and helpful content (e.g., Overduin & Furnham (2012) exclusively target and provide substantial detail about questionnaires; Grabill et al. summarize psychometric strengths and weaknesses). Overall, whereas the number of instruments complicates some issues in this domain, there is real benefit to having multiple options spanning multiple methods of assessment. The reader is unlikely to come away from this or any of the cited reviews concluding that Instrument X is the only one to use.

Conclusions

Assessment of OCD symptomatology is a particularly challenging endeavor. Symptom heterogeneity, matters of insight, the private/covert nature of symptoms, associated stigma and embarrassment, and cross-cultural issues combine to complicate an accurate and comprehensive evaluation. The process must begin by determining what *specific information* is sought through assessment. Researchers and clinicians are advised to identify a clear goal for the objective, and this goal should be matched with the best-available assessment tools. No one instrument can perform equally well for *all* objectives, so it may be necessary to understand the proper circumstances in which to use a given tool, and to use multiple measures when a comprehensive assessment is sought. Critical issues to consider include: the dimensional nature of OCD symptoms; assessment of the many OCD symptom manifestations; obtaining input from multiple sources/methods when necessary and available; distinguishing breadth or variety of symptoms from symptom severity; the potential influence of related disorders and cognitive underpinnings; and the potential role of culture and self-identity in symptom experience/presentation.

References

Abramowitz, J. S., Khandker, M., Nelson, C. A., Deacon, B. J., & Rygwall, R. (2006). The role of cognitive factors in the pathogenesis of obsessive-compulsive symptoms: A prospective study. *Behaviour Research and Therapy, 44*, 1361–1374.

Abramowitz, J. S., Deacon, B., Olatunji, B. O., Wheaton, M. G., Berman, N. C., Losardo, D., ... Hale, L. R. (2010). Assessment of obsessive-compulsive symptoms: Development and evaluation of the dimensional obsessive-compulsive scale. *Psychological Assessment, 22*, 180–198.

American Psychiatric Association. (2013). *Diagnostic and statistical manual of mental disorders* (5th ed.). Arlington, VA: Author.

Antony, M. (2001). Measures for obsessive-compulsive disorder. In M. M. Antony, S. M. Orsillo, & L. Roemer (Eds.), *Practitioner's guide to empirically based measures of anxiety* (pp. 219–243). New York: Kluwer.

Beck, A. T., Steer, R. A., & Brown, G. K. (1996). *Beck depression inventory manual* (2nd ed.). San Antonio, TX: The Psychological Corporation.

Bogetto, F., Venturello, S., Maina, A., & Ravizza, L. (1999). Gender-related clinical differences in obsessive-compulsive disorder. *European Psychiatry, 14*, 434–441.

Brown, T.A., & Barlow, D. H. (2014). *Anxiety and related disorders interview schedule for DSM-5*. New York: Oxford University Press.

Burns, G. L., Keortge, S. G., Formea, G. M., & Sternberger, L. G. (1996). Revision of the Padua Inventory of obsessive compulsive disorder symptoms: Distinctions between worry, obsessions, and compulsions. *Behaviour Research and Therapy, 34*, 163–173.

Carleton, R. N., Norton, M. A., & Asmundson, G. J. G. (2007). Fearing the unknown: A short version of the intolerance of uncertainty scale. *Journal of Anxiety Disorders, 21*, 105–117.

Clark, D. A., Antony, M. M.M., Beck, A. T., Swinson, R. P., & Steer, R. A. (2005). Screening for obsessive and compulsive symptoms: Validation of the Clark–Beck obsessive-compulsive inventory. *Psychological Assessment, 17*, 132–143.

Deacon, B. J., & Maack (2008). The effects of safety behaviours on the fear of contamination: An experimental investigation. *Behaviour Research and Therapy, 46*, 537–547.

DiNardo, P. A., Brown, T. A., & Barlow, D. H. (1994). *Anxiety disorders interview schedule for DSM-IV: Lifetime version (ADIS-IV-L)*.New York: Oxford University Press.

Eisen, J. L., Phillips, K. A., Baer, L., Beer, D. A., Atala, K. D., & Rasmussen, S. A. (1998). The Brown assessment of beliefs scale: Reliability and validity. *American Journal of Psychiatry, 155*, 102–108.

First, M. B., Spitzer, R. L., Gibbon M., & Williams, J. B. W. (2002). *Structured clinical interview for DSM-IV-TR axis I disorders, research version, patient edition*. New York: Biometrics Research, New York State Psychiatric Institute.

First, M. B., Williams, J. B. W., Karg, R. S., & Spitzer, R. L. (2015). Structured Clinical Interview for DSM-5 – Research Version (SCID-5 for DSM-5, Research Version; SCID-5-RV). Arlington, VA, American Psychiatric Association.

Foa, E. B., Huppert, J. D., Leiberg, S., Langner, R., Kichic, R., Hajcak, G., & Salkovskis, P. M. (2002). The obsessive-compulsive inventory: Development and validation of a short version. *Psychological Assessment, 14*, 485–496.

Frost, R. O., Steketee, G., & Grisham, J. (2004). Measurement of compulsive hoarding: Saving inventory – revised. *Behaviour Research and Therapy, 42*, 1163–1182.

Goodman, W. K., Price, L. H., Rasmussen, S. A., Mazure, C., Fleischmann, R. L., Hill, C. L., Heninger, G. R., & Charney, D. S. (1989). The Yale–Brown obsessive-compulsive scale: I. Development, use, and reliability. *Archives of General Psychiatry, 46*, 1006–1011.

Grabill, K., Merlo, L., Duke, D., Harford, K-L., Keeley, M. L., Geffken, G. R., & Storch, E. A., (2008). Assessment of obsessive-compulsive disorder: A review. *Journal of Anxiety Disorders, 22*, 1–17.

Grayson, J. B. (2010). OCD and intolerance of uncertainty: Treatment issues. *Journal of Cognitive Psychotherapy, 24*, 3–15.

Kuckertz, J. M., Amir, N., Tobin, A. C., & Najmi, S. (2013). Interpretation of ambiguity in individuals with obsessive-compulsive symptoms. *Cognitive Therapy and Research, 37*, 232–241.

Mehl, M. R., & Conner, T. S. (Eds.). (2012). *Handbook of research methods for studying daily life*. New York: Guilford.

Morrison, N., & Westbrook, D. (2004). Obsessive-compulsive disorder. In: J. Bennett-Levy, G. Butler, M. Fennell, A. Hackmann, M. Mueller, & D. Westbrook (Eds.), *Oxford guide to behavioural experiments in cognitive therapy* (pp. 101–118). New York: Oxford University Press.

Neziroglu, F., McKay, D., Yaryura-Tobias, J. A., Stevens, K. P., & Todaro, J. (1999). The overvalued ideas scale: Development, reliability and validity in obsessive-compulsive disorder. *Behaviour Research and Therapy, 37*, 881–902.

Obsessive Compulsive Cognition Working Group. (2005). Psychometric validation of the obsessive belief questionnaire and interpretation of intrusions inventory – Part 2: Factor analyses and testing of a brief version. *Behaviour Research and Therapy, 43*, 1527–1542.

Okazaki, S., & Sue, S. (1995). Methodological issues in assessment research with ethnic minorities. *Psychological Assessment, 7*, 367–375.

Olatunji, B. O., Williams, B. J., Haslam, N., Abramowitz, J. S., & Tolin, D. F. (2008). The latent structure of obsessive-compulsive symptoms: A taxometric study. *Depression and Anxiety, 25*, 956–968.

Overduin, M. K., & Furnham, A. (2012). Assessing obsessive-compulsive disorder (OCD): A review of self-report measures. *Journal of Obsessive-Compulsive and Related Disorders, 1*, 312–324.

Rachman, S., & de Silva, P. (1978). Abnormal and normal obsessions. *Behaviour Research and Therapy, 16*, 233–248.

Richter, M. A., Cox, B. J., & Direnfeld, D. M. (1994). A comparison of three assessment instruments for obsessive-compulsive symptoms. *Journal of Behavior Therapy and Experimental Psychiatry, 25*, 143–147.

Rosário-Campos, M. C., Miguel, E. C., Quatrano, S., Chacon, P., Ferrao, Y., Findley, D., ... Leckman, J. F. (2006). The dimensional Yale–Brown obsessive–compulsive scale (DY-BOCS): An instrument for assessing obsessive-compulsive symptom dimensions. *Molecular Psychiatry, 11*, 495–504.

Rotge, J. Y., Clair, A. H., Jaafari, N., Hantouche, E. G., Pelissolo, A., Goillandeau, M., ... Aouizerate, B. (2008). A challenge task for assessment of checking behaviors in obsessive-compulsive disorder. *Acta Psychiatrica Scandinavica, 117*, 465–473.

Ryder, A. G., Yang, J., Zhu, X., Yao, S., Yi, J., Heine, S. J., & Bagby, R. M. (2008). The cultural shaping of depression: Somatic symptoms in China, psychological symptoms in North America? *Journal of Abnormal Psychology, 117*, 300–313.

Salkovskis, P. M. (1985). Obsessional-compulsive problems: A cognitive-behavioural analysis. *Behaviour Research and Therapy, 23*, 571–583.

Salkovskis, P. M., Wroe, A., Gledhill, A., Morrison, N., Forrester, E., Richards, C., Reynolds, M., & Thorpe, S. (2000). Responsibility attitudes and interpretations are characteristic of obsessive compulsive disorder. *Behaviour Research and Therapy, 38*, 347–372.

Segal, D. L., & Coolidge, F. L. (2007). Structured and semistructured interviews for differential diagnosis: Issues and applications. In: M. Hersen, S. M. Turner, & D. C. Beidel (Eds.), *Adult psychopathology and diagnosis* (pp. 78–100) (5th ed.). Hoboken, NJ: Wiley.

Shafran, R., Thordarson, D. S., & Rachman, S. (1996). Thought–action fusion in obsessive-compulsive disorder. *Journal of Anxiety Disorders, 10*, 379–391.

Sheehan, D. V., Lecrubier, Y., Sheehan, K. H., Amorim, P., Janavs, J., Weiller, E., ... Dunbar, G. C. (1998). The mini international neuropsychiatric interview (MINI): The development and validation of a structured diagnostic psychiatric interview for DSM-IV and ICD-10. *Journal of Clinical Psychiatry, 59*, 22–33.

Steketee, G., Chambless, D. L., Tran, G. Q., Worden, H., & Gillis, M. M. (1996). Behavioral avoidance test for obsessive compulsive disorder. *Behaviour Research and Therapy, 34*, 73–83.

Storch, E. A., Bagner, D., Merlo, L. J., Shapira, N. A., Geffken, G. R., Murphy, T. K., & Goodman, W. K. (2007). Florida obsessive-compulsive scale: Development, reliability, and validity. *Journal of Clinical Psychology, 63*, 851–859.

Summerfeldt, L. J. (2001). Obsessive-compulsive disorder: A brief overview and guide to assessment. In: M. M. Antony, S. M. Orsillo, & L. Roemer (Eds.), *Practitioner's guide to empirically based measures of anxiety* (pp. 211–217). New York: Kluwer.

Taylor, S. (1995). Assessment of obsessions and compulsions: Reliability, validity, and sensitivity to treatment effects. *Clinical Psychology Review, 15*, 261–296.

Taylor, S., Abramowitz, J. S., & McKay, D. (2010). Obsessive-compulsive disorder. In: M. M. Antony & D. H. Barlow (Eds.), *Handbook of assessment and treatment planning for psychological disorders* (pp. 267–300) (2nd ed.). New York: Guilford.

Thordarson, D. S., Radomsky, A. S., Rachman, S., Shafran, R., Sawchuk, C. N., & Hakstian, A. R. (2004). The Vancouver obsessional compulsive inventory (VOCI). *Behaviour Research and Therapy, 42*, 1289–1314.

Van Oppen, P., Hoekstra, R. J., & Emmelkamp, P. M. G. (1995). The structure of obsessive-compulsive symptoms. *Behavior Research and Therapy, 33*, 15–23.

Washington, C. S., Norton, P. J., & Temple, S. (2008). Obsessive-compulsive symptoms and obsessive-compulsive disorder A multiracial/ethnic analysis of a student population. *Journal of Nervous and Mental Disease, 196*, 456–461.

Watson, D., Hubbard, B., & Wiese, D. (2000). General traits of personality and affectivity as predictors of satisfaction in intimate relationships: Evidence from self- and partner-ratings. *Journal of Personality, 68*, 413–449.

Watson, D., & Wu, K. D. (2005). Development and validation of the Schedule of Compulsions, Obsessions, and Pathological Impulses (SCOPI). *Assessment, 12*, 50–65.

Williams, M. T., & Turkheimer, E. (2007). Identification and explanation of racial differences on contamination measures. *Behaviour Research and Therapy, 45*, 3041–3050.

Wu, K. D. (2013). Contemporary personality disorder assessment in clients with anxiety disorders. In: D. McKay & E. A. Storch (Eds.), *Handbook of assessing variants and complications in anxiety disorders* (pp. 189–202). New York: Springer.

Wu, K. D., & Carter, S. A. (2008). Specificity and structure of obsessive-compulsive disorder symptoms. *Depression and Anxiety, 25*, 641–652.

6

Measures for Diagnosing and Measuring Severity of OCD Symptoms in Children

Hannah Frank, Elyse Stewart, Jennifer Herren, and Kristen Benito

Obsessive-Compulsive Disorder (OCD) is a neurobehavioral disorder characterized by anxiety-invoking thoughts or images (obsessions) and overt behaviors or mental rituals performed to reduce the distress caused by these thoughts (compulsions). OCD has been estimated to affect up to 2–3% of children (Rapoport & Inoff-Germain, 2000; Valleni-Basile, Garrison, Jackson, & Waller, 1994), with point prevalence estimates indicating that between .25 and 1% of the pediatric population suffers from OCD at any given moment (Flament, Whitaker, Rapoport, & Davies, 1988; Heyman et al., 2003).Formerly categorized in the *Diagnostic and Statistical Manual of Mental Disorders*, Fourth Edition, Text Revision (DSM-IV-TR) (American Psychological Association, 2000) as an anxiety disorder, OCD is newly classified under the DSM-5 category "Obsessive-Compulsive and Related Disorders" (American Psychiatric Association, 2013). This change reflects empirical support for behavioral and phenomenological similarities with "OC-spectrum" disorders (Van Ameringen, Patterson, & Simpson, 2014), such as Trichotillomania (hair-pulling disorder) and Excoriation (skin-picking disorder), which are also included in this category.

Without being properly assessed and treated, childhood OCD may have deleterious long-term effects, including disruptions to normative development (e.g., Piacentini, Bergman, Keller, & McCracken, 2003) and impairments in social, academic, and family functioning (Valderhaug & Ivarsson, 2005). In addition, untreated OCD often leads to greater severity of illness and a greater risk for developing comorbid disorders. This in turn leads to increased disability costs, decreased work productivity, and increased utilization of health care services (Knapp, Henderson, & Patel, 2000). Such consequences highlight the importance of careful screening and assessment for childhood OCD, so as to minimize the long-term burden of the disorder. Several studies have clearly demonstrated the efficacy of a specific type of Cognitive Behavioral Therapy (CBT) called Exposure with Response Prevention (ERP), or ERP plus a Serotonin Reuptake Inhibitor (SRI), in treating children and adolescents with OCD

The Wiley Handbook of Obsessive Compulsive Disorders, Volume I, First Edition.
Edited by Jonathan S. Abramowitz, Dean McKay, and Eric A. Storch.
© 2017 John Wiley & Sons Ltd. Published 2017 by John Wiley & Sons Ltd.

(American Academy of Child and Adolescent Psychiatry, 2012; Freeman et al., 2014), but appropriate, tailored treatment can only be provided with proper assessment.

This chapter outlines recommendations for measures that can be used to screen for and diagnose OCD, as well as to assess severity of symptoms. Factors that might affect assessment, including developmental considerations and differential diagnoses, are also discussed.

Screening for OCD

Children presenting with complaints of intrusive thoughts, recurrent worries, excessive reassurance-seeking, and repetitive rituals or behaviors should be screened for OCD (Keeley, Storch, Dhungana, & Geffken, 2007). Ideally, a comprehensive assessment with multiple informants (i.e., the child, parent(s), and possibly teachers) should be conducted to differentiate developmentally appropriate from pathological behaviors, as well as to make a distinction between possible functions of the behavior (i.e., OCD or other anxiety) (American Academy of Child and Adolescent Psychiatry, 2012). Additional information about functional assessment and developmental considerations are discussed below.

Prior to using any formal measures to assess OCD, pre-screening in the form of open-ended questions may be appropriate. Such questions might include asking about rituals or repetitive behaviors and intrusive worries. AACAP practice parameters (2012) suggest initially probing for OCD based on DSM-5 diagnostic criteria (e.g., Do you have worries that just will not go away? Do you have intrusive or unwanted thoughts, ideas, images, or urges that make you anxious and you cannot suppress?). If symptoms of OCD are endorsed in response to these questions, parent- and self-report measures are often recommended as an efficient and low-cost method of further OCD screening. Self-report measures might be helpful to gather information from parents and children who may otherwise be reticent to initially divulge symptom information directly to a provider. The measures described below are useful to gain a preliminary sense of elevated anxiety and OCD symptoms and to decide whether further assessment is warranted. These may be particularly helpful in settings such as pediatrician's offices or community mental health clinics, where children are likely to initially present with complaints about OCD symptoms.

Despite these advantages, it is important to note that self-report measures are most useful as a preliminary screen and/or to gain an initial understanding of a child's symptoms. Many of the measures described include subscales, which when scored, include clinical cut-offs. These are useful as a guide, but should not be used alone to make a diagnosis. It is also important to interpret scores with some caution, as responses to certain questions might be unclear without further functional assessment of symptoms. In addition, many of these screening measures include both child- and parent- report versions. Discrepant reports from children and parents are common (e.g., Choudhury, Pimentel, & Kendall, 2003), but might provide important and relevant information about behaviors across settings and from varying perspectives (Villabo, Gere, Torgersen, March, & Kendall, 2012). Specific measures recommended for OCD screening, as well as the empirical findings on each measure, are described below, with psychometric properties shown in Table 6.1.

Table 6.1 Pediatric OCD Measures

Measure	Citation	Reporter	Time to administer	Recommended assessment age of patient	Purpose	Psychometrics
Screening for OCD						
Child Behavior Checklist (CBCL)	Achenbach (1991)	Parent	20 min	Tested in ages 1.5–5; 6–18	Screening for OCD and other behavioral and emotional problems	Good reliability and validity. Very high sensitivity and specificity. Tested in children with OCD compared to psychiatric and normal controls.
Screen for Child Anxiety Related Disorders (SCARED)	Birmaher et al. (1997)	Child and parent	15 min	Tested in ages 9–18	Screening for anxiety disorders	Good internal consistency, test–retest reliability, discriminative validity, and parent–child agreement. Tested in children referred to an anxiety/mood clinic.
Children's Florida Obsessive-Compulsive Inventory (C-FOCI)	Storch et al. (2009)	Child	5–10 min	Tested in ages 7–20	Symptom severity	Internal consistency is acceptable, construct validity and discriminant validity is supported. Demonstrated convergent and divergent validity through correlations with other OCD impairment measures but not with general anxiety or depression measures. Evidence of treatment sensitivity. Tested in both clinical and community settings.

(Continued)

Table 6.1 (Continued)

Measure	Citation	Reporter	Time to administer	Recommended assessment age of patient	Purpose	Psychometrics
Leyton Obsessional Inventory Child Version Survey Form (LOI-CV Survey Form)	Berg, Whitaker, Davies, & Flament (1988)	Child	10 min	Tested in ages 6–18	Assesses symptoms	Demonstrated good internal consistency. Good to poor test–retest reliability based on age. Adequate concurrent validity. Not sensitive to treatment effects. Demonstrated high false-positive rates in other research. Tested in a community sample of high school students. Storch et al.'s (2011) research found it inadequate for the screening and assessment of pediatric OCD.
Short Leyton Obsessional Inventory Survey Form (Short LOI-CV Survey Form)	Bamber, Tamplin, Park, Kyte, & Goodyer (2002)	Child	5 min	Tested in ages 12–16	Assesses symptoms	Adequate internal consistency, sensitivity, and specificity. Storch et al.'s (2011) research found it inadequate for the screening and assessment of pediatric OCD.
Structured Interviews: Diagnosing OCD						
Schedule for Affective Disorders and Schizophrenia for School-Age Children (K-SADS)	Kaufman et al. (1997)	Clinician	75–90 min per reporter	Tested in ages 7–17	Diagnostic interview	Concurrent validity, interrater reliability, and test–retest reliability are supported. Highly correlated with other pediatric diagnostic interviews and psychopathology measures. Tested in psychiatric outpatients and normal controls.

Measure	Author	Reporter	Time	Ages	Type	Psychometric properties
Anxiety Disorders Interview Schedule (ADIS)	American Psychiatric Association 2013	Clinician	45–60 min per reporter	Tested in ages 7–17	Diagnostic interview	Excellent interrater agreement and test–retest reliability. In a clinical sample there was low agreement between parent-report and child-report which may demonstrate that parent-reports are considered more by clinicians.
Mini International Neuropsychiatric Interview Child/Adol Version (MINI)	Sheehan et al. (2006)	Clinician	30 min	Tested in ages 6–17. Parent presence recommended for younger children.	Diagnostic interview	Demonstrates adequate reliability and validity. Good interrater and test–retest reliability. Concordance with the KSADS has been established. Tested in outpatients and normal controls.
National Institute of Mental Health Diagnostic Interview Schedule for Children Version IV (NIMH DISC-IV)	Shaffer et al. (2000)	Clinician	70 min per reporter	Tested in ages 9–17	Diagnostic interview	No formal validity testing of this measure has occurred. Previous versions have shown moderate to good diagnostic reliability. Tested in a clinical sample. Previous versions have been tested in a community sample.

(Continued)

Table 6.1 (Continued)

Measure	Citation	Reporter	Time to administer	Recommended assessment age of patient	Purpose	Psychometrics
Assessing OCD Severity						
Children's Yale–Brown Obsessive Compulsive Scale (CY-BOCS)	Scahill et al. (1997)	Clinician	15–45 min	Tested in ages 8–17	Current OCD symptoms and severity	Internal consistency is high, good interrater reliability, mixed discriminant validity, divergent validity, and convergent validity. Demonstrates sensitivity to treatment effects. Considered the "gold standard" clinician-administered measure for assessing the severity of pediatric OCD. Tested in children with an OCD diagnosis.
Children's Yale–Brown Obsessive-Compulsive Scale-Child Report and Parent Report (CY-BOCS-CR; CY-BOCS-PR)	Storch et al. (2006)	Child, Parent	15 min	Tested in ages 8–17	Current OCD symptoms and severity	Satisfactory reliability, convergent and divergent validity. Demonstrated concurrent validity with the CY-BOCS. CY-BOCS-PR had slightly higher rates of correspondence with the CY-BOCS which may account for the clinical tendency to weigh more on the parent-report than the child-report. Further psychometric analysis is needed. Tested in children with an OCD diagnosis and their parents.

Measure	Reference	Administration	Time	Ages	Construct	Psychometrics/Notes
The Dimensional Yale–Brown Obsessive-Compulsive Scale (DY-BOCS)	Rosário-Campos et al. (2006)	Clinician		Tested in ages 6–69	Functional relationship between obsessions and compulsions	Excellent interrater reliability and internal consistency. Demonstrated convergent and divergent validity. Limited research on its use in children and adolescents.
Clinical Global Impressions – Improvement and Severity (CGI-I, CGI-S)	Guy (1976)	Clinician	1 min	All	Global severity and clinical improvement	Has been used successfully in patients with OCD and used extensively in treatment outcome studies.
Children's Global Assessment Scale (CGAS)	Schaffer et al. (1983)	Clinician	1 min	Tested in ages 4–16	Overall impairment	Established interrater reliability, test–retest reliability, sensitivity to change, and concurrent validity.
Global Assessment of Functioning (GAF)	APA (2000)	Clinician	1 min	All	Global impairment	Used in previous versions of the DSM corresponding to diagnoses.
National Institute of Mental Health-Global Obsessive-Compulsive Scale (NIMH-GOCS)	Insel et al. (1983); Murphy et al. (1982)	Clinician	1 min	All	Overall severity	Good interrater reliability.
Clinical Intake Interview	N/A	Clinician	Variable	Any age; often a different version for children 6 and under	Unstructured interview	No psychometrics. Used to conceptualize case and assign initial diagnoses.

(Continued)

Table 6.1 (Continued)

Measure	Citation	Reporter	Time to administer	Recommended assessment age of patient	Purpose	Psychometrics
Child Obsessive Compulsive Impact Scale-Revised (COIS-R)	Piacentini et al. (2007)	Parent, Child	10 min	Tested in ages 5–17	Psychosocial functioning	Good internal consistency, concurrent validity, and test–retest reliability. Sensitivity to treatment effects not yet established with this revised version. Tested in children with an OCD diagnosis.
Obsessive-Compulsive Inventory Child Version (OCI-CV)	Foa et al. (2010)	Parent, Child	15 min	Tested in ages 7–17	Assesses OCD symptoms and severity	Strong retest reliability, initial support for divergent validity and sensitivity to change. Tested in children with a primary OCD diagnosis.
Children's Obsessional Compulsive Inventory-Revised (ChOCI-R)	Uher et al. (2008)	Parent, Child	15 min	Tested in ages 9–18	Assesses symptoms	Good internal consistency, established convergent, divergent, and discriminant validity. No information on sensitivity to change and predictive validity. Tested in a clinical sample.
Family Accommodation Scale (FAS)	Calvocoressi et al. (1995, 1999)	Clinician	20 min	Tested in ages 7 to adult	Degree of family accommodation	Excellent interrater reliability, good internal consistency, convergent, and discriminant validity. Tested in relatives of OCD patients. Further research of its use with families and children with OCD is needed.

Family Accommodation Scale (FAS)	Flessner et al. (2011)	Parent	10 min	Tested in ages 7–17	Degree of family accommodation	Examined psychometrics of original clinician-administered version (Calvocoressi et al., 1995, 1999) with parent-report. Good convergent and discriminant validity and good internal consistency.
OCD Family Functioning Scale (OFF)	Stewart et al. (2011)	Child		Tested in ages 7–75	Family functioning	Demonstrated excellent internal consistency, adequate test–retest reliability, and excellent convergent validity with the Family Accommodation Scale and the Work and Social Adjustment Scale. Tested in OCD diagnosed children and adults.

OCD-Specific Screening Measures

Children's Florida Obsessive-Compulsive Inventory (C-FOCI). The C-FOCI (Storch et al., 2009) is a brief child self-report screening measure for OCD with good psychometric properties. The measure includes two parts, a symptom checklist and a severity scale. The symptom checklist includes questions about 17 obsessions and compulsions across three categories: unpleasant thoughts and images; worries about terrible things happening; and the need to perform certain acts over and over again. The severity scale portion of the measure, which is similar to the structure of the Children's Yale–Brown Obsessive Compulsive Scale (CY-BOCS) severity subscale, asks about the items endorsed in the symptom checklist. Questions include the amount of time occupied by the thoughts and behaviors endorsed, how much the thoughts and behaviors bother the child, amount of control over the thoughts and behaviors, level of avoidance and interference. Though this measure has demonstrated good psychometric properties and is brief and easy to administer, additional research is needed on its validity as a screener for OCD.

Leyton Obsessional Inventory – Survey Form (LOI-CV, survey form) and Survey Form, Short Version (LOI-CV, Survey Form, Short Version). Based on the LOI-CV card-sorting task (Berg, Rapoport, & Flament, 1986), the LOI-CV survey form (Bamber, Tamplin, Park, Kyte, & Goodyer, 2002; Berg, Whitaker, Davies, Flamentm & Rapoport, (1988) includes 20 OCD symptom items, which are rated as present or absent. A short version of the LOI-CV survey form includes 11 items. Both versions of the scale also assess interference of endorsed symptoms. Though initially validated in a large epidemiological study (Berg et al., 1988; Flament et al., 1988), further examination by Storch and colleagues (2011) suggest that the LOI-CV survey form and the LOI-CV short form do not have adequate psychometric properties to be used as a screening instrument or a symptom severity assessment measure in youth with OCD. Based on these findings, this measure should be used with significant caution.

Other Measures

As outlined by the AACAP practice parameters (2012), other non-OCD specific measures may also be useful to assess symptoms of OCD and other anxiety. Examples of such measures include the Child Behavioral Checklist (CBCL) (Achenbach 1991), n 118-item parent-report measure of behavioral and emotional problems in children, and the Screen for Anxiety Related Disorders – Revised (SCARED-R) (Muris et al. 1999), a 66-item child- and parent-report questionnaire that assesses for symptoms of several anxiety disorders.

Diagnosing OCD

If concerns about OCD persist after initial screening, further information should be gathered through a clinical interview in order to determine whether a diagnosis of OCD is warranted. The most comprehensive type of clinical interview is a structured interview. In contrast with screening measures, structured interviews are much more detailed and include diagnostic categories other than OCD and anxiety disorders. Structured interviews are designed as a valid and reliable method for assessing psychiatric disorders and assigning appropriate diagnoses. They allow for consistent administration across youth and systematic gathering of parent, child and combined reports of symptoms. Furthermore, clinician judgment in structured interviews minimizes errors when compared to self- or parent-report measures. In addition, structured interviews assess for comorbid disorders, which might be relevant in making differential diagnoses and recommendations for treatment.

In spite of the strengths of structured interviews, there are also several disadvantages (Lewin & Piacentini, 2010). First, structured interviews are costly to administer, both in terms of materials and clinician time. The briefest interviews take a minimum of 30 minutes, but most interviews approach closer to 90 minutes in administration time. In addition, administration of structured interviews requires a trained clinician or administrator, which is not always feasible in community settings. Structured interviews are most frequently used in research studies during which incorporating sufficient time and training is more feasible.

Though individual attributes of common structured interviews are discussed below, there are some components that are consistent across interviews. First, the child and parent are each interviewed, often separately. Second, most of these interviews are specific to DSM-IV diagnoses, with a DSM-5 version in development. Third, though assessment may focus on OCD if that is the reason for the referral, anxiety disorders and other childhood psychiatric disorders will also be assessed. Though input from multiple parties is important (i.e., parent, child), clinical judgment is ultimately used to make final decisions regarding diagnoses. A summary of diagnostic interviews and their psychometric properties is included in Table 6.1.

Structured Interviews

Anxiety Disorders Interview Scheduled for DSM-IV – Child and Parent Version (ADIS-C/P). The ADIS is a clinician-administered structured interview (Silverman & Albano, 1996), which was developed based on DSM-IV diagnostic criteria. It takes approximately 45–60 minutes to administer. The ADIS primarily focuses on diagnosing anxiety disorders, though it also includes screening questions for other disorders (e.g., mood disorders, disruptive behavior disorders). Individual disorders are assessed by preliminary screening questions, which, if endorsed, are followed up by more detailed questions. Typically, parents and children are interviewed separately and the clinician combines information obtained from both interviews to make a diagnosis. Diagnoses are determined by symptom endorsement and a clinician severity rating (CSR) higher than 4 (range: 0–8). Overall, the ADIS has excellent psychometric properties (Silverman, Saavedra, & Pina, 2001; Wood, Piacentini, Bergman, McCracken, & Barrios, 2002). Given its focus on anxiety disorders and OCD, the ADIS is often considered the strongest measure for clinical assessment and treatment outcome research among youth with OCD (Lewin & Piacentini, 2010). However, its lengthy administration makes it less feasible for some settings.

Schedule for Affective Disorders and Schizophrenia for School-Age Children (K-SADS-PL). The K-SADS-PL (Kaufman, Birmaher, Brent, & Rao, 1997) is a semi-structured diagnostic interview with excellent psychometric properties that assesses for current and lifetime symptoms of a wide range of childhood disorders. As with the ADIS, the K-SADS-PL is typically administered to the child and parent separately. Clinician judgment is used to make final diagnoses and impairment ratings. The interview begins with a 10–15 minute unstructured introductory interview, during which the clinician collects clinical and demographic information and builds rapport with the child. Similar to the ADIS, the K-SADS-PL includes screener questions, which allow the clinician to skip the supplemental questions if the screener questions are not endorsed. Unlike the ADIS, the structure of the K-SADS-PL is such that all screener questions are administered first, followed by the appropriate diagnostic supplements. These diagnostic supplements include Affective Disorders, Psychotic Disorders, Anxiety Disorders, Behavioral Disorders, and Substance Abuse, Eating, and Tic Disorders. Diagnoses are then scored as "definite," "probable" or "not present." Given the nature of this comprehensive diagnostic interview, the K-SADS-PL is lengthy to administer and requires substantial clinician training. Typically, administration takes up to 90 minutes with each reporter (i.e., parent, child), making it less feasible for use in many clinical settings.

Mini International Neuropsychiatric Interview (MINI-KID). The MINI-KID (Sheehan et al., 2010) is a brief structured diagnostic interview that assesses for psychiatric disorders in children and adolescents aged 6–17 years. It is designed to assess current symptoms of psychopathology for 24 disorders including OCD, social anxiety, GAD, depression, tics, and other possible psychiatric disorders. Unlike the ADIS and K-SADS-PL, the MINI-KID can be administered to the child and parent together, rather than separately. The interview is organized such that the clinician only proceeds with asking additional symptom questions for the disorder if screening questions are endorsed. Because the child and parent are both present during the interview, discrepancies are addressed as they arise, with clinical judgment being used for final decisions. Unlike the longer ADIS and K-SADS-PL, the MINI-KID only takes approximately 30 minutes to administer, which makes it a more feasible alternative to longer structured interviews. The MINI-KID has demonstrated adequate reliability and validity and is highly concordant with diagnoses found on the K-SADS-PL. Perhaps as a result of its brevity, the MINI-KID does provide less disorder subtyping and tends to identify more cases of disorders (possible "false-positives") than the K-SADS-PL. However, Sheehan and colleagues (2010) suggest that rather than the MINI-KID overestimating some disorders, it is also possible that the K-SADS-PL underestimates some conditions due to fatigue effects (i.e. interviewees know that endorsing additional symptoms will generate additional questions and lengthen the interview further).

NIMH Diagnostic Interview Schedule for Children Version IV (NIMH DISC-IV). The NIMH-DISC-IV (Shaffer, Fisher, Lucas, Dulcan, & Schwab-Stone, 2000) is a highly structured clinical interview that assesses over 30 DSM-IV and ICD-10 psychiatric disorders in children and adolescents. Categories of diagnoses assessed include anxiety disorders (including OCD), mood disorders, schizophrenia, disruptive behavior disorders, substance use disorders, and miscellaneous disorders (e.g., eating disorders, tic disorders). Unlike the structured interviews described above, the NIMH-DISC-IV was designed to be administered by nonclinicians. Initially designed for large-scale epidemiological studies, it has also been used as a screening tool and in clinical studies. To minimize training, questions are relatively short and simple and designed to be read verbatim by the interviewer. "Stem" questions, which ask about symptoms in broad terms, are asked of every respondent. Any symptoms that are endorsed are followed up by contingent questions that probe around frequency, duration and intensity. If a clinically significant number of diagnostic criteria are endorsed, questions about age of onset, impairment and treatment history are also asked. Overall, the NIMH-DISC-IV is an inexpensive and convenient structured interview that requires minimal training and can be administered by "lay interviewers." However, because it was developed for large epidemiological studies, it may not be as useful for making difficult differential diagnoses and does not have a specific emphasis on OCD or anxiety disorders. Administration time is approximately 70 minutes per reporter (e.g., parent, child), which is about equivalent to other structured interviews, such as the ADIS-C/P.

Unstructured Clinical Interview

An alternative to a structured diagnostic interview is an unstructured clinical interview. Unstructured, open-ended intake interviews are more commonly used in clinical settings than in research. They are briefer and less expensive than structured interviews and require less training and many of the same benefits. Unstructured interviews aim to conceptualize the case and take into consideration treatment history, family factors and the patient's symptoms (Lewin & Piacentini, 2010). Typically, an unstructured interview involves gathering information about the presenting problem and the role it has played in the patient's family history, developmental history, educational history, and other developmentally appropriate categories (e.g., substance use, employment history) (Jones, 2010). Ideally, questions about these areas should lead to "diagnostic clues," which a clinician should use to assign a diagnosis (Jones, 2010). In addition, questions about impairment are typically asked both to develop treatment goals and to help with patient motivation to engage in treatment. Strengths include faster administration and less clinician training, but minimizing time and training also leads to some disadvantages when using unstructured interviews. Because questions are not standardized, the clinician is entirely responsible for formulating relevant questions for each client and assigning an appropriate diagnosis based on this information. This may increase the likelihood of a diagnosis being missed or not being assessed, leading to overall lower diagnostic accuracy. Despite some of the drawbacks, unstructured interviews are the most frequently used diagnostic tool in clinical settings, but should ideally be augmented by additional measures and reports.

Assessing OCD Severity and Impairment

Once OCD has been identified as the working diagnosis, a number of additional measures are available to assess severity and impairment due to OCD symptoms (see Table 6.1 for psychometric properties). Though a formal assessment typically occurs during the first session, assessment of symptoms is an ongoing process throughout treatment.

Clinician-administered

Children's Yale–Brown Obsessive Compulsive Scale (CY-BOCS). The CY-BOCS (Scahill, Riddle, McSwiggin-Hardin, & Ort, 1997) is the child version of the adult Yale-Brown Obsessive-Compulsive Scale (Y-BOCS) and is considered the "gold standard" measure of OCD. Though its administration typically takes between 30 and 60 minutes, the CY-BOCS is highly recommended for use in clinical settings to diagnose and assess OCD.

The CY-BOCS includes a semi-structured list of common OCD symptoms called the CY-BOCS Symptom Checklist (CY-BOCS-SC). The first section includes a checklist of possible obsessive symptoms divided into categories, such as contamination and aggressive obsessions. Clinicians administering this measure should ask whether items on the checklist bother the child. Ideally, clinicians should also question how these obsessions map on to the second section of the measure, which is a checklist of common compulsive symptoms. As described in more detail in the "Functional Assessment" section below, both the obsessions and compulsions checklists are organized in topographical categories, but should be considered functionally as well. Gallant et al. (2008) demonstrated initial psychometric support for the CY-BOCS-SC, but research on the reliability and validity of the symptom checklist is otherwise limited.

Following the checklist portion of the measure, the third and fourth sections ask about the frequency, interference, distress, ability to resist and perceived control of obsessive and compulsive symptoms. Each of these categories is rated on a five-point Likert-type scale ranging from 0 (none) to 4 (extreme), except for the perceived control category, which is rated from 0 (complete control) to 4 (no control). Summed scores range from 0 to 20 on each subscale (obsessions severity and compulsions severity) and 0 (subclinical) to 40 (extreme) on the total scale. The CY-BOCS can be administered jointly with the child and parent or separately, depending on the clinician's judgment of developmental appropriateness. Psychometrics properties of the CY-BOCS obsessions and compulsions subscales and total score are excellent in school-age children and adolescents (Scahill et al., 1997; Storch et al., 2004). Preliminary findings on the reliability and validity of the CY-BOCS among younger children (ages 5–8) demonstrate adequate psychometric properties, except for the Obsessions subscale, which should be interpreted with caution (Freeman, Flessner, & Garcia, 2011).

In terms of its clinical utility, change in CY-BOCS score is among the most frequently used measures of symptom improvement and outcome in clinical trials. Ideally, many measures should be used together to measure symptom change and severity, but a 25–50% CY-BOCS reduction, often used to denote "treatment responder" status in research studies, might also be a useful clinical cut-off for judging improvement (Lewin & Piacentini, 2010).

Clinical Global Impressions (CGI) Scale: Improvement and Severity (CGI-I and CGI-S). The CGI (Guy, 1976) is a brief, stand-alone assessment of overall clinical improvement and severity based on symptoms observed and impairment reported.

Both the CGI-I and CGI-S include a seven-point clinician-rated scale, with the severity scale regarding level of mental illness and the improvement scale regarding change in symptoms during treatment. Though the CGI-I and CGI-S are not specific to OCD, they have been used successfully in patients with OCD (Garvey et al., 1999; Perlmutter et al., 1999) and are consistent with CY-BOCS severity scores (Lewin et al., 2014).

Children's Global Assessment Scale (CGAS). The CGAS (Shaffer et al., 1983) is a child-focused measure of global impairment and functioning based on the adult "Global Assessment Scale (GAS) (Endicott, Spitzer, Fleiss, & Cohen, 1976). Scores range from 1 (lowest functioning) to 100 (highest) and are assigned by a clinician. A hybrid of the CGAS and GAS, the Global Assessment of Functioning (GAF) (American Psychological Association, 2000), scale is a 100-point measure of functioning for all ages that was formerly tied to DSM diagnoses (Schorre & Vandvik, 2004), but is not included in DSM-5.

NIMH Global Obsessive-Compulsive Scale (NIMH Global OCS). The NIMH Global OCS (Insel et al., 1983) is a clinician-rated index of illness severity and functional impairment. Each scale is a single-item composite rating of illness severity ranging from 1 (normal) to 15 (very severe). A rating of 7 is the clinical severity threshold for the diagnosis of OCD. The measure has good interrater reliability and psychometric properties and is useful as a brief measure of OCD symptom severity and change.

Child/Parent Report

Child- and parent-report measures recommended for screening are reviewed above. The following measures are useful throughout treatment for OCD rather than during initial screening. At the beginning of treatment, some families are more comfortable completing self-report measures than divulging information to a clinician in a clinician-administered interview, which helps to combat under- (or over-) reporting that sometimes occurs (Merlo, Storch, Murphy, Goodman, & Geffken, 2005). Child and parent-report measures are also useful because they can easily be re-administered throughout treatment to see if there is a change in symptoms and impairment. However, findings from self-report measures must be interpreted with some caution. First, individual response style may affect assessment of symptoms on self-report measures (Merlo et al., 2005). In addition, self-report questionnaires may be confusing or difficult to understand. Respondents may not pay close attention or may underestimate impairment if questions are not phrased in a clearly applicable manner (Merlo et al., 2005).

Child Obsessive-Compulsive Impact Scale – Revised (COIS-R). The COIS-R (Piacentini, Peris, Bergman, Chang, & Jaffer, 2007), based on the original COIS (Piacentini et al., 2003), measures OCD-specific functional impairment across several domains. Parallel child- and parent-report versions assess academic, social, and family impairment. Questions address specific activities with which OCD may interfere (e.g., "Taking tests or exams," "Getting ready for bed at night"). Responses are rated on a four-point Likert scale, with 0 indicating "not at all" and 3 indicating "very much." Factor analysis of the parent-report version resulted in a four-factor solution including OCD-related impairment in daily living skills, school, social, and family/activities (Piacentini et al., 2007). Findings on the youth report produced a three-factor solution, including school, social, and activities (Piacentini et al., 2007). Both the parent- and child-report versions demonstrated good psychometric properties. The COIS is a useful measure for establishing target areas for functional improvement and assessing changes in impairment throughout the course of treatment.

Obsessive Compulsive Inventory – Child Report (OCI-CV). The OCI-CV (Foa et al., 2010) is a 21-item self-report measure that assesses child OCD symptom presence and dimensionality. Based on the OCI-Revised (OCI-R) (Foa et al., 2002) adult OCD measure, the OCI-CV has six factorially derived subscales, including doubting/checking, obsessions, hoarding, washing, ordering and neutralizing (Foa et al., 2010). Scores from each of these subscales are totaled to yield a total score. Individual items are rated on a three-point response scale (0 = never to 2 = always). Though the OCI-R includes frequency and distress ratings for each question, the OCI-CV only includes frequency ratings. Both Foa and colleagues (2010) and Jones and colleagues (2013) demonstrated adequate psychometric properties for the use of the OCI-CV to measure OCD symptom severity in children. Foa et al. (2010) also found that the OCI-CV demonstrates similar sensitivity to change as the CY-BOCS, meaning that re-administration of the OCI-CV later in treatment would be a useful method of measuring improvement. Despite its utility in this regard, the OCI should ideally be used in conjunction with other measures of OCD severity and treatment outcome from multiple reporters.

Children's Yale–Brown Obsessive Compulsive Scale – Child-Report and Parent-Report (CY-BOCS-CR and -PR). Though the CY-BOCS was originally developed as a clinician-administered measure (described above), child self-report and parent-report versions have also been developed with slight changes to wording specific to the reporter (Storch et al., 2006). Psychometric properties for the CYBOCS-CR and CYBOCS-PR are adequate (Storch et al, 2006). These self- and parent-report versions are most useful when brevity, minimizing clinician time, and assessing current severity are priorities. However, clinician administration is preferred in order to use the CY-BOCS for functional assessment and as a tool for treatment planning.

Children's Obsessional Compulsive Inventory-Revised (ChOCI-R). The ChOCI-R (Uher, Heyman, Turner, & Shafran, 2008), revised from the original CHOCI (Shafran et al., 2003), measures OCD symptom severity and content in youth. Parallel child- and parent-report versions allow for a more complete assessment of the youth's symptoms. The ChOCI is structured similarly to the CY-BOCS, with an initial list of 10 common compulsions, followed by a list of 10 common obsessions. Responses to these items are on a three-point scale ranging from 0 (not at all) to 2 (a lot). Each subscale (compulsions and obsessions) yields a score ranging from 0 to 20. Total scores are calculated by adding the compulsions and obsessions scores together (range 0–40). Also similar to the CY-BOCS, the symptom lists are followed by severity questions for compulsions and obsessions, which are each rated on a five-point scale. Severity items include time spent with the symptoms, interference with functioning, distress, resistance, control and avoidance. Severity scores are calculated by summing the item responses for obsessions (range 0–24), compulsions (range 0–24), and total (range 0–48). A confirmatory factor analysis resulted in poor factor loadings for the resistance items for both obsessions and compulsions. As a result, Uher et al. (2008) provide equivalent summed scores for the measure with and without resistance items, allowing researchers and clinicians to choose the 10- or -12-item version of the ChOCI.

The ChOCI-R was developed as a brief, self-report alternative to the CY-BOCS and is suggested for use as a routine measurement of OCD severity in clinical practice. In mild to moderate cases, Uher et al. (2008) found that the CHOCI might be better than the CY-BOCS at differentiating between mild symptoms and normative behaviors. However, the CY-BOCS is better at discriminating among severe cases. Given its brevity and good psychometric properties, the CHOCI is a time efficient alternative to clinician-administered interviews for mild to moderate cases. However, additional research on sensitivity to change on this measure is needed.

Dimensional Yale–Brown Obsessive-Compulsive Scale (DY-BOCS). The DY-BOCS (Rosário-Campos et al., 2006) is a dimensional measure of OCD. Given that OCD is such a heterogeneous disorder, attempts have been made to better understand symptom patterns that may apply across individuals. For example, several factor analytic studies have suggested common dimensions such as symmetry/ordering and contaminating/cleaning (e.g., Mataix-Cols, Rosário-Campos, & Leckman, 2005). A dimensional measure allows clinicians to ask more specific questions about these common symptom dimensions and to better understand the functional relationship between obsessions and compulsions (discussed in more detail in the "Functional Assessment" section below). Rosário-Campos and colleagues (2006) developed and examined the psychometric properties of the DY-BOCS in a combined child and adult sample, which yielded good psychometric properties. However, data on the psychometric properties of this scale have not been examined in a youth-only sample. Further research is needed to determine whether this is a useful measure for assessing symptom dimensions in children with OCD.

Assessing Family Accommodation and Family Functioning

Another important area to consider when assessing and treating OCD among youth is the role of the family. This may include family member involvement in rituals or overall impairment in family functioning. Providing reassurance and physically assisting in rituals, such as washing, are common types of parental involvement in OCD-related behaviors (e.g., Rettew, Swedo, Leonard, Lenane, & Rapoport, 1992). In addition, children's OCD symptoms may serve as significant stressors for parents, resulting in increased parental accommodation and negative affect (Futh, Simonds, & Micali, 2012). Further, parent accommodation has been found to mediate the relationship between OCD symptom severity and functional impairment, suggesting that it may be a critical target for treatment (Caporino et al., 2012). Overall, it is important to assess both the stressors caused by a child's OCD symptoms, as well as the role the parent may be playing in reinforcing symptoms.

Family accommodation refers to the extent to which family members (i.e., parents and siblings) alleviate a youth's symptoms by changing schedules, routines or partaking in rituals (Storch et al., 2007). Theoretically, family accommodation negatively reinforces a youth's symptoms by temporarily reducing OCD-related anxiety. Treatment studies have shown that, likely as a result of this negative reinforcement cycle, family accommodation has an adverse impact on treatment outcome (e.g., Garcia et al., 2010; Merlo et al., 2009).

Assessment Tools

Family Accommodation Scale (FAS). The FAS (Calvocoressi, Lewis, Harris, & Trufan, 1995; Calvocoressi et al., 1999) is a 13-item clinician-administered measure of family accommodation (Calvocoressi et al., 1995; Calvocoressi et al., 1999). Although the FAS was originally designed and tested as a clinician-administered measure, most studies have used the FAS as a family or parent-report measure. The FAS has been widely used for adults and youth with OCD and has excellent psychometric properties (e.g., Flessner et al., 2011; Merlo, Lehmkuhl, Geffken, & Storch, 2009; Peris et al., 2008; Storch et al., 2007), as shown in Table 6.1. The FAS consists of nine questions that assess the degree to which family members have accommodated the child's OCD symptoms in the last month and four items that assess the level of impairment or distress experienced by the family as a result of the need to accommodate. Items are rated on a five-point Likert-type scale ranging from 0 (none/never) to 4 (every day) and are summed to yield a total score. Example questions include, "Has ritual time increased when you have not participated?" and "How often did you modify the family's routine due to the patient's symptoms?" The majority of families of youth with OCD report some degree of accommodation to the youth's symptoms (Storch et al., 2007). Family accommodation is related to higher OCD symptom severity and functional impairment (Caporino et al., 2012; Lebowitz, Vitulano, & Omer, 2011; Storch et al., 2007), and reductions in accommodation are associated with better OCD treatment response among children (Merlo et al., 2009; Piacentini et al., 2011).

A recent investigation of the FAS factor structure further supports its validity as a parent-report measure (FAS-PR) (Flessner et al., 2011). The FAS-PR consists of two factor-analytically derived subscales, including parental involvement in the child's compulsions and family avoidance of OCD-related triggers (Flessner et al., 2011). Though studies have yet to directly compare clinician-administered and family-report versions of the FAS, using the clinician-administered version may be better suited for probing about behaviors that the family may recognize as accommodation. The parent-report measure is likely better suited to settings where brevity and minimizing clinician time is a priority. As demonstrated by findings in clinical trials (e.g. Garcia et al., 2010; Merlo et al., 2009) assessing and reducing family accommodation is crucial for improving treatment outcome among youth with OCD.

OCD Family Functioning Scale (OFF Scale). The OFF Scale (Stewart et al., 2011) is a 42-item self-report measure of OCD-related functional impairment. The measure contains 3 subscales including a family functioning impairment subscale, a symptom-specific impairment subscale, and a family role-specific impairment subscale. The family functioning impairment subscale asks about frequency of OCD-related impairment with response options including 0 (never), 1 (monthly), 2 (weekly), and 3 (daily). Scores for this subscale are calculated by summing the scores of all items (range 0–63). The other subscales contain the same response options, but are scored as dichotomous variables, with a response of 0 (never) being a considered a negative response and a score of 1 (monthly), 2 (weekly), or 3 (daily) being considered a positive response. Both the self-report and family-member-report (in the case of children, typically a parent) versions of the measure contain questions about family functioning impairment at the time of scale completion and during the "worst ever" OCD severity.

Findings from the development of this measure suggest that individuals with OCD and their relatives differentially rate the impact of OCD in various areas of family functioning (Stewart et al., 2011). Such discrepancies highlight the need to carefully assess areas of impairment from multiple perspectives and plan treatment goals accordingly. Though this is a promising measure of OCD-related impairment in family functioning, additional research needs to be conducted to replicate findings, examine sensitivity to change and to further examine the use of this scale among children.

Functional Assessment

The most critical factor to assess when planning for treatment of pediatric OCD is the functional relationship between obsessions and compulsions. All of the OCD measures discussed in this chapter can be used as part of a functional assessment to acquire an understanding of the patient's symptoms. These measures identify symptoms while the clinician works to interpret and investigate meaningful connections between them. A functional assessment of symptoms will further guide treatment since ERP, the empirically supported treatment for OCD, is dependent on the relation between obsessions and compulsions (Freeman et al., 2014).

To complete a thorough functional assessment, the patient's core obsessional fears must first be investigated. Research suggests two core dimensions linked to OCD obsessions: harm avoidance and incompleteness (Ecker & Gönner, 2008; Pietrefesa & Coles, 2009; Summerfeldt, 2004). Harm avoidance includes symptoms of exaggerated evasion of potential harm to one's self or others. The patient's obsessional content can be the fear of consequences, sensitivity to threats, and a sense of responsibility over preventing a possible catastrophic incidence. Generally, children with harm avoidance will report that "something bad might happen" if they do not complete their compulsions. Within harm avoidance, there are common subtypes of feared outcomes including scrupulosity, aggression and contamination concerns. Given the highly idiosyncratic nature of these fears, individualized functional assessment is particularly important. Unlike harm avoidance, incompleteness is not connected to fears of potential consequences. Children often cannot verbalize these specific obsessions other than feeling uncomfortable, distressed, or "not just right." The child will engage in their compulsions until the feeling of "completeness" or "perfection" is achieved. By categorizing the child's symptoms into these two core dimensions, the clinician will have a better understanding of the function that these behaviors serve. Children may present with both types of these core obsessions or just one.

To gain an effective understanding of symptoms, clinicians must establish a distinction between symptom topography and symptom function (Conelea, Freeman, & Garcia, 2012). Topography refers to what the behavior looks like during observation or while experiencing it (e.g., hand washing, repeating, ordering). Symptom topography plays a role in setting the scene with specific stimuli for exposure tasks. Function describes what drives the behavior within its context, including the antecedents and consequences of that behavior (e.g., just right, harm avoidance, attention). Symptom topography and symptom function should remain two separate entities, as they are often mistakenly fused during the assessment process. The following is an example of how the distinction between topography and function can be applied: a child is observed hand washing and seeking reassurance from his caregiver after throwing out the trash. The clinician completes a functional assessment and concludes that these compulsions (e.g., hand washing, reassurance-seeking) are related to the same core fear of harm avoidance related to illness; specifically, these behaviors are thought to prevent the child from contracting an illness. Even though the compulsions of hand washing and reassurance-seeking differ topographically, they both serve the same function of harm avoidance. Additionally, it is important to be cognizant that compulsions that are topographically the same across patients (i.e., the same behavior) do not necessarily serve the same function. For instance, ritualistic hand washing may occur for either harm avoidance or incompleteness purposes.

Conelea and colleagues (2012) propose a building block approach to administering the CY-BOCS checklist to better understand function. They advise to first collect information about the topography of symptoms. Once that is obtained, the next step is to connect specific obsessions to their corresponding compulsions. This is completed through understanding symptom topography versus symptom function and through asking functional assessment questions. Such questions may include: "If you didn't [do compulsion], what do you worry could happen? Do you feel like you will just keep feeling uncomfortable, like something is 'not just right' or 'incomplete'"? and "When you have [obsession], what makes it better/go away/reduces your anxiety?" (Conelea et al., 2012: 115). These focused questions can help elucidate functional relationship between obsessions and compulsions. The end result is a map of the child's symptoms starting with core obsession themes (harm avoidance or incompleteness) and the specific obsessions associated with them. These obsessions are then linked to compulsions that are associated with relieving anxiety from that fear. For example, one section of a map may contain the core obsession of harm avoidance, the specific obsession of getting oneself ill, and the associated compulsions of reassurance-seeking, hand washing, and avoidance of the trashcan. Given the idiosyncratic nature of OCD symptoms, investigative questions should not only be used in the assessment but throughout treatment.

A functional assessment is not only essential to the overall assessment of OCD, but can also aid in treatment planning and the use of ERP. Once the relationships between obsessions and compulsions are established, a treatment plan with meaningful exposures can be designed to best meet the child's individual needs. More specifically, a clinician can tailor an exposure to the individual patient to activate the appropriate fear structure and promote habituation through response prevention. For instance, exposures around harm avoidance (e.g., contamination) with hand washing will be much different than exposures around "not just right" feelings for hand washing. The assessment process of OCD should be ongoing and the clinician should constantly assess for functional relationships to optimize the patient's treatment.

Clinical Considerations for Using OCD Measures with Children and Adolescents Developmental Considerations

Obsessive-compulsive symptom expression can differ across age groups, which may be in part to due to developmental factors, such as cognitive maturation. Thus, developmental differences in symptom expression should be taken into account when using measure to assess pediatric OCD. In children, compulsions without expressed obsessions are common, and the compulsive behaviors themselves may be different than those observed in adolescents or adults (Freeman et al., 2012). For instance, early-onset cases tend to have increased sensory phenomena-related compulsions, such as the need to touch or tap things until they feel "just right" (Rosário-Campos et al., 2001). Young children with OCD, unlike older children or adults, may be unable to distinguish obsessional thoughts from other, nonintrusive recurring cognitions or images. Additionally, they may not understand or be able to identify the connection between obsessional thoughts and subsequent compulsions, or to verbally express this pattern to others. It is also important for assessors to be cognizant about typical developmental rituals when evaluating for pediatric OCD. Younger children will often have routines around bedtime, meals, and dressing that may look similar to compulsions. Generally, typical developmental routines do not result in interference or create significant distress for the child when interrupted (American Academy of Child and Adolescent Psychiatry, 2012). It might be helpful for an assessor to question whether such routines have an impact on family functioning and what happens if a child's routine is disrupted (e.g., child's emotional and/or behavioral response including duration and severity). Interviewers may also need to assess and help parents differentiate between rigid temperaments and compulsive behaviors (Freeman et al., 2012).

Based upon their experience assessing young children in the Pediatric Obsessive Compulsive Disorder Treatment Study for Young Children (POTS Jr), Freeman and colleagues (2012) provide assessment modifications to help facilitate obtaining accurate information for assessing younger children with OCD. These modifications may also be useful with other patients, such as those with cognitive delays, autism, or limited insight. When administering the CY-BOCS, youth and parents may find it easier to report on compulsions first, since these behaviors are typically observable and children tend to be more aware of them. Interviewers can then use information about the reported compulsions to gather more information about obsessions. For example, an assessor may ask the following sequence of questions to better understand a child's obsessions: "You said that you check to see if your brother is okay several times a day, but you are not sure how much you worry about something bad happening to your brother. Do you usually check on your brother when you're worried about him? Are there times you check on him when you aren't worried? Do you ever worry about him and not check?" Caregivers may also provide support during the assessment to help rephrase questions into more understandable language for their own child. Using concrete examples can often be helpful since children may have difficulty understanding questions related to thoughts or concepts about time or estimating time. Freeman and colleagues (2012) recommend integrating psychoeducation into the assessment process to ensure families understand the definitions of obsessions and compulsions and to help differentiate between behaviors that are and are not OCD symptoms. Lastly, it is important to be mindful of children's shorter attention spans and manage time appropriately. If using a structured interview, clinicians may choose a shorter interview, such as the MINI, and prioritize additional measures that assess OCD specifically, such as the CY-BOCS.

Differential Diagnoses

Many other childhood disorders have behaviors that are topographically similar to OCD, which may make differential diagnoses challenging for children with OCD. Additionally, many of these disorders are often comorbid with childhood OCD. In general, one should tailor the use of assessment measures to consider the context in which the symptoms occur, the function of the symptoms, and the history of symptoms. For instance, ritualized eating behaviors, touching or tapping, "just right" symptoms, and reassurance-seeking may topographically look like OCD but may reflect a different condition. Behavioral observations and utilizing other diagnostic tools as described earlier may be especially useful when seeking diagnostic clarity. Lastly, ongoing evaluation of symptoms in the context of therapeutic interactions may be necessary to determine an accurate diagnosis. The discussion below provides an overview of common overlapping symptoms with OCD and more specific considerations for differentiating OCD from other disorders when administering OCD measures. When deciding a differential diagnosis, it is important for assessors to keep in mind that individuals with OCD often have other psychiatric conditions, so it is possible that these conditions are comorbid with OCD.

Generalized Anxiety Disorder (GAD). GAD and OCD are highly comorbid and share phenomenological overlap, making it challenging to differentiate between the two disorders in youth (Comer, Kendall, Franklin, Hudson, & Pimentel, 2004; Lewin & Piacentini, 2010). Both obsessions in OCD and worry in GAD encompass repetitive cognitive activity that is perceived as uncontrollable and intrusive. Unfortunately, there is limited research examining the difference between worry and obsessions in youth samples; however, adult literature suggests that OCD obsessions are less likely to have a specific, identifiable trigger, tend to have an imaginal form, and are associated with a greater sense of responsibility or attached significance to the cognition (Comer et al., 2004). The content of GAD worries in children are typically related to everyday experiences (e.g., school, weather, performance, safety, health), whereas OCD obsessions can have more unusual content (e.g., scrupulosity, sexual, aggression) (Lewin & Piacentini, 2010).

Additionally, individuals with GAD may engage in compulsive-like behaviors, such as reassurance-seeking, which may be difficult to differentiate from compulsions in OCD. Comer and colleagues (2004) suggest that considering frequency, rigidity, quality, and function in compulsive behavior may be useful clinical considerations for making a differential diagnosis between OCD and GAD. One might find that OCD compulsions occur at a higher rate and are more rigid than GAD behaviors. For instance, children with GAD may seek reassurance around a variety of possible bad outcomes (e.g., Will I get sick? What if I get dehydrated and have to go to the hospital? What if I get sick and I can't call you because your cell phone battery is dead?) in contrast to repeated reassurance around the same feared outcome (e.g., Will I get sick?). Children with OCD may also require specific answers from another person (e.g., I *promise* you won't get sick) instead of a more general answer (e.g., You won't get sick). The quality of compulsive behavior should also be assessed. Children with GAD may be more likely to provide a feared outcome and make more logical connections between compulsive behaviors and feared outcomes (e.g., checking to ensure they wrote down the assignment correctly in order to not get a bad grade) as opposed to children with OCD who may have looser logical connections (e.g., erasing their name on their homework to prevent something bad from happening to their friend). Lastly, Comer and colleagues suggest considering the function of compulsive behaviors. Youth with GAD may be more likely to engage in certain behaviors to prevent the occurrence of a bad outcome, whereas youth with OCD may be more likely to engage in compulsive behaviors to relieve their immediate distress related to the thoughts of a bad event happening. While these guidelines may be helpful for differential diagnoses, it is important to note that empirical evidence to support such differences remains elusive (Comer et al., 2004).

Tic Disorders. A tic is a sudden rapid, recurrent, and nonrhythmic motor movement or vocalization (American Psychiatric Association, 2013). Differentiating tics from compulsions is often difficult and is further complicated by their common co-occurrence with OCD, up to 30% (American Psychiatric Association, 2013; Lewin & Piacentini, 2010). A simple tic can more easily be distinguished from compulsions due to the brevity of the tics and nature (e.g., eye blinking, kick, throat clearing); however, complex tics are often longer in duration, may combine multiple simple tics, and often seem purposeful. Observing the behavior alone is often insufficient to determine whether a movement is a tic or compulsion. OCD rituals and complex tics may topographically look the same, such as repeated tapping. Distinguishing these behaviors in children is further complicated by the fact that youth have more difficulty describing their internal experiences and obsessional content, if present.

On a broad level, compulsions typically occur as a neutralizing agent to an obsession, whereas tics do not. Tics are usually preceded by premonitory sensory urges and compulsions are preceded by obsessions (American Psychiatric Association, 2013). Assessment, therefore, should focus on the description of the experience prior to the behavior (e.g., tic or compulsion) and how the individual responds to not engaging in the behavior. Lewin and Piacentini (2010) provide guidelines to help assessors differentiate these two processes through understanding the function of the symptom, as well as what would happen if the child refrained from engaging in the symptom (see Table 6.2). Additionally, a child's history should be taken into consideration, such as a whether the child has a history of clear OCD symptoms or tics without anxiety. To assess tic severity and impairment, the Yale Global Tic Severity Scale (YGTSS) (Leckman et al., 1989) is a clinician-administered scale that has excellent psychometric properties.

Autism Spectrum Disorders. Autism Spectrum Disorders (ASD) can be challenging to determine a differential diagnoses from OCD, especially in young children, due to the core symptoms of repetitive behaviors and fixated interests. Obtaining a thorough developmental history assessing for other symptoms associated with ASD (e.g., deficits in social communication and interactions) is critical. Additionally, stereotypic behaviors in ASD are generally related to gratification and pleasure, whereas compulsions are typically ego dystonic and function to reduce anxiety or uncomfortable feelings (American Academy of Child and Adolescent Psychiatry, 2012). For example, a child with ASD may spin repeatedly for enjoyment or because he "likes it," whereas, a child with OCD may spin because he feels like he has to in order to prevent something bad from happening or to make an uncomfortable feeling go away. If a differential diagnosis is unclear, practitioners may consider referring the child for a more comprehensive evaluation by a developmental specialist.

Table 6.2 Differentiating Tics from Compulsions

Assessment	Compulsion	Tic
Trigger/preceding internal process	Obsession	Premonitory sensory urge
Function of the symptom or behavior	Relief of anxiety or distress	Reduction in urge or sensation
Restraint from symptom or behavior (e.g., what happens if you do not [tap the side of the chair]?).	1 Harm avoidance (e.g., something bad might happen) 2 Increased distress (e.g., "I'd be upset/uncomfortable") 3 Sense of incompleteness (e.g., does not feel right)	1 Increase in urge (e.g., urge would get stronger) 2 No outcome (e.g., nothing would happen) 3 Uncontrollable (e.g., cannot stop it, it would be too hard to control) 4 Sense of incompleteness (e.g., does not feel right)

Other differential disorders. Psychosis is sometimes a differential diagnosis from OCD, and it is not uncommon for more severe OCD to mimic schizophrenum spectrum diagnoses (Lewin & Piacentini, 2010). The "stretchy logic" and magical thinking found in OCD may present similarly to a psychotic process; however, psychosis in childhood is quite rare (American Academy of Child and Adolescent Psychiatry, 2012). Given that insight may be lacking in youth with OCD, it may be hard to distinguish these processes in early development. Treatment response and the manifestation of symptoms over time (e.g., emergence of other positive or negative psychotic symptoms) can assist in differentiating a psychotic process. Eating disorders, particularly Anorexia Nervosa, involve obsessional thinking and ritualistic behaviors. However, the content of such thinking and behaviors is related to body disturbance, food consumption, and weight, rather than other content areas found in OCD (e.g., avoidance of food due to contamination). Other disorders, such as trichotillomania (Hair-Pulling Disorder) and Body Dysmorphic Disorder, classified in DSM-5 under Obsessive-Compulsive and Related Disorders may result in diagnostic confusion for some children. For further descriptions of differential diagnoses, please refer to DSM-5 (American Psychiatric Association, 2013).

Conclusions

Overall, the measures and considerations included in this chapter highlight the importance of carefully assessing OCD – from initial suspicion of symptoms to the completion of treatment. Identifying OCD symptoms and providing appropriate referrals for treatment is important in minimizing the possible long-term negative consequences of pediatric OCD. Furthermore, monitoring symptoms throughout treatment will improve treatment planning and outcomes. Though further research is needed to refine existing measures and to more thoroughly understand the functional relationship of symptoms, using a combination of the measures described above will provide important guidelines and information for clinicians and referring providers.

References

Achenbach, T. M. (1991). *Manual for the child behavior checklist/4–18 and 1991 profile.* Burlington, VT: University of Vermont, Department of Psychiatry.

American Academy of Child and Adolescent Psychiatry. (2012). Practice parameters for the assessment and treatment of children and adolescents with obsessive-compulsive disorder. *Journal of the American Academy of Child & Adolescent Psychiatry, 51*(1), 98–113.

American Psychiatric Association. (2013). Diagnostic and statistical manual of mental disorders (5th ed.). Arlington, VA: American Psychiatric Publishing.

American Psychological Association. (2000). Diagnostic and statistical manual of mental disorders (4th ed.). Arlington, VA: American Psychiatric Publishing.

Bamber, D., Tamplin, A., Park, R. J., Kyte, Z. A., & Goodyer, I. M. (2002). Development of a short Leyton Obsessional Inventory for children and adolescents. *Journal of the American Academy of Child & Adolescent Psychiatry, 41*(10), 1246–1252.

Berg, C. J., Rapoport, J. L., & Flament, M. (1986). The Leyton Obsessional Inventory – Child Version. *Journal of the American Academy of Child Psychiatry, 25*(1), 84–91.

Berg, C. Z., Whitaker, A., Davies, M., Flament, M. F., & Rapoport, J. L. (1988). The survey form of the Leyton Obsessional Inventory – Child Version: Norms from an epidemiological study. *Journal of the American Academy of Child & Adolescent Psychiatry, 27*(6), 759–763.

Birmaher, B., Khetarpal, S., Brent, D., Cully, M., Balach, L., Kaufman, J., & Neer, S. M. (1997). The Screen for Child Anxiety Related Emotional Disorders (SCARED): Scale construction and psychometric characteristics. *Journal of the American Academy of Child & Adolescent Psychiatry, 36*(4), 545–553.

Calvocoressi, L., Lewis, B., Harris, M., & Trufan, S. J. (1995). Family accommodation in obsessive-compulsive disorder. *American Journal of Psychiatry, 152*(3), 441–443.

Calvocoressi, L., Mazure, C. M., Kasl, S. V., Skolnick, J., Fisk, D., Vegso, S. J., … Price, L. H. (1999). Family accommodation of obsessive-compulsive symptoms: Instrument development and assessment of family behavior. *Journal of Nervous and Mental Disease, 187*(10), 636–642.

Caporino, N., Morgan, J., Beckstead, J., Phares, V., Murphy, T., & Storch, E. (2012). A Structural equation analysis of family accommodation in pediatric obsessive-compulsive disorder. *Journal of Abnormal Child Psychology, 40*(1), 133–143.

Choudhury, M. S., Pimentel, S. S., & Kendall, P. C. (2003). Childhood anxiety disorders: Parent–child (dis)agreement using a structured interview for the DSM-IV. *Journal of the American Academy of Child & Adolescent Psychiatry, 42*(8), 957–964.

Comer, J. S., Kendall, P. C., Franklin, M. E., Hudson, J. L., & Pimentel, S. S. (2004). Obsessing/worrying about the overlap between obsessive-compulsive disorder and generalized anxiety disorder in youth. *Clinical Psychology Review, 24*(6), 663–683.

Conelea, C. A., Freeman, J. B., & Garcia, A. M. (2012). Integrating behavioral theory with OCD assessment using the Y-BOCS/CY-BOCS symptom checklist. *Journal of Obsessive Compulsive & Related Disorders, 1*(2), 112–118.

Ecker, W., & Gönner, S. (2008). Incompleteness and harm avoidance in OCD symptom dimensions. *Behaviour Research and Therapy, 46*(8), 895–904.

Endicott, J., Spitzer, R. L., Fleiss, J. L., & Cohen, J. (1976). The Global Assessment Scale: A procedure for measuring overall severity of psychiatric disturbance. *Archives of General Psychiatry, 33*(6), 766–771.

Flament, M. F., Whitaker, A., Rapoport, J. L., & Davies, M. (1988). Obsessive compulsive disorder in adolescence: An epidemiological study. *Journal of the American Academy of Child & Adolescent Psychiatry, 27*(6), 764–771.

Flessner, C. A., Sapyta, J., Garcia, A., Freeman, J. B., Franklin, M. E., Foa, E., & March, J. (2011). Examining the psychometric properties of the Family Accommodation Scale-Parent-Report (FAS-PR). *Journal of Psychopathology and Behavioral Assessment, 33*(1), 38–46.

Foa, E. B., Coles, M., Huppert, J. D., Pasupuleti, R. V., Franklin, M. E., & March, J. (2010). Development and validation of a child version of the Obsessive Compulsive Inventory. *Behavior Therapy, 41*(1), 121–132.

Foa, E. B., Huppert, J. D., Leiberg, S., Langner, R., Kichic, R., Hajcak, G., & Salkovskis, P. M. (2002). The Obsessive-Compulsive Inventory: Development and validation of a short version. *Psychological Assessment, 14*(4), 485–496.

Freeman, J., Flessner, C. A., & Garcia, A. (2011). The Children's Yale–Brown Obsessive Compulsive Scale: Reliability and validity for use among 5 to 8 year olds with obsessive-compulsive disorder. *Journal of Abnormal Child Psychology, 39*(6), 877–883.

Freeman, J., Garcia, A., Benito, K., Conelea, C., Sapyta, J., Khanna, M., ... Franklin, M. (2012). The Pediatric Obsessive Compulsive Disorder Treatment Study for Young Children (POTS jr): Developmental considerations in the rationale, design, and methods. *Journal of Obsessive Compulsive & Related Disorders, 1*(4), 294–300.

Freeman, J., Garcia, A., Frank, H., Benito, K., Conelea, C., Walther, M., & Edmunds, J. (2014). Evidence base update for psychosocial treatments for pediatric obsessive-compulsive disorder. *Journal of Clinical Child &Adolescent Psychology, 43*(1), 7–26.

Freeman, J., Sapyta, J., Garcia, A., Compton, S., Khanna, M., Flessner, C., ... Franklin, M. (2014). Family-based treatment of early childhood obsessive-compulsive disorder: The Pediatric Obsessive-Compulsive Disorder Treatment Study for Young Children (POTS Jr): A randomized clinical trial. *JAMA Psychiatry, 71*(6), 689–698.

Futh, A., Simonds, L. M., & Micali, N. (2012). Obsessive-compulsive disorder in children and adolescents: Parental understanding, accommodation, coping and distress. *Journal of Anxiety Disorders, 26*(5), 624–632.

Gallant, J., Storch, E. A., Merlo, L. J., Ricketts, E. D., Geffken, G. R., Goodman, W. K., & Murphy, T. K. (2008). Convergent and discriminant validity of the Children's Yale–Brown Obsessive Compulsive Scale-Symptom Checklist. *Journal of Anxiety Disorders, 22*(8), 1369–1376.

Garcia, A. M., Sapyta, J. J., Moore, P. S., Freeman, J. B., Franklin, M. E., March, J. S., & Foa, E. B. (2010). Predictors and moderators of treatment outcome in the Pediatric Obsessive Compulsive Treatment Study (POTS I). *Journal of the American Academy of Child & Adolescent Psychiatry, 49*(10), 1024–1033.

Garvey, M. A., Perlmutter, S. J., Allen, A. J., Hamburger, S., Lougee, L., Leonard, H. L., ... Swedo, S. E. (1999). A pilot study of penicillin prophylaxis for neuropsychiatric exacerbations triggered by streptococcal infections. *Biological Psychiatry, 45*(12), 1564–1571.

Grabill, K., Merlo, L., Duke, D., Harford, K-L., Keeley, M. L., Geffken, G. R., & Storch, E. A. (2008). Assessment of obsessive-compulsive disorder: A review. *Journal of Anxiety Disorders, 22*(1), 1–17.

Guy, W. (1976). *Clinical global impressions ECDEU Assessment Manual for Psychopharmacology* (pp. 218–222). Rockville, MD: National Institute for Mental Health.

Heyman, I., Fombonne, E., Simmons, H., Ford, T., Meltzer, H., & Goodman, R. (2003). Prevalence of obsessive-compulsive disorder in the British nationwide survey of child mental health. *International Review of Psychiatry, 15*(1/2), 178–184.

Insel, T., Murphy, D., Cohen, R., Alterman, I., Kilts, C., & Linnoila, M. (1983). Obsessive-compulsive disorder in five US communities. *Archives of General Psychiatry, 40*, 605–612.

Jones, A. M., De Nadai, A. S., Arnold, E. B., McGuire, J. F., Lewin, A. B., Murphy, T. K., & Storch, E. A. (2013). Psychometric properties of the Obsessive Compulsive Inventory: Child version in children and adolescents with obsessive-compulsive disorder. *Child Psychiatry& Human Development, 44*(1), 137–151.

Jones, K. D. (2010). The unstructured clinical interview. *Journal of Counseling & Development, 88*(2), 220–226.

Kaufman, J., Birmaher, B., Brent, D., & Rao, U. (1997). Schedule for Affective Disorders and Schizophrenia for School-Age Children – Present and Lifetime version (K-SADS-PL):

Initial reliability and validity data. *Journal of the American Academy of Child & Adolescent Psychiatry, 36*(7), 980–988.

Keeley, M. L., Storch, E. A., Dhungana, P., & Geffken, G. R. (2007). Pediatric obsessive-compulsive disorder: A guide to assessment and treatment. *Issues in Mental Health Nursing, 28*(6), 555–574.

Knapp, M., Henderson, J., & Patel, A. (2000). Costs of obsessive-compulsive disorder: A review. In M. Maj, N. Sartorius, A. Okasha & J. Zohar (Eds.), *Obsessive-compulsive disorder* (pp. 253–299). New York: Wiley.

Lebowitz, E. R., Vitulano, L. A., & Omer, H. (2011). Coercive and disruptive behaviors in pediatric obsessive compulsive disorder: a qualitative analysis. *Psychiatry, 74*(4), 362–371.

Leckman, J. F., Riddle, M. A., Hardin, M. T., Ort, S. I., Swartz, K. L., Stevenson, J., & Cohen, D. J. (1989). The Yale Global Tic Severity Scale: Initial testing of a clinician-rated scale of tic severity. *Journal of the American Academy of Child & Adolescent Psychiatry, 28*(4), 566–573.

Lewin, A. B., & Piacentini, J. (2010). Evidence-based assessment of child obsessive compulsive disorder: Recommendations for clinical practice and treatment research. *Child & Youth Care Forum, 39*(2), 73–89.

Lewin, A. B., Piacentini, J., De Nadai, A. S., Jones, A. M., Peris, T. S., Geffken, G. R., … Storch, E. A. (2014). Defining clinical severity in pediatric obsessive-compulsive disorder. *Psychological Assessment, 26*(2), 679–684.

March, J. S., Biederman, J., Wolkow, R., Safferman, A., Mardekian, J., Cook, E. H., … Steiner, H. (1998). Sertraline in children and adolescents with obsessive-compulsive disorder: A multicenter randomized controlled trial. *Journal of the American Medical Association, 280*(20), 1752–1756.

Mataix-Cols, D., Rosário-Campos, M. C., & Leckman, J. F. (2005). A multidimensional model of obsessive-compulsive disorder. *American Journal of Psychiatry, 162*(2), 228–238.

Merlo, L. J., Lehmkuhl, H. D., Geffken, G. R., & Storch, E. A. (2009). Decreased family accommodation associated with improved therapy outcome in pediatric obsessive-compulsive disorder. *Journal of Consulting & Clinical Psychology, 77*(2), 355–360.

Merlo, L. J., Storch, E. A., Murphy, T. K., Goodman, W. K., & Geffken, G. R. (2005). Assessment of pediatric obsessive-compulsive disorder: A critical review of current methodology. *Child Psychiatry and Human Development, 36*(2), 195–214.

Muris, P., Merckelbach, H., Van Brakel, A., & Mayer, A. B. (1999). The revised version of the Screen for Child Anxiety Related Emotional Disorders (SCARED-R): Further evidence for its reliability and validity. *Anxiety, Stress and Coping, 12*(4), 411–425.

Peris, T. S., Bergman, R. L., Langley, A., Chang, S., McCracken, J. T., & Piacentini, J. (2008). Correlates of accommodation of pediatric obsessive-compulsive disorder: parent, child, and family characteristics. *Journal of the American Academy of Child & Adolescent Psychiatry, 47*(10), 1173–1181.

Perlmutter, S. J., Leitman, S. F., Garvey, M. A., Hamburger, S., Feldman, E., Leonard, H. L., & Swedo, S. E. (1999). Therapeutic plasma exchange and intravenous immunoglobulin for obsessive-compulsive disorder and tic disorders in childhood. *Lancet, 354*(9185), 1153–1158.

Piacentini, J., Bergman, R. L., Chang, S., Langley, A., Peris, T., Wood, J. J., & McCracken, J. (2011). Controlled comparison of family cognitive behavioral therapy and psychoeducation/relaxation training for child obsessive-compulsive disorder. *Journal of the American Academy of Child & Adolescent Psychiatry, 50*(11), 1149–1161.

Piacentini, J., Bergman, R. L., Keller, M., & McCracken, J. (2003). Functional impairment in children and adolescents with obsessive-compulsive disorder. *Journal of Child & Adolescent Psychopharmacology, 13*(2 Suppl.), S61–S69.

Piacentini, J., Peris, T. S., Bergman, R. L., Chang, S., & Jaffer, M. (2007). Functional impairment in childhood OCD: Development and psychometrics properties of the Child

Obsessive-Compulsive Impact Scale-Revised (COIS-R). *Journal of Clinical Child & Adolescent Psychology, 36*(4), 645–653.

Pietrefesa, A. S., & Coles, M. E. (2009). Moving beyond an exclusive focus on harm avoidance in obsessive-compulsive disorder: Behavioral validation for the separability of harm avoidance and incompleteness. *Behavior Therapy, 40*(3), 251–259.

Rapoport, J. L., & Inoff-Germain, G. (2000). Treatment of obsessive-compulsive disorder in children and adolescents. *Journal of Child Psychology & Psychiatry, 41*(4), 419–431.

Rettew, D. C., Swedo, S. E., Leonard, H. L., Lenane, M. C., & Rapoport, J. L. (1992). Obsessions and compulsions across time in 79 children and adolescents with obsessive-compulsive disorder. *Journal of the American Academy of Child & Adolescent Psychiatry, 31*(6), 1050–1056.

Rosário-Campos, M. C., Leckman, J. F., Mercadante, M. T., Shavitt, R. G., Prado, H. S., Sada, P., ... Miguel, E. C. (2001). Adults with early-onset obsessive-compulsive disorder. *American Journal of Psychiatry, 158*(11), 1899–1903.

Rosário-Campos, M. C., Miguel, E. C., Quatrano, S., Chacon, P., Ferrao, Y., Findley, D., ... Leckman, J. F. (2006). The Dimensional Yale–Brown Obsessive-Compulsive Scale (DYBOCS): An instrument for assessing obsessive-compulsive symptom dimensions. *Molecular Psychiatry, 11*(5), 495–504.

Safford, S. M., Kendall, P. C., Flannery-Schroeder, E., Webb, A., & Sommer, H. (2005). A longitudinal look at parent–child diagnostic agreement in youth treated for anxiety disorders. *Journal of Clinical Child & Adolescent Psychology, 34*(4), 747–757.

Scahill, L., Riddle, M. A., McSwiggin-Hardin, M., & Ort, S. I. (1997). Children's Yale–Brown Obsessive Compulsive Scale: Reliability and validity. *Journal of the American Academy of Child & Adolescent Psychiatry, 36*(6), 844–852.

Schorre, B. E., & Vandvik, I. H. (2004). Global assessment of psychosocial functioning in child and adolescent psychiatry. A review of three unidimensional scales (CGAS, GAF, GAPD). *European Child & Adolescent Psychiatry, 13*(5), 273–286.

Shaffer, D., Fisher, P., Lucas, C. P., Dulcan, M. K., & Schwab-Stone, M. E. (2000). NIMH Diagnostic Interview Schedule for Children Version IV (NIMH DISC-IV): Description, differences from previous versions, and reliability of some common diagnoses. *Journal of the American Academy of Child & Adolescent Psychiatry, 39*(1), 28–38.

Shaffer, D., Gould, M. S., Brasic, J., Ambrosini, P., Fisher, P., Bird, H., & Aluwahlia, S. (1983). A Children's Global Assessment Scale (CGAS). *Archives of General Psychiatry, 40*(11), 1228–1231.

Shafran, R., Frampton, I., Heyman, I., Reynolds, M., Teachman, B., & Rachman, S. (2003). The preliminary development of a new self-report measure for OCD in young people. *Journal of Adolescence, 26*(1), 137–142.

Sheehan, D. V., Sheehan, K. H., Shytle, R. D., Janavs, J., Bannon, Y., Rogers, J. E., ... Wilkinson, B. (2010). Reliability and validity of the Mini International Neuropsychiatric Interview for Children and Adolescents (MINI-KID). *Journal of Clinical Psychiatry, 71*(3), 313–326.

Silverman, W. K., & Albano, A. M. (1996). *Anxiety disorders interview schedule for DSM-IV child version: Clinical manual*. Albany, NY: Graywind.

Silverman, W. K., Saavedra, L. M., & Pina, A. A. (2001). Test–retest reliability of anxiety symptoms and diagnoses with Anxiety Disorders Interview Schedule for DSM-IV: Child and parent versions. *Journal of the American Academy of Child & Adolescent Psychiatry, 40*(8), 937–944.

Stewart, S. E., Hu, Y. P., Hezel, D. M., Proujansky, R., Lamstein, A., Walsh, C., ... Pauls, D. L. (2011). Development and psychometric properties of the OCD Family Functioning (OFF) Scale. *Journal of Family Psychology, 25*(3), 434–443.

Storch, E. A., Geffken, G. R., Merlo, L. J., Jacob, M. L., Murphy, T. K., Goodman, W. K., ... Grabill, K. (2007). Family accommodation in pediatric obsessive-compulsive disorder. *Journal of Clinical Child & Adolescent Psychology, 36*(2), 207–216.

Storch, E. A., Khanna, M., Merlo, L. J., Loew, B. A., Franklin, M., Reid, J. M., ... Murphy, T. K. (2009). Children's Florida Obsessive Compulsive Inventory: Psychometric properties and feasibility of a self-report measure of obsessive-compulsive symptoms in youth. *Child Psychiatry & Human Development, 40*(3), 467–483.

Storch, E. A., Murphy, T. K., Adkins, J. W., Lewin, A. B., Geffken, G. R., Johns, N. B., ... Goodman, W. K. (2006). The Children's Yale–Brown obsessive-compulsive scale: Psychometric properties of child- and parent-report formats. *Journal of Anxiety Disorders, 20*(8), 1055–1070.

Storch, E. A., Murphy, T. K., Geffken, G. R., Soto, O., Sajid, M., Allen, P., ... Goodman, W. K. (2004). Psychometric evaluation of the Children's Yale–Brown Obsessive-Compulsive Scale. *Psychiatry Research, 129*(1), 91–98.

Storch, E. A., Park, J. M., Lewin, A. B., Morgan, J. R., Jones, A. M., & Murphy, T. K. (2011). The Leyton Obsessional Inventory – Child Version Survey Form does not demonstrate adequate psychometric properties in American youth with pediatric obsessive-compulsive disorder. *Journal of Anxiety Disorders, 25*(4), 574–578.

Summerfeldt, L. J. (2004). Understanding and treating incompleteness in obsessive-compulsive disorder. *Journal of Clinical Psychology, 60*(11), 1155–1168.

Uher, R., Heyman, I., Turner, C. M., & Shafran, R. (2008). Self-, parent-report and interview measures of obsessive-compulsive disorder in children and adolescents. *Journal of Anxiety Disorders, 22*(6), 979–990.

Valderhaug, R., & Ivarsson, T. (2005). Functional impairment in clinical samples of Norwegian and Swedish children and adolescents with obsessive-compulsive disorder. *European Child & Adolescent Psychiatry, 14*(3), 164–173.

Valleni-Basile, L. A., Garrison, C. Z., Jackson, K. L., & Waller, J. L. (1994). Frequency of obsessive-compulsive disorder in a community sample of young adolescents. *Journal of the American Academy of Child & Adolescent Psychiatry, 33*(6), 782–791.

Van Ameringen, M., Patterson, B., & Simpson, W. (2014). DSM-5 obsessive-compulsive and related disorders: Clinical implications of new criteria. *Depress and Anxiety, 31*(6), 487–493.

Wood, J. J., Piacentini, J., Bergman, R. L., McCracken, J., & Barrios, V. (2002). Concurrent validity of the anxiety disorders interview schedule for DSM-IV: Child and parent versions. *Journal of the American Academy of Child & Adolescent Psychiatry, 40*, 937–944.

7

Functional Assessment

Lillian Reuman, Shannon M. Blakey, Ryan J. Jacoby, and Jonathan S. Abramowitz

Whereas the DSM may provide a useful framework for identifying the *presence* of obsessive-compulsive disorder (OCD), the complexity, heterogeneity, and idiosyncratic presentation of this condition begs for a more in-depth assessment of an individual's obsessional fears, compulsive rituals, and other phenomena that go beyond what a descriptive diagnosis can offer. This fine-grained analysis is called a *functional assessment*, and it uses an empirically established conceptual model – the cognitive-behavioral framework – to organize and understand the processes that (a) maintain a given person's OCD symptoms and (b) are to be targeted in cognitive-behavioral therapy (CBT) (Follette, Naugle, & Linnerooth, 2000). Functional assessment relies on various techniques to identify the antecedents, behaviors, cognitions, and their consequences that serve as maintenance factors of OCD. Functional assessment contributes to a patient-specific case conceptualization, identification of targets for CBT, and a means of evaluating the treatment effects.

Different from diagnostic assessment, or the types of assessment that might accompany dynamically oriented therapies, functional assessment relies on the patient's expertise – it is assumed that she or he has the best knowledge of his or her own thoughts and psychological experiences. The clinician, meanwhile, wields knowledge regarding how to ask the right assessment questions and then to organize the data collected using the cognitive-behavioral model. This chapter is designed to aid the clinician in executing an effective functional assessment of OCD to help in treatment planning. We illustrate the use of this technique using a case example ("Adam") as described below.

Adam's Presenting Symptoms

Adam presented to our clinic with multiple types of obsessions and rituals. A highly functioning teacher, he had intense fears of contracting bacterial infections (i.e., staphylococcus) and consequently avoided numerous potentially "contaminated" situations (e.g., elevators, bathrooms). In response to these fears, he engaged in excessive hand washing, teeth brushing, and showering routines. Adam maintained his home in ways that "maximized cleanliness." For example, he excessively cleaned surfaces and kept his own bedroom – and especially his pillow – as a "safe haven" from

The Wiley Handbook of Obsessive Compulsive Disorders, Volume I, First Edition.
Edited by Jonathan S. Abramowitz, Dean McKay, and Eric A. Storch.
© 2017 John Wiley & Sons Ltd. Published 2017 by John Wiley & Sons Ltd.

"outside" contamination. That is, before entering his room, Adam would feel the urge to shower and change his clothes if he had been out of his home. He did not bring anything from outside his home into his bedroom unless it had undergone a ritualistic decontamination washing. He cleaned (usually by wiping down with a cleanser) mail, new clothes he had purchased, and other items such as books or trophies, before allowing them in his room.

Although Adam had no history of violence, he feared that he might bring direct physical harm to "vulnerable" individuals (i.e., young children, elderly individuals). As such, he avoided driving on streets with school bus stops and using knives out of fear that he might intentionally hit, shove, or stab someone. Relatedly, Adam expressed a pervasive fear of becoming a victim of harm; he repeatedly checked the locks of his car and home, avoided using his locked back door, stored all valuables next to his bed, and maintained the highest home alarm system settings. We will return to Adam's example throughout this chapter to illustrate the techniques of functional assessment.

Parameters of the Functional Assessment

Following the diagnostic assessment and a determination that the patient is suitable for treatment, the clinician should begin to collect specific information about all symptoms of OCD. Indeed, the obsessional triggers, thoughts, feared consequences, and the rituals and avoidance strategies for people with OCD may vary endlessly and might be very particular. Thus, we recommend against the clinician *assuming* that she or he knows the patient's OCD patterns without asking the patient to clarify that assumptions are correct. Although we describe the functional assessment format in an order likely to be the most efficient, and encourage the clinician to use a similarly structured approach to collecting functional assessment data, it is indeed fine if one ends up shifting the order with respect to assessing the various parameters discussed here. In fact, for some patients, a less structured approach might be best for maintaining rapport. What is most important is that a thorough assessment is conducted – not in what order the data are collected.

Review of Recent Episodes

To begin to ascertain information regarding the client's experience with OCD, the clinician may ask the client to provide a "play-by-play" of some recent instances of obsessional thoughts, ritualistic behavior, and avoidance patterns. For example, the clinician might ask, "When was a recent time that OCD became a problem for you? Can you walk me through what happened?" The goal of this technique is to provide the client with a concrete starting point. This strategy can be used throughout the assessment, particularly when the client is having difficulty articulating a particular constellation of symptoms.

Throughout this "play-by-play," the clinician should follow up with questions that will allow the client to elaborate upon their experience. For example, "Where were you, and what were you doing when your obsessions were triggered?" The clinician could follow up with questions about how the client responded (i.e., emotionally and cognitively) to the situation. For example, "What thoughts were going though your mind while this was happening … what were you feeling and thinking?," "how anxious did you become, and what did you do to reduce your anxiety?," and "how did this episode end and how did you feel afterwards?" The questioning and accompanying conversation provide opportunities for the patient to recognize how their obsessional thoughts increase distress and how avoidance and compulsive behavior leads to a reduction in anxiety.

By briefly summarizing the main points from the "play-by-play" for the client, the clinician can solidify the functional connections between the obsessions and compulsions. For example, Adam's therapist said the following: "That's an excellent example of how your intrusive fears about contracting an infection from the woman sneezing on the bus provoked a high degree of anxiety. It sounds like once you got off the bus at the next stop, you felt relieved and 'could finally breathe. And then once you got home and showered, you felt even more relaxed – like you could go into your bedroom safely' Do you see how your avoidance and rituals reduce your anxiety and make you feel safer?"

Identifying External Triggers

The clinician can begin by collecting information about stimuli and situations in the environment that trigger the client's obsessional fears. It may be helpful to ask "what types of situations do you avoid for fear of intrusive thoughts?," or "what types of thoughts trigger your compulsive rituals?" If an interview such as the Yale–Brown Obsessive Compulsive Symptom Checklist (YBOCS) (Goodman et al., 1989a; Goodman et al., 1989b) was previously used, data collected from this can be useful in making sure the functional assessment is thorough. It is important to remember that in a feared situation (i.e., leaving the house unalarmed) may be related to different feared consequences (i.e., causing harm to oneself vs. feelings of "not just right" experiences) and unique rituals (i.e., seeking reassurance vs. repetitive checking, respectively). As such, it is necessary to clarify why a given situation evokes fear.

Contamination. Patients with contamination symptoms often experience anxiety and obsessions as triggered by bodily waste or secretions (e.g., urine, saliva), dirt, germs, environmental contaminants (e.g., toxic waste), household items (e.g., cleaners, solvents), animals, and sticky residues. Relatedly, individuals may fear that they will contract an illness (i.e., the 'flu, cancer) upon coming into contact with a contaminant, or that they may bring illness upon others by spreading contamination. Patients commonly assume that contamination is spread through other people, objects, and surfaces (i.e., residue on a handrail); therefore, it is necessary to assess peripheral sources of contamination. Patients may also associate contamination fears with triggers that have little to no logical connection to a contaminant itself (e.g., the color brown as dirty). Questions such as, "What things make you feel contaminated or want to wash or clean?" are useful ways to elicit pertinent information.

For Adam, a host of potential contaminants triggered his obsessions. For example, hearing or seeing someone cough, certain putrid bathroom smells, and body odors triggered obsessional fears. More generally, traveling in small spaces with "recycled air" (i.e., buses, elevators) brought upon intrusive thoughts about contamination.

Responsibility for causing or preventing harm. Stimuli that trigger aggressive thoughts or those in which the patient may feel responsible for harm or mistakes are unique across individuals. Routine activities such as leaving the house ("What if I left the door open and a violent intruder enters?") might be cues. Other potential triggers include driving (for fear of hitting pedestrians), stairs or subways (for fear of pushing someone), and sending emails (e.g., a fear of attaching inappropriate media, such as pornographic images, resulting in negative consequences). Situations (e.g., driving past a school bus stop) can also trigger thoughts related to responsibility for harm. Words (e.g., "psychotic") or numbers (e.g., 6) that the patient associates with danger, harm, or bad luck may also trigger obsessional fear. Aspects of the stimuli (i.e., strength of the potential victim) may also contribute to the intensity of the intrusive thoughts. For example, Adam reported that young children and elders disproportionately triggered beliefs about causing physical harm (in comparison with able-bodied individuals, who did not elicit such thoughts). Additionally, the degree to which Adam "cared for" an individual contributed to the degree of fear that accompanied the trigger. Therefore, it is necessary to collect nuanced information about the potential triggers.

Incompleteness. Patients with concerns about incompleteness typically report the need for "order" and "symmetry" regarding feelings of imbalance or disorderliness. Objects, situations, words, numbers, and feelings can trigger these sensations. For example, pictures or window blinds that hang "unevenly" or clothes that are folded "sloppily" can trigger such thoughts. Past patients have reported distress upon being touched on one side of her body but not the other, or anxiety when paying a bill that did not end in an even "quarter amount" (e.g., $0.25, $0.50, $0.75). Patients may struggle to articulate a particular fear; rather, they will suggest that something is anxiety provoking if not "just right."

Unacceptable obsessional thoughts. Individuals with unacceptable obsessional thoughts pertaining to religious, sexual, or violent content may find external triggers such as religious icons, children, and (potential) weapons (i.e., knives) to be particularly anxiety-inducing (among other triggers). Clients may also fear certain holidays (i.e., Halloween), places of worship (i.e., churches), religious symbols (i.e., crosses), words, numbers, or visual stimuli (i.e., pornography, horror movies) that kindle thoughts of deviance (with regard to violence, sexuality, religion, etc.). Such concerns may also acquire secondary associations, by which individuals avoid anything related to primary external triggers. For example, a patient with blasphemous intrusions feared places of worship that evoked such thoughts *and* avoided conversation with others in the event that someone might blurt out "God damn."

Adam was afraid of knives and stairs, which served as external triggers for obsessions pertaining to harm. Specifically, he was concerned that he might accidentally cut himself or stab others with a knife; therefore, he hid his knives and refrained from cooking meals that required chopping or dicing. Adam's unwanted obsessional thoughts about pushing someone down the stairs led him to avoid walking down staircases while near anyone else or clasping his hands behind his back while repeating the mantra "I am a good person."

Identifying Obsessional Thoughts

Individuals with OCD experience intrusive, senseless thoughts in some form – this is a hallmark of the condition. Some patients go to extremes to conceal their intrusive thoughts, for fear that, for example, vocalizing a profane thought could increase the chance of the occurrence of the corresponding event. Patients may also believe that the mere presence of a bad thought indicates that she or he is a bad person. For example, one client refused to talk about her unwanted impulse to fondle her young nieces out of fear that sharing the thought would bring her closer to acting upon the intrusive belief. Nevertheless, it is important to skillfully encourage the client to divulge as many details as possible about their intrusions so that they can be incorporated into the conceptualization and addressed in treatment. Typically, clients are surprised to observe that their clinician is not alarmed by the content and frequency of their intrusive thoughts; and some find the functional assessment process therapeutic, in and of itself, as a therapist's compassionate response may help to normalize the obsessional intrusions. At times, a checklist (i.e., YBOCS) may be useful to elicit the client's endorsement of seemingly taboo thoughts. By responding in an objective manner, the clinician has the opportunity to further reinforce the notion that bizarre or rare obsessions are non-threatening and valid.

Contamination. Obsessions about contamination pertain to a client's fears that contact with a feared contaminant could bring illness or harm (short or long term) to themselves or others. A subtype of these beliefs, known as "mental contamination," refers to unwanted thoughts or images that evoke feelings of internal dirtiness, yet occur in the absence of a physical pollutant. Examples of such mental contaminants include traumatic memories and can be triggered by another's actions (i.e., humiliation). In the case of Adam, intrusive thoughts such as, "I will contract herpes if I don't wash my hands after using the public bathroom," served as exemplars for this contamination category.

Harm. Some individuals have intrusive thoughts and images about causing harm to themselves or others due to their mistakes or inadvertent negligence. Others constantly doubt whether or not they may have accidently offended (i.e., inserted inappropriate, hurtful behavior into an email message), injured, or killed someone (perhaps even themselves). For individuals with scrupulous concerns, intrusive thoughts about harm may pertain to doubts about whether they have followed religious doctrines to the letter of the law.

Adam experienced harm-related intrusions in various situations. For example, he had unwanted thoughts that he might inadvertently or intentionally stab a loved one with a knife while cooking. While driving, Adam experienced intrusive thoughts about accidentally swerving his car toward a group of innocent children waiting for a school bus: "what if I hit them?" At home, he had obsessions about bringing about his own violent death by mistakenly leaving his valuable belongings in plain view and leaving a door unlocked and the alarm unarmed.

Incompleteness. Intrusive thoughts in the context of incompleteness can be vague and are notoriously difficult to identify and articulate. Typically, clients report the need to have things "just right" in order to prevent imminent anxiety and distress. These intrusive thoughts – the sense that something is "awry" – may overlap with magical thinking and intrusive thoughts about harming others. For example, the obsessional thought that if the books are not arranged properly, a loved one will die.

Unacceptable thoughts. Intrusive thoughts, images, and impulses that the client deems "unacceptable" typically concern immoral or taboo topics, such as aggression, sex, and religion. Violent or aggressive obsessions include unwanted ideas such as "I could push my fiancé in front of this oncoming train," or "what if I blurt out profanities while teaching?" Sexual obsessions can entail unwanted images of pedophilia or raping others, thoughts of consensual yet personally undesirable sexual behavior (e.g., caressing one's mother), unwelcome thoughts of improper sexual activity (e.g., with a colleague), and unacceptable images such as that of one's partner having an affair. Scrupulous obsessions may include blasphemous images (e.g., of stabbing Jesus) or other doubts that create the feeling of having sinned (e.g., questioning the existence of Allah).

For example, one female patient reported unwanted intrusive thoughts about sexually molesting her young nieces. The most distressing images were those of fondling the young girls while they sat on her lap. The client equated such beliefs with the actual *act* of molestation. A male client who identified as a heterosexual and a devout Christian reported intrusive images about Jesus' penis repeatedly entering his mouth. Such obsessions were particularly distracting as they challenged his own notions about both his sexuality and his devotion to God. The client feared that he would be sent to hell for "allowing" such sacrilege.

Identifying Feared Consequences and Dysfunctional Beliefs

Cognitive behavioral models of OCD suggest that clients misinterpret the meaning of their obsessional thoughts and overestimate the danger associated with objectively safe situations and stimuli. Because such maladaptive cognitions and feared consequences are important to address in CBT, functional assessment includes gathering information about the content of these phenomena. The clinician might ask questions such as:

- *What is so bad for you about* riding public transportation: what bad things do you expect to happen?
- *What would be the worst part about* contracting a staph infection?
- *What do you tell yourself* before going to bed that makes you feel like you need to check all of the locks?
- *What might happen if* you tilt the picture hanging on the wall?
- *What do you think it means* that you're having this intrusive thought repeatedly?

The clinician can then use the downward arrow technique, as illustrated below, to identify the client's strongly held core beliefs to be challenged in treatment. Adam, for example, described a time in which he avoided eating his lunch outdoors with the rest of his colleagues. The clinician used the downward-arrow method in the following conversation to identify his feared consequences of eating lunch outside.

CLINICIAN: Can you tell me what was going through your mind when your coworkers invited you to eat outside?

ADAM: I was afraid that my sandwich would get contaminated. The air is always full of insects during the summer, and the rusty public picnic tables are a breeding ground for tetanus and other bacteria.

CLINICIAN: Alright, well what could have happened if you ate outside and your sandwich touched the table?

ADAM: My food would become covered in bacteria.

CLINICIAN: Okay. And exactly how would that become a problem? What do you think would happen next?

ADAM: I would ingest the toxins and contract tetanus or a host of other diseases.

CLINICIAN: And what would that be like? How bad would that be?

ADAM: It would be awful; I'd have no way of ridding my body of the contamination. I'd be imminently ill. I'd be permanently contaminated.

CLINICIAN: Imminently? Permanently?

ADAM: Yes. You don't know what's on these tables! Symptoms would appear within a few days, and there's no cure for tetanus.

CLINICIAN: How *likely* is it that you would get sick from eating lunch on a rusty table? What percent?

ADAM: Close to 90 percent. I can see the rust.

CLINICIAN: So it sounds like eating outdoors on a metal table is frightening because there's a high chance that you'd become permanently seriously ill.

ADAM: Yes, that's right.

Notice that in the functional assessment, the clinician does not challenge the client's clearly exaggerated beliefs and assumptions; rather, the clinician summarizes the client's beliefs and continues to collect information about the feared consequences. Although Adam was able to articulate his core fears, some clients are unable to articulate, or even identify, the perceived consequences of their intrusive thoughts. Even if the client's feared consequence is that "the anxiety will never subside," it is important for individuals to identify this. By identifying the fear, the clinician and client can jointly target these fears during treatment.

   Contamination. Contamination OCD symptoms often involve the belief that feared contaminants (i.e., household cleaners, dirt, germs) pose a significant threat to physical or mental well-being. Individuals often overestimate the likelihood of coming into contact with contaminants, the possibility of spreading contaminants to others (or contracting them from inanimate surfaces), and the severity of an accompanying illness. Clients with contamination concerns may believe that they are particularly susceptible to exposure (i.e., asbestos) or uniquely vulnerable to the harmful effects. Clients may also express the fear of feeling a sense of disgust, or physical or mental impurity, if contaminated. Such fear is based on the belief that the sense of disgust or impurity is "intolerable," or will persist indefinitely, or lead to more serious physical or mental consequences (e.g., throwing up, losing control). Adam's beliefs, as illustrated above, demonstrate overestimates of threat from and severity of a potential contaminant that is common within this symptom dimension.

   Harm. Although the belief that uncertainty is intolerable is a part of many OCD symptoms, it is most pronounced in obsessional thoughts and doubts about harm and mistakes. This symptom presentation often involves the belief that because harm *could* occur (no matter how small the possibility) one must act to prevent it or be responsible for it (e.g., "I can't take the chance that the feared outcome will occur"). The probability and severity of feared negative outcomes are also overestimated. Sometimes, the uncertainty is focused on consequences that might occur in the distant future (e.g., getting cancer 40 years from now), or that can never be confirmed (e.g., going to Hell when one dies).

Incompleteness. Obsessions involving the need for symmetry and order are often mediated by the need to have things perfect, balanced, or completely under control – what is sometimes termed *not just right experiences* (NJRE) (Coles, Frost, Heimberg, & Rhéaume, 2003). Some patients fear that the sense of uneasiness over having things incomplete will persist indefinitely or increase to unmanageable levels and result in physical or psychological harm. Exaggerated responsibility and intolerance of uncertainty cognitions might mediate some incompleteness obsessions where in the client associates NJREs with an increased chance that disastrous consequences (e.g., bad luck) will befall themselves or loved ones.

Unacceptable thoughts. It is important to assess how individuals with this presentation OCD appraise their obsessional thoughts. For example, clients may believe they are "depraved" for having thoughts about hurting loved ones or "freakish" for having thoughts about incest. They may equate their beliefs with actions (i.e., "Only bad people have bad thoughts"). Clients may fear that an inability to control their unacceptable thoughts may lead to eventual action. For example, "I'll become a pedophile if I don't control my sexual thoughts about my niece," or "I'll be sent to hell for having blasphemous thoughts about God."

Identifying Responses to Obsessional Anxiety

After developing a comprehensive understanding of the client's intrusive thoughts, fears, and the underlying dysfunctional beliefs, the clinician assesses behaviors performed in response to the obsessions, such as observable compulsive rituals, safety behaviors, overt and covert avoidance, and mental rituals (i.e., covert neutralizing). These types of behavior maintain obsessional fear and are thus critical to the functional assessment. Although topographically different, these behaviors all serve the same short-term function: to minimize the anxiety accompanying unwanted intrusive thoughts. Yet these behaviors prevent the correction of maladaptive beliefs and the extinction of obsessional anxiety in the long term.

Not only is it important to understand the specific form of the client's anxiety-reduction behaviors, but also therapists should assess the specific perceived benefits of engaging in rituals and safety behaviors (i.e., their *function*). Clients might, for example, believe that a ritual (or avoidance strategy) was responsible for preventing a feared outcome (i.e., checking the door 16 times prevented a potential burglary) or serving merely to reduce distress. Questions such as the following can be useful in this regard:

- What do you do when confronted with situations and thoughts that evoke obsessive fears?
- When you're feeling anxious about (fill in obsessional fear), how do you reduce your distress?
- Why do you perform this behavior (or avoid _____)?
- What might happen if you didn't complete this ritual?

Clients will rarely spontaneously describe their all avoidance and safety-seeking behaviors during the initial assessment. Many rituals are ingrained into the daily routine (i.e., taking a circuitous route to work in order to avoid left turns) such that the client does not recognize them as avoidance strategies or rituals. To facilitate the client's reporting, the clinician can provide examples of behaviors or mental strategies that might be performed to reduce obsessional distress.

Compulsive rituals. The majority of clients exhibit an array of ritualistic behaviors. During the functional assessment, the clinician should obtain information about the frequency and duration of each ritual. Certain rituals may be quite rigid and repetitive (i.e., tapping a surface in three sets of three upon entering a room), whereas others may be covert (i.e., repeating a "mantra" to myself). The clinician should also assess how variability in external triggers and intrusive thoughts influence the quality or quantity of the ritual, and what factors signify when the ritual has been completed. If possible, the clinician can ask the client to demonstrate the ritual. For example, "Adam, could you please demonstrate what you mean by 'turning off the faucet with the "clean" part of the handle?'" For rituals that may be considered private (e.g., routines prior to, or following, sexual intercourse), the clinician should ask for a thorough description of the behavior. For example, "Many people with fears of bodily secretions take a lot of time going through a routine to ensure that they feel pure and clean. Does that ring true for you? Would you feel comfortable describing what you do after sex?"

Lastly, clinicians should inquire about the clients' feelings after completing rituals.

For example, "How do you feel after you have checked?" or "When you finish checking that the appliances are turned off, how do you feel about the risk of bringing harm to others via a house fire?" Additionally, it is helpful to inquire about what the client would feel if prevented from (or interrupted while) completing the ritual.

Adam exhibited classic decontamination rituals: excessive hand washing, elaborate shower routines, extensive flossing, frequent cleansing or tossing of potentially "contaminated" objects, unique strategies for opening doors, and systematic breathing rituals. He detailed elaborate strategies for washing his hands so as not to touch the "dirty" left handle after cleaning. He also reported spending upwards of one hour showering each day and flossing his teeth for up to 90 minutes each day. He maintained a specific method of entering the shower, washing certain body parts in a given order, and wrapping up the routine. When in contained spaces (i.e., buses), Adam would calculate his breathing so as to systematically exhale as others nearby exhaled or sneezed (so as to not inhale their air). This sometimes resulted in his holding his breath when around others.

Checking responses and repeating/ordering rituals are prevalent among individuals with intrusive thoughts pertaining to harm. Adam repeatedly checked that the alarm was set, as he believed a tripped alarm could potentially ward off any potential intruders. He would check that all appliances had been shut off in order to prevent electrical fires. He would also repeatedly check to prevent loss (i.e., to make sure that his cell phone and wallet had not slipped out of his pocket). Although Adam did not exhibit the following classic symptoms, many individuals with OCD with fears of accidentally injuring or offending someone else may check to see that they have not caused harm (i.e., by retracing routes to ensure they did not accidentally hit someone while driving), compulsively checking over emails (for flagrant errors or profanity) before sending, or seeking reassurance. Typically, individuals will repeatedly ask their partners or relatives if that they are safe, if they have safely turned off an appliance, and/or if the door is locked.

Repeating and ordering rituals serve the purpose of reducing doubt about responsibility for harm. By completing a ritual "properly" or re-doing a ritual, the client may assure him- or herself that an error on their part is not responsible for someone else's harm. The client's repetition may be informed by his or her beliefs about certain lucky/unlucky numbers (i.e., rituals must be repeated in three sets of three or else something bad will happen). The clinician should collect information about the frequency and duration of these rituals.

In response to intrusive thoughts about harming a loved one or vulnerable individual, Adam engaged in a series of "competing responses." While traveling on an escalator, Adam would clasp his hands behind his back to minimize the chance that he might inadvertently push them.

Rituals targeting thoughts about "incompleteness" serve to achieve order and perfection. Individuals have reported the need to count letters in words and sentences, re-read emails or paragraphs a certain number of times, or re-write answers until they "look perfect." Additionally, patients may have rituals to re-order objects that "feel" out of place or to make minute adjustments to establish symmetry.

Individuals with unacceptable thoughts engage in a series of rituals to "cancel out" their intrusive, unwanted worry. Patients may engage in overt rituals (i.e., reassurance seeking, or checking) or repeat "safe" words, phrases, or prayers silently. Common mental rituals include mental reviewing (i.e., analyzing or replaying an event over and over to make sure nothing bad happened) or "testing," which refers to collecting evidence that supports the improbability of a feared event.

Avoidance. Passive avoidance, in this context, refers to the intentional failure to engage in a low-risk activity. Certain obsessional cues and catastrophic beliefs inform passive avoidance. For example, fear of knives may lead to avoidance of kitchens; fear of contamination may lead to avoidance of public bathrooms and hospitals; and fear of incest may result in avoidance of family events. Patients may insist that family members avoid feared stimuli, too; for example, a child might demand that her parents avoid saying the number "6" at any time for fear of bringing bad luck upon her. To obtain more information about passive avoidance, clinicians could ask:

- What kind of things do you not do because of your obsessional fears?
- Do you ask others (i.e., partner, parent) to avoid certain situations for you?

The clinician can use his or her intuition to help the patient expand upon related avoidance strategies. For example:

- You mentioned a fear of breathing in fumes from passing trucks. Do you also avoid gas stations because of this?

Commonly avoided situations due to contamination include unknown substances of a particular color (i.e., brown spots), certain surfaces (i.e., door knobs), animals, and public places (i.e., hospitals). Individuals may use only certain parts of an object or may employ "barriers" (i.e., latex gloves) to push an elevator button. Adam contorted his body into uncomfortable positions to open a door. The patient may also arbitrarily designate "safe" or "clean" areas (i.e., of the floor, of a faucet) that can be touched sparingly. Relatedly, clients may establish safety zones in their home or office in which foreign contaminants (i.e., people who have not showered recently, items from outside, etc.) are prohibited.

In response to intrusive thoughts about accidentally harming a loved one or vulnerable individual, Adam engaged in a series of avoidance behaviors. While at the grocery store, he devised alternate routes around the store to avoid shopping in aisles where children were present. Similarly, he took circuitous routes while driving to school so as to avoid passing any children waiting for the school bus.

Within the domain of "incompleteness," avoidance behaviors serve to reduce the need for rituals. By avoiding certain spaces (i.e., rooms in their house), clients may feel as though they are better able to control or avoid urges to rearrange objects, create "balance," or perform counting rituals.

Clients with unacceptable thoughts, images, or impulses tend to avoid stimuli that trigger such undesirable thoughts. Additionally, clients may avoid situations in which they fear they may act on these unwanted impulses. Individuals with violent intrusive thoughts may avoid triggers including potential weapons (i.e., knives, guns) or victims (i.e., loved ones). Additionally, they may avoid pictures, places, and movies associated with violence. For example, a client with concerns about accidentally stabbing her husband not only avoided knives in the kitchen, but also avoided movies with stabbing scenes and news articles about stabbing deaths. A client with violent thoughts about harming others avoided crowded spaces, as such areas had the tendency to intensify his intrusive worries.

Mental rituals. Mental rituals, also known as covert neutralizing, may pose a particular challenge to treatment, as they are often brief and unobservable. Most clinicians are unable to recognize these behaviors, and clients may have trouble articulating these rituals. The most common strategies include thought suppression and concealment. Some clients may fear that the act of verbalizing their thoughts may (a) get them into trouble (i.e., with the law) or with family members, and (b) bring them closer to acting upon the thoughts.

Self-Monitoring

Self-monitoring represents an important, complementary tool to gain additional information about the client's obsessions and rituals. A common procedure in CBT, self-monitoring refers to the detailed, in-the-moment recording of instances of obsessional fears, avoidance, and rituals. Such details include the date, time, frequency, intensity, and duration of the listed symptoms. This strategy is particularly beneficial if the clinician is concerned that the client may be underestimating the frequency or distress associated with each thought and behavior (Abramowitz & Jacoby, 2014).

The clinician can introduce the concept of self-monitoring by having the client record actual, recent examples. The clinician should acknowledge that self-monitoring requires great effort and detail. Particularly at the beginning of treatment, self-monitoring logs may be long; as such, the timely reporting of symptoms is crucial. The client should be instructed that she or he should use a watch (rather than guessing) to determine the exact amount of time spent ritualizing. A sample explanation follows:

CLINICIAN: Self-monitoring will not be easy at first. It is a seemingly foreign task, and it will take time to familiarize yourself with the procedure. Here are some reasons that I am asking that you self-monitor: first, it will give us accurate information about the ways OCD interferes with your routine. It will give us a sense of when various triggers arise, and how much time they tend to take. Second, it will help us to track your progress in treatment. Throughout therapy, we can check in and see how often you are ritualizing in comparison to when you started. Lastly, self monitoring can actually help you reduce your OCD symptoms right away. The very act of having to write down your rituals may help you resist doing them. So, I want you to collect complete and accurate data.

Upon jointly reviewing self-monitoring logs, the clinician can query for additional information: e.g., "Why did you wash your hands in that situation?" By gaining a better understanding of the client's triggers and urges, the clinician and client can jointly consider situations to be included as exercises for exposure.

Practical Considerations

Given the detailed nature of a functional assessment – and the potential for the need to discuss personal or sensitive information (e.g., sexual thoughts or behaviors, violent or blasphemous images, bathroom-related behaviors) – it is crucial to build positive rapport with the client. Clients may be reluctant to share sensitive thoughts that run counter to their true beliefs; so, a therapist's gentle, yet firm, encouragement is beneficial. Clients may also experience difficulty in describing their thoughts (i.e., thoughts of molesting their niece) due to embarrassment or shame. The clinician is advised to avoid appearing surprised when learning of disturbing, intrusive thoughts and ritualistic behaviors in order to reduce potential stigmatization.

Additionally, an exhaustive functional assessment can be time consuming, so it is important to be sensitive to the client's energy level throughout. Frequently, OCD features (i.e., need for reassurance, rigidity) may hamper the assessment process. Clinicians should allow time for the client to pause and reflect upon their courage for sharing openly and honestly. For example, the clinician could help the client process in vivo by querying, "What was this like for you? What does it suggest that an entire checklist of thoughts and behaviors exists?"

Insight among individuals with OCD can span the range from excellent to absent (American Psychiatric Association, 2013). A functional assessment for an individual with poor insight may necessitate multi-informant (i.e., family members) report. Information provided by an outside informant can aid the clinician in completing a thorough functional assessment. Low agreement between the client and an informant may reflect unique information that the clinician can later address in treatment.

Lastly, functional assessment is an ongoing, iterative process. After conducting the functional assessment and implementing a treatment protocol based on the functional assessment, the success of treatment can inform the degree to which the assessment was complete and accurate. Further assessment can be used to continuously revise the intervention and guide treatment.

Functional Assessment for Evaluating Treatment

Continuous functional assessment can assist the clinician in evaluating whether, or how, the client is responding to treatment. The clinician should not simply rely on the client's (or informant's) report of "feeling better." Progress should be measured systematically by comparing current functioning against the initial functional assessment.

Various strategies can accomplish this goal of determining whether (and which) additional treatment is necessary. Ideally, a multimethod, collaborative approach, involving the use of multiple informants, multiple measures, semi-structured questioning, and self-monitoring can be used. Informants can let the clinician know whether alternative maladaptive strategies (i.e., use of sanitizers) have replaced the initial hand-washing rituals. A self-monitoring log, as described earlier, is also a useful tool to track treatment progress. Visually, the log can demonstrate the extent to which urges and accompanying rituals are shifting in both quantity and quality.

Conclusions

This chapter has identified and elaborated on strategies and practical considerations for conducting a functional assessment for individuals with OCD. In order to optimize functional assessment, a multitrait, multimethod approach should be employed. In assessing OCD across the lifespan, a number of considerations must be made. Children may be particularly embarrassed by their obsessions and also may have difficulty describing their thoughts using words. Therefore, the clinician should be flexible in their way of assessing symptoms and associations between thoughts and behaviors. For example, clinicians might encourage a child to write down his or her fears or draw pictures of his or her thoughts. In older adults, fears of or actual decline in cognitive abilities may mediate OCD thoughts and symptoms. Such decline may not only be a focus of concern, but also impede the assessment process. Following the functional assessment, the therapist should have the information necessary to construct an individualized model of the patient's specific OCD symptoms and to begin to develop an exposure and response prevention plan. A number of manuals are available that detail the specific construction of a conceptualization and treatment plan (e.g., Abramowitz & Jacoby, 2014).

References

Abramowitz, J. S., & Jacoby, R. J. (2014). *Obsessive-compulsive disorder in adults*. Boston, MA: Hogrefe.

American Psychiatric Association. (2013). *Diagnostic and statistical manual of mental disorders* (5th ed.). Arlington, VA: American Psychiatric Publishing.

Coles, M. E., Frost, R. O., Heimberg, R. G., & Rhéaume, J. (2003). "Not just right experiences": Perfectionism, obsessive-compulsive features and general psychopathology. *Behaviour Research and Therapy, 41*(6), 681–700.

Follette, W., Naugle, A., & Linnerooth, P. (2000). Functional alternatives to traditional assessment and diagnosis. In M. Doughter (Ed.), *Clinical behavior analysis* (pp. 99–125). Reno, NV: Context Press.

Goodman, W. K., Price, L. H., Rasmussen, S. A., Mazure, C., Delgado, P., Heninger, G. R., & Charney, D. S. (1989a). The Yale–Brown Obsessive Compulsive Scale: II. Validity. *Archives of General Psychiatry*, *46*(11), 1012–1016. http://doi.org/10.1001/archpsyc.1989.01810110054008

Goodman, W. K., Price, L. H., Rasmussen, S. A., Mazure, C., Fleischmann, R. L., Hill, C. L., … Charney, D. S. (1989b). The Yale–Brown Obsessive Compulsive Scale: I. Development, use, and reliability. *Archives of General Psychiatry*, *46*(11), 1006–1011. doi. 1989.01810110048007

8

Assessment of Cognitive Distortions and Cognitive Biases

Patrick A. Vogel and Stian Solem

Cognitive distortions and biases are essential in understanding and treating obsessive-compulsive disorder (OCD) according to cognitive-behavioral treatment (CBT) models, which have dominated the understanding and treatment of OCD. Right from the beginning, the earliest evidence-based treatments for OCD have been hybrids of behavioral treatment methods combined with differing degrees of cognitive therapy elements (Meyer, 1966; Rachman, Hodgson, & Marks, 1971). The highly influential CBT model for the treatment of OCD, termed Exposure with Response Prevention (ERP), includes a clear focus on cognitive aspects of treatment although the emphasis in ERP is on the behavioral components (Foa, Yadin, & Lichner, 2012). OCD-related cognitions are usually "processed" after the fact and the exposures are not primarily designed, a priori, as tests of the validity of the cognitions.

Cognitive models of OCD have their origins within Beck's schema theory of emotional disorders (Beck, 1976) and view dysfunctional schemas, beliefs, and appraisals as core constituents of the disorder. Cognitive theories have often been termed "appraisal theories," given the significance of the subjective interpretation of intrusions. These theories postulate that intrusions can be placed on a dimension of normal cognitive phenomenon and that the appraisal is partly derived from more enduring underlying beliefs and determine whether or not intrusions develop into clinical obsessions. Cognitively-based OCD treatments explicitly derive the OCD-related appraisals behind the patient's symptoms and afterwards design behavioral experiments to test their validity. The disconfirmation of the fear provoking predictions and thoughts is given renewed emphasis in recent conceptualizations of the mechanisms involved in effective exposure therapy (Craske, Treanor, Conway, Zbozinek, & Vervliet, 2014). Since there is a good degree of overlap in behavioral and cognitive treatment, it is not surprising that it is difficult to prove the superiority of one intervention over another (e.g., Vogel, Stiles, & Götestam, 2004; Whittal, Thordarson, & McLean, 2005).

It is evident that some element of exposure is important to obtaining good treatment results for OCD (Abramowitz, 2006). There has long been evidence for successful treatment of anxiety disorders (Öst, 2008), but there has also been recent advances in our understanding of anxiety disorders (Shafran, Radomsky, Coughtrey, & Rachman, 2013). We are now able to successfully treat what were previously

The Wiley Handbook of Obsessive Compulsive Disorders, Volume I, First Edition.
Edited by Jonathan S. Abramowitz, Dean McKay, and Eric A. Storch.
© 2017 John Wiley & Sons Ltd. Published 2017 by John Wiley & Sons Ltd.

referred to as "pure obsessions," which historically have been an exclusion criterion for ERP trials (Marks, Hodgson, & Rachman, 1975). Also, attending to obsessions and dysfunctional beliefs related to OCD and achieving unambiguous testing of them in varied situations is likely to be important to obtaining good treatment results (Craske et al., 2014). All these developments underline the importance of obtaining good assessments of the cognitive aspects behind the OCD symptoms. This chapter will examine what measures of these beliefs are available that could aid in those assessments and what value they have demonstrated in the treatment of OCD.

Questionnaires Assessing Cognitive Distortions in OCD

Existing questionnaires that assess the most important cognitive beliefs and appraisals in OCD can be of use either after successful exposures in ERP to identify beliefs that have been disconfirmed or "up front" when designing behavioral experiments. The main part of this chapter describes the theoretical foundations for the most used, validated and researched questionnaires and presents information on their clinical utility.

Obsessive Beliefs Questionnaire (OBQ)

The OBQ (OCCWG, 2005) has been used extensively as a measure of cognitive beliefs relevant in OCD. The OBQ was developed collaboratively by members of the Obsessive Compulsive Cognitions Working Group consisting of over 40 investigators interested in cognitive aspects of OCD (Taylor, Kyrios, Thordarson, Steketee, & Frost, 2002). The OBQ assesses belief domains that have been proposed to be important in the etiology of OCD. The most commonly used questionnaire consists of 44 items (although a 20-item version has also been developed [Moulding, 2011]) rated on a scale from 1 (strongly disagree) to 7 (strongly agree). There are three subscales: (1) responsibility/threat (R/T); (2) perfectionism/certainty (P/C); and (3) importance/control of thoughts (I/C). These factors are all thought to be essential in a CBT understanding of OCD.

One of the most influential cognitive analyses of OCD was presented by Salkovskis (1985, 1999, 2007; Salkovskis, 1989). Central in this cognitive model is that faulty appraisal promotes the notion of exaggerated personal responsibility for events that will bring harm. The concept of responsibility concerns believing that one has power to bring about or prevent negative outcomes. The interpretation of an intrusion based on the belief of responsibility (i.e., responsible for harm to oneself or others) will result in emotional discomfort and will motivate attempts at neutralization aimed at reducing or avoiding the perceived responsibility (Salkovskis, Richards, & Forrester, 1995). In a review of the empirical findings regarding Salkovskis' theory, Clark (2004: 100) concluded that "appraisals/beliefs of responsibility and neutralization, are clearly core elements in the persistence of obsessions." Other scales for assessing responsibility also exist including the 26-item Responsibility Attitude Scale and the 22-item Responsibility Interpretations Questionnaire (Salkovskis et al., 2000).

Another central belief in OCD concerns the perceived likelihood and cost of aversive events (e.g., Foa & Kozak, 1986; Freeston, Rheume, & Ladoucer, 1996; Salkovskis, 1985). Examples of such beliefs could be, "I believe that the world is a dangerous place," and "bad things are more likely to happen to me than to other people." Related to overestimation of harm are beliefs about coping ability, low tolerance for uncertainty, and low tolerance for anxiety/discomfort. Such overestimation of threat has been linked with all anxiety disorders and may not be a unique cognitive distortion in OCD (Sookman & Pinard, 2002).

Contemporary cognitive theorists have also suggested a role for perfectionism in the understanding of OCD. Several studies have found that perfectionism is related to obsessive-compulsive symptoms (e.g., Frost, Novara & Rheaume, 2002). Similar to threat overestimation, perfectionism is not specific to OCD as elevated scores are also found in other psychiatric disorders (e.g., Frost & Steketee, 1997; Sassaroli et al., 2008). This observation has been discussed in terms of perfectionism being a necessary trait, but not a sufficient trait for the development of obsessive-compulsive symptoms (Frost & Steketee, 1997).

Individuals with OCD often exhibit pathological intolerance of uncertainty concerning the properties of stimuli, situations, and actions (e.g., Rasmussen & Eisen, 1988). Doubts are often seen in regard to whether hand washing has been performed or as to whether they have forgotten something important. Pathological doubt has been thought to be most evident among patients with checking compulsions (e.g., Radomsky, Shafran, Coughtrey, & Rachman, 2010), but has also been postulated to play a central role in many other anxiety disorders as well as in obsessive-compulsive personality disorder and dependent personality disorder (American Psychiatric Association, 1994). Intolerance for uncertainty is often observed in people having difficulty making decisions. It seems as if they are more cautious and use the longer time to categorize objects and wishes for information to be repeated. When a decision is made it often involves greater doubt about the correctness of this decision and uncertainty is interpreted as potentially dangerous. These experiences are quite similar to that observed in people with generalized anxiety disorder (Gentes & Ruscio, 2011). Difficulties with strong effect and confidence in the ability to cope with ambiguous situations may also be dimensions of this belief.

The misinterpretation of significance theory developed by Rachman (1997, 1998, 2003) suggests that catastrophic misinterpretations of importance of one's thoughts, images, and impulses both lead to and contributes to persistence of obsessions. The central premise is that normally occurring intrusions are catastrophically misinterpreted in terms of signifying to the person that they are "mad, bad, or dangerous." According to Rachman, these are signs of Thought–Action Fusion (TAF) where intrusive thoughts are interpreted as equivalent to the feared actions or that they can produce them or dangerous situations (Rachman, 1998). It has been suggested that there are similarities between the content of obsessions coming from OCD patients and normal controls (Rachman & de Silva, 1978) although more recent research suggest that some obsessions may be more abnormal than others (Rassin & Muris, 2007). The theory suggests that normal unwanted intrusive thoughts will develop into clinical obsessions if they are misinterpreted as personally important and threatening, given that the content of the intrusions is contrary to the individual's value system. When this occurs, frequency of the obsessions will increase because internal cues (i.e., anxiety sensations), with or without the presence of external cues (e.g., sharp objects), may be misinterpreted as threatening (i.e., "the terrible physical sensations indicate that I could lose my mind and end up hurting myself or others with that knife") instead of being of neutral significance. This in turn leads to increased persistence of the obsessions, since avoidance and attempts at neutralization will prevent disconfirmation and instead reinforce the catastrophic misinterpretation. Clark (2004) concluded that inflated misinterpretations of significance have empirical support in OCD.

The tendency to overestimate the significance of controlling one's thoughts, and the belief that this is attainable and desirable has also been given prominence with the theory regarding control of thoughts. This domain is largely based on cognitive control theory (Clark & Purdon, 1993; Purdon & Clark, 1994). In addition to the primary appraisal of intrusions based on importance, threat, and inflated responsibility, the model proposes that a faulty secondary appraisal of failed thought control plays an important role in OCD. Several features of this secondary misinterpretation contribute to escalation of obsessive-compulsive symptoms, including misinterpreting failed thought control as highly significant and/or as increasing the probability for future threat, believing that it is possible and desirable to achieve complete or perfect control, having an inflated sense of responsibility, and drawing faulty conclusions about uncontrollability (Clark, 2004). Clark (2004) reported that there is only indirect support for some parts of the cognitive control theory.

Using the OBQ in Clinical Practice

The OBQ demonstrates good internal consistency and criterion-related validity in both clinical and nonclinical samples (OCCWG, 2005). One study has suggested a four-factor solution instead of three factors with threat and responsibility forming separate dimensions (e.g., Myers, Fisher, & Wells, 2008; Moulding, 2011). Changes in OBQ scores also accompany changes in OCD symptoms (e.g., Solem, Håland, Vogel, Hansen, & Wells, 2009) and significant differences in obsessive beliefs were found between treatment responders and non-responders after treatment. Whittal and colleagues (2005) reported similar results for CT and ERP treatment with a significant correlation between residual change scores for obsessive beliefs and OCD symptoms. Whittal and colleagues found that cognitive change was associated with symptom improvement. There were no significant differences between the conditions (CT or ERP) on any of the specific cognitive beliefs and appraisals at treatment termination or follow-up suggesting that changes in cognitive distortions occur in both types of treatment. There are also studies indicating that the beliefs assessed with the OBQ function as a predictor (risk factor) of future OCD symptoms even after controlling for pre-existing OCD symptoms and depressive and anxious symptoms (e.g., Abramowitz, 2006). There might also be a differential response to SSRI treatment as patients with perfectionism/certainty tend to have poorer treatment response (Selvi, Atli, Besiroglu, Aydin, & Gulec, 2011).

A demonstration of the potential usefulness of assessing obsessive beliefs to aid in prevention of the development of OCD symptoms in high risk individuals has recently been completed in a study of a prevention program for postpartum obsessive-compulsive symptoms (Timpano, Abramowitz, Mahaffey, Mitchell, & Schmidt, 2011). Pregnant women with high scores on the importance and control subscale that received interventions that addressed these beliefs showed significantly less OCD symptoms at follow-up assessments than those not randomly assigned to receive those interventions.

A child version of the OBQ has been developed with promising qualities (Coles et al., 2010). One study examined different cognitive beliefs common in OCD (i.e.,

TAF, responsibility, and metacognitions), and found that levels of these beliefs were not significantly related to OCD symptoms before the age of 12, but they were after. However, there were no significant differences in age of onset or severity of the OCD symptoms between the samples of younger or older children (Farrell, Waters, & Zimmer-Gembeck, 2012). Thus, these differences may only indicate that the disorder has different expressions at different ages that do not play a role in the development of the disorder. Another explanation could be that small children lack the clear obsessive beliefs that are heavily represented on the OBQ. Measures more clearly related to the functionality of their rituals for them at relieving their anxiety would probably be more related to their obsessive-compulsive symptoms.

In summary, the OBQ assesses cognitive characteristics believed relevant in the pathogenesis and maintenance of obsessive-compulsive symptoms. These beliefs may not necessarily be specific to OCD as they also occur in other anxiety disorders, but studies suggest that increasing levels of such obsessive beliefs may be both a risk factor for developing OCD, that they are related to severity of OCD, and that improvement in OCD is accompanied by improvements in these beliefs. CBT provides several therapeutic interventions designed to promote change in these beliefs (e.g., Wilhelm & Steketee, 2006).

Interpretation of Intrusions Inventory (III) (OCCWG, 1997, 2001)

In contrast to the OBQ, which was designed to assess general beliefs (traits) relevant to OCD, the III is a semi-idiographic self-report questionnaire designed to measure immediate appraisals (states) or interpretations of intrusions. Respondents are first given a definition of unwanted ego-dystonic mental intrusions along with common examples. They are then asked to provide two unwanted intrusions they have recently experienced, followed by ratings of recency, frequency, and distress associated with these intrusions. The respondents are instructed to rate the level of appraisal associated with these intrusions for each of the 31 statements, ranging from a score of 0 ("I did not believe this idea at all") to 100 ("I was completely convinced this idea was true"). Appraisal is measured using 31 items that reflect three theoretically derived domains relevant in understanding the etiology and persistence of OCD: (1) inflated responsibility; (2) over-importance of thoughts; and (3) importance of controlling one's thoughts.

Use of the III in Clinical Settings

The III has shown good internal consistency and good test-retest reliability in both clinical and non-clinical populations (OCCWG, 2005). Validation studies of III (OCCWG. 2001, 2003) found high intercorrelations between the three subscales. In 2005, the OCCWG examined the factor structure of the III using a sample of individuals with OCD and the results of the factor analysis suggested a one-factor model. Similar to that of the OBQ, there are indications of elevated scores on the III also in other disorders such and general anxiety and depression.

The III is supposed to be more state-like while the OBQ is supposed to be trait-like, but research has not confirmed this. The III is less researched than the OBQ and there is significant overlap between the two which might be the reason for more the

OBQ being used more frequently. No known version of the III exists for use with children. Cognitive therapy techniques are well suited for dealing with these appraisals and provides several therapeutic interventions designed to promote change in these appraisals (e.g., Wilhelm & Steketee, 2006).

Thought–Action Fusion Scale (TAFS) (Shafran, Thordarson, & Rachman, 1996)

Thought–action fusion is defined as "a phenomenon in which people tend to regard their thoughts as being psychologically equivalent to the corresponding action, and/or believe that their thoughts of possible misfortunes actually increase the likelihood that the misfortune will occur" (Rachman, 2003: 12). The TAFS is a 19-item self-report measure of the tendency to believe that thoughts are equivalent to actions. Twelve items assess moral TAF, which is the belief that thoughts are the moral equivalent of actions (e.g., "Having a blasphemous thought is almost as sinful to me as a blasphemous action"). Three items assess likelihood-self TAF, which is the belief that merely thinking about harm coming to oneself increases the likelihood of being harmed (e.g., "If I think of myself being in a car accident this increases the risk that I will have a car accident"). The remaining four items assess likelihood-other TAF, which is the belief that thinking about harm coming to someone else increases the likelihood of that person being harmed (e.g., "If I think of a relative/friend losing their job, this increases the risk that they will lose their job). Agreement with each item is rated on a scale from 0 (disagree strongly) to 4 (agree strongly).

Use of the TAFS in clinical settings. The instrument's psychometric properties are good (Rassin, Merckelbach, Muris, & Schmidt, 2001; Shafran et al., 1996). TAF is associated with tendencies towards obsessive-compulsive symptoms. However, the literature investigating TAF and other variables implicated in OCD remains inconclusive (Berle & Starcevic, 2005). Moral TAF and depression are both likely to be strongly associated with blasphemous obsessions. A review of the status of TAFS concluded that: "The research to date has reinforced our early view that these scales may be best used as a starting point in identifying beliefs for a patient rather than as total scores to show the extent of TAF beliefs" (Shafran & Rachman, 2004: 104).

The TAFS has been used successfully in children with OCD (e.g., Barrett & Healy, 2003). Like the OBQ and III, TAF may not be specific to OCD, but could be associated with differences in negative affect. TAF may decrease with successful treatment of OCD even without addressing it. Mini surveys can be used to normalize obsessions and challenge TAF. One example of such a survey involves interviewing people on strange thoughts they may experience. Coming to realize that other people also experience intrusive thoughts could be a powerful normalizing strategy. Also, finding out how others could be unaffected by these thoughts may also provide the patient with advice with regard to dealing with such thoughts. Other interventions could involve behavioral experiments testing whether thinking about events can make them happen. The patient could attempt to make his or her therapist sick or be involved in an accident by thinking about it or writing in down. Other specific TAF interventions that could prove beneficial have been described by Rachman (2003).

Some divergence in beliefs is found in various cultures since ethnicity, religion, and other aspects of culture could influence the expression of OCD. Religion has been found to be related to TAFS scores (Rassin & Koster, 2003). However, the findings are mixed and may be specific to certain types of religion. Obtained differences on TAFS were not related to differences in prevalence rates of pathology among the religious groups that were studied (Siev & Cohen, 2007). In another study, moral TAF was only related to OCD symptoms among Jews, but not for Christians where these types of beliefs are more culturally normative (Siev, Chambliss, & Huppert, 2010). A study with a nonclinical sample utilizing a more idiographic rather than nomothetic approach to this issue, found more likelihood of harm estimates and more neutralizing behaviors among highly religious Protestant Christians when writing that a family member was involved in a car accident than among atheists/agnostics (Berman, Abramowitz, Pardue, & Wheaton, 2010). However, there were no differences between these two groups in the level of anxiety aroused by this task.

Not Just Right Experiences Questionnaire (NJRE-Q-R) (Coles, Frost, Heimberg, & Rheaume, 2003)

The NJREQ-R (Coles et al., 2003) consists of 19 items assessing feelings of incompleteness or "not just right" experiences. The first 10 items of the NJRE-Q-R provide examples of not just right experiences (e.g., sensation after getting dressed that parts of my clothes didn't feel just right) and respondents are to indicate whether they experienced each within the past month. The last seven items require respondents to rate frequency, intensity, immediate and delayed distress, related rumination, urge to respond, and responsibility.

Many individuals with OCD have a wish to have things perfect, certain, or under control and compulsive behaviors have been conceptualized as attempts to achieve the perfect and certain state. Not just right experiences represent a mismatch between perceptions of a current state and a desired state. The inability for individuals with OCD to fully attain their desired state purportedly leads them to continually experience not just right experiences, which in turn engenders further engagement in compulsive behaviors. The repetitive nature of compulsive behaviors is thus viewed, in part, as being the result of not just right experiences (Coles et al., 2003). Not just right experiences are identified as a common experience (Coles, Heimberg, Frost, & Steketee, 2005), with approximately 95% of nonclinical samples reporting at least one not just right experience in their lifetime (Coles et al. 2003; Fergus, 2014). Not just right experiences have been linked with OCD although no prevalence studies exist. However, not just right experiences are strongly related to OCD symptoms, especially with checking, ordering, and doubting, although less so with washing, obsessing, hoarding, and neutralizing (Coles et al., 2003).

Clinical Use of the NJRE-Q-R

Coles et al. (2003) found that the questionnaire had fair internal consistency and showed good convergent and discriminant validity. The NJRE-Q-R can be especially helpful with identifying beliefs in patients who report low scores on the OBQ or similar measures of cognitive beliefs in OCD. Not just right experiences could be a challenge for treatment since it is often more difficult to address obsessions of "incompleteness" because they are less concrete than those of "harm avoidance" and complete response prevention may be difficult for those with severe "just right" symptoms.

Not just right experiences have also been assessed in adolescents (Ravid, Franklin, Khanna, Storch, & Coles, 2014); adolescents endorse such experiences similar to adults, but OCD symptoms were not related to not just right experiences. More research is also needed on cultural and ethnic variations. However, some Italian studies have found that not just right experiences explain OCD symptoms variation over time even when general distress and looming style were controlled (Sica, Caudek, Chiri, Ghisi, & Marchetti, 2012), and that fathers' not just right experiences predicted OCD symptoms in their sons, but not in their daughters (Sica et al., 2013). The other Italian study found that not just right severity was associated with OCD symptoms and that scores on the NJRE-Q-R scale differentiated between OCD and non-OCD patients (Ghisi, Chiri, Marchetti, Sanavio, & Sica, 2010). Similar to previous findings on obsessive beliefs not being specific to OCD, there are also indications that not just right experiences are found in other disorders (Fergus, 2014).

Few studies have addressed how to best deal with these not just right beliefs, although one case-illustration using CT for this population exists (Summerfeldt, 2004). The aim of ERP for people with not just right experiences could be to habituate to feelings of sensory-affective discomfort and that these experiences should not guide behavior. Cognitive beliefs may be less important than the behavioral component of CBT in people with predominantly not just right experiences. Interventions that bolster the likelihood of habituation (e.g., longer sessions and more repetitive exposure tasks) and aim at tolerating distress tolerance (e.g., mindfulness) may be helpful in. Externalizing and reframing not just right experiences could also be potential beneficial interventions.

Metacognitive Questionnaires

A review on the role of metacognition in OCD concluded that metacognition has a key role in the etiology of OCD (Rees & Anderson, 2013). A number of studies have demonstrated that metacognitive beliefs are positively correlated with obsessive-compulsive symptoms even after controlling for worry and responsibility (e.g., Myers & Wells, 2005; Solem, Myers, Fisher, Vogel, & Wells, 2010).

Different metacognitive questionnaires exist which could be helpful in understanding and treating OCD. The most commonly used are the Metacognitions Questionnaire (MCQ) (Wells & Cartwright-Hatton, 2004) which measures generic metacognitive beliefs relevant to most emotional disorders, but there are also questionnaires more specific to OCD such as the thought-fusion questionnaire, beliefs about rituals instrument, and the stop signals questionnaire. Elements of these three OCD-specific metacognitive measures are also included in the obsessive-compulsive disorder scale (OCD-S) (Wells, 2009).

The MCQ is a 30-item self-report scale measuring beliefs about thinking. Responses are required on a four-point scale ranging from 1 (do not agree) to 4 (agree very much). A five-factor structure exists: (1) positive beliefs about worry; (2) negative beliefs about the controllability of thoughts and corresponding danger; (3) (low) cognitive confidence; (4) negative beliefs about thoughts in general/need to control thoughts; and (5) cognitive self-consciousness. High scores reflect more reported problems with the item in question (e.g., a high cognitive confidence score indicates less trust in one's memory). Negative metacognitive beliefs may be especially strongly related to OCD symptoms, but lack of cognitive confidence may also be particularly important in OCD. Processing biases documented in OCD may actually be consequences of OCD rather than causes. Studies have shown that people with OCD, mainly with the checking subtype, have low confidence in their memory abilities (e.g., Hermans, Martens, DeCort, Pieters, & Eelen, 2003; Tolin et al., 2001) and that this may be related to heightened CSC. For example, Exner and colleagues (2009) found high CSC mediated episodic memory difficulties in OCD. *The Memory and Cognitive Confidence Scale* (MACCS) (Nedeljkovic & Kyrios, 2007) also measures trait meta-memory, which encompasses four factors: concentration and attention, decision-making abilities, perfectionism regarding one's memory, and confidence in one's memory abilities. All of these factors have been associated with obsessive-compulsive symptoms, especially checking behavior (Nedeljkovic & Kyrios, 2007).

Building on and extending the concepts of thought-fusion and importance of thoughts, three types of thought-fusion beliefs can be assessed in the metacognitive model of OCD (Wells, 2009). TAF involves believing that a thought alone can cause a person to carry out an action, or that a thought is equivalent to an action. Thought–Event Fusions (TEF) involves thinking that having a thought can cause events. Thought–Object Fusions (TOF) involves the belief that thoughts and feelings can be transferred into objects. The thought-fusion beliefs can be measured with the Thought Fusion Instrument (TFI) (Wells, Gwilliam, & Cartwright-Hatton, 2001). TFI consist of 14 items rated on a 0–100 scale. Depending upon the strength of these fusion beliefs, the intrusions could be appraised as significant and possibly dangerous. According to the metacognitive model these fusion beliefs are activated following a trigger (usually an automatic thought) and will further give rise to beliefs about rituals.

Beliefs about rituals are similar to beliefs about the importance of controlling ones' thoughts as specified by the OBQ, and involves assumptions an individual holds about the need to carry out rituals and neutralising behaviour in response to intrusions. These are expressed in a declarative form and could either be positive, for example, "if I keep knives locked in the cupboard I will not hurt my children", or negative, for example, "my rituals could make me go crazy." These beliefs about rituals activate a metacognitive plan for reducing the perceived threat, which includes a wide range of overt and covert neutralizing strategies as well as perseverative thinking and monitoring for unwanted thoughts in an attempt to neutralize threat. The Beliefs About Rituals Inventory (BARI) (Wells & McNicol, 2004) assesses the strength of such beliefs about compulsions and consists of 14 items rated on a 1 (disagree) to 4 (agree very much) scale.

Rituals and neutralising behaviour are performed until an internal subjective criteria, or stop signal, is met. The stop signal is often a metacognitive experience such as a feeling of knowing or a feeling of satisfaction used by the individual to determine whether it is safe to terminate their neutralizing behavior. Examples of such subjective criteria are "having a perfect memory of the action" and "having performed the rituals in the correct order." These stop signals and others have been proposed and assessed with the Stop Signals Questionnaire (SSQ) (Myers, Fisher & Wells, 2009). SSQ is developed to capture the importance of certain stop criteria in deciding to stop carrying out rituals. The items are constructed based on a list of unhelpful stop signals prevalent in OCD patients as found in case-material (Myers et al., 2009). The questionnaire consists of 12 items and respondents are asked to rate how important each of these signals are for stopping their rituals on a five-point scale from 0 (not at all important) to 5 (extremely important). All items begin with "An important signal of when I can stop my rituals is when …" and one example of an item is " … I have replaced the intrusive thought with a positive image."

Clinical use of metacognitive questionnaires. Similar to other questionnaires mentioned in this chapter, the MCQ could also be relevant not only for OCD but for other disorders as well and metacognitive beliefs could be the same across subtypes (Irak & Tosun, 2008) suggesting that subtype specific therapy may not be necessary. The questionnaire has been found to be valid in different cultures such as Turkey, Iran, Netherlands, Norway, and Spain.

There are adaptations of the MCQ-30 which can be used for children and adolescents (Bacow, Pincus, Ehrenreich, & Brody, 2009). The fact that there were significant relationships between the metacognitive and cognitive biases of mothers with the same biases in their early onset children with OCD, suggests that cognitive and metacognitive interventions might be appropriate as part of family treatment interventions for OCD (Farrell et al., 2012). There is evidence that family accommodation to OCD rituals in both adult and children with OCD can interfere with treatment outcome (Abramowitz et al., 2013). Therefore identifying subclinical levels of obsessional beliefs in family members may well be an important task for therapy.

Metacognitive therapy (Wells, 2009) for OCD corresponds well with the beliefs specified by the MCQ, TFI, BARI, and SSQ and provides several therapeutic interventions designed to promote change in these beliefs. Metacognitive therapy aims at getting all metacognitive beliefs down to zero using techniques such as detached mindfulness to stop worrying and rumination, challenging metacognitive beliefs and abandoning all safety behaviors including threat monitoring. Patients with high scores on low cognitive confidence could be also be targeted with psychoeducation which could illustrate the detrimental aspects of repeated checking on actual memory retrieval performance and then appropriate behavioral tests of these beliefs could be designed (e.g., Radomsky et al., 2010).

Insight and Conviction of Beliefs

Patients with OCD can vary in their level of insight into the senselessness of their obsessions and compulsions. Poor insight might be related to earlier age-at-onset, longer duration of illness, higher severity, and more comorbid disorder. Different instruments exist that could assess insight. The most common are the Overvalued Ideas Scale (Neziroglu, McKay, Yaryura-Tobias, Stevens, & Todar, 1999) and the Brown Assessment of Beliefs Scale (BABS) (Eisen et al., 1998). All are interview based since insight is difficult to assess using self-report. The BABS is not disorder specific and questions have been raised whether it assesses delusionality or overvalued ideas, nonetheless it ostensibly measures insight into the senselessness of obsessions and compulsions. The BABS is a six-item semi-idiographic measure administered as a semi-structured interview. The patient and clinician first identify the patient's specific obsessional fears (e.g., "I will get AIDS from flushing a public toilet," "I will hit someone with my car without realizing it"). Next, these beliefs are rated according to: conviction in the belief, perception of others' views, explanation of differing views, fixity of the belief, attempts to disprove the belief, and insight. Insight could be considered a representation of the strength of belief about probability and severity of danger. Item scores range from 0 (normal) to 4 (pathological) and are summed to produce a total score ranging from 0 to 24. The scale has good psychometric properties as reported by Eisen et al. (1998).

Clinical Use of Measures of Insight

Patients with extremely low levels of insight have often a poorer treatment prognosis (Nezirolgu, Stevens, McKay, & Yaryura-Tobias, 2000), but they may still benefit from CBT for OCD and pharmacotherapy. The latest version of the *Diagnostic and Statistical Manual of Mental Disorders*, Fifth Edition (American Psychiatric Association, 2013), includes a specification of the degree of insight into the obsessional beliefs since it is thought to be important in treatment planning. OCD with poor insight has been described as having egosyntonic symptoms that might extend to delusions and psychosis (e.g., Matsunaga et al., 2002). Most likely, insight falls on a continuum. Insight has been associated with symptom severity and chronicity (including comorbidity), early symptom onset, and a positive family history of OCD (e.g., Bellino, Patria, Ziero, & Bogetto, 2005). Poor insight can be associated with less resistance to obsessive–compulsive symptoms and increases in externalizing symptoms (Storch et al., 2014). These associated features may interfere with successful CBT. The identification of obsessions as unrealistic is an important component of CBT for OCD in both children and adults. The identification of patients with lower levels of insight as shown on the BABS may alert the clinician to the need for modifications of the treatment rationale employed. The BABS can be used on adolescents, and a child version of the scale has been developed (Storch et al., 2014). There is a lack of research on possible cultural and ethnic variations in insight into OCD.

Although CBT for OCD is associated with improved insight in patients with OCD, patients with low insight are often unwilling to engage in treatment. Motivational interviewing-based interventions may be a necessary precursor that can prevent dropout and encourage completion of all items on an exposure hierarchy. Studies suggest that patients who initially refuse treatment because of their uncertainties about ERP could successfully complete therapy successfully following a motivational pre-therapy (Maltby & Tolin 2005; Simpson & Zuckoff, 2011). Related research findings have been found with pediatric OCD (Merlo et al., 2010). In extreme cases the underlying beliefs include pessimism about the patient's own perceived ability to change because of their underlying defectiveness. A direct attack on these beliefs may provoke more defensive resistance. A more profitable approach may be to ask the patient to suspend an immediate test of these beliefs, but to ask instead if they would be willing to attempt small behavioral changes to see if they can improve their total life functioning. Overvalued ideas can be challenged using CBT techniques although further research is necessary to develop better treatment strategies to address overvalued ideation. Some suggestions (e.g., psychoeducation, encourage them to research obsessive content, and consulting with "experts") for dealing with poor insight in pediatric OCD have been described (Adelman & Lebowitz, 2012).

Concluding Remarks

The last decades of research on cognitive biases in OCD have provided us with a better understanding of key cognitive and metacognitive beliefs of OCD and valid measures have been developed to assess these allowing for empirical investigations. How these beliefs develop and if there are any order effects remains to be investigated. It also remains to be proven that targeting these cognitions and metacognitions during treatment will improve treatment outcome. The role of beliefs and appraisals in OCD is complex and there are overlapping constructs. The large overlap could also suggest that they simply assess a general tendency to hold irrational beliefs. Focusing on a single domain in isolation from other constructs could prove fruitless. Some claim that certain cognitions are relevant to certain subtypes of OCD whilst others claim that a few beliefs are most important across subtypes.

Taylor et al. (2006) suggested that some OCD patients actually do not present with obsessional beliefs or have low levels of these. Similarly, Chik, Calamari, Rector, and Riemann (2010) found that OCD patients with low beliefs showed more not just right experiences, while OCD patients with high beliefs group were characterized by metacognitive beliefs. These findings suggest that some OCD patients present with low beliefs as a consequence of different factors. One possible factor is that the low belief group lack awareness in regard to their beliefs and appraisals as addressed by certain theories and assessed by certain questionnaires. It might be that for someone struggling with OCD over time the compulsions could become habitual and people could come to forget why one performs one's rituals. Also, young children that have OCD often do not have clear awareness of the content of their obsessions (American Psychiatric Association, 2013). It is not uncommon for patients with OCD to only report compulsions on certain self-report inventories and claim that they are not bothered with obsessions. This group would usually have low scores on questionnaires assessing cognitive biases. This could also be a matter related to measurement issues. Some questionnaires could be more relevant to this group such as those addressing not just right experiences and beliefs about their rituals. It is also possible that patients with low beliefs could experience increases in obsessive beliefs when they start treatment and face their fears and thus become more aware of their obsessions. Behavioral assessment/avoidance tasks (e.g., Steketee et al., 1996) could also be beneficial to elicit possible obsessions and associated beliefs in patients with low beliefs.

Many of the cognitive beliefs and biases addressed in this chapter may not be specific to OCD. Specificity could be important for understanding the etiology and perhaps for prevention, but may be less important when treating the problem. This is one of the bases for the growing interest in transdiagnostic approaches (e.g., Barlow, Allen, & Choate, 2004). Many of the measures reviewed here may be also relevant to comorbid disorders. If these beliefs are addressed appropriately, then existing comorbid conditions may also be more amenable for treatment after OCD symptoms are reduced because the underlying vulnerabilities have already been partially treated (e.g. undermining avoidance as a useful coping strategy).

References

Abramowitz, J. S. (2006). The psychological treatment of obsessive-compulsive disorder. *Canadian Journal of Psychiatry, 51*, 407–416.

Abramowitz, J. S., Baucom, D. H., Wheaton, M. G., Boeding, S., Fabricant, L. E., Paprocki, C., & Fischer, M. S. (2013). Enhancing exposure and response prevention for OCD: A couple-based approach. *Behavior Modification, 37*, 189–210.

Adelman, C. B., & Lebowitz, E. R. (2012). Poor insight in pediatric obsessive-compulsive disorder: Developmental considerations, treatment implications, and potential strategies for improving insight. *Journal of Obsessive-Compulsive and Related Disorders, 1*, 119–124.

American Psychiatric Association. (1994). *Diagnostic and statistical manual of mental disorders* (4th ed.). Washington, DC: Author.

American Psychiatric Association. (2013). *Diagnostic and statistical manual of mental disorders* (5th ed.). Washington, DC: Author.

Bacow, T. L., Pincus, D. B., Ehrenreich, J. T., & Brody, L. R. (2009). The Metacognitions Questionnaire for Children: Development and validation in a clinical sample of children and adolescents with anxiety disorders. *Journal of Anxiety Disorders, 23*, 727–736.

Barlow, D. H., Allen, L. B., & Choate, M. L. (2004). Toward a unified treatment for emotional disorders. *Behavior Therapy, 35*, 205–230.

Barrett, P. M., & Healy, L. (2003). An examination of the cognitive processes involved in childhood obsessive-compulsive disorder. *Behaviour, Research and Therapy, 41*, 285–299.

Beck, A. T. (1976). *Cognitive therapy and the emotional disorders.* New York: International Universities Press.

Bellino S, Patria, L., Ziero, S., & Bogetto, F. (2005). Clinical picture of obsessive–compulsive disorder with poor insight: A regression model. *Psychiatry Research, 136*, 223–231.

Berle, D., & Starcevic, V. (2005). Thought–action fusion: Review of the literature and future directions. *Clinical Psychology Review, 25*, 263–284.

Berman, N. C., Abramowitz, J. S., Pardue, C. M., & Wheaton, M. G. (2010). The relationship between religion and thought–action fusion: Use of an in vivo paradigm. *Behaviour Research and Therapy, 48*(7), 670–674.

Chik, H. M., Calamari, J. E., Rector, N. A., & Riemann, B. C. (2010). What do low-dysfunctional beliefs obsessive-compulsive disorder subgroups believe? *Journal of Anxiety Disorders, 24*, 837–846.

Clark, D. A. (2004). *Cognitive-behavioral therapy for OCD.* New York: Guilford Press.

Clark, D. A., & Purdon, C. (1993). New perspectives for a cognitive theory of obsessions. *Australian Psychologist, 28*, 161–167.

Coles, M. E., Frost, R. O., Heimberg, R. G., & Rheaume, J. (2003). "Not just right experiences": Perfectionism, obsessive-compulsive features and general psychopathology. *Behaviour Research and Therapy, 41*, 681–700.

Coles, M. E., Heimberg, R. G., Frost, R. O., & Steketee, G. (2005). Not just right experiences and obsessive-compulsive features: Experimental and self-monitoring perspectives. *Behaviour Research and Therapy, 43*, 153–167.

Coles, M. E., Wolters, L. H., Sochting, I. de Haan, E., Pietrefesa, A. S., & Whiteside, S. P. (2010). Development and initial validation of the Obsessive Belief Questionnaire – Child Version (OBQ-CV). *Depression and Anxiety, 27*, 982–991.

Craske, M. G., Treanor, M., Conway, C. C., Zbozinek, T., & Vervliet, B. (2014). Maximizing exposure therapy: An inhibitory learning approach. *Behaviour Research and Therapy, 58*, 10–23.

Eisen, J. L., Phillips, K. A., Baer, L., Beer, D. A., Atala, K. D., & Rasmussen, S. A. (1998). The Brown Assessment of Beliefs Scale: Reliability and validity. *American Journal of Psychiatry, 155*, 102–108.

Exner, C., Kohl, A., Zaudig, M., Langs, G., Lincoln, T. M., & Rief, W. (2009). Metacognition and episodic memory in obsessive-compulsive disorder. *Journal of Anxiety Disorders, 23,* 624–631.

Farrell, L. J., Waters, A. M., & Zimmer-Gembeck, M. J. (2012). Cognitive biases and obsessive-compulsive symptoms in children: Examining the role of maternal cognitive bias and child age. *Behavior Therapy, 43,* 593–605.

Fergus, T. A. (2014). Are "not just right experiences" (NJREs) specific to obsessive-compulsive symptoms?: Evidence that NJREs span across symptoms of emotional disorders. *Journal of Clinical Psychology, 70,* 353–363.

Foa, E. B., & Kozak, M. J. (1986). Emotional processing of fear: Exposure to corrective information. *Psychological Bulletin, 99,* 20–35.

Foa, E. B., Yadin, E., & Lichner, T. K. (2012). Exposure and response (ritual) prevention for obsessive-compulsive disorder. Therapist guide, 2nd edtion. *Treatments That Work.* Oxford: Oxford University Press.

Freeston, M. H., Rheume, J., & Ladoucer, R. (1996). Correcting faulty appraisals of obsessive thoughts. *Behaviour Research and Therapy, 34,* 443–446.

Frost, R. O., Novara, C., & Rheaume, J. (2002). Perfectionism in obsessive compulsive disorder. In R. O. Frost & G. Steketee (Eds.), *Cognitive approaches to obsessions and compulsions: Theory, assessment and treatment* (pp. 91–106). Oxford: Elsevier.

Frost, R. O., & Steketee, G. (1997). Perfectionism in obsessive-compulsive disorder patients. *Behaviour Research and Therapy, 35,* 291–296.

Gentes, E. L., & Ruscio, A. M., (2011). A meta-analysis of the relation of intolerance of uncertainty to symptoms of generalized anxiety disorder, major depressive disorder, and obsessive–compulsive disorder. *Clinical Psychology Review, 31,* 923–933

Ghisi, M., Chiri, L. R., Marchetti, I., Sanavio, E., & Sica, C. (2010). In search of specificity: "Not just right experiences" and obsessive-compulsive symptoms in non-clinical and clinical Italian individuals. *Journal of Anxiety Disorders, 24,* 879–886.

Hermans, D., Martens, K., De Cort, K., Pieters, G., & Eelen, P. (2003). Reality monitoring and metacognitive beliefs related to cognitive confidence in obsessive-compulsive disorder. *Behaviour Research and Therapy, 41,* 383–401.

Irak, M., & Tosun, A. (2008). Exploring the role of metacognition in obsessive-compulsive and anxiety symptoms. *Journal of Anxiety Disorders, 22,* 1316–1325.

Maltby, N., & Tolin, D. F. (2005). A brief motivational intervention for treatment-refusing OCD patients. *Cognitive Behavior Therapy, 34,* 176–184.

Marks, I. M., Hodgson, R., & Rachman, S. (1975). Treatment of chronic obsessive-compulsive neurosis by in vivo exposure. *British Journal of Psychiatry, 127,* 349–364.

Matsunaga, H., Kiriike, T., Matsui, T., Oya, K., Iwasaki, Y., Koshimune, K., Miyata, A., & Stein, D. J. (2002). Obsessive-compulsive disorder with poor insight. *Comprehensive Psychiatry, 43,* 150–157.

Merlo, L. J., Storch, E. A., Lehmkuhl, H. D., Jacob, M. L., Murphy, T. K, Goodman, W. K., & Geffken, G. R. (2010). Cognitive behavioral therapy plus motivational interviewing improves outcome for pediatric obsessive-compulsive disorder: A preliminary study. *Cognitive Behaviour Therapy, 39,* 24–27

Meyer, V. (1966). Modification of expectations in cases with obsessional rituals. *Behaviour Research and Therapy, 4,* 273–280.

Moulding, R. (2011). The Obsessive Beliefs Questionnaire (OBQ): Examination in nonclinical samples and development of a short version. *Assessment, 18,* 357–374.

Myers, S. G., Fisher, P. L., & Wells, A. (2008). Belief domains of the Obsessive Beliefs Questionnaire-44 (OBQ-44) and their specific relationship with obsessive-compulsive symptoms. *Journal of Anxiety Disorders, 22,* 475–484.

Myers, S. G., Fisher, P. L., & Wells, A. (2009). An empirical test of the metacognitive model of obsessive-compulsive symptoms: Fusion beliefs, beliefs about rituals, and stop signals. *Journal of Anxiety Disorders, 23,* 436–442.

Myers, S. G., & Wells, A. (2005). Obsessive-compulsive symptoms: The contribution of meta-cognitions and responsibility. *Journal of Anxiety Disorders, 19*, 806–817.

Nedeljkovic, M., & Kyrios, M (2007). Confidence in memory and other cognitive processes in obsessive-compulsive disorder. *Behaviour Research and Therapy, 45*, 2899–2914.

Neziroglu, F., McKay, D., Yaryura-Tobias, J. A., Stevens, K. P., & Todaro, J. (1999). The overvalued ideas scale: Development, reliability and validity in obsessive-compulsive disorder. *Behaviour Research and Therapy, 37*, 881–902.

Neziroglu, F., Stevens, K. P, McKay, D., & Yaryura-Tobias, J. A. (2000). Predictive validity of the overvalued ideas scale: Outcome in obsessive-compulsive and body of dysmorphic disorders. *Behaviour Research and Therapy, 39*, 745–756.

Obsessive Compulsive Cognitions Working Group. (1997). Cognitive assessment of obsessive-compulsive disorder. *Behaviour Research and Therapy, 35*, 667–681.

Obsessive Compulsive Cognition Working Group. (2001). Development and initial validation of the Obsessive Beliefs Questionnaire and the Interpretation of Intrusions Inventory. *Behaviour Research and Therapy, 39*, 987–1006.

Obsessive Compulsive Cognitions Working Group (2003). Psychometric validation of the Obsessive Beliefs Questionnaire and the Interpretation of Intrusions Inventory. *Part I. Behaviour Research and Therapy, 41*, 863–878.

Obsessive Compulsive Cognition Working Group (2005). Psychometric validation of the Obsessive Beliefs Questionnaire and the Interpretation of Intrusions Inventory. Part II: factor analyses and testing of a brief version. *Behaviour Research and Therapy, 43*, 1527–1542.

Öst, L-G. (2008). Cognitive behavior therapy for anxiety disorders: 40 years of progress. *Nordic Journal of Psychiatry, 62*(Suppl. 47), 5–10.

Purdon, C., & Clark, D. A. (1994). Obsessive intrusive thoughts in nonclinical subjects. Part II. Cognitive appraisal, emotional response and thought control strategies. *Behaviour Research and Therapy, 32*, 403–410.

Rachman, S. J. (1997). A cognitive theory of obsessions. *Behaviour Research and Therapy, 35*, 793–802.

Rachman, S. J. (1998). A cognitive theory of obsessions: Elaborations. *Behaviour Research and Therapy, 36*, 385–401.

Rachman, S. J. (2003). *The treatment of obsessions.* New York: Oxford University Press.

Rachman, S. J., & de Silva, P. (1978). Abnormal and normal obsessions. *Behaviour Research and Therapy, 16*, 233–238.

Rachman, S., Hodgson, R., & Marks, I. (1971). The treatment of obsessive-compulsive neurosis. *Behaviour Research and Therapy, 9*, 237–247.

Radomsky, A. S., Shafran, R., Coughtrey, A. E., & Rachman, S. (2010). Cognitive-behavior therapy for compulsive checking in OCD. *Cognitive and Behavioral Practice, 17*, 119–131

Rasmussen, S. A., & Eisen, J. L. (1988). Clinical and epidemiological findings of significance to neuropharmacologic trials in obsessive-compulsive disorder. *Psychopharmacology Bulletin, 24*, 466–470.

Rassin, E., & Koster, E. (2003). The correlation between thought–action fusion and religiosity in a normal sample. *Behaviour Research and Therapy, 41*(3), 361–368.

Rassin, E., Merckelbach, H., Muris, P., & Schmidt, H. (2001). The Thought–Action Fusion Scale: Further evidence for its reliability and validity. *Behaviour Research and Therapy, 39*, 537–544.

Rassin, E., & Muris, P. (2007). Abnormal and normal obsessions: A reconsideration. *Behaviour Research and Therapy, 45*, 1065–1070.

Ravid, A., Franklin, M. E., Khanna, M., Storch, E. A., & Coles, M. E. (2014). "Not just right experiences" in adolescents: Phenomenology and associated characteristics. *Child Psychiatry and Human Development, 45*, 193–200.

Rees, C. S., & Anderson, R. A. (2013). A review of metacognition in psychological models of obsessive-compulsive disorder. *Clinical Psychologist, 17*, 1–8.

Salkovskis, P. M. (1985). Obsessional-compulsive problems: a cognitive-behavioural analysis. *Behaviour Research and Therapy*, *23*, 571–583.

Salkovskis, P. M. (1999). Understanding and treating obsessive-compulsive disorder. *Behaviour Research and Therapy*, *37*, 29–52.

Salkovskis, P. M. (2007). Psychological treatment of obsessive-compulsive disorder. *Psychiatry*, *6*, 229–233.

Salkovskis, P. M., & Kirk, J. (1989). Obsessional disorders. In I. K. Hawton, P. M. Salkovskis, J. Kirk, & D. M. Clark (Eds.), *Cognitive-behavioural treatment for psychiatric disorders: A practical guide* (pp. 129–168). Oxford: Oxford University Press.

Salkovskis, P. M., Richards, C., & Forrester, G. (1995). The relationship between obsessional problems and intrusive thoughts. *Behavioural and Cognitive Psychotherapy*, *23*, 281–299.

Salkovskis, P. M., Wroe, A. L., Gledhill, N., Morrison, N., Forrester, E., Richards, M., Reynolds, M., & Thorpe, S. (2000). Responsibility attitudes and interpretations are characteristic of obsessive compulsive disorder. *Behaviour Research and Therapy*, *38*, 347–372.

Sassaroli, S., Lauro, L. J., Ruggiero, G. M., Mauri, M. C., Vinai, P., & Frost, R. (2008). Perfectionism in depression, obsessive-compulsive disorder and eating disorders. *Behaviour Research and Therapy*, *46*, 757–765.

Selvi, Y, Atli, A., Besiroglu, L., Aydin, A., & Gulec, M. (2011). The impact of obsessive beliefs on pharmacological treatment response in patients with obsessive-compulsive disorder. *International Journal of Psychiatry in Clinical Practice*, *15*, 209–213.

Shafran, R., & Rachman, S. (2004). Thought–action fusion: A review. *Journal of Behavior Therapy and Experimental Psychiatry*, *35*, 87–107.

Shafran, R., Radomsky, A. S., Coughtrey, A. E., & Rachman, S. (2013). Advances in the cognitive behavioural treatment of obsessive compulsive disorder. *Cognitive Behaviour Therapy*, *42*, 265–274.

Shafran, R., Thordarson, D.S., & Rachman, S. (1996). Thought–action fusion in obsessive–compulsive disorder. *Journal of Anxiety Disorders*, *10*, 379–391.

Sica, C., Caudek, C., Chiri, L. R., Ghisi, M., & Marchetti, I. (2012). "Not just right experiences" predict obsessive-compulsive symptoms in non-clinical Italian individuals: A one-year longitudinal study. *Journal of Obsessive-Compulsive and Related Disorders*, *1*, 159–167.

Sica, C., Caudek, C., Bottesi, G., De Fazio, E., Ghisi, M., Marchetti, I. & Orsucci, A. (2013). Fathers' "not just right experiences" predict obsessive-compulsive symptoms in their sons: Family study of a non-clinical Italian sample. *Journal of Obsessive-Compulsive and Related Disorders*, *2*, 263–272.

Siev, J., Chambless, D. L., & Huppert, J. D. (2010). Moral thought–action fusion and OCD symptoms: The moderating role of religious affiliation. *Journal of Anxiety Disorders*, *24*, 309–312.

Siev, J., & Cohen, A. B. (2007). Is thought–action fusion related to religiosity? Differences between Christians and Jews. *Behaviour Research and Therapy*, *45*(4), 829–837.

Simpson, H. B., & Zuckoff, A. (2011). Using motivational interviewing to enhance treatment outcome in people with obsessive-compulsive disorder. *Cognitive and Behavioral Practice*, *18*, 28–37

Solem, S., Håland, Å. T., Vogel, P. A., Hansen, B., & Wells, A. (2009). Change in metacognitions predicts outcome in obsessive–compulsive disorder patients undergoing treatment with exposure and response prevention. *Behaviour Research and Therapy*, *47*, 301–307.

Solem, S., Myers, S. G., Fisher, P. L., Vogel, P. A., & Wells, A. (2010). An empirical test of the metacognitive model of obsessive-compulsive symptoms: Replication and extension. *Journal of Anxiety Disorders*, *24*, 79–86.

Sookman, D., & Pinard, G. (2002). Overestimation of threat and intolerance of uncertainty in obsessive-compulsive disorder. In R. O. Frost & G. Steketee (Eds.), *Cognitive approaches to obsessions and compulsions: Theory, assessment and treatment* (pp. 63–89). Oxford: Elsevier.

Steketee, G. S., Chambless, D. L., Tran, G. Q., Worden, H., & Gillis, M. M. (1996). Behavioral avoidance test for obsessive compulsive disorder. *Behaviour Research and Therapy, 34,* 73–83.

Storch, E. A., De Nadaia, A. S., Jacob, M. L., Lewin, A. B., Muroff, J., Eisen, J., ... Murphy, T. K. (2014). Phenomenology and correlates of insight in pediatric obsessive-compulsive disorder. *Comprehensive Psychiatry, 55,* 613–620.

Summerfeldt, L. J. (2004). Understanding and treating incompleteness in obsessive-compulsive disorder. *Journal of Clinical Psychology, 60,* 1155–1168.

Taylor, S., Abramowitz, J. S., McKay, D., Calamari, J. E., Sookman, D., Kyrios, M., Wilhelm, S., & Carmin, C. (2006). Do dysfunctional beliefs play a role in all types of obsessive-compulsive disorder? *Journal of Anxiety Disorders, 20,* 85–97.

Taylor, S., Kyrios, M., Thordarson, D. S., Steketee, G., & Frost, R. O. (2002). Development and validation of instruments for measuring intrusions and beliefs in obsessive compulsive disorder. In R. O. Frost & G. Steketee (Eds.), *Cognitive approaches to obsessions and compulsions: Theory, assessment and treatment* (pp. 117–138). Oxford: Elsevier.

Tolin, D. F., Abramowitz, J. S., Brigidi, B. D., Amir, N., Street, G. P., & Foa, E. B. (2001). Memory and memory confidence in obsessive-compulsive disorder. *Behavior Research and Therapy, 39,* 913–927.

Timpano, K. R., Abramowitz, J. S., Mahaffey, B. L., Mitchell, M. A., & Schmidt, N. B. (2011). Efficacy of a prevention program for postpartum obsessive-compulsive symptoms. *Journal of Psychiatric Research, 45,* 1511–1517.

Vogel, P. A., Stiles, T. C., & Götestam, K. G. (2004). Adding cognitive therapy elements to exposure therapy for obsessive compulsive disorder: a controlled study. *Behavioural and Cognitive Psychotherapy, 32,* 275–290.

Wells, A. (2009). *Metacognitive therapy for anxiety and depression.* New York: Guilford Press.

Wells, A., & Cartwright-Hatton, S. (2004). A short form of the metacognitions questionnaire: Properties of the MCQ-30. *Behaviour Research and Therapy, 42,* 385–396.

Wells, A., Gwilliam, P. D. H., & Cartwright-Hatton, S. (2001). The thought fusion instrument. Unpublished scale, University of Manchester, Manchester.

Wells, A., & McNicol, K. (2004). *The beliefs about rituals inventory.* Unpublished self-report scale. University of Manchester, Manchester.

Whittal, M. L., Thordarson, D. S., & McLean, P. D. (2005). Treatment of obsessive-compulsive disorder: Cognitive behavior therapy vs. exposure and response prevention. *Behaviour Research and Therapy, 43,* 1559–1576.

Wilhelm, S., & Steketee, G. (2006). *Cognitive therapy for obsessive-compulsive disorder: A guide for professionals.* Oakland, CA: New Harbinger.

9

A Critical Review of Neuropsychological Functioning and Heterogeneity in Individuals with Obsessive-Compulsive Disorder

Michael J. Larson and Ann Clawson

Research on neuropsychological functioning in individuals with obsessive-compulsive disorder (OCD) has markedly increased in the last decade. Fueled by the idea of a heritable marker for the disorder, many studies are focused on broad neuropsychological deficits and cognitive functioning in first-degree relatives (Mataix-Cols et al., 2013; Rajender et al., 2011; Riesel, Endrass, Kaufmann, & Kathmann, 2011). The increase in focus on neuropsychological functioning in individuals with OCD, however, has revealed a complex and multifaceted picture that is belied by contradictory studies and null findings (Abramovitch, Abramowitz, & Mittelman, 2013). When looked at as a whole, an emerging theme from this literature is that frontostriatal mediated executive functioning abilities are impaired, but broader neuropsychological functioning is nuanced by specific individual differences and symptom profiles. Thus, we summarize the primary areas of neuropsychological dysfunction, outline the somewhat contradictory findings in domains such as memory and attention, and provide possible reasons for heterogeneity in research findings and symptom presentation across individuals and OCD subtypes. We focus primarily on the neuropsychological domains of executive functioning, memory, visuospatial skills, and attention/processing speed as these are the domains most commonly examined in the research literature. We then provide a critical analysis of the literature and provide suggestions for future research to advance our knowledge of OCD-related neuropsychological functioning.

Executive Functioning

There is a consistently replicated pattern of deficits in frontostriatal executive functioning abilities in individuals with OCD (e.g., Abramovitch et al., 2013; Gambini, Abbruzzese, & Scarone, 1993; Greisberg & McKay, 2003; Krishna et al., 2011; Maia,

The Wiley Handbook of Obsessive Compulsive Disorders, Volume I, First Edition.
Edited by Jonathan S. Abramowitz, Dean McKay, and Eric A. Storch.
© 2017 John Wiley & Sons Ltd. Published 2017 by John Wiley & Sons Ltd.

Cooney, & Peterson, 2008; Mataix-Cols, Jungque, & Sanchez-Turet, 1999; Veale, Sahakian, Owen, & Marks, 1996). The pattern of deficits in executive skills is demonstrated in multiple studies using a variety of executive-functioning tasks that show impairments in the ability to shift set, organize, plan, and quickly solve problems (Abramovitch et al., 2013). Symptoms of OCD such as impulse control and repetitive behaviors may be tied to abnormal executive and cognitive control functions, a broad category of higher-level processes necessary for behavioral regulation, internal and external monitoring, and goal-directed behavior (Botvinick, Carter, Braver, Barch, & Cohen, 2001). Specifically, executive functions such as set-shifting, inhibition, and planning may underlie the obsessive thoughts and compulsive behaviors associated with OCD, as deficits in these areas may result in an inability to appropriately monitor and adapt thoughts and behavioral responses (Chamberlain, Blackwell, Fineberg, Robbins, & Sahakian, 2005; Maia et al., 2008; Menzies et al., 2007).

Substantial research has been devoted to understanding the nature of executive functioning deficits in OCD in an attempt to link neurological abnormalities to characteristic OCD symptom behaviors. Indeed, some researchers have suggested that the clinical symptoms of OCD may reflect specific deficits in executive functions (Chamberlain et al., 2005; Maia et al., 2008; Menzies et al., 2007) emerging from neurophysiological abnormalities within the orbitofrontal cortex, anterior cingulate cortex, and caudate nucleus (Aouizerate et al., 2004; Friedlander & Desrocher, 2006; Maia et al., 2008). Nevertheless, the preponderance of research on executive functioning is mixed, indicating that OCD is associated with a diverse and complex cognitive profile. Below we outline the research on specific aspects of executive functions and cognitive control, including set shifting, inhibition, planning, and performance monitoring, in individuals with OCD followed by a brief discussion of the neuroanatomical substrates and sources of heterogeneity in executive functioning in individuals with OCD.

Set-shifting

Studies examining set shifting, the ability to adjust attentional focus based on relevant stimulus information and performance feedback, in individuals with OCD present varied results. In several studies, individuals with OCD performed comparably to controls (Abbruzzese, Ferri, & Scarone, 1995; Moritz et al., 2001a; Moritz et al., 2002). In addition, set-shifting abilities appear to be intact throughout development, as premorbid scores at age 13 did not significantly differentiate those who were diagnosed with OCD at age 32 (Grisham, Anderson, Poulton, Moffitt, & Andrews, 2009). However, other studies of set shifting reveal significantly lower performance in individuals with OCD relative to controls (de Geus, Denys, Sitskoorn, & Westenberg, 2007; Lacerda et al., 2003; Moritz, Fricke, & Hand, 2001b; Spitznagel & Suhr, 2002). Such discrepancies may reflect subtle task differences tied to underlying deficits in response inhibition (Chamberlain et al., 2005) or attention (de Geus et al., 2007). Also, there is great variability in the tasks used to measure set shifting, as some studies have used tasks potentially requiring high levels of activity from orbitofrontal (e.g., the Delayed Alternation Test and Object Alternation Test) or dorsolateral prefrontal cortex (e.g., Wisconsin Card Sorting Task) brain regions. Accordingly, group differences between those with OCD and controls may also indicate important functional neurological differences associated with the degree of neural involvement from prefrontal brain regions (Kuelz, Hohagen, & Voderholzer, 2004). Taken together, although an inability to shift set may be tied to the observed cognitive and behavioral rigidity of OCD, findings to date are mixed and further research is necessary to understand those specific processes involved in set-shifting that may be impaired in OCD, along with the neural activation underlying these differences.

Inhibition

Inhibition, the ability to suppress inappropriate thoughts and actions (Albert, López-Martín, & Carretié, 2010), may be reduced in people with OCD, as the compulsive and perseverative behaviors typically associated with OCD could reflect a reduced ability to inhibit intrusive and maladaptive response patterns. This executive dysfunction hypothesis is tied to neuroimaging findings revealing volume and meta-bolic abnormalities within frontostriatal circuits, including the caudate nucleus (Robinson et al., 1995), striatum (Bartha et al., 1998), thalamus (Alptekin et al., 2001; Kim et al., 2001; Lacerda et al., 2003), and the dorsolateral prefrontal cortex in children and adolescents with OCD (Lacerda et al., 2003). Response inhibition deficits are present across a variety of executive functioning tasks, implicating impaired response patterns in both children (Rosenberg et al., 1997) and adults (Aycicegi, Dinn, Harris, & Erkmen, 2003; Bannon, Gonsalvez, Croft, & Boyce, 2002; Kim, Kim, Yoo, & Kwon, 2006; Watkins et al., 2004). Menzies and colleagues (2007) pro-posed that such deficits in motor inhibition may qualify as heritable markers of OCD (i.e., an endophenotypic marker), as they observed impaired response inhibition in both patients and nonaffected relatives tied to patterns of abnormal grey matter density. Of note, however, Bedard, Joyal, Godbout, and Cantal (2009) suggest that most studies to date have not specifically separated the effects of information processing or motor speed from general response inhibition processes, meaning observed differences may not reflect true impairments specific to inhibitory control. A recent meta-analysis showed only a moderate effect size for deficits in response inhi-bition and noted differences in performance were related to the type of task used (e.g., Stroop versus Go/No-Go; Abramovitch et al., 2013). In sum, although symptom presentation and neural activation in OCD implicates deficits in behavioral inhibition, it is unclear to what extent these results reflect motor speed differences or abnormal cognitive functioning.

Planning

Most research indicates that cognitive planning is intact in adults and children with OCD (Bedard et al., 2009; Bohne et al., 2005; Purcell, Maruff, Kyrios, & Pantelis, 1998; Watkins et al., 2004). Cognitive planning involves behavioral control and problem solving abilities (Olley, Malhi, & Sachdev, 2007). Despite similar performance overall among those with and without OCD, there may be important differences in the way cognitive planning tasks are completed by individuals with OCD, as performance may be somewhat reduced due to poor spatial working memory and overall speed of completion (Chamberlain et al., 2005; Kuelz et al., 2004; Olley et al., 2007; Purcell et al., 1998). For example, Huyser, Veitman, Wolters, de Haan, and Boer (2010) observed similar but slower performance on a task designed to measure problem solving and planning (i.e., Tower of London task) in children with OCD relative to non-OCD controls. Importantly, these children with OCD displayed abnormal neural activation and slowed responses before, but not after, cognitive behavioral therapy. Thus, although overall performance may be comparable to non-psychiatric controls in those with OCD, underlying performance mechanisms may be abnormally activated during tasks that involve cognitive planning.

Performance Monitoring

Promising research reveals marked hyperactivity in performance-monitoring functions in individuals with OCD. Performance monitoring refers to the ability to monitor and regulate performance according to environmental demands or internal goals. Electroencephalogram and fMRI studies reveal that these performance monitoring processes are particularly enhanced in individuals with OCD during error trials, possibly revealing overactive cognitive control processes within the anterior cingulate cortex (ACC) (Carrasco et al., 2013; Endrass, Klawohn, Schuster, & Kathmann, 2008; Endrass et al., 2010; Gehring, Himle, & Nisenson, 2000; Hajcak, Franklin, Foa, & Simons, 2008; Maltby, Tolin, Worhunsky, O'Keefe, & Kiehl, 2005; Ruchsow et al., 2005; Ursu, Stenger, Shear, Jones, & Carter, 2003). This enhanced error-related neural activity is present in both children and adults (Hajcak et al., 2008), is manifest before and after treatment (Hajcak et al., 2008), and may also be present in non-affected relatives (Carrasco et al., 2013; Riesel et al., 2011), potentially qualifying as a heritable neural marker of OCD (Olvet & Hajcak, 2008; Riesel et al., 2011). In addition, in an event-related fMRI study, Maltby and colleagues (2005) observed greater ACC activation following error trials in individuals with OCD, but also observed frontal-striatal activation during high conflict correct trials requiring response inhibition. This hyperactive performance monitoring during correct trials may be tied to an inability to inhibit responding evident in the compulsive behaviors of OCD (Maltby et al., 2005). In sum, overactive performance monitoring in OCD during error and correct trials may be associated with a persistent drive to change or improve behavior, leading to subsequent compulsive behaviors (Ursu et al., 2003). Increased performance monitoring activity in individuals with OCD is a promising avenue for future research relating executive and cognitive control abilities to treatment compliance and outcomes.

Anatomical Abnormalities

Recent developments in neuroimaging technology have allowed researchers to associate executive and cognitive control processes with irregular structural and functional neural patterns in OCD. These abnormal neural activation patterns are correlated with symptom severity (Christian et al., 2008; Lacerda et al., 2003; Nakao et al., 2009) and differ based on symptom clusters within OCD (Aouizerate et al., 2004; Gilbert et al., 2009; Nakao et al., 2009). For example, Nakao and colleagues (2009) observed decreased neural activity in patients with obsessions/checking rituals relative to those with cleanliness/washing rituals, possibly indicating important neural deficits unique to this OCD symptom subtype. In addition, children may display unique activation patterns within the same neural regions, suggesting potential neurodevelopmental differences (Gilbert et al., 2009).

Common abnormalities appear in regions of the ACC and prefrontal cortex activated during error and conflict processing or reward and emotional regulation

(Aouizerate et al., 2004), consistent with the abovementioned executive and cognitive control abnormalities. Many electrophysiological (Endrass et al., 2008; Gehring et al., 2000; Hajcak et al., 2008; Ruchsow et al., 2007; Xiao et al., 2011) and neuroimaging (Ursu et al., 2003) studies confirm hyperactivation within the ACC, a brain region involved in self-regulation as well as conflict and emotional processing (Carter & van Veen, 2007; Posner, Rothbart, Sheese, & Tang, 2007; van Veen & Carter, 2002). Similar overactivation within the orbitofrontal cortex (Alptekin et al., 2001; Kwon et al., 2003; Ursu & Carter, 2009), involved in integrating emotional information from surrounding neural regions, may be associated with uncontrolled situational appraisal and inappropriate evaluation or suppression of behavior based on changing environmental rewards (Aouizerate et al., 2004; Krawczyk, 2002). Abnormal activation has also been documented within the dorsolateral prefrontal cortex (Nakao et al., 2009), associated with working memory and reasoning among response options for appropriate decision making (Krawczyk, 2002). These functional abnormalities likely reflect grey and white matter volume differences within these prefrontal regions (Christian et al., 2008; Togao et al., 2010) and hyperactivity of connections specifically within regions of the medial frontal cortex (Fitzgerald et al., 2010).

In light of these findings, several researchers have suggested that the executive deficits of OCD reflect interrupted neural circuitry involving frontostriatal–thalmacocortical networks. According to this model, impairments in the striatum (Whiteside, Port, & Abramowitz, 2004) and thalamus (Kim et al., 2001; Lacerda et al., 2003) may act in tandem with prefrontal cortex regions, leading to a reduced ability to relay information necessary for inhibitory and impulse control (Del Casale et al., 2011a; Friedlander & Desrocher, 2006). Indeed, one review paper proposes a causal role for the basal ganglia-thalamic loops, OFC, and ACC in the pathogenesis of OCD (Maia et al., 2008). Future research is necessary to determine whether these abnormal activation patterns are a consequence of OCD or a contributory mechanism leading to the symptoms of OCD (Aouizerate et al., 2004). Specifically, longitudinal studies examining the developmental trajectory of OCD may elucidate important cognitive changes as they occur throughout the course of the disorder.

Together, research findings to date on executive functioning abilities in OCD offer a diverse and inconsistent picture. Performance monitoring processes generally appear to be heightened in OCD, suggesting overactive error and conflict monitoring. Planning appears to be intact in OCD, though groups may differ in response strategies as evidenced by unique patterns of neural activation. Thus, greater methodological specificity is required in order to understand the specific cognitive processes and related neural networks that are impaired in OCD. For example, variability in research findings on measures of set shifting may be due in part to task differences involving orbitofrontal neural regions compared to tasks involving more dorsolateral prefrontal neural regions. Likewise, although measures of inhibition are less discrepant and point to reduced inhibitory control in OCD, current findings may reflect motor speed differences rather than differences in cognitive processes. Thus, although neuroimaging evidence points to specific neural abnormalities and impairments in basal ganglia-thalamic—cortical loops, variability in measures of executive functioning suggest a need for future research integrating neural and neuropsychological measures.

Memory

Neuropsychological performance of individuals with OCD is less clear in the research literature for cognitive domains outside of executive functions. Memory abilities are a frequent topic of research in individuals with OCD due to suggestions that OCD-related doubts or feelings of incompleteness associated with ritual behaviors are symptoms of poor memory. Termed the "forgetfulness hypothesis" or "memory deficit theory" by some researchers (e.g., Cuttler & Graf, 2009; Moritz, Ruhe, Jelinek, & Naber, 2009), the idea of memory impairment in OCD can be broken down into four potential main areas: (1) generalized memory deficits; (2) memory deficits for nonverbal, but not verbal material; (3) memory dysfunction that is secondary to executive dysfunction; and (4) meta-memory (remembering to remember) dysfunction (Moritz et al., 2009). These categories are not mutually exclusive, but represent the largest areas of research on memory functions reviewed in the OCD literature to date.

Generalized Memory

The empirical evidence for generalized memory impairment in individuals with OCD is weak. Several studies report no memory difficulties in individuals with OCD relative to controls (Moritz et al., 2009), show that any memory difficulties that are present can be accounted for by depression symptoms (Moritz, Kloss, Jahn, Schick, & Hand, 2003), or indicate that memory impairments that are present are not global, but occur in specific domains such as nonverbal memory or meta-memory (see Kuelz et al., 2004; Olley et al., 2007). Indeed, the preponderance of studies on memory functioning in individuals with OCD either do not suggest worse memory than that for other anxiety disorders or memory deficits that are secondary to other neuropsychological processes (Olley et al., 2007). Furthermore, studies indicate that even individuals with primarily checking OCD accurately remember whether or not an event has occurred (e.g., they are aware the door is locked); however, these individuals still check in an effort to relieve anxiety, rather than because they do not recall whether or not a task is completed (Tuna, Tekcan, & Topcuoglu, 2005). Indeed, a recent comprehensive review indicated that memory performance in individuals with primary checking symptoms do not differ from those with other subtypes of OCD (Cuttler & Graf, 2009). Thus, the preponderance of findings indicates that there is not generalized memory impairment in individuals with OCD.

Nonverbal Memory

There is a much stronger evidence base for OCD-related deficits specifically in nonverbal, but not verbal memory. Indeed, deficits in nonverbal memory are among the most consistently reported neuropsychological deficits associated with OCD (Anderson & Savage, 2004; Jang et al., 2010; Kuelz et al., 2004; Martinez-Gonzalez & Pigueras-Rodriguez, 2008). Early studies of nonverbal memory report preserved verbal memory abilities in the presence of impaired nonverbal memory skills (e.g., Boone, Ananth, Philpott, & Kaur, 1991; Zielinski, Taylor, & Juzwin, 1991). Subsequent replication of these findings, however, has come with several caveats. For example, Christensen, Kim, Dysken, & Hoover (1996) and Moritz et al. (2009)

indicate nonverbal memory difficulties are potentially the result of processing speed slowing. Moritz and colleagues (2003; Moritz et al., 2009) found nonverbal memory impairments only in individuals with OCD and comorbid depression, not those with only OCD, although Rampacher and colleagues (2010) show visual memory deficits in OCD beyond what is present in unipolar depression. Purcell and colleagues (1998) reported that nonverbal memory difficulties were present beyond what is seen in other psychiatric disorders, but were selective to tasks where recognition of spatial locations was required, rather than a generalized impairment. More recent work supports the idea of deficits in memory for spatial location in OCD, but does not show a relationship with dopaminergic mechanisms thought to be involved in OCD-related deficits (Morein-Zamir et al., 2010). In contrast, however, several studies report no differences between individuals with OCD and controls on measures of nonverbal memory (e.g., Berthier, Kulisevsky, Gironell, & Heras, 1996; Krishna et al., 2011; Moritz et al., 2009). When looked at meta-analytically, however, there is a large effect size for nonverbal memory impairments in those diagnosed with OCD relative to controls (Abramovitch et al., 2013). Memory for verbal information is better than for nonverbal memory in those with OCD, with only minor impairments and considerable heterogeneity between studies as to whether or not verbal memory deficits are present (Abramovitch et al., 2013). Thus, whereas nonverbal memory deficits are present, it appears there are additional contributing factors beyond nonverbal memory related to the presentation of deficits in OCD, including processing speed and the presence or absence of depression. Another area that appears to largely contribute to nonverbal memory difficulties in OCD is poor executive functioning.

Executive Function in Memory

Kuelz and colleagues (2004), in a thorough review of fifty studies reporting OCD-related neuropsychological data, indicated that research findings of poor verbal and nonverbal memory may be due to poor strategies for organizing and encoding material. This evidence of poor encoding in OCD may reflect a decreased ability to identify or regulate available information for storage, which is likely reflected in an overall reduced ability to identify and utilize relevant information to reduce obsessive thoughts or compulsive behaviors. For example, on the California Verbal Learning Test, a test of long-term memory with a list of items that can be semantically encoded, individuals with OCD showed decreased ability to integrate and utilize semantic information relative to controls (Cabrera, McNally, & Savage, 2001; Deckersbach, Otto, Savage, Baer, & Jenike, 2000; Deckersbach et al., 2005). Similarly, Savage and colleagues (1999, 2000) and others (Penedes, Catalan, Andres, Salamero, & Gasto, 2005) administered tests of verbal and nonverbal memory that required organization strategies for good performance and found individuals with OCD were impaired relative to controls and that memory impairments were generally the result of poor organizational strategies. In addition, children with OCD showed some organizational difficulties when copying complex nonverbal stimuli, although the differences between children with OCD and controls did not reach statistical significance (Shin et al., 2008).

Much of the research on nonverbal memory in individuals with OCD has utilized the Rey-Osterrieth Complex Figure (ROCF) (Kuelz et al., 2004; Olley et al., 2007; Rey, 1941). This task requires individuals to organize and copy a complex image, then draw that image from memory after a delay period. It is generally well accepted that individuals who are better at organizing their initial drawing show better retrieval skills after the delay and have better executive abilities than those with poor organizational strategies (Strauss, Sherman, & Spreen, 2006). Multiple studies show decreased nonverbal memory on the ROCF in individuals with OCD relative to controls (see Kuelz et al., 2004, for review). Researchers, however, suggest that the deficits present on ROCF performance can be attributed to poor ability to organize the material, leading to subsequent deficits in recall (e.g., Deckersbach et al., 2005; Savage et al., 1999; Shin et al., 2008). Such findings suggest that poor memory performance in individuals with OCD relative to controls could be due to executive difficulties in organizing data for encoding and subsequent retrieval (Deckersbach et al., 2000, 2005; Greisberg & McKay, 2003; Savage et al., 1999).

In contrast, some studies report no differences between individuals with OCD and controls for tasks that require organizational strategies or show no mediation between executive abilities and memory performance (see Moritz et al., 2009). The state of the research, therefore, suggests more specific individual difference and subtype factors may be contributing to the heterogeneity in findings. In this vein, studies suggest poor organizational strategies may be related to specific OCD subtypes such as symmetry/ordering and obsessions/checking (Jang et al., 2010), as the focus of obsessive and compulsive behaviors may reflect an inability to organize specific environmental information to regulate behavior. Shin et al. (2010) tested the hypothesis that organizational strategies would mediate nonverbal memory impairments in both drug-naive and medicated individuals with OCD. Their findings indicated impaired nonverbal memory abilities in both medicated and drug-naïve participants. Notably, however, organizational strategies mediated nonverbal memory impairments only in the medicated participants, thus suggesting a potential role of psychotropic medications in the relationship between nonverbal memory impairments and executive skills in OCD. Andres and colleagues (2007) showed a similar pattern in pediatric OCD, with drug-naive OCD participants showing slightly better organizational performance than those on medication.

When the evidence is examined together, it appears that there is a plausible role for a relationship between OCD-related memory difficulties and executive dysfunction associated with organization strategies for encoding and retrieval. Future studies of OCD subtypes, medication status, comorbidity, and other individual difference factors are needed to further clarify the relationship between organizational strategies and memory abilities in individuals with OCD.

Meta-Memory

The last category of potential memory impairments in people with OCD is in meta-memory, a category of memory referring to an individual's beliefs and perceptions regarding their memory abilities. Meta-memory is part of a broader category of meta-cognitive processes wherein individuals monitor and adjust their own cognitive processing (Exner et al., 2009; Nedeljkovic, Moulding, Kyrios, & Doron, 2009; Tuna et al., 2005). The concept of impaired meta-memory in OCD has received considerable recent attention due to consistent findings of low confidence and doubt in memory abilities and a heightened tendency to focus attention on thought processes and contents (Exner et al., 2009; Olley et al., 2007; Tuna et al., 2005), potentially contributing to the persistent patterns of anxiety seen in OCD. Indeed, low levels of memory confidence are inversely related to OCD-symptom severity (Nedeljkovic et al., 2009;

Tuna et al., 2005), suggesting that hyperactive meta-memory associated with levels of self-consciousness may mediate the relationship between the presence of OCD and more episodic memory deficits in individuals with OCD (Exner et al., 2009).

Meta-memory in individuals with primary checking symptoms is remarkably similar to meta-memory in individuals with other primary OCD symptoms, such as washing (Cuttler & Graf, 2009), suggesting that differential meta-memory performance is not the major difference between those with checking symptoms and other OCD subtypes. When subtypes are pooled, however, there appear to be more OCD-related impairments in meta-memory than in primary memory functions (Cuttler & Graf, 2009). We note, however, results of a study did not show any differences in memory confidence between individuals with OCD and controls (Moritz et al., 2009). The preponderance of findings in this nascent literature, however, suggests meta-memory deficits that may correspond with episodic memory difficulties. Thus, a potentially fruitful avenue of future research in OCD-related memory difficulties is in reducing meta-cognitive thoughts in order to reduce pathological doubt and improve subsequent memory abilities (Exner et al., 2009; Wells, 2007).

In summary, memory processes in individuals with OCD are highly heterogeneous across studies and riddled with caveats, despite theoretical links between memory impairment and the ritualistic behaviors that characterize OCD. There is not consistent replication across studies to clearly identify OCD-related impairments in specific memory processes. Research to date does not support the idea of a global memory deficit in individuals with OCD, but does provide some tenuous evidence for nonverbal memory difficulties. Memory difficulties that are present appear to be influenced by executive dysfunction related to organization of encoding and retrieval strategies, supporting the primary role of executive dysfunction in OCD. Future studies examining symptom subtypes and individual differences in meta-memory abilities are needed.

Visuospatial Abilities

Outside executive functions and memory, visuospatial abilities represent an area that has received considerable attention in individuals with OCD. Much of this interest has stemmed from the possibility of nonverbal memory impairments discussed above. Findings of visuospatial abilities not tied to memory performance suggest broad deficits in complex visuospatial skills (Anderson & Savage, 2004; Kuelz et al., 2004). For example, studies show deficits in integrating visuospatial parts into a whole (Boone et al., 1991), difficulties with left-right discrimination (Hymas, Lees, Bolton, Epps, & Head, 1991), decreased ability in accurately judging angles (Tukel et al., 2012a), poor three-dimensional visuospatial imagery (Abramovitch, Dar, Schweiger, & Hermesh, 2011), and impaired visuoconstruction abilities, including block design and the copy trial of the ROCF (see Anderson & Savage, 2004; Andres et al., 2007; Kuelz et al., 2004; Moritz et al., 2003). In contrast, some studies report intact aspects of visuospatial abilities, such as mental rotation and position discrimination in individuals with OCD (Moritz et al., 2003, 2005).

In one of the more thorough studies conducted on the specificity of visuospatial deficits in OCD, Moritz and colleagues (2005) compared individuals with OCD to healthy and psychiatrically diagnosed control participants on a series of visuospatial tasks. Findings indicated poor visuoconstruction abilities in individuals with OCD, but, importantly, none of the visuospatial measures completed discriminated the individuals with OCD from the psychiatric control group. This absence of discrimination between groups suggests that visuospatial deficits may be due to the presence of psychopathology in general, rather than OCD specifically. In contrast, Purcell et al. (1998) compared individuals with OCD to samples with depression, panic disorder, and psychiatrically healthy controls. Findings showed significant impairments in ability to accurately identify visuospatial locations that may be related to poor visuospatial memory abilities, but could also be the result of poor ability to synthesize and identify visuospatial information, again pointing to underlying deficits in organizing and appropriately utilizing environmental information. Other studies report that, relative to healthy controls, children with OCD showed higher levels of impairment on perceptual-organization tasks that require organization, planning, and rapid completion (Andres et al., 2007; Shin et al., 2008). Similarly, Behar and colleagues (1984) reported that adolescents with OCD have visuospatial organization difficulties similar to individuals with frontal lobe lesions, including poor visuospatial rotation ability and poor ability to learn rules in order to appropriately navigate mazes.

When findings are taken together, it appears that individuals with OCD have some difficulties with complex visuospatial abilities. Indeed, recent work even suggests that poor performance on the visuospatial block design task in children with OCD predicts persistence of OCD symptoms into adulthood (Bloch et al., 2011). It remains unclear, however, whether observed difficulties are specific to OCD and whether the difficulties are primary OCD-related deficits or whether these deficits are secondary to executive dysfunction (Moritz et al., 2005; Savage et al., 1999). Future studies designed to directly tease apart these possibilities with psychiatric comparison groups are clearly needed. From an anatomical perspective, findings of deficits in complex visuospatial skills and executive abilities have led some to suggest dysfunctional right hemisphere and frontostriatal basal ganglia mechanisms in individuals with OCD (Anderson & Savage, 2004; Boone et al., 1991; Del Casale et al., 2011b; Hollander et al., 1990; Lacerda et al., 2003; Savage et al., 1999; Zielinski et al., 1991). Such dysfunctional mechanisms would be consistent with the executive functioning research, although the heterogeneity in findings across studies indicates future research should focus on individual differences and OCD subtypes. In this regard, as noted above, Jang et al. (2010) looked at OCD symptom dimensions and showed poor visuospatial memory performance were related to symmetry/ordering and obsessions/checking dimensions. Future studies similar to that of Jang et al. are needed to replicate and further clarify visuospatial abilities in people with OCD.

Attention and Processing Speed

In the aforementioned comprehensive summary of the OCD and neuropsychology literature up until 2004, Kuelz and colleagues (2004) concluded that there is little evidence for basic attention dysfunction in individuals with OCD. This conclusion was based on many studies showing no differences between individuals with OCD and control participants on a range of tasks, including those designed to test attention span, sustained attention, and selective attention (Kuelz et al., 2004). Research since 2004 does not refute these conclusions. For example, a study in medication-naive participants with OCD and psychiatrically healthy controls showed no differences between groups on measures of attention span and sustained attention (Krishna et al., 2011). Moritz and Wendt (2006) did not show differences in attentional bias to specific versus overall gestalt features on the ROCF.

In contrast, there are studies that show poor attention in OCD, but most of these studies come with caveats. Roth, Milovan, Baribeau, & O'Connor (2005) found worse auditory attention abilities in individuals with late-onset OCD relative to early-onset OCD; however, there were no non-OCD comparison participants. Tukel et al. (2012a) and Abramovitch et al. (2011) reported decreased attention in OCD relative to controls, but the indices used were Stroop and Go-No-Go response times, tasks more related to processing speed and response inhibition than sustained attention (Perlstein, Carter, Barch, & Baird, 1998; Seignourel et al., 2005). Morein-Zamier and colleagues (2010) showed decreased sustained attention in individuals with OCD relative to psychiatrically healthy controls, but the sustained attention task required considerable processing speed demands. Thus, basic attention functions do not appear to be impaired in individuals with OCD.

There are several additional studies that either indicate slow processing speed or are confounded by slowed processing speed in individuals with OCD. Kuelz et al. (2004) report an inconsistent pattern of findings in studies of processing speed prior to 2004, ranging from slowed processing speed in motor and fluency tasks (e.g., Moritz et al., 2002) to no group differences in processing speed abilities (e.g., Aronowitz et al., 1994). It appears, however, that Kuelz et al. (2004) defined processing speed in a rather narrow fashion by equating it to performance on a limited number of motor-processing speed tasks. A broader look at the literature reveals several studies showing longer response times and slowed motor initiation across a variety of tasks (Abramovitch et al., 2011; Burdick, Robinson, Malhotra, & Szeszko, 2008; Christian et al., 2008; Morein-Zamir et al., 2010; Purcell et al., 1998; Rampacher et al., 2010; Soref, Dar, Argov, & Meiran, 2008; Tukel et al., 2012a). Other studies, however, do not support these differences between controls and those with OCD on processing speed measures (Martinez-Gonzalez & Pigueras-Rodriguez, 2008; Ornstein, Arnold, Manassis, Mendlowitz, & Schachar, 2010; Simpson et al., 2006). Our read of the literature on the whole suggests that OCD is generally associated with some slowing of motor and cognitive processing speed, although the mechanisms and reasons for such slowing are unclear. In our opinion, this is a fruitful area for future research and identification of specific areas of deficit and how such difficulties are related to treatment process and outcome.

Heterogeneity in Neuropsychological Findings

Although it is evident that OCD-related deficits in executive functioning exist and are tied to the clinical symptoms and underlying pathophysiology of OCD, there remains substantial heterogeneity with regard to both the consistency of these findings and OCD-related neuropsychological functioning in other domains of cognition such as memory, visuospatial abilities (including memory), and processing speed. Such diversity among current research findings may be explained by methodological discrepancies or may signify the important influence of other factors that must be examined further in the future. We outline some of these potential factors below.

First, many studies examining neuropsychological functioning in OCD include individuals with comorbid disorders such as depression and anxiety, meaning observed deficits may be more reflective of comorbid symptomology than OCD (Bedard et al., 2009; Chamberlain et al., 2005; Kuelz et al., 2004; Moritz et al., 2001a). Admittedly, the majority of children and adults with OCD exhibit comorbid symptoms, which are often associated with greater OCD severity (Miguel et al., 2011; Nestadt et al., 2001; Peris et al., 2010; Ruscio, Stein, Chiu, & Kessler, 2010), suggesting that research excluding comorbid symptoms may be less representative of the affected population. Indeed, the results from several studies suggest that cognitive deficits are nonexistent or significantly decreased in the absence of comorbid anxiety and depressive symptoms, possibly due to differential neural activation unique to each disorder (Aycicegi et al., 2003; Bedard et al., 2009; Beers et al., 1999; Moritz et al., 2001a; see Rao, Arasappa, Reddy, & Venkatasubramanian, 2010, for alternative findings). Thus, whereas it is necessary to consider OCD alone to accurately characterize deficits specific to OCD, it may also be important to consider the interaction between OCD and comorbid disorders (see Moritz et al., 2001a, 2009). In fact, a recent study in youth with OCD showed the presence of comorbid conditions and use of neuroleptic medications were among the strongest predictors of cognitive difficulties in those with OCD (Lewin et al., 2014). Studies specifying comorbid conditions, including studies with psychiatric non-OCD controls, will aid in identifying specific neuropsychological areas of impairment in OCD.

Second, observed differences across tasks putatively assessing a specific neuropsychological domain may indicate subtle differences in a broader range of cognitive abilities. For example, Bedard et al. (2009) hypothesized that lower-order cognitive functions involving basic executive abilities (e.g., inhibition, decision-making, etc.) may be impaired to a greater degree than more complex higher-order executive functions (e.g., planning, judging, etc.), explaining many of the observed differences in executive functioning. Alternatively, as noted by Kuelz et al. (2004), it may also be important to consider the neural circuits implicated in task performance. For example, tasks assessing set-shifting abilities that involve activation of the dorsolateral prefrontal cortex yielded no significant differences between groups (Abbruzzese et al., 1995; Kuelz et al., 2004; Moritz et al., 2001b, 2002). In contrast, group differences are present in set-shifting tasks involving greater recruitment from the orbitofrontal cortex (Abbruzzese et al., 1995; Kuelz et al., 2004; Moritz et al., 2001a; Spitznagel & Suhr, 2002). Thus, important differences may exist within range of neuropsychological domains based on the neural generators engaged by a task.

Third, discrepant findings may also reflect differences based on aggregation according to symptom clusters within OCD. Though diagnosis of OCD using the DSM-V does not include subcategories, several researchers have agreed that the behavioral symptoms of OCD can be grouped into broad symptom dimensions, such as contamination, harming, symmetry/ordering, pure obsessions, and hoarding (Markarian et al., 2010; Mataix-Cols, do Rosário-Campos, & Leckman, 2005). Though it may be limiting to divide OCD according to exclusive symptomatic categories, a dimensional approach based on these clusters may account for symptomatic differences in executive functioning while acknowledging common overlap among several symptom domains (Hashimoto et al., 2011). Indeed, Lawrence and colleagues (2006) observed greater deficits in decision making among hoarders and an inverse relationship between symmetry/ordering symptoms and set shifting. Likewise, others have observed differences in performance relative to controls on tasks as a function of OCD symptom dimension (Hashimoto et al., 2011; Omori et al., 2007), further supporting the presence of unique executive functioning profiles according to symptom-based subtypes within OCD. Recent work is most suggestive of increased cognitive sequelae in those with symmetry/ordering and hoarding-type difficulties (McGuire et al., 2014).

Obsessive-compulsive disorder may differ based on age of onset, implying important differences in the developmental trajectory of this disorder. Beers and colleagues (1999) observed no differences in performance between children with OCD and controls across several cognitive tasks, suggesting that the cognitive deficits may be minimal initially, but gradually worsen with development. Alternatively, early-onset OCD may be a distinct disorder associated with unique deficits (Beers et al., 1999). Cerebral blood flow in brain areas including the ACC, prefrontal cortex, and orbito-frontal cortex may differ based on age of onset (Busatto et al., 2001), implying that executive processes tied to these neural regions may also differ based on onset. Roth and colleagues (2005) confirmed this hypothesis, observing worse executive functioning in those with late-onset relative to early-onset OCD. Despite these findings, the developmental nature of these impairments remains largely unclear. Future research may aid in understanding whether early-onset or late-onset OCD represent distinct categories, or whether they are part of a continuum.

Conclusions and Future Directions

Neuropsychological functioning in individuals with OCD is complex, and the current literature offers a diverse pattern of findings highlighted by deficits in frontostriatal executive functions. Specific areas of executive dysfunction include set-shifting, inhibition, planning/organization, and performance monitoring. These deficits in executive abilities, particularly involved with planning and organizing, likely contribute to both nonverbal and verbal memory difficulties. An increased balance of research appears to support nonverbal- relative to verbal-memory difficulties; however, this remains unclear. Meta-memory functions appear to contribute to these memory problems, although the precise role meta-memory plays in symptomatic low confidence and doubt in memory abilities has yet to be elucidated. Research findings generally support the presence of complex visuospatial skill impairments and slowed processing speed, though basic attention processes are generally intact. It is possible that deficits may underlie OCD-related impairments in other domains, such as executive functions. Together, diverse and often contradictory evidence in the literature to date highlights the need for replication and extension in the future, focused on improved understanding of the concomitant relationship between these neuropsychological deficits.

Most notable, perhaps, in this review of neuropsychological functioning in individuals with OCD is the striking heterogeneity across studies and domains of cognition. The state of the literature is such that key steps are requisite to improve the specificity of findings. Specifically, there remains inadequate control for comorbid conditions. Too few studies utilize clinical comparison groups to ensure that deficits are specific to OCD, rather than general deficits related to psychiatric pathology. For example, one recent study comparing individuals with OCD to individuals with panic disorder found null differences between groups on measures of response inhibition (Thomas, Gonsalvez, & Johnstone, 2014), a surprising finding that suggests response inhibition problems may not be specific to OCD. Advances in neuroimaging provide the tools for improved investigation of the neural mechanisms underlying OCD-related impairments; however, there is a need for increased collaboration across disciplines, including neuroanatomy, genetics, and psychology to better understand the anatomical bases of these difficulties. For example, Tukel and colleagues (2012b) recently reported that individuals who carried the Met allele of the brain-derived neurotrophic factor (BDNF) gene Val66Met polymorphism had significantly worse performance on measures of executive functioning, memory, and processing speed relative to noncarriers and control carriers. Indeed, a large-scale review implicates specific genes in the serotonin, glutamate, and dopamine systems, as well as interactions between genes, in the expression of OCD (Pauls, Abramovitch, Rauch, & Geller, 2014). Such specificity is needed in the study of OCD-related neuropsychological functioning. In addition, investigations into the neuropsychological functions associated with OCD may be enhanced if specific dimensional clusters of symptoms, including the developmental course of OCD-related deficits, are included. The separation of hoarding into a separate disorder in DSM-V may help in this domain; however, treating OCD as a homogeneous construct is clearly restricting our ability to find specific neurocognitive effects (Abramovitch et al., 2013). These important methodological changes may provide needed clarity to elucidate the relationship between cognitive difficulties and the symptoms that characterize OCD.

References

Abbruzzese, M., Ferri, S., & Scarone, S. (1995). Wisconsin Card Sorting Test performance in obsessive-compulsive disorder: No evidence for involvement of dorsolateral prefrontal cortex. *Psychiatry Research, 58*, 37–43.

Abramovitch, A., Abramowitz, J. S., & Mittelman, A. (2013). The neuropsychology of adult obsessive-compulsive disorder: A meta-analysis. *Clinical Psychology Review, 33*, 1163–1171.

Abramovitch, A., Dar, R., Schweiger, A., & Hermesh, H. (2011). Neuropsychological impairments and their association with obsessive-compulsive symptom severity in obsessive-compulsive disorder. *Archives of Clinical Neuropsychology, 26*, 364–376.

Albert, J., López-Martín, S., & Carretié, L. (2010). Emotional context modulates inhibition: Neural and behavioral data. *Neuroimage, 49*, 914–921.

Alptekin, K., Degirmenci, B., Kivircik, B., Durak, H., Yemez, B., Derebek, E., & Tunca, Z. (2001). Tc-99 m HMPAO brain perfusion SPECT in drug-free obsessive-compulsive patients without depression. *Psychiatry Research, 107*, 51–56.

Anderson, K. E., & Savage, C. (2004). Cognitive and neurobiological findings in obsessive-compulsive disorder. *Psychiatric Clinics of North America, 27*, 37–47.

Andres, S., Boget, T., Lazaro, L., Penades, R., Morer, A., Salamero, M., & Castro-Fornieles, J. (2007). Neuropsychological performance in children and adolescents with obsessive-compulsive disorder and influence of clinical variables. *Biological Psychiatry, 61*, 946–951.

Aouizerate, B., Guehl, D., Cuny, E., Rougier, A., Bioulac, B., Tignol, J., & Burbaud, P. (2004). Pathophysiology of obsessive-compulsive disorder: A necessary link between neuropsychology, imagery, and physiology *Progress in Neurobiology, 72*, 195–221.

Aronowitz, B. R., Hollander, E., DeCaria, C., Cohen, L., Saoud, J. B., & Stein, D. (1994). Neuropsychology of obsessive-compulsive disorder: Preliminary findings. *Neuropsychiatry, Neuropsychology, & Behavioral Neurology, 14*, 241–245.

Aycicegi, A., Dinn, W. M., Harris, C. L., & Erkmen, H. (2003). Neuropsychological function in obsessive-compulsive disorder: Effects of comorbid conditions on task performance. *European Psychiatry, 18*, 241–248.

Bannon, S., Gonsalvez, C. J., Croft, R. J., & Boyce, P. M. (2002). Response inhibition deficits in obsessive-compulsive disorder. *Psychiatry Research, 110*, 165–174.

Bartha, R., Stein, M. B., Williamson, P. C., Drost, D. J., Neufeld, R. W. J., Carr, T. J., … Siddiqui, A. R. (1998). A short echo 1H spectroscopy and volumetric MRI study of the corpus striatum in patients with obsessive-compulsive disorder and comparison subjects. *American Journal of Psychiatry, 155*, 1584–1591.

Bedard, M. J., Joyal, C. C., Godbout, L., & Cantal, S. (2009). Executive functions and the obsessive-compulsive disorder: On the importance of subclinical symptoms and other concomitant factors. *Archives of General Neuropsychology, 24*, 585–598.

Beers, S. R., Rosenberg, D. R., Dick, E. L., Williams, T., O'Hearn, K. M., Birmaher, B., & Ryan, C. M. (1999). Neuropsychological study of frontal lobe function in psychotropic-naive children with obsessive-compulsive disorder. *American Journal of Psychiatry, 156*, 777–779.

Behar, D., Rapoport, J. L., Berg, C. J., Denekla, M. B., Mann, L., Cox, C., … Wolfman, M. G. (1984). Computerized tomography and neuropsychological test measures in adolescents with obsessive-compulsive disorder. *American Journal of Psychiatry, 141*, 363–369.

Berthier, M. L., Kulisevsky, J., Gironell, A., & Heras, J. A. (1996). Obsessive-compulsive disorder associated with brain lesions: clinical phenomenology, cognitive function, and anatomic correlates. *Neurology, 47*, 353–361.

Bloch, M. H., Sukhodolsky, D. G., Dombrowski, P. A., Panza, K. E., Craiglow, B. G., Landeros-Weisenberger, A., … Schultz, R. T. (2011). Poor fine-motor and visuospatial skills predict persistence of pediatric-onset obsessive-compulsive disorder into adulthood. *Journal of Child Psychology and Psychiatry, 52*, 974–983.

Bohne, A., Savage, C. R., Deckersbach, T., Keuthen, N. J., Jenike, M. A., Tuschen-Caffier, B., & Wilhelm, S. (2005). Visuospatial abilities, memory, and executive functioning in trichotillomania and obsessive–compulsive disorder. *Journal of Clinical and Experimental Neuropsychology, 27*, 385–399.

Boone, K. B., Ananth, J., Philpott, L., & Kaur, A. (1991). Neuropsychological characteristics of nondepressed adults with obsessive-compulsive disorder. *Neuropsychiatry, Neuropsychology, & Behavioral Neurology, 4*, 96–109.

Botvinick, M., Carter, C. S., Braver, T. S., Barch, D. M., & Cohen, J. D. (2001). Conflict monitoring and cognitive control. *Psychological Review, 108*, 624–652.

Burdick, K. E., Robinson, D. G., Malhotra, A. K., & Szeszko, P. R. (2008). Neurocognitive profile analysis in obsessive-compulsive disorder. *Journal of the International Neuropsychological Society, 14*, 640–645.

Busatto, G. F., Buchpiguel, C. A., Zamignani, D. R., Garrido, G. E. J., Glabus, M. F., Rosario-Campos, M. C., … Miguel, E. C. (2001). Regional cerebral blood flow abnormalities in early-onset obsessive-compulsive disorder: An exploratory SPECT study. *Journal of the American Academy of Child and Adolescent Psychiatry, 40*, 347–354.

Cabrera, A. R., McNally, R. J., & Savage, C. (2001). Missing the forest for the trees? Deficient memory for linguistic gist in obsessive-compulsive disorder. *Psychological Medicine, 31*, 1089–1094.

Carrasco, M., Harbin, S. M., Nienhuis, J. K., Fitzgerald, K. D., Gehring, W. J., & Hanna, G. L. (2013). Increased error-related brain activity in youth with obsessive-compulsive disorder and unaffected siblings. *Depression and Anxiety, 30*, 39–46.

Carter, C. S., & van Veen, V. (2007). Anterior cingulate cortex and conflict detection: An update of theory and data. *Cognitive Affective and Behavioral Neuroscience, 7*, 367–379.

Chamberlain, S. R., Blackwell, A. D., Fineberg, N. A., Robbins, T. W., & Sahakian, B. J. (2005). The neuropsychology of obsessive compulsive disorder: The importance of failures in cognitive and behavioral inhibition as candidate endophenotypic markers. *Neuroscience and Biobehavioral Reviews, 29,* 399–419.

Christensen, K. J., Kim, S. W., Dysken, M. W., & Hoover, K. M. (1996). Neuropsychological performance in obsessive-compulsive disorder. *Biological Psychiatry, 31,* 4–18.

Christian, C. J., Lencz, T., Robinson, D. G., Burdick, K. E., Ashtari, M., Malhotra, A. K., … Szeszko, P. R. (2008). Gray matter structural alterations in obsessive-compulsive disorder: Relationship to neuropsychological functions. *Psychiatry Research, 164,* 123–131.

Cuttler, C., & Graf, P. (2009). Checking-in on the memory deficit and meta-memory deficit theories of compulsive checking. *Clinical Psychology Review, 29,* 393–409.

de Geus, F. D., Denys, D. A. J. P., Sitskoorn, M. M., & Westenberg, H. G. M. (2007). Attention and cognition in patients with obsessive-compulsive disorder. *Psychiatry and Clinical Neurosciences, 61,* 45–53.

Deckersbach, T., Otto, M., Savage, C., Baer, L., & Jenike, M. A. (2000). The relationship between semantic organization and memory in obsessive-compulsive disorder. *Psychotherapy and Psychosomatics, 69,* 101–107.

Deckersbach, T., Savage, C., Dougherty, D. D., Bohne, A., Loh, R., Nierenberg, A., … Rauch, S. L. (2005). Spontaneous and directed application of verbal learning strategies in bipolar disorder and obsessive-compulsive disorder. *Bipolar Disorders, 7,* 166–175.

Del Casale, A., Kotzalidis, G. D., Rapinesi, C., Serata, D., Ambrosi, E., Simonetti, A., … Girardi, P. (2011a). Functional neuroimaging in obsessive-compulsive disorder. *Neuropsychobiology, 64,* 61–85.

Del Casale, A., Kotzalidis, G. D., Rapinesi, C., Serata, D., Ambrosi, E., Simonetti, A., … Girardi, P. (2011b). Functional neuroimaging in obsessive-compulsive disorder. *Neuropsychobiology, 64,* 61–85.

Endrass, T., Klawohn, J., Schuster, F., & Kathmann, N. (2008). Overactive performance monitoring in obsessive-compulsive disorder: ERP evidence from correct and erroneous reactions. *Neuropsychologia, 46,* 1877–1887.

Endrass, T., Schuermann, B., Kaufann, C., Spielberg, R., Kniesche, R., & Kathmann, N. (2010). Performance monitoring and error significance in patients with obsessive-compulsive disorder. *Psychophysiology, 84,* 257–263.

Exner, C., Kohl, A., Zaudig, M., Langs, G., Lincoln, T. M., & Rief, W. (2009). Metacognition and episodic memory in obsessive-compulsive disorder. *Journal of Anxiety Disorders, 23,* 624–631.

Fitzgerald, K. D., Stern, E. R., Angstadt, M., Nicholson-Muth, K. C., Maynor, M. R., Welsh, R. C., … Taylor, S. F. (2010). Altered function and connectivity of the medial frontal cortex in pediatric obsessive-compulsive disorder. *Biological Psychiatry, 68,* 1039–1047.

Friedlander, L., & Desrocher, M. (2006). Neuroimaging studies of obsessive-compulsive disorder in adults and children. *Clinical Psychology Review, 26,* 32–49.

Gambini, O., Abbruzzese, M., & Scarone, S. (1993). Smooth pursuit and saccadic eye movement and Wisconsin Card Sorting Test performance in obsessive-compulsive disorder. *Psychiatry Research, 48,* 191–200.

Gehring, W. J., Himle, J., & Nisenson, L. G. (2000). Action-monitoring dysfunction in obsessive-compulsive disorder. *Psychological Science, 11,* 1–6.

Gilbert, A. R., Akkal, D., Almeida, J. R., Mataix-Cols, D., Kalas, C., Delvin, B., … Phillips, M. L. (2009). Neural correlates of symptom dimensions in pediatric obsessive-compulsive disorder: A functional magnetic resonance imaging study. *Journal of the American Academy of Child and Adolescent Psychiatry, 48,* 936–944.

Greisberg, S., & McKay, D. (2003). Neuropsychology of obsessive-compulsive disorder: A review and treatment implications. *Clinical Psychology Reviews, 23,* 95–117.

Grisham, J. R., Anderson, T. M., Poulton, R., Moffitt, T. E., & Andrews, G. (2009). Childhood neuropsychological deficits associated with adult obsessive-compulsive disorder. *British Journal of Psychiatry, 195,* 138–141.

Hajcak, G., Franklin, M. E., Foa, E. B., & Simons, R. F. (2008). Increased error-related brain activity in pediatric obsessive-compulsive disorder before and after treatment. *American Journal of Psychiatry, 165*, 116–123.

Hashimoto, N., Nakaaki, S., Omori, I. M., Fujioi, J., Noguchi, Y., Murata, Y., … Furukawa, T. A. (2011). Distinct neuropsychological profiles of three major symptom dimensions in obsessive-compulsive disorder. *Psychiatry Research, 187*, 166–173.

Hollander, E., Schiffman, E., Cohen, B., Rivera-Stein, M. A., Rosen, W., Gorman, J. W., … Liebowitz, M. R. (1990). Signs of central nervous system dysfunction in obsessive-compulsive disorder. *Archives of General Psychiatry, 47*, 27–32.

Huyser, C., Veitman, D. J., Wolters, L. H., de Haan, É., & Boer, F. (2010). Functional magnetic resonance imaging during planning before and after cognitive-behavioral therapy in pediatric obsessive-compulsive disorder. *Journal of the American Academy of Child and Adolescent Psychiatry, 49*, 1238–1248.

Hymas, N., Lees, A., Bolton, D., Epps, K., & Head, D. (1991). The neurology of obsessional slowness. *Brain, 114*, 2203–2233.

Jang, J. J., Kim, H. S., Ha, T. H., Shin, N. Y., Kang, D. H., Choi, J. S., … Kwon, J. S. (2010). Nonverbal memory and organizational dysfunctions are related with distinct symptom dimensions in obsessive-compulsive disorder. *Psychiatry Research, 180*, 93–98.

Kim, J., Lee, M. C., Kim, J., Kim, I. Y., Kim, S. I., Han, M. H., … Kwon, J. S. (2001). Grey matter abnormalities in obsessive-compulsive disorder: Statistical parametric mapping of segmented magnetic resonance images. *British Journal of Psychiatry, 179*, 330–334.

Kim, M-S., Kim, Y. Y., Yoo, S. Y., & Kwon, J. S. (2006). Electrophysiological correlates of behavioral response inhibition in patients with obsessive-compulsive disorder. *Depression and Anxiety, 24*, 22–31.

Krawczyk, D. C. (2002). Contributions of the prefrontal cortex to the neural basis of human decision making *Neuroscience and Biobehavioral Reviews, 26*, 631–664.

Krishna, R., Udupa, S., George, C. M., Kumar, K. J., Viswanath, B., Kandavel, T., … Reddy, Y. C. (2011). Neuropsychological performance in OCD: A study in medication-naïve patients. *Progress in Neuropsychopharmacology and Biological Psychiatry, 35*, 1969–1976.

Kuelz, A. K., Hohagen, F., & Voderholzer, U. (2004). Neuropsychological performance in obsessive-compulsive disorder: A critical review. *Biological Psychology, 65*, 185–236.

Kwon, J. S., Kim, J., Lee, D. W., Lee, J. S., Lee, D. S., Kim, M-S., … Lee, M. C. (2003). Neural correlates of clinical symptoms and cognitive dysfunctions in obsessive-compulsive disorder. *Psychiatry Research, 122*, 37–47.

Lacerda, A. L. T., Dalgalarrondo, P., Caetano, D., Haas, G. L., Camargo, E. E., & Keshavan, M. S. (2003). Neuropsychological performance and regional cerebral blood flow in obsessive-compulsive disorder. *Progress in Neuro-Psychopharmacology & Biological Psychiatry, 27*, 657–665.

Lawrence, N. S., Wooderson, S., Mataix-Cols, D., David, R., Speckens, A., & Phillips, M. L. (2006). Decision-making and set-shifting impairments are associated with distinct symptom dimensions in obsessive-compulsive disorder. *Neuropsychology, 20*, 409–419.

Lewin, A. B., Larson, M. J., Park, J. M., McGuire, J. F., Murphy, T. K., & Storch, E. A. (2014). Neuropsychological functioning in youth with obsessive compulsive disorder: An examination of executive function and memory impairment. *Psychiatry Research, 216*, 108–115.

Maia, T. V., Cooney, R. E., & Peterson, B. S. (2008). The neural bases of obsessive-compulsive disorder in children and adults. *Developmental Psychopathology, 20*, 1251–1283.

Maltby, N., Tolin, D. F., Worhunsky, P., O'Keefe, T. M., & Kiehl, K. A. (2005). Dysfunctional action monitoring hyperactivates frontal-striatal circuits in obsessive-compulsive disorder: An event-related fMRI study. *Neuroimage, 24*, 495–503.

Markarian, Y., Larson, M. J., Aldea, M. A., Baldwin, S. A., Good, D. A., Berkeljon, A., … McKay, D. (2010). Multiple pathways to functional impairment in obsessive-compulsive disorder. *Clinical Psychology Review, 30*, 78–88.

Martinez-Gonzalez, A. E., & Pigueras-Rodriguez, J. A. (2008). Neuropsychological update on obsessive-compulsive disorder. *Revista de Neurologia, 46*, 618–625.

Mataix-Cols, D., Boman, M., Monzani, B., Ruck, C., Serlachius, E., Langstrom, N., & Lichtenstein, P. (2013). Population-based, multigenerational family clustering study of obsessive-compulsive disorder. *JAMA Psychiatry, 70*, 709–717.

Mataix-Cols, D., do Rosário-Campos, M. C., & Leckman, J. F. (2005). A multidimensional model of obsessive-compulsive disorder. *American Journal of Psychiatry, 162*, 228–238.

Mataix-Cols, D., Jungque, C., & Sanchez-Turet, M. (1999). Neuropsychological functioning in a subclinical obsessive-compulsive sample. *Biological Psychiatry, 45*, 898–904.

McGuire, J. F., Crawford, E. A., Park, J. M., Storch, E. A., Murphy, T. K., Larson, M. J., & Lewin, A. B. (2014). Neuropsychological performance across symptom dimensions in pediatric obsessive compulsive disorder. *Depression and Anxiety, 31*(12), 988–996.

Menzies, L., Achard, S., Chamberlain, S. R., Fineberg, N., Chen, C. H., del Campo, N., ... Bullmore, E. (2007). Neurocognitive endophenotypes of obsessive-compulsive disorder. *Brain, 130*, 3223–3236.

Miguel, E. C., Torres, A. R., Sampaio, A. S., Fossaluza, V., Mathis, M. A., do Rosário, M. C., ... Koenen, K. C. (2011). Comorbid major depression in obsessive-compulsive disorder patients *Comprehensive Psychiatry, 52*, 386–393.

Morein-Zamir, S., Craig, K. J., Ersche, K. D., Abbott, S., Muller, U., Fineberg, N. A., ... Robbins, T. W. (2010). Impaired visuospatial associative memory and attention in obsessive compulsive disorder but no evidence for differential dopaminergic modulation. *Psychopharmacology, 212*, 357–367.

Moritz, S., Birkner, C., Kloss, M., Jacobsen, D., Fricke, S., Böthern, A., & Hand, I. (2001a). Impact of comorbid depressive symptoms on neuropsychological performance in obsessive-compulsive disorder. *Journal of Abnormal Psychology, 110*, 653–657.

Moritz, S., Birkner, C., Kloss, M., Jahn, H., Hand, I., Haasen, C., & Krausz, M. (2002). Executive functioning in obsessive-compulsive disorder, unipolar depression and schizophrenia. *Archives of Clinical Neuropsychology, 17*, 477–483.

Moritz, S., Fricke, S., & Hand, I. (2001b). Further evidence for delayed alternation deficits in obsessive-compulsive disorder. *Journal of Nervous and Mental Disorders, 189*, 562–564.

Moritz, S., Kloss, M., Jacobsen, D., Kellner, M., Andresen, B., Fricke, S., ... Hand, I. (2005). Extent, profile and specificity of visuospatial impairment in obsessive-compulsive disorder (OCD). *Journal of Clinical and Experimental Neuropsychology, 27*, 795–814.

Moritz, S., Kloss, M., Jahn, H., Schick, M., & Hand, I. (2003). Impact of comorbid depressive symptoms on nonverbal memory and visuospatial performance in obsessive-compulsive disorder. *Cognitive Neuropsychiatry, 8*, 261–272.

Moritz, S., Ruhe, C., Jelinek, L., & Naber, D. (2009). No deficits in nonverbal memory, metamemory and internal as well as external source memory in obsessive-compulsive disorder (OCD). *Behaviour Research and Therapy, 47*, 308–315.

Moritz, S., & Wendt, M. (2006). Processing of local and global visual features in obsessive-compulsive disorder. *Journal of the International Neuropsychological Society, 12*, 566–569.

Nakao, T., Nakagawa, A., Nakatani, E., Nabeyama, M., Sanematsu, H., Yoshiura, T., ... Kanba, S. (2009). Working memory dysfunction in obsessive-compulsive disorder: A neuropsychological and functional MRI study. *Journal of Psychiatric Research, 43*, 784–791.

Nedeljkovic, M., Moulding, R., Kyrios, M., & Doron, G. (2009). The relationship of cognitive confidence to OCD symptoms. *Journal of Anxiety Disorders, 23*, 463–468.

Nestadt, G., Samuels, J., Riddle, M. A., Liang, K. Y., Bienvenu, O. J., Hoehn-Saric, R., ... Cullen, B. (2001). The relationship between obsessive-compulsive disorder and anxiety and affective disorders: Results from the Johns Hopkins OCD Family Study. *Psychological Medicine, 31*, 481–487.

Olley, A., Malhi, G., & Sachdev, P. (2007). Memory and executive functioning in obsessive-compulsive disorder: A selective review. *Journal of Affective Disorders, 104*, 15–23.

Olvet, D. M., & Hajcak, G. (2008). The error-related negativity (ERN) and psychopathology: Toward an endophenotype. *Clinical Psychology Review, 28*, 1343–1354.

Omori, I. M., Maurata, Y., Yamanishi, T., Nakaaki, S., Akechi, T., Mikuni, M., & Furukawa, T. A. (2007). The differential impact of executive attention dysfunction on episodic memory in obsessive-compulsive disorder patients with checking symptoms vs. those with washing symptoms. *Journal of Psychiatric Research, 41*, 776–784.

Ornstein, T. J., Arnold, P., Manassis, K., Mendlowitz, S., & Schachar, R. (2010). Neuropsychological performance in childhood OCD: A preliminary study. *Depression and Anxiety, 27*, 372–380.

Pauls, D. L., Abramovitch, A., Rauch, S. L., & Geller, D. A. (2014). Obsessive-compulsive disorder: An integrated genetic and neurobiological perspective. *Nature Reviews Neuroscience, 15*, 410–424.

Penedes, R., Catalan, R., Andres, S., Salamero, M., & Gasto, C. (2005). Executive function and nonverbal memory in obsessive-compulsive disorder. *Psychiatry Research, 133*, 81–90.

Peris, T. S., Bergman, R. L., Asarnow, J. R., Langley, A., McCracken, J. T., & Piacentini, J. (2010). Clinical and cognitive correlates of depressive symptoms among youth with obsessive compulsive disorder. *Journal of Clinical Child and Adolescent Psychology, 39*, 616–626.

Perlstein, W. M., Carter, C. S., Barch, D. M., & Baird, J. W. (1998). The Stroop task and attention deficits in schizophrenia: A critical evaluation of card and single-trial Stroop methodologies. *Neuropsychology, 12*, 414–425.

Posner, M. I., Rothbart, M. K., Sheese, B. E., & Tang, Y. (2007). The anterior cingulate gyrus and the mechanism of self-regulation. *Cognitive Affective and Behavioral Neuroscience, 7*, 391–395.

Purcell, R., Maruff, P., Kyrios, M., & Pantelis, C. (1998). Neuropsychological deficits in obsessive-compulsive disorder: a comparison with unipolar depression, panic disorder, and normal controls. *Archives of General Psychiatry, 55*, 415–423.

Rajender, G., Bhatia, M. S., Kanwal, K., Malhotra, S., Singh, T. B., & Chaudhary, D. (2011). Study of neurocognitive endophenotypes in drug-naïve obsessive-compulsive disorder patients, their first-degree relatives and healthy controls. *Acta Psychiatrica Scandinavia, 124*, 152–161.

Rampacher, F., Lennertz, L., Vogeley, A., Schulze-Rauschenbach, S., Kathmann, N., Falkai, P., & Wagner, M. (2010). Evidence for specific cognitive deficits in visual information processing in patients with OCD compared to patients with unipolar depression. *Progress in Neuropsychopharmacology and Biological Psychiatry, 34*, 984–991.

Rao, N. P., Arasappa, R., Reddy, N. N., & Venkatasubramanian, G. (2010). Emotional interference in obsessive-compulsive disorder: A neuropsychological study using optimized emotional Stroop test. *Psychiatry Research, 180*, 99–104.

Rey, A. (1941). L'examen psychologique dans les cas d'encephalopathie traumatique. *Archives de Psychologie, 28*, 286–340.

Riesel, A., Endrass, T., Kaufmann, C., & Kathmann, N. (2011). Overactive error-related brain activity as a candidate endophenotype for obsessive-compulsive disorder: Evidence from unaffected first-degree relatives. *American Journal of Psychiatry, 168*, 317–324.

Robinson, D., Wu, H., Munne, R., Ashtari, M., Alvir, J. J., Lerner, G., … Bogerts, B. (1995). Reduced caudate nucleus volume in obsessive–compulsive disorder. *Archives of General Psychiatry, 52*, 393–398.

Rosenberg, D. R., Averbach, D. H., O'Hearn, K. M., Seymour, A. B., Birmaher, B., & Sweeney, J. A. (1997). Oculomotor response inhibition abnormalities in pediatric obsessive compulsive disorder. *Archives of General Psychiatry, 54*, 831–838.

Roth, R. M., Milovan, D., Baribeau, J., & O'Connor, K. O. (2005). Neuropsychological functioning in early- and late-onset obsessive-compulsive disorder. *Journal of Neuropsychiatry and Clinical Neuroscience, 17*, 208–213.

Ruchsow, M., Grön, G., Reuter, K., Spitzer, M., Hermle, L., & Kiefer, M. (2005). Error-related brain activity in patients with obsessive-compulsive disorder and in healthy controls. *Journal of Psychophysiology, 19*, 298–304.

Ruchsow, M., Reuter, K., Hermle, L., Ebert, D., Kiefer, M., & Falkenstein, M. (2007). Executive control in obsessive-compulsive disorder: Event-related potentials in a Go/No-go task. *Journal of Neural Transmission, 114*, 1595–1601.

Ruscio, A. M., Stein, D. L., Chiu, W. T., & Kessler, R. C. (2010). The epidemiology of obsessive-compulsive disorder in the National Comorbidity Survey Replication. *Molecular Psychiatry, 15*, 53–63.

Savage, C. R., Baer, L., Keuthen, N. J., Brown, H. D., Rauch, S. L., & Jenike, M. S. (1999). Organizational strategies mediate nonverbal memory impairment in obsessive-compulsive disorder. *Biological Psychiatry, 45*, 905–916.

Savage, C. R., Deckersbach, T., Wilhelm, S., Rauch, S. L., Baer, L., Reid, T., & Jenike, M. A. (2000). Strategic processing and episodic memory impairment in obsessive compulsive disorder. *Neuropsychology, 14*, 1–11.

Seignourel, P. J., Robins, D. L., Larson, M. J., Demery, J. A., Cole, M., & Perlstein, W. M. (2005). Cognitive control in closed head injury: Context maintenance dysfunction or prepotent response inhibition deficit? *Neuropsychology, 19*, 578–590.

Shin, M. S., Choi, H., Kim, H., Hwang, J. W., Kim, B. N., & Cho, S. C. (2008). A study of neuropsychological deficit in children with obsessive-compulsive disorder. *European Psychiatry, 23*, 512–520.

Shin, N. Y., Kang, D. H., Choi, J. S., Jung, M. H., Jang, J. H., & Kwon, J. S. (2010). Do organizational strategies mediate nonverbal memory impairment in drug-naïve patients with obsessive-compulsive disorder? *Neuropsychology, 24*, 527–533.

Simpson, H. B., Rosen, W., Huppert, J. D., Lin, S. H., Foa, E. B., & Liebowitz, M. R. (2006). Are there reliable neuropsychological deficits in obsessive-compulsive disorder? *Journal of Psychiatric Research, 40*, 247–257.

Soref, A., Dar, R., Argov, G., & Meiran, N. (2008). Obsessive-compulsive tendencies are associated with a focused information processing strategy. *Behaviour Research and Therapy, 46*, 1295–1299.

Spitznagel, M. B., & Suhr, J. A. (2002). Executive function deficits associated with symptoms of schizotypy and obsessive-compulsive disorder. *Psychiatry Research, 110*, 151–163.

Strauss, E., Sherman, E. M. S., & Spreen, O. (2006). *A compendium of neuropsychological tests* (3rd ed.). New York: Oxford University Press.

Thomas, S. J., Gonsalvez, C. J., & Johnstone, S. J. (2014). How specific are inhibitory deficits to obsessive-compulsive disorder? A neurophysiological comparison with panic disorder. *Clinical Neurophysiology, 125*, 463–475.

Togao, O., Yoshiura, T., Nakao, T., Nabeyama, M., Sanematsu, H., Nakagawa, A., … Honda, H. (2010). Regional gray and white matter volume abnormalities in obsessive-compulsive disorder: A voxel-based morphoetry study. *Psychiatry Research, 184*, 29–37.

Tukel, R., Gurvit, H., Ertekin, B. A., Oflaz, S., Ertekin, E., Baran, B., … Atalay, F. (2012a). Neuropsychological function in obsessive-compulsive disorder. *Comprehensive Psychiatry, 53*, 167–175.

Tukel, R., Gurvit, H., Ozata, B., Ozturk, N., Ertekin, B. A., Ertekin, E., … Direskeneli, G. S. (2012b). Brain-derived neurotrophic factor gene Val66Met polymorphism and cognitive function in obsessive-compulsive disorder. *American Journal of Genetics Part B Neuropsychiatric Genetics, 159B*, 850–858.

Tuna, S., Tekcan, A. I., & Topcuoglu, V. (2005). Memory and metamemory in obsessive-compulsive disorder. *Behaviour Research and Therapy, 43*, 15–27.

Ursu, S., & Carter, A. (2009). An initial investigation of the orbitofrontal cortex hyperactivity in obsessive-compulsive disorder: exaggerated representations of anticipated aversive events? *Neuropsychologia, 47*, 2145–2148.

Ursu, S., Stenger, V. A., Shear, M. K., Jones, M. R., & Carter, C. S. (2003). Overactive action monitoring in obsessive-compulsive disorder: Evidence from functional magnetic resonance imaging. *Psychological Science, 14,* 347–353.

van Veen, V., & Carter, C. S. (2002). The anterior cingulate as a conflict monitor: fMRI and ERP studies. *Physiology & Behavior, 77,* 477–482.

Veale, D., Sahakian, B., Owen, A., & Marks, I. (1996). Specific cognitive deficits in tests sensitive to frontal lobe dysfunction in obsessive-compulsive disorder. *Psychological Medicine, 26,* 1261–1269.

Watkins, L. H., Sahakian, B. J., Robertson, M. M., Veale, D. M., Rogers, R. D., Pickard, K. M., … Robbins, T. W. (2004). Executive function in Tourette's syndrome and obsessive-compulsive disorder. *Psychological Medicine, 34,* 1–12.

Wells, A. (2007). Cognition about cognition: Metacognitive therapy and change in generalized anxiety disorder and social phobia. *Cognitive and Behavioral Practice, 14,* 18–25.

Whiteside, S. P., Port, J. D., & Abramowitz, J. S. (2004). A meta-analysis of functional neuroimaging in obsessive-compulsive disorder. *Psychiatry Research: Neuroimaging, 132,* 69–79.

Xiao, Z., Wang, J., Zhang, M., Li, H., Tang, Y., Wang, Y., … Fromson, J. A. (2011). Error-related negativity abnormalities in generalized anxiety disorder and obsessive-compulsive disorder. *Progress in Neuro-Psychopharmacology & Biological Psychiatry, 35,* 265–272.

Zielinski, C. M., Taylor, M. A., & Juzwin, K. R. (1991). Neuropsychological deficits in obsessive-compulsive disorder. *Neuropsychiatry, Neuropsychology, & Behavioral Neurology, 4,* 110–116.

10

An International Perspective on Obsessive-Compulsive Disorder Assessment

Miquel A. Fullana, Clara López-Sola, Lorena Fernández de la Cruz, and Pino Alonso

Introduction

Obsessive-compulsive (OC) symptoms do not only characterize obsessive-compulsive disorder (OCD), but are present in many different mental disorders and are also frequent in "healthy" individuals (Blom, Hagestein-de Bruijn, de Graaf, ten Have, & Denys, 2011; Fullana et al., 2009). As in many other forms of psychopathology, cross-cultural variables may complicate the assessment of OC symptoms/OCD. Differences in the frequency, expression, or associated characteristics of these phenomena across different cultures need therefore to be taken into account when they are assessed.

The goal of this chapter is to review the main instruments currently available to assess OC symptoms in different settings, with a special focus on cross-cultural issues (e.g., validation of assessment tools in different languages/cultural contexts, peculiarities in the assessment based on cultural aspects, etc.). To this end, a systematic review of articles focusing on assessment instruments published up to May 2014 was carried out in the databases Medline (Pubmed) and ScienceDirect by two of the authors (CLS and LFC). The following keywords were used: *self-report* or *questionnaire* or *inventory* or *checklist* or *test* or *scale* and *validation* or *validated* or *validity* or *reliability* or *sensitivity* or *specificity* or *psychometry* or *psychometric* and *OCD* or *obsessive compulsive disorder*. Additionally, manual searches of reference lists of empirical studies and review articles were conducted. The inclusion criteria specified that the article should present the description and/or psychometric properties of an assessment tool for OC symptoms or OCD.

Screening Instruments

Despite its prevalence and impact, which make it a public health concern, OCD is often under-recognized (Heyman, Mataix-Cols, & Fineberg, 2006). Reasons for this may include inadequate screening and hesitance to report certain symptoms because of their embarrassing nature (e.g., aggressive obsessions) (Grabill et al., 2008). Identifying OCD

The Wiley Handbook of Obsessive Compulsive Disorders, Volume I, First Edition.
Edited by Jonathan S. Abramowitz, Dean McKay, and Eric A. Storch.
© 2017 John Wiley & Sons Ltd. Published 2017 by John Wiley & Sons Ltd.

is important given that effective interventions are available (Franklin & Foa, 2011). However, very few screening instruments for OCD have been properly assessed. These include the Short Leyton Obsessional Inventory (Bamber, Tamplin, Park, Kyte, & Goodyer, 2002) and the Short OCD Screener (Uher, Heyman, Mortimore, Frampton, & Goodman, 2007), both developed for children/adolescents. The two instruments have sound psychometric properties, although the latter seems to have better discriminant properties and is also shorter (6 vs. 11 items). We are not aware of any screening instrument for OCD in adults with published psychometric properties to date.

Diagnostic Instruments

Diagnosis of OCD is mainly established through the use of structured diagnostic interviews. A section devoted to OCD appears in virtually all mental health diagnostic interviews, but the psychometric properties of the OCD section have been investigated only for a few of them. These include the Anxiety Disorders Interview Schedule (ADIS-IV) (Di Nardo, Brown, & Barlow, 1994) and the Structured Clinical Interview for DSM-IV-TR Axis I Disorders (SCID-I) (First, Spitzer, Gibbon, & Williams, 2002), both of which demonstrate excellent psychometrics (Brown, Di Nardo, Lehman, & Campbell, 2001; see www.scid4.org).

Previous research has suggested that, although different raters tend to agree on the presence of OC symptoms, they often do not coincide on whether the individual meets the clinical cut-off for the disorder (Brown et al., 2001). This is relevant given that, nowadays, OCD is seen as the extreme end of a continuum between "normal" and "pathological" symptoms – based on their frequency and associated distress – and that "subclinical" OCD is relatively common (Fullana et al., 2009; Grabe et al., 2001).

An important and scarcely investigated question is whether certain OC symptoms are more easily recognized (and labeled as OCD) by clinicians than others. Based on our clinical experience, we believe that individuals with typical OCD presentations (e.g., contamination symptoms) are more easily recognized as suffering from OCD than others (e.g., those presenting with obsessions of harm). Furthermore, the wording of the questions used in some structured interviews used to detect OCD may inadvertently contribute to a misdiagnosis of the disorder (e.g., when obsessions are called "worries") (Stein, Forde, Anderson, & Walker, 1997).

Finally, changes in our nosological systems may have an impact on the assessment of OCD. For example, the emergence of a new "hoarding disorder" category in the DSM-5 (American Psychiatric Association, 2013) may change the diagnosis of an individual presenting with hoarding symptoms for which so far the most likely diagnosis was OCD (Mataix-Cols et al., 2011).

Measures of Symptoms and Severity

Many assessment instruments have been developed to capture the core features of OCD and OC symptoms. They can be broadly divided into clinician-administered measures of severity and self-report measures of symptoms/severity. A summary of the psychometric properties of these instruments appears in Table 10.1 and descriptions of their structure and main characteristics are offered in this section.

Table 10.1 Clinician-administered instruments for obsessive-compulsive disorder (adults and children/adolescents)

Instrument[1] & reference	Validated versions	No. of items and approx. testing time	Factor structure	Internal consistency[2]	Test–retest reliability[2]	Convergent validity[3]	Divergent validity[3]	Sensitivity to treatment	Interrater reliability
GOCS NIMH Global Obsessive Compulsive Scale (Insel et al., 1983)	Brazilian-Portuguese, Chinese, Egyptian, English, Dutch, French, German, Italian, Japan, Korean, Norwegian, Spanish, Turkish.	Single-item	NA	NA	Good to excellent	Medium correlations with SCL-90-R OC scale, large with YBOCS (Taylor, 1995)	NA	NA	Excellent (Taylor, 1995)
Y-BOCS Yale-Brown Obsessive-Compulsive Scale (Goodman et al., 1989a, 1989b)	Brazilian-Portuguese, Chinese, Egyptian, English, Dutch, French, German, Italian, Japan, Korean, Norwegian, Spanish, Turkish.	10 items +11 investigational items 30–40 min	Obsessions; compulsions (Amir, Foa, & Coles, 1997). Disturbance; severity (McKay, Neziroglu, Stevens, & Yaryura-Tobias, 1998). Severity; resistance and control (Deacon & Abramowitz, 2005). Severity of obsessions; Severity of compulsions; control (Kim, Dysken, Pheley, & Hoover, 1994). Severity of obsessions; Severity of compulsions; resistance (Moritz et al., 2002).	Acceptable to good (OCD) (Woody, Steketee, & Chambless, 1995), Good in non-clinical samples (Frost, Steketee, Krause, & Trepanier, 1995).	Questionable to excellent depending on interval duration and raters (Woody, Steketee, & Chambless, 1995).	Excellent (large correlations with MOCI and clinician ratings of global OCD severity).	Poor (large correlations with HAS and HDRS) (Frost, Steketee, Krause, & Trepanier,1995; Price, Goodman, Chamey, Rasmussen, & Heninger, 1987; Woody, Steketee, & Chambless, 1995).	Yes (PF, CBT) (Taylor et al., 1995).	Good to excellent (Woody, Steketee, & Chambless, 1995).
Y-BOCS Symptom Checklist Yale-Brown Obsessive-Compulsive Scale Checklist (Goodman et al., 1989a, 1989b)	Brazilian-Portuguese, Chinese, Egyptian, English, Dutch, French, German, Italian, Japan, Korean, Norwegian, Spanish, Turkish.	74 examples	Contamination and cleaning; hoarding obsessions and compulsions; symmetry and ordering; sexual and religious; aggressive (Stewart et al., 2007). Not confirmed by latent class analysis (Delucchi et al., 2011).	NA	NA	Small to large correlations with MOCI – better for washing dimensions (Mataix-Cols et al., 2004).	Medium correlations with Y-BOCS global severity score and HDRS (Mataix-Cols et al., 2004).	NA	NA

CY-BOCS Children's Yale-Brown Obsessive-Compulsive Scale (Scahill et al., 1997)	English, French, Polish, Spanish, Turkish,	10 items 30–90 min	Disturbance (resistance and symptom control items); severity factors (frequency, distress and interference items) (McKay, et al., 2003; Storch et al., 2004).	Good (Storch et al., 2004).	Acceptable for obsessions, compulsions and total scores.	Excellent (large correlations with CGI and TODS-PR OCD) (Gallant et al., 2008).	Small correlations with MASC, but large with TODS-PR Total (Gallant et al., 2008).	Yes (PF, CBT) (Geller et al., 2003).	Excellent
DY-BOCS Dimensional Yale-Brown Obsessive-Compulsive Scale (Rosário et al., 2006).	Chinese, English, Japanese, Hungarian, Portuguese, Spanish,	88 items 40 min (self-report part) 49 min (clinician rating)	Aggression, injury, violence, natural disasters; sexual, moral, religious; symmetry, just-right, count, order, arrange; contamination, cleaning; hoarding; and miscellaneous (Pertusa et al., 2012).	Excellent (Pertusa et al., 2012).	NA	Large correlations with Y-BOCS.	Small to medium correlations with HAS and HDRS, large with YGTSS.	NA	Excellent
Y-BOCS II Yale-Brown Obsessive-Compulsive Scale second edition (Storch et al., 2010b)	English, Thai	10 items	Obsessions; compulsions	Excellent for total score; good for obsessions and compulsions (Hiranyatheb, Saipanish, & Lotrakul, 2014).	Good (Hiranyatheb, Saipanish, & Lotrakul, 2014).	Large correlations with CGI-S and NIMH-GOCS, small with OCI-R (Gallant et al., 2008).	Small correlations with PSWQ, medium with IDS-SR (Hiranyatheb, Saipanish, & Lotrakul, 2014).	NA	Excellent (Hiranyatheb, Saipanish, & Lotrakul, 2014).

(Continued)

Table 10.1 (Continued)

Instrument[1] & reference	Validated versions	No. of items and approx. testing time	Factor structure	Internal consistency[2]	Test–retest reliability[2]	Convergent validity[3]	Divergent validity[3]	Sensitivity to treatment	Interrater reliability
Y-BOCS-II Symptom Checklist Yale–Brown Obsessive-Compulsive Scale (2nd edition) Checklist (Storch et al., 2010a).	English, Thai	67 items	Symmetry and ordering; contamination and cleaning; hoarding; sexual and religious and aggressive.	Excellent for total scores; good for obsessions and compulsions; questionable for avoidance.	Excellent for total scores and compulsions, good for obsessions, acceptable for avoidance.	Medium correlations with Y-BOCS II and OCI-R.	Small correlations with PSWQ medium with IDS-SR.	NA	Excellent for total, obsessions and compulsions scores, good for avoidance.

Abbreviations: CBT = Cognitive-behavioral treatment; CGI = Clinical Global Impression; HAS = Hamilton Anxiety Scale; HDRS = Hamilton Depression Rating Scale; IDS-SR = Inventory Depressive Symptomatology Self-Report; MOCI = Maudsley Obsessive Compulsive Inventory; NA = Not available; OCD = Obsessive-Compulsive Disorder; OCI-R = Obsessive-Compulsive Inventory – Revised; PF = Psychopharmacological treatment; PSQW = Penn State Worry Questionnaire; SCL-90-R = Symptom Checklist-90 – Revised; TODS-PR = Tourette's Disorder Scale Parents Rated.

[1] Information on the psychometric properties of the measures in the table comes from the original reference, except when there is another reference cited, usually a further validation.

[2] Data on internal consistency and test –retest reliability follow this classification: ≥ .9 = excellent; .8–.89 = good; .7–.79 = acceptable, .6–.69 = questionable, .5–.59 = poor; ≤ .5 = unacceptable based on George and Mallery (2003).

[3] Judgment of validity (convergent and divergent) follows this classification: ≥ .10 = small; ≥ .30 = medium; ≥ .50 = large (Cohen, 1977). Note that for divergent validity the classification is reversed (i.e., high correlations with instruments measuring different constructs are noted as "medium", and low correlations are noted as "large").

Clinician-administered Measures of Severity

Yale–Brown Obsessive-Compulsive Scale (Y-BOCS). The Yale–Brown Obsessive-Compulsive Scale (Y-BOCS) (Goodman et al., 1989a, 1989b) is a semi-structured clinician-administered interview designed to assess the severity of OC symptoms in OCD. It is currently the "gold standard" to assess OCD severity, especially in treatment trials. However, it is important to note that it is *not* a diagnostic instrument.

The Y-BOCS consists of three parts. The first provides with definitions and examples of obsessions and compulsions. The second is the Y-BOCS Symptom Checklist (Y-BOCS-SC), which contains 74 examples of common obsessions and compulsions, organized into 13 categories based on content (contamination, aggression, sexual, hoarding, somatic, symmetry, and religious obsessions; and washing, checking, repeating, counting, ordering, and hoarding compulsions), as well as two ancillary miscellaneous categories. The patient is asked to identify the current or past presence of any of these symptoms and the most prominent obsessions, compulsions, and avoidance behaviors during the last week. Finally, five aspects of the main obsessions and compulsions, over the last week, are rated on a 0 (no symptoms) to 4 (extreme symptoms) scale: frequency or time spent, degree of interference, distress, resistance (with greater resistance assigned to lower scores), and perceived control over the symptoms. These two five-item subscale scores – one for obsessions and one for compulsions – are then summed to yield a maximum 40-points Y-BOCS Total Score. Probe questions and written definitions accompanying each point on the 0–4 scales are provided to facilitate the rating, which is based on patient reports, as well as other's accounts, and the clinician observations and judgment.

The Y-BOCS ends with 11 investigational items that assess amount of time free of obsessions or compulsions, insight into the irrationality of obsessions and compulsions, avoidance, degree of indecisiveness, overvalued sense of personal responsibility, obsessional slowness/inertia, pathological doubting, global severity, overall response to treatment, and reliability of information obtained from the patient. These are rated on 0–4 or 0–6 scales.

It has been suggested that clinical severity in OCD may be better evaluated by considering the subscales scores individually, since the global score might misrepresent symptom severity for some patients, that is, a person presenting only with compulsions would receive a maximum score of 20 (McKay, Danyko, Neziroglu, & Yaryura-Tobias, 1995). Moreover, resistance items show poor correlation with the total score and have been considered to poorly contribute to the assessment of OCD severity. Their replacement by items assessing avoidance has been proposed (Woody, Steketee, & Chambless, 1995).

The Y-BOCS has been criticized for underrepresenting particular symptoms, such as mental rituals, just-right experiences, or symptoms more relevant to pediatric populations, such as family accommodation or reassurance-seeking (Storch et al., 2007b). Nevertheless, it is overall considered a useful tool that allows a comprehensive assessment of OC symptoms, since many individuals may feel reluctant to discuss their obsessions and compulsions and they may not even mention some of them unless asked directly by the interviewer. Recent work also suggests the possibility of using the Y-BOCS-SC to assess not only the presence of certain symptoms but also the functional relationship between obsessions and compulsions (Conelea, Freeman, & Garcia, 2012).

Cross-cultural studies have demonstrated that the Y-BOCS is a valid measure in different geographical and cultural contexts (Arrindell, de Vlaming, Eisenhardt, ven Berkum, & Keww, 2002) as well as in different populations, including Asian, Hispanic, and White groups (Garnaat & Norton, 2010). Controversial results have been reported for African American populations, with some studies establishing it as a valid measure (Williams, Wetterneck, Thibodeau, & Duque, 2013), but others suggesting that it might under-estimate the interference, distress, and attempts at resistance due to obsessions among Black participants (Garnaat & Norton, 2010).

A limitation of the Y-BOCS is that it is both a time- and resource-consuming tool. The whole Y-BOCS requires an average of 30–40 minutes per individual and the use of trained raters (Grabill et al., 2008). Self-report versions of the Y-BOCS, some of them computer-administered, have been developed to solve this (Federici et al., 2010; Steketee, Frost, & Bogart, 1996; Warren, Zgourides, & Monto, 1993). Although they may be a more cost-effective alternative to the clinical interview, low convergence with the original Y-BOCS and potential discrepancies for overall severity classification suggest the need for revision and more detailed instructions to enhance their validity (Federici et al., 2010).

Yale–Brown Obsessive-Compulsive Scale – Second Edition (Y-BOCS-II). The Y-BOCS has several limitations. These include lower sensitivity to slight changes in the severity of symptoms, lack of integration of compulsive avoidance, ambiguity of some items, low correlation between resistance against obsessions and the total severity score. The second edition of the Y-BOCS (Y-BOCS-II) was developed to overcome some of these limitations (Storch et al., 2010b). Major changes from the original Y-BOCS include the replacement of the "resistance against obsessions" item for an "obsession-free interval" item; extending the scoring for each one of the obsessions and compulsions scales from 5 to 6 points (raising the upper limit on the total Y-BOCS-II scores to 50 instead of 40); integrating avoidance to the scoring of the severity scale items; and modifying the Symptom Checklist content and format (Storch et al., 2010a). The Y-BOCS-II has also shown good psychometric properties (see Table 10.1).

Child Yale–Brown Obsessive-Compulsive Scale (CY-BOCS). The Child Yale–Brown Obsessive-Compulsive Scale (CY-BOCS) (Scahill et al., 1997), adapted from the adult version in a child-friendly language, was developed in 1997. The overall structure, anchor points, and scoring were retained from the Y-BOCS, and therefore it provides with an obsession and a compulsion subscale score, as well as a total severity score. The CY-BOCS often involves two informants: the child and a parent/caregiver. Depending on the age and level of anxiety, the interview may be conducted jointly with the parent and the child, or sequentially. The clinician conducting the interview is called on to integrate data from both informants. A self-report measure, both for child- and parent-rated versions, has been developed (Storch et al., 2006a) (see Table 10.3), as well as a modified version for Pervasive Developmental Disorders (Scahill et al., 2006).

Dimensional Yale–Brown Obsessive-Compulsive Scale (DY-BOCS). OCD is currently conceptualized as a multidimensional disorder (Mataix-Cols, Rosario-Campos, & Leckman, 2005), consisting of three to five major clinical symptom dimensions (Bloch, Landeros-Weisenberger, Rosário, Pittenger, & Leckman, 2008). Accordingly, an effort has been made to develop tools that allow severity ratings for each OC symptom dimension, such as the Dimensional Yale–Brown Obsessive-Compulsive Scale (DY-BOCS) (Rosário et al., 2006). The DY-BOCS is a semi-structured interview that includes a self-report instrument and an interview by an expert rater (based on the self-report). The DY-BOCS self-report consists of an 88-item patient-friendly written checklist designed to provide a detailed description of obsessions and compulsions, that are divided into six different OC symptom dimensions: (1) harm due to aggression, injury, violence, natural disasters; (2) sexual, moral, religious; (3) symmetry, just-right, counting, ordering, arranging; (4) contamination, cleaning; (5) hoarding; and (6) miscellaneous obsessions and compulsions. Severity for each dimension is measured on three scales focusing on symptom frequency (0–5), associated distress (0–5), and interference with functioning (0–5) during the previous week. The raters are asked to estimate global OC symptom severity using the same three scales. Finally, they are asked to assess an individual's overall level of current impairment due to OC symptoms on a 0 (none) to 15 (severe) scale. The total global score is obtained by combining the sum of the global severity scores for frequency, distress, and interference, and the impairment score (0–15), yielding a maximum total severity score of 30. Data on an independent validation of the English DY-BOCS have been presented recently (Pertusa, Fernández de la Cruz, Alonso, Menchón, & Mataix-Cols, 2012).

Advantages of the D-YBOCS include the fact that each dimension assesses the severity of both thematically related obsessions and compulsions, eliminating the bias in collecting information from patients with either obsessions or compulsions only. Moreover, it does not include items about control and resistance, the two items of the Y-BOCS that do not seem to contribute meaningfully to severity assessment (Woody, Steketee, & Chambless, 1995). It also expands from five to six anchor points the ordinal scales, allowing for a better assessment of individuals with subclinical symptoms. Finally, it includes avoidance behaviors, one of the major shortcomings of the Y-BOCS. A limitation of the D-YBOCS is time burden, since it takes approximately 40 minutes to complete the self-report and slightly longer (*c.* 50 minutes) to complete the interview.

NIMH Global Obsessive-Compulsive Scale (GOCS). The GOCS (Taylor, 1995) is a clinician-rated single-item measure of the overall severity of OC symptoms, ranging from 1 (minimal symptoms or within normal range) to 15 (very severe). Severity levels are clustered into five main groups (i.e., ratings of 1–3, 4–6, 7–9, 10–12, and 13–15), with detailed descriptions for each cluster. Although it has been widely use in clinical trials, little is known about its psychometric properties.

Self-report Questionnaires

Table 10.2 offers a summary of the psychometric properties of the main self-report instruments assessing OC symptoms/OCD. Of those, the most widely used measures are described below.

Leyton Obsessional Inventory – Survey Form (LOI-Survey Form). The LOI-Survey Form (Kazarian, Evans, & Lefave, 1977) was developed to assess OC symptoms and obsessive traits. It includes four subscales and several questions devoted to assess resistance and interference. It has shown adequate psychometric properties. However, it is a time-consuming scale. For this reason, a reduced version was developed, the LOI – Short Form (Mathews, Jang, Hami, & Stein, 2004). The LOI-SF has demonstrated overall good psychometric properties, although convergent validity data are

Table 10.2 Self-report instruments for obsessive-compulsive symptoms and obsessive-compulsive disorder (adults)

Instrument[1] & reference	Validated versions	No. of items and approx. testing time	Factor structure	Internal consistency[2]	Test–retest reliability[2]	Convergent validity[3]	Divergent validity[3]	Sensitivity to treatment	Diagnostic sensitivity
LOI-Survey Form Leyton Obsessional Inventory (Kazarian et al., 1977; Cooper, 1970).	English	69 items 90 min	Clean and tidy; indecision; checking; orderliness; sensitization.	Good	Good (Stanley et al., 1993).	Large–medium (Stanley et al., 1993).	Large (Stanley et al., 1993).	Yes (PF) (Allen & Rack, 1975).	Cutoff = 15 Sensitivity = 80% Specificity = 88% (OCD vs. non-OCD) (Stanley et al., 1993).
LOCQ Lynfield Obsessional/ Compulsive Questionnaires (Allen & Tune, 1975)	English	20 items 15 min	Clean and tidy; incompleteness; checking; rumination.	NA	NA	NA	NA	NA	NA
CAC Compulsive Activities Checklist (Steketee & Freund, 1993; Philpott, 1975)	English, French.	38 items 5 min	Non-clinical sample: washing; checking; personal hygiene. OCD sample: washing-cleanliness; checking.	Excellent	Questionable	Medium	NA	Yes (CBT)	Sensitivity = 71% (OCD/anxiety) Sensitivity = 84% (OCD vs. controls).
MOCI Maudsley Obsessive Compulsive Inventory (Hodgson & Rachman, 1977)	Chinese, English, French, German, Icelandic, Italian Japanese, Korean, Norwegian, Spanish, Turkish.	30 items 10 min	Checking; cleaning; slowness; doubting.	Acceptable	Good (1 month)	Large	NA	Yes (PF, CBT) (Thordarson et al., 2004).	NA

Measure (reference)	Language	Items/Time	Content/subscales						
HSCL Hopkins Symptom Checklist (Steketee & Doppelt, 1986; Derogatis, Lipman, Rickels, Uhlenhuth, & Covi, 1974)	English	58 items 30 min	Obsessive-compulsive; anxiety; depression; somatization; interpersonal sensitivity.	Good	Unacceptable–poor	Poor	Medium with depression and anxiety.	Yes (CBT) (subscales marginally sensitive).	Cutoff = 16 (OCD vs. anxiety).
PI Padua Inventory (Sanavio, 1988)	Chinese, Dutch English, French, German, Italian, Japanese, Persian, Spanish, Turkish.	60 items 30 min	Impaired control of mental activity; contaminated; checking; urges & worries of losing control.	Acceptable– excellent	Good	Large	Large with extraversion and psychoticism. Medium with anxiety.	NA	NA
HOCI-S Hamburg Obsessive-Compulsive Inventory – Short form (Klepsch, Zaworka, Hand, Lünenschloss, & Jauernig, 1991)	German	72 items 23 min	Checking; cleaning; arranging; counting, touching, speaking; thoughts of words– pictures; thoughts about doing harm to oneself– others.	Acceptable	Acceptable– excellent (3 months, OCD). Poor–acceptable (neurotic syndromes).	Large	Medium with personality and anxiety.	NA	NA
CAC-R Compulsive Activities Checklist – Revised (Steketee & Freund, 1993)	English	28 items 3–5 min	NA	Good	NA	Large	NA	NA	NA

(Continued)

Table 10.2 (Continued)

Instrument[1] & reference	Validated versions	No. of items and approx. testing time	Factor structure	Internal consistency[2]	Test–retest reliability[2]	Convergent validity[3]	Divergent validity[3]	Sensitivity to treatment	Diagnostic sensitivity
SRS Self-Rated Scale for Obsessive-Compulsive Scale (Kaplan, 1994)	English	35 items 15–20 min	Obsessions; rituals; perfection; contamination.	Excellent	NA	Large	NA	NA	NA
PI-R Padua Inventory – Revised (Van Oppen et al., 1995)	Dutch, Turkish.	41 items 20–25 min	Impulses; washing; checking; rumination; precision.	Good–excellent	NA	Medium–large	Poor–medium	NA	NA
YBOCS-SR Yale–Brown Obsessive Compulsive Self-Report (Steketee, Frost, & Bogart, 1996; Baer, Brown-Beasley, Sorce, & Henriques, 1993)	English, Korean.	58 items 40 min	Time spent; interference; distress; resistance; control.	Acceptable (OCD) Good (controls)	Good (1 week, controls). (Warren, Zgourides, & Monto, 1993).	Large	NA	NA	Cut-off=16. Good. Sensitivity Poor Specificity (50% of the non-patients scored above the cut-off).
PI-WSUR Padua Inventory – Washington State University Revision (Burns et al., 1996)	English, German, Icelandic, Persian, Spanish, Turkish.	39 items 10 min	Obsessions about harm self/others; impulses to harm self-others; contamination/washing; checking; dressing-grooming.	Acceptable–excellent.	Questionable–acceptable.	Large (Jónsdóttir & Smári, 2000).	Medium–large	NA	NA

Measure	Languages	Items / time	Subscales			Effect size		Treatment sensitivity	Cut-off / Sensitivity / Specificity
OCI Obsessive-Compulsive Inventory (Foa et al., 1998)	English, Italian.	42 items 12–14 min	Washing; checking; doubting; ordering; obsessing; hoarding; mental neutralizing.	Acceptable–excellent (OCD, social phobia and controls).	Good except for ordering in OCD (acceptable); and doubting and hoarding in controls (questionable).	Medium–large	Medium with anxiety and depression	NA	NA
A-OCS Arabic Obsessive-Compulsive Scale (Abdel-Khalek, 1998)	Arabic, English.	32 items 15 min	Doubts, orderliness and discipline; slowness and hesitation; rumination and compulsion; meticulousness and repetition; checking; obsessive thoughts.	Acceptable	Good	Medium–large	Large	NA	NA
OCI-R Obsessive-Compulsive Inventory – Revised (Foa et al., 2002)	African Americans, Brazilian-Portuguese, Chinese, English, French, German, Icelandic, Italian, Korean, Norwegian, Persian, Spanish.	18 items 3–5 min	Washing; checking; obsessing; ordering; hoarding; mental neutralizing.	Good–excellent (OCD). Acceptable–good for controls except for checking (questionable) and neutralizing (unacceptable).	Acceptable–good (OCD). Questionable–good (controls).	Large	Large with depression.	Yes (CBT) (Belloch et al., 2013).	Cut-off=21 (OCD vs. non-anxious) Sensitivity=65% Specificity=64% Cut-off=18 (OCD vs. anxiety) Sensitivity=74%. Specificity=75%.

(*Continued*)

Table 10.2 (Continued)

Instrument[1] & reference	Validated versions	No. of items and approx. testing time	Factor structure	Internal consistency[2]	Test–retest reliability[2]	Convergent validity[3]	Divergent validity[3]	Sensitivity to treatment	Diagnostic sensitivity
OBS-SR Obsessive Compulsive Spectrum Self-Report Version (Dell'Osso et al., 2002)	Italian, English, Spanish.	195 items 90 min	Childhood–adolescence experiences; doubt; hypercontrol; attitudes toward time; perfectionism; repetion and automation; specific themes (contamination, cleaning, sexual, existential attitude toward religion, aggressive).	Good–excellent	NA	NA	NA	NA	NA
VOCI Vancouver Obsessive-Compulsive Inventory (Thordarson et al., 2004)	English, French, Italian, German, Spanish.	55 items 35–40 min	Contamination; checking; obsessions; hoarding; routine, counting, slowness; indecisiveness, perfection, concern over mistakes (just right).	Good–excellent (OCD). Acceptable–good (students).	Excellent (47 days, OCD). Poor (11 days, students).	Large except with Y-BOCS (poor). (OCD and students).	Medium (OCD) Medium–large (students).	NA	NA
LOI-Short Form Leyton Obsessional Inventory –Short Form (Mathews et al., 2004)	English	30 items 10 min	Contamination; repeating, doubts; checking; worries, just right.	Good	NA	NA	Medium–large	NA	NA
SCOPI Schedule of Compulsions, Obsessions, and Pathological Impulses (Watson & Wu, 2005)	English	45 items 10–15 min	Checking; cleanliness; pathological impulses; compulsive rituals; hoarding.	Good	Good (2 months)	Large (OCD and controls)	NA	NA	NA

	Language	Items & time	Content	Internal consistency	Test–retest	Effect size	Validity		
VOCI-MC Vancouver Obsessive-Compulsive Inventory – Mental Contamination (Rachman, 2006)	English	20 items 5 min	Mental contamination severity.	Excellent (OCD, anxiety and students).	NA	Medium–large.	Poor with anxiety and medium with depression.	NA	NA
CBOCI Clark–Beck Obsessive-Compulsive Inventory (Clark, Antony, Beck, Swinson, & Steer, 2005)	English.	25 items 5 min	Frequency and severity of obsessions and compulsions.	Good–excellent.	Acceptable (1 month, students).	High (OCD and controls).	Low (OCD and students).	NA	NA
FOCI Florida Obsessive-Compulsive Inventory (Storch et al., 2007)	English.	20 items & 5 dimensions of severity 5 min	Distress; interference; time occupied; resistance; degree of control.	Good	NA	Large	Checklist: Medium symptom severity; poor with depression	Yes (CBT) (Aldea et al., 2009)	NA
YBOCS-SR Checklist Yale–Brown Obsessive Compulsive Self-Report Checklist (Wu, Watson, & Clark, 2007)	English.	40 items 20 min	Obsessions: Aggressive; sexual; religious; somatic; symmetry; contamination; hoarding; miscellaneous. Compulsions: checking; ordering; counting; repeating; cleaning; hoarding; miscellaneous.	Acceptable–good	NA	NA	NA	NA	NA

(Continued)

Table 10.2 (Continued)

Instrument[1] & reference	Validated versions	No. of items and approx. testing time	Factor structure	Internal consistency[2]	Test–retest reliability[2]	Convergent validity[3]	Divergent validity[3]	Sensitivity to treatment	Diagnostic sensitivity
VOCI-R Vancouver Obsessive-Compulsive Inventory – Revised (Gönner, Ecker, Leonhart, & Limbacher, 2010)	German, English, French.	30 items 15 min	Contamination; checking; hoarding; symmetry-ordering; obsessions.	Good–excellent	Acceptable	Large except with Y-BOCS-SR (medium).	Medium	NA	NA
SOAQ Symmetry Ordering and Arranging Questionnaire (Gönner et al., 2010; Radomsky & Rachman, 2004)	English, French, German.	20 items 10 min	Developed as an optional module to supplement VOCI. Ordering and arranging behaviors.	Excellent	Excellent	Medium	Medium	NA	NA
PI-PR Padua Inventory – Palatine Revision (Gönner, Ecker, & Leonhart, 2010)	German	24 items 10–12 min	Contamination, washing, checking; numbers; dressing-grooming; rumination; harming.	Acceptable–excellent (OCD and anxiety).	NA	Large except with Y-BOCS (medium).	Medium–large (OCD & anxiety).	NA	Cut-off = 1.0 (OCD vs. anxiety). Sensitivity = 77%. Specificity = 76%.
DOCS Dimensional Obsessive-Compulsive Scale (Abramowitz et al., 2010)	English, Icelandic, Spanish, Swedish.	20 items 10 min	Contamination, cleaning; harm-checking; order-arranging; unacceptable intrusions – compulsive neutralizing.	Good–excellent (OCD and students).	Poor–questionable (12 weeks, students).	Large (OCD and students).	Medium (OCD, anxiety disorders and students).	Yes (CBT)	Cut-off = 21 (OCD vs. anxiety). Sensitivity = 70%. Specificity = 70%. Cut-off = 18 (OCD vs. controls). Sensitivity = 78%. Specificity = 78%.

Measure	Language	Items / time	Constructs						Cut-off / sensitivity / specificity
POCS Perinatal Obsessive-Compulsive Scale (Lord, Rieder, Hall, Soares, & Steiner, 2011)	English	Prenatal: 15 items. Postpartum: 33 items. 35 min	Severity; interference.	Excellent	NA	Large	NA	NA	Severity: Cut-off=9. Sensitivity=62%. Specificity=92%. Interference: cut-off=5.5. Sensitivity=64%. Specificity=94%.
BOCS Brief Obsessive-Compulsive Scale (Bejerot et al., 2014)	Swedish	16 checklist items & 6 severity items 20 min	Symmetry; forbidden thoughts; contamination; magical thoughts; dysmorphic thoughts.	Poor (checklist). Excellent (severity scale).	NA	NA	NA	Yes (CBT)	Checklist: Cut-off=0.15. Sensitivity=85% for OCD. Specificity=62–70% for other diagnoses. Severity: Cut-off=1.50. Sensitivity=72% for OCD. Specificity=75–84% for other disorders.

Abbreviations: NA=Not available; PF=Psychopharmacological treatment; CBT=Cognitive-behavioral treatment.

[1] Information on the psychometric properties of the measures in the table comes from the original reference, except when there is another reference cited, usually a further validation.

[2] Data on internal consistency and test–retest reliability follow this classification: ≥ .9 = excellent; .8–.89 = good; .7–.79 = acceptable; .6–.69 = questionable; .5–.59 = poor; ≤ .5 = unacceptable based on (George & Mallery, 2003).

[3] Judgment of validity (convergent and divergent) follows this classification: ≥ .10 = small; ≥ .30 = medium; ≥ .50 = large (Cohen, 1977). Note that for divergent validity the classification is reversed (i.e., high correlations with instruments measuring different constructs are noted as "small," moderate correlations are noted as "medium," and low correlations are noted as "large").

limited (Grabill et al., 2008). We did not identify validated versions of the LOI-SF in languages other than the English in our review.

Padua Inventory (PI).   The PI (Sanavio, 1988) is a widely used self-report of OC symptoms in research and clinical settings. It has a four-factor structure and, overall, excellent psychometric properties. It has been validated into several languages (see Table 10.2). The original PI has however been criticized because of possible confounding of obsessions and worries and also because it is time-consuming (around 30 minutes) (Grabill et al., 2008; Overduin & Furnham, 2012). Shorter versions have been developed, including the Padua Inventory – Washington State University Revision (PI-WSUR) (Burns, Keortge, Formea, & Sternberger, 1996), the Padua Inventory – Revised (PI-R) (Van Oppen, Hoekstra, & Emmelkamp, 1995) and, more recently, the Padua Inventory – Palatine Revision (PI-PR) (Gönner, Ecker, & Leonhart, 2010). Overall, there is consistency in the psychometric properties of the PI in different cultures. However, there have been some concerns about its factor structure and discriminant validity. The factor structure has been replicated in non-clinical samples of some (Gönner et al., 2010; Zhong et al., 2011), but not all (Besiroglu et al., 2005; Mataix-Cols et al., 2002) cultural contexts, and has not been confirmed in clinical or mixed samples (Gönner et al., 2010) There is also a need to further demonstrate its discriminant validity across different cultural contexts, particularly for the "Urges and Worries" subscale (Kyrios et al., 1996).

Obsessive-Compulsive Inventory – Revised (OCI-R).   The OCI-R (Foa et al., 2002) is another "classical" assessment instrument for OC symptoms, which has been validated into more than 10 languages (see Table 10.2) and has shown, overall, excellent psychometric properties in both clinical (Foa et al., 2002) and nonclinical samples (Fullana et al., 2005). The OCI-R was developed after the Obsessive-Compulsive Inventory (Foa, Kozak, Salkovskis, Coles, & Amir, 1998). Noted limitations of the OCI-R include the excessive weight of compulsions in comparison with obsessions and the lack of a separate severity scale (Grabill et al., 2008). In general, the OCI-R is a useful measure to assess OC symptoms in different cultural contexts, with sound psychometric properties, except for the neutralization subscale in non-OCD individuals (Foa et al., 2002; Fullana et al., 2005; Gönner et al., 2008; Sica et al., 2009; Woo et al., 2010). Cross-cultural validations (American, French, German, Icelandic, Italian, and Spanish versions) have confirmed the six-factor structure of the scale (Sica et al., 2009). However, differences have been found between university students and OCD patients from Korea compared with other cultures. Korean students and patients tend to score higher on the OCI total, neutralizing, washing, and obsessing subscales compared with French, Icelandic, and Spanish students, and also compared with German patients (Woo et al., 2010). On the other hand, the cut-off of 21 established by the original version to identify OCD cases does not seem to be high enough to detect cases among African Americans (cut-off = 36) (Williams et al., 2013).

Vancouver Obsessive-Compulsive Inventory (VOCI).   Developed to improve upon the Maudsley Obsessional Compulsive Inventory (MOCI) (Hodgson & Rachman, 1977), the VOCI (Thordarson et al., 2004) covers six different dimensions and its factor structure has been confirmed in OCD patients. Strengths of the VOCI include its coverage of cognitive and behavioral aspects of OCD. However, it does not cover dimensions such as ordering/symmetry, doubts, or mental ritualizing. To complement these missing dimensions, the use of the Symmetry, Ordering, and Arranging Questionnaire (SOAQ) (Radomsky & Rachman, 2004) has been proposed. The six-factor structure of the VOCI has been replicated in other languages, namely, French, German, Italian, and Spanish, and using clinical and nonclinical samples (see Table 10.2), with the exception of the German version, where the "Obsessions" subscale has not been replicated in a clinical sample. Two more narrowly defined obsessional dimensions were proposed ("Immoral Obsessions" and "Harming Obsessions") (Gönner et al., 2010). Finally, as in the original version, limited support for discriminant validity has been found in an Italian sample of non-clinical subjects (Chiorri et al, 2011).

Dimensional Obsessive-Compulsive Inventory (DOCS). The DOCS (Abramowitz et al., 2010) has been validated into at least four different languages and covers the four most replicated OC symptom dimensions (contamination/cleaning, harm/checking, order/arranging, and unacceptable intrusions/compulsive neutralizing). Following current developments in the OCD and related disorders field, hoarding symptoms were not included in the scale (Abramowitz et al., 2010). The original DOCS has shown good psychometric properties qualities in both clinical and non-clinical samples (Abramowitz et al., 2010). The Spanish and Icelandic versions of the DOCS (López-Solà et al., 2014; Ólafsson et al., 2013) have similar psychometric properties to the original American instrument. For the Spanish version, the psychometrics are somewhat better among OCD patients than among students (López-Solà, 2013). The Swedish version of the DOCS (Enander et al., 2012) gives support for the Internet administration of the scale to OCD patients.

Assessment in Children and Adolescents

Assessment of children and adolescents with OCD/OC symptoms can be specially challenging for a number of reasons. First, OC symptoms, especially obsessions, are usually not noticeable to others (Merlo, Storch, Murphy, Goodman, & Geffken, 2005). Although some OC symptoms have relatively clear behavioral signs, such as frequent hand washing, others may be more difficult to identify (Rapoport et al., 2000). This may lead to the disorder being underrecognized and underdiagnosed in this age group. This is especially relevant given the already mentioned embarrassing nature of the symptoms. OC symptoms, especially those from the "forbidden thoughts" dimension (i.e., aggressive, sexual, and religious obsessions) (Bloch et al., 2008), may remain undetected as young people would not want to disclose symptoms, which might be perceived as unacceptable and/or embarrassing (Canavera, Wilkins, Pincus, & Ehrenreich-May, 2009; Fernández de la Cruz et al., 2013). A second aspect to take into account has to do with the developmental stage of the child. Depending on the degree of maturity, self-report of symptoms (especially obsessions as compared with compulsions) may be difficult. Young people may lack the cognitive maturity to identify thoughts as unwanted or may feel that if they admit to wishing they did not have symptoms, they may be asked to stop ritualizing, which they fear would be difficult and anxiety-provoking (Veale, Freeston, Krebs, Heyman, & Salkovskis, 2009). Finally, the assessment of pediatric OCD is particularly difficult given the wide range of symptom presentation and the idiosyncratic nature of symptoms (Merlo et al., 2005).

Table 10.3 presents a summary of the psychometric properties of a number of self-report (and/or parent-report) tools to assess severity of OC symptoms in children and adolescents. As can be seen, in comparison with adults, there is a shortage of

Table 10.3 Self-report instruments for obsessive-compulsive symptoms and obsessive-compulsive disorder (children/adolescents)

Instrument[1]	Validated versions	No. of items and approx. testing time	Factor structure	Internal consistency[2]	Test–retest reliability[2]	Convergent validity[3]	Divergent validity[3]	Sensitivity to treatment	Diagnostic sensitivity
LOI-CV Survey Form Leyton Obsessional Inventory – Child Version, Survey Form (Berg et al., 1988)	English	20 items×2, if applicable (interference questions) 45–50 min	General obsessive; dirt–contamination; numbers–luck; school.	Good (Berg et al., 1988; Storch et al., 2011).	Poor–good based on child age (King, Inglis, Jenkins, Myerson, & Ollendick, 1995).	Low–medium (Berg et al., 1988; Stewart, Ceranoglu, O'Hanley, & Geller, 2005; Storch et al., 2011).	NA	Mixed results (Como & Kurlan, 1991; de Haan, Hoogduin, Buitelaar, & Keijsers, 1998; Geller et al., 2003; Storch et al., 2011).	Mixed evidence (Flament et al., 1988; Stewart et al., 2005; Storch et al., 2011; Wolff & Wolff, 1991).
Ch-OCI Children's Obsessional Compulsive Inventory (Shafran et al., 2003)	English	44 items 20 min	NA	Good	NA	Medium	NA	NA	Cut-off=17. Sensitivity=88%. Specificity=95%.
CHOCI-R Children's Obsessional Compulsive Inventory – Revised (Uher et al., 2008)	English	32 items 15 min	Unifactorial.	Acceptable–good.	NA	Medium–large.	Medium–large.	NA	NA
CY-BOCS-CR & CY-BOCS-PR Children's Yale–Brown Obsessive-Compulsive Scale – Child Report & Parent Report (Storch et al., 2006)	English, Spanish.	10 items 5 min	NA	Acceptable–good.	NA	Large.	Medium.	NA	NA

Measure	Language	Items / Time	Subscales	Internal consistency	Test-retest	Convergent validity	Divergent validity	Treatment sensitivity	Available treatment
C-FOCI Children's Florida Obsessive-Compulsive Inventory (Storch et al., 2009)	English	17 items 10 min	NA	Good.	NA	Medium-large.	Good (with externalizing symptoms).	Yes (CBT)	NA
OCI-CV Obsessive Compulsive Inventory – Child Version (Foa et al., 2010)	English, Spanish.	21 items 10 min	Doubting, checking; obsessing; hoarding; washing; ordering; neutralizing.	Good (Foa et al., 2010; A. M. Jones et al., 2013).	Good	Medium (Foa et al., 2010; A. M. Jones et al., 2013).	Medium-large (Foa et al., 2010; A. M. Jones et al., 2013).	Yes (CBT, PF, or combination).	NA

Note: All instruments consist of a child- and a parent-report version except for the LOI-CV Survey Form, the C-FOCI, and the OCI-CV.

Abbreviations: NA = Not available; PF = Psychopharmacological treatment; CBT = Cognitive-behavioral treatment.

[1] Information on the psychometric properties of the measures in the table comes from the original reference cited, usually a further validation.

[2] Data on internal consistency and test-retest reliability follow this classification: ≥ .9 = excellent; .8–.89 = good; .7–.79 = acceptable; .6–.69 = questionable; .5–.59 = poor; ≤ .5 = unacceptable based on George & Mallery (2003).

[3] Judgment of validity (convergent and divergent) follows this classification: ≥ .10 = small; ≥ .30 = medium; ≥ .50 = large (Cohen, 1977). Note that for divergent validity the classification is reversed (i.e., high correlations with instruments measuring different constructs are noted as "small," moderate correlations are noted as "medium," and low correlations are noted as "large").

assessment tools for pediatric OCD. These instruments include the Leyton Obsessional Inventory – Child Version (LOI-CV) Survey Form (Berg, Whitaker, Davies, Flament, & Rapoport, 1988), derived from the LOI-CV Card Sorting Task (Berg, Rapoport, & Flament, 1986); the Children's Obsessional Compulsive Inventory (Shafran et al., 2003), as well as its revised version (Uher, Heyman, Turner, & Shafran, 2008); the CY-BOCS Child-Report (CY-BOCS-CR) and Parent-Report (Storch et al., 2006b); the Obsessive-Compulsive Inventory – Child Version (OCI-CV) (Foa et al., 2010); and the Children's Florida Obsessive-Compulsive Inventory (C-FOCI) (Storch et al., 2009). Unfortunately, few validations of these assessment tools into different languages/cultures have been published so far. Our systematic review identified Spanish versions of the child reported CY-BOCS (Godoy et al., 2011) and the OCI-CV (Rosa-Alcazar et al., 2014) (see Table 10.3). Overall, both Spanish instruments showed similar psychometric characteristics as the original English version in population samples. Additionally, a Greek version of the LOI-CV has been standardized in a school-based sample of adolescents (Roussos et al., 2013).

Despite not being an instrument specifically designed to assess OC symptoms, an additional measure that deserves mention is the Obsessive Compulsive Scale of the Child Behavior Checklist (CBCL) (Achenbach, 1991), which has shown good psychometric properties (Geller et al., 2006; Hudziak et al., 2006; Nelson et al., 2001; Storch et al., 2006b). For a comprehensive review of these self-report questionnaires, see Merlo et al. (2005) and Storch et al. (2009).

Given the importance of the family involvement in the treatment of pediatric OCD (and often in its maintenance), scales that assess the role of family members in the disorder, such as the Family Accommodation Scale (Calvocoressi et al., 1999; Pinto, Van Noppen, & Calvocoressi, 2013), have a special relevance in children. Accommodation of OC symptoms refers to actions taken by the family members to facilitate rituals (e.g., provide objects needed for rituals), comply with the child's demands (e.g., following a certain routine to minimize anxiety), provide reassurance to the child (e.g., answer questions repeatedly), decrease child responsibility (e.g., minimize attempts at discipline), or assist with or complete tasks for the child (e.g., provide extra assistance with homework, chores, and so on). The parent-rated version of the FAS has shown good psychometric properties in pediatric populations (Flessner et al., 2011; Storch et al., 2007).

Another useful tool in the assessment of pediatric OCD is the Child Obsessive-Compulsive Impact Scale – Revised (COIS-R) (Piacentini, Bergman, Keller, & McCracken, 2003; Piacentini, Peris, Bergman, Chang, & Jaffer, 2007). This is a parent- and child-report questionnaire measuring to what extent pediatric OCD causes impairment in specific areas of child psychosocial functioning. The scale has shown good psychometric properties and low scores at baseline have been related to poorer treatment outcomes (Piacentini, Bergman, Jacobs, McCracken, & Kretchman, 2002). Moreover, it has shown to be sensitive to treatment effects (Geller et al., 2003; Liebowitz et al., 2002).

Measures of OCD-related Phenomena

The publication of the *Diagnostic and Statistical Manual of Mental Disorders* (Fifth Edition) (DSM-5) (American Psychiatric Association, 2013) has emancipated OCD from the anxiety disorders chapter to be part of an independent "OCD and related disorders" chapter, along with body dysmorphic disorder (BDD), hoarding disorder, trichotillomania (hair-pulling disorder), and excoriation (skin-picking) disorder, as well as other residual categories. Research into assessment tools for these conditions is certainly scarce and in need of further developments. However, there are some measures that have been developed and validated, showing adequate psychometric properties.

In the case of BDD, a modified version of the Y-BOCS, the Yale–Brown Obsessive Compulsive Scale modified for Body Dysmorphic Disorder (BDD-YBOCS) (Phillips et al., 1997; Phillips, Hart, & Menard, 2014) can be used to assess severity of the symptoms. Related self-report questionnaires with adequate psychometric properties include the Body Dysmorphic Disorder Questionnaire (BDDQ) (Dufresne, Phillips, Vittorio, & Wilkel, 2001; Phillips, 2009), the Dysmorphic Concern Questionnaire (DCQ) (Jorgensen, Castle, Roberts, & Groth-Marnat, 2001), or the Appearance Anxiety Inventory (AAI) (Veale et al., 2013).

Regarding hoarding disorder, despite its recent inclusion in the DSM-5, several assessment tools already exist. Among the most extensively used tools, we find the Hoarding Rating Scale (HRS) (Tolin, Frost, & Steketee, 2010), the Saving Inventory Revised (SI-R) (Frost, Steketee, & Grisham, 2004), and the Clutter Image Rating (CIR) (Frost, Steketee, Tolin, & Renaud, 2008) – the latter specifically designed to assess the level of clutter. All of them have shown to be valid and reliable to assess hoarding symptoms. More recently, a clinician-administered diagnostic interview, the Structured Interview for Hoarding Disorder (SIHD), has been developed and has shown good psychometric properties (Nordsletten et al., 2013).

Assessment tools for the so-called body-focused repetitive behavioral disorders (Stein et al., 2010), including hair-pulling and skin-picking disorders, are notably scarcer and, overall, present with more limited psychometric properties. The diagnostic, clinician-administered Yale–Brown Obsessive-Compulsive Scale modified for assessment of trichotillomania (Y-BOCS-TM) (Stanley, Prather, Wagner, Davis, & Swann, 1993) and the Y-BOCS modified for Neurotic Excoriation (NE-YBOCS) (Arnold et al., 1999) are generally used to assess severity of the symptoms. Regarding self-report measures, the Massachusetts General Hospital Hair Pulling Scale (MGH-HPS) (Keuthen et al., 2007), the Skin-Picking Scale (Keuthen et al., 2001) and the Skin-Picking Symptom Assessment Scale (Grant, Odlaug, & Kim, 2007) are probably the most widely used.

More recently, with the release of the DSM-5 and its requirement of dimensional assessments to supplement traditional categorical diagnoses, the DSM-5 subwork group on obsessive-compulsive spectrum disorders developed a set of brief self-rated scales for BDD, hoarding disorder, trichotillomania, and skin-picking disorder (the BDD-D, HD-D, TTM, and SPD-D, respectively). These scales are consistent in content and structure (with some exceptions, all of them enquire about time, distress, degree of control, avoidance, and interference), reflect the DSM-5 criteria, and can be used by clinicians to help generate a dimensional severity rating for the disorders. The scales have demonstrated good internal consistency and convergent and divergent validity in nonclinical samples and unidimensionality for each scale has been confirmed. Further evaluation of these scales in clinical samples is warranted (LeBeau et al., 2013).

Additionally, there are a handful of measures that, despite not being designed to assess OCD symptoms or severity, may become handy and relevant to assess other clinical aspects of OCD. These measures, which have mainly emerged from the cognitive-behavioral account of OCD (Taylor, Abramowitz, & McKay, 2007), aim to assess theoretically relevant dysfunctional beliefs found to be associated with the emergence and maintenance of OC symptoms or specific dysfunctional beliefs or appraisals. Some of these measures include the Obsessive Beliefs Questionnaire (OBQ) (Obsessive Compulsive Cognitions Working Group, 2005), the Interpretations of Intrusions Inventory (III) (Obsessive Compulsive Cognitions Working Group, 2005), the Meta-Cognitions Questionnaire (MCQ) (Cartwright-Hatton & Wells, 1997), the Responsibility Attitudes Questionnaire (RAQ) (Salkovskis et al., 2000), the Responsibility Interpretations Questionnaire (RIQ) (Salkovskis et al., 2000), the Thought–Action Fusion Scale (TAFS) (Shafran, Thordarson, & Rachman, 1996), the OCD Origins Questionnaire (OOQ) (M. K. Jones & Menzies, 1998), the Thought Control Questionnaire (TCQ) (Wells & Davies, 1994), the Intolerance of Uncertainty Scale (IUS) (Buhr & Dugas, 2002), and the Multidimensional Perfectionism Scale (MPS) (Frost, Marten, Lahart, & Rosenblate, 1990).

Some of these measures have also been validated in young people, including the Obsessive Beliefs Questionnaire – Child Version (Coles et al., 2010), the Metacognition Questionnaire in its children (Bacow, Pincus, Ehrenreich, & Brody, 2009) and adolescent (Cartwright-Hatton et al., 2004) versions, the Thought Action Fusion Inventory for Children (Evans, Hersperger, & Capaldi, 2011), the Thought–Action Fusion Questionnaire for Adolescents (Muris, Meesters, Rassin, Merckelbach, & Campbell, 2001), the OCD Origins Questionnaire for Adolescents (Lawrence & Williams, 2011), and the Intolerance of Uncertainty Scale for Children (IUSC) (Read, Comer, & Kendall, 2013).

Moreover, several measures assess specific OCD-relevant constructs. For example, the Not Just Right Experiences Questionnaire – Revised (Coles, Heimberg, Frost, & Steketee, 2005), the University of São Paulo Sensory Phenomena Scale (Rosário et al., 2009), and the Penn Inventory of Scrupulosity (Olatunji, Abramowitz, Williams, Connolly, & Lohr, 2007).

Summary

If we look at the number and diversity of instruments for the assessment of OCD and related constructs currently available, it seems that the OCD clinician/researcher is placed in a privileged position. Many different instruments are available in adults and, to a lesser extent, in children/adolescents. Moreover, adapted and validated versions of many instruments exist in different languages/cultures. Despite this, some areas – specially screening measures – are relatively underdeveloped. Also, the performance of current instruments (specially severity measures) in certain ethnic/cultural groups is still unknown or a matter of debate and further research seems warranted.

We believe that future developments in the assessment of OCD and related phenomena will closely follow advances in our psychopathological knowledge of these conditions. New instruments will be needed and "old" instruments will need to be refined. Cross-cultural perspectives may play a major role in this endeavor. Moreover, it is likely that in the following years we see important changes on how assessment instruments are applied, with an increasing use of "new" technologies that may facilitate clinicians and researchers the task of understanding better these highly prevalent phenomena.

References

Abdel-Khalek, A. M. (1998). The Development and Validation of the Arabic Obsessive Compulsive Scale. *European Journal of Psychological Assessment, 14,* 146–158.

Abramowitz, J. S., Deacon, B. J., Olatunji, B. O., Wheaton, M. G., Berman, N. C., Losardo, D., ... Hale, L. R. (2010). Assessment of obsessive-compulsive symptom dimensions: development and evaluation of the Dimensional Obsessive-Compulsive Scale. *Psychological Assessment, 22,* 180–198.

Achenbach, T. (1991). *Child behavior checklist (4–18).* Burlington: University of Vermont.

Allen, J. J., & Rack, P. H. (1975). Changes in obsessive/compulsive patients as measured by the Leyton Inventory before and after treatment with clomipramine. *Scottish Medical Journal, 20,* 41–44.

Allen, J. J., & Tune, G. S. (1975). The Lynfield Obsessional/Compulsive Questionnaires. *Scottish Medical Journal, 20,* 21–24.

American Psychiatric Association (2013). *The Diagnostic and Statistical Manual of Mental Disorders (Fifth Edition: DSM-5).* Washington, DC: American Psychiatric Association.

Amir, N., Foa, E. B., & Coles, M. E. (1997). Factor structure of the Yale–Brown Obsessive-Compulsive Scale. *Psychological Assessment, 9,* 312–316.

Arnold, L. M., Mutasim, D. F., Dwight, M. M., Lamerson, C. L., Morris, E. M., & McElroy, S. L. (1999). An open clinical trial of fluvoxamine treatment of psychogenic excoriation. *Journal of Clinical Psychopharmacology, 19,* 15–18.

Arrindell, W. A., de Vlaming, I. H., Eisenhardt, B. M., ven Berkum, D. E., & Keww, M. G. T. (2002). Cross-cultural validity of the Yale–Brown Obsessive Compulsive Scale. *Journal of Behavioral Therapy and Exposure Psychiatry, 33,*159–176.

Bacow, T. L., Pincus, D. B., Ehrenreich, J. T., & Brody, L. R. (2009). The metacognitions questionnaire for children: Development and validation in a clinical sample of children and adolescents with anxiety disorders. *Journal of Anxiety Disorders, 23,* 727–736.

Baer, L., Brown-Beasley, M. W., Sorce, J., & Henriques, A. I. (1993). Computer-assisted telephone administration of a structured interview for obsessive-compulsive disorder. *American Journal of Psychiatry, 150,* 1737–1738.

Bamber, D., Tamplin, A., Park, R. J., Kyte, Z. A., & Goodyer, I. M. (2002). Development of a short Leyton obsessional inventory for children and adolescents. *Journal of the American Academy of Child and Adolescent Psychiatry, 41,* 1246–1252.

Bejerot, S., Edman, G., Anckarsäter, H., Berglund, G., Gillberg, C., Hofvander, B., ... Frisén, L. (2014). The Brief Obsessive-Compulsive Scale (BOCS): A self-report scale for OCD and obsessive-compulsive related disorders. *Nordic Journal of Psychiatry, 68,* 549–559.

Belloch, A., Roncero, M., García-Soriano, G., Carrió, C., Cabedo, E., & Fernández-Álvarez, H. (2013). The Spanish version of the Obsessive-Compulsive Inventory-Revised (OCI-R): Reliability, validity, diagnostic accuracy, and sensitivity to treatment effects in clinical samples. *Journal of Obsessive-Compulsive and Related Disorders, 2,* 249–256.

Berg, C. J., Rapoport, J. L., & Flament, M. (1986). The Leyton Obsessional Inventory – Child Version. *Journal of the American Academy of Child Psychiatry, 25,* 84–91.

Berg, C. Z., Whitaker, A., Davies, M., Flament, M. F., & Rapoport, J. L. (1988). The Survey Form of the Leyton Obsessional Inventory – Child Version: Norms from an Epidemiological Study. *Journal of the American Academy of Child and Adolescent Psychiatry, 27,* 759–763.

Besiroglu, L., Yücelagargün, M., Boysan, M., Eryonucu, B., Gülec, M., & Selvi, Y. (2005). The assessment of obsessive-compulsive symptoms: Reliability and validity of the Padua Inventory in Turkish population. *Turkish Journal of Psychiatry, 16,* 1–11.

Bloch, M. H., Landeros-Weisenberger, A., Rosario, M. C., Pittenger, C., & Leckman, J. F. (2008). Meta-analysis of the symptom structure of Obsessive-Compulsive Disorder. *American Journal of Psychiatry, 165,* 1532–1542.

Blom, R. M., Hagestein-de Bruijn, C., de Graaf, R., ten Have, M., & Denys, D. A. (2011). Obsessions in normality and psychopathology. *Depression Anxiety, 28*, 870–875.

Brown, T. A., Di Nardo, P. A., Lehman, C. L., & Campbell, L. A. (2001). Reliability of DSM-IV anxiety and mood disorders: Implications for the classification of emotional disorders. *Journal of Abnormal Psychology, 110*, 49–58.

Buhr, K., & Dugas, M. J. (2002). The Intolerance of Uncertainty Scale: Psychometric properties of the English version. *Behaviour Research and Therapy, 40*, 931–945.

Burns, G. L., Keortge, S. G., Formea, G. M., & Sternberger, L. G. (1996). Revision of the Padua Inventory of obsessive compulsive disorder symptoms: Distinctions between worry, obsessions, and compulsions. *Behaviour Research and Therapy, 34*, 163–173.

Calvocoressi, L., Mazure, C. M., Kasl, S. V, Skolnick, J., Fisk, D., Vegso, S. J., ... Price, L. H. (1999). Family accommodation of obsessive-compulsive symptoms: instrument development and assessment of family behavior. *Journal of Nervous and Mental Disease, 187*, 636–642.

Canavera, K. E., Wilkins, K. C., Pincus, D. B., & Ehrenreich-May, J. T. (2009). Parent–child agreement in the assessment of obsessive-compulsive disorder. *Journal of Clinical Child and Adolescent Psychology, 38*, 909–915.

Cartwright-Hatton, S., Mather, A., Illingworth, V., Brocki, J., Harrington, R., & Wells, A. (2004). Development and preliminary validation of the Meta-cognitions Questionnaire – Adolescent Version. *Journal of Anxiety Disorders, 18*, 411–422.

Cartwright-Hatton, S., & Wells, A. (1997). Beliefs about worry and intrusions: The Meta-Cognitions Questionnaire and its correlates. *Journal of Anxiety Disorders, 11*, 279–296.

Chiorri, C., Melli, G., & Smurra, R. (2011). Second-order factor structure of the Vancouver Obsessive Compulsive Inventory (VOCI) in a non-clinical sample. *Behavioural and Cognitive Psychotherapy, 39*, 561–577.

Clark, D. A., Antony, M. M., Beck, A. T., Swinson, R. P., & Steer, R. a. (2005). Screening for obsessive and compulsive symptoms: Validation of the Clark–Beck Obsessive-Compulsive Inventory. *Psychological Assessment, 17*, 132–143.

Cohen, J. (Ed.). (1977). *Statistical power for the behavioral sciences* (Rev. ed.). Hillsdale, NJ: Lawrence Erlbaum.

Coles, M. E., Heimberg, R. G., Frost, R. O., & Steketee, G. (2005). Not just right experiences and obsessive-compulsive features: Experimental and self-monitoring perspectives. *Behaviour Research and Therapy, 43*, 153–167.

Coles, M. E., Wolters, L. H., Sochting, I., de Haan, E., Pietrefesa, A. S., & Whiteside, S. P. (2010). Development and initial validation of the Obsessive Belief Questionnaire – Child Version (OBQ-CV). *Depression and Anxiety, 27*, 982–991.

Como, P. G., & Kurlan, R. (1991). An open-label of fluoxetine for obsessive-compulsive disorder in Gilles de la Tourette's syndrome. *Neurology, 41*, 872–874.

Conelea, C. A., Freeman, J. B., & Garcia, A. M. (2012). Integrating behavioral theory with OCD assessment using the Y-BOCS/CY-BOCS symptom checklist. *Journal of Obsessive-Compulsive and Related Disorders, 1*, 112–118.

Cooper, J. (1970). The Leyton Obsessional Inventory. *Psychological Medicine, 1*, 48–64.

Deacon, B. J., & Abramowitz, J. S. (2005). The Yale–Brown Obsessive-Compulsive Scale: Factor analysis, construct validity, and suggestions for refinement. *Journal of Anxiety Disorders, 19*, 573–585.

De Haan, E., Hoogduin, K. A., Buitelaar, J. K., & Keijsers, G. P. (1998). Behavior therapy versus clomipramine for the treatment of obsessive-compulsive disorder in children and adolescents. *Journal of the American Academy of Child and Adolescent Psychiatry, 37*, 1022–1029.

Dell'Osso, L., Rucci, P., Cassano, G. B., Maser, J. D., Endicott, J., Shear, M. K., ... Frank, E. (2002). Measuring social anxiety and obsessive-compulsive spectra: Comparison of interviews and self-report instruments. *Comprehensive Psychiatry, 43*, 81–87.

Di Nardo, P. A., Brown, T. A., & Barlow, D. H. (1994). *Anxiety Disorders Interview Schedule for DSM-IV: Lifetime version (ADIS-1V-L)*. San Antonio, TX: Psychological Corporation.

Delucchi, K. L., Katerberg, H., Stewart, S. E., Denys, D. A., Lochner, C., Stack, D. E., den Boer, J. A., ... Mathews, C. A. (2011). Latent class analysis of the Yale–Brown Obsessive-Compulsive Scale symptoms in obsessive-compulsive disorder. *Comprehensive Psychiatry, 52*, 334–341.

Derogatis, L. R., Lipman, R. S., Rickels, K., Uhlenhuth, E. H., & Covi, L. (1974). The Hopkins Symptom Checklist (HSCL): A self-report symptom inventory. *Behavioral Science, 19*, 1–15.

Dufresne, R. G., Phillips, K. A., Vittorio, C. C., & Wilkel, C. S. (2001). A screening question- naire for body dysmorphic disorder in a cosmetic dermatologic surgery practice. *Dermatologic Surgery, 27*, 457–462.

Enander, J., Andersson, E., Kaldo, V., Lindefors, N., Andersson, G., & Rück, C. (2012). Internet administration of the Dimensional Obsessive-Compulsive Scale: A psychometric evaluation. *Journal of Obsessive-Compulsive and Related Disorders, 1*, 325–330.

Evans, D. W., Hersperger, C., & Capaldi, P. A. (2011). Thought–action fusion in childhood: Measurement, development, and association with anxiety, rituals and other compulsive-like behaviors. *Child Psychiatry and Human Development, 42*, 12–23.

Federici, A., Summerfeldt, L. J., Harrington, J. L., McCabe, R. E., Purdon, C. L., Rowa, K., & Antony, M. M. (2010). Consistency between self-report and clinician-administered ver- sions of the Yale–Brown Obsessive-Compulsive Scale. *Journal of Anxiety Disorders, 24*, 729–733.

Fernández de la Cruz, L., Barrow, F., Bolhuis, K., Krebs, G., Volz, C., Nakatani, E., ... Mataix- Cols, D. (2013). Sexual obsessions in pediatric obsessive-compulsive disorder: Clinical characteristics and treatment outcomes. *Depression and Anxiety, 30*, 732–740.

First, M. B., Spitzer, R. L., Gibbon, & Williams J. B. W. (2002). *Structured Clinical Interview for DSM-IV-TR Axis I Disorders, Research Version, Patient Edition*. (SCID-I/P) New York: Biometrics Research, New York State Psychiatric Institute.

Flament, M. F., Whitaker, A., Rapoport, J. L., Davies, M., Berg, C. Z., Kalikow, K., ... Shaffer, D. (1988). Obsessive compulsive disorder in adolescence: An epidemiological study. *Journal of the American Academy of Child and Adolescent Psychiatry, 27*, 764–771.

Flessner, C. A., Sapyta, J., Garcia, A., Freeman, J. B., Franklin, M. E., Foa, E. B., & March, J. (2011). Examining the psychometric properties of the Family Accommodation Scale – Parent-report (FAS-PR). *Journal of Psychopathology and Behavioral Assessment, 33*, 38–46.

Foa, E. B., Coles, M. E., Huppert, J. D., Pasupuleti, R. V., Franklin, M. E., & March, J. (2010). Development and validation of a child version of the Obsessive Compulsive Inventory. *Behavior Therapy, 41*, 121–132.

Foa, E. B., Huppert, J. D., Leiberg, S., Langner, R., Kichic, R., Hajcak, G., & Salkovskis, P. M. (2002). The Obsessive-Compulsive Inventory: Development and validation of a short version. *Psychological Assessment, 14*, 485–495.

Foa, E. B., Kozak, M. J., Salkovskis, P. M., Coles, M. E., & Amir, N. (1998). *The validation of a new Obsessive-Compulsive Disorder Scale: The Obsessive-Compulsive Inventory, 10*, 206–214.

Franklin, M. E., & Foa, E. B. (2011). Treatment of obsessive compulsive disorder. *Annual Review of Clinical Psychology, 7*, 229–243

Frost, R. O., Marten, P., Lahart, C., & Rosenblate, R. (1990). The dimensions of perfec- tionism. *Cognitive Therapy and Research, 14*, 449–68.

Frost, R. O., Steketee, G., & Grisham, J. (2004). Measurement of compulsive hoarding: Saving Inventory – Revised. *Behaviour Research and Therapy, 42*, 1163–1182.

Frost, R. O., Steketee, G., Krause, M., & Trepanier, K. L. (1995). The relationship of the Yale– Brown Obsessive-Compulsive Scale (YBOCS) to other measures of obsessive-compulsive symptoms in a nonclinical population. *Journal of Personality Assessment, 65*, 158–168.

Frost, R. O., Steketee, G., Tolin, D., & Renaud, S. (2008). Development and validation of the clutter image rating. *Journal of Psychopathology, 30,* 193–203.

Fullana, M. A., Mataix-Cols, D., Caspi, A., Harrington, H., Grisham, J. R., Moffitt, T. E., & Poulton, R. (2009). Obsessions and compulsions in the community: Prevalence, interference, help-seeking, developmental stability, and co-occurring psychiatric conditions. *American Journal of Psychiatry, 166,* 329–336.

Fullana, M. A., Tortella-Feliu, M., Caseras, X., Andión, O., Torrubia, R., & Mataix-Cols, D. (2005). Psychometric properties of the Spanish version of the Obsessive-Compulsive Inventory – revised in a non-clinical sample. *Journal of Anxiety Disorders, 19,* 893–903.

Gallant, J., Storch, E. A., Merlo, L. J., Ricketts, E. D., Geffken, G. R., Goodman, W. K., & Murphy, T. K. (2008). Convergent and discriminant validity of the Children's Yale–Brown Obsessive Compulsive Scale – Symptom Scale. *Journal of Anxiety Disorders, 22,* 1369–1376.

Garnaat, S. L., & Norton, P. J. (2010). Factor structure and measurement invariance of the Yale–Brown Obsessive-Compulsive Scale across four racial/ethnic groups. *Journal of Anxiety Disorders, 24,* 723–728.

Geller, D. A., Biederman, J., Stewart, S. E., Mullin, B., Martin, A., Spencer, T., & Faraone, S. V. (2003). Which SSRI? A meta-analysis of pharmacotherapy trials in pediatric obsessive-compulsive disorder. *American Journal of Psychiatry, 160,* 1919–1928.

Geller, D. A., Doyle, R., Shaw, D., Mullin, B., Coffey, B., Petty, C., … Biederman, J. (2006). A quick and reliable screening measure for OCD in youth: Reliability and validity of the obsessive compulsive scale of the Child Behavior Checklist. *Comprehensive Psychiatry, 47,* 234–240.

George, D., & Mallery, P. (2003). *SPSS for windows step by step: A sample guide & reference.* Boston: Allyn & Bacon.

Godoy, A., Gavino, A., Valderrama, L., Quintero, C., Cobos, M. P., Casado, Y., Sosa, M. D., & Capafons, J. I (2011). Factor structure and reliability of the Spanish adaptation of the Children's Yale–Brown Obsessive-Compulsive Scale – Self Report (CY-BOCS-SR). *Psicothema, 23,* 330–335.

Gönner, S., Ecker, W., & Leonhart, R. (2010). The Padua Inventory: Do revisions need revision? *Assessment, 17,* 89–106.

Gönner, S., Ecker, W., Leonhart, R., & Limbacher, K. (2010). Multidimensional assessment of OCD: Integration and revision of the Vancouver Obsessional – Compulsive Inventory and the Symmetry Ordering and Arranging Questionnaire. *Journal of Clinical Psychology, 66,* 739–757.

Goodman, W. K., Price, L. H., Rasmussen, S. A., Mazure, C., Delgado, P., Heninger, G. R., & Charney, D. S. (1989a). The Yale–Brown Obsessive-Compulsive Scale-II. *Validity. Archives of General Psychiatry, 46,* 1012–1016.

Goodman, W. K., Price, L. H., Rasmussen, S. A., Mazure, C., Fleischman, R. L., Hill, C. L., Heninger, G. R., & Charney, D. S. (1989b). The Yale–Brown Obsessive-Compulsive Scale-I: Development, use, and reliability. *Archives of General Psychiatry, 46,* 1006–1011.

Grabe, H. J., Meyer, C., Hapke, U., Rumpf, H. J., Freyberger, H. J., Dilling, H., & John, U. (2001). Lifetime-comorbidity of obsessive-compulsive disorder and subclinical obsessive-compulsive disorder in Northern Germany. *European Archives of Psychiatry and Clinical Neurosciences, 251,* 130–135.

Grabill, K., Merlo, L., Duke, D., Harford, K. L., Keeley, M. L., Geffken, G. R., & Storch, E. A. (2008). Assessment of obsessive-compulsive disorder: A review. *Journal of Anxiety Disorders, 22,* 1–17.

Grant, J. E., Odlaug, B. L., & Kim, S. W. (2007). Lamotrigine treatment of pathologic skin picking: An open-label study. *Journal of Clinical Psychiatry, 68,* 1384–1391.

Heyman, I., Mataix-Cols, D., & Fineberg, N.A. (2006). Obsessive-compulsive disorder. *British Medical Journal, 333,* 424–429.

Hiranyatheb, T., Saipanish, R., & Lotrakul, M. (2014). Reliability and validity of the Thai version of the Yale–Brown Obsessive-Compulsive Scale – Second Edition in clinical samples. *Neuropsychiatric Disease and Treatment, 10*, 471–477.

Hodgson, R. J., & Rachman, S. (1977). Obsessional-compulsive complaints. *Behaviour Research and Therapy, 15*, 389–395.

Hudziak, J. J., Althoff, R. R., Stanger, C., van Beijsterveldt, C. E. M., Nelson, E. C., Hanna, G. L., ... Todd, R. D. (2006). The Obsessive Compulsive Scale of the Child Behavior Checklist predicts obsessive-compulsive disorder: A receiver operating characteristic curve analysis. *Journal of Child Psychology and Psychiatry and Allied Disciplines, 47*, 160–166.

Jones, A. M., De Nadai, A. S., Arnold, E. B., McGuire, J. F., Lewin, A. B., Murphy, T. K., & Storch, E. A. (2013). Psychometric properties of the obsessive compulsive inventory: Child version in children and adolescents with obsessive-compulsive disorder. *Child Psychiatry and Human Development, 44*, 137–151.

Jones, M. K., & Menzies, R. G. (1998). The relevance of associative learning pathways in the development of obsessive-compulsive washing. *Behaviour Research and Therapy, 36*, 273–283.

Jónsdóttir, S. D., & Smári, J. (2000). Measuring obsessions without worry: Convergent and discriminant validity of the Revised Padua Inventory in an Icelandic student population. *Scandinavian Journal of Behaviour Therapy, 29*, 49–56.

Jorgensen, L., Castle, D., Roberts, C., & Groth-Marnat, G. (2001). A clinical validation of the Dysmorphic Concern Questionnaire. *Australian and New Zealand Journal of Psychiatry, 35*, 124–128.

Kaplan, S. L. (1994). A self-rated scale for obsessive-compulsive disorder. *Journal of Clinical Psychology, 50*, 564–574.

Kazarian, S. S., Evans, D. R., & Lefave, K. (1977). Modification and factorial analysis of the Leyton Obsessional Inventory. *Journal of Clinical Psychology, 33*, 422–425.

Keuthen, N. J., Flessner, C. A., Woods, D. W., Franklin, M. E., Stein, D. J., & Cashin, S. E. (2007). Factor analysis of the Massachusetts General Hospital Hairpulling Scale. *Journal of Psychosomatic Research, 62*, 707–709.

Keuthen, N. J., Wilhelm, S., Deckersbach, T., Engelhard, I. M., Forker, A. E., Baer, L., & Jenike, M. A. (2001). The Skin Picking Scale: Scale construction and psychometric analyses. *Journal of Psychosomatic Research, 50*, 337–341.

Kim, S. W., Dysken, M. W., Pheley, A. M., & Hoover, K. M. (1994) The Yale–Brown Obsessive-Compulsive Scale: Measures of internal consistency. *Psychiatry Research, 51*, 203–211.

King, N. J., Inglis, S., Jenkins, M., Myerson, N., & Ollendick, T. (1995). Test–retest reliability of the survey form of the Leyton Obsessional Inventory – Child Version. *Perceptual and Motor Skills, 80*, 1200–1202.

Klepsch, R., Zaworka, W., Hand, I., Lünenschloss, K., & Jauernig, G. (1991). Derivation and validation of the Hamburg Obsession/Compulsion Inventory – Short Form (HOCI-S): First results. *Psychological Assessment: A Journal of Consulting and Clinical Psychology, 3*, 196–201.

Kyrios, M., Bhar, S., & Wade, D. (1996). The assessment of obsessive-compulsive phenomena: Psychometric and normative data on the Padua Inventory from an Australian non-clinical student sample. *Behaviour Research and Therapy, 34*, 85–95.

Lawrence, P. J., & Williams, T. I. (2011). Pathways to inflated responsibility beliefs in adolescent obsessive-compulsive disorder: a preliminary investigation. *Behavioural and Cognitive Psychotherapy, 39*, 229–234.

LeBeau, R. T., Mischel, E. R., Simpson, H. B., Mataix-Cols, D., Phillips, K. A., Stein, D. J., & Craske, M. G. (2013). Preliminary assessment of obsessive-compulsive spectrum disorder scales for DSM-5. *Journal of Obsessive-Compulsive and Related Disorders, 2*, 114–118.

Liebowitz, M. R., Turner, S. M., Piacentini, J., Beidel, D. C., Clarvit, S. R., Davies, S. O., ... Simpson, H. B. (2002). Fluoxetine in children and adolescents with OCD: A placebo-controlled trial. *Journal of the American Academy of Child and Adolescent Psychiatry, 41*, 1431–1438.

López-Solà, C., Gutiérrez, F., Alonso, P., Rosado, S., Taberner, J., Segalàs, C., ... Fullana, M. A. (2014). Spanish version of the Dimensional Obsessive-Compulsive Scale (DOCS): Psychometric properties and relation to obsessive beliefs. *Comprehensive Psychiatry, 55*, 206–214.

Lord, C., Rieder, A., Hall, G. B. C., Soares, C. N., & Steiner, M. (2011). Piloting the perinatal obsessive-compulsive scale (POCS): Development and validation. *Journal of Anxiety Disorders, 25*, 1079–1084.

Mataix-Cols, D., Fernandez de la Cruz, L., Nakao, T., Pertusa, A., DSM-5 Obsessive-Compulsive Spectrum Sub-Work Group of the Anxiety, O.-C. S. P., & Dissociative Disorders Work, G. (2011). Testing the validity and acceptability of the diagnostic criteria for Hoarding Disorder: A DSM-5 survey. *Psychological Medicine, 41*, 2475–2484.

Mataix-Cols, D., Fullana, M. A., Alonso, P., Menchon, J. M., & Vallejo, J. (2004). Convergent and discriminant validity of the Yale–Brown Obsessive Compulsive Scale Symptom Checklist. *Psychotherapy and Psychosomatics, 73*, 190–196.

Mataix-Cols, D., Rosário-Campos, M. C., & Leckman, J. F. (2005). A multidimensional model of obsessive-compulsive disorder. *American Journal of Psychiatry, 162*, 228–238.

Mataix-Cols, D., Sánchez-Turet, M., & Vallejo, J. (2002). A Spanish version of the Padua Inventory: Factors structure and psychometric properties. *Behavioural and Cognitive Psychotherapy, 30*, 25–36.

Mathews, C. A., Jang, K. L., Hami, S., & Stein, M. B. (2004). The structure of obsessionality among young adults. *Depression and Anxiety, 20*, 77–85.

McKay, D., Danyko, S., Neziroglu, F., & Yaryura-Tobias, J. A. (1995). Factor structure of the Yale–Brown Obsessive-Compulsive Scale: A two-dimensional measure. *Behavior Research and Therapy, 33*, 865–869.

McKay, D., Neziroglu, F., Stevens, K., & Yaryura-Tobias, J. A. (1998). The Yale–Brown Obsessive-Compulsive Scale: Confirmatory factor analytic findings. *Journal of Psychopathology and Behavioral Assessment, 20*, 265–274.

McKay, D., Piacentini, J., Greisberg, S., Graae, F., Jaffer, M., Miller, J., Neziroglu, F., & Yaryura-Tobias, J. A. (2003). The Children's Yale–Brown Obsessive-Compulsive Scale: Item structure in an outpatient setting. *Psychological Assessment, 15*, 578–581.

Merlo, L. J., Storch, E. A., Murphy, T. K., Goodman, W. K., & Geffken, G. R. (2005). Assessment of pediatric obsessive-compulsive disorder: A critical review of current methodology. *Child Psychiatry and Human Development, 36*, 195–214.

Moritz, S., Meier, B., Kloss, M., Jacobsen, D., Wein, C., Fricke, S., & Hand, I. (2002). Dimensional structure of the Yale–Brown Obsessive Compulsive Scale (Y-BOCS). *Psychiatry Research, 109*, 193–199.

Muris, P., Meesters, C., Rassin, E., Merckelbach, H., & Campbell, J. (2001). Thought–action fusion and anxiety disorders symptoms in normal adolescents. *Behaviour Research and Therapy, 39*, 843–852.

Nelson, E. C., Hanna, G. L., Hudziak, J. J., Botteron, K. N., Heath, A. C., & Todd, R. D. (2001). Obsessive-compulsive scale of the child behavior checklist: Specificity, sensitivity, and predictive power. *Pediatrics, 108*, E14.

Nordsletten, A., Fernández de la Cruz, L., Pertusa, A., Reichenberg, A., Hatch, S. L., & Mataix-Cols, D. (2013). The Structured Interview for Hoarding Disorder (SIHD): Development, usage and further validation. *Journal of Obsessive-Compulsive and Related Disorders, 2*, 346–350.

Obsessive Compulsive Cognitions Working Group. (2005). Psychometric validation of the obsessive belief questionnaire and interpretation of intrusions inventory – Part 2: Factor analyses and testing of a brief version. *Behaviour Research and Therapy, 43*, 1527–1542.

Ólafsson, R. P., Arngrímsson, J. B., Árnason, P., Kolbeinsson, Þ., Emmelkamp, P. M. G., Kristjánsson, Á., & Ólason, D. Þ. (2013). The Icelandic version of the dimensional obsessive compulsive scale (DOCS) and its relationship with obsessive beliefs. *Journal of Obsessive-Compulsive and Related Disorders, 2,* 149–156.

Olatunji, B. O., Abramowitz, J. S., Williams, N. L., Connolly, K. M., & Lohr, J. M. (2007). Scrupulosity and obsessive-compulsive symptoms: Confirmatory factor analysis and validity of the Penn Inventory of Scrupulosity. *Journal of Anxiety Disorders, 21,* 771–787.

Overduin, M. K., & Furnham, A. (2012). Assessing obsessive-compulsive disorder (OCD): A review of self-report measures. *Journal of Obsessive-Compulsive and Related Disorders, 1,* 312–324.

Pertusa, A., Fernández de la Cruz, L., Alonso, P., Menchón, J. M., & Mataix-Cols, D. (2012). Independent validation of the dimensional Yale–Brown Obsessive-Compulsive Scale (DY-BOCS). *European Psychiatry, 27,* 598–604.

Phillips, K. A. (2009). *Understanding body dysmorphic disorder.* New York: Oxford University Press.

Phillips, K. A., Hart, A. S., & Menard, W. (2014). Psychometric evaluation of the Yale–Brown Obsessive-Compulsive Scale modified for body dysmorphic disorder (BDD-YBOCS). *Journal of Obsessive-Compulsive and Related Disorders, 3*(3), 205–208.

Phillips, K. A., Hollander, E., Rasmussen, S. A., Aronowitz, B. R., DeCaria, C., & Goodman, W. K. (1997). A severity rating scale for body dysmorphic disorder: Development, reliability, and validity of a modified version of the Yale–Brown Obsessive Compulsive Scale. *Psychopharmacology Bulletin, 33,* 17–22.

Philpott, R. (1975). Recent advances in the behavioural measurement of obsessional illness: Difficulties common to these and other measures. *Scottish Medical Journal, 20,* 33–40.

Piacentini, J., Bergman, R. L., Jacobs, C., McCracken, J. T., & Kretchman, J. (2002). Open trial of cognitive behavior therapy for childhood obsessive-compulsive disorder. *Journal of Anxiety Disorders, 16,* 207–219.

Piacentini, J., Bergman, R. L., Keller, M., & McCracken, J. (2003). Functional impairment in children and adolescents with obsessive-compulsive disorder. *Journal of Child and Adolescent Psychopharmacology, 13,* S61–S69.

Piacentini, J., Peris, T. S., Bergman, R. L., Chang, S., & Jaffer, M. (2007). Functional impairment in childhood OCD: Development and psychometrics properties of the Child Obsessive-Compulsive Impact Scale-Revised (COIS-R). *Journal of Clinical Child and Adolescent Psychology, 36,* 645–653.

Pinto, A., Van Noppen, B., & Calvocoressi, L. (2013). Development and preliminary psychometric evaluation of a self-rated version of the Family Accommodation Scale for Obsessive-Compulsive Disorder. *Journal of Obsessive-Compulsive and Related Disorders, 2,* 457–465.

Price, L. H., Goodman, W. R., Chamey, D. S., Rasmussen, S. A., & Heninger, G. R (1987). Treatment of severe obsessive-compulsive disorder with fluvoxamine. *American Journal of Psychiatry, 144,*1059–1661.

Rachman, S. J. (2006). *The fear of contamination: Assessment and treatment.* Oxford: Oxford University Press.

Radomsky, A. S., & Rachman, S. (2004). Symmetry, ordering and arranging compulsive behaviour. *Behaviour Research and Therapy, 42,* 893–913.

Rapoport, J. L., Inoff-Germain, G., Weissman, M. M., Greenwald, S., Narrow, W. E., Jensen, P. S., ... Canino, G. (2000). Childhood obsessive-compulsive disorder in the NIMH MECA study: Parent versus child identification of cases. *Journal of Anxiety Disorders, 14,* 535–548.

Read, K. L., Comer, J. S., & Kendall, P. C. (2013). The intolerance of uncertainty scale for children (IUSC): Discriminating principal anxiety diagnoses and severity. *Psychological Assessment, 25,* 722–729.

Rosa-Alcazar, A. I., Ruiz-Garcia, B., Iniesta-Sepulveda, M., Lopez-Pina, J. A., Rosa-Alcazar, A., & Parada-Navas, J. L. (2014). Obsessive Compulsive Inventory – Child Version (OCI-CV) in a Spanish community sample of children and adolescents. *Psicothema, 26,* 174–179.

Rosário, M. C., Miguel, E., Quatrano, A., Chacon, P., Ferrao, Y., Findley, D., Katsovich, L., … Leckman, J. F. (2006). The Dimensional Yale–Brown Obsessive Compulsive Scale (DY-BOCS): An instrument for assessing obsessive-compulsive symptom dimensions. *Molecular Psychiatry, 11,* 495–504.

Rosário, M. C., Prado, H. S., Borcato, S., Diniz, J. B., Shavitt, R. G., Hounie, A. G., … Miguel, E. (2009). Validation of the University of São Paulo Sensory Phenomena Scale: Initial psychometric properties. *CNS Spectrums, 14,* 315–323.

Roussos, Al., Francis, K., Koumoula, A., Richardson, C., Kabakos, C., Kiriakidou, T., Karagianni, S., & Karamolegou, K., (2003). The Leyton Obsessional Inventory – Child Version in Greek Adolescents. *European Child & Adolescent Psychiatry, 12,* 58–66.

Salkovskis, P. M., Wroe, A. L., Gledhill, A., Morrison, N., Forrester, E., Richards, C., … Thorpe, S. (2000). Responsibility attitudes and interpretations are characteristic of obsessive compulsive disorder. *Behaviour Research and Therapy, 38,* 347–372.

Sanavio, E. (1988). Obsessions and compulsions: The Padua Inventory. *Behaviour Research and Therapy, 26,* 169–177.

Scahill, L., McDougle, C. J., Williams, S. K., Dimitropoulos, A., Aman, M. G., McCracken, J. T., … Vitiello, B (2006). Children's Yale–Brown Obsessive Compulsive Scale modified for pervasive developmental disorders. *Journal of the American Academy of Child and Adolescent Psychiatry, 45,*1114–1123.

Scahill, L., Riddle, M. A., McSwiggin-Hardin, M., Ort, S. I., King, R. A., Goodman, W. K., Cicchetti, D., & Leckman, J. F. (1997) Children's Yale–Brown Obsessive Compulsive Scale: Reliability and validity. *Journal of the American Academy of Child and Adolescent Psychiatry, 36,* 844–852.

Shafran, R., Frampton, I., Heyman, I., Reynolds, M., Teachman, B., & Rachman, S. (2003). The preliminary development of a new self-report measure for OCD in young people. *Journal of Adolescence, 26,* 137–142.

Shafran, R., Thordarson, D. S., & Rachman, S. (1996). Thought–action fusion in obsessive compulsive disorder. *Journal of Anxiety Disorders, 10,* 379–391.

Sica, C., Ghisi, M., Altoè, G., Rocco Chiri, L., Franceschini, S., Coradeschi, D., & Melli, G. (2009). The Italian version of the Obsessive Compulsive Inventory: Its psychometric properties on community and clinical samples. *Journal of Anxiety Disorders, 23,* 204–211.

Stanley, M. A., Prather, R. C., Beck, J. G., Brown, T. C., Wagner, A. L., & Davis, M. L. (1993). Psychometric analyses of the Leyton Obsessional Inventory in patients with obsessive-compulsive and other anxiety disorders. *Psychological Assessment, 5,* 187–192.

Stanley, M. A., Prather, R. C., Wagner, A. L., Davis, M. L., & Swann, A. C. (1993). Can the Yale–Brown Obsessive-Compulsive Scale be used to assess trichotillomania? A preliminary report. *Behaviour Research and Therapy, 31,* 171–177.

Stein, M. B., Forde, D. R., Anderson, G., & Walker, J. R. (1997). Obsessive-compulsive disorder in the community: An epidemiologic survey with clinical reappraisal. *American Journal of Psychiatry, 154,* 1120–1126.

Stein, D. J., Grant, J. E., Franklin, M. E., Keuthen, N. J., Lochner, C., Singer, H. S., & Woods, D. W. (2010). Trichotillomania (hair pulling disorder), skin picking disorder, and stereotypic movement disorder: Toward DSM-V. *Depression and Anxiety, 27,* 611–626.

Steketee, G., & Doppelt, H. (1986). Measurement of obsessive-compulsive symptomatology: Utility of the Hopkins Symptom Checklist. *Psychiatry Research, 19,* 135–145.

Steketee, G., & Freund, B. (1993). Compulsive Activity Checklist (CAC): Further psychometric analyses and revision. *Behavioural Psychotherapy, 21,* 13–25.

Steketee, G., Frost, R., & Bogart, K. (1996). The Yale–Brown Obsessive Compulsive Scale: Interview versus self-report. *Behaviour Research and Therapy, 34,* 675–684.

Stewart, S. E., Ceranoglu, T. A., O'Hanley, T., & Geller, D. A. (2005). Performance of clinician versus self-report measures to identify obsessive-compulsive disorder in children and adolescents. *Journal of Child and Adolescent Psychopharmacology, 15,* 956–963.

Stewart, S. E., Rosário, M. C., Brown, T. A., Carter, A. S., Leckman, J. F., Sukhodolsky, D., Katsovitch, L., ... Pauls, D. L. (2007) Principal components analysis of obsessive-compulsive disorder symptoms in children and adolescents. *Biological Psychiatry, 61,* 285–291.

Storch, E. A., Bagner, D., Merlo, L. J., Shapira, N. A., Geffken, G. R., Murphy, T. K., & Goodman, W. K. (2007a). Florida Obsessive-Compulsive Inventory: Development, reliability, and validity. *Journal of Clinical Psychology, 63,* 851–859.

Storch, E. A., Geffken, G. R., Merlo, L. J., Jacob, M. L., Murphy, T. K., Goodman, W. K., ... Grabill, K. (2007b). Family accommodation in pediatric obsessive-compulsive disorder. *Journal of Clinical Child and Adolescent Psychology, 36,* 207–216.

Storch, E. A., Khanna, M., Merlo, L. J., Loew, B. A., Franklin, M., Reid, J. M., ... Murphy, T. K. (2009). Children's Florida Obsessive-Compulsive Inventory: Psychometric properties and feasibility of a self-report measure of obsessive-compulsive symptoms in youth. *Child Psychiatry and Human Development, 40,* 467–483.

Storch, E. A., Larson, M. J., Price, L. H., Rasmussen, S. A., Murphy, T. K., & Goodman, W. K. (2010a). Psychometric analysis of the Yale–Brown Obsessive-Compulsive Scale Second Edition Symptom Checklist. *Journal of Anxiety Disorders, 24,* 650–656.

Storch, E. A., Murphy, T. K., Adkins, J. W., Lewin, A. B., Geffken, G. R., Johns, N. B., Jann, K. E., & Goodman, W. K. (2006a). The Children's Yale–Brown Obsessive-Compulsive Scale: Psychometric properties of child- and parent-report formats. *Journal of Anxiety Disorders, 20,* 1055–1070.

Storch, E. A., Murphy, T. K., Bagner, D. M., Johns, N. B., Baumeister, A. L., Goodman, W. K., & Geffken, G. R. (2006b). Reliability and validity of the Child Behavior Checklist Obsessive-Compulsive Scale. *Journal of Anxiety Disorders, 20,* 473–485.

Storch, E. A., Murphy, T. K., Geffken, G. R, Soto, O., Sajid, M., Allen, P., ... Goodman, W. K. (2004). Psychometric evaluation of the Children's Yale–Brown Obsessive-Compulsive Scale. *Psychiatry Research, 129,* 91–98.

Storch, E. A., Park, J. M., Lewin, A. B., Morgan, J. R., Jones, A. M., & Murphy, T. K. (2011). The Leyton Obsessional Inventory – Child Version Survey Form does not demonstrate adequate psychometric properties in American youth with pediatric obsessive-compulsive disorder. *Journal of Anxiety Disorders, 25,* 574–578.

Storch, E. A., Rasmussen, S. A., Price, L. H., Larson, M. J., Murphy, T. K., & Goodman, W. K. (2010b). Development and psychometric evaluation of the Yale–Brown Obsessive-Compulsive Scale (Second Edition). *Psychological Assessment, 22,* 223–232.

Taylor, S. (1995). Assessment of obsessions and compulsions: Reliability, validity and sensitivity to treatment effects. *Clinical Psychology Review, 15,* 261–296.

Taylor, S., Abramowitz, J. S., & McKay, D. (2007). Cognitive-behavioral models of obsessive-compulsive disorder. In M. M. Antony, C. Purdon. & L. Summerfeldt (Eds.), *Psychological treatment of obsessive-compulsive disorder: Fundamentals and beyond.* (pp. 9–29). Washington, DC: American Psychological Association.

Thordarson, D. S., Radomsky, A. S., Rachman, S., Shafran, R., Sawchuk, C. N., & Ralph Hakstian, A. (2004). The Vancouver Obsessional Compulsive Inventory (VOCI). *Behaviour Research and Therapy, 42,* 1289–1314.

Tolin, D. F., Frost, R. O., & Steketee, G. (2010). A brief interview for assessing compulsive hoarding: The Hoarding Rating Scale – Interview. *Psychiatry Research, 178,* 147–152.

Uher, R., Heyman, I., Mortimore, C., Frampton, I., & Goodman, R. (2007). Screening young people for obsessive compulsive disorder. *British Journal of Psychiatry, 191,* 353–354.

Uher, R., Heyman, I., Turner, C. M., & Shafran, R. (2008). Self-, parent-report and interview measures of obsessive-compulsive disorder in children and adolescents. *Journal of Anxiety Disorders, 22,* 979–990.

Van Oppen, P., Hoekstra, R. J., & Emmelkamp, P. M. (1995). The structure of obsessive-compulsive symptoms. *Behaviour Research and Therapy, 33*, 15–23.

Veale, D., Eshkevari, E., Kanakam, N., Ellison, N., Costa, A., & Werner, T. (2013). The Appearance Anxiety Inventory: Validation of a process measure in the treatment of body dysmorphic disorder. *Behavioural and Cognitive Psychotherapy, 3*, 1–12.

Veale, D., Freeston, M., Krebs, G., Heyman, I., & Salkovskis, P. (2009). Risk assessment and management in obsessive-compulsive disorder. *Advances in Psychiatric Treatment, 15*, 332–343.

Warren, R., Zgourides, G., & Monto, M. (1993). Self-report versions of the Yale–Brown Obsessive-Compulsive Scale: An assessment of a sample of normals. *Psychological Reports, 73*, 574.

Watson, D., & Wu, K. D. (2005). Development and validation of the Schedule of Compulsions, Obsessions, and Pathological Impulses (SCOPI). *Assessment, 12*, 50–65.

Wells, A., & Davies, M. I. (1994). The Thought Control Questionnaire: A measure of individual differences in the control of unwanted thoughts. *Behaviour Research and Therapy, 32*, 871–878.

Williams, M., Davis D. M., Thibodeau, M. A., & Bach, N. (2013). Psychometric properties of the Obsessive-Compulsive Inventory Revised in African Americans with and without obsessive-compulsive disorder. *Journal of Obsessive-Compulsive and Related Disorders, 2*, 399–405.

Williams, M. T., Wetterneck, C. T., Thibodeau, M. A., & Duque, G. (2013). Validation of the Yale–Brown Obsessive-Compulsive Scale in African American with obsessive-compulsive disorder. *Psychiatry Research, 209*, 214–221.

Wolff, R. P., & Wolff, L. S. (1991). Assessment and treatment of obsessive-compulsive disorder in children. *Behavior Modification, 15*, 372–393.

Woo, C-W., Kwon, S-M., Lim, Y-J., & Shin, M-S. (2010). The Obsessive-Compulsive Inventory – Revised (OCI-R): Psychometric properties of the Korean version and the order, gender, and cultural effects. *Journal of Behavior Therapy and Experimental Psychiatry, 41*, 220–227.

Woody, S. R., Steketee, G., & Chambless, D. L. (1995). Reliability and validity of the Yale–Brown Obsessive-Compulsive Scale. *Behaviour Research Therapy, 33*, 597–605.

Wu, K. D., Watson, D., & Clark, L. A. (2007). A self-report version of the Yale–Brown Obsessive-Compulsive Scale Symptom Checklist: Psychometric properties of factor-based scales in three samples. *Journal of Anxiety Disorders, 21*, 644–661.

Zhong, J., Wang, C., Liu, J., Qin, M., Tan, J., & Yi, C. (2011). Psychometric properties of the Padua Inventory in Chinese college samples. *Psychological Reports, 109*, 803–818.

11

Using Objective Personality Assessment for Effective Treatment Planning

Caleb W. Lack and Brittany M. Riggin

The treatment of obsessive-compulsive disorder (OCD) by a mental health clinician is no easy task, despite the considerable amount of evidence showing that cognitive-behavioral therapy (CBT) emphasizing exposure and response prevention (EX/RP) is highly effective in both adult and pediatric populations (Eddy, Dutra, Bradley, & Westen, 2004; Mancuso, Faro, Joshi, & Geller, 2010). Best practice guidelines are often focused on the components of CBT for OCD, including psychoeducation, development of a hierarchy of feared situations, EX/RP, cognitive restructuring, and relapse prevention (Selles, Storch, & Lewin, 2014). However, in order for a clinician to undertake treatment, it is crucial to begin with a thorough assessment of the symptoms of OCD, other mental health symptoms, and factors associated with those symptoms, which will in turn inform effective treatment planning.

The most widely used assessment tools by clinicians treating those with OCD are either self-rating scales, such as the Obsessive-Compulsive Inventory – Revised (OCI-R) (Hajcak, Huppert, Simmons, & Foa, 2004), or clinician-administered rating scales, such as the adult and pediatric versions of the Yale–Brown Obsessive-Compulsive Scale (YBOCS) (Scahill et al., 1997; Storch et al., 2010). These scales and many others that are designed specifically to assess OCD symptomology (see Storch, Benito, & Goodman, 2011, for a review of the many different ones available) are extremely useful in treatment planning. Given their narrow focus, however, they do little to inform the clinician about issues such as comorbidity, personality, and others that can have a significant impact on treatment outcome. Broadening one's focus outside specific obsessions and compulsions only can have a significant benefit for the clinician and their patients.

The purpose of this chapter is to review the more widely-known and used global personality and psychopathology measures and show how they can help to better inform an individual's treatment plan. In doing so, we will discuss each measure in general, how each relates to or assesses OCD symptoms in particular, and then demonstrate specifically how each can be used in treatment planning for OCD treatment. Given the extensive coverage in the literature on the general uses for each instrument as well as their specific uses for anxiety disorders (e.g., Rogove, 2013), the focus of

The Wiley Handbook of Obsessive Compulsive Disorders, Volume I, First Edition.
Edited by Jonathan S. Abramowitz, Dean McKay, and Eric A. Storch.
© 2017 John Wiley & Sons Ltd. Published 2017 by John Wiley & Sons Ltd.

this chapter will be specifically on their use as concerns OCD symptoms and diagnosis. After covering objective measures, a brief section on the projective measures and the problems in using them for evidence-based assessment follows.

Symptom Checklist-90: Revised and Brief Symptom Inventory

The Symptom Checklist 90 – Revised (SCL-90-R) (Derogatis, 1994) is a self-report measure commonly used to screen for the presence or absence of nine dimensions of psychological distress. The measure consists of 90 items and uses a five-point Likert scale. Ten items are used to assess each of the measure's constructs, which are Somatization, Obsessive-Compulsive Symptoms, Interpersonal Sensitivity, Depression, Anxiety, Hostility, Phobic-Anxiety, Paranoid Ideation, and Psychoticism. Additionally, the SCL-90 includes three global indexes: the Global Severity Index, Positive Symptom Total, and Positive Symptom Distress Index. Completion of the measure takes roughly 10–15 minutes. The SCL-90-R can be administered to individuals aged 13 years or older and requires at least a 6th-grade reading level. Four norm types are available, including psychiatric outpatients, community nonpatients, psychiatric inpatients, and adolescent nonpatients. The SCL-90-R has been translated into over 20 languages, which makes it ideal for use in multicultural settings.

Overall, the SCL-90-R has shown quite high internal consistency, test–retest reliability, and overall validity (see Derogatis & Unger, 2010, for a review). Within the realm of OCD symptoms specifically, though, there have not been many investigations. Those that have taken place generally examine the Obsessive-Compulsive Symptoms (OC) scale in particular. This scale is described as focusing on thoughts, impulses, and actions that are experienced as irresistible, unremitting, and unwanted. However, behavior and experiences reflecting a more general deficit also contribute to the scale. Derogatis (1994) reported good internal consistency ($\alpha = 0.86$) and test–retest reliability ($r = 0.85$) for the OC scale. Additionally, Pedersen and Karterud (2004) found that the Obsessive-Compulsive Symptoms scale mean score was significantly different between those with and without a diagnosis of OCD, but concluded that due to high overlap with other anxiety symptoms, it was perhaps best used for screening out OCD rather than making diagnostic decisions.

In one of the only large studies to date, Woody, Steketee, and Chambless (1995) found that responses to several items on the OC scale were limited to the low severity range when assessing individuals who had already received a diagnosis of OCD from an experienced clinician. Specifically, items such as "the mind going blank" and "trouble remembering things," as well as "worried about sloppiness or carelessness" were all positively skewed in that the majority of ratings were 0 or 1 on level of severity. They did find that the SCL-90-R has good internal consistency ratings for the OCD population ($\alpha = 0.81$), however. Woody and colleagues assert that the SCL-90-R provides good construct validity in that the OC scale correlated highly with the Maudsley Obsessional Compulsive Inventory (MOCI) and the Yale–Brown Obsessive-Compulsive Scale (YBOCS). Divergent validity analyses, though, showed that the OC scale of the SCL-90-R is more strongly related to the measure's scales assessing depression and anxiety symptoms than to either the MOCI or the YBOCS.

Measures of symptoms prior to treatment and after treatment suggested that the SCL-90-R is highly sensitive to behavioral change. Overall, while the test is sensitive to changes in compulsive rituals associated with treatment, it does not appear to be sensitive to such changes in obsessions, and may instead be reflective of overall psychological distress as opposed to OCD symptoms specifically (Woody et al., 1995). These findings and more recent work (e.g., Grabill et al., 2008) suggest that the SCL-90-R is not well suited for diagnosis of OCD or for the measurement of OC symptoms.

Brief Symptom Inventory

The Brief Symptom Inventory (BSI) (Derogatis, 1993) is essentially the short-form version of the SCL-90-R. It was constructed in response to time limitations faced by those administering the parent measure. The BSI contains only 53 items and assesses psychological symptoms experienced by both psychological patients and community nonpatients. It is appropriate for use with individuals aged 13 years or older, requires a 6th-grade reading level, and requires approximately 8–10 minutes to complete. Similar to its parent measure, the BSI has strong overall reliability and broad validity as a measure of psychological distress.

In one study, the Obsessive-Compulsive (O-C) scale of the BSI had a .44 correlation with Scale 7: Psychasthenia of the MMPI (which is related to OCD symptoms) (Derogatis, 1993). Another study, however, reported this correlation to be as high as .54, suggestive of moderate convergent validity (Boulet & Boss, 1991). Unfortunately, the same study also suggests that the BSI is limited in its ability to discriminate between symptom dimensions. A principal components analysis of the subscales was also conducted and suggested that analysis of the subscales independently of one another (e.g., analysis of the O-C scale only) yields little information when compared wit an analysis of the overall global indices because each individual scale shares an significant portion of variance with the other scales. That said, the BSI's O-C scale showed the highest amount of intercorrelation with the Depression (.75) and Anxiety (.75) scales, symptoms not uncommon in individuals also reporting primary symptoms of OCD. Similarly, the BSI's O-C scale showed a .96 correlation with the SCL-90-R's OC scale (as would be expected given the near identical nature of the two assessments). With regard to the predictive validity of the BSI, one study showed that of the sample screened for psychological symptoms using the BSI, 80% were identified as psychiatrically positive, and 87% of these identified individual cases were later firmed to be experiencing psychological distress through subsequent diagnosis (Kuhn, Bell, Seligson, Laufer, & Lindner, 1988).

Given the above information, for assisting with treatment planning for those with OCD, the SCL-90-R and BSI can best be thought of and used as an overall measure of psychological distress. With the heterogeneity of OCD's presentation between individuals, it is often easy to get caught up in assessing the different potential obsessions and resultant compulsions a patient has and then ignore other potentially problematic behaviors, cognitions, and emotional states. Given the decrease in quality of life seen in OCD (Lack et al., 2009) and the very high rates of psychiatric comorbidity (Pallanti, Giacomo, Sarrecchia, Cantisani, & Pellegrini, 2011), it is important to take into account an individual's overall mental health and not focus exclusively on OC symptoms.

We know that the presence of affective disorders, such as depression and bipolar, are associated with higher levels of OCD symptoms compared with other kinds of comorbidity (Timpano, Rubenstein, & Murphy, 2013), and research has consistently found that comorbidity in general negatively impacts one's quality of life (Huppert, Simpson, Nissesnson, Liebowitz, & Foa, 2009). Since research shows that CBT for OCD often decreases comorbid symptoms even without specifically addressing them (Lack, Lehmkuhl-Yardley, & Dalaya, 2013), regular completion of the SCL-90-R or BSI can help a clinician quickly and reliably track various aspects of mental health to see if certain types of symptoms are decreasing across treatment.

The Minnesota Multiphasic Personality Inventory

The most commonly used psychological test in the United States, the Minnesota Multiphasic Personality Inventory, Second Edition (MMPI-2) (Butcher, Dahlstrom, Graham, Tellegen, & Kaemmer, 1989) is an extensive self-report questionnaire designed to assist in the diagnosis of psychological and personality disorders. The examinee is required to respond to 567 true–false statements that assess a variety of current psychological symptoms, as well as the validity and interpretability of the individual's scores. The MMPI-2 is designed for use with adults with at least a 6th-grade reading level. An additional version of this measure is available for individuals younger than 18 years of age: the Minnesota Multiphasic Personality Inventory – Adolescent (MMPI-A) (Butcher et al., 1992). A number of scores can be derived from the MMPI-2, several of which have direct relevance in the assessment of OCD and could be potentially useful in treatment planning.

Clinical scale 7 of the MMPI-2 was developed to assess the construct of Psychasthenia. While this term is not in common use today, the scale matches closely with a number of OCD symptoms through its measurement of obsessive thoughts, feelings of fear, and compulsions across 48 items. Scale 7 shows high internal consistency coefficients for both women ($\alpha = .87$) and men ($\alpha = .85$), as well as high test–retest coefficients for both women ($\alpha = .72$) and men ($\alpha = .68$) (Butcher et al., 2001). Several studies over the past 20 years have shown positive correlations between scores on scale 7 and measures of OCD (e.g., Graham, Ben-Porath, & McNulty, 1999; Tellegen et al., 2006). It is important to note, however, that people commonly diagnosed with OCD also tend to have elevated scores on scales 2 (depression), 4 (psychopathic deviance), and 8 (schizophrenia); thus taking any one scale as a "pure" measure of OCD is misguided (Carey et al., 1986; Graham et al., 1999).

In addition to the original clinical scales, MMPI-2 content scales were also developed to assess the content dimensions of the measure as a whole. Sixteen items on the MMPI-2 were found to assess levels of obsessive symptoms (OBS) specifically. Internal consistency for this content scale was high for both men and women in the normative sample, .74 and .77, respectively (Butcher, Graham, Williams, & Ben-Porath, 1990). Test–retest reliability for this content scale is also high for men and women, .83 and .85, respectively. Correlations between this content scale and the Psychasthenia clinical scale of the MMPI-2 were rather strong for both men (.77) and women (.79), suggesting that while the two scales are not necessarily interchangeable (as would be expected since the content scale purports to measure obsessive symptoms exclusively), they are both measures of OCD symptomology. Researchers have shown that combining both Clinical and Content scales results in an increase in prediction of scores on related self-report measures and clinician rating scales, thus improving the measure's overall convergent validity (Archer, Aiduk, Griffin, & Elkins, 1996; Ben-Porath, McCully, & Almagor, 1993).

While the MMPI-2 demonstrates acceptable convergent validity through its ability to correlate positive scores on clinical scales with other relevant extra-test factors, the MMPI-2 does not perform as well when issues of discriminate validity arise (Helmes & Reddon, 1993). Overall, test items are heterogeneous. Because test items for scales 7 and the OBS content scale overlap with test items for other scales, these seems to inadvertently assess symptomology belonging to other diagnoses rather than solely OCD (in this case, depression and other forms of anxiety) (Sellbom & Lee, 2013).

In addition to content scales, Restructured Clinical (RC) scales have also been developed for use with the assessment in an attempt to rectify issues surrounding discriminate validity and item heterogeneity. Van der Heijden, Egger, Rossi, Grundel, and Derksen (2013) assert that these scales demonstrate good convergent and discriminant validity with regard to the Structured Clinical Interview for the *Diagnostic and Statistical Manual of Mental Disorders* (Fourth Edition) (DSM-IV) (American Psychiatric Association, 2000). That said, while many of the RC scales demonstrate high convergent validity with corresponding clinical scales, there is not an RC scale developed specifically for assessment of OCD symptoms. In fact, the highest level of convergent validity for clinical scale 7 was a correlation of .83 with RC scale 7, which is supposed to measure symptoms of depression as well as feelings of insecurity, excessive sensitivity, and excessive rumination about perceived failures (Tellegen et al., 2003). Because the RC7 scale correlated highly with clinical scale 7, both scales likely measure similar, but not identical, constructs. This provides evidence for convergent validity of the RC scales, but calls into question the discriminant validity of clinical scale 7, which purports to assess OCD symptoms, symptoms that do not appear to be the focus of RC7. For these reasons, Sellbom and Lee (2013) emphasize that these parts of the MMPI-2 (scale 7, RC7, and the OBS content scale) do not seem to be adequate on their own to fully assess OCD symptomology or to accurately differentiate OCD from other kinds of anxiety disorders.

The MMPI-A assesses the same constructs as the MMPI-2, but the former is for use with a younger population. The MMPI-A also contains scales for assessing the validity and interpretability of the individual's scores. It is designed for use with individuals between 14 and 18 years of age and requires at least a 4th-grade reading level. It contains 478 true–false items and requires approximately 60 minutes to complete.

Similar to the MMPI-2, no specific MMPI-A scales have been found to be strongly related to the diagnosis of OCD exclusively. For example, Scale 7 of the MMPI-A, which is used to assess Psychasthenia, which matches closely to (OCD) symptomology, is identical to the scale used in the MMPI-2. As such, it can be suggested that validity measures for this scale are similar to Scale 7 in the MMPI-2. Content Scales were developed for the MMPI-A, but suffer from some of the same limitations as the ones on the MMPI-2. The A-obs (Adolescent-Obsessiveness) scale contains 15 items, 12 of which are also contained in the clinical scale of the adult version of the assessment. Data has shown high scores on this scale to be related to general maladjustment in males and females, anxious behavior in clinical boys, and suicidal ideation and gestures in clinical girls (Butcher et al., 1992; Veltri et al., 2009). However, more research needs to be conducted to better understand the scale's relationship to OCD specifically. For example, McGrath, Pogge, and Stokes (2002) found that Clinical Scale 7 better predicted OCD behaviors than the corresponding A-obs content scale.

For assisting with treatment planning, then, the MMPI-2 and the MMPI-A are best thought of as being measures of broad psychological functioning rather than as measures specific for assessing OC symptoms or tracking progress in treating OCD. The scales described above (Scale 7, RC7, OBS, A-obs) can be highly useful in tracking one's general anxious distress, either for initial assessment or as a measure of change over time. Further research could inform the use of these scales (or newly developed ones) for assisting with specific diagnostic categories, such as OCD, but as of now they do not.

Another potential use in treatment planning is examining the validity scales of the MMPI (F, L, and K) to help to gauge the extent of potential underreporting of symptoms in general as well as potential defensiveness. This knowledge would be useful in treatment planning, as the elevations could point to the need for particular attention to be paid by the clinician to an individual not revealing particularly "embarrassing" or "weird" obsessions or resultant compulsions. This is often seen in persons who have sexual obsessions and compulsions, as they can be very reluctant to admit certain types of "morally repugnant" thoughts or compulsions that they find uncomfortable to tell clinicians about.

The Millon Inventories

The Millon Clinical Multiaxial Inventory – III (MCMI-III) (Millon, 1994) is designed to identify pervasive personality characteristics underlying an individual's overt symptomology. The assessment was designed to parallel the criteria found within the third edition of the *Diagnostic and Statistical Manual of Mental Disorders* (DSM-III) (American Psychiatric Association, 1980) for various Axis I and Axis II disorders. While the DSM-III is not in current use, the central symptoms surrounding the diagnosis of (OCD) have experienced little change over this time. The MCMI-III consists of 175 true–false statements and requires approximately 20–30 minutes to complete. It is for use with individuals aged 18 years or older and requires an 8th-grade reading level. Because the MCMI-III has fewer than 200 items, it is considerably less time-consuming than other comparative broadband personality measures. Of note, given that it was normed on a clinical population, it is not a good measure to use with nonclinical individuals, as it tends to overpathologize people who do not have diagnosable disorders.

For the assessment of OCD, the most obvious aspect of the MCMI-III to examine would seem to be Scale 7 (Compulsive), which corresponds to the DSM diagnosis of obsessive-compulsive personality disorder (OCPD). However, OCD and OCPD are distinct diagnoses and appear to have little overlap (Wu, Clark, & Watson, 2006). People who have OCPD tend to have little insight into their behavior as being problematic, while those with OCD are highly distressed by it. In contrast to OCD, people with OCPD do not have intrusive and distressing obsessions and do not engage in compulsions to get rid of that distress. People with OCPD also tend to not seek treatment of their own accord, and instead believe that if others merely conformed to their rules and standards, things would be great.

Internal consistency ratings for the Compulsive scale are .66, the lowest of all 24 scales, but test–retest reliability is .92 (Millon, 1994) A study designed to assess external-criterion validity of the scales of the MCMI-III compared clinician's ratings of OCD symptoms with scores on the MCMI-III. It found 39 individuals from the sample who were rated as experiencing obsessive-compulsive symptoms as either a primary or secondary diagnosis by clinicians, and that 40 sample members were also found to be experiencing these symptoms as reported on the MCMI-III. This suggests overall agreement between the clinicians and the MCMI-III with regard to (OCD) (Millon, 1994). Other research, though, shows less support for this relationship.

For instance, correlations between other objective personality measures of obsessive-compulsive symptoms and the MCMI-III's Compulsive scale are not as expected. Instead, the MCMI-III shows significant *negative* correlations with other scales. Scale 7 of the MCMI-III exhibited a significant negative correlation (–.37) with the Obsessive-Compulsive Scale of the SCL-90-R and a significant negative correlation (–.47) with the Psychasthenia scale (scale 7) of the MMPI-2 (Millon, 1994). This could be explained by the fact that this is designed to measure OCPD, not necessarily OCD, or it could be that those MMPI scales are measuring general anxious distress (as reviewed above) more than measuring OCD symptoms specifically. Oddly, one of the only studies that we were able to find that used primarily an OCD population showed that people with an OCD diagnosis did not score differently on the MCMI Compulsive scale than did nonclinicals (Joffe, Swinson, & Regan, 1988). In fact, there is a large amount of work on prior versions of the MCMI showing that higher scores on the Compulsive scale are actually associated with *better* treatment outcomes and lower overall mental health problems (see Craig, 2005, for a review).

Another study on the MCMI examined how personality traits impacted treatment outcomes in people with OCD. It found that those with either no personality difficulties or dependent personality problems did the best in treatment, while histrionic and borderline traits apparently interfered with maintenance of gains across time (Fals-Stewart & Lucente, 1992). Unfortunately, however, this study used a prior version of the MCMI. Whether or not this research, and even that reviewed in the prior paragraph, are applicable to the MCMI-III, which has considerably less published research (even 20 years after its publication), is not known.

The Millon Pre-Adolescent Clinical Inventory (M-PACI) (Millon, Tringone, Millon, & Grossman, 2005) was developed as an extension of the MCMI-III in an effort to provide assessment for populations between the ages of 9 and 12. It is a self-report measure and requires a 3rd-grade reading level. It consists of 97 true–false items, requires approximately 15–20 minutes to complete, and contains 14 profile scales divided between two categories: Emerging Personality Disorders and Current Clinical Signs. The Obsessions-Compulsions Scale is a measure of current clinical signs of both intrusive thoughts and ritualistic behaviors as some children may ritualize, but be unaware of the thoughts that accompany such behaviors. A high score is suggestive of a possible emerging issue with OCD and should warrant a more comprehensive evaluation (Millon et al., 2005). Unfortunately, according to the M-PACI Manual, the Obsessions-Compulsions scale did not show a significant correlation with clinician ratings of similar symptoms. The Obsessions-Compulsions scale was shown however to have a significant correlation (.62) with the Anxiety scale of the Behavior Assessment System for Children: Self-Report of Personality Form C (BASC-SRP-C), which is expected as obsessive-compulsive symptoms are considered to be a manifestation of anxiety (Millon et al., 2005). Unfortunately, the authors were unable to find other research in the past 10 years examining the M-PACI as it relates to OCD, which likely points to it not being used often for the assessment of such symptoms.

The final Millon instrument, the Millon Adolescent Clinical Inventory (MACI) (Millon, Millon, Davis, & Grossman, 1993) was developed as an extension of the MCMI-III designed to assess common issues and concerns common within that age group. Unfortunately, the MACI does not contain a scale designed to assess obsessive-compulsive symptomology. Further, the authors were not able to identify any published literature using the MACI to assess for OCD.

Based on the paucity of recent research on the MCMI-III and the M-PACI with an obsessive-compulsive population, combined with the lack any work using the MACI, prevents us from recommending the Millon Inventories for specific assessment of OCD. Instead, it should be used to examine personality factors that could potentially impact treatment progress and outcome. For instance, it has been found that certain personality disorders (PD, particularly schizotypal and narcissistic), as well as the presence of multiple comorbid PDs, can significantly lower treatment outcome for persons with OCD (see Thiel et al., 2013, for a review). As such, specialized treatment planning is recommended for people with OCD and comorbid personality disorders. These patients will likely benefit from longer-term and more intense therapy (Fricke et al., 2006) and may benefit more from concurrent medication treatment than those with OCD alone or OCD and comorbid non-PD diagnoses (Catapano et al., 2006; Reich, 2003).

Five-Factor Model Assessment

The Five-Factor Model (FFM) is one of the most well-researched and well-supported trait theories of personality in psychological literature (Allik, Realo, & McCrae, 2013). It posits that humans tend to express their personality broadly in terms of five major factors (the "Big 5"): neuroticism, extraversion, openness-to-experience, agreeableness, and conscientiousness. The FFM defines these traits as follows:

> Neuroticism encompasses the predisposition to experience negative affectivity such as anxiety, depression, anger, guilt, and disgust. Extraversion includes sociability, cheerfulness and liveliness. Openness to experience consists of aesthetic sensitivity, intellectual curiosity, and need for variety. Agreeableness incorporates trust, altruism, and sympathy, and conscientiousness includes a strict adherence to principles and a desire to achieve goals. (Rector, Hood, Richter, & Bagby, 2002: 1207)

Several measures of the FFM have been developed over the past 30 years. The most commonly used commercial measure is the NEO Personality Inventory (NEO-PI). The latest version, the NEO-PI-3 (Costa & McCrae, 2005) is a self-administered questionnaire designed to assess the five major domains of personality (neuroticism, extraversion, openness-to-experience, agreeableness, and conscientiousness) by assessing six lower-order trait facets for each of the five domains. Separate self-report forms are available for use with adults (21 years and older) and adolescents (12–20 years old). The assessment contains 240 items, takes approximately 30–40 minutes to administer and requires at least a 4th-grade reading level. The major change from the prior version was that 38 items were made more readable and easier to understand.

A large body of research has explored the validity and reliability of the Five-Factor Model's relationship with OCD symptomology. While the five broad domains of personality do not necessarily represent a correlation with certain disorders, research has revealed that certain specific facets underlying these broad domains may be more salient in individuals suffering from specific types of mental illness. For example, Rector, Richter, and Babgy (2005) found that, in people with OCD, a low score on "openness to ideas" was significantly positively correlated with obsession severity, while low "openness to action" was significantly positively correlated with compulsion severity. A later study, however, found no differences on these facets between individuals with OCD and those with other mood and personality disorders (Rector, Bagby, Huta, & Ayearst, 2012). That said, they also discovered that only Post-Traumatic Stress Disorder and OCD were associated with low "openness to new ideas," which is not surprising as both are characterized by intrusive and unwanted cognitions. Furthermore, high scores on the "order" facet of the Conscientiousness domain was also correlated with a diagnosis of OCD.

Interestingly, a high level of Neuroticism has been linked to increased checking behaviors in both nonclinical (Wu & Watson, 2005) and clinical individuals (La-Salle-Ricci et al., 2006) who exhibit hoarding symptoms. Hoarding symptomology has been associated with several different disorders (most notably OCPD and the relatively new diagnosis of Hoarding Disorder), but is quite commonly associated with OCD. La-Salle-Ricci and colleagues' (2006) research has shown hoarding symptomology to be negatively correlated with the Conscientiousness domain and positively correlated with the Neuroticism domain of the NEO-PI.

With regard to OCD as a whole, research found that individuals with a diagnosis of OCD scored higher on all facets of the Neuroticism domain and lower on the Assertiveness facet of the Extraversion domain when compared to community participants without a diagnosis of OCD (Samuels et al., 2000). Rector and colleagues (2002) found similar results, with people who had OCD having high scores on the Neuroticism domain, low scores on the Extraversion domain, and low scores on the Conscientiousness domain. This pattern was similar to that seen in individuals with Major Depressive Disorder (MDD). Interestingly, people with OCD showed significantly higher scores on the domains of Extraversion, Agreeableness, and Conscientiousness than those with MDD. Scores for the Neuroticism domain were most notable for high scores on the facets of Trait Anxiety and Vulnerability. Scores for the Actions facet of Openness were in the low range and scores of the Tender-Mindedness facet of Agreeableness were high. While a significantly lower score on the Conscientiousness domain may be surprising (given that most people tend to have a schema of people with OCD being into cleanliness, order, and rules), this may be in part due to very low scores on the Self-Discipline domain. These findings were consistent with previous work (e.g., Samuels et al., 2000) and suggest that obsession and compulsion severity may be linked to low levels of Conscientiousness.

More understanding of lower-order facets of the symptomology of OCD is needed to better understand how this disorder correlates with the FFM. While promising exploration has been made into how an individual's broad domains of the FFM of personality may correlate with OCD symptomology through the use of assessments like the NEO-PI, it should be remembered that it is not a tool to diagnose OCD, but should be used to provide a more comprehensive treatment plan and understanding of an individual's symptomology. Knowing where your patients fall on the various facets and domains described above can help in nondiagnostic aspects of treatment planning as well. For instance, Wiggins (2003) heartily endorses the conclusions of Miller (1991), who found strong treatment implications for scores on each of the factors.

Adapting those general recommendations to someone who is coming in specifically for OCD treatment could be highly useful. For example, people with high Extraversion scores tend to show more interest in (and enthusiasm for) treatment. High Openness scores often result in more willingness to entertain interventions that seem as if they would be uncomfortable or new. Low scorers on E and O, then, might need to undergo motivational enhancement prior to beginning exposure therapy in order to potentially decrease drop-out rates. Therapists might also need to employ more of a story-driven and less of an evidence-driven explanation for how well exposure therapy works (e.g., discussing similar cases to the current patient and their positive outcomes more than talking about the research support). High Neuroticism scores tend to indicate patients will be less able to endure high levels of distress and discomfort. So, patients scoring highly on N might need to start with very low-level exposures in a highly controlled environment, or might need to have initial sessions planned to be longer than typical. People with low Agreeableness scores are more likely to resist forming a strong therapeutic alliance, so more emphasis on rapport-building at the start of therapy could be necessary in that case. Finally, Conscientiousness is related to one's willingness to do between-session assigned tasks (i.e., homework), which is a crucial aspect of positive treatment outcome. Someone who is low on C will need more of a support network around them to ensure that they follow through on exposures outside the therapy room, and may even need intensive treatment up front to make progress.

A Brief Note on Projective Measures

Among those who practice evidence-based psychology, many view the continued use of projective measures of personality to assess psychopathology as akin to a physician who uses trepanning to treat epilepsy – as a pseudoscientific practice which should have no place in a modern, scientific field. There are, however, numerous supporters of projective techniques and tests to assess for psychopathology in both clinical practice and academia (Hogan, 2005; Hojnoski, Morrison, Brown, & Matthews, 2006). As such, we wanted to briefly address the extant research on the use of projective measures for the assessment of OCD (for a thorough review of the topic, see Lack & Thomason, 2013).

Despite the long history of various projective tests, a review of the evidence does not support the routine usage of any projective measure in the assessment of anxiety symptoms or diagnostic constructs, including OCD. While certain measures have been found to be useful in examining overall adjustment (Rotter Incomplete Sentences Blank) (Lah, 1989), psychotic disorders (Rorschach Inkblot Method) (Wood, Nezworski, Lilienfeld, & Garb, 2003), personality disorders (Thematic Apperception Test) (Ackerman, Clemence, Weatherill, & Hilsenroth, 1999), or disruptive behavior and mood problems (global figure drawing scores) (Naglieri & Pfeffier, 1992), none have consistently been shown to be diagnostically useful for the assessment of anxiety, either alone or in addition to other measures. By this, we mean that the above-referenced measures do not display good reliability or validity when used in the assessment of anxiety and OCD. Although there was one study showing that responses on the Washington University Sentence Completion Task can differentiate between separation and generalized anxiety in children (Westenberg, Siebelink, Warmenhoven, & Treffers, 1999), no research examining OCD specifically has borne positive results.

Given the above information and dearth of research showing that projective assessment has incremental validity over more objective means, we do not support the use of any projective measures when assessing for obsessions or compulsions in child or adult populations. Instead, reliable and valid assessment tools, such as objective personality tests, diagnostic and severity measures, or functional assessment methods, should be used.

Conclusions

As reviewed above, broadband personality measures such as the MMPI and MCMI families, or those measuring Big 5 traits, do not have much support for their use as OCD symptoms specific assessments. This does not mean, however, that they cannot be useful in treatment planning for patients with OCD. Indeed, they can provide highly useful supplementary information on comorbid disorders that can impact treatment outcome, general distress levels, and even personality traits that can point to how the pace or style of treatment should proceed. The best treatment planning will take the information these types of measures provide and combine it with functional assessments, symptom-specific measures, and measures of functional impairment to form a complete picture of a particular patient's illness.

References

Ackerman, S. J., Clemence, A. J., Weatherill, R., & Hilsenroth, M. J. (1999). Use of the TAT in assessment of DSM-IV cluster B personality disorders. *Journal of Personality Assessment, 73*, 422–448.

Allik, J., Realo, A., & McCrae, R. (2013). Universality of the five-factor model of personality. In T. A., Widiger & P. T. Costa, Jr. (Eds.), *Personality disorders and the Five-Factor Model of Personality* (pp. 61–74) (3rd ed.). Washington, DC: American Psychological Association.

American Psychiatric Association. (1980). *Diagnostic and statistical manual of mental disorders* (3rd ed., text rev.). Washington, DC: Author.

American Psychiatric Association. (2000). *Diagnostic and statistical manual of mental disorders* (4th ed., text rev.). Washington, DC: Author.

American Psychiatric Association. (2013). *Diagnostic and statistical manual of mental disorders* (5th ed., text rev.). Washington, DC: Author.

Archer, R. P., Aiduk, R., Griffin, R., & Elkins, D. E. (1996). Incremental validity of the MMPI-2 content scales in a psychiatric sample. *Assessment, 3*, 79–90.

Ben-Porath, Y. S., McCully, E., & Almagor, M. (1993). Incremental validity of the MMPI-2 content scales in the assessment of personality and psychopathology by self-report. *Journal of Personality Assessment, 61*, 557–575.

Boulet, J., & Boss, M. W. (1991). Reliability and validity of the Brief Symptom Inventory. *Psychological Assessment: A Journal of Consulting and Clinical Psychology, 3*(3), 433–437.

Butcher, J. N., Dahlstrom, W. G., Graham, J. R., Tellegen, A., & Kaemmer, B. (1989). *Minnesota Multiphasic Personality Inventory-2 (MMPI-2): Manual for administration and scoring.* Minneapolis, MN: University of Minnesota Press.

Butcher, J. N., Graham, J. R., Williams, C. L., & Ben-Porath, Y.S. (1990). *Development and use of the MMPI-2 content scales.* Minneapolis, MN: University of Minnesota Press.

Butcher, J. N., Graham, J. R., Ben-Porath, Y. S., Tellegen, A., Dahlstrom, W. G., & Kaemmer, B. (2001). *MMPI-2 (Minnesota Multiphasic Personality Inventory–2): Manual for administration, scoring, and interpretation, revised.* Minneapolis, MN: University of Minnesota Press.

Butcher, J. N., Williams, C. L., Graham, J. R., Archer, R. P., Tellegren, A., Ben-Porath, Y. S., & Kaemmer, B. (1992). *Minnesota Multiphasic Personality Inventory – Adolescent (MMPI-A): Manual for administration, scoring and interpretation.* Minneapolis, MN: University of Minnesota Press.

Carey, R. J., Baer, L., Jenike, M. A., Minichiello, W. E., Schwartz, C., & Regan, N. (1986). MMPI correlates of obsessive-compulsive disorder. *Journal of Clinical Psychiatry, 47,* 371–372.

Catapano, F., Perris, F., Fabrazzo, M., Cioffi, V., Giacco, D., De Santis, V., & Maj, M. (2010). Obsessive-compulsive disorder with poor insight: A three-year prospective study. *Progress in Neuro-Psychopharmacology & Biological Psychiatry, 34,* 323–330

Costa, P. T., & McCrae, R. R. (1992). *Revised NEO Personality Inventory (NEO-PI-R) and NEO Five-Factor Inventory (NEO-FFI) professional manual.* Odessa, FL: Psychological Assessment Resources.

Craig, R. J. (2005). Alternative interpretations for the Histrionic, Narcissitic, and Compulsive Personality Disorder scales of the MCMI-III. In R. J. Craig (Ed.), *New Directions in interpreting the Millon Clinical Multiaxial Inventory-III* (pp. 71–93). Hoboken, NJ: Wiley.

Derogatis, L. R. (1993). *BSI Brief Symptom Inventory: Administration, scoring, and procedure manual* (4th ed.). Minneapolis, MN: National Computer Systems.

Derogatis, L. R. (1994). *Symptom Checklist-90-R: Administration, scoring, and procedures manual* (3rd ed.). Minneapolis, MN: National Computer Systems.

Derogatis, L. R., & Unger, R. (2010). Symptom Checklist-90 – Revised. In I. B. Weiner, & W. E. Craighead (Eds.), *Corsini encyclopedia of psychology* (pp. 81–84). Hoboken, NJ: Wiley.

Eddy, K. T., Dutra, L., Bradley, R., & Westen, D. (2004). A multidimensional meta-analysis of psychotherapy and pharmacotherapy for obsessive–compulsive disorder. *Clinical Psychology Review, 24,* 1011–1103

Fals-Stewart, W., & Lucente, S. (1993). An MCMI cluster typology of obsessive-compulsives: A measure of personality characteristics and its relationship to treatment participation, compliance and outcome in behavior therapy. *Journal of Psychiatric Research, 27*(2), 139–154.

Fricke, S., Moritz, S., Andresen, B., Jacobsen, D., Kloss, M., Rufer, M., & Hand, I. (2006). Do personality disorders predict negative treatment outcome in in obsessive-compulsive disorders? A prospective 6-month follow-up study. *European Psychiatry, 21*(5), 319–324

Grabill, K., Merlo, L., Duke, D., Harford, K., Keeley, M. L., Geffken, G. R., & Storch, E. A. (2008). Assessment of obsessive-compulsive disorder: A review. *Journal of Anxiety Disorders, 22*(1), 1–17.

Graham, J. R., Ben-Porath, Y. S., & McNulty, J. L. (1999). *MMPI-2 correlates for outpatient community mental health settings.* Minneapolis, MN: University of Minnesota Press.

Helmes, E., & Reddon, J. R. (1993). A perspective on developments in assessing psychopathology: A critical review of the MMPI and MMPI-2. *Psychological Bulletin, 113,* 453–471.

Hajcak, G., Huppert, J. D., Simons, R. F., & Foa, E. B. (2004). Psychometric properties of the OCI-R in a college sample. *Behaviour Research and Therapy, 42*(1), 115–123.

Hogan, T. P. (2005). 50 widely used psychological tests. In G. P. Koocher, J. C. Norcross, & S. S. Hill III (Eds.), *Psychologists: Desk reference* (2nd ed.) (pp. 101–104). New York: Oxford University Press.

Hojnoski, R. L., Morrison, R., Brown, M., & Matthews, W. J. (2006). Projective test use among school psychologists: A survey and critique. *Journal of Psychoeducational Assessment, 24,* 145.

Huppert, J. D., Simpson, H. B., Nissesnson, K. S., Liebowitz, M. R., & Foa, E. B. (2009). Quality of life and functional impariment in obsessive-compulsive disorder: A comparison of patients with and without comorbidity, patients in remission, and healthy controls. *Journal of Depression and Anxiety, 26*(1), 39–45.

Joffe, R. T., Swinson, R. P., & Regan, J. J. (1998). Personality features of obsessive-compulsive disorder. *American Journal of Psychiatry, 145*(9), 1127–1129.

Kuhn, W. F., Bell, R. A., Seligson, D., Laufer, S. T., & Lindner, J. E. (1998). The tip of the iceberg: Psychiatric consultations of an orthopedic service. *International Journal of Psychiatry in Medicine, 18*(4), 375–382.

Lack, C. W., Lehmkuhl-Yardley, H., & Dalaya, A. (2013). Treatment of multiple co-morbid anxiety disorders. In E. Storch & D. McKay (Eds.), *Handbook of treating variants and complications in anxiety disorders* (pp. 309–319). New York: Springer.

Lack, C. W., Storch, E. A., Keely, M., Geffken, G. R., Ricketts, E., Murphy, T. K., & Goodman, W. K. (2009). Quality of life in children and adolescents with Obsessive-Compulsive Disorder. *Social Psychiatry and Psychiatric Epidemiology, 44*, 935–942.

Lack, C. W., & Thomason, S. P. (2013). Projective personality assessment of anxiety: A critical appraisal. In D. McKay & E. Storch (Eds.), *Handbook of assessing variants and complications in anxiety disorders* (pp. 203–216). New York: Springer.

Lah, M. I. (1989). New validity, normative, and scoring data for the Rotter Incomplete Sentences Blank. *Journal of Personality Assessment, 53*(3), 607–620.

LaSalle-Ricci, V. H., Arnkoff, D. B., Glass, C. R., Crawley, S. A., Ronquillo, J. G., & Murphy, D. L. (2006). The hoarding dimension of OCD: Psychological comorbidity and the five-factor personality model. *Behaviour Research and Therapy, 44*, 1503–1512.

Mancuso, E., Faro, A., Joshi, G., & Geller, D. A. (2010). Treatment of pediatric obsessive-compulsive disorder: A review. *Journal of Child and Adolescent Psychopharmacology, 20*(4), 299–308.

McGrath, R. E., Pogge, D. L., & Stokes, J. M. (2002). Incremental validity of selected MMPI-A content scales in an inpatient setting. *Psychological Assessment, 14*(4), 401–409.

Miller, T. R. (1991). The psychotherapeutic utility of the five-factor model of personality: A clinician's experience. *Journal of Personality Assessment, 57*(3), 415–433

Millon, T., Millon, C., Davis, R., & Grossman, S. (1993). *Millon Adolescent Clinical Inventory (MACI) Manual* (2nd ed.). Minneapolis, MN: Pearson.

Millon, T. (1994). *The Millon Clinical Multiaxial Inventory-III manual.* Minneapolis, MN: National Computer Systems.

Millon, T., Tringone, R., Millon, C., & Grossman, S. (2005). *Million Pre-Adolescent Clinical Inventory (M-PACI) Manual* (3rd ed.). Minneapolis, MN: Pearson.

Naglieri, J. A., & Pfeffier, S. I. (1992). Performance of disruptive behavior-disordered and normal samples on the Draw-A-Person: Screening Procedure for Emotional Disturbance. *Psychological Assessment, 4*, 156–159.

Pallanti, S., Giacomo, G., Sarrecchia, E. D., Cantisani, A., & Pellegrini, M. (2011). Obsessive compulsive disorder comorbidity: Clinical assessment and therapeutic implications. *Frontiers in Psychiatry, 2*(70), 1–11.

Pedersen, G., & Karterud, S. (2004). Is SCL-90R helpful for the clinician in assessing DSM-IV symptom disorders? *Acta Psychiatrica Scandinavica, 110*(3), 215–224.

Rector, N. A., Bagby, R. M., Huta, V., & Ayearst, L. E. (2012). Examination of the trait facets of the five-factor model in discriminating specific mood and anxiety disorders. *Psychiatry Research, 199*, 131–139.

Rector, N. A., Hood, K., Richter, M. A., & Bagby, M. R. (2002). Obsessive-Compulsive Disorder and the five-factor model of personality: Distinction and overlap with major depressive disorder. *Behaviour Research and Therapy, 40*, 1205–1219.

Rector, N. A., Richter, M. A., & Bagby, R. M. (2005). The impact of personality on symptom expression in OCD. *Journal of Nervous and Mental Disease, 193*, 231–236.

Reich, J. (2003). The effect of Axis II disorders on the outcome of treatment of anxiety and uni-polar depressive disorders: A review. *Journal of Personality Disorders, 17*(5), 387–405.

Rogove, J. (2013). Anxiety disorders and evidence-based practice: The role of broadband self-report measures of personality in diagnosis, case conceptualization, and treatment planning. In D. McKay, & E. A. Storch (Eds.), *Handbook of assessing variants and complications in anxiety disorders* (pp. 163–188). New York: Springer.

Samuels, J., Nestadt, G., Bienvenu, O. J., Costa, P. T., Riddle, M. A., & Liang, K. (2000). Personality disorders and normal personality dimensions in obsessive-compulsive disorder. *British Journal of Psychiatry, 177*, 457–462.

Scahill, L., Riddle, M. A., McSwiggin-Hardin, M., Ort, S. I., King, R. A., Goodman, W. K., Cicchetti, D., & Leckman, J. F. (1997). Children's Yale–Brown Obsessive Compulsive Scale: Reliability and validity. *Journal of the American Academy of Child and Adolescent Psychiatry, 36*(6), 844–852.

Sellbom, M., & Lee, T. T. C. (2013). MMPI-2, MMPI-2-RF, MMPI-A, and anxiety. In D. McKay & E. Storch (Eds.), *Handbook of assessing variants and complications in anxiety disorders* (pp. 139–162). New York: Springer.

Selles, R. R., Storch, E. A., & Lewin, A. B. (2014). Variations in symptom prevalence and clinical correlates in younger versus older youth with obsessive-compulsive disorder. *Child Psychiatry & Human Development, 45*(6), 666–674.

Storch, E. A., Benito, K., & Goodman, W. (2011). Assessment scales for obsessive-compulsive disorder. *Neuropsychiatry, 1*(3), 243–250.

Storch, E. A., Larson, M. J., Price, L. H., Rasmussen, S. A., Murphy, T. K., & Goodman, W. K. (2010). Psychometric analysis of the Yale–Brown Obsessive-Compulsive Scale – Second Edition Symptom Checklist. *Journal of Anxiety Disorders, 24*(6), 650–656.

Tellegen, A., Ben-Porath, Y. S., NcNulty, J. L., Arbisi, P. A., Graham, J. R., & Kaemmer, B. (2003). *The MMPI-2 Restructured Clinical (RC) scales: Development, validation, and interpretation.* Minneapolis, MN: University of Minnesota Press.

Thiel, N., Hertenstein, E., Nissen, C., Herbst, N., Külz, A. K., & Voderholzer, U. (2013). The effect of personality disorders on treatment outcomes in patients with obsessive compulsive disorders. *Journal of Personality Disorders, 27*(6), 697–715.

Timpano, K. R., Rubenstein, L. M., & Murphy, D. L. (2012). Phenomenological features and clinical impact of affective disorders in OCD: A focus on the bipolar disorder and OCD connection. *Journal of Depression and Anxiety, 29*(3), 226–233.

Van der Heijden, P. T., Egger, J. I. M., Rossi, G. M. P., Grundel, G., & Derksen, J. J. L. (2013). The MMPI-2 restructured form and the standard MMPI-2 clinical scales in relation to DSM-IV. *European Journal of Psychological Assessment, 29*(3), 182–188.

Veltri, C.O., Graham, J. R., Sellbom, M., Ben-Porath, Y. S., Forbey, J. D., O'Connell, C., Rogers, R., & White, R. S. (2009). Correlates of MMPI-A scales in acute psychiatric and forensic samples. *Journal of Personality Assessment, 91*, 288–300.

Westenberg, P. M., Siebelink, B. M., Warmenhoven, N. J. C., & Treffers, P. D. A. (1999). Separation anxiety and overanxious disorders: Relations to age and psychosocial maturity. *Journal of the American Academy of Child and Adolescent Psychiatry, 38*(8), 1000–1007.

Wiggins, J. S. (2003). *Paradigms of personality assessment.* New York: Guilford Press.

Wood, J. M., Nezworski, M. T., Lilienfeld, S. O., & Garb, H. N. (2003). *What's wrong with Rorscach? Science confronts the controversial inkblot test.* New York: Jossey-Bass.

Woody, S. R., Steketee, G., & Chambliss, D. L. (1995). The usefulness of the obsessive-compulsive scale of the Symptom Checklist-90 – Revised. *Journal of Behavior Research and Therapy, 33*(5), 607–611.

Wu, K. D., Clark, L. A., & Watson, D. (2006). Relations between obsessive-compulsive disorder and personality: Beyond axis I–axis II comorbidity. *Journal of Anxiety Disorders, 20*, 695–717.

Wu, K. D., & Watson, D. (2005). Hoarding and its relation to obsessive-compulsive disorder. *Behaviour Research and Therapy, 43*, 897–921.

12

Psychological Models and Treatments of OCD for Adults

Noah C. Berman, Rachel Schwartz, and Jennifer Park

There are a number of theoretical explanations regarding the development, maintenance, and treatment of Obsessive Compulsive Disorder (OCD). Although a host of theories have been proposed over the past century, the behavioral, cognitive, and acceptance and commitment therapy (ACT) models have been extensively studied through multiple assessment and treatment trials and garnered significant empirical support. To provide a comprehensive overview, the present chapter will separately discuss the following for each model: (a) theoretical framework; (b) essential treatment components; and (c) empirical support. Moreover, for each model, we will apply the theoretical framework and treatment to a case example. Lastly, we will conclude by discussing similarities across the models, as well as how to integrate the three into treatment in clinical practice.

Behavioral Theory and Therapy for OCD

Behavioral Model

According to the behavioral model (see Figure 12.1), intrusions constitute previously neutral stimuli that elicit anxiety through classical conditioning (e.g., Mowrer, 1960). In essence, benign thoughts, images, impulses or ideas (e.g., hurting a child) become associated with escalating anxiety through repeated pairings. Compulsions, in turn, operate as attempts to escape the uncomfortable physiological effects of anxiety. These attempts, collectively characterized as safety behaviors, can be overt compulsions (e.g., hand washing), avoidance of threatening stimuli (e.g., sharp objects), or covert rituals (e.g., mental reviewing). For example, a parent who has an excessive fear of violently harming his or her child repeats a prayer every time the thoughts recur and avoids knives in the presence of his or her daughter. Her behavioral response leads to a temporary reduction in emotional arousal, which prevents the natural habituation of anxiety. As a result, the compulsive rituals and avoidance behaviors are negatively reinforced, thereby increasing the likelihood that the behaviors will be repeated when

The Wiley Handbook of Obsessive Compulsive Disorders, Volume I, First Edition.
Edited by Jonathan S. Abramowitz, Dean McKay, and Eric A. Storch.
© 2017 John Wiley & Sons Ltd. Published 2017 by John Wiley & Sons Ltd.

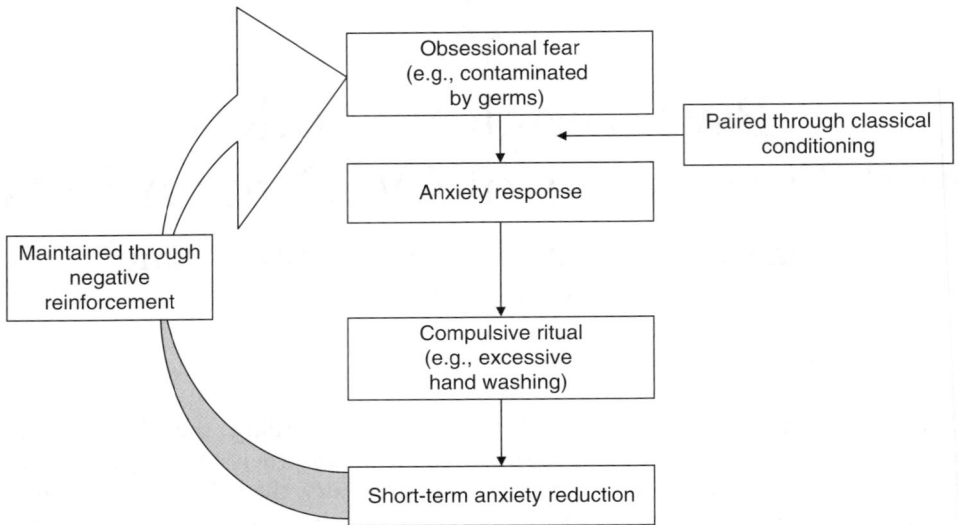

Figure 12.1   Behavioral model of OCD

similar anxiety-provoking stimuli are confronted in the future. Taken together, the behavioral model of OCD posits that avoidance and compulsive rituals interfere with the natural habituation of anxiety and ultimately maintain or exacerbate obsessive-compulsive symptomology.

Behavioral Therapy Overview

The behavioral model of OCD maps onto the two empirically supported treatment components of "exposure with response prevention" (ERP): (1) weakening the classically conditioned association between obsessions and anxiety by systematically confronting anxiety-provoking stimuli in a graduated fashion (termed "exposures"); and (2) refraining from performing the safety behaviors that would otherwise provide short-term anxiety relief, thereby disrupting the negative reinforcement cycle (termed "response prevention"). Typically, clinicians and patients collaboratively develop a "fear hierarchy" that ranks patients' feared or avoided situations. Initially, patients conduct exposures to situations perceived to be "low risk," which fosters self-efficacy and increases motivation for continued treatment (e.g., Zoellner, Echiverri, & Craske, 2000), and gradually approach more threatening situations in a systematic manner.

Two types of exposure are utilized in ERP: in vivo (real-life confrontation with feared stimuli); and imaginal (imagining confrontation with feared stimuli or consequences). In either case, the rationale for conducting the designated exposure is essential. For example, the patient should be aware that an in vivo exposure in which the house is purposely left unlocked directly challenges an expectation that doing so will lead to harm befalling the patient's family. Following the behavioral model, upon provoking the obsessional fear in the exposure, the clinician should allow the anxiety to habituate and retrigger the obsessional fear until its presentation no longer elicits significant anxiety. Doing so will likely lead to habituation within-session (fear responses gradually diminish during the exposure itself) and between-sessions (initial fear response at the beginning of each exposure declines across exposure sessions) (Foa & Kozak, 1986).

While many feared or avoided situations can be targeted behaviorally (e.g., touching a contaminated surface), imaginal exposures are especially useful: (a) when in vivo exposures are unavailable (e.g., violent obsessions of harming another individual); (b) if the therapist wants to expose a patient to a *particular* feared consequence (e.g., contracting a cold after not washing one's hands); or (c) as a supplement to in vivo exposures (Abramowitz, 2006). Imaginal exposures can be delivered via audio recorded loop tapes (approximately 45–60 seconds long) that describe the obsessional trigger, intrusive thought(s), emotional reaction, and prevention of safety behaviors. The loop tape is then listened to repeatedly (Abramowitz, 2006). For instance, an individual who is unprepared to confront potential contamination might record a story in which he or she walks barefoot in a public bathroom and becomes covered in germs. The patient then listens to the imaginal exposure repeatedly, which both facilitates habituation and acts as a first step toward engaging in the in vivo exposure.

While exposures constitute an essential component of ERP, response prevention – refraining from the use of safety behaviors or rituals – is critical for modifying maladaptive learning patterns and enacting behavioral change. Preventing the use of avoidance behaviors or ritualistic compulsions disrupts the negative reinforcement cycle that maintains OCD symptomology. By doing so, the patient learns to tolerate the physiological effects of anxiety and recognize that safety behaviors are redundant. Moreover, because an individual can no longer attribute his or her safety to the fulfillment of rituals or avoidance, response prevention weakens the conditioned relationship between safety-behaviors and anxiety reduction.

Advances to ERP: Inhibitory Learning Model. While the classical conceptualization of ERP hypothesizes that the habituation of anxiety is the driving mechanism by which change occurs (Himle & Franklin, 2009), recent research has highlighted the importance of inhibitory learning (i.e., the formation of secondary, non-threat associations to previously feared stimuli; Craske et al., 2008; Craske, Liao, Brown, & Verviliet, 2012). Given evidence that the degree to which one's anxiety habituates during an exposure trial does not predict overall symptom reduction (for a review, see Craske et al., 2008), the inhibitory model of ERP de-emphasizes weakening the association between obsessional triggers and anxiety. Instead, the development of alternative, non-threat associations to feared stimuli (e.g., "thoughts about being gay are normal and acceptable") that compete with the original threat association (e.g., "thoughts about being gay are threatening and intolerable) is encouraged. After habituation occurs during an exposure, the feared stimulus is thought to possess two meanings: the original excitatory meaning (obsession-anxiety) and a new inhibitory meaning (obsession-no anxiety). Thus, while the original threat association remains intact, the goal of the inhibitory learning approach is to maximize the likelihood that the new non-threat association will be activated in the presence of previously feared stimuli (Abramowitz & Arch, 2014; Deacon et al., 2013).

Recent work in neuroimaging, psychophysiology, and psychopharmacology increasingly lend support to the inhibitory learning model (Craske et al., 2012). Moreover, compared with the habituation-focused derivative, inhibitory learning is better able to account for documented phenomena such as spontaneous recovery (i.e., re-emergence of anxiety after time has elapsed since habituation), reinstatement (i.e., re-emergence of anxiety after the reinforcer is reintroduced), and context dependency (i.e., restoration of anxiety when the context differs from that where habituation learning took place) (Craske et al., 2012). Importantly, the inhibitory learning approach does not emphasize systematically approaching feared stimuli and awaiting habituation, but, instead, generating secondary non-threat associations (Abramowitz & Arch, 2014; Craske et al., 2008). For instance, when exposure to the feared stimulus (e.g., repeatedly checking whether the front door is locked) does not result in the feared consequence (e.g., being robbed), an alternative, non-threat meaning for the original stimulus develops (e.g., checking the door once is sufficient). Another method that promotes secondary associations is eliminating safety cues that signal the absence of the feared consequence (Abramowitz & Arch., 2014; Craske et al., 2008). Since certain stimuli (e.g., presence of the therapist) may become associated with a lack of catastrophic outcomes, it is important for patients to practice exposures independently and in the absence of other safety cues for novel associations to develop. Combining excitatory conditioners – that is, conducting exposures of feared stimuli individually, and then combining them – may also encourage secondary associations (Abramowitz & Arch, 2014; Craske et al., 2008; Craske et al., 2012).

The inhibitory learning model also strives to enhance the accessibility and retrievability of the secondary associations. Given evidence that spacing learning trials at increasingly larger intervals results in better long-term retention than massed or regularly spaced learning trials (at least for non-emotional material) (Bjork, 1988), scheduling ERP sessions at increasingly longer intervals (e.g., weekly sessions at first, then every two weeks, then once per month) may help consolidate long-term learning (Abramowitz & Arch, 2014). Moreover, maximizing variability in exposure content, context, and even levels of fear elicited may help newly formed secondary connections become readily accessible by creating a wide array of retrieval cues (Abramowitz & Arch, 2014; Craske et al., 2008; Craske et al., 2012). For instance, if exposure to the fear of becoming ill was originally accomplished by eating a cracker off of the floor of the therapist's office, the same exposure could then be implemented in different settings (e.g., off the floor of a grocery store or parking lot) or with different types of food (e.g., cookies or carrots).

In keeping with the goal of diversifying exposure conditions, random ordering of exposures, rather than a predictable and linear hierarchy, may result in superior retrievability of secondary associations (Abramowitz & Arch, 2014; Craske et al., 2008; Craske et al., 2012). Using this paradigm, a therapist might generate a hierarchy of feared situations with a patient, but randomly select the situation they will confront in that session. Further, during any given exposure, the therapist might vary the point at which the exposure is terminated, rather than allow anxiety to reach a negligible level. Although this conceptualization of treatment deviates from ERP as it is currently administered, it remains to be determined whether the theoretical implications of the inhibitory learning approach translate into significantly better treatment outcomes.

Empirical Evidence

Several meta-analyses (e.g., Abramowitz, 1996; Abramowitz, 1997; Eddy, Dutra, Bradley & Westen, 2004; Rosa-Alcázar, Sánchez-Meca, Gómez-Conesa, & Marín-Martínez, 2008; Ponniah, Magiati, & Hollon, 2013) and randomized controlled trials (e.g., Fals-Stewart, Marks, & Schafer, 1993; Lindsay, Crino, & Andrews, 1997; Foa et al., 2005) have demonstrated the efficacy of ERP. Moreover, studies indicate that ERP is an effective treatment for 60–90% of individuals with OCD, with a typical symptom reduction rate of 50–80% (Himle & Franklin, 2009) and treatment gains that are maintained long term (e.g., 2 years) (Whittal, Robichaud, Thordarson, & McLean, 2008). When compared against other established interventions for OCD, studies have shown ERP to be similarly or more effective than cognitive treatments (e.g., Olatunji, Davis, Powers, & Smits, 2013; Ponniah et al., 2013), and safer, more acceptable, and longer lasting than various forms of psychopharmacology (Foa et al., 2005; Kobak, Greist, Jefferson, Katzelnick, & Henk, 1998; Simpson et al., 2004). Given the multitude of studies demonstrating the efficacy and effectiveness of ERP, it is recognized as both the first-line intervention and psychological treatment of choice for individuals with OCD (National Institute for Health and Clinical Excellence, 2006; Olatunji, Cisler, & Deacon, 2010).

A large body of work has also investigated how ERP can be optimally delivered to maximize symptom improvement. Interventions that incorporate both in vivo and imaginal exposures consistently outperform treatments that use in vivo exposures alone, suggesting that imaginal exposure to (a) the consequences of not ritualizing or (b) otherwise inaccessible material is an important adjunct to in vivo exposure (e.g., Abramowitz, 1996; Abramowitz, Rosa-Alcázar et al., 2008). Furthermore, therapist-guided exposures (i.e., therapist is present), are associated with a better treatment response when compared wit therapist-assisted self-exposures (i.e., conducted as homework) (Abramowitz, 1996; Abramowitz 1997; Rosa-Alcázar et al., 2008). In terms of optimal session frequency, two meta-analytic studies found that multiple ERP sessions per week were associated with better outcomes than once-weekly sessions (Abramowitz, 1996; Abramowitz, 1997). Further, while there is evidence that intensive treatment (e.g., two hours daily for three weeks) has some advantage in symptom reduction over twice weekly sessions at post-treatment, the differences between the two approaches were no longer present after three months, suggesting that a twice weekly ERP schedule may provide clinicians with a more pragmatic, yet equally effective, alternative to intensive treatment (Abramowitz, Foa, & Franklin, 2003).

Case Study: Ellen

Ellen is a 22-year-old female whose primary obsessions involve contamination and a fear of contracting HIV. Ellen's symptoms started in high school, when she learned about the transmission of sexually transmitted diseases. In response to her budding fear of HIV, she began avoiding individuals she suspected might have the disease, specifically homosexual students and teachers. After one month, she was skipping all classes in which there was contact with a perceived homosexual. Not surprisingly, her grades plummeted. Gradually, in her first year of college, her avoidance behaviors began to generalize. She avoided hospitals and doctors' offices, even at the expense of her own health care. She believed that contaminants in these settings would be highly concentrated and that there was a higher likelihood of transmission. When Ellen encountered someone she perceived to be threatening (e.g., homosexual, drug user, the homeless), she covered her face, limited her breathing, and discontinued her current activity to vigorously wash her body in the shower. Moreover, despite being in a long-term monogamous relationship and previously having had sex with her boyfriend, her fear of HIV caused her to avoid any and all sexual contact. Ultimately, her contamination concerns, avoidance behaviors, and corresponding rituals became so disruptive that Ellen took a leave of absence from her undergraduate studies. She currently lives at home with her family.

Using the behavioral model, Ellen's symptoms can be conceptualized as maladaptive learning patterns. Her avoidance of threatening stimuli and use of compensatory rituals provided short-term anxiety relief, thereby perpetuating the negatively reinforcement cycle. Moreover, by avoiding "contaminated" objects and allowing rituals to abbreviate anxiety prematurely, Ellen deprived herself of the opportunity to learn that anxiety extinguishes naturally. At the onset of ERP, Ellen's behavioral therapist conducted a preliminary assessment of her obsessions, safety-seeking strategies, and avoidance behaviors using the Yale–Brown Obsessive Compulsive Scale (Y-BOCS) (Goodman et al., 1989), the gold standard instrument for assessing OCD symptoms and severity in adults. Ellen received a total score of 30, indicating that her symptoms were in the "severe" range. The therapist also conducted a functional assessment of Ellen's compulsive behaviors, by identifying the triggers for each safety behavior and a detailed description of each ritual and its purported utility (e.g., reduces the likelihood of harm). This targeted assessment is a critical first step toward developing Ellen's fear hierarchy, ensuring that exposures are engineered to match the specific elements that maintain her unique symptomology.

Following the diagnostic and functional assessment, the therapist provided two sessions of psychoeducation in which Ellen was introduced to the behavioral model and the rationale for ERP. Collaboratively, Ellen and her therapist then developed a hierarchy of 15 feared or avoided situations to confront over the course of treatment. Specifically, the therapist helped Ellen order the items on the hierarchy in a gradual fashion, such that the situations that provoked the least amount of anxiety would be approached first and would be followed by increasingly more difficulty scenarios. In order to help quantify her anxiety, Ellen's therapist taught her how to use the Subjective Units of Distress Scale (SUDS) and rate her anxiety on a 0–100 scale (0 indicated no distress and 100 indicating maximum distress; see abridged fear hierarchy).

Ellen and her therapist started with a low to moderate exposure of sitting in a hospital waiting room without wearing a mask or washing her hands or body after. Ellen's identified fears in this scenario were contracting HIV and not being unable to tolerate her anxiety without ritualizing. Ellen reported that she would "know whether she had contracted HIV because her throat would become sore and the glands would become

Table 12.1 Abridged Fear Hierarchy for Ellen

Fear hierarchy	SUDS
Sit outside hospital	30
Sit in hospital waiting room	35
Enter hospital waiting room + take deep breaths	40
Go on walk with boyfriend while holding hands	45
Sit next to stranger in a doctor's office	50
Kiss boyfriend on cheek	60
Sit next to stranger in a hospital + imagine he has HIV	70
Be intimate with boyfriend	75
Visit the home of her homosexual friend who may or may not have HIV	80
Visit patient with HIV in hospital	85
Visit friend who has HIV and kiss him on the cheek	95

swollen." Upon arriving at the hospital, Ellen reported an instantaneous spike in her anxiety (i.e., SUDS of 90) and an escalating urge to cover her face and wash her hands. For the next 45 minutes in the hospital waiting room, Ellen's therapist persistently monitored her SUDS ratings and re-oriented Ellen's attention to the exposure task (e.g., "We are sitting here in a hospital waiting room where someone with HIV might have been. We don't know whether the seat has been contaminated and we are sitting here with that uncertainty"), thereby limiting the possibility for distraction. Moreover, the therapist monitored Ellen's urge to engage in maladaptive avoidance or compensatory behaviors and reiterated the goal to refrain from engaging in such rituals. Near the end of the hour, Ellen's SUDS dropped to 30 (i.e., one-third of its initial level) and the therapist ended the exposure. The final ten minutes of the session: (a) consolidated her learning by making sense of the mismatch in expectancies (e.g., why didn't my throat become sore even though I might have been exposed to HIV); (b) assigned homework; and (c) discussed the next exposure exercise (Abramowitz, 2006).

Despite Ellen's success with the low to moderate item, she was resistant to engage in more difficult in vivo exposures involving her boyfriend. Ellen reported wanting to have sexual relations with her boyfriend again, but felt as though it was impossible due to her contamination concerns. Therefore, Ellen and her therapist started with an imaginal exposure. Together, they composed a 45-second story, in which she had sex with her boyfriend and resisted the urge to ask him whether he was HIV positive. Below is an abbreviated version of the script that Ellen read aloud and listened to on a loop recording:

> I am having dinner with Dave at his apartment. When we finished cleaning up he reaches for my hand and squeezes it tightly. He draws me in closer and puts his arms around my waist. He kisses me on the lips, and I suddenly think that he must have HIV. My thoughts are racing, but we continue into the bedroom. As we undress, I feel my anxiety spike and I continue to wonder if he has HIV. I want to ask him if he's been tested for HIV, but I resist. The anxiety is causing my heart to race and I feel panicky. I keep thinking that my anxiety will never come down. We have protected sex and I lie awake afterwards wondering whether we both have HIV. I suppose I have to sit with this uncertainty.

In all subsequent ERP sessions, the first 10 minutes were spent reviewing Ellen's homework assignment from the past week (i.e., repeating the exposure exercise in different contexts or slightly modifying the exposures to increase difficulty level) and the remainder was dedicated to therapist-guided exposure exercises of increasing difficulty. By session 14, Ellen had confronted a number of avoided situations and had successfully refrained from employing maladaptive compensatory behaviors. At this juncture, she reported confidence in her ability to tolerate the anxiety associated with difficult exposures and had even targeted the top of her hierarchy.

Throughout the course of ERP, Ellen had acquired the necessary skills for approaching feared or avoided stimuli and managing the associated distress. She strengthened her skill use through repeated practice and generalized the principles by varying the context (e.g., going to a methadone clinic) of the exposure exercises. To assist Ellen in maintaining her treatment gains, the last two sessions targeted relapse prevention strategies, such as developing specific response prevention instructions (e.g., not covering face in the hospital) and reviewing steps to take if she ritualizes (e.g., deliberately re-expose herself). The therapist concluded treatment with a re-assessment of Ellen's symptoms using the Y-BOCS. Ellen received a score of 15 (mild range), demonstrating a substantial decline in her OCD symptom severity. Ellen reported extreme satisfaction with her improvement and set up an appointment to follow up with her therapist in a month.

Cognitive Theory and Therapy for OCD

Cognitive Model

The cognitive model of OCD proposes that dysfunctional beliefs and maladaptive interpretations about intrusive thoughts, images, impulses, or ideas are a primary contributor to the development and maintenance of this disabling psychiatric condition (see Figure 12.2) (e.g., Rachman, 1997; 1998). Specifically, the cognitive model suggests that unwanted intrusions (e.g., sexual contact with a relative) are ubiquitous and normal (Rachman & de Silva, 1978). In fact, decades of research has demonstrated that nearly everyone experiences disturbing intrusions (e.g., Rachman, 1997; 1998; Rachman & de Silva, 1978; Rassin, Cougle, & Muris, 2007). Given their normalcy, it is not the presence of intrusions that differentiates individuals with OCD from those without, but rather the interpretation of the intrusion as overly significant, threatening or morally reprehensible (e.g., having an incest-related intrusion *means* I want to engage in the behavior and am therefore a disgusting person).

Considering that intrusions are unwanted and often disturbing, many try to suppress the thoughts; however, efforts to control intrusions paradoxically increases their frequency and salience (Purdon, 1999; Wegner, Schneider, Carter, & White 1987). When suppression is no longer successful at dismissing the unwanted intrusions, individuals then rely upon compulsive rituals (Clark & Purdon, 1993). Engaging in avoidant (e.g., not attending church) or compulsive rituals (e.g., excessive praying) reduces the heightened emotional arousal associated with the intrusions' misappraisal and also decreases the perceived likelihood that the feared outcome (e.g., going to Hell) will occur. While these maladaptive behaviors provide short-term relief, they simultaneously maintain or exacerbate the severity of obsessive compulsive symptoms and moreover, the individual does not have the opportunity to disconfirm faulty thinking.

While the misinterpretation of intrusions bears great significance to the cognitive model, it is important to note that long-standing dysfunctional belief systems underlie one's maladaptive appraisals. Factor analytic studies have identified that the following three obsessive beliefs give rise to the misinterpretation of unwanted thoughts, images, impulses or ideas: responsibility/threat estimation; perfectionism/certainty; and overimportance/control of thoughts (Obsessive Compulsive Cognitions Working Group [OCCWG], 2005).

Belief Systems

Inflated responsibility and threat estimation. Those with an exaggerated sense of responsibility and an overestimation of threat believe that they are responsible for preventing feared outcomes (from minor to disastrous) from occurring and are apt to inflate the likelihood of catastrophe (e.g., OCCWG, 1997; 2003; 2005; Salkovskis, 1985). For example, a 46-year-old male who has recently moved into a new apartment reports excessive fears that his family will be harmed because of his mistake or error

Internal or External Cue

Example: driving past a church.

⇩

Obsessive Beliefs

Thoughts are important and I need to control them.

Intrusive Thought, Image, Impulse or Urge

Example: unwanted thought that "God is dead".

⇩

Misappraisal of Intrusion

Example: having this thought *means* that I believe God is dead and am therefore an immoral person who is going to Hell.

Environment

Growing up with certain religious teachings.

⇧

⇩

Feeling(s)

Example: anxiety, embarrassment, guilt, sadness.

⇧

Biology

Family history of OCD and related disorders.

⇩

Avoidant or Ritualistic Behavior(s)

Example: avoid church, repeatedly pray for forgiveness, undo the effects of the intrusion through a tapping ritual.

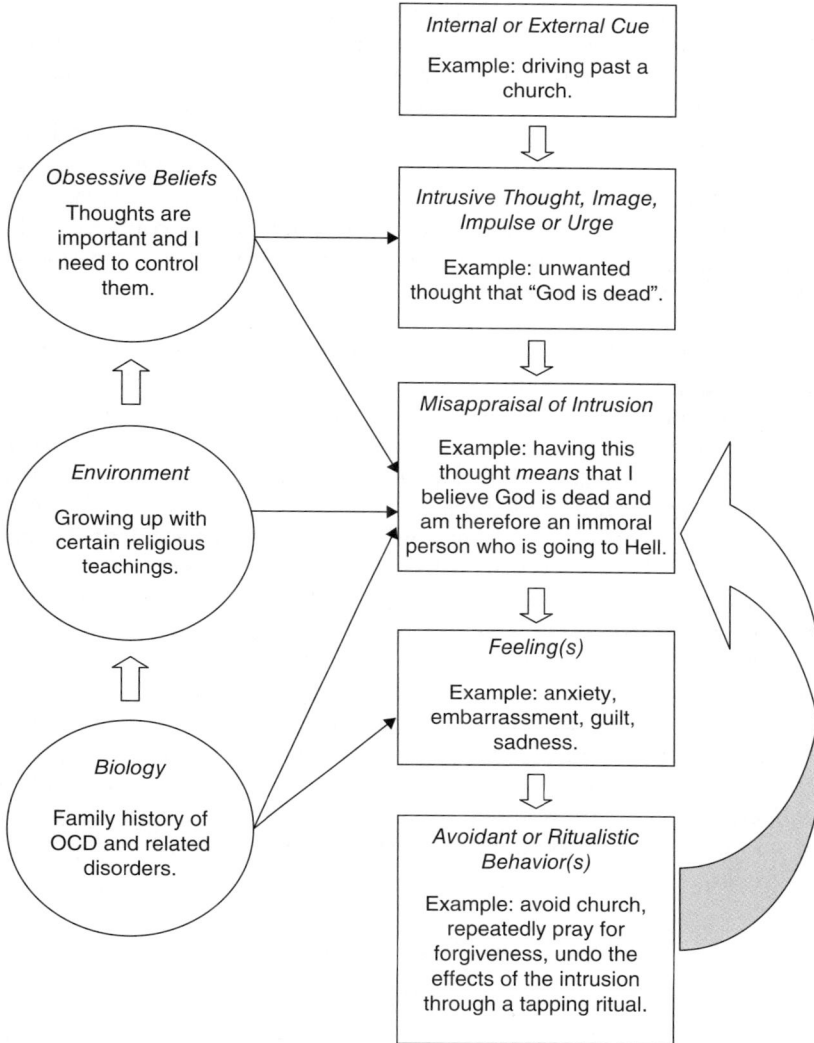

Figure 12.2 Cognitive model of OCD. Source: Adapted from Wilhelm and Steketee, 2006

(e.g., not locking all the doors and windows). Given his inflated sense of responsibility and exaggerated threat perception, he believes that the onus of protecting his family's safety rests upon him. As a result, he engages in multiple rituals to minimize the feared outcome from occurring, such as repeated checking of the locks. Additionally, he avoids leaving the house (unless absolutely necessary) because of the possibility that a disastrous event will occur in his absence.

Perfectionism/need for certainty. Individuals with elevated perfectionism concerns can believe that perfection and/or exact solutions to every problem are obtainable and necessary. For example, a 16-year-old high school student in AP Biology believes that one mistake on her final exam is tantamount to failing. Indeed, this belief system is associated with all-or-nothing thinking and the fear that minor mistakes can have catastrophic outcomes (e.g., if I don't do perfectly in this recital, then I will never be successful in my career). Associated with perfectionism concerns are dysfunctional beliefs about the need for certainty. Researchers have suggested that this belief system results from a perceived inability to manage ambiguity (Sookman, Pinard, & Beck, 2001). For example, an unemployed 58-year-old avoids applying for a job because he believes that he cannot cope with the ambiguity of the interview process (e.g., "If I can't prepare 100% for every interview question, then I will definitely make a mistake and will not be hired"). In response to excessive perfectionistic concerns and a need for certainty, individuals tend to engage in checking, mental reviewing, and reassurance seeking compulsions (Gershuny & Sher, 1995).

Overimportance/control of thoughts. The third belief domain identified by the OCCWG (2005) is the overimportance and control of thoughts. Individuals who overvalue the significance of their thoughts tend to ascribe greater threat to normally occurring intrusions and can even believe that merely having thoughts (a) is equivalent to engaging in the associated behavior (*moral thought action fusion*; e.g., thinking about having an abortion is the moral equivalent of having the procedure) or (b) increases the likelihood of the feared outcome occurring (*likelihood thought action fusion*; e.g., thinking about my mother in a fatal car accident increases the probability that this disastrous event will occur) (Shafran, Thodarson, & Rachman, 1996). Given the significance applied to these intrusions, it is not surprising that efforts to control the unwanted thoughts tend to accompany this set of distortions. For example, a 72-year-old grandfather has disturbing intrusive thoughts about molesting his grandchildren. He believes that having these thoughts means that he is immoral and more likely to act on the behavior. In response to these upsetting intrusions, he actively suppresses the thoughts and images; however, this active effort increases the frequency and strength of the intrusions. Therefore, he hides pictures of his grandchildren and ignores their phone calls to avoid triggering the obsessional thoughts and engages in elaborate mental rituals, such as prayer, to neutralize the perceived threat.

Cognitive Therapy Overview

Cognitive therapy (CT) begins with a thorough assessment of obsessive beliefs (Obsessive Belief Questionnaire [OBQ-44]) (OCCWG, 2005) and obsessive-compulsive symptoms (YBOCS) (Goodman et al., 1989) and progresses into psycho-education and self-monitoring. Upon demonstration that the patient understands the cognitive model and how to effectively track an obsessional trigger, intrusion, immediate interpretation, emotional response, and consequential behavior, then he or she is taught how to apply empirically supported cognitive strategies. In essence, CT targets the patient's immediate interpretations of intrusive thoughts, underlying obsessive beliefs, and deep-seated core beliefs about themselves, the world, and other people. CT does not aim to modify the intrusions themselves, as doing so can inadvertently provide them with validity and exacerbate OCD severity (van Oppen & Arntz, 1994; Wilhelm & Steketee, 2006). To facilitate successful delivery of this intervention, Wilhelm and Steketee (2006) outline how to apply cognitive techniques to each type of obsessive belief domain (e.g., perfectionism). We will walk through four of the most common strategies and then apply the techniques in a brief case example.

Continuum technique. For those with all-or-nothing thinking, the continuum technique (Beck, 1995) can effectively modify the patient's polarized distortions. To conduct this strategy, the clinician must help the patient identify a negative trait that is exaggerated (e.g., immoral). Next, the patient is asked to rate him- or herself on this trait from 0 to 100. For instance, a patient with aggressive fears might be asked to rate how immoral he or she is for having such intrusive thoughts. The clinician and therapist then create a list of other potentially immoral behaviors (e.g., molesting a child, beating your spouse, cheating on a test, murder) and subsequently rate each one on the continuum. The patient then re-rates his or her degree of immorality for having the intrusive thought. At the completion of the exercise, the patient should develop a more accurate perception of their innocuous intrusive thoughts and understand where this mental act falls in the wide range of human behavior.

Behavioral experiment. This useful CT technique tests the accuracy of patients' beliefs through data collection. Behavioral experiments are most effective when the patient can test specific hypotheses (e.g., I will become sick within the next 4 hours of entering the hospital), rather than vague future-oriented fears (e.g., I might get a brain tumor when I am older). To conduct the experiment, the patient should be treated as a co-investigator and reminded of the scientific method (e.g., defining hypotheses *a priori*). Collaboratively, the clinician and patient (a) determine the idiosyncratic feared predictions associated with an avoided (or feared) situation, (b) operationalize the procedure to test the validity of the prediction, (c) rate the likelihood that the feared outcome will occur, (d) complete the procedure in or outside of the office, (e) discuss how the data map onto the initial prediction, and (f) use Socratic questioning to make sense of the mismatch between the feared and actual outcome.

Courtroom technique. The courtroom technique challenges faulty beliefs through a role playing exercise. The patient acts as a prosecutor in a courtroom and presents the available evidence that supports his belief. Conversely, the therapist plays the role of the defense attorney presenting the opposing perspective. For instance, a 26-year-old female who believes she is responsible for her father's recent and sudden health decline would be asked to present why and how her thoughts can cause such disastrous outcomes using objective evidence that would "stand up in court." The therapist presents the contradictory perspective, such as "thoughts are just thoughts" and "she has had thoughts about catastrophic events in the past and the corresponding event never occurred." Once the patient demonstrates competency, then the roles should be reversed.

Advantages and disadvantages. This CT strategy can help individuals make decisions, evaluate the consequences of tolerating uncertainty, and examine the pros and cons of believing or "holding onto" certain thoughts. For example, a clinician treating a patient with sexual intrusions uses this technique to help her evaluate the pros and cons of believing that she is a dangerous person. Upon identification of various advantages and disadvantages, the clinician works with the patient to evaluate the validity of the advantages and develop an alternative (or more adaptive) viewpoint.

Empirical Support

Individual CT has been shown to be highly effective at reducing OCD symptom severity in multiple treatment trials (e.g., Emmelkamp & Beens, 1991; Emmelkamp, Visser, & Hoekstra, 1988; van Oppen et al., 1995). Specifically, maladaptive obsessive beliefs and OCD symptom severity were both found to significantly decrease following CT in an open trial (Wilhelm et al., 2005), waitlist controlled trial (Wilhem et al. 2009), and randomized-controlled trial (e.g., Cottraux et al., 2001; Whittal, Thordarson, & McLean, 2005). In fact, patients' improvement is comparable to exposure-based therapies and is maintained a full year following treatment (e.g., Foa et al., 2005; Wilhelm et al., 2009). In sum, a number of trials have demonstrated that CT is an acceptable and effective psychosocial intervention for OCD, with similar response rates and long-term gains to exposure-based therapies.

Case Example

Bonnie is a 42-year-old Hispanic female who is married and has one child. She has a successful career as a dentist and recently opened her own practice. Bonnie was raised in a strict Catholic home in New Jersey and attended a Catholic elementary and middle school. During her childhood, Bonnie was instructed that certain thoughts were immoral and needed to be controlled; however, if the thoughts occurred, confession could absolve her of sin. As Bonnie matured, she struggled to control unwanted intrusive thoughts that were blasphemous, sexual, or aggressive in nature. To avoid triggering the obsessional thoughts, she stopped attending church in college. Given the minimal interference caused by her intrusions, she never sought psychological treatment. However, after the birth of her child, the intrusive thoughts returned with greater strength and frequency. Despite her best efforts at distraction or suppression, the intrusions only became more interfering and disrupted her performance at work and her parenting at home. Therefore, Bonnie sought treatment from a local cognitive therapist.

Bonnie's cognitive therapist conducted a comprehensive assessment of obsessive beliefs and OCD symptoms (Y-BOCS score of 24 = moderately severe) before providing her with psychoeducation. Bonnie was relieved to learn about the normalcy of intrusions and the fact that their mere presence does not reflect her moral character. After being taught the cognitive model, Bonnie was able to apply it to her own symptoms (see Figure 12.2). Next, Bonnie's therapist taught her how to self-monitor and track her intrusions, immediate interpretations, emotional responses, and associated behaviors. After one week of dedicated practice, Bonnie's therapist began teaching cognitive strategies that targeted her dysfunctional beliefs related to the *Overimportance/control of thoughts*. Specifically, a thought-suppression experiment (Wegner et al., 1987) demonstrated the futility of suppressing certain thoughts (e.g., "I'm an Atheist"), given that doing so increased the salience of the intrusion. Additionally, Bonnie reported that the Continuum Technique effectively challenged her belief that having blasphemous thoughts makes her an immoral and dangerous person. Over the course of the next eight weeks, Bonnie acquired a number of other useful strategies (e.g., Courtroom Technique, Behavioral Experiment) to modify her faulty appraisals and learned how to generate more adaptive responses to her intrusions. Bonnie strengthened and generalized her skill use by completing homework nearly every day. At the completion of treatment, Bonnie completed a Y-BOCS with the clinician and her symptom severity score had dropped to 11 (well below the clinical cut-off).

Acceptance and Commitment Therapy (ACT) for OCD

ACT Model

Acceptance and commitment therapy (ACT) is a CBT-based intervention that is rooted in the philosophy of functional contextualism, which posits that cognitions, emotions and behaviors are influenced by ongoing processes and events (Hayes, Luoma, & Bond, 2006; Hayes, Strosahl, & Wilson, 1999). Unlike CT and ERP, ACT utilizes a top-down approach where the primary goal is to facilitate and encourage individuals to engage in behaviors that are consistent with their values. And, as a result of this process, symptom reduction is ultimately achieved. ACT emphasizes the counterproductive nature, and the potentially detrimental consequences of, engaging in experiential avoidance (i.e., avoidance of unwanted cognitions, physical sensations, emotions and memories) (Hayes, Wilson, Gifford, Follette, & Strosahl, 1996). In the context of OCD, ACT encourages individuals to manage obsessions by increasing their willingness to experience these unwanted thoughts, images, impulses, or ideas without becoming overwhelmed with distress (Twohig, Hayes, & Masuda, 2006; Twohig, 2008). Moreover, ACT emphasizes the futility of controlling obsessions by highlighting the paradoxical effects of thought suppression and the long-term effect on emotional distress (i.e., suffering) (Twohig et al., 2006).

ACT maintains that the presence of obsessions is not inherently bad or wrong; however, how an individual responds to these obsessions (i.e., engaging in compulsions that interfere with individual's ability to live a fulfilled life) may be harmful. To enhance quality of life and diminish impairment due to OCD, ACT focuses on increasing psychological flexibility by targeting six interacting psychological processes: acceptance, defusion, values, self as context, contact with the present moment, and committed action (Hayes et al., 1996). We will briefly present each of the psychological processes and highlight its application to an ACT conceptualization of treatment of OCD.

Acceptance

Counter to experiential avoidance, acceptance involves being aware of, and fully experiencing, the presence of aversive internal events (e.g., cognitions, physical sensations). Acceptance is rooted in the idea that although pain exists (either psychological or physical), suffering is optional. An elderly male with an intrusion that harm will befall others because of mistake or inaction will likely combat these thoughts by pushing them away or through neutralization. These efforts can actually increase distress, thereby creating more suffering for the individual and resulting in long-term harm and functional interference. Through acceptance, the individual minimizes this internal struggle and accepts the pervasiveness of uncertainty.

Defusion

Through the lens of cognitive defusion, obsessions and worries are considered to be the same as any other passing thought – an internal cognition that is not necessarily rooted in truth or reality. Individuals with OCD often perceive their intrusive thoughts to be literal and concrete and as a result, may be frightened or disturbed by their own intrusions. Cognitive defusion de-emphasizes attempts to understand the meaning of an intrusion, as this can inadvertently increase the perceived importance of the thought, and instead attempts to modify the context in which the intrusion is experienced (e.g., imagining the intrusion as a lyric in a pop song) (Hayes & Smith, 2005). By stripping meaning away from the obsessions, the weight and power of the thoughts can be dramatically reduced.

Values

Identifying personal values motivates individuals to engage in behaviors that will lead to a more fulfilled life. Upon determining their value system, individuals might be asked to consider: (a) how obsessions interfere with their ability to live a satisfying life; (b) the type of life they would prefer to lead; and (c) how they could change their behaviors to better align with their values. Emphasizing the importance of acting in line with one's value system provides individuals with an overarching goal for treatment that bolsters their motivation (and perceived ability) to approach fearful and avoided stimuli.

Self as Context

This ACT principle posits that each individual possesses a stable and unchanging self, which is not defined or altered by ongoing external and internal experiences. To access self as context, individuals are instructed to experience events as an observer, and to accept the emotions, cognitions, and sensations that come in and out of their lives. For example, rather than saying, "I am an anxious person," one would say "I am a person who experiences anxiety." By doing so, there is both an acceptance and distancing of the anxious experience and more importantly, the individual is no longer defined by his/her symptoms. Furthermore, changing how one defines this internal experience promotes the acceptance of the "pain that is" and minimizes suffering.

Contact with the Present Moment

Contact with the present moment incorporates mindfulness skills, such that individuals are taught to experience the "here and now" in a nonjudgmental manner. Mindfulness teaches individuals to observe and experience emotions, thoughts, and sensations without evaluation. Observing (and not judging) their internal experiences (e.g., "I am having a thought that my mother will be harmed") enhances the degree to which one accepts the continuous ebb and flow of ongoing events, highlights the potentially deleterious role of a cognitive evaluation (e.g., "having this thought must mean it's significant"), and increases the willingness to both dismiss innocuous intrusions and allow the escalating neutralization urge to pass.

Committed Action

Committed action involves engaging in the behaviors that lead towards a fulfilling and meaningful life. While behavioral change is the ultimate goal of committed action, this process relies upon the identification of one's value system, as well as acceptance and cognitive defusion, to spur behavioral responses. In regards to OCD, through committed action, compulsions should theoretically decrease as individuals disengage from experiential avoidance and move towards living a valued life.

ACT Therapy Overview

As symptom reduction is not the focus of treatment in ACT, evaluation of the severity, frequency and intensity of OCD symptoms is not as relevant as in CT and ERP. Rather, assessment of OCD focuses on the function of obsessions and compulsions, psychological flexibility (Acceptance and Action Questionnaire [AAQ]) (Hayes et al., 2004), and level of cognitive defusion (Thought Action Fusion Scale) (Shafran et al., 1996). Unlike CT and ERP, ACT guides the individual through a discussion that flows fluidly between the six psychological processes previously described. Therapy often begins with a dialogue in which the therapist assesses the various strategies the individual utilizes to combat OCD and the efficacy of their techniques. The over-arching goal of these early sessions is to highlight that attempts to control or suppress intrusions, as well as engaging in compulsions, may be helpful in the short-term, but in the long-term, these behaviors can be damaging.

Given that some ACT principles may be too abstract or confusing for patients, ACT often utilizes metaphors to facilitate the ease of comprehension. For example, the "person in the hole" metaphor presents the fruitlessness of struggle and the need for acceptance (Hayes et al., 1999). In this metaphor, the individual is asked to imagine falling in a hole and using a shovel as a tool to escape; the hole is conceptualized as the obsessions and the shovel is considered to be the compulsions. This description demonstrates the futility and further damage that transpires when compulsions are employed as a method of relieving the distress associated with obsessions.

In addition to the use of metaphors, much of the ACT treatment (as described in the Contact with the Present Moment process) rests upon mindfulness and distancing techniques. While specific strategies are not often highlighted in ACT, mindfulness is a skill that may require practice to fully understand and be able to utilize effectively. Mindfulness exercises may include deep breathing, where individuals are instructed to focus on the sensations of the breath, and in a non-evaluative manner, experience the breath as it enters and leaves the mouth and nostrils. Another mindfulness exercise is to imagine each thought, emotion, physiological experience, and urge as a car on a moving train. The patient is asked to identify the type of internal experience (e.g., thought) and subsequently place it on the train and watch it speed away. This task encourages the patient to label internal experiences, practice "letting them go," and fosters acceptance of a range of psychological phenomena.

Unlike ERP, ACT does not depend upon fear extinction (via exposure) as the primary mechanism of change and therefore, in-session exposures are not necessary. Rather, ACT seeks to improve quality of life by increasing psychological flexibility. Individuals are encouraged to utilize effective skills (e.g., recalling metaphors, mindfulness, defusion, acting in line with values) when confronting fearful stimuli, thereby engendering naturalistic exposures, rather than planned or structured exposures. Throughout the treatment, clinicians continue to emphasize how approaching fearful or avoided stimuli (i.e., exposure) and refraining from ritualistic behaviors (i.e., response prevention) aligns with the goal of living a valued and meaningful life.

Empirical Support

While the empirical literature regarding the efficacy of ACT for OCD is limited, the few published studies have promising results. In a pilot study of four individuals with OCD, eight sessions of ACT was efficacious in reducing OCD symptoms, as well as anxiety and depressive symptoms (Twohig et al., 2006). Additionally, participants reported a decrease in both experiential avoidance and the believability of obsessions (i.e., increased cognitive defusion). An eight-session, randomized controlled trial of ACT for 46 individuals with OCD found similar results where the ACT group had significantly greater reductions in OCD severity and depressive symptoms at post-treatment, relative to the progressive relaxation training group (Twohig et al., 2010). In both of these trials, ERP was purposefully not incorporated into the treatment, thereby permitting researchers to examine the efficacy of ACT as a stand-alone intervention. However, a remaining question is how ACT compares with ERP in the treatment of OCD and whether these treatments, in combination, provide maximal symptom reduction.

Case Example

Brad is a 19-year-old male who is a sophomore in college. Although he reported experiencing a relatively happy childhood, he described his single mother as "overprotective and a worrier." As a child, Brad's mother did not allow matches or lighters in the home and only had a single candle lighter in the residence. She also asked Brad to check in with her often when she was out with friends. Brad also described himself as an anxious child; however, he noted that his anxiety increased significantly once he left the home to live in the college dormitory. Brad felt overly responsible for the well-being of his college roommates and experienced intrusive thoughts that he may cause harm to others because of something he had done or had not done; he frequently checked the lights and stoves on all floors of the dorm to prevent an accidental electrical fire. Over time, these rituals caused him to be late for class, appointments, and social outings. By the time Brad sought treatment, his checking rituals lasted between 60–120 minutes, interfering with his academic achievement and interpersonal relationships. Brad sought treatment from an ACT therapist, who first administered a measure of experiential avoidance (AAQ) (Hayes et al., 2004), finding that Brad strongly avoided uncomfortable thoughts, feelings, and urges and possessed minimal psychological flexibility.

In Brad's first few therapy sessions, he expressed ambivalence about treatment, specifically regarding the acceptance of obsessions. To enhance his motivation, and in line with ACT principles, Brad's therapist asked him to track (over the week) his internal experiences, behavioral responses, the effectiveness of his efforts, and the associated degree of momentary pain and prolonged suffering. By asking Brad to judge "what works," he recognized that thought suppression and compulsive checking afforded him short-term relief, but over time, these responses increased his degree of suffering. Through further discussion with his therapist, Brad agreed that although he believes his worries are relatively realistic, the frequency and intensity of his obsessions were preventing him from living a valued life (e.g., engaging in college activities, making good grades). He further noted that changes in his perspective regarding the worries may be helpful in reducing his anxiety and distress.

The therapist and Brad then worked together to minimize battling or "falling into" the obsessions. To do so, Brad's therapist utilized a number of metaphors to target his willingness toward acceptance, such as the "Chinese Finger Trap." Brad learned that, just like the Chinese Finger Trap he played with as a child, persistently pulling away from internal experiences yields a paradoxical effect – the more he avoids distressing thoughts, emotions, and urges, the stronger these internal experiences become. Therefore, rather than trying to escape or "get free" from these uncomfortable internal experiences, he must accept their presence and move toward them; only by letting go of the struggle can he find the peace he desires (Hayes & Smith, 2005).

To bolster Brad's mindfulness skills (i.e., observe and describe internal experiences in a nonjudgmental manner), his therapist not only introduced the essential tenets, but began each session with a mindfulness exercise. For instance, for the first 10 minutes of session 4, Brad imagined each of his thoughts, physical sensations, emotions, and urges as passing clouds. He labeled each internal experience and practiced "letting it go" by watching it slowly drift away through the clear blue sky. If Brad's attention drifted during the activity, he congratulated himself for reorienting his attention to the mindfulness task and then continued the labeling and distancing of internal experiences. Brad reported "loving" this mindfulness activity as it enhanced his ability to objectively label thoughts, feelings, and urges as passing internal phenomena that do not need to be evaluated.

Upon demonstration of Brad's mindfulness skills, his therapist introduced cognitive defusion exercises. For instance, Brad chose a recurring intrusive thought (e.g., "I left the toaster on and as a result my dorm is going to burn down") and practiced changing the context in which this intrusion occurs in order to decrease its significance and degree of threat. Brad utilized a number of different playful defusion techniques, such as repeating the intrusion in "slow motion," in a different voice (e.g., high pitched or cartoonish), or as a lyric to an energetic song. During these exercises, his therapist encouraged Brad to immerse himself in the defusion exercise, rather than become trapped in its meaning or significance (Hayes & Smith, 2005).

Over the next eight weeks, Brad continued to engage in behaviors that were aligned with his ideas of a valued life. He started to engage in social outings, first for short time periods, and gradually into longer activities. Through his pursuit of values, and understanding the long-term futility of thought suppression and ritualistic behaviors, Brad slowly reduced the frequency of his checking compulsions. When he experienced an intrusion and his anxiety increased, he would (a) utilize mindfulness exercises to observe his worries and sensations and allow them to pass, (b) defuse the intrusion by playfully changing its presentation, or (c) consider how engaging the obsessional anxiety or utilizing ritualistic behaviors would move him toward his values of strength, respect, and bravery. At the end of treatment, Brad was re-administered the AAQ, finding that his psychological flexibility had significantly improved. Moreover, Brad reported an overall better quality of life that was marked by increased social interaction and satisfactory grades, decreased experiential avoidance, and a reduction in functional impairment.

Conclusion

The behavioral, cognitive, and ACT model of OCD possess many similarities in their conceptualization and treatment approach, but also maintain distinguishing characteristics. Broadly speaking, all three models are present focused, employ a functional assessment of obsessions and compulsions, and rely upon the identification of cognitions (e.g., feared consequences), and monitoring of emotional and behavioral responses. Upon detecting these internal experiences and behavioral responses, each model targets the symptoms in a unique fashion. In ERP, the patient systematically confronts their obsessional anxiety and refrains from engaging in compulsive rituals in the service of fear extinction. In CT, the emphasis rests upon the misinterpretation phase (e.g., the significance or threat applied to the innocuous thought). The clinician teaches skills, specific to the patients' dysfunctional belief domains, which modify the appraisal and ultimately lead to behavioral symptom reduction. In ACT, the labeling and description of internal experiences serves to distance the patient from the intrusion, emotion, or urge and facilitates acceptance of the uncomfortable experience. These mindfulness skills, along with defusion techniques and metaphors, provide patients with the necessary strategies to move toward, rather than away from, a meaningful life that aligns with one's values.

While the present chapter divided the three models into separate sections, many practitioners combine elements of these treatments in clinical practice. For example, a clinician may conceptualize patients from a comprehensive cognitive-behavioral model of OCD, in which innocuous intrusive thoughts (and their misinterpretation) lead to an anxious response. Rituals, in turn, provide a sense of short-term relief that negatively reinforce the use of maladaptive behaviors. Following psychoeducation, clinicians may choose to introduce cognitive restructuring prior to ERP and simultaneously incorporate acceptance-based strategies to manage intrusions. Throughout the exposure component of treatment, the mindfulness techniques of ACT are especially useful for staying present in the experience and monitoring one's cognitive, emotional, and physiological response. Moreover, many ACT strategies, such as cognitive defusion, parallel exposure-based processes. For instance, the overarching goal of both an imaginal exposure and cognitive defusion is to modify the patient's relationship with an intrusion, rendering it "boring" or even humorous. Taken together, the three empirically-supported psychological models and treatments for OCD can either be delivered independently or harmoniously integrated (depending on the clinician or patient preference). Regardless of the intervention choice, the patient is provided with a range of skills aimed at improving the patient's quality of life, decreasing functional interference, and ultimately reducing the severity of OCD symptomology.

References

Abramowitz, J. S. (1996). Variants of exposure and response prevention in the treatment of obsessive-compulsive disorder: A meta-analysis. *Behavior Therapy, 27*(4), 583–600.

Abramowitz, J. S. (1997). Effectiveness of psychological and pharmacological treatments for obsessive-compulsive disorder: A quantitative review. *Journal of Consulting and Clinical Psychology, 65*(1), 44–52.

Abramowitz, J. S. (2006). *Understanding and treating obsessive-compulsive disorder: A cognitive behavioral approach.* Mahwah, NJ: Lawrence Erlbaum.

Abramowitz, J. S., & Arch, J. J. (2014). Strategies for improving long-term outcomes in cognitive behavioral therapy for obsessive-compulsive disorder: Insights from learning theory. *Cognitive and Behavioral Practice, 21*(1), 20–31.

Abramowitz, J. S., Foa, E. B., & Franklin, M. E. (2003). Exposure and ritual prevention for obsessive-compulsive disorder: Effects of intensive versus twice-weekly sessions. *Journal of Consulting and Clinical Psychology, 71*(2), 394–398.

Abramowitz, J. S., Franklin, M. E., & Foa, E. B. (2002). Empirical status of cognitive-behavioral therapy for obsessive-compulsive disorder: A meta-analytic review. *Romanian Journal of Cognitive & Behavioral Psychotherapies, 2*, 89–104.

Bjork, R. A. (1988). Retrieval practice and the maintenance of knowledge. In M. M. Gruneberg, P. E. Morris, & R. N. Sykes (Eds.), *Practical aspects of memory: Current research and issues* (Vol. 1, pp. 396–401). Oxford: Blackwell.

Clark, D. A., & Purdon, C. (1993). New perspectives for a cognitive theory of obsessions. *Australian Psychologist, 28*, 161–167.

Cottraux, J., Note, I., Yao, S. N., Lafont, S., Note, B., Mollard, E., & Dartigues, J. F. (2001). A randomized controlled trial of cognitive therapy versus intensive behavior therapy in obsessive compulsive disorder. *Psychotherapy and Psychosomatics, 70*, 288–297.

Craske, M. G., Kircanski, K., Zelikowsky, M., Mystkowski, J., Chowdhury, N., & Baker, A. (2008). Optimizing inhibitory learning during exposure therapy. *Behaviour Research and Therapy, 46*(1), 5–27.

Craske, M., Liao, B., Brown, L., & Vervliet, B. (2012). The role of inhibition in exposure therapy. *Journal of Experimental Psychopathology, 3*(3), 322–345.

Deacon, B., Kemp, J. J., Dixon, L. J., Sy, J. T., Farrell, N. R., & Zhang, A. R. (2013). Maximizing the efficacy of interoceptive exposure by optimizing inhibitory learning: A randomized controlled trial. *Behaviour Research and Therapy, 51*(9), 588–596.

Eddy, K. T., Dutra, L., Bradley, R., & Westen, D. (2004). A multidimensional meta-analysis of psychotherapy and pharmacotherapy for obsessive-compulsive disorder. *Clinical Psychology Review, 24*(8), 1011–1030.

Emmelkamp, P. M. G., & Beens, H. (1991). Cognitive therapy with obsessive-compulsive disorder: A comparative evaluation. *Behaviour Research and Therapy, 29*, 293–300.

Emmelkamp, P. M., van Oppen, P., & van Balkom, A. J. (2002). Cognitive changes in patients with obsessive compulsive rituals treated with exposure in vivo and response prevention. In R. O. Frost, & G. Steketee (Eds.), *Cognitive approaches to obsessions and compulsions: Theory, assessment, and treatment* (pp. 391–401). Amsterdam: Elsevier.

Emmelkamp, P. M. G., Visser, S., & Hoekstra, R. J. (1988). Cognitive therapy vs. exposure in vivo in the treatment of obsessive-compulsives. *Cognitive Therapy and Research, 12*, 103–114.

Fals-Stewart, W., Marks, A. P., & Schafer, J. (1993). A comparison of behavioral group therapy and individual behavior therapy in treating obsessive-compulsive disorder. *Journal of Nervous and Mental Disease, 181*(3), 189–193.

Foa, E. B., & Kozak, M. J. (1986). Emotional processing of fear: Exposure to corrective information. *Psychological Bulletin, 99*, 20–35.

Foa, E. B., Liebowitz, M. R., Kozak, M. J., Davies, S., Campeas, R., Franklin, M. E., … Tu, X. (2005). Randomized, placebo-controlled trial of exposure and ritual prevention, clomipramine, and their combination in the treatment of obsessive-compulsive disorder. *American Journal of Psychiatry, 162*(1), 151–161.

Gershuny, B. S., & Sher, K. J. (1995). Compulsive checking and anxiety in a nonclinical sample: Differences in cognition, behavior, personality, and affect. *Journal of Psychopathology and Behavioral Assessment, 32*, 19–38.

Goodman, W. K., Price, L. H., Rasmussen, S. A., Mazure, C., Fleischmann, R. L., Hill, C. L., … & Charney, D. S. (1989). The Yale–Brown Obsessive Compulsive Scale: I. Development, use, and reliability. *Archives of General Psychiatry, 46*(11), 1006–1011.

Hayes, J. B., Luoma, J. B., & Bond, F.W. (2006). Acceptance and commitment therapy: Model, processes and outcomes. *Behaviour Research and Therapy, 44*, 1–25.

Hayes, S. C., & Smith, S. (2005). *Get out of your mind and into your life*. Oakland, CA: New Harbinger.

Hayes, S. C., Strosahl, K. D., & Wilson, K. G. (1999). *Acceptance and Commitment Therapy: An experiential approach to behavior change.* New York: Guilford Press.

Hayes, S. C., Strosahl, K. D., Wilson, K. G., Bissett, R. T., Pistorello, J., Toarmino, D., ... & McCurry, S. M. (2004). Measuring experiential avoidance: A preliminary test of a working model. *The Psychological Record, 54,* 553–578.

Hayes, S. C., Wilson, K. G., Gifford, E. V., Follette, V. M., & Strosahl, K. D. (1996). Emotional avoidance and behavior disorders: A functional dimensional approach to diagnosis and treatment. *Journal of Consulting and Clinical Psychology, 64,* 1152–1168.

Himle, M. B., & Franklin, M. E. (2009). The more you do it, the easier it gets: Exposure and response prevention for OCD. *Cognitive and Behavioral Practice, 16*(1), 29–39.

Kobak, K. A., Greist, J. H., Jefferson, J. W., Katzelnick, D. J., & Henk, H. J. (1998). Behavioral versus pharmacological treatments of obsessive compulsive disorder: A meta-analysis. *Psychopharmacology, 136*(3), 205–216.

Lindsay, M., Crino, R., & Andrews, G. (1997). Controlled trial of exposure and response prevention in obsessive-compulsive disorder. *British Journal of Psychiatry, 171*(2), 135–139.

Mowrer, O. (1960). *Learning theory and behavior.* New York: Wiley.

National Institute for Health and Clinical Excellence (NICE). (2006). Obsessive-compulsive disorder: Core interventions in the treatment of obsessive-compulsive disorder and body dysmorphic disorder. *British Psychological Society and the Royal College of Psychiatrists.* Retrieved from: www.nice.org.uk.

Obsessive Compulsive Cognitions Working Group. (1997). Cognitive assessment of obsessive-compulsive disorder. *Behaviour Research and Therapy, 35,* 667–681.

Obsessive Compulsive Cognitions Working Group. (2003). Psychometric validation of the Obsessive Beliefs Questionnaire and the Interpretation of Intrusions Inventory – Part I. *Behaviour Research and Therapy, 41*(8), 863–878.

Obsessive Compulsive Cognitions Working Group. (2005). Psychometric validation of the Obsessive Belief Questionnaire and Interpretation of Intrusions Inventory – Part 2: Factor analyses and testing of a brief version. *Behaviour Research and Therapy, 43*(11), 1527–1542.

Olatunji, B. O., Cisler, J. M., & Deacon, B. J. (2010). Efficacy of cognitive behavioral therapy for anxiety disorders: A review of meta-analytic findings. *Psychiatric Clinics of North America, 33*(3), 557–577.

Olatunji, B. O., Davis, M. L., Powers, M. B., & Smits, J. A. (2013). Cognitive-behavioral therapy for obsessive-compulsive disorder: A meta-analysis of treatment outcome and moderators. *Journal of Psychiatric Research, 47*(1), 33–41.

Ponniah, K., Magiati, I., & Hollon, S. D. (2013). An update on the efficacy of psychological treatments for obsessive-compulsive disorder in adults. *Journal of Obsessive-Compulsive and Related Disorders, 2*(2), 207–218.

Purdon, C. (1999). Thought suppression and psychopathology. *Behaviour Research and Therapy, 37,* 1029–1054.

Rachman, S. (1997). A cognitive theory of obsessions. *Behaviour Research and Therapy, 35,* 793–802.

Rachman, S. (1998). A cognitive theory of obsessions: Elaborations. *Behaviour Research and Therapy, 36*(4), 385–401.

Rachman, S., & de Silva, P. (1978). Abnormal and normal obsessions. *Behaviour Research and Therapy, 16,* 233–248.

Rassin, E., Cougle, J. R., & Muris, P. (2007). Content difference between normal and abnormal obsessions. *Behaviour Research and Therapy, 45*(11), 2800–2803.

Rosa-Alcázar, A. I., Sánchez-Meca, J., Gómez-Conesa, A., & Marín-Martínez, F. (2008). Psychological treatment of obsessive–compulsive disorder: A meta-analysis. *Clinical Psychology Review, 28*(8), 1310–1325.

Salkovskis, P. M. (1985). Obsessional-compulsive problems: A cognitive-behavioural analysis. *Behaviour Research and Therapy, 23,* 571–584.

Shafran, R., Thordarson, D., & Rachman, S. (1996). Thought–action fusion in obsessive-compulsive disorder. *Journal of Anxiety Disorders, 10*(5), 379–391.

Simpson, H. B., Liebowitz, M. R., Foa, E. B., Kozak, M. J., Schmidt, A. B., Rowan, V., … & Campeas, R. (2004). Post-treatment effects of exposure therapy and clomipramine in obsessive–compulsive disorder. *Depression and Anxiety, 19*(4), 225–233.

Sookman, D., Pinard, G., & Beck, A. T. (2001). Vulnerability schemas in obsessive-compulsive disorder. *Archives of General Psychiatry, 56*, 121–127.

Twohig, M. P. (2008). The application of acceptance and commitment therapy to obsessive-compulsive disorder. *Cognitive and Behavioral Practice, 16*, 18–28.

Twohig, M. P., Hayes, S. C., & Masuda, M. (2006). Increasing willingness to experience obsessions: Acceptance and commitment therapy as a treatment for obsessive-compulsive disorder. *Behavior Therapy, 37*, 3–13.

Twohig, M. P., Hayes, S. C., Plumb, J. C., Pruitt, L. D., Collins, A. B., Hazlett-Stevens, H., & Woidneck, M. R. (2010). A randomized clinical trial of acceptance and commitment therapy vs progressive relaxation training for obsessive compulsive disorder. *Journal of Consulting and Clinical Psychology, 78*, 705–716.

van Oppen, P., & Arntz, A. (1994). Cognitive therapy for obsessive-compulsive disorder. *Behaviour Research and Therapy, 32*, 79–87.

van Oppen, P., de Haan, E., van Balkom, A. J., Spinhoven, P., Hoogduin, K., & van Dyck, R. (1995). Cognitive therapy and exposure in vivo in the treatment of obsessive compulsive disorder. *Behaviour Research and Therapy, 33*, 379–390.

Wegner, D. M., Schneider, D. J., Carter, S. R., & White, T. L. (1987). Paradoxical effects of thought suppression. *Journal of Personality and Social Psychology, 53*, 5–13.

Whittal, M. L., Robichaud, M., Thordarson, D. S., & McLean, P. D. (2008). Group and individual treatment of obsessive-compulsive disorder using cognitive therapy and exposure plus response prevention: A 2-year follow-up of two randomized trials. *Journal of Consulting and Clinical Psychology, 76*(6), 1003–1014.

Whittal, M. L., Thordarson, D. S., & McLean, P. D. (2005). Treatment of obsessive-compulsive disorder: Cognitive behavior therapy vs. exposure and response prevention. *Behaviour Research and Therapy, 43*(12), 1559–1576.

Wilhelm, S., & Steketee, G. S. (2006). *Cognitive therapy for obsessive compulsive disorder: A guide for professionals.* Oakland, CA: New Harbinger.

Wilhelm, S., Steketee, G., Fama, J. M., Buhlmann, U., Teachman, B. A., & Golan, E. (2009). Modular cognitive therapy for obsessive compulsive disorder: A wait-list controlled trial. *Journal of Cognitive Psychotherapy, 23*, 294–305.

Wilhelm, S., Steketee, G., Reilly-Harrington, N. A., Deckersbach, T., Buhlmann, U., & Baer, L. (2005). Effectiveness of cognitive therapy for obsessive-compulsive disorder: An open trial. *Journal of Cognitive Psychotherapy, 19*, 173–179.

Zoellner, L. A., Echiverri, A., & Craske, M. G. (2000). Processing of phobic stimuli and its relationship to outcome. *Behaviour Research and Therapy, 38*(9), 921–931.

13

Psychological Models and Treatments for OCD in Children

Amy Przeworski and Jennifer M. Birnkrant

Obsessive-compulsive disorder (OCD) is a serious and often chronic condition in childhood and affects up to 0.25–4% of children (Douglass, Moffitt, Dar, McGee, & Silva, 1995; Flament et al., 1988; Heyman, Fombonne, Meltzer, & Goodman 2001; Zohar, 1999). Childhood OCD results in impairment in many areas, including school, peer relationships, and family functioning (Piacentini, Bergman, Keller, & McCracken, 2003). Models of OCD emphasize behavioral factors, memory biases, cognitive factors, and family factors. Many of these models have substantial research support in adults; few of these models have been developmentally adapted for children or examined in samples of children. Thus, it is difficult to know to what degree these models apply to children with OCD.

Emotional Processing

Foa and Kozak (1986) identified a model of fear that has been applied to all fear-based disorders. In this model, a fear network is created that includes information about the feared stimulus, responses to the stimulus, and the meaning of the stimulus and response. The theory states that individuals who have fear-related disorders have excessive responses to feared stimuli, including avoidance and extreme physiological activity. These excessive responses are generally resistant to change, therein maintaining the fear in response to the stimulus. However, the fear network may be changed if the fear memory and network are activated, and if information is made available that is incongruent with the fear structure. This is called emotional processing.

Emotional processing leads to new memory formation and associated emotional change. Emotional processing is indicated by physiological activation, habituation during exposure sessions, and a reduction in the initial fear to feared stimuli. Although this theory is not specific to OCD, it is the theoretical foundation for behavioral treatments for fear-based disorders, including exposure and response prevention (ERP). A significant research base supports the theory (see Foa & Kozak, 1986).

The Wiley Handbook of Obsessive Compulsive Disorders, Volume I, First Edition.
Edited by Jonathan S. Abramowitz, Dean McKay, and Eric A. Storch.
© 2017 John Wiley & Sons Ltd. Published 2017 by John Wiley & Sons Ltd.

Cognitive Biases

Some have theorized that attentional and memory biases may play an important role in OCD. Individuals with OCD, especially those with contamination fears, demonstrate attentional biases to threat (Foa, Ilai, McCarthy, Shoyer, & Murdock, 1993; Foa & McNally, 1986), specifically biases associated with their fears (Lavy, Van Oppen, & Van Den Hout, 1994; Tata, Leibowitz, Prunty, Cameron, & Pickering, 1996). Interestingly, these biases are no longer demonstrated after successful treatment (Foa & McNally, 1986). However, other studies have shown no attentional biases to threat (McNally, Kaspi, Riemann, & Zeitlin, 1990) or biases to threatening stimuli that are unrelated to OCD (McNally, Riemann, Louro, Lukach, & Kim, 1992). Currently, there is a lack of research regarding attentional and threat biases in childhood OCD. Research in child anxiety has found associations between anxiety and attentional biases (for a review, see Hadwin, Garner, & Perez-Olivas, 2006); however, the age at which these emerge is subject to controversy (e.g., Kindt, Bögels, & Morren, 2003; Kindt, Brosschot, & Everaerd, 1997), and no studies have examined attentional biases in childhood OCD.

With regard to memory biases, some have suggested that individuals who engage in compulsive checking may experience memory deficits in the ability to remember whether they checked in the past (McNally & Kohlbeck, 1993). Some data support an association between memory impairments and compulsive checking (e.g., Tallis, Pratt, & Jamani, 1999; Wilhelm, McNally, Baer, & Florin, 1997), as well as an association between immediate nonverbal and verbal memory deficits and OCD symptoms (Savage et al., 1999; Savage et al., 2000). Additionally, research suggests that with repetition of an action, the vividness of the memory and confidence in having completed the action both decrease (Van den Hout & Kindt, 2003a). This suggests that repetitive checking may actually maintain obsessions and lead to increased compulsions by impairing one's memory of checking.

Still other data suggest that individuals with OCD have no differences in recall than others (e.g., Macdonald, Antony, Macleod, & Richter, 1997; Maki, O'Neill, & O'Neill, 1994) or increased recall of threatening stimuli (Constans, Foa, Franklin, & Mathews, 1995; Radomsky & Rachman, 1999; Wilhelm, Mcnally, Baer, & Florin, 1996). Other data suggest that those with OCD may not experience memory impairments, but impaired *confidence* in their memory (MacDonald, Antony, MacLeod, & Richter, 1997; McNally & Kohlbeck, 1993; Van den Hout & Kindt, 2003b). Little data currently exist regarding potential memory impairments or confidence in memory in childhood OCD. Two studies have examined memory biases in children with high and low trait anxiety and have found conflicting results (Daleiden, 1998; Dalgleish et al., 2003). No studies have examined memory impairments or confidence in childhood memory in OCD. However, MRI studies in children with OCD have found negative correlations between OCD symptom severity and bilateral hippocampal gray matter volume, which may suggest more severe symptomatology is associated with memory deficits (Carmona et al., 2007). Other findings suggest that children and adolescents with OCD may experience deficits in verbal and visual memory compared with healthy controls, even after controlling for age and OCD symptom severity (Andrés et al., 2007).

Another type of cognitive bias that has been proposed in OCD is that there is a deficit in impulse control, mainly the ability to inhibit thoughts and behaviors that are not adaptive in specific situations (Rapoport, 1991; Rauch et al., 1994). Response inhibition, or the ability to inhibit stimuli and behavioral responses to them, is decreased in adults with OCD (e.g., Bannon, Gonsalvez, Croft, & Boyce, 2002; Chamberlain et al., 2006; Menzies et al., 2008; Penades et al., 2007) and children with OCD (Rosenberg et al., 1997). However, other studies of adults have found no deficits in response inhibition (Hollander et al., 1993).

Similarly, when examining the volume of regions of the brain responsible for inhibitory control, such as the caudate nucleus and dorsolateral frontal cortex, some studies have shown differences between those with OCD and control participants in adult samples (Lacerda et al., 2003; Lucey et al., 1997; Robinson et al., 1995; Scarone et al., 1992) and child samples (Luxemberg et al., 1988). However, other studies have shown no differences in the volume of the caudate nucleus in adults (Aylward et al., 1996) or in the dorsolateral frontal cortex in studies of adolescents (Szeszko et al., 2004). Studies examining functioning of the areas of the brain responsible for motor inhibition and cognitive inhibition have demonstrated dysregulation in the frontostriatothalamic, temporoparietal and frontocerebellar, and the right orbitofrontal and left dorsolateral prefrontal cortices in children with OCD (Woolley et al., 2008) which supports the notion of inhibitory deficits underlying OCD. Additional studies are necessary to determine whether inhibitory deficits underlie OCD in some, but not all cases, or whether differences in methodology have led to the conflicting results regarding inhibitory control and brain structures.

Trauma and Stressful Events

Trauma has been shown to be a risk factor for a variety of mental health disorders, including mood, anxiety, and personality disorders. Trauma may be related to the development of OCD in that ritualistic behaviors may be a response to stress due to individuals' desire to control unpredictable and stressful environments (Mineka & Hendersen, 1985). Data regarding childhood trauma as a precursor for later OCD symptoms has been mixed. One study by Mathews et al. (2008) found a significant association between obsessive compulsive symptoms and both a history of self-reported childhood emotional abuse as well as physical abuse, associations which remained significant even after controlling for comorbid non-obsessive compulsive anxiety symptoms (Mathews, Kaur, & Stein, 2008). Cromer and colleagues also examined self-reported traumatic life events in individuals with OCD (Cromer, Schmidt, & Murphy, 2007). Fifty-four percent of the sample of over 250 participants with OCD endorsed having experienced at least one traumatic life event at some point in their lifetime. Results indicated that the presence of at least one traumatic event in an individual's life was significantly associated with increased OCD symptom severity, a relationship that remained significant after controlling for age, comorbidities, and age of onset of OCD symptoms. The presence of checking, symmetry, and ordering compulsive symptoms were highly associated with a history of traumatic events, which may lend evidence to the idea that experiencing trauma or life stress results in an increased need for order and control. Similarly, Przeworski, Cain, and Dunbeck

(2014) found that 89.3% of those with elevated OCD symptoms had experienced at least one lifetime traumatic event; however, in this study OCD symptom severity was not associated with the number of traumatic events. It is important to note that these results are based on retrospective self-report data as opposed to prospective longitudinal studies and, therefore, it is unclear whether there is a causal link between trauma and the development of OCD. In a sample of individuals with OCD, Selvi and colleagues (2012) found that a retrospective self-report of traumatic childhood experiences including physical, emotional, and sexual abuse was not significantly related to current OCD symptoms, nor were traumatic experiences related to self-reported levels of metacognitions relevant to OCD such as positive beliefs about the function of worry and negative beliefs about controllability of one's thoughts (Selvi et al., 2012). Another large study of individuals with OCD found that traumatic childhood experiences including physical and sexual abuse, witnessing violence, and early parental separation were not significantly associated with OCD symptom severity nor length of illness (Visser et al., 2014). Results also failed to indicate a dose–response effect for number of childhood stressors. However, adverse childhood events were associated with diagnosis of comorbid mental health disorders, including mood, substance use, and eating disorders.

Cognitive Theories

Numerous theories emphasize cognitive factors that may lead to the development and maintenance of OCD. Freeston and colleagues identified five maladaptive types of cognitions that they theorized play a central role in OCD: perfectionism, inflated responsibility, overestimation of threat, overestimation of the importance of thoughts/ magical thinking/thought–action fusion, and intolerance of uncertainty (Freeston, Rhéaume & Ladouceur, 1996). The Obsessive-Compulsive Cognitions Working Group (OCCWG, 1997) identified six aspects of obsessive cognitions, those identified by Freeston and colleagues, as well as overestimation of the importance of controlling one's thoughts.

Perfectionism

Perfectionism has long been identified as a cognitive characteristic associated with OCD (Burns, 1980; Pacht, 1984). Some have suggested that perfectionism is due to difficulty tolerating uncertainty (Guidano & Liotti, 1983), while others have suggested that it is due to a belief that mistakes are intolerable or a desire to avoid criticism (e.g., Mallinger & DeWyze, 1992; Salzman, 1979). Perfectionism has been associated with OCD symptoms in many studies (e.g., Frost & Steketee, 1997; Frost, Steketee, Cohn, & Griess, 1994; Gershuny & Sher, 1995; Norman, Davies, Nicholson, Cortese, & Malla, 1998; Rhéaume, Freeston, Dugas, Letarte, & Ladouceur, 1995). High levels of perfectionism have been found in individuals with OCD relative to community controls (Antony, Purdon, Huta, & Swinson, 1998; Ladouceur, Léger, Rhéaume, & Dubé, 1996; Steketee & Frost, 2001), and in individuals with generalized anxiety disorder and panic disorder (Mavissakalian, Hamann, Abou Haidar, & De Groot, 1993). However, one study found no difference between those with anxiety disorders and those with OCD (Steketee & Frost, 2001), and yet another study found differences between those with anxiety disorders and those with OCD on some aspects of perfectionism but not on other aspects of perfectionism (Antony, Purdon, Huta, & Swinson, 1998). This calls into question the degree to which perfectionism is specific to OCD rather than a common factor among anxiety disorders.

To date, little research has examined perfectionism in children with OCD. In one study, children with OCD were found to have higher levels of concern for mistakes, one dimension of perfectionism, than a nonclinical comparison group but did not differ from an anxious control group (Libby, Reynolds, Derisley, & Clark, 2004). These results are consistent with those from the adult literature, which indicate that perfectionism may be common to anxious individuals, rather than specific to OCD. Another study in children with OCD (Ye, Rice, & Storch, 2008) found that perfectionistic beliefs accounted for significant variance in OCD and peer relationship difficulties. Consistent with the Libby and colleagues' study, sensitivity to mistakes was the aspect of perfectionism that was most highly associated with OCD and peer relationship problems. Additional research is necessary to examine the role that perfectionism may play in childhood OCD, as well as the specificity of perfectionism to OCD in children and adults.

Thought Suppression

Thought suppression, another cognitive variable theorized to be related to OCD, describes the process wherein an individual with OCD experiences an intrusive thought and attempts to push the thought out of awareness (Wegner, 1989). Once this attempt at thought suppression occurs, however, the individual experiences a rebound effect, wherein the thoughts return in greater frequency.

Research examining the association between thought suppression and OCD has led to conflicting results (for a review, see Abramowitz, Tolin, & Street, 2001). Questionnaire studies have indicated that individuals with OCD and analogue participants with subclinical OCD report attempts to suppress thoughts, and higher levels of suppression than nonanxious control participants (Amir, Cashman, & Foa, 1997). Attempts to suppress thoughts lead to tension, discomfort, anxiety, and negative mood (Bouman, 2003; Corcoran & Woody, 2009; Purdon, 1999). One study found that a higher percentage of individuals with OCD experienced a rebound effect than nonclinical controls (Janeck & Calamari, 1999). However, only 25% of the OCD sample was categorized as experiencing a rebound effect (vs. 0% of nonclinical control participants). Other studies have found no evidence of a rebound effect in undergraduates (e.g., Muris, Merckelbach, & De Jong, 1993; Smári, Birgisdóttir, & Brynjólfsdóttir, 1995) or individuals with OCD (Tolin, Abramowitz, Przeworski, & Foa, 2002), and no association or a negative association between OCD and the number of intrusions following suppression (Smári et al., 1995). Additionally, a meta-analysis supports the existence of a small to moderate rebound effect, but found no differences in the rebound effect in analogue participants versus clinical samples (Abramowitz et al., 2001). However, this meta-analysis included only one study of individuals with OCD. Very little research has examined thought suppression in children or adolescents. Gaskell, Wells, and Calam (2001) examined thought suppression in a large sample of school children and found no evidence of a rebound effect.

However, another study found that adolescents with OCD had higher scores on the White Bear Suppression Inventory (Wegner & Zanakos, 1994) than control adolescents, indicating that adolescents with OCD tended to suppress intrusive thoughts (Kadak, Balsak, Besiroglu, & Celik, 2014). Finally, Farrell, Waters, and Zimmer-Gembeck (2012) found that there was a positive association between child thought suppression and maternal metacognitions (consisting of a total score of cognitive confidence, positive beliefs about worry, cognitive self-consciousness, negative beliefs about the uncontrollability of thoughts, and beliefs about the need to control thoughts) in a sample of children and adolescents with OCD. These associations were negative in the adolescent sample, suggesting the importance of considering the child's developmental stage and parental beliefs as factors associated with child thought suppression in childhood OCD.

Excessive Responsibility

Obsessive thoughts occur in most individuals, with intrusive thoughts that are similar in content to that of clinical obsessions occurring in 90% of the population (Rachman & de Silva, 1978; Salkovskis & Harrison, 1984). However, what distinguishes those who have OCD from those who do not is the meaning attributed to the thoughts and the related level of processing of the thought. Individuals who have OCD believe that the presence of an intrusive thought indicates the potential for serious risk and that they are responsible for preventing the negative event from occurring (Salkovskis & McGuire, 2003; Salkovskis, Shafran, Rachman, & Freeston, 1999). This is in contrast to non-clinical individuals, who may see themselves as responsible for their actions, but not for the failure to prevent something from occurring (Salkovskis, 1996).

After engaging in a compulsion, the individual with OCD experiences a reduction in distress and in responsibility. Research suggests that beliefs regarding one's responsibility for causing and/or preventing harm to the self and others may play a crucial role in the maintenance of compulsive behaviors such as checking in OCD. Several studies have found increased sense of responsibility for harm in individuals with intrusive cognitions (Freeston & Ladouceur, 1997; Rhéaume et al., 1995; Salkovskis et al., 2000). Similarly, heightened sense of responsibility is one of the strongest predictors of obsessional symptoms over and above other variables (Salkovskis et al., 2000). Additionally, research suggests that responsibility beliefs have been shown to impact the frequency of obsessional behaviors (e.g., Bouchard, Rhéaume, & Ladouceur, 1999; Lopatka & Rachman, 1995; Shafran, 1997).

Unfortunately, the means by which inflated responsibility develops in individuals with OCD, including in children, have not been evaluated empirically before the development of OCD. Little research to date has focused on the presence and developmental nature of excessive responsibility in childhood OCD. Two studies of community-based samples of children found that inflated responsibility was associated with high levels of OCD symptoms (Magnusdottir & Smári, 2004; Matthews, Reynolds, & Derisley, 2007). Inflated responsibility completely mediated the effect of thought–action fusion and partially mediated the effect of metacognitive beliefs on OCD symptoms. Another study found that adolescents with OCD reported higher levels of inflated responsibility than those with anxiety disorders or nonclinical adolescents and inflated responsibility predicted OCD symptoms (Libby et al., 2004).

One study by Barrett and Healy (2003) examined cognitive processes in children with a diagnosis of OCD, a clinical control group of children with other anxiety diagnoses, and nonclinical control children between the ages of 7 and 13 years. Results indicated that children with OCD reported significantly higher ratings of feelings of responsibility specifically for OCD-relevant threats compared with the nonclinical control group. However, no significant differences in responsibility ratings were found between the OCD group and the anxious control group, nor were differences found between groups with regard to non-OCD-relevant stimuli. These findings suggest that excessive responsibility may be a common factor across different childhood anxiety disorders and may not be specific to OCD in childhood.

Only three other studies have examined perceived responsibility in children with OCD. Barrett and Healy (2003) experimentally manipulated perceived responsibility for threat in children and adolescents with OCD during a behavioral avoidance task. Although the manipulation was successful at increasing responsibility in children with OCD, inconsistent with what has been found in the adult literature, increased responsibility for harm did not lead to increased ratings of the likelihood of harm, severity of harm, or children's distress. In another study, Farrell and Barrett (2006) examined whether responsibility attitudes and probability estimates for threat varied by age in a cross-sectional study of children, adolescents, and adults with OCD. They found increasing responsibility attitudes and probability estimates in adolescents and adults with OCD relative to children with OCD. Similarly, Farrell et al. (2012) found that there was an association between child responsibility and OCD severity, but only in adolescents, not in younger children with OCD.

Thought–Action Fusion

Thought–action fusion (TAF) is a cognitive distortion that has been implicated in the development and maintenance of OCD. It has been proposed that thought–action fusion consists of two components: a belief that (a) thinking about an unacceptable or distressing event makes it more likely to occur, and (b) having an unacceptable thought is equivalent to carrying out the unacceptable action (Shafran, Thordarson, & Rachman, 1996). The presence of TAF has been found to be higher in individuals with OCD than in nonclinical control individuals. Individuals with OCD endorse higher likelihoods of negative events occurring as a direct result of their negative thoughts compared with nonclinical controls. Additionally, those with OCD have endorsed higher likelihoods of being able to prevent distressing events from occurring by way of their positive thoughts (Amir, Freshman, Ramsey, Neary, & Brigidi, 2001).

Little research to date has focused on thought–action fusion in children and adolescents. Two studies found an association between thought–action fusion and OCD symptoms in community samples of children (Bolton, Dearsley, Madronal-Luque, & Baron-Cohen, 2002; Matthews et al., 2007). Thought–action fusion is associated with subclinical OCD symptoms as well as generalized anxiety symptoms (Muris, Meesters, Rassin, Merckelbach, & Campbell, 2001). Three studies (Barrett & Healy, 2003; Kadak et al., 2014; Libby et al., 2004) found that children with OCD reported higher ratings of thought–action fusion compared with a nonclinical control group; however, no differences in TAF were found between the OCD and anxious control groups in Barrett and Healy's study (2003). In a cross-sectional study examining thought–action fusion across children, adolescents, and adults with OCD, Farrell and Barrett (2006) found no difference in levels of TAF across ages, suggesting that this cognitive bias may be present in anxious children from an early age. Additionally, Farrell and colleagues (2012) found that there was a positive association between child TAF and maternal metacognitions (consisting of a total score of cognitive confidence, positive beliefs about worry, cognitive self-consciousness, negative beliefs about the uncontrollability of thoughts, and beliefs about the need to control thoughts) in a sample of children with OCD. These associations were negative in the adolescent sample. This suggests more similarity between maternal and child beliefs about thoughts in children than in adolescents, suggesting the importance of considering the child's developmental stage and parental beliefs.

Intolerance of Uncertainty

It has been theorized that individuals with OCD have an elevated need for certainty to predict and control events (Makhlouf-Norris & Norris, 1973). Uncertainty may likely play a role in the development and maintenance of compulsive rituals in OCD in a number of ways. For example, Beech and Liddell (1974) suggested that compulsive rituals may in part be maintained through a need for certainty about when to end a behavior (compulsion) as well as due to the reduction in anxiety that occurs after completing a ritual. Uncertainty surrounding the potential danger involved in intrusive thoughts may also lead to anxiety in response to such thoughts in OCD (Langlois, Freeston, & Ladouceur, 2000).

Intolerance of uncertainty may be an especially salient factor in the maintenance of checking compulsions. Tolin, Abramowitz, Brigidi, and Foa (2003) found that those with checking compulsions exhibited significantly greater levels of intolerance for uncertainty compared with both OCD noncheckers as well as nonanxious controls (Tolin et al., 2003). Additionally, both repeating and checking rituals were significantly associated with levels of intolerance of uncertainty. Intolerance of uncertainty has also been implicated in other anxiety disorders such as GAD, with one meta-analysis (Gentes & Ruscio, 2011) finding a greater association between intolerance of uncertainty and GAD than OCD, while another study (Holaway, Heimberg, & Coles, 2006) found no difference between the two groups.

There is currently a dearth of published research regarding intolerance of uncertainty in childhood OCD. The construct of intolerance of uncertainty, however, has been studied in childhood anxiety broadly. Boelen, Vrinssen, and Van Tulder (2010) found that intolerance of uncertainty was significantly positively associated with clinically significant worry as well as social anxiety symptoms in a sample of adolescents. Clearly, additional research is required in order to examine the presence and effect of intolerance of uncertainty in childhood OCD.

Family Model of OCD

The family model of OCD suggests that family members contribute to the maintenance of OCD through criticism of the individual with OCD, emotional overinvolvement/intrusiveness, and family accommodation of OCD (Van Noppen & Steketee,

2009). This model emphasizes the importance of a relative's attributions regarding the controllability of OCD. If a relative believes that OCD symptoms are controllable, they are likely to respond to the individual with OCD with criticism and hostility, which may exacerbate OCD symptoms. Family members who believe that OCD symptoms are not controllable may accommodate OCD through participation in rituals. Research provides support for the role that family factors play in maintaining and exacerbating OCD symptoms in children and adolescents. The majority of parents of children with OCD engage in accommodation (Benito et al., 2015; Peris et al., 2008) with one study showing that more than 95% of parents reported some type of accommodation (Benito et al., 2015). Parent involvement in child OCD-related rituals was associated with higher levels of child OCD symptom severity, as well as increased parental psychopathology (Merlo, Lehmkuhl, Geffken, & Storch, 2009; Peris et al., 2008; Storch et al., 2007). Family factors have also been demonstrated to predict attenuated treatment response (Peris et al., 2012; Przeworski et al., 2012).

Treatment

The previously described models are the theoretical underpinnings for evidence-based treatments of OCD, including cognitive-behavioral therapy (CBT). CBT for OCD usually consists of psychoeducation about OCD, self-monitoring of obsessions and compulsions, graded and prolonged exposure to feared stimuli, ritual prevention, and cognitive techniques, such as cognitive restructuring (often shifting perceptions of responsibility for a dreaded outcome), increasing positive self-talk (e.g., "It's only OCD" or "I can beat OCD"), and having clients identify interpretations of intrusions that may increase their anxiety about the intrusions (thought–action fusion, exaggerated responsibility, etc.) (March & Mulle, 1998). However, some treatments emphasize behavioral techniques and limit the degree of cognitive techniques, whereas other treatments emphasize cognitive techniques and rely less on behavioral techniques.

Individual and Group Cognitive-Behavioral Treatment

Numerous studies have examined treatments consisting primarily of individual CBT, often with a few family-based sessions or additional family involvement on an as-needed basis (e.g., Pediatric OCD Treatment Study (POTS) Team, 2004; Franklin et al., 2011). CBT has been demonstrated to be efficacious relative to wait list (Bolton & Perrin, 2008; Williams et al., 2010). In one trial (POTS, 2004), CBT was equally efficacious compared to pharmacotherapy with an SSRI and the combination of CBT plus an SSRI was superior to either treatment alone. However, both the CBT alone condition and the CBT plus pharmacotherapy condition led to a greater number of children being considered to have had an "excellent" treatment response. In a follow-up study of partial responders to the SSRI condition, the addition of CBT to medication compared with medication alone led to significantly greater treatment response (POTS, 2011). Individual CBT and group CBT have been demonstrated to be equally efficacious (Barrett, Healy, Farrell, & March, 2004) and group CBT is equally efficacious as sertraline (Asbahr et al., 2005).

Family-based Behavior Therapy

Family-based cognitive behavioral therapy (FCBT) for childhood OCD typically consists of the same elements included in individual CBT, as well as techniques designed to reduce family accommodation and criticism and/or hostility of the child with OCD. FCBT has been found to be associated with symptom reduction and overall clinical improvement in children as young as 5 years of age in randomized controlled trials (Barrett, Farrell, Dadds, & Boulter, 2005; Barrett et al., 2004; Freeman et al., 2014; Storch et al., 2013). FCBT has been demonstrated to be superior to wait list (Barrett et al., 2004) as well as relaxation conditions (Freeman et al., 2008; Piacentini et al., 2011).

Meta-Analyses

Meta-analyses supported the efficacy of individual and family CBT (Abramowitz, Whiteside, & Deacon, 2005; Watson & Rees, 2008). One meta-analysis demonstrated a large effect sizes for CBT (effect size = 1.45, 95% CI = .68–2.22) and medium effect size pharmacotherapy (effect size = .48, 95% CI = .36–.61) (Watson & Rees, 2008).

Conclusions

Numerous models of OCD have been developed, emphasizing behavioral avoidance, attentional or memory biases, and/or cognitive factors such as exaggerated responsibility, perfectionism, and thought suppression. However, the majority of these models have been developed and tested in adults and there is a dearth of research evaluating whether these models apply to children and adolescents, and if so, at what age. Family-based models of OCD, which emphasize family accommodation and parental criticism and hostility have been the models most commonly applied to childhood and adolescent OCD. Similarly, treatment studies have either involved individual treatment with a few parent sessions or have involved consistent parental involvement to reduce accommodation and improve family dynamics. Despite the efficacy of cognitive behavioral therapy for childhood OCD, a significant portion of treated children remain symptomatic. Additional studies are necessary to improve treatment efficacy and to identify effective interventions for treatment refractory childhood OCD.

References

Abramowitz, J. S., Tolin, D. F., & Street, G. P. (2001). Paradoxical effects of thought suppression: A meta-analysis of controlled studies. *Clinical Psychology Review, 21*(5), 683–703.

Abramowitz, J. S., Whiteside, S. P., & Deacon, B. J. (2005). The effectiveness of treatment for pediatric obsessive-compulsive disorder: A meta-analysis. *Behavior Therapy, 36*, 55–63.

Amir, N., Cashman, L., & Foa, E. B. (1997). Strategies of thought control in obsessive-compulsive disorder. *Behaviour Research and Therapy, 35*(8), 775–777.

Amir, N., Freshman, M., Ramsey, B., Neary, E., & Brigidi, B. (2001). Thought–action fusion in individuals with OCD symptoms. *Behaviour Research and Therapy, 39*(7), 765–776.

Andrés, S., Boget, T., Lázaro, L., Penadés, R., Morer, A., Salamero, M., & Castro-Fornieles, J. (2007). Neuropsychological performance in children and adolescents with Obsessive-Compulsive Disorder and influence of clinical variables. *Biological Psychiatry, 61*(8), 946–951.

Antony, M. M., Purdon, C. L., Huta, V., & Swinson, R. P. (1998). Dimensions of perfectionism across the anxiety disorders. *Behaviour Research and Therapy, 36*(12), 1143–1154.

Asbahr, F. R., Castillo, A. R., Ito, L. M., de Oliveira Latorre, M. R. D., Moreira M. N., & Lotufo-Neto, F. (2005). Group cognitive-behavioral therapy versus sertraline for treatment of children and adolescents with obsessive-compulsive disorder. *Journal of the American Academy of Child and Adolescent Psychiatry, 44*, 1128–1136.

Bannon, S., Gonsalvez, C. J., Croft, R. J., & Boyce, P. M. (2002). Response inhibition deficits in obsessive-compulsive disorder. *Psychiatry Research, 110*(2), 165–174.

Barrett, P., Farrell, L., Dadds, M., & Boulter, N. (2005). Cognitive-behavioral family treatment of childhood obsessive-compulsive disorder: Long-term follow-up and predictors of outcome. *Journal of the American Academy of Child and Adolescent Psychiatry, 44*, 1005–1014.

Barrett, P., Healy, L. J., Farrell, L., & March, J. S. (2004). Cognitive-behavioral family treatment of childhood Obsessive-Compulsive Disorder: A controlled trial. *Journal of the American Academy of Child & Adolescent Psychiatry, 43*(1), 46–62.

Barrett, P. M., & Healy, L. J. (2003). An examination of the cognitive processes involved in childhood obsessive–compulsive disorder. *Behaviour Research and Therapy, 41*(3), 285–299.

Beech, A. R., & Liddell, A. (1974). Decision-making, mood states and ritualistic behavior among obsessional patients. In H. R. Beech (Ed.), *Obsessional States* (pp. 143–160). London: Methuen.

Benito, K. G., Caporino, N. E., Frank, H. E., Ramanujam, K., Garcia, A., Freeman, J., … Storch, E. A. (2015). Development of the pediatric accommodation scale: Reliability and validity of clinician- and parent-report measures. *Journal of Anxiety Disorders, 29*, 14–24.

Boelen, P. A., Vrinssen, I., & van Tulder, F. (2010). Intolerance of uncertainty in adolescents: Correlations with worry, social anxiety, and depression. *Journal of Nervous and Mental Disease, 198*(3), 194–200.

Bolton, D., Dearsley, P., Madronal-Luque, R., & Baron-Cohen, S. (2002). Magical thinking in childhood and adolescence: Development and relation to obsessive compulsion. *British Journal of Developmental Psychology, 20*(4), 479–494.

Bolton, D., & Perrin, S. (2008). Evaluation of exposure with response-prevention for obsessive-compulsive disorder in childhood and adolescence. *Journal of Behavior Therapy and Experimental Psychiatry, 39*, 11–22.

Bouchard, C., Rhéaume, J., & Ladouceur, R. (1999). Responsibility and perfectionism in OCD: An experimental study. *Behaviour Research and Therapy, 37*(3), 239–248.

Bouman, T. K. (2003). Intra- and interpersonal consequences of experimentally induced concealment. *Behaviour Research and Therapy, 41*(8), 959–968.

Burns, D. (1980). The perfectionist's script for self-defeat. *Psychology Today*, 34–51.

Carmona, S., Bassas, N., Rovira, M., Gispert, J. D., Soliva, J. C., Prado, M., …Vilarroya, O. (2007). Pediatric OCD structural brain deficits in conflict monitoring circuits: A voxel-based morphometry study. *Neuroscience Letters, 421*(3), 218–223.

Chamberlain, S. R., Fineberg, N. A., Blackwell, A. D., Robbins, T. W., & Sahakian, B. J. (2006). Motor inhibition and cognitive flexibility in obsessive-compulsive disorder and trichotillomania. *American Journal of Psychiatry, 163*, 1282–1284.

Constans, J. I., Foa, E. B., Franklin, M. E., & Mathews, A. (1995). Memory for actual and imagined events in OC checkers. *Behaviour Research and Therapy, 33*(6), 665–671.

Corcoran, K. M., & Woody, S. R. (2009). Effects of suppression and appraisals on thought frequency and distress. *Behaviour Research and Therapy, 47*(12), 1024–1031.

Cromer, K. R., Schmidt, N. B., & Murphy, D. L. (2007). An investigation of traumatic life events and obsessive-compulsive disorder. *Behaviour Research and Therapy, 45*(7), 1683–1691.

Daleiden, E. L. (1998). Childhood anxiety and memory functioning: A comparison of systemic and processing accounts. *Journal of Experimental Child Psychology, 68*(3), 216–235.

Dalgleish, T., Taghavi, R., Neshat-Doost, H., Moradi, A., Canterbury, R. & Yule, W. (2003). Patterns of processing bias for emotional information across clinical disorders: A comparison of attention, memory, and prospective cognition in children and adolescents with depression, generalized anxiety, and posttraumatic stress disorder. *Journal of Clinical Child & Adolescent Psychology, 32*(1), 10–21.

Douglass, H. M., Moffitt, T. E., Dar, R., McGee, R., & Silva, P. (1995). Obsessive-compulsive disorder in a birth cohort of 18-year-olds: Prevalence and predictors. *Journal of the American Academy of Child and Adolescent Psychiatry, 34*(11), 1424–1431.

Farrell, L., & Barrett, P. (2006). Obsessive-compulsive disorder across developmental trajectory: Cognitive processing of threat in children, adolescents and adults. *British Journal of Psychology, 97*(1), 95–114.

Farrell, L. J., Waters, A. M., & Zimmer-Gembeck, M. J. (2012). Cognitive biases and obsessive-compulsive symptoms in children: Examining the role of maternal cognitive bias and child age. *Behavior Therapy, 43*(3), 593–605.

Flament, M. F., Whitaker, A., Rapoport, J. L., Davies, M., Berg, C. Z., Kalikow, K., …Shaffer, D. (1988). Obsessive compulsive disorder in adolescence: An epidemiological study. *Journal of the American Academy of Child and Adolescent Psychiatry, 27*(6), 764–771.

Foa, E. B., Ilai, D., McCarthy, P. R., Shoyer, B., & Murdock, T. (1993). Information processing in obsessive-compulsive disorder. *Cognitive Therapy and Research, 17*(2), 173–189.

Foa, E. B., & Kozak, M. J. (1986). Emotional processing of fear: Exposure to corrective information. *Psychological Bulletin, 99*(1), 20–35.

Foa, E. B., & McNally, R. J. (1986). Sensitivity to feared stimuli in obsessive-compulsives: A dichotic listening analysis. *Cognitive Therapy and Research, 10*(4), 477–485.

Franklin, M. E., Sapyta, J., Freeman, J. B., Khanna, M., Compton, S., Almirall, D., … March, J. S. (2011). Cognitive behavior therapy augmentation of pharmacotherapy in pediatric obsessive-compulsive disorder: The Pediatric OCD Treatment Study II (POTS II) randomized controlled trial. *Journal of the American Medical Association, 306*(11), 1224–1232.

Freeman, J. B., Garcia, A. M., Coyne, L., Ale, C., Przeworski, A., Himle, M., … Leonard, H. L. (2008). Early childhood OCD: Preliminary findings from a family-based cognitive-behavioral approach. *Journal of the American Academy of Child & Adolescent Psychiatry, 47*(5), 593–602.

Freeman, J., Garcia, A., Frank, H., Benito, K., Conelea, C., Walther, M., & Edmunds, J. (2014). Evidence base update for psychosocial treatments for Pediatric Obsessive-Compulsive Disorder. *Journal of Clinical Child & Adolescent Psychology, 43*(1), 7–26.

Freeston, M. H., Ladouceur, R., Gagnon, F., Thibodeau, N., Rhéaume, J., Letarte, H., & Bujold, A. (1997). Cognitive-behavioral treatment of obsessive thoughts: A controlled study. *Journal of Consulting and Clinical Psychology, 65*(3), 405–413.

Freeston, M. H., Rhéaume, J., & Ladouceur, R. (1996). Correcting faulty appraisals of obsessional thoughts. *Behaviour Research and Therapy, 34*(5/6), 433–446.

Frost, R. O., & Steketee, G. (1997). Perfectionism in Obsessive-Compulsive Disorder patients. *Behaviour Research and Therapy, 35*(4), 291–296.

Frost, R. O., Steketee, G., Cohn, L., & Griess, K. (1994). Personality traits in subclinical and non-obsessive-compulsive volunteers and their parents. *Behaviour Research and Therapy, 32*(1), 47–56.

Gaskell, S. L., Wells, A., & Calam, R. (2001). An experimental investigation of thought suppression and anxiety in children. *British Journal of Clinical Psychology, 40*(1), 45–56.

Gentes, E. L., & Ruscio, A. M. (2011). A meta-analysis of the relation of intolerance of uncertainty to symptoms of generalized anxiety disorder, major depressive disorder, and obsessive–compulsive disorder. *Clinical Psychology Review*, *31*(6), 923–933.

Gershuny, B. S., & Sher, K. J. (1995). Compulsive checking and anxiety in a nonclinical sample: Differences in cognition, behavior, personality, and affect. *Journal of Psychopathology and Behavioral Assessment*, *17*(1), 19–38.

Guidano, V., & Liotti, G. (1983). *Cognitive processes and emotional disorders*. New York: Guilford Press.

Hadwin, J. A., Garner, M., & Perez-Olivas, G. (2006). The development of information processing biases in childhood anxiety: A review and exploration of its origins in parenting. *Clinical Psychology Review*, *26*(7), 876–894.

Heyman, I., Fombonne, E., Meltzer, H., & Goodman, R. (2001). Prevalence of obsessive-compulsive disorder in the British nationwide survey of child mental health. *British Journal of Psychiatry*, *179*, 324–329.

Holaway, R. M., Heimberg, R. G., & Coles, M. E. (2006). A comparison of intolerance of uncertainty in analogue obsessive-compulsive disorder and generalized anxiety disorder. *Journal of Anxiety Disorders*, *20*(2), 158–174.

Hollander, E., Cohen, L., Richards, M., Mullen, L., DeCaria, C., & Stern, Y. (1993). A pilot study of the neuropsychology of obsessive-compulsive disorder and Parkinson's disease: Basal ganglia disorders. *Journal of Neuropsychiatry and Clinical Neurosciences*, *5*(1), 104–107. doi: 10.1176/jnp.5.1.104.

Janeck, A. S., & Calamari, J. E. (1999). Thought suppression in Obsessive-Compulsive Disorder. *Cognitive Therapy and Research*, *23*(5), 497–509.

Kadak, M. T., Balsak, F., Besiroglu, L., & Celik, C. (2014). Relationships between cognitive appraisals of adolescents with OCD and their mothers. *Comprehensive Psychiatry*, *55*(3), 598–603.

Kindt, M., Bögels, S., & Morren, M. (2003). Processing bias in children with Separation Anxiety Disorder, Social Phobia and Generalised Anxiety Disorder. *Behaviour Change*, *20*(03), 143–150.

Kindt, M., Brosschot, J. F., & Everaerd, W. (1997). Cognitive processing bias of children in a real life stress situation and a neutral situation. *Journal of Experimental Child Psychology*, *64*(1), 79–97.

Lacerda, A. L. T., Dalgalarrondo, P., Caetano, D., Haas, G. L., Camargo, E. E., & Keshavan, M. S. (2003). Neuropsychological performance and regional cerebral blood flow in obsessive-compulsive disorder. *Progress in Neuropsychopharmacology and Biological Psychiatry*, *27*(4), 657–665.

Ladouceur, R., Léger, E., Rhéaume, J., & Dubé, D. (1996). Correction of inflated responsibility in the treatment of obsessive-compulsive disorder. *Behaviour Research and Therapy*, *34*(10), 767–774.

Ladouceur, R., Rhéaume, J., & Aublet, F. (1997). Excessive responsibility in obsessional concerns: A fine-grained experimental analysis. *Behaviour Research and Therapy*, *35*(5), 423–427.

Ladouceur, R., Rhéaume, J., Freeston, M. H., Aublet, F., Jean, K., Lachance, S., … De Pokomandy-Morin, K. (1995). Experimental manipulations of responsibility: An analogue test for models of Obsessive-Compulsive Disorder. *Behaviour Research and Therapy*, *33*(8), 937–946.

Langlois, F., Freeston, M. H., & Ladouceur, R. (2000). Differences and similarities between obsessive intrusive thoughts and worry in a non-clinical population: Study 2. *Behaviour Research and Therapy*, *38*(2), 175–189.

Lavy, E., Van Oppen, P., & Van Den Hout, M. (1994). Selective processing of emotional information in obsessive compulsive disorder. *Behaviour Research and Therapy*, *32*(2), 243–246.

Lebowitz, E. R. (2013). Parent-based treatment for childhood and adolescent OCD. *Journal of Obsessive-Compulsive and Related Disorders, 2*(4), 425–431.

Libby, S., Reynolds, S., Derisley, J., & Clark, S. (2004). Cognitive appraisals in young people with obsessive-compulsive disorder. *Journal of Child Psychology and Psychiatry, and Allied Disciplines, 45*(6), 1076–1084.

Lopatka, C., & Rachman, S. (1995). Perceived responsibility and compulsive checking: An experimental analysis. *Behaviour Research and Therapy, 33*(6), 673–684.

Lucey, J. V., Burness, C. E., Costa, D. C., Gacinovic, S., Pilowsky, L. S., Ell, P. J., … Kerwin, R. W. (1997). Wisconsin Card Sorting Task (WCST) errors and cerebral blood flow in obsessive-compulsive disorder (OCD). *British Journal of Medical Psychology, 70*(4), 403–411.

Luxemberg, J. S., Swedo, S. E., Flament, M. F., Friedland, R. P., Rapoport, J., & Rapoport, S. I. (1988). Neuroanatomical abnormalities in obsessive-compulsive disorder detected with quantitative X-ray computed tomography. *American Journal of Psychiatry, 145*(9), 1089–1093.

Macdonald, P. A., Antony, M. M., Macleod, C. M., & Richter, M. A. (1997). Memory and confidence in memory judgments among individuals with obsessive compulsive disorder and non-clinical controls. *Behaviour Research and Therapy, 35*(6), 497–505.

Magnusdottir, I., & Smári, J. (2004). Are responsibility attitudes related to obsessive-compulsive symptoms in schoolchildren? *Cognitive Behaviour Therapy, 33*(1), 21–26.

Makhlouf-Norris, F., & Norris, H. (1973). The obsessive compulsive syndrome as a neurotic device for the reduction of self-uncertainty. *British Journal of Psychiatry, 122*(568), 277–288.

Maki, W. S., O'Neill, H. K., & O'Neill, G. W. (1994). Do nonclinical checkers exhibit deficits in cognitive control? Tests of an inhibitory control hypothesis. *Behaviour Research and Therapy, 32*(2), 183–192.

Mallinger, A., & DeWyze, J. (1992). *Too perfect: When being in control gets out of control.* New York: Fawcett Columbine.

March, J. S., & Mulle, K. (1998). *OCD in children and adolescents: A cognitive-behavioral treatment manual.* New York: Guilford Press.

Mathews, C. A., Kaur, N., & Stein, M. B. (2008). Childhood trauma and obsessive-compulsive symptoms. *Depression and Anxiety, 25*(9), 742–751.

Matthews, L., Reynolds, S., & Derisley, J. (2007). Examining cognitive models of obsessive compulsive disorder in adolescents. *Behavioural and Cognitive Psychotherapy, 35*(2), 149–163.

Mavissakalian, M. R., Hamann, M. S., Abou Haidar, S., & De Groot, C. M. (1993). DSM-III personality disorders in generalized anxiety, panic/agoraphobia, and obsessive-compulsive disorders. *Comprehensive Psychiatry, 34*(4), 243–248.

McNally, R. J., Kaspi, S. P., Riemann, B. C., & Zeitlin, S. B. (1990). Selective processing of threat cues in posttraumatic stress disorder. *Journal of Abnormal Psychology, 99*(4), 398–402.

McNally, R. J., & Kohlbeck, P. A. (1993). Reality monitoring in obsessive-compulsive disorder. *Behaviour Research and Therapy, 31*(3), 249–253.

McNally, R. J., Riemann, B. C., Louro, C. E., Lukach, B. M., & Kim, E. (1992). Cognitive processing of emotional information in panic disorder. *Behaviour Research and Therapy, 30*(2), 143–149.

Menzies, L., Chamberlain, S. R., Laird, A. R., Thelen, S. M., Sahakian, B. J., & Bullmore, E. T. (2008). Integrating evidence from neuroimaging and neuropsychological studies of obsessive-compulsive disorder: The orbitofronto-striatal model revisited. *Neuroscience & Biobehavioral Reviews, 32*(3), 525–549.

Merlo, L. J., Lehmkuhl, H. D., Geffken, G. R., & Storch, E. A. (2009). Decreased family accommodation associated with improved therapy outcome in Pediatric Obsessive-Compulsive Disorder. *Journal of Consulting and Clinical Psychology, 77*(2), 355–360.

Mineka, S., & Hendersen, R. W. (1985). Controllability and predictability in acquired motivation. *Annual Review of Psychology, 36*(1), 495–529.

Muris, P., Meesters, C., Rassin, E., Merckelbach, H., & Campbell, J. (2001). Thought–action fusion and anxiety disorders symptoms in normal adolescents. *Behaviour Research and Therapy, 39*(7), 843–852.

Muris, P., Merckelbach, H., & De Jong, P. (1993). Verbalization and environmental cuing in thought suppression. *Behaviour Research and Therapy, 31*(6), 609–612.

Norman, R. M. G., Davies, F., Nicholson, I. R., Cortese, L., & Malla, A. K. (1998). The relationship of two aspects of perfectionism with symptoms in a psychiatric outpatient population. *Journal of Social and Clinical Psychology, 17*(1), 50–68.

Obsessive Compulsive Cognitions Working Group. (1997). Cognitive assessment of obsessive-compulsive disorder. Obsessive Compulsive Cognitions Working Group. *Behaviour Research and Therapy, 35*(7), 667–681.

Pacht, A. R. (1984). Reflections on perfection. *American Psychologist, 39*(4), 386–390.

Pediatric OCD Treatment Study (POTS) Team. (2004). Cognitive-behavior therapy, sertraline, and their combination for children and adolescents with obsessive-compulsive disorder: The Pediatric OCD Treatment Study (POTS) randomized controlled trial. *Journal of the American Medical Association, 292*(16), 1969–1976.

Penades, R., Catalan, R., Rubia, K., Andres, S., Salamero, M., & Gasto, C. (2007). Impaired response inhibition in obsessive compulsive disorder. *European Psychiatry, 22*(6), 404–410.

Peris, T. S., Bergman, R. L., Langley, A., Chang, S., Mccracken, J. T., & Piacentini, J. (2008). Correlates of accommodation of pediatric obsessive-compulsive disorder: Parent, child, and family characteristics. *Journal of the American Academy of Child & Adolescent Psychiatry, 47*(10), 1173–1181.

Peris, T. S., Sugar, C. A., Bergman, R. L., Chang, S., Langley, A., & Piacentini, J. (2012). Family factors predict treatment outcome for pediatric obsessive-compulsive disorder. *Journal of Consulting and Clinical Psychology, 80*(2), 255–263.

Piacentini, J., Bergman, R. L., Chang, S., Langley, A., Peris, T., Wood, J. J., & McCracken, J. (2011). Controlled comparison of family cognitive behavioral therapy and psychoeducation/relaxation training for child OCD. *Journal of the American Academy of Child and Adolescent Psychiatry, 50*(11), 1149–1161.

Piacentini, J., Bergman, R. L., Keller, M., & McCracken, J. (2003). Functional impairment in children and adolescents with obsessive-compulsive disorder. *Journal of Child and Adolescent Psychopharmacology, 13*(1), 61–69.

Przeworski, A., Cain, N., & Dunbeck, K. (2014). Traumatic life events in individuals with hoarding symptoms. obsessive-compulsive symptoms, and comorbid obsessive-compulsive and hoarding symptoms. *Journal of Obsessive-Compulsive Related Disorders, 3*, 52–59.

Przeworski, A., Zoellner, L. A., Franklin, M. E., Garcia, A., Freeman, J., March, J. S., & Foa, E. B. (2012). Maternal and child expressed emotion as predictors of treatment response in pediatric obsessive–compulsive disorder. *Child Psychiatry & Human Development, 43*(3), 337–353.

Purdon, C. (1999). Thought suppression and psychopathology. *Behaviour Research and Therapy, 37*(11), 1029–1054.

Rachman, S., & De Silva, P. (1978). Abnormal and normal obsessions. *Behaviour Research and Therapy, 16*(4), 233–248.

Radomsky, A. S., & Rachman, S. (1999). Memory bias in obsessive-compulsive disorder (OCD). *Behaviour Research and Therapy, 37*(7), 605–618.

Rapoport, J. L. (1991). Recent advances in obsessive-compulsive disorder. *Neuropsychopharmacology, 5*(1), 1–10.

Rauch, S. L., Jenike, M. A., Alpert, N. M., Baer, L., Breiter, H. C. R., Savage, C. R., & Fischman, A. J. (1994). Regional cerebral blood flow measured during symptom provocation in obsessive-compulsive disorder using oxygen 15: Labeled carbon dioxide and positron emission tomography. *Archives of General Psychiatry, 51*(1), 62–70.

Rhéaume, J., Freeston, M. H., Dugas, M. J., Letarte, H., & Ladouceur, R. (1995). Perfectionism, responsibility and obsessive-compulsive symptoms. *Behaviour Research and Therapy, 33*(7), 785–794.

Robinson, D., Wu, H., Munne, R. A., Ashtari, M., Alvir, J., Ma, J., Lerner, G., ... Bogerts, B. (1995). Reduced caudate nucleus volume in obsessive-compulsive disorder. *Archives of General Psychiatry, 52*(5), 393–398.

Rosenberg, D. R., Averbach, D. H., O'Hearn, K. M., Seymour, A. B., Birmaher, B., & Sweeney, J. A. (1997). Oculomotor response inhibition abnormalities in pediatric obsessive-compulsive disorder. *Archives of General Psychiatry, 54*(9), 831–838.

Salkovskis, P. M. (1996). Cognitive-behavioral approaches to the understanding of obsessional problems. In R. M. Rapee (Ed.), *Current controversies in anxiety disorders* (pp. 103–133). New York: Guilford Press.

Salkovskis, P. M., & Harrison, J. (1984). Abnormal and normal obsessions: A replication. *Behaviour Research and Therapy, 22*(5), 549–552.

Salkovskis, P. M., & McGuire, J. (2003). Cognitive-behavioural theory of OCD. In R. G. Menzies & P. De Silva (Eds.), *Obsessive-Compulsive Disorder: Theory, research and treatment* (Vol. 65, pp. 59–78). Chichester: Wiley.

Salkovskis, P. M., Wroe, A. L., Gledhill, A., Morrison, N., Forrester, E., Richards, C., ... Thorpe, S. (2000). Responsibility attitudes and interpretations are characteristic of obsessive compulsive disorder. *Behaviour Research and Therapy, 38*(4), 347–372.

Salkovskis, P., Shafran, R., Rachman, S., & Freeston, M. H. (1999). Multiple pathways to inflated responsibility beliefs in obsessional problems: Possible origins and implications for therapy and research. *Behaviour Research and Therapy, 37*(11), 1055–1072.

Salzman, L. (1979). Psychotherapy of the obsessional. *American Journal of Psychotherapy, 33*(1), 32–40.

Savage, C. R., Baer, L., Keuthen, N. J., Brown, H. D., Rauch, S. L., & Jenike, M. A. (1999). Organizational strategies mediate nonverbal memory impairment in obsessive-compulsive disorder. *Biological Psychiatry, 45*(7), 905–916.

Savage, C. R., Deckersbach, T., Wilhelm, S., Rauch, S. L., Baer, L., Reid, T., & Jenike, M A. (2000). Strategic processing and episodic memory impairment in obsessive compulsive disorder. *Neuropsychology, 14*(1), 141–151.

Scarone, S., Colombo, C., Livian, S., Abbruzzese, M., Ronchi, P., Locatelli, M., ... Smeraldi, E. (1992). Increased right caudate nucleus size in obsessive-compulsive disorder: Detection with magnetic resonance imaging. *Psychiatry Research: Neuroimaging, 45*(2), 115–121.

Selvi, Y., Besiroglu, L., Aydin, A., Gulec, M., Atli, A., Boysan, M., & Celik, C. (2012). Relations between childhood traumatic experiences, dissociation, and cognitive models in obsessive compulsive disorder. *International Journal of Psychiatry in Clinical Practice, 16*(1), 53–59.

Shafran, R. (1997). The manipulation of responsibility in obsessive-compulsive disorder. *British Journal of Clinical Psychology, 36*(3), 397–407.

Shafran, R., Thordarson, D. S., & Rachman, S. (1996). Thought–action fusion in obsessive compulsive disorder. *Journal of Anxiety Disorders, 10*(5), 379–391.

Smári, J., Birgisdóttir, A. B., & Brynjólfsdóttir, B. (1995). Obsessive-compulsive symptoms and suppression of personally relevant unwanted thoughts. *Personality and Individual Differences, 18*(5), 621–625.

Steketee, G., & Frost, R. (2001). Development and initial validation of the Obsessive Beliefs Questionnaire and the Interpretation of Intrusions Inventory. *Behaviour Research and Therapy, 39*(8), 987–1006.

Storch, E. A., Bussing, R., Small, B. J., Geffken, G. R., McNamara, J. P., Rahman, O., ... Murphy, T. K. (2013). Randomized, placebo-controlled trial of cognitive-behavioral therapy alone or combined with sertraline in the treatment of pediatric obsessive-compulsive disorder. *Behaviour Research and Therapy, 51*(12), 823–829.

Storch, E. A., Geffken, G. R., Merlo, L. J., Jacob, M. L., Murphy, T. K., Goodman, W. K., … Grabill, K. (2007). Family accommodation in pediatric Obsessive-Compulsive Disorder. *Journal of Clinical Child & Adolescent Psychology, 36*(2), 207–216.

Szeszko, P. R., MacMillan, S., McMeniman, M., Chen, S., Baribault, K., Lim, K. O., … Rosenberg, D. R. (2004). Brain structural abnormalities in psychotropic drug-naive pediatric patients with obsessive-compulsive disorder. *American Journal of Psychiatry, 161*, 1049–1056.

Tallis, F., Pratt, P., & Jamani, N. (1999). Obsessive compulsive disorder, checking, and nonverbal memory: A neuropsychological investigation. *Behaviour Research and Therapy, 37*(2), 161–166.

Tata, P. R., Leibowitz, J. A., Prunty, M. J., Cameron, M., & Pickering, A. D. (1996). Attentional bias in obsessional compulsive disorder. *Behaviour Research and Therapy, 34*(1), 53–60.

Tolin, D. F., Abramowitz, J. S., Brigidi, B. D., & Foa, E. B. (2003). Intolerance of uncertainty in obsessive-compulsive disorder. *Journal of Anxiety Disorders, 17*(2), 233–242.

Tolin, D. F., Abramowitz, J. S., Przeworski, A., & Foa, E. B. (2002). Thought suppression in obsessive-compulsive disorder. *Behaviour Research and Therapy, 40*(11), 1255–1274.

Van den Hout, M., & Kindt, M. (2003a). Phenomenological validity of an OCD-memory model and the remember/know distinction. *Behaviour Research and Therapy, 41*(3), 369–378.

Van den Hout, M., & Kindt, M. (2003b). Repeated checking causes memory distrust. *Behaviour Research and Therapy, 41*(3), 301–316.

Van Noppen, B., & Steketee, G. (2009). Testing a conceptual model of patient and family predictors of obsessive compulsive disorder (OCD) symptoms. *Behaviour Research and Therapy, 47*(1), 18–25.

Van Oppen, P., & Arntz, A. (1994). Cognitive therapy for obsessive-compulsive disorder. *Behaviour Research and Therapy, 32*(1), 79–87.

Visser, H. A., Van Minnen, A., Van Megen, H., Eikelenboom, M., Hoogendoorn, A. W., Kaarsemaker, M., … Van Oppen, P. (2014). The relationship between adverse childhood experiences and symptom severity, chronicity, and comorbidity in patients with obsessive-compulsive disorder. *Journal of Clinical Psychiatry, 75*(10), 1034–1039.

Watson, H. J., & Rees, C. S. (2008). Meta-analysis of randomized, controlled treatment trials for pediatric obsessive-compulsive disorder. *Journal of Child Psychology and Psychiatry, 49*, 489–498.

Wegner, D. M. (1989). *White bears and other unwanted thoughts: Suppression, obsession, and the psychology of mental control* (Vol. XII). New York: Penguin.

Wegner, D. M., & Zanakos, S. (1994). Chronic thought suppression. *Journal of Personality, 62*(4), 615–641.

Wilhelm, S., Mcnally, R. J., Baer, L., & Florin, I. (1996). Directed forgetting in obsessive-compulsive disorder. *Behaviour Research and Therapy, 34*(8), 633–641.

Wilhelm, S., McNally, R. J., Baer, L., & Florin, I. (1997). Autobiographical memory in obsessive-compulsive disorder. *British Journal of Clinical Psychology, 36*(1), 21–31.

Williams, T. L., Salkovskis, P. M., Forrester, L., Turner, S., White, H., & Allsopp, M. A. (2010). A randomized controlled trial of cognitive behavioral treatment for obsessive compulsive disorder in children and adolescents. *European Child and Adolescent Psychiatry, 19*, 449–456.

Woolley, J., Heyman, I., Brammer, M., Frampton, I., McGuire, P. K., & Rubia, K. (2008). Brain activation in paediatric obsessive-compulsive disorder during tasks of inhibitory control. *British Journal of Psychiatry, 192*(1), 25–31. doi: 10.1192/bjp.bp.107.036558.

Ye, H. J., Rice, K. G., & Storch, E. A. (2008). Perfectionism and peer relations among children with obsessive-compulsive disorder. *Child Psychiatry and Human Development, 39*(4), 415–426.

Zohar, A. H. (1999). The epidemiology of obsessive-compulsive disorder in children and adolescents. *Child and Adolescent Psychiatric Clinics of North America, 8*(3), 445–460.

14

Biological Models and Treatments for OCD in Adults

S. Evelyn Stewart and Adrian S. Loh

Obsessive-Compulsive Disorder (OCD) is one of the most common psychiatric disorders with a lifetime prevalence of 2.3% (using DSM-IV criteria) (Ruscio, Stein, Chiu, & Kessler, 2010). Whether presenting during childhood, adolescence, or adulthood, this disorder places a significant burden on affected individuals (Pinto, Mancebo, Eisen, Pagano, & Rasmussen, 2006). However, clinically significant differences between pediatric and adult-onset OCD have been identified with respect to symptom presentation, comorbidity, sex distribution (Bloch, Landeros-Weisenberger, Rosario, Pittenger, & Leckman, 2008), insight level, and etiology (Kalra & Swedo, 2009). While pediatric OCD emergence coincides during important phases of prefrontal cortex maturation, adult-onset OCD occurs subsequent to major neurodevelopmental phases and tends to demonstrate lower heritability and genetic influences.

To optimize the treatment of OCD, and with eventual goals of preventing its onset and associated morbidity, it is critical to have an understanding of OCD etiology. In recent decades various constructs have been proposed to help characterize OCD, including numerous biological models. While these should optimally be combined with cognitive-behavioral and other models to gain an integrated perspective of underlying influences and driving forces in OCD pathology, the current chapter will focus on summarizing current evidence for biological models, with an aim to understand their potential clinical relevance.

Biological Models

The following sections will describe biological models that incorporate contributing factors to OCD pathology across multiple perspectives as follows: neuroanatomy/neurocircuitry (i.e., gross anatomy), neurochemical/neurotransmitter (i.e., biochemistry and physiologic), genetic factors (i.e., cellular biology), and effects of autoimmune and systemic conditions. These models are not mutually exclusive, but provide complementary perspectives of OCD biology across macroscopic and microscopic levels. Via exploration of biological models within this chapter, as well as other models covered elsewhere in this book, we aim to enable a more informed understanding of this disease and its treatment.

The Wiley Handbook of Obsessive Compulsive Disorders, Volume I, First Edition.
Edited by Jonathan S. Abramowitz, Dean McKay, and Eric A. Storch.
© 2017 John Wiley & Sons Ltd. Published 2017 by John Wiley & Sons Ltd.

Neuroanatomy and Neurocircuitry

OCD is commonly described as a neuropsychiatric illness. Understanding of the neuroanatomy and neurocircuitry related to OCD has evolved via decades of research utilizing neuroimaging modalities, including Computed Tomography (CT), Magnetic Resonance Imaging (MRI), functional MRI (fMRI), Magnetic Resonance Spectroscopy (MRS), and Positron Emission Tomography (PET) scans. Neurobiological models of OCD have primarily focused on dysfunction within the circuits connecting more evolved, prefrontal cortical (PFC) and premotor cortical parts of the human brain (represented in blue and purple, respectively, in Figure 14.1) with the more primitive and reflexive structures contained closer to the brain's core (the basal ganglia, thalamus, amygdala, and hippocampus, represented in green, pink, orange, and yellow, respectively).

Specifically, the cortico-striatal-thalamo-cortical (CSTC) pathways have been repeatedly implicated (Kang et al., 2013). These complex pathways are reported to contain both a ventromedial "affective" circuit and a dorsolateral "cognitive" circuit (van den Heuvel et al., 2009). Nodes of these pathways are interconnected anatomically via two principal white-matter tracts: the cingulum bundle and the anterior limb of the internal capsule. More recently, models have been proposed to expand upon the two-circuit model, and to include a ventral cognitive circuit (Milad & Rauch, 2012).

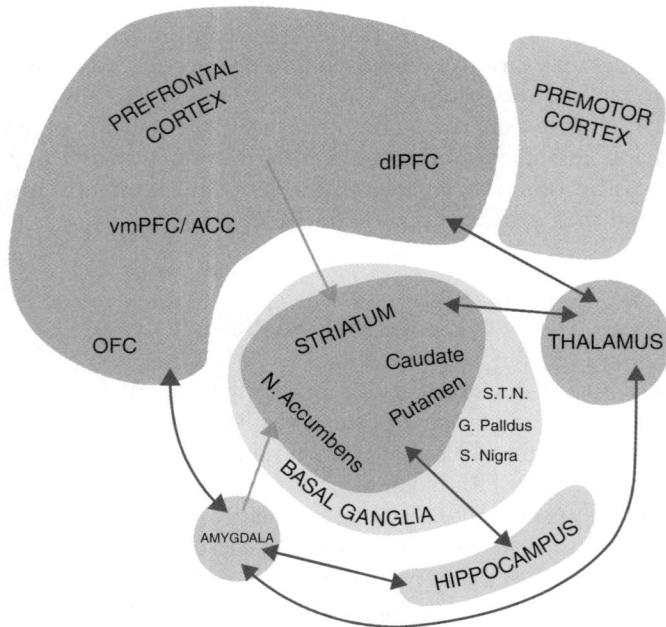

Figure 14.1   Schematic of implicate brain regions in OCD
Abbreviations: dlPFC = dorsolateral prefrontal cortex; vmPFC = ventromedial prefrontal cortex; ACC = anterior cingulate cortex; OFC = orbitofrontal cortex; G. Pallidus = globus pallidus; N. Accumbens = nucleus accumbens; S. Nigra = substantia nigra; S.T.N. = subthalamic nucleus.

The basal ganglia, as its name suggests, is a collection of neural nuclei located at the "base" of the brain, which consists of several subcortical nuclei (in light and dark green, Figure 14.1). These nuclei include the globus pallidus, the substantia nigra, the subthalamic nucleus (STN) and, most importantly from an OCD perspective, the striatum. The striatum contains the caudate nucleus, putamen and nucleus accumbens (in dark green, Figure 14.1), which appears to play a central role in OCD pathology.

The basal ganglia comprise a key node in a complex system of parallel CSTC loops that integrate motor and cognitive functions. Neurological conditions affecting the basal ganglia, such as multiple sclerosis (Foroughipour et al., 2012), Huntington's chorea (Cummings & Cunningham, 1992), and Parkinson's disease (Müller et al., 1997), often present with symptoms that include OCD-like compulsions. Degenerative lesions in this region have been found to result in compulsions in both human (Tonkonogy, Smith, & Barreira, 1994) and animal models (Rapoport, Ryland, & Kriete, 1992).

Regarding the neurocircuitry of obsessions, prefrontal and orbitofrontal brain regions have been implicated as brain regions charged with "making sense of the environment" via filtration of incoming stimuli and suppression of unnecessary responses. OCD neuroimaging studies have identified a combination of deficits in feedback inhibition circuits within the dorsolateral prefrontal cortical (DLPFC) parietal network, coupled with possible hyperactivation of orbital frontal (OFC) and anterior cingulate cortices (ACC) (Melloni et al., 2012). Resting-state fMRI studies have reported a model of hyperconnectivity between the OFC and the basal ganglia for unmedicated patients, which is reduced in medicated OCD patients (Beucke et al., 2013). A related recent study found that improvement of OCD symptoms significantly correlated with changes in connectivity in the right ventral frontal cortex following treatment (Shin et al., 2014).

OCD symptom dimensions may also be mediated by distinct, but partially overlapping, neural systems (Mataix-Cols & van den Heuvel, 2006; Rauch & Britton, 2010). As demonstrated via PET imaging, striatal blood flow increased with checking and decreased with symmetry/ordering, while bilateral ACC and left OFC blood flow increases correlated with washing symptoms (Rauch et al., 1998).

Beyond specific anatomical brain region abnormalities, various OCD studies have demonstrated increased overall grey matter volume, and decreased white matter volume and integrity, highlighting the important role of neurodevelopment in OCD etiology (Jenike, Rauch, Cummings, Savage, & Goodman, 1996; Szeszko et al., 2005). They have also demonstrated more dramatic involvement of right versus left hemispheric structures (Hansen, Hasselbalch, Law, & Bolwig, 2002; Shin et al., 2014; Swedo et al., 1992). Potentially related to this, OCD studies reporting neurological examination findings have shown subtle left hemi-body signs and dyskinesias (Behar & Rapoport, 1984; Hollander et al., 1990). In addition, nonlocalizing abnormalities called neurological soft signs have been studied in OCD (Hollander et al., 2005), with a meta-analysis reporting increased deficits in sensory integration, primitive reflexes, and motor coordination compared with healthy controls (Jaafari et al., 2013). Moreover, sensory difficulties have been reported in two-thirds of OCD cases (Miguel et al., 2000; Prado et al., 2008), leading to the development of a sensory responsiveness scale for this population (Sampaio, McCarthy, Mancuso, Stewart, & Geller, 2014).

Neurotransmitters/Neurochemicals

Among neurotransmitter models of OCD, those involving serotonin system have historically received the most attention. Serotonergic networks appear to mediate effectiveness of first-line pharmacologic agents for OCD (Murphy et al., 1989), with early studies suggesting serotonergic subsystem dysfunction (Insel, Mueller, Alterman, Linnoila, & Murphy, 1985; Murphy & Pigott, 1990), and serotonergic involvement in OCD-related decision-making deficits (Homberg, 2012). However, numerous inconsistencies remain unresolved, and the role of serotonin in OCD pathophysiology has not been proven.

Dopaminergic mechanisms have also been implicated in OCD pathogenesis (Zohar, Chopra, Sasson, Amiaz, & Amital, 2000), with reports of decreased D2 and D3 receptor availability in OCD as well as TS, potentially reflecting higher endogenous dopamine levels in both disorders (Denys et al., 2013). More recently, glutamatergic systems have also been implicated in OCD (Pittenger, Bloch, & Williams, 2011) and a glutamate transporter gene is suspected to play a role in OCD (Stewart et al., 2007). Converging evidence for the role of glutamate in OCD has led to the development of a glutamate hypothesis for OCD and new proposed treatment strategies involving glutamatergic compounds (Wu, Hanna, Rosenberg, & Arnold, 2012).

With an increasing body of research, the complexity of interplay between neurotransmitter systems in OCD has become more greatly appreciated (Pittenger et al., 2011). Improved understanding of this interplay may help the development of new treatment targets.

Genetic

Family and twin studies have demonstrated that genetic factors predispose certain individuals to OCD. A meta-analysis of five family OCD studies revealed a summary odds ratio (OR) of 4.0 (95% CI: 2.2–7.1) for OCD in first-degree relatives (Hettema, Neale, & Kendler, 2001). Twin studies have shown elevated concordance (80–87%) among monozygotic (MZ) twin pairs compared with dizygotic (DZ) twin pairs (47–50%) (Pauls, 2010). While genetic influence is stronger in child-onset OCD (heritability estimate = 0.45–0.65), there is also evidence for a moderate genetic influence in adult-onset OCD in adult samples (heritability estimate 0.27–0.47) (van Grootheest, Cath, Beekman, & Boomsma, 2005). Consistent with these findings, adult twin studies have demonstrated that environmental factors play a somewhat larger role than genetic influences (Van Grootheest, Cath, Beekman, & Boomsma, 2007).

The genetic influence on OCD transmission has also been supported by several complex segregation analyses, linkage studies, candidate gene studies and genome-wide association studies, which have confirmed the complexity of genetic vulnerability in OCD (Pauls, 2010). Similar to other psychiatric disorders, it is likely that numerous gene variants are implicated in the genetics of this disorder.

The search for candidate genes has utilized functional, positional, and whole genome approaches. Genes of ongoing interest include the glutamate transporter gene, SLC1A1 (71), glutamate gene GRIK2 (Sampaio et al., 2011), and other candidate genes (Pauls, 2010) focused primarily on the serotonergic and dopaminergic system-related genes, such as serotonin receptor/transporter, dopamine receptor/transporter, Catechol-O-Methyltransferase (COMT), and Monoamine Oxidase A (MAO-A) genes. However, to date, no OCD vulnerability genes have been confirmed; almost certainly due to underpowered sample sizes. While the first genome-wide association study in

OCD did not find significant association ($P < 5 \times 10^{-8}$) with any common alleles, enrichment for alleles associated with frontal lobe gene expression was identified (Stewart et al., 2013), converging with neuroimaging findings (e.g., the centrality of the frontal lobe within the CSTC circuit for OCD) (Kang et al., 2013).

Improved understanding of environmental triggers, OCD subtypes and overlapping genetic vulnerability with other psychiatric illnesses is necessary. The identification of endophenotypes, or genetic trait markers, may help to detect individuals at risk of OCD before it manifests. For example, surface expansion of the ventromedial caudate, the right thalamus, and the right OFC have been demonstrated in both OCD-affected individuals and in their unaffected first-degree siblings compared with healthy controls (Shaw et al., 2015). However, much larger sample sizes and collaboration across international OCD research programs will also be required to achieve this goal (Murphy et al., 2014).

Autoimmune and Other Medical Causes

Within the pediatric OCD literature, the role of autoimmune reactions have been proposed as etiologic factors in a minority of affected youth (Murphy, Kurlan, & Leckman, 2010). The diagnosis labeled Pediatric Autoimmune Neuropsychiatric Disorders Associated with Streptococcal infections (PANDAS) attributed abrupt onset of OCD and tics to basal ganglia inflammation. A broader entity labeled as Pediatric Acute-onset Neuropsychiatric Syndrome (PANS) (Murphy, Gerardi, & Leckman, 2014) has more recently been proposed, focusing on the acuity of OCD or eating-related syndrome presentation rather than requiring proof of presumptive infectious/autoimmune etiology.

More broadly across the lifespan, autoimmune diseases have also been implicated as a biological etiological factor contributing to OCD. A chart review of adult OCD patients found increased immune-related disease comorbidity compared with other psychiatric disorders (Dinn, Harris, McGonigal, & Raynard, 2001). Contamination and aggression obsessions in Sydenham's Chorea (SC), resemble those of primary OCD (Asbahr, Ramos, Costa, & Sassi, 2005; de Alvarenga et al., 2009; Murphy et al., 2010). Increased OCD incidence also occurs in Rheumatic Fever (RF) without chorea (Mercadante et al., 2000). Adult OCD studies have been inconsistent with respect to detecting immune dysfunction, suggesting the need for further investigation of this topic (Murphy et al., 2014).

Potential biological underpinnings are also demonstrated in other uncommon causes of OCD. For example, brain insults arising from trauma, inflammation, and infection have preceded the development of OCD according to case reports (Jenike, 1998; Muir, McKenney, Connolly, & Stewart, 2013). In addition to the above, hormonal influences have been reported, including links onset and exacerbation during menarche, pregnancy and postpartum time periods (Forray, Focseneanu, Pittman, McDougle, & Epperson, 2010; Labad et al., 2005).

Biological Treatments

Appropriate management of OCD often involves a multifaceted approach, illustrating how biological and psychosocial treatments have efficacy when used alone or in combination. The current section primarily focuses on biological medication treatment, while other OCD treatments such as cognitive-behavior therapy will be discussed in other parts of this book. As previously noted, however, the labeling of etiologic and treatments as "biological" versus "non-biological" is somewhat misguided, given that nonmedicinal and noninvasive approaches such as CBT have demonstrated associated structural and functional brain changes that are observable from a "biological" perspective (Nakao, Okada, & Kanba, 2014). First-line OCD medications may be used as monotherapy, in combination with augmenting medications, or with other modalities. Given suboptimal response and remission rates for OCD with medications and CBT, second- and third-line or alternate approaches have also been studied and are available.

This section primarily draws upon treatment guidelines of the American Psychiatric Association (Koran, Hanna, Hollander, Nestadt, & Simpson, 2007). In addition, the UK-based National Institute for Health and Care Excellence (NICE) issued 2005 guidelines for the management of OCD and Body Dysmorphic Disorder (BDD) (NICE, 2005), which largely align with APA guidelines (Koran et al., 2007). Please refer to Tables 14.1, 14.2, and 14.3 for summary tables on dosing information for OCD monotherapy agents, augmenting agents, and special circumstances, respectively.

Monotherapy

In accordance with the etiologic model of OCD implicating serotonergic dysregulation (Jenike et al., 1990), first-line OCD medications are serotonergic agents, also known as serotonin reuptake inhibitors (SRIs). They include selective serotonin reuptake inhibitors (SSRIs) and the serotonergic tricyclic antidepressant (TCA), clomipramine. While serotonin–noradrenaline reuptake inhibitors (SNRIs) have been used in the treatment of OCD, evidence for this family of medications is much weaker than that for SSRIs and clomipramine.

SSRIs. SSRIs are widely recognized as the most appropriate first-line OCD medication (Van Ameringen et al., 2014). The selection of an SSRI should be based on best clinical judgment, balancing factors such as past individual and family treatment response, tolerability, drug interactions, and cost. The most recent Cochrane review meta-analysis of OCD medication RCTs confirmed superior efficacy of SSRIs over placebo in reducing OCD symptom severity (Soomro, Altman, Rajagopal, & Oakley-Browne, 2008). In the 17 studies meeting inclusion criteria, comprising a combined total of 3,097 participants, all SSRIs included (citalopram, fluoxetine, fluvoxamine, paroxetine, and sertraline) were found to have comparable efficacy. With the exception of citalopram and escitalopram, all of the SSRIs have been approved by the US Food and Drug Administration (FDA) for OCD treatment. Nevertheless, citalopram and escitalopram are widely used in an "off-label" fashion in OCD treatment.

One distinct aspect of SSRI use in the treatment of OCD is often overlooked. A meta-analysis of nine studies involving 2,268 OCD subjects, found a linear dose–response curve, such that higher SSRI doses were associated with improved treatment efficacy (Bloch, McGuire, Landeros-Weisenberger, Leckman, & Pittenger, 2010). This is in sharp contrast to recommended SSRI dosages for treatment depression and anxiety, which are often successfully used at low dose. Recommended starting and target doses for specific SSRIs in OCD are found in Table 14.1.

Table 14.1 OCD monotherapy

Drug (generic name)	Drug (trade name)	APA-defined Start dose (mg/d)	APA-defined target dose (mg/d)	Adverse effects [special considerations]
Monotherapy agents (SRIs) SSRIs				
Citalopram	Celexa	20	Up to 40	Common: insomnia, sedation,
Escitalopram	Lexapro	10	30	GI upset, decreased sexual
Fluoxetine	Prozac	20	40–80	function, dizziness, weight
Fluvoxamine	Luvox	50	200–300	gain.
Paroxetine	Paxil	20	40–60	Rare: Hypomania. Citalopram
Sertraline	Zoloft	50	200	dosages exceeding 40 mg/day may also cause arrythmia, black box warning in place [*monitor weight*]
Tricyclic antidepressants				
Clomipramine	Anafranil	25	50–250*	Common: anticholinergic, dry mouth, blurred vision, constipation dizziness, decreased sexual function, antihistamine (sedation weight gain), tremor. Rare: ECG changes, seizures [*monitor weight, vitals, ECG and serum total, and metabolite levels*]

* Lower dose required if given with fluvoxamine.

SSRIs are generally well tolerated, a feature supporting their widespread use. Common adverse effects include gastrointestinal discomfort (e.g., nausea, diarrhea), activation (e.g., tremor, insomnia), sedation, headache, and dizziness, which often self-resolve. Longer-term side effects include weight gain, apathy, and sexual effects, such as decreased libido and anorgasmia. While SSRIs are generally considered safe from a cardiovascular standpoint, some evidence has indicated a potential risk for QTc prolongation, and the Food and Drug Administration recommended limiting dosage of citalopram to 40 mg daily (Stern, Fava, Wilens, & Rosenbaum, 2015). Rare adverse effects include serotonin syndrome and, in youth, suicidality (Hammad, Laughren, & Racoosin, 2006), although for adults treated for nonmood disorders, there does not appear to be an increased risk of treatment-emergent suicidality (Tauscher-Wisniewski, Disch, Plewes, Ball, & Beasley, 2007).

While SSRIs within their class have been shown to be equally effective for OCD, there are clear variations in their individual pharmacodynamic and pharmacokinetic profiles that may guide selection. Clinically relevant examples include sertraline's relative potency for dopamine reuptake inhibition, citalopram and fluoxetine being racemic mixtures with differing isomers (explaining how escitalopram came to be marketed separately), fluoxetine's unusually long-acting pharmacologically active metabolite, and individual SSRIs varying effects on the Cytochrome P450 (CYP) system (Goodnick & Goldstein, 1998).

Table 14.2   OCD SRI augmentation

Atypical antipsychotics				Adverse effects [special considerations]
Risperidone*	Risperdal	1 (qd or divided bid)	0.5–6	Common: weight gain, dizziness, sedation, constipation, sexual.
Olanzapine	Zyprexa	5	5–20 (qd or divided bid)	Rare: hyperglycemia, elevated prolactin, extrapyramidal symptoms [monitor weight, abdominal circumference lipids, cholesterol and ECG]
Quetiapine	Seroquel	50 (divided bid)	500 (divided bid)	
Aripiprazole	Abilify	10	10–30	
Ziprasidone	Geodon	40 (divided bid)	40–160 (divided bid)	
Benzodiazepines				
Clonazepam	Klonopin	0.25–0.5 (qd or divided bid)	0.5–3 (qd or divided bid)	Common: sedation. Rare: impaired cognition, disinhibition, ataxia [potential for tolerance – monitor for escalating dose, rebound anxiety]
Lorazepam	Ativan	0.5 (divided bid-tid)	0.5-4 (divided bid-tid)	Generally for short-term use, while establishing stabilization.
Glutamatergic agents				
Memantine	Namenda	10 (divided BID)	20 (divided BID)	Common: dizziness, drowsiness, headache, insomnia, confusion. Rare: vomiting, increased libido, cystitis.
N-acetyl cysteine	Mucomyst	1200 (divided BID)	2,400 (divided BID)	Common: dizziness, drowsiness, nausea, vomiting, diarrhea, heartburn. Rare: headache, increased ICP.
Riluzole	Rilutek		100 (divided BID)	Common: nausea, sedation. Rare: liver toxicity. [monitor liver function]
Other agents				
Buspirone	Buspar	10 (divided bid)	10–45 (divided bid)	Common: dizziness, headache, nausea Rare: sedation, rash.

* this medication has the best level of evidence among anti-psychotics.

Clomipramine. TCAs as a class act by inhibiting serotonin and norepinephrine reuptake. However, the only TCA indicated for use in OCD is clomipramine (CMI), which is significantly more serotonergic compared with other TCAs. No other TCAs have been found to be effective in the treatment of OCD. The most recent meta-analysis of seven randomized trials and 392 OCD patients concluded that CMI reduces OCD symptoms compared with placebo (Ackerman & Greenland, 2002).

Table 14.3 Practical suggestions for SRI timing and augmentation with comorbid conditions/special circumstances in OCD treatment

	Class/drug	Timing	Considerations
Comorbid MDD	Bupropion (Wellbutrin).	Post-SRI initiation	Dopaminergic effects; seizure risk increased (caution with comorbid bulimia).
Medication-induced weight gain	Topiramate (Topamax).	Post-weight gain	Aim for 1–2 lb loss weekly.
Mood instability	Lamotrigine (Lamictal).	Pre-SRI initiation	May reduce risk of SRI-induced mood switch.
Comorbid ADHD	Stimulant, alpha-agonist, atomoxetine.	Post-SRI stabilization.	Timing may reduce risk of stimulant-induced anxiety/disinhibition/activation.
Comorbid impairing tics	Alpha-agonist.	Pre-SRI initiation.	Alpha-agonists may reduce risk of SRI-induced tic worsening.

A meta-analysis of randomized trials not directly comparing CMI with SSRIs demonstrated that CMI had a greater effect size than SSRIs (Decloedt & Stein, 2010). In general, SSRIs and CMI lead to improvement in 40–60% of cases, while total elimination of symptoms is less common. Treatment doses for CMI range between 100 and 250 mg/day, according to the APA Guidelines, although the required effective dose may be lower when initiated in combination with fluvoxamine, as explained in the following paragraph.

The adverse effects most commonly associated with CMI are anticholinergic in mechanism, including sedation, dry mouth, blurred vision, constipation, urinary hesitancy, and arrhythmias. For the latter reason, patients on clomipramine should undergo electrocardiogram (ECG) screening prior to treatment initiation. These anticholinergic side effects are attributed largely to its metabolite desmethyl-clomipramine (dm-CMI), as opposed to the therapeutic effects of CMI. Hence, monitoring the serum ratio of dm-CMI to CMI is strongly recommended, with a goal of maintaining a ratio of < 0.3. Fast metabolizers of the Cytochrome P450 system less easily achieve higher serum levels of CMI, and will thus have a higher dm-CMI to CMI ratio, resulting in a greater likelihood of adverse effects. While not discussed in APA or AACAP guidelines, we assert that clinicians prescribing clomipramine should actively manage the dm-CMI to CMI ratio, even during an initial CMI trial. The authors suggest that this ratio would be kept to a minimum by initiating CMI only in the presence of fluvoxamine, a potent inhibitor of the P450 enzyme CYP1A2 that metabolizes CMI. This approach enables higher serum levels of CMI with lower dosage and related side effects. Moreover, by adding fluvoxamine to clomipramine rather than vice versa, the potential for exceeding safe levels of clomipramine is prevented. Monitoring serum levels of clomipramine as well as performing an ECG 7–10 days following each dose adjustment of fluvoxamine and clomipramine is advisable. Blood samples should be collected 12 hours post-clomipramine dose.

Please refer to Figure 14.2 for an example of how fluvoxamine co-administration alters the dm-CMI to CMI ratio in favor of CMI, with higher resultant CMI serum levels at a dose of 100 mg daily (with concurrent fluvoxamine) compared with 150 mg of clomipramine daily alone.

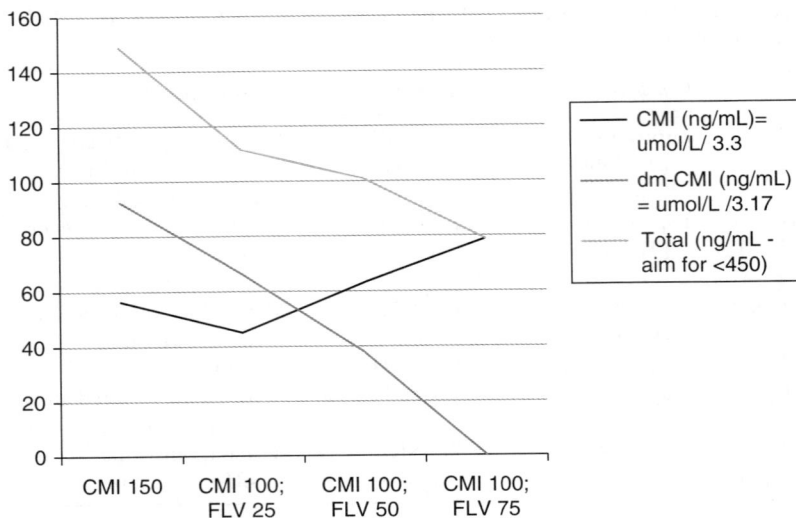

Figure 14.2 Effects of fluvoxamine co-administration on serum levels of clomipramine and desmethyl-clomipramine

SNRIs.   Because of their serotonin reuptake inhibition activity, SNRIs such as venlafaxine and duloxetine might be anticipated to be active in OCD. However, evidence from studies to support this has been limited and, to date, they have not received FDA approval for OCD treatment (Dell'Osso, Nestadt, Allen, & Hollander, 2006). In addition, as OCD treatment doses for serotonergic agents are generally higher than treatment doses for depression, the need to use SNRIs at higher dose ranges not only gives rise to adverse effects similar to SSRIs, but may also incur a risk of significant adverse effects in the sympathetic nervous system, such as blood pressure elevation.

Other medications.   Agents that have demonstrated possible benefits in OCD include mirtazapine (Koran, Gamel, Choung, Smith, & Aboujaoude, 2005) and psychostimulants (Joffe, Swinson, & Levitt, 1991). However, randomized controlled trials of these medications have not been conducted to date; nor have they been labeled by the FDA for use in OCD.

Treatment Trials and Duration

SSRIs are considered to be the best choice as a first-line OCD medication, unless contraindications present. While higher doses are required in OCD, as compared with their use in mood disorders (Bloch et al., 2010; Hollander et al., 2003), this should be balanced against tolerability. Hence, patients should be initiated at a low dose to minimize initial adverse effects, and gradually titrated upwards over an 8–12-week period. If an SSRI trial has continued with an adequate duration of treatment (at least three weeks at maximally tolerated dose with total trial > 8–12 weeks), and treatment response is poor or tolerability becomes an issue that limits dosing, a second SSRI monotherapy trial is advisable (Koran et al., 2007). In contrast to a frequent misapprehension that SSRIs are equally effective at an individual patient level, a 40% response rate can be expected for a second SSRI trial. However, the likelihood of treatment response diminishes as the number of failed adequate trials increases (Koran et al., 2007).

SRI Augmentation

SRI augmentation may be considered when monotherapy elicits only partial response (Table 14.2). Options for augmentation include the following:

1   *CBT.* Where CBT has not been used in combination with a first-line medication that resulted in partial or nonresponse, it should be used as an augmentation approach (Simpson et al., 2008; Tenneij, van Megen, Denys, & Westenberg, 2005). CBT augmentation of SSRIs was found to be more effective than augmentation with risperidone, especially among younger patients and those with increased OCD severity (Wheaton, Rosenfield, Foa, & Simpson, 2015).
2   *Atypical antipsychotics.* A number of studies have concluded that both first- and second-generation antipsychotics have efficacy in reducing OCD symptoms when used as augmenting agents (Bystritsky et al., 2004; Carey et al., 2005; McDougle et al., 1994). Two meta-analyses found that the evidence for efficacy was strongest for risperidone (Bloch et al., 2006; Dold, Aigner, Lanzenberger, & Kasper, 2013), with low required doses, although side effects such as metabolic syndrome and movement disorders were not uncommon. While the former meta-analysis suggested good evidence for haloperidol as an augmenting agent, the latter stated that evidence for this medication was inconsistent, in addition to findings regarding aripiprazole. Both stated that significant efficacy was not determined for olanzapine or quetiapine. However, uncontrolled studies (Connor, Payne, Gadde, Zhang, & Davidson, 2005) as well as two RCTs (Muscatello et al., 2011; Sayyah, Sayyah, Boostani, Ghaffari, & Hoseini, 2012) indicate that aripiprazole, with less associated weight gain, may also be a useful augmentation strategy. Overall, the meta-analysis by Dold et al. (2013) found that approximately one-third of SSRI resistant patients responded to antipsychotic augmentation.
3   *Benzodiazepines.* Clonazepam has not demonstrated effectiveness as OCD monotherapy in one RCT (Hollander, Kaplan, & Stahl, 2003). However, a cross-over study comparing clomipramine, clonazepam, and clonidine concluded that clonazepam may be useful (Hewlett, Vinogradov, & Agras, 1992).
4   *Glutamatergic agents.* Pharmacologic modulation of glutamatergic systems has been increasingly studied in OCD (Pittenger, 2015). Related options include: N-acetylcysteine (Lafleur et al., 2006), memantine (Aboujaoude, Barry, & Gamel, 2009; Kariuki-Nyuthe, Gomez-Mancilla, & Stein, 2014; Poyurovsky, Weizman, Weizman, & Koran, 2005; Stewart et al., 2010), riluzole (Coric et al., 2005), and minocycline (Rodriguez et al., 2010). At present, evidence supporting glutamatergic augmentation remains limited, and none of these have been FDA approved for OCD. A review of glutamergic agents published in 2014 concluded that while this class of agents held potential, further studies are needed (Kariuki-Nyuthe et al., 2014).
5   Other augmentation options with limited evidence include lithium, buspirone, clonazepam, L-triiodothyronine, pindolol, desipramine topiramate, d-amphetamine, and ondansetron. While the evidence supporting use of such augmentation agents is weak compared to antipsychotics, they may be preferable when antipsychotic-related adverse effects are problematic.

Somatic and Other Treatments

Somatic treatments.   In cases of treatment resistance and marked OCD severity, use of nonpharmacological physical treatment approaches may be considered, including electroconvulsive therapy (ECT) (only case studies and series published) ((Fontenelle et al., 2015), repetitive transcranial magnetic stimulation (rTMS) (Slotema, Blom, Hoek, & Sommer, 2010), deep brain stimulation (DBS) (Blomstedt, Sjöberg, Hansson, Bodlund, & Hariz, 2013; Goodman et al., 2010) and ablative psychosurgery, such as cingulotomy and anterior capsulotomy, which can now be performed using modern stereotactic gamma knife techniques (Sheehan, Patterson, Schlesinger, & Xu, 2013). A review by Atmaca (2013) summarizes evidence for these treatments.

Psychosocial and other treatments.   While this chapter does not aim to detail treatments utilizing psychological and social approaches to OCD management, it is pertinent to note that practical OCD management extensively involves such treatments, often in combination with medication. These include the following:

1   CBT is a first-line treatment option alongside serotonin agents, with approaches including exposure and response prevention (ERP) and cognitive therapy. A history of CBT is reported to increase clomipramine response rates, as well as reducing relapse rates from 45% to 12% (Foa et al., 2005).
2   D-Cycloserine, a partial agonist at the N-methyl-D-aspartate (NMDA) receptor, has been reported to reduce response time to ERP (Wilhelm et al., 2008). It is thought that this may be linked to enhanced fear extinction, as demonstrated by animal models. However, recent work suggests that its facilitating effect on fear extinction may be blocked by interaction with antidepressants, making its use more appropriate in the absence of SSRIs (Andersson et al., 2015).
3   Psychoeducation by the treatment provider is an important part of a clinical consultation.
4   Other therapies that have been studied include acceptance and commitment Therapy (ACT) (Twohig, 2012), motivational interviewing (Simpson et al., 2010), and intensive treatment (Brennan et al., 2014; Stewart et al., 2009).

Other Practical Aspects

Comorbidities.   The presence of comorbidities is the rule rather than the exception in OCD. OCD is a condition known to have a multitude of comorbidities, including anxiety, mood and psychotic disorders, tic disorders, and attention deficit-hyperactivity disorder (ADHD). It is important that comorbid conditions are identified early on such that treatment is planned accordingly to facilitate overall recovery. Fortuitously, antidepressants used for their antiobsessive effect are often helpful for some comorbidities such as depressive disorders and anxiety disorders. Table 14.3 lists suggestions for comorbidity management in OCD, based upon the authors' clinical experience.

Maintenance/Discontinuation

Extended trials of SSRIs and clomipramine have established that patients who continue taking medication experience lower rates of relapse than those who are switched to placebo. APA practice guidelines recommend that OCD patients responding to an adequate SRI trial of a serotonergic agent should continue maintenance medications for at least one to two years (Koran et al., 2007). Should discontinuation be chosen, the guidelines advise a gradual tapering of medications. Those benefitting from antipsychotic augmentation should be closely monitored during dose tapering and discontinuation due to associated risks of relapse (Maina, Albert, Ziero, & Bogetto, 2003).

Perhaps most important of all in optimizing long-term outcome is the effort to achieve full remission during initial OCD treatment, whether it be via CBT, SRI, or augmenting approaches. Illustrating this, the Brown Longitudinal Obsessive Compulsive Study (BLOCS) found that full remission following initial treatment had the largest impact on prevention of long-term relapse (Eisen et al., 2013).

Conclusion

OCD is a complex disease with biologic underpinnings that have been identified at macroscopic and microscopic levels. In contrast to outdated theories, biologic, environmental, learning and other contributors to OCD expression are not mutually exclusive. This chapter summarizes research findings related to the "biologic" etiology and treatment of OCD, which must be read in conjunction with other chapters of this book to gain a balanced understanding of this disease.

References

Aboujaoude, E., Barry, J. J., & Gamel, N. (2009). Memantine augmentation in treatment-resistant obsessive-compulsive disorder: An open-label trial. *Journal of Clinical Psychopharmacology, 29*(1), 51–55. doi: 10.1097/JCP.0b013e318192e9a4.

Ackerman, D. L., & Greenland, S. (2002). Multivariate meta-analysis of controlled drug studies for obsessive-compulsive disorder. *Journal of Clinical Psychopharmacology, 22*(3), 309–317. Retrieved from http://www.ncbi.nlm.nih.gov/pubmed/12006902.

Allen, A. J., Leonard, H. L., & Swedo, S. E. (1995). Case study: A new infection-triggered, autoimmune subtype of pediatric OCD and Tourette's syndrome. *Journal of the American Academy of Child and Adolescent Psychiatry, 34*(3), 307–311. doi: 10.1097/00004583-199503000-00015.

Alsobrook II, J. P., Leckman, J. F., Goodman, W. K., Rasmussen, S. A., & Pauls, D. L. (1999). Segregation analysis of obsessive-compulsive disorder using symptom-based factor scores. *American Journal of Medical Genetics, 88*(6), 669–675. Retrieved from http://www.ncbi.nlm.nih.gov/pubmed/10581488.

Andersson, E., Hedman, E., Enander, J., Radu Djurfeldt, D., Ljótsson, B., Cervenka, S., … Rück, C. (2015). d-Cycloserine vs. placebo as adjunct to cognitive behavioral therapy for obsessive-compulsive disorder and interaction with antidepressants: A randomized clinical trial. *JAMA Psychiatry, 72*(7), 659–667. doi: 10.1001/jamapsychiatry.2015.0546.

Asbahr, F. R., Ramos, R. T., Costa, A. N., & Sassi, R. B. (2005). Obsessive-compulsive symptoms in adults with history of rheumatic fever, Sydenham's chorea and type I diabetes mellitus: Preliminary results. *Acta Psychiatrica Scandinavica*, *111*(2), 159–161. doi: 10.1111/j.1600-0447.2004.00455.x.

Atmaca, M. (2013). Somatic treatments excluding psychopharmacology in obsessive-compulsive disorder: A review. *Review of Recent Clinical Trials*, *8*(2), 119–123.

Baxter, L. R., Thompson, J. M., Schwartz, J. M., Guze, B. H., Phelps, M. E., Mazziotta, J. C., … Moss, L. (1987). Trazodone treatment response in obsessive-compulsive disorder: Correlated with shifts in glucose metabolism in the caudate nuclei. *Psychopathology*, *20*(Suppl. 1), 114–122. Retrieved from http://www.ncbi.nlm.nih.gov/pubmed/3501130.

Behar, D., & Rapoport, J. L. (1984). Computer tomography and neuropsychological test measures in adolescents with obsessive compulsive disorder. *American Journal of Psychiatry*, *141*(3), 363–369. Retrieved from http://journals.psychiatryonline.org/data/Journals/AJP/3348/363.pdf.

Beucke, J. C., Sepulcre, J., Talukdar, T., Linnman, C., Zschenderlein, K., Endrass, T., … Kathmann, N. (2013). Abnormally high degree connectivity of the orbitofrontal cortex in obsessive-compulsive disorder. *JAMA Psychiatry*, *70*(6), 619–629. doi: 10.1001/jamapsychiatry.2013.173.

Bisserbe, J., Lane, R., & Flament, M. (1997). A double-blind comparison of sertraline and clomipramine in outpatients with obsessive-compulsive disorder. *European Psychiatry*, *12*(2), 82–93. doi: 10.1016/S0924-9338(97)89646-0.

Bloch, M. H., Landeros-Weisenberger, A., Kelmendi, B., Coric, V., Bracken, M. B., & Leckman, J. F. (2006). A systematic review: antipsychotic augmentation with treatment refractory obsessive-compulsive disorder. *Molecular Psychiatry*, *11*(7), 622–632. doi: 10.1038/sj.mp.4001823.

Bloch, M. H., Landeros-Weisenberger, A., Rosario, M. C., Pittenger, C., & Leckman, J. F. (2008). Meta-analysis of the symptom structure of obsessive-compulsive disorder. *American Journal of Psychiatry*, *165*(12), 1532–1542. doi: 10.1176/appi.ajp.2008.08020320.

Bloch, M. H., McGuire, J., Landeros-Weisenberger, A., Leckman, J. F., & Pittenger, C. (2010). Meta-analysis of the dose-response relationship of SSRI in obsessive-compulsive disorder. *Molecular Psychiatry*, *15*(8), 850–855. doi: 10.1038/mp.2009.50.

Blomstedt, P., Sjöberg, R. L., Hansson, M., Bodlund, O., & Hariz, M. I. (2013). Deep brain stimulation in the treatment of obsessive-compulsive disorder. *World Neurosurgery*, *80*(6), e245–e253. doi: 10.1016/j.wneu.2012.10.006.

Brennan, B. P., Lee, C., Elias, J. A., Crosby, J. M., Mathes, B. M., Andre, M-C., … Hudson, J. I. (2014). Intensive residential treatment for severe obsessive-compulsive disorder: Characterizing treatment course and predictors of response. *Journal of Psychiatric Research*, *56*, 98–105. doi: 10.1016/j.jpsychires.2014.05.008.

Bystritsky, A., Ackerman, D. L., Rosen, R. M., Vapnik, T., Gorbis, E., Maidment, K. M., & Saxena, S. (2004). Augmentation of serotonin reuptake inhibitors in refractory obsessive-compulsive disorder using adjunctive olanzapine: a placebo-controlled trial. *Journal of Clinical Psychiatry*, *65*(4), 565–568. Retrieved from http://www.ncbi.nlm.nih.gov/pubmed/15119922.

Cannistraro, P. A., Wright, C. I., Wedig, M. M., Martis, B., Shin, L. M., Wilhelm, S., & Rauch, S. L. (2004). Amygdala responses to human faces in obsessive-compulsive disorder. *Biological Psychiatry*, *56*(12), 916–920. doi: 10.1016/j.biopsych.2004.09.029.

Carey, P. D., Vythilingum, B., Seedat, S., Muller, J. E., van Ameringen, M., & Stein, D. J. (2005). Quetiapine augmentation of SRIs in treatment refractory obsessive-compulsive disorder: A double-blind, randomised, placebo-controlled study (ISRCTN83050762). *BMC Psychiatry*, *5*, 5. doi: 10.1186/1471-244X-5-5.

Carpenter, L. L., Heninger, G. R., McDougle, C. J., Tyrka, A. R., Epperson, C. N., & Price, L. H. (2002). Cerebrospinal fluid interleukin-6 in obsessive-compulsive disorder and trichotillomania. *Psychiatry Research, 112*(3), 257–262. Retrieved from http://www.ncbi. nlm.nih.gov/pubmed/12450635.

Cavallini, M. C., Pasquale, L., Bellodi, L., & Smeraldi, E. (1999). Complex segregation analysis for obsessive compulsive disorder and related disorders. *American Journal of Medical Genetics, 88*(1), 38–43. Retrieved from http://www.ncbi.nlm.nih.gov/pubmed/10050965.

Chamberlain, S. R., & Menzies, L. (2009). Endophenotypes of obsessive-compulsive disorder: rationale, evidence and future potential. *Expert Review of Neurotherapeutics, 9*(8), 1133–1146. doi: 10.1586/ern.09.36.

Chambert-Loir, C., Ouachee, M., Collins, K., Evrard, P., & Servais, L. (2009). Immediate relief of Mycoplasma pneumoniae encephalitis symptoms after intravenous immunoglobulin. *Pediatric Neurology, 41*(5), 375–377. doi: 10.1016/j.pediatrneurol.2009.05.008.

Connor, K. M., Payne, V. M., Gadde, K. M., Zhang, W., & Davidson, J. R. T. (2005). The use of aripiprazole in obsessive-compulsive disorder: Preliminary observations in 8 patients. *Journal of Clinical Psychiatry, 66*(1), 49–51. Retrieved from http://www.ncbi.nlm.nih. gov/pubmed/15669888.

Coric, V., Taskiran, S., Pittenger, C., Wasylink, S., Mathalon, D. H., Valentine, G., ... Krystal, J. H. (2005). Riluzole augmentation in treatment-resistant obsessive-compulsive disorder: An open-label trial. *Biological Psychiatry, 58*(5), 424–428. doi: 10.1016/j. biopsych.2005.04.043.

Cummings, J. L., & Cunningham, K. (1992). Obsessive-compulsive disorder in Huntington's disease. *Biological Psychiatry, 31*(3), 263–270. Retrieved from http://www.ncbi.nlm.nih. gov/pubmed/1532132.

Da Rocha, F. F., Correa, H., & Teixeira, A. L. (2008). Obsessive-compulsive disorder and immunology: A review. *Progress in Neuro-Psychopharmacology & Biological Psychiatry, 32*(5), 1139–1146. doi: 10.1016/j.pnpbp.2007.12.026.

Davis, L. K., Yu, D., Keenan, C. L., Gamazon, E. R., Konkashbaev, A. I., Derks, E. M., ... Scharf, J. M. (2013). Partitioning the heritability of Tourette syndrome and obsessive compulsive disorder reveals differences in genetic architecture. *PLoS Genetics, 9*(10), e1003864. doi: 10.1371/journal.pgen.1003864.

De Alvarenga, P. G., Floresi, A. C., Torres, A. R., Hounie, A. G., Fossaluza, V., Gentil, A. F., ... Miguel, E. C. (2009). Higher prevalence of obsessive-compulsive spectrum disorders in rheumatic fever. *General Hospital Psychiatry, 31*(2), 178–180. doi: 10.1016/j. genhosppsych.2008.11.003.

Decloedt, E. H., & Stein, D. J. (2010). Current trends in drug treatment of obsessive-compulsive disorder. *Neuropsychiatric Disease and Treatment, 6,* 233–242. Retrieved from http://www.pubmedcentral.nih.gov/articlerender.fcgi?artid=2877605&tool=pmcentrez&rendertype=abstract.

Dell'Osso, B., Nestadt, G., Allen, A., & Hollander, E. (2006). Serotonin–norepinephrine reuptake inhibitors in the treatment of obsessive-compulsive disorder: A critical review. *Journal of Clinical Psychiatry, 67*(4), 600–610. Retrieved from http://www.ncbi.nlm.nih. gov/pubmed/16669725.

Denys, D., de Vries, F., Cath, D., Figee, M., Vulink, N., Veltman, D. J., ... van Berckel, B. N. M. (2013). Dopaminergic activity in Tourette's syndrome and obsessive-compulsive disorder. *European Neuropsychopharmacology, 23*(11), 1423–1431. doi: 10.1016/j. euroneuro.2013.05.012.

Dinn, W. M., Harris, C. L., McGonigal, K. M., & Raynard, R. C. (2001). Obsessive-compulsive disorder and immunocompetence. *International Journal of Psychiatry in Medicine, 31*(3), 311–320. Retrieved from http://www.ncbi.nlm.nih.gov/pubmed/11841128.

Dold, M., Aigner, M., Lanzenberger, R., & Kasper, S. (2013). Antipsychotic augmentation of serotonin reuptake inhibitors in treatment-resistant obsessive-compulsive disorder: A meta-analysis of double-blind, randomized, placebo-controlled trials. *International Journal of Neuropsychopharmacology*, *16*(3), 557–574. doi: 10.1017/S1461145712000740.

Eisen, J. L., Sibrava, N. J., Boisseau, C. L., Mancebo, M. C., Stout, R. L., Pinto, A., & Rasmussen, S. A. (2013). Five-year course of obsessive-compulsive disorder: Predictors of remission and relapse. *Journal of Clinical Psychiatry*, *74*(3), 233–239. doi: 10.4088/JCP.12m07657.

Fallon, B. A., & Nields, J. A. (1994). Lyme disease: A neuropsychiatric illness. *American Journal of Psychiatry*, *151*(11), 1571–1583. Retrieved from http://www.ncbi.nlm.nih.gov/pubmed/7943444.

Fontenelle, L. F., Coutinho, E. S., Lins-Martins, N. M., Fitzgerald, P. B., Fujiwara, H., & Yücel, M. (2015). Electroconvulsive therapy for obsessive-compulsive disorder: A systematic review. *Journal of Clinical Psychiatry*, *76*(7), 949–957. doi: 10.4088/JCP.14r09129.

Foroughipour, M., Behdani, F., Hebrani, P., Marvast, M. N., Esmatinia, F., & Akhavanrezayat, A. (2012). Frequency of obsessive-compulsive disorder in patients with multiple sclerosis: A cross-sectional study. *Journal of Research in Medical Sciences*, *17*(3), 248–253. Retrieved from http://www.pubmedcentral.nih.gov/articlerender.fcgi?artid=3527042&tool=pmcentrez&rendertype=abstract.

Forray, A., Focseneanu, M., Pittman, B., McDougle, C. J., & Epperson, C. N. (2010). Onset and exacerbation of obsessive-compulsive disorder in pregnancy and the postpartum period. *Journal of Clinical Psychiatry*, *71*(8), 1061–1068. doi: 10.4088/JCP.09m05381blu.

Goodman, W. K., Foote, K. D., Greenberg, B. D., Ricciuti, N., Bauer, R., Ward, H., ... Okun, M. S. (2010). Deep brain stimulation for intractable obsessive compulsive disorder: Pilot study using a blinded, staggered-onset design. *Biological Psychiatry*, *67*(6), 535–542. doi: 10.1016/j.biopsych.2009.11.028.

Goodnick, P. J., & Goldstein, B. J. (1998). Selective serotonin reuptake inhibitors in affective disorders – I: Basic pharmacology. *Journal of Psychopharmacology*, *12*(3 Suppl. B), S5–S20. Retrieved from http://www.ncbi.nlm.nih.gov/pubmed/9808077.

Grados, M. A., Riddle, M. A., Samuels, J. F., Liang, K. Y., Hoehn-Saric, R., Bienvenu, O. J., ... Nestadt, G. (2001). The familial phenotype of obsessive-compulsive disorder in relation to tic disorders: The Hopkins OCD family study. *Biological Psychiatry*, *50*(8), 559–565. Retrieved from http://www.ncbi.nlm.nih.gov/pubmed/11690590.

Grados, M. A., Walkup, J., & Walford, S. (2003). Genetics of obsessive-compulsive disorders: New findings and challenges. *Brain & Development*, *25* (Suppl. 1), S55–S61. Retrieved from http://www.ncbi.nlm.nih.gov/pubmed/14980374.

Hammad, T. A., Laughren, T., & Racoosin, J. (2006). Suicidality in pediatric patients treated with antidepressant drugs. *Archives of General Psychiatry*, *63*(3), 332–339. doi: 10.1001/archpsyc.63.3.332.

Hansen, E. S., Hasselbalch, S., Law, I., & Bolwig, T. G. (2002). The caudate nucleus in obsessive-compulsive disorder: Reduced metabolism following treatment with paroxetine: a PET study. *International Journal of Neuropsychopharmacology*, *5*(01), 1–10. doi: 10.1017/S1461145701002681.

Hettema, J. M., Neale, M. C., & Kendler, K. S. (2001). A review and meta-analysis of the genetic epidemiology of anxiety disorders. *American Journal of Psychiatry*, *158*(10), 1568–1578. Retrieved from http://www.ncbi.nlm.nih.gov/pubmed/11578982.

Hewlett, W. A., Vinogradov, S., & Agras, W. S. (1992). Clomipramine, clonazepam, and clonidine treatment of obsessive-compulsive disorder. *Journal of Clinical Psychopharmacology*, *12*(6), 420–430. Retrieved from http://www.ncbi.nlm.nih.gov/pubmed/1474179.

Hollander, E., Allen, A., Steiner, M., Wheadon, D. E., Oakes, R., & Burnham, D. B. (2003). Acute and long-term treatment and prevention of relapse of obsessive-compulsive disorder with paroxetine. *Journal of Clinical Psychiatry, 64*(9), 1113–1121. Retrieved from http://www.ncbi.nlm.nih.gov/pubmed/14628989.

Hollander, E., Kaplan, A., Schmeidler, J., Yang, H., Li, D., Koran, L. M., & Barbato, L. M. (2005). Neurological soft signs as predictors of treatment response to selective serotonin reuptake inhibitors in obsessive-compulsive disorder. *Journal of Neuropsychiatry and Clinical Neurosciences, 17*(4), 472–477. doi: 10.1176/appi.neuropsych.17.4.472.

Hollander, E., Kaplan, A., & Stahl, S. M. (2003). A double-blind, placebo-controlled trial of clonazepam in obsessive-compulsive disorder. *World Journal of Biological Psychiatry, 4*(1), 30–34. Retrieved from http://www.ncbi.nlm.nih.gov/pubmed/12582975.

Hollander, E., Schiffman, E., Cohen, B., Rivera-Stein, M. A., Rosen, W., Gorman, J. M., ... Liebowitz, M. R. (1990). Signs of central nervous system dysfunction in obsessive-compulsive disorder. *Archives of General Psychiatry, 47*(1), 27–32. Retrieved from http://www.ncbi.nlm.nih.gov/pubmed/2294853.

Homberg, J. R. (2012). Serotonin and decision making processes. *Neuroscience and Biobehavioral Reviews, 36*(1), 218–236. doi: 10.1016/j.neubiorev.2011.06.001.

Insel, T. R., Mueller, E. A., Alterman, I., Linnoila, M., & Murphy, D. L. (1985). Obsessive-compulsive disorder and serotonin: Is there a connection? *Biological Psychiatry, 20*(11), 1174–1188. Retrieved from http://www.ncbi.nlm.nih.gov/pubmed/2413912.

Jaafari, N., Fernández de la Cruz, L., Grau, M., Knowles, E., Radua, J., Wooderson, S., ... Mataix-Cols, D. (2013). Neurological soft signs in obsessive-compulsive disorder: Two empirical studies and meta-analysis. *Psychological Medicine, 43*(5), 1069–1079. doi: 10.1017/S0033291712002012.

Jenike, M. A. (1998). Neurosurgical treatment of obsessive-compulsive disorder. *British Journal of Psychiatry, 35*(Suppl.), 79–90. Retrieved from http://www.ncbi.nlm.nih.gov/pubmed/9829030.

Jenike, M. A., Hyman, S., Baer, L., Holland, A., Minichiello, W. E., Buttolph, L., ... Ricciardi, J. (1990). A controlled trial of fluvoxamine in obsessive-compulsive disorder: implications for a serotonergic theory. *American Journal of Psychiatry, 147*(9), 1209–1215. Retrieved from http://www.ncbi.nlm.nih.gov/pubmed/2143637.

Jenike, M. A., Rauch, S. L., Cummings, J. L., Savage, C. R., & Goodman, W. K. (1996). Recent developments in neurobiology of obsessive-compulsive disorder. *Journal of Clinical Psychiatry, 57*(10), 492–503. Retrieved from http://www.ncbi.nlm.nih.gov/pubmed/8909341.

Joffe, R. T., Swinson, R. P., & Levitt, A. J. (1991). Acute psychostimulant challenge in primary obsessive-compulsive disorder. *Journal of Clinical Psychopharmacology, 11*(4), 237–241. Retrieved from http://www.ncbi.nlm.nih.gov/pubmed/1680885.

Kalra, S. K., & Swedo, S. E. (2009). Children with obsessive-compulsive disorder: Are they just "little adults"? *Journal of Clinical Investigation, 119*(4), 737–746. doi: 10.1172/JCI37563

Kang, D-H., Jang, J. H., Han, J. Y., Kim, J-H., Jung, W. H., Choi, J-S., ... Kwon, J. S. (2013). Neural correlates of altered response inhibition and dysfunctional connectivity at rest in obsessive-compulsive disorder. *Progress in Neuro-Psychopharmacology & Biological Psychiatry, 40*, 340–346. doi: 10.1016/j.pnpbp.2012.11.001.

Kariuki-Nyuthe, C., Gomez-Mancilla, B., & Stein, D. J. (2014). Obsessive compulsive disorder and the glutamatergic system. *Current Opinion in Psychiatry, 27*(1), 32–37. doi: 10.1097/YCO.0000000000000017.

Koran, L. M., Gamel, N. N., Choung, H. W., Smith, E. H., & Aboujaoude, E. N. (2005). Mirtazapine for obsessive-compulsive disorder: An open trial followed by double-blind discontinuation. *Journal of Clinical Psychiatry, 66*(4), 515–520. Retrieved from http://www.ncbi.nlm.nih.gov/pubmed/15816795.

Koran, L. M., Hanna, G. L., Hollander, E., Nestadt, G., & Simpson, H. B. (2007). Practice guideline for the treatment of patients with obsessive-compulsive disorder. *American Journal of Psychiatry*, *164*(7 Suppl.), 5–53. Retrieved from http://www.ncbi.nlm.nih.gov/pubmed/17849776.

Koran, L. M., McElroy, S. L., Davidson, J. R., Rasmussen, S. A., Hollander, E., & Jenike, M. A. (1996). Fluvoxamine versus clomipramine for obsessive-compulsive disorder: A double-blind comparison. *Journal of Clinical Psychopharmacology*, *16*(2), 121–129. Retrieved from http://www.ncbi.nlm.nih.gov/pubmed/8690827.

Labad, J., Menchón, J. M., Alonso, P., Segalàs, C., Jiménez, S., & Vallejo, J. (2005). Female reproductive cycle and obsessive-compulsive disorder. *Journal of Clinical Psychiatry*, *66*(4), 428–435, quiz 546. Retrieved from http://www.ncbi.nlm.nih.gov/pubmed/15816784.

Lafleur, D. L., Pittenger, C., Kelmendi, B., Gardner, T., Wasylink, S., Malison, R. T., … Coric, V. (2006). N-acetylcysteine augmentation in serotonin reuptake inhibitor refractory obsessive-compulsive disorder. *Psychopharmacology*, *184*(2), 254–256. doi: 10.1007/s00213-005-0246-6.

López-Ibor, J. J., Saiz, J., Cottraux, J., Note, I., Viñas, R., Bourgeois, M., … Gómez-Pérez, J. C. (1996). Double-blind comparison of fluoxetine versus clomipramine in the treatment of obsessive compulsive disorder. *European Neuropsychopharmacology*, *6*(2), 111–118. Retrieved from http://www.ncbi.nlm.nih.gov/pubmed/8791036.

Maina, G., Albert, U., Ziero, S., & Bogetto, F. (2003). Antipsychotic augmentation for treatment resistant obsessive-compulsive disorder: What if antipsychotic is discontinued? *International Clinical Psychopharmacology*, *18*(1), 23–28. doi: 10.1097/01.yic.0000047784.24295.2b.

Marazziti, D., Presta, S., Pfanner, C., Gemignani, A., Rossi, A., Sbrana, S., … Cassano, G. B. (1999). Immunological alterations in adult obsessive-compulsive disorder. *Biological Psychiatry*, *46*(6), 810–814. Retrieved from http://www.ncbi.nlm.nih.gov/pubmed/10494449.

Mataix-Cols, D., & van den Heuvel, O. A. (2006). Common and distinct neural correlates of obsessive-compulsive and related disorders. *Psychiatric Clinics of North America*, *29*(2), 391–410, viii. doi: 10.1016/j.psc.2006.02.006.

McDougle, C. J., Goodman, W. K., Leckman, J. F., Lee, N. C., Heninger, G. R., & Price, L. H. (1994). Haloperidol addition in fluvoxamine-refractory obsessive-compulsive disorder: A double-blind, placebo-controlled study in patients with and without tics. *Archives of General Psychiatry*, *51*(4), 302–308. Retrieved from http://www.ncbi.nlm.nih.gov/pubmed/8161290.

Melloni, M., Urbistondo, C., Sedeño, L., Gelormini, C., Kichic, R., & Ibanez, A. (2012). The extended fronto-striatal model of obsessive compulsive disorder: Convergence from event-related potentials, neuropsychology and neuroimaging. *Frontiers in Human Neuroscience*, *6*, 259. doi: 10.3389/fnhum.2012.00259.

Mercadante, M. T., Busatto, G. F., Lombroso, P. J., Prado, L., Rosário-Campos, M. C., do Valle, R., … Miguel, E. C. (2000). The psychiatric symptoms of rheumatic fever. *American Journal of Psychiatry*, *157*(12), 2036–2038. Retrieved from http://www.ncbi.nlm.nih.gov/pubmed/11097972.

Miguel, E. C., do Rosário-Campos, M. C., Prado, H. S., do Valle, R., Rauch, S. L., Coffey, B. J., … Leckman, J. F. (2000). Sensory phenomena in obsessive-compulsive disorder and Tourette's disorder. *Journal of Clinical Psychiatry*, *61*(2), 150–156, quiz 157. Retrieved from http://www.ncbi.nlm.nih.gov/pubmed/10732667.

Milad, M. R., & Rauch, S. L. (2012). Obsessive-compulsive disorder: Beyond segregated cortico-striatal pathways. *Trends in Cognitive Sciences*, *16*(1), 43–51. doi: 10.1016/j.tics.2011.11.003.

Mittleman, B. B., Castellanos, F. X., Jacobsen, L. K., Rapoport, J. L., Swedo, S. E., & Shearer, G. M. (1997). Cerebrospinal fluid cytokines in pediatric neuropsychiatric disease. *Journal of Immunology*, *159*(6), 2994–2999. Retrieved from http://www.ncbi.nlm.nih.gov/pubmed/9300724.

Monteleone, P., Catapano, F., Fabrazzo, M., Tortorella, A., & Maj, M. (1998). Decreased blood levels of tumor necrosis factor-alpha in patients with obsessive-compulsive disorder. *Neuropsychobiology*, 37(4), 182–185. Retrieved from http://www.ncbi.nlm.nih.gov/pubmed/9648125.

Muir, K. E., McKenney, K. S., Connolly, M. B., & Stewart, S. E. (2013). A case report of obsessive-compulsive disorder following acute disseminated encephalomyelitis. *Pediatrics*, 132(3), e771–e774. doi: 10.1542/peds.2012-2876.

Müller, N., Putz, A., Kathmann, N., Lehle, R., Günther, W., & Straube, A. (1997). Characteristics of obsessive-compulsive symptoms in Tourette's syndrome, obsessive-compulsive disorder, and Parkinson's disease. *Psychiatry Research*, 70(2), 105–114. Retrieved from http://www.ncbi.nlm.nih.gov/pubmed/9194204.

Murphy, D. L., & Pigott, T. A. (1990). A comparative examination of a role for serotonin in obsessive compulsive disorder, panic disorder, and anxiety. *Journal of Clinical Psychiatry*, 5 (Suppl.), 53–58, discussion 59–60. Retrieved from http://www.ncbi.nlm.nih.gov/pubmed/2139026.

Murphy, D. L., Zohar, J., Benkelfat, C., Pato, M. T., Pigott, T. A., & Insel, T. R. (1989). Obsessive-compulsive disorder as a 5-HT subsystem-related behavioural disorder. *British Journal of Psychiatry*. Supplement 8, 15–24. Retrieved from http://www.ncbi.nlm.nih.gov/pubmed/2692636.

Murphy, T. K., Gerardi, D. M., & Leckman, J. F. (2014). Pediatric Acute-Onset Neuropsychiatric Syndrome. *Psychiatric Clinics of North America*, 37(3), 353–374. doi: 10.1016/j.psc.2014.06.001.

Murphy, T. K., Kurlan, R., & Leckman, J. (2010). The immunobiology of Tourette's disorder, pediatric autoimmune neuropsychiatric disorders associated with streptococcus, and related disorders: A way forward. *Journal of Child and Adolescent Psychopharmacology*, 20(4), 317–331. doi: 10.1089/cap.2010.0043.

Muscatello, M. R. A., Bruno, A., Pandolfo, G., Micò, U., Scimeca, G., Romeo, V. M., … Zoccali, R. A. (2011). Effect of aripiprazole augmentation of serotonin reuptake inhibitors or clomipramine in treatment-resistant obsessive-compulsive disorder: A double-blind, placebo-controlled study. *Journal of Clinical Psychopharmacology*, 31(2), 174–179. doi: 10.1097/JCP.0b013e31820e3db6.

Nakao, T., Okada, K., & Kanba, S. (2014). Neurobiological model of obsessive-compulsive disorder: Evidence from recent neuropsychological and neuroimaging findings. *Psychiatry and Clinical Neurosciences*, 68(8), 587–605. doi: 10.1111/pcn.12195.

Nestadt, G., Lan, T., Samuels, J., Riddle, M., Bienvenu, O. J., Liang, K. Y., … Shugart, Y. Y. (2000). Complex segregation analysis provides compelling evidence for a major gene underlying obsessive-compulsive disorder and for heterogeneity by sex. *American Journal of Human Genetics*, 67(6), 1611–1616. doi: 10.1086/316898.

Pauls, D. L. (2010). The genetics of obsessive-compulsive disorder: A review. *Dialogues in Clinical Neuroscience*, 12(2), 149–163. Retrieved from http://www.pubmedcentral.nih.gov/articlerender.fcgi?artid=3181951&tool=pmcentrez&rendertype=abstract.

Pauls, D. L., Towbin, K. E., Leckman, J. F., Zahner, G. E., & Cohen, D. J. (1986). Gilles de la Tourette's syndrome and obsessive-compulsive disorder: Evidence supporting a genetic relationship. *Archives of General Psychiatry*, 43(12), 1180–1182. Retrieved from http://www.ncbi.nlm.nih.gov/pubmed/3465280.

Pinto, A., Mancebo, M. C., Eisen, J. L., Pagano, M. E., & Rasmussen, S. A. (2006). The Brown Longitudinal Obsessive Compulsive Study: Clinical features and symptoms of the sample at intake. *Journal of Clinical Psychiatry*, 67(5), 703–711.

Pittenger, C., Bloch, M. H., & Williams, K. (2011). Glutamate abnormalities in obsessive-compulsive disorder: Neurobiology, pathophysiology, and treatment. *Pharmacology & Therapeutics*, 132(3), 314–332. doi: 10.1016/j.pharmthera.2011.09.006.

Pittenger, C. (2015). Glutamate modulators in the treatment of obsessive-compulsive disorder. *Psychiatric Annals*, 45(6), 308–315. doi: 10.3928/00485713-20150602-06.

Poyurovsky, M., Weizman, R., Weizman, A., & Koran, L. (2005). Memantine for treatment-resistant OCD. *American Journal of Psychiatry, 162*(11), 2191–2192. doi: 10.1176/appi.ajp.162.11.2191-a.

Prado, H. S., Rosário, M. C., Lee, J., Hounie, A. G., Shavitt, R. G., & Miguel, E. C. (2008). Sensory phenomena in obsessive-compulsive disorder and tic disorders: A review of the literature. *CNS Spectrums, 13*(5), 425–432. Retrieved from http://www.ncbi.nlm.nih.gov/pubmed/18496480.

Rapoport, J. L., Ryland, D. H., & Kriete, M. (1992). Drug treatment of canine acral lick: An animal model of obsessive-compulsive disorder. *Archives of General Psychiatry, 49*(7), 517–521. Retrieved from http://www.ncbi.nlm.nih.gov/pubmed/1385694.

Rauch, S. L., & Britton, J. C. (2010). Developmental neuroimaging studies of OCD: The maturation of a field. *Journal of the American Academy of Child and Adolescent Psychiatry, 49*(12), 1186–1188. doi: 10.1016/j.jaac.2010.08.016.

Rauch, S. L., Whalen, P. J., Curran, T., McInerney, S., Heckers, S., & Savage, C. R. (1998). Thalamic deactivation during early implicit sequence learning: A functional MRI study. *Neuroreport, 9*(5), 865–870. Retrieved from http://www.ncbi.nlm.nih.gov/pubmed/9579681.

Rodriguez, C. I., Bender, J., Marcus, S. M., Snape, M., Rynn, M., & Simpson, H. B. (2010). Minocycline augmentation of pharmacotherapy in obsessive-compulsive disorder: An open-label trial. *Journal of Clinical Psychiatry, 71*(9), 1247–1249. doi: 10.4088/JCP.09l05805blu.

Ruscio, A. M., Stein, D. J., Chiu, W. T., & Kessler, R. C. (2010). The epidemiology of obsessive-compulsive disorder in the National Comorbidity Survey Replication. *Molecular Psychiatry, 15*(1), 53–63. doi: 10.1038/mp.2008.94.

Sampaio, A. S., Fagerness, J., Crane, J., Leboyer, M., Delorme, R., Pauls, D. L., & Stewart, S. E. (2011). Association between polymorphisms in GRIK2 gene and obsessive-compulsive disorder: A family-based study. *CNS Neuroscience & Therapeutics, 17*(3), 141–147. doi: 10.1111/j.1755-5949.2009.00130.x.

Sampaio, A. S., McCarthy, K. D., Mancuso, E., Stewart, S. E., & Geller, D. A. (2014). Validation of the University of São Paulo's Sensory Phenomena Scale – English version. *Comprehensive Psychiatry, 55*(5), 1330–1336. doi: 10.1016/j.comppsych.2014.02.008.

Saxena, S., & Rauch, S. L. (2000). Functional neuroimaging and the neuroanatomy of obsessive-compulsive disorder. *Psychiatric Clinics of North America, 23*(3), 563–586. Retrieved from http://www.ncbi.nlm.nih.gov/pubmed/10986728.

Sayyah, M., Sayyah, M., Boostani, H., Ghaffari, S. M., & Hoseini, A. (2012). Effects of aripiprazole augmentation in treatment-resistant obsessive-compulsive disorder (a double blind clinical trial). *Depression and Anxiety, 29*(10), 850–854. doi: 10.1002/da.21996.

Shapira, N. A., Ward, H. E., Mandoki, M., Murphy, T. K., Yang, M. C. K., Blier, P., & Goodman, W. K. (2004). A double-blind, placebo-controlled trial of olanzapine addition in fluoxetine-refractory obsessive-compulsive disorder. *Biological Psychiatry, 55*(5), 553–555. doi: 10.1016/j.biopsych.2003.11.010.

Shaw, P., Sharp, W., Sudre, G., Wharton, A., Greenstein, D., Raznahan, A., ... Rapoport, J. (2015). Subcortical and cortical morphological anomalies as an endophenotype in obsessive-compulsive disorder. *Molecular Psychiatry, 20*(2), 224–231. doi: 10.1038/mp.2014.3.

Sheehan, J. P., Patterson, G., Schlesinger, D., & Xu, Z. (2013). γ knife surgery anterior capsulotomy for severe and refractory obsessive-compulsive disorder. *Journal of Neurosurgery, 119*(5), 1112–1118. doi: 10.3171/2013.5.JNS13201.

Shin, D-J., Jung, W. H., He, Y., Wang, J., Shim, G., Byun, M. S., ... Kwon, J. S. (2014). The effects of pharmacological treatment on functional brain connectome in obsessive-compulsive disorder. *Biological Psychiatry, 75*(8), 606–614. doi: 10.1016/j.biopsych.2013.09.002.

Simpson, H. B., Foa, E. B., Liebowitz, M. R., Ledley, D. R., Huppert, J. D., Cahill, S., ... Petkova, E. (2008). A randomized, controlled trial of cognitive-behavioral therapy for augmenting pharmacotherapy in obsessive-compulsive disorder. *American Journal of Psychiatry, 165*(5), 621–630. doi: 10.1176/appi.ajp.2007.07091440.

Simpson, H. B., Slifstein, M., Bender, J., Xu, X., Hackett, E., Maher, M. J., & Abi-Dargham, A. (2011). Serotonin 2A receptors in obsessive-compulsive disorder: A positron emission tomography study with [11C]MDL 100907. *Biological Psychiatry, 70*(9), 897–904. doi: 10.1016/j.biopsych.2011.06.023.

Simpson, H. B., Zuckoff, A. M., Maher, M. J., Page, J. R., Franklin, M. E., Foa, E. B., ... Wang, Y. (2010). Challenges using motivational interviewing as an adjunct to exposure therapy for obsessive-compulsive disorder. *Behaviour Research and Therapy, 48*(10), 941–948. doi: 10.1016/j.brat.2010.05.026.

Slotema, C. W., Blom, J. D., Hoek, H. W., & Sommer, I. E. C. (2010). Should we expand the toolbox of psychiatric treatment methods to include Repetitive Transcranial Magnetic Stimulation (rTMS)? A meta-analysis of the efficacy of rTMS in psychiatric disorders. *Journal of Clinical Psychiatry, 71*(7), 873–884. doi: 10.4088/JCP.08m04872gre.

Soomro, G. M., Altman, D., Rajagopal, S., & Oakley-Browne, M. (2008). Selective serotonin re-uptake inhibitors (SSRIs) versus placebo for obsessive compulsive disorder (OCD). *Cochrane Database of Systematic Reviews, (1)*, CD001765. doi: 10.1002/14651858. CD001765.pub3

Stern, T. A., Fava, M., Wilens, T. E., & Rosenbaum, J. F. (2015). *Massachusetts General Hospital comprehensive clinical psychiatry.* Oxford: Elsevier Health Sciences.

Stewart, S. E., Fagerness, J. A., Platko, J., Smoller, J. W., Scharf, J. M., Illmann, C., ... Pauls, D. L. (2007). Association of the SLC1A1 glutamate transporter gene and obsessive-compulsive disorder. *American Journal of Medical Genetics. Part B, Neuropsychiatric Genetics, 144B*(8), 1027–1033. doi: 10.1002/ajmg.b.30533.

Stewart, S. E., Jenike, E. A., Hezel, D. M., Stack, D. E., Dodman, N. H., Shuster, L., & Jenike, M. A. (2010). A single-blinded case-control study of memantine in severe obsessive-compulsive disorder. *Journal of Clinical Psychopharmacology, 30*(1), 34–39. doi: 10.1097/JCP.0b013e3181c856de.

Stewart, S. E., Stack, D. E., Tsilker, S., Alosso, J., Stephansky, M., Hezel, D. M., ... Jenike, M. A. (2009). Long-term outcome following intensive residential treatment of obsessive-compulsive disorder. *Journal of Psychiatric Research, 43*(13), 1118–1123. doi: S0022-3956(09)00072-7 [pii]10.1016/j.jpsychires.2009.03.012.

Stewart, S. E., Yu, D., Scharf, J. M., Neale, B. M., Fagerness, J. A., Mathews, C. A., ... Pauls, D. L. (2013). Genome-wide association study of obsessive-compulsive disorder. *Molecular Psychiatry, 18*(7), 788–798. doi: 10.1038/mp.2012.85.

Swedo, S. E., Pietrini, P., Leonard, H. L., Schapiro, M. B., Rettew, D. C., Goldberger, E. L., ... Grady, C. L. (1992). Cerebral glucose metabolism in childhood-onset obsessive-compulsive disorder: Revisualization during pharmacotherapy. *Archives of General Psychiatry, 49*(9), 690–694. Retrieved from http://www.ncbi.nlm.nih.gov/pubmed/1514873.

Szeszko, P. R., Ardekani, B. A., Ashtari, M., Malhotra, A. K., Robinson, D. G., Bilder, R. M., & Lim, K. O. (2005). White matter abnormalities in obsessive-compulsive disorder: a diffusion tensor imaging study. *Archives of General Psychiatry, 62*(7), 782–790. doi: 10.1001/archpsyc.62.7.782.

Tauscher-Wisniewski, S., Disch, D., Plewes, J., Ball, S., & Beasley, C. M. (2007). Evaluating suicide-related adverse events in clinical trials of fluoxetine treatment in adults for indications other than major depressive disorder. *Psychological Medicine, 37*(11), 1585–1593. doi: 10.1017/S0033291707001146.

Tenneij, N. H., van Megen, H. J. G. M., Denys, D. A. J. P., & Westenberg, H. G. M. (2005). Behavior therapy augments response of patients with obsessive-compulsive disorder responding to drug treatment. *Journal of Clinical Psychiatry, 66*(9), 1169–1175. Retrieved from http://www.ncbi.nlm.nih.gov/pubmed/16187776.

Tonkonogy, J. M., Smith, T. W., & Barreira, P. J. (1994). Obsessive-compulsive disorders in Pick's disease. *Journal of Neuropsychiatry and Clinical Neurosciences*, *6*(2), 176–180. Retrieved from http://www.ncbi.nlm.nih.gov/pubmed/8044041.

Van Ameringen, M., Simpson, W., Patterson, B., Dell'Osso, B., Fineberg, N., Hollander, E., … Zohar, J. (2014). Pharmacological treatment strategies in obsessive compulsive disorder: A cross-sectional view in nine international OCD centers. *Journal of Psychopharmacology*, *28*(6), 596–602. doi: 10.1177/0269881113517955.

Van den Heuvel, O. A., Remijnse, P. L., Mataix-Cols, D., Vrenken, H., Groenewegen, H. J., Uylings, H. B. M., … Veltman, D. J. (2009). The major symptom dimensions of obsessive-compulsive disorder are mediated by partially distinct neural systems. *Brain: A Journal of Neurology*, *132*(4), 853–868. doi: 10.1093/brain/awn267.

Van Grootheest, D. S., Cath, D. C., Beekman, A. T., & Boomsma, D. I. (2005). Twin studies on obsessive-compulsive disorder: A review. *Twin Research and Human Genetics*, *8*(5), 450–458. doi: 10.1375/183242705774310060.

Van Grootheest, D. S., Cath, D. C., Beekman, A. T., & Boomsma, D. I. (2007). Genetic and environmental influences on obsessive-compulsive symptoms in adults: A population-based twin-family study. *Psychological Medicine*, *37*(11), 1635–1644. doi: 10.1017/S0033291707000980.

Wheaton, M. G., Rosenfield, D., Foa, E. B., & Simpson, H. B. (2015). Augmenting Serotonin reuptake inhibitors in obsessive-compulsive disorder: What moderates improvement? *Journal of Consultative & Clinical Psychology*. doi: 10.1037/ccp0000025.

Wilhelm, S., Buhlmann, U., Tolin, D. F., Meunier, S. A., Pearlson, G. D., Reese, H. E., … Rauch, S. L. (2008). Augmentation of behavior therapy with D-cycloserine for obsessive-compulsive disorder. *American Journal of Psychiatry*, *165*(3), 335–341, quiz 409. doi: 10.1176/appi.ajp.2007.07050776.

Wu, K., Hanna, G. L., Rosenberg, D. R., & Arnold, P. D. (2012). The role of glutamate signaling in the pathogenesis and treatment of obsessive-compulsive disorder. *Pharmacology, Biochemistry, and Behavior*, *100*(4), 726–735. doi: 10.1016/j.pbb.2011.10.007.

Zohar, J., Chopra, M., Sasson, Y., Amiaz, R., & Amital, D. (2000). Obsessive compulsive disorder: Serotonin and beyond. *World Journal of Biological Psychiatry*, *1*(2), 92–100. Retrieved from http://www.ncbi.nlm.nih.gov/pubmed/12607204.

Zohar, J., & Judge, R. (1996). Paroxetine versus clomipramine in the treatment of obsessive-compulsive disorder: OCD Paroxetine Study Investigators. *British Journal of Psychiatry*, *169*(4), 468–474. Retrieved from http://www.ncbi.nlm.nih.gov/pubmed/8894198.

15

Neurobiological and Neurodevelopmental Perspectives on OCD and their Clinical Implications

Tord Ivarsson, Bernhard Weidle, Gudmundur Skarphedinsson, and Robert Valderhaug

In this chapter, we will first consider what is known about the phenomenology of obsessive compulsive disorder (OCD), its course, and what model or understanding of OCD pathogenesis is most appropriate. Then, we will discuss what implications this understanding has for the way we should organize the care of our patients. Our understanding of pediatric OCD has undergone decisive changes across the last 50 years. Emminghaus' (1887) descriptions of child cases with OCD, showed phenomenological precision and interesting speculations on etiology that could even be taken from current literature, particularly his realization that the brain engagement was diffuse or widespread rather than focal. However, the first half of the twentieth century with its psychoanalytic period has left little impact, and it was not until the second half the century that psychological thinking based on learning theory became the main basis for understanding OCD (Foa, 2010). Its success was based on its usefulness; cognitive behavior therapy is unrivalled as a clinical tool with impressive efficacy (Abramowitz, Whiteside, & Deacon, 2005a; Watson & Rees, 2008). (See also Chapter 12 in this volume and a critical review by Skarphedinsson et al., 2015b). However, even though learning theory gives a fair understanding of what maintains, or worsens, OCD (Rachman, De Silva, & Roper, 1976), it provides no understanding of its onset or pathogenesis (Abramowitz, Taylor, & McKay, 2007; Carr, 1974; Rachman & Hodgson, 1980).

OCD Phenomenology and Neurobiology

Our current definition of OCD in accordance with the DSM-5 is that OCD rituals are goal-directed behaviors aimed at neutralizing (perceived) dangers and/or reducing anxieties, disgust, and other unpleasant feelings (American Psychiatric Association, 2013).

The Wiley Handbook of Obsessive Compulsive Disorders, Volume I, First Edition.
Edited by Jonathan S. Abramowitz, Dean McKay, and Eric A. Storch.
© 2017 John Wiley & Sons Ltd. Published 2017 by John Wiley & Sons Ltd.

The obsessions are thus embedded within the "goals" of the ritual, for example, fear of bacilli are an integral part of the rituals goal to rid the hands of the bacilli. Moreover, some rituals have little cognitive content, such as repetitions, touching, or arranging things until "it feels right" or has to be done in accordance to strict rules (American Psychiatric Association, 2013). The latter two examples show less cognitive content and are not typical goals within goal-directed behaviors. In this chapter, we focus on those OCD symptoms that fit in well with the first definition, that is, rituals as goal directed behavior and discuss how neurobiology provides valuable perspectives.

Goal-directed Behaviors

The human capacity for goal-directed behaviors developed as the frontal lobes became enlarged across evolution. It is a multipurpose system that satisfies many different needs (access to food and water, sex, social relations, security, etc.) and flexibly takes into account the risk or cost of different actions and the need to change behavior as circumstances demand (S. de Wit et al., 2012; Dickinson, 1985; Haber & Knutson, 2010; Teffer & Semendeferi, 2012). Goal-directed behaviors are more characteristic of humans than other animals, including the primates. The system that enables these behaviors has been defined to "encode the relationship between actions and their consequences" (S. de Wit et al., 2012). It promotes the flexibility to behave to achieve what is regarded by the individual as desirable, that is, to what is rewarding taking potential risks into consideration.

A goal-directed behavior is characterized by a goal that replaces the more direct instinct or need-driven drives that is typical for most animals. It differs as well from habit-driven behaviors, that is, instrumental behaviors that have been conditioned repeatedly so the presence of the stimulus triggers the behavior automatically. Thus, it is cognitively labeled, and provided with an affect that is associated with the ultimate "goal" of the goal, be it avoiding a fearsome situation, gaining food, or access to a sexual partner. The positive affects/emotions are part of the reward "system" that provides powerful incentives for behaviors (Haber, 2011; Haber & Knutson, 2010). Many different behaviors may lead to the ultimate goal, and a choice has to be made as to which behavior, which then is disinhibited, is most likely to reach the goal. Moreover, the person needs to inhibit behaviors that are unlikely to reach the goal, or which are in conflict with other important goals, for example, leading to conflict, jail, or to being socially outcast. It is a complicated computational problem to reach a suitable compromise, and it is not strange that many child psychiatric syndromes are characteristic of failures of different kinds on the way to these compromises. Finally, once the goal has been reached, it must be recognized as a fact, and all behaviors leading to the goal are inhibited again. A review of this system can be found in several papers, for example, C. A. de Wit & Dickinson (2009),; Grahn, Parkinson, & Owen (2009); Gremel & Costa (2013); Haber (2011); and Haber & Rauch (2010).

Goal-directed behaviors are resource-demanding, not the least of attention and of working memory. Thus, in accordance with the "dual theory" for human behavior, a complementary and computationally simpler system – the habit-based system – takes over once complex behaviors have been mastered (C. A. de Wit & Dickinson, 2009). Such habits are effective in stable situations. However, they can easily be decoupled from their original usefulness and be repeated (often unawares) in spite of changing circumstances, for example, when you drive the usual way to work though you know that road work makes another route faster.

The brain systems that underlie the capacity for goal-directed behaviors are connected into loops (Alexander & Crutcher, 1990). A detailed description of these loops and how they function is beyond the scope of this chapter (see a cognitive neuroscience text, e.g., Gazzaniga, Ivry, and Mangun (2013). Shortly, each loop, has a cortical node (e.g., the orbitofrontal cortex [OFC]), a connection to a specific part of striatum (e.g., the caudate nucleus), which connects to a specific part of the thalamus. Thalamus connects back to the same cortical region (e.g., OFC). Each loop has specific functional significance(s) and does not work in isolation, their integration toward smooth functioning is done through the different cortical nodes' connection to other loops' striatal areas (Haber & Knutson, 2010). Moreover, some corticostriatal loops control, and are involved in the shift between, habitual and goal-directed actions. OFC activation leads to increased goal-directed behaviors, while inhibition of the OFC disrupts goal-directed behavior (Gremel & Costa, 2013).

OCD: A Disorder of the Goal-directed Behavioral System

It has been argued, based on imaging data and neuropsychological tests, that OCD (in adults) should be explained on the basis of a deficit in the goal-directed system (Boulougouris, Chamberlain, & Robbins, 2009; Haber & Heilbronner, 2013; Joel, Doljansky, Roz, & Rehavi, 2005; Pauls, Abramovitch, Rauch, & Geller, 2014; Rotge et al., 2009). Such a dysfunction would lead to an overreliance on the simpler habit system, something that has been observed in adult OCD (Gillan et al., 2011). These patients show broader dysfunctions of goal-directed behavior as well on psychological tests, including value-based goals and the effects of punishments (Gillan et al., 2013; Morein-Zamir et al., 2013). Interestingly, the proposal and findings have been corroborated by animal studies using a compulsive animal model, showing that an OFC lesion produces such a shift from goal-directed toward habit-directed behaviors, a shift that could be reversed through an SSRI (Joel et al., 2005).

However, data from research on pediatric patients with OCD is lacking, even though it seems reasonable to presume that, in this respect, children with OCD have symptoms based on a similar basis. The presumption is supported by the fact that a majority of adult patients with OCD have their onset in childhood (Rasmussen & Eisen, 1992). Thus, the question of how the capacities for goal-directed behaviors develop is of special importance.

Developmental Disorders

Late childhood and adolescence is the period in life when behavior changes from being impulse- and affect-driven, to being to a greater part driven by goals (Haber & Rauch, 2010; Teffer & Semendeferi, 2012). Many child psychiatric syndromes that usually have their onset before or early in this period are today viewed as developmental disorders and classified in the DSM-5 as such, for example, autism, ADHD, Tourette's syndrome, as well as the "classical" developmental disorders, such as learning disorders and dyslexia (American Psychiatric Association, 2013). We will argue here that pediatric OCD should be seen as a developmental disorder in the development of goal-directed behaviors. The arguments for this view will be based on the following considerations: neurobiological findings, including some neuropsychological findings (albeit a recent review shows findings to be inconsistent) (Abramovitch et al., 2015); cognitive neuroscience findings; clinical aspects like comorbidity; inferences from treatment; and the natural course of pediatric OCD.

A "developmental disorder" is defined by a delay in development based on that expected for a given age level or stage of development, that originates before age 18, may be expected to continue indefinitely, and constitutes a substantial impairment. Biological and nonbiological factors are involved in these disorders. The definition is narrow compared with the definition that has been accepted among child psychiatric researchers. Most see developmental disorders as disorders of brain function that affect emotion, learning ability, self-control, and memory unfolding as the individual grows. Examples include, as mentioned above, autism, ADHD, and Tourette's syndrome. OCD is not on the list, and today occupies a unique position outside, but following the anxiety disorders, in DSM-5. DSM-5 recognized the "close relationship" with these disorders, among which it was classified earlier, but placed it into a new obsessive-compulsive spectrum group that includes hoarding disorder, trichotillomania, skin picking disorder, and a few other related disorders. OCD is subclassified into tics and non-tic related OCD, as well as with regard to the level of insight. Tic disorders are, on the other hand, classified among the neurodevelopmental disorders. The DSM-5 classification (American Psychiatric Association, 2013) may, we believe, need a nosological reclassification in the future.

Current Findings in the Neurobiology of Pediatric OCD

Research has repeatedly shown that the parts of the brain associated with pediatric OCD (Arnsten & Rubia, 2012; Brem et al., 2012) are the same structures that in cognitive neuroscience have been shown to support goal-directed behaviors (S. de Wit et al., 2012; Tanaka, Balleine, & O'Doherty, 2008). Thus, parts of the frontal lobes that have specific roles in such behaviors, the OFC and dorsolateral prefrontal cortex (dlPFC), respectively, are cortical nodes of specific loops implied as dysfunctional in pediatric OCD (Britton et al., 2010; Huey et al., 2008). In pediatric OCD, the seminal papers from Rosenberg and colleagues focused interest on one of the neuro-circuits involving prefrontal cortex, that is, the OFC (MacMaster, O'Neill, & Rosenberg, 2008; Wu, Hanna, Rosenberg, & Arnold, 2012). The OFC loop has been described as the part of the brain that ascribes a value or a valence (e.g., reward or fear) to the goal to be reached (Haber & Knutson, 2010). However, the value in its wider sense includes not only the OFC, but parts of the ventromedial prefrontal cortex (vmPFC), putting potential rewarding situations in context. Moreover, the OFC loop is widely connected, among other regions to the amygdala and to the insula where fear/anxiety and disgust, respectively, are thought to be underpinned, thus providing links to affects that are salient values and especially important in OCD (Amaral, 2002; Husted, Shapira, & Goodman, 2006). The belief that the OFC loops parts of the brain are hyperactivated are based on the Rosenberg studies and has been widely accepted (MacMaster et al., 2008; Pittenger, Bloch, & Williams, 2011). The difficulty a child has in refraining from an OCD behavior could consequently in some part be explained by the set value of the goal as being unusually "hot."

However, other tasks of the OCD loops, that of unattaching the value from a goal that does not provide goal fulfillment and which might reflect a measure of cognitive inflexibility, might as well be involved in pediatric OCD (Britton et al., 2010; Elliott,

Dolan, & Frith, 2000). The capacity to shift mental sets (i.e., cognitive flexibility) is part of a wider spectrum of executive functions that cover abilities, such as the ability to update information, monitor, and inhibit responses (Miyake, Kakimoto, & Sorimachi, 1981). Executive functioning is dependent on smooth and functional frontostriatal loop activities as research suggest that both basal ganglia and the pre-frontal cortex (OFC and dlPFC) play a major role in tasks related to cognitive flexi-bility such as mental task-switching (Alvarez & Emory, 2006; Monchi, Petrides, Strafella, Worsley, & Doyon, 2006). Deficits in cognitive flexibility are linked to less activity in frontal-striatal regions (Britton et al., 2010; Gu et al., 2008; Page et al., 2009; Remijnse et al., 2006). Furthermore, the vmPFC also seems to be important in this respect, relating responses to both earlier experience and the internal situation. It is engaged as earlier learning must be suppressed because responses are not suitable any more (Haber, 2011).

The presence of deficits in cognitive flexibility and response inhibition in OCD has been shown in different neuropsychological tests such as the Wisconsin Card Sort, reversal learning, task-switching, set-shifting, and response inhibition tasks (Bannon, Gonsalvez, Croft, & Boyce, 2006; Chamberlain, Fineberg, Blackwell, Robbins, & Sahakian, 2006; Gu et al., 2008; Kuelz, Hohagen, & Voderholzer, 2004; Lawrence et al., 2006; Lewin et al., 2014; Remijnse et al., 2006; Watkins et al., 2005). The stability, and presumably antecedent status of these dysfunctions, is shown in that OCD patients still have a considerable impairment in cognitive flex-ibility (measured with set shifting tasks) after being treated and achieving symptom remission (Bannon et al., 2006).

However, as observed above, a goal may be reached through multiple ways, and the striatum has the task to choose the behavior that is best. A dysfunction in these sys-tems leading to disinhibition problems has been shown in children with OCD, that is, in a way that is similar to the more pervasive problem with disinhibition that charac-terize children with ADHD (Arnsten & Rubia, 2012). The loops that enable this function have their cortical node in the dlPFC, and their function has been likened to that of a dam, withholding waters, and just disinhibiting the particular behavior that is suitable (see Gazzaniga, 2013, for a description).

The cortical node of this loop shows reduced activity when the child is confronted with something that arouses obsessions (but as well concerning neutral objects) (Gilbert et al., 2009). It is important with regard to the capacity for "response inhi-bition," that is, the ability to inhibit a behavior that is inappropriate given the wider context. In pediatric OCD, a lack of response inhibition goes beyond the OCD symp-toms and has been found as well in motor inhibition, reflexes, and verbal behavior (Menzies et al., 2008). It seems probable that this type of dysfunction is the reason for the comorbidity with ADHD, which is present in a sizable minority (about 10%), as well as the presence of subclinical ADHD-type symptoms, which are common in pediatric OCD (D. A. Geller et al., 2002; Ivarsson, Melin, & Wallin, 2008). Such problems are also found in neuropsychological tests (Andres et al., 2008), although negative findings have been reported as well (Chang, McCracken, & Piacentini, 2007). As noted by Abramowitz et al. (2015), a new generation of studies are needed to clarify the inconsistent results.

The findings of Hajcak et al. (2008) and Huyser et al. (2011) showing that the error circuit may be dysfunctional in pediatric OCD are very important as well. Error in this context is an overactive cingulate cortex (ACC) loop that does not signal the fact that a behavior has reached its set goal (e.g., in OCD clean hands), thus probably contributing to the persistent and repetitive behaviors that we call OCD rituals. Whether such a dysfunction is correlated with specific OCD symptom types is unknown. Possibly, it might be especially severe in repeating or arranging compulsions without a cognitive content (except the sense of incompleteness).

Comorbidity

The pattern of comorbidity varies between child-, adolescent-, and adult-onset OCD. Childhood-onset, particularly very early-onset OCD, has more developmental disorders for example, ADHD (10–33%), tics/Tourette's disorder (27–34%), separation anxiety (8–33%), and ASD (6–8%) (D. A. Geller, Biederman, Griffin, Jones, & Lefkowitz, 1996b; Ivarsson et al., 2008; Weidle, Melin, Drotz, Jozefiak, & Ivarsson, 2012) than expected from their respective prevalence in the general population. Adult- and adolescent-onset OCD (i.e., not adolescents with a childhood onset of OCD), in contrast, has more depression, other anxiety disorders, and drug abuse (the latter particularly in adults) (Abramowitz, Storch, Keeley, & Cordell, 2007; LaSalle et al., 2004).

In summary, the type and prevalence of comorbidity indicates that OCD, in addition to itself being a disorder of goal-directed behavior, frequently has associated problems that show a wider presence of disordered goal-directed behavior, all of which have been labeled developmental disorders. At least 40–50% of children with OCD have one of these (D. A. Geller et al., 2001a; Ivarsson et al., 2008).

Course of Pediatric OCD

OCD long-term follow-up studies, almost regardless of whether patients were treated or untreated (Stewart et al., 2004; Thomsen, 1994) show that roughly 25% of the patients become well, and that about 40% have clinical OCD. The remaining patients have subclinical OCD, or OCD that waxes to clinical level and then wanes to subclinical symptoms depending on the level of stress and other adversities (Thomsen & Mikkelsen, 1995). The level of residual symptoms is in line with findings from other developmental disorders, for example ADHD and Tourette's syndrome (Gorman et al., 2010; Shaw et al., 2012). Moreover, 50–80% of adults with OCD have pediatric onset of their disorder (Rasmussen & Eisen, 1992), indicating the continuity of pediatric OCD in many cases.

Conclusion

Based on the findings from studies of the neurological underpinnings of OCD that show dysfunctions in frontal cortex disrupting goal-directed behavior similar to other disorders considered as developmental (e.g., ADHD, Tourette's, and ASD), the presence of neuropsychological problems seen both in OCD and in these developmental disorders, the type of comorbidities (which in pediatric OCD to a significant extent is developmental disorders); and finally the course of the disorder, we conclude that pediatric OCD is best understood as a developmental disorder, an idea that was expressed more than a decade ago by Geller and colleagues (2001a). Later, Huyser et al. (2009) proposed even more explicitly the likelihood of OCD being best understood as a developmental disorder (Huyser, Veltman, de Haan, & Boer, 2009). We share this conclusion and believe it is of importance because it has implications for treatment and how to organize clinics that serve these children. However, we want to make clear that regarding pediatric OCD as a developmental disorder does not contradict the importance of learning-based theory and treatments in clinical work. Learning in accordance with learning theory has started and continues across the period when goal-directed behavioral system has being developed. Presumably, such learning affects, and is affected by, these developmental problems in a reciprocal way. Moreover, much of learning in this sense, that is, classical conditioning, and operant conditioning is achieved through systems that are evolutionarily old, that is, the amygdala and the associated fear system, orchestrating behavioral responses both to concrete and immediate dangers (through the direct link to thalamus mediating sensory information) as well as to more abstract dangers (through cortical links mediating processed information) (Johansen, Cain, Ostroff, & LeDoux, 2011; LeDoux, 2012).

Implications for Treatment

The advantage of the view of OCD as a developmental disorder is that it acknowledges the way that comorbidity occurs and the complications for treatment that ensues. We believe that clinics caring for children and adolescents with OCD need to be organized with a longitudinal and persistent perspective in mind so that the child's needs are considered throughout treatment and as development unfolds. These aspects include the sequencing of treatments, the use of concomitant treatments for comorbidities, and the follow-up structure needed to discover complications or relapse into OCD and complications as patients' lives go on to developmental periods, taxing their developmental resources based on both the OCD and the different comorbidities.

Treatment

European clinical guidelines state that CBT should be the first intervention irrespective of severity (NICE, 2005). This is in contrast to the AACAP Practice parameter, that recommend that in cases with moderate to severe OCD, CBT should be combined with a SSRI, (D. Geller et al., 2012). In this recommendation (No. 9), the authors refer to the larger effect size of combination treatment (combo) over unimodal therapy in the POTS. CBT is also unrivalled as a treatment in pediatric OCD with a larger effect size than SSRI (Ivarsson et al., 2015). CBT poses demands on the child's developmental level, for example, executive resources and as well on the families' resources in cooperating with the therapists. Drug treatment, on the other hand, is challenging in other ways. Below, we will discuss these problems. There are some, although too limited, research data providing guidance for the clinician, so that the following recommendations are largely based on clinical experience.

CBT. CBT is a challenging treatment, and clinicians confront challenges that are conditional upon the patient's personality and development, the comorbidities, and the family. First, a challenge for many patients is that CBT demands the ability to make plans, to follow them, and to keep the goal of treatment alive (an EF task) in trying circumstances when anxiety soars. It is a particular challenge to patients with large problems in EF. This will be described below in the section on ADHD and also Tourette's syndrome as it is most evident in those patients. CBT aims to restore functional goal-directed behavior as OCD rituals, albeit defined as goal-directed behaviors, are nonfunctional and whose goals (i.e., immediately neutralizing anxiety and dangers) merely reinforce the OCD and lead to functional impairments. In CBT better goals (e.g., peer and parental relations and school attainments) are defined and plans laid for their realization, as incentives for ERP tasks that may be unpalatable in the short range.

Second, some patients show a lack of "ordinary" incentives to cooperate in treatment as is mostly associated with ASD. Another aspect, which is more extreme in ASD, and which contributes to OCD phenomenology is the ability for cognitive set-shift, that is, in OCD seen as cognitive inflexibility. Traditional CBT does not focus on this ability to any great extent, but the CBT adaptations to patients with OCD and ASD proposed below will provide some advice which can be helpful also in patients with ASD traits without an ASD diagnosis. High levels of aggressive behavior forcing families to accommodate to the child's demands is a problem that is more common than the comorbidity with oppositional defiant disorder (ODD) indicates and will too be discussed below.

   Drug treatment.

SSRI actions. How SRI drugs bring about their OCD-relieving action is not fully understood. It is known that the serotonin reuptake pump is blocked by these drugs leading to increased transmission, which subsequently leads to down-regulation of the receptors of first the presynaptic, and then the postsynaptic neuron. However, doses above a threshold dose (usually corresponding to 75–125 mg sertraline) used during a few weeks are needed before reduced side effects and a decrease of OCD symptoms are obtained (Stahl, 2013). As described earlier, obsessions and the OCD rituals' intentions are thought to be expressed through loops involving the OFC. The OFC and thalamus nodes of these loops use glutamate, an excitatory acid, in their pathways to the striatum and OFC, respectively, and are believed to be hyperactive (Pittenger et al., 2011). However, signaling from the striatum to thalamus is two-way, using GABA (an inhibitory amino acid), thorough a direct (go) and an indirect (no-go) path with two or three neurons, respectively, in a series. The loops are modulated at all levels by serotonergic neurons, and also innervate the PFC richly from their origin in the raphe region of the brain stem (Celada, Puig, & Artigas, 2013; Kandel & Hudspeth, 2012). However, the modulation is dependent on a complex interaction between different serotonin receptor subtypes, each with a unique topographical distribution in the PFC. Moreover, using SSRI to modulate excitatory neurons (e.g., in the thalamus or OFC) or inhibitory neurons (in the striatum) may have markedly different net effects on the loop. In addition, serotonin has different actions on the PFC neurons, for example, an inhibitory effect via the 5-HT1A receptors, which are mostly expressed on the axon hillock of the pyramidal neurons (the output neuron of the cortex). Furthermore, serotonin has excitatory actions as well through the 5-HT2A receptor, which are strongly expressed in these neurons dendritic tree, and also on 5HT3 receptors on GABA inhibitory interneurons acting on the dendrites. The functional consequences of shifts in the balance between excitation and inhibition is not well understood, nor which response will dominate as a consequence of serotonin activation, although the inhibitory effects may be dominant (Celada et al., 2013). Currently, it is believed that relief from OCD symptoms depends on the OFC loop decreasing its activation (Pittenger et al., 2011), a process that has been observed in a study using paroxetine, a SSRI (Bolton, Moore, MacMillan, Stewart, & Rosenberg, 2001).

However, as described above, other loops, for example, those based in the dlPFC, are important in OCD pathogenesis as well. A serotonin activation effect there, analogous to those of OFC loops, with a weakened net effect, and poorer EF as a result might be problematic. On the other hand, if the ACC loop, observed to be hyperactive as well (Hajcak et al., 2008; Huyser et al., 2011), decreased its activation, the net result might be beneficial. The caveat is that the details of how these loops work and interact, and how serotonin modulates them is not well known, and further research is necessary. Findings from drug trials indicate, furthermore, that OCD which is comorbid with tics or ADHD, may show a weaker response to serotonin reuptake-inhibiting drugs than those without tics (see below in the section on ADHD and tics/ Tourette's syndrome) (D. A. Geller et al., 2003; Ginsburg, Kingery, Drake, & Grados, 2008; March et al., 2007). This may be due to the patients not tolerating high enough doses, due to the side effects on EF, but other pharmacodynamical effects are possible, although not, to our knowledge investigated. These aspects, we believe, may show that OCD, tics, and ADHD share neuro-developmental pathways, and that better response to psychopharmacology in CBT nonresponders with these comorbidities may be developed once we have a better understanding of the pathways.

Psychiatric side effects. The vicissitudes of SSRI treatment with regard to its effects on these systems discussed above is shown by the psychiatric side effects that may be more prominent than the OCD-relieving effect. In OCD drug treatment (using the upper dose range) we aim at a strong antiobsessional effect targeting and decreasing the OFC loop's activity. In a significant minority we see a side effect called the "demotivation syndrome," with apathy, affective blunting, and forgetfulness (Murphy, Segarra, Storch, & Goodman, 2008), and in interviewing these patients it appears as though long-term goals have lost their value. Does it signify a too strong, perhaps inhibitory, effect on the OFC "goal-directed behavior loop"? Another side effect, called "activation," may point to a vulnerability with regard to the dorsal-cognitive (dlPFC) loop showing as EF deficits (Kuelz et al., 2004). It is more often seen in younger than in older subjects, more often in those with than those without comorbid ADHD and/or Tourette's syndrome (Murphy et al., 2008). Activation is a nonspecific increase of all behaviors, goal-directed as well as not goal directed, and is often a reason for not increasing drug doses to levels that affect the OCD symptoms. Second, an increase of impulsive and thoughtless behaviors, for example, saying hurtful or inappropriate things, acting aggressively for insufficient reasons (as compared with before SSRI treatment), or acting inappropriately in other respects (sexual jokes with the teacher), as well point to SSRI increasing the vulnerability to EF dysfunction.

Evidence for the SRI drugs' efficacy. The first effective drug to be used in pediatric OCD (as well as adult OCD) was clomipramine, (Rapoport, Elkins, & Mikkelsen, 1980; Thoren, Asberg, Cronholm, Jornestedt, & Traskman, 1980), and its was shown that its efficacy was related to its ability to inhibit serotonin reuptake (SRI) in the synapses (Thoren, Asberg et al., 1980a), and not due to a general antidepressive effect through a cross-over trial versus desipramine, a non-adrenergic antidepressant drug (Leonard, Swedo, Rapoport, Coffey, & Cheslow, 1988). Its efficacy was subsequently tested in a traditional double-blind placebo-controlled trial (DeVeaugh-Geiss et al., 1992). However, clomipramine was a drug with many pharmacological properties and thus had many side effects. New compounds that were more specific with regard to their SRI properties were developed and a number of randomized placebo controlled trials of the specific SRIs (SSRI) in pediatric OCD were performed (D. A. Geller et al., 2001b; D. A. Geller et al., 2004; Liebowitz et al., 2002; March et al., 1998; Riddle et al., 2001; Riddle et al., 1992; The Pediatric OCD Treatment Study (POTS) Team, 2004). These studies, using meta-analytic techniques, were shown to correspond to a moderate effect size (0.43) (D. A. Geller et al., 2003) or stated in another way such that the response rate, for example, a reduction of scores of at least 25%, is attained by just half the group across the usual study time of three months (for sertraline, see March et al., 1998). Furthermore, few reach full remission (about 20%) (The Pediatric OCD Treatment Study Team, 2004). Even more problematic is the significant proportion of treatment refractory cases to SSRI treatment. Even when sertraline treatment was prolonged for up to a year, Wagner (2003) found that more than every fourth patient was a non-remitter (a CY-BOCS of 8 or less). However, among study completers, fewer did not remit (14%). Even so, SRI drugs are the psychopharmacological treatment in OCD that are available. However, as Haynes (2006) has pointed out, when there are other safe and effective treatments for a disorder, placebo has played out its role, trials should be direct comparisons between the treatments, in this case (S)SRI vs. CBT. Based on meta-analyses, using both indirect (Abramowitz, Whiteside, & Deacon, 2005b; Sanchez-Meca, Rosa-Alcazar, Iniesta-Sepulveda, & Rosa-Alcazar, 2014; Watson & Rees, 2008) extant data and the three direct comparisons between CBT and SRI that exist (Ivarsson et al., 2015), it is clear that CBT has the superior effect and better tolerability. The NICE guidelines (NICE, 2005) are well in consonance with these findings.

Combinations and sequencing of SRI drugs and CBT. The view that combination treatment is preferable in moderate–severe OCD was stated in the US OCD Practice parameter (D. Geller et al., 2012), based on the findings of the POTS study (2004), and endorsed in two recent meta-analyses, one based on child-only studies (Sanchez-Meca et al., 2014) and one based on both adult and child studies (Romanelli, Wu, Gamba, Mojtabai, & Segal, 2014). However, the conclusion is not unproblematic due to the heterogeneous outcome in the COMBO group, with the superiority of COMBO dependent on one site, while another site had equally high efficacy in CBT only as in COMBO. The latter findings are in line with a recent study by Storch et al. (2013). Ivarsson (2015), using a meta-analytic approach, combined the available data on COMBO vs. CBT and found no superiority for COMBO over CBT. Thus, we believe, it has not been proved that sertraline enhances CBT efficacy. On the other hand, when Franklin studied SSRI partial responders, adding CBT to the SSRI, this form of COMBO was significantly superior to optimized SSRI treatment. Sequencing of these treatment was investigated with regard to CBT non- or partial responders by Skarphedinsson et al. (2015c), who showed that continued CBT was as effective as switching to sertraline. We regard the findings as an indication of the robustness of CBT efficacy as compared with that of SSRI.

We conclude that SSRI treatment should be reserved for patients with pediatric OCD who are true CBT non-responders (i.e. CBT should not have a fixed length), or for those who cannot tolerate CBT, cooperate with the demands in CBT, or fail to make progress. However, the evidence for SSRI response in CBT non- or partial responders is limited, just the study by Skarphedinsson cited above, showing equal response for sertraline and CBT. Moreover, we do not know whether SSRI (and continued CBT) are superior to placebo as no placebo control was used in the study.

ADHD. Patients with comorbid ADHD have problems in executive functioning (EF) inherent in the diagnostic criteria, and ADHD ought maybe to be renamed as such (Hosenbocus & Chahal, 2012). Deficient EF is antithetical to adequate goal-directed behavior, which has long range rather than short-term perspectives, and complex and sophisticated goals (sometimes even abstract) divided into subgoals rather than simple and concrete goals. ADHD is a common comorbidity in OCD with a prevalence from just under 10% (D. A. Geller et al., 2004; Ivarsson et al., 2008) to about 30% of patients (D. A. Geller et al., 1996b). Less serious forms of attention deficits are common as well, in many patients on a subclinical level, and particularly in patients with ASD and with more severe OCD (Ivarsson et al., 2008). Patients with OCD+ADHD often benefit from treatment for ADHD symptoms in their ability to cooperate with the CBT demands on EF, according to clinical experience (a study is much needed). In contrast to the US Practice parameter (D. Geller et al., 2012), stating that in patients with OCD+ADHD the OCD should be treated first, we argue that the disorder with the most pervasive effect on executive function, that is, ADHD, should be treated first, or concurrently, to provide optimal grounds for the success of CBT. This is important given the advantage of CBT over SSRI treatment with regard to effect size and patient preference. For patients with the least EF deficits, CBT is an excellent training ground for EF, and no additional treatment might be needed. However, in between these two extremes there is a wide gray zone, in the borderline between subclinical (although significant) ADHD symptoms, and a full-blown ADHD diagnosis, where there may be both the need for psychological training of EF (see a review on such methods by Daley, 2014) and for drug treatment. We believe that this treatment should be planned before CBT for OCD is started. In fact, the clinical experience of the authors is that many children with OCD+ADHD improve from stimulant treatment not only with regard to the ADHD symptoms, but that OCD-symptoms decrease as well, often to a significant degree. This issue needs to be studied empirically. Adaptations of the OCD CBT program for children with different levels of executive dysfunction are often applied in practice to enhance patience and tolerance for anxiety. A more formally adapted program is still to be developed and evaluated scientifically.

Practical consequences for the adjustment of treatment for OCD with comorbid ADHD. Adaptations of CBT to comorbid ADHD are necessary, otherwise the treatment may become chaotic and unstructured. However, clinical experience indicates that CBT can be successful in the presence of milder ADHD symptoms if treatment is adapted to the patient's shorter attention span, impulsivity, and limited patience, for example, reduced length of treatment sessions, pauses with more pleasurable activities (play or games) during sessions, and a firm and foreseeable structure for sessions. However, findings have not been consistent (Ginsburg et al., 2008; Storch et al., 2008; Torp et al., 2015), and these adaptations to CBT need to be empirically tested.

With regard to drug treatments most patients with ADHD respond well to drug treatments such as stimulants, noradrenaline reuptake inhibitors or alpha-adrenergic agonists. The response of EF to psychopharmacological interventions may, however, need to go beyond the common drugs described above, see a review by Hosenbocus (2012) for examples. In all cases the treatments need to be coordinated so that CBT for the OCD starts when adequate compliance based on better EF in the child is established.

Tics/Tourette disorder. The onset of OCD, when associated with TS is on average two years later than the onset of tics (Leckman, 2002). Patients with tic-related OCD report more aggressive, religious, and sexual obsessions, as well as checking, counting, ordering, touching, and symmetry compulsions than do patients with non-tic-related OCD (Leckman et al., 1994; Worbe et al., 2010), findings that have been confirmed in children and adolescents (Masi et al., 2005). However, in line with the developmental view, younger patients with OCD and TS report more problems with impulse control, while older patients report more checking, arranging, and fear of contamination (Frankel et al., 1986). Moreover, underlining the role of deficient response inhibition, the comorbidity of TS with OCD is associated with elevated levels of ADHD and ODD, although not necessarily as a more severe condition compared with either disorder alone (Lewin, Chang, McCracken, McQueen, & Piacentini, 2010). The differentiation between tic-related and non-tic-related OCD, is clinically important, as both choice of, and response to, treatment might diverge. This is demonstrated in medication trials, and to a lesser extent, in CBT trials. Studies of the influence of comorbid tic disorders on OCD treatment outcome have shown ambiguous results. First, with regard to CBT, comorbid TS seem to have little impact (Himle, Fischer, Van Etten, Janeck, & Hanna, 2003; Piacentini, Bergman, Jacobs, McCracken, & Kretchman, 2002; Torp et al., 2015). However, in drug trials comorbid tics have been associated with poorer response (Ginsburg et al., 2008; March et al., 2007). In the NordLOTS we found no significant difference between treatment response to CBT in children with OCD only and those with comorbid TS (Torp et al., 2015). However, among CBT non-responders, sertraline was superior to continued CBT in patients with comorbid TS (Skarphedinsson, et al., 2015a), a finding that needs to be replicated.

Differentiation between tic-related and non-tic-related OCD. To differentiate between compulsions and tics might be difficult especially in cases with repetition rituals and "just right" perceptions, because of the similarity and overlap of symptoms. In clinical context, a careful evaluation of the antecedents of the phenomenon is crucial. Compulsions are anteceded by cognitions in most cases and hence typical goal-directed behaviors. The patient has extensive anxiety-provoking thoughts or preoccupations in the mind, but not a physical sensation, tension, etc. in the whole or in parts of the body. These sensations, usually described as "premonitory urges," are common antecedents before a tic, and hence a habit-like unconditioned response. Another cue to delineate a tic from a compulsion is an analysis of the function of the action. If a movement or an action is performed in order to avoid anxiety, disgust, or other unpleasant thoughts, it is likely to be a compulsion. To explore the nature of perceptions just before the action or movement in question together with the young patient will be helpful to distinguishing the symptoms. In cases where a differentiation is very difficult or impossible, a practical approach could be to classify the behavior in the context of and according to the prevalence and the degree of the symptoms. If the repetitive movement or action is rare or isolated and the child has no other tics, it is clinically appropriate to regard the disorder as OCD. Likewise, when the child has many other tics and only a few compulsions, the behavior could be regarded as a tic. However, there will be a considerable number of children presenting with both conditions, or developing the other comorbid condition after a previous period with only one of them.

Practical consequences for the adjustment of treatment for OCD with comorbid TS. Comprehensive Behavioral Intervention for Tics (CBIT) is a treatment package where the central component, Habit Reversal Training (HRT), consisting of training in tic awareness and competing response, is extended with relaxation training, functional interventions, and social support (Piacentini et al., 2002). A treatment manual for CBIT is available (Woods et al., 2008), which has showed good efficacy as compared with a psychological placebo treatment (Piacentini et al., 2010). Behavioral interventions such as CBIT aiming to reduce tics are recommended as first-line treatment in clinical guidelines (Verdellen, van de Griendt, Hartmann, Murphy, & Group, 2011). The effectiveness of CBIT/HRT in the treatment of Tourette's syndrome has been evaluated in, to date, three reviews. The most recently published (McGuire et al., 2014) identified eight RCTs comprising 438 participants. A random effects meta-analysis found a medium to large effect size for behavioral therapy relative to comparison conditions. When examining comorbidity, no significant association was identified between the percent of study participants with OCD and effect size. However, a small negative association between the percent of study participants with ADHD and effect size was identified, suggesting that these patients may need other or concomitant treatment.

Exposure and response prevention (ERP) vs. CBIT/HRT. ERP has been applied successfully in the treatment of tics. Verdellen and colleagues (2004) evaluated treatment outcome of ERP compared with HRT. Both treatment strategies resulted in significant improvement, that is, reduction of tics without differences between treatment conditions. The common denominator for both interventions, aiming to reduce tics as well as compulsions, is to interrupt the stimulus–response sequences that maintain the behavior. However, in a clinical context the difference between the methods might be important, at least in some patients. In ERP we teach the child that the obsessions are only false alarms. For example, in a patient with compulsions driven by the fear of contamination, the therapist conveys a technique to identify these thoughts as false alarm, allowing the patient to resist the urge. To convey this technique to a patient with tics seems to be more challenging, because most patients with tics experience the urge as a "real" intolerable tension. Contrary to the insight that the compulsive behavior is an exaggerated and unreasonable reaction, which is typical for OCD patients, a comparable cognition is lacking in TS. Probably the majority of children with tics have been told previously, several times and from different people in their environment that they should just stop the tics, without succeeding in this attempt. To introduce a therapeutic tool as HRT, helping them to resist the tics, is something quite different. Of course, therapeutic sessions with psychoeducation about the nature of tics and the maintaining mechanisms including follow-up, which is provided during a CBT course, is a different setting than "just telling to stop tics," and more likely to induce changes. Nevertheless, based on clinical experience, it seems to be easier to motivate children with tics for HRT, where the competing response technique offers an alternative behavior. This might provide a better tool to fight against tics, than just to resist the urge. If none of the behavioral interventions, despite of adequate delivering, had been effective, the addition of a pharmacological compound should be considered.

Practical approach. As a rule of thumb the main treatment strategy is chosen based on the prevalence of symptoms and degree of impairment in parents' and the child's perception. If OCD symptoms are dominating the clinical presentation, ERP should be offered. Accordingly, when tics are dominating the clinical picture and constitute the impairing symptoms, CBIT should be offered. If there are a few symptoms on the list that resemble more tic-like behavior, they could be treated with ERP as well. If the child does not succeed with the ERP technique, it is of crucial importance to differentiate between OCD symptoms and tics. If not, it will deprive the child of the experience of having defeated OCD, maintaining cognitions that some of the "OCD symptoms" might be invincible, or at least more difficult to overcome. It would be more helpful, rather, to convey an attitude that the child has succeeded and defeated OCD, but that tics are a different foe that need a different strategy, namely HRT (or the addition of pharmacologic therapy). In children with TS as the primary disorder, the situation could be the opposite: Both child and parents (and even an inexperienced therapist) may think that all the presented symptoms are derived from TS. To overlook compulsions, which often are more impairing than tics, may prevent the child from an effective course of ERP.

In addition to the practical considerations above, the developmental aspects of both disorders should inform all therapeutic interventions. TS and OCD have a somewhat different developmental course. Tics have the greatest effect on a patient's self-esteem and peer and family relationships from the ages 7 of 12 years, with an exacerbation period between the ages of 10–13 years, and a possible remission from age 16 to 20 years (Leckman, 2002). To have the natural course of TS in mind, and to inform the child and parents about the prognosis, adjusting therapeutic interventions accordingly is of crucial importance.

Autism Spectrum Disorders

As outlined above, ASD is by definition the disorder most frequently conceived as developmental, together with the specific developmental disorders. Impairment of executive functions, including cognitive flexibility, ability to inhibit behaviors, and goal-directed behavior, are core deficits in children with ASD and constitute a considerable overlap between ASD and OCD symptoms (Hosenbocus & Chahal, 2012). In addition, the lack (or at least severe delay) in the understanding of social cues and the inability to comply with social demands from the environment enhances the problems. Furthermore, in 50% of cases with ASD, ADHD is present as well aggravating the problems to a great extent (Mattila et al., 2010). Studies showing abnormal neural connectivity patterns and imbalances of excitatory and inhibitory neurotransmitters underline problems with the process of filtering out signals from noise (Hollander et al., 2005). To avoid sensory overload and overstimulation as many children with ASD report must be addressed in a therapeutic context. Therefore, to adjust therapeutic interventions to the needs of this subgroup with OCD and ASD is a challenging task.

Many OCD therapists will meet patients with autistic traits in their clinical practice, both with established diagnoses of ASD and with unrecognized ASD symptoms. Elevated comorbidity of OCD and symptom overlap with ASD has been reported both in adult (Cath, Ran, Smit, van Balkom, & Comijs, 2008) and pediatric populations, and may be challenging to recognize. Of children and adolescents treated for OCD, 8% fulfilled the diagnostic criteria for ASD (Ivarsson et al., 2008), and subclinical ASD symptoms are very common in children with OCD (Arildskov et al., 2015) as well when compared with controls (Weidle et al., 2012). The other way round is even more likely: ASD therapists will certainly meet patients with OCD, as OCD is a frequent comorbidity in ASD. Epidemiologic studies describe OCD prevalence in ASD to range from 8 to 37%. (Leyfer et al., 2006; Simonoff et al., 2008). Therefore, OCD symptoms should be distinguished from repetitive behaviors and special interests and diagnosed, as patients with ASD and OCD may benefit from standard treatments. Without a good understanding of both conditions, OCD therapists may overlook ASD cases, misinterpreting the symptoms as OCD. In the same way, ASD therapists may regard comorbid OCD as a part of ASD, preventing the patient from adequate therapeutic interventions. Successfully treated OCD can lead to a markedly improvement of functioning and quality of life in affected individuals, even when the basic ASD symptoms remain unchanged.

Assessment: Differentiation between OCD and ASD symptoms. A diagnosis of OCD should be established based on the same criteria as in children without ASD, including functional impairment, that is, OCD symptoms interfere with the patient's daily life. However, rigidity with inflexible adherence to routines, repetitive and ritualized patterns of behavior, preoccupation with details, and a near-obsessive interest in restricted, areas or topics of interests that are abnormal in intensity or focus are a part of the clinical picture of ASD. Literally interpretation of facts is common in children with ASD and could be misinterpreted as obsessions (e.g., information about toxicity of the environment, nutrition principles, or the need of infection prevention). Rigidity in ASD is egosyntonic (unlike compulsions) and usually not perceived as unpleasant by the child, often in vivid contrast to the perception of the parents. Similarly to the distinction between tics and OCD, the key to differentiate between rigidity and OCD again is to carefully evaluate the antecedents and the function of the phenomenon. As outlined above, compulsions are anteceded by cognitions such as anxiety provoking thoughts or images, and compulsions are performed in order to avoid anxiety or disgust. Repetitive behavior and rigidity rituals in ASD are probably driven by the need for sameness, and perceived as pleasant and definitely not performed to avoid adversities or a catastrophe. Rigidity in ASD does not lead to avoidance behavior and subjective impairment. In addition, rigidity is a more stable trait of the child's personality, which always has been present to a certain degree, while OCD symptoms are developing with a point of onset, although sometimes insidious. To assess time for onset of OCD symptoms may be useful in the differentiation of rigidity and OCD; if OCD symptoms are developing without having being present previously or to a low degree only, this is an indicator for comorbid OCD in the presence of ASD.

Growing evidence for treatment effectiveness. Successful treatment of OCD in adolescents with ASD has been reported (Lehmkuhl, Storch, Bodfish, & Geffken, 2008; Reaven & Hepburn, 2003), although less symptom relief has been noted as compared with OCD without ASD. The first randomized treatment study with adolescents and young adults with ASD and OCD compared CBT and "anxiety management" (Russell et al., 2013). Both treatments resulted in a significant reduction of OCD symptoms, assessed with the YBOCS. The CBT group had more responders to the treatment, but between-group differences were not significant. Eight other controlled trials have examined the use of CBT- based approaches for mainly non-OCD anxiety disorders in ASD in children and adolescents, all of which found that CBT was superior to control conditions (Sukhodolsky, Bloch, Panza, & Reichow, 2013). Selles and colleagues (2014) showed the problem of maintenance of CBT gains for anxiety in youth with ASD. At posttreatment evaluation after 10–26 months, on average treatment gains were well maintained, but a considerable group of participants experienced symptom relapse. Five participants (16%) in this study had OCD.

Practical considerations and adjustments for therapy. The deficits in most areas of development in children and adolescents with ASD and comorbid OCD demand an adaption of the concepts and routines for therapeutic interventions. Treatment of OCD in children with ASD needs to be adjusted to the deficits in executive functioning, social development and their perception of the environment. A precondition for proper delivering of these treatment interventions is that the therapist is not only experienced in CBT, but also in communication with children with ASD, or at least has access to the required supervision. To adjust CBT/ERP to the needs of children with ASD the following considerations are important:

(1) **Adjustment of communication.** Communication needs to be succinct, clear and concrete without ambiguity. Sentences with metaphors and implicit messages can be interpreted literally and should be explained. Small talk should be avoided. Precise expression in few words with a focus on the essential messages with a clear expression of what is expected helps the child to understand the processes during therapy. In view of the deficits in executive functioning, it is necessary to allow additional time and repeated explanations including checking whether the content was understood.

(2) **Motivation.** An important reward for children with OCD engaging in successful ERP is allowing them to participate in a social life with their friends and peers again, which is often hampered by OCD. Because of the lack of social motivation, children with ASD might perceive their OCD symptoms as less dysfunctional than their parents. Therefore, assessing individual motivation factors, beyond just getting better from OCD, is important. Examples can be that the child will be able to avoid stress when accidentally in contact with germs, to avoid fuss from parents, or to gain more time for other areas of interest when OCD is conquered. In addition, rewards using areas of special interest or other ways to make therapy interesting for example reframing exposure as "scientific experiment" can be helpful.

(3) **Poor insight.** Children with ASD frequently lack insight into the true nature of their obsessions (DSM-5, poor or absent insight). Impaired ability to introspection, literal perception of language (e.g., exaggerated alerts of danger in the media) and impaired social judgment may reduce their insight into the irrational and unreasonable nature of the obsessions. More psychoeducation, CBT techniques such as "Socratian" questioning, thought experiments, calculations of likelihood, and exploration of cognitions are needed in order to enhance insight.

(4) **Concrete and clear treatment goals.** Implicit treatment goals such as "OCD-symptom reduction" might be unclear for the child. To negotiate and agree upon clear treatment goals and repeat them as often as needed is a strong motivational factor.

(5) **Fixed schedule and structure for the sessions.** CBT is highly structured with clear routines and roles. This structure suits the need of children with ASD. To adhere to, to visualize, and to repeat the structure in the sessions, using written working schedules, symptom mapping, homework assignment, etc. compensates for the developmental problems in terms of impaired goal-directed behavior and enhances the child's compliance to treatment.

(6) **Time schedule.** Intensive social interaction during CBT sessions is challenging. In addition, reduced attention span demands processing time and repetitions. Sessions duration need to be adjusted, that is, reduced in most cases, while additional sessions might be needed. However, even more than in standard CBT for children with OCD, without ASD it is important to emphasize the need for progression and to focus on goal direction, even when treatment progress might be slow in periods. If this aspect is missed out, CBT sessions itself might turn into a ritual with only minimal or no progression toward the goal to defeat OCD and both patient and therapist lose their motivation.

(7) **Generalization problems and parental involvement.** Generalization of training gains to real-life situations have generally been a problem in children with ASD (Golan & Baron-Cohen, 2006). To solve, or at least to mitigate, this problem, more parents' involvement and education as the therapist's co-workers will often be required in order to provide a scaffolding frame in order to support and to maintain motivation, to encourage and facilitate ERP exercises, and to supervise and monitor homework assignments.

Aggressive Behavior

Aggressive behavior is prevalent in pediatric OCD, both in general (Ivarsson et al., 2008) and as aggressive storms or violent outbursts (Krebs et al., 2013; Storch et al., 2012). Aggression is mostly best understood within the framework of a functional analysis with OCD as learning-based behavior, that is, the behavior has the goal to avert contact with an obsessional stimulus or to prevent the need of compulsions. A differential diagnosis is ODD that is found with prevalence below 10% in most studies (Ivarsson et al., 2008; Piacentini et al., 2011), with few exceptions (D. A. Geller, Biederman, Griffin, Jones, & Lefkowitz, 1996a).

The motivation for outbreaks of aggression in ODD differs from those in OCD. Rather than the urge to neutralize or avoid anxiety or danger, in ODD the refusal is to recognize authority and the goal usually to do pleasurable activities. A careful interview with both the child and parent is needed for a judgment. However, comorbid ODD is associated with high levels of aggression, negativity, oppositionality, and hostility, and is a challenge to the therapeutic alliance. The exposure tasks will not be performed, parental monitoring will be obstructed, and a common ground for establishing therapeutic goals jeopardized. A solution is the use of a stepwise treatment approach analogously to the situation with ADHD, that is, to start out with treatment for the comorbid ODD, for example, Parent Management Training (PMT) (Drugli, Larsson, Fossum, & Morch, 2010). Sukhodolsky and colleagues (2013) used 6 hours PMT for the ODD, followed by 12 hours ERP for the OCD, while controls received ERP for the OCD only. Those who received the combination did better than the controls. The study needs to be replicated using a bigger sample, but it shows the way.

However, aggressive behavior is not only a question of OCD. In a study by Ivarsson et al. (2008), comorbid developmental disorders (i.e., ADHD, ASD, and TS) predicted higher aggression levels, particularly in those individuals who had both ASD and TS. Moreover, girls with ADHD+OCD had high levels of aggression too. So, the learning perspective explains why children with OCD are aggressive, but the developmental perspective may explain why some children reach very high levels, probably due to behavior inhibition deficits in some children associated with comorbidity. Thus, parental accommodation, which is a known cause of treatment resistance, is higher in families with a patient with higher levels of aggression (Garcia et al., 2010). This may need to be addressed not only through parental training and guidance, but by treatment of the comorbidity. Again, a study investigating whether such experience stands the test of a trial is much needed.

How to Organize Clinics

Recognizing OCD as a developmental disorder has several practical implications for how to design services for these children and adolescents. First, assessment procedures need to be broad enough to cover both OCD and comorbidities. Using a semi-structured interview such as K-SADS or ADIS is necessary both from the differential diagnostic point of view and also for a clear understanding of treatment demanding comorbidities, particularly those mentioned above, but also depression and other anxiety disorders. Moreover, assessments may need to include screening for cognitive level and for neuropsychological dysfunctions. Diagnostic reassessments need to be done when CBT outcome is insufficient. Clinical experience shows that ADHD can go undetected across psychiatric interviews, because both the child and the parents are so overwhelmed with the impact of the OCD-symptoms that previously existing ADHD symptoms are forgotten or regarded as insignificant.

Second, CBT must not have a fixed length. As our NordLOTS study showed, about half of the patients who were non-responders to 14 sessions of CBT responded to 10 more sessions. The new sessions may need to be geared to problems, many of them developmental, that complicated the first CBT step, for example, a need for shorter ERP episodes intermixed with moving around or play in children with ADHD symptoms, a new approach to motivation in children with ASD-problems, or combining ERP with HRT in children with tics and OCD symptoms that overlap.

Third, an OCD treatment with CBT may not be durable for all youth. Relapse in OCD may have different causes. In addition to classical stress or adverse event-related incidents (such as peer cruelty), some patients relapse following positive stressors in adolescence like love affairs. However, we also see cases with childhood onset that relapse as school becomes more challenging in the early teens when less obvious learning difficulties may interfere with adaptation to school. Thus, apart from treating the relapse, we may need to assess the background of the problems at school.

As described earlier, comorbidities in OCD are frequent and have profound impact on treatment, and therapists with good insight into both the treatment of OCD and the comorbidities are needed. Thus, specialist centers for OCD need general child psychiatric competence as well.

In Norway, the development of specialized OCD units has occurred within recent years, following a directive from the Norwegian Directorate of Health. The directive states that every region must establish both pediatric and adult subspecialized OCD treatment units. The spread of CBT competence has been a primary objective during the implementation. With regard to pediatric OCD, these clinics follow the NICE guidelines, recommending that CBT should be the first intervention for

OCD symptoms requiring treatment. In the years to come, as more cases are treated, and relapse, we expect to see a development where CBT non-responders, as well as CBT plus (S)SRI non-responders will be increasingly observed. A consequence will be that more of these cases will need treatment and, we hope, move through a treatment chain where a university-based OCD clinic will be the final step for the non-responding patient. It is vital that treatment failure is no longer accepted at the district level, as is now mostly the case in generalized CAP clinics. A system is needed where experts in the complications of OCD treatment, take over based on their competence, not geography.

Conclusion

OCD is a multifaceted disorder best understood as a developmental disorder based on the neurophysiological correlates, clinical features, comorbidities course, and on experience from the treatment of comorbid cases. Future research needs to focus on what factors promote maturation of the neuropsychological and developmental underpinnings of the disorder. Thus, other types of assessment, tapping these areas, need to be done apart from the classical outcome variables such as symptoms and psychosocial functioning.

We conclude that teams that assess and treat child and adolescent patients with OCD need to have access to good CBT therapists and psychopharmacologists, but also to have a wider perspective on the care of the patient. We argue that the comorbidities as well as other developmental problems need to be assessed and treated, and that a capacity to cooperate with the care-takers and schools needs to be in place across longer developmental periods then just the period when OCD symptoms are rampant.

References

Abramovitch, A., Abramowitz, J. S., Mittelman, A., Stark, A., Ramsey, K., & Geller, D. A. (2015). Research review: Neuropsychological test performance in pediatric obsessive-compulsive disorder: A meta-analysis. *Journal of Child Psychology and Psychiatry and Allied Disciplines, 56*(8), 837–847.

Abramowitz, J. S., Storch, E. A., Keeley, M., & Cordell, E. (2007). Obsessive-compulsive disorder with comorbid major depression: What is the role of cognitive factors? *Behavorial Research Therapy, 45*(10), 2257–2267.

Abramowitz, J. S., Taylor, E., & McKay, D. (2007). Psychological theories of obsessive-compulsive disorder. In E. A. Storch, G. R. Geffken, & D. G. Murphy (Eds.), *Handbook of child and adolescent obsessive-compulsive disorder* (pp. 109–130). Mahwah, NJ: Lawrence Erlbaum.

Abramowitz, J. S., Whiteside, S. P., & Deacon, B. J. (2005a). The effectiveness of treatment for pediatric obsessive-compulsive disorder. *Behavior Therapy, 36*, 55–63.

Abramowitz, J. S., Whiteside, S. P., & Deacon, B. J. (2005b). The Effectiveness of treatment for pediatric obsessive-compulsive disorder: A meta-analysis. *Behavior Therapy, 36*(1), 55–63.

Alexander, G. E., & Crutcher, M. D. (1990). Functional architecture of basal ganglia circuits: Neural substrates of parallel processing. *Trends in Neurosciences, 13*(7), 266–271.

Alvarez, J. A., & Emory, E. (2006). Executive function and the frontal lobes: A meta-analytic review. *Neuropsychology Review, 16*(1), 17–42.

Amaral, D. G. (2002). The primate amygdala and the neurobiology of social behavior: Implications for understanding social anxiety. *Biological Psychiatry, 51*(1), 11–17.

American Psychiatric Association. (2013). *Diagnostic and statistical manual of mental disorders (DSM-5)* (5th ed.). Washington, DC: American Psychiatric Publishing.

Andres, S., Lazaro, L., Salamero, M., Boget, T., Penades, R., & Castro-Fornieles, J. (2008). Changes in cognitive dysfunction in children and adolescents with obsessive-compulsive disorder after treatment. *Journal of Psychiatric Research, 42*(6), 507–514.

Arildskov, T., Højgaard, D. M. A., Skarphedinsson, G., Thomsen, P., Ivarsson, T., Weidle, B., Melin, K. H., & Hybel, K. A. (2015). Subclinical autism spectrum symptoms in pediatric obsessive-compulsive disorder. *European Child and Adolescent Psychiatry, 25*(7), 711–723.

Arnsten, A. F., & Rubia, K. (2012). Neurobiological circuits regulating attention, cognitive control, motivation, and emotion: Disruptions in neurodevelopmental psychiatric disorders. *Journal of the American Academy of Child and Adolescent Psychiatry, 51*(4), 356–367.

Bannon, S., Gonsalvez, C. J., Croft, R. J., & Boyce, P. M. (2006). Executive functions in obsessive-compulsive disorder: State or trait deficits? *Australian and New Zealand Journal of Psychiatry, 40*(11/12), 1031–1038.

Bolton, J., Moore, G. J., MacMillan, S., Stewart, C. M., & Rosenberg, D. R. (2001). Case study: Caudate glutamatergic changes with paroxetine persist after medication discontinuation in pediatric OCD. *Journal of the American Academy of Child and Adolescent Psychiatry, 40*(8), 903–906.

Boulougouris, V., Chamberlain, S. R., & Robbins, T. W. (2009). Cross-species models of OCD spectrum disorders. *Psychiatry Research, 170*(1), 15–21.

Brem, S., Hauser, T. U., Iannaccone, R., Brandeis, D., Drechsler, R., & Walitza, S. (2012). Neuroimaging of cognitive brain function in paediatric obsessive compulsive disorder: A review of literature and preliminary meta-analysis. *Journal of Neural Transmission, 119*(11), 1425–1448.

Britton, J. C., Rauch, S. L., Rosso, I. M., Killgore, W. D., Price, L. M., Ragan, J., ... Stewart, S. E. (2010). Cognitive inflexibility and frontal-cortical activation in pediatric obsessive-compulsive disorder. *Journal of the American Academy of Child and Adolescent Psychiatry, 49*(9), 944–953.

Carr, A. T. (1974). Compulsive neurosis: A review of the literature. *Psychological Bulletin, 81*(5), 311–318.

Cath, D. C., Ran, N., Smit, J. H., van Balkom, A. J., & Comijs, H. C. (2008). Symptom overlap between autism spectrum disorder, generalized social anxiety disorder and obsessive-compulsive disorder in adults: A preliminary case-controlled study. *Psychopathology, 41*(2), 101–110.

Celada, P., Puig, M. V., & Artigas, F. (2013). Serotonin modulation of cortical neurons and networks. *Frontiers in Integrated Neuroscience, 7*, 25.

Chamberlain, S. R., Fineberg, N. A., Blackwell, A. D., Robbins, T. W., & Sahakian, B. J. (2006). Motor inhibition and cognitive flexibility in obsessive-compulsive disorder and trichotillomania. *American Journal of Psychiatry, 163*(7), 1282–1284.

Chang, S. W., McCracken, J. T., & Piacentini, J. C. (2007). Neurocognitive correlates of child obsessive compulsive disorder and Tourette's syndrome. *Journal of Clinical and Experimental Neuropsychology, 29*(7), 724–733.

Daley, D., van der Oord, S., Ferrin, M., Danckaerts, M., Doepfner, M., Cortese, S., et al. (2014). Behavioral Interventions in attention-deficit/hyperactivity disorder: A meta-analysis of randomized controlled trials across multiple outcome domains. *Journal of the American Academy of Child and Adolescent Psychiatry, 53*(8), 835–847.

de Wit, C. A., & Dickinson, A. (2009). Associative theories of goal-directed behaviour: A case for animal–human translational models. *Psychological Research, 73*, 463–476.

de Wit, S., Watson, P., Harsay, H. A., Cohen, M. X., van de Vijver, I., & Ridderinkhof, K. R. (2012). Corticostriatal connectivity underlies individual differences in the balance between habitual and goal-directed action control. *Journal of Neuroscience, 32*(35), 12066–12075.

DeVeaugh-Geiss, J., Moroz, G., Biederman, J., Cantwell, D., Fontaine, R., Greist, J. H., … Landau, P. (1992). Clomipramine hydrochloride in childhood and adolescent obsessive-compulsive disorder: A multicenter trial. *Journal of the American Academy of Child and Adolescent Psychiatry, 31*(1), 45–49.

Dickinson, A. (1985). Actions and habits: The Development of behavioural autonomy. *Philosophical Transactions of the Royal Society of London. Series B, Biological Sciences, 308,* 67–68.

Drugli, M. B., Larsson, B., Fossum, S., & Morch, W. T. (2010). Five- to six-year outcome and its prediction for children with ODD/CD treated with parent training. *Journal of Child Psychology and Psychiatry and Allied Disciplines, 51*(5), 559–566.

Elliott, R., Dolan, R. J., & Frith, C. D. (2000). Dissociable functions in the medial and lateral orbitofrontal cortex: Evidence from human neuroimaging studies. *Cerebral Cortex, 10*(3), 308–317.

Emminghaus, H. (1887). *Die psychischen störungen des kinderalters.* Tf bingen: H. Laupp'schen Buchhandlung.

Foa, E. B. (2010). Cognitive behavioral therapy of obsessive-compulsive disorder. *Dialogues in Clinical Neuroscience, 12*(2), 199–207.

Frankel, M., Cummings, J. L., Robertson, M. M., Trimble, M. R., Hill, M. A., & Benson, D. F. (1986). Obsessions and compulsions in Gilles de la Tourette's syndrome. *Neurology, 36*(3), 378–382.

Garcia, A. M., Sapyta, J. J., Moore, P. S., Freeman, J. B., Franklin, M. E., March, J. S., & Foa, E. B. (2010). Predictors and moderators of treatment outcome in the Pediatric Obsessive Compulsive Treatment Study (POTS I). *Journal of the American Academy of Child and Adolescent Psychiatry, 49*(10), 1024–1033.

Gazzaniga, M. E., Ivry, R. B., & Mangun, G. R. (2013). *Cognitive neuroscience: The biology of the mind* (2nd ed.). New York: W.W. Norton.

Geller, D., March, J. S., & (CQI), t. A. C. o. Q. I. (2012). Practice parameter for the assessment and treatment of children and adolescents with Obsessive Compulsive Disorder. *Journal of the American Academy of Child and Adolescent Psychiatry, 51*(1), 98–113.

Geller, D. A., Biederman, J., Faraone, S., Agranat, A., Cradock, K., Hagermoser, L., … Coffey, B. J. (2001a). Developmental aspects of obsessive compulsive disorder: Findings in children, adolescents, and adults. *Journal of Nervous and Mental Disease, 189*(7), 471–477.

Geller, D. A., Biederman, J., Faraone, S. V., Cradock, K., Hagermoser, L., Zaman, N., … Golvinsky, I. (2002). Attention-deficit/hyperactivity disorder in children and adolescents with obsessive-compulsive disorder: Fact or artifact? *Journal of the American Academy of Child and Adolescent Psychiatry, 41*(1), 52–58.

Geller, D. A., Biederman, J., Griffin, S., Jones, J., & Lefkowitz, T. R. (1996a). Comorbidity of juvenile obsessive-compulsive disorder with disruptive behavior disorders. *Journal of the American Academy of Child and Adolescent Psychiatry, 35*(12), 1637–1646.

Geller, D. A., Biederman, J., Griffin, S., Jones, J., & Lefkowitz, T. R. (1996b). Comorbidity of juvenile obsessive-compulsive disorder with disruptive behavior disorders. *Journal of the American Academy of Child and Adolescent Psychiatry, 35*(12), 1637–1646.

Geller, D. A., Biederman, J., Stewart, S. E., Mullin, B., Farrell, C., Wagner, K. D., Elmslie, G., & Carpenter, D. (2003). Impact of comorbidity on treatment response to paroxetine in pediatric obsessive-compulsive disorder: Is the use of exclusion criteria empirically supported in randomized clinical trials? *Journal of Child and Adolescent Psychopharmacology, 13*(Suppl. 1), S19–S29.

Geller, D. A., Biederman, J., Stewart, S. E., Mullin, B., Martin, A., Spencer, T., & Farone, S. V. (2003). Which SSRI? A meta-analysis of pharmacotherapy trials in pediatric obsessive-compulsive disorder. *American Journal of Psychiatry, 160*(11), 1919–1928.

Geller, D. A., Hoog, S. L., Heiligenstein, J. H., Ricardi, R. K., Tamura, R., Kluszynski, S., & Jacobson, J. G. (2001b). Fluoxetine treatment for obsessive-compulsive disorder in children and adolescents: A placebo-controlled clinical trial. *Journal of the American Academy of Child and Adolescent Psychiatry, 40*(7), 773–779.

Geller, D. A., Wagner, K. D., Emslie, G., Murphy, T., Carpenter, D. J., Wetherhold, E., ... Gardiner, C. (2004). Paroxetine treatment in children and adolescents with obsessive-compulsive disorder: A randomized, multicenter, double-blind, placebo-controlled trial. *Journal of the American Academy of Child and Adolescent Psychiatry, 43*(11), 1387–1396.

Gilbert, A. R., Akkal, D., Almeida, J. R., Mataix-Cols, D., Kalas, C., Devlin, B., ... Phillips, M. L. (2009). Neural correlates of symptom dimensions in pediatric obsessive-compulsive disorder: A functional magnetic resonance imaging study. *Journal of the American Academy of Child and Adolescent Psychiatry, 48*(9), 936–944.

Gillan, C. M., Morein-Zamir, S., Kaser, M., Fineberg, N. A., Sule, A., Sahakian, B. J., Cardinal, R. N., & Robbins, T. W. (2013). Counterfactual processing of economic action-outcome alternatives in obsessive-compulsive disorder: Further evidence of impaired goal-directed behavior. *Biological Psychiatry, 75*(8), 639–646.

Gillan, C. M., Papmeyer, M., Morein-Zamir, S., Sahakian, B. J., Fineberg, N. A., Robbins, T. W., & de Wit, S. (2011). Disruption in the balance between goal-directed behavior and habit learning in obsessive-compulsive disorder. *American Journal of Psychiatry, 168*(7), 718–726.

Ginsburg, G. S., Kingery, J. N., Drake, K. L., & Grados, M. A. (2008). Predictors of treatment response in pediatric obsessive-compulsive disorder. *Journal of the American Academy of Child and Adolescent Psychiatry, 47*(8), 868–878.

Golan, O., & Baron-Cohen, S. (2006). Systemizing empathy: Teaching adults with Asperger syndrome or high-functioning autism to recognize complex emotions using interactive multimedia. *Development and Psychopathology, 18*(2), 591–617.

Gorman, D. A., Thompson, N., Plessen, K. J., Robertson, M. M., Leckman, J. F., & Peterson, B. S. (2010). Psychosocial outcome and psychiatric comorbidity in older adolescents with Tourette's syndrome: Controlled study. *British Journal of Psychiatry, 197*(1), 36–44.

Grahn, J. A., Parkinson, J. A., & Owen, A. M. (2009). The role of the basal ganglia in learning and memory: Neuropsychological studies. *Behavioural Brain Research, 199*(1), 53–60.

Gremel, C. M., & Costa, R. M. (2013). Orbitofrontal and striatal circuits dynamically encode the shift between goal-directed and habitual actions. *Nature Communications, 4*, 2264.

Gu, B-M., Park, J-Y., Kang, D-H., Lee, S. J., Yoo, S. Y., Jo, H. J., ... Kwon, J. S. (2008). Neural correlates of cognitive inflexibility during task-switching in obsessive-compulsive disorder. *Brain, 131*(1), 155–164.

Haber, S. N. (2011). Neuroanatomy of reward: A view from the ventral striatum. In J. A. Gottfried (Ed.), *Neurobiology of Sensation and Reward*. Boca Raton, FL: CRC Press.

Haber, S. N., & Heilbronner, S. R. (2013). Translational research in OCD: Circuitry and mechanisms. *Neuropsychopharmacology, 38*(1), 252–253.

Haber, S. N., & Knutson, B. (2010). The reward circuit: Linking primate anatomy and human imaging. *Neuropsychopharmacology, 35*(1), 4–26.

Haber, S. N., & Rauch, S. L. (2010). Neurocircuitry: A window into the networks underlying neuropsychiatric disease. *Neuropsychopharmacology, 35*(1), 1–3.

Hajcak, G., Franklin, M. E., Foa, E. B., & Simons, R. F. (2008). Increased error-related brain activity in pediatric obsessive-compulsive disorder before and after treatment. *American Journal of Psychiatry, 165*(1), 116–123.

Haynes, R. B., Sackett, D. L., Guyatt, H. H., & Tugwell, P. (2006). *Clinical epidemiology: How to do clinical practise research* (Vol. 3). Philadelphia, PA: Lippincott Williams & Wilkins.

Himle, J. A., Fischer, D. J., Van Etten, M. L., Janeck, A. S., & Hanna, G. L. (2003). Group behavioral therapy for adolescents with tic-related and non-tic-related obsessive-compulsive disorder. *Depression and Anxiety, 17*(2), 73–77.

Hollander, E., Phillips, A., Chaplin, W., Zagursky, K., Novotny, S., Wasserman, S., & Ivengar, R. (2005). A placebo controlled crossover trial of liquid fluoxetine on repetitive behaviors in childhood and adolescent autism. *Neuropsychopharmacology, 30*(3), 582–589.

Hosenbocus, S., & Chahal, R. (2012). A review of executive function deficits and pharmacological management in children and adolescents. *Journal of the Canadian Academy of Child and Adolescent Psychiatry, 21*(3), 223–229.

Huey, E. D., Zahn, R., Krueger, F., Moll, J., Kapogiannis, D., Wassermann, E. M., & Grafman. J. (2008). A psychological and neuroanatomical model of obsessive-compulsive disorder. *Journal of Neuropsychiatry and Clinical Neurosciences, 20*(4), 390–408.

Husted, D. S., Shapira, N. A., & Goodman, W. K. (2006). The neurocircuitry of obsessive-compulsive disorder and disgust. *Progress in Neuro-Psychopharmacology and Biological Psychiatry, 30*(3), 389–399.

Huyser, C., Veltman, D. J., de Haan, E., & Boer, F. (2009). Paediatric obsessive-compulsive disorder, a neurodevelopmental disorder?: Evidence from neuroimaging. *Neuroscience and Biobehavioral Reviews, 33*(6), 818–830.

Huyser, C., Veltman, D. J., Wolters, L. H., de Haan, E., & Boer, F. (2011). Developmental aspects of error and high-conflict-related brain activity in pediatric obsessive-compulsive disorder: A fMRI study with a Flanker task before and after CBT. *Journal of Child Psychology and Psychiatry, 52*(12), 1251–1260.

Ivarsson, T., Melin, K., & Wallin, L. (2008). Categorical and dimensional aspects of co-morbidity in obsessive-compulsive disorder (OCD). *European Child and Adolescent Psychiatry, 17*(1), 20–31.

Ivarsson, T., Skarphedinsson, G., Kornør, H., Axelsdottir, B., Biedilæ, S., Heyman, I., … March, J. (2015). The place of and evidence for serotonin reuptake inhibitors (SRIs) in obsessive compulsive disorder (OCD) in children and adolescents: Views based on a systematic review and meta-analysis. *Psychiatry Research, 227*(1), 93–103.

Joel, D., Doljansky, J., Roz, N., & Rehavi, M. (2005). Role of the orbital cortex and of the serotonergic system in a rat model of obsessive compulsive disorder. *Neuroscience, 130*(1), 25–36.

Johansen, J. P., Cain, C. K., Ostroff, L. E., & LeDoux, J. E. (2011). Molecular mechanisms of fear learning and memory. *Cell, 147*(3), 509–524.

Kandel, E. R., & Hudspeth, A. J. (2012). The brain and behavior. In E. Kandel, J. H. Schwartz, T. M. Jessell, S. A. Siegelbaum & A. J. Hudspeth (Eds.), *Principles of neural science* (5th ed.). New York: McGraw-Hill.

Krebs, G., Bolhuis, K., Heyman, I., Mataix-Cols, D., Turner, C., & Stringaris, A. (2013). Temper outbursts in paediatric obsessive-compulsive disorder and their association with depressed mood and treatment outcome. *Journal of Child Psychology and Psychiatry and Allied Disciplines, 54*(3), 313–322.

Kuelz, A. K., Hohagen, F., & Voderholzer, U. (2004). Neuropsychological performance in obsessive-compulsive disorder: A critical review. *Biological Psychology, 65*(3), 185–236.

LaSalle, V. H., Cromer, V. R., Nelson, K. N., Kazuba, D., Justemente, L., & Murphy, D. L. (2004). Diagnostic interview assessed neuropsychiatric disorder comorbidity in 334 individuals with obsessive-compulsive disorder. *Depression and Anxiety, 19*, 163–173.

Lawrence, N. S., Wooderson, S., Mataix-Cols, D., David, R., Speckens, A., & Phillips, M. L. (2006). Decision-making and set shifting impairments are associated with distinct symptom dimensions in obsessive-compulsive disorder. *Neuropsychology, 20*(4), 409–419.

Leckman, J. F. (2002). Tourette's syndrome. *Lancet, 360*(9345), 1577–1586.

Leckman, J. F., Grice, D. E., Barr, L. C., de Vries, A. L., Martin, C., Cohen, D. J., … Rassmuessen, S. A. (1994). Tic-related vs. non-tic-related obsessive compulsive disorder. *Anxiety, 1*(5), 208–215.

LeDoux, J. E. (2012). Evolution of human emotion: a view through fear. *Progress in Brain Research, 195*, 431–442.

Lehmkuhl, H., Storch, E., Bodfish, J., & Geffken, G. (2008). Brief report: Exposure and response prevention for obsessive compulsive disorder in a 12-year-old with autism. *Journal of Autism and Developmental Disorders, 38*(5), 977–981.

Leonard, H. L., Swedo, S., Rapoport, J. L., Coffey, M., & Cheslow, D. (1988). Treatment of childhood obsessive compulsive disorder with clomipramine and desmethylimipramine: a double-blind crossover comparison. *Psychopharmacology Bulletin, 24*(1), 93–95.

Lewin, A. B., Chang, S., McCracken, J., McQueen, M., & Piacentini, J. (2010). Comparison of clinical features among youth with tic disorders, obsessive-compulsive disorder (OCD), and both conditions. *Psychiatry Research, 178*(2), 317–322.

Lewin, A. B., Larson, M. J., Park, J. M., McGuire, J. F., Murphy, T. K., & Storch, E. A. (2014). Neuropsychological functioning in youth with obsessive compulsive disorder: An examination of executive function and memory impairment. *Psychiatry Research, 216*(1), 108–115.

Leyfer, O. T., Folstein, S. E., Bacalman, S., Davis, N. O., Dinh, E., Morgan, J., Tager-Flusberg, H., & Lainhart, J. E. (2006). Comorbid psychiatric disorders in children with autism: Interview development and rates of disorders. *Journal of Autism and Developmental Disorders, 36*(7), 849–861.

Liebowitz, M. R., Turner, S. M., Piacentini, J., Beidel, D. C., Clarvit, S. R., Davies, S. O., ... Simpson, H. B. (2002). Fluoxetine in children and adolescents with OCD: A placebo-controlled trial. *Journal of the American Academy of Child and Adolescent Psychiatry, 41*(12), 1431–1438.

MacMaster, F. P., O'Neill, J., & Rosenberg, D. R. (2008). Brain imaging in pediatric obsessive-compulsive disorder. *Journal of the American Academy of Child and Adolescent Psychiatry, 47*(11), 1262–1272.

March, J. S., Biederman, J., Wolkow, R., Safferman, A., Mardekian, J., Cook, E. H., ... Steiner, H. (1998). Sertraline in children and adolescents with obsessive-compulsive disorder: A multicenter randomized controlled trial. *Journal of the American Medical Association, 280*(20), 1752–1756.

March, J. S., Franklin, M. E., Leonard, H., Garcia, A., Moore, P., Freeman, J., & Foa, E. (2007). Tics moderate treatment outcome with sertraline but not cognitive-behavior therapy in pediatric obsessive-compulsive disorder. *Biological Psychiatry, 61*(3), 344–347.

Masi, G., Millepiedi, S., Mucci, M., Bertini, N., Milantoni, L., & Arcangeli, F. (2005). A naturalistic study of referred children and adolescents with obsessive-compulsive disorder. *Journal of the American Academy of Child and Adolescent Psychiatry, 44*(7), 673–681.

Mattila, M. L., Hurtig, T., Haapsamo, H., Jussila, K., Kuusikko-Gauffin, S., Kielinen, M., ... Moilanen, J. (2010). Comorbid psychiatric disorders associated with Asperger syndrome/ high-functioning autism: A community- and clinic-based study. *Journal of Autism and Developmental Disorders, 40*(9), 1080–1093.

McGuire, J. F., Piacentini, J., Brennan, E. A., Lewin, A. B., Murphy, T. K., Small, B. J., & Storch, E. A. (2014). A meta-analysis of behavior therapy for Tourette syndrome. *Journal of Psychiatric Research, 50*, 106–112.

Menzies, L., Chamberlain, S. R., Laird, A. R., Thelen, S. M., Sahakian, B. J., & Bullmore, E. T. (2008). Integrating evidence from neuroimaging and neuropsychological studies of obsessive-compulsive disorder: The orbitofronto-striatal model revisited. *Neuroscience BiobehavioralReview, 32*(3), 525–549.

Miyake, M., Kakimoto, Y., & Sorimachi, M. (1981). A gas chromatographic method for the determination of N-acetyl-l-aspartic acid, N-acetyl-aspartylglutamic acid and -citryl-l-glutamic acid and their distributions in the brain and other organs of various species of animals. *Journal of Neurochemistry, 36*(3), 804–819.

Monchi, O., Petrides, M., Strafella, A. P., Worsley, K. J., & Doyon, J. (2006). Functional role of the basal ganglia in the planning and execution of actions. *Annals of Neurology, 59*(2), 257–264.

Morein-Zamir, S., Papmeyer, M., Gillan, C. M., Crockett, M. J., Fineberg, N. A., Sahakian, B. J., & Robbins, T. W. (2013). Punishment promotes response control deficits in obsessive-compulsive disorder: Evidence from a motivational go/no-go task. *Psychological Medicine, 43*(2), 391–400.

Murphy, T. K., Segarra, A., Storch, E. A., & Goodman, W. K. (2008). SSRI adverse events: How to monitor and manage. *International Review of Psychiatry, 20*(2), 203–208.

National Institute for Care and Excellence (NICE). (2005). Obsessive compulsive disorder (OCD) and body dysmorphic disorder (BDD). London: NICE.

Page, L. A., Rubia, K., Deeley, Q., Daly, E., Toal, F., Mataix-Cols, D., … Murphy, D. G. (2009). A functional magnetic resonance imaging study of inhibitory control in obsessive-compulsive disorder. *Psychiatry Research, 174*(3), 202–209.

Pauls, D. L., Abramovitch, A., Rauch, S. L., & Geller, D. A. (2014). Obsessive-compulsive disorder: An integrative genetic and neurobiological perspective. *Nature Reviews Neuroscience, 15*(6), 410–424.

Piacentini, J., Bergman, R. L., Chang, S., Langley, A., Peris, T., Wood, J. J., & McCracken, J. (2011). Controlled comparison of family cognitive behavioral therapy and psychoeducation/relaxation training for child obsessive-compulsive disorder. *Journal of the American Academy of Child and Adolescent Psychiatry, 50*(11), 1149–1161.

Piacentini, J., Bergman, R. L., Jacobs, C., McCracken, J. T., & Kretchman, J. (2002). Open trial of cognitive behavior therapy for childhood obsessive-compulsive disorder. *Journal of Anxiety Disorders, 16*(2), 207–219.

Piacentini, J., Woods, D. W., Scahill, L., Wilhelm, S., Peterson, A. L., Chang, S., … Walkup, J. T. (2010). Behavior therapy for children with Tourette disorder: A randomized controlled trial. *Journal of American Medical Association, 303*(19), 1929–1937.

Pittenger, C., Bloch, M. H., & Williams, K. (2011). Glutamate abnormalities in obsessive compulsive disorder: Neurobiology, pathophysiology, and treatment. *Pharmacology and Therapeutics, 132*(3), 314–332.

Rachman, S., De Silva, P., & Roper, G. (1976). The spontaneous decay of compulsive urges. *Behaviour Research and Therapy, 14*(6), 445–453.

Rachman, S., & Hodgson, R. J. (1980). *Obsessions and compulsions.* Englewood Cliffs, NY: Prentice-Hall.

Rapoport, J., Elkins, R., & Mikkelsen, E. (1980). Clinical controlled trial of chlorimipramine in adolescents with obsessive-compulsive disorder. *Psychopharmacology Bulletin, 16*(3), 61–63.

Rasmussen, S. A., & Eisen, J. L. (1992). The epidemiology and clinical features of obsessive-compulsive disorder. *Psychiatric Clinics of North America, 15,* 743–758.

Reaven, J., & Hepburn, S. (2003). Cognitive-behavioral treatment of obsessive-compulsive disorder in a child with Asperger syndrome: a case report. *Autism, 7*(2), 145–164.

Remijnse, P. L., Nielen, M. M., van Balkom, A. J., Cath, D. C., van Oppen, P., Uylings, H. B., & Veltman, D. J. (2006). Reduced orbitofrontal-striatal activity on a reversal learning task in obsessive-compulsive disorder. *Archives of General Psychiatry, 63*(11), 1225–1236.

Riddle, M. A., Reeve, E. A., Yaryura-Tobias, J. A., Yang, H. M., Claghorn, J. L., Gaffney, G., … Walkup, J. T. (2001). Fluvoxamine for children and adolescents with obsessive-compulsive disorder: A randomized, controlled, multicenter trial. *Journal of the American Academy of Child and Adolescent Psychiatry, 40*(2), 222–229.

Riddle, M. A., Scahill, L., King, R. A., Hardin, M. T., Anderson, G. M., Ort, S. I., … Cohen, D. J. (1992). Double-blind, crossover trial of fluoxetine and placebo in children and adolescents with obsessive-compulsive disorder. *Journal of the American Academy of Child and Adolescent Psychiatry, 31*(6), 1062–1069.

Romanelli, R. J., Wu, F. M., Gamba, R., Mojtabai, R., & Segal, J. B. (2014). Behavioral therapy and serotonin reuptake inhibitor pharmacotherapy in the treatment of obsessive-compulsive disorder: A systematic review and meta-analysis of head-to-head randomized controlled trials. *Depression and Anxiety, 31*(8), 641–52.

Rotge, J. Y., Guehl, D., Dilharreguy, B., Tignol, J., Bioulac, B., Allard, M., Burboaud, P., & Aouizerate, B. (2009). Meta-analysis of brain volume changes in obsessive-compulsive disorder. *Biological Psychiatry, 65*(1), 75–83.

Russell, A. J., Jassi, A., Fullana, M. A., Mack, H., Johnston, K., Heyman, I., Murphy, D. J., & Mataix-Cols, D. (2013). Cognitive behavior therapy for comorbid obsessive-compulsive disorder in high-functioning autism spectrum disorders: A randomized controlled trial. *Depression and Anxiety, 30*(8), 697–708.

Sanchez-Meca, J., Rosa-Alcazar, A. I., Iniesta-Sepulveda, M., & Rosa-Alcazar, A. (2014). Differential efficacy of cognitive-behavioral therapy and pharmacological treatments for pediatric obsessive-compulsive disorder: A meta-analysis. *Journal of Anxiety Disorders, 28*(1), 31–44.

Selles, R. R., Arnold, E. B., Phares, V., Lewin, A. B., Murphy, T. K., & Storch, E. A. (2014). Cognitive-behavioral therapy for anxiety in youth with an autism spectrum disorder: A follow-up study. *Autism, 19*(5), 613–621.

Shaw, M., Hodgkins, P., Caci, H., Young, S., Kahle, J., Woods, A. G., & Arnold, L. E. (2012). A systematic review and analysis of long-term outcomes in attention deficit hyperactivity disorder: Effects of treatment and non-treatment. *BMC Medicine, 10*, 99.

Simonoff, E., Pickles, A., Charman, T., Chandler, S., Loucas, T., & Baird, G. (2008). Psychiatric disorders in children with autism spectrum disorders: Prevalence, comorbidity, and associated factors in a population-derived sample. *Journal of the American Academy of Child and Adolescent Psychiatry, 47*(8), 921–929.

Skarphedinsson, G., Compton, S., Thomsen, P. H., Weidle, B., Dahl, K., Nissen, J. B., ... Iversson, T. (2015a). Tics moderate sertraline, but not cognitive-behavior therapy response in pediatric obsessive-compulsive disorder patients who do not respond to cognitive-behavior therapy. *Journal of Child and Adolescent Psychopharmacology, 25*(5), 432–439.

Skarphedinsson, G., Hanssen-Bauer, K., Kornor, H., Heiervang, E. R., Landro, N. I., Axelsdottir, B., ... Ivarsson, T. (2015b). Standard individual cognitive behaviour therapy for paediatric obsessive-compulsive disorder: A systematic review of effect estimates across comparisons. *Nordic Journal of Psychiatry, 69*(2), 81–92.

Skarphedinsson, G., Weidle, B., Thomsen, P. H., Dahl, K., Torp, N. C., Nissen, J. B., ... Ivarsson, T. (2015c). Continued cognitive behavior therapy versus sertraline for children and adolescents with obsessive-compulsive disorder that were non-responders to cognitive behavior therapy: A randomized controlled trial. *European Child and Adolescent Psychiatry, 24*(5), 591–602.

Stahl, S. M. (2013). *Stahl's essential psychopharmacology: Neuroscientific basis and practical applications* (4th ed.). Cambridge: Cambridge University Press.

Stewart, S. E., Geller, D. A., Jenike, M., Pauls, D., Shaw, D., Mullin, B., & Farone, S. V. (2004). Long-term outcome of pediatric obsessive-compulsive disorder: A meta-analysis and qualitative review of the literature. *Acta Psychiatrica Scandinavica, 110*(1), 4–13.

Storch, E. A., Bussing, R., Small, B. J., Geffken, G. R., McNamara, J. P., Rahman, O., ... Murphy, T. K. (2013). Randomized, placebo-controlled trial of cognitive-behavioral therapy alone or combined with sertraline in the treatment of pediatric obsessive-compulsive disorder. *Behaviour Research and Therapy, 51*(12), 823–829.

Storch, E. A., Jones, A. M., Lack, C. W., Ale, C. M., Sulkowski, M. L., Lewin, A. B., ... Murphy, T. K. (2012). Rage attacks in pediatric obsessive-compulsive disorder: Phenomenology and clinical correlates. *Journal of the American Academy of Child and Adolescent Psychiatry, 51*(6), 582–592.

Storch, E. A., Merlo, L. J., Larson, M. J., Geffken, G. R., Lehmkuhl, H. D., Jacob, M. L., ... Goodman, W. K. (2008). Impact of comorbidity on cognitive-behavioral therapy response in pediatric obsessive-compulsive disorder. *Journal of the American Academy of Child and Adolescent Psychiatry, 47*(5), 583–592.

Sukhodolsky, D. G., Bloch, M. H., Panza, K. E., & Reichow, B. (2013). Cognitive-behavioral therapy for anxiety in children with high-functioning autism: A meta-analysis. *Pediatrics, 132*(5), e1341–e1350.

Sukhodolsky, D. G., Gorman, B. S., Scahill, L., Findley, D., & McGuire, J. (2013). Exposure and response prevention with or without parent management training for children with obsessive-compulsive disorder complicated by disruptive behavior: A multiple-baseline across-responses design study. *Journal of Anxiety Disorders, 27*(3), 298–305.

Tanaka, S. C., Balleine, B. W., & O'Doherty, J. P. (2008). Calculating consequences: Brain systems that encode the causal effects of actions. *Journal of Neuroscience, 28*(26), 6750–6755.

Teffer, K., & Semendeferi, K. (2012). Human prefrontal cortex: Evolution, development, and pathology. *Progress in Brain Research, 195,* 191–218.

The Pediatric OCD Treatment Study (POTS) Team. (2004). Cognitive-behavior therapy, sertraline, and their combination for children and adolescents with obsessive-compulsive disorder: The Pediatric OCD Treatment Study (POTS) randomized controlled trial. *Journal of the American Medical Association, 292*(16), 1969–1976.

Thomsen, P. H. (1994). Obsessive-compulsive disorder in children and adolescents. A 6–22 year follow-up study: Clinical descriptions of the course and continuity of obsessive-compulsive symptomatology. *European Child and Adolescent Psychiatry, 3,* 82–96.

Thomsen, P. H., & Mikkelsen, H. U. (1995). Course of obsessive-compulsive disorder in children and adolescents: A prospective follow-up study of 23 Danish cases. *Journal of the American Academy of Child and Adolescent Psychiatry, 34,* 1432–1440.

Thoren, P., Asberg, M., Bertilsson, L., Mellstrom, B., Sjoqvist, F., & Traskman, L. (1980a). Clomipramine treatment of obsessive-compulsive disorder. II: Biochemical aspects. *Archives of General Psychiatry, 37*(11), 1289–1294.

Thoren, P., Asberg, M., Cronholm, B., Jornestedt, L., & Traskman, L. (1980b). Clomipramine treatment of obsessive-compulsive disorder. I: A controlled clinical trial. *Archives of General Psychiatry, 37*(11), 1281–1285.

Torp, N. C., Dahl, K., Skarphedinsson, G., Compton, J. S., Thomsen, P. H., Weidle, B., … Ivarsson, T. (2015). Predictors associated with improved cognitive behaviour therapy outcome in pediatric obsessive-compulsive disorder. *Journal of the American Academy of Child and Adolescent Psychiatry, 54*(3), 200–207.

Verdellen, C., van de Griendt, J., Hartmann, A., Murphy, T., & Group, E. G. (2011). European clinical guidelines for Tourette's syndrome and other tic disorders. Part III: Behavioural and psychosocial interventions. *European Child and Adolescent Psychiatry, 20*(4), 197–207.

Verdellen, C. W., Keijsers, G. P., Cath, D. C., & Hoogduin, C. A. (2004). Exposure with response prevention versus habit reversal in Tourettes's syndrome: A controlled study. *Behaviour Research and Therapy, 42*(5), 501–511.

Wagner, K. D., Cook, E. H., Chung, H., & Messig, M. (2003). Remission status after long-term sertraline treatment of pediatric obsessive-compulsive disorder. *Journal of Child and Adolescent Psychopharmacology, 13*(Suppl. 1), S53–S60.

Watkins, L. H., Sahakian, B. J., Robertson, M. M., Veale, D. M., Rogers, R. D., Pickard, K. M., … Robbins, T. W. (2005). Executive function in Tourette's syndrome and obsessive-compulsive disorder. *Psychological Medicine, 35*(4), 571–582.

Watson, H. J., & Rees, C. S. (2008). Meta-analysis of randomized, controlled treatment trials for pediatric obsessive-compulsive disorder. *Journal of Child Psychology and Psychiatry, 49*(5), 489–498.

Weidle, B., Melin, K., Drotz, E., Jozefiak, T., & Ivarsson, T. (2012). Preschool and current autistic symptoms in children and adolescents with obsessive-compulsive disorder (OCD). *Journal of Obsessive-Compulsive and Related Disorders, 1,* 168–174.

Woods, D. W., Piacentini, J., Chang, S. W., Deckersbach, T., Ginsburg, G., & Peterson, A. L. (2008). *Managing Tourette's syndrome: A Behavioral intervention for children and adults (therapist guide)*. New York: Oxford University Press.

Worbe, Y., Mallet, L., Golmard, J. L., Behar, C., Durif, F., Jalenques, I., ... Hartmann, A. (2010). Repetitive behaviours in patients with Gilles de la Tourette syndrome: Tics, compulsions, or both? *PLoS One, 5*(9), e12959.

Wu, K., Hanna, G. L., Rosenberg, D. R., & Arnold, P. D. (2012). The role of glutamate signaling in the pathogenesis and treatment of obsessive-compulsive disorder. *Pharmacology, Biochemistry and Behavior, 100*(4), 726–735.

16

Pharmacological Augmentations of SRIs for Obsessive Compulsive Disorder

Eric W. Leppink and Jon E. Grant

Selective serotonin reuptake inhibitors (SSRIs) and serotonin reuptake inhibitors (SRIs) have been consistently supported as a first-line pharmacological treatment for obsessive compulsive disorder (OCD). Fluoxetine, fluvoxamine, paroxetine, citalopram, escitalopram, and sertraline are the SSRIs and this class of medications primarily affect only serotonin. Clomipramine is a nonselective SRI, which means that it affects many other neurotransmitters besides serotonin. and because of this it has a more complicated set of side effects than the SSRIs. (Fineberg, Bullock, & Montgomery, 1992; Jenike et al., 1990; Smeraldi, Erzegovesi, Bianchi, & Pasquali, 1992; Thorén, Åsberg, Cronholm, Jörnestedt, & Träskman, 1980; Tollefson et al., 1994). Previous studies have noted, however, that as many as 40–60% of patients with OCD do not respond to typical SSRI/SRI treatments, or do not respond as quickly as necessary (Alarcon, Libb, & Spitler, 1993; Erzegovesi, Martucci, Heinin, & Bellodi, 2001; Ravizza, Barzega, Bellino, Bogetto, & Mai, 1995). In these cases, it may be necessary to supplement ongoing treatment with further medications, using these augmentations to elicit a higher response than was possible with SSRI/SRI monotherapy.

Numerous agents have been tested in this capacity and demonstrated varying degrees of success. Meta-analyses assessing atypical antipsychotics have frequently shown the highest degrees of success (Bloch et al., 2006; Dold, Aigner, Lanzenberger, & Kasper, 2012; Skapinakis, Papatheodorou, & Mavreas, 2007). However, with significant concerns regarding discontinuation from these medications, side effects, and contraindications, numerous alternative agents, with divergent mechanisms of action, have been examined in OCD (Arumugham & Reddy, 2013; Maina, Albert, Ziero, & Bogetto, 2003; Ramasubbu, Ravindran, & Lapierre, 2000). Both serotonergic and glutamatergic agents have been proposed as alternative augmentation options, and each category includes numerous medications with slightly different mechanisms of action (Marek, Carpenter, McDougle, & Price, 2003; Pittenger, Bloch, & Williams, 2011). Additionally, the available data for the various augmentation strategies ranges widely from several studies (e.g., risperidone, olanzapine, and ondansetron) to only limited support (Abdel-Ahad & Kazour, 2013; Albert, Barbaro, Aguglia, Maina, & Bogetto, 2012; Lack, 2012).

The Wiley Handbook of Obsessive Compulsive Disorders, Volume I, First Edition.
Edited by Jonathan S. Abramowitz, Dean McKay, and Eric A. Storch.
© 2017 John Wiley & Sons Ltd. Published 2017 by John Wiley & Sons Ltd.

This chapter will examine the published data regarding augmentation strategies for SSRI/SRIs in the treatment of OCD. Due to the number of studies currently available, the chapter will limit itself to only those double- and single-blind studies that used a controlled or comparative design. One issue that arises is how to examine whether an agent is successful as an augmentation. In general, response rates for OCD studies have examined the percent of subjects who experience a reduction in scores on the Yale–Brown Obsessive Compulsive Scale (Y-BOCS) (Goodman et al., 1989) relative to baseline. The criteria most commonly used have been either a 35% or 25% decrease, depending on the given study's methodology (Pallanti et al., 2002). The specific 35% and 25% criteria reflect "partial responses" and "complete responses," respectively. The criteria use by each study is specifically noted in the relevant section. However, this information was not available for all studies, with some instead reporting overall reduction in Y-BOCS scores or other measures. Studies missing this information are specifically indicated in the applicable table. These numbers should be considered within the context of each study's methodology, as the presence of a lead-in period, subject population, and permitted concomitant medications can alter baseline response rates, and could prove misleading without careful consideration.

The information provided in this chapter is intended to provide a general summary of available data from blinded, controlled studies assessing augmentation efficacy; thus, it does not include evidence from open-label trials, case reports, or retrospective analyses. Dosing information provided for each agent reflects the current levels reported in available studies meeting inclusion criteria, as is the case with treatment duration.

Antipsychotic Augmentations

Although not approved by the FDA for this purpose, antipsychotic medications are often used as augmentations for standard SSRI/SRI treatments of OCD (detailed list in Table 16.5; all tables can be found following the text). Early promising responses with antipsychotics (both typical and atypical) may indicate that dopaminergic abnormalities are a core neural underpinning in OCD (Billett et al., 1998; Hesse et al., 2005). Support from both individual studies and meta-analyses provide additional support for this theory (Bloch et al., 2006; Dold et al., 2013; Skapinakis et al., 2007). Although atypical antipsychotics affect both serotonergic and dopaminergic systems, their efficacy in patients with only limited responses to typical SSRI/SRI monotherapies may indicate an interconnection between the two systems (Olijslagers, Werkman, McCreary, Kruse, & Wadman, 2006). Research with typical antipsychotics has also supported this possibility, with one augmentation study using haloperidol, a dopamine inverse agonist, showing promising improvements in symptom severity and response rates (McDougle et al., 1994). Due to the number of possible side effects with antipsychotic medications (e.g., metabolic syndrome, hypercholesterolemia, diabetes, obesity), side-effect risks need to be weighed against the possibility of significant reductions in OCD symptom severity, as is the case with all of the atypical psychotics discussed in this chapter. For a brief summary of the medications discussed in this section, see Table 16.1.

Atypical Antipsychotics

Risperidone. Arguably one of the most extensively supported augmentation strategies for OCD, risperidone is a second-generation atypical antipsychotic and has previously been approved for use with schizophrenia, bipolar mania, and irritability associated with autistic disorder. Three separate double-blind, placebo-controlled studies found that risperidone augmentation produced greater improvements on target measures relative to placebo (Erzegovesi, Guglielmo, Siliprandi, & Bellodi, 2005; Hollander, Baldini Rossi, Sood, & Pallanti, 2003; McDougle, Epperson, Pelton, Wasylink, & Price, 2000). Two of these studies also reported improvement on secondary measures assessing depression and anxiety (Erzegovesi et al., 2005; McDougle et al., 2000). Available comparison and cross-over studies have also shown improvements on OCD severity in groups taking active risperidone augmentation. In two single-blind comparison studies and one double-blind, placebo-controlled cross-over study, risperidone showed significant improvement relative to baseline scores for target measures. However, risperidone was not shown to be more effective than olanzapine (Maina, Pessina, Albert, & Bogetto, 2008), or haloperidol (Li et al., 2005) in reducing target measures, and showed only secondary advantages over aripiprazole (Selvi et al., 2011).

Response rates ranged from 40% (0% placebo, ≥ 25% Y-BOCS improvement) (Hollander et al., 2003), to 50% (0% placebo, ≥ 25% Y-BOCS improvement) (Erzegovesi et al., 2005; McDougle et al., 2000) across all studies reporting response rates. Dosing ranged from 0.5 mg/day (Erzegovesi et al., 2005) to 3 mg/day (Maina et al., 2008; Selvi et al., 2011). Studies using risperidone augmentations have reported some of the most consistent results in controlled studies, with all controlled studies finding improvements relative to placebo.

Quetiapine. Quetiapine is also a second-generation atypical antipsychotic and has previously been approved for use with schizophrenia, bipolar mania, and bipolar depression. Studies on quetiapine augmentation have shown mixed results on efficacy using multiple designs, with different methods and populations eliciting variations in the results.

Of seven double-/single-blind, placebo-controlled studies, three showed improvements with quetiapine augmentation relative to placebo on target measures, including Y-BOCS scores (Atmaca, Kuloglu, Tezcan, & Gecici, 2002; Denys, de Geus, van Megen, & Westenberg, 2004; Vulink, Denys, Fluitman, Meinardi, & Westenberg, 2009). The remaining four studies found no improvement over placebo, with one comparison study finding that both placebo and clomipramine augmentations were superior to quetiapine in this capacity (Carey et al., 2005; Diniz et al., 2011; Fineberg, Sivakumaran, Roberts, & Gale, 2005; Kordon et al., 2008). However, several of the investigators reporting nonsignificant findings either specifically noted methodological limitations that may have obscured the possible efficacy of quetiapine, or noted trends that did not reach significance upon further analysis (Carey et al., 2005; Fineberg et al., 2005).

Response rates ranged from 27% (10% placebo, ≥ 35% Y-BOCS reduction) (Fineberg et al., 2005) to 65% (44% placebo, ≥ 35% Y-BOCS reduction) (Kordon et al., 2008) across all studies reporting response rates. Dosing ranged from 91 mg/day (±41.1) (Atmaca et al., 2002) to 600 mg/day (Kordon et al., 2008). Various studies assessing quetiapine augmentation for OCD have yielded some positive results, with all available controlled studies reporting at least a 25% response rate amongst active treatment subjects. However, these findings are tempered by additional controlled studies that report no observed advantage of quetiapine over placebo under comparable study conditions.

Olanzapine. Olanzapine, another second-generation atypical antipsychotic, has previously been approved for use with schizophrenia, bipolar manic/mixed episodes, and as augmentation for resistant depression and bipolar depression. However, fewer studies in OCD have been conducted with olanzapine compared with either risperidone or quetiapine, and results have been mixed regarding its efficacy. Although as we stated above all the antipsychotic medications have been associated with serious side effects, olanzapine appears to have an even more pronounced association with the risk of hyperlipidemia, cardiovascular consequences, metabolic syndrome, and thereby warrants serious consideration of its risk-benefit ratio.

Two double-blind, placebo-controlled studies have assessed olanzapine augmentation, but the results of these two studies are contradictory, with Bystritsky and colleagues (2004) finding significant improvement relative to the control group, and Shapira et al. (2004) finding no significant improvements relative to controls. It should be noted that Shapira et al. (2004) asserted that the short lead-in period and lower dose used in their methodology may have confounded results. Supplemental findings from a single-blind study comparing olanzapine and risperidone augmentation indicated that both treatments produced significant improvements on Y-BOCS scores relative to baseline, with both agents eliciting a comparable degree of improvement (Maina et al., 2008).

Response rates ranged from 23% (18% placebo, ≥ 35% Y-BOCS reduction) (Shapira et al., 2004) to 57.1% (50% risperidone, ≥ 35% Y-BOCS reduction) (Maina et al., 2008) across all studies reporting response rates. Dosing ranged from 3.5 mg/day (Maina et al., 2008) to 11.2 mg/day (±6.5) (Bystritsky et al., 2004). As was the case with quetiapine, results from controlled studies have indicated mixed findings regarding olanzapine's potential efficacy as an augmentation for OCD. Additionally, the research base for olanzapine augmentation in OCD is significantly smaller than what is available for both risperidone and quetiapine.

Aripiprazole. Aripiprazole is a more recent option in the line of atypical antipsychotics, and has previously been approved for use with schizophrenia, bipolar mania, bipolar mixed episodes, irritability associated with autistic disorder, and as an augmentation for major depressive disorder. Only a few double-blind, placebo-controlled studies have been conducted with aripiprazole, but they have consistently shown improvement in target symptoms relative to placebo.

Three studies have assessed the efficacy of aripiprazole as an augmentation, of which the two double-blind studies found significant improvements on target measures relative to placebo (Muscatello et al., 2011; Sayyah, Olapour, Saeedabad, Yazdan Parast, & Malayeri, 2012b). In the third, a single-blind comparison study, both aripiprazole and risperidone produced significant improvements on target measures (Selvi et al., 2011). Improvements did not differ between the two groups, except for on Y-BOCS obsession scores, with risperidone showing a significantly greater reduction during the course of the study.

Response rates ranged from 25% (0% placebo, ≥ 35% Y-BOCS reduction) (Muscatello et al., 2011) to 72.2% (50% risperidone, ≥ 35% Y-BOCS reduction) (Selvi et al., 2011) across all studies reporting response rates. Dosing ranged from 10 mg/day

(Sayyah et al., 2012b) to 15 mg/day (Muscatello et al., 2011; Selvi et al., 2011). Overall, controlled studies assessing aripiprazole as an augmentation for OCD have shown promising results on Y-BOCS score reduction relative to placebo conditions. Additionally, comparable results between risperidone and aripiprazole in a direct comparison study may indicate additional commonalities between the two agents.

Paliperidone. The final atypical antipsychotic is paliperidone, which has previously been approved for use with schizophrenia and schizoaffective disorder. There has only been one controlled study looking at paliperidone as an augmentation strategy for OCD. This double-blind, placebo-controlled study did not show any improvement over placebo on target measures (Storch et al., 2013). The authors of the study noted that there were select nonsignificant trends in the data which may support further studies on the medication. The response rate for this study was 35% (29% placebo, ≥ 35% Y-BOCS reduction). The mean ending dose for the treatment group was 4.94 mg/day (±2.36). Results reported by Storch and colleagues (2013) do not indicate significant differences on target measures between paliperidone and placebo augmentations. However, only this one controlled study has assessed paliperidone's potential efficacy as an augmentation for OCD.

Typical Antipsychotics

Haloperidol. Haloperidol is a first-generation typical antipsychotic and has previously been approved for use with schizophrenia and Tourette's Disorder. Few double-blind, placebo-controlled studies have assessed haloperidol's efficacy as an augmenting medication in OCD. However, the primary study assessing its utility as an augmentation noted marked improvements specifically in patients whose OCD symptoms included tics, a subset of patients with OCD that may share similarities with Tourette's Disorder (McDougle et al., 1994).

Only two double-blind, placebo-controlled studies have been conducted with haloperidol. Both of these studies showed that haloperidol produced significant symptom reduction relative to placebo (Li et al., 2005; McDougle et al., 1994). One of these studies, a cross-over study with haloperidol and risperidone, showed that both drugs elicited significant improvements on target measures relative to placebo, but did not differ from each other (Li et al., 2005). The other also assessed haloperidol's efficacy in OCD patients with and without tics, showing improved results for those with tics (McDougle et al., 1994). In this study, 100% percent of patients with tics who received the haloperidol augmentation showed at least a 35% reduction in Y-BOCS scores.

Response rates for haloperidol come from one double-blind, placebo-controlled study in which 64.7% of subjects responded to the treatment (0% placebo, ≥ 35% Y-BOCS reduction). Dosing ranged from 2 mg (Li et al., 2005) to 10 mg (McDougle et al., 1994) in the two available studies. Although controlled studies assessing haloperidol augmentation are limited, positive findings in treatment-resistant cases of OCD with accompanying tics are particularly notable. In many studies, patients whose OCD is accompanied by tics are identified as particularly treatment resistant, and are often excluded from augmentation studies for this reason. Thus, the findings reported by McDougle and colleagues (1994), namely, high response rates to haloperidol augmentation amongst patients with OCD related tics, may be an indication of haloperidol's utility in the treatment of OCD.

Serotonergic Agents

As noted previously, SSRIs/SRIs are currently the most common pharmaceutical options for OCD (Fineberg et al., 1992; Jenike et al., 1990; Smeraldi et al., 1992; Thorén et al., 1980; Tollefson et al., 1994) (detailed list in Table 16.6). Following from these findings, a number of studies have examined serotonergic agents as augmentations for standard regimens of SSRIs/SRIs. The majority of these studies, however, have not elicited the level of symptom reduction that might be expected (Marek et al., 2003). Although there are some notable exceptions, such as ondansetron (discussed below), very few serotonergic medications have been tested with the same rigor, or positive results, as antipsychotic augmentations. Promising results with a number of agents have not been confirmed in later trials, emphasizing the importance of retesting medications in a number of subgroups to establish a baseline of efficacy (Arumugham & Reddy, 2013). None of these medications are FDA-approved as augmentation agents for OCD (although clomipramine is approved as a monotherapy for OCD). For a brief summary of the medications discussed in this section, see Table 16.2.

Ondansetron. Ondansetron, a 5-HT_3 antagonist and weak 5-HT_4 antagonist (Hasler, Hirt, Ridolfi Luethy, Leibundgut, & Ammann, 2008), has previously been approved to prevent nausea and vomiting from various causes such as chemotherapy. Of the serotonergic agents, ondansetron has been assessed in the largest number of controlled studies and shown consistently positive results across these trials.

Two double-blind, placebo-controlled studies have assessed ondansetron as an augmentation strategy for typical SSRI/SRI treatment in OCD. Both studies found that it was associated with significant improvements relative to placebo on target measures (Heidari et al., 2014; Soltani et al., 2010). Additionally, two single-blind studies demonstrated significant improvement relative to baseline in subjects treated with ondansetron augmentation (Pallanti, Bernardi, Antonini, Singh, & Hollander, 2009, 2014). One of these studies specifically used ondansetron as a tertiary medication for preexisting antipsychotic augmentation, a use not commonly explored for other agents (Pallanti et al., 2009). It should be noted that the high response rate reported by Heidari and colleagues (2014) reflects both responders to the augmentation and to standard treatment with fluvoxamine, as treatment with both medications was initiated at the beginning of the study.

Response rates ranged from 57% (≥25% Y-BOCS reduction) (Pallanti et al., 2014) to 90.9% (31.8% placebo, ≥ 25% Y-BOCS reduction) (Heidari et al., 2014) across all studies reporting response rates. Dosing ranged from 1 mg/day (Pallanti et al., 2009, 2014) to 8 mg/day (Heidari et al., 2014). Available studies using ondansetron as an augmentation for OCD have shown consistent improvements on OCD symptom severity. Even with these findings, ondansetron is less commonly used as augmentation than the antipsychotics. Reasons for this are unclear. Additionally, findings from Pallanti and colleagues (2009) showing significant improvements when using ondansetron as a tertiary augmentation may some utility as an additive for existing augmentations, potentially increasing the efficacy of antipsychotic augmentations in select patients with OCD.

Granisetron. Granisetron is another 5-HT_3 antagonist that has previously been approved to treat nausea and vomiting, particularly after chemotherapy treatments. Granisetron is thought to have a similar mechanism as ondansetron, but may avoid alterations to cytochrome P450 activity. Although similar to ondansetron, granisetron augmentation for OCD has not been well studied in double-blind, placebo-controlled studies.

In the only available study on granisetron augmentation, Askari and colleagues (2012) assessed granisetron's efficacy as an augmentation for fluvoxamine relative to placebo. The study reported significant improvement with granisetron over placebo on response rates during the course of the study. Adverse events were also equally common between the two groups, suggesting that granisetron was well tolerated during the study. Treatment with granisetron and fluvoxamine were started concurrently at the beginning of the study, thus the response rates reported do not solely reflect the efficacy of granisetron.

Response rate for the study reached 100% by the end of week 8 (35% placebo, ≥ 35% Y-BOCS reduction). Dosing was set at 1 mg/12 hours for the duration of the study. The results of this study suggest that granisetron may be an effective augmentation for fluvoxamine. Although this is the only study examining granisetron as an augmentation for OCD, its high response rates merit further investigation to confirm these findings.

Clomipramine. Although primarily used as a primary medication or monotherapy for OCD, clomipramine has also been proposed as an augmentation strategy for OCD. Clomipramine is a serotonin reuptake inhibitor (as opposed to selective serotonin reuptake inhibitors) commonly used in the treatment of OCD. Additionally, clomipramine has frequently been used as an acceptable primary medication in the majority of studies noted in this chapter. However, there has only been one double-blind, placebo-controlled study using clomipramine as the augmenting medication.

In the one available double-blind, placebo-controlled study conducted by Diniz and co-workers (2011), clomipramine was used as an augmentation for fluoxetine and compared with quetiapine and placebo augmentations. The study found that both clomipramine and placebo showed significantly greater reductions in Y-BOCS score relative to quetiapine. These results do not necessarily support the efficacy of clomipramine as an augmentation strategy, but may need to be considered in the context of other efficacy studies on clomipramine as a monotherapy. Response rates for the study were only reported using Clinical Global Improvement (CGI) scores ("much improved" or "very much improved"), with 44% of subjects classified as responders according to this criterion (33% quetiapine, 56% placebo). Dosing for the study was 55 mg/day (±20), but it was noted that plasma clomipramine levels were well below toxic limits and likely could have been increased.

Mirtazapine. Mirtazapine is an antidepressant that may also indirectly affect the serotonergic system by disinhibiting the norepinephrine activation of 5-HT neurons. It has previously been approved for use with major depressive disorder. There is preliminary data that mirtazapine as monotherapy may be beneficial for the treatment of OCD (Koran, Gamel, Choung, Smith, & Aboujaoude, 2005). Only one controlled study has assessed mirtazapine as an augmentation strategy for OCD.

In this study, Pallanti, Quercioli, and Bruscoli (2004) compared mirtazapine and placebo in patients starting a new citalopram regimen. The study showed no significant differences in symptom reduction between the two groups. However, the study did note that the active augmentation group showed a faster response rate to the citalopram treatment relative to the placebo group. Mirtazapine and citalopram treatment were initiated concurrently at the beginning of the study. The response rate for this study was 61.7% at the end of 12 weeks (61.9% placebo, ≥ 35% Y-BOCS reduction).

Dosing ranged from 15 to 30 mg/day over the course of the 12-week period. In the available controlled study, mirtazapine augmentation was associated with faster response rates relative to placebo. However, no significant results were reported for measures of symptom severity.

Buspirone. Buspirone is an anti-anxiety medication that is thought to be a 5-HT$_1$A receptor partial agonist. It has previously been approved for use with anxiety disorders, specifically generalized anxiety disorder. When considering double-blind, placebo-controlled studies, buspirone has not shown significant efficacy as an augmentation strategy for OCD.

Three available double-blind studies have examined buspirone augmentation using various placebo-controlled methods. Of these studies, none have found significant improvement with buspirone relative to placebo (Grady et al., 1993; McDougle et al., 1993; Pigott et al., 1992). All three studies used different primary SSRI/SRI medications, including clomipramine (Pigott et al., 1992), fluoxetine (Grady et al., 1993), and fluvoxamine (McDougle et al., 1993). Additionally, Pigott and colleagues (1992) reported that 21% of subjects in their study reported a 25% or greater worsening of symptoms over the course of the study.

Response rates ranged from 7% (0% placebo, ≥ 25% Y-BOCS reduction) (Grady et al., 1993) to 28.6% (≥25% Y-BOCS reduction) (Pigott et al., 1992) across available studies. Dosing for each study was as follows: Pigott et al. (1992), 57 mg/day (±7); Grady et al. (1993), 60 mg/day; McDougle et al. (1993), 59.2 mg/day (±3.4). Evidence from double-blind, controlled studies has consistently found buspirone to be ineffective as an augmentation strategy for primary SSRI/SRI treatment for OCD. Evidence from three separate studies has shown no improvement over placebo, with one of these studies reporting significant worsening in 20% of subjects.

Glutamatergic Agents

Although the exact role of glutamate in OCD is still an ongoing question, a number of trials testing glutamatergic augmentations have shown promising results (Afshar et al., 2012; Bruno et al., 2012; Ghaleiha et al., 2013; Haghighi et al., 2013; Mowla, Khajeian, Sahraian, Chohedri, & Kashkoli, 2010) (detailed list in Table 16.7). These findings are supported by additional genetics and imaging work implicating glutamate, along with serotonin and dopamine, in the neurobiology of OCD (Pittenger et al., 2011; Simpson et al., 2012; Wu, Hanna, Rosenberg, & Arnold, 2012).

The complexity of these interactions on a neurobiological level, and their influences on the severity and course of OCD, make specific claims of causality tenuous assertions. Various reviews of glutamatergic abnormalities have consistently suggested an interactive theory between glutamate, serotonin and dopamine. However, the exact mechanism by which glutamatergic agents impact OCD symptomology remains an ongoing point of investigation (Wu et al., 2012). For a brief summary of the medications discussed in this section, see Table 16.3.

Memantine. Memantine, a NMDA receptor antagonist, is FDA-approved for the treatment of Alzheimer-type dementia. Of the glutamatergic augmentations, memantine is one of the few that has shown significant reductions on target measures in at least two separate controlled studies. Two double-blind, placebo-controlled augmentation studies have been conducted using memantine to complement standard SSRI/SRI regimens.

Both of these augmentations studies indicated that memantine augmentation produced significant improvements on target measures relative to placebo (Ghaleiha et al., 2013; Haghighi et al., 2013). Ghaleiha and colleagues (2013) reported that during the course of their study 89% of subject taking active memantine achieved remission (Y-BOCS < 16). It should be noted that treatment with memantine was started co-currently with fluvoxamine for this study, and thus some of the response must be attributed to improvement from the fluvoxamine.

Response rates ranged from 64.3% (0% placebo, ≥ 35% Y-BOCS reduction) (Haghighi et al., 2013) to 100% (32% placebo, ≥ 25% Y-BOCS reduction) (Ghaleiha et al., 2013) for the two available studies. Dosing ranged from 5–10 mg/day (Haghighi et al., 2013) to 20 mg/day (Ghaleiha et al., 2013). Results from available controlled studies using memantine as an augmentation have reported significant improvements on target measures relative to control conditions. High response rates relative to placebo may suggest that memantine's role as an NMDA antagonist positively influences the effects of SSRI/SRI treatment for OCD symptoms.

N-Acetylcystine. N-acetylcystine (NAC) is an antioxidant and natural supplement that affects glutamate within the ventral striatal region of the brain. Additionally, NAC has been used as a primary treatment for various impulse control disorders, including pathological gambling and trichotillomania (Grant, Kim, & Odlaug, 2007; Grant, Odlaug, & Kim, 2009; Odlaug & Grant, 2007). Success with these disorders may indicate that NAC is a viable augmentation option for the treatment of OCD. Research on NAC remains limited and will require further investigation to confirm the results of the one available controlled study.

Only one double-blind, placebo-controlled study has assessed NAC's efficacy as an augmentation specifically in the context of OCD. In this study, Afshar and colleagues (2012) found that NAC augmentation showed improvement on target symptoms relative to placebo. NAC was also well tolerated. The response rate for this study was reported as 52.6% (15% placebo, ≥ 35% Y-BOCS reduction). Dosing ranged from 600 to 2,400 mg during the 12-week study. The available controlled study reported improvements on target symptoms when using NAC as an augmentation for OCD.

Topiramate. Topiramate, an anticonvulsant medication, is a glutamate inhibitor that affects the voltage-gated sodium and calcium ion channels. This mechanism of action distinguishes topiramate from other glutamatergic options, such as memantine and NAC, which could impact which patients will benefit most from its effects. Trials using anticonvulsants as augmentations for SSRI/SRI treatment of OCD have noted some significant improvements, and may indicate efficacy as augmentations for OCD (Berlin et al., 2011; Bruno et al., 2012; Mowla et al., 2010).

In both available double-blind, placebo-controlled studies using topiramate to augment SSRI/SRIs, the treatment groups showed significant improvements on clinical measures (Berlin et al., 2011; Mowla et al., 2010). The two studies, however, did not find the same improvements between treatment groups. Mowla and colleagues (2010) reported improvements on total Y-BOCS scores (reported in responder rate), while Berlin and colleagues (2011) only reported improvements on Y-BOCS compulsion scores, and further found that topiramate was not well tolerated, with 28% of subjects dropping out of the study due to side effects and 39% requiring a dose reduction.

Response rate was only available for one study, and reached 60% by the end of 12 weeks (0% placebo, ≥ 25% Y-BOCS reduction) (Mowla et al., 2010). Dosing means ranged from 177.8 mg/day (Berlin et al., 2011) to 180.15 mg/day (Mowla et al., 2010). Results from controlled studies assessing topiramate augmentation noted select improvements over placebo.

Lamotrigine. Lamotrigine is another anticonvulsant, the net effect of which is an overall reduction in excessive glutamate. However, the manner by which it affects glutamate may differentiate it from other anticonvulsants, such as topiramate (Burstein, 1995). Current research on lamotrigine augmentation for OCD is limited, but findings with topiramate may indicate possible benefits from anticonvulsant augmentation. This is tempered by select inconsistencies in the previous findings with topiramate, thus further research will be necessary to clarify efficacy (Berlin et al., 2011; Mowla et al., 2010).

Only one double-blind, placebo controlled study has been conducted with lamotrigine. In this study, Bruno and colleagues (2012) found that lamotrigine produced significant improvements on target symptoms relative to placebo. Additionally, this study noted that lamotrigine augmentation was associated with significant improvements on Semantic fluency tasks at the end of the study, relative to baseline. The reported response rate for the study was 35% on target measures (0% placebo, ≥ 35% Y-BOCS reduction). The final dosing for the study was 100 mg/day.

Riluzole. Riluzole is a glutamatergic modulator that affects glutamate release and other aspects of the glutamate system (Bellingham, 2011). Currently, riluzole is approved for use with amyotrophic lateral sclerosis. Unlike the other glutamatergic augmentations listed in this section, riluzole specifically affects the release of glutamate, a mechanism of action that may distinguish it from other glutamatergic agents. One double-blind, placebo-controlled study has been conducted on riluzole's efficacy in OCD, but the methods of the study limit the conclusions that can be drawn from its results.

Grant and colleagues (2014) assessed riluzole's efficacy as a treatment for OCD in a sample of children and adolescents aged 7–17 years, and found no improvements over placebo on target measures. However, their results are confounded by a number of variables that limit its applicability to discussions of augmentation. In the study's sample, only 77% of the treatment subjects were currently taking any type of SSRI or SRI, and of those, only 13% were taking only an SSRI or SRI. These concomitant medications could have significantly influenced the results of the study, a problem that the authors note in their discussion. Additionally, comorbidities were common in the sample, with a mean of 2.33 comorbid disorders per subject in the active treatment group. The response rate for the study was 16% (18% placebo, ≥ 35% Y-BOCS reduction). Dosing for the study was set at 100 mg/day.

Glycine. The final glutamatergic agent, glycine, is an allosteric NMDA agonist. Glycine is thought to produce neurobiological effects by altering levels of NMDA. There is only one study examining this type of medication as an augmentation strategy for OCD. In the one double-blind, placebo-controlled study available, Greenberg and colleagues (2009) found no significant improvement with glycine augmentation relative to controls. Additionally, 66.7% of active subjects discontinued from the study due to side effects or aversion to the taste of the medication. The response rate for completers was reported as 40% (two out of five subjects) (0% placebo, ≥ 35% Y-BOCS reduction). Dosing was set at 60 g/day.

Other Agents

The following medications represent a wide variety of different mechanisms (detailed list in Table 16.8). Summaries of each agent are provided under its respective heading. A number of treatments on this list have shown promising results, but few have more than one trial or have shown consistency across trials. For a brief summary of the medications discussed in this section, see Table 16.4.

Lithium. Lithium is well established as a treatment for bipolar disorder, affecting a number of different neurotransmitters, producing notable decreases in norepinephrine and increases in serotonin synthesis. Lithium was one of the first augmentations assessed for the treatment of OCD, and contrary to expectations, studies to date have not supported lithium augmentation for the treatment of OCD. In the only available double-blind, placebo-controlled study, McDougle, Price, Goodman, Charney, and Heninger (1991) found that lithium augmentation of fluvoxamine produced small, significant improvements relative to placebo. However, the authors deemed this difference clinically insignificant. In line with these findings, Pigott and colleagues (1991) found no improvement with either lithium or thyroid hormone in a double-blind, cross-over study assessing the two in conjunction with clomipramine.

Response rates ranged from 12.5% (6.3% placebo, ≥ 25% Y-BOCS reduction) (Pigott et al., 1991) to 13% (0% placebo, ≥ 35% Y-BOCS reduction) (McDougle et al., 1991). Dosing ranged from 900 mg/day (McDougle et al., 1991) to 1,500 mg/day (Pigott et al., 1991). Neither study showed clinically significant improvement using lithium augmentation for OCD. Although lithium could offer some benefit to patients with other comorbid disorders, it has not shown efficacy as a general augmentation for OCD

Pindolol. Pindolol is primarily a nonselective beta-blocker with an additional antagonistic effect on pre-synaptic 5-HT$_{1A}$ receptors. Pindolol's primary approved use is to control arterial hypertension. Two studies have been conducted assessing pindolol's efficacy as an augmentation for either fluvoxamine or paroxetine.

Results from these two studies are mixed. In one study, Mundo, Guglielmo, and Bellodi (1998) reported that pindolol did not produce significant improvements over placebo on target measures. This study began fluvoxamine treatment at the same time as pindolol or placebo augmentation. The response rate in the placebo group reached 85% in this study, which is much higher than comparable studies using treatment-resistant cases of OCD. This could have limited findings, as the fluvoxamine treatment produced high response rates regardless of condition. Countering this, Dannon et al. (2000) reported that pindolol produced significant reductions on the Y-BOCS relative to the placebo group. These results were achieved in only 6 weeks, as opposed to 8 weeks in the preceding study. The authors of this study also suggested that using pindolol as an augmentation for paroxetine may have been a more effective combination, as opposed to fluvoxamine. Response rates were only available for one study, in which 75% responded to the medication (85% placebo, ≥ 35% Y-BOCS reduction) (Mundo et al., 1998). Dosing for both studies was set as 7.5 mg/day.

Caffeine and d-amphetamine. In one double-blind study, Koran, Aboujaoude, and Gamel (2009) compared caffeine and d-amphetamine as augmentations for standard SSRI/SRI/SNRI treatments of OCD in a double-blind, cross-over procedure. In the study, caffeine was intended to act as a placebo condition, although its efficacy in this role is not well supported.

During the study, both the caffeine and the d-amphetamine augmentations produced significant reductions on the target measures. However, no differences were found between the final Y-BOCS scores for the two treatment groups. In the discussion, the authors note that caffeine was most likely not an effective placebo control, as its effects on a neurobiological level may have elicited positive responses similar to those expected from the d-amphetamine. Response rates for the two conditions were as follows: caffeine, 91.7%; d-amphetamine, 66.7% (≥25% Y-BOCS reduction). Dosing for the two conditions was as follows: caffeine, 300 mg/day; d-amphetamine, 30 mg/day.

Morphine. The opioid analgesic morphine has also been suggested as a possible augmentation for OCD. Koran et al. (2005b) conducted a double-blind, placebo-controlled cross-over study in which they compared once-weekly morphine, lorazepam (a benzodiazepine), and placebo augmentations in conjunction with set SSRI/SRIs and augmenting medications.

In the study, Koran et al. (2005b) found that morphine produced significant improvements relative to placebo and lorazepam on target measures. Some worsening of symptoms was reported in both of the active medication groups, but overall the treatments were well tolerated. Response rates for the study were as follows: morphine, 30.4%; lorazepam, 18.1% (0% placebo, ≥ 25% Y-BOCS reduction). Dosing was as follows: morphine, 30–45 mg/week; lorazepam, .5–2 mg/day. These results suggest indicate significant reductions in OCD symptom severity following morphine augmentation, even without controlling for concomitant augmentations. This may reflect a unique mechanism of action that has yet to be fully explored.

Zinc Sulfate. Zinc sulfate is a naturally occurring compound that has been associated with various roles in numerous biological processes (Nowak & Szewczyk, 2002; Takeda, 2000). Due to this varied role, Sayyah, Olapour, Saeedabad, Yazdan Parast, and Malayeri (2012a) assessed zinc sulfate's efficacy as an augmentation for the treatment of OCD. This double-blind, placebo-controlled study found that zinc sulfate was associated with both improvement on final Y-BOCS scores and faster response rates relative to placebo. Zinc sulfate augmentation was started concurrently with a fluoxetine regimen, and thus had no lead in period during which subjects could adjust to the medication prior to augmentation. Response rates were not reported for this study. Dosing was set at 40 mg/day for the duration of the study.

Celecoxib. Celecoxib is a non-steroidal anti-inflammatory drug (NSAID) that may selectively inhibit prostaglandin synthesis. Some data have suggested that inflammation from certain infections could result in OCD-like symptoms, which could then be treated with an NSAID such as celecoxib (Kurlan, 1998; Swedo et al., 1997). In response to this theory, Sayyah, Boostani, Pakseresht, and Malayeri (2011) conducted a double-blind, placebo-controlled study on celecoxib as an adjunct treatment option for OCD. In the one available double-blind study, results indicated that the celecoxib produced improvements on target measures in addition to shortened delays prior to response. Augmentation with celecoxib was started concurrently with fluoxetine, thus some degree of response would be expected solely in response to the SSRI treatment. Response rates were not reported for this study. Dosing was set at 400 mg/day for the duration of the study. As is the case with zinc sulfate, the exact manner though which celecoxib affects neurobiological factors remains a point of investigation.

Clonazepam. Clonazepam is a benzodiazepine that is thought to affect GABA levels by modulating the $GABA_A$ receptor. Although imaging studies have implicated GABA levels as another potential factor in the neurobiology of OCD, pharmaceutical implementations of this possibility have yet to show positive or consistent results (Nikolaus et al., 2012). In the one available double-blind, placebo-controlled study, Crocket, Churchill, and Davidson (2004) found no significant improvements with clonazepam augmentation relative to the placebo. In the study, clonazepam was initiated in conjunction with sertraline, thus response to sertraline likely accounts for a significant portion of subjects characterized as responders. The response rate for clonazepam in this study was 54.5% (45.5% placebo, ≥ 25% Y-BOCS reduction). Dosing for the study reached a mean of 2.7 mg/day.

Inositol. Inositol is a natural supplement that was found to be effective as a monotherapy for OCD (Fux, Levine, Aviv, & Belmaker, 1996). Its use as an augmenting agent has not elicited the same level of success. In a double-blind, placebo-controlled, cross-over study, Fux, Benjamin, and Belmaker (1999) found that inositol augmentation did not produce significant improvements relative to placebo. This is contrary to their findings on inositol as a monotherapy, and may suggest that inositol's mechanism of action as a monotherapy is not effective in conjunction with standard SSRI/SRI treatments. Response rates for the study were not reported. Dosing was set at 18 g/day for the duration of the study. Despite its support as a monotherapy, the available controlled study on inositol augmentation did not shown significant improvements relative to placebo.

Naltrexone. Naltrexone, an opioid antagonist, was also proposed as an augmentation for standard SSRI/SRI treatment. Naltrexone has shown promising results with impulse control disorders such as pathological gambling and trichotillomania (Grant et al., 2009; Kim, Grant, Adson, & Shin, 2001). Only one double-blind, placebo-controlled, cross-over study has assessed naltrexone's efficacy as an augmentation for OCD treatment (Amiaz, Fostick, Gershon, & Zohar, 2008). This study found that naltrexone augmentation produced no significant improvements on target measures relative to the placebo. Furthermore, the study found that the naltrexone group had higher rates of anxiety and depression relative to healthy controls.

No subjects in either the placebo or active groups were classified as responders (≥35% Y-BOCS reduction). Dosing ranged from 50 to 100 mg/day over the course of the study. This study showed no significant advantages when using naltrexone as an augmentation for OCD. Response rates in this sample were the lowest of any available study, with no subject reporting response to the augmentation.

Desipramine. Desipramine is a tricyclic antidepressant FDA-approved for the treatment of major depressive disorder. Unlike the other medications in this list, desipramine is thought to primarily affect norepinephrine transport, rather than directly influencing the serotonergic system. Only one double-blind, placebo-controlled study has been conducted on desipramine's efficacy as an augmentation for standard SSRI/SRI treatment for OCD. The one available double-blind, placebo-controlled study showed no improvements with desipramine augmentation relative to placebo (Barr, Goodman, Anand, McDougle, & Price, 1997). These findings have not been replicated or refuted in any further controlled studies. Response rates were 7% for the study (0% placebo, ≥ 35% Y-BOCS reduction). Dosing was set at 150 mg/day (±69.7).

Final Notes

A large body of research has emerged regarding medication augmentations for the treatment of OCD, and Table 16.9 provides a summary of the various categories of medications described in this chapter. As research has elaborated current conceptions of OCD's neurobiological profile, new treatments have emerged or been rejected

Table 16.1   Brief summary of studies assessing antipsychotic augmentation of SRIs in obsessive compulsive disorder

Agent	Studies reporting improvement/total studies	Agent	Studies reporting improvement/total studies
Risperidone	6/6	Aripiprazole	3/3
Quetiapine	3/7	Haloperidol	2/2
Olanzapine	2/3	Paliperidone	0/1

Table 16.2   Brief summary of studies assessing serotonergic augmentation of SRIs in obsessive compulsive disorder

Agent	Studies reporting improvement/total studies	Agent	Studies reporting improvement/total studies
Ondansetron	4/4	Buspirone	0/3
Granisetron	1/1	Mirtazapine	1/1 (mixed)
Clomipramine	1/1 (mixed)		

Table 16.3   Brief summary of studies assessing glutamatergic augmentation of SRIs in obsessive compulsive disorder

Agent	Studies reporting improvement/total studies	Agent	Studies reporting improvement/total studies
Memantine	2/2	Lamotrigine	1/1
NAC	1/1	Riluzole	0/1
Topiramate	2/2 (mixed)	Glycine	0/1

Table 16.4   Brief summary of studies assessing additional augmentations of SRIs in obsessive compulsive disorder

Agent	Studies reporting improvement/total studies	Agent	Studies reporting improvement/total studies
Pindolol	1/2	Lithium	0/2
Caffeine	1/1	Clonazepam	0/1
D-Amphetamine	1/1	Inositol	0/1
Morphine	1/1	Naltrexone	0/1
Zinc sulfate	1/1	Desipramine	0/1
Celecoxib	1/1		

Table 16.5 Double- and single-blinded studies with antipsychotic augmentation

Study	Design	Augmenting drug(s), dose (± SD), duration	Primary drug/ lead-in duration	N	Response rate (% of N)	Findings
		Risperidone				
McDougle et al. (2000)**	DB, PC	Risperidone 2.2 mg (.7) 6 weeks	SSRI 12 weeks	T: 20 P: 16	T: 50% P: 0%	Improvement vs. placebo on target measures and secondary measures.
Hollander et al. (2003)**	DB, PC	Risperidone 2.25 mg (.86) 8 weeks	SRI 12 weeks	T: 10 P: 6	T: 40% P: 0%	Improvement vs. placebo on target measures and secondary measures.
Li et al. (2005)	DB, PC, CR	Risperidone 1 mg Haloperidol 2 mg 2 week each	SRI 12 weeks	T: 16	Not reported/ assessed	Both drugs showed improved vs placebo. Secondary measures differed by drug.
Erzegovesi et al. (2005)**	DB, PC	Risperidone .5 mg 6 weeks	Fluvoxamine 12 weeks	T: 20 P: 19	T: 50% P: 20%	Significant improvement only in SRI-resistant subject. SRI responders showed no effect.
Maina et al. (2008)**	SB	Risperidone[1] 1–3 mg Olanzapine[2] 3.5–10 mg 8 weeks	SRI 16 weeks	T[1]: 25 T[2]: 25	T[1]: 50% T[2]: 57.1%	Both groups improved significantly. No differences between groups.
Selvi et al. (2011)**	SB	Risperidone[1] 3 mg Aripiprazole[2] 15 mg 8 weeks	SRI 12 weeks	T[1]: 20 T[2]: 21	T[1]: 50% T[2]: 72.2%	Both groups showed improvement, but risperidone showed greater reduction in Y-BOCS obsession scores.

(Continued)

Table 16.5 (Continued)

Study	Design	Augmenting drug(s), dose ($\pm$ SD), duration	Primary drug/ lead-in duration	N	Response rate (% of N)	Findings
		Quetiapine				
Atmaca et al. (2002)**	SB, PC	Quetiapine 91.1 mg (41.1) 8 weeks	SRI 12 weeks	T: 14 P: 13	T: 64.4% P: 0%	Improvement vs. placebo on target measures.
Denys et al. (2004)**	DB, PC	Quetiapine 300 mg 8 weeks	SRI 8 weeks	T: 20 P: 20	T: 40% P: 10%	Improvement vs. placebo on target measures.
Carey et al. (2005)**	DB, PC	Quetiapine 168.75 mg (120.82) 6 weeks	SRI 12 weeks	T: 20 P: 21	T: 40% P: 47.6%	No improvement vs. placebo on target measures. Design limitations may have significantly impacted results.
Fineberg et al. (2005) **	DB, PC	Quetiapine 215 mg (124) 16 weeks	SRI 12 weeks	T: 11 P: 10	T: 27% P: 10%	No improvement vs. placebo. Y-BOCS trends were noted but did not reach significance.
Kordon et al. (2008) **	DB, PC	Quetiapine 400–600 mg 12 weeks	SRI 12 weeks	T: 20 P: 20	T: 65% P: 44%	No improvement vs. placebo on target measures.
Vulink et al. (2009)	DB, PC	Quetiapine 300–450 mg 10 weeks	Citalopram No lead-in phase	T: 39 P: 37	Not reported/ assessed	Improvement vs. placebo on Y-BOCS scores. Subjects were non-refractory cases.
Diniz et al. (2011)	DB, PC	Quetiapine[1] $\leq$142 mg (65) Clomipramine[2] 55 mg (20) 12 weeks	Fluoxetine 8 weeks	T[1]: 18 T[2]: 18 P: 18	Not reported/ assessed	Both Clomipramine and placebo augmentations showed higher Y-BOCS reductions vs. quetiapine.

Olanzapine						
Bystritsky et al. (2004)*	DB, PC	Olanzapine 11.2 mg (6.5) 6 weeks	SRI 12 weeks	T: 13 P: 13	T: 46% P: 0%	Improvement vs. placebo on target measures.
Shapira et al. (2004)**	DB, PC	Olanzapine 10 mg 6 weeks	Fluoxetine 8 weeks	T: 22 P: 22	T: 23% P: 18%	No improvement vs. placebo on target measures. Short lead-in and lower dose may have confounded results.
Maina et al. (2008)**	SB	Risperidone[1] 1–3 mg, Olanzapine[2] 3.5–10 mg 8 weeks	SRI 16 weeks	T[1]: 25 T[2]: 25	T[1]: 50% T[2]: 57.1%	Both groups improved on target measures. No differences between groups.
Aripiprazole						
Muscatello et al. (2011)**	DB, PC	Aripiprazole 15 mg 16 weeks	SRI 12 weeks	T: 16 P: 14	T: 25% P: 0%	Improvement vs. placebo on target measures.
Selvi et al. (2011)**	SB	Risperidone[1] 3 mg Aripiprazole[2] 15 mg 8 weeks	SRI 12 weeks	T[1]: 20 T[2]: 21	T[1]: 50% T[2]: 72.2%	Both groups showed improvement, but risperidone showed greater reduction in Y-BOCS obsession scores.
Sayyah et al. (2012)*	DB, PC	Aripiprazole 10 mg	SRI 12 weeks	T: 15 P: 17	T: 53% P: 17.6%	Improvement vs. placebo on target measures.
Paliperidone						
Storch et al. (2013)**	DB, PC	Paliperidone 4.94 mg (2.36) 8 weeks	SRI 12 weeks	T: 17 P: 17	T: 35% P: 29%	No improvement vs. placebo on target measures. Select non-significant trends may support further studies.

(Continued)

Table 16.5 (Continued)

Study	Design	Augmenting drug(s), dose (± SD), duration	Primary drug/ lead-in duration	N	Response rate (% of N)	Findings
			Haloperidol			
McDougle et al. (1994)**	DB, PC	Haloperidol 10 mg 4 weeks	Fluvoxamine 7 weeks	T: 17 P: 17	T: 64.7% P: 0%	Improvement vs. placebo on target measures.
Li et al. (2005)	DB, PC, CR	Risperidone 1 mg Haloperidol 2 mg 2 week each	SRI 12 weeks	T: 16	Not reported/ assessed	Both drugs showed improved vs placebo. Secondary measures differed by drug.

* Response defined as ≥ 25% reduction on Y-BOCS.
** Response defined as ≥ 35% reduction on Y-BOCS.

Abbreviations: DB = double blind, SB = single blind, PC = placebo controlled, CR = cross-over study, T = treatment group, P = placebo group.
Super text (e.g. "1") = group related to indicated agent.

Table 16.6 Double- and single-blinded studies on serotonergic augmentations

Study	Design	Augmenting drug(s), dose (± SD), duration	Primary drug/ lead-in duration	N	Response rate (% of N)	Findings
Pallanti et al. (2009)*	SB	Ondansetron 1 mg 12 weeks	SRI + antipsychotic 12 weeks	T: 14	T: 64.3%	Significant improvement vs. baseline. All subjects had current SRI + antipsychotic treatment during the study.
Soltani et al. (2010)	DB, PC	Ondansetron 4 mg 8 weeks	Fluoxetine No lead-in	T: 20 P: 20	Not reported/ assessed	Improvement vs. placebo on Y-BOCS scores at weeks two and eight.
Pallanti et al. (2014)*	SB	Ondansetron 1 mg 12 weeks	SRI 12 weeks	T: 20	T: 57%	Improvement vs. baseline on target measures. 8/12 relapsed post discontinuation.
Heidari et al. (2014)*	DB, PC	Ondansetron 8 mg 8 weeks	Fluvoxamine No lead-in	T: 23 P: 23	T: 90.9% P: 31.8%	Improvement vs. placebo on target measures.
Askari et al. (2012)**	DB, PC	Granisetron 1 mg/12 hr. 8 weeks	Fluvoxamine No lead-in	T: 21 P: 21	T: 100% P: 35%	Improvement vs. placebo on target measures.
Diniz et al. (2011)	DB, PC	Quetiapine[1] ≤142 mg (65) Clomipramine[2] 55 mg (20) 12 weeks	Fluoxetine 8 weeks	T[1]: 18 T[2]: 18 P: 18	Not reported/ assessed	Both Clomipramine and placebo augmentations showed higher Y-BOCS reductions vs. quetiapine.

(Continued)

Table 16.6 (Continued)

Study	Design	Augmenting drug(s), dose (± SD), duration	Primary drug/ lead-in duration	N	Response rate (% of N)	Findings
Pigott et al. (1992)*	DB, 2 week PC lead-in	Buspirone 57 mg (7) 10 weeks	Clomipramine 10 weeks	T: 14	T: 28.6%	Augmented treatment showed no significant advantage vs. CMI alone.
Grady et al. (1993)*	DB, PC, CR	Buspirone 60 mg 8 weeks	Fluoxetine 10 weeks	T: 14	T: 7%	No improvement vs. placebo on target measures.
McDougle et al. (1993)*	DB, PC	Buspirone 59.2 mg (3.4) 6 weeks	Fluvoxamine 8 weeks	T: 19 P: 14	T: 10.5% P: 14.3%	No significant improvement vs. placebo on target measures.
Pallanti et al. (2004)**	SB, PC	Mirtazapine 15–30 mg 12 weeks	Citalopram No lead-in	T: 21 P: 28	T: 61.7% P: 61.9%	No improvement vs. placebo on symptom measures. Treatment produced earlier response vs. placebo.

* Response defined as ≥25% reduction on Y-BOCS.
** Response defined as ≥35% reduction on Y-BOCS.
Abbreviations: DB = double blind, SB = single blind, PC = placebo controlled, CR = cross-over study, T = treatment group, P = placebo group.
Super text (e.g. "[1]") = group related to indicated agent.

Table 16.7 Double- and single-blinded studies on glutamatergic augmentations

Study	Design	Augmenting drug(s), dose (± SD), duration	Primary drug/ lead-in duration	N	Response rate (% of N)	Findings
Ghaleiha et al. (2013)*	DB, PC	Memantine 20 mg 8 weeks	Fluvoxamine No lead-in	T: 19 P: 19	T: 100% P: 32%	Improvement vs. placebo on target measures. 89% achieved remission with memantine.
Haghighi et al. (2013)**	DB, PC	Memantine 5–10 mg 12 weeks	SRI 12 weeks	T: 14 P: 15	T: 64.3% P: 0%	Improvement vs. placebo on target measures.
Afshar et al. (2012)**	DB, PC	NAC 600–2,400 mg 12 weeks	SRI 12 weeks	T: 19 P: 20	T: 52.6% P: 15%	Improvement vs. placebo on target measures.
Mowla et al. (2010)**	DB, PC	Topiramate 180.15 mg 12 weeks	SRI 12 weeks	T: 20 P: 21	T: 60% P: 0%	Improvement vs. placebo on target measures.
Berlin et al. (2011)	DB, PC	Topiramate 177.8 mg (134.2) 12 weeks	SRI 12 weeks	T: 13 P: 14	Not reported/ assessed	Decrease in YBOCS compulsions vs. placebo, but no other measures. 28% of subjects discontinued due to side effects.
Bruno et al. (2012)**	DB, PC	Lamotrigine 100 mg 16 weeks	SRI 12 weeks	T: 17 P: 16	T: 35% P: 0%	Improvement vs. placebo on target measures.
Grant et al. (2014)**	DB, PC	Riluzole 100 mg 12 weeks	77% SRI. 8 weeks constant dose for concomitant medications	T: 29 P: 30	T: 16% P: 18%	No improvement vs. placebo on target measures. Numerous limitations noted by authors. Concomitant medications. Limited to children/ adolescents.
Greenberg et al. (2009)**	DB, PC	Glycine 60 g 12 weeks	Stabilized treatment 12 weeks	T: 12 P: 12	T: 40% (2/5) P: 0%	No significant improvement vs. placebo target measures. 66.7% (8/12) of active subjects discontinued the study due to side effects or aversion to the taste.

* Response defined as ≥25% reduction on Y-BOCS.

** Response defined as ≥35% reduction on Y-BOCS.

Abbreviations: DB = double blind, SB = single blind, PC = placebo controlled, CR = cross-over study, T = treatment group, P = placebo group.

Super text (e.g. "1") = group related to indicated agent.

Table 16.8 Double- and single-blinded studies on other augmentations

Study	Design	Augmenting drug(s), dose (± SD), duration	Primary drug/ lead-in duration	N	Response Rate (% of N)	Findings
Mundo et al. (1998)**	DB, PC	Pindolol 7.5 mg 8 weeks	Fluvoxamine No lead-in	T: 8 P: 6	T: 75% P: 85%	No improvement vs. placebo on target measures.
Dannon et al. (2000)	DB, PC	Pindolol 7.5 mg 6 weeks	Paroxetine 17.4 ± 2.1 weeks	T: 8 P: 6	Not reported/ assessed	Improvement vs. placebo on YBOCS scores.
Koran et al. (2009)**	DB	Caffeine[1] 300 mg D-amphetamine[2] 30 mg 5 weeks	SRI/SNRI 12 weeks	T[1]: 12 T[2]: 12	T[1]: 91.7% T[2]: 66.7%	Both groups improved significantly. No difference between groups.
Koran et al. (2005b)*	DB, PC, CR	Morphine[1] 30–45 mg 1×/week Lorazepam[2] .5–2.0 mg 2 weeks each	Current medications stable for 8 weeks	T[1]: 23 T[2]: 22 P: 23	T[1]: 30.4% T[2]: 18.1% P: 0%	Improvement vs. placebo and lorazepam on target measures. Select subjects reported worsening of symptoms.
Sayyah et al. (2012)	DB, PC	Zinc sulfate 40 mg 8 weeks	Fluoxetine No lead-in	T: 12 P: 11	Not reported/ assessed	Improvement on final YBOCS scores and rate of improvement vs placebo.
Sayyah et al. (2011)	DB, PC	Celecoxib 400 mg 8 weeks	Fluoxetine No lead-in	T: 27 P: 25	Not reported/ assessed	Improvement vs placebo on target measures and delay to response onset.
McDougle et al. (1991)**	DB, PC	Lithium 900 mg 2 weeks	Fluvoxamine 8 weeks	T: 16 P: 14	T: 13% P: 0%	Small improvement vs. placebo deemed clinically insignificant by authors.

Study	Design	Agent	Comparator	N	Response	Outcome
Pigott et al. (1991)*	DB, CR	Lithium[1] 1,500 mg Thyroid Hormone[2] 25 mg 4 weeks each	Clomipramine 6 months	T: 16	T[1]: 12.5% T[2]: 6.3%	No significant improvement on target measures.
Crockett et al. (2004)*	DB, PC	Clonazepam 2.7 mg 12 weeks	Sertraline No lead-in	T: 20 P: 17	T: 54.5% P: 45.5%	No significant improvement on target measures.
Fux et al. (1999)	DB, PC CR	Inositol 18 g 6 weeks	SRI 12 weeks	T: 10	Not reported/assessed	No significant improvement on target measures.
Amiaz et al. (2008)**	DB, PC, CR	Naltrexone 50–100 mg 5 weeks each	Set SRI and augmentations for 8 weeks	T: 10	T: 0% P: 0%	No significant improvement on target measures.
Barr et al. (1997)	DB, PC	Desipramine 150 mg (69.7) 10 weeks	SRI 10 weeks	T: 10 P: 13	Not reported/assessed	No improvement vs. placebo on target measures

* Response defined as ≥25% reduction on Y-BOCS.

** Response defined as ≥35% reduction on Y-BOCS.

Abbreviations: DB = double blind, SB = single blind, PC = placebo controlled, CR = cross-over study, T = treatment group, P = placebo group.
Super text (e.g. "[1]") = group related to indicated agent.

Table 16.9 Summary of augmenting agents with SRIs for obsessive compulsive disorder

Agents showing significant effects on OCD symptom severity in *two or more* blinded trials:

Antipsychotics (typical and atypical)
- risperidone, quetiapine, olanzapine, aripiprazole, haloperidol

Serotonergic Agents
- ondansetron

Glutamatergic agents
- memantine, topiramate

Agents showing significant effects on OCD symptom severity in *one* blinded trial:

Serotonergic agents
- granisetron, clomipramine, mirtazapine

Glutamatergic agents
- N-acetylcystine, lamotrigine

Other agents
- pindolol, caffeine, d-amphetamine, morphine, zinc sulfate, celecoxib

Agents showing significant effects on OCD symptom severity in *no* blinded trials:

Antipsychotics (typical and atypical)
- paliperidone

Serotonergic agents
- buspirone, desipramine

Glutamatergic agents
- riluzole, glycine

Other agents
- lithium, clonazepam, inositol, naltrexone

accordingly (Arumugham & Reddy, 2013). However, there are a number of factors that will impact the utility of these various medications. As was the case with haloperidol augmentation in patients with comorbid OCD and tics, some augmenting agents may function best within a select subgroup of patients (McDougle et al., 1994). When deciding on the best course of augmentation, it is important to consider the specific needs of the patient, side effect profiles of the various agents, and what factors might complicate the apparent efficacy of a given augmentation. Due to the increasing number of augmenting agents, it is possible to individualize treatment plans to fit the specific needs of the patient, potentially increasing treatment efficacy and tolerability. As research progresses, it will ideally shed more light on the specific benefits of each agent, allowing for even higher responder rates in targeted treatment.

References

Abdel-Ahad, P., & Kazour, F. (2013). Non-antidepressant pharmacological treatment of obsessive compulsive disorder: A comprehensive review. *Current Clinical Pharmacology*, Epub ahead of print.

Afshar, H., Roohafza, H., Mohammad-Beigi, H., Haghighi, M., Jahangard, L., Shokouh, P., Sadeghi, M., & Hafezian, H. (2012). N-acetylcysteine add-on treatment in refractory obsessive-compulsive disorder: A randomized, double-blind, placebo-controlled trial. *Journal of Clinical Psychopharmacology, 32*, 797–803.

Alarcon, R., Libb, J., & Spitler, D. (1993). A predictive study of obsessive compulsive response to clomipramine. *Journal of Clinical Psychopharmacology, 13*, 210–213.

Albert, U., Barbaro, F., Aguglia, A., Maina, G., & Bogetto, F. (2012). Combined treatments in obsessive-compulsive disorder: Current knowledge and future prospects. *Rivista di Psichiatria, 47*, 255–268.

Amiaz, R., Fostick, L., Gershon, A., & Zohar, J. (2008). Naltrexone augmentation in OCD: A double-blind placebo-controlled cross-over study. *European Neuropsychopharmacology, 18*, 455–461.

Arumugham, S., & Reddy, J. (2013). Augmentation strategies in obsessive-compulsive disorder. *Expert Reviews, 13*, 187–202.

Askari, N., Min, M., Sanati, M., Tajdini, M., Hosseini, S., Modabbernia, A., ... Akondzadeh S. (2012). Granisetron adjunct to fluvoxamine for moderate to severe obsessive-compulsive disorder: A randomized, double-blind, placebo-controlled trial. *CNS Drugs, 26*, 883–892.

Atmaca, M., Kuloglu, M., Tezcan, E., & Gecici, O. (2002). Quetiapine augmentation in patients with treatment resistant obsessive-compulsive disorder: A single-blind, placebo-controlled study. *International Journal of Psychopharmacology, 17*, 115–119.

Barr, L., Goodman, W., Anand, A., McDougle, C., & Price, L. (1997). Addition of desipramine to serotonin reuptake inhibitors in treatment-resistant obsessive-compulsive disorder. *American Journal of Psychiatry, 154*, 1293–1295.

Bellingham, M. (2011). A review of the neural mechanisms of action and clinical efficiency of riluzole in treating amyotrophic lateral sclerosis: What have we learned in the last decade? *CNS Neuroscience & Therapeutics, 17*, 4–31.

Berlin, H., Koran, L., Jenike, M., Shapira, N., Chaplin, W., Pallanti, S., & Hollander, E. (2011). Double-blind, placebo-controlled trial of topiramate augmentation in treatment-resistant obsessive-compulsive disorder. *Journal of Clinical Psychiatry, 72*, 716–721.

Billett, E., Richter, M., Sam, F., Swinson, R., Dai, X., King, N., ... Kennedy, J. (1998). Investigation of dopamine system genes in obsessive-compulsive disorder. *Psychiatric Genetics, 8*, 163–169.

Bloch, M., Landeros-Weisenberger, A., Kelmendi, B., Coric, V., Bracken, M., & Leckman, J. (2006). A systematic review: Antipsychotic augmentation with treatment refractory obsessive-compulsive disorder. *Molecular Psychiatry, 11*, 795.

Bruno, A., Micò, U., Pandolfo, G., Mallamace, D., Abenavoli, E., Di Nardo, F., ... Muscatello, M. (2012). Lamotrigine augmentation of serotonin reuptake inhibitors in treatment-resistant obsessive-compulsive disorder: A double-blind, placebo-controlled study. *Journal of Psychopharmacology, 26*, 1456–1462.

Burstein, A. (1995) Lamotrigine. *Pharmacotherapy, 15*, 129–143.

Bystritsky, A., Ackerman, D., Rosen, R., Vapnik, T., Gorbis, E., Maidment, K., & Saxena, S. (2004). Augmentation of serotonin reuptake inhibitors in refractory obsessive-compulsive disorder using adjunctive olanzapine: A placebo-controlled trial. *Journal of Clinical Psychiatry, 65*, 565–568.

Carey, P., Vythilingum, B., Seedat, S., Muller, J., van Ameringen, M., & Stein, D. (2005). Quetiapine augmentation of SRIs in treatment refractory obsessive-compulsive disorder: A double-blind, randomized, placebo-controlled study [ISRCTN83050762]. *BMC Psychiatry, 5*, 5.

Crocket, B., Churchill, E., & Davidson, J. (2004) A double-blind combination study of clonazepam with sertraline in obsessive-compulsive disorder. *Annals of Clinical Psychiatry, 16*, 127–132.

Dannon, P., Sasson, Y., Hirschmann, S., Iancu, I., Grunhaus, L., & Zohar, J. (2000). Pindolol augmentation in treatment-resistant obsessive compulsive disorder: A double-blind placebo controlled trial. *European Neuropsychopharmacology, 10*, 165–169.

Diniz, J., Shavitt, R., Fossaluza, V., Koran, L., Pereira, C., & Miguel, E. (2011). A double-blind, randomized, controlled trial of fluoxetine plus quetiapine or clomipramine versus fluoxetine plus placebo for obsessive-compulsive disorder. *Journal of Clinical Psychopharmacology, 31*, 763–768.

Denys, D., de Geus, F., van Megen, H., & Westenberg, H. (2004). A double-blind, randomized, placebo-controlled trial of quetiapine addition in patients with obsessive-compulsive disorder refractory to serotonin reuptake inhibitors. *Journal of Clinical Psychiatry, 65,* 1040–1048.

Dold, M., Aigner, M., Lanzenberger, R., & Kasper, S. (2013). Antipsychotic augmentation of serotonin reuptake inhibitors in treatment-resistant obsessive-compulsive disorder: A meta-analysis of double-blind, randomized, placebo-controlled trials. *International Journal of Neuropsychopharmacology, 16*(3), 557–574

Erzegovesi, S., Guglielmo, E., Siliprandi, F., & Bellodi, L. (2005). Low-dose risperidone augmentation of fluvoxamine treatment in obsessive-compulsive disorder: A double-blind, placebo-controlled study. *European Journal of Neuropsychopharmacology, 15,* 69–74.

Erzegovesi, S., Martucci, L., Heinin, M., & Bellodi, L. (2001). Low versus standard dose mCPP challenge in obsessive-compulsive patients. *Neuropsychopharmacology, 24,* 31–36.

Fineberg, N., Bullock, D., & Montgomery, S. (1992). Serotonin reuptake inhibitors are the treatment of choice in obsessive-compulsive disorder. *International Journal of Clinical Psychopharmacology, 7,* 43–47.

Fineberg, N., Sivakumaran, T., Roberts, A., & Gale, T. (2005). Adding quetiapine to SRI in treatment-resistant obsessive-compulsive disorder: A randomized controlled treatment study. *International Journal of Neuropsychopharmacology, 20,* 223–226.

Fux, M., Benjamin, J., & Belmaker, R. (1999). Inositol versus placebo augmentation of serotonin reuptake inhibitors in the treatment of obsessive-compulsive disorder: a double-blind cross-over study. *International Journal of Neuropsychopharmacology, 2,* 193–195.

Fux, M., Levine, J., Aviv, A., & Belmaker, R. (1996). Inositol treatment of obsessive-compulsive disorder. *American Journal of Psychiatry, 153,* 1219–1221.

Ghaleiha, A., Entezari, N., Modabbernia, A., Najand, B., Akari, N., Tabrizi, M., ... Akhondzadeh. S. (2013). Memantine add-on in moderate to severe obsessive-compulsive disorder: Randomized double-blind placebo-controlled study. *Journal of Psychiatric Research, 47,* 175–180.

Goodman, W., Price, L., Rasmussen, S., Mazure, C., Fleischmann, R., Hill, C., Heninger, G., & Charney, D. (1989). The Yale–Brown Obsessive Compulsive Scale, I: Development, use, and reliability. *Archives of General Psychiatry, 46,* 1006–1011.

Grady, T., Pigott, T., L'Heureux, F., Hill, J., Bernstein, S., & Murphy, D. (1993). Double-blind study of adjuvant buspirone for fluoxetine-treated patients with obsessive-compulsive disorder. *American Journal of Psychiatry, 150,* 819–821.

Grant, P., Joseph, L., Farme, C., Luckenbaugh, D., Lougee, L., Zarate, C., & Swedo, S. (2014). 12-week, placebo-controlled trial of add-on riluzole in the treatment of childhood-onset obsessive-compulsive disorder. *Neuropsychopharmacology, 39,* 1453–1459.

Grant, J., Kim, S., & Odlaug, B. (2007). N-acetyl cysteine, a glutamate-modulating agent, in the treatment of pathological gambling a pilot study. *Biological Psychiatry, 62,* 652–657.

Grant, J., Kim, S., & Odlaug, B. (2009). A double-blind, placebo-controlled study of the opiate antagonist, naltrexone, in the treatment of kleptomania. *Biological Psychiatry, 65,* 600–606.

Grant, J., Odlaug, B., & Kim, S. (2009). N-acetylcysteine, a glutamate modulator, in the treatment of trichotillomania: a double-blind, placebo-controlled study. *Archive of General Psychiatry, 66,* 756–763.

Greenberg, W., Benedict, M., Doerfer, J., Perrin, M., Panek, L, Cleveland, W., & Javitt, D. (2009). Adjunctive glycine in the treatment of obsessive-compulsive disorder in adults. *Journal of Psychiatric Research, 43,* 664–670.

Haghighi, M., Jahangard, L., Mohammed-Beigi, H., Bajoghli, H., Hafezian, H., Rahimi, A., ... Brand, S. (2013). In a double-blind, randomized and placebo-controlled trial, adjuvant memantine improved symptoms in patients suffering from refractory obsessive-compulsive disorder (OCD). *Psychopharmacology (Berl), 228,* 633–640.

Hasler, S., Hirt, A., Ridolfi Luethy, A., Leibundgut, K., & Ammann, R. (2008). Safety of ondansetron loading doses in children with cancer. *Supportive Care in Cancer, 16,* 469–475.

Heidari, M., Zarei, M., Hosseini, S., Taghvaei, R., Maleki, H., Tabrizi, M., Fallah, J., & Akhondzadeh, S. (2014). Ondansetron or placebo in the augmentation of fluvoxamine response over 8 weeks in obsessive-compulsive disorder. *International Journal of Clinical Psychopharmacology, 29,* 344–350.

Hesse, S., Müller, U., Lincke, T., Barthel, H., Villmann, T., Angermeyer, M., Sabri, O., & Stengler-Wenzke, K. (2005). Serotonin and dopamine transporter imaging in patients with obsessive-compulsive disorder. *Journal of Psychiatric Research, 140,* 63–72.

Hollander, E., Baldini Rossi, N., Sood, E., & Pallanti, S. (2003) Risperidone augmentation in treatment-resistant obsessive-compulsive disorder: A double-blind, placebo-controlled study. *International Journal of Neuropsychopharmacology, 6,* 397–401.

Jenike, M., Hyman, S., Baer, L., Holland, A., Minichiello, W., Buttolph, L., ... Ricciardi, J. (1990). A controlled trial of fluvoxamine in obsessive-compulsive disorder: Implications for a serotonergic theory. *American Journal of Psychiatry, 147,* 1209–1215.

Kim, S., Grant, J., Adson, D., & Shin, Y. (2001). Double-blind naltrexone and placebo comparison study in the treatment of pathological gambling. *Biological Psychiatry, 49,* 914–921.

Koran, L., Aboujaoude, E., Bullock, K., Franz, B., Gamel, N., & Elliott, M. (2005b) Double-blind treatment with oral morphine in treatment-resistant obsessive-compulsive disorder. *Journal of Clinical Psychiatry, 66,* 353–359.

Koran, L., Aboujaoude, E., & Gamel, N. (2009) Double-blind study of dextroamphetamine versus caffeine augmentation for treatment-resistant obsessive-compulsive disorder. *Journal of Clinical Psychiatry, 70,* 1530–1535.

Koran, L., Gamel, N., Choung, H., Smith, E., & Aboujaoude, E. (2005a). Mirtazapine for obsessive-compulsive disorder: An open trial followed by double-blind discontinuation. *Journal of Clinical Psychiatry, 66,* 515–520.

Kordon, A., Wahl, K., Koch, N., Zurowski, B., Anlauf, M., Vielhaber, K., ... Hohagen, F. (2008). Quetiapine addition to serotonin reuptake inhibitors in patients with severe obsessive-compulsive disorder: A double-blind, randomized, placebo-controlled study. *Journal of Clinical Psychopharmacology, 28,* 550–554.

Kurlan, R. (1998). Tourette's syndrome and "PANDAS": will the relation bear out? Pediatric autoimmune neuropsychiatric disorders associated with streptococcal infections. *Neurology, 50,* 1530–1534.

Lack, C. (2012). Obsessive-compulsive disorder: Evidence-based treatments and future directions for research. *World Journal of Psychiatry, 2,* 86–90.

Li, X., May, R., Tolbert, L., Jackson, W., Flournoy, J., & Baxter, L. (2005). Risperidone and haloperidol augmentation of serotonin reuptake inhibitors in refractory obsessive-compulsive disorder: A crossover study. *Journal of Clinical Psychiatry, 66,* 736–743.

Maina, G., Albert, U., Ziero, S., & Bogetto, F. (2003). Antipsychotic augmentation for treatment resistant obsessive-compulsive disorder: What if antipsychotic is discontinued? *International Journal of Clinical Psychopharmacology, 18,* 23–28.

Maina, G., Pessina, E., Albert, U., & Bogetto, F. (2008). An 8-week, single-blind, randomized trial comparing risperidone versus olanzapine augmentation of serotonin reuptake inhibitors in treatment-resistant obsessive-compulsive disorder. *European Neuropsychopharmacology, 18,* 364–372.

Marek, G., Carpenter, L., McDougle, C., & Price, L. (2003). Synergistic action of 5-HT2A antagonists and selective serotonin reuptake inhibitors in neuropsychiatric disorders. *Neuropsychopharmacology, 28,* 402–412.

McDougle, C., Epperson, C., Pelton, G., Wasylink, S., & Price, L. (2000). A double-blind, placebo-controlled study of risperidone addition in serotonin reuptake inhibitor-refractory obsessive-compulsive disorder. *Archives of General Psychiatry, 57*, 794–801.

McDougle, C., Goodman, W., Leckman, J., Holzer, J., Barr, L., McCance-Katz, E., Heninger, G., & Price, L. (1993). Limited therapeutic effect of addition of buspirone in fluvoxamine-refractory obsessive-compulsive disorder. *American Journal of Psychiatry, 150*, 647–649.

McDougle, C., Goodman, W., Leckman, J., Lee, N., Heninger, G., & Price, L. (1994). Haloperidol addition in fluvoxamine-refractory obsessive-compulsive disorder: A double-blind, placebo-controlled study in patients with and without tics. *Archives of General Psychiatry, 51*, 302–308.

McDougle, C., Price, L., Goodman, W., Charney, D., & Heninger, G. (1991). A controlled trial of lithium augmentation in fluvoxamine-refractory obsessive-compulsive disorder: Lack of efficacy. *Journal of Clinical Psychopharmacology, 11*, 175–184.

Mowla, A., Khajeian, A., Sahraian, A., Chohedri, A., & Kashkoli, F. (2010). Topiramate augmentation in resistant OCD: A double-blind placebo-controlled clinical trial. *CNS Spectrums, 15*, 613–617.

Mundo, E., Guglielmo, E., & Bellodi, L. (1998). Effect of adjuvant pindolol on the antiobsessional response to fluvoxamine: A double-blind, placebo-controlled study. *International Journal of Psychopharmacology, 13*, 219–224.

Muscatello, M., Bruno, A., Pandolfo, G., Micò, U., Scimeca, G., Romeo, V., … Zoccali, R. (2011). Effect of aripiprazole augmentation of serotonin reuptake inhibitors or clomipramine in treatment-resistant obsessive-compulsive disorder: A double-blind, placebo-controlled study. *Journal of Clinical Psychopharmacology, 31*, 174–179.

Nikolaus, S., Beu, M., De Souza Silva, A. M., Huston, J. P., Hautzel, H., Chao, O. Y., … Müller, H-W. (2014). Relationship between L-DOPA-induced reduction in motor and exploratory activity and degree of DAT binding in the rat. *Frontiers in Behavioral Neuroscience, 8*. doi: 10.3389/fnbeh.2014.00431.

Nowak, G., & Szewczyk, B. (2002). Mechanisms contributing to antidepressant zinc actions. *Polish Journal of Pharmacology, 54*, 587–592.

Odlaug, B., & Grant, J. (2007). N-acetyl cysteine in the treatment of grooming disorders. *Journal of Clinical Psychopharmacology, 27*, 227–229.

Olijslagers, J., Werkman, T., McCreary, A., Kruse, C., & Wadman, W. (2006). Modulation of midbrain dopamine neurotransmission by serotonin, a versatile interaction between neurotransmitters and significance for antipsychotic drug interaction. *Current Neuropsychopharmacology, 4*, 59–68.

Pallanti, S., Bernardi, S., Antonini, S., Singh, N., & Hollander, E. (2009). Ondansetron augmentation in treatment-resistant obsessive-compulsive disorder: a preliminary, single-blind, prospective study. *CNS Drugs, 23*, 1047–1055.

Pallanti, S., Bernardi, S., Antonini, S., Singh, N., & Hollander, E. (2014). Ondansetron augmentation with obsessive-compulsive disorder who are inadequate responders to serotonin reuptake inhibitors: Improvement with treatment and worsening following discontinuation. *European Neuropsychopharmacology, 24*, 375–380.

Pallanti, S., Hollander, E., Bienstock, C., Koran, L., Leckman, J., Marazziti, D., … International Treatment Refractory OCD Consortium. (2002). Treatment non-response in OCD: Methodological issues and operational definitions. *International Journal of Neuropsychopharmacology, 5*, 181–191.

Pallanti, S., Quercioli, L., & Bruscoli, M. (2004). Response acceleration with mirtazapine augmentation of citalopram in obsessive-compulsive disorder patients without comorbid depression: A pilot study. *Journal of Clinical Psychiatry, 65*, 1394–1399.

Pigott, T., L'Heureux, F., Hill, J., Bihari, K., Bernstein, S., & Murphy, D. (1992). A double-blind study of adjuvant buspirone hydrochloride in clomipramine-treated patients with obsessive-compulsive disorder. *Journal of Clinical Psychopharmacology, 12*, 11–18.

Pigott, T., Pato, M., L'Heureux, F., Hill, J., Grover, G., Bernstein, S., & Murphy, D. (1991). A controlled comparison of adjuvant lithium carbonate or thyroid hormone in clomipramine-treated patients with obsessive-compulsive disorder. *Journal of Clinical Psychopharmacology, 11*, 242–248.

Pittenger, C., Bloch, M., & Williams, K. (2011). Glutamate abnormalities in obsessive compulsive disorder: Neurobiology, pathophysiology, and treatment. *Pharmacology & Therapeutics, 132*, 314–332.

Ramasubbu, R., Ravindran, A., & Lapierre, Y. (2000). Serotonin and dopamine antagonism in obsessive-compulsive disorder: Effect of atypical antipsychotic drugs. *Pharmacopsychiatry, 33*, 236–238.

Ravizza, L., Barzega, G., Bellino, S., Bogetto, F., & Maina, G. (1995). Predictors of drug treatment response in obsessive-compulsive disorder. *Journal of Clinical Psychiatry, 56*, 368–373.

Sayyah, M., Boostani, H., Pakseresht, S., & Malayeri, A. (2011). A preliminary randomized double-blind clinical trial on the efficacy of celecoxib as an adjunct in the treatment of obsessive-compulsive disorder. *Psychiatry Research, 189*, 403–406.

Sayyah, M., Olapour, A., Saeedabad, Y., Yazdan Parast, R., & Malayeri, A. (2012a). Evaluation of oral zinc sulfate effect on obsessive-compulsive disorder: A randomized placebo-controlled clinical trial. *Nutrition, 28*, 892–895.

Sayyah, M., Sayyah, M., Boostani, H., Ghaffari, S., & Hoseini, A. (2012b). Effects of aripiprazole augmentation in treatment-resistant obsessive-compulsive disorder (a double blind trial). *Depression and Anxiety, 29*, 850–854.

Selvi, Y., Atli, A., Aydin, A., Besiroglu, L., Ozdemir, P., & Ozdemir, O. (2011). The comparison of aripiprazole and risperidone augmentation in selective serotonin reuptake inhibitor-refractory obsessive-compulsive disorder: A single-blind, randomized study. *Human Psychopharmacology, 26*, 51–57.

Shapira, N., Ward, H., Mandoki, M., Yang, M., Blier, P., & Goodman, W. (2004). A double-blind, placebo-controlled trial of olanzapine addition in fluoxetine-refractory obsessive-compulsive disorder. *Biological Psychiatry, 55*, 553–555.

Simpson, H., Shungu, D., Bender, J., Mao, X., Xu, X., Slifstein, M., & Kegeles, L. (2012). Investigation of cortical glutamate-glutamine and y-aminobutyric acid in obsessive-compulsive disorder by proton magnetic resonance spectroscopy. *Neuropsychopharmacology, 37*, 2684–2692.

Skapinakis, P., Papatheodorou, T., & Mavreas, V. (2007). Antipsychotic augmentation of serotonergic antidepressants in treatment-resistant obsessive-compulsive disorder: A meta-analysis of the randomized controlled trials. *European Neuropsychopharmacology, 17*, 79–93.

Smeraldi, E., Erzegovesi, S., Bianchi, I., & Pasquali, L. (1992). Fluvoxamine versus clomipramine for obsessive-compulsive disorder: A preliminary study. *New Trends Experimental and Clinical Psychiatry, 8*, 63–65.

Soltani, F., Sayyah, M., Feizy, F., Malayeri, A., Siahpoosh, A., & Motlagh, I. (2010). A double-blind, placebo-controlled pilot study of ondansetron for patients with obsessive-compulsive disorder. *Human Psychopharmacology, 25*, 509–513.

Storch, E., Goddard, A., Grant, J., De Nadai, A., Goodman, W., Mutch, P., ... Murphy, T. (2013). Double-blind, placebo-controlled, pilot trial of paliperidone augmentation in serotonin reuptake inhibitor-resistant obsessive-compulsive disorder. *Journal of Clinical Psychiatry, 74*, e527–e532.

Swedo, S., Leonard, H., Mittleman, B., Allen, A., Rapaport, J., Dow, S., ... Zabriskie, J. (1997). Identification of children with pediatric autoimmune neuropsychiatric disorders associated with streptococcal infections by a marker associated with rheumatic fever. *American Journal of Psychiatry, 154*, 110–112.

Takeda, A. (2000). Movement of zinc and its functional significance in the brain. *Brain Research Reviews, 34*, 137–148.

Thorén, P., Åsberg, M., Cronholm, B., Jörnestedt, L., & Träskman, L. (1980). Clomipramine treatment of obsessive-compulsive disorder. *Archives of General Psychiatry, 37,* 1289–1294.

Tollefson, G., Rampey, A., Potvin, J., Jenike, M., Rush, A., Dominguez, R., … Genduso, L. (1994). A multi-center investigation of fixed-dose fluoxetine in the treatment of obsessive-compulsive disorder. *Archives of General Psychiatry, 51,* 559–567.

Vulink, N., Denys, D., Fluitman, S., Meinardi, J., & Westenberg, H. (2009). Quetiapine augments the effect of citalopram in non-refractory obsessive-compulsive disorder: A randomized, double-blind, placebo-controlled study of 76 patients. *Journal of Clinical Psychiatry, 70,* 1001–1008.

Wu, K., Hanna, G., Rosenberg, D., & Arnold, P. (2012). The role of glutamate signaling in the pathogenesis and treatment of obsessive-compulsive disorder. *Pharmacology Biochemistry and Behavior, 100,* 726–735.

17

Contamination Fear
and Avoidance in Adults

Dean McKay and Sean Carp

Contamination fear, and associated cleaning rituals, is considered a core symptom of obsessive-compulsive disorder (OCD). The frequency of contamination fear in epidemiology samples has varied, with some research suggesting this is the most common presenting problem in OCD (see McKay et al., 2004) and other recent research suggesting it is a common symptom but not the most highly prevalent (i.e., Fullana et al., 2010). The epidemiology survey conducted by Fullana and colleagues spanned six countries, and found that contamination fear was three times more frequent in women than in men diagnosed with the disorder. Further, in factor analytic research contamination fear was found to be distinct from other psychopathology, unlike other symptoms of OCD, which was frequently comorbid with other conditions (Cullen et al., 2007). Accordingly, contamination fear and cleaning rituals warrant special attention. The aims of this chapter are to describe the various ways contamination fear and cleaning rituals may manifest in OCD, describe the underlying cognitive-behavioral features of this symptom, consider emotional determinants other than fear that contribute to the symptoms, and cover treatment approaches.

Nature of Contamination Fear

Contamination fear is a communicable fear. That is, the capacity for stimuli to evoke contamination fear is contagious, in that otherwise neutral objects can take on the fear-evoking properties after contact with stimuli that are feared. This is unique among fears, and is in line with a disgust evoking properties referred to as sympathetic magic (Rozin & Fallon, 1987). Sympathetic magic refers to the degree that neutral objects, or objects that are neutral but resemble disgust-evoking stimuli, can elicit disgust. The Law of Contagion governs the manner in which stimuli that are contaminated infect otherwise neutral objects. The Law of Similarity is the contamination-eliciting feature of objects that resemble contaminated stimuli, or are closely associated with contaminated stimuli, but are in fact neutral. These broad properties will be discussed further later in this chapter.

The Wiley Handbook of Obsessive Compulsive Disorders, Volume I, First Edition.
Edited by Jonathan S. Abramowitz, Dean McKay, and Eric A. Storch.
© 2017 John Wiley & Sons Ltd. Published 2017 by John Wiley & Sons Ltd.

Rachman (2004) described the phenomenon of contamination fear as also encompassing a memory for contaminated objects and situations, including precise locations. Further, individuals with contamination fear often do not experience degradation in the level of contamination at the source of the places and situations evoking contamination fear (see Rachman, 2004: 1231).

Concerns with Harm to Self

The most common expression of contamination fear involves concerns with oneself becoming contaminated. Further, individuals with contamination fear show automatic biases for contamination information, and the extent this bias predicts degree of avoidance in behavioral tasks. To illustrate, Armstrong, Sarawgi, and Olatunji (2012) found that contamination fearful individuals showed biases for tracking contamination stimuli compared with noncontamination fearful individuals, and this predicted their avoidance of stimuli in a bathroom behavioral avoidance test (touching toilet seats). Interestingly, while Rachman (2004) suggests a persistence of memory for contamination, suggesting an emotional memory bias, experimental research has not supported this (Charash & McKay, 2009). Instead, it appears that the biases are restricted to implicit processing and judgment tasks (Armstrong et al., 2012; Charash & McKay, 2009).

In addition to demonstrating implicit biases toward contamination fear stimuli, individuals with this symptom presentation of OCD also show a persistence of this bias. In one experiment using an implicit bias modification task, Green and Teachman (2012) showed that the implicit biases were resistant to modification. This purely cognitive intervention may therefore lack sufficient clinical potency to alter biases and associated behaviors in contamination fear. There are no studies to our knowledge, however, that examine changes in implicit bias following other cognitive interventions such as cognitive therapy derived from Salkovskis' (1985) model.

Mental Contamination. A few studies have illuminated a less common manifestation of contamination fear that involves contact with nonphysical pollutants. Fear of mental contamination shares much in common with fear of contact contamination, including the law of similarity, but is associated with threats to moral uprightness or mental purity rather than physical contact with contagions. It is evidenced in nonclinical populations in lexical semantics and religious cleansing rituals. Zhong and Liljenquist (2006) point out that words like "pure" and "clean" can be used to describe both physical assessments of cleanliness and moral purity, and they cite examples of idioms that use words like "dirty" to describe ethical delinquency. They also highlight several religious traditions including Christianity, Islam, and Hinduism in which various forms of ritualized bathing are regarded as essential to spiritual continence or unity. Further, preserving a sense of cleanliness has strong sociological implications, as evidenced in classic illustrations with native populations. These native peoples exhibit a wide range of culturally embedded rituals designed to maintain, preserve, or re-capture cleanliness; further, perceived lack of cleanliness, including culturally embedded moral transgressions are considered both impure and dangerous (cf. Douglas, 1966).

In clinical populations, fear of mental contamination has been correlated with OCD and PTSD (Cougle et al, 2008; Fairbrother & Rachman, 2004). Researchers have suggested that the relationship between OCD and mental contamination fear may be rooted in a clinical cognitive phenomenon called thought–action fusion (TAF). TAF has characterized as a persistent belief that thinking about an unacceptable event will cause it to happen and that having an unacceptable thought is equivalent to committing an disturbing action (Shafran, Thordarson, & Rachman, 1996). Fear of mental contamination likely originates in an intrusive feeling that thoughts about unfavorable events will lead them to occur in real life. Coughtrey, Shafran, Knibbs, and Rachman (2012) found that severity of mental contamination was correlated with severity of OCD and TAF. Interestingly, 10.2% of patients with mental contamination fear did not demonstrate contact contamination fear, suggesting that mental contamination may be related to but separate from contact contamination.

Underlying Cognitive-Behavioral Features

At the present time, the most extensive conceptualization of contamination fear has come from cognitive-behavior research. One model considered in this regard involves avoidance learning that motivates cleaning rituals, which serve to reinforce the behavior through negative reinforcement. Further, given the challenges in washing (i.e., time consuming, red and sore skin from excessive cleaning), many sufferers avoid situations that might lead to feelings of dirt and contamination.

Cognitive Avoidance

Perhaps the clearest account related to cognitive avoidance comes from Foa and Kozak (1986), wherein the individuals with contamination fear "freeze" contaminated sites. This creates "contaminated" and "clean" zones. Foa and Kozak describe this process as follows:

> An illustrative example of distortion is the cognitive avoidance practiced by a patient who felt contaminated by urine. During exposure sessions urine was put on several places on his arm. A strong initial fear reaction was manifested in nervous movements, blushing, and a very high anxiety rating. However, unlike the gradual reduction of anxiety observed in most patients, a sharp response decrement (within 3–5 min) was observed with this patient. This pattern of high initial response followed by rapid decline was repeated daily: Long-term habituation was not evident. Inquiry revealed a curious avoidance technique: In his imagination this patient first "froze" the contaminated spots to prevent their "spread"; having controlled them he stopped attending to them. In this case, the observed response decrease seemed not to reflect therapeutic emotional processing but rather, successful avoidance of the contaminant. Despite repeated presentations of potentially corrective information, emotional processing did not occur because the patient reformed potentially incompatible information ("urine is spread but I am not harmed") into compatible information ("urine is contained and I am not harmed").
>
> (Foa & Kozak, 1986: 30)

This process of cognitive avoidance is a common one among individuals with contamination fear, and should be assessed in evaluating any client presenting with this specific symptom. Aside from this specific point noted in Foa and Kozak, virtually no research has been conducted on this related specifically to contamination fear in particular, and OCD in general.

The conditioning models of OCD in general and contamination fear in particular have been inadequate in depicting the onset and maintenance of symptoms (Taylor, Abramowitz, & McKay, 2007). Briefly, the conditioning models have failed to adequately account for OCD due to a consistent lack of learning history among sufferers, there is little in these models that accounts for the heterogeneity of varied intrusive thoughts, they do not account for the malleability of symptoms over time in the absence of intervening environmental events, and these models does not account for the high levels of insight evident in most sufferers as to the senselessness of their symptoms. In order to address the shortcomings of purely behavioral models, cognitive features of contamination fear have been depicted.

Safety Signals and Behaviors. Safety signals are specific environmental stimuli that alert an individual that otherwise dangerous stimuli are not harmful. Safety behaviors involve specific actions designed to reduce the fear-inducing properties of any stimuli. Controversy exists over whether treatment models emphasizing extinction (i.e., exposure therapy) should work to eliminate safety signals and behaviors, or whether these should be accommodated into treatment (Helbig-Lang & Petermann, 2010). This controversy has persisted given that safety signals and behaviors have not consistently been associated with treatment outcome. In the case of individuals with contamination fear, safety signals are relevant given the aforementioned cognitive avoidance, where sufferers seek information that confers a sense of safety as a specific means of avoiding anxiety. Accordingly, individuals with contamination fear are attuned to information in the environment that might pose harm, and by extension, sources of safety from the perceived harmful objects. For example, Olatunji, Connolly, Lohr, and Elwood (2008) found that contamination fearful participants were able to generate significantly more reasons a public restroom might be harmful compared with noncontamination fearful participants. However, no differences were found between these groups for noncontamination based situations (i.e., cliff diving, going to the museum).

As will be discussed in the section related to treatment, exposure with response prevention is the most efficacious intervention for contamination fear. However, many clients are reluctant to participate in this form of therapy. Levy and Radomsky (2014) recently found that inclusion of a participant-selected safety signal enhanced the acceptability of exposure therapy. As an additional sign that safety behaviors work to facilitate outcome in a single session of exposure treatment (Goetz & Lee, 2015). It should be noted that all the research conducted examining safety signals and behaviors have been with non-clinical or undergraduate participants. Accordingly, the degree this line of research is generalizable to clinical samples is not known.

Intolerance of Uncertainty. Intolerance of uncertainty has been shown to be a liability for generalized anxiety and for OCD generally (Gentes & Ruscio, 2011). Most of the research examining intolerance of uncertainty centers on correlations with symptom severity of OCD. In the context of contamination fear, the findings are inconsistent in showing a relation with intolerance of uncertainty. For example, Brakoulias and colleagues (2014) did not find individuals with contamination fear had greater intolerance of uncertainty generally. On the other hand, Jensen and Heimberg (2015) found that individuals with contamination fear showed high levels of intolerance of uncertainty for contamination-based situations, but not for other situations.

Emotional Concomitants

Emerging research suggests that contamination fear interacts with other emotive and cognitive responses in multidimensional symptomatic constellations (Cisler, Brady, Olatunji, & Lohr, 2010; Moretz & McKay, 2008). Elevated levels of disgust sensitivity have been correlated with heightened contamination fear, and disgust has presented as an underlying process of contamination-based obsessions when controlling for trait anxiety (OCCWG, 2007; Tsao & McKay, 2004). This relationship is not surprising because sensitivity to contamination threat is characterized by persistent feelings of vulnerability to pollution by a person or object that has been in contact with contagions, and disgust has been conceptualized similarly as a contamination-avoidant adaptive process (Rachman, 2004). Obsessive beliefs, a symptom of OCD defined by dysfunctional perceptions such as overestimation of threat, has also correlated with contamination-based OCD (Tolin, Woods, & Abramowitz, 2003). The complex synthesis of affective and cognitive mechanisms involved in contamination-based OCD seem to be rooted in exaggerated impulses to avoid contact with contagions, and this interactive co-occurrence of emotions invalidates current etiological models.

The "disease-avoidance" model describes disgust as an adaptive affective mechanism that serves to elicit avoidant behavior towards potentially pathogenic substances (Matchett & Davy, 1991; Rozin & Fallon 1987). OCD patients with distress induced by contamination fear report intrusive feelings that contact with contaminated objects will lead to infection or other harms, which prompts excessive washing after incidental contact with potentially contaminating objects (Olatunji et al., 2010). Disgust and fear have been observed to correlate in nonclinical populations and in other psychopathologies, especially specific phobias (Sawchuk, Lohr, Tolin, Lee, & Kleinknech, 2000). Woody and Teachman (2006) reviewed literature comparing disgust and fear in measures of behavioral intention, acquisition, and operative role in phobic responses to better distinguish underlying emotive processes. They determined that disgust was more narrowly associated with fear of contagion than with general bodily threat. Some evidence suggests that disgust is correlated with a decline in heart rate, and that fear is associated with accelerated heart rate, but evidence is not conclusive (Ekman, Levenson, & Friesen, 1983).

Disgust has been conceptualized as a complex emotion with several subtypes that elicit distinct co-emotions and associate with specific items (Simpson, Carter, Anthony, & Overton, 2006). Much remains unknown about the domains of disgust that play a role in the etiology and maintenance of contamination fear in OCD. Olatunji, Sawchuk, Lohr, and Jong (2004) explored dimensional distinctions of disgust sensitivity relative to contamination fear. Three hundred and twenty-three subjects were classified as "high" or "low" in scales of contamination fear before completing multidomain measures of disgust sensitivity. Contamination fear was correlated with several disgust domains, most strongly with the disgust domain of sympathetic magic, also referred to as the "law of contagion." Disgust in the domain of sympathetic magic occurs when an object elicits a disgust response after it has been associated with contamination, even when no threat of contamination exists (Rozin & Nemeroff, 1990). Many patients with contamination fear avoid places or experiences because of incidental association with a contagion. In some cases avoidant behavior becomes so extreme that patients develop geographical networks of avoidance, often causing high levels of impairment (Risking et al., 1997). Correlations between fear and the disgust domain of sympathetic magic concur with the disease-avoidant mechanism believed to underlie both emotions.

Synthesis of fear and disgust in contamination-based OCD may be mediated by obsessive beliefs, a symptom of OCD characterized by persistent cognitive misconceptions. Cisler and colleagues (2010) found that contamination fear was nearly as strongly correlated with obsessive beliefs as with disgust, and they postulated that obsessive beliefs might augment disgust appraisals. Cognitive models for OCD have highlighted the significance of self-appraisals in the maintenance of obsessions (Rachman, 1998). Obsessive beliefs seem to originate in the overestimation of threat of contagion, contributing a cognitive element to the dynamic processes involved in contamination fear.

More research is needed to develop comprehensive models for contamination fear that synthesize contributing emotive and cognitive processes. Some research suggests that other subtypes of OCD may also involve disgust. For example, "not just right experiences" (NJREs) are characterized by intrusive feelings that tasks are incomplete, resulting in compulsive behaviors aimed at reducing discomfort by achieving completion (Coles, Frost, Heimberg, & Rhéaume, 2003). A common compulsion associated with NJREs is excessive hand washing, which may indicate a latent fear of contagion that correlates with disgust. Better characterizations of fear and disgust could facilitate the development of more comprehensive etiological models for contamination fear. More accurate taxonomies will allow for the development of more effective therapies.

Treatment Approaches

Cognitive-behavioral therapies (CBT) have consistently been shown to effectively alleviate general symptoms of OCD associated with all subtypes in clinical studies. This method addresses pathological anxiety and dysfunctional behavioral avoidance through exposure to distress elicitors (Abramowitz, 2006). Exposure with response prevention (ERP), a CBT method first developed in the 1960s, is currently utilized in OCD therapy almost exclusively, sometimes in conjunction with cognitive therapies (Rowa, Antony, & Swinson, 2007). ERP involves exposing patients to distress evoking stimuli while simultaneously preventing typical dysfunctional responses such as compulsive washing or avoidance. It is designed to gradually alleviate symptoms by habituation to distress evoking stimuli. A meta-analysis of empirically tested OCD therapies found ERP to be significantly more effective than relaxation, anxiety management training, and pill placebo (Olatunji, Davis, Powers, & Smits, 2013). Although the method has been proven effective in empirical research, studies demonstrate relapse or discontinuation of treatment in 25–50% of patients (Franklin & Foa, 2002). Due to high degrees of heterogeneity in OCD symptoms, and the existence of several distinct symptomatic subtypes, therapies might be more effective if they were designed to address specific symptomatic constellations such as contamination fear (McKay et al., 2004). Outcomes of treatments for contamination fear might be improved through the development of symptom specific therapies.

Researchers applying CBT to the treatment of contamination fear have highlighted variations in response among patients with contamination-based OCD. In an investigation of habituation in CBT treatment of contamination-based OCD, subjects with primary contamination fear (C-OC) and without primary contamination fear (O-OC) were exposed to distress evoking stimuli (McKay, 2006). Patients were exposed to disgust and anxiety eliciting stimuli for separate intervals of 30 minutes. Non-anxiety-inducing disgust elicitors were utilized, such as used garbage cans and cigarette ashes. Anxiety elicitors were geared towards the specific vulnerabilities of each participant. Results indicated that both groups habituated more quickly to disgust elicitors than anxiety elicitors, and that the C-OC group habituated more slowly than the O-OC group. This indicates etiological differences and treatment outcomes in OCD subtypes, and supports the development of subtype specific treatments for OCD.

Recent research has indicated that methods of cognitive restructuring such as inhibitory learning used in conjunction with ERP improve efficacy and reduce relapse rates in OCD, and may be especially effective for subjects with contamination fear. In a meta-analysis of studies evaluating the efficacy of ERP alone and ERP in conjunction with cognitive restructuring, Rosa-Alcázar and colleagues found evidence that ERP plus inhibitory learning was more effective than ERP alone in treating OC symptoms (Rosa-Alcázar et al., 2008). Riskind, Wheeler, and Picerno (1996) noted the apparent significance of looming threat and fear of contagion in the etiology of contamination fear, and developed a therapy designed to "freeze" or slow down the progress of obsessive fear of threat. Clinical OCD subjects were instructed to imagine their feelings of impending threat to be frozen in time and unable to move. The "freeze" method was effective at reducing fear in predominantly obsessive patients, and reducing fear and avoidant behavior in patients with relatively higher scores of dysfunctional imagination. Major deficits in understanding persist in the treatment of OC subtypes, and more research is needed to develop therapies that address specific symptoms. Systematic guidelines for treatment of subtypes would allow for more effective application of therapies.

Conclusions and Future Directions

At present, contamination fear is characterized by features associated with phobic responses as well as those associated with disgust. Treatment research shows robust response to exposure with response prevention (Abramowitz, Franklin, Schwartz, & Furr, 2004). Less well understood is whether several variations on the manifestation of contamination fear might impact treatment outcome. In preparing this chapter, no investigations were identified that examined clinical presentations of fear of contaminating others, yet include the same compulsions (excessive washing of oneself, avoiding places and situations with contaminants). Also worthy of further investigation is symptom presentation involving moral disgust. There is one highly cited investigation where individuals exposed to morally compromising information engage in greater handwashing (Zhong & Liljenquist, 2006). However, there have been significant problems in replicating this effect (Zuckerman & Siev, 2014).

Managing Disgust versus Fear

While the emphasis in treatment for contamination fear has been anxiety response, comparably little attention has been paid to how to address disgust reactions. At the present time, it appears that disgust reactions take longer to respond to intervention (McKay, 2006). Recently, a variety of alternative approaches to alleviating disgust responses were put forth by Mason and Richardson (2012). Among these approaches are cognitive interventions and response devaluation. However, none of these approaches have been subject to empirical tests.

A possible route for alleviating disgust reactions could be culled from the recent inhibitory learning model of exposure (i.e., Abramowitz, 2013; Craske et al., 2014). This model suggests that clinical efforts at altering fear responses (or in this case, disgust) involves any or all of the following: altering expectations around the stimuli and then engaging in exposure; deepened extinction (exposure to multiple individual conditioned stimuli prior to exposure to the stimulus complex); periodic reinforcement for engaging in exposure; removal of safety signals; and exposure in multiple contexts. Given the prevalence of contamination fear, and the growing research support that there is a prominent role for disgust, the inhibitory learning approach is a promising line of additional investigation worthy of pursuing.

Social Challenges

Given the aforementioned information processing bias for contamination fear, individuals at risk for developing this specific problem may develop symptoms based on several environmental predictors. For example, health scares can produce spikes in contamination fear in the public, and a growing frequency of contagious epidemics complicates clinical attempts to distinguish between rational hygienic vigilance and clinical contamination fear or health anxiety. As demonstrated by Woody and Teachman (2006), excessive contamination fear in clinical cases likely results from the intensification of universal affective mechanisms that serve to elicit avoidant behavior towards potentially harmful substances.

In recent years, in the wake of unprecedented globalization, greater frequency of disease outbreaks has lead to warnings about the possibility of cataclysmic contagious epidemics. Ebola virus, Severe Acute Respiratory Syndrome (SARS), Middle Eastern Respiratory Syndrome (MERS), and E. Coli have all been implicated in widespread outbreaks that led to containment measures by governmental agencies. This has led to the more widespread use of hand sanitizers, mandatory fever checkpoints in certain transit hubs, and other public measures for containing outbreaks. Individuals with clinical contamination fear may assess their symptoms as rational and justifiable in light of these outbreaks and may opt out of treatment. Indeed, a recent investigation showed that individuals with heightened contamination fear had greater fears of contracting H1N1 (commonly referred to as swine 'flu) (Wheaton, Abramowitz, Berman, Fabricant, & Olatunji, 2011), and that the relationship between contamination fear and swine 'flu fear was mediated by anxiety sensitivity and disgust (Brand, McKay, Wheaton, & Abramowitz, 2013). Public health policymakers would do well to better educate the public rather than provide sensationalized information in order to minimize the degree of ancillary contamination symptoms provoked in the general population.

References

Abramowitz, J. S. (2006). *Understanding and treating obsessive-compulsive disorder: A cognitive behavioral approach*. New York: Routledge.

Abramowitz, J. S. (2013). The practice of exposure therapy: Relevance of cognitive-behavioral theory and extinction theory. *Behavior Therapy, 44*, 548–558.

Abramowitz, J. S., Franklin, M. S., Schwartz, S. A., & Furr, J. M. (2004). Symptom presentation and outcome of cognitive-behavioral therapy for obsessive-compulsive disorder. *Journal of Consulting and Clinical Psychology, 71*, 1049–1057.

Armstrong, T., Sarawgi, S., & Olatunji, B. O. (2012). Attention bias toward threat in contamination fear: Overt components and behavioral correlates. *Journal of Abnormal Psychology, 121*, 232–237.

Brakoulias, V., Starcevic, V., Berle, D., Milicevic, D., Hannon, A., & Martin, A. (2014). The relationships between obsessive-compulsive symptom dimensions and cognitions in obsessive-compulsive disorder. *Psychiatric Quarterly, 85*, 133–142.

Cisler, J., Brady, R., Olatunji, B., & Lohr, J. (2010). Disgust and obsessive beliefs in contamination-related OCD. *Cognitive Therapy and Research, 34*, 439–448.

Brand, J., McKay, D., Wheaton, M. G., & Abramowitz, J. (2013). The relationship between obsessive-compulsive beliefs and symptoms, anxiety and disgust sensitivity, and swine flu fears. *Journal of Obsessive Compulsive and Related Disorders, 2*, 200–206.

Charash, M., & McKay, D. (2009). Disgust and contamination fear: Attention, memory, and judgment of stimulus situations. *International Journal of Cognitive Therapy, 2*, 53–65.

Coles, M. E., Frost, R. O., Heimberg, R. G., & Rhéaume, J. (2003). "Not just right experiences": Perfectionism, obsessive-compulsive features and general psychopathology. *Behaviour Research and Therapy, 41*, 681–700.

Coughtrey, A., Shafran, R., Knibbs, D., & Rachman, S. (2012). Mental contamination in obsessive-compulsive disorder. *Journal of Obsessive-Compulsive and Related Disorders, 1*(4), 244–250.

Cougle, J., Lee, H., Horowitz, J., Wolitzky-Taylor, K., & Telch, M. (2008). An exploration of the relationship between mental pollution and OCD symptoms. *Journal of Behavior Therapy and Experimental Psychiatry, 39*, 340–353.

Craske, M. G., Kircanski, K., Zelikowsky, M., Mystkowski, J., Chowdhury, N., & Baker, A. (2008). Optimizing inhibitory learning during exposure therapy. *Behaviour Research and Therapy, 46*, 5–27.

Cullen, B., Brown, C. H., Riddle, M. A., Grados, M., Bienvenu, O J., Hoehn-Saric, R., … Nestadt, G. (2007). Factor analysis of the Yale–Brown Obsessive-Compulsive Scale in a family study of obsessive-compulsive disorder. *Depression & Anxiety, 24*, 130–138.

Deacon, B., & Olatunji, B. (2007). Specificity of disgust sensitivity in the prediction of behavioral avoidance in contamination fear. *Behaviour Research and Therapy, 21*, 10–21.

Douglas, M. (1966). *Purity and danger*. New York: Routledge.

Ekman, P., Levenson, R. W., & Friesen, W. V. (1983). Autonomic nervous system activity distinguishes among emotions. *Science, 221*,1208–1210.

Fairbrother, N., & Rachman, S. (2004). Feelings of mental pollution subsequent to sexual assault. *Behaviour Research and Therapy, 42*(2), 173–189.

Foa, E. B., & Kozak, M. (1986). Emotional processing of fear: Exposure to corrective information. *Psychological Bulletin, 99*, 20–35.

Franklin, M. E., & Foa, E. B. (2002). Cognitive behavioral treatments for obsessive compulsive disorder. *A Guide to Treatments that Work, 2*, 367–386.

Fullana, A. M., Vilagut, G., Rojas-Farreras, S., Mataix-Cols, D., de Graaf, R., Demyttenaere, K., Hara, J. M., … Alonso, J. (2010). Obsessive-compulsive symptom dimensions in the general population: Results from an epidemiological study in six European countries. *Journal of Affective Disorders, 124*, 291–299.

Gentes, E. L., & Ruscio, A. M. (2011). A meta-analysis of the relation of intolerance of uncertainty to symptoms of generalized anxiety disorder, major depressive disorder, and obsessive-compulsive disorder. *Clinical Psychology Review, 31,* 923–933.

Goetz, A. R., & Lee, H. J. (2015). The effects of preventative and restorative safety behaviors on a single-session of exposure therapy for contamination fear. *Journal of Behavior Therapy and Experimental Psychiatry, 46,* 151–157.

Green, J. S., & Teachman, B. A. (2012). Is "cootie" in the eye of the beholder? An experimental attempt to modify implicit associations tied to contamination fear. *Journal of Experimental Psychopathology, 3,* 479–495.

Helbig-Lang, S., & Petermann, F. (2010). Tolerate or eliminate? A systematic review on the effects of safety behavior across anxiety disorders. *Clinical Psychology: Science & Practice, 17,* 218–233.

Jensen, D., & Heimberg, R. G. (2015). Domain-specific intolerance of uncertainty in socially anxious and contamination-focused obsessive-compulsive individuals. *Cognitive Behaviour Therapy, 44,* 54–62.

Levy, H. C., & Radomsky, A. S. (2014). Safety behaviour enhances the acceptability of exposure. *Cognitive Behaviour Therapy, 43,* 83–92.

Matchett, G., & Davey, G. C. (1991). A test of a disease-avoidance model of animal phobias. *Behaviour Research and Therapy, 29*(1), 91–94.

Mason, E. C., & Richardson, R. (2012). Treating disgust in anxiety disorders. *Clinical Psychology: Science & Practice, 19,* 180–194.

McKay, D. (2006). Treating disgust reactions in contamination-based obsessive-compulsive disorder. *Journal of Behavior Therapy and Experimental Psychiatry, 37*(1), 53–59.

McKay, D., Abramowitz, J., Calamari, J., Kyrios, M., Radomsky, A., Sookman, D., Taylor, S., & Wilhelm, S. (2004). A Critical evaluation of obsessive-compulsive disorder subtypes: Symptoms versus mechanisms. *Clinical Psychology Review, 24,* 283–313.

Moretz, M., & McKay, D. (2008). Disgust sensitivity as a predictor of obsessive-compulsive contamination symptoms and associated cognitions. *Journal of Anxiety Disorders, 22,* 707–715.

Olatunji, B. O., Connolly, K., Lohr, J. M., & Elwood, L.S. (2008). Access to information about harm and safety in contamination-related obsessive-compulsive disorder. *Journal of Cognitive Psychotherapy, 22,* 57–67.

Olatunji, B. O., Davis, M. L., Powers, M. B., & Smits, J. A. (2013). Cognitive-behavioral therapy for obsessive-compulsive disorder: A meta-analysis of treatment outcome and moderators. *Journal of Psychiatric Research, 47*(1), 33–41.

Olatunji, B., Moretz, M., Wolitzky-Taylor, K., McKay, D., Mcgrath, P., & Ciesielski, B. (2010). Disgust vulnerability and symptoms of contamination-based OCD: Descriptive tests of incremental specificity. *Behavior Therapy, 41*(4), 475–490.

Olatunji, B., Sawchuk, C., Lohr, J., & Jong, P. (2004). Disgust domains in the prediction of contamination fear. *Behaviour Research and Therapy, 42,* 93–104.

Rachman, S. (1998). A cognitive theory of obsessions: Elaborations. *Behaviour Research and Therapy, 36,* 385–401.

Rachman, S. (2004). Fear of contamination. *Behaviour Research and Therapy, 42,* 1227–1255.

Riskind, J., Wheeler, D., & Picerno, M. (1996). Using mental imagery with subclinical OCD to "freeze" contamination in its place: Evidence for looming vulnerability theory. *Behaviour Research and Therapy, 33*(2), 757–768.

Rosa-Alcázar, A. I., Sanchez-Meca, J., Gomez-Conesa, A., & Marin-Martinez, F. (2008). Psychological treatment of obsessive-compulsive disorder: A meta-analysis. *Clinical Psychology Review, 28*(8), 1310–1325.

Rowa, K., Antony, M. M., & Swinson, R. P. (2007). Exposure and response prevention. In M. M. Antony, C. Purdon, & L. Summerfeldt (Eds.), *Psychological treatment of obsessive-compulsive disorder: Fundamentals and beyond* (pp. 79–109). Washington, DC: American Psychological Association.

Rozin, P., & Fallon, A. E. (1987). A perspective on disgust. *Psychological Review, 94,* 23–41.

Rozin, P., & Nemeroff, C. (1990). The laws of sympathetic magic: A psychological analysis of similarity and contagion. In J. W. Stigler, R. A. Shweder, & G. Herdt (Eds.), *Cultural psychology: Essays on comparative human development* (pp. 205–232). New York: Cambridge University Press.

Sawchuk, C., Lohr, J., Tolin, D., Lee, T., & Kleinknecht, R. (2000). Disgust sensitivity and contamination fears in spider and blood–injection–injury phobias. *Behaviour Research and Therapy, 38,* 753–762.

Shafran, R., Thordarson, D., & Rachman, S. (1996). Thought–action fusion in obsessive compulsive disorder. *Journal of Anxiety Disorders, 10,* 379–391.

Simpson, J., Carter, S., Anthony, S. H., & Overton, P. G. (2006). Is disgust a homogeneous emotion? *Motivation and Emotion, 30,* 31–41.

Taylor, S., Abramowitz, J. S., & McKay, D. (2007). Cognitive-behavioral models of OCD. In M. M. Antony, C. Purdon, & L. Summerfeldt (Eds.), *Psychological treatment of OCD: Fundamentals and beyond* (pp. 9–29). Washington, DC: American Psychological Association.

Tolin, D. F., Woods, C. M., & Abramowitz, J. S. (2003). Relationship between obsessive beliefs and obsessive-compulsive symptoms. *Cognitive Therapy and Research, 27,* 657–669.

Tsao, S., & Mckay, D. (2004). Behavioral avoidance tests and disgust in contamination fears: Distinctions from trait anxiety. *Behaviour Research and Therapy, 42,* 207–216.

Wheaton, M. G., Abramowitz, J. S., Berman, N. C., Fabricant, L. E., & Olatunji, B. O. (2012). Psychological predictors of anxiety in response to the H1N1 (swine flu) pandemic. *Cognitive Therapy and Research, 36,* 210–218.

Woody, S., & Teachman, B. (2006). Intersection of disgust and fear: Normative and pathological views. *Clinical Psychology: Science and Practice, 7,* 291–311.

Zhong, C. B., & Liljenquist, K. (2006). Washing away your sins: Threatened morality and physical cleansing. *Science, 313,* 1451–1452.

Zuckerman, S. E., & Seiv, J. (2014). *The relationship between immorality and cleansing: A meta-analysis of the MacBeth Effect.* Paper presented at the annual meeting of the International Obsessive Compulsive Disorder Foundation, Los Angeles, CA.

18

Contamination Concerns in Children and Adolescents

Robert R. Selles, Elysse A. Arnold, and Eric A. Storch

Youth with obsessive-compulsive disorder (OCD) can present with obsessive-compulsive symptoms across a number of domains (e.g., aggressive obsessions, symmetry and arranging); however, many youth with OCD demonstrate symptoms of the contamination subtype at some point in their lifetime (Hanna, 1995; Riddle et al., 1990; Swedo, Rapoport, Leonard, Lenane, & Cheslow, 1989). Relative to other symptom domains, contamination symptoms may be especially problematic, as youth with contamination symptoms demonstrate increased avoidance behaviors and overall obsessive-compulsive symptom severity (Mataix-Cols, Nakatani, Micali, & Heyman, 2008). These data suggest that contamination symptoms are an important area of consideration in the assessment and treatment of OCD in youth. Therefore, the following chapter is designed to inform clinicians on the variations in which contamination symptoms present, as well as considerations that should be taken during both the assessment and treatment of youth with contamination obsessive-compulsive symptoms.

Contamination Symptoms

While seemingly straightforward, contamination concerns manifest in a diverse array of potential triggers, fears, avoidance behaviors, and compulsions. Youth present with an array of symptoms that vary in specificity as well as logicality. While not a complete list, the following section outlines some of the various ways in which contamination symptoms present.

Triggers

In general, youth's triggers take two forms. First, youth may express a fear of a relatively tangible contaminant. This group includes those who express fears of germs, dirt, illnesses (e.g., stomach viruses, AIDS), bodily fluids, residues, and potentially harmful substances (e.g., x-ray radiation, toxic waste, bleach). In general, these concerns have some basis in reality that has become exaggerated. Given their tangible

The Wiley Handbook of Obsessive Compulsive Disorders, Volume I, First Edition.
Edited by Jonathan S. Abramowitz, Dean McKay, and Eric A. Storch.
© 2017 John Wiley & Sons Ltd. Published 2017 by John Wiley & Sons Ltd.

nature, youth with these concerns often see them as highly logical and in some instances they may have initially been, or continue to be, encouraged by family members. In contrast, youth may express a fear of being contaminated by certain things without a direct tangible contaminant, a phenomenon often referred to as "mental pollution" (Rachman, 1994). Here, youth often make an association with a specific person, place, thing, such as a family member (e.g., sibling) or location (e.g., school). Other examples may include individuals of a certain race or specific pieces of furniture. Youth with mental pollution may not be able to provide a specific reason for why the trigger is contaminated; however, in some cases youth may express specific reasons, like the target being unclean, impure, immoral, or hostile (Coughtrey, Shafran, Lee, & Rachman, 2012; Rachman, 2004). In addition, mental pollution may be triggered by memories or other obsessions the youth experiences (e.g., intrusive taboo thoughts, aggressive obsessions) (Coughtrey et al., 2012). The most frequent triggering mechanism for youth is direct contact with the contaminant (e.g., germs on the door handle, being at school). However, particularly as symptom severity increases, youth may also become contaminated by cross-contaminated objects (e.g., touched clothes after touching the door handle, a piece of schoolwork touched the chair), proximity (e.g., being in the same room as a contaminated object/person), and associated items (e.g., pictures of contaminated person/place).

Fears

Similar to triggers, contact with a feared contaminant is associated with one of two feared outcomes (although youth may endorse both) (Feinstein, Fallon, Petkova, & Liebowitz, 2003). The first, is that exposure to a trigger will result in harm. Typically, the resulting harm is directly related to the nature of the contaminant. For example, children afraid of germs often fear that the germs will make them sick. However, in some cases, the feared outcome of contamination may be less related to the trigger, less pragmatic, or may be related to other OCD symptom domains. For example, we have seen youth who have been worried that contact with a feared contaminant may make their OCD symptoms worse, may result in them going to hell (i.e., connected to religious obsessions), or may result in a loss of certain abilities (e.g., athletic performance). The latter is consistent with what Volz and Heyman (2007) describe as "transformation obsessions"; intrusive thoughts and fear that contact with a contaminant will alter the youth in some domain (e.g., less popular, become an animal). The second type of feared outcome, which frequently occurs in response to nontangible triggers, is a fear of the feeling of being contaminated. In these cases, it is the resulting anxiety/discomfort of contamination that is the feared outcome, as most youth believe it will not naturally subside. As stated above, these fears are not necessarily mutually exclusive and youth may exhibit a variety of trigger and fear combinations.

Avoidance

Since contamination concerns are brought on by contact (or perceived contact) with a physical trigger, avoidance frequently plays a key role in a youth's symptoms. In fact, among other subtypes, contamination symptoms are most commonly associated with avoidance and the contamination subtype is a significant predictor of OCD-related avoidance (Mataix-Cols et al., 2008; Starcevic et al., 2011).

Youth may develop extensive rules regarding where they refuse to go (e.g., public bathrooms, school) and what they will not touch (e.g., door handles, microwave). In addition, they may set up rules to establish "safe" zones (e.g., child's bedroom) where contaminants may not enter (e.g., contaminated school books remain in living room). Other than complete avoidance, youth may develop strategies to minimize contact with contaminants. For example, many youth may avoid contamination by using a barrier when touching contaminated objects (e.g., shirt sleeve) or may only use new objects (e.g., plastic silverware, new toothbrush). They may also employ the help of others, typically parents, in order to ensure avoidance.

If successful in avoiding triggers, a child often demonstrates reduced frequency/ intensity of distress and reduced engagement in compulsive behavior compared with when triggers are not avoided. As a result, avoidance behaviors are often perceived as beneficial and frequently accommodated by family members (Albert et al., 2010; Caporino et al., 2012). However, avoidance behaviors contribute to symptom severity over time (Starcevic et al., 2011) and in more severe youth, avoidance and accommodation can become an area of particular concern. For example, youth who believe school is contaminated, if permitted, may withdrawal from school, or youth afraid of contamination via germs may employ their parents to contribute significantly to their avoidance (e.g., turn on/off sinks, continually buy disposable dishware).

Compulsions

The majority of compulsions associated with contamination concerns are external in nature and involve removal of, or prevention of contact with, the contaminant, typically through washing or cleaning (Mataix-Cols et al., 2008; Rachman, 2004). Depending on the severity of the compulsions, youth may vary in the length of the behavior, the frequency of the behavior, the method used (e.g., certain number of times, specific order), and the number/amount of additional components (e.g., soap, fresh towels). In many youth, washing serves as the primary behavior and may extend to varied body parts. Often hand sanitizer is employed in lieu of, or addition to, hand washing. Youth may also (or recruit others to) excessively clean objects and/or areas believed to be contaminated, such as their clothes, school items, phones, toys, and rooms.

In contrast, youth may also exhibit internal compulsions that are designed to internally reduce fear, distress and/or the sense of contamination (Rachman, 2004). This is particularly common in cases of mental pollution, where, given the nontangible nature of the trigger, the individual cannot modify his or her environment to eliminate the contaminant. For one, youth may attempt to obtain reassurance from others or may attempt to reassure themselves mentally. Youth frequently request reassurance regarding being contaminated (e.g., "this isn't dirty right?") or not getting sick (e.g., "I won't get sick if I eat this right?"). Contamination compulsions also often overlap with somatic compulsions, with reassurance questions regarding already being sick (e.g., "my stomach hurts, am I sick?"), as well as checking behaviors (e.g., temperature-taking). Other checking behaviors, such as checking if something is contaminated, checking that something is new, checking successful completion of washing/ cleaning, and checking expiration dates are also common. Superstitious behaviors, which typically involve doing something a certain way or certain number of times in order to prevent the feared outcome, may also overlap with washing/cleaning compulsions (i.e., hands have to be washed a certain way) or present separately (e.g., walking on certain tiles will prevent contamination).

Assessment Considerations for Contamination

Accurate and thorough assessment is critical as it dictates treatment plans and tracks symptoms and associated impairment/interference. In general, use of validated measures of obsessive-compulsive symptoms (e.g., Children's Yale–Brown Obsessive Compulsive Scale) (Scahill et al., 1997), along with a knowledge of the ways in which contamination concerns can present, will be sufficient for an accurate assessment of a majority of youth. In addition, familiarity with behaviors and cognitions that are developmentally appropriate aids a clinician in gauging which of the child's thoughts and behaviors may be excessive and qualify as potential obsessions and compulsions. However, given the varieties in possible symptom presentations, certain factors may lead to a more difficult assessment of symptoms. Therefore, practical and theoretical considerations in assessing children with contamination symptoms are discussed below.

Mental Compulsions

Most children and parents can accurately report on aspects of the child's compulsions when overt; however, children may employ subtle mental compulsions that they do not recognize as such and that escape parents' attention. In the case of contamination concerns, mental compulsions involve the child engaging in some mental activity (e.g., self-reassurance, counting, praying) to neutralize, avoid, or remove a contaminant. Given their internal nature, mental compulsions pose a number of challenges to assessment. Clinicians should take care in determining the function of the mental act (e.g., reduce distress, distract, resist obsessions) as some mental acts (e.g., that is an OCD thought) can present as positive symptom resistance (i.e., child uses labeling to reject obsessive thoughts) or problematic compulsive rituals (i.e., child repetitively recites phrase to temporarily reduce distress associated with perceived exposure).

Disgust

While definitions vary, disgust involves the withdrawal from a stimulus that is perceived to be objectionable to the senses and has been suggested to be a biologically evolved emotion aimed at self-protection (Olatunji & Sawchuk, 2005). In the case of OCD, disgust is often experienced in the place of, or in combination with, fear and can result in avoidant and compulsive behavior. Interestingly, research implicates disgust as playing a unique role in the presence of contamination symptoms (Olatunji, 2010; Olatunji, Sawchuk, Lohr, & de Jong, 2004); however, disgust in the context of obsessive-compulsive symptoms can be easily overlooked. In many cases, feelings of disgust appear to be experienced at a visceral level that evades conscious thought, limiting the individual's ability to report a conspicuous, intrusive thought/fear regarding his or her aversion. As a result, clinicians should take care to distinguish disgust-driven symptoms from to more "classic" contamination obsessions (e.g., fear of getting sick).

Sensory Symptoms

Sensitivity and intolerance of sensory stimuli (e.g., clothes, sounds, textures) is common among youth, particularly young children, and is hypothesized to decrease with age because children develop more adaptive coping techniques (Baranek, David, Poe, Stone, & Watson, 2006). Many children engage in oppositional behaviors (e.g., temper tantrums) in response to their sensory distress; however, some children develop rituals as a mechanism to cope with the distress. It is the latter case that has been conceptualized as a subtype of OCD (Hazen et al., 2008) and specific to contamination symptoms, children may engage in rituals such as hand washing or cleaning. Similar to disgust, the trigger is not perceived as a source of contamination, but rather the fear of experiencing distress associated with the physical properties of a stimulus prompts a child to engage in behavior aimed at reducing the anxiety.

Family Accommodation

The extent to which a family member participates in obsessive-compulsive symptoms has important assessment implications. This is particularly relevant for youth with contamination concerns as the existing literature youth with contamination obsessions and compulsions may be more prone to receive accommodation than other OCD subtypes (Lebowitz, Panza, Su, & Bloch, 2012; Wu, Lewin, Murphy, Geffken, & Storch, 2014). For all youth with OCD, parental involvement in rituals is associated with increased symptom severity, functional impairment, and externalizing and internalizing problems (Peris et al., 2008; Storch et al., 2007). Further, it may be difficult to gauge impairment and symptom severity if family members assume the child's responsibilities, participate in compulsions, facilitate compulsions, or facilitate avoidance of triggers. Parents may be unaware of the extent to which they accommodate their children's symptoms and the negative consequences of accommodation. In the case of contamination, given that symptoms can frequently stem from rational and legitimate concerns (some of which the parent may share), parents may not identify their accommodation as excessive. Parents may also be afraid of the consequences of reducing accommodation, particularly in youth with coercive and disruptive behaviors (Lebowitz, Vitulano, & Omer, 2011). As a result, it is important to be sensitive and nonaccusatory when assessing family accommodation.

Treatment Considerations

Treatment for individuals with contamination concerns should be appropriately tailored to their specific fears and triggers. As with all symptom areas, clinicians should work with the child to develop a comprehensive fear hierarchy that can be used to guide therapy sessions through exposures of gradually increasing difficulty. For youth with contamination concerns, exposures should encompass exercises focused on: increasing contact with/reducing avoidance of contaminated items; delaying, reducing, and eliminating compulsive behaviors such as washing or cleaning; and eliminating family accommodation. While exposures can be successfully used with the wide variety of triggers, fears, and behaviors present in youth with contamination concerns, the following strategies can be helpful in tailoring treatment to youth:

Modifying Contamination Levels

Some youth, particularly those with tangible triggers, may be able to identify varying levels of contaminated objects (e.g., door handles are not as contaminated as toilet seats). However, other youth may feel that all contaminated objects are equally contaminated and daunting. In these cases, clinicians may be able to use various strategies with the child to "modify" the level of contamination of the objects. Cross-contaminating a new object and having the child come in contact with the secondary, rather than primary, contaminated object (e.g., you touch the contaminated object on the desk, then they touch the desk) can reduce the level of contamination perceived. The extent of contamination associated with an exposure can also be modified through gradual modification to the extent of protections used during contact (e.g., paper towels, articles of clothing), the length of contact, or the surface area of contact (e.g., pinky, whole hand). If youth express that an object's level of contamination reduces over time, delaying contact with the contaminated object until some contamination has "worn off" slightly may also reduce the difficulty of the exposure for youth (e.g., the youth touches the contaminated object well after initial contamination occurs).

As youth become successful at coming in contact with the contaminant, exposures can be increased in intensity by having the youth cross contaminate other areas or objects they regularly come in contact with. For example, after touching a contaminated object, you may encourage youth to use their phone, enter their room, or hug their parent. Additionally, "ingesting" a contaminant (e.g., eating food off the floor) can function as a powerful exposure.

Modifying Compulsions

While ideally, increasing contact with contaminants would be followed by complete resistance against engaging in the prototypical compulsion, this may be too difficult for many youth. Therefore, a variety of modifications can be made to compulsions in order to make exposures successful. First, working with the youth to delay the immediacy of their completion can be effective. Delaying the compulsion forces the youth to begin habituate to the anxiety and as the speed of habituation increases, youth may delay for long enough that they no longer feel the need to complete the compulsion. Second, clinicians can work with youth to reduce time spent on, or reduce aspects of, the compulsion. For example, a youth with a washing compulsion may require others to turn the tap on and off for him or her, use five pumps of soap, wash for a set period, and need a freshly washed hand towel to dry. Completely eliminating the washing behavior may be extremely difficult for the youth; however, they may be amenable to make small changes over time. Some examples could include moving from five to three pumps of soap, reducing the washing time by some amount, or turning the tap on and off themselves. This type of exposure can be set independent of contact with contaminants (i.e., every time youth engages in compulsion they attempt to reduce a specific aspect).

Occasionally youth may display engagement in compulsions independent of clear triggering contact (i.e., youth feels contaminated and therefore engages in compulsion). In these cases, in addition to the strategies above aimed at reducing the extent of the compulsion, it can be helpful to set specific limits on the frequency of compulsions. For example, if currently the youth washes hands approximately five times per hour, you may work with the parent and child to reduce hand washing to three times per hour. The youth is encouraged to "save" compulsions for when they feel they really need to engage in them.

Modifying Parental Behaviors

As mentioned in the assessment section, families of youth with contamination concerns are often highly accommodating of youth's symptoms, whether by facilitating avoidance, providing reassurance, or completing compulsions for the child. Often for youth, particularly those with limited insight and/or motivation for treatment, working with parents to reduce their behaviors and impose limits can be an extremely important aspect of treatment. Often these exposures are set similarly to those directly aimed at the child. For example, parents may be instructed to reduce the extent or frequency of the compulsions they are engaging in for their child or clinicians may work to have families gradually reduce the number of times reassurance is provided to the child.

Targeting Thoughts

Given that triggers and fears can vary considerably for individuals with contamination concerns, utilization of cognitive techniques with youth may require modification. For youth who fear harm as a result of contamination, cognitive techniques will likely primarily focus on improving their appraisals of threat (Sookman, Abramowitz, Calamari, Wilhelm, & McKay, 2005). Conversely, youth who primarily fear feelings of contamination, benefit from improving labeling of feelings as fear and increasing distress tolerance (Sookman et al., 2005).

Disgust

Disgust reactions frequently occur in youth with contamination concerns and represent an important consideration for treating clinicians. On the one hand, disgust does appear to habituate in response to exposure (McKay, 2006) and successful reductions in disgust mediate symptom reductions over the course of treatment (Olatunji, Tart, Ciesielski, McGrath, & Smits, 2011). Conversely, feelings of disgust appear more resistant to extinction than fear and individuals with contamination concerns appear to take longer to habituate to feelings of disgust than those without contamination concerns (McKay, 2006; Olatunji, Wolitzky-Taylor, Willems, Lohr, & Armstrong, 2009). Therefore, for individuals with disgust driven symptoms, increased length and intensity of exposure sessions may be needed to ensure successful habituation (Olatunji et al., 2009). Finally, the importance of anxiety versus disgust in predicting change in urge to wash may be dependent on the primary threat of the exposure (i.e., illness-related threats versus non-illness threats) (Cougle, Wolitzky-Taylor, Lee, & Telch, 2007).

Careful consideration of the patient's contamination theme may aid in appropriately targeting exposures and ensuring effective treatment (Cougle et al., 2007).

Conclusion

Contamination concerns are a common symptom domain of OCD that result in a wide array of symptoms and are frequently associated with increased severity, avoidance and family accommodation. The information and special considerations outlined in this chapter are intended to aid in accurate assessment and effective intervention; however, unique presentations and additional assessment/treatment challenges may face clinicians working with youth with contamination concerns.

References

Albert, U., Bogetto, F., Maina, G., Saracco, P., Brunatto, C., & Mataix-Cols, D. (2010). Family accommodation in obsessive-compulsive disorder: Relation to symptom dimensions, clinical and family characteristics. *Psychiatry Research, 179*, 204–211.

Baranek, G. T., David, F. J., Poe, M. D., Stone, W. L., & Watson, L. R. (2006). Sensory Experiences Questionnaire: Discriminating sensory features in young children with autism, developmental delays, and typical development. *Journal of Child Psychology and Psychiatry, 47*, 591–601.

Caporino, N. E., Morgan, J., Beckstead, J., Phares, V., Murphy, T. K., & Storch, E. A. (2012). A structural equation analysis of family accommodation in pediatric obsessive-compulsive disorder. *Journal of Abnormal Child Psychology, 40*, 133–143.

Coughtrey, A. E., Shafran, R., Lee, M., & Rachman, S. J. (2012). It's the feeling inside my head: A qualitative analysis of mental contamination in obsessive-compulsive disorder. *Behavioural and Cognitive Psychotherapy, 40*, 163–173.

Cougle, J. R., Wolitzky-Taylor, K. B., Lee, H. J., & Telch, M. J. (2007). Mechanisms of change in ERP treatment of compulsive hand washing: does primary threat make a difference? *Behaviour Research and Therapy, 45*, 1449–1459.

Feinstein, S. B., Fallon, B. A., Petkova, E., & Liebowitz, M. R. (2003). Item-by-item factor analysis of the Yale–Brown Obsessive Compulsive Scale Symptom Checklist. *Journal of Neuropsychiatry and Clinical Neuroscience, 15*, 187–193.

Hanna, G. L. (1995). Demographic and clinical features of obsessive-compulsive disorder in children and adolescents. *Journal of the American Academy of Child and Adolescent Psychiatry, 34*, 19–27.

Hazen, E. P., Reichert, E. L., Piacentini, J. C., Miguel, E. C., do Rosario, M. C., Pauls, D., & Geller, D. A. (2008). Case series: Sensory intolerance as a primary symptom of pediatric OCD. *Annals of Clinical Psychiatry, 20*, 199–203.

Lebowitz, E. R., Panza, K. E., Su, J., & Bloch, M. H. (2012). Family accommodation in obsessive-compulsive disorder. *Expert Review of Neurotherapeutics, 12*, 229–238.

Lebowitz, E. R., Vitulano, L. A., & Omer, H. (2011). Coercive and disruptive behaviors in pediatric obsessive compulsive disorder: a qualitative analysis. *Psychiatry, 74*, 362–371.

Mataix-Cols, D., Nakatani, E., Micali, N., & Heyman, I. (2008). Structure of obsessive-compulsive symptoms in pediatric OCD. *Journal of the American Academy of Child and Adolescent Psychiatry, 47*, 773–778.

McKay, D. (2006). Treating disgust reactions in contamination-based obsessive-compulsive disorder. *Journal of Behavior Therapy and Experimental Psychiatry, 37*, 53–59.

Olatunji, B. O. (2010). Changes in disgust correspond with changes in symptoms of contamination-based OCD: a prospective examination of specificity. *Journal of Anxiety Disorders, 24*, 313–317.

Olatunji, B. O., & Sawchuk, C. N. (2005). Disgust: Characteristic features, social manifestations, and clinical implications. *Journal of Social and Clinical Psychology, 24*, 932–962.

Olatunji, B. O., Sawchuk, C. N., Lohr, J. M., & de Jong, P. J. (2004). Disgust domains in the prediction of contamination fear. *Behaviour Research and Therapy, 42*, 93–104.

Olatunji, B. O., Tart, C. D., Ciesielski, B. G., McGrath, P. B., & Smits, J. A. (2011). Specificity of disgust vulnerability in the distinction and treatment of OCD. *Journal of Psychiatric Research, 45*, 1236–1242.

Olatunji, B. O., Wolitzky-Taylor, K. B., Willems, J., Lohr, J. M., & Armstrong, T. (2009). Differential habituation of fear and disgust during repeated exposure to threat-relevant stimuli in contamination-based OCD: An analogue study. *Journal of Anxiety Disorders, 23*, 118–123.

Peris, T. S., Bergman, R. L., Langley, A., Chang, S., McCracken, J. T., & Piacentini, J. (2008). Correlates of accommodation of pediatric obsessive-compulsive disorder: Parent, child, and family characteristics. *Journal of the American Academy of Child and Adolescent Psychiatry, 47*, 1173–1181.

Rachman, S. (1994). Pollution of the mind. *Behaviour Research and Therapy, 32*, 311–314.

Rachman, S. (2004). Fear of contamination. *Behaviour Research and Therapy, 42*, 1227–1255.

Riddle, M. A., Scahill, L., King, R., Hardin, M. T., Towbin, K. E., Ort, S. I., ... Cohen, D. J. (1990). Obsessive compulsive disorder in children and adolescents: Phenomenology and family history. *Journal of the American Academy of Child and Adolescent Psychiatry, 29*, 766–772.

Scahill, L., Riddle, M. A., McSwiggin-Hardin, M., Ort, S. I., King, R. A., Goodman, W. K., ... Leckman, J. F. (1997). Children's Yale–Brown Obsessive Compulsive Scale: Reliability and validity. *Journal of the American Academy of Child and Adolescent Psychiatry, 36*, 844–852.

Sookman, D., Abramowitz, J. S., Calamari, J. E., Wilhelm, S., & McKay, D. (2005). Subtypes of obsessive-compulsive disorder: Implications for specialized cognitive behavior therapy. *Behavior Therapy, 36*, 393–400.

Starcevic, V., Berle, D., Brakoulias, V., Sammut, P., Moses, K., Milicevic, D., & Hannan, A. (2011). The nature and correlates of avoidance in obsessive-compulsive disorder. *Australian & New Zealand Journal of Psychiatry, 45*, 871–879.

Storch, E. A., Geffken, G. R., Merlo, L. J., Jacob, M. L., Murphy, T. K., Goodman, W. K., ... Grabill, K. (2007). Family accommodation in pediatric obsessive-compulsive disorder. *Journal of Clinical Child and Adolescent Psychology, 36*, 207–216.

Swedo, S. E., Rapoport, J. L., Leonard, H., Lenane, M., & Cheslow, D. (1989). Obsessive-compulsive disorder in children and adolescents. Clinical phenomenology of 70 consecutive cases. *Archives of General Psychiatry, 46*, 335–341.

Volz, C., & Heyman, I. (2007). Case series: Transformation obsession in young people with obsessive-compulsive disorder (OCD). *Journal of the American Academy of Child and Adolescent Psychiatry, 46*, 766–772.

Wu, M. S., Lewin, A. B., Murphy, T. K., Geffken, G. R., & Storch, E. A. (2014). Phenomenological considerations of family accommodation: Related clinical characteristics and family factors in pediatric obsessive-compulsive disorder. *Journal of Obsessive-Compulsive and Related Disorders, 3*(3), 228–235.

19

Responsibility, Checking, and Reassurance-seeking in OCD

Rachael L. Neal, Gillian M. Alcolado, and Adam. S. Radomsky

According to cognitive theory, inflated responsibility plays a central role in the onset and maintenance of obsessive-compulsive disorder (OCD) (e.g., Salkovskis, 1985). In this chapter, we discuss the relationships between heightened responsibility appraisals and two characteristic symptoms of OCD: compulsive checking and reassurance-seeking (RS). Throughout the chapter, relevant historical and contemporary research studies are highlighted. In addition, we identify cognitive-behavioral techniques which clinicians may find useful when addressing responsibility appraisals, compulsive checking, and RS, respectively.

In advance of our discussion of the relationships between responsibility, compulsive checking, and RS, we define these key concepts. A broad term such as "responsibility" can have many meanings. In the context of OCD, inflated responsibility is "the belief that one has power which is pivotal to bring about or prevent subjectively crucial negative outcomes. These outcomes are perceived as essential to prevent. They may be actual, that is, having consequences in the real world, and/or at a moral level" (Salkovskis, Richards, & Forrester, 1995: 285). In response to excessive feelings of responsibility, individuals with OCD may feel compelled to engage in compulsive checking, a repetitive verification behavior or mental act that an individual feels driven to perform in order to neutralize anxiety or distress and/or to prevent perceived harm (e.g., Rachman, 2002; Rachman & Hodgson, 1980; van den Hout & Kindt, 2003b). Similar to checking, RS is defined as "the *repeated* solicitation of safety-related information from others about a threatening object, situation or interpersonal characteristic, despite having already received this information" (Parrish & Radomsky, 2010, emphasis added).

Role of Inflated Responsibility Beliefs and Appraisals in OCD Onset and Maintenance

Why do some individuals develop obsessions, while others do not? Intrusive thoughts are an extremely common experience (Rachman & de Silva, 1978; Radomsky et al., 2014a), yet only 2% of the population will develop OCD (Kessler et al., 2005).

The Wiley Handbook of Obsessive Compulsive Disorders, Volume I, First Edition.
Edited by Jonathan S. Abramowitz, Dean McKay, and Eric A. Storch.
© 2017 John Wiley & Sons Ltd. Published 2017 by John Wiley & Sons Ltd.

Obsessional thoughts differ compared with typical thoughts in the extent to which the person feels that they are intrusive, is aware of the thoughts, and feels that the thoughts are ego-dystonic (i.e., the person feels that the thoughts are inconsistent with his belief systems) (Salkovskis, 1985). Cognitive theory suggests that there are a number of biased belief domains that are central to OCD which may predispose certain individuals to experience intrusive thoughts as unwanted and distressing, one of which is inflated responsibility (e.g., Obsessive Compulsive Cognitions Working Group [OCCWG], 1997; Rachman, 1993, 1997, 1998; Salkovskis, 1985, 1996, 1999).

Research aimed at understanding the role of responsibility in the aetiology of OCD symptomatology began several decades ago. Drawing on initial work by Carr (1974) and Rachman and Hodgson (1980), Salkovskis (1985) theorized that for individuals with OCD, negative automatic thoughts often concern one's personal responsibility for preventing harm. Importantly, his theory also proposed that an individual's *interpretation* or *appraisal* of a thought's meaning, rather than the specific content of the thought, determines whether an individual will experience negative mood states and/ or feel driven to perform a compulsive behavior in response to the thought's occurrence (Salkovskis, 1985, 1989).

Consistent with cognitive theory, findings collectively suggest that attributions of personal responsibility are indeed heightened in individuals with OCD relative to anxious and healthy controls (e.g., OCCGW, 2003, 2005; Rachman, Thordarson, Shafran, & Woody, 1995; Salkovskis et al., 2000). Specifically, individuals with OCD (a) have beliefs about personal responsibility that differ from healthy controls, and which predispose them to feel excessively responsible (e.g., "I am more personally responsible than others for preventing harm"); and (b) tend to appraise the occurrence or content of specific intrusive thoughts as signaling that they have responsibility to act to prevent a feared outcome (e.g., "having a thought about harm means I am now responsible for preventing that harm") (Cougle, Lee, & Salkovskis, 2007; OCCWG, 1997; Salkovskis et al., 2000). As such, if an individual believes that a thought is meaningless, she or he is likely to disregard it with little concern. On the other hand, if the individual interprets the thought to mean something terrible about her or him as a person (e.g., "having a thought about pushing an elderly man in front of the subway means that I am a danger to society"), or that the thought is a warning of something terrible to come, then s/he may feel responsible to act to prevent the feared outcome (Ashbaugh, Gelfand, & Radomsky, 2006; OCCWG, 1997; Rachman, 1993; Salkovskis, 1985, 1999; Salkovskis et al., 2000; Wilson & Chambless, 1999).

Based on these theories, a number of creative studies have been conducted to examine how feelings of high versus low responsibility relate to OCD symptomatology. For instance, Ladouceur and colleagues (1995) conducted a manual pill-sorting/classification study and found that individuals under a high-responsibility condition showed more hesitations and checks than did those under low responsibility, and also reported greater anxiety and concern about errors. Similarly, Lopatka and Rachman (1995) found that individuals whose perceived responsibility was experimentally reduced experienced decreased negative affect and urges to check, relative to those whose perceived responsibility was experimentally increased. Moreover, Shafran (1997) found that individuals felt greater responsibility for preventing feared outcomes when they were alone versus when with a responsible person. Shafran (1997) also found that participants in a high-responsibility condition gave higher ratings of urges to check, anxiety/distress, and perceived threat than did individuals in a low-responsibility condition. Additionally, Ashbaugh and colleagues (2006) examined how individuals who are high versus low in OCD symptomatology construe responsibility interpersonally for different kinds of outcomes, and found that those who had higher scores on measures of OCD symptomatology rated themselves as having more responsibility than others for negative (including harmful) and neutral (but not positive) outcomes. Interestingly, responsibility manipulations have also been shown to impact upon memory appraisals among those who compulsively check; high responsibility is associated with greater memory for threat relevant information, yet lower memory confidence, compared to lower responsibility (Radomsky, Rachman, & Hammond, 2001). These findings are consistent with theory that heightened responsibility is associated with negative affect and compulsive urges.

In addition to the research showing that inflated responsibility is associated with aspects of OCD symptomatology, responsibility attributions are thought to be related to a number of other cognitive biases in OCD, including overestimation of threat (e.g., Foa, Sacks, Tolin, Prezworski, & Amir, 2002; OCCWG, 2003, 2005). For instance, Menzies, Harris, Cumming, and Einstein (2000) found that individuals tended to rate potential outcomes as being more harmful (i.e., threatening) when they were responsible, relative to when others were responsible. In addition, inflated responsibility is often associated with the belief that having a thought about a negative event is the same as it occurring (referred to as "thought–action fusion," (TAF) (e.g., Amir, Freshman, Ramsey, Neary, & Brigidi, 2001; Rachman, 1993; Shafran & Rachman, 2004). Individuals with OCD who have a thought about a bad event may believe that it is more likely to happen, and/or that the thought's occurrence is morally equivalent to engaging in a reprehensible act; as such, TAF is associated with increased distress and urges to engage in compulsive acts to prevent the feared occurrence (Amir et al., 2001).

Although responsibility attributions have been implicated in the aetiology of OCD in general (e.g., Salkovskis, 1985), several researchers (e.g., Lopatka & Rachman, 1995; Rachman, 1993; Rachman & Hodgson, 1980) have suggested that inflated responsibility has a more prominent role in certain subtypes of OCD (i.e., checking) than in others. Rachman and Hodgson (1980), for instance, reported that patients may decrease their checking behavior upon admittance to a hospital because they do not feel responsible for their environment; yet, patients may resume their compulsions over time as they become more familiarized with, and thus responsible for, the environment. Although research suggests that responsibility appraisals are not *confined* to checking (e.g., Shafran, 1997; Wilson & Chambless, 1999), they are considered to be a central component in the aetiology of compulsive checking (Rachman, 2002, see below).

Psychological Theories of Compulsive Checking in OCD

Who among us has never stopped to verify that their travel documents are in the bag on the way to the airport? Or that the alarm has been set properly the night before an important early morning appointment? Certainly, the occasional act of checking is fairly common; in fact, having thoughts of doubt that might lead people to check seems to be an almost universal experience (Rachman & de Silva, 1978; Radomsky et al., 2014a). In particular, unwanted intrusive thoughts of *doubt*, such as with respect to objects such as appliances, locks, or important personal belongings are the most common type of intrusive thought worldwide (Radomsky et al., 2014a). What, however, turns the occasional check into multiple checks which take up hours of one's time, accompanied by great distress and interference? Luckily, as one of the most commonly occurring compulsions (Ruscio, Stein, Chiu, & Kessler, 2010), checking has received much research attention over time from those who wish to better understand and treat it.

Historically, Freud regarded compulsive acts as defense mechanisms which guarded against anxiety, inevitably occurring as the result of an "anal-erotic" personality (Freud, 1908, as cited in Rachman & Hodgson's 1980 review). Mowrer's (1947) two-process theory has also been applied to understand compulsive behaviors such as checking. In situations in which one feels fearful, behaviors which reduce that anxiety are reinforced (as per the principals of operant conditioning). Therefore, individuals who react fearfully to intrusive thoughts of doubt will be likely to check again if doing so temporarily reduces that fear.

It was not until much more recently that a cognitive theory centered specifically on compulsive checking was proposed (Rachman, 2002). Drawing from previous work (Salkovskis, 1985), and clinical observations (Rachman & Hodgson, 1980), Rachman outlined three cognitive multipliers which determine the length of a given check. The first is the extent of the responsibility felt. With increasing responsibility, there will be an increase in the amount and duration of checking. Second, the perceived probability of the event will determine the amount of checking. When it comes to checking behavior, a functioning appliance, which represents a high probability of harm, is likely to receive more attention than a broken one, which is associated with a low probability of harm. Third, the severity of the harm also determines the duration and intensity of the check. Wasting electricity (a relatively nonharmful outcome), for example, might induce less checking than avoiding a potential fire (an extremely harmful outcome). Rachman also described a "self-perpetuating mechanism" of checking (Rachman, 2002: 629) to explain why one check is not enough. The mechanism was proposed to comprise four factors: (1) an unsuccessful search for certainty; (2) increased feelings of personal responsibility; (3) increased perceived probability of the harm caused by checking; and (4) the paradoxical effect of checking whereby the more one checks, the less certain they are about the check.

Many elements of Rachman's (2002) theory have been corroborated by research. Evidence for the role of responsibility specifically in checking (and RS, see below) was demonstrated many times, including in an experimental pill-sorting task with nonclinical participants (Parrish & Radomsky, 2006). Individuals under elevated levels of responsibility had higher urges to check aspects of the task. A vignette study administered to students included manipulations of responsibility *and* the seriousness of the threat and examined their impact on checking (and on RS, see below) (Parrish & Radomsky, 2011). When students imagined themselves in these varying situations, increased responsibility and seriousness were both associated with greater urges to check (and to seek RS, see below). A recent investigation has manipulated responsibility, seriousness, and probability of harm within the same experimental paradigm. In both students and compulsive checkers, the multipliers interacted to increase the duration of time spent checking real appliances, such that those who felt more responsible checked more, particularly for objects that were high in threat (i.e., a stove that could cause a fire), and functionality (i.e., working appliances) (Radomsky, Alcolado, Dugas, & Lavoie, 2014b).

Rachman (2002) initially theorized that repeated checking erodes memory confidence. Notably, van den Hout and Kindt (2003b) postulated that this occurs because as the act of checking becomes habitual, fewer attentional resources are devoted to it (van den Hout & Kindt, 2003b). Consequently, less vividness and detail is encoded, as the memory shifts from "remembering" to "knowing" (Tulving, 1985). Seminal work by this group demonstrated that repeated checking does indeed erode memory confidence for the check (van den Hout & Kindt, 2003a), and, furthermore, that individuals who repeatedly check rely increasingly on a feeling of "knowing" as compared with "remembering" (van den Hout & Kindt, 2003b). For instance, after repeatedly checking virtual stove burners or light bulbs prior to making one final check of the stove, nonclinical participants who had repeatedly checked the stove had much less confidence for a final check of the stove as compared with those who had checked light bulbs (van den Hout & Kindt, 2003a, 2003b, 2004). This finding has been replicated using real and functional appliances (Radomsky, Gilchrist, & Dussault, 2006), and is robust, regardless of whether attentional focus is allocated in a diffuse (peripheral) versus focused (central) manner (Ashbaugh & Radomsky, 2007). Further investigations have demonstrated that memory confidence begins to erode after as few as two checks of an object (Coles, Radomsky, & Horng, 2006), and that repeated *mental* checking has the same detrimental effects as repeated physical checking (Radomsky & Alcolado, 2010). Investigations using heterogeneous OCD samples (Boschen & Vuksanovic, 2007) and compulsive checkers specifically (Radomsky et al., 2014b) have found the same results.

In addition to the above studies of how repeated checking can cause low memory confidence, it has been further proposed that the low memory confidence/ maladaptive beliefs about memory may contribute toward compulsive checking (Alcolado & Radomsky, 2011). Psychometric work has shown that low memory confidence predicts checking symptoms in nonclinical participants over and above depression, anxiety, and other known obsessive-compulsive beliefs, including responsibility in nonclinical and OCD samples (Nedeljkovic & Kyrios, 2007; Nedeljkovic, Moulding, Kyrios, & Doron, 2009). More recently, the interaction between obsessive-compulsive belief domains and memory confidence has been shown to predict checking in a nonclinical sample (Cuttler, Alcolado, & Taylor, 2013). Experimental studies wherein individuals' memory confidence/beliefs about memory was/were manipulated via false feedback showed the same effect. Individuals who were led to believe they had a poor memory had greater urges to check their performance on subsequent tasks than those who were led to believe they had an excellent memory (Alcolado & Radomsky, 2011). This finding has been replicated in the context of prospective memory confidence/beliefs (Cuttler, Sirois-Delisle, Alcolado, Radomsky, & Taylor, 2013).

Regardless of the means by which one comes to compulsively check, this behaviour is closely tied to RS as this act can be considered to be checking "by proxy" (Rachman, 2002: 627). In RS another person is asked to provide information which one would otherwise glean through personally checking. Therefore, the multipliers and self-perpetuating mechanism identified above are also likely to contribute to the duration and intensity of RS (see below).

Psychological Theories of Reassurance-Seeking

Reassurance-seeking is now understood to be a commonly used strategy by individuals with OCD to diminish anxiety or distress (Freeston & Ladouceur, 1997; Starcevic et al., 2012). Studies of RS began in the context of depression, wherein researchers found that depressed individuals tend to seek reassurance when their interpersonal connections are uncertain, in order to reduce feelings of relational anxiety and distress (e.g., "How can I really be sure that you won't leave me?") (see Coyne, 1976). Excessive RS has since been identified as a problematic behavior in numerous mental disorders, including health anxiety disorder (e.g., Salkovskis & Warwick, 1986), social anxiety disorder (Heerey & Kring, 2007), generalized anxiety disorder (Beesdo-Baum et al., 2012), and OCD (e.g., Kobori & Salkovskis, 2013; Parrish & Radomsky, 2010, 2011).

In the context of OCD, RS is thought to arise due to overestimations of threat and danger, and underestimation of one's ability to cope with the perceived threat (Rector, Kamkar, Cassin, Ayearst, & Laposa, 2011). Since RS has been conceptualized as a type of compulsive checking, as noted above, it is thought to function similarly to decrease anxiety, distress, and uncertainty, which may be triggered by feelings of excessive personal responsibility for preventing feared outcomes (e.g., Kobori & Salkovskis, 2013; Kobori, Salkovskis, Read, Lounes, & Wong, 2012; Parrish & Radomsky, 2010, 2011; Rachman, 2002; Rector et al., 2011; Starcevic et al., 2012).

As heightened responsibility beliefs are thought to be a primary motivating factor in RS (e.g., Kobori et al., 2012; Parrish & Radomsky, 2010; Salkovskis, 1985), theory suggests that individuals should feel greater urges to engage in RS under conditions of high responsibility. In a similar paradigm to that used by Ladouceur and colleagues (1995) to examine responsibility and checking, Parrish and Radomsky (2006) allocated a sample of nonclinical participants to complete a manual pill-sorting task under conditions of either high or low responsibility. These researchers found that participants who were told that their results would have implications for improving methods of dispensing pharmaceuticals in third-world countries (i.e., high-responsibility condition) reported greater urges to check and seek reassurance than did those who were told that they were participating in a study of shape and color perception (i.e., low-responsibility condition).

Both checking and RS are thought to decrease perceptions of responsibility for preventing feared outcomes, but only RS is thought to also *transfer* feelings of responsibility to another person (e.g., a person seeking reassurance may feel less solely responsible for preventing a feared outcome after receiving reassurance because the other person has been made aware of the perceived threat, and should therefore share in the blame if anything bad were to happen) (e.g., Kobori et al., 2012; Kobori & Salkovskis, 2013; Salkovskis, 1985). Anecdotal evidence supports the occurrence of a transfer of responsibility following RS (e.g., Kobori et al., 2012; Parrish & Radomsky, 2010). For instance, one individual reported that, "the worst could happen and it would still be awful but at least I could say well, it wasn't just my own bad judgment" (Kobori et al., 2012: 28).

Kobori and colleagues (2012) propose three primary motivations which may lead individuals to seek reassurance: a need to feel certain or perfect; a need to feel right, safe, or comfortable; and/or a need to diffuse responsibility to others. These researchers suggest that when individuals seek reassurance, they put forth "ceaseless and careful effort ... to find the right reassurance given by the right person" (Kobori et al., 2012: 28), such that they can trust and understand the reassurance; hence, individuals may seek reassurance from a number of sources. In addition, and similar to checking, many people seeking reassurance simply want to feel "sure" or confident about something they doubt. This desire for certainty is likely motivated by feelings of responsibility and/or a fear of failing to prevent harm.

Research has demonstrated that when individuals with OCD sought reassurance they tended to do so from trusted others, to seek it multiple times, and to become very careful when receiving the reassurance (e.g., controlling the environment to minimize distractions) (Kobori & Salkovskis, 2013). These researchers found that RS was most strongly related to checking, doubting, and obsessions, whereas other types of OCD were less strongly related to the behavior. Other researchers found that RS is related to uncertainty about actions/decisions, and perfectionism about making mistakes (Kobori et al., 2012; Parrish & Radomsky, 2010; Rector et al., 2011). Correspondingly, ambiguous feedback has been shown to increase urges to seek reassurance (Parrish & Radomsky, 2011). These findings support the theorized link between heightened responsibility appraisals and neutralizing behaviors, and also support the proposed functional similarities between compulsive checking and RS (e.g., Kobori et al., 2012; Kobori & Salkovskis, 2013; Parrish & Radomsky, 2010, 2011; Rachman, 2002).

In a qualitative study aimed at better understanding why and how individuals seek RS, researchers found that participants' desire to decrease anxiety and prevent the occurrence of feared outcomes motivated their RS behavior (Parrish & Radomsky, 2010). Participants with OCD and participants with depression reported higher anxiety, negative affect, and perceptions of threat in association with RS than did healthy controls. Participants with OCD, however, reported seeking reassurance primarily about general perceived threats (e.g., the stove, locks), whereas participants with depression were more likely to report that concern about social bonds (e.g., being rejected) was their chief reason for seeking reassurance. These findings support the distinctions made in the literature regarding differing motivations for seeking reassurance across mental health disorders.

Despite feeling highly motivated to seek reassurance due to the aforementioned factors, individuals may hesitate to seek reassurance because they are aware of the self-perpetuating nature of RS, do not want to embarrass themselves, or because they do not want to burden others (Kobori et al., 2012). As a means of lessening the strain of RS on others, individuals may attempt to seek reassurance in more subtle, or *covert* ways (Kobori et al., 2012; Parrish & Radomsky 2010; Rachman & Hodgson, 1980). For instance, a person may say to their partner, "You saw me turn off the stove, so it's okay to leave now" and examine the partner's reactions for evidence that they disagree (e.g., Parrish & Radomsky, 2010). Thus, both overt and covert RS must be addressed in treatment.

Existing Treatment Frameworks for OCD

The first-line intervention for OCD (NICE, 2005; Podea, Suciu, Suciu, & Ardelean, 2009) is exposure and response prevention (ERP), an empirically validated treatment (Chambless et al., 1998). This intervention involves asking individuals to face their feared situations while refraining from engaging in any compensatory or compulsive behavior. Using a customized, graded exposure hierarchy, individuals typically begin by repeatedly attempting tasks that are only mildly or moderately anxiety-provoking until their anxiety is reduced. They progress through successive steps of anxiety-provoking situations until they are able to attempt those situations that are the most distressing with diminished anxiety. For example, if one's goal were to stop checking a door, the individual might first agree to reduce the duration of or delay the commencement of a bout of checking, perhaps in the presence of a loved one (a moderately anxiety-provoking feared situation). She or he would gradually progress to not checking the door at all while at home alone (a maximally feared situation). Over time, and with repeated exposure to the feared situation, anxiety typically reduces as the individual learns not to fear the situation, and the compulsion subsides (see Kozak & Coles, 2005, for a review). This largely behavioral and broad approach, most easily applicable to overt compulsions, has been found to be a highly effective intervention including for checking symptoms (e.g., Abramowitz, Franklin, Schwartz, & Furr, 2003). This makes logical sense, as checking and RS are behaviors from which one can refrain. Indeed, when clustered with other miscellaneous symptoms, these dimensions of OCD were found to respond well to ERP (Abramowitz et al., 2003). It should be noted that because reassurance typically comes from loved ones not involved in the therapeutic intervention, this may present its own set of challenges (see below). With respect to responsibility beliefs, while not overtly targeted/challenged through straightforward ERP, a patient or client might come to their own new beliefs about how responsible they feel through learning that takes place as they become better able to refrain from checking; in fact, there is some evidence suggesting that changes in responsibility beliefs precede symptom change in ERP (Rhéaume & Ladouceur, 2000).

In attempts to further improve upon and refine existing treatments (see Clark, 2005), more cognitive approaches have been developed (e.g., Clark, 2003; Rachman, 2003; Radomsky, Shafran, Coughtrey, & Rachman, 2010). These may typically include targeting cognitive change via guided discovery and behavioral experiments designed to directly tackle the maladaptive beliefs central to OCD. The beliefs targeted may include those that have been investigated empirically, including (a) overestimation of threat/responsibility, (b) importance of/control over thoughts, and (c) perfectionism/intolerance of uncertainty (OCCWG, 2005). For instance, Rachman (1993, 1997, 1998) proposed that obsessions will continue as long as catastrophic misinterpretations of the significance of one's thoughts continue. Unwanted, intrusive thoughts should therefore diminish if an individual reappraises the thoughts as having decreased personal significance. Cognitive interventions can be designed to target responsibility directly, and specific examples are given below. Similarly, other beliefs related to the urge to begin and continue checking, and seeking reassurance, can be modified through this type of protocol.

Although there is evidence to suggest that cognitive interventions can be just as effective as behavioral ones (e.g., Rosa-Alcásar, Sánchez-Meca, Gómez-Conesa, & Marín-Martínez, 2008), as well as preliminary evidence proposing that cognitive approaches are more acceptable (Levy & Radomsky, 2014; Milosevic & Radomsky, 2013), they have not improved the overall efficacy of treatments for OCD (Clark, 2005). For example, a recent intervention had only a 59% response rate (Whittal, Woody, McLean, Rachman, & Robichaud, 2010). There is evidence that cognitive therapy can successfully target responsibility within the context of checking (Rhéaume & Ladouceur, 2000), but to our knowledge, this type of intervention has not been specifically examined for its impact on RS.

What has been lacking until this point are specifically tailored treatments for different symptom types and maladaptive beliefs that are idiosyncratic to the presenting individual. As such, our recommendations will allow for concrete ways to intervene with individuals with an inflated sense of responsibility, who check and/ or engage in problematic RS.

Targeted Interventions for Responsibility, Checking, and Reassurrance Seeking

The first step for intervening with responsibility, compulsive checking, or RS is to address the nature of the intrusive thoughts. Individuals with OCD are often distressed in part because they feel that they are alone in experiencing these often unexpected, horrifying, and ego-dystonic obsessions. Therefore, it can be immensely helpful to explain the ubiquitous nature of unwanted intrusive thoughts.

A landmark study by Rachman and de Silva (1978) found that, across three experiments, normal intrusive thoughts are similar to obsessions in content, although not as frequent, long lasting, or associated with as much distress. Thus, it is the *misinterpretation*, rather than the actual thoughts, that renders them obsessive in nature (Rachman, 1997, 1998). These studies, and the subsequent model of obsessive thoughts, are described in lay terms in a resource book (Rachman & de Silva, 2009), which may be useful as a between-session reading assignment for some clients.

A recent international investigation has found that doubt is the most common intrusive thought worldwide (Radomsky et al., 2014a). Accordingly, for some clients it may be useful to begin a therapeutic discussion with this topic. Clients who are upset by intrusive doubting thoughts (which often lead to checking and RS) will likely have also experienced other intrusive thoughts that did not bother them, for example, the thought of jumping in front of a train. Discussion of this discrepancy can help elucidate for the client the ways in which interpretations of thoughts can cause or diminish problems. Thus, clients may realize that although everyone has these thoughts of doubt, not everyone reacts to them as they do, for example by checking or seeking reassurance (which, of course, may be due in part to their feelings of responsibility).

Inflated responsibility appraisals have been highlighted by cognitive theory and research for their role in maintaining OCD symptomatology, including compulsive checking and RS. As such, this type of appraisal is likely to be a key target of treatment for many clients. When addressing heightened responsibility appraisals a number of techniques may be employed successfully, including pie charts, contracts, and the "double standard" technique.

First, responsibility pie charts may be useful in helping a client to visualize the discrepancy between their subjective feelings of personal responsibility for preventing feared outcomes, and a more realistic attribution of responsibility (e.g., van Oppen & Arntz, 1994). The client is first asked to complete a pie chart depicting how she or he feels responsibility for preventing a feared outcome (e.g., a fire caused by leaving the stove on) is distributed (e.g., 95% to him- or herself, 5% to their cat). Next, the clinician and client brainstorm a list of other individuals/factors that may also be responsible for preventing a fire. For instance, the list could be expanded to include neighbors, the landlord, the electrician who installed the stove, the company that manufactured the stove, the building inspector, the fire department, the company that made the fire alarm, etc. The client should then complete a new pie chart by filling in each other individual/factor with its associated responsibility, and ending with a (usually) greatly diminished amount of responsibility that remains for her or him. The clinician and client can then have a discussion of the discrepancy between the client's initial feelings of responsibility and the more realistic estimate, and how the inflated initial attribution could be influencing their thoughts/feelings/behaviors. This should lead to reductions in targeted symptoms, including any checking and reassurance seeking which was fueled by inflated responsibility beliefs.

Another technique which may be useful in targeting responsibility is the use of contracts. The clinician and client collaboratively generate a written, signed agreement that for a certain period of time (e.g., one day, one hour), the client will assume responsibility for a specified feared outcome; then, at a subsequent time, they make another written, signed agreement giving the therapist full responsibility for the feared occurrence. The clinician could then explore with the client what their experience was under differing levels of responsibility, particularly with regard to distress, anxiety, and drive to perform compulsions.

An additional technique that may be useful for targeting overestimations of responsibility is termed the "double standard" technique (van Oppen & Arntz, 1994). The clinician asks the client how he or she would respond if the feared outcome happened to someone else (e.g., "Would the consequences be as terrible if your sister were to be responsible?"). Typically, clients state that the feared consequences would be worse when they (versus others) were responsible. This "double standard" is then highlighted and discussed.

In addition to addressing compulsive checking by altering appraisals of inflated responsibility, the behaviour can be targeted directly in other ways. For example, some of the above findings about repetition and doubt can lead to a particularly potent behavioral experiment in which clients are asked to record their levels of memory confidence, doubt, and urges to check, after checking for several minutes and after checking for a few minutes. It is important not to count out a precise number of checks, as that might render each memory more distinct and the point of the exercise will be lost (Radomsky et al., 2010; Shafran, Radomsky, Coughtrey, & Rachman, 2013). Most clients find that when they check for several minutes, they experience quite low levels of memory confidence, and correspondingly high levels of doubt and urges to check. In contrast, clients generally find that they actually feel more confident in their memory and experience lower levels of doubt and urges to check when they spend less time checking. Discussions about how more checking has made them *less* confident are often highly productive.

Another approach for reducing compulsive checking is a newly proposed intervention, which targets the belief that one has a bad memory (Alcolado & Radomsky, under review). Clients are first given the psychoeducation that some people may check in part because they believe they have a bad memory. They are then asked to make predictions before they check as to the state of the object (e.g., "I think the light is still on"), and record the outcome afterwards (e.g., "Actually, the light was off"). This will allow the clients to discover that regardless of their previous beliefs about their memory ability (whether they stemmed from repeated checking leading to subsequent decreases memory confidence, or from beliefs which may have preceded their symptoms), their memory for checking situations is, in actuality, perfectly fine. Second, psychoeducation can be provided about the nature of serious memory deficits occurring in the context of neurodegenerative diseases (e.g., Alzheimer's disease). The client then records how often they have these problems (e.g., forgetting the name of a typically checked object, or how to use the object). Thus, whatever memory problems one might perceive one-self to have, the infrequency of objective memory deficits will allow the client to see that the facets of their memory implicated in checking are actually intact. Overall, this information should help the client come to believe their memory for checking may be far better than they thought, and that therefore they might not need to check.

In targeting RS, clinicians may find it beneficial to use interventions similar to those used to address checking, such as behavioral experiments. For instance, clients could be asked find out whether or not they already know what another person will say in response to their RS attempts by writing down a prediction of what the person's response will be; afterwards, they can record whether or not they were correct. If they are correct, clinicians can help clients to reconceptualize RS as a comfort-seeking behavior in response to anxiety, as opposed to an information-seeking behavior, which can be helpful moving forward.

Another primary target in many interventions for RS in OCD is to decrease symptom accommodation by significant others, that is, when a family member helps an individual with OCD carry out compulsive behaviors by actively participating (providing reassurance), taking on responsibilities for the individual, or helping to fix problems brought on by the individual's OCD symptoms (Abramowitz et al., 2013). Family members and close friends may provide reassurance because they do not know what else to do to help their loved one feel less anxious (Pagdin, Kobori, Salkovskis, & Read, 2011). Family accommodation is, however, related to a number of negative outcomes (e.g., Abramowitz et al., 2013). Therefore, clinicians may meet with clients and significant others to identify situations in which the individual is likely to seek reassurance, as well as to discuss any accommodation behaviors by significant others and how they may interfere with corrective learning. Strategies are then developed that the clients and their significant others *agree* upon for the significant others to use when reassurance is sought. For example, they may agree that a partner will validate the individual's feelings of anxiety and distress instead of providing reassurance. It is important to make the discussion collaborative, in order to minimize negative feelings if and when reassurance is denied.

Notably, clinicians should also be aware of RS attempts by clients, so as not to provide any inadvertent reassurance. If such behavior is noted in therapy, the clinician can point out the RS to the client and engage the client in a collaborative discussion of how the clinician will react when and if reassurance is sought in the future. Together with the techniques described above, it is hoped that these suggestions will provide new options to facilitate interventions for inflated responsibility, compulsive checking, and RS.

Conclusion

In summary, contemporary theory proposes that inflated responsibility for prevent-ing harm is a core cognitive bias underlying the perpetuation of OCD symptom-atology (e.g., Rachman, 1993, 1997, 1998; Rachman & Hodgson, 1980; Salkovskis, 1985, 1999). Research now supports the assertion that beliefs and appraisals regarding inflated responsibility are associated with increased negative affectivity and urges to engage in neutralizing behaviors, including checking and reassurance seeking. Theories of compulsive checking and RS suggest that both behaviors function to decrease feelings of anxiety, distress, or uncertainty in the short term (with RS also being theorized to transfer responsibility to others), but perpetuate symptoms of OCD in the long term by preventing corrective learning. As theory and research have evolved, clinicians have correspondingly developed increasingly effective cognitive intervention techniques to better target these facets of the disorder during treatment. This work continues, as CBT was designed to be self-improving. It is our hope that the above strategies and information will be helpful to therapists and clients alike.

References

Abramowitz, J. S., Baucom, D. H., Wheaton, M. G., Boeding, S., Fabricant, L. E., Paprocki, C., & Fischer, M. S. (2013). Enhancing exposure and response prevention for OCD: A couple-based approach. *Behavior Modification, 37*, 189–210.

Abramowitz, J. S., Franklin, M. E., Schwartz, S. A., & Furr, J. M. (2003). Symptom presentation and outcome of cognitive-behavioral therapy for obsessive-compulsive disorder, *Journal of Consulting and Clinical Psychology, 71*, 1049–1057.

Alcolado, G. M., & Radomsky, A. S. (2011). Believe in yourself: Manipulating beliefs about memory causes checking. *Behaviour Research and Therapy, 49*, 42–49.

Alcolado, G. M., & Radomsky, A. S. (Under review). A novel cognitive intervention for compulsive checking: Targeting maladaptive beliefs about memory.

Amir, N., Freshman, M., Ramsey, B., Neary, E., & Brigidi, B. (2001). Thought–action fusion in individuals with OCD symptoms. *Behaviour Research and Therapy, 39*, 765–776.

Ashbaugh, A. R., Gelfand, L. A., & Radomsky, A. S. (2006). Interpersonal aspects of responsibility and obsessive compulsive symptoms. *Behavioural and Cognitive Psychotherapy, 34*, 151–163.

Ashbaugh, A. R., & Radomsky, A. S. (2007). Attentional focus during repeated checking influences memory but not metamemory. *Cognitive Therapy and Research, 31*, 273–289.

Beesdo-Baum, K., Jenjahn, E., Höfler, M., Lueken, U., Becker, E. S., & Hoyer, J. (2012). Avoidance, safety behavior, and reassurance seeking in generalized anxiety disorder. *Depression and Anxiety, 29*, 948–957.

Boschen, M. J., &Vuksanovic, D. (2007). Deteriorating memory confidence, responsibility perceptions and repeated checking: Comparisons in OCD and control samples. *Behaviour Research and Therapy, 45*, 2098–2109.

Carr, A. T. (1974). Compulsive neurosis: A review of the literature. *Psychological Bulletin, 81*, 311–318.

Chambless, D. L., Baker, M. J., Baucom, D. H., Beutler, L. E., Calhoun, K. S., Crists-Christoph, P., … Woody, S. R. (1998). Update on empirically validated therapies – II. *The Clinical Psychologist, 51*, 3–16.

Clark, D. A. (2003). *Cognitive-behavioural therapy for OCD*. New York: Guilford Press.

Clark, D. A. (2005). Focus on "cognition" in cognitive behavior therapy for OCD: Is it really necessary? *Cognitive Behavior Therapy, 34*, 131–139.

Coles, M. E., Radomsky, A. S., & Horng, B. (2006). Exploring the boundaries of memory distrust from repeated checking: Increasing external validity and examining thresholds. *Behaviour Research and Therapy, 44*, 995–1006.

Cougle, J. R., Lee, H., & Salkovskis, P. M. (2007). Are responsibility beliefs inflated in non-checking OCD patients? *Journal of Anxiety Disorders, 21*, 153–159.

Coyne, J. C. (1976). Toward an interactional description of depression. *Psychiatry, 39*, 28–40.

Cuttler, C., Alcolado, G. M., & Taylor, S. (2013). Mediation and interaction effects of doubt, dysfunctional beliefs, and memory confidence on the compulsion to check. *Journal of Obsessive-Compulsive and Related Disorders, 2*, 157–166.

Cuttler, C. Sirois-Delisle, V., Alcolado, G. M., Radomsky, A. S., & Taylor, S. (2013). Diminished confidence in prospective memory causes doubts and urges to check. *Journal of Behaviour Therapy and Experimental Psychiatry, 44*, 329–334.

Foa, E. B., Sacks, M. B., Tolin, D. E., Prezworski, A., & Amir, N. (2002). Inflated perception of responsibility for harm in OCD patients with and without checking compulsions: A replication and extension. *Journal of Anxiety Disorders, 16*, 443–453.

Freeston, M. H., & Ladouceur, R. (1997). What do patients do with their obsessive thoughts? *Behaviour Research and Therapy, 35*, 335–348.

Heerey, E. A., & Kring, A. M. (2007). Interpersonal consequences of social anxiety. *Journal of Abnormal Psychology, 116*, 125–134.

Kessler, R. C., Berglund, P., Demler, O., Jin, R., Merikangas, K. R., & Walters, E. E. (2005). Lifetime prevalence and age-of-onset distributions of DSM-IV disorders in the National Comorbidity Survey replication. *Archives of General Psychiatry, 62*, 593–602.

Kobori, O., & Salkovskis, P. M. (2013). Patterns of reassurance seeking and reassurance-related behaviours in OCD and anxiety disorders. *Behavioural and Cognitive Psychotherapy, 41*, 1–23.

Kobori, O., Salkovskis, P. M., Read, J., Lounes, N., & Wong, V. (2012). A qualitative study of the investigation of reassurance seeking in obsessive-compulsive disorder. *Journal of Obsessive-Compulsive and Related Disorders, 1*, 25–32.

Kozak, M. J., & Coles, M.E. (2005). Treatment for OCD: Unleashing the power of exposure. In J. S. Abramowitz, & A. C. Houts (Eds.), *Concepts and controversies in OCD* (pp. 263–282). New York: Springer.

Ladouceur, R., Rhéaume, J., Freeston, M. H., Aublet, F., Jean, K., Lachance, S., … de Pokomandy-Morin, K. (1995). Experimental manipulations of responsibility: An analogue test for models of Obsessive-Compulsive Disorder. *Behaviour Research and Therapy, 33*, 937–946.

Levy, H. C., & Radomsky, A. S. (2014). Safety behaviour enhances the acceptability of exposure. *Cognitive Behaviour Therapy, 43*, 83–92.

Lopatka, C., & Rachman, S. (1995). Perceived responsibility and compulsive checking: An experimental analysis. *Behaviour Research and Therapy, 33*, 673–684.

Menzies, R. G., Harris, L. M., Cumming, S. R., & Einstein, D. A. (2000). The relationship between inflated personal responsibility and exaggerated danger expectancies in obsessive-compulsive concerns. *Behaviour Research and Therapy, 38*, 1029–1037.

Milosevic, I., & Radomsky, A. S. (2013). Incorporating the judicious use of safety behaviour into exposure-based treatments for anxiety disorders: A study of treatment acceptability. *Journal of Cognitive Psychotherapy, 27*, 155–174.

Mowrer, O. H. (1947). On the dual nature of learning: A reinterpretation of "conditioning" and "problem solving". *Harvard Educational Review, 17*, 102–148.

Nedeljkovic, M., & Kyrios, M. (2007). Confidence in memory and other cognitive processes in obsessive-compulsive disorder. *Behaviour Research and Therapy, 45*, 2899–2914.

Nedeljkovic, M., Moulding, R., Kyrios, M., & Doron, G. (2009). The relationship of cognitive confidence to OCD symptoms. *Journal of Anxiety Disorders, 23*, 463–468.

NICE (2005). Obsessive compulsive disorder: Core interventions in the treatment of obses-sive-compulsive disorder and body dysmorphic disorder. Retrieved from: http://www.nice.org.uk/cg31.

Obsessive Compulsive Cognitions Working Group (1997). Cognitive assessment of obsessive-compulsive disorder. *Behaviour Research and Therapy, 35*, 667–681.

Obsessive Compulsive Cognitions Working Group (2003). Psychometric validation of the Obsessive Beliefs Questionnaire and the Interpretation of Intrusions Inventory – Part I. *Behaviour Research and Therapy, 41*, 863–878.

Obsessive Compulsive Cognitions Working Group (2005). Psychometric validation of the obsessive belief questionnaire and interpretations of intrusions inventory – Part 2: Factor analyses and testing of a brief version. *Behaviour Research and Therapy, 43*, 1527–1542.

Pagdin, R., Kobori, O., Salkovskis, P. M., & Read, J. (2011, September). Cognitive behavioural treatment for Obsessive Compulsive Disorder: Developments and enhancements. *Carer's perception of and reaction to reassurance seeking in OCD*. Symposium conducted at the meeting of the European Association for Behavioural and Cognitive Therapies, Reykjavík, Iceland.

Parrish, C. L., & Radomsky, A. S. (2006). An experimental investigation of responsibility and reassurance: Relationships with compulsive checking. *International Journal of Behavioural and Consultation Therapy, 2*, 174–191.

Parrish, C. L., & Radomsky, A. S. (2010). Why do people seek reassurance and check repeatedly? An investigation of factors involved in compulsive behaviour in OCD and depression. *Journal of Anxiety Disorders, 24*, 211–222.

Parrish, C. L., & Radomsky, A. S. (2011). An experimental investigation of factors involved in excessive reassurance seeking: The effects of perceived threat, responsibility and ambiguity on compulsive urges and anxiety. *Journal of Experimental Psychopathology, 2*, 44–62.

Podea, D. Suciu, R., Sucui, C., & Ardelean, M. (2009). An update on the cognitive behavior therapy of obsessive compulsive disorder in adults. *Journal of Cognitive and Behavioral Psychotherapies, 9*, 221–233.

Rachman, S. (1993). Obsessions, responsibility and guilt. *Behaviour Research and Therapy, 31*, 149–154.

Rachman, S. (1997). A cognitive theory of obsessions. *Behaviour Research and Therapy, 35*, 793–802.

Rachman, S. (1998). A cognitive theory of obsessions: Elaborations. *Behaviour Research and Therapy, 36*, 385–401.

Rachman, S. (2002). A cognitive theory of compulsive checking. *Behaviour Research and Therapy, 40*, 625–639.

Rachman, S. (2003). *The treatment of obsessions*. New York: Oxford University Press.

Rachman, S., & Hodgson, R. J.(1980). *Obsessions and compulsions*. Englewood Cliffs, NJ: Prentice-Hall.

Rachman, S., & de Silva, P. (1978). Abnormal and normal obsessions. *Behaviour Research and Therapy, 16*, 233–248.

Rachman, S., & de Silva, P. (2009). *Obsessive-compulsive disorder: The facts* (4th ed.). New York: Oxford University Press.

Rachman, S., Thordarson, D. S., Shafran, R., & Woody, S. R. (1995). Perceived responsibility: Structure and significance. *Behaviour Research and Therapy, 33*(7), 779–784.

Radomsky, A. S., Alcolado, G. M., Abramowitz, J., Belloch, A., Bouvard, M., Clark, D. A., … Wong, W. (2014a). You can run but you can't hide: Intrusive thoughts across 13 cities on 6 continents – Part 1. *Journal of Obsessive-Compulsive and Related Disorders, 3*, 269–279.

Radomsky, A. S., & Alcolado, G. M. (2010). Don't even *think* about checking: Repeated checking causes memory distrust. *Journal of Behaviour Therapy and Experimental Psychiatry, 41*, 345–351.

Radomsky, A. S., Dugas, M. J., Alcolado, G. M., & Lavoie, S. (2014b). When more is less: Doubt, repetition, memory, metamemory, and compulsive checking in OCD. *Behaviour Research and Therapy, 59*, 30–39.

Radomsky, A. S., Gilchrist, P. T., & Dussault, D. (2006). Repeated checking really does cause memory distrust. *Behaviour Research and Therapy, 44*, 305–316.

Radomsky, A. S., Rachman, S., & Hammond, D. (2001). Memory bias, confidence and responsibility in compulsive checking. *Behaviour Research and Therapy, 39*(7), 813–822.

Radomsky, A. S., Shafran, R., Coughtrey, A. E., & Rachman, S. (2010). Cognitive-behavior therapy for compulsive checking in OCD. *Cognitive and Behavioral Practice, 17*, 119–131.

Rector, N. A., Kamkar, K., Cassin, S. E., Ayearst, L. E., & Laposa, J. M. (2011). Assessing excessive reassurance seeking in the anxiety disorders. *Journal of Anxiety Disorders, 25*, 911–917.

Rhéaume, J., & Ladouceur, R. (2000). Cognitive and behavioural treatments of checking behaviours: An examination of individual cognitive change. *Clinical Psychology and Psychotherapy, 7*, 118–127.

Rosa-Alcásar, A. I., Sánchez-Meca, J., Gómez-Conesa, A., & Marín-Martínez, F. (2008). Psychological treatment of obsessive-compulsive disorder: A meta-analysis. *Clinical Psychology Review, 28*, 1310–1325.

Ruscio, A. M. Stein, D. J., Chiu, W. T., & Kessler, R. C. (2010). The epidemiology of obsessive-compulsive disorder in the national comorbidity survey replication. *Molecular Psychiatry, 15*, 53–63.

Salkovskis, P. M. (1985). Obsessive-compulsive problems: A cognitive-behavioral analysis. *Behaviour Research and Therapy, 23*, 571–583.

Salkovskis, P. M. (1989). Cognitive-behavioural factors and the persistence of intrusive thoughts in obsessional problems. *Behaviour Research and Therapy, 27*(6), 677–682. doi: 10.1016/0005-7967(89)90152-6.

Salkovskis, P. M. (1996). Cognitive-behavioral approaches to the understanding of obsessional problems. In R. M. Rapee (Ed.), *Current controversies in the anxiety disorders* (pp. 103–133). New York: Guilford Press.

Salkovskis, P. M. (1999). Understanding and treating obsessive-compulsive disorder. *Behaviour Research and Therapy, 37*, S29–S52.

Salkovskis, P. M., Richards, H., & Forrester, E. (1995). The relationship between obsessional problems and intrusive thoughts. *Behavioural and Cognitive Psychotherapy, 23*, 281–299.

Salkovskis, P. M., & Warwick, H. M. C. (1986). Morbid preoccupations, health anxiety and reassurance: A cognitive-behavioural approach to hypochondriasis. *Behaviour Research and Therapy, 24*, 597–602.

Salkovskis, P. M., Wroe, A. L., Gledhill, A. A., Morrison, N. N., Forrester, E. E., Richards, C. C., … Thorpe, S. S. (2000). Responsibility attitudes and interpretations are characteristic of obsessive compulsive disorder. *Behaviour Research and Therapy, 38*, 347–372.

Shafran, R. (1997). The manipulation of responsibility in obsessive-compulsive disorder. *British Journal of Clinical Psychology, 36*, 397–407.

Shafran, R., & Rachman, S. (2004). Thought–action fusion: A review. *Journal of Behavior Therapy and Experimental Psychiatry, 35*, 87–107.

Shafran, R., Radomsky, A. S., Coughtrey, A. E., & Rachman, S. (2013). Advances in the cognitive behavioral treatment of Obsessive Compulsive Disorder. *Cognitive Behaviour Therapy, 42*, 265–274.

Starcevic, V., Berle, D., Brakoulias, V., Sammut, P., Moses, K., Milicevic, D., & Hannan, A. (2012). Interpersonal reassurance seeking in obsessive-compulsive disorder and its relationship with checking compulsions. *Psychiatry Research, 200*, 560–567.

Tulving, E. (1985). Memory and consciousness. *Canadian Psychology, 26*, 1–12.

van den Hout, M., & Kindt, M. (2003a). Repeated checking causes memory distrust. *Behaviour Research and Therapy, 41*, 301–316.

van den Hout, M., & Kindt, M. (2003b). Phenomenological validity of an OCD-memory model and the remember/know distinction. *Behaviour Research and Therapy, 41*, 369–378.

van den Hout, M., & Kindt, M. (2004). Obsessive-compulsive disorder and the paradoxical effects of perseverative behaviour on experienced uncertainty. *Journal of Behavior Therapy and Experimental Psychiatry, 35*, 165–181.

van Oppen, P., & Arntz, A. (1994). Cognitive therapy for obsessive-compulsive disorder. *Behaviour Research and Therapy, 32*, 79–87.

Whittal, M. L., Woody, S. R., McLean, P. D., Rachman, S. J., & Robichaud, M. (2010). Treatment of obsessions: A randomized controlled trial. *Behaviour Research and Therapy, 48*, 295–303.

Wilson, K. A., & Chambless, D. L. (1999). Inflated perceptions of responsibility and obsessive-compulsive symptoms. *Behaviour Research and Therapy, 37*, 325–335.

20

Harm Avoidance and Checking Rituals in Pediatric Obsessive Compulsive Disorder

Michelle Rozenman, Allison Vreeland, and Tara S. Peris

Obsessive Compulsive Disorder (OCD) is a heterogeneous condition, with symptom presentations that can vary widely from one individual to another. One of the most common symptom clusters found in both adults and youth with OCD involves fears of perceived harm and related checking compulsions (e.g., Stewart et al., 2007). Harm avoidance typically refers to intrusive thoughts that the individual will engage in violent or otherwise harmful acts, including inadvertently or purposefully harming oneself or another person. It may also include fears of being harmed by another person. Sometimes referred to as "aggressive" obsessions, these intrusive thoughts may include fears of thinking, speaking, or behaving in a way that might result in a harmful outcome. The corresponding compulsions attempt to ensure the safety of affected individuals and those around them. Such compulsions may include avoiding use of sharp objects (e.g., knives, scissors), needing to engage in mental rituals to neutralize the intrusive thoughts, or taking other active measures to prevent harm. Checking rituals often accompany harm avoidance, and they emerge as another strategy for preventing feared catastrophic outcomes.

In this chapter, we review the empirical literature on harm avoidance and checking in youth with OCD. We then describe an evidence-based approach to assessment and treatment for use in both research and clinical practice, focusing on developmental issues that arise in working with children and adolescents. Finally, we provide illustrative examples of how different variations of these symptoms may be addressed within the context of exposure-based cognitive behavior therapy (CBT). We conclude with considerations for future research.

Harm Avoidance and Checking Rituals as a Clinical Subtype

In the adult psychopathology literature, "harm avoidance" is viewed broadly as a temperamental trait that is associated with anxiety and with exaggerated concern about threat or danger in the environment (e.g., Ettelt et al., 2008). The repetitive

The Wiley Handbook of Obsessive Compulsive Disorders, Volume I, First Edition.
Edited by Jonathan S. Abramowitz, Dean McKay, and Eric A. Storch.
© 2017 John Wiley & Sons Ltd. Published 2017 by John Wiley & Sons Ltd.

checking behavior that harm obsessions frequently elicit has also been associated with biased cognitions that the individual has a responsibility to prevent harm to him or herself and/or others (e.g., Rachman, 2002). These features intersect with common cognitive biases associated with OCD. First, both adults and children with harm avoidance symptoms tend to overestimate the likelihood of threat or harm in their environment, and subsequently, to experience an inflated sense of responsibility to prevent harm by checking, engaging in other rituals, or even attempting to control their own thoughts (e.g., Lewin, Caporino, Murphy, Geffken, & Storch, 2010; Rachman, 2002). Second, individuals with OCD are more likely to view their intrusive thoughts as actual events that occur in the real world than individuals without the disorder (Rachman, 1993; Shafran, Thordarson, & Rachman, 1996). Fusing action and thought may lead individuals to feel personal responsibility that they caused a negative or catastrophic event in the real world. Thus, an individual with harm avoidance symptoms may feel a moral obligation to think "pure" or "good" thoughts in order to prevent negative outcomes from occurring, and may believe that the experience of intrusive thoughts related to harm will result in the occurrence of negative events in their immediate environment or elsewhere in the world. Researchers studying thought–action fusion have found that adults with OCD tend broadly to exhibit this cognitive bias, even when the thought content is not specific to the individual's OCD symptoms (Shafran et al., 1996). This finding suggests that individuals experiencing thought-action fusion in relation to harm avoidance will also likely experience thought–action fusion for other symptoms or fears as well.

Consistent with the heterogeneity observed across symptom subtypes in OCD, there is considerable variability in how symptoms manifest *within* a given cluster. Harm avoidance and checking are no exception. Some individuals may experience obsessions about harming others with sharp objects (i.e., stabbing someone with knives, scissors, or pencils) and may feel that thinking or speaking of those objects makes them more likely to act upon their obsessions. They may respond by avoiding sharp objects altogether or by being particularly vigilant for them throughout the day. Others may worry that a loved one will suffer catastrophic harm and respond with compulsive checking behavior. As we detail later, the diverse topography of these symptoms is mirrored by considerable variability in how they present across the lifespan, with noteworthy differences observed among children and adults. This variability notwithstanding, harm avoidance and checking emerge as one of the most common symptom subtypes in adults (e.g., Rachman, 2003) and youth (Storch et al., 2007; Summerfeldt, Richter, Antony, & Swinson, 1999; Toro, Cervera, Osejo, & Salamero 1992). Studies of OCD symptoms in pediatric samples have found that these symptoms are endorsed by 23–71% of children and adolescents with OCD (Garcia et al., 2009; Nikolajsen, Nissen, & Thomsen, 2011; Scahill et al., 2003; Stewart et al., 2007).

Efforts to understand the phenomenology of this group of symptoms consistently find that intrusive thoughts about harm, violence, and aggression cluster with checking compulsions in both adult and youth OCD (e.g., Stewart et al., 2007). However, the individual symptoms included in this cluster vary across studies. Studies of adult OCD symptom dimensions have found a group of symptoms that includes aggressive, sexual, religious, and somatic obsessions, with related checking compulsions (Delorme et al., 2006; Hasler et al., 2005; Leckman et al., 1997). Findings with pediatric samples parallel those findings in adults with OCD, such that obsessions about harm, violence, and aggression consistently present with harm-avoidant and checking behavior. Some investigations with youth have directly replicated this cluster found in adult samples (e.g., Stewart et al., 2008; Summerfeldt et al., 1999). Others have found that this group of aggressive, sexual, and somatic obsessions is part of the same cluster as counting compulsions, and that checking is relevant to both to harm and symmetry/ordering symptoms (Delorme et al., 2006; Stewart et al., 2007).

It is unclear whether the harm avoidance and checking symptom dimension is stable in pediatric OCD samples. Only two studies have attempted to examine the developmental trajectory of OCD symptom clusters, with discrepant findings. While Delorme and colleagues (2006) found this subtype of aggressive, sexual, somatic, counting, and checking symptoms in children and adolescents with OCD to be relatively unchanged after a four-year follow-up, Rettew and colleagues (1992) reported that youth experienced symptom change of current harm avoidance symptoms and the addition of new symptoms over a two–seven-year follow-up period. Further research in this area may provide a more comprehensive understanding of the stability of the harm avoidance and checking symptom cluster over the course of development and into adulthood.

Clinical Characteristics Relevant to the Harm Avoidance and Checking Subtype

Harm avoidance and checking have been linked to a variety of clinical characteristics in youth. The subtype has been linked to earlier age of onset of OCD symptomatology (Leckman, Zhang, Alsobrook, & Pauls, 2001), and several studies have found that older youth report more checking compulsions compared with their younger counterparts (Farrell, Barrett, & Piacentini, 2006; Garcia et al., 2009; Selles, Storch, & Lewin, 2014). The harm avoidance and checking subtype has also been associated with hoarding symptoms in children and adolescents with OCD (Mataix-Cols, Nakatani, Micali, & Heyman, 2008). Finally, the subtype has been found to co-occur in youth with tic-related OCD symptoms and tic disorders (Leckman et al., 2001; Nikolajsen et al., 2011), as well as in youth with panic and depressive symptoms (Masi et al., 2010).

In addition, genetic and familial characteristics have been identified as relevant to the harm avoidance and checking symptom domain. Relatives of adults with harm avoidance symptoms are at significantly higher risk of developing OCD themselves, compared with relatives of adults who have OCD comprised of other symptom subtypes (e.g., Alsobrook, Leckman, Goodman, Rasmussen, & Pauls, 1999; Ettelt et al., 2008). This suggests that a parent with OCD that includes harm avoidance and checking symptoms may be more likely to have a child who develops OCD. This may be due to both genetic and neurobiological factors, as well as parental modeling of fearful behavior relevant to harm or danger to the child (e.g., Ettelt et al., 2008).

Finally, the experience harm avoidance and checking symptoms may be a predictor of treatment response. While some studies of adult OCD have found that individuals with checking compulsions do not respond as well to behavior therapy as compared with individuals without checking rituals (Basoglu, Lax, Kasvikis, & Marks, 1988; Rachman & Hodgson, 1980), other studies have found no differences in treatment response between checkers and non-checkers (Foa & Goldstein, 1978). Interestingly, one pediatric OCD treatment study found that youth with checking compulsions tied to harm-related obsessions were more likely to respond to cognitive behavioral therapy (CBT) than youth who endorsed only nonaggressive-related checking symptoms (Storch et al., 2008). It may be possible that the feared outcomes of youth with harm avoidance symptoms are more immediate (e.g., "if I hold a knife, I will stab my therapist"), whereas the feared outcomes of youth with nonaggressive checking might be more temporally distant (e.g., "if I don't check my homework tonight, I will get a bad grade once the teacher grades the assignment"). Thus, youth with harm avoidance symptoms may quickly learn during exposures that the feared outcome does not occur (e.g., "I've been holding the knife for five minutes and have not stabbed anyone"), while engaging in exposures may not necessarily provide immediate learning for non-aggressive checkers (e.g., "I purposefully incorrectly answered math questions during therapy, but that doesn't have the same kind of consequence as getting a bad grade in school"). Further study of this cluster of symptoms is warranted to explore this symptom subtype as a potential moderator/predictor of treatment response.

Assessment of Harm Avoidance and Checking Rituals

As described previously, checking rituals are preventative in intent, with the goal of ensuring that no harm or tragedy occurs to the self or others. Checking compulsions and other ritualistic or avoidant behaviors can be in response to a number of intrusive thoughts. To determine whether a youth's avoidance or checking is related to fears of harm or aggression, one might inquire as to the intention of the behavior. Does the youth check his or her body because of fear a mole will turn into cancer, or do they check to ensure that they did not stab themselves? Does the adolescent avoid his or her parent because they worry about getting contaminated, or do they believe they will injure or inappropriately touch their parent if they are in close proximity? Does the child confess their intrusive thoughts because they have concerns about offending religious figures and will be punished, or do they seek reassurance from others that they have not acted aggressively?

Several standardized assessment tools may be helpful in evaluating symptom clusters of OCD in pediatric samples. Here we outline three of the more common measures, which have demonstrated strong psychometric properties in youth with clinically significant OCD. These questionnaires can be especially useful in normalizing symptoms, as well as to track symptom change over the course of treatment.

Considered the "gold standard" dimensional measure of pediatric OCD symptoms, the Children's Yale–Brown Obsessive Compulsive Scale (CY-BOCS) (Scahill et al., 1997) is a semi-structured, clinician-rated clinical interview assessing OCD symptoms and severity. The CY-BOCS consists of a 62-item symptom checklist covering the major subtypes of obsessions and compulsions, including aggressive obsessions, harm-avoidant compulsions, and checking compulsions. The CY-BOCS also includes separate obsession and compulsion severity scores, which are each the sum of five items assessing time spent, distress, impairment, resistance against, and ability to control symptoms. Total scores range from 0 to 40, with totals above 12 suggesting clinically significant symptoms (e.g., Stewart, Ceranoglu, O'Hanley, & Geller, 2005). The CY-BOCS has demonstrated strong psychometric properties (e.g., Scahill et al., 1997; Stewart et al., 2005; Storch et al., 2004). Parent and child self-report versions of the CY-BOCS is also available, and they provide a more efficient and accessible way of assessing OCD in youth (Storch et al., 2006).

In addition to clinician-rated assessment, two questionnaires may be particularly relevant to assessing for harm avoidance in research and clinical practice settings alike. The Children's Florida Obsessive Compulsive Inventory (C-FOCI) (Storch et al., 2009) is a self-report questionnaire to be completed by children and adolescents. The C-FOCI provides an overall symptom severity score and also queries common OCD symptom domains, including several items querying harm avoidance and checking. It has demonstrated good psychometric properties (Storch et al., 2007) and may be especially useful as a brief screening tool.

The Child Obsessive-Compulsive Impact Scale-Revised (COIS-R) (Piacentini, Peris, Bergman, Chang, & Jaffer, 2007) is a psychometrically sound youth- and parent-reported questionnaire of the degree to which OCD symptoms cause impairment in school, social, and home activities. Although the COIS-R does not specifically query about impairment related to OCD subtypes, it may provide useful information about the youth's impairment from both youth and parent perspectives, which in turn may inform treatment planning.

Treatment

As detailed elsewhere in this volume (see Chapters 12 and 13), the treatment of choice for child and adolescent OCD is exposure-based CBT administered alone for youth with symptoms in the mild to moderate range, or in conjunction with pharmaco-therapy (selective serotonin reuptake inhibitors; SSRIs) (Freeman et al., 2014; POTS Team, 2004) for youth with moderate to severe symptoms and/or who do not demonstrate response to CBT alone (Geller & March, 2012). Briefly, exposure-based CBT involves psychoeducation about the cycle of OCD and how rituals serve to strengthen the relationship between intrusive thoughts and distress intolerance. It provides the youth with adaptive coping skills so that they learn to approach feared situations and triggering intrusive thoughts while refraining from engaging in compulsions (e.g., Piacentini, Langley, & Roblek, 2007). These core treatment components may be supplemented with cognitive restructuring, relaxation training, mindfulness skills, and behavioral rewards. These strategies, while typically implemented in the context of individual child treatment, work best when families maintain active involvement in treatment. Indeed, families play a central role in the treatment process, and it is expected that they will participate in the treatment process by working with the therapist to reduce patterns of family accommodation and to facilitate exposure practice at home (Peris & Piacentini, 2013).

For harm avoidance and checking rituals in particular, the goal of exposure is to create scenarios where the child fears that he or she may be in danger or cause danger or harm to others. Following standard ERP procedures, exposures proceed in a gradual manner, and the therapist must strike a balance between being creative in designing exposures to trigger intrusive thoughts and recognizing what is appropriate for the youth's age and development. Throughout therapy, the clinician must continue to provide psychoeducation and a clear rationale to both child and parent about how engaging in exposures that trigger harm- and aggression-related obsessions will aid in symptom reduction. See Table 20.1 for some common types of intrusive thoughts, related rituals, and sample exposures.

The practice of exposures themselves can emphasize distress tolerance as well as evaluation of whether a feared outcome occurred. Indeed, this may be particularly important in cases where obsession involve fears of poor outcomes at unspecified points in the future.

It should be noted that new theories of fear acquisition and extinction no longer suggest the need for strictly following an exposure hierarchy from least to most distressing or difficult exposures. Rather, new scientific evidence suggests that varying exposure intensity and mixing exposures within sessions may help to maximize extinction of fear associations in session, with better generalization of in-session gains to real-world functioning (e.g., Abramowitz, 2013; Kircanski et al., 2012; Kircanski & Peris, 2014). Practically, this may involve combining two or more exposures together into a larger exposure, doing a more difficult exposure, followed by an easier exposure and then again a more difficult exposure, and focusing on distress tolerance rather than anxiety reduction as the goal of therapy. For example, an adolescent with fears of stabbing herself or ingesting pills may engage in exposures later in therapy where she holds a knife to her wrist with one hand and holds a handful of pills in the other. A child with fears of punching his mother may engage in early exposures

Table 20.1 Sample exposures for harm avoidance and checking symptoms

Obsession	Compulsion	Exposure
Fear of harming self with sharp objects.	Stay away from sharp objects, check room to ensure no sharp objects present.	Hold scissors in hand, hold sharp objects to own skin.
Fear of harming self by playing outdoors (e.g., sports, bike).	Avoids outdoor activities, checks body for cuts/bruises after playing outdoors.	Play dodgeball and allow self to be hit by ball, refrain from checking body or seeking reassurance.
Fear of harming another person by bumping into them.	Avoidance of crowded places, looking backward when walking to ensure that did not cause injury for another.	Walk through very crowded grocery store or mall, attend concert, purposefully bump into others.
Fear parent will have car accident if child does not do a ritual.	Say "I love you" when parent drops off at school or when parent drives without child.	Write "I hope mom has a car accident," refrain from "I love you" compulsion.
Violent or horrific images.	Attempt to avoid thoughts by replacing with pleasant thought or doing mental ritual.	Write detailed script of violent images and read over and over many times.
Fear of blurting out obscenities.	Avoiding certain words that may sound like obscenities.	Write, state, yell words that sound like obscenities.
Fear will engage in sexual behavior towards others.	Checking to ensure did not touch others, avoidance.	Engage in social activities with others. If appropriate, give them a hug/hold their hand, sit next to them.

walking next to and bumping into strangers, then move up the hierarchy to walking next to and bumping into his mother, whereas later on in therapy the session may start with exposures with his mother, then move to exposures with strangers, then again exposures with his mother. The goal is to teach children and adolescents that, no matter what the situation, they are able to tolerate distress and anxiety associated with intrusive thoughts.

Developmental Considerations in Assessment and Treatment of Harm Avoidance and Checking Rituals

Several developmental features merit consideration when assessing and treating harm avoidance and checking behavior. First, as with all symptoms of OCD, the youngster's level of cognitive and social development will influence the child's ability to report on symptoms and participate in treatment. Second, the nature of family involvement (both in the symptoms themselves and in treatment planning) may shift based on developmental status. Finally, depending on the content of the harm obsessions, affected youngsters may feel uncomfortable, and, in some cases, unwilling to discuss their worries. Symptoms that involve graphic violent and disturbing imagery, detailed thoughts involving sexual activity, and aggressive thoughts may be especially difficult to disclose. By virtue of their developmental status and limited insight, children and adolescents may be particularly prone to believing that when they think such thoughts, they will certainly act on them. Alternatively, they may think that the thoughts reflect a purposeful intent and a desire to harm themselves or others. Moreover, youth may believe that the process of thinking such thoughts is equivalent to engaging in aggressive or violent behavior, or otherwise causing negative events in the world. The clinician's ability to be delicate during the initial evaluation, as well as to normalize the symptoms for both youth and family, will set the stage for more open and reliable reporting, and, in turn, produce a clearer case conceptualization and treatment plan. It will also create an open and trusting environment for the youth and family to communicate with one another and the therapist during treatment. In this next section, we review some of the developmental considerations that are particularly relevant when working with youth with harm avoidance and checking rituals.

Assessing for Associated Symptoms

As described above, harm avoidance and checking occur in both youth and adults with OCD. However, other symptoms found to be associated with the harm avoidance cluster in children and adolescents have not been found in adult samples; these include repeating, symmetry, and ordering rituals (Stewart et al., 2007). These associated compulsions may occur specifically in response to harm obsessions in pediatric patients. That is, youngsters may engage in repeating, symmetry, and arranging compulsions in response to aggressive or violent thoughts because they have not yet developed the abstract thinking skills to engage in mental compulsions or avoidance behaviors specifically geared toward preventing harm or violence. The treating clinician should assess for the full spectrum of OCD symptoms, and consider that possibility that repeating, symmetry, and/or arranging compulsions may relieve anxiety or discomfort that occurs when the youth experiences intrusive thoughts about harm or aggression.

In assessment with the youth and primary caregiver, the therapist should carefully query symptom content and consequences. However, we note that the clinician need not push the child to divulge all symptoms at once. It is often the case that youngsters become more willing to talk as rapport and trust in the ERP process build. When symptoms are eventually acknowledged they can be added to the existing hierarchy following the procedure with any other symptom subtype. As described previously, checking rituals may be done with a variety of intentions. A youth may check to see whether they came into physical contact with others because they are concerned about contamination, refuse to use certain objects unless they have a "just right" or "positive" thought, or engage in other checking behaviors to ensure that they completed a task correctly – these checking rituals are not specific to harm avoidance. Checking related to harm avoidance may involve checking one's body to see whether they are bruised or otherwise injured, asking for reassurance that one did not hurt themselves or another person, examining sharp objects to see whether the objects have blood on them, and so forth. Youth may also report a constellation of magical thinking and other symptoms or beliefs related to the checking compulsions that may be perceived as delusional if taken out of the context of OCD as the primary problem area. Assessing *why* the youth engages in checking and other avoidance rituals will help to identify appropriate obsessions to target in treatment. At the same time, developmental considerations may make it difficult for younger youth to answer this question. There may simply be a sense of needing to check to neutralize an unpleasant feeling. In such situations, emphasis on the compulsions rather than obsessions may be more fruitful.

Age and Cognitive Development

As with all child and adolescent intervention, youth age and cognitive development should always be included in the case conceptualization and treatment plan. Several specific challenges may arise based on developmental status. First, youth may experience special difficulty understanding the abstract concept that thoughts are not equivalent to behavior (i.e., "just because I have an intrusive thought about harming someone does not mean that I have actually harmed them"). Similarly, some youth may have difficulty with discussions in which the therapist asks about frequency of low-likelihood events (e.g., "How often do kids actually break a bone when they bump into someone walking on the street?") due to relatively limited life experience and understanding of life events. Second, younger children may also have an incomplete or inaccurate understanding of topics surrounding physical development and harm related to sex. Adolescents, on the other hand, may be especially triggered by their own physical development, discussions with peers about romantic relationships, and content in their environment (e.g., movies, music, books, news) that may be relevant to sex and interpersonal aggression. Third, as noted earlier, youth of all ages may be embarrassed, confused, and upset by such thoughts, particularly if they feel that discussion of self- or other-harm is taboo or stigmatizing. Finally, the exposures required for these symptoms may appear to conflict with developmental issues (e.g., write a sentence about punching mom; think about sibling dying).

Treatment Considerations

How are these challenges described above best addressed in treatment? Recognizing the child's cognitive and social development, the treating clinician should normalize the experience of harm-related obsessions, harm avoidance, and checking rituals and to indicate that they are quite common in OCD. The clinician should be sensitive to the youth's reluctance to report such symptoms, and take care not to invalidate the child if his or her understanding of life experience is limited or inaccurate. For example, a female child may believe that she will become pregnant by sitting in a chair where a male previously sat. Debunking myths in a developmentally appropriate, gentle, and sensitive way may provide the child with useful and accurate information that provides contrary evidence to the child's intrusive thoughts. The clinician might also consider, and consult with a primary caregiver, about whether and what type of corrective information might be provided to a child, as compared to an adolescent. For example, if the abovementioned female child has not yet received sex education in school or by her parents, she may not need detailed and specific information about exactly *how* one becomes pregnant. Conversely, an adolescent who has already has an understanding of sex may be able to engage in more detailed or advanced conversations about pregnancy, and also be able to participate in more complex exposures that may even assume accuracy in the myths (e.g., sitting in chairs where men previously sat and creating imaginal exposure scripts about being the first female to become pregnant in this way.)

Safety

Issues of safety may also be raised in working with youth with harm avoidance and checking symptoms. Many individuals with harm avoidance symptoms report intrusive thoughts about harming themselves or others, and/or thoughts that others will behave in an aggressive or sexual way toward them. They may endorse distress related to thoughts about touching or being touched by others in inappropriate ways. The challenge for the clinician is to carefully distinguish between an obsession consistent with OCD and actual events in the environment, a distinction which is often aided by report from parents or teachers, as well as prior developmental and psychiatric history and behavior. As part of soliciting information from these sources, the clinician should provide education on the difference between an intrusive thought (e.g., "an obsession pops into your head and sometimes you can't make go away even if you try") and events (e.g., "if there was a video camera filming what happened, and someone was watching the film, would they see that person touch you?"). Similarly, if a youth reports a desire to harm themselves (e.g., cut themselves with a knife, run into traffic), the distinction between obsessions and suicidal or nonsuicidal injurious thoughts is typically made when a youth describes that the intrusive thoughts are upsetting and distressing, and/or that they do not want to harm themselves but feel as though they might during experience of the intrusive thought. Youth with harm avoidance symptoms will often avoid using objects about which they experience intrusive thoughts (e.g., knives, scissors, pens), rather than attempt to use the objects when they think about self- or other-harm. In all of the above discussions, therapists are advised to remember their roles as mandated reporters and to do their due diligence in assessing actual threat/danger to youth clients and possible history of abuse.

The Role of the Family

The involvement of family members in symptoms (i.e., accommodation), the family belief system, and the emotional climate of the home environment are critical to treating all youth with OCD. Growing evidence underscores the importance of assessing family accommodation for developing a treatment plan where gains will generalize into the home, school, and social contexts (e.g., Peris et al., 2008; Peris et al., 2012). The challenge for youth who present with harm avoidance/checking symptoms is that families may have limited knowledge of symptoms, particularly obsessions which cannot be observed. Youth may feel ashamed or uncomfortable about the content of harm avoidance symptoms and thus be secretive with family members and reluctant to have even the therapist divulge information. The result is that families may be unaware of the specific intrusive thoughts or the youth's specific distress and impairment. The clinician should query the youth about how much parents or other family members know about their symptoms, and always include the youth in conversations involving psychoeducation and discussion of symptom content. The therapist might also meet with family members separately to reiterate this information, and make clear that the youth should not be punished or embarrassed because of his or her symptoms, no matter the nature of their content. The therapist might also ask family members about their broader community, religious, or other belief systems that might make it difficult for family members to be understanding about harm, aggressive, and sexual intrusive thoughts.

The Role of the Clinician

Finally, the clinician should be aware of his or her own comfort level with and response to harm avoidance symptom content. Intrusive thoughts about harm, aggression, and of a sexual nature can be graphic and disturbing. As youth and their family members may already feel anger, embarrassment, shame, and stigma, the therapist should take care to demonstrate a neutral and matter-of-fact response to hearing about these symptoms. Providing a safe therapeutic context for the youth to disclose their harm-related obsessions goes hand-in-hand with normalization and psychoeducation about this very common OCD subtype. As we discuss later, treatment of these symptoms also requires that the therapist be comfortable with crafting and implementing exposures that directly address taboo or difficult topics.

Illustrative Case Examples

These treatment principles are illustrated in our work with two youths who presented to our university-based specialty clinic for the treatment of OCD: an 8-year-old girl and a 16-year-old boy. The core features of disorder for both youths included frequent, distressing intrusive thoughts related to harm and aggression, accompanied by avoidance and checking rituals. Yet each youth reported quite distinct symptoms within the harm avoidance subtype. In the vignettes that follow, we provide background information on each youth and his or her primary symptoms. We then discuss applications of exposure-based CBT.

Maria

Maria, an 8-year-old Mexican American female, was brought by her mother and father to our specialty treatment clinic for evaluation of fears that she might hurt herself and others and significant checking behavior to ensure that she was not near sharp objects. During the initial evaluation, Maria reported that she experienced frequent thoughts that she would stab herself or her two younger brothers with sharp objects (e.g., scissors, knives, pens), that she would drop her youngest brother if she was holding him, and that she could not hug her parents because she might inadvertently hit them in some way that would cause internal bleeding. Maria described these thoughts in graphic detail; for example, she reported that the intrusive thoughts related to stabbing herself and others involved her taking the butcher's knife from the kitchen, stabbing herself or others, first in the hands, and then stabbing in the stomach, causing bleeding and death. Maria endorsed these thoughts as occurring hourly and causing significant distress because, as she reported, she did not want to harm herself or her family. She also reported several types of compulsive behavior in attempts to keep herself and her loved ones safe: checking for and avoidance of sharp objects when she entered rooms, standing with her hands clasped behind her back, sitting on her hands while seated, and no longer playing with her brothers.

Maria denied any history of aggressive or self- or other-harm behavior, but reported that thinking about doing something "bad" meant that she would certainly engage in aggressive behavior. During this conversation, Maria became increasingly fidgety and tearful, and subsequently began to endorse intrusive thoughts that were of a sexually aggressive nature. She reported that she had thoughts that a knife would stab her in her groin and that she was especially afraid of touching her mother anywhere near her mother's groin because of intrusive thoughts that she might hit or stab her mother in that area. After careful assessment with both Maria and her parents, the therapist determined that Maria had not experienced any abuse or other trauma and that these symptoms were part of her harm avoidance. Maria was embarrassed about these thoughts and asked the therapist not to share the information with her parents, as she was concerned that her parents would be disgusted by and negatively judge her. Eventually, during treatment, the therapist was able to coach Maria to share some of these thoughts with her mother in order to appropriately address them as part of the treatment plan.

When the therapist met with Maria's parents, they reported that Maria's concerns about harming herself and her family members began one year prior. They also reported that Maria's avoidance and checking had led to significant conflict and disruption in family life. Her parents were unable to report on the specific thought content, other than what they had heard Maria state about being "a dangerous girl" and her fears that she would stab herself or hurt her family members. Her parents were much more aware of the checking behaviors, and reported that Maria would not enter the kitchen, became upset if anyone in the family left scissors on the counter, refused to use pens or sharp pencils to complete school assignments, had stopped hugging anyone in the family, had stopped playing with her brothers, and even physically kept a distance from her friends on the school playground. Her mother also reported that Maria had told her teacher that she could not concentrate in class, and asked the teacher to move her to a desk at the very back away from where her classmates sat. Maria's father reported that Maria's paternal great-uncle was extremely preoccupied with cleanliness; her father wondered whether Maria's concerns about harm were related to her great-uncle's contamination concerns.

Throughout the evaluation, and during the feedback session, the therapist provided psychoeducation to normalize Maria's symptoms within the OCD framework and outlined that her compulsive behaviors were triggered by intrusive thoughts. The therapist reiterated to Maria and her parents that many children came to the specialty clinic for evaluation of very similar concerns that they would harm others, and that what Maria described did not make the therapist think that she was strange, abnormal, or dangerous. The therapist framed Maria's intrusive thoughts as "false alarms" (Piacentini et al., 2007) and that the OCD bully was trying to trick her into doing things that were not necessary or important to do. The therapist conceptualized Maria's primary OCD symptoms as consistent with the harm avoidance and checking rituals cluster.

Justin

Justin, a Caucasian adolescent male, lived with both of his parents and two younger sisters in a large urban city. Recently having celebrated his sixteenth birthday, Justin's mother brought him for evaluation to our specialty clinic because he refused to take driving lessons and had begun isolating from his family and peers. Justin's mother reported that he had always been a sensitive child, prone to worry about a variety of situations that he might hear about on the news or in the local community. His mother also reported that, in recent years, Justin had become especially concerned with community violence, and spent a substantial amount of time looking for news stories online about violent crime in their city.

When the therapist met individually with Justin during the initial interview, he reported a variety of OCD symptoms that began when he started middle school, and had increased substantially in the last two years, as he transitioned from middle to high school. Justin reported that he was perfectionistic about school assignments, sometimes checking and rechecking assignments late into the night, checked doors and windows to ensure they were locked at night, wanted items in his bedroom to be arranged in a specific organized fashion, and became upset if family members moved books on his shelves or if his mother put his laundry away incorrectly, and felt that he had to count up to the number seven until it felt "just right" before he allowed himself to watch television or use the internet.

Justin's primary concern was his belief that he was responsible for crime in his city and that he was causing aggression and violence because he experienced recurrent, intrusive thoughts about beating up and raping people he knew, as well as strangers. Justin reported that he experienced violent and bloody images of physically beating or raping others, including his loved ones. He was most disturbed by graphic images of raping his sisters, for which he felt shame, disgust, and self-hatred. He told the therapist that any time he was unable to "get rid of" the aggressive thoughts with checking rituals (i.e., counting to seven until it felt "just right" and then asking the individual if they felt "okay"), he was convinced that either he or someone else in his city would perpetrate a violent crime. He also reported being terrified at the thought of driving because he felt certain that he would physically lose control of himself, turn the wheel, and run over a pedestrian with his car.

These intrusive thoughts and related checking rituals had caused Justin significant impairment in the last two years. At home, Justin spent nearly all of his free time searching for news stories involving violent crime, never came near or touched his sisters because he was afraid he might hit and/or rape them, and refused to take driving lessons despite his parents offering to buy him a new car once he had his license. Academically, Justin had difficulty completing assignments on time, both because of the intrusive aggressive thoughts and also because he felt the need to check his assignments many times over. He also reported that he had quit his swim team because he would sometimes have thoughts of drowning his teammates in the pool. Socially, Justin had all but isolated from his peers, and his refusals to hang out with his friends over the last two years had resulted in his friends no longer inviting Justin to get together.

Justin was convinced that he was a terrible person because he feared that someday he would start acting on the thoughts. He reported that his checking rituals, including asking others if they were okay, and searching for violent crime stories on the news and Internet, were the only reason that he had not yet behaved in a physically aggressive way toward others. Justin had found articles about OCD, and specifically the harm avoidance symptom cluster, on the Internet. He described to the therapist that individuals with OCD were not actually violent people, and simply experienced frightening obsessive thoughts, but that he was "a bad guy" responsible for interpersonal violence and aggression in his community. Justin also asked the therapist several times during the initial interview to refrain from disclosing to his mother that he believed he was a violent, aggressive person who caused physical pain and suffering for others.

Although initially resistant to the information that the therapist provided to Justin during psychoeducation, he became more accepting of the idea that his symptoms might fall within the OCD harm avoidance subtype when the therapist provided information about other youths she had treated with similar symptoms. The therapist was sensitive to Justin's request to not share his symptoms with his mother, and negotiated with him such that, at the end of the evaluation, Justin himself provided a broad description of his symptoms to his mother without providing specific detailed content of his intrusive thoughts. As described below, treatment with Justin was not without its challenges given his inflated responsibility for negative events and hesitation to accept that his experience was consistent with OCD.

Treatment for Maria and Justin

Treatment for both Maria and Justin was exposure-based, following a cognitive-behavioral framework as described above. With their therapists, Maria and Justin completed some very similar exposures to address their overlapping symptoms. For example, during the course of treatment, both youths practiced standing close to the therapist and family members to challenge the notion that they would harm others if in close proximity. The therapists also asked these two youths to hold sharp objects (pens, scissors, paperclips, and, eventually, a butter knife, a steak knife, and a butcher's knife) to the therapists' arms, neck, throat, and torso. As the exposures became more difficult and involved sharp objects, the therapists aided the youths in describing to their parents the content of some of their intrusive thoughts to explain the reason for such exposures. Both youths spent time with their younger siblings as treatment progressed, with homework assigned to hug the siblings each night without engaging in compulsions. Both youths also participated in imaginal exposures, where they wrote stories with intense and graphic details about how they would cause harm to their loved ones, and then read the script many times over each day until they were able to tolerate the distress associated with reading the scripts. Near the end of treatment, both youths cut vegetables in their kitchens with all family members present in the kitchen; for Justin, this resulted in learning that he loved to cook, and he began participating in preparing the family's dinner each evening.

There were also central differences in Maria's therapy as compared with Justin's. Maria quickly learned to trust her therapist, and, even when she was afraid of and reluctant to participate in exposures, she would always eventually agree to participate in the exposure after the therapist had reviewed psychoeducation with her about the OCD cycle and purpose of therapy. Because of Maria's young age, her therapist checked in with parents at the start and end of every session and often asked Maria's mother to join them in session for exposures involving knives and other sharp objects. The therapist also spent a substantial amount of time explaining accommodation to Maria's parents and assigning the parents homework to reduce provision of reassurance, require that Maria use pencils and pens for her school homework assignments, and so on. Although Maria's parents were very concerned that other members of their family and community would find out that Maria was in treatment for OCD, and feared negative evaluation by other members of their community, they actively participated in Maria's treatment. Between Maria's hard work and her parents' support in therapy, she completed a course of CBT and experienced significant remission of her harm avoidance and checking symptoms within three months.

Justin, on the other hand, had more difficulty during his treatment course. Although he had other symptoms of OCD (e.g., checking schoolwork, arranging and organizing his room, etc.), he and the therapist agreed that they would first focus on his harm avoidance and checking, as these symptoms caused much more distress and impairment. Some of his exposures involved reconnecting and spending time with his friend group, participating in activities where he might be in possession of a potential weapon (e.g., going to the batting cage and playing golf with his father), holding hands with his sisters and mother, and stating some of his aggressive thoughts aloud to the therapist (e.g., "I'm going to punch you in the head until you lose consciousness"). Additionally, the therapist asked Justin to slowly begin tapering his online searches for violent crime (e.g., only searching 1x/day for 20 minutes, then only searching three days per week for 10 minutes each time, and eventually not searching online at all).

The two biggest challenges in working with Justin were his mental compulsions and his fears of involving his parents in the treatment plan. As the therapist could not see when Justin was engaging in mental compulsions (i.e., counting to seven), she asked him to tell her when he was doing a compulsion. Along these lines, several weeks into treatment, Justin confided that he had been doing mental compulsions during their exposures until that point, and that he was afraid of what might happen if he did not do the mental counting compulsion. To address this issue, the therapist returned to psychoeducation about the OCD cycle, reminding him that he would not improve in his ability to tolerate the intrusive thoughts if he continued to do the mental counting. This included a gentle, Socratic discussion of the short- versus long-term benefits of his choices. The discussion helped Justin to consider the value of practicing somewhat easier exposures without ritualizing until he was able to take on more difficult tasks without compensating or attempting to neutralize his anxiety.

Justin was also extremely resistant to involving his parents in treatment. At the start of treatment, the therapist met with Justin's parents individually and asked them to stop providing reassurance if Justin asked "are you okay?" and also to not watch the news for several weeks. Over the course of treatment, Justin became more open with his parents, sharing with them the content of several obsessions. Justin's disclosures provided his parents with a better awareness of his compulsions, and they became more vigilant about complying with the treatment plan in reducing accommodation. Finally, for the majority of treatment, Justin expressed beliefs that his symptoms were an indicator that he was an inherently aggressive person responsible for local community violence. Rather than arguing with him, the therapist simply asked Justin to remind her of the rationale for exposures at the start and end of every session. The therapist also told Justin that if he were a violent person, engaging in exposures without being violent might help him develop new habits in his social relationships. Justin generally complied with participating in exposures in-session and at home and eventually, as he began to report symptom reduction, his inflated sense of responsibility began to decrease. Over several months, Justin was able to increasingly tolerate distress associated with his intrusive thoughts without engaging in compulsions. By the end of treatment, he experienced symptom remission, no longer searched the news for stories of violence, and spent much of his free time with family and friends.

Concluding Remarks

Harm avoidance and checking behavior occur commonly in child and adolescent OCD. Yet, systematic empirical examination of this subset of symptoms remains sparse. It is unknown whether it is a stable aspect of the clinical presentation as youth progress through childhood and adolescence, and it is unclear how the focus of these particular symptoms shifts with changing developmental status. Perhaps more importantly, understanding of how the presence of this particular symptom cluster relates to treatment outcome for youth with OCD is limited. Despite these gaps in scientific understanding, clinical experience suggests that ERP works well in addressing both harm avoidance and checking. Certainly, the field is ripe for future work aimed at better understanding how distinct symptom profiles predict or moderate clinical outcomes. As the field moves toward more personalized approaches to treating OCD, such work will be crucial in matching affected individuals to optimal interventions.

References

Abramowitz, J. S. (2013). The practice of exposure therapy: Relevance of cognitive-behavioral theory and extinction theory. *Behavior Therapy, 44,* 548–558.

Alsobrook II, J. P., Leckman, J. F., Goodman, W. K., Rasmussen, S. A., & Pauls, D. L. (1999). Segregation analysis of obsessive-compulsive disorder using symptom-based factor scores. *American Journal of Medical Genetics, 88*(6), 669–675.

Basoglu, M., Lax, T., Kasvikis, Y., & Marks, I. M. (1988). Predictors of improvement in obsessive-compulsive disorder. *Journal of Anxiety Disorders, 2*(4), 299–317.

Delorme, R., Bille, A., Betancur, C., Mathieu, F., Chabane, N., Mouren-Simeoni, M. C., & Leboyer, M. (2006). Exploratory analysis of obsessive compulsive symptom dimensions in children and adolescents: A prospective follow-up study. *BMC Psychiatry, 6*(1). doi:10.1186/1471-244X-6-1.

Ettelt, S., Freyberger, H. J., Ruhrmann, S., Grabe, H. J., Wagner, M., John, U., … Wagner, M. (2008). Harm avoidance in subjects with obsessive-compulsive disorder and their families. *Journal of Affective Disorders*, *107*(1/3), 265–269.

Farrell, L. J., Barrett, P., & Piacentini, J. (2006). Obsessive-compulsive disorder across the developmental trajectory: Clinical correlates in children, adolescents and adults. *Behaviour Change*, *23*(2), 103–120.

Foa, E. B., & Goldstein, A. (1978). Continuous exposure and complete response prevention in the treatment of obsessive-compulsive neurosis. *Behavior Therapy*, *9*(5), 821–829.

Freeman, J., Garcia, A., Frank, H., Benito, K., Conelea, C. Walther, M., & Edmunds, J. (2014). Evidence base update for psychosocial treatments for pediatric obsessive-compulsive disorder. *Journal of Clinical Child & Adolescent Psychology*, *43*(1), 7–26.

Garcia, A. M., Freeman, J. B., Himle, M. B., Berman, N. C., Ogata, A. K., Ng, J., … Leonard, H. (2009). Phenomenology of early childhood onset obsessive compulsive disorder. *Journal of Psychopathology and Behavioral Assessment*, *31*(2), 104–111.

Geller, D. A. (2012). Practice parameter for the assessment and treatment of children and adolescents with obsessive-compulsive disorder. *FOCUS*, *10*(3), 360.

Geller, D., & March, J. (2012). Practice parameter for the assessment and treatment of children and adolescents with obsessive-compulsive disorder. *Journal of the American Academy of Child and Adolescent Psychiatry*, *51*, 98–113.

Hasler, G., Lasalle-Ricci, V. H., Ronquillo, J. G., Crawley, S. A., Cochran, L. W., Kazuba, D., … Murphy, D. L. (2005). Obsessive-compulsive disorder symptom dimensions show specific relationships to psychiatric comorbidity. *Psychiatry Research*, *135*(2), 121–132.

Kircanski, K., Mortazavi, A., Castriotta, N., Baker, A. S., Mystkowski, J. L., Yi, R., & Craske, M. G. (2012). Challenges to the traditional exposure paradigm: Variability in exposure therapy for contamination fears. *Journal of Behavior Therapy and Experimental Psychiatry*, *43*(2), 745–751.

Kircanski, K., & Peris, T. S., (2014). Exposure and response prevention process predicts treatment outcome in youth with OCD. *Journal of Abnormal Child Psychology*,*43*(3), 543–552. doi: 10.1007/s10802-014-9917-2.

Leckman, J., Grice, D., Boardman, J., Zhang, H., Vitale, A., Bondi, C., … Pauls, D. L. (1997). Symptoms of obsessive-compulsive disorder. *American Journal of Psychiatry*, *154*(7), 911–917.

Leckman, J. F., Zhang, H., Alsobrook, J. P., & Pauls, D. L. (2001). Symptom dimensions in obsessive-compulsive disorder: Toward quantitative phenotypes. *American Journal of Medical Genetics*, *105*(1), 28–30.

Lewin, A. B., Caporino, N., Murphy, T. K., Geffken, G. R., & Storch, E. A. (2010). Understudied clinical dimensions in pediatric obsessive compulsive disorder. *Child Psychiatry & Human Development*, *41*(6), 675–691.

Masi, G., Millepiedi, S., Perugi, G., Pfanner, C., Berloffa, S., Pari, C., Mucci, M., & Akiskal, H. S. (2010). A naturalistic exploratory study of the impact of demographic, phenotypic and comorbid features in pediatric obsessive-compulsive disorder. *Psychopathology*, *43*(2), 69–78.

Mataix-Cols, D., Nakatani, E., Micali, N., & Heyman, I. (2008). Structure of obsessive-compulsive symptoms in pediatric OCD. *Journal of the American Academy of Child & Adolescent Psychiatry*, *47*(7), 773–778.

Nikolajsen, K. H., Nissen, J. B., & Thomsen, P. H. (2011). Obsessive-compulsive disorder in children and adolescents: Symptom dimensions in a naturalistic setting. *Nordic Journal of Psychiatry*, *65*(4), 244–250.

Pediatric OCD Treatment Study Team. (2004). Cognitive-behavior therapy, sertraline, and their combination for children and adolescents with obsessive-compulsive disorder: The Pediatric OCD Treatment Study (POTS) randomized controlled trial. *Journal of the American Medical Association*, *292*(16), 1969–1976

Peris, T. S., Bergman, R. L., Langley, A., Chang, S., McCracken, J. T., & Piacentini, J. (2008). Correlates of family accommodation of childhood obsessive compulsive disorder: Parent, child, and family characteristics. *Journal of the American Academy of Child & Adolescent Psychiatry, 47*, 1173–1181. doi: 10.1097/CHI.0b013e3181825a91.

Peris, T. S., & Piacentini, J. (2013). Optimizing treatment for complex cases of childhood obsessive compulsive disorder: A preliminary trial. *Journal of Clinical Child & Adolescent Psychology, 42*(1), 1–8.

Peris, T. S., Sugar, C. A., Bergman, R. L., Chang, S., Langley, A., & Piacentini, J. (2012). Family factors predict treatment outcome for pediatric obsessive-compulsive disorder. *Journal of Consulting and Clinical Psychology, 80*, 255–223. doi: 10.1037/a0027084.

Piacentini, J., Langley, A., & Robleck, T. (2007). *Cognitive behavioral treatment of childhood OCD: It's only a false alarm.* New York: Oxford University Press.

Piacentini, J., Peris, T. S., Bergman, R. L., Chang, S., & Jaffer, M. (2007). Brief Report: Functional impairment in childhood OCD: Development and psychometrics properties of the Child Obsessive-Compulsive Impact Scale-Revised (COIS-R). *Journal of Clinical Child & Adolescent Psychology, 36*(4), 645–653.

Rachman, S. (1993). Obsessions, responsibility, and guilt. *Behavior Research and Therapy, 31*, 149–154.

Rachman, S. (2002). A cognitive theory of compulsive checking. *Behaviour Research and Therapy, 40*(6), 625–639.

Rachman, S. (2003). Compulsive checking. In R. B. Menzies & P. de Silva (Eds.), *Obsessive compulsive disorder theory, research, and treatment* (pp. 138–180). Chichester: Wiley.

Rachman, S., & Hodgson, R. J. (1980). *Obsessions and compulsions.* Englewood Cliffs, NJ: Prentice-Hall.

Rettew, D. C., Swedo, S. E., Leonard, H. L., Lenane, M. C., & Rapoport, J. L. (1992). Obsessions and compulsions across time in 79 children and adolescents with obsessive-compulsive disorder. *Journal of the American Academy of Child & Adolescent Psychiatry, 31*(6), 1050–1056.

Scahill, L., Kano, Y., King, R. A., Carlson, A., Peller, A., Lebrun, U., … Leckman, J. F. (2003). Influence of age and tic disorders on obsessive-compulsive disorder in a pediatric sample. *Journal of Child and Adolescent Psychopharmacology, 13*(Suppl. 1), 7–17.

Scahill, L., Riddle, M. A., Mcswiggin-Hardin, M., Ort, S. I., King, R. A., Goodman, W. K., … Leckman, J. F. (1997). Children's Yale–Brown Obsessive Compulsive Scale: Reliability and validity. *Journal of the American Academy of Child & Adolescent Psychiatry, 36*(6), 844–852.

Selles, R., Storch, E., & Lewin, A., (2014). Variations in symptom prevalence and clinical correlates in younger versus older youth with obsessive-compulsive disorder. *Child Psychiatry and Human Development, 45*(6), 666–674. doi: 10.1007/s10578-014-0435-9.

Shafran, R., Thordarson, D. S., & Rachman, S. (1996). Thought–action fusion in obsessive compulsive disorder. *Journal of Anxiety Disorders, 10*(5), 379–391.

Stewart, S. E., Ceranoglu, T. A., O'Hanley, T., & Geller, D. A. (2005). Performance of clinician versus self-report measures to identify obsessive-compulsive disorder in children and adolescents. *Journal of Child and Adolescent Psychopharmacology, 15*(6), 956–963.

Stewart, S. E., Rosário, M. C., Brown, T. A., Carter, A. S., Leckman, J. F., Sukhodolsky, D., … Pauls, D. L. (2007). Principal components analysis of obsessive-compulsive disorder symptoms in children and adolescents. *Biological Psychiatry, 61*(3), 285–291.

Stewart, S. E., Rosário, M. C., Baer, L., Carter, A. S., Brown, T. A., Scharf, J. M., … Pauls, D. L. (2008). Four-factor structure of obsessive-compulsive disorder symptoms in children, adolescents, and adults. *Journal of the American Academy of Child & Adolescent Psychiatry, 47*(7), 763–772.

Storch, E. A., Murphy, T. K., Adkins, J. W., Lewin, A. B., Geffken, G. R., Johns, N. B., Jann, K. E., & Goodman, W. K. (2006). The Children's Yale–Brown Obsessive-Compulsive

Scale: Psychometric properties of child- and parent-report formats. *Journal of Anxiety Disorders, 20*(8), 1055–1070.

Storch, E. A., Lack, C., Merlo, L., Marien, W., Geffken, G., Grabill, K., ... Goodman, W. K. (2007). Associations between miscellaneous symptoms and symptom dimensions: An examination of pediatric obsessive-compulsive disorder. *Behaviour Research and Therapy, 45*(11), 2593–2603.

Storch, E. A, Merlo, L. J., Larson, M. J., Geffken, G. R., Lehmkuhl, H. D. Jacob, M. L., ... Goodman, W. K. (2008). Impact of comorbidity on cognitive-behavioral therapy response in pediatric obsessive-compulsive disorder. *Journal of the American Academy of Child & Adolescent Psychiatry, 47*(5), 583–592.

Storch, E. A., Khanna, M., Merlo, L. J., Leow, B. A., Franklin, M., Reid, J. M., ... Murphy, T. K. (2009). Children's Florida Obsessive Compulsive Inventory: Psychometric properties and feasibility of a self-report measure of obsessive-compulsive symptoms in youth. *Child Psychiatry and Human Development, 40*(3), 467–483.

Storch, E. A., Murphy, T. K., Geffken, G. R., Soto, O., Sajid, M., Allen, P., ... Goodman, W. K. (2004). Psychometric evaluation of the Children's Yale–Brown Obsessive-Compulsive Scale. *Psychiatry Research, 129*(1), 91–98.

Summerfeldt, L. J., Richter, M. A., Antony, M. M., & Swinson, R. P. (1999). Symptom structure in obsessive-compulsive disorder: A confirmatory factor-analytic study. *Behaviour Research and Therapy, 37*(4), 297–311.

Summerfeldt, L. J., Kloosterman, P. H., Antony, M. M., Richter, M. A., & Swinson, R. P. (2004). The relationship between miscellaneous symptoms and major symptom factors in obsessive-compulsive disorder. *Behaviour Research and Therapy, 42*(12), 1453–1467.

Toro, J., Cervera, M., Osejo, E., & Salamero, M. (1992). Obsessive-compulsive disorder in childhood and adolescence: A clinical study. *Journal of Child Psychology and Psychiatry, 33*(6), 1025–1037.

21

Symmetry, Ordering, and Arranging Symptoms in Adults

Steven Taylor

The preference for order and symmetry is a robust bias found throughout the animal kingdom; humans, just like bumblebees, prefer orderly, symmetric environments (Shepherd & Bar, 2011). For humans, the reason for this esthetic preference is not entirely clear, although it has been proposed that symmetric or orderly environments are preferred because the features of such environments are detected and processed more efficiently by the visual system (Shepherd & Bar, 2011). In some cases of obsessive-compulsive disorder (OCD), the preference for order and symmetry is taken to excessive levels, leading to distress and impairment.

The focus of this chapter is on symmetry, ordering, and arranging obsessions and compulsions (SOA) in adults diagnosed with OCD. We will review the descriptive psychopathology of SOA, discuss what is known about the biopsychosocial etiology, review the empirical literature on the treatment, and describe cognitive-behavioral interventions. Assessment of SOA is covered elsewhere in this volume. Excluded from this review are SOA phenomena as they occur in children and in people with autism spectrum disorder. Although our focus is on SOA in adults, these symptoms commonly develop in childhood and persist into adulthood.

Descriptive Psychopathology

Clinical Features

SOA involves obsessions and compulsions about symmetry, orderliness, and exactness. The person may spend hours each day arranging objects in their living space or place of work, to the point that social and occupational functioning is impaired. Perceived disorganization evokes distress and urges to order or arrange objects (Fitch & Cougle, 2013; Radomsky & Rachman, 2004). Examples of SOA include the following:

- organizing cans in the pantry so that the labels are all pointing in the same direction;
- organizing shirts in one's closet so that all shirts are perfectly straight on their hangers, and organized as to color and purpose (e.g., work shirts separated from casual shirts);

The Wiley Handbook of Obsessive Compulsive Disorders, Volume I, First Edition.
Edited by Jonathan S. Abramowitz, Dean McKay, and Eric A. Storch.

- arranging books or compact disks according to specific rules (e.g., height and color of books, artist and year of publication of compact disks);
- aligning pencils and other items on one's desk;
- straightening wall hangings or arranging furniture or other items in one's house according to specific rules (e.g., arranging remote control devices so that they are perfectly aligned and equidistant from one another);
- meticulous organization and filing of documents;
- organization of kitchen utensils;
- balancing sensations or stimuli; for example, ensuring that shoelaces are tied such that shoes are of the same tension; or saying "left" after one has said "right."

SOA has long been observed to be a feature of OCD. To illustrate, over a century ago Janet (1908) described a patient for whom it was:

> Always necessary for her to line up objects, half to her right, half to her left … If she steps on a little protruding stone, she feels forced to search the other foot for an analogous sensation. When she has placed a hand on some marble or on any other cold object she is forced to inflict a similar impression to the other symmetrical body part. (p. 122)

Avoidance of stimuli that trigger obsessions or compulsions is not a prominent feature of SOA, as compared with other types of OC symptoms (Starcevic et al., 2011b). However, avoidance does occur and it can be subtle. For example, the person might avoid having wall hangings, so as not to be preoccupied and distressed about whether a picture frame, for example, is askew.

Rules for arranging objects can involve simple rules of symmetry and orderliness (e.g., books arranged in a bookcase in descending order of height). Rules can also stem from superstitious beliefs (e.g., lining up objects on one's desk to face northwest, because this direction is believed to be associated with good luck). Some of these beliefs may concern good or bad luck to the person or can concern harm to loved ones (e.g., "If my guitar pick is not arranged at 45 degrees to my desk, then my mother could die").

Age of Onset

Evidence suggests that early and late onset OCD are distinct subtypes, with early onset tending to be associated with greater symptom severity and a greater prevalence of comorbid tics (Taylor, 2011a). There are conflicting findings as to whether SOA is more prevalent in early than late onset OCD (Kichuk et al., 2013; Taylor, 2011a; Wang et al., 2012). SOA can be found in both forms of OCD. SOA appear to be equally common in women and men (Fullana et al., 2010).

Co-occurrence with Other Forms of Psychopathology

Factor analytic studies show that symmetry, ordering, and arranging symptoms are particularly likely to co-occur with one another, but also commonly co-occur with other OC symptoms, particularly checking-related symptoms such as repeating and counting compulsions (Bloch et al., 2008). Longitudinal research suggests that SOA symptoms, but not other obsessive-compulsive (OC) symptoms, predict suicide attempts, even after controlling for baseline depression and baseline suicidal ideation (Alonso et al., 2010).

Differential Diagnosis

The distinction between normal or subclinical SOA versus clinical SOA is largely arbitrary, based on current conventions for diagnosing mental disorders (e.g., American Psychiatric Association, 2013). Clinically significant SOA meet criteria for OCD; that is, the obsessions and compulsions are time consuming (more than an hour per day), and associated with distress and impairment in functioning. Subclinical SOA might be somewhat distressing and impairing, but not meet the full criteria for OCD. Clinical and subclinical SOA should not be confused with normal symmetry, ordering, or arranging behaviors, which may be socially pre-scribed among some cultural groups (e.g., following the practices of Feng Sui or adhering to the organizing guidelines advocated in various lifestyle and housekeeping magazines).

Distinguishing SOA in OCD versus obsessive-compulsive personality disorder (OCPD) can be more challenging. OCPD is associated with preoccupations with order and organization, to the extent that the major point of the activity is lost. DSM-5 claims that "OCD is usually easily distinguished from obsessive-compulsive personality disorder by the presence of true obsessions and compulsions in OCD" (American Psychiatric Association, 2013: 681). However, the notion of "true obses-sions and compulsions" is vague. Although most OC symptoms in OCD are ego-dystonic, this is not the case when the person has poor insight. DSM-5 has specifiers for OCD, which include poor insight and absent insight. In cases in which a person performs symmetry, ordering, or arranging behaviors in order to achieve a "just right" experience (discussed below), it can be difficult to distinguish OCD from OCPD. Such cases underscore the limits in the utility of current diagnostic schemes.

Biopsychosocial Etiology

If SOA and other OC symptoms had simple etiologies, then the causes would have been identified decades ago. Evidence suggests that OCD has a complex biopsycho-social etiology (Taylor, 2011b). There is no unified theory of OCD, although research suggests that three groups of etiologic factors are involved in OCD in general, including SOA: genetic and environmental factors, motivational factors, and dysregu-lated neurocircuitry.

Genetic and Environmental Factors

Behavioral–genetic (twin) studies show that SOA, just like other OC symptoms, are strongly heritable and arise from the interaction between environmental factors and additive (i.e., nondominance) genetic factors (Taylor, 2011b). Behavioral–genetic studies show that SOA symptoms are caused by genetic and environmental factors specific to SOA, along with nonspecific genetic and environmental factors, which influence other OC symptoms and other forms of psychopathology (Taylor, 2011b). SOA symptoms are also genetically related to OCPD traits (Taylor et al., 2011).

Little is known about the specific genes involved in SOA or about the learning experiences or other environmental events that shape SOA. A meta-analysis genetic association studies suggests that OCD in general is associated with multiple genes, which each having a small impact on the person's risk of the developing the disorder (Taylor, 2013). The same is likely to be the case for SOA.

Much remains to be learned about the types of environmental events that increase a person's of developing SOA. Preliminary research suggest that SOA is associated with a past history of traumatic life events (Cromer et al., 2007). There is also suggestive evidence that SOA symptoms are influenced by perinatal insults (e.g., maternal hypertension, antepartum hemorrhage) (Grisham et al., 2011).

Motivational Factors

Contemporary cognitive-behavioral models of OCD propose that various types of dysfunctional beliefs play an etiologic role (Frost & Steketee, 2002). Three main sets of factor-analytically derived beliefs have been proposed: (a) perfectionism and intolerance of uncertainty; (b) overimportance and need to control thoughts; and (c) inflated responsibility and overestimation of threat. Research suggests that SOA is most closely related to perfectionism and intolerance of uncertainty (Fitch & Cougle, 2013; Sarawgi et al., 2013; Taylor et al., 2010, 2011). Research further suggests that genetic and environmental factors influence perfectionism and intolerance of uncertainty, which in turn influence SOA (Taylor & Jang, 2011). In some cases, SOA may be driven by magical ideation about perfectionism or harm, such as the need to order or align items to prevent harm befalling loved ones (Rasmussen & Eisen, 1992).

Other research suggests that the sense of incompleteness plays an etiologic role in OCD. Incompleteness is a form of sensory perfectionism; that is, the sense that one's actions, intentions, or experiences have not been done "just right." This can occur in the apparent absence of beliefs about feared consequences. SOA, like other OC symptoms, is significantly correlated with incompleteness, even after controlling for the effects of dysfunctional beliefs (Taylor et al., 2014). Incompleteness is a commonly reported reason given by people who engage in symmetry, ordering, or arranging rituals, although in other cases such rituals may also be performed to avoid feared consequences (Starcevic et al., 2011a). Little is known about the causes of incompleteness, or why some people with OCD have a persistent sense that a given action (e.g., arranging items on one's desk) has not been properly performed. Theories have been proposed that attempt to explain incompleteness and related phenomena (e.g., Szechtman & Woody, 2004), but such theories suffer from empirical and conceptual problems (Taylor et al., 2005). Much remains to be learned about incompleteness, as it occurs in OCD in general, and in SOA in particular.

Neurocircuitry

Cortico-striatal-thalamo-cortical models are the leading neuroanatomic conceptualizations of OCD (Graybiel & Rauch, 2000; Milad & Rauch, 2012). Such models propose that OCD arises from dysregulated circuits connecting structures in the prefrontal cortex, striatum, and thalamus. These include circuits involved in error detection, decision making, and response inhibition. Consistent with these models, SOA is associated with subtle neuropsychological deficits on tasks involving set shifting, motor inhibition, and decision making (Dittrichet et al., 2011; Hashimoto et al., 2011; Lawrence et al., 2006). However, current neuroanatomic models do not explain why some cases of OCD are characterized by SOA whereas other cases are characterized by other types of symptoms, such as checking, washing, and doubting. It may be that the various symptoms arise from partially distinct neural systems. There is preliminary support for this conjecture. Preliminary neuroimaging research suggests that SOA severity is inversely correlated with global gray matter volume, and with regional gray matter volumes in some brain areas, including in the motor, insula, and parietal cortices (van den Heuvel et al., 2009). Neuroimaging research on the micro-structure of white matter further suggests that SAO is associated with alterations in visual processing tracts (Koch et al., 2012). Koch and colleagues speculated that this might be part of the neural basis for attention to irrelevant detail that characterizes SAO. It remains to be determined whether the neuroimaging findings are robust (replicable).

Treatment

Treatment Efficacy Studies

First-line treatments for OCD include (a) exposure and response prevention (ERP), which is often combined with cognitive restructuring, to form cognitive-behavior therapy (CBT), and (b) serotonin reuptake inhibitors (SRIs) (Abramowitz et al., 2009). There is no persuasive evidence that SOA is associated with a poorer response to treatment than other OC symptoms. Clinical trials indicate that ERP and SRIs are generally efficacious for SOA, and that SOA is no more difficult to treat than proto-typic OC symptoms such as washing and checking (Abramowitz et al., 2003; Mataix-Cols et al., 2002; Starcevic & Brakoulias, 2008). Nevertheless, there is room for improvement in the efficacy of the current first-line treatments for all OC symptoms, including SOA.

For patients who fail to benefit from either SRIs or ERP, a common strategy is to combine the two treatments. There is evidence that for SRI nonresponders, treatment outcome is enhanced by adding ERP (Simpson et al., 2013). There are mixed find-ings as to whether outcome for SRI nonresponders is enhanced by adding antipsy-chotic medication (Carey et al., 2012; Simpson et al., 2013). There is no evidence that the efficacy of ERP is be enhanced by adding SRIs. These findings apply to OC symptoms in general, and are likely to apply to SOA, given that the treatment response for SOA is about the same as the response for most other OC symptoms.

Cognitive-Behavioral Interventions

The treatment of SOA is much the same as the treatment of other OC symptoms, with some exceptions, most notably the use of time limits to complete tasks such as tidying one's desk or placing groceries in the pantry. For a description of the nuts and bolts of cognitive-behavioral interventions for OCD in general, see Abramowitz (2009). The following sections illustrate cognitive-behavioral interventions, as applied to SOA.

Treatment-related assessment. Although the assessment of SOA is discussed elsewhere in this volume, as part of treatment it is important for the therapist to conduct a functional analysis, to identify the person's motivation for engaging in ordering and arranging rituals. Such motivators could be perfectionism, incompleteness, or magical beliefs. Treatment differs, to some extent, depending on the nature of the motivator, as illustrated below.

ERP exercises. ERP for SOA is much the same as ERP for other types of OC symptoms (see Abramowitz, 2009). That is, exposure can be imaginal or in vivo, with the latter being conducted in the therapist's office and in the patient's home. A hierarchy of distressing stimuli can be created, for which treatment consists of progressing up the hierarchy. Response prevention involves delaying or, preferably, refraining from engaging in ordering or arranging compulsions. Such exercises can lead to the habituation of distress associated with exposure to imperfection or incompleteness in one's activities and environment.

The nature of ERP exercises depends on the nature of the person's concerns. Exposure exercises in the therapist's office might involve exposure to "disarray" or objects in the "wrong" order; a patient might be asked to deliberately tilt a picture frame on the wall so it is askew. The patients might be asked to "disorganize" books on the therapist's bookshelf; for example, arranging books so that they are not arranged according to height, topic, or color. The patient would then be asked to refrain from ordering the items and sit with their discomfort for the duration of the therapy session, which might involve a discussion of topics as homework assignments. The usefulness of such in-session exercises depends on the nature of the patient's problems. Some patients are acutely distressed by any type of disorder in their environment, and so making the therapist's office "messy," without tidying up the "mess," can be a useful ERP exercise. Other patients are focused entirely on the orderliness of their personal work or home environment, and are unconcerned about spaces outside their personal territory. In these cases, in-session ERP exercises might not be useful, unless they involved exercises aimed at disorganizing the patient's possessions (e.g., mixing up the order of the contents of a patient's wallet or purse, such as messing up the order in which the patient keeps credit cards or bank notes, or pressing one side of one's body against a wall without evening it up on the other side).

In-session ERP likely to be insufficient for SOA. ERP in the patient's home or work environment is likely to be required. This can involve homework assignments (e.g., tilt all the pictures on the walls in your house) or therapist-assisted exposure in the patient's home. The latter is likely to be more effective because the therapist can examine the home environment to identify potential targets of ERP. A therapist visit to the patient's place of work, for the purpose of therapist-assisted ERP, is usually not feasible. During a home visit, the therapist and patient can create a hierarchy of distressing stimuli and the patient can be asked to work up the hierarchy deliberately disorganizing his or her possessions, such as items on a coffee table or on shelves, and then refraining from reorganizing as his or her distress gradually subsides.

Homework assignments for SOA should also take time into consideration. For example, for the task of unpacking groceries and placing them in the refrigerator and pantry, or folding laundry, or making the bed, reasonable time limits should be set for such activities. It should not take an hour to place a dozen cans in the pantry; the patient should be prompted to complete this activity within minutes, and then proceed to some other activity. Setting time limits is important because patients with SOA can spend inordinate amounts of time on trivial tasks such as placing items in a pantry. Letting one's spouse and children to be "messy" can also be a useful part of ERP.

Cognitive interventions. Cognitive interventions can be used to addressed patients' ambivalence or concerns about entering treatment (e.g., "The therapist will make me mess up my house, and that would be awful"). Psychoeducation can be offered to provide guidelines about normal ordering and arranging behaviors; for example, most people do not arrange soup cans so that the labels are perfectly aligned, and most people require only minutes to put groceries in the pantry. Such information can be used to set goals for completing tasks such as unpacking groceries.

For patients with perfectionistic beliefs related to SOA, cognitive restructuring can be useful. Examples of cognitive restricting for perfectionism in OCD are presented in detail elsewhere (Wilhelm & Steketee, 2006). Behavioral experiments can be set up to test magical beliefs about SOA. These need to be very specific in terms of pre-dicted outcomes, because patients who engage in magical thinking can be overly liberal in the evidence that they regard as supporting their beliefs. For a patient, for example, who believed that his iPhone had to face northwest on his desk in order to prevent bad luck, the therapist could set up a behavioral experiment in which the iPhone was set to face another direction. But in order to successfully conduct such a behavioral experiment, it is necessary for the patient and therapist to arrange at a shared understanding of what would constitute a "bad luck" outcome.

Cognitive restructuring can be useful even when SOA appears to be driven by incompleteness (sensory perfectionism). The therapist can examine the patient's interpretations and beliefs about the meaning of his or her sense of incompleteness when completing tasks (Summerfeldt, 2008). Patients can be informed that the sense of incompleteness is a false message from the brain, and not an indication that a task has been improperly performed. With continued practice at ERP and completing tasks within specified time limits, patients can learn to accept that they might have a lingering sense of incompleteness after performing a task, but that abates as one moves on to other tasks or activities.

Other interventions. Family-based interventions can also be useful, because family members sometimes react to the patient's symptoms and associated problems (e.g., procrastination, slowness) with frustration, criticism, and anger (Summerfeldt, 2007). It can be helpful to interview the patient's significant other(s) (e.g., spouse) and pro-vide them with psychoeducation about the nature, causes, and treatment of SOA. Significant others can be educated that the patient is not to blame for the symptoms, and that hostility and criticism often makes matters worse, because OC symptoms can worsen under stress.

Conclusion

SOA appears to be an extreme form of the normal human preference for order and symmetry. Evidence suggests that SOA, like other OC symptoms, has a complex bio-psychosocial etiology. Genetic and environmental factors play a role, in addition to motivational factors such as dysfunctional beliefs, particularly beliefs about perfectionism, and also sensory perfectionism (incompleteness phenomena). Dysregulated neurocircuitry may also place a role, although the dysregulations specifically associated with SOA have yet to be delineated. Treatments for SOA involve the first-line treatments for OCD in general; that is, ERP, with or without cognitive restructuring, and SRIs. There is no evidence that SOA is more difficult to treat than other OC symptoms. Nevertheless, the first-line treatments for OCD are not cures. They reduce the severity and impact of OC symptoms such as SOA, but not all patients benefit from these treatments, and even treatment responders may have residual symptoms at the end of a course of treatment. Advances in treating SOA and other OC symptoms will likely require a better understanding of the causes of these phenomena.

References

Abramowitz, J. S. (2009). *Getting over OCD*. New York: Guilford Press.

Abramowitz, J. S., Franklin, M. E., Schwartz, S. A., & Furr, J. M. (2003). Symptom presentation and outcome of cognitive-behavioral therapy for obsessive-compulsive disorder. *Journal of Consulting and Clinical Psychology*, 71, 1049–1057.

Abramowitz, J. S., Taylor, S., & McKay, D. (2009). Obsessive-compulsive disorder. *Lancet*, 374, 491–499.

Alonso, P., Segalàs, C., Real, E., Pertusa, A., Labad, J., Jiménez-Murcia, S., … Menchón, J. M. (2010). Suicide in patients treated for obsessive-compulsive disorder: A prospective follow-up study. *Journal of Affective Disorders*, 124, 300–308.

American Psychiatric Association. (2013). *Diagnostic and statistical manual of mental disorders* (5th ed.). Arlington, VA: Author.

Bloch, M. H., Landeros-Weisenberger, A., Rosário, M. C., Pittenger, C., & Leckman, J. F. (2008). Meta-analysis of the symptom structure of obsessive-compulsive disorder. *American Journal of Psychiatry*, 165, 1532–1542.

Carey, P. D., Lochner, C., Kidd, M., van Ameringen, M., Stein, D. J., & Denys, D. (2012). Quetiapine augmentation of serotonin reuptake inhibitors in treatment-refractory obsessive–compulsive disorder: Is response to treatment predictable? *International Clinical Psychopharmacology*, 27, 321–325.

Cromer, K. R., Schmidt, N. B., & Murphy, D. L. (2007). An investigation of traumatic life events and obsessive-compulsive disorder. *Behaviour Research and Therapy*, 45, 1683–1691.

Dittrich, W. H., Johansen, T., Landrø, N. I., & Fineberg, N. A. (2011). Cognitive performance and specific deficits in OCD symptom dimensions – III: Decision-making and impairments in risky choices. *German Journal of Psychiatry*, 14, 13–25.

Fitch, K. E., & Cougle, J. R. (2013). An evaluation of obsessive beliefs as predictors of performance on in vivo assessments of obsessive–compulsive symptoms. *Cognitive Therapy and Research*, 37, 207–220.

Frost, R. O., & Steketee, G. (2002). *Cognitive approaches to obsessions and compulsions: Theory, assessment and treatment*. Oxford: Elsevier.

Fullana, M. A., Vilagut, G., Rojas-Farreras, S., Mataix-Cols, D., de Graaf, R., Demyttenaere, K., … Alonso, J. (2010). Obsessive-compulsive symptom dimensions in the general population: Results from an epidemiological study in six European countries. *Journal of Affective Disorders*, 124, 291–299.

Graybiel, A. M., & Rauch, S. L. (2000). Toward a neurobiology of obsessive-compulsive disorder. *Neuron*, 28, 343–347.

Grisham, J. R., Fullana, M. A., Mataix-Cols, D., Moffitt, T. E., Caspi, A., & Poulton, R. (2011). Risk factors prospectively associated with adult obsessive–compulsive symptom dimensions and obsessive–compulsive disorder. *Psychological Medicine*, 41, 2495–2506.

Hashimoto, N., Nakaaki, S., Omori, I. M., Fujioi, J., Noguchi, Y., Murata, Y., … Furukawa, T. A. (2011). Distinct neuropsychological profiles of three major symptom dimensions in obsessive-compulsive disorder. *Psychiatry Research*, 187, 166–173.

Janet, P. (1908). *Les obsessions et la psychasthénie* (2nd ed.), trans. M. W. Adamowicz. Paris: Alcan.

Kichuk, S. A., Torres, A. R., Fontenelle, L. F., Rosário, M. C., Shavitt, R. G., Miguel, E. C., … Bloch, M. H. (2013). Symptom dimensions are associated with age of onset and clinical course of obsessive-compulsive disorder. *Progress in Neuro-Psychopharmacology & Biological Psychiatry*, 44, 233–239.

Koch, K., Wagner, G., Schachtzabel, C., Christoph Schultz, C., Straube, T., Güllmar, D., … Schlösser, R. G. M. (2012). White matter structure and symptom dimensions in obsessive-compulsive disorder. *Journal of Psychiatric Research*, 46, 264–270.

Lawrence, N. S., Wooderson, S., Mataix-Cols, D., David, R., Speckens, A., & Phillips, M. L. (2006). Decision making and set shifting impairments are associated with distinct symptom dimensions in obsessive-compulsive disorder. *Neuropsychology*, 20, 409–419.

Mataix-Cols, D., Marks, I. M., Greist, J. H., Kobak, K. A., & Baer, L. (2002). Obsessive-compulsive symptom dimensions as predictors of compliance with and response to behaviour therapy. *Psychotherapy & Psychosomatics*, 71, 255–262.

Milad, M. R., & Rauch, S. L. (2012). Obsessive-compulsive disorder: Beyond segregated cortico-striatal pathways. *Trends in Cognitive Sciences*, 16, 43–51.

Radomsky, A. S., & Rachman, S. (2004). Symmetry, ordering and arranging compulsive behaviour. *Behaviour Research and Therapy*, 42, 893–913.

Rasmussen, S. A., & Eisen, J. L. (1992). The epidemiology and clinical features of obsessive compulsive disorder. *Psychiatric Clinics of North America*, 15, 743–758.

Sarawgi, S., Oglesby, M. E., & Cougle, J. R. (2013). Intolerance of uncertainty and obsessive-compulsive symptom expression. *Journal of Behavior Therapy and Experimental Psychiatry*, 44, 456–462.

Shepherd, K., & Bar, M. (2011). Preference for symmetry. *Perception*, 40, 1254–1256.

Simpson, H. B., Foa, E., Liebowitz, M. R., Huppert, J., Cahill, S., Maher, M. J., … Campeas, R. (2013). Cognitive-behavioral therapy vs risperidone for augmenting serotonin reuptake inhibitors in obsessive-compulsive disorder: A randomized clinical trial. *JAMA Psychiatry*, 70, 1190–1199.

Starcevic, V., Berle, D., Brakoulias, V., Sammut, P., Moses, K., Milicevic, D., … Hannan, A. (2011a). Functions of compulsions in obsessive-compulsive disorder. *Australian and New Zealand Journal of Psychiatry*, 45, 449–457.

Starcevic, V., Berle, D., Brakoulias, V., Sammut, P., Moses, K., Milicevic, D., & Hannan, A. (2011b). The nature and correlates of avoidance in obsessive-compulsive disorder. *Australian and New Zealand Journal of Psychiatry*, 45, 871–879.

Starcevic, V., & Brakoulias, V. (2008). Symptom subtypes of obsessive-compulsive disorder: Are they relevant for treatment? *Australian and New Zealand Journal of Psychiatry*, 42, 651–661.

Summerfeldt, L. J. (2007). Treating incompleteness, ordering, and arranging concerns. In M. M. Antony, C. Purdon & L. J. Summerfeldt (Eds.), *Psychological treatment of obsessive-compulsive disorder: Fundamentals and beyond* (pp. 187–207). Washington, DC: American Psychological Association.

Summerfeldt, L. J. (2008). Ordering, incompleteness, and arranging. In J. S. Abramowitz, D. McKay & S. Taylor (Eds.), *Clinical handbook of obsessive-compulsive and related phenomena* (pp. 44–60). Baltimore, MD: Johns Hopkins University Press.

Szechtman, H., & Woody, E. (2004). Obsessive-compulsive disorder as a disturbance of security motivation. *Psychological Review*, 111, 111–127.

Taylor, S. (2011a). Early versus late onset obsessive-compulsive disorder: Evidence for distinct subtypes. *Clinical Psychology Review*, 31, 1083–1100.

Taylor, S. (2011b). Etiology of obsessions and compulsions: A meta-analysis and narrative review of twin studies. *Clinical Psychology Review*, 31, 1361–1372.

Taylor, S. (2013). Molecular genetics of obsessive-compulsive disorder: A comprehensive meta-analysis of genetic association studies. *Molecular Psychiatry*, 18, 799–805.

Taylor, S., Asmundson, G. J. G., & Jang, K. L. (2011). Etiology of obsessive-compulsive symptoms and obsessive-compulsive personality traits: Common genes, mostly different environments. *Depression and Anxiety*, 28, 863–869.

Taylor, S., Coles, M. E., Abramowitz, J. S., Wu, K. D., Olatunji, B. O., Timpano, K. R., ... Tolin, D. F. (2010). How are dysfunctional beliefs related to obsessive-compulsive symptoms? *Journal of Cognitive Psychotherapy*, 24, 165–176.

Taylor, S., & Jang, K. L. (2011). Biopsychosocial etiology of obsessions and compulsions: An integrated behavioral–genetic and cognitive-behavioral analysis. *Journal of Abnormal Psychology*, 120, 174–186.

Taylor, S., McKay, D., & Abramowitz, J. S. (2005). Is obsessive-compulsive disorder a disturbance of security motivation? *Psychological Review*, 112, 650–657.

Taylor, S., McKay, D., Crowe, K. B., Abramowitz, J. S., Conelea, C. A., Calamari, J. E., ... Sica, C. (2014). The sense of incompleteness as a motivator of obsessive-compulsive symptoms: An empirical analysis of concepts and correlates. *Behavior Therapy*, 45, 254–262.

van den Heuvel, O. A., Remijnse, P. L., Mataix-Cols, D., Vrenken, H., Groenewegen, H. J., Uylings, H. B. M., ... Veltman, D. J. (2009). The major symptom dimensions of obsessive-compulsive disorder are mediated by partially distinct neural systems. *Brain*, 132, 853–868.

Wang, X., Cui, D., Wang, Z., Fan, Q., Xu, H., Qiu, J., ... Xiao, Z. (2012). Cross-sectional comparison of the clinical characteristics of adults with early-onset and late-onset obsessive compulsive disorder. *Journal of Affective Disorders*, 136, 498–504.

Wilhelm, S., & Steketee, G. (2006). *Cognitive therapy for obsessive-compulsive disorder*. Oakland, CA: New Harbinger.

22

Symmetry and Ordering in Youth with Obsessive Compulsive Disorder

Amy M. Jacobsen and Ashley J. Smith

Although OCD is considered a unitary disorder, it consists of a heterogeneous group of symptom phenotypes. Numerous factor and cluster–analytical studies have evaluated symptom heterogeneity and identified four relatively distinct symptom dimensions, including harming obsessions with checking compulsions, symmetry obsessions with ordering/repeating/counting compulsions, contamination obsessions with washing compulsions, and hoarding (e.g., Bloch, Landeros-Weisenberger, Rosario, Pittenger, & Leckman, 2008; Mataix-Cols, Rosario-Campos, & Leckman, 2005). Research examining the structure of OCD symptoms among pediatric samples has yielded less consistent results (e.g., Ivarsson & Valderhaug, 2006; McKay et al., 2006), yet most studies have replicated adult studies to reveal similar symptom phenotypes for youth (Delorme et al., 2006; Mataix-Cols, Nakatami, Micali, & Heyman, 2008; Stewart et al., 2007). The aim of this chapter is to provide a clinical description of the symmetry/ordering dimension in children and adolescents, and to summarize correlates and diagnostic considerations. Case examples will be used to illustrate the clinical presentation and treatment of youth with symmetry/ordering symptoms. In addition, challenging clinical issues and strategies for overcoming these obstacles will be discussed.

Clinical Presentation

Epidemiological studies indicate that the symmetry/ordering dimension is one of the most common presentations of OCD across the lifespan (e.g., Summerfeldt, Richter, Antony, & Swainson, 1999; Valleni-Bassile et al., 1994). Indeed, the symmetry/ordering dimension is one of the most frequent phenotypes among youth with OCD (Masi et al., 2010). Ivarsson and Valderhaug (2006) reported that arranging and ordering occurred in approximately 35% of their pediatric sample, while other studies have found even higher frequencies (e.g., Labad et al., 2008; Masi et al., 2010; Mataix-Cols et al., 2008), particularly in youth with earlier onset OCD (Kichuk et al., 2013).

The Wiley Handbook of Obsessive Compulsive Disorders, Volume I, First Edition.
Edited by Jonathan S. Abramowitz, Dean McKay, and Eric A. Storch.
© 2017 John Wiley & Sons Ltd. Published 2017 by John Wiley & Sons Ltd.

The thematic presentations within the symmetry/ordering dimension can vary widely. It is primarily characterized by obsessions that concern incompleteness and exactness, which often involve a need for order, neatness, symmetry, and having things "just right." The accompanying compulsions often consist of repeating, arranging, and ordering behaviors. Examples include the child who feels the need to repeatedly erase and rewrite letters until they look and/or feel "just right," and the adolescent who feels the need to touch items with his left hand after touching them with his right in order to "even out" the feeling. It may also involve the need to line up toys, complete a routine in exactly the right order, and maintain excessive order and neatness in the bedroom while not allowing others to enter or disturb that environment. Many youth experiencing these symptoms, especially young children, openly engage in rituals, and expect parents to similarly conform to the "rules" of the compulsions. If ritualizing is interrupted, the child may become agitated and angry without recognizing this response as unusual or excessive.

Empirical research has attempted to learn more about the particular symptoms captured within this subtype. Storch and colleagues (2007) evaluated the predictive value of the miscellaneous items on the Children's Yale–Brown Obsessive Compulsive Scale (CY-BOCS) (Scahill et al., 1997). Results identified seven symptoms significantly associated with the symmetry/ordering dimension: a need to know or remember; a fear of not saying just the right thing; intrusive sounds, words, music, or numbers; ritualized eating behaviors; a need to touch, tap, or rub; a need to do things until it feels "just right"; and rituals involving blinking or staring. These authors noted that their results made conceptual sense given that this factor largely reflects the need for things to feel "just right" and to do things exactly or thoroughly. Although the cognitive content may be sparse, it is believed that these compulsions serve the same purpose as other compulsions, which is to neutralize and reduce distress related to the obsession (Rachman & Hodgson, 1980). Therefore, these compulsions are employed in the child's efforts to obtain control and achieve an internal sense of being "just right," which provides a feeling of safety and/or control over her environment (Radomsky & Rachman, 2004).

When evaluating symptoms involving the need for symmetry and order, the function of the compulsion should be identified. For some youth, the symmetry and exactness symptoms are associated directly with the need to neutralize "not just right experiences" (NJREs) (Coles, Heimberg, Frost, & Steketee, 2005), which can be visual, proprioceptive, tactile, and/or cognitive (Summerfeldt, 2007). In these instances, the feeling of incompleteness or imperfection is the feared consequence, and compulsions are completed in an effort to decrease the discomfort caused by the NJREs (Summerfield, 2004). Other patients experience incompleteness symptoms associated with magical thinking. This presentation is characterized by a belief that a disastrous conclusion (e.g., death of a parent, bad luck) will occur if the "just right" state is not achieved. Clarifying the underlying feared outcome(s) and the function of compulsions will be important factors in determining exposure and response prevention goals to include in the youth's treatment plan.

Case Vignettes

The hypothetical cases of Gregor and Jamie (pseudonyms), who represent amalgamations of actual patients with symmetry/ordering symptoms seen in our clinic, will be introduced to illustrate symptom profiles.

Gregor, an 8-year-old boy, presented for treatment because parents, teachers, and peers noticed that he walked in an unusual way at school and in the kitchen at home. Others observed that, at times, he walked on his toes, turned sideways, appeared to march in place, and had an uneven gait; these oddities were not present when he walked on carpet or in the grass. Gregor was able to explain that he felt "bad" (i.e., experienced an uncomfortable sensation in his body) whenever he stepped on a crack (e.g., in the sidewalk, grouting between tiles). He experienced unpleasant sensations of unevenness with one leg feeling "heavy" while the other felt "light." These uncomfortable sensations persisted until he evened out his body by stepping on the same crack with the other foot. As a result, he made great efforts to avoid stepping on cracks altogether, which resulted in his unusual walking patterns.

Jamie, a 15-year-old girl, presented for treatment because she was struggling in school. While historically a strong student, her grades had declined over the past year because of failure to turn in homework assignments. Some completed schoolwork was found in her backpack, but she did not turn it in because it was imperfect. Many other assignments were not completed at all, despite Jamie's time and effort given to them. Incompletion was due, in part, to the amount of time she spent erasing and rewriting words and sentences in an attempt to make them look "right." In addition, she found it difficult to initiate homework if her workspace was not perfectly arranged (e.g., books straightened, pens and pencils precisely organized). Jamie described feeling annoyed and unable to focus if her workspace was not neat or her writing was imperfect.

Jamie's parents recounted that she always preferred neatness and routine, yet the severity and associated distress had escalated over time. They also reported excessive rigidity in her night-time routine, which involved getting ready for bed in a particular order and repeating the phrase, "I love you. Good night. I'll see you in the morning," to her parents until she achieved exactly the right voice inflection, volume, and rate of speech. She also demanded that her parents do the same, directing them to modify and repeat the same phrase numerous times. Her parents helped her to perform the routine and accommodated her requests to prevent the inevitable meltdown and repetition of actions that occurred if the routine was not done correctly. Jamie feared that something bad would happen to her parents or siblings during the night if she did not complete her nighttime rituals in this "just right" manner.

Clinical Correlates

Several studies have examined correlates of the symmetry and ordering dimension among youth. Findings on the age of onset have primarily demonstrated a relation between earlier age of onset (i.e., at or before 9 years old) and the presence of symmetry/ordering symptoms (Labad et al., 2008; Nakatani et al., 2011), although such findings have not been consistent (Mataix-Cols et al., 2008). There also is some evidence of the magical thinking component becoming more prevalent with age. Examining the phenomenology of OCD in younger children (3–9 years) compared with older children (10–18 years), Selles, Storch, and Lewin (2014) found that older youth evidenced an increased occurrence of magical thinking, with 32% of older youth endorsing this experience compared with 17% of younger children. This difference may be explained by the less well-developed cognitive abilities of younger children. It may be difficult for youth to articulate reasons for engaging in rituals other than endorsing a need to do things until it feels "just right" (Storch et al., 2007). Additionally, it may be that this dimension lessens in intensity and frequency over time and is replaced or overshadowed by the surfacing of more intrusive cognitive symptoms (Radomsky & Rachman, 2004). Examination of gender differences within this dimension has similarly yielded inconsistent results, with some evidence that male youth more frequently present with symmetry and ordering symptoms (Masi et al., 2010), while other studies show no difference (e.g., Mataix-Cols, Nakatani, Micali, & Heman, 2008).

For family factors, there has been no relation found for this symptom dimension and particular parental child-rearing behaviors (Alonso et al., 2004). Family history of OCD, however, does appear to be related (Nikolajsen, Nissen, & Thomsen, 2011), with high scores on the symmetry/ordering dimension positively correlated with OCD in first-degree relatives.

Neuroimaging research has demonstrated neural correlates of symmetry and ordering (Lawrence et al., 2006), although findings do not appear to be specific to this dimension. Of note, the presence and the region of the functional abnormalities appear to be similar across adult and pediatric studies, yet the direction of the abnormality seems to be reversed. Specifically, comparing a pediatric OCD sample to a control sample, Gilbert and colleagues (2009) identified abnormalities in the dorsal prefrontal cortex during a symmetry/ordering provocation task, with the OCD sample exhibiting reduced activity in the insula and thalamus. This is in contrast to results from adult studies, which demonstrated increased activity in the region in response to symmetry/ordering provocation (Lawrence et al., 2006). The authors suggested that their findings support important developmental differences and reflect a possible delay in insular development in OCD youths or aberrant development in the cortico-striatal-thalamic pathway. Findings were consistent across other symptom-specific provocations, suggesting that this is a nonspecific neural correlate of pediatric OCD.

Diagnostic Considerations and Comorbidities

Developmentally Normative Behaviors

When assessing repetitive behaviors in youth, several factors should be considered through the differential diagnostic process. One factor pertains to the severity and functional impairment associated with these behaviors. Certainly, ritualistic, repetitive behaviors, including a desire for sameness, a preference for symmetry, and a system for arranging preferred objects, are normative phenomena among children (e.g., Evans et al., 1997). Even "just right" behaviors are considered normative among typically developing children. Transition times, such as bedtime, tend to be characterized by ritualized behaviors, and indeed, parents are encouraged to implement structured routines to promote compliance, mastery of skills, and healthy adjustment in children. While nonclinical routines can be viewed as adaptive, several factors differentiate OCD from these normative ritualizations. Such factors include the child's developmental age, the level of distress associated with the need to engage in the behavior, and the degree of impairment if the behavior is disrupted. Evidence of magical thinking tied to the need to engage in the behavior would also suggest an OCD presentation.

Overlap with Autism Spectrum Disorders

Another diagnostic consideration is the overlap in clinical presentation across autism spectrum disorders (ASD) and OCD. A high prevalence of autistic traits has been identified in youth with OCD (e.g., Ivarsson & Melin, 2008), as well as a high frequency of OCD symptoms in youth with ASD compared with non-ASD children (Ruta, Mugno, D'Arrigo, Vitiello, & Mazzone, 2010). At a basic level, our diagnostic system identifies ASD as being characterized by repetitive motor behaviors and stereotypies, need for sameness, ritualized routines, ordering, and lining up of objects (American Psychiatric Association, 2013). Even in the ASD literature, such behaviors have been broadly considered obsessive compulsive traits consistent with the physical manifestations of the symmetry/ordering dimension of OCD. In their review, Fischer-Terworth and Probst (2009) explain the different cognitive, motivational, and functional underpinnings that are believed to distinguish these diagnostic groups, despite the comparable behaviors and clinical phenomenology. Specifically, youth with ASD tend not to show distress associated with their behaviors and, in fact, are believed to engage in these activities willingly and to receive pleasure or a self-soothing response from them (i.e., positive reinforcement) (Baron-Cohen, 1989). In contrast, youth with OCD perform these rituals in the service of alleviating anxiety or discomfort (i.e., negative reinforcement) and, in the case of magical thinking, preventing harm. Despite these identified functional differences (e.g., McDougle, Kresch, Goodman, & Naylor, 1995), it can be difficult to discern repetitive behaviors from obsessions and compulsions associated with OCD, and dual diagnoses must be considered.

To distinguish between purely OCD profiles and ASD-related repetitive behaviors, Cath, Ran, Smit, van Balkom, and Comijs (2008) suggested that clinicians include an assessment of autism domains. Using a translated version of the Autism Spectrum Questionnaire (AQ) (Baron-Cohen, Wheelwright, Skinner, Martin, & Clubley, 2001) with an adult population, these authors found that individuals with comorbid OCD and ASD scored higher on subscales assessing communication problems and lack of imagination compared with adults with purely OCD profiles and controls. Child and adolescent versions of the AQ are available (Auyeung, Baron-Cohen, Wheelwright, & Allison, 2008; Baron-Cohen, Hoekstra, Knickmeyer, & Wheelwright, 2006). The Social Communication Questionnaire (SCQ) (Rutter, Bailey, & Lord, 2003), a parent-report screening questionnaire, has also been employed to discriminate between diagnostic profiles. For example, Weidle, Melin, Drotz, Jozefiak, and Ivarsson (2012) examined the prevalence of autistic behaviors in OCD youth using the SCQ. Excluding items assessing OCD- and tic-like symptoms, results identified only a subgroup of OCD youth (i.e., 1 in 6) actually evidencing a more significant level of other autistic behaviors. Another distinguishing factor appears to be age. Zandt, Prior, and Kyrios (2007) found similar rates of ordering and sameness behaviors among ASD and OCD, yet sameness behaviors occurred at significantly higher rates in younger children with OCD compared to older children, whereas the prevalence of these behaviors remained stable for ASD youth.

Overlap with Tic Disorders

The clinical overlap of OCD and tics has received particular attention and interest in recent years. Reasons for this include the common occurrence of symmetry and exactness symptoms in youth with Tourette's Disorder (TD) (Cardona, Romano,

Bollea, & Chiarotti, 2004) and the commonalities across the clinical features of these diagnoses. The differential diagnostic process can prove especially challenging in the case of complex motor tics that may be indistinguishable from compulsions, such as the child who engages in repetitive behaviors a specific number of times or until it feels "just right" (Castellanos, 1998). Indeed, repetitive behaviors, including the need for symmetry and touching, are estimated to occur in as many as 65% of patients with TD (Worbe et al., 2010).

It has been specifically debated whether NJREs belong more to the "tic-like" versus "OCD-like" symptom groups (Eapen, Robertson, Alsobrook, & Pauls, 1997; Worbe et al., 2010), or whether these experiences are most common among a subset of patients with co-occurring tic disorders (e.g., Leckman, Walker, Goodman, Pauls, & Cohen, 1994). Leckman and colleagues (2000) identified a unique subgroup of patients who experience "tic-related OCD." In their analysis, they suggested that this subgroup is distinguished from non-tic-related OCD based on several characteristics, including earlier age of onset, male preponderance, and symptomatology that often includes repetitive behaviors (e.g., touching, tapping, rubbing) and concerns with symmetry and exactness. Mansueto and Keuler (2005) extended this work in their proposal of the term "Tourettic OCD" (TOCD) as a conceptual framework to describe a subgroup of patients who experience a blend of OCD and TD. In their description, patients with TOCD engage in repetitive behaviors commonly associated with OCD, such as symmetry, touching, and NJREs, yet these behaviors are largely driven by experiences of sensory discomfort associated with TD. Although this theory remains under investigation, these authors underscore the importance of a functional analysis to assess the patient's subjective experiences and problematic repetitive behaviors to inform both the diagnostic profile and identify the types of treatment components from both the OCD and TD literature that may be beneficial.

Treatment

Empirical research examining treatment outcomes for this subtype, especially among pediatric populations, is sparse (e.g., Storch et al., 2008). Extant adult treatment outcome literature for symmetry and ordering symptoms has mostly suggested that established treatments for OCD, including cognitive behavioral therapy with exposure/response prevention (CBT/ERP) and serotonin reuptake inhibitors (e.g., Foa et al., 2005), yield a less favorable response compared with other manifestations of OCD. In this section, we present an overview of the scientific outcome data examining the effectiveness of these interventions for this symptom subtype, discuss cognitive behavioral treatment strategies for symmetry and ordering symptoms in youth, and illustrate treatment in case examples.

Pharmacological Treatment

Findings on response to pharmacotherapy for this symptom dimension have been inconsistent. In the adult literature, most studies suggest that patients with symmetry and ordering symptoms respond similarly to pharmacotherapy compared with patients with other subtypes (e.g., Denys, Burger, van Megen, de Geus, & Westenberg, 2003), yet other studies have yielded a poorer response to SRI treatment (e.g., Landeros-Weisenberger et al., 2010). To our knowledge, there are no pediatric studies investigating medication response by symptom dimension.

Psychological Treatment

Studies examining associations between OCD subtypes and CBT/ERP response rates for adults have identified a modest response to treatment for symmetry and ordering symptoms. While research does not suggest that these patients respond worse to CBT/ERP than patients with other subtypes (e.g., Abramowitz, Franklin, Schwartz, & Furr, 2003; Rufer, Fricke, Moritz, Kloss, & Hand, 2006), they do not seem to achieve the same robust treatment response as other symptom subtypes, excluding hoarding. Abramowitz and colleagues (2003) found that hoarding symptoms alone predicted poorer response to ERP, yet the response rate for the symmetry domain was most similar to hoarding than all remaining manifestations (e.g., harming, contamination, unacceptable thoughts).

Several factors have been identified as likely contributing to the modest treatment response for this subtype. Patients with symmetry and ordering symptoms have been underrepresented in outcome trials (e.g., Ball, Baer, & Otto, 1996), limiting the reliability of these findings. This underrepresentation may reflect their lower likelihood to seek treatment and the experience of egosyntonia with these symptoms. In their review, Starcevic and Brakoulias (2008) also noted several features associated with this subtype that may place these patients at risk for poorer response, including the higher prevalence of co-occurring tic disorders and the absence of a specific feared consequence with NJREs. Given these challenges, Summerfeldt (2007) proposed modifications to CBT/ERP for patients with symmetry, ordering, and arranging when compulsions are completed in an effort to neutralize an NJRE, with a greater emphasis on behavioral intervention through ERP strategies aimed at modifying the patient's response to the disturbing sensory–affective experiences.

We are only aware of one study examining CBT/ERP response rates across symptom dimensions with a pediatric OCD population. This study by Storch et al. (2008) did not reveal substantial differences across symptom dimensions, although there was some evidence of youth with checking rituals and harm obsessions demonstrating a better response. Perhaps certain features of CBT/ERP for pediatric OCD can enhance the response rate for symmetry and ordering symptoms, although further research is needed to ascertain this. Specifically, a family-based format with active parent participation, as used in the Storch et al. study, can promote the child's effort and treatment adherence. Additionally, the greater emphasis on the behavioral aspects of treatment, as is typical of treatment with youth, may be particularly beneficial for this symptom subtype, as proposed by Summerfeldt (2007).

A typical CBT protocol for pediatric OCD includes the following components: psychoeducation, cognitive training, hierarchy development, (ideally therapist-directed) exposure with response prevention (ERP), and relapse prevention (March & Mulle, 1998; Pediatric OCD Treatment Study Team, 2004), with the emphasis on implementation of ERP. A family-based approach is particularly recommended (e.g., Freeman et al., 2014). Highlights of psychoeducation include teaching youth and families to conceptualize OCD within a neurobiological framework, increasing their understanding of the functional relationship between obsessions and compulsions, and providing the rationale for ERP (essentially that changing behaviors allows for the reduction of obsessive thoughts and related distress and that habituation occurs with the passage of time alone). Cognitive training includes techniques such as positive self-talk, cognitive restructuring, and labeling/dismissing OCD (i.e., developing a "nonattachment" to OCD in which obsessions are acknowledged, then attention is refocused on the task at hand without any further active response to OCD). The key treatment component, ERP, involves systematically activating obsessive fears, then refraining from rituals or avoidance to encourage tolerance and modification of the fear response. ERP tasks are typically conducted in a graduated manner, starting with targets in the moderately distressing range and working up the hierarchy to the highest degree of anxiety-provoking situations as ERP mastery and anxiety modification occur.

Applying CBT to Symmetry/Ordering Symptoms

Developing effective exposure tasks hinges on a strong conceptualization of symptoms and understanding of the core fears that drive compulsive behaviors. The same compulsion may occur in response to different obsessional themes (e.g., tapping items to achieve a "just right" feeling versus to prevent harm), and yet the response prevention guidelines may be similar (e.g., resist tapping). The structure of exposure exercises, however, would differ depending on whether they are designed to target NJRE-related symptoms or those related to magical thinking. For example, the boy who feels like he must evenly stretch his muscles may engage in compulsions involving stretching one side and then the other, repeating until the "just right" or even feeling is achieved. Exposures may include stretching one leg for 10 seconds, and the other for 5 seconds or stretching one leg only. By activating the NJRE and refraining from compulsions, a tolerance for the discomfort can develop, and he learns that it gradually dissipates with the passage of time alone. The girl who erases and rewrites letters because they do not look right may engage in exposures focused on resisting urges to erase, then writing in pen (which prevents erasing), and finally writing messily on purpose. The teen with magical thinking who believes that he will have bad luck if he does not line up his belongings according to size and color may test out his OCD predictions by swapping two items in line, mixing up the order completely, and keeping items in a pile rather than a line; in addition, he may try other exposures to "bad luck" by trying to bring on bad luck intentionally through activities such as walking under a ladder or another task that he associates with bad luck.

Instructing patients in what to do with their thoughts and attention during exposures is important. Youth will benefit most from ERP efforts when they fully confront anxious thoughts and feelings. Therefore, imaginal or thought exposure strategies should be incorporated into in vivo exposures. For example, the girl who wrote messily on purpose would then be instructed to focus her attention on the parts of her writing that are most bothersome to OCD, maintaining attention while resisting rituals, to modify her response to this experience. Structuring her exposure in this manner allows for a more robust learning experience than simply writing messily and immediately putting away the paper. In contrast, the teen who feared bad luck may be asked to conduct an imaginal exposure to his most feared scenario: not lining up his belongings, incurring bad luck, and experiencing the feared outcomes of that luck. In addition, during in vivo exposures, such as messing up the order of his items, he may be asked to focus on the anxious thought (e.g., "I will have bad luck") and feared outcome; this added component can enhance the learning effect, promote tolerance of the thought, and correct the level of belief in the obsession.

Through combined in vivo and imaginal/thought exposures with response prevention, youth with OCD can learn several important lessons. First, they learn that anxiety/distress will decrease without the completion of compulsions, which directly challenges commonly held beliefs that distress will continue to escalate and/or never dissipate until the compulsion is completed. Youth also learn that they are capable of handling distress, even at high levels, contrary to what many individuals with anxiety disorders believe. In addition, ERP allows for a shift in cognitions that is often not achievable through more formal cognitive restructuring techniques alone. Testing out the validity of anxious beliefs provides corrective experiences. Moreover, properly conducted ERP takes the "power" and meaning out of obsessive thoughts, allowing youth to recognize that they do not have to attend to or act on intrusive thoughts or urges.

Case Vignettes: Illustration of Treatment

The following is a description of the course of treatment for Gregor and Jamie, including modifications to the treatment protocol often made to increase active participation, adherence, and outcome.

Gregor's OCD symptoms were quite circumscribed, yet his distress was immediate and intense when triggered. That is, if he did not immediately even out his steps when he stepped on a crack, he experienced extreme distress, and consequently construction of a hierarchy proved to be challenging. Initially, a goal was set for him to step on a crack with one foot and resist evening out for 1 minute with the plan of lengthening the duration of time resisting as toleration improved. Early ERP efforts resulted in uncontrollable crying episodes, suggesting that even a short delay was beyond his working range (i.e., not in the moderate level of distress, or one that he could reasonably tolerate). His hierarchy was reworked to include the use of a distracting activity to help increase his tolerance for distress. For example, during sessions, he initially played catch with the therapist during the delay period. This activity was distracting enough that it reduced his level of distress to a manageable level, and he was able to resist rituals. This allowed him to learn that he did not have to immediately even out his steps. As the delay period was extended, he noted that he "got used to" the physical sensations he experienced upon stepping on a crack and no longer felt the need to even out. He was then willing and able to complete the ERP process without the use of distraction; instead, he was instructed to focus on the sensations until toleration naturally occurred. These experiences directly challenged his underlying beliefs that his distress would last forever and that he would be unable to handle it. He is now able to walk normally, without paying attention to whether he steps on cracks or not.

Jamie's treatment plan also focused primarily on implementation of ERP, though her hierarchy was more complex given the presence of both NJRE and magical thinking obsessional themes. In the course of developing the exposure hierarchy, she indicated that targeting NJRE-related symptoms would be less distressing, as these tasks felt less threatening given that they did not elicit fears of harm befalling her family. Her hierarchy included the following, from least to most anxiety provoking:

1 writing in pen without marking out letters or starting over (not schoolwork);
2 writing messily on purpose (not schoolwork);
3 starting homework with pens and pencils messed up on her desk;
4 completing homework with a messy desk;
5 writing messily on purpose on schoolwork;
6 mixing up the order of two steps of her bedtime routine;
7 eliminating one step of her bedtime routine;
8 completely re-ordering her bedtime routine;
9 parents saying, "I love you. Good night. I'll see you in the morning," one time only, regardless of whether it was "right" or not;
10 parents saying a different phrase every night;
11 saying, "I love you. Good night. I'll see you in the morning," one time only to parents;
12 saying, "I'll see you in the morning. Good night. I love you" (mixed up order) one time only to parents;
13 not saying anything to parents before going to bed.

Upon starting treatment, Jamie reported motivation to overcome OCD because she wanted to earn better grades. As she started lower level exposures, however, she expressed reluctance to participate. To promote her willingness to engage in ERP, a reward system was implemented. She was able to earn points each time she completed an exposure, and points were redeemed for additional privileges such as staying up 30 minutes late, extra allowance, and a pass on doing specific chores. These extra incentives enhanced her motivation to participate in exposures.

As Jamie transitioned from NJRE-related ERP targets to magical thinking-related ERP goals, she again became reluctant to engage in exposure work. In addition, she had a tendency to meltdown at night when rituals were interrupted or parents did not readily accommodate. Through prior ERP experiences, she fully understood the rationale for treatment and had first-hand experience with the process of habituation, yet she feared the risk of harm coming to her loved ones. Several strategies were employed to re-engage her in the treatment process, including bolstering the incentive plan, increasing parental involvement, and incorporating imaginal exposures.

A new behavior plan was developed with enhanced rewards and consequences. Specifically, access to daily privileges, such as spending time with friends, electronics, and activities that cost money (e.g., eating out), were made contingent upon completing treatment activities and refraining from meltdowns through the use of coping strategies. Parents were also trained to work consistently with Jamie to adjust the night-time routine, withdraw their accommodations according to her hierarchy, and effectively respond to meltdowns; this also allowed all changes to occur expectedly and collaboratively.

In addition to in vivo ERP targets, imaginal exposure helped Jamie address her fears. She developed an exposure script describing a scenario in which she did not complete her night-time routine perfectly and her parents died during the night (the feared outcome according to her OCD). Repeated exposure to the script fostered a modification of her belief in this feared outcome and a reduction in her anxiety. She was then able to pair the imaginal exposure with in vivo targets, fully confronting the feared thoughts that drove her compulsive behaviors and enhancing her learning effect.

Clinical Issues and Troubleshooting

Treating children and families affected by OCD presents unique challenges, regardless of the particular symptom presentation. With the symmetry/ordering subtype, differences between developmentally appropriate and excessive engagement in routine or repetitive behaviors must be carefully considered. Families should understand that the intention of CBT is to reestablish a normative degree of routine and structure that is helpful to a child's development versus disruptive and impairing. For many children, limited insight into the impairing or excessive nature of these symptoms hinders their motivation to engage in CBT. Moreover, family accommodation often reinforces the pattern of obsessive-compulsive symptoms. Identifying strategies to promote motivation and eliminate OCD accommodations are crucial for the child's success during and after treatment. This section offers some strategies to address such potential challenges.

Most youth with the need for symmetry or order hold a belief that they must engage in "just right" behaviors or their distress will persist forever and possibly lead to catastrophic outcomes (e.g., lose control) until the "just right" feeling is achieved. Parents often adopt a similar belief based on the severity of distress and disruptive behaviors observed in their child when compulsions are interrupted. Naturally, such beliefs may lead parents to postpone seeking CBT due to concerns that the child is too fragile and that it would be better to wait until the child actively requests treatment to address these behaviors. Alternatively, parents may view symmetry/ordering symptoms as "quirky," but not pathological. An example is a child who experiences severe distress if her shoes are not lined up perfectly before going to bed at night. Whatever the reason parents may delay intervention, the family response is often to accommodate the child's need for symmetry and order, which unfortunately serves to reinforce and often exacerbate symptoms. Important messages to parents are that excessive rigidity, with rules and routines that lead to extreme distress, is not developmentally normative, that symptoms are likely to worsen over time without proper intervention, and that CBT is a safe, evidence-based treatment for all ages. Also, early intervention is recommended (e.g., Freeman et al., 2014), and helping children build flexibility and learn to cope with adversity promotes resilience, even beyond OCD management.

Parents and clinicians alike should also understand that treatment participation does not rely on the youth's insight or internal motivation. Indeed, behavior modification methods are regularly a part of OCD treatment to promote motivation and participation. There are a plethora of resources on contingency management (e.g., Kazdin, 2013) that are commonly incorporated into treatment plans within our clinic. As with any behavior modification plan, parents and therapists alike should be aware of the "extinction burst" process that involves a temporary "burst" (i.e., increase) of disruptive/noncompliant behavior that initially occurs when the response to a behavior is modified. This can understandably, yet also mistakenly, be viewed as a child's poor response to the plan and lead parents to discontinue such efforts. This also can have the adverse effect of further entrenchment in the maladaptive beliefs about the child's need to engage in symmetry/ordering symptoms and incapacity to cope. Thus, for behavior modification to be successful, consistent implementation of a structured plan through this process is crucial. Of course, therapists must also consider the function and severity of the child's symptoms as well as rewards and consequences that will effectively promote behavior change when developing a plan to foster its success. A behavior modification plan may target any of the following goals: (1) the youth's participation in exposures; (2) ritual prevention adherence; (3) goals toward eliminating family accommodations; and (4) use of established coping skills to manage emotions. These are considered the child's "earning power" toward incentives. Parents at the same time are taught specific parental response strategies (e.g., direct commands, active ignoring, praise, time out, job grounding) to shape their child's compliance.

Several other strategies have proven beneficial in encouraging youth's participation in CBT. One strategy involves externalizing the child's OCD by giving it a name (e.g., March & Mulle, 1998). This allows a separation of OCD from the child, empowers his or her ability to "take on" OCD, and offers a language for the family to discuss symptoms. One family in our clinic chose to call the daughter's OCD "Mr. Bossy Pants." She was able to recognize OCD and employ ERP to challenge (i.e., "boss back") Mr. Bossy Pants when she felt the need to turn in the opposite direction to "even out" this experience. Older youth may not want to name their OCD; externalizing, nonetheless, can be helpful (e.g., teen versus "OCD").

Another strategy for promoting active engagement in treatment is to start with minor modifications to ritual prevention. As in the case of ordering rituals and rigid routines, adolescents may start by adding in or removing one step or changing the order in which steps are completed (i.e., "messing it up"), rather than eliminating the entire ritual. This can increase confidence in their ability to make greater changes over time. In the case of magical thinking, it may be useful to start with a mock exposure or experiment. An example was an adolescent male who feared that his mother would die if he did not engage in behaviors to maintain symmetry (e.g., pulling his socks up to the same point). We identified a separate behavior that he paired with the idea of his mother finding a $100 bill in the community to test out the validity of his beliefs. Corrective information from this experiment enhanced his readiness and confidence to proceed with active ERP targeting the anxiety-provoking triggers.

Consistent with other subtypes of OCD, therapists should assess both overt and covert forms of avoidance and ritualizing, including subtle mental rituals or physical acts to achieve symmetry and order. Further, it should be explained to patients that subtle avoidance and ritualizing interfere with the modification of obsessive-compulsive symptoms, and therefore patients should be encouraged to communicate with parents and therapists if they notice such symptoms occurring. Such awareness is also important to relapse prevention. Youth who can more readily recognize OCD symptoms can in turn "catch" these opportunities to apply CBT/ERP in the moment and promote long-term maintenance of gains. Additionally, families who understand the nature of OCD and how to make ERP a "lifestyle" can better manage lapses, even when the type of symptoms experienced by the patient shifts over time.

References

Abramowitz, J. S., Franklin, M. E., Schwartz, S. A. & Furr, J. M. (2003). Symptom presentation and outcome of cognitive-behavioral therapy for obsessive-compulsive disorder. *Journal of Consulting & Clinical Psychology, 71*, 1049–1057.

Alonso, P, Menchon, J. M., Mataix-Cols, D., Pifarre, J., Urretavizcaya, M., Crespo, J. M., … Vallejo, J. (2004). Perceived parental rearing style in obsessive-compulsive disorder: Relation to symptom dimensions. *Psychiatry Research, 127*, 267–278.

American Psychiatric Association, DSM-5 Task Force. (2013). *Diagnostic and statistical manual of mental disorders: DSM-5*. Arlington, VA: American Psychiatric Publishing.

Auyeung, B., Baron-Cohen, S., Wheelwright, S., & Allison, C. (2008). The Autism Spectrum Quotient: Children's Version (AQ-Child). *Journal of Autism and Developmental Disorders, 38*, 1230–1240.

Ball, S. G., Baer, L., & Otto, M. W. (1996). Symptom subtypes of obsessive-compulsive disorder in behavioral treatment studies: A quantitative review. *Behaviour Research and Therapy, 34*, 47–51.

Baron-Cohen, S. (1989). Do autistic children have obsessions and compulsions? *British Journal of Clinical Psychology, 28*, 193–200.

Baron-Cohen, S., Hoekstra, R. A., Knickmeyer, R., & Wheelwright, S. (2006). The Autism-Spectrum Quotient (AQ): Adolescent version. *Journal of Autism and Developmental Disorders, 36*, 343–350.

Baron-Cohen, S., Wheelwright, S., Skinner, R., Martin, J., & Clubley, E. (2001). The autism-spectrum quotient (AQ): Evidence from Asperger syndrome/high-functioning autism, males and females, scientists and mathematicians. *Journal of Autism and Developmental Disorders, 31*, 5–17.

Bloch, M. H., Landeros-Weisenberger, A., Rosario, M. C., Pittenger, C., & Leckman, J. F. (2008). Meta-analysis of the symptom structure of obsessive-compulsive disorder. *American Journal of Psychiatry, 165*, 1532–1542.

Cardona, F., Romano, A., Bollea, L., & Chiarotti, F. (2004). Psychopathological problems in children affected by tic disorders: Study on a large Italian population. *European Child and Adolescent Psychiatry, 13*, 166–171.

Castellanos, F. X. (1998). Tic disorders and obsessive compulsive disorder. In B. T. Walsh (Ed.), *Child Psychopharmacology* (pp. 1–28). Arlington, VA: American Psychiatric Association.

Cath, D. C., Ran, N., Smit, J. H., van Balkom, A. J., & Comijs, H. C. (2008). Symptom overlap between autism spectrum disorder, generalized social anxiety disorder and obsessive-compulsive disorder in adults: A preliminary case-controlled study. *Psychopathology, 41*, 101–110.

Coles, M., Heimberg, R., Frost, R., & Steketee, G. (2005). Not just right experiences and obsessive-compulsive features: Experimental and self-monitoring perspectives. *Behaviour Research and Therapy, 43*, 153–167.

Delorme, R., Bille, A., Betancur, C., Mathieu, F., Chabane, N., Mouren-Simeoni, M. C., & Leboyer, M. (2006). Exploratory analysis of obsessive compulsive symptom dimensions in children and adolescents: A prospective follow-up study. *BMC Psychiatry, 6*, 1–10.

Denys, D., Burger, H., van Megen, H., de Geus, F., & Westenberg, H. (2003). A score for predicting response to pharmacotherapy in obsessive-compulsive disorder. *International Clinical Psychopharmacology, 18*, 315–322.

Eapen, V., Robertson, M., Alsobrook, J. P., & Pauls, D. L. (1997). Obsessive compulsive symptoms in Gilles de la Tourette syndrome and obsessive compulsive disorder: Differences by diagnosis and family history. *American Journal of Medical Genetics, 74*, 432–438.

Evans, D., Leckman, J. F., Carter, A., Reznick, J. S., Henshaw, D., King, R. A., & Pauls, D. (1997). Ritual, habit, and perfectionism: The prevalence and development of compulsive-like behavior in young children. *Child Development, 68*, 58–68.

Fischer-Terworth, C., & Probst, P. (2009). Obsessive-compulsive phenomena and symptoms in Asperger's disorder and high-functioning autism: An evaluative literature review. *Life Span and Disability, 7*, 5–27.

Foa, E. B., Liebowitz, M. R., Kozak, M. J., Davies, S., Campeas, R., Franklin, M. E., … Tu, X. (2005). Randomized, placebo-controlled trial of exposure and ritual prevention, clomipramine, and their combination in the treatment of obsessive-compulsive disorder. *American Journal of Psychiatry, 162*(1), 151–161.

Freeman, J., Sapyta, J., Garcia, A., Compton, S., Khanna, M., Flessner, C., ... Franklin, M. (2014). Family-based treatment of early childhood obsessive-compulsive disorder: The Pediatric Obsessive-Compulsive Disorder Treatment Study for Young Children (POTS Jr) – a randomized clinical trial. *JAMA Psychiatry, 71*, 689–698.

Gilbert, A. R., Akkal, D., Almeida, J. R., Mataix-Cols, D., Kalas, C., Devlin, B., ... Phillips, M. L. (2009). Neural correlates of symptom dimensions in pediatric obsessive-compulsive disorder: A functional magnetic resonance imaging study. *Journal of the American Academy of Child and Adolescent Psychiatry, 48*, 936–944.

Ivarsson, T., & Melin, K. (2008). Autism spectrum traits in children and adolescents with obsessive-compulsive disorder. *Journal of Anxiety Disorders, 22*, 969–978.

Ivarsson, T., & Valderhaug, R. (2006). Symptom patterns in children and adolescents with obsessive-compulsive disorder. *Behaviour Research and Therapy, 44*, 1105–1116.

Kazdin, A. (2013). *The everyday parenting toolkit: The Kazdin method for easy, step-by-step, lasting change for you and your child.* New York Houghton Mifflin Harcourt.

Kichuk, S. A., Torres, A. R., Fontenelle, L. F., Rosário, M. C., Shavitt, R. G., Miguel, E. C., Pittenger, C. & Bloch, M. H. (2013). Symptom dimensions are associated with age of onset and clinical course of obsessive-compulsive disorder. *Progress in Neuro-Psychopharmacology and Biological Psychiatry, 44*, 233–239.

Labad, J., Mencho, J. M., Alonso, P., Segalas, C., Jimenez, S., Jaurrieta, N., ... Vallego, J. (2008). Gender differences in obsessive-compulsive symptom dimensions. *Depression and Anxiety, 25*, 832–838.

Landeros-Weisenberger, A., Bloch, M. H., Kelmendi, B., Wegner, R., Nudel, J., Dombrowski, P., ... Coric, V. (2010). Dimensional predictors of response to SRI pharmacotherapy in obsessive–compulsive disorder. *Journal of Affective Disorders, 121*, 175–179.

Lawrence, N. S., Wooderson, S., Mataix-Cols, D., David, R., Speckens, A., & Phillips, M. L. (2006). Decision making and set shifting impairments are associated with distinct symptoms dimensions in obsessive-compulsive disorder. *Neuropsychology, 20*, 409–419.

Leckman, J. F., McDougle, C. J., Pauls, D. L., Peterson, B. S., Grice, D. E., King, R. A., ... Rasmussen, S. A. (2000). Tic-related versus non-tic-related obsessive-compulsive disorder. In W. K. Goodman, M. V. Rudorter, & J. D. Maser (Eds.), *Obsessive-compulsive disorder: Contemporary issues in treatment* (pp. 43–68). Mahwah, NJ: Lawrence Erlbaum.

Leckman, J. F., Walker, D. E., Goodman, W. K., Pauls, D. L., & Cohen. D. J. (1994). "Just right" perceptions associated with compulsive behavior in Tourette's syndrome. *American Journal of Psychiatry, 151*, 675–680.

Leonard, H. L., Lenane, M. C., Swedo, S. E., Rettew, D. C., Gershon, E. S., & Rapaport, J. L. (1992). Tics and Tourette's disorder: A 2–7 year follow-up of 54 obsessive compulsive children. *American Journal of Psychiatry, 149*, 1244–1251.

Mansueto, C. S., & Keuler, D. J. (2005). Tic or compulsion?: It's Tourettic OCD. *Behavior Modification, 29*, 784–799.

March, J. S., & Mulle, K. (1998). *OCD in children and adolescents: A cognitive-behavioral treatment manual.* New York: Guilford Press.

Masi, G., Millepiedi, S., Perugi, G., Pfanner, C., Berloffa, S., Pari, C., ... Akiskal, H. S. (2010). A naturalistic exploratory study of the impact of demographic, phenotypic, and comorbid features in pediatric obsessive-compulsive disorder. *Psychopathology, 43*, 69–78.

Mataix-Cols, D., Nakatani, E., Micali, N., & Heyman, I. (2008). Structure of obsessive-compulsive symptoms in pediatric OCD. *Journal of the American Academy of Child and Adolescent Psychiatry, 47*, 773–778.

Mataix-Cols, D., Rosário-Campos, M. C., & Leckman, J. F. (2005). A multidimensional model of obsessive-compulsive disorder. *American Journal of Psychiatry, 162*, 228–238.

McDougle, C., Kresch, L., Goodman, W. K., & Naylor, S. T. (1995). A case controlled study of repetitive thoughts and behavior in adults with autistic disorder and obsessive compulsive disorder. *American Journal of Psychiatry, 152*, 772–777.

McKay, D., Piacentini, J., Greisberg, S., Graae, F., Jaffer, M., & Miller, J. (2006). The structure of childhood obsessions and compulsions: Dimensions in an outpatient sample. *Behaviour Research and Therapy, 44,* 137–146.

Nakatani, E., Krebs, G., Micali, N., Turner, C., Heyman, I., & Mataix-Cols, D. (2011). Children with very early onset obsessive-compulsive disorder: Clinical features and treatment outcome. *Journal of Child Psychology and Psychiatry, 52,* 1261–1268.

Nikolajsen, K. H., Nissen, J. B., & Thomsen, P. H. (2011). Obsessive-compulsive disorder in children and adolescents. Symptom dimensions in a naturalistic setting. *Nordic Journal of Psychiatry, 65,* 244–250.

Pediatric OCD Treatment Study (POTS) Team. (2004). Cognitive-behavioral therapy, sertraline, and their combination for children and adolescents with obsessive-compulsive disorder: The Pediatric OCD Treatment Study (POTS) randomized controlled trial. *Journal of the American Medical Association, 292*(16), 1969–1976.

Rachman, S., & Hodgson, R. J. (1980). *Obsessions and compulsions.* Englewood Cliffs, NJ: Prentice-Hall.

Radomsky, A. S., & Rachman, S. (2004). Symmetry, ordering and arranging compulsive behaviour. *Behaviour Research and Therapy, 42,* 893–913.

Rufer, M., Fricke, S., Moritz, S., Kloss, M., & Hand. I. (2006). Symptom dimensions in obsessive-compulsive disorder: Prediction of cognitive-behavior therapy outcome. *Acta Psychiatrica Scandinavica, 113,* 440–446.

Ruta, L., Mugno, D., D'Arrigo, V. G., Vitiello, B., & Mazzone, L. (2010). Obsessive-compulsive traits in children and adolescents with Asperger syndrome. *European Child and Adolescent Psychiatry, 19,* 17–24.

Rutter, M., Bailey, A., & Lord, C. (2003). *Social Communication Questionnaire.* Los Angeles, CA: Western Psychological Services.

Scahill, L., Riddle, M. A., McSwiggin-Hardin, M., Ort, S. I., King, R. A., Goodman, W. K., … Leckman, J. F. (1997). Children's Yale–Brown Obsessive Compulsive Scale: Reliability and validity. *Journal of the American Academy of Child and Adolescent Psychiatry, 36,* 844–852.

Selles, R. R., Storch, E. A., & Lewin, A. B. (2014). Variations in symptom prevalence and clinical correlates in younger versus older youth with obsessive-compulsive disorder. *Child Psychiatry and Human Development.* Retrieved from http://www.ncbi.nlm.nih.gov/pubmed/24549726.

Starcevic, V., & Brakoulias, V. (2008). Symptom subtypes of obsessive-compulsive disorder: Are they relevant for treatment? *Australian and New Zealand Journal of Psychiatry, 42,* 651–661.

Stewart, S. E., Rosario, M. C., Brown, T. A., Carter, A. S., Leckman, J. F., Sukhodolsky, D., … Pauls, D. L. (2007). Principal components analysis of obsessive-compulsive disorder symptoms in children and adolescents. *Biological Psychiatry, 61,* 285–291.

Storch, E. A., Lack, C., Merlo, L. J., Marien, W. E., Geffken, G. R., Grabill, K., … Goodman, W. K. (2007). Associations between miscellaneous symptoms and symptom dimensions: An examination of pediatric obsessive-compulsive disorder. *Behaviour Research and Therapy, 45,* 2593–2603.

Storch, E. A., Merlo, L. J., Larson, M. J., Bloss, C. S., Geffken, G. R., Jacob, M. L., … Goodman, W. K. (2008). Symptom dimensions and cognitive behavioural therapy outcome for pediatric obsessive-compulsive disorder. *Acta Psychiatrica Scandinavica, 117,* 67–75.

Summerfeldt, L.J. (2004). Understanding and treating incompleteness in obsessive-compulsive disorder. *Journal of Clinical Psychology, 60,* 1155–1168.

Summerfeldt, L. J. (2007). Treating incompleteness, ordering, and arranging concerns. In M. M. Antony, C. Purdon, & L. J. Summerfeldt (Eds.), *Psychological Treatment of Obsessive-Compulsive Disorder: Fundamentals and Beyond* (pp. 187–207). Washington, DC: American Psychological Association.

Summerfeldt, L. J., Richter, M. A., Antony, M. M., & Swinson, R. P. (1999). Symptom structure in obsessive-compulsive disorder: A confirmatory factor-analytic study. *Behaviour Research and Therapy, 37*, 297–311.

Valleni-Basile, L. A., Garrison, C. Z., Jackson, K. L., Waller, J. L., McKeown, R. E., Addy, C. L., & Cuffe, S. P. (1994). Frequency of obsessive-compulsive disorder in a community sample of young adolescents. *Journal of the American Academy of Child and Adolescent Psychiatry, 33*, 782–791.

Weidle, B., Melin, K., Drotz, E., Jozefiak, T., & Ivarsson, T. (2012). Preschool and current autistic symptoms in children and adolescents with obsessive-compulsive disorder. *Journal of Obsessive-Compulsive and Related Disorders, 1*, 168–174.

Worbe, Y., Mallet, L., Golmard, J., Behar, C., Durif, F., Jalenques, I., … Hartmann, A. (2010). Repetitive behaviors in patients with Gilles de la Tourette Syndrome: Tics, compulsions, or both? *PLoS One, 5*(9), e12959. doi: 10.1371/journal.pone.0012959.

Zandt, F., Prior, M., & Kyrios, M. (2007). Repetitive behaviour in children with high functioning autism and obsessive compulsive disorder. *Journal of Autism and Developmental Disorders, 37*, 251–259.

23

Repugnant Obsessions
Phenomenology, Etiology, and Treatment
David A. Clark and Catherine A. Hilchey

John, a 38-year-old father with two children, was first diagnosed with obsessive compulsive disorder (OCD) 15 years ago when he started having highly upsetting repugnant sexual obsessions that became so persistent that he could hardly think of anything else. His main obsession was an unrelenting self-doubt about his sexual impulses and whether he was sexually attracted to little girls. If he saw a prepubescent girl in person or was even exposed to the image of a little girl on television or in the media, he had the unwanted thought "I am noticing this little girl is cute; does this mean I'm sexually attracted to her?" The intrusion always took the form of a question like "is that little girl cute?" "do I find her physically attractive"?, or the obsession could be an assertion "she's a cute little girl." Immediately John was seized with anxiety, guilt and disgust. He became fixated on the thought, spending hours and sometimes days asking himself over and over whether he really did find the little girl attractive, and if he did find her attractive what did this mean about him as a person.

John would try to neutralize the obsession not through overt compulsions, but by reassuring himself that he was not physically attracted to little girls. Of course his underlying core fear was a concern that he might have unconscious pedophilic tendencies. This filled him with horror and disgust because of his moral outrage at the thought of causing harm to a child. John avoided female children as much as possible and would even avoid pictures, movies, or any other medium that depicted little girls. John was anxious in social or public situations, always vigilant to whether he might accidentally see a little girl and the obsessive thinking would start all over again. John had recently become more generally anxious, withdrawn, and dysphoric because of these obsessive episodes.

Over the years, John was treated with a variety of pharmacological agents, but with limited success. At the best of times, he experienced a reduction in anxiety, but his sexual obsession never disappeared completely. At the time of referral, John stated that now he was ready to try a cognitive-behavioral approach. Clinical history revealed that John had a solid adult heterosexual orientation, with no indication of actual attraction to children. In fact he had the extreme opposite reaction to children; he was anxious and avoidant of them because of a fear of triggering his obsessive thinking. The sexual obsession had a strong doubting element since John would obsessively question himself whether he really thought the little girl was physically attractive and

The Wiley Handbook of Obsessive Compulsive Disorders, Volume I, First Edition.
Edited by Jonathan S. Abramowitz, Dean McKay, and Eric A. Storch.
© 2017 John Wiley & Sons Ltd. Published 2017 by John Wiley & Sons Ltd.

whether there was anything sexual in his judgment of her appearance. Psychometric testing revealed mild depressive symptoms (Beck Depression Inventory-II = 13, Beck Anxiety Inventory Total = 10, Beck Hopelessness Score = 2). Only two current symptoms were endorsed on the Yale–Brown Obsessive Compulsive Scale, sexual obsessions with content involving children or incest and mental compulsions.

This case illustrates a special subtype of OCD called repugnant obsessions. Unwanted sexual, religious, and harm/aggression obsessions are usually categorized under this subtype. In this chapter we begin with a consideration of the phenomenology of repugnant obsessions and whether they are distinct from other types of obsessional content. We then discuss three theoretical accounts of repugnant obsessions that help to explain their pathogenesis. The chapter concludes with a focus on treatment issues, such as the status of empirical outcome research, issues of assessment and case conceptualization, and suggestions for specific treatment elements that should be included in cognitive behavior therapy for repugnant obsessions.

Phenomenology

Repugnant obsessions are known by various labels such as unacceptable/taboo thoughts, forbidden thoughts or "pure obsessions", and they refer to unwanted thoughts of harm, aggression, sex, or religion. Some have included somatic obsessions and checking compulsions within this symptom subtype (i.e., Bloch, Landeros-Weisenberger, Rosário, Pittenger, & Leckman, 2008). The term pure obsessional or "Pure-O" (OCD-UK, 2013), which refers to obsessions without overt compulsions, is often used in reference to repugnant obsessions (Insel, 1990; Rachman, 1971). Although this is entirely appropriate given that mental compulsions are most frequent in repugnant obsessions (Sibrava, Boisseau, Mancebo, Eisen, & Rasmussen, 2011; Williams et al., 2011), the term "pure" is misleading since mental neutralization and reassurance seeking, often seen in pure obsessions, serve the same function as overt behavioral compulsions.

The content of repugnant obsessions tends to revolve around themes of significant violation of moral principles or standards of personal integrity and so often concern issues of (a) uncontrolled aggression, harm, or injury toward others, (b) violation of religious or ethical convictions, or (c) forbidden, even disgusting, sexual thoughts or images. Examples are thoughts of stabbing your much-loved child with a knife, swerving your car into oncoming traffic, engaging in a disgusting sexual act, running over a pedestrian, blaspheming God or the Prophet, failing to fully confess sin, and the like. Williams and colleagues describe a special type of repugnant obsession called sexual-orientation fears in which the individual fears (a) an unwanted change in sexual orientation, (b) that others might perceive he is homosexual, or (c) that he has latent homosexual desires (Williams, Crozier, & Powers, 2011). They note that individuals with homosexual OCD experience genuine anxiety and distress, not pleasure, when they have doubtful thoughts about their sexual orientation, and so should not be confused as having conflicts over their sexual orientation or an underlying wishful attraction to the same sex. Based on a re-analysis of the DSM-IV Field Trial for OCD (Foa & Kozak, 1995), Williams and Farris (2011) found that 8% of the sample had current obsessions about sexual orientation, with presence of sexual-orientation obsessions associated with significantly greater intensity, interference, and avoidance. Although sexual-orientation obsessions may respond to standard exposure/response prevention treatment (Williams et al., 2011), there is so little research on this type of obsessional thinking that no definitive conclusions can be reached about treatment efficacy at this time.

Prevalence and Cultural Differences

Although once considered rare, more recent studies indicate that repugnant obsessions occur in 20–30% of OCD samples (Moulding, Aardema, & O'Connor, 2014). In the DSM-IV Field Trial, fear of harming self or others was the primary obsession in 23.6% of the sample, with religious and sexual obsessions trailing at 5.9% and 5.5%, respectively (Foa & Kozak, 1995). If we broaden our inquiry to include individuals with lifetime OCD who report any repugnant obsessions, whether they are primary or secondary symptoms, the frequency jumps to 50–60% (Pinto et al., 2008). However, in nonclinical samples unwanted intrusive thoughts of harm, sex, and religion are relatively infrequent (Radomsky et al., 2014). Clearly, then, repugnant obsessions are more pervasive than first thought, at least in OCD samples.

Cultural differences have a significant effect on the prevalence and content of repugnant obsessions. In a large review study, religious and aggressive obsessions were more prominent in Brazilian and Middle Eastern OCD samples (Fontelle, Mendlowicz, Marques, & Versiani, 2004). Religious obsessions are much more prevalent in countries with strong religious values, such as Egypt or Iran (Ghassemzadeh et al., 2002; Okasha, Saad, Khalil, Dawla, & Yehia, 1994). Strict religious adherence can influence the form and content of repugnant obsessions, with devoted Muslims and ultra-orthodox Jews with OCD more concerned about contamination and impurity (see Ciarrocchi, 1995). An extension downward to nonclinical individuals reveals that highly religious individuals have more frequent unwanted religious, but not more sexual or harm intrusive thoughts than the nonreligious (Altin, Clark, & Karanci, 2007). Research and treatment of repugnant obsessions in OCD patients must be particularly cognizant of the role of cultural factors in the symptom presentation.

Clinical Severity, Comorbidity, and Symptom Differentiation

One of the striking features of repugnant obsessions is their egodystonicity (Purdon, 2004). Egodystonicity is the extent that the theme of an obsession is inconsistent or in conflict with a person's self-view as reflected in his or her core values, ideals, or moral tenets (Clark, 2004). For example, repeated thoughts or images of molesting a child would be highly egodystonic for a person who places high value on protecting the innocence of children and upholding the rule of law. Such a thought would be egosyntonic or consistent with the moral values of a convicted pedophile. Thus, the egodystonicity of a thought is a defining feature of its repugnancy, and so is critical for differentiating unacceptable or taboo obsessions from other types of repetitive thought (Purdon, 2004). In clinical and nonclinical samples, moral-based obsessions or unwanted intrusive thoughts are rated as more egodystonic (Belloch, Roncero & Perpiná, 2012; Purdon et al., 2007). As discussed below, egodystonicity plays an important role in self-construct models of repugnant obsessions.

There is some evidence that repugnant obsessions are associated with greater clinical severity, higher co-morbidity, and poorer treatment outcome (see Moulding et al., 2014). Based on a principal components analysis of the YBOCS Symptom Checklist, Brakoulias and colleagues found that higher scores on the YBOCS unacceptable/taboo dimension (i.e., aggression, sex, and religious thoughts) were associated with greater obsessionality, distress, time spent on obsessions, hostility, prior treatment, being male, and a past diagnosis of nonalcohol substance dependence (Brakoulias et al., 2013). Likewise, Williams and Farris (2011) found positive correlations between presence of sexual-orientation obsessions and time spent on obsessions, interference and distress. Comorbidity is another indicator of clinical severity, and once again, repugnant obsessions are associated with more comorbidity for anxiety, depression, and alcohol dependence than other OCD symptom subtypes (Hasler et al., 2005).

Given the heterogeneity of OCD, numerous studies have examined whether individuals with repugnant obsessions might constitute a distinct subtype of OCD. A meta-analysis of 21 studies involving 5,124 participants concluded that four factors reliably emerged from factor analyses of the YBOCS Symptom Checklist (Bloch et al., 2008). One of these factors was labeled "forbidden thoughts" and included aggression, sexual, religious, and somatic obsessions, and checking compulsions. Generally, these analyses tend to find that aggressive, sexual, and religious obsessions load together quite consistently, whereas there is less agreement on whether somatic obsessions and checking also define this symptom dimension (i.e., Pinto et al., 2008). Miscellaneous compulsions like mental rituals and reassurance-seeking sometimes load on an unacceptable thoughts dimension (e.g., Abramowitz, Franklin, Schwartz, & Furr, 2003). In sum there is sufficient empirical evidence to conclude that repugnant obsessions do form a distinct symptom subtype of OCD.

Conceptual Models of Repugnant Obsessions

A specific theory of repugnant obsessions has not yet been formulated. Accordingly, we consider three perspectives that have particular relevance to the topic at hand: cognitive appraisal, self-construal, and the autogenous vs reactive distinction. In addition we discuss O'Connor and associates inferential confusion theory under the cognitive appraisal theory of obsessions (Aardema & O'Connor, 2003).

Cognitive Appraisal of Repugnancy

Rachman (2003) provides the most succinct account of the cognitive appraisal theory of obsessions, based on Salkovskis' (1985) cognitive-behavioral formulation of OCD and D. M. Clark's (1986) theory of panic. Rachman argues that obsessions have their origin in the universal experience of unwanted intrusive thoughts. The core pathologic process responsible for the escalation from normal intrusion to clinical obsession is "the misinterpretation of the intrusive thoughts as being very important, personally significant, revealing, and threatening or even catastrophic ..." for the individual (Rachman, 2003: 14). The catastrophic misinterpretation can give rise to additional fears about the consequences of the obsession. The mere occurrence of the intrusion, as well as its content, feed into the faulty threat interpretation. Cognitive biases such as an inflated sense of personal responsibility and thought–action fusion (TAF) increase the likelihood that unwanted intrusions will be misinterpreted in a catastrophic manner (Rachman, 2003). (Rachman and Shafran [1998] define TAF as the belief that obsessional thinking increases the probability of a feared event [i.e., TAF-Likelihood] or that the obsessional thought is morally equivalent to the forbidden action [i.e., TAF- Morality.) Other dysfunctional beliefs are also implicated in the pathogenesis of obsessions such as need to control (i.e., overvaluing the importance of exerting complete control over intrusive thoughts), overimportance of thoughts (i.e., the mere occurrence of unwanted thoughts implies their importance), and intolerance of uncertainty (i.e., that certainty is a necessity and unpredictability or ambiguity must be avoided) (Taylor, 2002).

Rachman (2003) noted that attempts to neutralize the obsession or diminish its anticipated effects are an additional element in the cognitive behavioral model of obsessions. Neutralization can take a variety of forms from compulsive rituals to reassurance seeking and self-rationalization. However, neutralization is difficult, exhausting, and short-lived at best. The obsession and its associated discomfort return, often within a few minutes in severe OCD. Efforts to control the obsession are bound to fail, thereby increasing the salience of the obsessional thought. Clark (2004) noted that faulty appraisals of failed thought control can also contribute to the escalation of the obsession.

We can use the case example presented at the beginning of this chapter to illustrate how the cognitive appraisal model would explain the rise of repugnant obsessions. John's repugnant obsession occurs as the unwanted intrusive thought "what an attractive little girl." At the outset we note that having the thought "what a cute little girl" is quite normal. Who has not seen a child and thought that the child was physically attractive (i.e., cute)? In fact, we might even say to a parent "your child looks so cute," knowing the parent would consider this a compliment. So the thought "what a cute little girl" begins as a perfectly normal intrusive thought. But John did not interpret the thought as normal or complimentary. John misinterpreted the origins of the intrusion, questioning whether it meant he was sexually attracted to the child. Of course, child molestation was as repugnant to John as it is to society at large, thus his misinterpretation of the intrusion entailed a catastrophic implication. Several cognitive biases and faulty beliefs accentuated the misinterpretation such as inflated responsibility ("I must prevent any possibility of harming a child"), TAF-Likelihood ("The more I think about physical attraction, the more I am likely to commit this terrible crime"), overimportance of thought ("The fact that I am repeatedly thinking about little girls means there is something wrong with me"), and need to control ("I must stop thinking about the physical attractiveness of children"). John tried to neutralize the obsession by avoiding any situations where he might see a child, reassuring himself he was not physically attracted to little girls, and rationalizing the occurrence of the thought. However, his inability to control the obsession became the overwhelming proof there was something terribly wrong with him, that he had weak mental control. John worried that he might eventually snap; that the anxiety and distress caused by the obsession would be too much to bear. He was not concerned about harming a child because he was repulsed by such a thought. However, he was concerned that the obsession would cause a "nervous breakdown" if it did not stop. In sum, John's cognitive biases and faulty beliefs, along with failed neutralization efforts, led to the catastrophic misinterpretation that the "cute little girl" thought was a significant personal threat.

Very few empirical studies have investigated the cognitive basis of repugnant obsessions. Williams, Mugno, Franklin, and Faber (2013) noted that individuals with unacceptable (repugnant) obsessions often appraise their thoughts as overly important and dangerous, and so devote considerable mental effort in attempting to suppress the obsession. Brakoulias and associates (2013) found that higher scores on the unacceptable/taboo dimension of the YBOCS was associated with stronger beliefs in the importance of controlling unwanted thoughts as measured by the 44-item Obsessive Beliefs Questionnaire (OBQ-44) (OCCWG, 2003). Another study found that religious obsessions were correlated with a broad range of dysfunctional beliefs (e.g., overimportance of thought, need to control, inflated responsibility and threat estimation), but sexual obsessions were only associated with overimportance and control of thoughts (Siev, Steketee, Fama, & Wilhelm, 2011). Finally, we found indirect support for the cognitive appraisal model in two studies in which highly religious nonclinical individuals reported more guilt-related intrusive thoughts and greater endorsement of beliefs about the threat, inflated responsibility, and control of unwanted intrusions (Hale & Clark, 2013; Inozu, Karanci, & Clark, 2012).

O'Connor and colleagues propose an alternative cognitive model of obsessions they termed the inference-based approach to OCD (O'Connor, Aardema, & Pélissier, 2005). They argue that the core cognitive process in the pathogenesis of obsessions is not the faulty appraisal of unwanted intrusive thoughts, but rather that obsessions involve a problematic inference in which the individual confuses imagined possibilities with reality (Moulding et al., 2014). This inferential confusion gives rise to doubt in which the individual focuses on the possibility of the imagined state despite contradictory real-life evidence (O'Connor et al., 2005). Several erroneous inferential processes are thought to give rise to inferential confusion, such as category errors, selective use of out-of-context facts, inverse inference, and the like. In this model, intrusions are the product of inferential confusion and doubt. It is these processes, rather than the occurrence of intrusions and their appraisals, that are key to the etiology of obsessions. In our case example, then, John considers himself a caring, conscientious, and morally upright individual. Part of this self-view is never causing harm to children, but then John notices a child and wonders if he is having "bad thoughts about children." He then confuses this question, the possibility of a bad thought, with reality "this means I might be a child molester" even though there is no external evidence that he would ever harm children. So John is confusing the possibility ("any adult could be capable of harming a child") with a horrific reality ("I could be a latent child molester"). Inference-based therapy for obsessions differs from appraisal-based CBT, adopting a singular focus on correcting the primary inferential confusion that underlies obsessional thinking.

Self-Construal Theory

Recently several researchers within the cognitive appraisal perspective have emphasized the importance of self-perceptions in the etiology of obsessions (see Moulding et al., 2014, for review). The role of the self in the pathogenesis of obsessions has been examined from a number of different perspectives, which reflect the complex and varied nature of selfhood theory and research.

Bhar and Kyrios (2007) proposed that the problem in OCD is an *ambivalent self-view*. Based on Guidano and Liotti's (1983) concept of self-ambivalence, Bhar and Kyrios argued that individuals with OCD may be especially prone to interpret egodystonic intrusions (i.e., repugnant thoughts) as meaningful threats to valued aspects of the self, whereas nonobsessional individuals with a more established self-view would reject such self-recriminating or contradictory thinking in order to protect their positive sense of self-worth. Moreover, self-ambivalent individuals are thought to hold contradictory and opposing self-views so an unwanted intrusion becomes evidence for the negative as opposed to positive self-view. In a study of self-ambivalence in clinical and nonclinical samples, Bhar and Krios (2007) found that both self-worth ambivalence and moral ambivalence were significant unique predictors of OC symptoms and beliefs, but there was no significant difference in self-ambivalence scores between the OCD and anxious control samples. So self-ambivalence may be relevant but not specific to obsessional concerns.

Offering a slightly different perspective on self-perception in OCD, Doron and Kyrios (2005) proposed that selfhood vulnerability in OCD is characterized by a self-concept that involves relatively few domains of competence. Intrusive thoughts representing failure in these "sensitive domains" threaten an individual's self-worth and so have processing priority in terms of heightened attention, evaluation, and associated distress (Moulding et al., 2014). The presence of these sensitive domains of competence combined with beliefs that the world is dangerous but controllable constitutes an underlying vulnerability to misinterpret mental intrusions and their control in a pathologic fashion. As predicted, Doron, Kyrios, and Moulding (2007) found that sensitivity in the moral and job-competence domains was related to OC symptoms and beliefs in a nonclinical sample. Overall, there is emerging evidence that low moral self-perception, in particular, may be relevant in the etiology of OCD. As discussed below, this research could be especially important in understanding the pathogenesis of repugnant obsessions.

Another approach to selfhood processes in OCD is based on Crocker and Wolfe's (2001) self-worth contingency theory. Here global self-esteem is considered contingent on perceived success or failure in seven domain-specific categories, such as family support, appearance, competition with others, approval from others, and the like. Research on self-worth contingency in OC relevant domains have found that perceived failure in maintaining moral standards is associated with OC symptoms (García-Soriano, Clark, Belloch, del Palacio, & Castañeiras, 2012), although this findings was not replicated in an OCD sample (García-Soriano & Belloch, 2012).

Finally Aardema and O'Connor (2007) offered a perspective on selfhood themes in obsessions that is linked to their inference-based theory of OCD. They begin by noting that obsessional concerns center on a possible cognitive or mental state in which the person with obsessions makes an inferential error that assumes the cognitive intrusion (obsession) is an accurate reflection of the self. It is noted that we all construct a narrative about ourselves that is an attempt to explain our behavior and the nonconscious processes that operate outside conscious awareness. However, what is unique in obsessional states is that discordant self-representations play an integral role in self-representation. This occurs because individuals with OCD commit a number of reasoning errors that renders thoughts of a possible self into a reality. A negative self-representation that involves a possibility (e.g., "What if I lose control and harm my children?") becomes confused with a reality (e.g., "Because I am thinking this way,

I must be capable of harming my children"), so the individual acts as if the possible were a real probability. The individual then becomes immersed in "a fear of who they could be or might become …" (Aardema & O'Connor, 2007: 191). In the obsessional sense of self, the individual is heavily invested in the "self-as-could-be" and less invested in the self-as-is. The end result is a strong sense of self-doubt and a distrust of the self-as-is (i.e., the actual or real self). In sum, the obsession is always objectively discordant with the actual self (i.e., egodystonic) because it is based on a faulty inference involving a fear of a nonexistent self (Aardema and O'Connor, 2007). Recently, a Fear of Self Questionnaire was developed that showed strong correlations with OC symptoms, beliefs and inferential confusion in nonclinical samples (Aardema et al., 2013).

The study of selfhood processes in OCD is in its infancy and a variety of perspectives have been offered. It could be that the most distal contributor to these forbidden thoughts is an inadequately formed sense of self, or self-ambivalence, that is rooted in early developmental experiences. In such individuals, learning experiences could contribute to sensitivities in the moral self-domain or lead to a perceived lack of self-contingent moral attainment. Within this context a distrusted sense of self develops, along with a predilection to construct a self-representational narrative in which the possibility of a feared state of mind is erroneously construed as a real probability and so takes precedence in self-representation. In our case example, John has doubts about his moral integrity. Noticing the physical appearance of a child is misconstrued as the possibility that he is a child molester. With a heightened sensitivity to failure in moral integrity, John commits errors in deductive reasoning, constructing a self-representational narrative in which the nonexistent act of molesting children becomes a real probability rather than a feared imagined possibility. In time, John acquires an obsessional sense of self in which "the self-as-could be" becomes the defining feature of his self-identity (Aardema & O'Connor, 2007).

Autogenous Obsessions

Lee and Kwon (2003) proposed that obsessions could be categorized into two subtypes, autogenous and reactive, which were thought to differ in evoking stimuli, content, and cognitive processing. The autogenous subtype bears a close resemblance to repugnant obsessions, consisting of unwanted intrusive thoughts of harm/aggression, impulsive acting out, embarrassment, and unacceptable sexual activities. The reactive obsessions consist of doubts about mistakes, dirt, and contamination.

Since Lee and Kwon's (2003) autogenous category applies to repugnant obsessions, their research does have relevance to the topic at hand. It is evident that obsessions with a mainly internal origin are qualitatively different from obsessions with an external referent (e.g., Lee, Kwon, Kwon, & Telch, 2005). This distinction appears to be associated with different etiological and phenomenological characteristics, and could have important treatment implications. Moreover, it is clear that the autogenous/reactive differentiation is relevant in both clinical and nonclinical samples, supporting the notion of a continuum between "normal" and abnormal obsessions. We might also expect autogenous and reactive intrusions to have a different selfhood profile, although the only study to investigate this possibility found no difference between the two subtypes. In the end, support for considering repugnant obsessions a unique subtype of OCD, worthy of a distinct case conceptualization and treatment protocol, can be found in Lee and Kwon's research.

Treatment Outcome

Several reviewers have noted that pharmacotherapy and exposure response prevention (ERP) may be less effective in the treatment of repugnant obsessions than other OCD subtypes (e.g., Starcevric & Brakoulias, 2008; Williams et al., 2013). However, the findings for ERP treatment of repugnant obsessions are not uniformly dismal. Abramowitz and colleagues did not find a significant treatment outcome for their cluster of participants with unacceptable/taboo obsessions (Abramowitz et al., 2003). Several reasons have been cited for the longer and possibly less encouraging outcomes for repugnant obsessions. ERP tends to focus on overt compulsions, which is less common in repugnant obsessions. It may be harder to use exposure because repugnant obsessions are a threat to the individual's self-view (Moulding et al., 2014). As discussed previously, repugnant obsessions can play an integral role in self-definition and so become fused with exaggerated beliefs and appraisals of significance and need to control. It can be especially difficult for such individuals to relinquish their control over the obsession, which is fundamental to the response prevention component of ERP. Consequently, it has been suggested that cognitive interventions might be better suited to the treatment of obsessions without overt compulsions more generally, and repugnant obsessions specifically (Rachman, 2003; Williams et al., 2011). Likewise, Lee and colleagues (2005) concluded that autogenous obsessions might respond better to a cognitive approach than to ERP because of the absence of external target stimuli.

Only a handful of treatment outcome trials of CBT for obsessions without overt compulsions have been reported (e.g., Freeston et al., 1997), with few based on repugnant obsessions alone. Collectively, these studies suggest that pharmacotherapy and standard ERP may be of some benefit for this presentation of OCD, but they are clearly not the optimal treatment protocol for repugnant obsessions. Psychological treatments that emphasize cognitive interventions are promising, but the significant improvement is only seen in 40–65% of individuals who complete therapy. Some data even suggest that the inclusion of ERP could detract from the effectiveness of CBT for repugnant obsessions. Whatever the case, there is obviously considerable room for improvement in CBT treatment of repugnant obsessions. In the remainder of this chapter we consider several avenues in which CBT case conceptualization and treatment of repugnant obsessions might be modified to improvement treatment effectiveness.

Cognitive Behavioral Case Formulation

Over the years much has been written about assessment and case formulation of obsessions from a cognitive-behavioral perspective (e.g., Clark, 2004; Rachman, 2003; Wilhelm & Steketee, 2006). These sources should be consulted when developing a treatment plan for repugnant obsessions. In this section we highlight several constructs that are specific to repugnant obsessions that should be included in the case formulation. Table 23.1 summarizes the seven features of repugnant obsessions that the CBT practitioner should consider when developing a case formulation and treatment plan.

Table 23.1 Specific constructs in the case conceptualization of repugnant obsessions

Construct	Explanation
Concealment	Given the overimportance and self-representational significance of the repugnant thoughts and images, individuals will be reluctant to admit to their occurrence.
Egodystonicity	The extent that the obsession contradicts, or is at least inconsistent with, valued selfhood domains and therefore represents a threat to self-representation (Purdon et al., 2007).
Thought–action fusion: morality	The extent that the mere occurrence of the obsession is as morally reprehensible as acting on the obsession (Shafran & Rachman, 2004).
Importance/ control of thoughts	The belief that the mere occurrence of the obsession confers it with personal significance that necessitates heightened mental control effort.
Reasoning errors	Errors that result in an inferential confusion in which an imagined negative possible self is assumed to represent real aspects of the actual self (Aardema & O'Connor, 2007).
Heightened selfhood sensitivity	A general ambivalence or distrust in the self coupled with negative evaluation in certain sensitive self domains such as moral virtue.
Feared self	The extent that self-representation involves self-relevant qualities that the person does not want to possess; that represent a threat or danger to personal integrity.

Concealment

Purdon (2004) emphasized the importance of obtaining a full description of the obsession content. However, given the highly distressing, repulsive nature of repugnant obsessions, many clients try to conceal their obsessional concerns from others. They can also be very reluctant to disclose their repugnant obsessions to their therapist (Newth & Rachman, 2001). This is understandable since individuals believe their repugnant thoughts represent significant, albeit highly negative, aspects of the self and that therapists have an obligation to break confidentiality if they believe the person represents a danger to self or others (Purdon, 2004). Thus, it is incumbent on the cognitive behavioral therapist to build trust early in therapy and to conduct a risk assessment of danger to self and others. Once the therapist is confident that the obsessions are egodystonic and the client poses no danger to others, then efforts should be made to encourage full disclosure of the obsession content. This can be done in a gradual fashion, recognizing that the mere mention of the repugnant obsession can be anxiety-provoking for the individual. In our experience, the therapist can begin by referring to the obsession in general terms (e.g., the "sexual thought," or the "blasphemous image"). Over time discussion of the obsession becomes more detailed and graphic, which acts as a type of cognitive exposure to the obsession.

In his treatment manual on obsessions, Rachman (2003) describes a therapeutic use of concealment. He suggests that the therapist ask a client if he told anyone about his obsession. If yes, then the therapist questions whether the friend's subsequent behavior changed toward the client, and if the client had a friend who disclosed the obsession, would he change his behavior toward the friend. It is expected that the individual will deny any behavioral change with disclosure, which provides disconfirming evidence of the personal meaningfulness of the obsession. Individuals with repugnant obsessions will vary greatly in their level of concealment. CBT will be sabotaged early in treatment if a therapist is too confrontational with a high conceal-ment client. Thus, it is imperative to determine the role of concealment early in the therapy process.

Egodystonicity

One of the most critical features of repugnant obsessions is their level of egodystonic-ity. How inconsistent is the obsessional content with the person's sense of self as reflected in the client's core values, ideals and moral attributes (Clark, 2004)? Purdon and colleagues (2007) stated that an egodystonic thought is perceived as having little or no context within the self, whereas Aardema and O'Connor (2007) argued that repugnant obsessions are a feared state of mind associated with imagined negative self-representations that are misconstrued as real possibilities. In this context, the egodystonic obsessional content is not irrelevant to the person's self-definition, but instead becomes misconstrued as a feared possible self. For John, the obsessional content "what a cute little girl" is significant because it represents a repulsive aspect of the self which is that of a child molester. At one level, it is entirely inconsistent with John's sense of self as a moral, trustworthy, and law-abiding citizen, and yet John con-fuses the obsession with a feared possibility that he is a "latent child molester". In sum assessment of egodystonicity can be complicated but a critical element of the case conceptualization for repugnant obsessions.

A knowledgeable clinical interview can determine level of egodystonicity. Initially the clinician identifies the goals, principles, and moral attributes valued by the individual, as well as behavior that is consistent with the person's moral tenets. This information is then contrasted to the obsessional content to determine their similar-ities and differences. Several years ago, one of us (DAC) was treating an individual with OCD who had a repugnant sexual obsession of exposing himself in public, while at the same time treating another client charged with sexually exposing himself to young women. The thought of sexual exposure was clearly egodystonic for the OCD client, who experienced great distress and embarrassment when he had a sexual exposure intrusion, and he would avoid public places as a result. For the sex offender, on the other hand, the sexual exposure thought was clearly egosyntonic. He experi-enced pleasure and excitement at the thought of exposing himself, and he would pur-posely seek out exposure opportunities. Of course, the individual with OCD was a law-abiding citizen who had an outstanding reputation in his community, whereas the sexual offence client had a long criminal record and was again facing a court appear-ance. The experienced clinician, then, can establish the egodystonicity of the obses-sion by determining its juxtaposition with the person's moral imperatives. As an alternative, Purdon et al. (2007) developed the 37-item Egodystonicity Questionnaire, which holds promise of providing a more accurate assessment of egodystonicity. Unfortunately, there is insufficient empirical research on the measure to recommend its use in clinical practice at this time.

Thought–Action Fusion (TAF) – Morality

Moral TAF is "the belief that having an unacceptable intrusive thought is almost the moral equivalent of carrying out that particular act" (Shafran & Rachman, 2004: 88). An example would be a highly religious individual with OCD who believes that his unwanted intrusive sexual images are almost as morally wrong as engaging in adulterous sex. Most likely his sexual obsessions would be associated with intense guilt and ritualistic confession. Moral TAF involves an inflated sense of responsibility for harm and is one of the ways that individuals place undue significance on the obsession.

Moral TAF can be assessed with the 19-item TAF Scale (Shafran, Thordarson, & Rachman, 1996). Scores in the mid to upper 20s could be indicative of heightened Moral TAF (Shafran & Rachman, 2004). Alternatively, the clinician can ask about the extent that individuals with repugnant obsessions believe their unwanted thoughts are highly unacceptable, even immoral. Does the individual feel a heightened sense of responsibility to control the unacceptable intrusions? What is the feared consequence of these thoughts? Is there an intense feeling of guilt and, if so, what is the meaning of this guilt; that is, how is it interpreted or understood? To what extent does the client believe her private mental state is a true reflection of her moral character? As can be seen, the presence of Moral TAF will contribute to the individual's belief in the importance and need to control the repugnant obsession.

Importance/Control of Thoughts

As previously reviewed, beliefs about the importance and need to control obsessions is a significant cognitive dysfunction in repugnant obsessions. It is important that the therapist thoroughly assess control beliefs, effort to control, perceived consequences of control failures, and actual neutralization or control strategies employed in response to the obsession. This information will be useful in identifying the key cognitive dysfunction that contributes to the persistence of the repugnant obsessions.

Although various self-report questionnaires have been developed to assess OC-related beliefs, the most extensively researched measure is the 44-item Obsessional Beliefs Questionnaire (OBQ) (OCCWG, 2005). This can be administered to assess endorsement of importance and control beliefs, although the OBQ instructs respondents to base their answers on beliefs associated with unwanted intrusive thoughts more generally, and not just beliefs related to the repugnant obsession. The clinical assessment interview should also include questions about importance and control beliefs specific to the obsession. Below is a list of some key questions about need to control. See also the semi-structured interview on obsessions developed by Rachman (2003).

a   When the intrusive thought (obsession) pops into your mind, is your attention fully drawn to the thought? Are you able to think about other things or engage in activities, or does the thought capture your full attention?
b   What makes this thought so important or significant to you? Are you concerned that its mere occurrence will cause harm, or are you more concerned about what you are thinking about its content?
c   How critical is it to stop thinking about the obsession? What are you afraid will happen if the obsession persists, or you cannot get it out of your mind?
d   Imagine you are working hard on a project, focusing your entire attention on the task at hand. You are putting a great deal of mental effort into focusing your thoughts on this task. Compared with this focused work, how much effort do you put into controlling the obsession?

e   Why do you think you appear to have lost control over your obsessional thinking? What do you think is wrong with you? What do you think needs to be done to remedy your obsessional thinking?

Reasoning Errors

O'Connor and colleagues have written extensively about an inferential-based therapy for treatment of obsessions (O'Connor et al., 2005; O'Connor & Aardema, 2011). We recommend that therapists consult these resources for instructions on how to assess the faulty reasoning responsible for misconstruing an imagined negative possibility (e.g., "What if I really enjoyed harming others?") as an actual attribute of the real self (e.g., "I must be a violent person who needs to keep strict control over her thoughts and impulses"). Based on inference-based theory, the following reasoning errors should be assessed within the context of the repugnant obsession (see O'Connor et al., 2005: 117):

a   *category errors:* confusing two logical or ontologically distinct properties or objects;
b   *apparently comparable events:* confusing two distinct events;
c   *selective use of out-of-context facts:* such as selective abstraction in which abstract facts are inappropriately applied to personal contexts;
d   *purely imaginary sequences:* living out imagined stories;
e   *idiosyncratic associational networks:* creating chains of arbitrary associations;
f   *distrust of normal perception:* disregard one's sensory information in favor of a personally constructed abstraction of reality;
g   *inverse inference:* instead of inferences based on observations of reality, inferences are formed prior to reality-based observations.

Heightened Selfhood Sensitivity

There are two approaches to the assessment of self-definition. The first involves a more general assessment of self-worth in various life domains such as work, family, morality, intimate relationships, physical appearance, and the like. Various self-report measures are available, such as the Adult Self-Perception Profile (see Doron, Moulding, Kyrios, & Nedeljkovic, 2008), the Obsessional Concerns and Self Questionnaire (García-Soriano et al., 2012), or the Self-Ambivalence Measure (Bhar & Kyrios, 2007). These measures can be helpful, although the availability of clinical norms is limited to nonexistent. Therefore, caution must be exercised when used in the clinical setting.

It will be more important to obtain a specific selfhood assessment that focuses on the self in relation to the repugnant obsession. Questions should focus on the perceived importance and competence associated with various domains that may be especially relevant to repugnant obsessions such as morality, relationships, and spirituality. The following are some illustrative questions that can be used to determine an individual's sense self-worth in these various domains:

a   What do you consider the most important characteristics, values, or attributes of a moral person? How important are morality, ethical behavior, and virtue in defining your self-worth?

b   Do you consider yourself a moral person? Thinking back to the characteristics of
    a moral person, where do you think you have succeeded and where do you feel
    you have fallen short?
c   Does the obsession threaten your sense of personal morality, or at least make you
    question whether you are a moral person? If so, explain how the obsession poses
    a threat to your morality? Has the obsession become the main indicator for how
    moral you feel?

This line of inquiry can be repeated for each of the most relevant selfhood domains
for repugnant obsessions: family, relationships, spirituality, etc.

Feared Self

A final construct in the case conceptualization of repugnant obsessions is the feared
self, which is a specific aspect of heightened selfhood sensitivity. The Fear of Self
Questionnaire (FSQ) developed by Aardema et al. (2013) can be used to assess this
construct, although once again it currently exists as a research rather than clinical
instrument. When used clinically, caution must be exercised because a clinical scoring
range has not been established. Also the FSQ is a single factor measure so it does not
assess the feared self in specific domains. Instead, it will provide a general measure of
the extent that one's self-view is defined by a fear of negative characteristics or
possibilities.
      When developing the case formulation for repugnant obsessions, the clinician could
ask more specific questions about what aspects of the obsession are most fearful and
how these dreaded characteristics relate to a sense of self. For example, John's repugnant obsession was "Am I sexually attracted to little girls?" The feared self was that he
might be a "latent child molester," that harming children might be an underlying
characteristic. He began to see himself as a "potential child molester" who needed to
maintain strict control to prevent his deviance from breaking out. The constant preoccupation with sexual attraction to children confirmed to John that what he feared
most about himself, that he was a latent pedophile, might be true. For John, this
feared self became the most influential stimulus for self-definition.

Cognitive Behavior Treatment: Special Considerations

Much has been written about CBT for obsessions (e.g., Clark, 2004; Rachman,
2003), including some consideration of the treatment of repugnant obsessions
(Moulding et al., 2014; Purdon, 2004; Williams et al., 2013). In this section we offer
a few additional suggestions about particular topics that should be considered in CBT
for repugnant obsessions.

Imaginal Exposure

Imaginal exposure will be particularly important in the treatment of repugnant obsessions, especially given the prominence of Moral TAF, egodystonicity, and overimportance beliefs. In many cases the mere occurrence of the obsession elicits significant

anxiety and guilt. Repeated intentional and sustained exposure to the obsession can be a critical empirical hypothesis-testing experience that challenges the client's belief in the significance and need to control the obsession. The first step in exposure is the construction of an exposure narrative in which clients write a detailed account of the obsessional content in their own words. The therapist might need to adopt a graduated approach over several sessions depending on the degree of concealment and fear associated with talking about the repugnant content.

Once a detailed narrative is constructed, the therapist should do several in-session imaginal exposures with the narrative so it is clear how to conduct exposure. This also insures therapist support and guidance through the initial exposure sessions that can be highly distressing for individuals. Then a variety of recording approaches can be used to facilitate imaginal exposure as a homework assignment. Moulding and colleagues (2014) discuss several approaches, including audio recording, intentionally verbalizing the obsession while preventing any neutralizing response, and exposing oneself to external obsession triggers that were previously avoided. Another possibility is use of a smartphone app that could be programmed to repeatedly present the obsession throughout the day. Whatever methodology employed, imaginal exposure is a critical element of CBT for repugnant obsessions because it provides direct experience that the obsession is not dangerous, nor does it need to be avoided or suppressed in order to engage in the normal activities of daily living.

Neutralization Prevention

Any neutralization response associated with the repugnant obsession must be eliminated (Moulding et al., 2014; Williams et al., 2013). Mental compulsions are often present so these need to be a particular focus for change. The therapist must work on response prevention strategies directly in the therapy session by provoking the obsession and then discussing various strategies that might be used to prevent neutralization. For example, reassurance seeking is a common response to religious obsessions. Individuals who are irrationally obsessed with whether they have sinned, offended God, or truly confessed will repeatedly ask family or a religious leader(s) whether they have sinned or offended God. An important element of the therapy is to work with the client to cease all reassurance seeking activities.

Collaborating with the client in the development of alternative strategies to neutralization is an important part of neutralization prevention. This can include cognitive or behavioral competing activities that demand attentional resources, making it difficult to also engage in neutralization. For example when the urge to seek reassurance arises, the client could engage in physical exercise, read a novel, answer email, cook, work on a puzzle, etc. The intention is not to distract the client from the obsession, but rather to provide a competing response to neutralization.

It may be necessary to take a graduated approach to response prevention (Clark, 2004; Moulding et al., 2014). The client can be encouraged to delay neutralization, at first for a brief time, and then gradually lengthening the delay period so that eventually the neutralization response is suppressed entirely. One of John's most frequent neutralization responses was self-rationalization. Whenever his doubt about sexual attraction to little girls arose, he would try to convince himself he was not a pedophile. He would go through all the reasons why he was sexually attracted to adult women and not children. John found the self-rationalization extremely difficult to stop, so it was important to introduce a graduated approach, first delaying neutralization 5 minutes, then 10 minutes, and so on until John stopped neutralizing entirely. As well, during the delay period John had a list of behavioral activities he was to attentively complete. To encourage attentive engagement, John could write a brief description of the activity and rate it along several dimensions such as degree of enjoyment, sense of accomplishment, usefulness, etc. When using this approach it is important to spend time each session expanding the list of alternative activities, increasing the delay interval, and problem-solving any difficulties the client might have with neutralization prevention.

Cognitive Restructuring: Normalization

Most individuals with repugnant obsessions believe that the occurrence of the abhorrent intrusion is the main source of their emotional turmoil. They are convinced they must be abnormal for having repugnant thoughts since most people are not plagued by such bizarre thinking. An important aspect of CBT for obsessions is correcting these dysfunctional beliefs of significance by *normalizing the obsession*; that is, the occurrence of even repugnant thoughts is normal but it is the appraisal or interpretation of the intrusion that causes an escalation in its frequency and intensity.

As described in more detail elsewhere (Clark, 2004), the therapist begins by showing the client a list of unwanted intrusive thoughts (see Clark, 2004; Rachman, 2003, for such lists). The client selects an intrusion he or she has experienced only occasionally, but with no distress. The therapist explores with the client how he or she makes a benign interpretation of the intrusion (e.g., "I tell myself this is stupid, I would never do such an awful thing"). Then, the client and therapist discuss how this intrusion could be interpreted differently so it is turned into a distressing obsession (e.g., "well, if I believed that I might act on the intrusion, I suppose it would bother me"). Finally, the therapist and client collaboratively explore how he or she is generating a faulty interpretation of the repugnant obsession that makes it worse and whether an alternative benign interpretation could reduce the distressing quality of the intrusion. A useful homework assignment is to ask the client to conduct a mini-survey among family or close friends, showing them the list of unwanted intrusions and asking whether they have ever experienced such thoughts. If so, do they take the thoughts seriously or not? The objective of this exercise is to help clients accept the normality of even repugnant intrusions and to realize that it is the faulty interpretation, and not the intrusion itself, that is maintaining its persistence and distress.

Cognitive Restructuring: Self-construal Modification

It was noted that the etiology of repugnant obsessions might have their origins in a dysfunctional self-construal process in which imagined negative possibilities about the self, or the feared self, come to play a major role in self-definition. Morality and integrity, for example, were important self-attributes for John. These attributes played a critical role in John's feeling of self-worth. Yet over the years, with the persistence of the sexual obsession, John had come to see himself as failing in his morality. He increasingly saw himself as an immoral individual for having such abhorrent, disgusting thoughts of harming children. He became convinced that the repugnant obsessions were proof of his failings, and he came to the conclusion that he was not a good person. His greatest fear was that his moral failings might lead to an utter loss of control over his behavior.

There are a couple of therapeutic implications of this self-construal conceptualization. First, the above formulation can be woven into the psychoeducation phase of treatment. Collaboratively the therapist and client can explore how the "feared self" and loss of self-worth contingency have created a false self-representation in the moral or relationship domains. Second, the therapist can compare the client's self-representation in a non-OCD domain with the self-representational processes in the OCD-related domain. Once the client recognizes the dysfunction, a more constructive, alternative self-representation can be developed. For example, John could see that his fear "what if I am a latent child molester" was clouding his ability to consider himself a moral person. We compared this with how John views himself as a competent, hard-working, and reliable person. The therapist asked John "you see yourself as competent and hard-working, how do you know this?" John then listed several indicators of his strong work ethic. We then compared these reality-based indicators with his "what if" indicators he used to define his moral identity. Once the faulty nature of his moral self-construal process was identified, the therapist then worked with John to shift the emphasis from a "possibility basis" to a real basis (e.g., "what would you think of a wealthy person who thought about giving to the needy, versus a wealthy person who actually gave to the needy?"). On the basis of this reasoning, John and his therapist could then search for real-life indicators of his moral character.

In the third phase of this therapeutic work, it is important to assign empirical hypothesis-testing homework that would help consolidate the new sense of self. In John's case his homework involved collecting information from family and close friends on what indicators they used to form their judgments of other people's moral character. John and his therapist then used this information to gauge his actual level of moral standing. Over several weeks John was to record real-life indicators of moral character (e.g., "yesterday I spent an hour assisting a co-worker with a problem he could not solve"; "I opened the door for a woman struggling with a stroller and many parcels, etc.). With time John was able to recover a since of confidence and self-worth in his moral character.

References

Aardema, F., Moulding, R., Radomsky, A. S., Doron, G., Allamby, J., & Souki, E. (2013). Fear of self and obsessionality: Development and validation of the Fear of Self Questionnaire. *Journal of Obsessive-Compulsive and Related Disorders, 2*, 306–315.

Aardema, F., & O'Connor, K. (2003). Seeing white bears that are not there: Inference processes in obsessions. *Journal of Cognitive Psychotherapy, 17*, 23–37.

Aardema, F., & O'Connor, K. (2007). The menace within: Obsessions and the self. *Journal of Cognitive Psychotherapy: An International Quarterly, 21*, 182–197.

Abramowitz, J. S., Franklin, M. E., Schwartz, S. A., & Furr, J. M. (2003). Symptom presentation and outcome of cognitive-behavioral therapy for obsessive-compulsive disorder. *Journal of Consulting and Clinical Psychology, 71*, 1049–1057.

Altin, M., Clark, D. A., & Karanci, N. (2007). *The impact of religiosity on obsessive-compulsive cognitions and symptoms in Christian and Muslim students.* Paper presented at the World Congress of Behavioural and Cognitive Therapies, Barcelona, Spain.

Belloch, A., Roncero, M., & Perpiná, C. (2012). Ego-syntonicity and ego-dystonicity associated with upsetting intrusive cognitions. *Journal of Psychopathology and Behavioral Assessment, 34*, 94–106.

Bhar, S. S., & Kyrios, M. (2007). An investigation of self-ambivalence in obsessive-compulsive disorder. *Behaviour Research and Therapy, 45*, 1845–1857.

Bloch, M. H., Landeros-Weisenberger, A., Rosário, M. C., Pittenger, C., & Leckman, J. F. (2008). Meta-analysis of the symptom structure of obsessive-compulsive disorder. *American Journal of Psychiatry, 165*, 1532–1542.

Brakoulias, V., Starcevic, V., Berle, D., Milicevic, D., Moses, K., Hannan, A., Sammut, P., & Martin, A. (2013). The characteristics of unacceptable/taboo thoughts in obsessive-compulsive disorder. *Comprehensive Psychiatry, 54*, 750–757.

Ciarrocchi, J. W. (1995). *The doubting disease: Help for scrupulosity and religious compulsions.* New York: Paulist Press.

Clark, D. A. (2004). *Cognitive-behavioral therapy for OCD.* New York: Guilford Press.

Clark, D. A., & García-Soriano, G. (2010). *Development of the Obsessional Concerns and Self Questionnaire (OCSQ).* Unpublished manuscript, University of New Brunswick, Canada.

Clark, D. M. (1986). A cognitive approach to panic. *Behaviour Research and Therapy, 24*, 461–470.

Doron, G., & Kyrios, M. (2005). Obsessive compulsive disorder: A review of possible specific internal representations within a broader cognitive theory. *Clinical Psychology Review, 25*, 415–432.

Doron, G., Kyrios, M., & Moulding, R. (2007). Sensitive domains of self-concept in obsessive-compulsive disorder (OCD): Further evidence for a multidimensional model of OCD. *Journal of Anxiety Disorders, 21*, 433–444.

Doron, G., Moulding, R., Kyrios, M., & Nedeljkovic, M. (2008). Sensitivity of self-beliefs in obsessive compulsive disorder. *Depression and Anxiety, 25*, 874–884.

Foa, E. B., & Kozak, M. J. (1995). DSM-IV field trial: Obsessive-compulsive disorder. *American Journal of Psychiatry, 152*, 90–96.

Fontenelle, L. F., Mendlowicz, M. V., Marques, C., & Versiani, M. (2004). Trans-cultural aspects of obsessive-compulsive disorder: A description of a Brazilian sample and a systematic review of international clinical studies. *Journal of Psychiatric Research, 38*, 403–411.

Freeston, M. H., Ladouceur, R., Gagnon, F., Thibodeau, N., Rheaume, J., Letarte, H., & Bujold, A. (1997). Cognitive-behavioral treatment of obsessive thoughts: A controlled study. *Journal of Consulting and Clinical Psychology, 65*, 405–413.

García-Soriano, G., Clark, D. A., Belloch, A., del Palacio, A., & Castañeiras, C. (2012). Self-worth contingencies and obsessionality: A promising approach to vulnerability? *Journal of Obsessive Compulsive and Related Disorders, 1*, 196–202.

Ghassemzadeh, H., Mojtabai, R., Khamseh, A., Ebrahimkhani, N., Issazadegan, A-A., & Saif-Nobakht, Z. (2002). Symptoms of obsessive-compulsive disorder in a sample of Iranian patients. *International Journal of Social Psychiatry, 48*, 20–28.

Guidano, V., & Liotti, G. (1983). *Cognitive processes and emotional disorders.* New York: Guilford Press.

Hale, M. A., & Clark, D. A. (2013). When good people have bad thoughts: Religiosity and the emotional regulation of guilt-inducing intrusive thoughts. *Journal of Psychology & Theology, 41*, 24–35.

Hasler, G., LaSalle-Ricci, V. H., Ronquillo, J. G., Crawley, S. A., Cochran, L. W., Kazuba, D., Greenberg, D. B., & Murphy, D. L. (2005). Obsessive-compulsive disorder symptom dimensions show specific relationships to psychiatric comorbidity. *Psychiatry Research, 135*, 121–132.

Insel, T. R. (1990). Phenomenology of obsessive compulsive disorder. *Journal of Clinical Psychiatry, 51*(Suppl.), 4–8.

Inozu, M., Karanci, A. N., & Clark, D. A. (2012). Why are religious individuals more obsessional? The role of mental control beliefs and guilt in Muslims and Christians. *Journal of Behavior Therapy and Experimental Psychiatry, 43*, 959–966.

Lee, H-J., & Kwon, S-M. (2003). Two different types of obsession: autogenous and reactive obsessions. *Behaviour Research and Therapy, 41*, 11–29.

Lee, H-J., Kwon, S-M., Kwon, J. S., & Telch, M. J. (2005). Testing the autogenous-reactive model of obsessions. *Depression and Anxiety, 21*, 118–129.

Moulding, R., Aardema, F., & O'Connor, K. P. (2014). Repugnant obsessions: A review of the phenomenology, theoretical models, and treatment of sexual and aggressive obsessional themes in OCD. *Journal of Obsessive-Compulsive and Related Disorders, 3*, 161–168.

Newth, S., & Rachman, S. (2001). The concealment of obsessions. *Behaviour Research and Therapy, 39*, 457–464.

OCCWG (Obsessive Compulsive Cognitions Working Group). (2003). Psychometric validation of the Obsessive Beliefs Questionnaire and the Interpretations of Intrusions Inventory: Part I. *Behaviour Research and Therapy, 41*, 863–878.

OCCWG (Obsessive Compulsive Cognitions Working Group). (2005). Psychometric validation of the Obsessive Beliefs Questionnaire and the Interpretations of Intrusions Inventory – Part 2: Factor analyses and testing a brief version. *Behaviour Research and Therapy, 43*, 1527–1542.

OCD-UK. (2013). What is Pure-O? Retrieved from: http://www.ocduk.org/pure-o, January 9, 2015.

O'Connor, K., & Aardema, F. (2011). *Clinician's handbook for obsessive-compulsive disorder: Inference-based therapy.* Chichester: Wiley.

O'Connor, K., Aardema, F., & Pélissier, M-C. (2005). *Beyond reasonable doubt: Reasoning processes in obsessive-compulsive disorder and related disorders.* Chichester: Wiley.

OKasha, A., Saad, A., Khalil, A. H., Dawla, S. E., & Yehia, N. (1994). Phenomenology of obsessive-compulsive disorder: A transcultural study. *Comprehensive Psychiatry, 25*, 191–197.

Purdon, C. (2004). Cognitive-behavioral treatment of repugnant obsessions. *Journal of Clinical Psychology, In Session, 60*, 1169–1180.

Purdon, C., Cripps, E., Faull, M., Joseph, S., & Rowa, K. (2007). Development of a measure of egodystonicity. *Journal of Cognitive Psychotherapy, 21*, 198–216.

Pinto, A., Greenberg, B. D., Grados, M. A., Bienvenu, O. J., Samuels, J. F., Murphy, D. L., ... Nestadt, G. (2008). Further development of YBOCS dimensions in the OCD Collaborative Genetics Study: Symptoms vs. categories. *Psychiatry Research, 160*, 83–93.

Rachman, S. J. (1971). Obsessional ruminations. *Behaviour Research and Therapy, 9*, 229–235.

Rachman, S. (2003). *The treatment of obsessions.* Oxford: Oxford University Press.

Rachman, S., & Shafran, R. (1998). Cognitive and behavioral features of obsessive-compulsive disorder. In R. P. Swinson, M. M. Antony, S. Rachman, & M. A. Richter (Eds.), *Obsessive-compulsive disorder: Theory, research and practice* (pp. 51–78). New York: Guilford Press.

Radomsky, A. S., Alcolado, G. M., Abramowitz, J., Alonso, P., Belloch, A., Bouvard, M., ... Wong, W. (2014). You can run but you can't hide: Intrusive thoughts on six continents – Part 1. *Journal of Obsessive-Compulsive and Related Disorders, 3*, 269–279.

Salkovskis, P. M. (1985). Obsessive-compulsive problems: A cognitive-behavioural analysis. *Behaviour Research and Therapy, 23*, 571–583.

Shafran, R., & Rachman, S. (2004). Thought–action fusion: A review. *Journal of Behavior Therapy and Experimental Psychiatry, 35*, 87–107.

Shafran, R., Thordarson, D. S., & Rachman, S. J. (1996). Thought–action fusion in obsessive compulsive disorder. *Journal of Anxiety Disorders, 10*, 379–391.

Sibrava, N. J., Boisseau, C. L., Mancebo, M. C., Eisen, J. L., & Rasmussen, S. A. (2011). Prevalence and clinical characteristics of mental rituals in a longitudinal clinical sample of obsessive-compulsive disorder. *Depression and Anxiety, 28*, 892–898.

Siev, J., Steketee, G., Fama, J. M., & Wilhelm, S. (2011). Cognitive and clinical characteristics of sexual and religious obsessions. *Journal of Cognitive Psychotherapy, 25*, 167–176.

Taylor, S. (2002). Cognition in obsessive compulsive disorder: An overview. In R.O. Frost, & G. Steketee (Eds.), *Cognitive approaches to obsessions and compulsions: Theory, assessment, and treatment* (pp. 1–12). Amsterdam: Elsevier Science.

Wilhelm, S., & Steketee, G. (2006). *Cognitive therapy for obsessive compulsive disorder: A guide for professionals.* Oakland, CA: New Harbinger.

Williams, M. T., Crozier, M., & Powers, M. (2011). Treatment of sexual orientation obsessions in obsessive-compulsive disorder using exposure and ritual prevention. *Clinical Case Studies, 10*, 53–66.

Williams, M. T., & Farris, S. (2011). Sexual orientation obsessions in obsessive-compulsive disorder: Prevalence and correlates. *Psychiatry Research, 187*, 156–159.

Williams, M. T., Farris, S. G., Turkheimer, E., Pinto, A., Ozanick, K., Franklin, M. F., Simpson, H. B., & Foa, E. B. (2011). Myth of the pure obsessional type in obsessive-compulsive disorder. *Depression and Anxiety, 28*, 495–500.

Williams, M. T., Mugno, B., Franklin, M., & Faber, S. (2013). Symptom dimensions in obsessive-compulsive disorder: Phenomenology and treatment outcomes with exposure and ritual prevention. *Psychopathology, 46*, 365–376.

24

Unacceptable Obsessional Thoughts in Children and Adolescents

Carly Johnco and Eric A. Storch

"Unacceptable" or "forbidden" obsessions typically refer to thoughts and images with aggressive/harm, sexual, and religious or moral content (Bloch, Landeros-Weisenberger, Rosario, Pittenger, & Leckman, 2008; Mataix-Cols, Rosário-Campos, & Leckman, 2005; Moulding, Aardema, & O'Connor, 2014; Purdon, 2004). So-called "aggressive" or "harm" obsessions are typically characterized by obsessional thinking about behaving in a way that would purposefully or unintentionally cause harm to oneself or others (Moulding et al., 2014; Purdon, 2004). Sexual obsessions generally refer to unwanted sexual thoughts, often involving family members, friends, or children, and violent or homosexual activities (Fernandez de la Cruz et al., 2013; Grant et al., 2006; Williams & Farris, 2011). Religious obsessions can include a pre-occupation with blasphemous thoughts, death, unwarranted fears of having sinned, and religious of moral judgment that are often overly focused on a narrow or insignificant aspect of religious doctrines or moral standards (Ciarrocchi, 1995; Miller & Hedges, 2008). Although characterized by qualitatively different preoccupations, factor analytic studies consistently group these types of obsessions as relating to the same underlying factor (Bloch et al., 2008). The reason that these obsessions are classified or termed as "unacceptable," or "forbidden," or "taboo" is that they frequently encompass thoughts and images that are egodystonic in nature, and violate a range of moral and social standards. Individuals who experience these type of obsessions usually hold a belief that their experience of having the thought or image is morally equivalent to engaging in the overt actions; that these thoughts symbolize their actual desire for such events to occur; or that having the thought will somehow increase the likelihood that they will engage in such acts. This failure to differentiate thoughts from behaviors is referred to as thought–action fusion (Amir, Freshman, Ramsey, Neary, & Brigidi, 2001; Rachman, 1998; Shafran, Thordarson, & Rachman, 1996). These type of obsessions are highly distressing for individuals and often go undetected given the high levels of associated embarrassment and shame.

Although these obsessions are discussed more often in the context of adult OCD, these symptoms do present in childhood and adolescent OCD. Clinical studies have reported that 25–41% of youth with OCD report sexual and/or religious obsessions

The Wiley Handbook of Obsessive Compulsive Disorders, Volume I, First Edition.
Edited by Jonathan S. Abramowitz, Dean McKay, and Eric A. Storch.
© 2017 John Wiley & Sons Ltd. Published 2017 by John Wiley & Sons Ltd.

(Geller et al., 2001; Hanna, 1995; Mancebo et al., 2008; Storch et al., 2007) and as many as 70% report aggressive obsessions (Geller et al., 2001; Storch et al., 2007). Reported rates sometimes differ in child samples, with rates of religious obsessions around 15% and sexual obsessions around 11% (Geller et al., 2001). Given the nature of the obsessional thoughts, parental reactions to the disclosure of these symptoms can be extremely varied, ranging from a supportive response and aware-ness of the underlying pathology to critical and punitive reactions and an attribution of deviance. Parental reactions can have considerable impact on the child's level of embarrassment and shame about discussing and treating their symptoms, as well as on the type of help-seeking sought by the family (e.g., religious advisors or mental health services). Compulsions can often be more covert or mental in comparison to other stereotyped obsessions (e.g., contamination), and often include confessing, repeating rituals, superstitious games, mental rituals, reassurance-seeking and avoid-ance (Fernandez de la Cruz et al., 2013). This chapter will discuss the phenome-nology and clinical presentation of aggressive/harm, sexual and religious/moral obsessions, as well as issues relating to assessment and treatment of these conditions in youth.

Phenomenology

Aggressive Obsessions

Aggressive obsessions vary considerably in content, and can include graphic thoughts or images about injuring or killing oneself or others, often when in proximity to a situation or object that can inflict harm, for example, a knife or staircase (Milliner-Oar, Cadman, & Farrell, 2016; Moulding et al., 2014; Purdon, 2004). These can also include violent sexual thoughts, such as assaulting a family member, friend, or stranger. In youth, these thoughts or images often incorporate fears of harming a family member, and fears that they will succumb to these thoughts and perpetrate acts of violence against their will. Youth may also experience pervasive fears about blurting out obscene, insulting or offensive things, or engaging in aggressive or antisocial acts, such as stealing or setting a fire. They may also perseverate on thoughts or images of death or injury, or about harm coming to a loved one. Unlike youth with suicidal or homicidal intentions, youth with aggressive/harm obsessions find these thoughts highly distressing and, generally, do not want to cause harm to others or themselves. To the contrary, these youth typically feel an inflated sense of responsibility to prevent harm and may go to great lengths to avoid being in situations where they perceive that they may inflict harm, that harm may be inflicted upon them, or to prevent harm coming to others. For example, youth may avoid using knives or scissors, being in proximity to certain family members, or touching certain body parts on themselves of others (e.g., necks). They may insist upon family member altering their behavior to avoid harm, and become distressed if they refuse to accommodate this request. Aggressive obsessions are commonly endorsed by children and adolescents with OCD, with some studies suggesting rates as high as 80% (Hanna, 1995; Mataix-Cols, Nakatani, Micali, & Heyman, 2008). Aggressive and harm obsessions have been asso-ciated with increased levels of functional impairment in youth with OCD (Storch et al., 2010a).

Sexual Obsessions

Sexual obsessions include unwanted sexual thoughts, images, and impulses. Common obsessions include ideas of engaging in inappropriate sexual acts with family, friends, young children or animals, sexually aggressive behavior and infidelity (Grant et al., 2006; Williams & Farris, 2011). These type of obsessions can also include sexual orientation obsessions, where individuals doubt their sexual preference, or perseverate on whether their outward appearance and behavior may be perceived by others as homosexual/heterosexual (i.e., the opposite of their identified sexual orientation). With the onset of puberty and adolescence, individuals can experience sexual arousal in response to a range of stimuli or fantasies in which they would not actually engage. However, individuals with sexual obsessions may ruminate about their physiological reactions and the meaning of them, and in particular, fear that this is either a reflection of their inner desires or that this will influence their likelihood of engaging in such acts. Parental attributions often erroneously attribute these obsessions to inner desire, and may question the level of risk their child poses to others (Fernandez de la Cruz et al., 2013). Conversely, parents and clinicians may mistakenly attribute the child's preoccupation with sexual themes to some form of abuse (Veale, Freeston, Krebs, Heyman, & Salkovskis, 2009), delaying access to evidence-based treatments.

Youth with unwanted sexual obsessions typically find the thoughts upsetting and distressing, and are fearful of losing control and engaging in these acts. They may also feel dirty or impure for having these types of thoughts. In an attempt to neutralize or compensate for these thoughts, youth may engage in a range of covert or overt compulsions. For example, youth may repeat certain activities to neutralize the perceived likelihood of engaging in the behavior, such as needing to generate "good" thoughts to compensate for the bad thoughts, counting, repeating phrases, or praying. Youth with these types of obsessions may try to control their thoughts, or avoid situations that may trigger the obsessions, such as avoiding being near or being alone with certain people, avoiding looking at certain body parts, seeking excessive reassurance, confessing (Fernandez de la Cruz et al., 2013). Sexual obsessions can be particularly impairing for youth when they are triggered or involve friends or classmates at school, and be compounded by hormonal and physiological changes during adolescence and puberty.

Religious and Moral Obsessions

Religious and moral obsessions, known as scrupulosity, include excessive preoccupations about having committed a sin, blasphemy, going to hell, concern one's behavior will condemn a loved one to hell, death, judgment from god, purity, potential loss of impulse control, and behaving morally (Abramowitz, Huppert, Cohen, Tolin, & Cahill, 2002; Ciarrocchi, 1995; Miller & Hedges, 2008). Obsessions that the child might have somehow cheated is a particularly common imagined sin among youth. Interestingly, youth who experience religious obsessions also commonly experience sexual and/or aggressive obsessions (Bloch et al., 2008) and may fear judgement as a result of having these thoughts. For example, seeing an attractive stranger may trigger a sexual thought, which may be deemed sinful by the youth who adheres to religious doctrines that condemn lust. Furthermore, aggressive obsessions or aggressive sexual obsessions may be considered extremely sinful. Obsessions often take the form of doubting whether one has sinned or been immoral, or whether a thought or action might have constituted a sin, and engaging in the compulsion "just in case" to avoid eternal condemnation.

While some compulsions to neutralize these obsessional thoughts are overt behaviors, others are more covert, and in many cases are consistent with religious practice (although usually excessive or extreme). For example, youth may seek excessive religious advice, utilize excessive confession or prayer (often with a need for the prayer to be repeated until it is "just right"), ritualized or repeated use of religious phrases or images, bargaining with God, or find ways to punish themselves for their imagined sins (Ciarrocchi, 1995; Miller & Hedges, 2008). Youth may also avoid certain situations or objects where they may sin or cause something bad to happen, and family members may engage in various forms of family accommodation to reduce the child's exposure to triggers and subsequent distress. Although youth will report a desire to be "perfect" in their religion and moral doctrines, their practices and preoccupations are often extreme, overly literal, or focused on a trivial area, even in the context of other more important areas of their religion or morals being largely ignored. For example, youth may say their prayers over and over for fear of having accidentally omitted a loved one, or have not said their prayer "just right." They may worry about making morally correct decisions in every circumstance, or take excessive responsibility for the actions of others (e.g., accepting incorrect change from a cashier).

Around 23% of children and adolescents with OCD endorse religious and moral obsessions (Hanna, 1995). These can occur in youth with strong religious ties to any faith, including youth of nondenominational, agnostic, or atheist beliefs. Scrupulous youth often do not recognize the inappropriate nature of their religious and moral preoccupations. Unlike aggressive or sexual obsessions, attempts to follow religious and moral doctrines are often viewed as virtuous and respectable. These beliefs are often central to the child's spiritual beliefs and often those of their family, and challenging the religious obsessions can be mistakenly viewed as challenging the faith itself (which in turn is interpreted by the youth as sinful or blasphemous). However scrupulosity is quite different from devout or extreme religiosity, and youth feel increasingly insecure in their faith and fear a punitive outcome despite their attempts to become less sinful or "pure."

Clinical Features of Youth Who Experience Aggressive, Sexual or Religious Obsessions

The effect of age on the presentation and incidence of unacceptable obsessional thoughts varies considerably between studies. Some studies have found similarly higher rates of aggressive and harm obsessions in children and adolescents in comparison with adults (Geller et al., 2001), while other studies have found higher rates of aggressive obsessions in adolescents compared with children, with similar rates between adolescents and adults (Mancebo et al., 2008). Similarly, studies vary in whether they find age differences in sexual and religious obsessions, with some suggesting higher rates of sexual obsessions in adolescents compared with children (Fernandez de la Cruz et al., 2013; Geller et al., 2001), and higher rates of sexual and religious obsessions in adolescents compared with adults (Butwicka & Gmitrowicz, 2010), while other studies have found similar rates of sexual and religious obsessions between children, adolescents, and adults (Mancebo et al., 2008).

In terms of gender, higher rates of aggressive obsessions have been noted in women with OCD (Lensi et al., 1996) and in girls (Mataix-Cols et al., 2008), although other studies have not found a gender difference in adolescents with OCD (Zohar et al., 1997). Sexual obsessions are documented in both men and women, with some studies suggesting similar rates (Grant et al., 2006) and others suggesting higher rates in males (Labad et al., 2008), particularly in references to sexual orientation obsessions (Williams & Farris, 2011). Studies with youth tend to suggest higher rates of sexual and religious obsessions in boys with OCD relative to girls (Mataix-Cols et al., 2008).

In terms of comorbidity and clinical course, aggressive, sexual, and religious obsessions are more common in early-onset OCD that later-onset OCD (Leckman, Bloch, & King, 2009; Rosário-Campos et al., 2005), and are frequently comorbid with tic disorders in youth (Masi et al., 2005; Zohar et al., 1997). In adults, individuals who experience these types of obsessions have been found to exhibit more severe symptom severity in comparison with other OCD subtypes (Abramowitz, Franklin, Schwartz, & Furr, 2003). In youth, sexual obsessions are associated with more severe OCD symptomatology and increased depressive symptoms (Fernandez de la Cruz et al., 2013). Similarly, the presence of sexual obsessions in adults with OCD is associated with increased suicidal thoughts and plans (Torres et al., 2011), suggesting high levels of distress among individuals with this clinical presentation.

Assessment of Aggressive, Sexual, and Religious/Moral Obsessions in Youth

Routine assessment of aggressive, sexual, and religious obsessions is important in youth, especially given that many individuals will not voluntarily report these symptoms. Youth may fail to volunteer this information as a result of high levels of shame and embarrassment about their symptoms; they may lack of awareness that these experiences are symptomatic of OCD; or especially in the case of religious obsessions, youth may not recognize the inappropriate or excessive nature of their symptoms. In the case of each unacceptable obsessional subtype, differential diagnostic considerations are important to consider, and, namely, need to focus on whether the obsessions are repetitive, unwanted and upsetting to the individual. For example, aggressive thoughts may be a brief reactive phenomenon in the context of conflict between parent and child, although the youth may not fear engaging in the behavior, or may even find some comfort in this brief fantasy. In contrast, repetitive unprompted and distressing thoughts or images about hurting someone when the child bears no ill-will, and fears engaging in these acts involuntarily, are more consistent with OCD. Similarly, some youth may experience shame surrounding sexual fantasies that the child or adolescent derives pleasure from, and differentiating these sexual paraphilias or fetishes from unwanted and distressing sexual obsessions is warranted. In the case of religious obsessions, youth may find it difficult to endorse distress relating to their scrupulosity, as this may in itself be perceived to be sinful.

Methods of Assessment

Standardized assessment measures allow clinicians to ask about a range of OCD symptoms, and can help to normalize and educate youth about symptoms of OCD. The Children's Yale–Brown Obsessive Compulsive Scale (CY-BOCS) (Scahill et al., 1997) is the preferred clinical interview for assessing obsessive-compulsive symptoms in children and adolescents. This measure consists of a 62-item symptom checklist that includes semi-structured questions about a broad range of aggressive, sexual, and religious or moral obsessions. For example, items assessing religious and moral concerns include asking whether the child is "overly concerned with offending God or other religious object (e.g., having blasphemous thoughts, saying blasphemous things, or being punished for these things)" or experiences "Excessive concern with right/wrong, morality (e.g., worries about always doing the right thing, worries about having told a lie of having cheated someone)." Items that assess sexual obsessions include "Forbidden or upsetting sexual thoughts, images, or impulses (e.g., unwanted images of violent sexual behavior towards others, or unwanted sexual urges towards family members of friends)," and "Obsessions about sexual orientation (e.g., that he or she may be gay or may become gay when there is no basis for these thoughts)." A number of items assess aggressive obsessions, including asking about whether they "Fear [they] might harm self (e.g., using kitchen knives or other sharp objects)," experiences "Violent or horrific images (e.g., images or murders, dismembered bodies, other disgusting images)," has a "Fear of blurting out obscenities or insults," or "Fear will steal things against his/her will (e.g., accidentally "cheating" cashier or shoplifting something)." Symptom severity can be calculated as a composite of the time occupied, distress, resistance against, and degree of control over obsessions and compulsions.

There are some self-report measures that provide some assessment of aggressive, sexual, or religious OCD symptoms in youth; the Children's Florida Obsessive Compulsive Inventory (C-FOCI) (Storch et al., 2009) and either the Children's Obsessional Compulsive Inventory (ChOCI) (Shafran et al., 2003) or the revised version (ChOCI-R) (Uher, Heyman, Turner, & Shafran, 2008), and to some extent, the Obsessive Compulsive Inventory – Child Version (OCI-CV) (Foa et al., 2010). While these self- and parent-report measures provide some examination of, primarily, harm symptoms, there is little examination of religious or sexual obsessions. The C-FOCI consists of a 17-item symptom checklist of common obsessions and compulsions, as well as a symptom severity scale. The C-FOCI shows sensitivity to treatment effects and good convergent validity (Storch et al., 2009). The C-FOCI includes some assessment of harm-related and aggressive obsessions using items such as "Frequent images of death or other horrible things," "Accidentally hitting a pedestrian with your car or hurting someone," and "Harm coming to a loved one because you weren't careful enough." However, there is no explicit examination of religious or sexual obsessions.

The ChOCI is a child- and parent-report measure that follows that format of the CY-BOCS interview. The measure has two sections assessing compulsions and obsessions respectively, along with the accompanying time spent on the symptoms, interference, distress, resistance, control, and avoidance. The original version of the ChOCI includes a couple of additional items assessing aggressive and harm obsessions that were not retained in the revised version, however, overall the items and structure of the two versions is very similar. This measure yields a score for impairment related to obsessions, compulsions, and a total score. The ChOCI-R demonstrates adequate internal consistency, convergent and divergent validity (Uher et al., 2008), however does not provide particularly strong measurement of OCD subtypes (Foa et al., 2010). Items on the ChOCI-R include questions assessing aggressive and harm obsessions, such as "I can't stop upsetting thoughts about death from going round in my head, over and over again," "I can't stop thinking upsetting thoughts about an accident, I keep on having frightening thoughts that something terrible is going to happen and it will be my fault." This ChOCI-R also has one item assessing religious obsessions, "I am very frightened that I will think something (or do something) that will upset God." However there is no explicit examination of moral obsessions. While more generic items such as "I often have bad thoughts that make me feel like a terrible person" may be answered in reference to sexual, aggressive or religious obsessions, sexual obsessions unfortunately are not explicitly assessed.

The OCI-CV includes a number of more generic obsession items that may capture aggressive, sexual, and scrupulosity obsessions when individuals identify these type of thoughts as "bad." For example, items such as "I'm upset by bad thoughts," "If a bad thought comes into my head I need to say certain things over and over," "I get upset by bad thoughts that pop into my head when I don't want them to" (Foa et al., 2010) may be endorsed in the context of these type of obsessions, however, items do not explicitly ask about, or refer to, harm, sexual, or religious content.

With the limitations of existing self-report measures for identifying aggressive, sexual, and religious/moral obsessions in youth, it is important for clinicians to conducted detailed assessment using standardized clinical assessment techniques and conduct a thorough functional analysis of factors that precipitate and maintain the individual's OCD symptoms, with particular sensitivity to developmental issues. Self-monitoring is also important early in treatment, where youth track the triggers, frequency, intensity, and reactions to their obsessions in order to enhance functional analysis of maintaining factors, and enhance assessment of baseline severity.

Assessment Challenges and Considerations with Youth

The issue of shame and embarrassment has already been discussed above, however, there are a number of other considerations to take into account when assessing unacceptable obsessions in children and adolescents. It is important to tailor assessment to the developmental age of the child when phrasing questions. For example, younger children may have less awareness about sex, and the choice of language or examples provided during assessment is important to adjust accordingly. Similarly, depending on the age, developmental stage, and family relationships, the young person may feel more or less comfortable discussing certain obsessional thoughts with their parent present. Clinicians should consider these dynamics, or could explicitly ask the child their preferences for parental presence or absence.

In contrast to the underreporting of symptoms common in the context of shame and embarrassment, many youth are uncomfortable at the prospect of participating in a clinical assessment, and may be unsure of what is expected of them. Youth may answer positively to questions in an effort to "please" the interviewer, and/or may also lack the cognitive capacity and insight to differentiate obsessions from fleeting thoughts. Accordingly, it is important to ask the child open-ended, follow-up questions to try to gauge the severity of obsessions, their distress and resistance, and to differentiate the presence of a fleeting thought or worry from genuine repetitively and intrusive obsession. The clinician may need to provide psychoeducation about the nature or distinction of obsessions, as well as some initial education about the format of the assessment (e.g., there are no right or wrong answers, some of these questions might apply to you and some might not). It is important to note, that in many cases youth are relieved to disclose their symptoms to a non-judgmental clinician, and to have these symptoms normalized.

Further inquiry into mental compulsions is also important, and can have important implications for later treatment. Mental and overt compulsive behaviors can have a variety of triggers. For example, mentally repeating a phrase may be an attempt to neutralize an aggressive or blasphemous thought, or may be the result of doubting whether this was said correctly and needing to repeat until it feels "just right." Distinguishing mental compulsions that are linked with unacceptable obsessions and those that are not can be helpful for directing exposure and response prevention treatment targets.

Family accommodation is a core area to assess for when youth present with aggressive, sexual, and scrupulosity symptoms. In most cases, asking parents about specific behaviors is sufficient, or this information may be elicited during a functional analysis (e.g., "When your child engages in [compulsion] or tells you about [obsession] what do you do?"). Family accommodation is a key maintaining factor in pediatric OCD that needs to be targeted in treatment (Lebowitz & Bloch, 2012; Merlo, Lehmkuhl, Geffken, & Storch, 2009), correcting misattribution of OCD symptoms while still remaining sensitive to familial belief systems that may be connected to the child's symptoms. Common forms of family accommodation when youth present with aggressive and/or harm obsessions include hiding sharp knives and scissors; cutting the child's food for them; providing excessive reassurance that nothing bad will happen, allowing or facilitating avoidance of certain people, and screening or recording nontriggering television and movies; checking online newspapers for reports of accidents; and avoiding certain colors or numbers in the house (e.g., black or red, the number 6). Family accommodation of sexual obsessions can include providing excessive reassurance about a child's sexual orientation; facilitating avoidance of certain people or remaining in the child's presence when they are near particular individuals; altering their clothing to reduce potential triggers for the child (e.g., wearing conservative clothing or covered certain body parts); screening or altering the television, magazines and books that a child is exposed to (including at school or avoiding certain stores, such as the grocery store); or facilitating or participating in compensatory compulsions such as repeating certain phrases or behaviors. In the case of scrupulosity, family members may take the child to multiple religious services or confessions; praise their excessive praying or bible study; reassure the child that their actions were not sinful or that they are "good" after the child "confesses"; repeat certain religious phrases or prayers at the child's request; or alter certain family routines and practices, such as recycling or reducing shower durations in the case of moral obsessions about wastefulness, or not eating meat, eggs or milk, or wearing leather in the case of moral obsessions about harming animals.

Given the high rates of comorbidity in pediatric OCD, it is important to assess for a range of associated symptoms. As discussed above, youth who experience one type of taboo obsession often experience others (Bloch et al., 2008; Leckman et al., 2009). There is also a high rate of comorbid tic disorders in youth who experience aggressive, religious, and sexual obsessions (Masi et al., 2005; Zohar et al., 1997). Very notably, when youth disclose the presence of aggressive or sexual obsessions, it is particularly important to examine risk and safety issues. Distinguishing between obsessions and suicidal, homicidal, or aggressive desires is important, and is generally done via assessing whether youth who experience these obsessions and are fearful of them, do not desire to hurt themselves/others, and try to avoid being in situations where they fear they might cause themselves or others harm (e.g., being near sharp objects, moving cars or high places). This provides the clinician with different information about risk and safety compared with the youth who is preoccupied with thoughts of harm or death, is depressed and/or has current suicidal ideation. The distinction between obsessions and suicidal or nonsuicidal injurious thoughts is typically made when a youth describes that the intrusive thoughts are upsetting and distressing, and/ or that they do not want to harm themselves but feel as though they might during experience of the intrusive thought.

Treatment

As with other subtypes of OCD, cognitive behavioral therapy (CBT) with a focus on exposure and response prevention (ERP) is the first-line treatment for aggressive, religious/moral and sexual obsessions in youth (Abramowitz, Whiteside, & Deacon, 2005; Fernandez de la Cruz et al., 2013; Lewin, Storch, Geffken, Goodman, & Murphy, 2006; Watson & Rees, 2008). Several studies in adults with OCD have suggested that adults who present with sexual and religious obsessions show poorer treatment response (Alonso et al., 2001; Mataix-Cols, Marks, Greist, Kobak, & Baer, 2002; Rufer, Fricke, Moritz, Kloss, & Hand, 2006); however, these results were not been replicated in studies with youth (Fernandez de la Cruz et al., 2013; Storch et al., 2008), suggesting no evidence to impediments to standard treatment for youth presenting with these types of obsessions. Even in nonclinical individuals, unusual or intrusive thoughts are a common phenomenon (Brewin, 1996; Rachman & de Silva, 1978; Rassin & Muris, 2007), many of which may resemble the content of OCD obsessions; however, individuals without OCD generally dismiss these thoughts while those with OCD engage with the thought in an attempt to remove, control, avoid, understand, interpret, or find meaning in the thought (Purdon & Clark, 1993, 1994; Salkovskis & Campbell, 1994). In general, the goal of ERP with individuals who experience aggressive, sexual, and religious obsessions is to allow the individual to see intrusive thoughts as "just thoughts." These thoughts do not represent any deep-seated unconscious desires (despite some psychoanalytic theories), will not influence behavior, and do not need to be controlled. The format and procedures of ERP are discussed elsewhere in this book (see Chapters 13 and 31), so we will focus on the specifics of implementing ERP with youth presenting with aggressive, religious/ moral and sexual obsessions.

Types of Exposure Tasks

As with ERP for other symptom dimensions, treatment for aggressive, sexual, and religious obsessions typically involves graded exposure to increasingly distressing situations, however, there is an increased emphasis on managing covert or mental compulsions as well as reducing family accommodation. For example, youth with aggressive obsessions may increase their exposure to being around dangerous objects, for example, standing on a bridge with another person, holding scissors, saying aggressive phrases out loud. The tasks generally serve to test out the belief that the young person will lose control of their behavior as a result of the thought. In many cases "overlearning" can be helpful, where extreme behavioral tasks are used to test the OCD predictions (e.g., holding a sharp knife to a confederate's neck). Discussing the rationale for ERP tasks with youth and their parents can be especially important for harm exposures, as many parents and youth will have a high level of fear about engaging in these "risky" exposure tasks, and often the therapist will be involved in the initial tasks to model their confidence in the perceived probability of the harmful outcome occurring.

In the case of sexual obsessions, it can be important to discuss familial beliefs around sexuality with the young person, as well as their parents prior to initiating treatment. Families where there is a high level of shame or secrecy around sexuality may foster the child's negative interpretations and shame around these thoughts, and increase their desire to avoid or neutralize the "bad" thoughts. Normalizing sexuality and age-appropriate sexual development can be important when working with these youth, but should be respectful of family and parental values. Exposure tasks with these youth with typically involves triggering a sexual thought and not neutralizing with a compulsion, and reducing behavioral avoidance of people/situations to decreasing thought–action fusion. For example, being alone with the person involved in their obsessional thought or viewing pictures that "make them gay."

Treating religious and moral obsessions also requires a great deal of sensitivity. Clinicians need to remain respectful of the family and young person's faith and beliefs, while also highlighting incompatibilities between the youth's obsessions and the general beliefs, behaviors, and doctrines of their faith (Huppert & Siev, 2010; Peris & Rozenman, 2016). Motivation to engage in treatment for scrupulosity can vary between clients, and even if youth are motivated to reduce their symptoms, parental and family influences may need to be addressed. It can be challenging when family members not only accommodate the child's religious obsessions, but actually rein-force them. As discussed already, the involvement of clergy can be useful in some cases where OCD scrupulosity can be differentiated from religious doctrines, however, in many cases, clergy and religious leaders also reinforce symptoms. Family sessions and parent sessions that involve psychoeducation about OCD and scrupulosity may help to increase parental insight and provide a rationale for reducing accommodation. Careful psychoeducation about scrupulosity symptoms can incorporate a stance that OCD has attached itself to religion (rather than other domains) because that area has some core importance to the child, and OCD uses these beliefs against them (Huppert & Siev, 2010). However, the obsessions and compulsions are fear-governed rather than faith-based. If the young person is motivated to address their symptoms, but parental involvement is counterproductive, it may be possible to work with the child alone and reduce parental participation.

Differentiating OCD and religious beliefs can be complex. Feared outcomes are often difficult to directly test with scrupulosity given that individuals may fear judgment and condemnation from their God, or going to hell. Given that these events are proposed to occur after death, it can be difficult to directly test or logically dispute these feared outcomes. Individuals with scrupulosity typically desire certainty regarding their actions and eternity, which cannot be achieved. Treatment for scrupulosity involves ERP as the main treatment component, where individuals are repeatedly exposed to triggers while refraining from compulsions in order to learn that the feared outcome does not happen, as well as to habituate to the triggers by reducing avoidance. Religious exposures may also involve deliberately engaging in blasphemous acts to assess the outcome (e.g., tearing a page out of the bible and writing curse words). Participating in ERP requires the individual to be able to take a risk about their future, learning to tolerate uncertainty, and to set achievable and meaningful goals for their lifestyle and religious practices. Involvement of clergy in the treatment of scrupulosity should be carefully considered. In some cases, seeking advice or guidance from religious advisors to differentiate which aspects of their obsessions are inconsistent with the general beliefs of their faith can be useful. However, unfortunately, some clergy and religious leaders may actually encourage compulsive behaviors, misidentifying them as being signs of devout religious practice (Huppert & Siev, 2010). Similarly, patients often consider the advice of religious or spiritual leaders to be superior to that of a mental health professional. Feedback from clergy that the youth is not sinning, or that their God (or equivalent) is compassionate and forgiving can often be important corrective information to be used during ERP when sought once, especially early in treatment. However repeated reassurance-seeking from clergy tends to serve as accommodation, perpetuating OCD symptomatology. It is important to consider the relative benefits and challenges of involving religious leaders in treatment, particularly when their spiritual advice may be incompatible with ERP (Deacon, Vincent, & Zhang, 2013). Where possible, collaborative efforts are ideal (Siev & Huppert, 2016). Similarly, working with youth to identify whether their religious practices are in fact faith-based or OCD-based can also help to build motivation for treating their OCD. Once the young person is willing to engage in treatment, ERP tasks usually involve deliberately engaging in certain mental or overt behaviors (e.g., thinking or saying blasphemous things, purposely not saying prayers "right") without engaging in compulsions until they habituate to the distress. This can also include moderating the frequency of certain religious practices (e.g., excessive use of confession or prayer) or eliminating others (e.g., self-punishment).

Themes of morality can be somewhat more complex to work with. Morality is often viewed as a punitive externalized standard that the young person fails to live up to. Cognitive therapy tends to involve developing an internalized belief system about morality and to develop goals about the acts and actions that are deemed moral by the individual. As with religious obsessions, ERP typically involves reducing compulsive responses, excessive preoccupations (via habituation), and reducing avoidance. Individuals may be encouraged to engage in actions or activities that would support their internalized beliefs about morality (e.g., voluntary work, being a kind friend), reduce perfectionism and to learn self-forgiveness or self-compassion.

Role of Family

As with other types of pediatric presentations, working solely with the young person is likely to result in barriers to generalization of skills outside of session, compliance with homework practice, and motivation. Depending on the child's age, parental insight into (and attribution of) their child's symptoms, and the relationship between the parent and child, parents can be a strong support for treatment or can present a significant clinical obstacle.

Parental reactions to their child's symptoms can be important to consider and manage if necessary for successful treatment. Critical parental reactions in response to a child's aggressive, religious, or sexual obsessions may arise for a number of reasons. For example, parents may mistakenly believe that their child is deviant, or is likely to engage in these behaviors (Fernandez de la Cruz et al., 2013); the parent may not understand that these obsessional thought and/or images are symptomatic of OCD; they may feel powerless to help their child; or feel a level of shame and embarrassment themselves. Unfortunately, critical reactions are likely to increase the child's level of shame and embarrassment, and to be an obstacle to youth feeling comfortable discussing these symptoms in treatment. Psychoeducation about OCD can be important for parents and family members, in addition to the presenting child, in order to correct any misunderstandings and misattributions, and to address unhelpful reactions.

For ethical reasons, it is also important to have parental consent and close involvement when engaging in exposure tasks for aggressive, sexual, and religious obsessions, necessitating a shared understanding of the underlying pathology (Ung, Ale, & Whiteside, 2016). Parents are usually relieved to understand their child's symptoms and to learn that there are effective treatments to work with these symptoms. Reinforcing the importance of a supportive and nonjudgmental parental reaction toward obsessions will encourage children to be more open about their symptoms, and potentially allow them to engage more effectively with treatment.

Parents may also accommodate their child's OCD-related avoidance of certain situations or stimuli, or partake in compulsive behaviors (e.g., providing reassurance, encouraging excessive religious counsel, or allowing avoidance of certain situations) (Lebowitz & Bloch, 2012; Storch et al., 2010b). Family accommodation is associated with poorer treatment response for pediatric OCD (Lebowitz & Bloch, 2012; Merlo, Lehmkuhl, Geffken, & Storch, 2009), and needs to be directly targeted in treatment. Parents who understand the nature of their child's symptoms can help to facilitate or support the implementation of treatment strategies during out-of-session practice tasks. They can also work at reducing parental accommodation behaviors that maintain their child's symptoms. Educating parents about unacceptable obsessional thoughts and reducing their accommodation of symptoms can also improve the accuracy of parental feedback to therapist about the young person's progress, and facilitate increased discussion of obsessional topics within the family (which can serve as a form of ERP in and of itself).

References

Abramowitz, J. S., Franklin, M. E., Schwartz, S. A., & Furr, J. M. (2003). Symptom presentation and outcome of cognitive-behavioral therapy for obsessive-compulsive disorder. *Journal of Consultative and Clinical Psychology, 71*(6), 1049–1057. doi: 10.1037/0022-006x.71.6.1049.

Abramowitz, J. S., Huppert, J. D., Cohen, A. B., Tolin, D. F., & Cahill, S. P. (2002). Religious obsessions and compulsions in a non-clinical sample: The Penn Inventory of Scrupulosity (PIOS). *Behaviour Research and Therapy, 40*(7), 825–838.

Abramowitz, J. S., Whiteside, S. P., & Deacon, B. J. (2005). The effectiveness of treatment for pediatric obsessive-compulsive disorder: A meta-analysis. *Behavior Therapy, 36*(1), 55–63. doi: 10.1016/S0005-7894(05)80054-1.

Alonso, P., Menchon, J. M., Pifarre, J., Mataix-Cols, D., Torres, L., Salgado, P., & Vallejo, J. (2001). Long-term follow-up and predictors of clinical outcome in obsessive-compulsive patients treated with serotonin reuptake inhibitors and behavioral therapy. *Journal of Clinical Psychiatry*, 62(7), 535–540.

Amir, N., Freshman, M., Ramsey, B., Neary, E., & Brigidi, B. (2001). Thought–action fusion in individuals with OCD symptoms. *Behaviour Research and Therapy*, 39(7), 765–776. doi: 10.1016/S0005-7967(00)00056-5.

Bloch, M. H., Landeros-Weisenberger, A., Rosário, M. C., Pittenger, C., & Leckman, J. F. (2008). Meta-analysis of the symptom structure of Obsessive-Compulsive Disorder. *American Journal of Psychiatry*, 165(12), 1532–1542. doi: 10.1176/appi.ajp.2008.08020320.

Brewin, C. R. (1996). Brief report: Intrusive Thoughts and Intrusive Memories in a Nonclinical Sample. *Cognition and Emotion*, 10(1), 107–112. doi: 10.1080/026999396380411.

Butwicka, A., & Gmitrowicz, A. (2010). Symptom clusters in obsessive-compulsive disorder (OCD): Influence of age and age of onset. *European Child and Adolescent Psychiatry*, 19(4), 365–370. doi: 10.1007/s00787-009-0055-2

Ciarrocchi, J. W. (1995). *The doubting disease: Help for scrupulosity and religious compulsions.* Mahwah, NJ: Integration Books.

Deacon, B. J., Vincent, A. M., & Zhang, A. R. (2013). Lutheran clergy members' responses to scrupulosity: The effects of moral thought–action fusion and liberal vs. conservative denomination. *Journal of Obsessive-Compulsive and Related Disorders*, 2(2), 71–77. doi: 10.1016/j.jocrd.2012.12.003.

Fernandez de la Cruz, L., Barrow, F., Bolhuis, K., Krebs, G., Volz, C., Nakatani, E., ... Mataix-Cols, D. (2013). Sexual obsessions in pediatric obsessive-compulsive disorder: Clinical characteristics and treatment outcomes. *Depression and Anxiety*, 30(8), 732–740. doi: 10.1002/da.22097.

Foa, E. B., Coles, M., Huppert, J. D., Pasupuleti, R. V., Franklin, M. E., & March, J. (2010). Development and validation of a child version of the obsessive compulsive inventory. *Behavior Therapy*, 41(1), 121–132. doi: 10.1016/j.beth.2009.02.001.

Geller, D. A., Biederman, J., Faraone, S., Agranat, A., Cradock, K., Hagermoser, L., ... Coffey, B. J. (2001). Developmental aspects of obsessive compulsive disorder: Findings in children, adolescents, and adults. *Journal of Nervous and Mental Disorders*, 189(7), 471–477.

Grant, J. E., Pinto, A., Gunnip, M., Mancebo, M. C., Eisen, J. L., & Rasmussen, S. A. (2006). Sexual obsessions and clinical correlates in adults with obsessive-compulsive disorder. *Comprehensive Psychiatry*, 47(5), 325–329. doi: 10.1016/j.comppsych.2006.01.007.

Hanna, G. L. (1995). Demographic and clinical features of obsessive-compulsive disorder in children and adolescents. *Journal of the American Academy of Child and Adolescent Psychiatry*, 34(1), 19–27. doi: 10.1097/00004583-199501000-00009.

Huppert, J. D., & Siev, J. (2010). Treating scrupulosity in religious individuals using cognitive-behavioral therapy. *Cognitive and Behavioral Practice*, 17(4), 382–392. doi: 10.1016/j.cbpra.2009.07.003.

Labad, J., Menchon, J. M., Alonso, P., Segalas, C., Jimenez, S., Jaurrieta, N., ... Vallejo, J. (2008). Gender differences in obsessive–compulsive symptom dimensions. *Depression and Anxiety*, 25(10), 832–838. doi: 10.1002/da.20332.

Lebowitz, E. R., & Bloch, M. (2012). Family Accommodation in pediatric obsessive compulsive disorder. *Expert Review of Neurotherapeutics*, 12(2), 229–238. doi: 10.1586/ern.11.200.

Leckman, J. F., Bloch, M. H., & King, R. A. (2009). Symptom dimensions and subtypes of obsessive-compulsive disorder: A developmental perspective. *Dialogues in Clinical Neuroscience*, 11(1), 21–33.

Lensi, P., Cassano, G. B., Correddu, G., Ravagli, S., Kunovac, J. L., & Akiskal, H. S. (1996). Obsessive-compulsive disorder: Familial-developmental history, symptomatology, comorbidity and course with special reference to gender-related differences. *British Journal of Psychiatry*, 169(1), 101–107.

Lewin, A. B., Storch, E. A., Geffken, G. R., Goodman, W. K., & Murphy, T. K. (2006). A neuropsychiatric review of pediatric obsessive-compulsive disorder: Etiology and efficacious treatments. *Neuropsychiatric Disease and Treatment, 2*(1), 21–31.

Mancebo, M. C., Garcia, A. M., Pinto, A., Freeman, J. B., Przeworski, A., Stout, R., … Rasmussen, S. A. (2008). Juvenile-onset OCD: Clinical features in children, adolescents and adults. *Acta Psychiatrica Scandinavica, 118*(2), 149–159. doi: 10.1111/j.1600-0447.2008.01224.x.

Masi, G., Millepiedi, S., Mucci, M., Bertini, N., Milantoni, L., & Arcangeli, F. (2005). A naturalistic study of referred children and adolescents with obsessive-compulsive disorder. *Journal of the American Academy of Child and Adolescent Psychiatry, 44*(7), 673–681. doi: 10.1097/01.chi.0000161648.82775.ee.

Mataix-Cols, D., Marks, I. M., Greist, J. H., Kobak, K. A., & Baer, L. (2002). Obsessive-compulsive symptom dimensions as predictors of compliance with and response to behaviour therapy: Results from a controlled trial. *Psychotherapy and Psychosomatics, 71*(5), 255–262.

Mataix-Cols, D., Nakatani, E., Micali, N., & Heyman, I. (2008). Structure of obsessive-compulsive symptoms in pediatric OCD. *Journal of the American Academy of Child and Adolescent Psychiatry, 47*(7), 773–778. doi: 10.1097/CHI.0b013e31816b73c0.

Mataix-Cols, D., Rosário-Campos, M. C., & Leckman, J. F. (2005). A multidimensional model of obsessive-compulsive disorder. *American Journal of Psychiatry, 162*(2), 228–238. doi: 10.1176/appi.ajp.162.2.228.

Merlo, L. J., Lehmkuhl, H. D., Geffken, G. R., & Storch, E. A. (2009). Decreased family accommodation associated with improved therapy outcome in pediatric obsessive-compulsive disorder. *Journal of Consulting and Clinical Psychology, 77*(2), 355–360. doi: 10.1037/a0012652.

Miller, C. H., & Hedges, D. W. (2008). Scrupulosity disorder: An overview and introductory analysis. *Journal of Anxiety Disorders, 22*(6), 1042–1058. doi: 10.1016/j.janxdis.2007.11.004.

Milliner-Oar, E. L., Cadman, J. H., & Farrell, L. J. (2016). Treatment of Aggressive obsessions in childhood obsessive-compulsive disorder. In E. A. Storch, & A. B. Lewin (Eds.), *Clinical handbook of obsessive-compulsive and related disorders* (pp. 149–169). Cham, Switzerland: Springer.

Moulding, R., Aardema, F., & O'Connor, K. P. (2014). Repugnant obsessions: A review of the phenomenology, theoretical models, and treatment of sexual and aggressive obsessional themes in OCD. *Journal of Obsessive-Compulsive and Related Disorders, 3*(2), 161–168. doi: 10.1016/j.jocrd.2013.11.006.

Peris, T. S., & Rozenman, M. (2016). Treatment of Scrupulosity in childhood obsessive-compulsive disorder. In E. A. Storch, & A. B. Lewin (Eds.), *Clinical handbook of obsessive-compulsive and related disorders* (pp. 131–147). Cham, Switzerland: Springer

Purdon, C. (2004). Cognitive-behavioral treatment of repugnant obsessions. *Journal of Clinical Psychology, 60*(11), 1169–1180. doi: 10.1002/jclp.20081.

Purdon, C., & Clark, D. A. (1993). Obsessive intrusive thoughts in nonclinical subjects. Part I: Content and relation with depressive, anxious and obsessional symptoms. *Behaviour Research and Therapy, 31*(8), 713–720. doi: 10.1016/0005-7967(93)90001-B.

Purdon, C., & Clark, D. A. (1994). Obsessive intrusive thoughts in nonclinical subjects. Part II: Cognitive appraisal, emotional response and thought control strategies. *Behaviour Research and Therapy, 32*(4), 403–410. doi: 10.1016/0005-7967(94)90003-5.

Rachman, S. (1998). A cognitive theory of obsessions: elaborations. *Behaviour Research and Therapy, 36*(4), 385–401.

Rachman, S., & de Silva, P. (1978). Abnormal and normal obsessions. *Behaviour Research and Therapy, 16*(4), 233–248. doi: 10.1016/0005-7967(78)90022-0.

Rassin, E., & Muris, P. (2007). Abnormal and normal obsessions: A reconsideration. *Behaviour Research and Therapy, 45*(5), 1065–1070. doi: 10.1016/j.brat.2006.05.005.

Rosário-Campos, M. C., Leckman, J. F., Curi, M., Quatrano, S., Katsovitch, L., Miguel, E. C., & Pauls, D. L. (2005). A family study of early-onset obsessive-compulsive disorder. *American Journal of Medical Genetics Part B Neuropsychiatric Genetics, 136B*(1), 92–97. doi: 10.1002/ajmg.b.30149.

Rufer, M., Fricke, S., Moritz, S., Kloss, M., & Hand, I. (2006). Symptom dimensions in obsessive-compulsive disorder: Prediction of cognitive-behavior therapy outcome. *Acta Psychiatrica Scandinavica, 113*(5), 440–446. doi: 10.1111/j.1600-0447.2005.00682.x.

Salkovskis, P. M., & Campbell, P. (1994). Thought suppression induces intrusion in naturally occurring negative intrusive thoughts. *Behaviour Research and Therapy, 32*(1), 1–8. doi: 10.1016/0005-7967(94)90077-9.

Scahill, L., Riddle, M. A., McSwiggin-Hardin, M., Ort, S. I., King, R. A., Goodman, W. K., … Leckman, J. F. (1997). Children's Yale–Brown Obsessive Compulsive Scale: Reliability and validity. *Journal of the American Academy of Child and Adolescent Psychiatry, 36*(6), 844–852. doi: 10.1097/00004583-199706000-00023.

Shafran, R., Frampton, I., Heyman, I., Reynolds, M., Teachman, B., & Rachman, S. (2003). The preliminary development of a new self-report measure for OCD in young people. *Journal of Adolescence, 26*(1), 137–142.

Shafran, R., Thordarson, D. S., & Rachman, S. (1996). Thought–action fusion in obsessive compulsive disorder. *Journal of Anxiety Disorders, 10*(5), 379–391. doi: 10.1016/0887-6185(96)00018-7.

Siev, J., & Huppert, J. D. (2016). Treatment of scrupulosity-related obsessive-compulsive disorder. In E. A. Storch, & A. B. Lewin (Eds.), *Clinical handbook of obsessive-compulsive and related disorders* (pp. 39–54). Cham, Switzerland: Springer.

Storch, E. A., Khanna, M., Merlo, L. J., Loew, B. A., Franklin, M., Reid, J. M., … Murphy, T. K. (2009). Children's Florida Obsessive Compulsive Inventory: Psychometric properties and feasibility of a self-report measure of obsessive-compulsive symptoms in youth. *Child Psychiatry and Human Development, 40*(3), 467–483. doi: 10.1007/s10578-009-0138-9.

Storch, E. A., Lack, C. W., Merlo, L. J., Geffken, G. R., Jacob, M. L., Murphy, T. K., & Goodman, W. K. (2007). Clinical features of children and adolescents with obsessive-compulsive disorder and hoarding symptoms. *Comprehensive Psychiatry, 48*(4), 313–318. doi: 10.1016/j.comppsych.2007.03.001.

Storch, E. A., Larson, M. J., Muroff, J., Caporino, N., Geller, D., Reid, J. M., … Murphy, T. K. (2010a). Predictors of functional impairment in pediatric obsessive-compulsive disorder. *Journal of Anxiety Disorders, 24*(2), 275–283. doi: 10.1016/j.janxdis.2009.12.004.

Storch, E. A., Larson, M. J., Muroff, J., Caporino, N., Geller, D., Reid, J. M., … Murphy, T. K. (2010b). Predictors of functional impairment in pediatric obsessive-compulsive disorder. *Journal of Anxiety Disorders, 24*(2), 275–283. doi: 10.1016/j.janxdis.2009.12.004.

Storch, E. A., Merlo, L. J., Larson, M. J., Marien, W. E., Geffken, G. R., Jacob, M. L., … Murphy, T. K. (2008). Clinical features associated with treatment-resistant pediatric obsessive-compulsive disorder. *Comprehensive Psychiatry, 49*(1), 35–42. doi: 10.1016/j.comppsych.2007.06.009.

Torres, A. R., Ramos-Cerqueira, A. T., Ferrao, Y. A., Fontenelle, L. F., do Rosário, M. C., & Miguel, E. C. (2011). Suicidality in obsessive-compulsive disorder: Prevalence and relation to symptom dimensions and comorbid conditions. *Journal of Clinical Psychiatry, 72*(1), 17–26, quiz 119–120. doi: 10.4088/JCP.09m05651blu.

Uher, R., Heyman, I., Turner, C. M., & Shafran, R. (2008). Self-, parent-report and interview measures of obsessive-compulsive disorder in children and adolescents. *Journal of Anxiety Disorders, 22*(6), 979–990. doi: 10.1016/j.janxdis.2007.10.001.

Ung, D., Ale, C. M., & Whiteside, S. P. H. (2016). Treatment of sexual obsessions in childhood obsessive-compulsive disorder. In E. A. Storch, & A. B. Lewin (Eds.), *Clinical handbook of obsessive-compulsive and related disorders* (pp. 117–130). Cham, Switzerland: Springer.

Veale, D., Freeston, M., Krebs, G., Heyman, I., & Salkovskis, P. (2009). Risk assessment and management in obsessive-compulsive disorder. *Advances in Psychiatric Treatment, 15*, 332–343.

Watson, H. J., & Rees, C. S. (2008). Meta-analysis of randomized, controlled treatment trials for pediatric obsessive-compulsive disorder. *Journal of Child Psychology and Psychiatry, 49*(5), 489–498. doi: 10.1111/j.1469-7610.2007.01875.x.

Williams, M. T., & Farris, S. G. (2011). Sexual orientation obsessions in obsessive-compulsive disorder: Prevalence and correlates. *Psychiatry Research, 187*(1/2), 156–159. doi: 10.1016/j.psychres.2010.10.019.

Zohar, A. H., Pauls, D. L., Ratzoni, G., Apter, A., Dycian, A., Binder, M., … Cohen, D. J. (1997). Obsessive-compulsive disorder with and without tics in an epidemiological sample of adolescents. *American Journal of Psychiatry, 154*(2), 274–276. doi: doi:10.1176/ajp.154.2.274.

25

Mental Contamination

Anna E. Coughtrey, Roz Shafran, and Sophie Bennett

Mental contamination is the experience of feeling dirty and polluted in the absence of physical contact with a contaminant. It has been the focus of considerable recent clinical and research interest. Unlike the traditional concept of contact contamination – where contamination fears are evoked by direct physical contact with a dirty, dangerous, or harmful item or place associated with disease, dirt, or harmful substances – mental contamination evokes predominately internal feelings of dirtiness and pollution, and thus will often appear elusive, obscure, and intangible. One of the most famous literary examples of mental contamination is Shakespeare's Lady Macbeth, who, after ordering the brutal murder of King Duncan, compulsively washes her hands saying "will these hands ne'er be clean?" Despite not committing the murder herself, she still experiences a sense of internal pollution and feels tainted by King Duncan's blood. Similarly, sufferers of mental contamination often attempt to cleanse and wash away their internal sense of pollution, and for this reason mental contamination is thought to be particularly relevant to obsessive-compulsive disorder (OCD) where compulsive washing driven by a fear of contamination is one of the most common symptom subtypes.

Contamination fears in OCD have traditionally been treated using exposure and response prevention (ERP), where the patient is repeatedly exposed to the feared contaminant and is asked to not engage in washing behavior. ERP is an effective treatment for OCD, with around half of patients showing clinically significant change (e.g., Eddy, Dutra, Bradley, & Western, 2004; Foa et al., 2005). However, there is room for improvement, and the overall success rates for the treatment of OCD have not improved during the last 25 years (Eddy et al., 2004; Foa et al., 2005). As a result, calls have been made to better understand the psychopathology of OCD and enhance treatment efficacy (Ponniah, Magiati, & Hollon, 2013). We consider that advances in the understanding and treatment of contamination fears, particularly mental contamination, have the potential to improve outcome (Rachman, 2006; Rachman, Coughtrey, Shafran, & Radomsky, 2015).

This chapter will introduce the main forms of contamination and review the current evidence regarding the characteristics, assessment, and treatment of mental contamination.

The Wiley Handbook of Obsessive Compulsive Disorders, Volume I, First Edition.
Edited by Jonathan S. Abramowitz, Dean McKay, and Eric A. Storch.
© 2017 John Wiley & Sons Ltd. Published 2017 by John Wiley & Sons Ltd.

Forms of Contamination

Mental contamination and contact contamination regularly co-occur, due to a number of overlapping features. In both forms of contamination, clients report feelings of discomfort and dread that generate strong urges to wash, clean, and avoid re-contamination. However, the key distinguishing feature is that mental contamination arises without physical contact with a contaminant and that the primary source is human. The key features of mental and contact contamination are shown in Table 25.1.

According to the cognitive-behavioral theory of contamination fears (Rachman, 2004, 2010), the source of mental contamination is usually human and can take a number of related forms, including contamination after psychological or physical violation; self-contamination by one's own thoughts, images, and memories; and visual contamination and morphing into someone viewed as undesirable. It is understandable to initially feel dirty following a physical violation such as a sexual assault. However, in some cases, victims continue to experience feelings of internal dirtiness and an urge to wash for many years. This persistent sense of internal pollution, combined with re-evocations in the absence of physical contact, is indicative of mental contamination. Mental contamination can also arise following a psychological or emotional violation, including personal betrayal and perceived ill-treatment. Both victims and perpetrators of these humiliating, shaming, or degrading experiences may experience subsequent feelings of internal dirtiness and compulsive washing, and are commonly unable to even speak the name of the violator, see Table 25.2.

Mental contamination can be a direct product of a person's own mind, arising from unwanted, unacceptable, and repugnant thoughts, images, memories, and urges, known as self-contamination. The defining features of self-contamination are shown in Table 25.3. Sufferers tend to have high personal standards, are scrupulous, and strive to maintain their moral and physical purity. Thus, unacceptable and repugnant thoughts and acts lead to mental contamination, guilt and shame.

Some people are contaminated merely by the sight of a person viewed as immoral, disreputable, or bizarre. This visual contamination is closely linked to *morphing*, the fear of becoming contaminated, tainted, or somehow altered, by close association with a person perceived to be undesirable. In extreme cases, a person may fear that they may acquire these unpleasant characteristics and morph into the undesirable person themselves. The features of morphing are shown in Table 25.4.

Case Illustration of Mental Contamination

Caroline, a young woman in her twenties, experienced a fear of morphing. Specifically, she feared that she could catch cancer from being near people who she thought had cancer, and she felt "dirty" when she looked at or spoke to people she believed to be immoral. When she was near someone who she thought was immoral, she reported feeling vicariously guilty, as if she herself had done something wrong. For Caroline, feelings of dirtiness were akin to feelings of shame and guilt. Being near these undesirable people would leave her feeling dirty under her skin, which she described felt like an itch inside her body and left her with an urge to drink water, wash her hands, and to shower.

Table 25.1   Key features of contact and mental contamination

Contact contamination	Mental contamination
Feelings of discomfort, dread.	Feelings of discomfort, uneasiness, dread.
Provoked by contact with dirt, disease.	Physical contact not necessary.
Dominates other behavior.	Dominates other behavior.
Not applicable.	Can be generated internally.
Feelings evoked instantly with contact.	Occasionally.
Concentrated mainly on skin, especially the hands; localized.	No typical focus; diffuse; internal.
Generated by contact with external stimuli.	Can be generated internally (e.g., urges, thoughts, memories, images).
Not generated by ill-treatment.	Usually generated by perceived violation.
Contaminants are dirty, harmful substances.	Primary source is a person not a substance.
Feeling dirty, infected.	Internal dirtiness, pollution predominantly.
Spreads widely.	Some generalization.
Easily transmissible to others.	Rarely transmissible to others.
Other people are vulnerable to the contaminants.	Unique to the affected person.
Source of contamination is known.	Source of contamination obscure to affected person.
Site identifiable.	Site inaccessible.
Tangible contaminants.	Intangible contaminants.
Contamination re-evocable by contact with dirty, diseased source.	Contamination re-evocable by contact with human source.
Contamination evocable by secondary "carriers."	Contamination evocable by secondary sources, "carriers."
Common in childhood OCD.	Rarely occurs in childhood.
Pollution seldom re-evoked by mental events.	Pollution re-evocable by relevant mental events.
Anxiety evocable by relevant mental events.	Anxiety evocable by relevant mental events.
Lacks a moral element.	Moral element common.
Revulsion, disgust, nausea, fear.	Anxiety, revulsion, anger, shame, guilt, disgust common.
Not applicable.	Level/range of contamination fluctuates in response to changes in attitude to contaminator.
Generates urges to wash.	Generates urges to wash.
Generates urges to avoid.	Generates urges to avoid.
Transiently responsive to cleaning.	Cleaning is ineffective.
Treatment moderately effective.	Promising, specific treatment for mental contamination.

Source: Rachman 2014. Reproduced with permission of Oxford University.

Table 25.2 The features of mental contamination following physical and psychological violation

- The primary source of the contamination is a person(s), not a harmful or disgusting, inanimate substance.
- Items, places, or people associated with the primary person(s) can turn into secondary sources of contamination.
- The feelings of contamination seldom degrade spontaneously.
- The feelings of contamination spread.
- The feelings instigate urges to clean away the perceived contamination.
- The feelings promote avoidance of cues of contamination and avoidance of reminders of the incident/perpetrator and any cues/memories that are associated with the incident/ period/perpetrator.
- The feelings of contamination can be induced, and revived, with or without direct physical contact with items/places/people associated with the perpetrator.
- These feelings of contamination are often accompanied by more familiar forms of contact contamination (from sources such as dirt, germs).
- The affected person is uniquely, specifically, vulnerable to the primary source of the contamination.
- Fluctuations in the affected person's feelings/attitudes to the contaminator are followed by fluctuations in the level and range of contamination.
- The contamination is associated with a range of negative emotions and reactions that include anger, self-criticism, guilt, damaged self-esteem, general anxiety.
- The transmissibility of the contamination has three facets: other people are not vulnerable to becoming contaminated by contact with the primary source, but are vulnerable to secondary contamination, usually via the affected patient; people who come into contact with the primary source of the contamination can become secondary sources of contamination (carriers) for the affected patient.

Source: Rachman 2014. Reproduced with permission of Oxford University.

Table 25.3 The features of self-contamination

- The person him- or herself is the source of the contamination.
- Hence, the opportunities for contamination and re-contamination are constantly present.
- Unwanted, intrusive, repugnant thoughts, urges are a major source of the feelings of contamination.
- Many of the repugnant intrusions involve unwanted sexual or religious thoughts.
- Thoughts or harming other people, especially those who are unable to defend themselves, can evoke shame and feelings of pollution.
- Intrusive, repugnant thoughts that cause feelings of self-contamination are concealed.
- Feelings of self-contamination are influenced by mood states, especially depression.
- There usually is an (im)moral element.
- Repugnant habits (e.g., watching pornography) can cause feelings of contamination or pollution.
- Shame, guilt, self-distrust often accompany self-contamination.
- The contamination is relevant to the patient, but not to anyone else.
- The appraisals of the contaminants, and their threat, are unique.

Source: Rachman 2014. Reproduced with permission of Oxford University.

Table 25.4 The main features of a fear of morphing

- The person fears that he or she might unwillingly pick up undesirable characteristics from people whom they regard as weird, mentally unstable, marginal, immoral, shabby, drug-addicted, low status, and/or that they will be adversely changed by contact with such people.
- The assimilation of the unacceptable characteristics can occur as a result of touching the undesirable person or his or her clothing, or other possessions.
- The assimilation can also occur without physical contact – notably by visual contamination.
- Assimilation/exacerbation can be produced by remote cues, such as television, newspaper stories, etc.
- In extreme cases the affected person fears that he or she will lose his or her own identity and morph into the undesirable personality.
- The fear of morphing is sometimes accompanied by a belief that there are contagious germs which can transfer mental instability from person to person.
- The affected person feels uniquely threatened.
- Recognizes the irrationality of the fear.
- Resists the idea.
- Is not delusional.
- Usually the person has concurrent or past fears of contact contamination.
- In most cases, the affected person continues to function at least moderately well.
- The fear is accompanied by shame and/or embarrassment.
- It impairs the ability to concentrate.
- It generates avoidance behaviour, mental cleansing, neutralizing, washing.

Source: Rachman 2014. Reproduced with permission of Oxford University.

Caroline explained that her fear of morphing had intensified when she had discovered that her partner had cheated while he was away with friends. Following this incident, Caroline had felt very upset and angry with her partner, but had agreed to continue with the relationship. She described how she began to avoid all contact with her partner's friends, who she regarded as highly immoral as they all regularly cheated on their partners. Caroline reported that if she did come into contact with these people, even indirectly through her partner, she would wash and shower to prevent her from becoming tainted by their immorality.

In addition to morphing fear and visual contamination, Caroline also explained that the feelings of mental contamination and urges to wash could be evoked by unwanted intrusive thoughts and images about abusing children and incest. Caroline experienced these cognitions as highly repugnant, particularly as she regarded herself as a highly moral person. When she experienced these thoughts, Caroline would sip water and wash her hands in order to prevent the contamination and immorality from spreading to her loved ones and personal possessions. Despite medication and a previous course of cognitive-behavioral therapy (CBT) for OCD, which had focused mainly on systematic, graded ERP, Caroline continued to experience severe and debilitating mental contamination. We worked with Caroline over 12 sessions, during which she made significant progress. A description of the course of treatment is provided at the end of this chapter.

Current Evidence

Sometimes a clinical phenomenon is so striking that it captures the imagination and interest of clinicians and researchers alike. This has been our experience with thought–action fusion, a cognitive distortion in OCD that has been the subject of 58 papers by a wide variety of research groups around the globe. We have had a similar experience with mental contamination. In workshops, clinicians nod their heads in recognition of the clinical phenomenon, researchers ask for copies of the instrument we use to assess it, and cases that previously failed to respond to treatment are reconsidered. Such is the extent of interest, that despite the full theory first being posited only a decade ago, a systematic search of the literature yielded 32 papers, 18 using nonclinical participants, and the remainder using clinical populations. Two of the papers on mental contamination are the most downloaded in a leading journal of OCD research (Coughtrey, Shafran, Knibbs, & Rachman, 2012; Coughtrey, Shafran, & Rachman, 2013b). The aim of the remainder of this chapter is to summarize the current evidence regarding the clinical characteristics of mental contamination, its assessment, and treatment.

Phenomenology

Evoked in the absence of contact. The fundamental aspect of mental contamination is that it is evoked in the absence of physical contact with a contaminant. Early studies used the "dirty kiss" method to evoke feelings of mental contamination in nonclinical participants. In these studies, healthy university students listened to audio descriptions of scenarios involving a nonconsensual kiss and were asked to vividly imagine the experience.

In the original study of 121 females, Fairbrother, Newth, and Rachman (2005) found that participants who imagined receiving a nonconsensual kiss reported significant increases in feelings of mental contamination and urges to wash, compared with participants who imagined receiving a consensual kiss. Additionally, eight participants in the nonconsensual condition subsequently washed out their mouths. The key finding that imagining a violating and distressing experience evokes feelings of contamination in the absence of physical contact and can result in actual washing behavior has been replicated in four subsequent studies, including in an independent sample of Japanese students (Elliott & Radomsky, 2009, 2012; Herba & Rachman, 2007; Ishikawa, Kobori, Komuro, & Shimizu, 2014). Additionally, a variant of the dirty-kiss task during which males were asked to imagine being the perpetrator of a nonconsensual kiss, has demonstrated that imagining and thinking about an unacceptable, nonconsensual experience can also evoke mental contamination (Rachman, Radomsky, Elliott, & Zysk, 2012). The magnitude of induced mental contamination was strongest when an element of betrayal was introduced into the imagined scenario, and when the participant appraised themselves as having personal responsibility for the occurrence of the kiss (Elliott & Radomsky, 2013; Radomsky & Elliott, 2009), highlighting possible cognitive targets in the treatment of mental contamination.

These early studies, however, were criticized on the grounds that participants were being asked to recall an event in which there had originally been physical contact. In response to these criticisms, different methods were developed to evaluate whether feelings of dirtiness could be evoked in the absence of imagined interpersonal contact.

These studies have robustly demonstrated that mental contamination can indeed be evoked following an autobiographical memory task (Coughtrey, Shafran & Rachman, 2014a, 2014b), imagery tasks (Lee et al., 2013), and by playing a violent video game (Gollwitzer & Melzer, 2012).

The experience of mental contamination is often difficult for patients to articulate. Often patients are baffled by the elusive, pervasive, and persistent sense of dirtiness and discomfort. Nevertheless, when gently probed, patients are able to recall times when they had felt dirty or contaminated in the absence of physical contact with a contaminant. Consistent with the theory, patients describe how their feelings of contamination are primarily associated with a human source, generate internal dirtiness, cause emotional distress, and evoke an urges to wash, neutralize, and avoid (Coughtrey, Shafran, Lee, & Rachman, 2012b).

Two studies have investigated the role of imagery in mental contamination. A qualitative study has demonstrated that people with contamination-related OCD report intrusive images of contamination that are vivid, distressing, and evoke feelings of dirtiness and trigger subsequent washing behavior (Coughtrey, Shafran, & Rachman, 2014c). A brief 20-item questionnaire measure has been developed to assess mental contamination imagery, and has demonstrated that compared with non-clinical controls, people with contamination OCD experience imagery that is more vivid, distressing, and harder to dismiss, and are more likely to experience images that directly evoke feelings of contamination and a subsequent urge to wash (Coughtrey et al., 2013a). In both studies, a small number of participants reported experiencing images (e.g., of mental shields) that were beneficial in reducing feelings of mental contamination and protecting them from future harm.

Persistence. One of the key aspects of mental contamination is its remarkable persistence. We recently had a patient, aged 54, whose specific contamination began when he was only 14 and living on a different continent. Interestingly, the phenomenon of mental contamination in the laboratory experiments described above was at odds with the clinical phenomenon, and instead was transient, with feelings of mental contamination naturally declining over time (Ishikawa et al., 2014). The same phenomenon of transience was found by Coughtrey and colleagues (2014c), who demonstrated that feelings of mental contamination in nonclinical participants lasted for a mere 3 minutes. However, repeatedly triggering of the feelings of mental contamination or repeatedly re-evoking the feelings and then washing with antibacterial wipes led to the persistence of mental contamination. This interesting finding suggests that the feelings of mental contamination might not be persistent per se, but instead are repeatedly triggered by repeated memories and experiences.

Associated with moral violations. Unlike contact contamination, mental contamination has been hypothesized to have a close relationship to moral violations. Initial findings supported this relationship. Using the dirty kiss paradigm, Elliott and Radomsky (2009), for example, found that a kiss from a man described as immoral led to increased mental contamination compared with a kiss from a man described as moral. Zhong and Liljenquist (2006) conducted four interconnected experiments and demonstrated that participants who were asked to recall an unethical memory (vs. recall of an ethical memory) were significantly more likely to generate more cleaning-related words in a word-fragment completion task, and were more likely to select an antibacterial hand wipe over a pencil as a choice of free gift, than participants who were asked to recall an ethical memory. Similarly, participants who copied out a story describing an unethical event rated cleansing products as significantly more desirable than participants who copied a story of an ethical event. Finally, in the fourth experiment, participants who washed their hands using an antibacterial hand wipe after recalling an unethical deed were significantly more likely to help a graduate student in a subsequent research task than participants who did not wash after recalling an unethical memory. Participants who washed reported significantly reduced feelings of guilt, shame, disgust, regret, embarrassment, and anger compared with participants who were not given the opportunity to wash their hands. Despite these promising initial findings of the relationship between feelings of dirtiness and moral violation, and a successful replication with participants with OCD (Reuven, Liberman, & Dar, 2013), subsequent replications of these four studies in samples of students in India, Spain, the United Kingdom and the United States have not found significant results (Earp, Everett, Madva, & Hamlin, 2014; Gamez, Diaz, & Marrero, 2011).

Spreading. One of the notable characteristics of conventional contact contamination is that it spreads. With physical dirt, the rationale behind such spreading is clear, although it takes on an element of magical thinking (Tolin, Worhunsky, & Matlby, 2004). Clinically, many patients show significant amounts of magical thinking when explaining how mental contamination spreads. In an experimental task, feelings of mental contamination were evoked in nonclinical participants. They were then asked to spread the contamination to a previously uncontaminated object (a pencil) without touching (no-contact condition) and with physical contact (contact condition). Almost half (48%) were able to magically spread mental contamination to the previously uncontaminated pencil, compared with 72% who could spread contact contamination. Participants were also able to subsequently transfer the mental contamination from the pencil to 12 subsequent neutral pencils, without degradation, thus replicating the clinical phenomenon that mental contamination can be transferred and spread without physical contact (Coughtrey et al., 2013).

Associations with Psychopathology

Most work on mental contamination has focused on its relationship with OCD. In a sample of patients with OCD at a university clinic in the United Kingdom, 46% reported clinically relevant levels of mental contamination; and mental contamination in the absence of contact contamination was reported by 10% of participants (Coughtrey et al., 2012a). Estimates of the presence of clinically relevant mental contamination symptoms in patients with OCD at an Italian outpatient clinic ranged between 12% and 61% (Carraresi, Bulli, Melli, & Stopani, 2013; Melli, Bulli, Carraresi, & Stopani, 2014). In all three studies, mental contamination severity was significantly correlated with symptoms of OCD, even after controlling for anxiety and depression (Carraresi et al., 2013; Coughtrey et al., 2012a; Melli et al., 2014). Additionally, mental contamination has been shown to mediate the relationships between disgust propensity and symptoms of OCD and fear of contamination (Carraresi et al., 2013; Melli et al., 2014). A phenomenon similar to morphing, known as "transformation obsession," has been reported in a series of nine cases of pediatric OCD (Volz & Heyman, 2007), where children described a fear of turning into someone else or taking on undesirable characteristics.

Prior to the development of the cognitive-behavioral theory of mental contamination, a number of case histories of individuals with comorbid posttraumatic stress disorder (PTSD) and OCD, demonstrated the presence of contamination-related symptoms (de Silva & Marks, 1999; Gershuny, Baer, Radomsky, Wilson, & Jenike, 2003). Subsequent research has indicated that experiences of sexual assault can evoke feelings of mental contamination, and that these feelings of internal dirtiness and disgust may mediate the relationship between sexual assault and PTSD symptoms (Adams, Badour, Cisler, & Feldner, 2014; Badour, Feldner, Blumenthal, & Bujarski, 2013; Badour, Feldner, Babdson, Blumenthal, & Dutton, 2013; Fairbrother & Rachman, 2004; Ishikawa, Kobori, & Shimizu, 2013).

Assessment of Mental Contamination

We have developed three questionnaires to assess different aspects of mental contamination: (a) the Mental Contamination addition to the VOCI (VOCI-MC); (b) the Contamination Thought–Action Fusion Scale (CTAF); and (c) the Contamination Sensitivity Scale (CSS). A psychometric analysis of these three scales has demonstrated that they have excellent internal consistency, convergent and divergent validity, and discriminant validity. The three scales accounted for significant unique variation in OCD symptoms beyond that accounted for by contact contamination, OCD-related cognitive distortions, general anxiety symptoms, and depression (Radomksy, Rachman, Shafran, Coughtrey, & Barber, 2014), indicating that they assess something that other measures cannot capture. An alternative measure of mental contamination is the Mental Pollution Questionnaire (MPQ), developed by Cougle, Lee, Horowitz, Wolitzky-Taylor, and Telch (2008). This eight-item measure has adequate item validity, good test–retest reliability, and predicted OCD symptoms over and above what was predicted by measures of guilt and disgust (Cougle et al., 2008). In a subsequent study of a sample of religious students, scores on the MPQ were not associated with religiosity, but were significantly correlated with childhood trauma and maladaptive guilt induction strategies used by parents (Berman, Wheaton, Fabricant, & Abramowitz, 2012). The availability of psychometrically sound self-report measures is critical both to supporting future research on mental contamination, but also in clinical applications in order to guide treatment.

Treatment of Mental Contamination

The motivation to develop a theoretical model, assessment instruments, and treatment for mental contamination was fueled by our clinical observation that many patients with this presentation of OCD appear to benefit from specific cognitive therapy techniques to directly address the particular beliefs and appraisals associated with mental contamination, for example, mislabeling of mood states, discussion of the meaning of betrayal, adjustment of moral standards, and imagery rescripting. Accordingly, the treatment for mental contamination that we have developed focuses on changing the meaning of mental contamination. Examples of common beliefs and appraisals associated with mental contamination are shown in Table 25.5.

More specifically, our psychological treatment for mental contamination involves approximately 12 one-hour sessions of individual CBT. The process of treatment is the same as CBT for contact contamination, but the content is different and tailored specifically for mental contamination. Although we do not incorporate systematic, graded exposure or response prevention behavioral experiments to test beliefs are a mainstay of the intervention. In addition to generic therapeutic and CBT skills such as engagement, setting goals, instilling hope, and reflecting and summarizing, treatment is tailored specifically for mental contamination.

Table 25.5 Beliefs and appraisals about mental contamination

- Many things look clean but feel dirty.
- People should be pure in mind and in body.
- Some people think I am weird because I am a clean freak.
- I must always avoid people with low morals.
- Before leaving home, I need to make sure that I am absolutely clean.
- If I think about contamination, it will increase my risk of actually becoming contaminated.
- Seeing disgusting pornographic material would make me feel sick, dirty.
- If I touched the possessions or clothing of someone who had treated me very badly, I would need to have a good wash.
- People who do something immoral will be punished.
- Sometimes I have a need to wash even though I know that I haven't touched anything dirty or dangerous.
- If I was touched by someone who had treated me very badly, it would make me feel unclean.
- People who read pornography must be avoided.
- Mixing with immoral people would definitely make me feel unclean.
- I will never be forgiven for my horrible thoughts.
- If I am touched by a nasty or immoral person, it makes me feel very unclean.
- It is quite possible to feel contaminated even without touching any contaminated material.
- It is immoral for me to use bad language at any time.
- Simply thinking about contamination can make me feel actually contaminated.
- No matter how hard I try with my washing, I never feel completely clean.
- If I cannot control my nasty thoughts I will go crazy.
- Simply remembering a contaminating experience can make me feel actually contaminated.
- It is completely wrong for me to tell dirty jokes.
- I am responsible for other people's bad behavior toward me.
- When I am in a low mood, I am far more sensitive to feelings of being contaminated.
- I will never get rid of the feeling that I am unclean, dirty.
- I definitely avoid movies that contain foul language and explicit sex scenes.
- I have a hard time getting rid of the feeling that I am unclean.
- People think I am weird because of my worries about dirt and diseases.
- If I did something immoral it would make me feel unclean.
- When I feel bad about myself, having a shower makes me feel better.
- Having to listen to someone making disgusting, nasty remarks makes me feel tainted, dirty.
- People will reject me if they find out about my nasty thoughts.
- If a nasty, immoral person touched me I would have to wash myself thoroughly.
- If I do not overcome my feelings of dirtiness, I will become sick.
- If I was touched by someone who behaved badly, I would need to wash myself.
- People who use disgusting language make me feel dirty, tainted

Source: Rachman 2014. Reproduced with permission of Oxford University.

Our initial evaluation of this treatment program was conducted with 12 patients who had failed to respond to conventional psychological treatment including ERP, all of whom had OCD with strong features of mental contamination. Following our treatment program, these patients reported reductions in mental contamination, other OCD symptoms, and seven no longer met the diagnostic criteria for OCD. These gains were maintained over a three- and six-month follow-up period (Coughtrey, Shafran, Lee, & Rachman, 2013a).

The initial treatment sessions are devoted to developing a detailed formulation of the patient's mental contamination fear. The nature and development of the mental contamination fears is analyzed and particular attention is given to the reasons why the patient currently feels under serious threat. Patients are asked to monitor and record contaminating triggers (in particular, human sources and their own thoughts and images), the intensity of mental contamination, location of pollution within themselves, and subsequent behaviors (e.g., forming a protective image, avoidance, washing, drinking water). This self-monitoring is used to increase a patient's general understanding and insight into mental contamination. In addition, personalized session-by-session monitoring of symptoms is utilized throughout treatment (e.g., recording the frequency and intensity of contaminating and protective images).

The next step involves a semi-didactic component to provide psychoeducation and corrective information about mental contamination. The different types of contamination are described and the human source of mental contamination is explained. A further area of discussion was mislabeling mood states and separating feelings of anger, aversion, and disgust from feelings of mental contamination. The ex-consequentia or emotional reasoning bias, when people infer the presence of danger from their feelings of fear (Arntz, Raunder, & Van den Hout, 1995), was also explained to clients. With mental contamination, the perceived contaminant evokes strong feelings of fear/disgust, and these feelings are interpreted in signaling the presence of significant danger of pollution. This component of treatment can help normalize patients' fears and provide assurance that such experiences are not a sign of impending doom or indicative that the patient is going mad.

Surveys are used to collect personally relevant information relating to mental contamination. In some cases, this is used to normalize the fears (e.g., by asking people how they would feel wearing a dead man's clothing), but they can also be related to more specific concerns, such as moral standards, reaction to particular categories of people, or ways of coping with emotions, such as guilt and depression.

Behavioral experiments, often incorporating exposure, but not necessarily, are a fundamental component of treatment and are used to test beliefs about contamination and to reduce maintaining behaviors (e.g., avoidance and washing behaviors). They are particularly helpful because they provide the patient with direct, vivid, and up-to-date information through personal experiences – which has greater weight than more distal information sources, such as reading or others' perspectives. The evidence is fed into the competing explanations, and, not infrequently, tips the balance (notably, say, in treating a fear of morphing). Technically it is important for the patient and therapist to formulate competing, unambiguous (written) predictions for each behavioral experiment. Unlike exposure exercises, which are deliberate, planned, repeated, prolonged confrontations with the same situation or to contaminated items (e.g., a hierarchy of fear contaminants), behavioral experiments are *circumscribed information-gathering exercises*. We do not use fear hierarchies in behavior experiments.

Cognitive-behavioral techniques are used to change the meaning of the source of contamination, modify self-generated contamination feelings by reinterpreting the significance of such feelings, address the meaning of dirtiness, and link this to issues of self-esteem and self-identity. Typical methods would include helping the patient see it from another perspective through discussions and cognitive restructuring.

A significant amount of treatment is devoted to understanding the role of images in triggering and maintaining mental contamination. The occurrence, nature, frequency, and effects of the unwanted intrusive images are assessed and rescripted as necessary (e.g., Arntz, 2012). The patient and therapist establish the content of the disturbing intrusive images and then assess the effects of the selected image(s) by using test probes. After establishing a baseline level of contamination, the therapist asks the client to form a vivid image of the primary source of mental contamination. They are then asked to report any feelings of contamination or dirtiness, and any urges to wash. Currently, the most effective method of dealing with unwanted intrusive images is to work with the image by changing its meaning via rescripting it and arriving at an alternative, more benign image (e.g., Arntz, 2012; Holmes, Arntz, & Smucker, 2007). The original image is not avoided, but rather changed. For example, Caroline experienced an intrusive image of her boyfriend cheating, which made her feel internally dirty and resulted in compulsive washing. Using rescripting techniques, Caroline updated the image to include new information (e.g., of her boyfriend saying that he had made a mistake and loved his girlfriend). The technique is enhanced by discussing how the patient construes the original and then the alternative image.

A relapse prevention plan is drawn up at the end of therapy. The plan includes a description of the factors that had maintained the client's contamination fear (e.g., beliefs that they were still in danger of contamination from the violator, mislabeling of mood states, beliefs about betrayal, and moral values), the techniques the client had found useful in treatment, identifying potential triggers for setbacks, and considering ways of resolving future difficulties.

A Case Illustration of the Treatment of Mental Contamination

Earlier, we introduced you to Caroline, a young woman with severe mental contamination and morphing fear. We worked with Caroline over 12 sessions, during which she made excellent progress. During the initial assessment and formulation sessions, the focus was on betrayal, guilt, and a fear of morphing into undesirable, immoral people. From this, it was established that Caroline held extremely high moral standards. Therefore, the majority of work from sessions 3–7 centered on testing her beliefs about morals, guilt, and omission/commission bias. Caroline conducted a survey of moral standards of people she held in high regard, and from this was able to rewrite a more realistic list of moral standards. These standards were then used in "old mindset vs. new mindset" experiments in which she acted "as if" she had the same moral standards as a close friend (who she regarded as an extremely kind and ethical person) for one full day, and then on the next day, reverted to her previously held higher moral standards. She assessed feelings of contamination, guilt, and washing behaviors on both days and discovered that her high moral standards were driving her feelings of mental contamination and urge to wash. Caroline also conducted behavioral experiments in which she deliberately tried to cause harm to others.

Table 25.6 Caroline's scores on outcome measures at pretreatment, posttreatment, and follow-up

	Pretreatment	*Posttreatment*	*3-month follow-up*	*6-month follow-up*
Y-BOCS	29	1	1	1
OCI-R	36	5	7	9
VOCI-MC	52	8	9	8
C-TAF	26	5	10	11
CSS	32	24	28	11
BDI-II	26	3	0	2
BAI	24	14	12	9

Note: Y-BOCS = Yale–Brown Obsessive-Compulsive Scale (Goodman et al., 1989); OCI-R = Obsessional Compulsive Inventory – Short Version (Foa et al., 2002); VOCI-MC = Mental Contamination subscale of the VOCI (Rachman, 2006; Radomsky et al., 2014); C-TAF = Contamination Thought–Action Fusion Scale (Radomsky et al., 2014); CSS = Contamination Sensitivity Scale (Radomsky et al., 2014); BDI-II = Beck Depression Inventory (Beck, Steer, & Brown, 1996); BAI = Beck Anxiety Inventory (Beck & Steer, 1990).

In these experiments, she deliberately tried to harm others by thinking about physically hurting them, betraying them, or wishing their relationship to break-up. She discovered that thinking something bad or immoral did not cause something bad or immoral to happen. Caroline also conducted "contrast behavioral experiments" in which she compared her feelings of contamination and guilt on days where she washed compulsively for one day and then washed only when she was physically dirty for the next; this was repeated throughout the week to obtain multiple data points for the experiment..

Sessions 8–11 focused on addressing the meaning of mental contamination and linking this with self-efficacy and self-esteem. This included discussions about misappraisal of mood states and cognitive restructuring of beliefs about the source of mental contamination. For example, at the start of therapy, Caroline believed that she was a bad person for thinking unkindly about others. At the end of therapy, she believed that it is normal to think unkind thoughts about other people, and that this did not make her an immoral person. The final treatment session focused on relapse prevention and Caroline developed a "blueprint for the future." This included a summary of the formulation of her difficulties, the results of key behavioral experiments that she had found helpful, a list of new helpful beliefs, and a message in a bottle: that thinking something "bad" did not make her "dirty." At the end of treatment, Caroline no longer required medication and did not meet the diagnostic criteria for mental contamination or any mental health problem. These gains were maintained over a six-month follow-up period, see Table 25.6.

Conclusions and Future Research

Recent clinical and research interest in mental contamination has resulted in a developing evidence base supporting Rachman's theory of contamination fears (1994, 2004, 2006), which postulates that feelings of dirtiness could arise in the absence of physical contact with a contaminant. The main findings of the evidence reviewed in this chapter indicate that mental contamination is a separate but overlapping construct from contact contamination, which is associated with diffuse feelings of internal dirtiness that can spread widely and rapidly without decline. Estimates in clinical samples indicate that it is an often unrecognized form of OCD and may also occur with PTSD symptoms in some victims of sexual assault. New measures developed to assess mental contamination have been shown to have excellent psychometric properties, but further research is needed to establish clinical norms.

Experimental studies in multiple countries have indicated that feelings of mental contamination can be evoked in nonclinical populations. This suggests that mental contamination exists on a continuum, with milder forms common in society, for example, following a bitter divorce (Rachman, 2013). However, the findings of these experiments indicate that the emotions evoked were intense yet fleeting. For example, in one study, the induced mental contamination was measurable only for around three minutes (Coughtrey et al., 2014a). This is in contrast to the theory and clinical reports that suggest that mental contamination is pervasive and stable. The transient nature of induced mental contamination may partially explain the nonsignificant findings in replications of Zhong and Liljenquist's (2006) original Macbeth effect experiment (Earp et al., 2014; Gamez et al., 2011). In the experiment by Coughtrey and colleagues (2014a), participants who repeatedly re-evoked their feelings of contamination or engaged in repeated washing using antibacterial hand wipes did not report a decline in their feelings of contamination. This suggests that compulsive washing and repeated triggering of contamination may possibly be maintaining fear and preventing its natural spontaneous decay. Further research is needed to explore the factors that maintain mental contamination fear in clinical populations. Furthermore, future research would benefit from developing a method for maintaining the induced feelings of mental contamination in healthy participants (e.g., by repeatedly re-triggering the feelings) over a longer time period, in order to investigate the differential effects of various methods on the reduction of feelings of dirtiness and urges to wash.

One motivation for the development of the theory of contamination was to ultimately improve treatment efficacy for OCD (Rachman, 2006). Mental contamination is essentially a cognitive problem and therefore may be responsive to a cognitive intervention (Rachman, 2006). Given the potential roles of maladaptive interpretations of responsibility, violation, and immorality in mental contamination (Elliott & Radomsky, 2013; Radomsky & Elliott, 2009), cognitive-based approaches which help the client to generate alternate interpretations are likely to be promising. Initial case reports indicate that mental contamination is responsive to a brief CBT intervention adapted specifically to address mental contamination concerns. Further research using randomized designs is needed to establish the effectiveness of this intervention in comparison with control groups, including ERP and treatment-as-usual.

Preliminary research findings indicate that mental contamination imagery is a useful mechanism for assessing mental contamination transdiagnostically. Mental contamination imagery is also a potential target for treatment intervention via imagery rescripting to change the content and meanings of unwanted images. It is also of note that some participants reported experiencing imagery that had a positive protective role, warding off feelings of contamination and preventing future harm. This is an important area to explore in the future, as it is likely to provide potentially useful information for developing therapeutic techniques for mental contamination. It would also be of use to examine whether this protective "positive" imagery is actually a maladaptive form of safety behavior or mental cleansing that maintains the feelings of mental contamination and whether it is specific to OCD.

We consider that the research into mental contamination has considerable clinical utility and can provide clinicians with novel options for successfully addressing this complex, disabling, and often misunderstood phenomenon. Awareness of the idea that feelings of pollution and contamination can be evoked in the absence of physical contact with a contaminant is important and necessary in order for it to be correctly assessed and addressed in treatment.

Acknowledgments

We would like to thank Professors S. Rachman and A. Radomsky for their conceptual input and contributions to this work.

References

Adams, T. G., Badour, C. L., Cisler, J. M., & Feldner, M. T. (2014). Contamination aversion and posttraumatic stress symptom severity following sexual trauma. *Cognitive Therapy and Research, 38*(4), 449–457.

Arntz, A. (2012). Imagery rescripting as a therapeutic technique: Review of clinical trials, basic studies and research agenda. *Journal of Experimental Psychopathology, 3,* 189–208.

Arntz, A., Rauner, M., & van den Hout, M. (1995). "If I feel anxious, there must be danger": Ex-consequentia reasoning in inferring danger in anxiety disorders. *Behaviour Research and Therapy, 33,* 917–925.

Badour, C. L., Feldner, M. T., Babson, K. A., Blumenthal, H., & Dutton, C. E. (2013). Disgust, mental contamination, and posttraumatic stress: Unique relations following sexual versus non-sexual assault. *Journal of Anxiety Disorders, 27,* 155–162.

Badour, C. L., Feldner, M. T., Blumenthal, H., & Bujarski, S. J. (2013). Examination of increased mental contamination as a potential mechanism in the association between disgust sensitivity and sexual assault-related posttraumatic stress. *Cognitive Therapy and Research, 37,* 697–703.

Beck, J. S., & Steer, R. A. (1990). *Beck anxiety inventory manual.* San Antonio, TX: Psychological Corp.

Beck, J. S., Steer, R. A., & Brown, G. K. (1996). *Manual for the Beck depression inventory – II.* San Antonio, TX: Psychological Corp.

Berman, N. C., Wheaton, M. G., Fabricant, L. E., & Abramowitz, J. S. (2012). Predictors of mental pollution: The contribution of religion, parenting strategies, and childhood trauma. *Journal of Obsessive-Compulsive and Related Disorders, 1,* 153–158.

Carraresi, C., Bulli, F., Melli, G., & Stopani, E. (2013). Mental contamination in OCD: Its role in the relationship between disgust propensity and fear of contamination. *Clinical Neuropsychiatry, 10,* 13–19.

Coughtrey, A. E., Shafran, R., Knibbs, D., & Rachman, S. J. (2012a). Mental contamination in obsessive-compulsive disorder. *Journal of Obsessive-Compulsive and Related Disorders, 1,* 244–250.

Coughtrey, A. E., Shafran, R., Lee, M., & Rachman, S. J. (2012b). It's the feeling inside my head: A qualitative analysis of mental contamination in obsessive-compulsive disorder. *Behavioural & Cognitive Psychotherapy, 40,* 163–173.

Coughtrey, A. E., Shafran, R., Lee, M., & Rachman, S. J. (2013a). The treatment of mental contamination: A case series. *Cognitive and Behavioral Practice, 20,* 221–231.

Coughtrey, A. E., Shafran, R., & Rachman, S. J. (2013b). Imagery in mental contamination: A questionnaire study. *Journal of Obsessive-Compulsive and Related Disorders, 2,* 385–390.

Coughtrey, A. E., Shafran, R., & Rachman, S. J. (2014a). The spontaneous decay and persistence of mental contamination: An experimental analysis. *Journal of Behaviour Therapy and Experimental Psychiatry, 45,* 90–96.

Coughtrey, A. E., Shafran, R., & Rachman, S. J. (2014b). The spread of mental contamination. *Journal of Behaviour Therapy and Experimental Psychiatry, 45,* 33–38.

Coughtrey, A. E., Shafran, R., & Rachman, S. J. (2014c). Imagery in mental contamination. *Behavioural and Cognitive Psychotherapy, 20,* 1–13.

Cougle, J. R., Lee, H. J., Horowitz, J. D., Wolitzky-Taylor, K. B., & Telch, M. J. (2008). An exploration of the relationship between mental pollution and OCD symptoms. *Journal of Behavior Therapy & Experimental Psychiatry, 39,* 340–353.

de Silva, P., & Marks, M. (1999). The role of traumatic experiences in the genesis of obsessive-compulsive disorder. *Behaviour Research and Therapy, 37*(10), 941–951. doi: 10.1016/S0005-7967(98)00185-5.

Earp, B. D., Everett, J. A., Madva, E. N., & Hamlin, J. (2014). Out, damned spot: Can the "Macbeth effect" be replicated? *Basic and Applied Social Psychology, 36,* 91–98.

Eddy, K., Dutra, L., Bradley, R., & Westen, D. (2004). A multi-dimensional meta-analysis of psychotherapy and pharmacotherapy for OCD. *Clinical Psychology Review, 24,* 1011–1030.

Elliott, C. M., & Radomsky, A. S. (2009). Analyses of mental contamination – Part I: Experimental manipulations of morality. *Behaviour Research & Therapy, 47,* 995–1003.

Elliott, C. M., & Radomsky, A. S. (2012). Mental contamination: The effects of imagined physical dirt and immoral behaviour. *Behaviour Research and Therapy, 50,* 422–427.

Elliott, C. M., & Radomsky, A. S. (2013). Meaning and mental contamination: Focus on appraisals. *Clinical Psychologist, 17,* 17–25.

Fairbrother, N., Newth, S. J., & Rachman, S. (2005). Mental pollution: Feelings of dirtiness without physical contact. *Behaviour Research & Therapy, 43,* 121–130.

Fairbrother, N., & Rachman, S. (2004). Feelings of mental pollution subsequent to sexual assault. *Behaviour Research & Therapy, 42,* 173–189.

Foa, E. B., Huppert, J. D., Leiberg, S., Langner, R., Kichic, R., Hajcak, G., & Salkovskis, P. M. (2002). The obsessive-compulsive inventory: Development and validation of a short version. *Psychological Assessment, 14,* 485–496.

Foa, E. B., Liebowitz, M. R., Kozak, M. J., Davies, S., Campeas, R., Franklin, M. E., … Tu, X. (2005). Randomized, placebo-controlled trial of exposure and ritual prevention, clomipramine, and their combination in the treatment of obsessive-compulsive disorder. *American Journal of Psychiatry, 162,* 151–161.

Gamez, E., Diaz, J. M., & Marreo, H. (2011). The uncertain universality of the Macbeth effect with a Spanish sample. *Spanish Journal of Psychology, 14,* 156–162.

Goodman, W. K., Price, L. H., Rasmussen, S. A., Mazure, C., Fleischmann, R. L., Hill, C. L., Heninger, G. R., & Charney, D. S. (1989). The Yale–Brown Obsessive Compulsive Scale: Development, use and validity. *Archives of General Psychiatry, 46,* 1006–1011.

Gershuny, B. S., Baer, L., Radomsky, A. S., Wilson, K. A., & Jenike, M. A. (2003). Connections among symptoms of obsessive-compulsive disorder and posttraumatic stress disorder: A case series. *Behaviour Research and Therapy, 41*(9), 1029–1041.

Herba, J. K., & Rachman, S. (2007). Vulnerability to mental contamination. *Behaviour Research & Therapy, 45,* 2804–2812.

Holmes, E. A., Arntz, A., & Smucker, M. R. (2007). Imagery rescripting in cognitive behaviour therapy: Images, treatment techniques and outcomes. *Journal of Behaviour Therapy and Experimental Psychiatry, 38,* 297–305.

Ishikawa, R., Kobori, O., Komuro, H., & Shimizu, E. (2014). Comparing the roles of washing and non-washing behaviour in the reduction of mental contamination. *Journal of Obsessive-Compulsive and Related Disorders, 3,* 60–64.

Ishikawa, R., Kobori, O., & Shimizu, E. (2013). Unwanted sexual experiences and cognitive appraisals that evoke mental contamination. *Behavioural and Cognitive Psychotherapy, 7*, 1–15.

Gollwitzer, M., & Melzer, A. (2012). Macbeth and the joystick: Evidence for moral cleansing after playing a violent video game. *Journal of Experimental Social Psychology, 48*, 1356–1360.

Lee, M., Shafran, R., Burgess, C., Carpenter, J., Millard, E., & Thorpe, S. (2013). The induction of mental and contact contamination. *Clinical Psychologist, 17*, 9–16.

Melli, G., Bulli, F., Carraresi, C., & Stopani, E. (2014). Disgust propensity and contamination-related OCD symptoms: The mediating role of mental contamination. *Journal of Obsessive-Compulsive and Related Disorders, 3*, 77–82.

Ponniah, K., Magiati, I., & Hollon, S. D. (2013). An update on the efficacy of psychological treatments for obsessive-compulsive disorder in adults. *Journal of Obsessive-Compulsive and Related Disorders, 2*(2), 207–218.

Rachman, S. J. (1994). Pollution of the mind. *Behaviour Research and Therapy, 32*, 311–314.

Rachman, S. J. (2004). Fear of contamination. *Behaviour Research and Therapy, 42*, 1227–1255.

Rachman, S. J. (2006). *The fear of contamination: Assessment and treatment.* Oxford: Oxford University Press.

Rachman, S. J. (2010). Betrayal: A psychological analysis. *Behaviour Research and Therapy, 48*, 304–311.

Rachman, S. J. (2013). Cleaning damned spots from the obsessive mind. *Nature, 503*, 7.

Rachman, S. J., Coughtrey, A. E., Shafran, R., & Radomsky, A. S. (2015). *Oxford guide to the treatment of mental contamination.* Oxford: Oxford University Press.

Rachman, S. J., Radomsky, A. S., Elliott, C. M., & Zysk, E. (2012). Mental contamination: The perpetrator effect. *Journal of Behaviour Therapy & Experimental Psychiatry, 43*, 587–593.

Radomsky, A. S., & Elliott, C. M. (2009). Analyses of mental contamination – Part II: Individual differences. *Behaviour Research & Therapy, 47*, 1004–1011.

Radomsky, A. S., Rachman, S. J., Shafran, R., Coughtrey, A. E., & Barber, K. C. (2014). The nature and assessment of mental contamination: A psychometric analysis. *Journal of Obsessive Compulsive and Related Disorders, 3*, 181–187.

Reuven, O., Liberman, N., & Dar, R. (2013). The effect of physical cleaning on threatened morality in individuals with obsessive-compulsive disorder. *Clinical Psychological Science, 2*, 224–229.

Tolin, D. F., Worhunsky, P., & Maltby, N. (2004). Sympathetic magic in contamination-related OCD. *Journal of Behaviour Therapy and Experimental Psychiatry, 35*, 193–205.

Volz, C., & Heyman, I. (2007). Case series: Transformation obsession in young people with obsessive-compulsive disorder (OCD). *Journal of the American Academy of Child and Adolescent Psychiatry, 46*, 766–772.

Zhong, C. B., & Liljenquist, K. (2006). Washing away your sins: Threatened morality and physical cleansing. *Science, 313*, 1451–1452.

26

Obsessive-Compulsive Problems in Very Young Children

Tommy Chou, Mariah DeSerisy, Abbe M. Garcia, Jennifer B. Freeman, and Jonathan S. Comer

Obsessions refer to recurrent and typically senseless intrusive thoughts, images, urges, or impulses that are not experienced as under one's direct control, whereas *compulsions* refer to repetitive, purposeful behaviors and activities performed to reduce anxiety, tension, or distress. Although obsessions and compulsions are ubiquitous in the general population, when they encroach upon functioning, cause marked distress, and/or interfere with major life roles, a diagnosis of obsessive-compulsive disorder (OCD) is warranted (American Psychiatric Association [APA], 2013). Epidemiologic research suggests that between 1.6% and 2.5% of the general population will meet criteria for OCD at some point in their lifetime (Canino et al., 1987; Comer & Olfson, 2010; Kessler et al., 2005a; Weissman et al., 1994), and between 0.7% and 2.0% have met criteria within the past year (Kessler, Chiu, Demler, Merikangas, & Walters, 2005b; Jacobi et al., 2004). Across health conditions, OCD is the tenth leading cause of disability, as it is associated with considerable family burdens and impaired quality of life (Jacoby, Leonard, Riemann, & Abramowitz, 2014; Storch, Abramowitz, & Keeley, 2009).

In the majority of OCD cases onset is prior to age 18 years (Comer & Olfson, 2010), and among youth-onset cases there is a bimodal age of onset, with one modal onset peak occurring before age 9 years and one occurring in later childhood and adolescence (Garcia et al., 2009; Geller, 2006). Earlier onset is associated with more complex and atypical presentations (Garcia et al., 2009; Gellar et al., 2001), higher rates of familial aggregation, and a more intractable course in adulthood (Comer & Olfson, 2010; de Mathis et al., 2008). Despite misguided notions that early child cases of OCD may be less severe, or may be more circumscribed in nature, research on clinical samples finds that roughly three-quarters of early-onset OCD cases show multiple obsessions, and over 95% show multiple compulsions (Garcia et al., 2009). As such, OCD in very young children (i.e., < 9 years) merits special consideration. This chapter covers the small but growing literature on the phenomenology, assessment, and recent advances in treatment of obsessive-compulsive problems in very young children, and concludes with a discussion of future directions and areas in need of focused empirical attention.

The Wiley Handbook of Obsessive Compulsive Disorders, Volume I, First Edition.
Edited by Jonathan S. Abramowitz, Dean McKay, and Eric A. Storch.
© 2017 John Wiley & Sons Ltd. Published 2017 by John Wiley & Sons Ltd.

Phenomenology of Obsessive-Compulsive Problems in Very Young Children

Obsessive-compulsive (OC) symptoms in early childhood tend to onset gradually (Garcia et al., 2009). Acute onset of OC symptoms in childhood has been reported, but is quite rare and is typically associated with a clear psychosocial stressor or traumatic event (Coskun, Zoroglu, & Ozturk, 2012), or an infectious trigger that results in sudden neuropsychiatric symptoms. Whereas such rare Pediatric Acute-onset Neuropsychiatric Syndrome (PANS) cases are characterized by a "sawtooth" remitting-relapsing episodic course (Murphy et al., 2014; Swedo et al., 1998), the majority of early child OCD cases show a progressive trajectory of OC symptoms that worsen steadily across time in the absence of treatment. Gradual, and sometimes subtle, symptom onset can interfere with timely recognition of and insight into OC problems, as slowly progressing OC symptoms go untreated for considerable lengths of time before families come to recognize their severity and associated family burdens (Garcia et al., 2009; Nakatani, et al., 2011). In fact, the mean age of OCD onset in early child samples is 4.95 years, but the average delay between OCD onset and initial presentation for treatment is roughly 2 years (Garcia et al., 2009).

Whereas research with adolescents and adults typically finds a preponderance of females among OCD sufferers (Comer & Olfson, 2010; Horwath & Weissman, 2000; Rasmussen & Tsuang, 1986), in early childhood there appears to be no gender effect, with young boys and girls presenting for OCD treatment at comparable rates (Garcia et al., 2009). Moreover, higher familial aggregation is typically found in cases of earlier-onset OCD than among cases of later-onset OCD. For example, Garcia and colleagues (2009) found roughly 20% of young children below the age of 9 years with OCD had a first-degree relative with OCD, whereas only 12% of adults with OCD have a first-degree relative with OCD (Nestadt et al., 2000) – and only less than 3% of the general population meets the criteria for OCD. Garcia and colleagues also found that 14% of very young children with OCD had a first-degree relative with a tic disorder, and roughly one-third had a first degree relative with a non-OCD anxiety disorder, providing further indication of particularly high familial aggregation of OCD and related disorders among early childhood OCD cases. Links between younger age of OCD onset and elevated family aggregation of related disorders may reflect a particularly strong genetic component to early child OCD (Coskun et al., 2012; Nestadt et al., 2000), but importantly no twin studies or molecular genetics research have been conducted with regard to early-onset OCD.

There is some evidence that the topographical nature of obsessions and compulsions in early childhood OCD differs relative to later childhood OCD. For example, earlier-onset OCD cases show higher rates of compulsion-only OCD (Geller, Biederman, Griffin, Jones, & Lefkowitz, 1996; Geller et al., 1998; Rettew, Swedo, Leonard, Lenane, & Rapoport, 1992), with roughly one-fifth of Garcia and colleagues' (2009) sample of early-onset OCD cases showing no evidence of obsessional problems. Checking behaviors appear to be the most common compulsions among early-onset OCD cases (~70%), but rates of checking are significantly lower among younger, relative to older, sufferers (Garcia et al., 2009). In contrast, "tic-like compulsions" are found nearly exclusively in young children and adults with very early onset OC symptoms. These compulsions include touching, tapping, rubbing, blinking, or staring rituals that children feel compelled to perform "until it feels just right" (Garcia et al., 2009; Hanna et al., 2002).

These "tic-like compulsions" often appear before the development of obsessions, suggesting that formal obsessions as well as more complex rituals may evolve later in young children and be associated with advances in cognitive development that come with age (Garcia et al., 2009). The limited capacities in metacognition, abstract thought, and casual reasoning that characterize early childhood may actually protect the youngest OCD sufferers from obsessions and complex compulsions. Such findings run counter to popular misconceptions that obsessions onset first in the development of OCD, and that compulsions develop strictly as reactions to obsessions. In addition, more atypical OCD presentations, such as breathing rituals or blinking compulsions, are more frequent among OCD sufferers whose symptoms onset before the age of 6 years (Rettew et al., 1992). Moreover, earlier-onset OCD is also more commonly associated with higher rates of sexual/religious, hoarding, and symmetry compulsions, contamination fears among females, and poorer insight (Narayanaswamy et al., 2012; Prabhu et al., 2013; Selles, Storch, & Lewin, 2014).

Generally speaking, comorbidity in most children with OCD is exceptionally high, with early-onset OCD cases more likely showing comorbid tic disorders, anxiety disorders, and disruptive behavior disorders (Coskun et al., 2012; Garcia et al., 2009; Geller, 2006). Comorbid anxiety diagnoses among children with earlier-onset OCD tend to be associated with more severe OC symptoms and greater treatment resistance (Krebs et al., 2013). Tic disorders are commonly comorbid with very early onset OCD symptoms, particularly among males (Hanna et al., 2002), and, in fact, comorbid tics tend to predate the onset of OC symptoms. Some tic disorders among OCD youth tend to abate by adolescence, whereas many tics associated with OCD will persist into adulthood (Diniz et al., 2006; Geller et al., 2001).

Comorbid disruptive behavior disorders (DBDs) among youth with OCD are most common in earlier-onset OCD cases, tend to emerge prior to the presentation of OCD symptoms, and are generally associated with lower child insight into OC symptoms (Bipeta et al., 2013; Garcia et al., 2009; Geller, 2006; Storch et al., 2010). Relative to children with only an OCD diagnosis, children with comorbid OCD and DBD diagnoses tend to display higher levels of impairment, more severe OCD symptoms, and greater family dysfunction (Lebowitz, Omer, & Leckman, 2011). Disruptive behaviors in young children with DBDs and comorbid OCD look somewhat different than disruptive behaviors found in children showing just DBDs. For example, children with DBDs and comorbid OCD actually show lower rates of conduct disorder than found in children with just DBDs, and these comorbid youth's externalizing presentations are characterized less by aggression and rule breaking than in classic DBD presentations (Lebowitz et al., 2011). Instead, the externalizing behavior of children with comorbid DBDs and OCD is more likely to reflect coercive and disruptive behavior patterns. Whereas youth with comorbid DBDs and OCD show lower levels of violence than youth with just DBDs, these comorbid youth are more likely to forbid certain family actions because of extreme feelings, or to impose strict rules or behaviors on others due to various sensitivities, and to then go into disruptive rages when their strict rules are broken (Lebowitz et al., 2011).

Tantrums and rage attacks are not uncommon in children with OCD and subclinical OC symptomology (Krebs et al., 2013; Storch et al., 2012), particularly in children below the age of 9. The irritability and tantrums found in earlier-onset OCD are most commonly directed exclusively at parents and siblings in the home, rather than more broadly directed at all authority figures and peers. Outbursts and tantrums in child OCD typically present in reaction to instances of ritual interference or refusal of OCD-related demands (Krebs et al., 2013; Storch et al. 2012), and less commonly reflect a general and proactive child pattern of oppositionality, noncompliance, and resistance to authority figures. Temper outbursts in child OCD can range in severity from slight irritability and verbal outbursts to (more rarely) violent and sometimes premeditated acts of aggression directed at those involved in ritual interference or compulsion demands (Krebs et al., 2013; Storch et al., 2009). In earlier-onset OCD, these outbursts are often associated with general temperamental characteristics such as general irritability and subclinical depressive symptoms (Krebs et al., 2013; Stringaris & Goodman, 2009).

Although OCD and anxiety comorbidities in young children are linked with higher OCD symptom severity than found in cases of OCD and DBD comorbidity, children with OCD and comorbid externalizing problems demonstrate the highest level of overall functional impairment, regardless of absolute OCD severity (Langley, Lewin, Bergman, Lee, & Piacentini, 2010). This greater functional impairment found in cases of comorbid OCD and externalizing problems has been linked to greater maternal accommodation of both OC symptoms and disruptive behaviors (Flessner et al., 2011).

Parental accommodation – referring to parental behavior modifications that attempt to prevent or reduce child distress associated with participation in age-appropriate activities and/or exposure to feared or avoided stimuli (Flessner et al., 2011; Thompson-Hollands, Kerns, Pincus, & Comer, 2014b) – can be more common, and more impairing, in families with earlier-onset OCD. Parental accommodation focused on reducing age-appropriate child distress in OCD youth is most prominent in the context of OCD symptoms and OCD-related demands. Parental accommodation is common across many child anxiety-spectrum disorders (see Thompson-Hollands et al., 2014b), but is particularly central to the functioning of families affected by child OCD. Parental accommodation is linked with greater functional impairment and poorer treatment response in child OCD cases (Bipeta et al., 2013; Caporino et al., 2012; Lebowitz, 2013; Merlo et al., 2009; Peris et al., 2008).

Family accommodation often entails the direct or passive involvement of family members in a young child's OCD symptoms, which can range from modification of family routines in order to avoid anxiety-provoking situations to providing active reassurance or assisting in ritual completion (Lebowitz, 2013; Lewin et al., 2014). Compulsion severity, child oppositional behaviors, and parental anxiety each predict the extent of family accommodation (Flessner et al., 2011). Importantly, although family accommodation of OCD symptoms can reduce a child's short-term distress, in the longer term it tends to maintain child OC patterns through negative reinforcement processes (Bipeta et al., 2013, Flessner et al., 2011).

Assessment of Obsessive-Compulsive and Related Problems in Very Young Children

Accurate identification and assessment of OCD in very young children presents multiple unique challenges. First, OCD is a relatively low base rate disorder, and early-onset OCD is even less common. Consequently, school personnel, pediatricians, and even mental health providers working with young children typically have very limited experience with early OCD. Professionals working with young children can, thus, be relatively poor at accurately recognizing emerging OCD symptoms, relative to recognizing other early child problems such as ADHD and autism-spectrum disorders.

Second, young children are typically poor self-reporters of their own symptoms and behavioral patterns. Limited metacognitive capacities found in early childhood (Flavell, Green & Flavell, 2000) interfere with young children's ability to reflect on their own mental content and report on their obsessions. Limited causal reasoning that characterizes early child cognition (Flavell et al., 2001) can interfere with young children's ability to link their thoughts and behaviors, which can compromise young children's self-reports of cognitive antecedents of behavior and relationships between compulsions and obsessions. Accordingly, it is essential to secure parent-reports as well in the assessment of early child OCD. Importantly, however, parents themselves may have limited awareness of child OCD problems – particularly symptoms reflecting unobservable or internal child phenomena such as obsessions, mental rituals, and covert compulsions. As such, a multi-informant assessment strategy (see Comer & Kendall, 2004), in which reports are obtained from both parents and children, is critical in the assessment of OCD in very young children.

Third, as noted above, family accommodation of early child OCD is common in which family members assist in ritual completions, family routines are modified in order to avoid overly distressing the child, or excessive reassurance is provided to the child. Family accommodation can be so effective in reducing child distress in the short term that it can even mask the presence of child difficulties altogether. In the context of modified family routines that considerably accommodate child OCD, young children can appear to be functioning remarkably well. As such, when interviewing parents of young children with OCD, it is critical to conduct a thorough assessment of family functioning and the presence of family accommodation. It is also critical to have parents go beyond considering how the child is presently functioning in the context of various accommodations, and to consider how the child would be functioning if there were not so many accommodations in place to optimize the child's comfort.

Fourth, as also noted above, early-onset OCD is commonly accompanied by comorbidities – such as disruptive behavior disorders and anxiety disorders – which in turn can receive more attention than the OCD symptoms. Tantrums and behavioral outbursts in young children can be more obvious and observable than many OCD symptoms, and as such may themselves prompt better identification and treatment than the OCD symptoms. On a related note, many OCD symptoms in young children can be difficult to distinguish from other early child problems. For example, differential diagnosis between early OCD and autism-spectrum disorders can prove difficult when primary child concerns are excessive inflexibility and rigidity accompanied by special routines and circumscribed interests. Similarly, the phenomenological overlap between OCD and generalized anxiety disorder (GAD), which can both be characterized by repetitive and interfering cognitive activity about negative circumstances, make differential diagnostic decisions between child OCD and GAD complicated (Comer, Kendall, Franklin, Hudson, & Pimentel, 2004). Moreover, when a young child with OCD shows serious disruptive behaviors that result in considerable impairment when rituals are interrupted or others do not abide by the child's strict rules (see Krebs et al., 2013; Storch et al., 2012), it is not readily apparent whether a primary diagnosis of OCD or a primary diagnosis of a DBD is warranted.

Finally, it can be hard to distinguish some features of OCD from normative developmental functioning in very young children. For example, the majority of very young children show some magical thinking and rigidity, whereas many compulsions such as repetitive checking are much more rare in preschool youth (Evans, Milanak, Medeiros, & Ross, 2002; Spence, Rapee, McDonald, & Ingram, 2001). In addition, it is not uncommon for individuals with OCD to believe that thinking of an unacceptable behavior is as bad as actively engaging in that behavior, or that thinking of an aversive event increases the likelihood that the event will actually occur (i.e., "thought-action fusion") (Shafran, Thordarson, & Rachman, 1996). However, at earlier stages of cognitive development, *all* children may exhibit somewhat high levels of thought-action fusion (Comer et al., 2004).

For these reasons, it is critical for providers to use an evidence-based assessment strategy when identifying and evaluating early child OCD. Such a strategy should include a structured diagnostic interview (ideally conducted by a professional with OCD experience) complemented by parent- and child-report measures that have demonstrated reliability and validity for assessing child OCD symptoms and related problems, the impact of OCD, and patterns of family accommodation. Below we review several key assessment instruments used in leading research on OCD in very young children.

OCD and Related Disorders in Very Young Children

Structured diagnostic interviewing conducted by a trained professional is an essential component for evidence-based assessment, although many providers hold negative attitudes about their merits (see Jensen-Doss & Hawley, 2010). Many leading structured diagnostic interviews with OCD sections, regrettably, have not been validated for use in very young children. However, the Schedule for Affective Disorders and Schizophrenia in School-Aged Children (KSADS) (Kaufman, Birmaher, Brent, & Rao, 1997) and the Anxiety Disorders Interview Schedule for Children and Parents for DSM-IV (ADIS-IV-C/P) (Silverman & Albano, 1996) have both been used successfully in research to assess OCD in children as young as 4 years (e.g., Comer et al., 2014; Freeman et al., 2012; Freeman et al., 2014b). Both are semi-structured interviews evaluating the full range of mental disorders in children and have demonstrated very strong psychometric properties, including retest reliability and concurrent validity (Kaufman et al., 1997; Silverman, Saavedra, & Pina, 2001; Silverman & Ollendick, 2005; Wood, Piacentini, Bergman, McCracken, & Barrios, 2002) – although further empirical work is needed to formally evaluate the reliability and validity of these structured interviews in younger children. Both the KSADS and the ADIS-IV-C/P typically require the combination of parent- and child-reports to confer diagnoses. In practice, evaluators may utilize clinical skill and experience to modify items for more developmentally appropriate delivery, and with children below the age of 6 years it is likely that only a parent interview will yield meaningful information.

The Children's Yale–Brown Obsessive-Compulsive Scale (CY-BOCS) (Scahill et al., 1997) is one of the few diagnostic measures with formal research directly providing empirical support for its validity and reliability in assessing obsessions and compulsions in very young children (Freeman, Flessner, & Garcia 2011). The CY-BOCS is a 10-item clinician-administered assessment tool examining OCD obsessions, compulsions, and overall severity. When conducting this interview, the evaluator first assesses the overall presence of common obsessions and compulsions with the family, and then inquires further about the time, interference, distress, resistance, and persistence associated with these symptoms. Scores on the obsessions and compulsions subscales each range from 0 to 20 (total symptoms scores range from 0 to 40), with higher scores indicating greater severity. Though the CY-BOCS was originally developed for use with older children and adolescents, Freeman and colleagues (2011) showed that it demonstrates good overall internal consistency, temporal stability, construct validity, and sensitivity to change when administered with children aged 5–8 years. A number of modifications, however, are recommended when using the CY-BOCS with younger children (see Freeman et al., 2011), including: (1) increasing reliance on parent report to address children's difficulties verbalizing anxiety symptoms; (2) using developmentally appropriate language to assess certain symptoms, such as those related to urine, feces, saliva, or violent or sexual content; and (3) administering the compulsions subscale prior to the obsessions subscale despite their reversed order in the standard measure. Administering the compulsions subscale first allows the assessment to begin with more objective, observable, and describable behaviors, and to then move on to obsessional thoughts and images that may be more abstract and difficult for young children to comprehend.

Impact of OCD

Comprehensive assessment of OCD in young children must include evaluation of functional impairment associated with the OCD symptoms (Piacentini et al., 2007b). Because of the heterogeneity of OCD and the wide range of associated impact across youth, it is critical to ascertain the main domains in which OCD affects each young child in order to guide decisions regarding treatment priorities and targets, and to identify specific areas in which young children and their families may be particularly motivated to change. The Child Obsessive-Compulsive Impact Scale – Revised (COIS-R) evaluates both setting-specific and overall impact of OCD symptoms in children as young as 5 years of age. The instrument consists of 52 Likert-scale items with response rating options ranging from 0 (not at all) to 3 (very much) that evaluate the functional cost of obsessions and compulsions in the school, social, and family/home domains. Research has demonstrated strong psychometric properties of the COIS-R, including internal consistency and retest reliability, in samples of OCD youth aged 5–17 years (Piacentini et al., 2007b).

Family Accommodation

Assessing family accommodation is critical in order to evaluate the impact of OCD symptoms on the broader family context, but also to identify potential targets for behavioral interventions designed to disrupt maintaining environmental factors of child OCD symptoms. The Family Accommodation Scale (Calvocoressi et al., 1999) can be completed by parents and assesses reassurance provided by family members, active and passive participation in compulsions by family members, avoidance promoted or enabled by family members, and modifications of family routines designed to accommodate OCD symptoms and relieve OCD-related distress. Slightly modified wordings can be used for improved compatibility with early-onset OCD populations (Freeman et al., 2012). In addition to assessing family accommodation directly related to OCD symptoms, it can also be helpful to assess family accommodation associated with child anxiety more broadly. The Family Accommodation Checklist and Interference Scale (FACLIS) (Thompson-Hollands et al., 2014b) assesses the scope and associated impact of family accommodation to child anxiety in children as young as 4 years, and can be useful for assessing the scope and interference of family accommodation more broadly in families of young children with OCD.

Treatment of Obsessive-Compulsive Problems in Very Young Children

Despite the severity and impairment associated with OCD in very young children, recent years have witnessed enormous advances in the evidence-based treatment of early-onset OCD (e.g., Freeman et al., 2014a). Until recently, there were no trials evaluating effective treatments for OCD in very young children, although over the past several decades there have been enormous advances demonstrating the efficacy of cognitive-behavioral therapy and antidepressant medications for treating OCD in *later* childhood and adolescence (e.g., Pediatric OCD Treatment Study Team, 2004; Piacentini et al., 2011; Storch et al., 2013). Despite support for pharmacologic interventions for OCD in older children and adolescents, medication has not been evaluated in the treatment of OCD in very young children and is not recommended as a first-line treatment for preschool OCD (Gleason et al., 2007), nor do the majority of parents of children in this very young age group have preferences for pharmacologic interventions over behavioral/psychosocial options. Building on the very strong evidence in older children and adolescents for cognitive-behavioral protocols for managing OCD, Freeman and Garcia (2008) developed a family-based cognitive-behavioral treatment specifically geared toward the needs of very young children with OCD, and have shown strong support for this protocol in a series of increasingly rigorous clinical trials (Freeman et al., 2008; Freeman et al., 2014a).

Family-based CBT for very young children with OCD (Freeman & Garcia, 2008) consists of four main components: (1) psychoeducation, (2) parent tools largely focused on behavior management training, (3) child tools consisting of behavioral components (i.e., exposure with response prevention, or EX/RP) and cognitive strategies to externalize OCD, and (4) family process components (Freeman et al., 2012). In early sessions, clinicians provide psychoeducation regarding the neurobiological underpinnings of OCD and help to differentiate OCD symptoms from non-OCD and developmentally normative behaviors. Clinicians also correct any misunderstandings and misattributions of OCD. Additionally, parents learn the general outline, major components, and goals of CBT for child OCD. These early informational sessions are instrumental in providing the rationale for treatment and exposure, and provide a forum in which to identify and pre-emptively address potential barriers to treatment or obstacles that could result in treatment drop-out (Choate-Summers et al., 2008).

Parent-focused efforts for behavioral management include training in differential attention (i.e., reward and praise for exposure attempts and child use of positive coping, versus active ignoring of anxious avoidance or OCD-related behaviors), modeling of appropriate and adaptive approach behaviors, and scaffolding to aid in child development of emotional awareness and regulation (Freeman et al., 2012). To address oppositional behaviors that commonly accompany OCD in very young children, clinicians also teach and coach parents in contingency management, as needed.

Given the high parental and family involvement in child symptoms that is typically found in families of very young children with OCD, parent-focused efforts also aim to reduce family accommodation and negative attention to OCD thoughts and behaviors. Parents learn to utilize differential attention to praise and promote positive behaviors, such as approach to anxiety-provoking situations, resistance of compulsions, and child efforts to "boss back" OCD. Additionally, clinicians guide parents in utilizing active ignoring strategies to remove attention to avoidance and reassurance-seeking, and reduce participation in obsessions and compulsions. Often, the introduction of these skills and new family exchanges can prompt considerable family disruption – and child symptoms may initially get worse – as the child becomes adjusts to reduced accommodations. For some parents, this may require some training and education in tolerating their own distress and anxiety about their child's exposure tasks. Clinicians also coach parents in using appropriate modeling and scaffolding to teach the child to identify his or her own emotional reactions to anxiety-provoking situations, resist maladaptive responses, and implement positive and productive self-regulation.

Child-focused efforts in family-based CBT for very young children with OCD focus on helping the child to understand OCD and the function and importance of exposure tasks, and to rate their anxiety during these tasks (Choate-Summers et al. 2008). The child is taught to externalize, or "boss back," OCD. Externalizing OCD for young children advances their understanding of obsessions and compulsions as simply illogical mental blips or "hiccups" in order to remove any associated self-blame and reduce negative self-evaluations. Externalizing the OCD also helps to clarify for the child that OCD – and not the child – is the target of change, and creates an opportunity for the clinician to serve as a coach for the child and family's "team" as they all work together to overcome OCD. In addition, the child is oriented to an anxiety/distress rating scale that is presented in a concrete form such as a "fear thermometer." This fear thermometer allows parents and the clinician understand how difficult or upset each situation makes the child, much like a physical thermometer helps parents and doctors understand how severe and uncomfortable a fever might be.

Early in family-based CBT for early-onset OCD, the clinician collaborates with the family to create a hierarchy of anxiety-provoking situations (Freeman & Garcia, 2008). This fear ladder provides a working "road map" for sequencing graduated EX/RP activities in which children confront increasingly feared situations without avoidance or engagement in rituals. Exposure tasks begin at the bottom of the fear ladder and gradually increase in difficulty as the child masters approach and resistance of compulsions in each situation. Parents actively participate in each EX/RP task to help improve family motivation, to identify targets of change in parental reactions to child anxiety, and to improve the likelihood of successful home practice. After the child has successfully navigated the highest items on his or her fear ladder, treatment shifts to focus on relapse prevention.

Although family-based CBT for early childhood OCD retains the core components of CBT for older children and adolescents (see March & Mulle, 1998; Piacentini, Langley, & Roblek, 2007a), several specific areas of increased emphasis, and several areas of modifications made to meet the unique developmental capacities of very young children, merit specific attention (see Choate-Summers et al., 2008). First, given limitations in cognitive development that characterize early childhood, very young children may experience difficulties engaging in the more cognitive aspects of treatment (see Carpenter, Puliafico, Kurtz, Pincus, & Comer, 2014; Comer et al., 2012), thus increasing the importance of full parent participation throughout the entire course of treatment. Although meta-analytic research underscores the value of some degree of family involvement in the treatment of OCD at any age (Thompson-Hollands, Edson, Tompson, & Comer, 2014a), family involvement appears to be particularly essential in the treatment of early child OCD.

Second, some content areas found in treatments for older children with OCD can receive somewhat greater emphasis in the treatment of very young children with OCD, due to their increased relevance in early childhood. For example, given the increased dependency that normatively characterizes early childhood, very young children with OCD may involve parents and other family members in their compulsive behaviors, rituals, and routines even more so than do older youth with OCD. Further, parents of very young children may be especially prone to accommodation and demonstrate particularly poor problem-solving, decreased confidence in child autonomy, and increased catastrophic thinking. In addition, differentiating between OCD behaviors and developmentally normative routines such as those surrounding school, meals, hygiene, and sleep, may be more difficult in early child populations (Freeman et al., 2012). To help parents draw these boundaries, clinicians may underscore the tremendous utility of normal routines for aiding developmentally appropriate socialization and then clarify the substantial differences in time, interference, and distress caused by compulsions relative to useful child and family routines (Choate-Summers et al., 2008).

Third, the large focus on parents in family-based CBT for very young children with OCD provides a valuable format for managing the disruptive behaviors that typically accompany early-onset OCD. Meta-analytic work highlights the high efficacy of family-based treatments for managing externalizing problems in very young children (e.g., Comer et al., 2013), and thus the contingency management and differential attention skills taught to parents in family-based CBT for early OCD allow parents to simultaneously address child OCD symptoms while also targeting disruptive behavior problems.

Fourth, parents are encouraged to take an active role in guiding treatment early on, and are seen as experts in their young child's behaviors and abilities. Clinicians work to boost parents' confidence in their ability to help address their young child's symptoms and pre-emptively address child-specific barriers to treatment. For example, parents who identify their child's limited attention span as potentially interfering to session participation may work with their clinician to incorporate small, periodic rewards to maintain child engagement. Additionally, the clinician may structure sessions with child participation such that the child is only present for relevant portions.

Fifth, child tools and their presentation are typically modified to increase their compatibility with early child cognitive development (Choate-Summers et al. 2008). When teaching a young child to externalize OCD, clinicians will often present obsessions and compulsions as the product of bullying and coercion of a "Worry Monster." To make OCD more concrete and digestible for younger children, in-session activities call for the child to draw and name his or her own Worry/OCD Monster. Moreover, whereas "bossing back" strategies used with older children typically involve coping thoughts and internal dialogues, clinicians may have younger children crumple, hit, rip, or otherwise destroy pictures of their Worry Monster.

Finally, younger children participating in family-based CBT for OCD may have difficulty recognizing and rating anxiety due to their limited cognitive capacities. Consequently, ratings preceding and during exposures may be inaccurate, and children can find themselves prematurely entering very difficult exposure tasks thought to be less distressing. Clinicians can help to improve the accuracy of fear ratings by modifying the fear thermometer (e.g., adding imagery/cartoons representing low distress and high distress, reducing the number of rating options, etc.) and may work with parents to adjust ratings based on the child's behaviors and nonverbal cues. Additionally, clinicians may prepare families for the unpredictable nature of exposures by explaining to parents and young children that OCD is "tricky"; modeling the calm use of skills taught in treatment to navigate unexpectedly difficult situations can provide opportunities to demonstrate anxiety and distress tolerance and model confidence in the child and parents' ability to handle such situations. The latter point is especially important, as control of exposures and OCD management are incrementally transferred from the clinician to the family over the course of treatment (Choate-Summers et al., 2008).

Expanding the Reach of Family-based CBT for OCD in Very Young Children

Regrettably, gaps persist between supported treatment in specialty care settings and services broadly available in the community (Comer & Barlow, 2014; Sandler et al., 2005). Although the inadequate availability of supported care for early-onset OCD is due, in part, to the fact that there has only *recently* been an empirical focus on early-onset OCD, several other key obstacles to effective care remain, including inadequate numbers of trained professionals, poor quality of available services for OCD, long wait lists at underfunded and overburdened facilities, and regional mental health workforce shortages (Comer & Barlow, 2014). These problems plague the availability of quality care for all mental health problems, but are particularly problematic for low-base rate disorders, such as OCD in very young children (see Comer & Barlow, 2014, for a full discussion).

In recent years, research has begun to evaluate how technological innovations and the Internet may offer transformative solutions to overcoming traditional barriers to effective care for early-onset OCD. For example, Comer and colleagues (e.g., Comer et al., 2014; Crum & Comer, 2016) have been specifically evaluating the potential of using videoconferencing to expand the reach of family-based CBT for early-onset OCD. Videoconferencing methods can overcome geographical obstacles to care by extending the availability of expert services and addressing regional workforce shortages in mental health care (Comer & Barlow, 2014; Storch et al., 2011). Families in rural or other underserved regions can participate in real-time treatment conducted by experts, regardless of their geographic proximity to an expert child OCD facility. In addition, treating families in their homes can overcome transportation issues that traditionally hinder treatment accessibility. Furthermore, harnessing technology to deliver expert care directly to families in their natural settings may extend the ecological validity of treatment, as services can be delivered in the very context in which many child OCD symptoms typically occur.

In an initial family-based CBT case series of five children with OCD between the ages of 4 and 8 years treated fully with videoconferencing methods, Comer and colleagues (2014) found all five children completed a full course of treatment, all showed OCD symptom improvements and global severity improvements, and all showed at least partial diagnostic response. Most of these children no longer met diagnostic criteria for OCD at posttreatment. Further, all mothers in this case series characterized the quality of services received as "excellent."

Building on this promising preliminary work, Comer and colleagues are currently evaluating Internet-delivered family-based CBT relative to standard in-clinic family-based CBT in a randomized clinical trial for OCD in very young children. If successful, a real-time, Internet-based interactive videoconferencing format may prove to be a valuable vehicle for meaningfully broadening the availability of family-based CBT for OCD in very young children by offering a comparable quantity of therapist contact and expertise to standard family-based CBT. Additional research examining the merits of videoconferencing methods for the treatment of OCD in very young children is needed, but this work is part of a growing body of research (e.g., Comer et al., 2015; Khanna & Kendall, 2010; Storch et al., 2011), suggesting that behavioral telehealth methods can remotely deliver evidence-based treatments for a range of child disorders with the same speed, facility, acceptability, and potentially effectiveness afforded in traditional in-clinic care.

Conclusions

OCD in very young children is associated with significant severity and burden, and earlier onset may portend greater impairment and treatment resistance across the lifespan. Accordingly accurate identification and effective treatment for early-onset OCD is critical, although research evaluating evidence-based assessment and intervention for early child OCD has lagged behind assessment and intervention research for OCD presenting in later childhood and adolescence. Recent years, however, have witnessed exciting advances in the psychometric evaluation of measures that can evaluate OCD and its associated features and impacts in very young children. Similarly the development of family-based CBT for early child OCD (Freeman & Garcia, 2008), as well as its recent evaluation in a rigorous multi-site controlled trial (Freeman et al., 2014b), has filled a critical gap in our understanding of best practices for treating OCD in very young children. Future work is now needed to evaluate potential mediators, mechanisms, and moderators of response to family-based CBT, in order to identify how and for whom treatment works best. Recent work evaluating the potential of videoconferencing methods for remotely delivering family-based CBT (e.g., Comer et al., 2014) may offer transformative solutions for meaningfully expanding the reach and scope of supported care for very young children with OCD, although continued research in this area is needed. At the same time, incorporating technological innovations into the treatment of early child OCD will require careful considerations with regard to privacy, security, competency, and liability, and will require guidance from the broader professional telemedicine community.

References

American Psychiatric Association. (2013). *Diagnostic and statistical manual of mental disorders* (5th ed.). Washington, DC: Author. doi: 10.1176/appi.books.9780890425596.249120.

Bipeta, R., Yerramilli, S. S., Pingali, S., Karredla, A. R., & Ali, M. O. (2013). A cross-sectional study of insight and family accommodation in pediatric obsessive-compulsive disorder. *Child and Adolescent Psychiatry and Mental Health, 7*(1), 20. doi: 10.1186/1753-2000-7-20.

Calvocoressi, L., Mazure, C.M., Kasl, S. V., Skolnick, J., Fisk, D., Vegso, S. J. ... Price, L. H. (1999). Family accommodation of obsessive compulsive symptoms: Instrument development and assessment of family behavior. *Journal of Nervous and Mental Disease, 187*(10), 636–642.

Canino, G. J., Bird, H. R., Shrout, P. E., Rubio-Stipec, M., Bravo, M., Martinez, R., ... Guevara, L. M. (1987). The prevalence of specific psychiatric disorders in Puerto Rico. *Archives of General Psychiatry, 44*(8), 727–735. doi: 10.1001/archpsyc. 1987.01800200053008.

Caporino, N. E., Morgan, J., Beckstead, J., Phares, V., Murphy, T. K., & Storch, E. A. (2012). A structural equation analysis of family accommodation in pediatric obsessive-compulsive disorder. *Journal of Abnormal Child Psychology, 40*, 133–143.

Carpenter, A., Puliafico, A. C., Kurtz, S. M. S., Pincus, D. B., & Comer, J. S. (2014). Extending Parent–Child Interaction Therapy for early childhood internalizing problems: New advances for an overlooked population. *Clinical Child and Family Psychology Review, 17*(4), 340–356. doi: 10.1007/s10567-014-0172-4.

Choate-Summers, M., Freeman, J. B., Garcia, A. M., Coyne, L., Przeworski, A., & Leonard, H. L. (2008). Clinical considerations when tailoring cognitive behavioral treatment for young children with obsessive compulsive disorder. *Education and Treatment of Children, 31*(3), 395–416. doi: 10.1353/etc.0.0004.

Comer, J. S., & Barlow, D. H. (2014). The occasional case against broad dissemination and implementation: Retaining a role for specialty care in the delivery of psychological treatments. *American Psychologist, 69*(1), 1–18. doi: 10.1037/a0033582.

Comer, J. S., Chow, C., Chan, P., Cooper-Vince, C., & Wilson, L. A. S. (2013). Psychosocial treatment efficacy for disruptive behavior problems in young children: A meta-analytic examination. *Journal of the American Academy of Child and Adolescent Psychiatry, 52*(1), 26–36. doi: 10.1016/j.jaac.2012.10.001.

Comer, J. S., Furr, J. M., Cooper-Vince, C., Kerns, C., Chan, P. T., Edson, A. L., ... Freeman, J. B. (2014). Internet-delivered, family-based treatment for early-onset OCD: A preliminary case series. *Journal of Clinical Child and Adolescent Psychology, 43*(1), 74–87. doi: 10.1080/15374416.2013.855127.

Comer, J. S., Furr, J. M., Cooper-Vince, C., Madigan, R. J., Chow, C., Chan, P. T., ... Eyberg, S. M. (2015). Rationale and considerations for the Internet-based delivery of Parent–Child Interaction Therapy. *Cognitive and Behavioral Practice, 22*(3), 302–316. doi: 10.1016/j.cbpra.2014.07.003.

Comer, J. S., & Kendall, P. C. (2004). A symptom-level examination of parent–child agreement in the diagnosis of anxious youths. *Journal of the American Academy of Child and Adolescent Psychiatry, 43*(7), 878–886. doi: 10.1097/01.chi.0000125092.35109.c5.

Comer, J. S., Kendall, P. C., Franklin, M. E., Hudson, J. L., & Pimentel, S. S. (2004). Obsessing/worrying about the overlap between obsessive-compulsive disorder and generalized anxiety disorder in youth. *Clinical Psychology Review, 24*(6), 663–683. doi: 10.1016/j.cpr.2004.04.004.

Comer, J. S., & Olfson, M. (2010). The epidemiology of anxiety disorders. In H. B. Simpson, F. Schneier, Y. Neria, & R. Lewis-Fernandez (Eds.), *Anxiety disorders: Theory, research, and clinical perspectives* (pp. 6–19). New York: Cambridge University Press.

Comer, J. S., Puliafico, A. C., Aschenbrand, S. G, McKnight, K., Robin, J. A., Goldfine, M., & Albano, A. M. (2012). A pilot feasibility evaluation of the CALM Program for anxiety disorders in early childhood. *Journal of Anxiety Disorders, 26*(1), 40–49. doi: 10.1016/j.janxdis.2011.08.011.

Coskun, M., Zoroglu, S., & Ozturk, M. (2012). Phenomenology, psychiatric comorbidity and family history in referred preschool children with obsessive-compulsive disorder. *Child and Adolescent Psychiatry and Mental Health, 6*(1), 36. doi: 10.1186/1753-2000-6-36.

Crum, K. I., & Comer, J.S. (2016). Using synchronous videoconferencing to deliver family-based mental health care. *Journal of Child and Adolescent Psychopharmacology, 26*(3), 229–234.

de Mathis, M. A., do Rosário, M. C., Diniz, J. B., Rodrigues Torres, A., Shavitt, R. G., Arzeno Ferrao, Y., ... Miguel, E. C. (2008). Obsessive-compulsive disorder: Influence of age at onset on comorbidity patterns. *European Psychiatry, 23*(3), 187–194. doi: 10.1016/j.eurpsy.2008.01.002.

Diniz, J. B., Rosário-Campos, M. C., Hounie, A. G., Curi, M., Shavitt, R. G., Lopes, A. C., & Miguel, E. C. (2006). Chronic tics and Tourette syndrome in patients with obsessive-compulsive disorder. *Journal of Psychiatric Research, 40*(6), 487–493. doi: 10.1016/j.jpsychires.2005.09.002.

Evans, D. W., Milanak, M. E., Medeiros, B., & Ross, J. L. (2002). Magical beliefs and rituals in children. *Child Psychiatry and Human Development, 33*(1), 43–58. doi: 10.1023/A:1016516205827.

Flavell, J. H., Green, F. L., & Flavell, E. R. (2000). Development of children's awareness of their own thoughts. *Journal of Cognition and Development, 1*(1), 97–112. doi: 10.1207/S15327647JCD0101N_10.

Flavell, J. H., Miller, P. H., & Miller, S. A. (2001). *Cognitive development* (4th ed.). New York: Prentice-Hall.

Flessner, C. A., Freeman, J. B., Sapyta, J., Garcia, A., Franklin, M. E., March, J. S., & Foa, E. (2011). Predictors of parental accommodation in pediatric obsessive-compulsive disorder: Findings from the pediatric obsessive-compulsive disorder treatment study (POTS) trial. *Journal of the American Academy of Child and Adolescent Psychiatry, 50*(7), 716–725. doi: 10.1016/j.jaac.2011.03.019.

Freeman, J., Flessner, C. A., & Garcia, A. (2011). The Children's Yale–Brown Obsessive Compulsive Scale: Reliability and validity for use among 5 to 8 year olds with obsessive-compulsive disorder. *Journal of Abnormal Child Psychology, 39*(6), 877–883. doi:10.1007/s10802-011-9494-6.

Freeman, J., & Garcia, A. M. (2008). *Family-based treatment for young children with OCD: Therapist guide.* New York: Oxford University Press.

Freeman, J., Garcia, A., Benito, K., Conelea, C., Sapyta, J., Khanna, M., ... Franklin, M. (2012). The Pediatric Obsessive-compulsive Disorder Treatment Study for young children (POTS Jr): Developmental considerations in the rationale, design, and methods. *Journal of Obsessive-Compulsive and Related Disorders, 1*(4), 294–300. doi: 10.1016/j.jocrd.2012.07.010.

Freeman, J. B., Garcia, A. M., Coyne, L., Ale, C., Przeworski, A., Himle, M., ... Leonard, H. L. (2008). Early childhood OCD: Preliminary findings from a family-based cognitive-behavioral approach. *Journal of the American Academy of Child and Adolescent Psychiatry, 47*(5), 593–602. doi: 10.1097/CHI.0b013e31816765f9

Freeman, J., Garcia, A., Frank, H., Benito, K., Conelea, C., Walther, M., & Edmunds, J. (2014a). Evidence base update for psychosocial treatments for pediatric obsessive-compulsive disorder. *Journal of Clinical Child And Adolescent Psychology, 43*(1), 7–26. doi: 10.1080/15374416.2013.804386.

Freeman, J., Sapyta, J., Garcia, A., Compton, S., Khanna, M., Flessner, C., ... Franklin, M. (2014b). Family-based treatment of early childhood obsessive-compulsive disorder: The

Pediatric Obsessive-Compulsive Disorder Treatment Study for Young Children (POTS Jr) – A randomized clinical trial. *JAMA Psychiatry, 71*(6), 689–698. doi: 10.1001/jamapsychiatry.2014.170.

Garcia, A. M., Freeman, J. B., Himle, M. B., Berman, N. C., Ogata, A. K., Ng, J., ... Leonard, H. (2009). Phenomenology of early childhood onset obsessive-compulsive disorder. *Journal of Psychopathology and Behavioral Assessment, 31*(2), 104–111. doi: 10.1007/s10862-008-9094-0.

Geller, D. A. (2006). Obsessive-compulsive and spectrum disorders in children and adolescents. *Psychiatric Clinics of North America, 29*(2), 353–370. doi: 10.1016/j.psc.2006.02.012.

Geller, D. A., Biederman, J., Faraone, S., Agranat, A., Cradock, K., Hagermoser, L., ... Coffey, B. J. (2001). Developmental aspects of obsessive-compulsive disorder: Findings in children, adolescents, and adults. *Journal of Nervous and Mental Disease, 189*(7), 471–477.

Geller, D. A., Biederman, J., Griffin, S., Jones, J., & Lefkowitz, T. R. (1996). Comorbidity of juvenile obsessive-compulsive disorder with disruptive behavior disorders. *Journal of the American Academy of Child and Adolescent Psychiatry, 35*(12), 1637–1646. doi: 10.1097/00004583-199612000-00016.

Geller, D. A., Biederman, J., Jones, J., Park, K., Schwartz, S., Shapiro, S., & Coffey, B. (1998). Is juvenile obsessive-compulsive disorder a developmental subtype of the disorder? A review of the pediatric literature. *Journal of the American Academy of Child and Adolescent Psychiatry, 37*(12), 420–427. doi: 10.1097/00004583-199804000-00020.

Gleason, M. M., Egger, H. L., Emslie, G. J., Greenhill, L. L., Kowatch, R. A., Lieberman, A. F., ... Zeanah, C. H. (2007). Psychopharmacological treatment for very young children: Contexts and guidelines. *Journal of the American Academy of Child and Adolescent Psychiatry, 46*(12), 1532–1572. doi: 10.1097/chi.0b013e3181570d9e.

Hanna, G. L., Piacentini, J., Cantwell, D. P., Fischer, D. J., Himle, J. A., & Van Etten, M. (2002). Obsessive-compulsive disorder with and without tics in a clinical sample of children and adolescents. *Depression and Anxiety, 16*(2), 59–63. doi: 10.1002/da.10058.

Horwath, E., & Weissman, M. M. (2000). The epidemiology and cross-national presentation of obsessive-compulsive disorder. *Psychiatric Clinics of North America, 23*(3), 493–507. doi: 10.1016/S0193-953X(05)70176-3.

Jacobi, F., Wittchen, H. U., Holting, C., Hofler, M., Pfister, H., Muller, N., & Lieb, R. (2004). Prevalence, comorbidity and correlates of mental disorders in the general population: Results from the German Health Interview and Examination Survey (GHS). *Psychological Medicine, 34*(4), 597–611. doi: 10.1017/S0033291703001399.

Jacoby, R. J., Leonard, R. C., Riemann, B. C., & Abramowitz, J. S. (2014). Predictors of quality of life and functional impairment in obsessive-compulsive disorder. *Comprehensive Psychiatry, 55*(5), 1195–1202. doi: 10.1016/j.comppsych.2014.03.011.

Jensen-Doss, A., & Hawley, K. M. (2010). Understanding barriers to evidence-based assessment: Clinician attitudes toward standardized assessment tools. *Journal of Clinical Child and Adolescent Psychology, 39*(6), 885–896. doi: 10.1080/15374416.2010.517169.

Kaufman, J., Birmaher, B., Brent, D., Rao, U., Flynn, C., Moreci, P., ... Ryan, N. (1997). Schedule for Affective Disorders and Schizophrenia for School-Age Children – Present and Lifetime version (K-SADS-PL): Initial reliability and validity data. *Journal of the American Academy of Child and Adolescent Psychiatry, 36*(7), 980–988.

Kessler, R. C., Berglund, P., Demler, O., Jin, R., Merikangas, K. R., & Walters, E. E. (2005a). Lifetime prevalence and age-of-onset distributions of DSM-IV disorders in the National Comorbidity Survey Replication. *Archives of General Psychiatry, 62*(6), 593–602. doi: 10.1001/archpsyc.62.6.593.

Kessler, R. C., Chiu, W. T., Demler, O., Merikangas, K. R., & Walters, E. E. (2005b). Prevalence, severity, and comorbidity of 12-month DSM-IV disorders in the National Comorbidity Survey Replication. *Archives of General Psychiatry, 62*(6), 617–627. doi: 10.1001/archpsyc.62.6.617.

Khanna, M. S., & Kendall, P. C. (2010). Computer-assisted cognitive behavioral therapy for child anxiety: Results of a randomized clinical trial. *Journal of Consulting and Clinical Psychology, 78*(5), 737–745. doi: 10.1037/a0019739.

Krebs, G., Bolhuis, K., Heyman, I., Mataix-Cols, D., Turner, C., & Stringaris, A. (2013). Temper outbursts in paediatric obsessive: Compulsive disorder and their association with depressed mood and treatment outcome. *Journal of Child Psychology and Psychiatry, 54*(3), 313–322. doi: 10.1111/j.1469-7610.2012.02605.x.

Langley, A. K., Lewin, A. B., Bergman, R. L., Lee, J. C., & Piacentini, J. (2010). Correlates of comorbid anxiety and externalizing disorders in childhood obsessive-compulsive disorder. *European Child and Adolescent Psychiatry, 19*(8), 637–645. doi: 10.1007/s00787-010-0101-0.

Lebowitz, E. R. (2013). Parent-based treatment for childhood and adolescent OCD. *Journal of Obsessive-Compulsive and Related Disorders, 2*(4), 425–431. doi: 10.1016/j.jocrd.2013.08.004.

Lebowitz, E. R., Omer, H., & Leckman, J. F. (2011). Coercive and disruptive behaviors in pediatric obsessive-compulsive disorder. *Depression and Anxiety, 28*(10), 899–905. doi: 10.1002/da.20858.

Lewin, A. B., Park, J. M., Jones, A. M., Crawford, E. A., DeNadai, A. S., Menzel, J., ... Storch, E. A. (2014). Family-based exposure and response prevention therapy for preschool-aged children with obsessive-compulsive disorder: A pilot randomized controlled trial. *Behaviour Research and Therapy, 56*, 30–38. doi: 10.1016/j.brat.2014.02.001.

March, J. S., & Mulle, K. (1998). *OCD in children and adolescents: A cognitive-behavioral treatment manual.* New York: Guilford Press.

Merlo, L. J., Lehmkuhl, H. D., Geffken, G. R., & Storch, E. A. (2009). Decreased family accommodation associated with improved therapy outcome in pediatric obsessive-compulsive disorder. *Journal of Consulting and Clinical Psychology, 77*, 355–360.

Murphy, T. K., Patel, P. D., McGuire, J. F., Kennel, A., Mutch, P. J., Athill, E. P., ... Rodriquez, C. A. (2014). Characterization of the Pediatric Acute-Onset Neuropsychiatric Syndrome phenotype. *Journal of Child and Adolescent Psychopharmacology, 25*(1), 14–25.

Nakatani, E., Krebs, G., Micali, N., Turner, C., Heyman, I., & Mataix-Cols, D. (2011). Children with very early onset obsessive-compulsive disorder: Clinical features and treatment outcome. *Journal of Child Psychology and Psychiatry, 52*(12), 1261–1268. doi: 10.1111/j.1469-7610.2011.02434.x.

Narayanaswamy, J. C., Viswanath, B., Veshnal Cherian, A., Bada Math, S., Kandavel, T., & Janardhan Reddy, Y. C. (2012). Impact of age of onset of illness on clinical phenotype in OCD. *Psychiatry Research, 200*(2/3), 554–559. doi: 10.1016/j.psychres.2012.03.037.

Nestadt, G., Samuels, J., Riddle, M., Bienvenu, O. J., Liang, K. Y., LaBuda, M., ... Hoehn-Saric, R. (2000). A family study of obsessive-compulsive disorder. *Archives of General Psychiatry, 57*(4), 358–363. doi: 10.1001/archpsyc.57.4.358.

Pediatric OCD Treatment Study (POTS) Team (2004). Cognitive-behavior therapy, sertraline, and their combination for children and adolescents with obsessive-compulsive disorder: The Pediatric OCD Treatment Study (POTS) randomized controlled trial. *Journal of the American Medical Association, 27*(16), 1969–1976. doi: 10.1001/jama.292.16.1969.

Peris, T. S., Bergman, R. L., Langley, A., Chang, S., McCracken, J. T., & Piacentini, J. (2008). Correlates of accommodation of pediatric obsessive-compulsive disorder: Parent, child, and family characteristics. *Journal of the American Academy of Child & Adolescent Psychiatry, 47*(10), 1173–1181. doi: 10.1097/CHI.0b013e3181825a91.

Piacentini, J., Bergman, R. L., Chang, S., Langley, A., Peris, T., Wood, J. J., & McCracken, J. (2011). Controlled comparison of family cognitive behavioral therapy and psychoeducation/relaxation training for child obsessive-compulsive disorder. *Journal of the American Academy of Child and Adolescent Psychiatry, 50*(11), 1149–1161. doi: 10.1016/j.jaac.2011.08.003.

Piacentini, J., Langley, A., & Roblek, T. (2007a). *Cognitive-behavioral treatment of childhood OCD: It's only a false alarm.* New York: Oxford University Press.

Piacentini, J., Peris, T. S., Bergman, R., Chang, S., & Jaffer, M. (2007b). Functional impairment in childhood OCD: Development and psychometrics properties of the Child Obsessive-Compulsive Impact Scale – Revised (COIS-R). *Journal of Clinical Child and Adolescent Psychology, 36*(4), 645–653. doi: 10.1080/15374410701662790.

Prabhu, L., Cherian, A. V., Viswanath, B., Kandavel, T., Math, S. B., & Reddy, Y. C. J. (2013). Symptom dimensions in OCD and their association with clinical characteristics and comorbid disorders. *Journal of Obsessive-Compulsive and Related Disorders, 2*(1), 14–21. doi: 10.1016/j.jocrd.2012.10.002.

Rasmussen, S. A., & Tsuang, M. T. (1986). Clinical characteristics and family history in DSM-III obsessive-compulsive disorder. *American Journal of Psychiatry, 143*(3), 317–382.

Rettew, D. C., Swedo, S. E., Leonard, H. L., Lenane, M. C., & Rapoport, J. L. (1992). Obsessions and compulsions across time in 79 children and adolescents with obsessive-compulsive disorder. *Journal of the American Academy of Child and Adolescent Psychiatry, 31*(6), 1050–1056. doi: 10.1097/00004583-199211000-00009.

Sandler, I., Ostrom, A., Bitner, M. J., Ayers, T. S., Wolchik, S., & Daniels, V. S. (2005). Developing effective prevention services for the real world: A prevention service development model. *American Journal of Community Psychology, 35*(3), 127–142. doi: 10.1007/s10464-005-3389-z.

Scahill, L., Riddle, M. A., McSwiggan-Hardin, M., Ort, S. I., King, R. A., Goodman, W. K., … Leckman, J. F. (1997). Children's Yale–Brown Obsessive-Compulsive Scale: Reliability and validity. *Journal of the American Academy of Child and Adolescent Psychiatry, 36*(6), 844–852. doi: 10.1097/00004583-199706000-00023.

Selles, R. R., Storch, E. A., & Lewin, A. B. (2014). Variations in symptom prevalence and clinical correlates in younger versus older youth with obsessive-compulsive disorder. *Child Psychiatry and Human Development, 45*(6), 666–674. doi: 10.1007/s10578-014-0435-9.

Shafran, R., Thordarson, D. S., & Rachman, S. (1996). Thought–action fusion in obsessive-compulsive disorder. *Journal of Anxiety Disorders, 10*(5), 379–391. doi: 10.1016/0887-6185(96)00018-7.

Silverman, W. K., & Albano, A. M. (1996). *The Anxiety Disorders Interview Schedule for Children for DSM-IV: Child and parent versions.* San Antonio, TX: Psychological Corp.

Silverman, W. K., & Ollendick, T. H. (2005). Evidence-based assessment of anxiety and its disorders in children and adolescents. *Journal of Clinical Child and Adolescent Psychology, 34*(3), 380–411. doi: 10.1207/s15374424jccp3403_2.

Silverman, W. K., Saavedra, L. M., & Pina, A. A. (2001). Test–retest reliability of anxiety symptoms and diagnoses with anxiety disorders interview schedule for DSM-IV: Child and parent versions. *Journal of the American Academy of Child and Adolescent Psychiatry, 40*(8), 937–944. doi: 10.1097/00004583-200108000-00016.

Spence, S. H., Rapee, R., McDonald, C., & Ingram, M. (2001). The structure of anxiety symptoms among preschoolers. *Behaviour Research and Therapy, 39*(11), 1293–1316. doi: 10.1016/S0005-7967(00)00098-X.

Storch, E. A., Abramowitz, J. S., & Keeley, M. (2009). Correlates and mediators of functional disability in obsessive-compulsive disorder. *Depression and Anxiety, 26*(9), 806–813. doi: 10.1002/da.20481.

Storch, E. A., Bussing, R., Small, B. J., Geffken, F.R., McNamara, J. P., Rahman, O., … Murphy, T. K. (2013). Randomized, placebo-controlled trial of cognitive-behavioral therapy alone or combined with sertraline in the treatment of pediatric obsessive-compulsive disorder. *Behaviour Research and Therapy, 51*(12), 823–829. doi: 10.1016/j.brat.2013.09.007.

Storch, E. A., Caporino, N. E., Morgan, J. R., Lewin, A. B., Rojas, A., Brauer, L., … Murphy, T.K. (2011). Preliminary investigation of web-camera delivered cognitive-behavioral therapy for youth with obsessive-compulsive disorder. *Psychiatry Research, 189*(3), 407–412. doi: 10.1016/j.psychres.2011.05.047.

Storch, E. A., Jones, A. M., Lack, C. W., Ale, C. M., Sulkowski, M. L., Lewin, A. B., ... Murphy, T. K. (2012). Rage attacks in pediatric obsessive-compulsive disorder: Phenomenology and clinical correlates. *Journal of the American Academy of Child & Adolescent Psychiatry*, 51(6), 582–592. doi: 10.1016/j.jaac.2012.02.016.

Storch, E. A., Lewin, A. B., Geffken, G. R., Morgan, J. R., & Murphy, T. K. (2010). The role of comorbid disruptive behavior in the clinical expression of pediatric obsessive-compulsive disorder. *Behaviour Research and Therapy*, 48(12), 1204–1210. doi: 10.1016/j.brat.2010.09.004.

Stringaris, A., & Goodman, R. (2009). Longitudinal outcome of youth oppositionality: Irritable, headstrong, and hurtful behaviors have distinctive predictions. *Journal of the American Academy of Child & Adolescent Psychiatry*, 48(4), 404–412. doi: 10.1097/CHI.0b013e3181984f30.

Swedo, S. E., Leonard, H. L., Garvey, M., Mittleman, B., Allen, A. J., Perlmutter, S., ... Lougee, L. (1998). Pediatric autoimmune neuropsychiatric disorders associated with streptococcal infections: Clinical description of the first 50 cases. *American Journal of Psychiatry*, 155(2), 264–271.

Thompson-Hollands, J., Edson, A., Tompson, M. C., & Comer, J. S. (2014a). Family involvement in the psychological treatment of obsessive-compulsive disorder: A meta-analysis. *Journal of Family Psychology*, 28(3), 287–298. doi: 10.1037/a0036709.

Thompson-Hollands, J., Kerns, C. E., Pincus, D. B., & Comer, J. S. (2014b). Parental accommodation of child anxiety and related symptoms: Range, impact, and correlates. *Journal of Anxiety Disorders*, 28(8), 765–773. doi: 10.1016/j.janxdis.2014.09.007.

Weissman, M. M., Bland, R. C., Canino, G. J., Greenwald, S., Hwu, H. G., Lee, C. K., ... Wickramaratne, P. J. (1994). The cross national epidemiology of obsessive compulsive disorder: The Cross National Collaborative Group. *Journal of Clinical Psychiatry*, 55(Suppl. 3), 5–10.

Wood, J. J., Piacentini, J. C., Bergman, R. L., McCracken, J., & Barrios, V. (2002). Concurrent validity of the anxiety disorders section of the Anxiety Disorders Interview Schedule for DSM-IV: Child and parent versions. *Journal of Clinical Child and Adolescent Psychology*, 31(3), 335–342. doi: 10.1207/S15374424JCCP3103_05.

27

Insight in Obsessive-Compulsive Disorder

Monica S. Wu and Adam B. Lewin

For individuals with obsessive-compulsive disorder (OCD), insight is generally characterized as the degree to which one recognizes the irrational and excessive nature of the OCD symptomology (American Psychiatric Association, 2013). On one end, individuals with poor insight are strongly convinced of the accuracy of their beliefs. For instance, a patient with poor insight may be highly certain that a feared outcome will ensue if the compulsions are not completed (e.g., a life-threatening illness will be contracted each time a doorknob is touched, and the excessive hand-washing rituals serve as a failsafe method to prevent illnesses from spreading). At the other end, a patient with good insight may present with the same OCD symptoms (i.e., engage in hand-washing compulsions to neutralize contamination fears), but will realize the intrinsic irrational nature of the obsessions and compulsions. Indeed, individuals possessing higher levels of insight tend to display more flexibility in their beliefs, and realize the excessive and irrational nature of their OCD symptoms.

Historically, insight has been described by a variety of terminology. First, Kozak and Foa (1994) characterized poor insight as overvalued ideation. Thereafter, the *Diagnostic and Statistical Manual of Mental Disorders* (DSM-IV) field trials described low levels of insight as fixed beliefs (Foa et al., 1995). Presently, poor insight is simply stated as such, with various gradations (i.e., poor insight, absent insight) allowed in its specification (American Psychiatric Association, 2013). Until recently, insight has been conceptualized as a requirement for a diagnosis of OCD (American Psychiatric Association, 2000), except in pediatric OCD. That is, the individual must realize, at some point during the course of the disorder, that their symptoms are excessive and unreasonable. Additionally, it was also considered as a dichotomous, categorical construct, where the individual either had insight into their symptoms or had "poor insight," representing individuals that failed to recognize the irrational nature of their symptoms for the majority of the time. However, clinical experience and a growing research base dictate otherwise, shifting the field toward a conceptualization of insight on a continuum.

Insight is more appropriately conceptualized as existing on a continuum (Kozak & Foa, 1994), which is reflected by the expanding literature, new diagnostic criteria, and empirically validated measures assessing insight. To reflect this new conceptualization, the DSM-5 no longer requires individuals to have insight into their symptoms in order to receive an OCD diagnosis, and allows the three insight specifiers to range

The Wiley Handbook of Obsessive Compulsive Disorders, Volume I, First Edition.
Edited by Jonathan S. Abramowitz, Dean McKay, and Eric A. Storch.
© 2017 John Wiley & Sons Ltd. Published 2017 by John Wiley & Sons Ltd.

from "good or fair insight," to "poor insight," to "absent insight" (American Psychiatric Association, 2013). Insight is also considered to be multifaceted, including components that consider the fixity, conviction, and stability of the beliefs, among other constructs, and these properties are reflected in the numerous assessment devices used to examine insight. Additionally, insight may not only range interindividually, but it is likely to fluctuate intraindividually as well. It is often observed that insight into the OCD symptoms is situation-dependent, where insight is higher when the individual is in a non-threatening situation and lower when the individuals is in a "dangerous" situation (Kozak & Foa, 1994; O'Dwyer, 2000). As such, clinicians should be cognizant of the fluctuating property of insight, as individuals often display more awareness into the senselessness of their symptoms when in non-threatening situations (e.g., the therapist's office). This highlights the importance of conducting in vivo exposures in various real-life situations to promote generalization and in-session practice of cognitive-behavioral skills (Lewin & Piacentini, 2009).

Differential diagnosis may be particularly difficult among individuals lacking insight and may require ongoing assessment, often in the context of intervention. On initial presentation, it can be difficult to accurately diagnose and differentiate between OCD devoid of insight versus delusions more consistent with psychosis/delusional disorders (Lewin, 2014; Poyurovsky & Koran, 2005). Generally, awareness regarding the (in)accuracy of an obsessional belief can be particularly difficult for individuals with OCD, but these individuals tend to present with lower fixity and conviction regarding the beliefs, as well as greater intraindividual fluctuation in contrast to an individual with psychotic delusions (Brakoulias & Starcevic, 2011). Indeed, in extreme cases, once the obsessions become egosyntonic and fully accepted, individuals may cross over into being delusional (Insel & Akiskal, 1986). However, even chronic, severe OCD with poor insight does not generally evolve into psychosis.

Insight is being increasingly studied given numerous implications for the assessment and treatment of OCD (Lewin, 2014). Specifically, insight may serve as a risk factor for numerous problems including (but not limited to) delaying treatment seeking in OCD (Demet et al., 2010), compounded impairment, treatment refractoriness (Erzegovesi et al., 2001; Prasko et al., 2009; Raffin, Guimaraes Fachel, Ferrao, Pasquoto de Souza, & Cordioli, 2009), and increased comorbidities (Catapano, Sperandeo, Perris, Lanzaro, & Maj, 2001; Ravi Kishore, Samar, Janardhan Reddy, Chandrasekhar, & Thennarasu, 2004). Given the relationships between insight and various deleterious outcomes, it is important to consider different factors that may impact an individual's clinical presentation and treatment response. Consequently, research findings and clinical implications of specific variables related to insight are explored in detail below.

Clinical Characteristics and Phenomenology

Demographic Variables

Investigations into the relationship between insight and various demographic variables have elicited differential findings. Not surprisingly, age is associated with level of insight among children. Findings suggest that younger age is associated with poorer insight (Bipeta, Yerramilli, Pingali, Karredla, & Ali, 2013; Lewin et al., 2010a; Lewin, Caporino, Murphy, Geffken, & Storch, 2010b; Nikolajsen, Nissen, & Thomsen,

2011; Selles, Storch, & Lewin, 2014). When compared across all age groups, children with OCD displayed poorer insight than adolescents and adults (Geller et al., 2001), and adolescents and adults exhibited similar levels of insight with one another (Mancebo et al., 2008). When investigating adults with OCD, researchers have largely found no impact of age on levels of insight (Karadag et al., 2011; Marazziti et al., 2002; Matsunaga et al., 2002; Onen, Karakas Ugurlu, & Caykoylu, 2013; Ravi Kishore et al., 2004; Tumkaya et al., 2009; Türksoy, Tükel, Ozdemir, & Karali, 2002).

Taken together, it appears that there is larger variation and relatively poorer insight among children, and less variability when considering older age groups (i.e., adolescents, adults). This may be attributed to the developmental maturity of the individual, as younger children are still undergoing considerable cognitive developments at a young age, whereas older youth/adolescents reach a cognitive level that is more comparable to that of an adult. As such, younger children may have increased challenges with recognizing the irrationality of their symptoms and thus display poorer insight (Lewin et al., 2014b). Accordingly, clinicians should be cognizant of the age and developmental level of the individual with OCD, as younger patients may be at risk for exhibiting relatively poorer insight into their OCD symptoms. Consistent with established assessment (Lewin & Piacentini, 2010) and treatment recommendations for pediatric OCD (Kircanski, Peris, & Piacentini, 2011), therapy should be conducted and explained in developmentally appropriate terms to maximize the child's ability to understand the rationale behind exposure and response prevention and to increase their awareness into their symptomology.

When considering the relationship between insight and sex, findings suggest that there are no significant differences between males and females (Karadag et al., 2011; Lewin et al., 2010a; Marazziti et al., 2002; Matsunaga et al., 2002; Onen et al., 2013; Ravi Kishore et al., 2004; Türksoy et al., 2002). Years of education also failed to show an impact on insight (Karadag et al., 2011; Matsunaga et al., 2002; Onen et al., 2013; Türksoy et al., 2002), with the exception of one study (Alonso et al., 2008). It appears that age is the most pertinent demographic variable when considering the effects on insight in younger children, but is less relevant with older ages (i.e., adolescents and adults).

Familial Variables

Given the broader impact of family functioning on OCD phenomenology and treatment response, it is important to consider the familial contributors to insight. Family psychiatric history has been related to levels of insight among patients with OCD, as lower levels of insight were related to the occurrence of OCD (Bellino, Patria, Ziero, & Bogetto, 2005) and/or schizophrenia spectrum disorders (Catapano et al., 2001) in family members. However, other investigations have failed to find a relationship between insight and family history of OCD (Elvish, Simpson, & Ball, 2010; Lewin et al., 2010a; Matsunaga et al., 2002) and/or broader family psychiatric history (Elvish et al., 2010; Marazziti et al., 2002; Onen et al., 2013; Ravi Kishore et al., 2004). Clinicians should remain vigilant for a family history of OCD and/or schizophrenia spectrum disorders, as they may be related to an individual's level of insight. However, findings are largely mixed and the majority of findings failed to find a significant relationship; future research is needed to garner a clearer picture of the relationship between insight and family psychiatric history.

While some investigations have failed to find any effect of marital status on insight (Ravi Kishore et al., 2004; Türksoy et al., 2002), Shimshoni, Reuven, Dar, and Hermesh (2011) reported that individuals currently not in a romantic relationship demonstrated poorer insight. Additionally, youth with poorer insight may experience greater family accommodation (Bipeta et al., 2013; Storch et al., 2008), though Lewin and colleagues (2010a) did not observe these differences. Although the findings for relationship status and family accommodation are not definitive, the potential impact of the respective variables has potential clinical implications. First, those in romantic relationships may benefit from interacting with a significant other that is able to challenge irrational thought processes and increase insight into the illogical nature of their OCD symptoms. Conversely, increased family involvement and engagement in accommodating behaviors can serve to increase OCD-related functional impairment (Calvocoressi et al., 1995). Individuals with lower levels of insight often display decreased resistance and control over OCD symptomology, potentially triggering family members to engage in increased accommodation. Unfortunately, family accommodation leads to symptom maintenance and exacerbation, contributing to poorer treatment response (Cherian et al., 2012; Garcia et al., 2010; Lewin et al., 2014b). Thus, it is essential for clinicians to assess the impact of insight on the family, and consequently convey the importance of utilizing more adaptive strategies to respond to OCD symptoms; emphasis on tactful ways of raising awareness and increasing insight into the symptoms should be highlighted, and accommodating behaviors should be identified and discontinued in a graduated manner.

Functional Impairment

The relationship between insight and functional impairment is not completely clear. Some studies have reported significantly poorer adaptive functioning (Lewin et al., 2010a; Matsunaga et al., 2002) and higher OCD-related impairment (Storch et al., 2008), even after controlling for OCD symptom severity in individuals with lower insight. Specifically, increased difficulties with maintaining gainful employment and poorer functioning in the social and familial domains occur in individuals with poorer insight (Fontenelle et al., 2013), even after controlling for potentially confounding variables (e.g., OCD symptom severity, gender, age) (Jakubovski et al., 2011). Other studies did not find group differences in OCD-related functional impairment between patients with lower and higher levels of insight on OCD-related impairment (Bipeta et al., 2013; Lewin, et al., 2010b). Methodological limitations regarding both assessment of insight and degree of functional impairment (e.g., OCD-specific or broader adaptive disabilities) may explain discrepant findings. For instance, Lewin and colleagues (2010a) found that general adaptive functioning was poorer in individuals with poorer insight, but no significant relationship was found between insight and OCD-related functional impairment. Future research should seek to clarify the relationship between insight and functional impairment with clear delineations of what aspect of functioning is being examined using evidence-based assessment tools (Lewin & Piacentini, 2010). Furthermore, clinicians should consider the impact of insight on the accuracy of reporting. That is, individuals with poorer insight may fail to accurately report on the functional impairment related to their OCD symptoms. As such, the reliability of patient self-report responses can be impacted, so clinicians should be vigilant when assessing the levels of functional impairment in individuals with poorer insight. In these cases, reports from individuals knowledgeable of the patient's symptomology (e.g., parents, significant others) will need to be gathered and weighed more heavily.

Association with OCD Symptoms

OCD Symptom Onset and Chronicity

Levels of insight may be related to the timing of OCD symptom onset, as well as the chronicity of the disorder. Based on adult samples, it is possible that individuals with lower levels of insight present with more chronic courses of OCD when compared with their counterparts (Bellino et al., 2005; Matsunaga et al., 2002; Ravi Kishore et al., 2004), but other investigations have been unable to replicate this finding (Catapano et al., 2001; De Berardis et al., 2005; Elvish et al., 2010; Jakubovski et al., 2011; Karadag et al., 2011; Marazziti et al., 2002; Onen et al., 2013; Türksoy et al., 2002). Additionally, adults with worse insight into their symptoms may have an earlier age of OCD symptom onset (Catapano et al., 2010; Matsunaga et al., 2002; Ravi Kishore et al., 2004), though Shimshoni and colleagues (2011) found that poor insight was associated with a later onset of symptoms. However, other investigations did not find any significant relationships between insight and age of onset (Catapano et al., 2001; De Berardis et al., 2005; Elvish et al., 2010; Jakubovski et al., 2011; Karadag et al., 2011; Marazziti et al., 2002; Onen et al., 2013; Türksoy et al., 2002). Given the discrepant findings, it may be important to consider the age range that is investigated and the types of OCD symptoms that are affected. Indeed, a pilot study by Fontenelle and colleagues (2013) reported lower insight for a sample of 60 adults experiencing an onset of OCD symptoms prior to age 10 or after age 18. In sum, when working with individuals with poorer insight, clinicians should be particularly watchful for more chronic courses of OCD and potential difficulties recognizing the irrationality behind certain OCD symptomology, depending on their age of onset.

OCD Symptom Severity

The relationship between insight and OCD severity has not been definitive. Some investigations demonstrate significant relationships between insight and the severity of obsessions (Karadag et al., 2011; Matsunaga, 2012; Türksoy et al., 2002), compulsions (Bellino et al., 2005; Cherian et al., 2012; Karadag et al., 2011; Matsunaga et al., 2002; Türksoy et al., 2002), and the combination of obsessions and compulsions (Catapano et al., 2001; Catapano et al., 2010; De Berardis et al., 2005; Fontenelle et al., 2013; Himle, Etten, Janeck, & Fischer, 2006; Ravi Kishore et al., 2004). On the other hand, a group of studies did not find a significant relationship between insight and OCD symptom severity (Eisen, Phillips, Coles, & Rasmussen, 2004; Lewin et al., 2010a; Marazziti et al., 2002; Onen et al., 2013; Shimshoni et al., 2011; Storch et al., 2014a; Tumkaya et al., 2009).

Although the findings have been inconclusive, it is important to consider the potential relationship between insight and OCD symptom severity from a clinical perspective. Specifically, the relationship between low insight and heightened OCD symptom severity may be largely driven by poor resistance and control over the symptoms (Alonso et al., 2008). Lower levels of insight have been consistently associated with lower ability to resist/control OCD symptoms (Jakubovski et al., 2011; Ravi Kishore et al., 2004; Storch et al., 2014a). As such, clinicians must exercise extra care in treating individuals with lower insight, emphasizing the importance of resisting the obsessions and refraining from engaging in compulsions.

OCD Symptom Dimensions

Levels of insight may be related to specific types of OCD symptoms, though findings are mixed. Individuals with poorer insight may display more health and somatic concerns (Abramowitz, Brigidi, & Foa, 1999; De Berardis et al., 2005), contamination symptoms (Cherian et al., 2012), aggressive and religious concerns (Tolin, Abramowitz, Kozak, & Foa, 2001), checking behaviors and uncertainty (Jaafari et al., 2011), repeating compulsions (Storch et al., 2008), ordering symptoms (Elvish et al., 2010; Storch et al., 2014a), hoarding/saving obsessions (De Berardis et al., 2005; Fontenelle et al., 2013; Ravi Kishore et al., 2004; Samuels et al., 2007; Torres et al., 2012), and "miscellaneous" symptoms (Fontenelle et al., 2013; Ravi Kishore et al., 2004; Türksoy et al., 2002). Alternatively, other studies reported that individuals with higher levels of insight may present with heightened contamination symptoms (Alonso et al., 2008), as well as "forbidden" and aggressive concerns (Cherian et al., 2012). Given the contradictory findings, further research is needed to clarify the impact of insight and specific OCD symptom dimensions. However, hoarding and "miscellaneous" symptoms appear to garner relatively more empirical support than the other symptom dimensions (with the exception of Storch et al. (2014a) who did not find a significant relationship between insight and hoarding). As such, clinicians may need to specifically focus on hoarding and "miscellaneous" symptoms (e.g., need to know, doing things until it feels "just right," need to touch/tap, ritualized eating behaviors) when they present in individuals with poorer insight, as they may demonstrate increased resistance and greater difficulty with recognizing the irrationality of the symptoms.

Impact of Comorbidities

Individuals with poorer insight may be at risk for various psychiatric comorbidities when compared to those with higher insight into OCD symptoms, necessitating examinations into this potential relationship. Some investigations yielded increased rates of present (Ravi Kishore et al., 2004) and past (childhood) psychiatric comorbidities (Catapano et al., 2001) in individuals with poor insight, while others failed to find any significant differences in comorbidities based on level of insight (Jakubovski et al., 2011; Marazziti et al., 2002). As these general findings remain mixed, targeted investigations into specific psychiatric conditions may elucidate more nuanced, valuable information.

Specifically, increased depressive symptoms and comorbid depressive disorders have shown higher representation in individuals with lower levels of insight (Alonso et al.,

2008; Bipeta et al., 2013; Catapano et al., 2010; De Berardis et al., 2005; Elvish et al., 2010; Fontenelle et al., 2013; Himle et al., 2006; Lewin et al., 2010a; Matsunaga et al., 2002; Ravi Kishore et al., 2004; Türksoy et al., 2002), though other investigations have failed to replicate this relationship (Jakubovski et al., 2011; Shimshoni et al., 2011). These discrepant findings may be attributed to varying levels of depressive symptom severity across samples. Additionally, there may also be differences in conceptualizing depression; some researchers examined the comorbid diagnosis of a depressive disorder, while others investigated the presence of depressive symptoms on a continuous measure. Indeed, Peris and colleagues (2010) detected significant differences in depressive symptoms in individuals with higher versus lower levels of insight, but the relationship was nonsignificant when depressive symptoms were considered categorical (i.e., high versus low levels of depressive symptoms). Additionally, depressive symptoms may uniquely affect insight into certain symptom dimensions, such as those related to aggression and checking (Fontenelle et al., 2013); future research should seek to evaluate the respective impact of insight on various types of OCD symptoms. Ultimately, given the potential relationship between insight and depressive symptomology, clinicians should consider the consequent implications for care of individuals with poorer insight. As individuals exhibiting depressive symptoms experience increased OCD-related functional impairment (Eisen et al., 2006; Huppert, Simpson, Nissenson, Liebowitz, & Foa, 2009; Storch et al., 2014b), clinicians should employ increased vigilance for at-risk individuals. Patients with poorer insight into their OCD may require extra attention and care in targeting depressive symptoms, as they may present with compounded difficulties and decreased motivation.

The relationship between insight and anxiety has also been investigated, and findings are mixed. Some investigators have reported that individuals with poorer insight more frequently present with comorbid anxiety disorders (Shimshoni et al., 2011), while others failed to report these group differences (Lewin et al., 2010a; Türksoy et al., 2002). Similarly, various reports indicate that individuals with lower levels of insight demonstrate higher state anxiety and anxiety symptomology (Türksoy et al., 2002), but other findings demonstrate no group differences in state or trait anxiety (Matsunaga et al., 2002), nor in anxiety symptomology (Storch et al., 2008). Collectively, it is difficult to determine whether or not varying levels of insight influence the presence of co-occurring anxiety, so future research should seek to further investigate potential group differences through differing measures that allow the data to be analyzed categorically and continuously. Nevertheless, should individuals with poorer insight more frequently present with comorbid anxiety, clinicians should be conscientious of potentially increased anxiety sensitivity and compounded worries. CBT can be similarly employed for the co-occurring anxiety, with a primary emphasis on exposures, and cognitive restructuring as needed.

At a broader level, the relationships between insight and internalizing/externalizing symptoms have been examined. Lewin and colleagues (2010a) did not find significant group differences for internalizing or externalizing symptoms, but Storch and colleagues (2014a) found increased externalizing symptoms in youth with poor insight. However, it appears that results vary depending on how the variables are analyzed; youth with poorer insight displayed higher levels of internalizing symptoms only when considered categorically, but they demonstrated higher internalizing and externalizing symptoms when considered continuously (Storch et al., 2008).

Furthermore, youth with varying levels of insight did not exhibit differences in rates of comorbid attention deficit hyperactivity disorder or tic disorders (Lewin et al., 2010a). Although evidence is mixed, clinicians should be vigilant for externalizing symptoms in youth with poorer insight. Externalizing symptoms and anger outbursts contribute to increased family accommodation and compounded OCD-related functional impairment (Wu, Lewin, Murphy, Geffken, & Storch, 2014). As such, clinicians should aim to preventatively target maladaptive externalizing behaviors in treatment, teaching more adaptive responses to obsessional distress and limiting family accommodation.

When considering the continuum of insight, the severe end of the spectrum has often been compared with delusions, making differential diagnosis difficult (Poyurovsky & Koran, 2005). Indeed, individuals with poor insight have demonstrated relatively more comorbid personality disorders than individuals with better insight, especially schizotypal personality disorder (Alonso et al., 2008; Catapano et al., 2010; Matsunaga et al., 2002), as well as borderline and narcissistic personality disorders (Türksoy et al., 2002). In a related vein, individuals with poor insight demonstrated more alexithymia than individuals with relatively better insight, suggesting difficulties with identifying and expressing emotions (De Berardis et al., 2005). Conversely, individuals with better insight were more likely to have comorbid obsessive-compulsive personality disorder (Bellino et al., 2005) and avoidant personality disorder (Türksoy et al., 2002). As such, depending on the individual's level of insight, they may be at risk for various personality disorders; clinicians are advised to assess for these potential comorbidities and determine if they will be contraindicated with OCD treatment.

Neuropsychological/Neurobiological Implications

Neuropsychological impairments, especially in executive functioning and working memory domains, are common among youth (Lewin et al., 2014a) and adults (Kuelz, Hohagen, & Voderholzer, 2004) with OCD. There are several investigations examining the potential relationship between levels of insight and various neuropsychological variables. Children with lower levels of insight may generally demonstrate poorer intellectual functioning (Lewin et al., 2010a). Adults with poorer insight may also exhibit poorer verbal memory (Kitis et al., 2007; Tumkaya et al., 2009) and fluency, executive functioning (Tumkaya et al., 2009), and conflict resolution (Kashyap, Kumar, Kandavel, & Reddy, 2012). Youth with poorer insight also generally exhibited relatively poorer verbal and non-verbal abilities (Lewin et al., 2010a) as measured by the Kaufman Brief Intelligence Test (K-BIT) (Kaufman, 1990). Taken together, Kashyap and colleagues (2012) conceptualized individuals with poorer insight as having increased difficulties with processing contradictory information, maintaining the newly learned information, accessing these memories, and associating and manipulating them. These impairments may partly explain why individuals with poorer insight can struggle with obtaining and integrating new information achieved through exposure exercises. When engaging in exposures, individuals are purposely provided with information that generally contradicts their feared beliefs, allowing them to form more realistic and more readily accessible associations with the feared stimuli (Craske et al., 2008). However, with the aforementioned difficulties, individuals with poorer insight may demonstrate trouble with integrating this new information into their belief schema, preventing them from effectively experiencing inhibitory learning from the situations.

Levels of insight may also be associated with various neurobiological variables. First, Aigner and colleagues (2005) conducted magnetic resonance imaging (MRI) with individuals with OCD that presented with varying levels of insight. When examining the frequency of abnormalities detected by MRI, individuals with poor insight more frequently displayed abnormalities (83%) than did their counterparts with intact insight (21%). Abnormalities were found in various brain structures, but the basal ganglia and parietal lobe were the structures that were most frequently reported as abnormal, which corroborates extant literature on the implications of basal ganglia dysfunction and OCD (Rapoport, 1991). Next, Karadag et al. (2011) examined neurobiological soft signs, or minor neurodevelopmental impairments typically pertaining to motor or somatosensory domains, in individuals with varying levels of insight. While all individuals with OCD displayed significantly more neurological soft signs than healthy controls, individuals with OCD exhibiting poorer insight displayed significantly poorer motor coordination and sensory integration when compared to those with good insight. This may be related to difficulties with sensory over-responsivity, or exaggerated responses to various sensory stimuli, in individuals with OCD, which is a relatively common phenomenon in youth with OCD (Lewin, Wu, Murphy, & Storch, 2015). Increased difficulties with sensory integration may need to be specially targeted in treatment, as it may exacerbate certain OCD symptomology and augment distress during sensory-related exposures. To date, there is a paucity of studies examining the efficacy of exposure and response prevention therapy for sensory-based OCD, illustrating potential difficulties with treating individuals with sensory over-responsivity.

Collectively, individuals with poorer insight may present with a different neuropsychological profile and possibly neurostructural and/or neurological abnormalities. While the chicken-or-egg dilemma applies to the above relationships, poor insight among individuals with OCD may suggest neuropsychological sequelae that may require adjustments in treatment. For example, difficulties with executive functioning and verbal memory have been documented in individuals with lower levels of insight, potentially impeding their ability to optimally integrate information learned through exposures. Similarly, clinicians may wish to closely assess insight among patients with histories of executive functioning problems and/or abnormal neurological examinations. Consequently, interventions may need modification in order to accommodate the additional difficulties (both low insight and/or neuro-executive deficits) in these patients. As such, clinicians should be conscientious of these potential complexities in individuals with poorer insight.

Assessment of Insight

Impact of Insight on Assessments

Much data about individuals' OCD symptomology are gathered through clinician-rated measures and/or self-report questionnaires, allowing individuals to provide subjective information about their respective experiences with OCD. There are naturally interindividual variations in how individuals report their symptoms, but their level of insight can influence the reliability of the given reports considerably.

Specifically, individuals with lower insight may experience difficulty with providing an accurate clinical picture of their OCD symptomology. For instance, younger children may lack insight into the presence of specific obsessions, making it challenging for clinicians to assess the content and severity of various symptoms. As such, it is clinically indicated to obtain supplemental reports from alternative informants (e.g., parents, significant others), allowing for corroboration of existing information and the attainment of a more comprehensive repertoire of OCD symptoms.

Measures to Assess Levels of Insight

Children's Yale–Brown Obsessive Compulsive Scale/Yale–Brown Obsessive Compulsive Scale Item No. 11 (CYBOCS/YBOCS). Given that the CYBOCS and YBOCS (Goodman, Price, Rasmussen, Mazure, Delgado, et al., 1989; Goodman, Price, Rasmussen, Mazure, Fleischmann, et al., 1989; Scahill et al., 1997) are considered the gold standard clinician-administered measurement tools for assessing OCD symptom presence and severity (Lewin et al., 2014c), many clinicians and researchers utilize item No. 11 for the examination of insight (Catapano et al., 2010; Cherian et al., 2012; De Berardis et al., 2005; Himle et al., 2006; Hollander, Baldini Rossi, Sood, & Pallanti, 2003; Lewin et al., 2010b; Raffin et al., 2009; Shimshoni et al., 2011; Storch et al., 2014b; Wu et al., 2014). Specifically, it is a one-item question examining the individual's level of insight on scale from 0 to 4, 0 meaning "excellent" insight and 4 meaning "lacking" insight. Prompts for the question assess the individual's insight into the reasonableness of their symptoms, ability to recognize contrary evidence, and conviction in their beliefs (e.g., that something bad really would happen if they did not carry out their compulsions).

Fixity of Beliefs Scale. The Fixity of Beliefs Scale (Foa et al., 1995) is a five-item face-valid measure that was designed for the DSM-IV field trial. It assesses the individual's insight into the unreasonableness of their obsessions and compulsions. Specifically, it examines how strongly the individual believes that feared consequences will truly happen if compulsions are not carried out. Inter-rater reliability has been low (Intraclass Correlation Coefficient [ICC] = .54) in the past (Foa et al., 1995), though studies utilizing this questionnaire have historically selected specific questions (rather than employing the whole scale) (Abramowitz et al., 1999; Garcia et al., 2010).

Brown Assessment of Beliefs Scale (BABS). The BABS (Eisen et al., 1998) is a seven-item clinician-administered measure that assesses the level of insight and degree of conviction an individual has regarding their symptoms during the past week. It conceptualizes insight as a multidimensional construct that occurs on a continuum. As such, the BABS assesses various dimensions of insight: conviction, perception of others' views of beliefs, explanation of differing views, fixity of ideas, attempt to disprove beliefs, insight, and ideas/delusions of reference (Eisen et al., 1998). Items are scored on a scale from 0 to 4. The first six items are summed to make a total score, with higher scores indicating poorer insight. The last item is a measure of the clinician's overall impression of the individual's level of insight. The BABS possesses good psychometric properties, demonstrating excellent internal consistency (Cronbach's α = .87), inter-rater reliability (ICCs = .78–.96), and test–retest reliability (ICCs = .79–.98), as well as good convergent and divergent validity (Eisen et al., 1998). Additionally, it demonstrated excellent sensitivity and specificity in identifying "delusional" patients, and exhibited good sensitivity to change in a sample of patients receiving sertraline, showing a correlated but not identical change in insight when compared to change in OCD symptom severity (Eisen et al., 1998).

Child Assessment of Beliefs Scale (CABS). The CABS (Storch et al., 2014a) is a three-item clinician-administered measure that assesses the level of insight regarding the excessiveness and unreasonableness of the individual's OCD symptoms. It is based on the BABS, but is adapted to be developmentally appropriate for youth. Specifically, items were either removed or reworded to be comprehensible for a younger population. Items are scored on a scale from 0 to 4 (higher scores indicating poorer insight), and items are summed to form a total score. After a comprehensive psychometric analysis, the retained items in the final measure examine the individual's beliefs regarding the rationality of the thoughts and behaviors, the fixity of the beliefs, as well as the cause of the symptoms. It demonstrated acceptable internal consistency ($\rho = .80$), as well as good divergent and convergent validity, exhibiting a strong correlation ($r = .70$, $p < .01$) with the insight question on the CYBOCS (Storch et al., 2014a).

Overvalued Ideas Scale (OVIS). The OVIS (Neziroglu, McKay, Yaryura-Tobias, Stevens, & Todaro, 1999) is an 11-item clinician-administered measure that assesses the degree of overvalued ideation related to the individual's OCD symptoms in the past week. Each item can be rated on a scale from 1 to 10. The total score is achieved by taking the mean of all item scores, with higher scores indicating greater overvalued ideation. The questions assess multidimensional aspects of overvalued ideation, such as the strength behind the beliefs, accuracy of the individual's obsessional beliefs, utility of compulsions, and strength of resistance against the beliefs. The scale possesses acceptable psychometric properties, demonstrating good internal, test–retest, and interrater reliability, as well as good convergent validity. However, there is a relative lack of strong evidence for the discriminant validity (especially with depressive and anxiety symptoms), and OVIS scores tend to demonstrate stronger stability for individuals with greater overvalued ideation (Neziroglu et al., 1999). Furthermore, the OVIS exhibited better predictive validity when compared to item No. 11 on the Y-BOCS (Neziroglu, Stevens, McKay, & Yaryura-Tobias, 2001).

DSM-IV Criterion. The DSM-IV (American Psychiatric Association, 2000) allows an individual to be diagnosed with OCD "with poor insight." This specifier is reserved for individuals that are not able to recognize the excessiveness and unreasonableness of their OCD symptoms for the majority of the time during their current episode, and is typically determined based on clinical impressions (Aigner et al., 2005; Shimshoni et al., 2011). While no studies have utilized the DSM-5 specifiers to investigate insight in OCD to date, future studies will likely use these criteria based on clinical impressions, categorizing various patients as having a "good or fair insight," "poor insight," or "absent insight/delusional" beliefs (American Psychiatric Association, 2013).

Ultimately, there are several clinician-administered and self-report measures that are specifically designed to assess insight in the OCD population. Depending on the measure, insight is assessed as a one-dimensional or a multidimensional construct, and is conceptualized as either dichotomous or continuous. Shimshoni and colleagues (2011) compared all of the aforementioned measures in 60 adults with OCD who were part of an Israeli clinical sample. Collectively, all measures demonstrated good correlations with one another, but depending on the measure that was used, different clinical correlates (e.g., onset age, comorbidity) were found. Given the multitude of measures, it is important for researchers and clinicians to consider what they are hoping to examine, the utility and feasibility of the respective measures, as well as the respective psychometric properties of each questionnaire.

Treatment Implications

Insight has potential implications for treatment response to pharmacological and/or cognitive behavioral interventions for OCD. When considering an individual's level of insight, cognitive-behavioral interventions may be less efficacious for those who do not perceive their symptoms as being problematic. Motivation and commitment to therapy may be stunted, suggesting consequential difficulties with homework compliance and lower engagement in exposure exercises (Tolin, Maltby, Diefenbach, Hannan, & Worhunsky, 2004). This can be particularly problematic, given the link between homework completion and treatment gains (Lewin, Peris, Lindsey Bergman, McCracken, & Piacentini, 2011; Simpson et al., 2011; Simpson, Marcus, Zuckoff, Franklin, & Foa, 2012). Additionally, individuals with decreased levels of insight fail to recognize the irrational nature of their symptoms and may not view them as problematic, causing them to engage in less resistance and control over their symptoms (Alonso et al., 2008; Insel & Akiskal, 1986; Jakubovski et al., 2011; Storch et al., 2014a; Storch et al., 2014b). This can unfortunately lead to attenuated motivation to engage in ritual prevention, thereby maintaining symptomology and contributing to increased OCD-related functional impairment (Lewin, 2014). Additionally, lower levels of insight may be associated with more severe pathology (Catapano et al., 2001; Catapano et al., 2010; Cherian et al., 2012; De Berardis et al., 2005; Fontenelle et al., 2013; Himle et al., 2006; Jakubovski et al., 2011; Karadag et al., 2011; Kashyap et al., 2012; Matsunaga et al., 2002; Ravi Kishore et al., 2004; Türksoy et al., 2002), compounding the difficulties with achieving treatment gains. Ultimately, the literature is mixed on the definitive impact of insight on treatment response; the findings are summarized below.

Pharmacotherapy

The literature is mixed on the relationship between poor insight and attenuated response to pharmacotherapy. Some researchers find no significant differences in treatment response between individuals with varying levels of insight (Alonso et al., 2008), reporting that poorer baseline levels of insight did not predict response to medication for OCD (Eisen et al., 2001). However, a relatively larger base of findings supports the notion that individuals with lower levels of insight attain poorer pharmacological treatment response (Catapano et al., 2001; Erzegovesi et al., 2001; Hollander et al., 2003; Karadag et al., 2011; Ravi Kishore et al., 2004; Shetti et al., 2005), and require additional medication trials and/or augmentation with antipsychotics (Catapano et al., 2010; Onen et al., 2013). Furthermore, individuals historically refusing medication at least once exhibited poorer insight than their counterparts, suggesting poorer adherence to pharmacotherapy (Santana, Fontenelle, Yucel, & Fontenelle, 2013). However, insight has been shown to improve following a course of pharmacotherapy for OCD (Alonso et al., 2008), particularly when a decrease in OCD symptom severity is observed (Eisen et al., 2001). Indeed, individuals currently on medication for OCD display higher levels of insight compared to their counterparts (Shimshoni et al., 2011). Taken altogether, clinicians should examine an individual's level of insight when considering pharmacological treatment for OCD, as varying levels of insight may yield differential responses to pharmacotherapy.

Cognitive-Behavioral Therapy

The findings on attenuated response to cognitive-behavioral therapy due to varying levels of insight are also mixed. Lower levels of insight are theoretically considered to be related to poorer treatment outcome (Kozak & Foa, 1994), which is also supported by extant empirical findings. Indeed, poorer insight is related to poorer treatment outcome and diminished ability to achieve remission (Prasko et al., 2009; Raffin et al., 2009), even after controlling for various baseline variables such as OCD severity, comorbid depression, and medication (Himle et al., 2006). For individuals receiving CBT after failing to respond to medication, levels of insight also predicted the degree of improvement following CBT (Tolin et al., 2004). Additionally, insight demonstrates improvement following CBT, and is not directly related to changes in OCD symptom severity (Lewin et al., 2010b). Although Shimshoni et al. (2011) failed to find deleterious effects of insight on psychotherapeutic treatment response, the predominant use of dynamic psychotherapy in the study's geographical location may have limited the ability to detect a potential deleterious effect of poor insight on outcome.

Collectively, much evidence suggests the deleterious effects of insight on CBT response. Given these findings, clinicians should consider the individual's level of insight when conducting CBT, given the probability of decreased effort in therapy and difficulties with compliance (Tolin et al., 2004). Consequential decreased resistance against and control over OCD symptomology contribute to heightened functional impairment and symptom maintenance, conveying the importance of targeting an individual's level of awareness and insight into their symptoms. Subsequent increases in homework compliance and motivation to engage in therapy should be targeted, with the goal of improving treatment response (Simpson et al., 2011; Simpson et al., 2012).

Combination Treatment

There have been few studies investigating the comparative effects of pharmacotherapy versus cognitive-behavioral therapy on levels of insight. Garcia and colleagues (2010) demonstrated that individuals with higher levels of insight enjoyed treatment gains, regardless of treatment assignment. When investigating the augmenting effect of various treatment modalities (i.e., exposure and response prevention, risperidone, and placebo) to serotonin reuptake inhibitors (SRIs), exposure and response prevention demonstrated superiority over risperidone and placebo in improving levels of insight (Simpson et al., 2013). Alternatively, insight failed to predict treatment response in individuals receiving CBT (49%) and/or SRIs (88%), though the sample was mostly represented by those receiving pharmacological treatment (Eisen et al., 2010). Ultimately, given the paucity of literature on this subject, results are preliminary and future research should investigate the potentially disparate effects of insight on various modalities of treatment. Regardless, insight remains an important variable to consider when working with individuals with OCD, as it has been shown to improve throughout treatment and serve as a predictor of treatment response. As such, it could be valuable to test potential modifications to treatment for individuals with low insight. For instance, decreased emphasis on cognitive therapeutic tools in the treatment of OCD for these individuals may be helpful, given their low levels of awareness and poor insight regarding their OCD symptoms. Additionally, increased family involvement may help with heightening awareness of obsessive-compulsive symptomology and bolster treatment compliance.

Conclusion

Insight is an influential factor that has various implications for the assessment and treatment of OCD. Numerous patterns of associations between lower levels of insight and several variables have emerged; individuals with lower levels of insight tended to be of a younger age, and more likely presented with increased comorbidities, OCD symptom severity, functional impairment, treatment refractoriness, and various neuropsychological/neurobiological abnormalities. Indeed, individuals with poorer insight may present with more complex clinical presentations, rendering assessments and therapy to become more difficult. Specifically, reliable reports from the individual may be challenging to obtain, and attenuated motivation and resistance against symptoms will likely be observed, stunting progress in therapy. While increasing attention has been garnered for this construct, further research still needs to be conducted, as many of the results are mixed. Given the impactful nature of insight, more nuanced and standardized investigations are pertinent to help clinicians and researchers better understand its mechanism of influence. Future studies should seek to fill the gaps by examining the construct in under-researched populations (e.g., youth), standardizing the method of assessing insight, exploring the mechanism through which insight impacts therapeutic outcome, and determining how to effectively target it in treatment.

References

Abramowitz, J., Brigidi, B. D., & Foa, E. B. (1999). Health concerns in patients with obsessive-compulsive disorder. *Journal of Anxiety Disorders, 13*(5), 529–539.

Aigner, M., Zitterl, W., Prayer, D., Demal, U., Bach, M., Prayer, L., ... Lenz, G. (2005). Magnetic resonance imaging in patients with obsessive-compulsive disorder with good versus poor insight. *Psychiatry Research: Neuroimaging, 140*(2), 173–179. doi: 10.1016/j.pscychresns.2005.03.002.

Alonso, P., Menchon, J. M., Segalas, C., Jaurrieta, N., Jimenez-Murcia, S., Cardoner, N., ... Vallejo, J. (2008). Clinical implications of insight assessment in obsessive-compulsive disorder. *Comprehensive Psychiatry, 49*(3), 305–312. doi: 10.1016/j.comppsych.2007.09.005.

American Psychiatric Association. (2000). *Diagnostic and statistical manual of mental disorders* (4th ed., Rev. text). Washington, DC: American Psychiatric Association.

American Psychiatric Association. (2013). *Diagnostic and statistical manual of mental disorders* (5th ed.). Arlington, VA: American Psychiatric Publishing.

Bellino, S., Patria, L., Ziero, S., & Bogetto, F. (2005). Clinical picture of obsessive-compulsive disorder with poor insight: A regression model. *Psychiatry Research*, *136*(2/3), 223–231. doi: 10.1016/j.psychres.2004.04.015.

Bipeta, R., Yerramilli, S. S., Pingali, S., Karredla, A. R., & Ali, M. O. (2013). A cross-sectional study of insight and family accommodation in pediatric obsessive-compulsive disorder. *Child and Adolescent Psychiatry and Mental Health*, *7*(20). doi: 10.1186/1753-2000-7-20.

Brakoulias, V., & Starcevic, V. (2011). The characterization of beliefs in obsessive-compulsive disorder. *Psychiatric Quarterly*, *82*(2), 151–161. doi: 10.1007/s11126-010-9157-8.

Calvocoressi, L., Lewis, B., Harris, M., Trufan, S. J., Goodman, W. K., McDougle, C. J., & Price, L. H. (1995). Family accommodation in Obsessive-Compulsive Disorder. *American Journal of Psychiatry*, *152*, 441–443.

Catapano, F., Perris, F., Fabrazzo, M., Cioffi, V., Giacco, D., De Santis, V., & Maj, M. (2010). Obsessive-compulsive disorder with poor insight: A three-year prospective study. *Progress in Neuro-Psychopharmacology & Biological Psychiatry*, *34*(2), 323–330. doi: 10.1016/j.pnpbp.2009.12.007.

Catapano, F., Sperandeo, R., Perris, F., Lanzaro, M., & Maj, M. (2001). Insight and resistance in patients with obsessive-compulsive disorder. *Psychopathology*, *34*(2), 62–68.

Cherian, A. V., Narayanaswamy, J. C., Srinivasaraju, R., Viswanath, B., Math, S. B., Kandavel, T., & Reddy, Y. C. (2012). Does insight have specific correlation with symptom dimensions in OCD? *Journal of Affective Disorders*, *138*(3), 352–359. doi: 10.1016/j.jad.2012.01.017.

Craske, M. G., Kircanski, K., Zelikowsky, M., Mystkowski, J., Chowdhury, N., & Baker, A. (2008). Optimizing inhibitory learning during exposure therapy. *Behaviour Research and Therapy*, *46*(1), 5–27. doi: 10.1016/j.brat.2007.10.003.

De Berardis, D., Campanella, D., Gambi, F., Sepede, G., Salini, G., Carano, A., … Ferro, F. M. (2005). Insight and alexithymia in adult outpatients with obsessive-compulsive disorder. *European Archives of Psychiatry and Clinical Neuroscience*, *255*(5), 350–358. doi: 10.1007/s00406-005-0573-y.

Demet, M. M., Deveci, A., Taskin, E. O., Erbay Dundar, P., Turel Ermertcan, A., Mizrak Demet, S., … Ozturkcan, S. (2010). Risk factors for delaying treatment seeking in obsessive-compulsive disorder. *Comprehensive Psychiatry*, *51*(5), 480–485. doi: 10.1016/j.comppsych.2010.02.008.

Eisen, J. L., Mancebo, M. A., Pinto, A., Coles, M. E., Pagano, M. E., Stout, R., & Rasmussen, S. A. (2006). Impact of obsessive-compulsive disorder on quality of life. *Comprehensive Psychiatry*, *47*(4), 270–275. doi: 10.1016/j.comppsych.2005.11.006.

Eisen, J. L., Phillips, K. A., Baer, L., Beer, D. A., Atala, K. D., & Rasmussen, S. A. (1998). The Brown Assessment of Beliefs Scale: Reliability and validity. *American Journal of Psychiatry*, *155*(1), 102–108.

Eisen, J. L., Phillips, K. A., Coles, M. E., & Rasmussen, S. A. (2004). Insight in obsessive compulsive disorder and body dysmorphic disorder. *Comprehensive Psychiatry*, *45*(1), 10–15. doi: 10.1016/j.comppsych.2003.09.010.

Eisen, J. L., Pinto, A., Mancebo, M. C., Dyck, I. R., Orlando, M. E., & Rasmussen, S. A. (2010). A 2-year prospective follow-up study of the course of obsessive-compulsive disorder. *Journal of Clinical Psychiatry*, *71*(8), 1033–1039. doi: 10.4088/JCP.08m04806blu.

Eisen, J. L., Rasmussen, S. A., Phillips, K. A., Price, L. H., Davidson, J., Lydiard, R. B., … Piggott, T. (2001). Insight and treatment outcome in obsessive-compulsive disorder. *Comprehensive Psychiatry*, *42*(6), 494–497. doi: 10.1053/comp.2001.27898.

Elvish, J., Simpson, J., & Ball, L. J. (2010). Which clinical and demographic factors predict poor insight in individuals with obsessions and/or compulsions? *Journal of Anxiety Disorders*, *24*(2), 231–237. doi: 10.1016/j.janxdis.2009.11.001.

Erzegovesi, S., Cavallini, M. C., Cavedini, P., Diaferia, G., Locatelli, M., & Bellodi, L. (2001). Clinical predictors of drug response in obsessive-compulsive disorder. *Journal of Clinical Psychopharmacology*, *21*(5), 488–492.

Foa, E. B., Kozak, M. J., Goodman, W. K., Hollander, E., Jenike, M. A., & Rasmussen, S. A. (1995). DSM-IV field trial: Obsessive-compulsive disorder. *American Journal of Psychiatry*, *152*(1), 90–96.

Fontenelle, J. M., Harrison, B. J., Santana, L., Rosario, M. C., Versiani, M., & Fontenelle, L. F. (2013). Correlates of insight into different symptom dimensions in obsessive-compulsive disorder. *Annals of Clinical Psychiatry*, *25*(1), 11–16.

Garcia, A. M., Sapyta, J. J., Moore, P. S., Freeman, J. B., Franklin, M. E., March, J. S., & Foa, E. B. (2010). Predictors and moderators of treatment outcome in the Pediatric Obsessive Compulsive Treatment Study (POTS I). *Journal of the American Academy of Child and Adolescent Psychiatry*, *49*(10), 1024–1033.

Geller, D. A., Biederman, J., Faraone, S., Agranat, A., Cradock, K., Hagermoser, L., ... Coffey, B. J. (2001). Developmental aspects of obsessive compulsive disorder: Findings in children, adolescents, and adults. *Journal of Nervous and Mental Disease*, *189*(7), 471–477.

Goodman, W. K., Price, L. H., Rasmussen, S. A., Mazure, C., Delgado, P., Heninger, G. R., & Charney, D. S. (1989). The Yale–Brown Obsessive Compulsive Scale – II. *Validity*. *Archives of General Psychiatry*, *46*(11), 1012–1016.

Goodman, W. K., Price, L. H., Rasmussen, S. A., Mazure, C., Fleischmann, R. L., Hill, C. L., ... Charney, D. S. (1989). The Yale–Brown Obsessive Compulsive Scale – I. Development, use, and reliability. *Archives of General Psychiatry*, *46*(11), 1006–1011.

Himle, J. A., Etten, M. L., Janeck, A. S., & Fischer, D. J. (2006). Insight as a predictor of treatment outcome in behavioral group treatment for obsessive-compulsive disorder. *Cognitive Therapy and Research*, *30*(5), 661–666. doi: 10.1007/s10608-006-9079-9.

Hollander, E., Baldini Rossi, N., Sood, E., & Pallanti, S. (2003). Risperidone augmentation in treatment-resistant obsessive-compulsive disorder: A double-blind, placebo-controlled study. *International Journal of Neuropsychopharmacology*, *6*(4), 397–401. doi: 10.1017/S1461145703003730.

Huppert, J. D., Simpson, H. B., Nissenson, K. J., Liebowitz, M. R., & Foa, E. B. (2009). Quality of life and functional impairment in obsessive-compulsive disorder: A comparison of patients with and without comorbidity, patients in remission, and healthy controls. *Depression and Anxiety*, *26*(1), 39–45. doi: 10.1002/da.20506.

Insel, T. R., & Akiskal, H. S. (1986). Obsessive-compulsive disorder with psychotic features: A phenomenologic analysis. *American Journal of Psychiatry*, *143*(12), 1527–1533.

Jaafari, N., Aouizerate, B., Tignol, J., El-Hage, W., Wassouf, I., Guehl, D., ... Insight Study Group. (2011). The relationship between insight and uncertainty in obsessive-compulsive disorder. *Psychopathology*, *44*(4), 272–276. doi: 10.1159/000323607.

Jakubovski, E., Pittenger, C., Torres, A. R., Fontenelle, L. F., do Rosario, M. C., Ferrao, Y. A., ... Bloch, M. H. (2011). Dimensional correlates of poor insight in obsessive-compulsive disorder. *Progress in Neuro-Psychopharmacology & Biological Psychiatry*, *35*(7), 1677–1681. doi: 10.1016/j.pnpbp.2011.05.012.

Karadag, F., Tumkaya, S., Kirtas, D., Efe, M., Alacam, H., & Oguzhanoglu, N. K. (2011). Neurological soft signs in obsessive compulsive disorder with good and poor insight. *Progress in Neuro-Psychopharmacology & Biological Psychiatry*, *35*(4), 1074–1079. doi: 10.1016/j.pnpbp.2011.03.003.

Kashyap, H., Kumar, J. K., Kandavel, T., & Reddy, Y. C. (2012). Neuropsychological correlates of insight in obsessive-compulsive disorder. *Acta Psychiatrica Scandinavica*, *126*(2), 106–114. doi: 10.1111/j.1600-0447.2012.01845.x.

Kaufman, A. S. (1990). *K-BIT: Kaufman brief intelligence test*. Circle Pines, MN: American Guidance Service.

Kircanski, K., Peris, T. S., & Piacentini, J. C. (2011). Cognitive-behavioral therapy for obsessive-compulsive disorder in children and adolescents. *Child and Adolescent Psychiatric Clinics of North America, 20*(2), 239–254. doi: 10.1016/j.chc.2011.01.014.

Kitis, A., Akdede, B. B., Alptekin, K., Akvardar, Y., Arkar, H., Erol, A., & Kaya, N. (2007). Cognitive dysfunctions in patients with obsessive-compulsive disorder compared to the patients with schizophrenia patients: Relation to overvalued ideas. *Progress in Neuro-Psychopharmacology & Biological Psychiatry, 31*(1), 254–261. doi: 10.1016/j.pnpbp.2006.06.022.

Kozak, M. J., & Foa, E. B. (1994). Obsessions, overvalued ideas, and delusions in obsessive-compulsive disorder. *Behaviour Research and Therapy, 32*(3), 343–353.

Kuelz, A. K., Hohagen, F., & Voderholzer, U. (2004). Neuropsychological performance in obsessive-compulsive disorder: A critical review. *Biological Psychology, 65*(3), 185–236. doi: S0301051103001558 [pii].

Lewin, A. B. (2014). Tractable impediments to cognitive behavioral therapy for pediatric obsessive compulsive disorder. In D. McKay & E. A. Storch (Eds.), *Obsessive-compulsive disorder and its spectrum: A lifespan approach.* Washington, DC: American Psychological Association Press.

Lewin, A. B., Bergman, R. L., Peris, T. S., Chang, S., McCracken, J. T., & Piacentini, J. (2010a). Correlates of insight among youth with obsessive-compulsive disorder. *Journal of Child Psychology and Psychiatry, 51*(5), 603–611. doi: 10.1111/ j.1469-7610.2009.02181.x.

Lewin, A. B., Caporino, N., Murphy, T. K., Geffken, G. R., & Storch, E. A. (2010b). Understudied clinical dimensions in pediatric obsessive compulsive disorder. *Child Psychiatry and Human Development, 41*(6), 675–691. doi: 10.1007/s10578-010-0196-z.

Lewin, A. B., Larson, M. J., Park, J. M., McGuire, J. F., Murphy, T. K., & Storch, E. A. (2014a). Neuropsychological functioning in youth with obsessive compulsive disorder: An examination of executive function and memory impairment. *Psychiatry Research, 216*(1), 108–115. doi: 10.1016/j.psychres.2014.01.014.

Lewin, A. B., Park, J. M., Jones, A. M., Crawford, E. A., DeNadai, A. S., Menzel, J., … Storch, E. A. (2014b). Family-based exposure and response prevention therapy for preschool-aged children with obsessive-compulsive disorder: A pilot randomized controlled trial. *Behaviour Research and Therapy, 56*, 30–38.

Lewin, A. B., Peris, T. S., Lindsey Bergman, R., McCracken, J. T., & Piacentini, J. (2011). The role of treatment expectancy in youth receiving exposure-based CBT for obsessive compulsive disorder. *Behaviour Research and Therapy, 49*(9), 536–543. doi: 10.1016/j.brat.2011.06.001.

Lewin, A. B., & Piacentini, J. (2009). Obsessive-compulsive disorder in children. In B. J. Sadock, V. A. Sadock, & P. Ruiz (Eds.), *Kaplan & Sadock's comprehensive textbook of psychiatry* (9th ed.) (Vol. 2, pp. 3671–3678). Philadelphia, PA: Lippincott Williams & Wilkins.

Lewin, A. B., & Piacentini, J. (2010). Evidence-based assessment of child obsessive compulsive disorder: Recommendations for clinical practice and treatment research. *Child Youth Care Forum, 39*(2), 73–89. doi: 10.1007/s10566-009-9092-8.

Lewin, A. B., Piacentini, J., De Nadai, A. S., Jones, A. M., Peris, T. S., Geffken, G. R., … Storch, E. A. (2014c). Defining clinical severity in pediatric obsessive-compulsive disorder. *Psychological Assessment, 26*(2), 679–684. doi: 10.1037/a0035174.

Lewin, A. B., Wu, M. S., Murphy, T. K., & Storch, E.A. (2015). Sensory over-responsivity in pediatric obsessive compulsive disorder. *Journal of Psychopathology and Behavioral Assessment.* doi: 10.1007/s10862-014-9442-1.

Mancebo, M. C., Garcia, A. M., Pinto, A., Freeman, J. B., Przeworski, A., Stout, R., … Rasmussen, S. A. (2008). Juvenile-onset OCD: Clinical features in children, adolescents and adults. *Acta Psychiatrica Scandinavica, 118*(2), 149–159. doi: 10.1111/j.1600-0447.2008.01224.x.

Marazziti, D., Dell'Osso, L., Nasso, E. D., Pfanner, C., Presta, S., Mungai, F., & Cassano, G. B. (2002). Insight in obsessive-compulsive disorder: A study of an Italian sample. *European Psychiatry, 17*, 407–410.

Matsunaga, H. (2012). Current and emerging features of obsessive-compulsive disorder: Trends for the revision of DSM-5. *Seishin Shinkeigaku Zasshi, 114,* 1023–1030.

Matsunaga, H., Kiriike, N., Matsui, T., Oya, K., Iwasaki, Y., Koshimune, K., ... Stein, D. J. (2002). Obsessive-compulsive disorder with poor insight. *Comprehensive Psychiatry, 43*(2), 150–157. doi: 10.1053/comp.2002.30798.

Neziroglu, F., McKay, D., Yaryura-Tobias, J. A., Stevens, K. P., & Todaro, J. (1999). The Overvalued Ideas Scale: Development, reliability and validity in obsessive-compulsive disorder. *Behaviour Research and Therapy, 37,* 881–902.

Neziroglu, F., Stevens, K. P., McKay, D., & Yaryura-Tobias, J. A. (2001). Predictive validity of the Overvalued Ideas Scale: Outcome in obsessive-compulsive and body dysmorphic disorders. *Behaviour Research and Therapy, 39,* 745–756.

Nikolajsen, K. H., Nissen, J. B., & Thomsen, P. H. (2011). Obsessive-compulsive disorder in children and adolescents: Symptom dimensions in a naturalistic setting. *Nordic Journal of Psychiatry, 65*(4), 244–250. doi: 10.3109/08039488.2010.533386.

O'Dwyer, A. M. (2000). Obsessive-compulsive disorder and delusions revisited. *British Journal of Psychiatry, 176*(3), 281–284. doi: 10.1192/bjp.176.3.281.

Onen, S., Karakas Ugurlu, G., & Caykoylu, A. (2013). The relationship between metacognitions and insight in obsessive-compulsive disorder. *Comprehensive Psychiatry, 54*(5), 541–548. doi: 10.1016/j.comppsych.2012.11.006.

Peris, T. S., Bergman, R. L., Asarnow, J. R., Langley, A., McCracken, J. T., & Piacentini, J. (2010). Clinical and cognitive correlates of depressive symptoms among youth with obsessive compulsive disorder. *Journal of Clinical Child and Adolescent Psychology, 39*(5), 616–626. doi: 10.1080/15374416.2010.501285.

Poyurovsky, M., & Koran, L. M. (2005). Obsessive-compulsive disorder (OCD) with schizotypy vs. schizophrenia with OCD: Diagnostic dilemmas and therapeutic implications. *Journal of Psychiatric Research, 39*(4), 399–408. doi: 10.1016/j.jpsychires.2004.09.004.

Prasko, J., Raszka, M., Adamcova, K., Grambal, A., Koprivova, J., Hudrnovska, H., ... Vyskocilova, J. (2009). Predicting the therapeutic response to cognitive behavioural therapy in patients with pharmacoresistant obsessive-compulsive disorder. *Neuroendocrinology Letters, 30*(5), 615–623.

Raffin, A. L., Guimaraes Fachel, J. M., Ferrao, Y. A., Pasquoto de Souza, F., & Cordioli, A. V. (2009). Predictors of response to group cognitive-behavioral therapy in the treatment of obsessive-compulsive disorder. *European Psychiatry, 24*(5), 297–306. doi: 10.1016/j.eurpsy.2008.12.001.

Rapoport, J. L. (1991). Recent advances in obsessive-compulsive disorder. *Neuropsychopharmacology, 5*(1), 1–10.

Ravi Kishore, V., Samar, R., Janardhan Reddy, Y. C., Chandrasekhar, C. R., & Thennarasu, K. (2004). Clinical characteristics and treatment response in poor and good insight obsessive-compulsive disorder. *European Psychiatry, 19*(4), 202–208. doi: 10.1016/j.eurpsy.2003.12.005.

Samuels, J. F., Bienvenu, O. J., Pinto, A., Fyer, A. J., McCracken, J. T., Rauch, S. L., ... Nestadt, G. (2007). Hoarding in obsessive-compulsive disorder: Results from the OCD Collaborative Genetics Study. *Behaviour Research and Therapy, 45*(4), 673–686. doi: 10.1016/j.brat.2006.05.008.

Santana, L., Fontenelle, J. M., Yucel, M., & Fontenelle, L. F. (2013). Rates and correlates of nonadherence to treatment in obsessive-compulsive disorder. *Journal of Psychiatric Practice, 19*(1), 42–53. doi: 10.1097/01.pra.0000426326.49396.97.

Scahill, L., Riddle, M. A., McSwiggin-Hardin, M., Ort, S.I., King, R.A., Goodman, W. K., ... Leckman, J. F. (1997). Children's Yale–Brown Obsessive Compulsive Scale: Reliability and validity. *Journal of the American Academy of Child and Adolescent Psychiatry, 36*(6), 9.

Selles, R. R., Storch, E. A., & Lewin, A. B. (2014). Variations in symptom prevalence and clinical correlates in younger versus older youth with obsessive-compulsive disorder. *Child Psychiatry and Human Development.* doi: 10.1007/s10578-014-0435-9.

Shetti, C. N., Reddy, Y. C., Kandavel, T., Kashyap, K., Singisetti, S., Hiremath, A. S., ... Raghunandanan, S. (2005). Clinical predictors of drug nonresponse in obsessive-compulsive disorder. *Journal of Clinical Psychiatry*, 66(12), 1517–1523.

Shimshoni, Y., Reuven, O., Dar, R., & Hermesh, H. (2011). Insight in obsessive-compulsive disorder: A comparative study of insight measures in an Israeli clinical sample. *Journal of Behavior Therapy and Experimental Psychiatry*, 42(3), 389–396. doi: 10.1016/j.jbtep.2011.02.011.

Simpson, H. B., Foa, E. B., Liebowitz, M. R., Huppert, J. D., Cahill, S., Maher, M. J., ... Campeas, R. (2013). Cognitive-behavioral therapy vs risperidone for augmenting serotonin reuptake inhibitors in obsessive-compulsive disorder: A randomized clinical trial. *JAMA Psychiatry*, 70(11), 1190–1199. doi: 10.1001/jamapsychiatry.2013.1932.

Simpson, H. B., Maher, M. J., Wang, Y., Bao, Y., Foa, E. B., & Franklin, M. (2011). Patient adherence predicts outcome from cognitive behavioral therapy in obsessive-compulsive disorder. *Journal of Consulting and Clinical Psychology*, 79(2), 247–252. doi: 10.1037/a0022659.

Simpson, H. B., Marcus, S. M., Zuckoff, A., Franklin, M., & Foa, E. B. (2012). Patient adherence to cognitive-behavioral therapy predicts long-term outcome in obsessive-compulsive disorder. *Journal of Clinical Psychiatry*, 73(9), 1265–1266. doi: 10.4088/JCP.12l07879.

Storch, E. A., De Nadai, A. S., Jacob, M. L., Lewin, A. B., Muroff, J., Eisen, J., ... Murphy, T. K. (2014a). Phenomenology and correlates of insight in pediatric obsessive-compulsive disorder. *Comprehensive Psychiatry*, 55(3), 613–620. doi: 10.1016/j.comppsych.2013.09.014.

Storch, E. A., Milsom, V. A., Merlo, L. J., Larson, M., Geffken, G. R., Jacob, M. L., ... Goodman, W. K. (2008). Insight in pediatric obsessive-compulsive disorder: Associations with clinical presentation. *Psychiatry Research*, 160(2), 212–220. doi: 10.1016/j.psychres.2007.07.005.

Storch, E. A., Wu, M. S., Small, B. J., Crawford, E. A., Lewin, A. B., Horng, B., & Murphy, T. K. (2014b). Mediators and moderators of functional impairment in adults with obsessive-compulsive disorder. *Comprehensive Psychiatry*, 55(3), 489–496.

Tolin, D. F., Abramowitz, J. S., Kozak, M. J., & Foa, E. B. (2001). Fixity of belief, perceptual aberration, and magical ideation in obsessive-compulsive disorder. *Journal of Anxiety Disorders*, 15, 501–510.

Tolin, D. F., Maltby, N., Diefenbach, G. J., Hannan, S. E., & Worhunsky, P. (2004). Cognitive-behavioral therapy for medication nonresponders with obsessive-compulsive disorder: A wait-list-controlled open trial. *Journal of Clinical Psychiatry*, 65(7), 922–931.

Torres, A. R., Fontenelle, L. F., Ferrao, Y. A., do Rosario, M. C., Torresan, R. C., Miguel, E. C., & Shavitt, R. G. (2012). Clinical features of obsessive-compulsive disorder with hoarding symptoms: A multicenter study. *Journal of Psychiatric Research*, 46(6), 724–732. doi: 10.1016/j.jpsychires.2012.03.005.

Tumkaya, S., Karadag, F., Oguzhanoglu, N. K., Tekkanat, C., Varma, G., Ozdel, O., & Atesci, F. (2009). Schizophrenia with obsessive-compulsive disorder and obsessive-compulsive disorder with poor insight: A neuropsychological comparison. *Psychiatry Research*, 165(1/2), 38–46. doi: 10.1016/j.psychres.2007.07.031.

Türksoy, N., Tükel, R., Ozdemir, O., & Karali, A. (2002). Comparison of clinical characteristics in good and poor insight obsessive-compulsive disorder. *Journal of Anxiety Disorders*, 16, 413–423.

Wu, M. S., Lewin, A. B., Murphy, T. K., Geffken, G. R., & Storch, E. A. (2014). Phenomenological considerations of family accommodation: Related clinical characteristics and family factors in pediatric OCD. *Journal of Obsessive-Compulsive and Related Disorders*, 3(3), 228–235.

28

Postpartum Obsessive-Compulsive Disorder

Shannon M. Blakey and Jonathan S. Abramowitz

For the majority of expecting parents, the perinatal period is an exciting time. Anticipation of the baby's arrival is followed by jubilation when the infant is finally born into his or her loving family. However, some new parents experience the onset (or intensification) of severe emotional distress during this time period. A great deal of attention has been paid to postpartum depression and psychosis, with much less attention paid to perinatal anxiety disorders – postpartum obsessive-compulsive disorder (ppOCD) in particular. Additionally, the majority of research has focused on *maternal* ppOCD, despite ppOCD symptoms also being documented among new fathers. Although early research suggested that pregnancy *protects* women from emotional disorders (Elliot, Rugg, Watson, & Brough, 1983), more recent evidence suggests that women are in fact at an *increased* risk of developing OCD during pregnancy and the postpartum period (e.g., Buttolph & Holland, 1990; Maina, Albert, Bogetto, Vaschetto, & Ravizza, 2000; for a review, see Abramowitz, Schwartz, Moore, & Luenzmann, 2003).

The opening section of this chapter provides clinicians with an overview and description of ppOCD, including a case example to illustrate the cardinal features of this presentation or "subtype" of OCD. We then consider the prevalence of perinatal and postpartum OCD and the relationship between ppOCD and OCD in general, highlighting their similarities and distinctions. Theoretical perspectives on ppOCD are presented in the third section of the chapter. The fourth section includes a discussion of two effective interventions for ppOCD: pharmacotherapy and cognitive-behavioral therapy (CBT). A treatment vignette is presented, along with a section on important clinical considerations specific to the population of new parents. We then conclude with a summary and discussion of future directions.

Clinical Presentation

Description of Symptoms

A number of studies have examined the presentation of OCD symptoms occurring in the context of pregnancy and the postpartum. In many cases, ppOCD symptoms appear strongly related to pregnancy-related factors, such as responsibility for the care

The Wiley Handbook of Obsessive Compulsive Disorders, Volume I, First Edition.
Edited by Jonathan S. Abramowitz, Dean McKay, and Eric A. Storch.
© 2017 John Wiley & Sons Ltd. Published 2017 by John Wiley & Sons Ltd.

and protection of an otherwise helpless unborn or newborn child. Table 28.1 lists the characteristic signs and symptoms of this presentation of OCD.

Buttolph and Holland (1990) provided the first report of ppOCD in the literature. They described two women whose OCD symptoms began during pregnancy and were characterized by obsessional fear of the unborn baby becoming contaminated by toxic agents and concurrent compulsive washing and cleaning rituals. These authors also described three cases in which rapid onset occurred soon *after* childbirth; postpartum symptoms concerned unwanted obsessional thoughts of harming the child with a knife and of contaminating the baby. Sichel Cohen, Dimmock, and Rosenbaum (1993a) reported a case series of 15 women with ppOCD, all of whom reported intrusive anxiety-evoking obsessional thoughts related to harming the infant (e.g., while the infant was sleeping). None of these patients evidenced overt compulsive rituals such as washing or checking; rather, they appeared to manage their obsessions via avoidance of the infant and of triggers, such as potential weapons (e.g., knives). In a second report, Sichel, Cohen, Rosenbaum, and Driscoll (1993b) described two ppOCD cases that involved unwanted obsessional thoughts of stabbing the newborn. Both of these women also developed phobic avoidance of the child and of knives. Although neither of these women reported observable rituals, covert (i.e., mental) rituals were not ruled out; as such, it is unclear whether or not these women performed a number of other strategies in order to prevent feared outcomes and/or alleviate associated distress. Diaz and colleagues (1997) described five women with perinatal onset OCD. In three of these cases, where onset coincided with pregnancy, the major symptoms were contamination obsessions and washing or cleaning compulsions. For the remaining two women – who experienced onset soon after childbirth – the main symptoms were upsetting thoughts of harming (e.g., sexually molesting or stabbing) the infant.

Thus, women developing OCD symptoms *during* pregnancy appear to experience contamination obsessions and washing or cleaning rituals, yet those who first report OCD symptoms *following* childbirth tend to experience unwelcome,

Table 28.1 Characteristic signs and symptoms of perinatal obsessive-compulsive disorder

Characteristic	Pregnancy	Postpartum
Onset	Gradual onset.	Rapid onset.
Content	Obsessional content involving contamination and illness.	Obsessional content involving harm, accidents, or loss.
Avoidance	Avoidance of contaminants.	Avoidance of obsessional cues, sometimes including avoidance of the newborn.
Rituals	Overt rituals (e.g., washing and checking).	Overt rituals (e.g., checking); covert mental rituals, neutralizing.
Comorbidity	Often associated with depressive symptoms.	Often associated with depressive symptoms.
Differentiation	Despite superficial similarity of thought content, not associated with postpartum psychosis.	Despite superficial similarity of thought content, not associated with postpartum psychosis.

distressing intrusive obsessional thoughts of harming the infant. Additionally, phobic avoidance of situations and stimuli that trigger such obsessions is frequent among affected individuals. In contrast, there is little, if any, mention in the ppOCD literature of perfectionism or symmetry/ordering symptoms that are often present in other forms of OCD.

Consistent with research on the occurrence of intrusive thoughts in the general population (e.g., Rachman & de Silva, 1978), clinical observations suggest that postpartum obsessional intrusions may be either transitory or persistent, and may even prompt actions designed to prevent disastrous consequences. For example, one of the authors (JSA) treated a woman who spent several hours each day praying that she would not act on her violent thoughts related to her infant. Another woman never allowed herself to be alone with her infant for fear that she might poison the child with household items such as bleach or lye by mistake. Finally, clinical research highlights the swift onset of postpartum obsessional symptoms, which is in contrast to the typically gradual onset of OCD symptoms that occur either *during* pregnancy or outside the context of pregnancy and childbirth altogether.

Comorbidity

Postpartum depression. There is evidence of a relationship between postpartum depression and ppOCD symptoms, particularly when the obsessions involve unwanted thoughts of hurting the newborn (Jennings, Ross, & Elmore, 1999; Wisner, Peindl, Gigliotti, & Hanusa, 1999). However, it is unknown whether these OCD symptoms are a cause or effect of the depressive symptoms. Given that depression often involves unwanted negative thoughts, it is possible that obsessional problems (e.g., unwanted aggressive thoughts) are symptoms of postpartum depression. Alternatively, it is plausible that the presence of distressing, recurrent, intrusions gives rise to depressive symptoms (e.g., hopelessness, dysphoria, social isolation). Indeed, OCD in general is typically associated with secondary depressive symptoms (Nestadt et al., 2001).

Although the symptoms of postpartum depression and OCD are highly distinct, one-quarter to one-half of OCD sufferers also meet criteria for depression (Abramowitz, Storch, Keeley, & Cordell, 2007). Evidence suggests that, in the majority of cases, symptoms of OCD predate the depression (Bellodi, Scuito, Diaferia, & Ronchi, 1992; Demal, Lenz, Mayrhofer, & Zapotoczky, 1993). Further, a large proportion of women with ppOCD subsequently develop depression (Sichel et al., 1993a). In the context of postpartum depression, obsessions are common, with the content typically involving thoughts of harm related to the infant (Jennings et al., 1999; Wenzel, Gorman, O'Hara, & Stuart, 2001; Wisner et al., 1999). To our knowledge, no formal diagnostic assessment of the development of OCD and depression from pregnancy to the postpartum has been conducted. Such an assessment would provide much needed information about the timing of onset (i.e., OCD preceding depression, depression preceding OCD, concurrent development) of these two conditions.

Postpartum psychosis. It is important to distinguish between the symptoms of ppOCD and those of postpartum psychosis considering that both conditions can involve ideation regarding harming the newborn. Despite the topographical similarity in thought content, there are key functional distinctions between the two conditions. First, hallucinations (e.g., "I saw smoke and fire coming from the baby's nose and ears") and delusions (e.g., persecutory delusions, "The Devil is out to get the baby"), which characterize postpartum psychosis, are quite rare generally, and usually absent in ppOCD. Second, such symptoms are usually accompanied by stereotypically psychotic symptoms, such as loose associations, labile mood, agitation, and other "bizarre" behaviors. Most importantly, the aggressive ideation in psychosis is experienced as consistent with the person's delusional thinking and behavior (*egosyntonic*), is not subjectively resisted (i.e., not associated with fears or compulsive rituals), and is associated with an increased risk of aggressive behavior.

In contrast, ppOCD symptoms (even violent and horrific obsessions; e.g., the thought to suffocate the baby) are *not* associated with an increased risk of committing harm. This is because obsessional thoughts are experienced as senseless, unwanted and inconsistent with the person's sense of self (*egodystonic*). Those with OCD recognize that the intrusive thoughts are contrary to their better judgment and report *fear* of engaging in unacceptable behavior (including fears of even *thinking* about engaging in such behavior). Moreover, individuals with ppOCD engage in excessive resistance, avoidance, and ritualizing in attempt to control or suppress obsessional thoughts and ensure that feared consequences do not occur. In short, parents with ppOCD present with severe anxiety complaints (e.g., worry over whether or not they will harm), as opposed to psychotic symptoms.

Case Vignette

"Lucy," a 28-year-old computer technician, had given birth to her son Andy two months previously. The pregnancy and delivery were uncomplicated. Although Lucy had no previous psychiatric history, she informed the pediatrician that she now was feeling "down" most of the day and sometimes felt afraid of interacting with Andy. The pediatrician recognized these symptoms as a postpartum psychiatric disorder and referred Lucy for psychological evaluation. At her initial assessment with one of the authors (JSA), Lucy described recurrent unwanted thoughts of harming Andy, including the idea that she could suffocate him with his blanket, put him in the microwave, or stab him with a knife while her husband, who worked as a layer full-time, would not be there to stop her. These intrusive thoughts were abhorrent to Lucy, who considered herself a "moral and gentle person" and reported no history of violent behavior and no intent to act on these intrusions. In fact, Lucy spent inordinate amounts of time praying for the thoughts to go away and avoided being alone with her infant. Lucy also admitted that whenever she tried to dismiss the terrible ideas of hurting Andy, they seemed to recur with greater intensity. Lucy's intrusive thoughts about harming Andy caused her a great deal of distress. She believed that because she was unsuccessful at getting rid of her thoughts, she was clearly "losing her sanity" and would be more likely to "do something terrible." Lucy's rituals and her avoidance of being alone with Andy for fear of "losing control" and harming him were interfering with her family functioning as well as with her relationship with her newborn.

Prevalence

Prenatal OCD Prevalence

Three studies have assessed prenatal OCD incidence and prevalence via gold standard diagnostic interviews. Zar, Wijma, and Wijma (2002) assessed 506 women during the third trimester (week 32) of pregnancy using the Anxiety Disorders Interview Schedule – Revised (ADIS-R) (Di Nardo & Barlow, 1988). Less than 1% (0.2%) of the sample met criteria for OCD at the time of the interview. Sutter-Dallay Giaconne-Marcesche, Glatigny-Dallay, and Verdoux (2004) later interviewed 497 women (using the Mini International Neuropsychiatric Interview for DSM-IV (MINI for DSM-IV) (Sheehan, et al., 1998) in the third trimester (week 31) of pregnancy. They found a pre-natal OCD prevalence of 1.2%. In the most recent study, Uguz and colleagues (2007) collected data from 434 women in the third trimester of pregnancy using the Structured Clinical Interview for DSM-IV, Clinician Version (SCID-I/CV) (First, Spitzer, Gibbon & Williams, 1997; Özkürkçügil, Aydermir, Yildiz, Danaci, & Koroglu, 1999). The authors reported a prenatal OCD prevalence of 3.5% and an incidence of 0.5%.

Postpartum OCD Prevalence

Studies in which the incidence of ppOCD has been assessed provide evidence of an increased risk of OCD development and exacerbation during the postpartum period (Uguz, Akman, Kaya, & Cilli, 2007; Wenzel, Haugen, Jackson, & Brendle, 2005; Zambaldi et al., 2009). Wenzel and colleagues (2005) interviewed 147 women at 8-weeks postpartum using a semi-structured diagnostic interview for DSM-IV (the SCID), reporting a sample ppOCD incidence of 2.0%. Given that more than three-quarters (78%) of the sample were multiparous (i.e., had given birth to multiple chil-dren), and risk for ppOCD appears to be greatest for primiparous women (i.e., women who had only given birth to one child), this is likely an underestimate of the actual incidence of ppOCD among new mothers. Uguz and colleagues (2007) conducted postpartum diagnostic assessments on 302 randomly sampled Turkish women at 6-weeks postpartum, also using the SCID. They reported an overall 4% ($n=12$) inci-dence of ppOCD: 6.57% among primiparous women and 1.81% among multiparous women. Symptoms began by four weeks postpartum for all of the diagnosed women. The largest and most recent study to date was carried out by Zambaldi and colleagues (2009). These authors assessed a sample of 400 women between 2 and 26 weeks post-partum using the MINI for DSM-IV and found a ppOCD incidence of 2.3% and a prevalence of 9%. Unfortunately, no information about the incidence among primip-arous compared with multiparous women was provided.

Collectively, these findings provide evidence that the early postpartum period is a time of increased risk for the onset of OCD, particularly among first time mothers. Specifically, the weighted mean prevalence of ppOCD based on the three studies dis-cussed above is 6.1% – notably higher than the 12-month prevalence rate of OCD among adult women in the general population (which is estimated at 1.5%) (Ruscio, Stein, Chiu, & Kessler, 2010). Research also supports the notion that pregnancy and childbirth influence the theme of OCD symptoms, which typically focus on harm befalling the infant (Abramowitz et al., 2003; Abramowitz, Khandker, Nelson, Deacon, & Rygwall, 2006; Wisner et al., 1999).

Theoretical Models

A number of etiological models have been presented to account for the development of OCD symptoms during and shortly following pregnancy, which are discussed below.

Biological Models

The temporal relationship between OCD onset or worsening and childbirth has prompted biological researchers to search for neurochemical explanations for this phenomenon. One such model derives from the "serotonin hypothesis" of OCD (Barr, Goodman, & Price, 1993), which implicates a dysregulation of the serotonin system. Specifically, there is evidence that fluctuations in estrogen and progesterone levels (as occur in late pregnancy) alter serotonergic transmission, reuptake, and binding (e.g., Stockert & deRobertis, 1985). Thus, the onset or exacerbation of OCD symptoms during or immediately following pregnancy may result from the effects of rapid changes in these two hormones on serotonin functioning. It is important to note, however, that researchers have long questioned the validity of the serotonin hypothesis of OCD on the basis of largely inconsistent research findings (Rausch & Jenike, 1993).

Another biological theory implicates the hormone oxytocin, which, in late pregnancy, plays a role in uterine contractions and lactation (Leckman et al., 1994a). Leckman and colleagues (1994b) found correlations between OCD severity and cerebrospinal fluid oxytocin levels among untreated OCD patients. Although there is no direct evidence that hormonal imbalances play a causal role in ppOCD (i.e., the data are merely correlational), these data are consistent with the idea that ppOCD is triggered by increased concentrations of oxytocin (Diaz et al., 1997). Additional research in this area is needed since much of the existing work is preliminary, and the precise neurobiological mechanisms of OCD have not been well explicated. Moreover, the presence of ppOCD symptoms among new *fathers* challenges biological models linked to biological changes that occur during pregnancy.

Cognitive-Behavioral Models

Cognitive-behavioral models of ppOCD derive from models of obsessional problems in general (e.g., Salkovskis, 1996), which highlight that intrusions (i.e., egodystonic and uncontrollable thoughts, images, and impulses) are normal experiences that most people have from time to time (e.g., Rachman & de Silva, 1978). The cognitive-behavioral model of ppOCD (Fairbrother & Abramowitz, 2007) proposes that such normal intrusions develop into highly distressing and time-consuming clinical obsessions when the intrusions are appraised as highly significant, or as posing a threat for which the individual is personally responsible (e.g., "even *thinking* about fondling my infant's genitals means I am an immoral person"). Cognitive theory (e.g., Beck & Emory, 1985) suggests that misinterpretations of harmless intrusions about the newborn arise due to certain core beliefs related to the baby: namely, inflated responsibility and threat estimates (i.e., overestimating the probability and cost of feared outcomes). Such appraisals evoke distress and motivate the parent to try to suppress or neutralize the unwanted thought (e.g., by praying), alleviate associated distress (e.g., by seeking spousal reassurance that they are *not* immoral), and attempt to prevent any harmful events associated with the intrusion (e.g., phobic avoidance).

Compulsive rituals, avoidance, and other "safety behaviors" are conceptualized as overt or covert attempts to prevent a feared consequence and/or reduce associated distress. There are several ways in which such responses are ultimately counterproductive. First, because safety behaviors are technically "effective" in the moment, these strategies are negatively reinforced and evolve into routines that consume substantial time and effort. Second, because avoidance and rituals reduce anxiety in the short term, they prevent the natural abatement of anxiety that typically occurs when individuals stay in feared situations for sufficiently long periods of time (i.e., *habituation*). Third, the availability and/or performance of rituals may lead to increased frequency of obsessions by serving as reminders of obsessional intrusions. To illustrate, a father who keeps a crucifix by his bedside table to facilitate praying to God for forgiveness for his unwanted, distressing images of molesting his newborn may experience intrusive thoughts upon merely seeing the crucifix incidentally. In this sense, aids designed to prevent harm or reduce anxiety may in in fact become triggers (retrieval cues) of obsessional fears themselves. Finally, rituals have the capacity to preserve maladaptive beliefs (e.g., "I will act on urges to harm my baby if I am left alone with him/her long enough") and misinterpretations of obsessional thoughts. That is, when feared consequences do not occur after performance of a ritual, the person attributes this to his or her having ritualized, instead of coming to the more adaptive (and accurate) conclusion that feared outcomes are, in fact, unlikely. As discussed later, rituals and other safety-seeking strategies are key targets in cognitive-behavioral interventions due to research consistently demonstrating their role in the maintenance of obsessional fears.

Finally, it is not uncommon for individuals with ppOCD to conceal their obsessional thoughts and associated distress from others. For example, in the case presented above, Lucy purposely did not divulge the contents of her obsessional thoughts to others because she was concerned that she would be labeled as "crazy" and subsequently be hospitalized. Concealment may be of particular importance in ppOCD because of fears of being viewed as an unfit parent and of having the child removed from the home. However, this type of concealment insidiously maintains ppOCD by preventing the individual from correcting his or her mistaken appraisals of the innocuous (if unpleasant) intrusions. That is, individuals who conceal their obsessional thoughts are denied the opportunity to see that others (a) also have unwanted intrusive thoughts, and (b) do not find him or her "dangerous" or "immoral" for having these thoughts.

To summarize, cognitive-behavioral models posit that when a new parent (regardless of gender) appraises an otherwise normally occurring mental intrusion about the unborn or newborn baby as overly meaningful or significant, he or she becomes distressed and tries to remove the intrusion and/or prevent disastrous consequences. Rituals and other attempts to reduce distress paradoxically prevent self-correction of mistaken appraisals.

Treatment

Treatments that are effective for OCD in general are similarly effective in reducing ppOCD symptoms. Thus, exposure-based cognitive-behavioral therapy (CBT) should be considered the first-line treatment, with serotonergic medications as the second-line. However, before treatment begins, a thorough review of the patient's medical records and complete medical evaluation is recommended to rule out coexisting or confounding organic bases for anxiety-related symptoms. Additionally, because severe depression may interfere with response to CBT or pharmacotherapy (Abramowitz, 2004), comorbid mood disorders should be assessed and treated appropriately. Below, we discuss effective treatment strategies for ppOCD, consider the effectiveness of these interventions, and illustrate treatment in a case example. Other important considerations in the treatment of ppOCD are also discussed.

Pharmacological Treatment

Pharmacotherapy with serotonin reuptake inhibitors (SRIs) (e.g., fluoxetine, citalopram) is a widely used treatment for OCD, yet clinical remission is rare. Approximately half of those taking SRIs achieve a clinical response ranging from 20% to 40% symptom reduction (Kaplan & Hollander, 2003). The remaining 50%, however, do not respond to SRI treatment, and most experience a relapse of symptoms upon medication discontinuation (Kaplan & Hollander, 2003). Nevertheless, several case histories have reported improvement in ppOCD symptoms following SRI use: Buttolph and Holland (1990) described four women whose ppOCD symptoms improved with fluoxetine; Sichel and colleagues (1993) reported that 15 women treated with various SRIs all had symptom reduction that was maintained after one year of continued medication; and Arnold (1999) reported positive response among three women during an open trial of fluvoxamine treatment.

Pharmacotherapy for ppOCD has advantages and disadvantages. The main advantage of SRI treatment pertains to the ease of access and administration. SRIs are easy to obtain with prescription and pharmacotherapy does not require frequent weekly meetings with a treatment provider (as is often the case with psychological treatments). Disadvantages of this approach include the somewhat modest mean symptom improvement (which occurs in about 50% of patients who take these medicines) and the need for long-term (perhaps indefinite) continuation of pharmacotherapy to avoid a return of symptoms, as relapse rates following pharmacotherapy discontinuation are unfortunately high (Abramowitz et al., 2003). Adverse effects can also be a substantial problem, especially for perinatal women who are already coping with physical symptoms of pregnancy and childbirth. The most common adverse effects of SRIs include headaches, nausea, changes in sleep patterns, changes in weight, and loss of sex drive.

Pregnancy-related adverse effects are of particular concern in the pharmacological treatment of ppOCD. For instance, there is a controversy regarding the possibility that SRI use during the third trimester of pregnancy is associated with perinatal syndromes. In fact, in the summer of 2004, the Food and Drug Administration (FDA) instructed antidepressant manufacturers to place warnings on SRI package inserts describing the possible occurrence of neurobehavioral symptoms in neonates exposed to these medications late in the third trimester and through labor and delivery. The FDA also recommended changes to the dosage and administration section of the drug label, advising physicians to consider tapering and discontinuing these agents prior to labor and delivery. Concerning symptoms among infants of mothers taking SRIs during the third trimester include feeding difficulties, agitation, irritability, sleep disturbance, respiratory distress, cyanosis, apnea, seizures, hypertonia, hyperflexia, and tremor. It is not clear whether these symptoms represent a type of withdrawal reaction or overstimulation of the serotonin system.

The decision to use SRIs during pregnancy should be approached on an individual basis, with discussion between the patient, her partner if appropriate, and her health-care provider. If pharmacotherapy is considered, the associated risks and benefits (especially those relative to psychological treatments, as discussed below) must be weighed and discussed openly and carefully with the patient. General guidelines for treatment include using the lowest effective dose of medication and avoiding consumption during the first trimester of pregnancy.

Psychological Treatment

The most effective treatment for OCD (regardless of childbirth status) is exposure-based CBT (for a complete description, see Abramowitz & Jacoby, 2014). The intervention involves four core procedures.

Functional assessment. The initial stage is a thorough assessment of obsessional thoughts (e.g., thoughts of harming the infant), stimuli that cue these thoughts (e.g., knives), feared consequences of the thoughts (e.g., "This means I am a terrible mother"), avoidance (e.g., refraining from bathing the child), and behavioral or mental rituals (e.g., praying, asking for assurances, checking for cuts on the baby's body).

Psychoeducation. The second stage focuses on teaching the patient the cognitive-behavioral model of OCD as well as normalizing obsessional thoughts. Specifically, it is stressed that many expectant and new parents experience unwelcome intrusions about their infant that, while upsetting, are not harmful or indicative of danger. The paradoxical effects of avoidance, rituals, and other safety behaviors in the maintenance of symptoms are also highlighted.

Exposure. The third procedure – and primary ingredient in CBT for ppOCD – is exposure. Broadly, exposure involves the systematic, repeated, and prolonged confrontation of patients with situations, people, objects, and/or thoughts that cue obsessional anxiety, but that are otherwise safe. When the patient deliberately confronts his or her fears (e.g., taking a nap home alone with the baby), he or she learns that feared outcomes (e.g., suffocating the baby) are unlikely to occur and that he or she can manage the associated uncertainty and distress. In this way, exposure weakens the association between feared stimuli and obsessional fear. Exposure also facilitates cognitive restructuring, in that exposures generally afford patients with corrective information regarding their incorrect appraisals of their unwanted intrusions (e.g., "Thinking about suffocating the baby means I *will* suffocate the baby").

Response prevention. The final strategy focuses on the elimination of rituals, avoidance, and other safety behaviors during planned exposures (e.g., bathing the baby without requiring the supervision of the co-parent) or spontaneous anxiety-provoking situations (e.g., chopping vegetables to prepare for dinner even when the baby is also in the kitchen). Response prevention during exposure maximizes the chances for cognitive change; that is, implementing response prevention ensures that the only explanation for the nonoccurrence of feared consequences of exposure is that such consequences are unlikely. Although some patients are willing to resist rituals more readily than others, clinicians should provide their patients with sufficient psychoeducation, control, and encouragement in order to fade safety behaviors as quickly as the patient is willing.

CBT is a time-limited treatment that typically involves 12–16 sessions for perinatal OCD. Exposure tasks might be in vivo, in which the patient actually confronts a feared stimulus in real life (e.g., holding the baby while walking down a flight of stairs), or imaginal (e.g., imagining dropping or throwing the baby down the steps). Interoceptive exposure to feared physical sensations associated with anxious arousal (e.g., increased heart rate, dizziness) might also be appropriate for certain patients, given his or her specific concern. For example, a father who worries that muscle tension or trembling forecasts his "losing control" and strangling the baby might conduct exposures to muscular fatigue (e.g., a series of pushups) while in the presence of the baby. Ultimately, the selection of the type of exposure is dictated by the characteristics of the patient's obsessional fears. Between treatment sessions, the patient reviews the psychoeducational material, practices exposure and response prevention exercises as assigned by the clinician, and self-monitors any problems with obsessional fear or compulsive behavior to aid in targeting the treatment plan appropriately.

Numerous well-conducted studies demonstrate the short- and long-term efficacy of CBT for OCD in general (a recent meta-analysis of 16 controlled trials reported a large between-group effect size of 1.39) (Olatunji, Davis, Powers, & Smits, 2013). Although many study samples include women with postpartum onset OCD (e.g., Abramowitz, Franklin, & Foa, 2002), there are few data on the efficacy of this treatment specifically for perinatal OCD. In a single case study, Christian and Storch (2009) described CBT for ppOCD in which gradual in vivo exposure (i.e., starting with exposures evoking moderate distress and working up to highly distressing tasks) composed the crux of treatment. These authors reported a 72% symptom reduction after only eight sessions. Clearly, studies examining the effectiveness of exposure therapy for the population of expecting or new parents in particular are needed.

Like any treatment approach, there are advantages and disadvantages to the use of CBT in treating perinatal or postpartum OCD. CBT is a highly effective and time-limited treatment for OCD that produces durable improvement. Further, it does not produce the adverse effects that often accompany pharmacological treatment. CBT requires a great deal of effort to be effective, however, and its success is dependent on the patient's willingness to endure the short-term increased anxiety elicited during exposures. Perinatal women in particular might have less time or energy to devote to attending treatment sessions, completing homework assignments, and tolerating the short-term distress associated with CBT. Finally, CBT is generally delivered by a trained mental health professional (e.g., a behaviorally oriented psychologist); although there has been a recent emphasis on training primary care and paraprofessionals to disseminate CBT, CBT may nevertheless be difficult to access in certain areas (Taylor & Chang, 2008).

Many clinicians express reservations about purposefully eliciting emotional and/or physiological arousal in pregnant women (e.g., Meyer et al., 2014). Although exposure-based CBT involves deliberate induction of intense anxiety symptoms, there is insufficient evidence to suggest that exposure therapy is contraindicated for pregnant women (e.g., Arch, Dimidjian, & Chessick, 2012; Beijers, Buitelaar, & de Weerth, 2005). Arch and colleagues (2012) offer adaptive strategies for modifying anxious arousal–induction tasks to accommodate pregnancy, such as monitoring heart rate in relation to a maximal threshold recommended by the pregnant mother's physician and sitting down to prevent the risk of a physical fall.

Case Illustration

In this section, we describe the treatment of Lucy, who was introduced at the beginning of this chapter:

Because Lucy was breast-feeding her infant Andy, she expressed a preference to first try CBT to manage her OCD instead of medication. During the first therapy session, the CBT clinician assessed Lucy's intrusive thoughts, inquiring about (a) the content of the thoughts and stimuli that trigger them, (b) her interpretations of the unwanted thoughts, and (c) her mental and behavioral responses to the thoughts and associated distress. Lucy reported that she believed the thoughts meant that she was "evil at heart" and that their presence was a sign that she might act on them at any moment. She believed she had to take precautions to prevent acting on her obsessions, such as having others nearby to stop her if she "lost control." When the thoughts came to mind, Lucy repeated certain prayers in sets of three, which she believed kept her from acting out her violent thoughts, and so consequently alleviated some of her anxiety. She had also been concealing the content and frequency of her obsessions from others (including her husband) for fear that they would think she was "an evil monster." Because Lucy's mood symptoms began only after she had been experiencing obsessions, her depression was conceptualized as secondary to the OCD symptoms. It was conjectured that successful treatment of her OCD would lead to an improvement in her mood.

Psychoeducation began after the assessment and case formulation was complete. The clinician normalized the experience of intrusive "bad" thoughts by teaching Lucy that practically everyone from time to time experiences ideas, images, or impulses that are upsetting or inconsistent with how they usually think. The clinician even provided examples of his own unwanted intrusive thoughts. Lucy had never considered that others also had similar kinds of intrusion, and said that she was quite relieved to find this out. The clinician discussed how Lucy's concealment of her thoughts, while understandable given Lucy's interpretation of the thoughts, prevented her from finding out how common such experiences are. Lucy was helped to see that her mistaken appraisals of her intrusive thoughts as very meaningful and dangerous, immoral, and needing to be controlled were the *real* problem. That is, her otherwise "normal intrusions" likely escalated into clinical obsessions because she misinterpreted them as dangerous. By trying to suppress and control these thoughts, she was making herself even more preoccupied, which accounted for their persistence and development of a "life of their own."

Lucy was also helped to see that she was unlikely to act on her unwanted thoughts if she did not *wish* to act on them. A discussion of the relationship between thoughts and actions was followed by an experiment in which Lucy was asked to hold a paperweight from the clinician's desk. The clinician turned his back and then asked Lucy to vividly imagine throwing this object at the clinician. Of course, Lucy did not throw the paperweight – even after visualizing this action for several minutes and even saying "I want to hurt you" and "I'm going to throw this at you." The results of this experiment (i.e., demonstrating that thoughts do not necessarily lead to corresponding actions) were discussed in terms of the improbability that Lucy would ever act on thoughts to harm Andy.

After a few sessions, Lucy found herself feeling less distressed by her intrusive thoughts, yet they still evoked moderate levels of anxiety. Lucy also remained fearful of having the thoughts while she was with Andy – especially if she was *alone* with

Andy – and continued to use prayer rituals to reduce her fears of disastrous consequences. Thus, the clinician introduced exposure and response prevention as exercises for weakening Lucy's patterns of (a) becoming anxious when such thoughts arose, and (b) engaging in deleterious rituals to reduce her anxiety. After providing a rationale for purposely confronting her unwanted thoughts without engaging in any safety behaviors, Lucy and the clinician constructed a hierarchy consisting of situations for Lucy to practice both in-session and at home. This list is shown in Table 28.2. Lucy agreed to practice the situations without saying the prayers. She realized that she needed to prove to herself that these thoughts were not indicative of danger and that her prayers were not actually keeping her from acting on them.

During the first exposure session, Lucy and the clinician collaboratively created an audio recorded scenario of Lucy's intrusive thought about stabbing Andy:

> You've just started cutting the vegetables and you see little Andy lying on the floor on his blanket. He's cooing and very content. Then you have the idea that you could easily stab him to death with the knife you are using. He is so small and defenseless. He wouldn't be able to stop you. You want to push the thought away, but instead allow yourself to just "go with it." Then, you feel the urge to pray growing stronger and stronger. You want to say the prayers, but you know you are not supposed to because of the therapy instructions. So, you refrain from praying. Then, you feel yourself going over to Andy and you begin stabbing him over and over. There is blood everywhere. What are you doing … this is your own son! Andy is crying, but then he goes limp as he dies on the blanket. You can't believe what you've just done. What will your husband say? If only you had said those prayers. Now, Andy is dead.

Lucy practiced listening to the scenario on an audio recording saved to her smartphone in the session. The clinician kept track of Lucy's anxiety level on a scale from 0 (none) to 100 (extreme). As the exposure began, Lucy's anxiety reached 75%, but decreased to 40% after listening to the recording repeatedly for 15 minutes. After another 10 minutes, the recording evoked mild anxiety (25%). Next, Andy (who had been in the waiting room with his father) was brought into the office and Lucy retrieved a large knife that she had brought from home. Andy was placed on the floor next to Lucy, and Lucy practiced holding the knife while listening to the audio recording. At first, Lucy felt uncomfortable, but after about 15 minutes, her distress subsided somewhat even while she held the knife. She also refrained from

Table 28.2 Lucy's exposure therapy hierarchy

Situation	Anxiety level %
1. Think about stabbing Andy.	40
2. Think about stabbing Andy while holding a knife with her husband nearby.	50
3. Think about putting Andy in the microwave.	55
4. Hold Andy in the kitchen while thinking about putting him in the microwave.	65
5. Think about suffocating Andy.	65
6. Watch Andy sleeping, hold a pillow, and think about suffocating him.	75
7. Think about stabbing Andy while holding a knife alone with Andy.	95

prayer rituals. Then, after obtaining Lucy's permission, the clinician left Lucy and Andy alone in the office. Again, Lucy's distress level increased, but soon declined somewhat as she realized that she could tolerate having the unpleasant thoughts and cope with the feelings of anxiety. Lucy also benefitted from learning that she did not need an absolute guarantee that she would not act on her obsessional thoughts; that is, Lucy learned that she could engage with anxiety-provoking situations even if feeling uncertain. She was then instructed to practice the same tasks once each day with Andy, including using the smartphone recording, between sessions.

Over the course of the next month, Lucy practiced similar exposure exercises while refraining from rituals and other avoidance strategies. This was extremely helpful; after only two months of treatment (eight therapy sessions), Lucy was no longer avoiding being alone with Andy, and her prayer rituals had reduced substantially. Although Lucy still experienced occasional unwanted intrusive violent thoughts, she was able to correctly appraise these experiences as normal and harmless – she reported "knowing in her gut" that she did not have to worry about acting violently. Lucy's depressive symptoms had also abated and she reported being much happier about being a new mother. For the next three months, the clinician saw Lucy on a monthly basis for follow-up sessions. Lucy maintained her treatment gains through the three-month discontinuation period and treatment was therefore terminated.

Special Considerations

There are a number of additional issues unique to the treatment of OCD in new parents that deserve consideration. Given that ppOCD is typically characterized by thoughts of harming one's infant, special care needs to be taken to ensure that there are no actual risk factors for child harm separate from the obsessional thoughts (which in themselves are not related to an increased risk of harming one's infant). Other areas that deserve special attention include social support for the parent with OCD and the parent–infant relationship. Social support is of particular importance in the early postpartum period as this is a highly demanding time in a parent's life. Given that ppOCD can lead to avoidance of one's infant, attention should be given to the mother– or father–infant relationship (including ways to systematically facilitate healthy parent–infant relationships into treatment).

The clinician must weigh the pros and cons of available treatment approaches and discuss these with the patient (and the patient's partner, if appropriate). As discussed above, both pharmacotherapy and psychotherapy are associated with certain advantages and disadvantages. It is also possible that a parent presenting with perinatal or postpartum OCD may face practical obstacles to receiving the best treatment. That is, at present, knowledgeable treatment providers who are trained to deliver exposure-based CBT are somewhat few and far between (although this is changing in many areas). Excellent resources for clinicians looking to refer patients for CBT include the Association for Behavioral and Cognitive Therapies (formerly the Association for Advancement of Behavior Therapy, www.aabt.org), the Anxiety Disorders Association of America (www.adaa.org), and the International OCD Foundation (www.iocdf.org). Each of these three organizations' websites includes helpful resources for locating a trained provider.

Summary and Conclusions

Perinatal and postpartum anxiety disorders have received little empirical attention relative to other conditions that affect expectant and new parents, such as depression and psychosis. In the case of OCD, the perinatal period appears to be a time of increased risk for the development of this disorder. Further, available evidence suggests that ppOCD presents a distinctive clinical picture, with prenatal onset characterized most often by contamination fears, and postpartum onset characterized by unwanted thoughts of harm befalling one's infant. However, evidence for ppOCD being a distinct OCD subtype is mixed (McGuinness, Blissett, & Jones, 2011).

Continued research in this area is vital, as many scientific questions regarding perinatal and postpartum OCD remain. First, no definitive incidence studies have been carried out; studies of this type would provide information on the relative risk of developing OCD during the perinatal period compared with other points in life. Additionally, the majority of ppOCD research has examined symptomatology among heterosexual female patients, effectively ignoring obsessional experiences among expectant or new fathers, nonbiological guardians (i.e., adoptive parents), and homosexual co-parents. Therefore, more research into perinatal and postpartum OCD symptoms among males and nontraditional parents is warranted. As intrusive thoughts of harm related to one's infant occur with some frequency among women with postpartum-onset depression, studies exploring the relationship between perinatal OCD and perinatal depression are also needed. Research furthering our understanding how ppOCD affects parenting behavior, infant development, and the mother–infant relationship have yet to be carried out. Finally, treatment efficacy and effectiveness studies aimed at identifying specific approaches and components most helpful for treating perinatal and postpartum OCD will be required in order to optimally meet the mental health needs of new parents.

References

Abramowitz, J. S. (2004). Treatment of obsessive-compulsive disorder in patients who have comorbid major depression. *Journal of Clinical Psychology, 60,* 1133–1141.

Abramowitz, J. S., Franklin, M. E., & Foa, E. B. (2002). Empirical status of cognitive-behavior therapy for obsessive-compulsive disorder: A meta-analytic review. *Romanian Journal of Cognitive and Behavioral Psychotherapies, 2,* 89–104.

Abramowitz, J. S., & Jacoby, R. J. (2015). *Obsessive-compulsive disorder in adults.* Boston, MA: Hogrefe.

Abramowitz, J. S., Khandker, M., Nelson, C. A., Deacon, B. J., & Rygwall, R. (2006). The role of cognitive factors in the pathogenesis of obsessive-compulsive symptoms: A prospective study. *Behaviour Research and Therapy, 44,* 1361–1374.

Abramowitz, J. S., Schwartz, S., Moore, K., & Luenzmann, K. (2003). Obsessive-compulsive symptoms in pregnancy and the puerperium: A review of the literature. *Journal of Anxiety Disorders, 17,* 461–478.

Abramowitz, J. S., Storch, E. A., Keeley, M., & Cordell, E. (2007). Obsessive-compulsive disorder with comorbid major depression: What is the role of cognitive factors? *Behaviour Research and Therapy, 45,* 2257–2267.

Arnold, L. M. (1999). A case series of women with postpartum-onset obsessive-compulsive disorder. *Primary Care Companion to the Journal of Clinical Psychiatry, 1*(4), 103–108.

Barr, L. C., Goodman, W. K., & Price, L. H. (1993). The serotonin hypothesis of obsessive-compulsive disorder. *International Clinical Psychopharmacology, 8*(Suppl. 2), 79–82.

Beck, A. & Emery, G. (1985). *Anxiety disorders & phobias: A cognitive perspective.* New York: Basic Books.

Beijers, R., Buitelaar, J. K., & de Weerth, C. (2014). Mechanisms underlying the effects of pre-natal psychosocial stress on child outcomes: Beyond the HPA axis. *European Child & Adolescent Psychiatry, 23*, 943–956.

Bellodi, L., Scuito, G., Diaferia, G., & Ronchi, P. (1992). Psychiatric disorders in the families of patients with obsessive-compulsive disorder. *Psychiatry Research, 42*, 111–120.

Buttolph, M. L., & Holland, A. D. (1990). Obsessive-compulsive disorders in pregnancy and childbirth. In M. Jenike, L. Baer, & W. Minichiello (Eds.), *Obsessive-compulsive disorders: Theory and management* (pp. 89–97). Chicago, IL: Year Book Medical.

Christian, L. M., & Storch, E. A. (2009). Cognitive behavioural treatment of postpartum onset: Obsessive-compulsive disorder with aggressive obsessions. *Clinical Case Studies, 8*, 72–83.

Di Nardo, P. A., & Barolw, D. H. (1988). Anxiety Disorders Interview Schedule – Revised (ADIS-R). *Phobia and Anxiety Disorders Clinic, Center for Stress and Anxiety Disorders,* State University of New York at Albany.

Demal, U., Lenz, G., Mayrhofer, A., & Zapotoczky, H. (1993). Obsessive-compulsive disorder and depression: A retrospective study on course and interaction. *Psychopathology, 26*, 145–150.

Diaz, S. F., Grush, L. R., Sichel, D. A., & Cohen, L. S. (1997). In L. J. Dickstein, M. B. Riba, & J. M. Oldham (Eds.), *Review of Psychiatry* (Vol. *16*, pp. 97–112). Washington, DC: American Psychiatric Press.

Elliot, S. A., Rugg, A. J., Watson, J. P., & Brough, D. I. (1983). Mood changes during preg-nancy and after the birth of a child. *British Journal of Psychiatry, 22*, 295–308.

Fairbrother, N., & Abramowitz, J. S. (2007). New parenthood as a risk factor for the development of obsessional problems. *Behaviour Research and Therapy, 45*, 2155–2163

First, M. B., Spitzer, R. L., Gibbon, M., Williams, J. B. W. (1997). *Structured Clinical Interview for DSM-IV – Clinical version (SCID-I-CV).* Washington, DC: American Psychiatric Press.

Foa, E. B., & Kozak, M. J. (1986). Emotional processing of fear: Exposure to corrective information. *Psychological Bulletin, 99*, 20–35.

Jennings, K. D., Ross, S., Popper, S., & Elmore, M. (1999). Thoughts of harming infants in depressed and nondepressed mothers. *Journal of Affective Disorders, 54*, 21–28.

Kaplan, A., & Hollander, E. (2003). A review of pharmacologic treatments for obsessive-com-pulsive disorder. *Psychiatric Services, 54*, 1111–1118.

Leckman, J., Goodman, W., North, W., Chappell, P., Price, L., Pauls, D., ... Barr, L. C. (1994a). The role of central oxytocin in obsessive-compulsive disorder and related normal behavior. *Psychoneuroendocrinology, 19*, 723–749.

Leckman, J., Goodman, W., North, W., Chappell, P., Price, L., Pauls, D., ... McDougle, C. J. (1994b). Elevated cerebrospinal fluid levels of oxytocin in obsessive-compulsive disorder. *Archives of General Psychiatry, 51*, 782–792.

McGuinness, M., Blissett, J., & Jones, C. (2011). OCD in the perinatal period: Is postpartum OCD (ppOCD) a distinct subtype? A review of the literature. *Behavioural and Cognitive Psychotherapy, 39*, 285–310.

Maina, G., Albert, U., Bogetto, F., Vaschetto, P., & Ravizza, L. (2000). Recent life events and obsessive-compulsive disorder (OCD): The role of pregnancy/delivery. *Psychiatry Research, 89*, 49–58.

Meyer, J. M., Farrell, N. R., Kemp, J. J., Blakey, S. M., & Deacon, B. J. (2014). Why do cli-nicians exclude anxious clients from exposure therapy? *Behaviour Research and Therapy, 54*, 49–53.

Nestadt, G., Samuels, J., Riddle, M. A., Liang, K-Y., Bienvenu, O. J., Hoehn-Saric, R., Grados, M., & Cullen, B. (2001). The relationship between obsessive-compulsive disorder and anxiety and affective disorders: Results from the Johns Hopkins OCD Family Study. *Psychological Medicine, 31*, 481–487.

Olatunji, B., Davis, M., Powers, M., & Smits, J. (2013). Cognitive-behavioral therapy for obsessive-compulsive disorder: A meta-analysis of treatment outcome and mediators. *Journal of Psychiatric Research, 47*, 33–41.

Özkürkçügil A., Aydermir, Ö., Yildiz, M., Danaci, E., Koroglu, E. (1999). Adaptation and reliability study of Structured Clinical Interview for DSM-IV Axis I disorders. *Turkish Journal of Drugs and Therapeutics, 12*, 233–236.

Pato, T. A., Zohar-Kadouch, R., Zohar, J., & Murphy, D. L. (1988). Return of symptoms after discontinuation of clomipramine in patients with obsessive-compulsive disorder. *American Journal of Psychiatry, 145*, 1521–1525.

Rachman, S. J., & de Silva, P. (1978). Abnormal and normal obsessions. *Behaviour Research and Therapy, 16*, 233–238.

Rauch, S., & Jenike, M. (1993). Neurobiological models of obsessive-compulsive disorder. *Psychosomatics, 34*, 20–32.

Ruscio, A. M., Stein, D. J., Chiu, W. T., & Kessler, R. C. (2010). The epidemiology of obsessive-compulsive disorder in the national comorbidity survey replication. *Molecular Psychiatry, 15*, 53–63.

Salkovskis, P. (1996). Cognitive-behavioral approaches to the understanding of obsessional problems. In R. M. Rapee (Ed.), *Current controversies in the anxiety disorders* (pp. 103–133). New York: Guilford Press.

Sheehan, D. V., Lecrubier, Y., Sheehan, K. H., Amorim, P., Janavs, J., Weiller, E., ... Dunbar, G. C. (1998). The Mini-International Neuropsychiatric Interview (MINI): The development and validation of a structured diagnostic psychiatric interview for DSM-IV and ICD-10. *Journal of Clinical Psychiatry, 59*, 22–33.

Sichel, D., A., Cohen, L. S., Dimmock, J. A., & Rosenbaum, J. F. (1993a). Postpartum obsessive-compulsive disorder: A case series. *Journal of Clinical Psychiatry, 54*, 156–159.

Sichel, D. A., Cohen, L. S., Rosenbaum, J. F., & Driscoll, J. D. (1993b). Postpartum onset of obsessive-compulsive disorder. *Psychosomatics, 34*, 277–279.

Stockert, M., & deRobertis, E. (1985). Effect of ovariectomy and estrogen on [^{3}H]imipramine binding on different regions of the rat brain. *European Journal of Pharmacology, 199*, 255–257.

Sutter-Dallay, A. L., Giaconne-Marcesche, V., Glatigny-Dallay, E., & Verdoux, H. (2004). Women with anxiety disorders during pregnancy are at increased risk of intense postnatal depressive symptoms: A prospective survey of the MATQUID cohort. *European Psychiatry, 19*, 459–463.

Taylor, C. B., & Chang, V. Y. (2008). Issues in the dissemination of cognitive-behavior therapy. *Nordic Journal of Psychiatry, 62*(Suppl. 47), 37–44.

Uguz, F., Akman, C., Kaya, N., & Cilli, A. S. (2007). Postpartum-onset obsessive-compulsive disorder: Incidence, clinical features, and related factors. *Journal of Clinical Psychiatry, 68*, 132–138.

Uguz, F., Gezginc, K., Zeytinci, I. E., Karatayli, S., Askin, R., Guler, O., ... Gecici, O. (2007). Obsessive-compulsive disorder in pregnant women during the third trimester of pregnancy. *Comprehensive Psychiatry, 48*, 441–445.

Wenzel, A., Gorman, L., O'Hara, M. W., & Stuart, S. (2001). The occurrence of panic and obsessive compulsive symptoms in women with postpartum dysphoria: A prospective study. *Archives of Women's Mental Health, 4*, 5–12.

Wenzel, A., Haugen, E. N., Jackson, L. C., & Brendle, J. R. (2005). Anxiety symptoms and disorders at eight weeks postpartum. *Journal of Anxiety Disorders, 19*, 295–311.

Wisner, K. L., Peindl, K. S., Gigliotti, T., & Hanusa, B. H. (1999). Obsessions and compulsions in women with postpartum depression. *Journal of Clinical Psychiatry, 60*, 176–180.

Zambaldi, C. F., Cantilino, A., Montenegro, A. C., Paes, J. A., de Albuquerque, T. L. C., & Sougey, E. B. (2009). Postpartum obsessive-compulsive disorder: Prevalence and clinical characteristics. *Comprehensive Psychiatry, 50*, 503–509.

Zar, M. M., Wijma, K., & Wijma, B. (2002). Relations between anxiety disorders and fear of childbirth during late pregnancy. *Clinical Psychology and Psychotherapy, 9*, 122–130.

29

Understanding and Treating Scrupulosity

Jedidiah Siev, Jonathan D. Huppert, and Shelby E. Zuckerman

Scrupulosity is a manifestation of obsessive-compulsive disorder (OCD) characterized by religious or moral fears. Religious obsessions are evident in 10–33% of individuals with OCD in Western cultures (Eisen et al., 1999; Mataix-Cols, Marks, Greist, Kobak, & Baer, 2002), and they are the primary obsessional fears for 5–6% (Foa & Kozak, 1995; Tolin, Abramowitz, Kozak, & Foa, 2001). They are even more common in religious cultures and subcultures, however, where they are sometimes present in the majority of cases (for a review, see Greenberg & Huppert, 2010).

Scrupulosity can take many forms and variations. Individuals with scrupulosity prototypically have excessive religious fears or doubts about sin; however, individuals may have secular moral scrupulosity, fearing being immoral, bad, or evil without any religious component. In fact, a recent study found that 18% of those with scrupulosity identified as having no religious affiliation (Siev, Baer, & Minichiello, 2011a), although some of those participants reported having been raised in a religious tradition that influenced their symptoms. Among those with religious scrupulosity, obsessional themes seem to vary as a function of religious affiliation. For example, Protestant Christians commonly have obsessions about sin, hell, devil worship, offending God, and Divine punishment (e.g., Ciarrocchi, 1995; Purdon & Clark, 2005). In contrast, Jews often obsess about violating or not adequately fulfilling behavioral proscriptions and requirements, for example, dietary laws, prayer, Sabbath observance, and ritual purity laws (Greenberg & Shefler, 2002, 2008). Catholics demonstrate a combination of these belief-based and behavioral fears, with obsessions similar to Protestant Christians, such as about hell and committing the unpardonable sin, as well as fears related to confession, the Eucharist, and adequate articulation of prayers (e.g., Ciarrocchi, 1995; Huppert & Siev, 2010).

To complicate matters further, many obsessional fears not commonly thought of as scrupulous have moral elements. For example, an individual with obsessions about murdering his family would typically be classified as having aggressive harm obsessions – not scrupulosity – despite the nearly universal judgment that murder is immoral and sinful. Not only do obsessions about committing immoral behaviors not necessarily imply scrupulosity, obsessions about secular or everyday behaviors may indicate scrupulosity.

The Wiley Handbook of Obsessive Compulsive Disorders, Volume I, First Edition.
Edited by Jonathan S. Abramowitz, Dean McKay, and Eric A. Storch.
© 2017 John Wiley & Sons Ltd. Published 2017 by John Wiley & Sons Ltd.

For instance, an individual with contamination fears about ritual purity or religious die-tary laws would be described as scrupulous even though the specific symptoms relate to contamination. The implication is that we consider symptoms across any OCD symptom dimension scrupulous if the underlying core fear is religious or moral. Therefore, although often grouped together with sexual and aggressive harm symptoms in a cate-gory of "unacceptable thoughts," scrupulosity can be thought of as a category of core fears rather than an OCD subtype (Siev & Huppert, 2016). Indeed, recent research indicates that sexual and harm thoughts do not co-occur with scrupulosity more than with other types of OCD symptoms in non-Christian patients (Huppert & Fradkin, 2016). In addition, religious obsessions seem related to a wider range of obsessional cognitions than are other types of cognitions (sexual and contamination), bolstering the idea that scrupulosity manifests across different symptom dimensions (Siev, Steketee, Fama, & Wilhelm, 2011b).

It is worth acknowledging that others have argued that scrupulosity is distinct from OCD and warrants a unique diagnostic category (Miller & Hedges, 2008). They base this assertion on several features of scrupulosity that may differ at least by a matter of degree from features of other OCD presentations. Like most others, however, we believe that overwhelming clinical and empirical evidence indicates that scrupulosity is a manifestation of OCD. The putative evidence in support of a separate scrupulosity disorder is addressed and refuted comprehensively by Greenberg and Huppert (2010) and Abramowitz and Jacoby (2014).

Religion and OCD

Religion does not cause OCD, but rather influences its manifestation. First, preva-lence rates of OCD are remarkably consistent across cultures, except where overall prevalence rates for psychopathology differ (e.g., Horwath & Weissman, 2000; Weissman et al., 1994). In contrast, among those with OCD, religious individuals are more likely to experience religious symptoms and obsessional themes (e.g., Greenberg, 1984; Greenberg & Witzum, 1994; Khanna & Channabasavanna, 1988; Okasha, Saad, Khalil, El-Dawla, & Yehia, 1994; Rasmussen & Tsuang, 1986). Similarly, rates of scrupulosity are much higher among those with OCD in religious cultures than those with OCD in less religious cultures (for a review, see Greenberg & Huppert, 2010).

Several studies have attempted and failed to demonstrate an association between the presence of OCD and religion. In two studies, individuals with OCD were no more religious than were those with other anxiety disorders (Hermesh, Masser-Kavitzky, & Gross-Isseroff, 2003; Steketee, Quay, & White, 1991), and in another study, religiosity was not related to OCD behavior (Zohar, Goldman, Calamary, & Mashiah, 2005). Two other studies found small differences on OCD variables as a function of religiosity in nonclinical samples (Abramowitz, Deacon, Woods, & Tolin, 2004; Sica, Novara, & Sanavio, 2002); however, there were no differences on the majority of variables, and for those variables that did differ, the mean scores for the more religious participants were lower than the means reported for nonclinical groups in normative data. In sum, there is compelling evidence that religious indi-viduals with OCD are more likely that nonreligious individuals with OCD to have religious themes to their symptoms, and no evidence that religious individuals are more likely to have OCD.

At face value, many scrupulous individuals seem to fear a harsh and punitive God. After all, they worry that God might respond to minor or accidental transgressions with extreme – even eternal – punishments. Two studies investigated concepts of God and scrupulosity. Siev and colleagues (2011a) found that among individuals with scrupulous OCD, severity of scrupulosity was associated with a more negative concept of God (as punishing, fearsome, jealous, terrifying, angry, vengeful), but uncorrelated with a positive concept of God (as peaceful, kind, comforting, gentle, compassionate, and loving). However, explicit ratings about God are limited by the possibility that participants know the "right answer" when asked things such as whether God is loving and compassionate, whether or not they experience Him as such. In a follow-up study, Pirutinsky, Siev, and Rosmarin (2015) examined both explicit beliefs and implicit associations, and found that only participants with both a highly negative explicit concept of God and a relatively more negative implicit association had more severe symptoms of scrupulosity.

Conceptualizations of Scrupulosity

Cognitive-Behavioral Model

Abramowitz and Jacoby (2014) propose a cognitive-behavioral model of scrupulosity that stresses the significance of dysfunctional and intrusive beliefs, the uncertain nature of many facets of religion, and the role of compulsive behaviors in the development and maintenance of scrupulosity. Their conceptualization essentially adapts existing cognitive-behavioral models of OCD in general to account for specific characteristics of scrupulosity. They argue that scrupulosity develops when intrusive and undesirable thoughts or images are perceived as significant, meaningful, and distressing. Religion may cultivate religious-based obsessions due to several factors including rules about the equivalence of thoughts and behaviors (thought–action fusion), the emphasis on thought control to prevent sin, the existence of important religious leaders, and fear of possible punishment. Thus, according to this model, the observance of strong religious beliefs and practices predisposes one to develop the types of thoughts that can be problematic in scrupulosity. These thoughts create uncertainty, anxiety, and distress.

Clearly, however, most religious individuals do not suffer from scrupulosity. According to Abramowitz and Jacoby (2014), intolerance of religious uncertainty is a distinguishing factor between religious people with and without scrupulosity. Those who accept religious uncertainty and participate in religious activities without proof that they are doing so acceptably typically do not suffer from scrupulosity. Instead, people who cannot tolerate religious uncertainty and require proof or validation of their religious beliefs or actions experience significant distress because there is no such certainty. Essentially, religious individuals with scrupulosity have "lost their faith in faith" (Abramowitz & Jacoby, 2014: 145). In sum, the authors argue that intolerance of uncertainty mediates the relationships between scrupulosity and both thought–action fusion and religious concerns.

Similar to others with OCD, individuals with scrupulosity engage in a realm of behaviors intended to reduce distress associated with obsessions, including ritualizing, attempting to suppress thoughts, and avoidance. These behaviors are often aimed at reducing anxiety or preventing a feared consequence. However, these actions provide negative reinforcement and maintain the cycle of symptoms. By engaging in compulsions, individuals with scrupulosity do not learn that their distress will subside without the rituals and that they can tolerate the distress associated with obsessive thoughts. Further, attempting to rid oneself of obsessive thoughts increases the frequency of the thoughts. Given that religious certainty can never be obtained, individuals with scrupulosity become entangled in a cycle of doubt, anxiety, attempts to neutralize distress, and uncertainty, which activates the sequence again.

Treatment goals are to address dysfunctional beliefs that are related to – but incongruent with – the individual's religion, increase the ability to tolerate uncertainty, and decrease compulsive behaviors and avoidance. Ultimately, treatment allows the individual to practice their religious beliefs in way that is fulfilling and not anxiety-driven. In fact, Siev et al. (2011a) found that the large majority of individuals with scrupulosity experience their symptoms as interfering with their religious observance. Promoting healthy religious practice can be accomplished by challenging and restructuring the patient's unwanted extreme, maladaptive, and rigid beliefs about their religion, engaging in in vivo and imaginal exposure and response (ritual) prevention (ERP), and distinguishing healthy religious practices and beliefs from those that create distress and harm and ultimately lead to pathology. Abramowitz and Jacoby (2014: 147) describe this last important process as deciding which practices are "fear-based" versus those that are "faith-based," although the clinician must be careful to ensure that efforts to make this decision do not become compulsive.

Existential and Self-threat

Some researchers have introduced an existential conceptualization of scrupulosity. According to terror management theory (TMT), religion is a means of coping with anxiety associated with fears of death and mortality. In response to this anxiety, people engage in a realm of behaviors and adopt a variety of beliefs as a means of reducing distress. TMT may relate to scrupulosity because scrupulosity is characterized by compulsive behaviors aimed at reducing distress and anxiety surrounding religious-based obsessions, which may function to buffer against existential fears. Consistent with this possibility, Fergus and Valentiner (2012) found that undergraduate students who scored higher on a measure of scrupulosity were more likely to respond to reminders of death by engaging in mistake-checking behaviors, as well as experiences of shame, guilt, and not just right experiences when checking.

Others assert that threats to self-competence lead individuals with insecure attachments to seek ways to restore a sense of competence in the threatened domain, sometimes resulting in obsessions and compulsions (e.g., Doron & Kyrios, 2005). In the context of scrupulosity, which is often associated with threats about sin or one's relationship with God, Fergus and Rowatt (2014a) suggest that attachment insecurities in relation to God might predict scrupulous obsessions and compulsions. Indeed, they found in a nonclinical sample that symptoms of scrupulosity were associated with attachment anxiety (i.e., distress regarding the unavailability of attachment figures during difficult times), although not attachment avoidance (i.e., distrust regarding attachment figures' goodwill).

Finally, personal uncertainty – different from informational uncertainty – is a sense of doubt regarding one's self or one's world views. Similar to the anxiety produced by fear of mortality in TMT, uncertainty about one's views can cause distress, which may lead individuals to engage in behaviors aimed at reducing anxiety. In two experimental studies with nonclinical participants, Fergus and Rowatt (2014b) demonstrated that increasing personal uncertainty strengthened the association between scrupulosity and (a) moral appraisals of intrusive thoughts (Study 1), and (b) the belief that God was upset with personal sin, among those with greater scrupulous symptoms (Study 2).

Taken together, these studies indicate that existential concerns, as well as experiences that threaten the self, may contribute to the manifestation of scrupulosity, perhaps among those with other OCD-relevant vulnerability factors. Measures of scrupulosity are difficult to interpret in nonclinical samples, however, because concern and anxiety about sin and God may indicate religiosity, religious struggles, and existential struggles, rather than symptoms of OCD. Therefore, although suggestive, these constructs await evaluation in clinical samples.

Treatment of Scrupulosity

Treatment Outcome

Data are mixed with respect to the impact of scrupulosity on treatment outcome. Several studies found that the presence of religious obsessions predicts poorer outcome for CBT and pharmacotherapy for OCD (e.g., Alonso et al., 2001; Ferrão et al., 2006; Mataix-Cols et al., 2002; Rufer, Grothusen, Maß, Peter, & Hand, 2005); however, others did not (e.g., Abramowitz, Franklin, Schwartz, & Furr, 2003). Nevertheless, clinicians are faced with several challenges when working with a scrupulous patient. They need to understand the patient's religious and cultural context, religious beliefs, and normative non-OCD-driven religious practice, and help the patient disentangle OCD from religion (e.g., compulsive rituals from religious rituals). Scrupulous fears are often less easy to test, and the patient may not receive any concrete evidence about the accuracy of his or her fears (e.g., whether it was sinful, offended God, she or he will suffer in Hell, etc.). Religious obsessions are also associated with poor insight and magical thinking (Tolin et al., 2001). Finally, individuals with scrupulosity may view their symptoms as religious rather than OCD (Huppert & Siev, 2010). Not surprisingly, those with scrupulous OCD are more likely than those with other types of OCD to seek pastoral counseling and less likely to receive pharmacotherapy (Siev et al., 2011a).

Overall Treatment Approach

Exposure and response (ritual) prevention (ERP) is a form of CBT tailored to address the factors that maintain OCD (for a treatment manual, see Foa, Yadin, & Lichner, 2012). ERP is identified as a first-line treatment for OCD (e.g., March, Frances, Kahn, & Carpenter, 1997; National Institute for Health and Clinical Excellence, 2006) with response rates as high as 86% among those who complete an adequate course of treatment (e.g., Foa et al., 2005). OCD is characterized by obsessions that generate anxiety and compulsions that aim to provide anxiety relief, and ERP is designed to break the connections between obsessions and anxiety, and between compulsions and anxiety relief. In so doing, the patient learns that obsessions and obsessional triggers do not result in never-ending anxiety, and that compulsions are not necessary to experience anxiety relief. Furthermore, the patient often learns that his or her obsessional fears do not actualize, or that she or he is capable of tolerating the associated risk and discomfort. At its core, ERP requires the patient to engage in prolonged in vivo and imaginal exposure to situations that provoke obsessions. However, in light of the aforementioned challenges in working with scrupulous patients, a number of adaptations to standard ERP are advisable, and several articles and books offer suggestions for tailoring ERP for use with scrupulous patients (e.g., Abramowitz, 2001, Bonchek, 2009; Bonchek & Greenberg, 2009; Ciarrocchi, 1995; Deacon & Nelson, 2008; Huppert & Siev, 2010; Huppert, Siev, & Kushner, 2007; Siev & Huppert, 2016).

There are actually several reasons to tailor standard ERP protocols for individuals with scrupulosity. First, as noted above, very religious patients are likely to have symptoms of scrupulosity if they have OCD. Therefore, some modifications are not due to scrupulosity, per se, but rather as efforts toward improving treatment acceptability and effectiveness for religious patients more generally (the principle of considering patient values as an essential aspect of evidence based practice) (Sackett, Rosenberg, Gray, Haynes, & Richardson, 2000). For example, discussing the evolutionary function of anxiety with a devout Fundamentalist Christian, who may be offended by the notion of evolution is not therapeutic and could even be counterproductive. Second, scrupulosity itself, particularly for the religious patient, is often tied up with the patient's value-based belief system, and requires work to help the patient differentiate between his or her beliefs and OCD. This typically involves helping the patient articulate, and thereby become more aware of, differences between his or her beliefs and those of others in their faith community. Third, in addition to beliefs, treatment requires the patient to behave in ways that are seen as not fully normative, yet which also do not violate the basic tenets of their faith. For example, an Orthodox Jewish patient may be asked to hold a jar of canned ham and to keep it in his or her office. This would be atypical, but not violate the laws of keeping kosher. In the following sections, we elaborate on these issues and review important modifications with respect to assessment, the therapeutic stance, psychoeducation, working with clergy, exposure work, and prayer.

ERP Modified

What is religion and what is OCD and how to tell. How does one distinguish between OCD and normative religion? Consider: (1) a man wakes up in the morning and will not touch food until he washes his hands by pouring water over his hands, alternating right hand then left three times each (normative in Orthodox Judaism); (2) another individual uses a compass to determine in what direction to pray (normative in some Muslim communities); (3) a woman avoids anything with the number 666 (normative in some fundamentalist Christian groups). Greenberg, Witztum, and Pisante (1987) suggest a number of questions that help the clinician differentiate between scrupulosity and normative religious practice: (1) is the behavior more extreme than typical in the community and in terms of how others interpret the requirements of religious law?; (2) does the behavior seem to be extremely narrow or overly trivial in comparison with the behavior of the individual's peers?; (3) are work, prayer, and family functioning impaired due to a focus on the scrupulous issue? We would add another possible indication: does the person seem overly distressed about his or her inability to practice as she or he believes she or he should? This potential index of pathology is tempered by the recognition that religious individuals may feel distressed by concerns that they cannot perform their religious obligations or rituals, which can be normative.

It is important to note that familiarity with specific group norms is often essential to make finer distinctions, and the particular practices of any given religious sect can differ from those in other subgroups within the same religion. Rosmarin, Pirutinsky, and Siev (2010) have shown that individuals within a community are typically able to differentiate normative from pathological OCD practice, even when people outside the community are unable to do so. Therefore, family members, friends, and clergy can all help provide information on normative practices of the community. Considerations for including clergy effectively in treatment are discussed below.

Considering how likely it is that religious patients with OCD will have religious obsessional fears (e.g., Greenberg & Shefler, 2002), it is important to evaluate all religious OCD patients for scrupulous symptoms. The Yale–Brown Obsessive Compulsive Scale (YBOCS) (Goodman et al., 1989) is the most commonly used interviewer rating scale for OCD; however, its checklist includes only a single item about religious obsessions and one other about moral obsessions. We find it useful to elaborate on various religious obsessions the individual may have in order to obtain a comprehensive clinical picture of the patient's OCD. Thus, it is often useful to start by asking globally about the patient's religion. Depending on the patient's responses, one can start probing about scrupulous obsessions by asking general questions such as: "Do you have any intrusive thoughts related to blasphemy or heresy? How about intrusive thoughts that you may have offended God or not fulfilled His wishes sufficiently? Perhaps even thoughts that you don't think are true, such as 'God is going to punish me for my thoughts or actions?'" Then, in the context of the patient's religious beliefs and general concerns, the therapist asks more detailed questions about intrusions such as about sin, blasphemy, and offending God. For example, if the patient identifies as a devout Protestant Christian and reports blasphemous thoughts, asking about intrusive thoughts of cursing Jesus or intrusive images of a cross smeared with feces are two of many possibilities. If the patient is a devout Catholic, images of sex with the Virgin Mary, fears of dropping the Eucharist, and thoughts about incomplete confessional are similar to the types of obsessions that may be more in line with his or her beliefs. For devout Jews, issues of prayer, dietary laws, family purity, and precision of daily rituals are more pertinent. For Muslims, proper thoughts about God and Muhammad, direction of prayer, cleanliness before prayer, complete fasting during Ramadan, and ensuring that one did not eat pork are concerns about which OCD may manifest. For Hindus, issues of portions and sufficient sacrifices, not eating beef, and reading the Bagavad Gita with sufficient attention may be prominent. Although these are only several examples of many possibilities, we find that by probing with concrete and specific examples, the therapist communicates knowledge, expertise, and professionalism, all of which normalize religious obsessions and allow the scrupulous patient to feel understood. In addition to the interview, there Penn Inventory of Scrupulosity (Abramowitz, Huppert, Cohen, Tolin, & Cahill, 2002) is a self-report measure of scrupulosity. This measure does particularly well at identifying Christians with scrupulosity, but is less effective in discriminating individuals with scrupulosity from those with sexual or aggressive thoughts in other religions (although it sufficiently differentiates between scrupulosity and contamination, doubts about actions, and ordering obsessions) (Huppert & Fradkin, 2016).

Individuals with scrupulosity often have poor insight (e.g., Tolin et al., 2001), and it is our clinical impression that in those cases the therapist needs to be knowledgeable about the individual's religious practices and also to involve clergy. This allows the therapist to speak with authority (by having authority by proxy) and confidence, without belittling or seeming arrogant. In addition, one needs to be clear and explicit about the goals of therapy (and of the therapist) because religious patients are frequently concerned that the therapist's goal is to reduce the person's religiosity or to challenge the basis of his or her religious beliefs. These concerns are first addressed indirectly by the clinician's therapeutic stance, and then in the formulation of the treatment rationale.

Therapeutic stance. The therapeutic stance in CBT for scrupulosity is, in most ways, similar to that in other forms of CBT. That is, the therapist is collaborative, uses Socratic questioning, and tries to see him- or herself as an ally of the patient against the patient's problem. Externalizing the disorder is useful, as well, but often more difficult at the beginning for many religious patients, as they may have trouble accepting that there is a distinction between their religious/spiritual lives and their OCD. On this issue, the therapist's stance is essential. By taking a clear and firm – though empathic – stance that scrupulosity is not true religious practice, the therapist helps the patient begin to distinguish religious from scrupulous beliefs. At the same time, the therapist avoids theological debates, as many religious patients are well versed in scripture and likely more knowledgeable about the areas about which they obsess than most individuals. When this is not the case, clear information can occasionally facilitate a major shift in beliefs; however, patients have often consulted with highly knowledgeable co-religionists and clergy before commencing ERP, to no avail.

Importantly, the religious patient may be skeptical about whether a nonfaith-based practitioner can treat them. This is due to a number of issues. First, there is a perception within many religious cultures that psychologists are anti-religious and see religion as a cause of pathology. This is particularly the case with OCD, both due to Freud's conceptualization (Freud, 1927) as well as a general cultural belief that religious ritual is almost a form of compulsive ritual. Thus, the therapist is explicit that the goal of therapy is to help the patient have a more fulfilling religious life. Inquiry into what that would mean for the patient, what his or her ideal religious life would be like, and what she or he thinks life would be like without OCD are good ways to explore these issues and demonstrate an openness and desire to help the patient live as she or he chooses. In fact, the therapist can reinforce this message and bolster its credibility by referring to research that most people with scrupulosity report that their symptoms interfere with their religious observance or relationship with God (Siev et al., 2011a). Similarly, for some patients, examining how they would describe their current relationship with God in comparison with their desired relationship can provide important cognitive and motivational information. Ultimately, many individuals want to derive from religious practice a sense of inner peace, connection with God, and fulfillment (and ultimately transcendence).

The therapist can also convey this therapeutic stance while simultaneously establishing a benchmark for normative and even admirable religious behavior by asking the patient to describe a religious figure she or he emulates. As with many OCD treatment strategies, one needs to be vigilant that the patient does not start to use this exercise as a mental ritual (e.g., comparing repeatedly to the religious figure in an effort to determine proper belief or behavior). Usually, useful strategies include limiting the frequency and duration of such comparisons and helping the patient to consider the issue flexibly (not every time the issue arises) and using different phrasing (that is, not by rote).

Ultimately, the therapist carefully infers and adapts to the scrupulous patient's needs and sensitivities while retaining the overarching goal of CBT for OCD: exposure to feared thoughts, response prevention, and work on metacognitive beliefs, especially related to thought–action fusion, responsibility, evaluations of threat, and tolerance of uncertainty. We find it useful to note to patients that their suffering from scrupulosity is not some kind of unconscious response to their ambivalence about religion or what religion represents, but rather reflects their core values which OCD "gloms onto" and attacks (Huppert & Siev, 2010; Huppert & Zlotnick, 2012). The implication is that the patient does not have an unconscious or latent desire to sin, just as the individual with obsessions about stabbing his child does not have a latent desire to do so. To the contrary, the patient cares so much about serving God properly that OCD opportunistically uses the inherent uncertainty about one's success to suggest that one is not doing so sufficiently. That is, the obsessions specifically target things most disturbing or concerning, not most secretly desired (e.g., Baer, 2002). As such, OCD can be described as bully, who says things just to be provocative. Often the most effective response is to agree with the bully or disengage, whatever one actually believes. That is, if the bully says, "You are stupid," you might simply respond, "That's right, I am really dumb." This disarms the bully, particularly if the person responding does so with the appearance of confidence and not fear. Thus, the scrupulous patient does not try to convince the OCD, as it were, that she or he truly does not desire to sin, but rather responds dispassionately with feigned (or even mock) acceptance or disengagement.

A few additional caveats arise when discussing acceptance of thoughts of sin with religious patients. First, most frequently, it is sufficient to discuss accepting the risk or possibility of sin rather than sin, per se. This may, in fact, generate even more anxiety because the patient's core fears are often about risk and possibility rather than certain sin, about which she or he may be more confident. Religious patients usually believe that engaging in acts with the purpose to sin is unacceptable. However, there are always conflicting values that require one to accept an elevated risk of sin of one kind in order to serve God properly in another way. Praying longer might come at the cost of helping one's spouse with the children or other religious obligations and opportunities. Attending a bible study class to discuss the Trinity may increase the possibility of committing the unpardonable sin with blasphemous thoughts against the Holy Ghost. Charitable work in a soup kitchen may increase the likelihood of causing others to eat food one accidentally made non-kosher. This means that accepting the risk of sin is different from accepting sin (although most religions also acknowledge that all people sin, there is a difference between accepting this fact and embracing sin). Second, by framing the acceptance of risking sin in the context of competing values within the patient's religious belief system, it is clear that one is not trying to prioritize secular or nonreligious beliefs over religious ones.

Note that the stance described in this section is highly respectful of the patient's religious beliefs, without any indication that the therapist shares those beliefs. In fact, the therapist adopts a value-neutral stance toward each religion. This allows a therapist of a different belief (or nonbelief) to engage effectively with the scrupulous patient. Sometimes there is benefit if the therapist is religious (even of a different religion), in terms of the patient feeling comfortable that the therapist will be respectful. However, there is also a risk that the patient may form certain expectations of the therapist's beliefs or behaviors that are inaccurate (especially when the patient is from a similar religious background).

Rationale/psychoeducation. Having a good understanding of the rationale for treatment is an essential ingredient in CBT for OCD (Abramowitz, Franklin, Zoellner, & Dibernardo, 2002). However, scientific language may not be the best method to help the patient understand and internalize the rationale. This is not to say that a psychobiobehavioral rationale cannot work with religious patients. In fact, some find the scientific rationale very persuasive. However, others may find a rationale expressed using metaphors and familiar language more convincing. For example, while therapists typically speak to patients about the goal of therapy as increasing functioning and quality of life, as previously mentioned, it can be meaningful to the scrupulous patient to state that one of the goals is to help him or her have a more fulfilling spiritual religious life and potentially feel closer to God. The notion is that scrupulosity interferes with "true" practice and belief, therefore making the patient feel more disconnected from co-religionists and God.

The therapist should also be sensitive to language issues that could raise skepticism and damage the alliance, but are also opportunities to improve the alliance and solidify shared goals, such as when speaking about the adaptive function of anxiety and communicating about treatment technique. Regarding the former, given that the function of anxiety is really the substantive matter, there is no therapeutic advantage to referencing evolution when discussing when and how anxiety is adaptive. One could even use religious language, such as asking the patient, "Why did God create the emotion of anxiety? How do you think it serves us as humans?" Regarding the latter, ERP is structured on the assumption that if one is pathologically avoidant of something, by practicing at the opposite extreme of (safe and acceptable) behavior, one learns to live comfortably in the middle. For example, one who is overconcerned about being impure for prayer and therefore washes excessively becomes comfortable with regular, hygiene for prayer by engaging in minimalist washing even after exposure to contaminants before prayer. This idea of overcorrection is echoed in many religious texts that discuss a version of the golden mean, such as those authored by Aquinas in Christianity, Maimonides in Judaism, and Al Ghazali in Islam. In the context of religious writings, for example, if a person is quick tempered and too easily upset or angered, she or he is advised to err to the opposite extreme by acting even more calm than desired. Ultimately, by overcorrecting, this opposite action results in the individual comfortably residing in the desired range vis-à-vis whatever target behavior, emotional response, or character trait. More generally, we recommend drawing on religious sources that are consistent with ERP when possible (e.g., see Besiroglu, Karaca, & Keskin, 2014, for Islamic sources; Ciarrocchi, 1995, for writings of Saint Ignatius Loyola and John Bunyan; and Greenberg & Shefler, 2008, for sources in the rabbinic literature).

An important issue that can arise in treating scrupulosity is the importance of thoughts (i.e., moral thought–action fusion). We do not suggest getting into lengthy discussions about whether thoughts can be immoral, which are normative beliefs in some religions, at least in principle. Rather, it is important to consider possible differences between intentional and unintentional thoughts, and between fantasies and thoughts that cause anxiety. Sometimes, it is helpful to emphasize the egodystonic nature of most scrupulous thoughts. Similarly, the patient should consider the religious acceptability of inducing otherwise discouraged thoughts for the purpose of treatment, when doing so is intended to improve one's spiritual and mental health, and will actually decrease the frequency of those same thoughts in the long run. These distinctions are often supported by clergy, who may suggest that unintentional or distressing thoughts can be distinguished from other fantasies, and may be accepted or even purposefully provoked.

Clergy attitudes and working with clergy. Data are limited about how clergy view OCD, but the general impression is that whereas most clergy have the ability to differentiate between OCD and normative religious practice, they vary in their attributions about the cause of the pathology. There is a more fundamentalist view that all pathology of the soul comes from insufficient piety and guilt (or from improper religious guidance, see Mowrer, 1963). Two recent studies suggest that clergy can indeed recognize scrupulosity, but vary in their treatment recommendations. In a study of Catholic priests, Hepworth, Simonds, and Marsh (2010) interviewed 11 priests to determine their understanding of scrupulosity, as well as their attitudes regarding treatment of scrupulous individuals who seek their help. They found that priests have a clear understanding that scrupulosity is in fact a religious manifestation of OCD and not a religious phenomenon, per se. Moreover, the priests reported feeling that they were not able to deal with such problems adequately, as their professional domain is spirituality not mental health. In a similar study, Horwitz (2013) interviewed 15 ultra-Orthodox rabbis in Israel regarding their views of scrupulosity. He also found that the rabbis were quick to identify scrupulosity as distinct from religious normative behavior such that the former was not a true expression of spirituality. They did not view scrupulous compulsions as admirable or positive. Slightly differently from the Catholic Priests, most rabbis believed that they had an important role in guiding the patient spiritually around the scrupulosity, while also acknowledging the potential helpful role of a mental health practitioner. In terms of cause, one rabbi described the causes of OCD as spiritual, while the rest suggested biological and psychological reasons. In a third study, Deacon, Vincent, and Zhang (2013) found that pastors in more conservative Lutheran denominations offered responses to a theoretical scrupulous parishioner that may increase fear of sin and encourage compulsive behavior. Overall, these studies suggests that clergy can often identify OCD in their religious parishioners, but may not have the tools to treat them or offer effective guidance.

Collaboration with clergy can be especially important. Clergy have knowledge and authority that most therapists do not have, and many scrupulous patients initially or simultaneously seek counsel or counseling from a religious authority, especially when these problems appear to be religious in nature (Huppert & Siev, 2010; Siev et al., 2011a). It is therefore necessary to avoid conflicting messages, as the therapist may unwittingly contradict religious authority, resulting in a loss of trust in the therapist by the patient, his or her family and community. It is our stance that it is best for the therapist to work directly with the patient's chosen clergy and not to "shop" for the most treatment-friendly religious figure. This is more respectful of the patient's values, and the patient typically already has a strong alliance and a baseline of trust with his or her chosen religious authority, whereas a member of the clergy selected by the therapist has less perceived credibility and may even appear to work more for the therapist than the patient. In consultations with religious authorities, the therapist's role is to explain the treatment rationale with the explicit goal of formulating a way to conduct treatment within the boundaries of religious requirements and proscriptions.

By conveying this message clearly, the therapist is able to explain that permissible and normative practice are not synonymous, and the goal is to push the boundaries of normative practice without either violating or being absolved of religious obligations. Therapists and even clergy sometimes suggest that patients abdicate those obligations during the course of treatment, and this is actually a common complaint of the religious patient, who does not seek exemption, desiring to fulfill religious obligations properly (and not be treated differently from others). Although ERP requires the patient to engage in non-normative but permissible behavior, we content that complete exemption from religious obligations is counterproductive because it does not allow the patient to learn to tolerate the possibility of performing religious acts imperfectly, the patient does not learn to cope with the feeling of uncertainty, and it removes responsibility and agency from the patient. In fact, absolution from standard religious obligations in the name of treatment can function as compulsive reassurance, in the sense that the patient cannot fail to fulfill an obligation from which she or he is altogether exempt.

Compulsive reassurance-seeking is common in scrupulosity, frequently in the form of repeated requests for information and clarification from clergy, as well as consultation and confession. Effective collaboration with clergy often includes a discussion of how to eliminate such reassurance-seeking, both in terms of guidelines from the clergy that allow the patient to cease compulsive consultation, as well as suggestions from the therapist to the clergy about how to refer the reassurance-seeking patient back to the therapist. However, when the religious authority considers the patient's question and recommends that the patient discuss the matter with the therapist, there is the potential risk of inadvertently providing implicit reassurance to the patient, who may infer that the question must not impact a true religious issue. Thus, sometimes it is best to guide the cleric to respond with statements such as, "I am sorry, but we have discussed this before and I cannot help you understand any further," or, "I am sorry, but I am not able to discuss this with you any longer. I am sorry this still plagues you, but you will need to manage the question without me." In this case, the cleric does not even suggest that the patient discuss the matter with the therapist.

In vivo exposure: how to violate OCD but not religious dictates. Although helping extricate religious figures from OCD to the extent that they enable or reinforce compulsions is an important aspect of successful treatment, this is balanced by the need to ensure that the ideas and exposures developed are truly within the framework of the patient's religious beliefs and practices. For example, how may the therapist expose a scrupulous patient to fears of cursing God, spitting on a church, or worshiping the devil? Direct exposure may represent an outright defiance of religious law. Religious authorities have the ability to assist in designing exposures that activate the patient's core fears without breaking religious code (Huppert et al., 2007).

As in most OCD treatment, one needs to tailor exposures to the patient's core beliefs (see Huppert & Zlotnick, 2012). Only after clarifying the context of the fears, the parameters and experiences that will trigger them, and the associated feared consequences can one determine the proper exposure hierarchy (which, in turn, also helps to clarify each of the aforementioned issues). In terms of determining the consequences of sin, it is important to consider that religious individuals may view sin as inherently bad and wrong regardless and independent of resultant consequences (e.g., even if they were not punished). At the same time, many individuals have received messages in their places of worship and in their religious education that sin leads to dire consequences. Allowing the patient to clarify his or her perceptions of those consequences both helps the patient feel understood and reveals the target exposure. The therapist probes with questions that encourage the patient to articulate what will happen if she or he sins. Will God punish him or her or his or her family (and if so, how?)? Will she or he end up causing the whole community to sin (*almost a form of contagion*)? And if the fear is that she or he will end up sinning, how will that happen? What are all of the steps that would necessarily have to occur to lead to the sin? All of this information is used to have the patient articulate the risk taken during in vivo exposures, and to construct effective imaginal exposures (see below). For example, during an in vivo exposure, the patient might say, "I am having this thought (or doing this act) knowing that I am risking sinning, and that by doing so, I risk that I will burn in Hell eternally." This type of explicit acknowledgment of the risk highlights the uncertainty that the patient is learning to tolerate, and precludes the possibility of subtle mental rituals that are designed to negate or downplay that uncertainty.

In a sense, any exposure to potential sin is inherently riskier than avoidance of the situation altogether. Therefore, when encouraging a religious patient to do in vivo exposures that elevate the risk of sin, one encounters a complicated, core issue at the interface between religion and OCD. That is, the individual is simultaneously motivated by both religion and OCD to avoid sin, and the patient needs to foster the former and violate the latter. This is where the issue of risk is essential. The therapist is explicit that the goal is not to engage in definitive sin. Rather, the patient uses others in their peer group as a benchmark of necessary and acceptable risks of sin, and deliberately risks sin by engaging in similar, normative behaviors. In contrast, the patient is not encouraged to sin definitively, or to say (inaccurately) that she or he is actually sinning when she or he is not (with the exception of acceptance-type statements in the face of a bully, as described above). Note that this is consistent with exposures for most types of obsessions, whether violent harm or sexual thoughts or obsessions about contamination or other catastrophes; the patient does not engage in acts that definitively cause the feared outcomes (e.g., stabbing a friend, molesting a child) or even cause an unacceptably elevated risk (e.g., injecting oneself with a contaminated needle), but rather practices normative behaviors that include an acceptable risk of the possibility of those feared outcomes. Even when exposures exceed normative behavior – in the treatment of scrupulosity and all other OCD manifestations – they are still constrained to behaviors someone without OCD *would* do if there were reason to, even if one does not do so under typical circumstances (e.g., touching the inside of a toilet to remove a fallen piece of expensive jewelry).

Devout patients may find difficult even approaching a risk of sin. In such situations, it is useful to discuss whether affirmative acts of serving God or avoidant acts to prevent sin are more important in most people's views of their religion. Is engaging in some positive act/commandment (e.g., helping others, praying, etc.) more important than avoiding the risk of a sin (e.g., risking harming poor people, or cursing God, etc.)? In addition, one can ask the patient to consider the roles of repentance and forgiveness of sin in religion, and under what circumstances inadvertent sinful acts are irreversible or unforgivable. Patients may distinguish, however, between inadvertent sin and sin that potentially results from intentional choices to risk sin, and it is often best to continue to emphasize the patient's choice between (a) striving to achieve good acts and a positive relationship with God by accepting a risk of sin, versus (b) excessive and distressing pursuit of absolute avoidance of one sin at the expense of other sins or missed opportunities for positive religious experiences.

Imaginal exposure: things that cannot be disconfirmed. Imaginal exposure is particularly indicated when OCD fears are difficult to confront or disconfirm in vivo, and it is helpful in leading patients to tolerate acceptable risks. In such cases, the goal of imaginal exposure is to develop very specific, patient-oriented scenarios that depict the patient engaging in relatively low-risk behaviors without ritualizing, but consistent with obsessional fears, cause extreme, negative consequences. For example, the therapist might create a scenario in which the patient refrains from cancelling a heretical intrusive thought with a reaffirmation of belief, opting for the goal of living a fulfilling religious life without OCD. The scenario would continue to unfold in the manner of the patient's specific obsessional fears. In this example, perhaps the patient's decision not to cancel his or her thought is seen as suspicious, the patient's religious leaders question his or her faith, and ultimately the community rejects him or her for being evil. The patient is ostracized, alone, and rejected by all, including family. The patient's existence feels meaningless and she or he lives out the rest of his or her life feeling disconnected from God. She or he dies and is judged to eternal damnation for not having repented for the one thought.

Fundamentally, a well-designed imaginal exposure that accurately reflects the patient's obsessional fears is an exercise in exposure to thoughts that trigger anxiety (just as in vivo exposures allow the patient to confront external stimuli that trigger anxiety). Conducted as such, imaginal exposure is an exposure to the feared consequence (which can never be tested in vivo), and also a means for cognitive work within the context of strong emotional responses (i.e., "hot" cognitions). Furthermore, when imagining the scenario, the patient may recognize efforts to avoid the possibility of inadvertent sin as excessive or inconsistent with religious beliefs, which may facilitate motivation to engage in response prevention.

The imaginal scenario should accurately reflect the obsessional fears. Elements that are unrealistically extreme or includes intentional sin may interfere with the ability of the patient to engage in the scenario (because it is too unrealistic), which prevents activation of the pathological fear (because it does not match the core fear), and thereby renders the exposure ineffective. Those elements also likely do not represent the patient's true core fears, which in many cases relate to uncertain risks and fears of not ritualizing, rather than extreme or intentional sin. Instead, the scenario should depict realistic behavior (engaging in typical behavior without compulsions, and incorporating risk-taking in service of fighting OCD) that results in an unlikely feared consequence. Although it should not be unrealistically extreme, imaginal exposure works well when the patient realizes that the likelihood of the feared consequence is much lower than originally thought and becomes more willing to tolerate that risk (e.g., with in vivo exposures). Therefore, the therapist is advised to construct scenarios that are expected to be recognized as unlikely, but which still reflect the patient's actual fears.

Prayer. Of all religious rituals, prayer is the likely most ubiquitous (particularly if one includes meditation). Thus, prayer is a common obsessional trigger (e.g., "Did I pray properly?") and can be used as a compulsive ritual (e.g., prayers to negate bad thoughts or avoid negative consequences, repetition of prayers) in scrupulosity. The notion of pathological prayer may be one of the most contentious issues in terms of distinguishing religiosity from scrupulosity for clergy and therapists. We have, on more than one occasion, had patients and their spiritual advisors question what authority the therapist has in discussing the nature and execution of prayer.

Prayer in the context of OCD is different from excessive prayer conducted by devout individuals who are striving to improve their spiritual lives (which can be normative in some circles, but is more likely to be compulsive in OCD; more on this below). First, being immersed in prayer more than the norm does not necessarily signify OCD. If one derives pleasure or a feeling of spirituality/transcendence without fear, and if the individual and important peers do not view the behavior as excessive, then the prayer is not pathological. Second, even if the prayer is excessive and/or fear driven, it can be driven by psychosis or bipolar disorder (often with grandiose intent, e.g., to be a saint), obsessive-compulsive personality disorder (feeling there is only one, perfect way to pray that is described by the religion as necessary rather than aspirational), or depression (via ruminative, brooding prayer, repeatedly beseeching God to end one's misery).

We first describe issues in identifying and treating obsessions related to prayer and then in addressing compulsions. OCD-related prayer obsessions can have many forms and core fears. Obsessions can include whether one prayed the proper words (e.g., saying all of the prescribed words), at the proper time, with the proper intent (intensity or meaning), with enough focus on God (and without focus on heretical thoughts, Satan, or any other figure), without forbidden content (e.g., sexual), in the appropriate direction (e.g., toward Mecca or Jerusalem), with sufficient purity (physical, such as uncontaminated with feces, or spiritual, such as having said confessional completely), and more. From a different perspective, obsessions about prayer can take the form of standard subtypes of OCD. That is, individuals can be concerned about contamination and therefore not want to pray, they can be concerned that if they do not pray properly, harm will come to others, they can be concerned with the order of prayer (or that they did not pray just right), and they can have intrusive thoughts of aggression or sex that can interfere with prayer. As with other symptoms of scrupulosity, this suggests that in scrupulosity, religion colors the OCD, which itself is manifest in the form of any general OCD symptom dimension. However, given religious dictates and proscriptions, some methods such as exposure to contamination or to harm thoughts are less feasible for the religious patient. Thus, approximations, such as allowing such thoughts to exist but not purposefully initiating them, or having such thoughts during "practice" prayers can be useful. In the case of fears that if one prays improperly then bad things will happen, one can have the patient pray minimally (here, permission from a religious authority can be helpful). For example, the patient might start with a single line of a prayer or pray quickly, without ritualizing afterward. A nonbelieving OCD therapist might view prayer as magical thinking or perhaps thought–action fusion – that is, as a manifestation of pathological thinking – and be tempted to suggest praying for things that clearly are futile (e.g., to turn into a pumpkin, to fly). Exercises such as these are essentially designed to suggest to the patient that prayer is just words, and are in principle not much different from other common CBT behavioral experiments in the context of other obsessional fears such as wishing harm upon passing vehicles or wishing that someone win the lottery. Nevertheless, we contend that it is counterproductive to dispute the efficacy of prayer. These types of "exposures" are more likely to elicit distrust and even distain from the patient, who may feel mocked or belittled. Moreover, many individuals without OCD believe that prayer has an effect, which is an indication that a belief in the utility of prayer is not obsessional. This attitude is similar to the idea that it is unnecessary and unhelpful to debate whether thoughts can ever have moral import with someone whose religious teachings assert that they do (see above).

Similarly, compulsive prayer can take many forms that may necessitate different intervention methods. Most commonly, we ask patients to pray for circumscribed amounts of time and the minimal way that peers do, until they have recovered. Prayers can be compulsive via praying very slowly, repeating prayers, praying at times that are not typical (usually to neutralize obsessions), or praying in a specific, idiosyncratic order. Response prevention is the main method in dealing with compulsions, but just as in other necessary acts (eating, drinking, breathing, etc.), for the religious patient, prayer is often seen as a necessary part of (spiritual) sustenance. This should not be challenged in principle, but instead the patient who uses prayer as a ritual limits prayer to the required minimum until the compulsive elements are effectively eliminated. Another common issue that arises in the treatment compulsive prayer relates to the boundaries of overcorrection. For example, if a patient prays excessively for the health of his or her children every time he or she sees red (the color of the devil), should he or she go to the opposite extreme and pray for his or her child to get sick and die? Praying for negative outcomes is often incompatible with the religious patient's beliefs, and there are reasonable alternatives. For example, instead of praying compulsively for the child's health, the patient can pray that God execute His will: "May whatever Your will dictates happen to my child, whether it be health or sickness, life or death." Whether this should be repeated in the same format (which can become compulsive) depends on the patient. Often, the patient can create differently worded statements that have a similar content, but include flexibility that decreases the likelihood of it turning into a compulsion.

Summary

Scrupulous OCD can manifest in many religious aspects of life. Although nonreligious individuals can also suffer from scrupulosity, many of the issues discussed in this chapter are more easily addressed with such patients. Given the high percentage of individuals who believe in a higher power throughout the world, it is important to learn to address such issues within various religious belief systems and cultural contexts. In this chapter, we discussed the phenomenology of scrupulosity, its diagnosis across cultures and religions, and the relationship between religion and OCD. We identified ERP as the fundamental treatment modality, and discussed how to address a number of unique challenges that arise in applying ERP for OCD to scrupulosity regarding (a) how to distinguish religion from OCD, (b) the therapeutic stance, (c) communicating the treatment rationale and psychoeducation, (d) involving and interacting effectively with clergy, (e and f) implementing in vivo and imaginal exposures, and (g) prayer. More generally, OCD is heterogeneous and therefore all effective treatments require careful consideration of each patient's idiosyncratic symptoms and fears. At its core, ERP for scrupulosity is the same as for other forms of OCD; the adaptations discussed in this chapter are intended to allow the therapist to implement ERP successfully with a symptom presentation many find particularly difficult to treat.

Acknowledgment

The authors thank Victoria Schlaudt for her assistance with preparing the manuscript.

References

Abramowitz, J. (2001). Treatment of scrupulous obsessions and compulsions using exposure and response prevention: a case report. *Cognitive and Behavioral Practice, 8,* 79–85. doi: 10.1016/S1077-7229(01)80046-8

Abramowitz, J. S., Deacon, B. J., Woods, C. M., & Tolin, D. F. (2004). Association between Protestant religiosity and obsessive-compulsive symptoms and cognitions. *Depression and Anxiety, 20,* 70–76. doi: 10.1002/da.20021.

Abramowitz, J. S., Franklin, M. E., Schwartz, S. A., & Furr, J. M. (2003). Symptom presentation and outcome of cognitive-behavioral therapy for obsessive-compulsive disorder. *Journal of Consulting and Clinical Psychology, 71,* 1049–1057. doi: 10.1037/0022-006X.71.6.1049.

Abramowitz, J. S., Franklin, M. E., Zoellner, L. A., & Dibernardo, C. L. (2002). Treatment compliance and outcome in obsessive-compulsive disorder. *Behavior Modification, 26,* 447–463. doi: 10.1177/0145445502026004001.

Abramowitz, J. S., Huppert, J. D., Cohen, A. B., Tolin, D. F., & Cahill, S. P. (2002). Religious obsessions and compulsions in a non-clinical sample: the Penn Inventory of Scrupulosity (PIOS). *Behaviour Research and Therapy, 40,* 825–838. doi: 10.1016/S0005-7967(01)00070-5.

Abramowitz, J. S., & Jacoby, R. J. (2014). Scrupulosity: A cognitive-behavioral analysis and implications for treatment. *Journal of Obsessive-Compulsive and Related Disorders, 3,* 140–149. doi: 10.1016/j.jocrd.2013.12.007

Alonso, P., Menchon, J. M., Pifarre, J., Mataix-Cols, D., Torres, L., Salgado, P., & Vallejo, J. (2001). Long-term follow-up and predictors of clinical outcome in obsessive-compulsive patients treated with serotonin reuptake inhibitors and behavioral therapy. *Journal of Clinical Psychiatry, 62,* 535–540. doi: 10.4088/JCP.v62n07a06.

Baer, L. (2002). *The imp of the mind: Exploring the silent epidemic of obsessive bad thoughts.* New York: Plume.

Besiroglu, L., Karaca, S., & Keskin, I. (2014). Scrupulosity and obsessive compulsive disorder: The cognitive perspective in Islamic sources. *Journal of Religion and Health, 53,* 3–12. doi: 10.1007/s10943-012-9588-7.

Bonchek, A. (2009). *Religious compulsions and fears: A guide to treatment.* Jerusalem: Feldheim.

Bonchek, A., & Greenberg, D. (2009). Compulsive prayer and its management. *Journal of Clinical Psychology, 65,* 396–405.

Ciarrocchi, J. W. (1995). *The doubting disease: Help for scrupulosity and religious compulsions.* New York: Paulist Press.

Deacon, B., & Nelson, E. A. (2008). On the nature and treatment of scrupulosity. *Pragmatic Case Studies in Psychotherapy, 4,* 39–53. doi: 10.14713/pcsp.v4i2.932.

Deacon, B. J., Vincent, A. M., & Zhang, A. R. (2013). Lutheran clergy members' responses to scrupulosity: The effects of moral thought-action fusion and liberal vs. conservative denomination. *Journal of Obsessive-Compulsive and Related Disorders, 2,* 71–77. doi: 10.1016/j.jocrd.2012.12.003.

Doron, G., & Kyrios, M. (2005). Obsessive compulsive disorder: A review of possible specific internal representations within a broader cognitive theory. *Clinical Psychology Review, 25,* 415–432. doi: 10.1016/j.cpr.2005.02.002.

Eisen, J. L., Sibrava, N. J., Boisseau, C. L., Mancebo, M. C., Stout, R. L., Pinto, A., & Rasmussen, S. A. (2013). Five-year course of obsessive-compulsive disorder: Predictors of remission and relapse. *Journal of Clinical Psychiatry, 74,* 233–239. doi: 10.4088/JCP.12m07657.

Fergus, T. A., & Rowatt, W. C. (2014a). Examining a purported association between attachment to God and scrupulosity. *Psychology of Religion and Spirituality, 6,* 230–236. doi: 10.1037/a0036345.

Fergus, T. A., & Rowatt, W. C. (2014b). Personal uncertainty strengthens associations between scrupulosity and both the moral appraisals of intrusive thoughts and beliefs that God is upset with sins. *Journal of Social and Clinical Psychology*, *33*, 51–74. doi: 10.1521/jscp.2014.33.1.51.

Fergus, T. A., & Valentiner, D. P. (2012). Terror management theory and scrupulosity: An experimental investigation. *Journal of Obsessive Compulsive and Related Disorders*, *1*, 104–111. doi: 10.1016/j.jocrd.2012.01.003.

Ferrão, Y., Shavitt, R., Bedin, N., Demathis, M., Carloslopes, A., Fontenelle, L., ... Miguel, E. (2006). Clinical features associated to refractory obsessive-compulsive disorder. *Journal of Affective Disorders*, *94*, 199–209. doi: 10.1016/j.jad.2006.04.019.

Foa, E. B., Hembree, E. A., Cahill, S. P., Rauch, S. A. M., Riggs, D. S., Feeny, N. C., & Yadin, E. (2005). Randomized trial of prolonged exposure for posttraumatic stress disorder with and without cognitive restructuring: Outcome at academic and community clinics. *Journal of Consulting and Clinical Psychology*, *73*, 953–964. doi: 10.1037/0022-006X.73.5.953.

Foa, E. B., & Kozak, M. J. (1995). DSM-IV field trial: Obsessive-compulsive disorder. *American Journal of Psychiatry*, *152*, 90–96.

Foa, E. B., Yadin, E., Lichner, T. K. (2012). *Exposure and response (ritual) prevention for obsessive-compulsive disorder*. New York: Oxford University Press.

Freud, S. (1927). *The future of an illusion* (trans. J. Starchey). New York: Norton.

Goodman, W. K., Price, L.H., Rasmussen, S. A., Mazure, C., Delgado, P., Heninger, G. R., & Charney, D. S. (1989). The Yale–Brown Obsessive Compulsive Scale – II: Validity. *Archives of General Psychiatry*, *46*, 1012. doi: 10.1001/archpsyc.1989.01810110054008.

Greenberg, D. (1984). Are religious compulsions religious or compulsive? A phenomenological study. *American Journal of Psychotherapy*, *38*, 524–532.

Greenberg, D., & Huppert, J. D. (2010). Scrupulosity: A unique subtype of obsessive-compulsive disorder. *Current Psychiatry Reports*, *12*, 282–289. doi: 10.1007/s11920-010-0127-5.

Greenberg, D., & Shefler, G. (2002). Obsessive compulsive disorder in ultra-orthodox Jewish patients: A comparison of religious and non-religious symptoms. *Psychology and Psychotherapy: Theory, Research and Practice*, *75*, 123–130. doi:10.1348/147608302169599.

Greenberg, D., & Shefler, G. (2008). Ultra-Orthodox rabbinic responses to religious obsessive compulsive disorder. *Israel Journal of Psychiatry*, *45*, 183–192.

Greenberg, D., & Witztum, E. (1994). The influence of cultural factors on obsessive compulsive disorder: Religious symptoms in a religious society. *Israel Journal of Psychiatry and Related Sciences*, *31*, 211–220.

Greenberg, D., Witztum, E., & Pisante, J. (1987). Scrupulosity: Religious attitudes and clinical presentations. *British Journal of Medical Psychology*, *60*, 29–37. doi: 10.1111/j.2044-8341.1987.tb02714.x.

Hermesh, H., Masser-Kavitzky, R., & Gross-Isseroff, R. (2003). Obsessive-compulsive disorder and Jewish religiosity. *Journal of Nervous and Mental Disease*, *191*, 201–203. doi: 10.1097/01.NMD.0000055083.60919.09.

Hepworth, M., Simonds, L. M., & Marsh, R. (2010). Catholic priests' conceptualisation of scrupulosity: A grounded theory analysis. *Mental Health, Religion & Culture*, *13*, 1–16. doi: 10.1080/13674670903092177.

Horwath, E., & Weissman, M. M. (2000). The epidemiology and cross-national presentation of obsessive-compulsive disorder. *Psychiatric Clinics of North America*, *23*, 493–507. doi: 10.1016/S0193-953X(05)70176-3.

Horwitz, B. (2013). *A qualitative analysis of contemporary rabbinical perspectives on scrupulosity*. (Unpublished Master of Psychology thesis). Hebrew University, Jerusalem, Israel.

Huppert, J. D., & Fradkin, I. (2016). Validation of the Penn Inventory of Scrupulosity (PIOS) in scrupulous and nonscrupulous patients: Revision of factor structure and psychometrics. *Psychological Assessment*, *28*(6), 639–650. doi: 10.1037/pas0000203.

Huppert, J. D., & Siev, J. (2010). Treating scrupulosity in religious individuals using cognitive-behavioral therapy. *Cognitive and Behavioral Practice, 17*, 382–392. doi: 10.1016/j.cbpra.2009.07.003.

Huppert, J. D., Siev, J., & Kushner, E. S. (2007). When religion and obsessive-compulsive disorder collide: Treating scrupulosity in ultra-orthodox Jews. *Journal of Clinical Psychology, 63*, 925–941. doi: 10.1002/jclp.20404.

Huppert, J. D., & Zlotnick, E. (2012). Core fears, values, and obsessive-compulsive disorder: A preliminary clinical–theoretical outlook. *Psicoterapia Cognitive e Comporamentale, 18*, 91–102.

Khanna, S., & Channabasavanna, S. M. (1988). Phenomenology of obsessions in obsessive-compulsive neurosis. *Psychopathology, 21*, 12–18. doi: 10.1159/000284534.

March, J. S., Frances, A., Kahn, D. A., & Carpenter, D. (1997). The expert consensus guideline series: Treatment of obsessive-compulsive disorder. *Journal of Clinical Psychiatry, 58*, 1–72.

Mataix-Cols, D., Marks, I. M., Greist, J. H., Kobak, K. A., & Baer, L. (2002). Obsessive-compulsive symptom dimensions as predictors of compliance with and response to behaviour therapy: Results from a controlled trial. *Psychotherapy and Psychosomatics, 71*, 255–262. doi: 10.1159/000064812.

Miller, C. H., & Hedges, D. W. (2008). Scrupulosity disorder: An overview and introductory analysis. *Journal of Anxiety Disorders, 22*, 1042–1058. doi: 10.1016/j.janxdis.2007.11.004.

Mowrer, O. H. (1963). Transference and scrupulosity. *Journal of Religion and Health, 2*, 313–343.

National Institute for Health and Clinical Excellence. (2006). *Obsessive-compulsive disorder: Core interventions in the treatment of obsessive-compulsive disorder and body dysmorphic disorder*. NICE clinical guideline 31. Leicester: British Psychological Society.

Okasha, A., Saad, A., Khalil, A. H., El-Dawla, A. S., & Yehia, N. (1994). Phenomenology of obsessive-compulsive disorder: A transcultural study. *Comprehensive Psychiatry, 35*, 191–197. doi: 10.1016/0010-440X(94)90191-0.

Purdon, C., & Clark, D. A. (2005). *Overcoming obsessive thoughts: How to gain control of your OCD*. Oakland, CA: New Harbinger.

Pirutinsky, S., Siev, J., & Rosmarin, D. H. (2015). Scrupulosity and implicit and explicit beliefs about God. *Journal of Obsessive-Compulsive and Related Disorders, 6*, 33–38. doi: 10.1016/j.jocrd.2015.05.002.

Rasmussen, S. A., & Tsuang, M. T. (1986). Clinical characteristics and family history in DSM-III obsessive- compulsive disorder. *American Journal of Psychiatry, 143*, 317–322. doi: 10.1176/ajp.143.3.317.

Rosmarin, D. H., Pirutinsky, S., & Siev, J. (2010). Recognition of scrupulosity and non-religious OCD by orthodox and non-orthodox Jews. *Journal of Social and Clinical Psychology, 29*, 930–944. doi: 10.1521/jscp.2010.29.8.930.

Rufer, M., Grothusen, A., Maß, R., Peter, H., & Hand, I. (2005). Temporal stability of symptom dimensions in adult patients with obsessive-compulsive disorder. *Journal of Affective Disorders, 88*, 99–102. doi: 10.1016/j.jad.2005.06.003.

Sackett, D. L., Rosenberg, W. M. C., Gray, J. A. M., Haynes, R. B., & Richardson, W. S. (1996). Evidence-based medicine: What it is and what it isn't. *British Medical Journal, 312*, 169–171.

Sica, C., Novara, C., & Sanavio, E. (2002). Religiousness and obsessive-compulsive cognitions and symptoms in an Italian population. *Behaviour Research and Therapy, 40*, 813–823. doi: 10.1016/S0005-7967(01)00120-6.

Siev, J., Baer, L., & Minichiello, W. E. (2011a). Obsessive-compulsive disorder with predominantly scrupulous symptoms: Clinical and religious characteristics. *Journal of Clinical Psychology, 67*, 1188–1196. doi: 10.1002/jclp.20843.

Siev, J., & Huppert, J. D. (2016). Treatment of scrupulosity-related obsessive-compulsive disorder. In E. A. Storch, & A. B. Lewin (Eds.), *Clinical handbook of obsessive-compulsive and related disorders: A case-based approach to treating pediatric and adult populations* (pp. 39–54). New York: Springer.

Siev, J., Steketee, G., Fama, J. M., & Wilhelm, S. (2011b). Cognitive and clinical characteristics of sexual and religious obsessions. *Journal of Cognitive Psychotherapy, 25,* 167–176. doi: 10.1891/0889-8391.25.3.167.

Steketee, G., Quay, S., & White, K. (1991). Religion and guilt in OCD patients. *Journal of Anxiety Disorders, 5,* 359–367. doi: 10.1016/0887-6185(91)90035-R.

Tolin, D. F., Abramowitz, J. S., Kozak, M. J., & Foa, E. B. (2001). Fixity of belief, perceptual aberration, and magical ideation in obsessive-compulsive disorder patients. *Journal of Anxiety Disorders, 15,* 501–510. doi: 10.1016/S0887-6185(01)00078-0.

Weissman, M. M., Bland, R. C., Canino, G. J., Greenwald, S., Hwu, H. G., Lee, C. K., ... Wickramaratne, P. J. (1994). The cross-national epidemiology of obsessive compulsive disorder. *The Cross National Collaborative Group. Journal of Clinical Psychiatry, 55,* S5–S10.

Zohar, A. H., Goldman, E., Calamary, R., & Mashiah, M. (2005). Religiosity and obsessive-compulsive behavior in Israeli Jews. *Behaviour Research and Therapy, 43,* 857–868. doi: 10.1016/j.brat.2004.06.009.

30

Assessment and Treatment of Relationship-Related OCD Symptoms (ROCD)
A Modular Approach
Guy Doron and Danny Derby

Lilly,[1] a 30-year-old woman, in her third year of medical residency, living with her current partner for the last year, seeks treatment for what she calls ROCD. She describes her problem: "I've been in a relationship for the last two years and my partner (Rob) has recently asked me to marry him. I am not sure about what to do. I love Rob; I think he is great. However, I imagined being in love differently. I thought that I would be thinking about my partner all the time; I would be euphoric, 'living in the clouds.' It is not at all like that. Every time I notice that I don't think of him constantly or that I am irritated, stressed or uneasy in his company, I start doubting whether he is the right one for me and whether I am in the right relationship. Recently, I've also begun thinking that he may not be interesting or intelligent enough for me. I know it is not true. Rob has a PhD; he is witty and easy going, but I can't stop thinking about whether this is the right relationship for me. I check what I feel for him all the time, how I feel when I am with him, whether he is smart enough. I know I love him, but these doubts haunt me. I find it hard to concentrate on my studies and it really affects my mood."

Lilly suffers from what is commonly referred to as Relationship Obsessive Compulsive Disorder (ROCD): obsessive-compulsive symptoms that center on close or intimate relationships, an OCD presentation that has been receiving increasing research and clinical attention (Doron, Derby, Szepsenwol, & Talmor, 2012a, 2012b; Doron, Derby, & Szepsenwol, 2014a). Relationship obsessions may occur in various types of close relationships, such as parent–child, relationship with a supervisor, and even relationship with one's God. Current research, however, has mainly focused on ROCD in the context of romantic relationships. In this chapter, we therefore refer to ROCD within romantic relationships.

---

[1] Lilly's details and characteristics are fictional, and dialogues are representative examples of sessions with different clients.

The Wiley Handbook of Obsessive Compulsive Disorders, Volume I, First Edition.
Edited by Jonathan S. Abramowitz, Dean McKay, and Eric A. Storch.
© 2017 John Wiley & Sons Ltd. Published 2017 by John Wiley & Sons Ltd.

One common presentation of ROCD involves doubts and preoccupations centered on the perceived suitability of the relationship itself (e.g., the strength of a person's feelings toward his or her partner, the "rightness" of the relationship), and on the perceived nature of one's partner's feelings towards oneself. This presentation has been referred to as *relationship-centered* OC symptoms (Doron et al., 2012a). Relationship obsessive-compulsive disorder may also involve disabling preoccupation with perceived deficits of the relationship partner (e.g., not being intelligent enough). Such symptoms have been referred to as *partner-focused* OC symptoms (Doron et al., 2012b). Although similar in some ways to what has been referred to in the literature as Body Dysmorphic Disorder by Proxy (i.e., obsessional focus on perceived physical flaws in others) (see Greenberg et al., 2013; Josephson & Hollander, 1997), partner-focused OC symptoms refer to obsessional preoccupation with a wider variety of the partner's "flawed" characteristics (e.g., morality, sociability, success) (Doron et al., 2014a).

ROCD symptoms have been linked with significant personal (e.g., mood, anxiety, other OCD symptoms) (Doron et al., 2012a, 2012b) and dyadic difficulties (e.g., relationship and sexual dissatisfaction) (Doron et al., 2012a, 2012b; Doron, Mizrahi, Szepsenwol, & Derby, 2014b). For instance, results from a recent study comparing OCD, ROCD, and community controls indicated similar levels of interference in functioning, distress, resistance attempts, and degree of perceived control in both clinical groups (Doron, Derby, Szepsenwol, Nahaloni, & Moulding, 2016).

ROCD-related intrusions often come in the form of thoughts such as "Is he the right one?" or "She is not beautiful," and images such as visualization of the face of the relationship partner or of an awkward moment associated with the partner. ROCD intrusions can also occur in the form of urges; for instance, the urge to leave one's current partner. Such intrusions are generally egodystonic, as they contradict the individual's personal values (e.g., "appearance should not be important in selecting a relationship partner") and/or subjective experience of the relationship (e.g., "I know I love her, but I can't stop questioning my feelings"). Hence, they are perceived as unacceptable and unwanted, and often bring about feelings of guilt and shame regarding their occurrence and/or content.

ROCD may also involve a wide range of compulsive behaviors and other maladaptive responses (see Table 30.1). Examples may include reassurance-seeking, repeated checking of one's own feelings, comparisons of one's partner's characteristics with those of other potential partners, and avoidance behaviors. Neutralizing behaviors may include visualizing being happy together and sustaining a positive thought about the partner. These compulsive behaviors are aimed at alleviating the significant distress caused by the unwanted intrusions (Doron et al., 2014a).

Development and Maintenance Mechanisms in ROCD

In this section, we present a summary of our ROCD model and supporting research (for a more extensive review, see Doron et al., 2014a). Cognitive-behavioral theories of OCD assert that most individuals experience a range of intrusive doubts, thoughts, urges, and images (Rachman & de Silva, 1978; Radomsky et al., 2014). In OCD and related disorders, the misappraisal and mismanagement of such intrusions lead to their escalation into obsessions (OCCWG, 2005; Storch, Abramowitz, & Goodman,

Table 30.1 Examples of ROCD related compulsions and maladaptive responses

Compulsions and maladaptive responses	Examples
Checking	Looking for information about relationships or about partner qualities on the Internet/Internet forum (e.g., "I am not sure about my feelings"; "not sure my partner is smart enough") or testing of the partner's behaviors (e.g., Do I think about my partner enough? Does my partner answer questions intelligently? Does my partner react properly in social situations?).
Monitoring (internal states)	Monitoring for current feelings (e.g., What am I feeling right now? Am I attracted to my partner?), their strength and their extent (e.g., Is this feeling "right" or "strong" enough?).
Neutralizing	Holding the opposite thought in mind, recalling situations where expectations were met, elaborating and reanalyzing the potential negative consequences of making the wrong decision (catastrophic scripts).
Comparison	Comparing qualities of the partner to other potential partners (e.g., colleagues, partners of her friends, acquaintances, or an internal image of ideal partner) or feelings toward past partners.
Reassurance	Consulting with friends, family, therapists, and even fortune tellers and psychics.
Self-criticism	Degrading self-talk (e.g., "I am selfish," "I am unappreciative," "I am stupid for thinking like this").
Avoidance	Avoiding social situations (e.g., meeting with certain friends) or particular leisure activities (e.g., going to romantic movies, watching romantic comedies on television).

2008). Consistent with this, Doron and Szepsenwol (2015) have suggested several mechanisms that perpetuate a vicious cycle of increased attention and reactivity to relationship-related concerns, the mismanagement of such intrusions and their escalation into relationship-related obsessions. These include particular self-vulnerabilities, OCD-related, and relationship-related unhelpful beliefs, attachment insecurities, compulsive behaviors, and dysfunctional commitment processes.

Self-vulnerabilities in ROCD

According to Doron and Kyrios (2005), pre-existing vulnerabilities in specific self-domains such as morality increase attention and vigilance to events related to these domains. Individuals whose self-esteem is highly dependent upon the relationship domain, for instance, may be hypervigilant to any slight relationship concern (e.g., feeling of boredom) as it has significant implications for their own feelings of worth (Doron, Szepsenwol, Karp, & Gal, 2013). Similarly, individuals who perceive their partner's deficiencies or flaws as reflecting on their own worth (i.e., partner–value contingent self-worth) are expected to be more sensitive to thoughts or events pertaining to their partner's qualities and characteristics (Doron et al., 2014a).

Consistent with this, recent findings indicate that self-esteem which is highly dependent on the relational domain (i.e., relationship contingent self-esteem) and attachment anxiety jointly contribute (i.e., double-relationship vulnerability) to increased ROCD behavioral tendencies (Doron et al., 2013). Likewise, self-esteem levels in individuals with high partner-focused obsessions have been found to be more susceptible to thoughts threatening positive views of their partner (e.g., she or he is not "as good" as others), relative to individuals with low partner-focused symptoms (Doron & Szepsenwol, 2015). Thus, particular self-sensitivities may increase attention and vigilance toward unwanted relationship-related intrusions thereby perpetuating the ROCD cycle.

Maladaptive Beliefs in ROCD

In OCD-related disorders, maladaptive beliefs, such as intolerance of uncertainty, importance of thoughts and their control, and inflated responsibility, increase the likelihood of catastrophic appraisals of intrusions (OCCWG, 2005; Storch et al., 2008). In ROCD, such maladaptive beliefs may play a similar role. For instance, attributing importance to thoughts and their control may increase unhelpful interpretations of the occurrence of commonly occurring relationship doubts. Similarly, difficulty with uncertainty may increase distress and maladaptive management of inherently elusive internal states such as love and passion. Indeed, findings suggest that ROCD symptoms are associated with OC-related beliefs in clinical and nonclinical samples (Doron et al., 2012a, 2012b; Doron et al., 2014a).

Beliefs regarding the potential negative consequences of relationships and unrealistic perceptions regarding the relationship experience may be particularly relevant to the development and maintenance of relational OCD. For instance, beliefs regarding the harmfulness of staying in a relationship one has doubts about or acute fears of discontinuing an existing relationship may provoke relationship-related "catastrophic scripts." Such scripts often include fears of being forever trapped in an unsatisfying and distressing relationship that one was not initially sure about. Other scripts include fears of missing "The One" and regretting it forever.

Extreme romantic beliefs including unrealistic perceptions of what love should be, feel and look like may also contribute to the misinterpretation of relationship events. ROCD clients often describe beliefs as, for example, "If I am not euphoric when I am with her, it is not true love" or "If I do not think about her all the time, she is not the one." Such beliefs, particularly when coinciding with a pre-existing fear of experiencing regret (e.g., "The feeling after making a wrong decision is intolerable for me") or fear of future regret (i.e., "I won't be able to cope with the thought that I have made a wrong decision"), frequently increase distress following relationship events pertaining to partner or relationship suitability.

Consistent with these suggestions, ROCD symptoms have been linked with relationship-related maladaptive beliefs. For instance, in a recent study using the Relationship Catastrophization Scale (RECATS) (Doron et al., 2014a), ROCD clients showed higher levels of relationship maladaptive beliefs than OCD clients and community controls (Doron et al., 2014a). Initial findings from our ongoing research using our Extreme Love Belief Scale (EXL) and Fear of Regret Scale (FOR) suggest increased ROCD symptoms are associated with higher endorsement of such beliefs.

Attachment Insecurities and ROCD

According to Doron, Sar-El, and Mikulincer (2012), for most people, the distress caused by maladaptive interpretation of intrusions results in the activation of distress-regulation strategies that restore emotional calmness. In ROCD, however, attachment insecurity, particularly attachment anxiety, has been suggested to hinder such adaptive emotional regulations strategies (Doron et al., 2013). According to attachment theory (Bowlby, 1973; Mikulincer & Shaver, 2007), interpersonal interactions with protective others ("attachment figures") early in life are internalized in the form of mental representations of self and others ("internal working models"). Interactions with attachment figures that are available and supportive in times of need foster the development of both a sense of attachment security and positive internal working models of self and others. Attachment security is undermined, however, when attachment figures are rejecting or unavailable in times of need, leading to the formation of negative representations of self and others (Mikulincer & Shaver, 2007).

Attachment orientations can be organized around two orthogonal dimensions, representing the two insecure attachment patterns of anxiety and avoidance (Brennan, Clark, & Shaver, 1998; reviewed by Mikulincer & Shaver, 2007). The first dimension, attachment anxiety, reflects the degree to which an individual worries that a significant other will not be available or adequately responsive in times of need, and the extent to which the individual adopts "hyperactivating" attachment strategies (i.e., insistent attempts to obtain care, support, and love from relationship partners) as a means of regulating distress and coping with threats and stressors. The second dimension, attachment avoidance, reflects the extent to which a person distrusts a relationship partner's good will and strives to maintain autonomy and emotional distance from him or her. An avoidantly attached individual relies on "deactivating" strategies, such as denial of attachment needs and suppression of attachment-related thoughts and emotions. Individuals who score low on both dimensions are said to hold a stable sense of attachment security (Mikulincer & Shaver, 2007).

According to Doron and colleagues (2014a), anxiously attached individuals' hypervigilance toward real or imagined relationship threats may make them especially vulnerable to intrusive thoughts that challenge self-perceptions in the relational domain. Moreover, their reliance on hyperactivating strategies may predispose such individuals to compulsive reassurance-seeking and checking behaviors, particularly in the context of intimate relationships. Further, anxiously attached individuals tend to react to such negative relationship experiences with the activation of maladaptive beliefs and hyperactivating attachment-relevant fears (Mikulincer & Shaver, 2003).

Indeed, previous findings have linked attachment insecurities with maladaptive beliefs and ROCD symptoms (Doron et al., 2012a, 2012b). For instance, subtle hints of incompetence in the relational self-domain (i.e., mildly negative feedback regarding the capacity to maintain long-term intimate relationships) were found to lead to increased ROCD tendencies mainly among individuals high in both attachment anxiety and relationship-contingent self-worth (Doron et al., 2013).

Compulsive Behaviors and ROCD Symptoms

Like in other OCD presentations, compulsive behaviors play a curial role in the maintenance of ROCD symptoms. ROCD-related compulsive behaviors include a wide variety of strategies aimed to reduce distress following the negative interpretations of relationship-related intrusions. These may include self-criticism (e.g., I am stupid to think like that, so the thought is not important), increased monitoring of internal states (e.g., scanning the body for feelings), reassurance-seeking behaviors (e.g., seeking reassurance that the relationship is going right), comparisons (e.g., Are we as happy as they are?) and neutralizing (e.g., recalling positive experiences with the partner). Importantly, such strategies paradoxically increase pre-existing vulnerabilities, maintain maladaptive beliefs and self-perpetuate. For instance, critical self-talk may increase self-vulnerabilities by reducing feelings of self-worth and self-confidence. Repeated recollection of positive relational situations or feelings (i.e., neutralizing) may prevent the assimilation of new information regarding one's ability to cope with uncertainty or regret. Compulsive monitoring of internal states is likely to self-perpetuate by decreasing accessibility to such states. Thus, identification and reduction of compulsive behaviors is crucial for successful therapeutic interventions.

Relational Commitment and ROCD

According to Rusbult, Martz, and Agnew (1998) one's intention to preserve an existing relationship (i.e., commitment) is highly influenced by relationship satisfaction, the perceived quality of potential alternatives, and one's investment in the current relationship. These three commitment components, however, significantly impact, and are impacted by ROCD symptoms. ROCD doubts, for instance, often reduce relational satisfaction. Lower relational satisfaction, however, may also increase relationship doubts. Indeed, ROCD symptoms have been linked with lower relationship satisfaction (Doron et al., 2012a, 2012b).

ROCD: Assessment and Treatment

Often clients and therapists are unaware of ROCD and related phenomena, and tend to mistake ROCD symptoms for "life dilemmas" or dyadic difficulties. Conversely, worries and doubts regarding relationships are common, particularly during relationship conflict, and may indeed reflect problematic couple interactions. Further, ROCD-like behaviors may occur during the normal course of a developing relationship, mainly during the flirting and dating stages or prior to relational commitment. Diagnosing ROCD, therefore, may be a complicated endeavor.

Like other OCD symptoms, relationship-related OC symptoms require psychological intervention when causing significant distress and when incapacitating. Relational obsessions tend to begin in the early stages of a relationship and exacerbate as the relationship progresses or reaches decision points (e.g., cohabitation, marriage). Clinicians should keep in mind that such relationship obsessions persist regardless of relationship conflict. When suspecting ROCD, initial evaluation should include a clinical interview to ascertain the diagnosis of OCD and coexisting disorders or medical conditions.

A thorough history would include the presenting problem(s), background of the problem(s), and personal history, with specific emphasis on relational history, family history, and family environment. It is of the utmost importance to gain a clear understanding of the nature, pattern, and duration of the client's symptoms within the current relationship context and in previous relationships. Therapists should collect detailed information about triggers of obsessions, their frequency and duration, the expected feared outcome or worry about the obsessions, and the responses to these intrusions. Responses include emotions (e.g., anxiety, guilt), overt compulsions (e.g., checking, comparing, reassurance-seeking), covert compulsions (e.g., thought suppression, monitoring of internal states, self-reassurance), and avoidance or safety behaviors.

To ascertain diagnosis of OCD and/or related conditions, it is strongly recommended to use structured interviews, such as the Mini International Neuropsychiatric Interview (MINI) (Sheehan et al., 1998) or the SCID (First, Spitzer, Gibbon, & Williams, 2012). Additional instruments should be used to quantify OCD symptoms (e.g., Obsessive-Compulsive Inventory-Revised [Foa et al., 2002]; Yale–Brown Obsessive Compulsive Scale [Goodman et al., 1989]), mood (depression, anxiety; Depression, Anxiety and Stress Scale [Lovibond & Lovibond, 1995]), body dysmorphic symptoms (e.g., DCQ [Oosthuizen, Lambert, & Castle, 1998]), and other symptoms identified in the clinical interview.

In the following sections of this chapter, we suggest assessment and intervention procedures that follow the theoretical model presented earlier. We use Lilly's case to exemplify these procedures. Importantly, each client shows different patterns of vulnerability and maintenance factors. The aim of the initial assessment, therefore, is to provide idiosyncratic case conceptualization that will allow a modular client-tailored treatment interventions focused on client-specific susceptibilities (see Table 30.2, for suggested assessment tools of ROCD).

The proposed intervention for ROCD follows cognitive behavioral therapy for OCD. Treatment includes assessment and information gathering, psychoeducation and case formulation, identification, and challenge of core ROCD-maintaining mechanisms and relapse prevention. We used cognitive-behavioral technics such as cognitive reconstruction, behavioral experiments and exposure and response prevention (ERP), as well as experiential interventions such as imagery rescripting to challenge dysfunctional self-perceptions, maladaptive beliefs, attachment-related fears, and commitment-related behaviors.

Psychoeducation and Case Formulation

The psychoeducation and case formulation component sets the tone of treatment and covers the cognitive model of ROCD with client-specific hypothesized maintenance mechanisms. It is important to provide the client with the rationale for the therapeutic process and discuss the course of therapy. In Lilly's case, following the clinical interview, the therapist summarized her reasons for attending therapy, and discussed the course of therapy. Lilly was haunted by fears relating to her relationship. She was unable to decide what was to be done? Was she the problem? Did her difficulties reflect "real" issues relating to the partner or to the relationship? She spent over three hours per day thinking about her relationship decisions. She also described a variety of behaviors she performed in response to these doubts (e.g., reassurance-seeking, checking information on the web).

Further probing led Lilly to realize, however, that the way she was trying to resolve her problem (i.e., repetitive thinking and related behaviors) may not have been very

Table 30.2 Suggested tools for assessment of ROCD symptoms and related phenomena*

Domain	Questionnaire	Item examples
Symptoms Relationship-centered	Relationship Obsessive-Compulsive Inventory (ROCI) (Doron et al., 2012a).	"I check and recheck whether my relationship feels 'right.'"
Partner-focused	Partner-related Obsessive-Compulsive Symptoms Inventory (PROCSI) (Doron et al., 2012b).	"When I am with my partner I find it hard to ignore her physical flaws."
Self Relationship contingencies	Relationship contingent self-esteem (RCSW) (Knee et al., 2008).	"My feelings of self-worth are based on how well things are going in my relationship."
Partner value contingency**	Partner-value contingent self-esteem (PVCSW).	"When others perceive my partner negatively, I feel like I am perceived in the same way."
Beliefs Catastrophic relationship beliefs	Relationship Catastrophization Scale (RECATS) (Doron et al., 2014b).	"For me, being in an imperfect relationship is like betraying myself."
Extreme love beliefs**	Extreme Love Beliefs scale (EXL).	"If the relationship is not completely harmonious, it is unlikely to be 'true love.'"
Fear of regret**	Fear of anticipated regret (FOR)	"I avoid decisions because I fear the feelings that may follow."
Attachment insecurities	Experience of close relationships (ECR) (Brennan et al., 1998)	"I find that my partners don't want to get as close as I would like."
Commitment	The investment model scale (Rusbult et al., 1998)	"I want our relationship to last for a very long time."

* See at: http://rocd.net/helpful-measures, for full questionnaires.
** Currently undergoing psychometric validation.

useful. On the contrary, over time she had become increasingly preoccupied, confused, distressed, and anxious. Discussing her troubled state and the impact it had on her ability to reach an informed conclusion, Lilly agreed to postpone her decision regarding the relationship for six months or until the obsessions were sufficiently reduced. The therapist and Lilly agreed that just as a thick fog tends to diminish our ability to see afar, obsessional thinking decreases our capacity to judge our relational experience.

Lilly did not want her partner to be involved in the therapy process. In other cases, however, one should consider involving the partner in the therapeutic process. In such cases, the partner's symptom accommodation should be assessed, ROCD psychoeducation should be provided, and strategies for reducing dyadic influences suggested.

Symptom Evaluation and Monitoring

Assessing the severity and focus of ROCD symptoms is important for the formulation of client-specific interventions. Monitoring of obsessions and compulsions also assist the client in managing the reduction of compulsions and avoidance behaviors. In her initial assessment session, Lilly described being distressed by obsessional thoughts regarding the relationship and her partner. The therapist used the Relationship Obsessive Compulsive Inventory (ROCI) (Doron et al., 2012a) to assess her levels of relationship-centered symptoms. The ROCI is used to evaluate individuals' ROCD symptoms in three dimensions: one's feelings toward one's partner, the "rightness" of the relationship, and the perceived nature of the partner's feelings toward oneself. Indeed, Lilly showed elevated scores on items such as "I continuously doubt my love for my partner" and "I check and recheck whether my relationship feels 'right.'" Lilly's relationship-centered symptoms seemed to be focused on her feelings toward her partner and the rightness of the relationship, rather than on her partner's feelings toward her.

The therapist then asked Lilly to complete the Partner-Related Obsessive-Compulsive Symptoms Inventory (PROCSI) (Doron et al., 2012b). The PROCSI was designed to measure obsessions (i.e., preoccupations and doubts) and neutralizing behaviors (i.e., checking) focused on the perceived flaws of one's relationship partner in six character domains: physical appearance, sociability, morality, emotional stability, intelligence, and competence. Lilly's strong adherence to items such as "I am constantly questioning whether my partner is deep and intelligent enough" echoed her severe preoccupation with her partner's intelligence and complexity.

Self-monitoring sheets were then used to identify Lilly's triggers and compulsive behaviors (see Table 30.1, for examples of ROCD maladaptive behaviors). Lilly's triggers were numerous. Some triggers she tried to avoid (e.g., meeting with certain friends, going to romantic movies, watching romantic comedies on television). It was harder for her to deal with other triggers such doubts "popping" into her head. Lilly described monitoring her feelings and attraction toward her partner numerous times a day. She also observed how "witty" he was in the company of friends, and compared his reactions to others (to assess his "depth"). Lilly's compulsive behaviors included sitting for hours, searching on Google for information such as "what to do when your partner is not smart enough" or "how do you know when your partner is right one," and lengthy participation on Internet-based relationship forums. She asked her friends for reassurance regarding the "normality" of her worries and the qualities of her partner.

Although she now realized that her response to triggers (e.g., monitoring, comparing, searching on the web) might not be useful in the long term, she still felt somewhat reluctant to cease performing them. The therapist, therefore, suggested a behavioral experiment – Lilly was to increase her web searching for information about relationships every second day (i.e., search for at least an hour). On the other days, she was to decrease these behaviors. During the week of the experiment, Lilly had to monitor her overall well-being, intensity of doubts, clarity of emotions, and overall satisfaction with the relationship. The following session, Lilly reported becoming increasingly aware of the negative effects of her searching on the web. Searching actually made her feel worse, caused her to doubt herself more, and amplified her confusion. Based on this understanding, Lilly and the therapist agreed on identifying additional unhelpful responses (e.g., self-reassurance) and using similar behavioral experiments to evaluate them. They would then think of ways to reduce such unhelpful behaviors.

In order to get a better understanding of her obsessional cycle, Lilly and the therapist examined the chain of events linking triggers to responses. They found that a triggering event (e.g., a couple kissing) often brought about an intrusion (e.g., "they look euphoric" or "we don't look this happy") that was followed by thoughts about the intrusion (e.g., "Rob, therefore, is not the ONE"). Thoughts about the intrusions or the meaning we give to intrusive thoughts, Lilly acknowledged, made her feel very anxious and guilty (emotional response) and she immediately responded by telling herself "We are very happy. He is smart and I love him." Following several such examples, they determined that Lilly's unhelpful responses were driven, at least to some extent, by her need to reduce anxiety, provoked by the meaning she gave to intrusions.

ROCD and Maladaptive Beliefs

The therapist explained that maladaptive beliefs might lead to negative and even catastrophic interpretations of commonly occurring intrusive thoughts. Such interpretations often lead to dysfunctional responses that maintain, or even increase, the distress associated with the intrusions. The therapist then asked Lilly to complete several questionnaires assessing her most prominent maladaptive beliefs. She showed high scores on the Extreme Love Beliefs scale (EXL) (see Table 30.1), Importance of Thoughts scale of the Obsessive Beliefs Questionnaire-Short (OBQ-S) (Moulding et al., 2011), the overestimation of the consequences of being in the wrong relationship subscale of the Relationship Catastrophization Scale (RECATS) (see Table 30.1) and the Fear of Regret scale (FOR) (see Table 30.1).

Lilly's obsessive peaks often followed thoughts relating to daily events contradicting her beliefs about how she should feel (e.g., euphoric, relaxed, without any negative feelings), think (e.g., constantly thinking about the partner, having no critical thoughts) and act (e.g., never look at other men) in the "right" relationship. Such relational events, therefore, would be interpreted as signs that she might not be "truly in love" with her partner and that her partner was not the Right One. The therapist and Lilly, therefore, decided to start by focusing on Lilly's extreme love beliefs.

High scores on items such as "If the relationship is not completely harmonious, it is unlikely to be 'true love'" and "It is not 'true' love, if you do not feel good all the time" on the EXL resonated Lilly's extreme love expectations. Lilly was, therefore, asked to note her beliefs regarding how one should feel, think and behave during relationships. Lilly then took it upon herself to survey her friends regarding their relational views. Contrary to her expectation, most respondents of the survey did not show extreme relational beliefs. More importantly, responses from the friends she viewed as having a "perfect" relationship considered emotional fluctuations and negative emotions a natural part of romantic relationships. They reported regularly experiencing different degrees of negative (e.g., anger, frustration, and apathy) and positive emotions (e.g., affection, attraction, and tenderness) during their relationship. They also recalled having a wide range of thoughts, including doubts regarding their relationship and criticism of their partner. Importantly, these friends also described a less stringent interpretation of their own behaviors (e.g., looking at other men is not harmful). The therapist then asked Lilly to consider scenarios whereby her extreme relational beliefs (e.g., of continuously thinking about one's partner) were to materialize. What would she expect the impact of such scenarios to have on her social, work, and family functioning and on the relationship itself? On second thought, Lilly declared, such relational expectations might be neither realistic nor desirable.

Lilly and the therapist decided to summarize these conclusions on a card or what they called a CBT-note. On one side of the card, Lilly wrote beliefs: "If the relationship is not completely harmonious, it is unlikely to be 'true love'" or "If you don't continuously think about your partner, he is not the ONE." Challenging these beliefs, on the other side of the card she wrote: "Does a completely harmonious relationship exist? Are feelings constant? Do I really want to think about my partner all the time? What would the impact of that be?"

Lilly believed that having doubts regarding the relationship might suggest that this relationship was not right for her. She therefore constantly attempted to suppress her thoughts, contradict them (using reassurance), and recall situations where she was sure about her partner. Challenging Lilly's beliefs regarding the importance and control of thoughts, the therapist proposed an alternative interpretation – Lilly's attempts to control her thoughts and doubts increased their frequency and associated distress. In order to test this hypothesis, the therapist and Lilly undertook the "Pink Elephant" behavioral experiment (see Bennett-Levy et al., 2004, for detailed description). As expected, trying "not to think" about a pink elephant made the thoughts more noticeable and frequent. Lilly and the therapist agreed to write another CBT-note to summarize this conclusion. On one side of this note Lilly wrote: "If I have doubts, there is a problem with the relationship or my partner is not the one." On the other side of the card she wrote: "My mishandling of intrusions may increase doubts – Pink Elephant."

For the next several sessions, Lilly and the therapist used a variety of exposure and response prevention (ERP) exercises in order to break the link between her maladaptive appraisals and unhelpful responses. For instance, Lilly was asked to repeatedly trigger her doubts and preoccupations by having sentences, such as "I don't feel euphoric" and "I have doubts," as frequent reminders on her phone. She was then to avoid using unhelpful responses (e.g., searching on the web for answers or use self-reassurance), but rather experience how the anxiety dissipated after a while.

Although somewhat reduced, Lilly's reaction to relationship doubts seemed to persist. Fear of regret was identified as an additional maintaining factor of the distress following relationship doubts. Indeed, Lilly endorsed items such as "I find the feelings after I make a wrong decision hard to tolerate" and "The thought that I may have made a better choice is distressing to me" on the FOR scale (see Table 30.1). The therapist and Lilly, therefore, decided to work on attenuating Lilly's fear of regret and the experience of regret. Initially, Lilly and the therapist built an exposure hierarchy of regret exposures whereby she was asked to purposely make wrong choices in everyday decisions (e.g., about shoes, food, movies, and books). This led Lilly to slightly revise her expectations of not being able to cope with the experience of regret.

Lilly's fear of regret, however, often expressed itself in "catastrophic relational scripts" – abstract mental images of hypothetical worst-case scenarios of making the wrong relational decision and the distress associated with them. She feared that remaining with Rob was the "wrong" relational choice that would lead her to a miserable life. Conversely, she dreaded leaving Rob as she might later realize she missed the "love of her life." Thus, Lilly was faced with "catastrophic relational scripts" irrespective of her relational decision. Moreover, Lilly felt that these catastrophic relational scripts were beyond her control, that they were automatic.

As a first step, the therapist introduced to Lilly the Identify, Delay, And Respond (I DARE) technique. Once identifying her relational intrusion, Lilly was taught to wait 10 seconds and only then (if she chose) start the elaboration of her scripts. During these 10 seconds, she was asked to consider whether she was interested in articulating (again) to herself the possible negative consequences of a wrong relational decision. Lilly quickly learned that such ruminations were deliberate actions under her control and that she could choose whether to initiate them. She also felt she could apply this method to many of her other maladaptive interpretations of intrusions.

Getting more control over the formation of catastrophic scripts was useful for Lilly's sense of competency and self-efficacy. Overcoming fear of regret, however, had to involve "facing" her catastrophic scripts. To better understand and deal with these scripts, Lilly and the therapist decided on repeated and systematic imagined exposure. Exposure for Lilly included writing (and then reading) these catastrophic scripts in as much emotional detail as possible, in the first person, and in the present tense. Lilly wrote the following script: "All I have is my work. My personal life is a mess. I live with Rob, but I do not want to be with him. I don't want to spend time with him. I thought he was not intelligent enough, but this is far worse. I can't talk to Rob, I find him so dull. It is like we are having the same conversations again and again. I go to work and complain to my friends about him. I feel trapped. I have the children at home, but I do not want to come home and have to face him. I am ashamed to socialize with others while with him. I want out of this horrible relationship, but I can't leave because of the children. I ask myself 'How did I marry this man?' I feel sorry for myself and I regret every moment I am in this relationship. I think to myself that 'this was a terrible mistake.'"

These exposure exercises followed by a discussion of the meanings and emotions associated with them (i.e., emotional processing) helped diminish Lilly's fears by facilitating the incorporation of new information regarding her role as an agent in her own life (i.e., the course of relationships is not predetermined), her capabilities (e.g., tolerating uncertainty and negative emotions), and the skills she felt she needed to improve (e.g., assertiveness). "Now," Lilly announced, "I feel more confident that I can reduce the chances of such situations occurring and I feel strong enough to cope with them if they do."

ROCD-related Self-vulnerabilities

Lilly attributed extreme importance to the success of her romantic relationships. She described being attuned and emotionally responsive to most relational events. Indeed, self-vulnerability in the relationship domain increases attention and hypervigilance to relationship-related occurrences. To evaluate this potential susceptibility, the therapist used the Relationship Contingent Self-Esteem questionnaire (RCSE) (Knee, Canevello, Bush, & Cook, 2008). The RCSE assesses the extent to which one's self-regard is dependent on the nature, process, and outcome of one's relationship. Lilly showed very high scores on items such as "An important measure of my self-worth is how successful my relationship is" and "I feel better about myself when it seems like my partner and I are emotionally connected," suggesting high contingency in this self-domain.

Lilly's self-esteem was also very much influenced by the way she viewed Rob's attributes and the way in which she believed others perceived him. Lilly was particularly sensitive to Rob's level of intelligence and "complexity." This self-esteem contingency was evident in her high scores on items such as "My partner's flaws reflect on me" and "My self-esteem suffers when my partner fails" on the partner-value contingent self-worth scale (PVCSW). This recently developed measure (currently undergoing psychometric validation) assesses the extent that perceived failures or flaws of the partner impact on one's own self-esteem.

Lilly and her therapist examined and challenged the links between her feelings of self-worth and perceived relational failures. They identified the rules of competence she applied to this self-domain (e.g., How is one expected to act in relationships? How would you expect a good relationship to be?) and examined the boundary of this domain (e.g., To what extent do romantic relationships have to dominate one's life?). Lilly and her therapist also explored other sources of self-worth (e.g., professional, academic, social, creative. and artistic) and she was encouraged to reconnect to activities neglected since the beginning of the current relationship.

The therapist and Lilly then tried to understand her reactions to Rob's perceived deficiencies, particularly in the intellectual domain. Lilly described becoming increasingly perfectionistic and attuned to criticism of her own intelligence following several incidents in her childhood and early adulthood. During these distressing and shame-provoking incidents, Lilly felt that others had underestimated her intelligence and competence. Her preoccupation with her partner's intelligence, she realized, was partly due to her own sensitivity and increased monitoring in this domain. The therapist and Lilly went on to explore her perception of Rob. Lilly discovered what she already knew – although Rob had a tendency to make a "fool" of himself, she did not perceive him as being less intelligent than her. The therapist and Lilly decided to add another CBT-note. On one side of the card Lilly wrote unwanted thoughts relating to her partner's value: "He is not intelligent," "People judge me based on my partner." On the other side of the same card, Lilly noted reminder phrases of what she felt were important insights from her discussions with the therapist: "That is his sense of humor," "I am sensitive and hypervigilant to criticism in this domain," and questions that challenged her current beliefs: "Am I acting from my own sensitivities?," "Do I judge my friends based on their partners?." Lilly was asked to go over all her CBT-notes regularly, preferably in the morning, but not following intrusion and obsessive spikes (e.g., for self-reassurance). These daily reminders reduced Lilly's tendency to over-monitor her partner's behavior and to engage in maladaptive reactions to intrusions (e.g., over-analyzing, compulsive doubts, and catastrophizing scripts).

Identifying and challenging Lilly's self-sensitivities and their impact helped Lilly cope with her reactivity to relational events. Increased attention to particular intrusions, however, does not inevitably lead to anxiety, distress and other negative responses. We all have intrusive thoughts and we all pay attention to some intrusions more than to others. Attachment insecurities may hinder adaptive coping with unwanted intrusions.

ROCD and Attachment Insecurities

Lilly described an intense apprehension of being trapped in a relationship that was not suitable for her. This anxiety was echoed in her strong adherence to items such as "I believe that making the wrong romantic choice is often a terrible thing" and "I believe that being in the wrong relationship almost always leads to a wasted life" on the RECATS (see Table 30.1). Lilly's fear of being in the "wrong" relationship, however, seemed to be fueled by dread that her partner would not be available or adequately responsive in times of need (i.e., attachment anxiety). Indeed, Lilly strongly endorsed items such as "I worry that romantic partners won't care about me as much as I care about them" and "I get frustrated when my partner is not around as much as I would like" on the anxiety scale of the Experience of Close Relationship scale (see Table 30.1).

Lilly's early life experiences had been dominated by frequent parental conflict. More specifically, her parents had shown mutual disrespect and, at times, even contempt during her childhood years. They had criticized each other in public and at home, often abusing each other verbally. During these frequent episodes, Lilly recalled hoping her parents would get divorced, feeling frightened, alone, and helpless. At the same time, these incidents were associated with intense fear of her parent's separating and her mother abandoning them.

Lilly's memories of her parents' relationship seemed to fuel her attachment insecurities and catastrophic perception of relationships. One incident seemed to particularly stand out for her, encapsulating the meaning of these early experiences – her mother repeatedly calling her father a "nobody" and a "loser," and stating that she would have left already had it not been for the children. Her father had done nothing and had just stared at the opposite wall. The therapist, therefore, decided to use Imagery Rescripting (Holmes, Arntz, & Smucker, 2007) in order to provide Lilly with a more realistic (e.g., "Some people are more predictable than others," "One can end a relationship that I am is not happy with") and less toxic (e.g., "I do not have to be like my parents") appraisal of these experiences.

In the imagery rescripting session, Lilly was instructed to bring up the memory of this specific incident. She was then asked to describe in detail what was occurring (in present tense and first person perspective) and elaborate on her thoughts, feelings, sensations, and needs. Lilly, imagining herself as a child, expressed a strong sense of injustice about her mother's behavior toward her father, whom she viewed as kindhearted. She was distressed at the unpredictability of her mother's outbursts, thinking: "Not again. This time she is going to leave. This is terrible. Why don't they break up? Why do they have to continue like this? I feel tense all over; everything is loud; I want to hide and I know I will never get married!" Lilly was then asked to enter the imagery as her own adult self and tell her mother what she felt and needed. Lilly entered the imagery, confronted her mother, and told her how her behavior had made "little Lilly" feel and what she needed. She asked her mother to "stop exploding" and to promise she would never abandon her. She also asked her mother to be more respectful toward her father "because he is my father and a kind man."

During the debriefing, Lily described feeling empowered when she confronted her mother, sheltered by her older self. She also described the attenuation of her anxiety of being abandoned and of being unprotected. Encouraged by the effects of this exercise, Lilly wanted to use imagery rescripting to express her needs to her father. In the following session, therefore, Lilly entered the imagery and told her father she needed him to be "stronger," more active in her life and show her that he could protect her and her mother.

The imagery rescripting sessions attenuated Lilly's core fears by enabling more adaptive appraisals of early experiences. Lilly was now able to see how being exposed to parental conflict contributed to her fear of being trapped in a failed relationship.

These exercises also allowed Lilly to better recognize how different she was from her mother in terms of emotional regulation skills and personality attributes. Although her critical voice was similar to her mother's, she was very different from her. Rob, Lilly also realized, was very different from her father – her was assertive and gave her a feeling of security. Finally, Lilly's fears of not being able to get out of a "bad" relationship were attenuated by learning to identify when "things go wrong" in the relationship and how to express her needs assertively (but not aggressively) when they do.

ROCD and Relational Commitment

Relational commitment is an important aspect of intimate relationships (Rusbult et al., 1998). ROCD symptoms may impact directly on commitment related processes by increasing preoccupation with potential alternative partners and indirectly by decreasing relationship satisfaction and relational investment.

Lilly still showed some sensitivity to potential alternative partners. The therapist and Lilly therefore decided on some ERP exercises for her to deal with the compulsion to check on potential partners on the web (e.g., Facebook photos and statuses, Tweets, and others). For instance, Lilly was to go over her Facebook feed, recognize potential partners (i.e., looked good or shared interesting statuses), but avoid further checking. Initially, this exercise proved difficult for Lilly as she believed she would not be able to resist the strong urge check and "to know" a little more about the person. With time, however, these behavioral exercises challenged this belief. The urge to check subsided and Lilly could more easily look at other potential partners and her Facebook feed without fear.

Lilly's level of investment in the relationship was low. She had feared that initiating fun activities such as going out to a bar, going to the movies, or even having sex would give Rob the wrong impression that she was ready to commit. More quality time with Rob, she feared, might also lead to a clearer understanding that he was not the One. Moreover, such activities often triggered intrusive thought and compulsive behaviors (e.g., overmonitoring of her feelings and comparing). This apparent lack of investment in the relationship and reduced sexual activity had led to relational conflict and had reduced relationship satisfaction for both Lilly and Rob. The therapist suggested testing an alternative strategy. Now that Lilly's ROCD symptoms and cognitions were significantly attenuated, interaction with Rob would allow her to experience the relationship more fully and make more informed decisions about the future of the relationship.

Lilly's increased level of investment in the relationship and associated time spent with Rob was a positive experience for both of them. Lilly and the therapist then went on to examine which qualities and characteristics Lilly believed to be essential for a potential partner, and which were less important. Lilly was happy to discover that Rob had many of the crucial qualities, although not all of the desired characteristics. Lilly decided that she was willing to accept and mourn the lack of these desired characteristics. She felt that she wanted Rob and loved him.

At the end of therapy, some clients choose to pursue the current relationship others end up breaking up. Successful treatment would substantially reduce ROCD symptoms and cognitions and promote relational decisions based on factors related to the quality of the relationship including mutual trust, feelings of closeness, communication, similar values, and relational expectations.

Concluding Remarks

In this chapter, we have presented an integrative, modular, CBT approach to the treatment of ROCD. We used the character of Lilly in order to exemplify assessment and interventions strategies we found useful in our dealings with ROCD within romantic relationships. ROCD symptoms, however, may occur in a variety of relational contexts including parent–child and individual–God relationships. Future research would benefit from exploring similar processes in such relational context, adjusting and refining the model accordingly. This new body of literature would also benefit from using larger clinical samples and the examination of different clinical groups. This would facilitate the identification of specific factors associated with ROCD symptoms. Longitudinal designs and more experimental manipulations would help establish causal between the hypothesized processes in the proposed ROCD model.

In our experience, a client-tailored modular approach is useful with ROCD clients. The goal of therapy is to reduce ROCD such that the client is able to reach an informed decision regarding his/her relationship. Back to Lilly: as therapy progressed, Lilly's sensitivities shifted and her extreme views about love and relationships weakened. Triggers became less frequent and distressing, her catastrophizing scripts were reduced, and her relational fears significantly attenuated. When therapy neared its end, Lilly was able to make the decision to marry Rob. Although Lilly still deals with obsessive spikes every now and then, she manages them well. Lilly is happy and is pleased with her relational choice.

References

Bennett-Levy, J., Butler, G., Fennell, M., Hackmann, A., Mueller, M., & Westbrook, D. (Eds.). (2004). *Oxford guide to behavioural experiments in cognitive therapy*. Oxford: Oxford University Press.

Bowlby, J. (1973). *Attachment and loss. Vol. 2: Separation: Anxiety and anger*. New York: Basic Books.

Brennan, K. A., Clark, C. L., & Shaver, P. R. (1998). Self-report measurement of adult attachment. In J. A. Simpson & W. S. Rholes (Eds.), *Attachment theory and close relationships* (pp. 46–76). New York: Guilford Press.

Doron, G., Derby, D., Szepsenwol. O., & Talmor. D. (2012a). Tainted love: Exploring relationship-centered obsessive compulsive symptoms in two non-clinical cohorts. *Journal of Obsessive-Compulsive and Related Disorders, 1*, 16–24.

Doron, G., Derby, D., Szepsenwol. O., & Talmor. D. (2012b). Flaws and all: Exploring partner-focused obsessive-compulsive symptoms. *Journal of Obsessive-Compulsive and Related Disorders, 1*, 234–243.

Doron, G., Derby, D., & Szepsenwol. O. (2014a). Relationship obsessive compulsive disorder (ROCD): A conceptual framework. *Journal of Obsessive-Compulsive and Related Disorders, 3*, 169–180.

Doron, G., Derby, D., Szepsenwol. O., Nahaloni. E, & Moulding. R. (2016). Relationship Obsessive-Compulsive Disorder (ROCD): Interference, symptoms and maladaptive beliefs. *Psychopathology, 58*, 1–9. doi: 10.3389/fpsyt.2016.00058.

Doron, G., & Kyrios, M. (2005). Obsessive compulsive disorder: A review of possible specific internal representations within a broader cognitive theory. *Clinical Psychology Review, 25*, 415–432.

Doron, G., Sar-El, D., & Mikulincer, M. (2012). Threats to moral self-perceptions trigger obsessive compulsive contamination-related behavioral tendencies. *Journal of Behavior Therapy and Experimental Psychiatry, 43,* 884–890.

Doron, G., Mizrahi, M., Szepsenwol, O., & Derby, D. (2014b). Right or flawed: Relationships, obsessions and sexual satisfaction. *Journal of Sexual Medicine, 11,* 2218–2224.

Doron, G., & Szepsenwol, O. (2015). Partner-focused obsessions and self-esteem: An experimental investigation. *Journal of Behavior Therapy and Experimental Psychiatry, 49*(B), 173–179. doi: 10.1016/j.jbtep.2015.05.007.

Doron, G., Szepsenwol. O., Karp. E., & Gal. N. (2013). Obsessing about intimate-relationships: Testing the double relationship-vulnerability hypothesis. *Journal of Behavior Therapy and Experimental Psychiatry, 44,* 433–440.

First, M. B., Spitzer, R. L., Gibbon, M., & Williams, J. B. (2012). Structured Clinical Interview for DSM-IV Axis I Disorders (SCID-I) – Clinician Version: Administration booklet. Arlington, VA: American Psychiatric Association Publishing.

Foa, E. B., Huppert, J. D., Leiberg, S., Langner, R., Kichic, R., Hajcak, G., & Salkovskis, P. M.. (2002). The Obsessive-Compulsive Inventory: Development and validation of a short version. *Psychological Assessment, 14,* 485–496.

Goodman, W. K., Price, L. H., Rasmussen, S. A., Mazure, C., Fleischmann, R. L., Hill, C. L., Heninger, G. R., & Charney, D. S. (1989). The Yale–Brown Obsessive-Compulsive Scale – I: Development, use, and reliability. *Archives of General Psychiatry, 46*(11), 1006–1011.

Greenberg, J. L., Falkenstein, M., Reuman, L., Fama, J., Marques, L., & Wilhelm, S. (2013). The phenomenology of self-reported body dysmorphic disorder by proxy. *Body Image, 10*(2), 243–246. doi: 10.1016/j.bodyim.2013.01.001.

Holmes, E. A., Arntz, A., & Smucker, M. R. (2007). Imagery rescripting in cognitive behaviour therapy: Images, treatment techniques and outcomes. *Journal of Behavior Therapy and Experimental Psychiatry, 38*(4), 297–305.

Josephson, S. C., & Hollander, E. (1997). Body dysmorphic disorder by proxy. *Journal of Clinical Psychiatry, 58*(2), 86–87.

Knee, C. R., Canevello, A., Bush, A. L., & Cook, A. (2008). Relationship-contingent self-esteem and the ups and downs of romantic relationships. *Journal of Personality and Social Psychology, 95,* 608–627.

Lovibond, P. F., & Lovibond, S. H. (1995). The structure of negative emotional states: Comparison of the Depression Anxiety Stress Scales (DASS) with the Beck Depression and Anxiety inventories. *Behaviour Research and Therapy, 33*(3), 335–343.

Mikulincer, M., & Shaver, P. R. (2007). *Attachment in adulthood: Structure, dynamics, and change.* New York: Guilford Press.

Moulding, R., Anglim, J., Nedeljkovic, M., Doron, G., Kyrios, M., & Ayalon, A. (2011). The Obsessive Beliefs Questionnaire (OBQ): Examination in non-clinical samples and development of a short version. *Assessment, 18,* 357–374.

Obsessive Compulsive Cognitions Working Group (OCCWG) (2005). Psychometric validation of the Obsessive Beliefs Questionnaire: Factor analyses and testing of a brief version. *Behaviour Research and Therapy, 43,* 1527–1542.

Oosthuizen, P., Lambert, T., & Castle, D. J. (1998). Dysmorphic concern: Prevalence and associations with clinical variables. *Australian and New Zealand Journal of Psychiatry, 32*(1), 129–132.

Rachman, S., & de Silva, P. (1978). Abnormal and normal obsessions. *Behaviour Research and Therapy, 16,* 233–248.

Radomsky, A. S., Alcolado, M. G., Abramowitz, J. S., Alonso, P., Belloch, A., Bouvard, M., ... Wong, W. (2014). Part 1. You can run but you can't hide: Intrusive thoughts on six continents. *Journal of Obsessive-Compulsive and Related Disorders, 3,* 269–279.

Rusbult, C. E., Martz, J. M., & Agnew, C. R. (1998). The investment model scale: Measuring commitment level, satisfaction level, quality of alternatives, and investment size. *Personal Relationships, 5*, 357–391.

Sheehan, D. V., Lecrubier, Y., Sheehan, K. H., Amorim, P., Janavs, J., Weiller, E … Dunbar, G. C. (1998). The Mini-International Neuropsychiatric Interview (MINI): The development and validation of a structured diagnostic psychiatric interview for DSM-IV and ICD-10. *Journal of Clinical Psychiatry, 59*, 22–33.

Storch, E. A., Abramowitz, J. S., & Goodman, W. K. (2008). Where does obsessive compulsive disorder belong in DSM-V?. *Depression and Anxiety, 25*, 226–247.

31

Exposure Therapy

Shannon M. Blakey, Lillian Reuman, Ryan J. Jacoby, and Jonathan S. Abramowitz

Carrie presented to our anxiety clinic with distressing, unwanted thoughts and images of stabbing, suffocating, or otherwise harming her husband. Her greatest fear was that she would experience an intrusion and get so anxious that she would eventually "break" and end up killing him. As a result, she engaged in avoidance strategies, such as running in the neighborhood if she woke up before her husband (to avoid harming him in his sleep) and not working with kitchen knives while he was home. Because Carrie interpreted anxious body sensations as signs that she might act on impulses to harm, she also avoided caffeinated drinks that made her feel "wound up" like she might lose control. Carrie sought treatment because she "couldn't handle the anxiety." She had also never told her husband about these intrusive thoughts and fears, and was running out of excuses for her unusual behaviors

Prior to the 1960s, obsessive-compulsive disorder (OCD) was considered an untreatable condition with a poor prognosis (e.g., Kringlen, 1965; Rasmussen & Eisen, 2002). Yet this perception has changed in the ensuing half century, such that OCD is now considered highly manageable. Translational research has been key in developing the most effective psychosocial treatment for OCD – exposure and response prevention (ERP) – which, broadly speaking, entails the guided, systematic, repeated confrontation with situations and stimuli that trigger obsessional fear. Exposure might take the form of repeated actual confrontation with feared low-risk situations (in vivo exposure), induction of feared body sensations (interoceptive exposure), or imaginal confrontation with feared thoughts or disastrous consequences associated with feared stimuli and situations (imaginal exposure). For example, Carrie might practice handling knives while standing close to her husband and imagining losing control and stabbing. During exposure, the client refrains from performing anxiety-reducing behaviors such as compulsive rituals and other subtle "safety behaviors." Ceasing rituals (response prevention) is a vital component of treatment because rituals block individuals from learning that their obsessional fears are excessive and unreasonable. For Carrie, response prevention might entail refraining from competing responses (e.g., clasping her hands behind her back) and from actively avoiding her husband in vulnerable situations (e.g., when he is sleeping).

There are multiple ERP delivery formats. One that is highly successful and "user-friendly" involves a few hours of assessment and treatment planning, followed by 16 twice-weekly treatment sessions lasting about 60–90 minutes each,

The Wiley Handbook of Obsessive Compulsive Disorders, Volume I, First Edition.
Edited by Jonathan S. Abramowitz, Dean McKay, and Eric A. Storch.
© 2017 John Wiley & Sons Ltd. Published 2017 by John Wiley & Sons Ltd.

spaced over about eight weeks (Abramowitz, Foa, & Franklin, 2003). Generally, the therapist supervises the client's exposures during therapy sessions and assigns self-exposure practice to be completed between appointments. Depending on the client's OCD symptoms – and the practicality of confronting actual feared situations – treatment sessions might involve varying amounts of in vivo and imaginal exposure practice. Leaving the therapist's office to confront stimuli for exposure (e.g., items in a grocery store) may also be warranted.

In this chapter, we (a) discuss the mechanisms by which ERP is thought to exert its effects on OCD symptoms, (b) provide an overview of the procedures involved in implementing ERP, (c) review the treatment outcome literature for this intervention, and (d) describe various obstacles to successful treatment. Abramowitz and Jacoby (2015) provide a more in-depth description of how to implement ERP for OCD; readers interested in a treatment manual for the use of this intervention should refer to this work.

How Does ERP Work?

Emotional processing theory (EPT), as initially outlined by Rachman (1980), elaborated upon by Foa and Kozak (1986), and subsequently revised by Foa and McNally (1996), has traditionally been the dominant theoretical model for explaining how ERP works. EPT posits that symptom reduction results from the activation of a fear structure (a fear-based association between a stimulus and its significance, such as Carrie's equating thoughts of harming her husband with the fear of acting on violent impulses) paired with corrective information that is incompatible with the fear structure (e.g., thinking of losing control and harming her husband does not lead to the corresponding behavior). Integral to this model are the concepts of within- and between-session habituation. Within-session habituation (WSH) represents the decline in fear in the presence of a feared stimulus (i.e., the gradual decline from peak fear over the course of a single exposure task) and is a prerequisite for between-session habituation (BSH; the reduction in peak fear reached between trials over the course of therapy). According to EPT, WSH and BSH indicate modification of the fear structure, and, therefore, therapeutic success.

Despite the popularity of EPT, research suggests that habituation is not a reliable predictor of extinction learning – the type of learning that occurs with ERP (Craske et al. 2008). Furthermore, the return of fear (and ultimately relapse) following an apparently successful course of ERP in which both WSH and BSH consistently occur cannot be adequately explained by EPT. In response to these theoretical challenges, inhibitory learning theory (ILT) (e.g., Craske et al., 2008) has been proposed to better account for the effects of ERP. ILT posits that during exposure, previously learned fear associations (e.g., thoughts are dangerous) are not "unlearned," but instead forced to compete with newly acquired (via exposure) safety associations (e.g., thoughts are not necessarily dangerous). Accordingly, following ERP, a feared stimulus is associated with *both* the original excitatory (danger) meaning and the new inhibitory (safety) meaning. Therefore, the aim of ERP from an ILT perspective is to help clients generate safety-based associations and enhance the accessibility of these new associations relative to older (obsessional) associations. This is accomplished by ensuring that ERP is conducted in such a way that the safety learning inhibits the older fear-based associations, resulting in long-term fear extinction (as described below). Treatment success, therefore, is demonstrated by the superior long-term recall of the safety-based inhibitory association during retest (e.g., when confronting the feared stimulus during or after therapy) (Craske et al., 2008; Laborda & Miller, 2012).

Fear extinction achieved through ILT-guided ERP largely relies on two mechanisms: expectancy violation and distress tolerance. Expectancy violation refers to the discrepancy between a client's anticipated consequence (e.g., becoming sick after touching a public door knob) and the actual consequence (e.g., not becoming sick). ERP can be engineered to repeatedly violate Carrie's fear-based expectations that she will act on the thought to harm her husband. Repeated violations of this expectancy (i.e., finding that thoughts do not necessarily lead to actions) might facilitate the learning of new information that competes with her older, fear-based associations. According to learning theory, extinction learning is best achieved when expectations are violated repeatedly and in diverse contexts (e.g., location, time of day, etc.). Distress tolerance refers to an individual's ability to withstand aversive emotional and physical states. As opposed to distress *reduction* (via habituation), distress tolerance is an important goal of ERP as learning that one can withstand distress itself helps to inhibit fear-based associations and guard against the return of fear.

Implementing ERP

Psychoeducation and Presenting the Treatment Rationale

Upon completing a functional assessment (see Chapter 7) to determine the client's fear triggers, cognitive basis for the obsessional fear, and safety behaviors (e.g., compulsive rituals), the therapist begins intervening with psychoeducation about OCD and the rationale for ERP. Psychoeducation entails providing accurate information about the nature of anxiety, normalizing a client's experiences with intrusive thoughts, and explaining how anxiety-reducing and other safety behaviors counterintuitively maintain OCD. Anxiety is explained as a natural and often adaptive response to perceived threat. The problem is not that clients with OCD experience anxiety per se, but that they frequently experience anxiety "false alarms" and respond as if actual danger is present. Consequently, the goal of ERP is to weaken connections between (a) obsessional stimuli and anxiety and (b) compulsive rituals and anxiety reduction by forming new safety-based associations regarding their feared stimuli.

A second component of psychoeducation involves normalizing distressing (obsessional) thoughts, images, and impulses. Indeed, unwanted, intrusive thoughts are universal experiences (e.g., Rachman & de Silva, 1978; Radomsky et al., 2014). Further, reported intrusions in healthy individuals are nearly identical in content to that reported by clinical samples (Rachman & de Silva, 1978). Therefore, it is the quantitative (i.e., frequency and intensity) rather than qualitative aspects that discriminate OCD and nonclinical intrusions. For many clients, learning that they are "not alone" in having such thoughts may be helpful.

After clients understand the nature of anxiety and intrusive thoughts, therapists should explain the cognitive-behavioral model of OCD *as it applies to them*. This involves helping the client recognize that their underlying beliefs, interpretations of fear triggers, and consequent safety behaviors interact to generate the "vicious cycle" of OCD (as explained by the cognitive-behavioral model of OCD; see Chapter 12). Therapists should emphasize that although compulsions reduce obsessional anxiety in the short term, they maintain OCD in the long term. That is, because clients engage in preventative and reactive safety behaviors, they do not have opportunities to learn that (a) feared outcomes are less likely and severe than anticipated, (b) anxiety naturally declines over time, and (c) obsessional doubts, uncertainty, and distress are tolerable experiences.

Although psychoeducation risks being purely didactic, therapists may practice Socratic questioning (e.g., Beck, 2011) to elicit examples from the client's own experience to demonstrate the way in which the cognitive-behavioral processes maintain his or her OCD. The client should be able to independently explain the conceptual model of OCD and the rationale for ERP. Most clients recognize that although ERP seems daunting, the treatment is face valid. Therapists should empathize with the client's nervous apprehension, but reinforce willingness to engage in ERP.

After the client has consented to beginning ERP, the therapist should explain his or her role in therapy. In ERP (like most cognitive-behavioral approaches), the therapist's role is similar to that of a "coach" or "teacher." Although the therapist may provide instruction and strongly encourage the client to face challenges previously avoided, the therapist will never force the client to engage in any exposure task. The therapist also functions as a "cheerleader," ever praising the client for working hard and providing support when the going gets tough.

Devising an Exposure Task List

An exposure task list is a written record of the feared stimuli and situations to be systematically confronted during ERP. Traditionally, items on the list are confronted in a hierarchical fashion. Clients may rank-order feared stimuli, beginning with moderately feared tasks, and working up to their most feared exposure task until all have been successfully encountered and practiced in a variety of contexts. Some research, however, suggests that hierarchical progression through exposure task lists is unnecessary, and perhaps suboptimal (Craske, Treanor, Conway, Zbozinek, & Vervliet, 2014; Lang & Craske, 2000). Rather, *variable* progression (e.g., randomly ordering items) through an exposure task list may enhance distress tolerance (i.e., help individuals learn to tolerate feared stimuli of varying difficulties) and maximize long-term treatment gains (as multiple internal states become associated with extinction learning and present more opportunities for expectancy violation; Lang & Craske, 2000; Rowe & Craske, 1998). Clinical experience reveals that not all clients feel comfortable with a variable approach, and early mastery experiences gained from successful easier exposures can be powerful currency for exposure therapists when helping clients face difficult tasks later in treatment. Accordingly, we suggest that while variable exposure is most optimal, it is certainly preferable to use a hierarchical approach (if necessary) than not use ERP at all.

Types of Exposure

Exposures may take one of three general forms, depending on the client's main concerns. In vivo exposure involves confronting actual distressing situations or stimuli (e.g., touching contaminated objects). Interoceptive exposure (exposure to feared body sensations) may also be relevant for clients who fear somatic experiences such as the physical sensations associated with anxiety. For example, Carrie might be encouraged to drink a caffeinated beverage to confront feared somatic sensations (e.g., increased heart rate) that, to her, forecast a "break" and acting on impulses to harm. Finally, imaginal exposure involves engaging with distressing thoughts or images. Imaginal exposure is appropriate when a client's fear cues are his or her own thoughts (e.g., the thought "God is dead"), involve uncertainty (e.g., "What if I 'snap' and act on my obsessions one day"), or are associated with consequences that are either impossible to evoke within an exposure session (e.g., killing a loved one, hitting someone with an automobile), or are impossible to determine (e.g., "I might go to Hell after I die").

Imaginal exposure can be further delineated based on therapeutic function. *Primary imaginal exposure* involves deliberately inducing distressing and unwanted thoughts, images, and urges (i.e., violent, sexual, or blasphemous obsessions). This may be done through repeated visual imagery, verbalizing the feared hypothetical scenario, writing down and repeatedly reading the scenario, or recording and repeatedly playing an audio file of the narrated scenario. *Secondary imaginal exposure* is used when situational exposure evokes fears of disastrous consequences. In such instances, imaginal exposure is begun during or after situational exposure and entails visualizing the feared outcomes or focusing on uncertainty associated with the risk of feared outcomes. Secondary imaginal exposure is especially useful when clients anticipate consequences of not ritualizing. For example, Carrie may be instructed to forgo her morning run, and then imagine the possibility of becoming so "wound up" that she suffocates her sleeping husband.

Finally, *preliminary imaginal exposure* involves clients imagining confronting a feared stimulus as a preliminary step in preparing for in vivo exposures (e.g., imagining using knives before actually using them). Although this type of exposure might be used as an intermediate step in preparing a client to confront a particularly difficult situation, therapists should consider whether an easier situational exposure task may be preferred. For example, if Carrie is unwilling to hold a knife near her husband, she might be asked to hold a sharp pen in the presence of her husband instead of *imagining* holding a sharp knife. Table 31.1 offers possible exposure tasks to illustrate what tasks might be appropriate given Carrie's symptoms.

Treatment is further enhanced by varying the context, state, duration, cue, task difficulty, and other aspects of the exposure (Golkar, Bellander, & Ohman, 2013; Hermans, Craske, Mineka, & Lovibond, 2006; Laborda & Miller, 2012; Lang & Craske, 2000). That is, a single successful in-session exposure under close therapist supervision is unlikely to result in long-term fear extinction. As such, varied and repeated practice of exposure tasks is necessary (see "Out of Session Exposures," below). There is also benefit to combining previously conducted exposure tasks (i.e., *deepened extinction*; Rescorla, 2006), as this more completely violates negative expectancies for harm (i.e., patients learn they can handle these fear cues alone *and* in combination with one another). For instance, Carrie might hold a knife nearby her husband while drinking coffee, imagine killing her sleeping husband when in bed, or imagine suffocating her sleeping husband while holding a pillow over him after drinking a cup of coffee.

It is worth noting that devising exposure tasks to be completed over the course of treatment affords opportunities for the client and therapist to collaborate and be

Table 31.1 Example exposures for Carrie's fear of stabbing her husband

Type of exposure	Example task	Concern addressed
In vivo	Hold a knife while standing behind blindfolded, seated husband.	"I might act on my distressing impulses to stab my husband."
Interoceptive	Consume a caffeinated beverage.	"I might become so 'wound up' that I may lose control and harm my husband."
Imaginal		
Primary	Repeatedly imagine fatally stabbing husband.	"I cannot tolerate the distress associated with having impulses to stab my husband."
Secondary	Consume a caffeinated beverage and imagine the possibility of "losing control."	"I might become so 'wound up' that I may lose control and harm my husband."
Preliminary	Imagine holding a knife while standing behind blindfolded, seated husband.	"I might act on my distressing impulses to stab my husband" and/or "I cannot tolerate the distress associated with having impulses to stab my husband."
Combined		
In vivo + imaginal	Imagine stabbing husband with a knife while standing behind blindfolded, seated husband and holding a knife.	"I might lose control and act on my distressing urges to stab my husband."
In vivo + interoceptive	Hold a knife while standing behind blindfolded, seated husband after drinking caffeinated beverage.	
In vivo + imaginal + interoceptive	Imagine stabbing husband with a knife after drinking a caffeinated beverage while standing behind blindfolded, seated husband and holding a knife.	

creative in designing a treatment plan. This teamwork is important for rapport building, which certainly plays a role in outcome. It also becomes clear during this treatment stage that a full exposure task list is difficult to create if not equipped with a thorough functional assessment of a client's OCD-related concerns, triggers, and safety rituals.

Response Prevention

Response prevention (RP) refers to the cessation of client safety behaviors (e.g., compulsive rituals) performed to prevent feared outcomes or reduce anxiety associated with feared stimuli. Despite the term "prevention," RP does not entail physically restraining the client in any way; rather, clients are helped and encouraged to choose for themselves to resist performing behaviors that effectively reduce anxiety in the short term but maintain OCD symptoms in the long term. In many cases, RP may be an exposure task in itself (e.g., Carrie's refraining from her morning run was an exposure to experiencing obsessions around her sleeping husband). Clients should also be encouraged to resist urges to perform rituals between treatment sessions, but report any rituals (i.e., violations of RP) to their therapist for troubleshooting. Chapter 12 describes the use of self-monitoring forms for keeping real-time records of any rituals performed between sessions.

It may not be necessary to eliminate all safety behaviors during ERP. Rachman, Radomsky, and Shafran (2008), for example, highlight the positive consequences of some safety behaviors, such as enhanced treatment acceptability (e.g., Levy & Radomsky, 2014) and approach behavior (e.g., Hood, Antony, Koerner, & Monson, 2010). That is, if clients feel safer knowing they may perform rituals, they might be more willing to complete more challenging exposure tasks. Correspondingly, some research shows that allowing clients to engage in some safety behaviors during exposure trials may actually enhance outcomes (e.g., Sy, Dixon, Lickel, Nelson, & Deacon, 2011). Other studies have not supported this view (e.g., Powers, Smits, & Telch, 2004). Although safety behaviors may not always be deleterious, we suggest that they should be discouraged in most cases (for reviews, see Helbig-Lang & Petermann, 2010; Telch & Lancaster, 2012). ERP therapists are advised to help clients resist whatever rituals they can at first (without demanding complete RP from the start), with the aim of achieving full RP as soon as possible.

Out of Session Exposures

It is also critical that clients complete exposure practices between sessions (daily, if not more frequently). Not only is such "homework" compliance a reliable predictor of treatment outcome (e.g., Abramowitz, Franklin, Zoellner, & Di Bernardo, 2002; de Araujo, Ito, & Marks, 1996), but repeated and varied exposure practices facilitate more generalized and enduring fear extinction. Some clients find the concept of homework aversive, yet it is important to explain the reason for conducting exposure tasks outside the session. Consider a man who wishes to learn to play the piano. He may register for piano lessons with a trained instructor in order to achieve his goal of becoming a proficient pianist, but as anyone who has taken music lessons knows, it is the practice invested between lessons that truly makes a performer. An instructor offers valuable praise and constructive feedback for improvement, but a great degree of learning and skills development occurs outside of the session. Such is the case in ERP – therapists provide expert guidance, but it is the way clients use opportunities to confront their fears and resist ritualizing between sessions that ultimately determines the degree of improvement. Framing out of session exposures as "practices" instead of "homework" may also mitigate clients' potential resistance to scheduling time to complete exposure assignments between sessions.

In early stages of treatment before exposure tasks have been introduced, assigned work may include self-monitoring of obsessions and compulsions to identify triggers to be encountered and safety behaviors to be eliminated later in treatment. Conventionally, clients are only expected to conduct out of session exposures that have already been practiced in some form with the therapist (e.g., Abramowitz, Deacon, & Whiteside, 2011). Some clients, however, are able to successfully design and implement novel exposure tasks independently. An appropriate compromise may be for therapists to encourage the client to conduct as many exposure tasks as he or she is willing as long as the therapist is confident that the client can properly design and implement the task. This recommendation is consistent with the goal for clients to adopt ERP as a lifestyle. Although ERP is designed to be a time-limited therapy, the exposure lifestyle entails a generalized willingness to approach obsessional triggers, in contrast to avoidant tendencies characteristic of OCD. Clients can be reminded that life presents daily opportunities to overcome OCD by encountering corrective information and developing greater distress tolerance. By being opportunistic and approaching distressing situations as spontaneous exposure tasks, clients are better equipped to "become their own therapist," which may increase their odds of a more complete treatment response.

Therapists are advised to review completed (or partially completed) homework at the start of each session to reinforce the importance of assigned tasks. Reviewing out of session exposures also alerts the therapist to a client's treatment progress as well as areas needing continued attention. Discussing possible explanations for unsuccessful exposure tasks (e.g., the task was too frightening) may also benefit both parties. If noncompliance becomes an issue, therapists should (a) make sure the client understands the rationale for assigned work, (b) troubleshoot homework completion obstacles with the client, or, ultimately, (c) consider stopping therapy until the client is ready to invest the time and energy necessary to benefit from ERP.

Ending an Exposure Task

There are three indicators of when it is appropriate to end an individual exposure session. In many instances, the initial distress that occurs when exposure begins declines over the course of the trial (i.e., habituation). Although this is one desirable outcome of exposure, and a reasonable terminus, habituation is neither necessary nor sufficient for the long-term success of ERP. More important than habituation, a second marker that an exposure session can be ended is the violation of the client's anxious expectations of what will occur during or because of the exposure. For example, Carrie would continue her exposure practice of holding a knife while feeling "wound up" in the presence of her husband until she realizes – contrary to her prediction – that she is unlikely to lose control and act on her impulse to stab him. Abramowitz and Arch (2014) have described how to arrange exposure tasks to violate client expectations. The third indicator that an exposure may be stopped is when the client appears to effectively manage the distress associated with the exposure task. For example, the therapist might stop the exposure practice when Carrie recognizes that although anxiety and obsessional thoughts are *unpleasant*, she is still able to engage in activities that are meaningful to her. This idea is consistent with Acceptance and Commitment Therapy's notions regarding the importance of moving toward values as a goal of treatment (Twohig et al., 2015).

Concluding Treatment

A course of ERP can be terminated when the client demonstrates fear extinction as indicated by a number of indices, which are discussed below.

Successful exposure to the most difficult feared stimuli in varied contexts. Completing the most difficult exposure tasks once is unlikely to be sufficient for long-term fear extinction for most clients. It is therefore recommended that clients conduct exposures to the most difficult tasks in a variety of settings (e.g., different locations and times of day), mood states (e.g., anxious, calm), and audiences (e.g., alone, accompanied) as many times as possible. If a client can handle *any* feared stimulus in *any* scenario at *any* time in *any* state of readiness *without* engaging in rituals, it is likely that ERP can be terminated without concern.

Correction of maladaptive beliefs. ERP bestows information that challenges maladaptive beliefs (e.g., threat overestimations) and thus, with repeated practice, offers experiences that cumulatively provide clients with a sense of unconditional learned safety. For example, by chopping vegetables with a butcher's knife in the kitchen while her husband sat at the table blindfolded and wearing headphones, Carrie was able to learn that (a) she was not likely to stab her husband even when she had full opportunity, (b) prolonged and intense anxiety was tolerable, (c) her anxiety did not cause her to "lose control," and (d) her distress declined naturally over time. Thus, when previously feared stimuli are no longer interpreted as dangerous, it may be appropriate to consider ending ERP. In addition to behavioral evidence for corrected beliefs (e.g., no longer avoiding certain stimuli or situations), therapists may administer psychometrically validated self-report measures of OCD and related cognitions (see Chapter 5) to determine whether such beliefs have shifted.

Eradication of safety behaviors. Another indication of sufficient ERP is complete RP across all life domains. Indeed, full ritual (and other safety behavior) abstinence implies sufficient safety learning, fear extinction, and changes in fear-based cognitions.

Enhanced quality of life and lack of functional impairment. The final – and perhaps most meaningful – index of a client's treatment success is enhanced quality of life and a reduction of functional impairment. Many individuals with OCD begin treatment unable to pursue rewarding activities, maintain employment, or sustain meaningful relationships with others due to their symptoms. Unsurprisingly, many clients also report low self-efficacy, depression, and poor physical health as a result of their OCD. Quality of life and self-efficacy can also be enhanced by participating in previously avoided activities. That is not to say that life after ERP will be without its challenges; rather, life after ERP will probably be more fulfilling and consistent with one's own values (e.g., Eifert & Forsyth, 2005).

Termination and Relapse Prevention

After determining that a client has received a sufficient dose of ERP, the therapist may terminate therapy and offer relapse prevention strategies. General termination procedures are beyond the scope of this chapter (readers are encouraged to consult general clinical guides, see, e.g., Beck, 2011; Ledley, Marx, & Heimberg, 2010), yet a number of considerations relevant to long-term maintenance of treatment following ERP for OCD exist (e.g., Hiss, Foa, & Kozak, 1994). Therapists should remind clients that the goal of ERP was not to eliminate anxious experiences altogether but to recalibrate anxiety (i.e., experience appropriate levels of anxiety in the appropriate circumstances); therefore, anxious experiences after ERP do not mean ERP was a failure. Therapists should also provide psychoeducation regarding the difference between a "lapse" (re-experiencing of some symptoms) and a "relapse" (a full return of symptoms and functional impairment), communicating that the former is common, yet does not have to lead to the latter if the client quickly implements ERP practice. Clients should be encouraged to contact their therapist to schedule a "booster session" if they struggle to independently implement ERP after a lapse.

How Effective is ERP?

ERP has demonstrated consistent efficacy and effectiveness in treatment outcome studies; consequently, it is considered the first-line psychological treatment for OCD (APA, 2007; March, Frances, Carpenter, & Kahn, 1997). Meta-analytic studies (e.g., Abramowitz, 1996, 1997; Abramowitz, Franklin, & Foa, 2002; Eddy, Dutra, Bradey, & Weston, 2004) consistently show that exposure-based cognitive-behavioral therapy produces large reductions in OCD, anxiety, and depressive symptoms. Randomized controlled trials have also shown that ERP produces statistically and clinically significant reductions in OCD symptoms as measured by the Yale–Brown Obsessive Compulsive Scale (YBOCS) (Goodman et al., 1989a, 1989b) – the gold standard therapist-rated measure of OCD severity.

Although efficacy studies (i.e., randomized controlled trials) provide the most compelling scientific evidence that the specific procedures of ERP can be advantageous for OCD treatment, most "real-world" practice settings are dissimilar from the controlled settings in which these trials are conducted. Accordingly, it is appropriate to examine whether ERP conducted in more representative (i.e., nonresearch) environments (e.g., with more typical clients and therapists) is also the treatment of choice. The findings from effectiveness studies, which aim to address this very question, indeed corroborate evidence that ERP as a highly robust intervention for OCD (e.g., Franklin, Abramowitz, Foa, Kozak, & Levitt, 2000).

Number of sessions. The number of exposure sessions required for successful treatment will depend on the length of the exposure task list as well as the rate of progress. Although a number of studies demonstrate large treatment effects in 12–16 weeks, other clients may require fewer or more sessions to maximally respond. Ideally, clients should attend ERP sessions as long as needed to achieve desired symptom reduction; however, not all clients have the financial or logistic flexibility to attend the ideal number of sessions. It is also worth noting that continued improvement after 20 sessions may be unlikely; in these instances, therapists should ensure that (a) the OCD diagnosis is accurate, (b) ERP is being implemented effectively, (c) ERP is the best treatment approach for the client, (d) the client is not engaging in counterproductive actions (e.g., substance abuse), and (e) the client is sufficiently motivated for behavioral change at the time.

Intersession interval. A second question concerns the intersession interval: the time frame in which exposure sessions should occur. Abramowitz and colleagues (2003) found that the robust effects of 15 intensive (daily) therapy sessions were not compromised by reducing session frequency to twice-weekly. Thus, a twice-weekly therapy schedule may be an equally effective approach as intensive treatment. Additional research shows that ERP may also be effective when delivered in a weekly format (e.g., Storch et al., 2007). Ultimately, therapists are advised to prioritize the quality, rather than quantity or frequency, of sessions when delivering ERP.

Combining ERP and medication. Although ERP has demonstrated superiority over pharmacotherapy as a stand-alone intervention for OCD (e.g., Foa et al., 2005; Nakatani et al., 2005), most clients with OCD will already be taking medication (e.g., serotonin reuptake inhibitors [SRIs]) when they seek psychological treatment. Although studies comparing ERP to SRIs are limited by their complex designs, the available research suggests that (a) combined ERP and SRI treatment yields superior outcome compared to SRIs alone, but (b) combined treatment does not lead to superior outcome relative to ERP monotherapy (e.g., Franklin, 2005). Thus, if ERP has not been tried, it is usually worth considering this option even if there has not been a successful response to one or more SRIs. Typically it is recommended that clients stabilize medication before beginning ERP so they and their treatment providers can better attribute symptom changes during ERP.

Although SRIs are unlikely to interfere with the effects of ERP, other types of medication often prescribed for OCD can attenuate the outcome of exposure therapy. Specifically, benzodiazepines – fast-acting agents that reduce anxious arousal – can interfere with extinction learning (especially when prescribed to be taken "as needed when feeling anxious") by preventing clients from experiencing the natural decline of anxiety over time during exposure (Westra & Stewart, 1998). Thus, these agents prevent the maximal violation of expectancies for harm (e.g., the expectation that anxiety is dangerous and will persist indefinitely) and do not allow clients to fully develop tolerance for prolonged and intense distress. Even more, encouraging benzodiazepine use may inadvertently communicate that anxiety is dangerous in and of itself, and must be neutralized if it becomes "too intense."

Barriers to Treatment Success

Client Factors

Client-related obstacles to effective ERP include factors such as ambivalence regarding treatment engagement, homework noncompliance, and other prognostic variables. For example, many clients express ambivalence regarding participating in therapy due to apprehensions about "facing one's fears," relinquishing perceived benefits of OCD (e.g., attention and social support), or a questioning of their "sense of self" without the disorder. Fortunately, motivational interviewing techniques (e.g., Westra, 2012) may help encourage clients to fully engage in ERP. Additional treatment-interfering behaviors such as homework noncompliance, frequently missing therapy sessions, and engaging in tangential discussions during therapy sessions may also attenuate outcome (e.g., Sánchez-Meca, Rosa-Alcázar, Marín-Martínez, & Gómez-Conesa, 2010; Schmidt & Wollaway-Bickel, 2000; Van Dyke & Pollard, 2005). Reviewing the rationale for ERP and emphasizing the importance of engaging in all aspects of therapy may ameliorate these problems. Finally, poor insight, comorbid depression, higher initial symptom severity, negative life events, and certain personality traits have negative prognostic implications (Abramowitz, Franklin, Street, Kozak, & Foa, 2000; Durham, Chambers,

Macdonald, & Fisher, 2009; Foa, Abramowitz, Franklin, & Kozak, 1999), although ERP may still be somewhat effective. Therapists are advised to assess for possible client-related barriers to effective ERP at intake and plan accordingly.

Therapist Factors

A number of therapist variables regarding the perceived safety, ethicality, and tolerability of ERP have also been documented as potential obstacles to its delivery (e.g., Deacon & Farrell, 2013), such that ERP is often underutilized despite its strong evidence base (e.g., Becker, Zayfert, & Andersen, 2004; Freiheit, Vye, Swan, & Cady, 2004; van Minnen, Hendriks, & Olff, 2010). Therapists with exaggerated concerns regarding the appropriateness of ERP often exclude clients from ERP for reasons that are unwarranted, such as a client's "emotional fragility" or comorbid psychotic disorder (e.g., Meyer, Farrell, Kemp, Blakey, & Deacon, 2014; Olatunji, Deacon, & Abramowitz, 2009). Fortunately, research suggests that didactic interventions can alleviate therapists' reservations about ERP (Deacon et al., 2013a) and perhaps lead to more confident delivery (e.g., Farrell, Deacon, Dixon, & Lickel, 2013).

A final category of barriers to therapeutic improvement is the manner in which therapists deliver ERP. For example, failure to accurately and effectively convey to a client the conceptual model of the problem and the rationale for ERP may result in a lack of client engagement with or adherence to treatment (Abramowitz, 2013). Additionally, relaxation techniques and concurrent use of anxiolytic medications (as previously mentioned, e.g., benzodiazepines) act on mechanisms that are incompatible with maximizing extinction learning (Deacon et al., 2013; Siev & Chambless, 2007). Therapists should prioritize clients' need to violate negative expectancies and develop greater distress tolerance and avoid prescribing arousal-reduction strategies.

Conclusions and Future Directions

Prior to the arrival of ERP, the prognosis for clients with OCD was poor. Fortunately, this approach has emerged as a highly efficacious intervention. We have provided an overview of the procedures and obstacles to implementing these techniques in the present chapter. It is important for the reader to understand that translational research has been key in developing exposure-based treatments for OCD. Early models of extinction learning in animals (Solomon, Kamin, & Wynne, 1953) and humans (Dollard & Miller, 1950) led to the development of ERP as an intervention for compulsive behavior that is motivated by irrational (obsessional) fear. Later work on fear extinction further informed the refinement of this approach, such as research indicating that exposure would be most effective if conducted under multiple contexts (e.g., Bouton, 2002). There remain, however, significant groups of OCD sufferers for whom ERP has limited efficacy. Research into how this intervention may be modified to address the needs of specific subgroups (i.e., individuals with higher overvalued ideas) is still needed. The inhibitory learning theory of ERP is promising, yet most of the research on inhibitory learning in exposure has focused on individuals with panic and specific phobias. It is clear that more work is needed to examine how well this model generalizes to the treatment of individuals with OCD.

References

Abramowitz, J. S. (1996). Variants of exposure and response prevention in the treatment of obsessive-compulsive disorder: A meta-analysis. *Behavior Therapy, 27*, 583–600.

Abramowitz, J. S. (1997). Effectiveness of psychological and pharmacological treatments for obsessive-compulsive disorder: A quantitative review. *Journal of Consulting and Clinical Psychology, 65*, 44–52.

Abramowitz, J. S. (2013). The practice of exposure therapy: Relevance of cognitive-behavioral theory and extinction theory. *Behavior Therapy, 44*, 548–558.

Abramowitz, J. S., & Arch, J. J. (2014). Strategies for improving long-term outcomes in cognitive behavioral therapy for obsessive-compulsive disorder: Insights from learning theory. *Cognitive and Behavioral Practice, 21*, 20–31.

Abramowitz, J. S., Deacon, B. J., & Whiteside, S. P. H. (2011). *Exposure therapy for anxiety: Principles and practice.* New York: Guilford Press.

Abramowitz, J. S., Foa, E. B., & Franklin, M. E. (2003). Exposure and ritual prevention for obsessive-compulsive disorder: Effects of intensive versus twice-weekly sessions. *Journal of Consulting and Clinical Psychology, 71*, 394–398.

Abramowitz, J. S., Franklin, M. E., & Foa, E. B. (2002). Empirical status of cognitive-behavioral therapy for obsessive-compulsive disorder: A meta-analytic review. *Romanian Journal of Cognitive and Behavioral Psychotherapies, 2*, 89–104.

Abramowitz, J. S., Franklin, M. E., Street, G. P., Kozak, M. J., & Foa, E. B. (2000). Effects of comorbid depression on response to treatment for obsessive-compulsive disorder. *Behavior Therapy, 31*, 517–528.

Abramowitz, J. S., Franklin, M. E., Zoellner, L. A., & DiBernardo, C. L. (2002). Treatment compliance and outcome of cognitive-behavioral therapy for obsessive-compulsive disorder. *Behavior Modification, 26*, 447–463.

Abramowitz, J. S., & Jacoby, R. J. (2015). *Obsessive-compulsive disorder in adults: Advances in psychotherapy: Evidence-based practice.* Gottingen: Hogrefe.

American Psychiatric Association (APA). (2007). Practice guideline for the treatment of patients with obsessive-compulsive disorder. *American Journal of Psychiatry, 164*, 1–56.

de Araujo, L.A., Ito, L. M., & Marks, I. M., (1996). Early compliance and other factors predicting outcome of exposure for obsessive-compulsive disorder. *British Journal of Psychiatry, 169*, 747–752.

Beck, J. S. (2011). *Cognitive behavioral therapy: Basics and beyond* (2nd ed.). New York: Guilford Press.

Becker, C., Zayfert, C., & Anderson, E. (2004). A survey of psychologists' attitudes toward utilization of exposure therapy for PTSD. *Behaviour Research and Therapy, 42*, 277–292.

Bouton, M. E. (2002). Context, ambiguity, and unlearning: Sources of relapse after behavioral extinction. *Biological Psychiatry, 52*, 976–986.

Craske, M. G., Kitcanski, K., Zelokowsky, M., Mystkowski, J., Chowdhury, N., & Baker, A. (2008). Optimizing inhibitory learning during exposure therapy. *Behavior Research and Therapy, 46*, 5–27.

Craske, M. G., Treanor, M., Conway, C. C., Zbozinek, T., & Vervliet, B. (2014). Maximizing exposure therapy: An inhibitory learning approach. *Behaviour Research and Therapy, 58*, 10–23.

Deacon, B. J., & Farrell, N. R. (2013). Therapist barriers in the dissemination of exposure therapy. In E. Storch, & D. McKay (Eds.), *Treating variants and complications in anxiety disorders* (pp. 363–373). New York: Springer.

Deacon, B. J., Farrell, N. R., Kemp, J. J., Dixon, L. J., Sy, J. T., Zhang, A. R., & McGrath, P. B. (2013a). Assessing therapist reservations about exposure therapy for anxiety disorders: The therapist beliefs about exposure scale. *Journal of Anxiety Disorders, 27*, 772–780.

Deacon, B. J., Kemp, J., Dixon, L. J., Sy. J. T., Farrell, N. R., & Zhang, A. (2013b). Maximizing the efficacy of interoceptive exposure by optimizing inhibitory learning: A randomized controlled trial. *Behaviour Research and Therapy, 51*, 588–596.

Dollard, J., & Miller, N. E. (1950). *Personality and psychotherapy: An analysis in terms of learning, thinking and culture.* New York: McGraw-Hill.

Durham, R. C., Chambers, J. A., Macdonald, R. R., & Fisher, P. L. (2009). Predictive validity of two prognostic indices for generalized anxiety disorder. *International Journal of Cognitive Therapy, 2*, 383–399.

Eddy, K., Dutra, L., Bradley, R., & Weston, D. (2004). A multidimensional meta-analysis of psychotherapy and pharmacotherapy for obsessive-compulsive disorder. *Clinical Psychology Review, 24*, 1011–1030.

Eifert, G. H., & Forsyth, J. P. (2005). *Acceptance and Commitment Therapy for anxiety disorders: A practitioner's treatment guide to using mindfulness, acceptance, and values-based behavior change strategies.* Oakland: New Harbinger.

Farrell, N. R., Deacon, B. J., Dixon, L. J., & Lickel, J. J. (2013). Theory-based training strategies for modifying practitioner concerns about exposure therapy for anxiety. *Journal of Anxiety Disorders, 27*, 781–787.

Foa, E. B., Abramowitz, J. S., Franklin, M. E., & Kozak, M. J. (1999). Feared consequences, fixity of belief, and treatment outcome in patients with obsessive-compulsive disorder. *Behavior Therapy, 30*, 717–724.

Foa, E. B., & Kozak, M. J. (1986). Emotional processing of fear: Exposure to corrective information. *Psychological Bulletin, 99*, 20–35.

Foa, E., Liebowitz, M. R., Kozak, M. J., Davies, S., Campeas, R., Franklin, M. E., … Tu, X. (2005). Randomized, placebo-controlled trial of exposure and ritual prevention, clomipramine, and their combination in the treatment of obsessive-compulsive disorder. *American Journal of Psychiatry, 162*, 151–161.

Foa, E. B., & McNally, R. J. (1996). Mechanisms of change in exposure therapy. In M. Rapee (Ed.), *Current controversies in the anxiety disorders* (pp. 329–343). New York: Guilford Press.

Franklin, M. E. (2005). Combining serotonin medication with cognitive-behavior therapy: Is it necessary for all OCD patients? In J. S. Abramowitz, & A. C. Houts (Eds.), *Concepts and controversies in Obsessive-Compulsive Disorder.* New York: Springer.

Franklin, M. E., Abramowitz, J. S., Foa, E. B., Kozak, M. J., & Levitt, J. T. (2000). Effectiveness of exposure and ritual prevention for obsessive-compulsive disorder: Randomized compared with nonrandomized samples. *Journal of Consulting and Clinical Psychology, 68*, 594–602.

Freiheit, S. R., Vye, C., Swan, R., & Cady, M. (2004). Cognitive-behavioral therapy for anxiety: Is dissemination working? *The Behavior Therapist, 27*, 25–32.

Golkar, A., Bellander, M., & Ohman, A. (2013). Temporal properties of fear extinction: Does time matter? *Behavioural Neuroscience, 127*, 59–69.

Goodman, W. K., Price, L. H., Rasmussen, S. A., Mazure, C., Delgado, P., Heninger, G. R., & Charney, D. S. (1989a). The Yale–Brown Obsessive Compulsive Scale: Validity. *Archives of General Psychiatry, 46*, 1012–1016.

Goodman, W. K., Price, L. H., Rasmussen, S. A., Mazure, C., Fleischmann, R. L., Hill, C. L., … Charney, D. S. (1989b). The Yale–Brown Obsessive Compulsive Scale: Development, use, and reliability. *Archives of General Psychiatry, 46*, 1006–1011.

Helbig-Lang, S., & Petermann, F. (2010). Tolerate or eliminate? A systematic review on the effects of safety behavior across anxiety disorders. *Clinical Psychology: Science and Practice, 17*, 218–233.

Hermans, D., Craske, M. G., Mineka, S., & Lovibond, P. F. (2006). Extinction in human fear conditioning. *Biological Psychiatry, 60*, 361–368.

Hiss, H., Foa, E. B., & Kozak, M. J. (1994). Relapse prevention program for treatment of obsessive-compulsive disorder. *Journal of Consulting and Clinical Psychology, 62*, 801–808.

Hood, H. K., Antony, M. M., Koerner, N., & Monson, C. M. (2010). Effects of safety behaviors on fear reduction during exposure. *Behavior Research and Therapy, 48*, 1161–1169.

Kringlen, E. (1965). Obsessional neurotics: A long-term follow-up. *British Journal of Psychiatry*, *111*, 709–722.

Laborda, M. A., & Miller, R. R. (2012). Reactivated memories compete for expression after Pavolovian extinction. *Behavioural Processes*, *90*, 20–27.

Lang, H. J., & Craske, M. G. (2000). Manipulations of exposure-based therapy to reduce fear: A replication. *Behaviour Research and Therapy*, *38*, 1–12.

Ledley, D. R., Marx, B. P., & Heimberg, R. G. (2010). *Making cognitive-behavioral therapy work* (2nd ed.). New York: Guilford Press.

Levy, H., & Radomsky, A. S. (2014). Safety behaviour enhances the acceptability of exposure. *Cognitive Behaviour Therapy*, *43*, 83–92.

March, J. S., Frances, A., Carpenter, D., & Kahn, D. (1997). The expert consensus guidelines series: Treatment of obsessive-compulsive disorder. *Journal of Clinical Psychiatry*, *58*, (Suppl. 4).

Meyer, J. M., Farrell, N. R., Kemp, J. J., Blakey, S. M., & Deacon, B. J. (2014). Why do clinicians exclude anxious clients from exposure therapy? *Behaviour Research and Therapy*, *54*, 49–53.

van Minnen, A., Hendriks, L., & Olff, M. (2010). When do trauma experts choose exposure therapy for PTSD patients? A controlled study of therapist and patient factors. *Behaviour Research and Therapy*, *48*, 312–320.

Nakatani, E., Nakagawa, A., Nakoa, T., Yoshizato, C., Nabeyama, M., Kudo, A., ... Kawamoto, M. (2005). A randomized controlled trial of Japanese patients with obsessive-compulsive disorder: Effectiveness of behavior therapy and fluvoxamine. *Psychotherapy and Psychosomatics*, *74*, 269–276.

Olatunji, B. O., Deacon, B. J., & Abramowitz, J. S. (2009). The cruelest cure? Ethical issues in the implementation of exposure-based treatments. *Cognitive and Behavioral Practice*, *16*, 172–180.

Powers, M. B., Smits, J. A., & Telch, M. J. (2004). Disentangling the effects of safety-behavior utilization and safety-behavior availability during exposure-based treatment: A placebo-controlled trial. *Journal of Consulting and Clinical Psychology*, *72*, 448–454.

Rachman, S. (1980). Emotional processing. *Behaviour Research and Therapy*, *18*, 51–60.

Rachman, S., & de Silva, P. (1978). Abnormal and normal obsessions. *Behaviour Research and Therapy*, *16*, 233–238.

Rachman, S., Radomsky, A. S., & Shafran, R. (2008). Safety behaviour: A reconsideration. *Behaviour Research and Therapy*, *46*, 163–173.

Radomsky, A. S., Alcolado, G. M., Abramowitz, J. S., Alonso, P., Belloch, A., Bouvard, M., ... Wong, W. (2014). Part 1 – You can run but you can't hide: Intrusive thoughts on six continents. *Journal of Obsessive-Compulsive and Related Disorders*, *3*, 269–279.

Rasmussen, S. A., & Eisen, J. L. (2002). The course and clinical features of obsessive-compulsive disorder. In K. L. Davis, D. Charney, J. T. Coyle, & C. Nemeroff (Eds.), *Neuropsychopharmacology: The fifth generation of progress* (pp. 1593–1608). Philadelphia, PA: Lippincott, Williams, & Wilkins.

Rescorla, R. A. (2006). Deepened extinction from compound stimulus presentation. *Journal of Experimental Psychology: Animal Behavior Processes*, *32*, 135–144.

Rowe, M. K., & Craske, M. G. (1998). Effects of varied stimulus exposure training on fear reduction and return of fear. *Behaviour Research and Therapy*, *36*, 719–734.

Sánchez-Meca, J., Rosa-Alcázar, A. I., Marín-Martínez, F., & Gómez-Conesa, A. (2010). Psychological treatment of panic disorder with or without agoraphobia: A meta-analysis. *Clinical Psychology Review*, *30*, 37–50.

Schmidt, N. B., & Woolaway-Bickel, K. (2000). The effects of treatment compliance on outcome in cognitive-behavioral therapy for panic disorder: Quality versus quantity. *Journal of Consulting and Clinical Psychology*, *68*, 13–18.

Siev, J., & Chambless, D. L. (2007). Specificity of treatment effects: Cognitive therapy and relaxation for generalized anxiety and panic disorders. *Journal of Consulting and Clinical Psychology*, *75*, 513–522.

Solomon, R. L., Kamin, L. J., & Wynne, L. C. (1953). Traumatic avoidance learning: The outcomes of several extinction procedures with dogs. *Journal of Abnormal and Social Psychology, 48,* 291–302.

Storch, E. A., Merlo, L. J., Bengston, M., Murphy, T. K., Lewis, M. H., Yang, M. C., … Goodman, W. K. (2007). D-cycloserine does not enhance exposure-response prevention therapy in obsessive-compulsive disorder. *International Clinical Psychopharmacology, 22,* 230–237.

Sy, J. T., Dixon, L. J., Lickel, J. J., Nelson, E. A., & Deacon, B. J. (2011). Failure to replicate the deleterious effects of safety behaviors in exposure therapy. *Behaviour Research and Therapy, 49*(5), 305–314. doi: 10.1016/j.brat.2011.02.005.

Telch, M. J., & Lancaster, C. L. (2012). Is there room for safety behaviors in exposure therapy for anxiety disorders? In P. Neudeck, & H. Wittchen (Eds.), *Exposure therapy: Rethinking the model – refining the method.* New York: Springer.

Twohig, M. P., Abramowitz, J. S., Bluett, E. J., Fabricant, L. E., Jacoby, R. J., Morrison, K. L., … Smith, B. M. (2015). Exposure therapy for OCD from an Acceptance and Commitment Therapy (ACT) framework. *Journal of Obsessive-Compulsive and Related Disorders, 6,* 167–173.

Van Dyke, M., & Pollard, C. A. (2005). Psychosocial treatment of refractory OCD: The St. Louis Model. *Cognitive and Behavioral Practice, 12,* 30–39.

Westra, H. A. (2012). *Motivational interviewing in the treatment of anxiety.* New York: Guildford Press.

Westra, H. A., & Stewart, S. H. (1998). Cognitive behavioural therapy and pharmacotherapy: Complementary or contradictory approaches to the treatment of anxiety? *Clinical Psychology Review, 18,* 307–340.

Cognitive Therapy for Obsessive-Compulsive Disorder

Morag Yule and Maureen L. Whittal

Like many innovations in science, cognitive therapy for OCD was introduced with the aim to improve upon the status quo. Rachman (1985) identified early on that the field was lacking appropriate strategies for some OCD presentations, namely obsessions. Salkovskis (1985) also noted that exposure and response prevention (ERP), while undoubtedly effective, is a technique that leads to improvement but does not directly address why change is occurring (i.e., the cognitive shifts that are associated with symptom improvement). It was thought that cognitive therapy (CT) could facilitate assessment, prevent premature discontinuation of therapy, and maximize adherence to challenging ERP exercises (Salkovskis & Warwick, 1985; Vogel, Stiles, & Götestam, 2004). Further, cognitive therapy could help to loosen the hold of dysfunctional beliefs surrounding the meaning of obsessions such that patients can more easily engage in exposures (Abramowitz, 2006).] p[In this chapter we describe the procedures of cognitive therapy for OCD, which are derived from cognitive models of the disorder. Research evaluating the effectiveness of these strategies are summarized followed by ideas for future directions.

Overview of Cognitive Therapy for OCD

Overall, the goal of cognitive therapy is to identify, challenge, and correct dysfunctional interpretations of intrusive thoughts, replacing them with more helpful, realistic, and benign interpretations. The cognitive theory of OCD posits that adjusting interpretations is a prerequisite to reducing persistence of obsessions. Although it is tempting to challenge patients on the content of their intrusions, this strategy may actually serve as reassurance and strengthen dysfunctional beliefs. It is essential to focus on the appraisal without attempting to alter the intrusion itself (Whittal & McLean, 2002).

Treatment duration and spacing of sessions varies according to a number of factors, but in uncomplicated cases weekly treatment is recommended in initial sessions. As is the case in all forms of CBT, the goal is to have the patient become their own therapist. Toward this goal, spacing sessions out as the therapy progresses

The Wiley Handbook of Obsessive Compulsive Disorders, Volume I, First Edition.
Edited by Jonathan S. Abramowitz, Dean McKay, and Eric A. Storch.
© 2017 John Wiley & Sons Ltd. Published 2017 by John Wiley & Sons Ltd.

is also recommended. In uncomplicated cases the total number of sessions could be as few as six–eight 1-hour sessions, whereas more severe presentations may necessitate upwards of 20–30 sessions.

Following assessment, treatment begins with psychoeducation. Self-monitoring of obsessions, compulsions and appraisals occurs throughout. Each individual session begins with a review of homework (and problem solving if homework was not completed), review of the cognitive conceptualization of maintenance of obsessions and compulsions, and challenging appraisals, which naturally leads into homework assignments. Throughout treatment the therapist assumes an inquisitive stance and refrains from being directive, but rather assists the patient in coming to conclusions on their own based upon the content of the discussion.

Cognitive therapy for OCD is best considered as a modular treatment. Following psychoeducation, there is no specified order of challenging appraisals. Self report assessment measures that include the Obsessional Belief Questionnaire (OBQ) (OCCWG 2005) identify the cognitive domains (i.e., overimportance/control of thoughts, overestimation of threat/responsibility, perfectionism/certainty) that are of primary importance to understanding an individual patient's presentation of OCD.

Psychoeducation about the Cognitive Model

Obsessions are "intrusive, repetitive thoughts, images or impulses that are unacceptable and/or unwanted and give rise to subjective resistance … the necessary and sufficient conditions … are intrusiveness, internal attribution, unwantedness and difficulty of control" (Rachman & Hodgson, 1980: 251). The cornerstone of the cognitive model is based upon research indicating that unwanted thoughts or intrusions are nearly ubiquitous and experienced by a large proportion of the nonclinical population (Rachman & de Silva, 1978). Rachman and de Silva (1978) found that 83% of "normal" participants admitted to having intrusive thoughts, that people vary in their level of tolerance toward these thoughts, and that clinical populations have a lower tolerance. These initial findings were supported by Salkovskis and Harrison (1984), who found that 88% of nonclinical individuals have intrusive thoughts.

The difference between "normal" intrusions and clinical obsessions is generally that clinical obsessions tend to last longer and are more discomforting, intense, and frequent compared with nonclinical obsessions. The *form* and *content* of obsessive thoughts, however, are similar between clinical and nonclinical groups (Rachman & de Silva, 1978; Salkovskis & Harrison, 1984). Importantly, the ease of dismissal is one of the crucial differences between obsessions among nonclinical and clinical individuals (Salkovskis & Harrison, 1984).

The content of one's intrusive thoughts is not random, but rather a reflection of what is important and meaningful to the patient, such that intrusions are related to the person's value system (Rachman, 1998) and often contradict the sense of self (Purdon & Clark, 1999). For an intrusion to be interpreted as "bad" or wrong, there must be some pre-existing notion of what is "good" or right (Whittal, Robichaud, & Woody, 2010a). If a thought is consistent with one's personal values, it causes no distress. If, on the other hand, an intrusive thought is *inconsistent* with one's personal values (e.g., a new mother who has aggressive intrusions against her child, or a highly religious person who has blasphemous thoughts), it is much more likely to cause distress and subsequent neutralizing or suppression, which may then lead to development of an obsession (Rowa, Purdon, & Summerfeldt, 2005). Upsetting intrusions often involve a vulnerable person (or group of people) who is significant to the patient in some way. It may actually be the case that the patient finds the intrusion so distasteful and horrific precisely because they are a kind, sensitive, and caring person, which is the opposite of their initial appraisal of the thought (Whittal et al., 2010a). A discussion of this nature can be very revealing for the patient, and can reduce distress significantly.

Cognitive models of obsessions propose that it is not the intrusive thought itself that is instrumental in the development of obsessions, but rather the misinterpretation of the significance of the intrusive thought (Rachman, 1997; Salkovskis, 1985). If an intrusive thought is misinterpreted as highly important ("this thought could be an omen") or of great personal significance ("this thought means I am a bad person"), it can morph from a slight nuisance into a clinical obsession that causes great distress and provokes compulsive behavior to neutralize this distress. Put simply, if the person interprets the thought as indicating he or she is "mad, bad, or dangerous" the thought is likely to become problematic (Rachman, 1997, 1998). Research supports the hypothesis that appraisals of intrusive thoughts contribute to the frequency and controllability of thoughts (Clark, Purdon, & Byers, 2000; Freeston, Ladouceur, Thibodeau, & Gagnon, 1991; Purdon & Clark, 1994). For example, Freeston, Ladouceur, Gagnon, and Thibodeau (1991) found that individuals with recurrent obsessions often attach an exaggerated significance to these thoughts, regarding them as horrific, disgusting, dangerous, and/or threatening. Once a thought is negatively evaluated, the individual may begin to use avoidance, compulsive rituals, or neutralizing strategies as a safety-seeking response to decrease the distress or anxiety associated with the thought. However, these neutralizing strategies have the opposite effect as intended, and actually maintain the fear. They increase the importance given to the thought, while at the same time disallowing disconfirmation of negative predictions associated with the thought. In this way, the safety behavior does not allow the patient to learn that the feared outcome would have never occurred in the first place (Abramowitz, 2006). An additional complication is that failure to control the thought will actually increase the perceived importance of the thought, thus strengthening the cycle (Purdon, 1999).

Cognitive models also assert that obsessions will persist as long as the misinterpretations continue, and that they will weaken once the misinterpretations are weakened (Rachman, 1997). Thus, the focus of cognitive therapy is on the reappraisal of intrusions, rather than on the intrusion itself. It begins with an educational component where the ubiquity of unwanted intrusive thoughts is discussed. Discovering and believing that unwanted thoughts are common can provide considerable relief for those suffering from OCD, and prepare the groundwork for less catastrophic interpretations of intrusive thoughts. Further, providing an understanding that the content of unwanted intrusive thoughts among a nonclinical population is not remarkably different from the content of clinical obsessions can be greatly relieving. Not only are patients often relieved of some level of guilt, but they are also relieved to hear that intrusive thoughts are not a sign of mental illness, nor do they lead to disaster or mean anything about them as a person. Rachman and de Silva's (1978) article included a list of "normal" intrusions that can be helpful to show in these early stages of treatment.

Patients may also find it helpful to poll a few acquaintances on whether they some-times experience intrusive or upsetting unwanted thoughts. This list of normal intru-sions can also be helpful in identifying the unwanted experiences that are easily dismissed (i.e., asking the patient to identify an intrusion they have experienced but were able to easily dismiss). Invariably the appraisal associated with said intrusion is relatively benign (e.g., "It's just a thought," "I know I won't do it," etc.). As an explanation for why negative intrusive thoughts arise, it may be helpful to explain that they seem to be the result of a highly developed human brain that is capable of a great amount of creativity. Just as we may at times imagine positive events (such as winning the lottery), our brain is also developed to be able to imagine negative scenarios that may be senseless and unpleasant (Abramowitz, 2006).

Strategies for Addressing Cognitive Domains

In addition to measures such as the OBQ, it may be helpful to use the "downward arrow" technique (Burns, 1980) to identify dysfunctional appraisals that will be chal-lenged throughout treatment. This technique involves asking the patient to describe a situation that triggered obsessions and compulsive behavior, and then using probing questions to identify the dysfunctional belief that evokes fear or discomfort (e.g., "What would be the worst thing that could happen?," "What would be so bad about that?"). While carrying out this type of questioning, the patient should be helped to focus not on their feared consequences, but on the meaning associated with these consequences (e.g., "If that were true, what would that mean about you?").

Overimportance of Thoughts and Need to Control Thoughts

Rachman initially described thought–action fusion (TAF) as being "the psychological fusion of the thought and the action, in which the person thinks that having an obses-sional thought is as bad as carrying out the action itself" (Rachman, 1993). The con-cept of TAF was later expanded to include two components: moral TAF (the belief that having an undesirable thought is the moral equivalent of carrying that thought out), and likelihood TAF (the belief that thinking about an undesirable event or behavior makes it more likely to happen) (Rachman, Thordarson, Shafran, & Woody, 1995; Shafran, Thordarson, & Rachman, 1996). Overall, fusion can serve to increase the perceived significance of a thought or obsession, and learning to defuse an obses-sional thought from its action can reduce the importance of the obsession itself.

Challenging likelihood of TAF. Behavioral experiments can be used to challenge likelihood TAF, such that patients can begin to consider that thinking about an event or behavior does not make it more likely to occur. In these experiments, the patient deliberately brings a negative thought to mind (e.g., someone the patient routines sees chipping a tooth, getting a black eye, breaking a bone), and monitors whether or not this thought results in a real-world outcome. The therapist can be an ideal target for these experiments, as he or she is someone the patient sees on a weekly basis, but is not a close friend or family member. The general guideline of TAF experiments is that the thought should be about something that is *uncommon*, but not *rare*. Thinking about common things occurring, such as catching the 'flu during the winter season, or very rare things, such as polio, will not tell us much about the power of thoughts. For example, if the patient experiments with the thought "my therapist will get the flu," during the winter months and this actually does occur, it will not necessarily be convincing since the base rate of the flu virus during the winter is elevated and coming down with the flu would not be surprising. Likewise having the patient think about something rare such as the therapist getting west Nile virus becomes too easy for the patient to negate the nonoccurrence of the event given the base rate.

The potential outcome of the thought should also be *observable*, and it is best if the therapist does not know the thought or potential outcome. This helps create an unambiguously belief-altering experience. For example, if the patient practices thinking that the therapist will break his or her leg in the coming week, and the therapist knows about this, an alternate explanation when no broken leg occurs is that the therapist was deliberately more careful to avoid an accident. These experiments should be engineered in ways that unequivocally provide evidence against the TAF belief. If the patient's TAF is directed toward him- or herself, a slightly different behavioral experiment could be used: because people generally feel that they have some control of their surroundings, directing the TAF experiment toward an inanimate object that directly affects the patient may be useful, for example having a toilet overflow, or getting a flat tire. If the patient has very strongly held TAF beliefs and is too fearful of the types of experiments mentioned previously, they might begin with testing whether thoughts of something positive will cause such events to occur (e.g., winning the lottery) (Freeston, Rhéaume, & Ladouceur, 1996).

Challenging moral TAF. In the case of moral TAF it might be helpful to begin by discussing a definition of morality as involving the choice of whether or not to act on a set of possibilities based on values and principles, rather than the occurrence of thoughts themselves (Freeston et al., 1996). The use of a "morality continuum" also may be beneficial. Anchors of "least moral" and "most moral" are established and are illustrated using classic examples of people often portrayed as "good" and "evil" (e.g., Mother Teresa and Hitler). The patient then places him- or herself on the continuum. Patients with unacceptable obsessional intrusions commonly see themselves close to the least moral end. Subsequent examples are then provided to help the patient separate thought from action for other people (e.g., people who *complete* infanticide compared with people who merely *think about* committing harm when they are frustrated) and notice how intentionality influences their judgments of morality. Then, the therapist can relate this back to the patient's own obsessions; For example, thoughts of killing another person while driving could be intentional (e.g., using the car as a weapon to purposely kill someone) or unintentional (e.g., accidentally killing someone who happened to walk in front of the vehicle by mistake). Often, varying intentionality results in differences on the continuum, thereby identifying a double standard. Questioning these differences can result in the patient altering moral judgments of themselves.

Challenging circular reasoning about thoughts. Individuals with OCD sometimes fall prey to the cognitive error of circular reasoning when misinterpreting intrusive thoughts (e.g., "A thought is important because it occurred, and it occurs because it is important") (Freeston et al., 1996). This is also reflected in the concept that because one has a particular thought, it must mean something about them (i.e., "If I have a thought about harming someone else, it must mean that I am a horrible person"). Techniques to challenge this circular reasoning include sampling thoughts that are present in any particular moment and using thought records to illustrate the sheer number of unimportant thoughts that occur. For example, the patient might observe and record all thoughts that occur in a 5-minute time span. This exercise will highlight the fact that there are a large number of thoughts that are occurring at any one time, and that the vast majority of these are meaningless. Attentional experiments (described later in this chapter) can also be used to demonstrate that arbitrarily believing something to be important can increase its salience (Freeston et al., 1996).

Thought sampling. Thought sampling can also be a useful method to challenge the belief that a thought is important solely because one thinks of it, as it can show that many unimportant thoughts occur and have no consequence. In this technique, the patient is instructed to think of a nonobsessive thought that does not cause distress, and reflect on why this thought is not perceived as significant. The abovementioned list of intrusive thoughts reported by non-OCD patients provided by Rachman and de Silva (1978) may be useful here. Patients can use the list to identify intrusions that they may have but that do not bother them and then discuss associated appraisals which are typically quite innocuous (e.g., "I know it's only a thought," "I know I would never do it"). For example, a patient whose obsessions focus on contamination, and who also has an occasional, nondistressing intrusive thought about physically harming other people, may benefit from a discussion about why this second thought does not cause distress. The patient will likely argue that the thought is not important because they would never harm anyone. This can reveal to the patient that, despite the thought being present, the interpretation of the thought is benign, and thus the thought is of no consequence to the patient. It follows that their problematic intrusion also does not have meaning solely because they have thought it.

Addressing thought suppression. If thoughts are perceived as important, and potentially a harbinger of future negative indicators, the need to control such thoughts will become paramount. One version of thought control, thought suppression, is a common strategy used in an attempt to gain relief from the distress associated with obsessions. Unfortunately, this tactic has a paradoxical effect: suppression of thoughts actually *increases* the frequency of that thought (Wegner, Schneider, Carter, & White, 1987) as well as the tendency toward preoccupation, which can lead to the thought becoming an obsession.

Thought suppression experiments can allow patients to register the negative effects of thought suppression, which opens the door to a discussion of how the patient might respond differently to intrusive thoughts (Wilhelm & Steketee, 2006). The "pink elephant" experiment is commonly used in cognitive therapy to illustrate this concept to patients. The patient is invited to think about anything they wish, *except* for a pink elephant for a certain period of time (usually around 30–60 seconds). Before launching into the experiment, the patient is asked to predict how many times they expect to think about a pink elephant, and then during the allotted time they are asked to indicate when a thought or image of a pink elephant arises (perhaps by lifting a finger). Patients usually find that suppressing the thought of a pink elephant is much more difficult than they imagined. The patient is then asked to think of *nothing but a pink elephant* – to keep the thought of a pink elephant in their mind as much as possible for the allotted time. Invariably, he or she finds that their mind wanders away from this thought despite their best efforts to remain with it. This experiment nicely illustrates the paradoxical effects of thought suppression.

The in-session discussion of the paradox of thought control naturally leads to a homework exercise. Specifically, patients are asked to alternate between letting thoughts come and go (similar to Trial 2 of the pink elephant demonstration) and compare it with fighting, dwelling on, or suppressing their thoughts (similar to Trial 1 of the pink elephant). Typically, the two strategies are alternated on a daily basis but if an entire day is too long, any time period can be used. The goal of the alternating exercise is to determine if the pattern observed in the session with the pink elephant experiment holds true when the content that is either suppressed or not are the obsessions in question. Patients are asked at the end of each day to record the overall severity of OCD and the success they had with the strategy of the day. If patients are successful at dropping control strategies they invariably observe the paradox of thought control (i.e., suppression generally leads to more intrusions and is more effortful).

Attentional experiments. As mentioned above, attention plays an important role in the prominence of thoughts, both for nonclinical and clinical populations. When something has meaning for us, we see more of it. This is true for benign situations, such as seeing more red cars when we have newly purchased a cherry red convertible, or noticing an increased number of pregnant women when a baby is on the way. It is also true if we are vigilant for threat. If a person is afraid of dogs, they will tend to notice a greater number of dogs than they would have otherwise. This phenomenon also applies to intrusive unwanted thoughts – the more meaning an intrusive thought has for a patient, the more likely he or she will be to notice such thoughts.

Attentional experiments, therefore, can be a powerful cognitive therapy tool. One easily conducted experiment requires the patient to pay particular attention to any "for sale" signs she or he comes across for a week. Prior to embarking on this experiment, the patient should estimate how many "for sale" signs she or he usually sees in a week. In the subsequent week, she or he is asked to no longer seek out these signs, but to make a note of when she or he does happen to see them (Whittal & McLean, 2002). Patients predictably find that they notice a higher number of the target object after training themselves to look out for them, even after they attempt to stop looking for them. Overall, these experiments can demonstrate to the patient that it may be their efforts at thought suppression and ensuing increased attention that increases the frequency of an intrusion, rather than the intrusion being present because it is fundamentally important.

Overestimation of Threat and Inflated Responsibility

Salkovskis (1985) postulated that people with OCD tend to feel an exaggerated sense of responsibility for actual, imagined, or anticipated misfortunes. This inflated sense of responsibility leads to increased obsessional thoughts, distress, and compulsive behavior. There is some overlap between overimportance of thoughts and inflated responsibility, which is based on the premise that thinking about something necessarily makes someone implicitly responsible for it (Freeston et al., 1996; Salkovskis, Richards, & Forrester, 1995). Thus, there are two sources of inflated responsibility: (a) TAF, in which feelings of responsibility are triggered by the patient's own thoughts; and (b) external sources, such as stoves and door locks, which may trigger compulsive checking. It is useful to address these sources separately in therapy. Further, overestimation of responsibility is comprised of two separate distortions: an exaggerated sense of the amount of responsibility one has in a situation (e.g., "If someone slips on that wet floor, it will be completely my fault"); and an inflated sense of the consequences of being responsible ("If someone slips and hurts herself, I will be legally liable"). Regardless of its source, inflated responsibility promotes urges and actions to prevent risk, such as checking or neutralizing (Shafran et al., 1996). Lopatka and Rachman (1995) found that patients with OCD tend to believe that the probability of misfortune increases when they are in a position of control or responsibility. Even if the chance of a catastrophe occurring remains very low, if the consequence of the catastrophe is high, the risk may be unacceptable to the patient. For example, the chance of contracting an illness such as HIV/AIDS may been seen by the patient to be quite low, however, if they perceive the consequence of infection with HIV/AIDS to be catastrophic they may struggle to decrease compulsive behavior related to this fear (van Oppen & Arntz, 1994).

Transferring responsibility. One method of addressing the exaggerated sense of responsibility is for the patient to briefly transfer (or share) the responsibility of a specific action onto the therapist, on the understanding that this transfer does not alter the patient's responsibility in other areas. This transfer of responsibility can produce drastic and sometimes immediate change in behavior, such that a person who has been anguished for years by the need to carry out numerous, time-consuming checks on their stove may be quickly able to return to normal use of the appliance. This exercise can foster increased understanding of the thoughts (i.e., "if someone falls, it will be all my fault") that drive related behaviors, with the goal of obtaining long-term reduction of inflated responsibility (Rachman, 1993). In fact, there is evidence that individuals with OCD reported a significant drop in compulsive urges to check when an experimental manipulation produced a temporary reduction in their sense of responsibility (Lopatka & Rachman, 1995).

Pie chart technique. "Pie charting" is another method of challenging exaggerated responsibility. In this technique, the patient lists all possible factors, no matter how small, that might contribute to the feared catastrophic event (including the patient him- or herself). Figure 32.1 illustrates this "pie-chart method" in the case of a patient who was concerned about being responsible for his child becoming ill. After a circle (the pie) was drawn, the patient estimated factors that might lead to his child becoming ill. He mentioned caught something at school, experiencing stress or being run down, eating something bad, allergies, and the patient not washing his own hands. He then estimated the importance or "weight" of each of these contributing factors (30%, 25%, 10%, 15%, and 10%, respectively) and filled these in as pieces of the pie (which was drawn on a white board). This exercise often helps patients to step back and see that their own degree of responsibility is often far less than originally estimated. This allows them to re-conceptualize their perception of responsibility (van Oppen & Arntz, 1994).

Overestimation of threat. At this point in therapy, it may be useful to introduce the patient to the concept of logical probability. For example, a patient who is concerned that she has not turned off the stove, and repeatedly returns home to check on it, might be asked to estimate how many times she left her home in the past six months (e.g., 300) and the number of times she had found that the stove had actually been left on (0). Based on this patient's experience, the logical probability of leaving the stove on the next time she leaves the house is 1/301 (0.3%). In keeping with the tendency to overestimate threat, patients can jump to the conclusion that leaving the

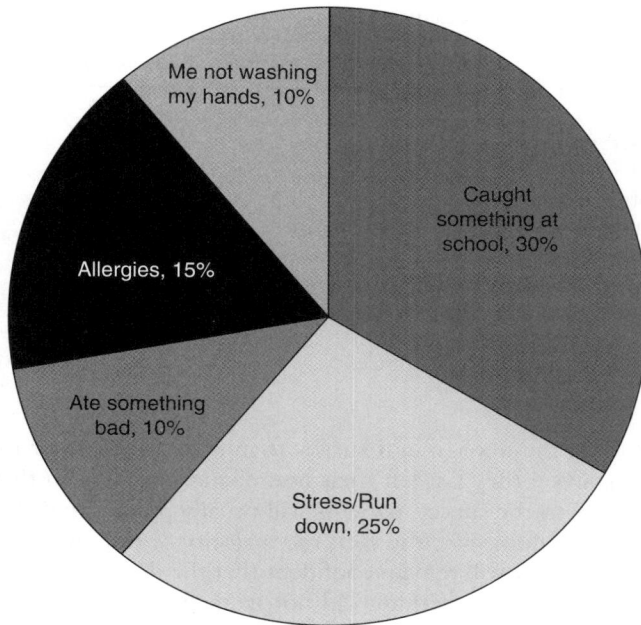

Figure 32.1   The "pie chart" of factors which might contribute to child's illness

stove on will immediately lead to an uncontrollable fire. Helping them to see that there are many steps that lead to the final feared outcome, and that each of these steps come with their own probability, is crucial in providing accurate estimates of threat. That is, the probability of the final feared outcome is the multiplicative property of the prior steps. Table 32.1 illustrates this exercise. Although it seems on the surface that this strategy is challenging the intrusion thereby amounting to reassurance, it is specifically designed to target the tendency to overestimate threat. We acknowledge that threat is not zero but that it is much lower than their anxiety makes them believe.

Need for Certainty and Perfectionism

Intolerance of uncertainty is often an important cognitive domain in OCD (Straus, 1948). This might lead to the need for perfection (i.e., the belief that there is a "right way" for things to be done) (Guidano, Liotti, & Mahoney, 1983) and difficulty with not knowing things *for sure*, leading to compulsive checking behavior. Because even a small amount of uncertainty leaves room for error (no matter how small), and the potential consequences of that error are estimated as catastrophic, the risk is also perceived as extremely high. Accordingly, there are a number of cognitive techniques that can help patients challenge and modify the intolerance of uncertainty.

Normalizing. The goal of normalizing the experience of uncertainty is to help the patient understand that uncertainty is ubiquitous, and that certainty is more or less an illusion. Accordingly, uncertainty does not indicate danger in and of itself, and thus does not need to be a cue for checking. One useful experiment to demonstrate this is to have the patient conduct a survey of ten friends or family members to see if they have similar uncertainties. For example, a patient who is concerned with whether or

Table 32.1 Logical probability calculations for catastrophic house fire

Step	Probability
Stove left on	1/500
Flammable item left near the element	1/50
Item catches fire	1/5
Fire spreads to other nearby items or walls	1/5
Smoke alarm not working	1/500
Fire not noticed by anyone	1/5
Fire department does not arrive in time	1/100
Catastrophic house fire	*

* Logical probability = $1 \times 1 \times 1 \times 1 \times 1 \times 1 \times 1$ divided by $500 \times 50 \times 5 \times 5 \times 500 \times 5 \times 100$ = a very small fraction of 1%.

not he or she locked the door, might survey friends to ask whether they remember locking their door when they last left their house; and how certain they are that the door is locked. Prior to the survey, patients will usually predict that their friends will remember locking the door, when in fact, the majority of respondents will likely *not* remember this action, but will remain confident that the door is locked. Not remembering does not mean that something did not happen (Whittal & McLean, 2002). A distinction can be made between "knowing" and being "certain." Many people will answer affirmatively when the question "is your door locked?" is posed. This affirmative response is often based on knowing rather than certainty. The latter assumes 100% confidence, which is a difficult standard to maintain on a daily basis, but is the goal for many OCD patients.

One useful analogy for normalizing uncertainty and perfectionism is as follows: imagine you are sitting in front of a large white cauldron of water. You would like to see the bottom of the cauldron, but there is some sort of brown substance on the bottom obstructing the view. The brown substance looks like brown sugar, so you decide to stir the water to see if the substance will dissolve. The brown substance, however, is not sugar, it is silt, and stirring the water actually makes the water more opaque and it is now more difficult to see the bottom. Thinking that stirring more vigorously will help dissolve the substance, you stir and stir, only making the bottom of the cauldron even more and more difficult to see. The only way to see the bottom of the cauldron at all is to stop stirring so that all the silt settles on the bottom. While you cannot see the entire bottom of the cauldron, as it is slightly obscured by the settled silt, you can now see much more than you could while you were stirring. The point of this analogy is to illustrate that in order to reach one's goals, one must accept that things will not be perfect, realize that there is no such thing as perfect certainty, and stop analyzing or thinking so that you do not make things worse.

Exploring advantages and disadvantages. The therapist can guide the patient in recognizing the disadvantage of the "black-and-white thinking" that accompanies perfectionism (e.g., "either it is perfect or it is not good enough"), including its ineffectiveness given that attaining absolute perfection is very difficult, if not impossible. It will also be beneficial to discuss other non-OCD related situations in which the patient does not require perfectionism, and does not experience associated distress. It is very likely the case that the patient already "knows" how to deal with imperfection in other areas of their lives, and guiding them to use some of these techniques to address their OCD anxieties may be helpful. Assigning the patient between-session tasks to complete imperfectly can be useful, as they will be given an opportunity to observe whether this leads to their feared outcome (e.g., not making gains in treatment).

It is important to have the patient weigh the advantages and disadvantages of living with uncertainty. Although it can be unpleasant to be unsure about the future it is futile to try to ensure certainty in most situations. Because there are so many different possible outcomes in a situation, trying to prepare for each possible outcome can take a tremendous amount of energy, and can greatly increase the amount of time spent worrying about possible outcomes, which are usually imagined to be catastrophic.

Concealment

Because of the abhorrent nature of intrusive thoughts, the patient may try to conceal the content of their obsessions from others, perhaps due to fear of judgment. This typically occurs in obsessions relating to religious, sexual, and aggressive obsessions, rather than those that involve checking, contamination, or perfectionism. If a patient believes that he or she is a terrible person for having aggressive thoughts about harming their children, he or she will be highly motivated to hide the content of these thoughts from others for fear of catastrophic repercussions. Unfortunately, habitual concealment has a maintaining role in obsessions (Newth & Rachman, 2001), as patients continue to believe that they are the only person who experiences such thoughts.

Discussion of concealment is an important component of cognitive therapy. Because it is a highly protective factor, often associated with the fear that others will judge the patient the same way that he or she judges him- or herself, breaking concealment can cause significant anxiety and distress, and thus should be undertaken only in the latter part of therapy. Moreover, if patients are reticent about dropping concealment the process can be completed in smaller steps (e.g., telling a loved one that they have unacceptable thoughts, but not immediately revealing the content). In dropping concealment the therapist should hopefully at this point be able to identify a close, supportive person in the patient's life with whom to gradually disclose the content of intrusions. Once such a person is identified, the patient should be encouraged to share Rachman and de Silva's (1978) list of "normal" intrusions with them. It is often the case that the friend or loved one endorses having experienced a number of these intrusions, but does not find these intrusions to be meaningful or upsetting in any way, which may be comforting to the patient. The next step in reducing concealment is for the patient to reveal some information about the content of their obsessions to their trusted person. A complete revealing of the obsessive content may be too distressing to the patient, in which case a slight unveiling of the content is an appropriate first step to test the reaction of the loved one. For example, if the obsessions involve sexual aggression toward the patient's children, she might initially reveal to her husband only that she is receiving treatment for obsessions related to the children, but that she would never act on these obsessions. The sexual content of the obsessions is withheld, at least for the time being, to allow a step-wise approach that is more acceptable to the patient. The next step for this patient may be to reveal further details about her obsessions, while being clear that the thoughts are unwanted. As the de-concealment process unfolds, the patient may find that her husband is more accepting of her obsessive content and understanding of her behaviors than she expected, and can perhaps even relate to some of the thoughts. The length of time required for this process depends on the client and his or her level of comfort at each stage. Although dropping concealment is important, if the therapist is not confident that the family member or friend will respond in a positive manner (e.g., be likely to take the obsessions on face value), dropping concealment should not be undertaken.

Review of the Treatment Outcome Studies on Cognitive Therapy

Research has provided some support for the cognitive model and its utility. Early studies comparing various forms of CT alone or with ERP typically found no group differences, but these sample sizes were small and the exposure therapy was always assigned as homework, rather than being supervised by a therapist, making group differences difficult to perceive (Emmelkamp & Beens, 1991; Emmelkamp, Visser, & Hoekstra, 1988). Freeston and Ladouceur (1997) found that changing beliefs that were specifically related to an obsession was significantly more effective in decreasing obsessive symptoms than changing general irrational beliefs. Van Oppen and colleagues (1995) provided some early evidence that individual CBT for OCD had greater gains than traditional ERP, but this was contradicted by McLean and colleagues (2001) whose controlled trial of group therapy for OCD found that those patients treated with ERP did significantly better than those treated with CBT.

More recently, Whittal and colleagues have conducted several outcome studies on individual and group treatments for OCD using cognitive therapy. Overall, this research has found comparable outcomes of ERP and CT treatments (and in one case no difference from an active stress management control; Whittal et al., 2010a), with generally no differences in Y-BOCS scores between groups (Whittal et al., 2005; Whittal, Robichaud, Thordarson, & McLean, 2008; Whittal, Woody, McLean, Rachman, & Robichaud, 2010b). One long-term study, however, did find that an ERP group had lower Y-BOCS scores over time than a CT group after two years (Whittal et al., 2008). Importantly, however, this study found tentative evidence that CT was better tolerated and had a lower dropout rate than the ERP group.

Overall, research shows that contemporary CT has comparable rates of efficacy compared to traditional ERP, but it may be the case that CT is more acceptable to patients, which leads to lower dropout rates (Whittal et al., 2008). Of course, these cognitive treatments do not work each and every time they are undertaken. There are some OCD presentations (e.g., "feel right" that is not accompanied by magical thinking) that are more challenging from a cognitive perspective and may better be addressed with traditional ERP. Like all forms of treatment with all disorders, patient's willingness and motivation to change along with nonspecific factors that include interpersonal fit with the therapist all potentially contribute change or lack thereof. Additionally, the strategies presented in this chapter are not necessarily stand alone procedures and can be combined with ERP to optimize outcomes.

Conclusions

The development of cognitive approaches to treat OCD came about secondary to the partial treatment response and the high drop out and refusal rates of earlier treatments. In the 30 years since the publication of the seminal article discussing a cognitive approach to the treatment of OCD (Salkovskis, 1985), much work has been done in developing the treatment and testing the efficacy of it. Although it is seen to be an effective treatment, it appears as if those efficacy rates are not significantly higher than those attributed to ERP. However a cognitive approach may be more tolerable for patients leading to a treatment that may overall be more effective.

Given the plateauing of treatment response for OCD, we need to turn our attention as researchers and clinicians to modifying our existing treatments in the hopes that it will confer benefit to those who require it the most. On the cognitive front there is exciting work in the early stages on a subset of people with contamination concerns (i.e., mental contamination; see Coughtrey, Shafran, & Rachman, 2014; Coughtrey, Shafran, Knibbs, & Rachman, 2012, Rachman, Coughtrey, Shafran & Radomsky, 2015, for more information). It is with these innovative approaches that we may move off our plateau and resume an upward treatment trajectory.

References

Abramowitz, J. S. (2006). *Understanding and treating obsessive-compulsive disorder.* Mahwah, NJ: Lawrence Erlbaum.

Burns, D. D. (1980). *Feeling good: The new mood therapy.* New York: New American Library.

Clark, D. A., Purdon, C., & Byers, E. S. (2000). Appraisal and control of sexual and non-sexual intrusive thoughts in university students. *Behaviour Research and Therapy, 38,* 439–455.

Coughtrey, A. E., Shafran, R., & Rachman, S. J. (2014). The spread of mental contamination. *Journal of Behavior Therapy and Experimental Psychiatry, 45*(1), 33–38. doi: 10.1016/j.jbtep.2013.07.008.

Coughtrey, A. E., Shafran, R., Knibbs, D., & Rachman, S. J. (2012). Mental contamination in obsessive-compulsive disorder. *Journal of Obsessive-Compulsive and Related Disorders, 1*(4), 244–250. doi: 10.1016/j.jocrd.2012.07.006.

Emmelkamp, P. M. G., & Beens, H. (1991). Cognitive therapy with obsessive-compulsive disorder: A comparative evaluation. *Behaviour Research and Therapy, 29*(3), 293–300. doi: 10.1016/0005-7967(91)90120-R.

Emmelkamp, P., Visser, S., & Hoekstra, R. J., (1988). Cognitive therapy vs exposure in vivo in the treatment of obsessive-compulsives. *Cognitive Therapy and Research, 12*(1), 103–114.

Freeston, M. H., & Ladouceur, R. (1997). What do patients do with their obsessive thoughts? *Behaviour Research and Therapy, 35*(4), 335–348. doi: 10.1016/S0005-7967(96)00094-0.

Freeston, M. H., Ladouceur, R., Thibodeau, N., & Gagnon, F. (1991). Cognitive intrusions in a non-clinical population – I: Response style, subjective experience, and appraisal. *Behaviour Research and Therapy, 29*(6), 585–597. doi: 10.1016/0005-7967(91)90008-Q.

Freeston, M. H., Rhéaume, J., & Ladouceur, R. (1996). Correcting faulty appraisals of obsessional thoughts. *Behaviour Research and Therapy, 34*(5/6), 433–446. doi: 10.1016/0005-7967(95)00076-3.

Guidano, V. F., Liotti, G., & Mahoney, M. J. (1983). *Cognitive processes and emotional disorders: A structural approach to psychotherapy.* New York: Guilford Press.

Lopatka, C., & Rachman, S. (1995). Perceived responsibility and compulsive checking: An experimental analysis. *Behaviour Research and Therapy, 33*(6), 673–684. doi: 10.1016/0005-7967(94)00089-3.

McLean, P. D., Whittal, M. L., Thordarson, D. S., Taylor, S., Söchting, I., Koch, W. J., Paterson, R., & Anderson, K. W. (2001). Cognitive versus behavior therapy in the group treatment of obsessive-compulsive disorder. *Journal of Consulting and Clinical Psychology*, *69*(2), 205–214. doi: 10.1037/0022-006X.69.2.205.

Newth, S., & Rachman, S. (2001). The concealment of obsessions. *Behaviour Research and Therapy*, *39*(4), 457–464.

Obsessive Compulsive Cognitions Working Group (OCCWG). (2005). Psychometric validation of the obsessive belief questionnaire and interpretation of intrusions inventory – Part 2: Factor analyses and testing of a brief version. *Behaviour Research and Therapy*, *43*(11), 1527–1542. doi: 10.1016/j.brat.2004.07.010.

Purdon, C. (1999). Thought suppression and psychopathology. *Behaviour Research and Therapy*, *37*, 1029–1054.

Purdon, C., & Clark, D. A. (1994). Perceived control and appraisal of obsessional intrusive thoughts: A replication and extension. *Behavioural and Cognitive Psychotherapy*, *22*(4), 269–285. doi: 10.1017/S1352465800013163.

Purdon, C., & Clark, D. A. (1999). Metacognition and obsessions. *Clinical Psychology & Psychotherapy*, *6*(2), 102–110.

Rachman, S. (1985). An overview of clinical and research issues in obsessional-compulsive disorder. In M. Mavissakalian, S. M. Turner, & L. Michelson (Eds.), *Obsessive-compulsive disorder: Psychological and pharmacological treatment* (pp. 1–47). New York: Plenum.

Rachman, S. (1993). Obsessions, responsibility and guilt. *Behaviour Research and Therapy*, *31*(2), 149–154. doi: 10.1016/0005-7967(93)90066-4.

Rachman, S. (1997). A cognitive theory of obsessions. *Behaviour Research and Therapy*, *35*(9), 793–802. doi: 10.1016/S0005-7967(97)00040-5.

Rachman, S. (1998). A cognitive theory of obsessions: elaborations. *Behaviour Research and Therapy*, *36*(4), 385–401. doi: 10.1016/S0005-7967(97)10041-9.

Rachman, S., Coughtrey, A., Shafran, R., & Radomsky, A (2015). *Oxford guide to the treatment of mental contamination*. Oxford: Oxford University Press.

Rachman, S., & de Silva, P. (1978). Abnormal and normal obsessions. *Behaviour Research and Therapy*, *16*(4), 233–248. doi: 10.1016/0005-7967(78)90022-0.

Rachman, S., & Hodgson, R. J. (1980). *Obsessions and compulsions*. Englewood Cliffs, NJ: Prentice-Hall.

Rachman, S., Thordarson, D. S., Shafran, R., & Woody, S. R. (1995). Perceived responsibility: Structure and significance. *Behaviour Research and Therapy*, *33*(7), 779–784.

Rowa, K., Purdon, C., & Summerfeldt, L. (2005). Why are some obsessions more upsetting than others? *Behaviour Research and Therapy*, *43*(11), 1453–1465. doi: 10.1016/j. brat.2004.11.003.

Salkovskis, P. (1985). Obsessional-compulsive problems: A cognitive-behavioural analysis. *Behaviour Research and Therapy*, *23*(5), 571–583. doi: 10.1016/0005-7967(85)90105-6.

Salkovskis, P. M., & Harrison, J. (1984). Abnormal and normal obsessions: A replication. *Behaviour Research and Therapy*, *22*(5), 549–552. doi: 10.1016/0005-7967(84)90057-3.

Salkovskis, P. M., Richards, H., & Forrester, E. (1995). The relationship between obsessional problems and intrusive thoughts. *Behavioural and Cognitive Psychotherapy*, *23*(3), 281–299.

Salkovskis, P. M., & Warwick, H. M. C. (1985). Cognitive therapy of obsessive-compulsive disorder: Treating treatment failures. *Behavioural and Cognitive Psychotherapy*, *13*(3), 243–255. doi: 10.1017/S0141347300011095.

Shafran, R., Thordarson, D. S., & Rachman, S. (1996). Thought–action fusion in obsessive compulsive disorder. *Journal of Anxiety Disorders*, *10*(5), 379–391. doi: 10.1016/ 0887-6185(96)00018-7.

Straus, E. W. (1948). On obsession: A clinical and methodological study. *Nervous and Mental Disease Monograph*, *73*, 1948. doi: 10.1007/BF01172967.

van Oppen, P., & Arntz, A. (1994). Cognitive therapy for obsessive-compulsive disorder. *Behaviour Research and Therapy, 32*(1), 79–87. doi: 10.1016/0005-7967(94)90086-8.

van Oppen, P., de Haan, E., van Balkon, A. J. L. M., Spinhoven, P., Hoogduin, K., & van Dyck, R. (1995). Cognitive therapy and exposure *in vivo* in the treatment of obsessive compulsive disorder. *Behaviour Research and Therapy, 33*(4), 379–390.

Vogel, P. A., Stiles, T. C., & Götestam, K. G. (2004). Adding cognitive therapy elements to exposure therapy for obsessive compulsive disorder: A controlled study. *Behavioural and Cognitive Psychotherapy, 32*(3), 275–290. doi: 10.1017/S1352465804001353.

Wegner, D. M., Schneider, D. J., Carter, S. R., & White, T. L. (1987). Paradoxical effects of thought suppression. *Journal of Personality and Social Psychology, 53*(1), 5–13. doi: 10.1037/0022-3514.53.1.5.

Whittal, M. L., & McLean, P. D. (2002). Group cognitive behavioral therapy for obsessive compulsive disorder. In R. O. Frost and G. S. Steketee (Eds.), *Cognitive approaches to obsessions and compulsions: Theory, assessment and treatment* (pp. 417–433). Oxford: Elsevier Science.

Whittal, M. L., Robichaud, M., & Woody, S. R. (2010a). Cognitive treatment of obsessions: Enhancing dissemination with video components. *Cognitive and Behavioral Practice, 17*, 1–8.

Whittal, M. L., Robichaud, M., Thordarson, D. S., & McLean, P. D. (2008). Group and individual treatment of obsessive-compulsive disorder using cognitive therapy and exposure plus response prevention: A 2-year follow-up of two randomized trials. *Journal of Consulting and Clinical Psychology, 76*(6), 1000–1014. doi: 10.1037/a0013076.

Whittal, M. L., Thordarson, D. S., & McLean, P. D. (2005). Treatment of obsessive-compulsive disorder: Cognitive behavior therapy vs. exposure and response prevention. *Behaviour Research and Therapy, 43*(12), 1559–1576. doi: 10.1016/j.brat.2004.11.012.

Whittal, M. L., Woody, S. R., McLean, P. D., Rachman, S. J., & Robichaud, M. (2010b). Treatment of obsessions: A randomized controlled trial. *Behaviour Research and Therapy, 48*(4), 295–303. doi: 10.1016/j.brat.2009.11.010.

Wilhelm, S., & Steketee, G. S. (2006). *Cognitive therapy for Obsessive-Compulsive Disorder*. Oakland, CA: New Harbinger.

33

Acceptance and Commitment Therapy for OCD

Brooke M. Smith, Ellen J. Bluett, Eric B. Lee, and Michael P. Twohig

Acceptance and commitment therapy (ACT) is a contextual, experiential model of psychotherapy that incorporates principles of behavioral psychology with mindfulness processes, emphasizing language and cognition as key factors in the etiology, maintenance, and treatment of psychopathology (Hayes, Strosahl, & Wilson, 2012). Because of the attention paid to cognition, ACT is considered one member of the broader class of cognitive and behavioral therapies (CBT) (Herbert & Forman, 2013; Twohig, Woidneck & Crosby, 2013). ACT is linked to the basic science of behavior analysis and its more recent branch relational frame theory (RFT) (Hayes, Barnes-Holmes, & Roche, 2001) and is founded upon a specific philosophy of science, functional contextualism (Hayes, 1993). ACT therefore resides at the level of applied theory and intervention within a larger, multilevel, and integrated program of psychological science known as contextual behavioral science (CBS) (Hayes, Levin, Plumb-Vilardaga, Villatte, & Pistorello, 2013).

Functional Contextualism

ACT is rooted in a pragmatic philosophy of science known as functional contextualism (Hayes, 1993). From this perspective, no event – including thoughts, emotions, and behaviors – is inherently problematic. Everything depends on context. The "truth" of any behavior is determined by *effective action*, or the degree to which it helps further a predetermined purpose. As applied clinically, "purpose" is synonymous with an individual's values and leads to a focus on valued living. As applied to psychological science, the specific purpose of CBS is *prediction and influence of behavior with precision, scope, and depth* (Hayes, Barnes-Holmes, & Wilson, 2012). *Prediction* of behavior is a goal that is shared with other philosophical approaches. However, functional contextualism's emphasis on the *influence* of behavior leads to a focus on stimuli that can be directly manipulated (Hayes & Brownstein, 1986). Related to this is an emphasis on the *function* of behavior – *why* a particular behavior occurs – rather than its topography, or form. The term "contextual" refers to the historical and situational setting of any

The Wiley Handbook of Obsessive Compulsive Disorders, Volume I, First Edition.
Edited by Jonathan S. Abramowitz, Dean McKay, and Eric A. Storch.
© 2017 John Wiley & Sons Ltd. Published 2017 by John Wiley & Sons Ltd.

event. Events are interdependent with their contexts, meaning they can only be ana-lyzed in terms of those contexts. The primary unit of analysis within functional contextualism is therefore the *ongoing act-in-context* (Hayes et al., 2012).

Foundations in Basic Science

The relationship between ACT and basic science is bidirectional; basic science provides empirically derived principles of behavior upon which clinical techniques are based; clinical issues help inform many of the basic science questions asked (Hayes et al., 2013).

Behavior Analysis

The behavior change techniques used in ACT are based on operant conditioning and are similar to the methods of traditional behavior therapy, such as skills training, goal setting, contingency management, behavioral activation, and exposure. RFT extends this analysis of behavior, showing how verbal processes are always operating on tradi-tional basic processes.

Relational Frame Theory

As conceptualized through RFT, language consists of the ability to respond to stimuli based upon arbitrary features, to derive relations between those stimuli that have never been directly trained, and to change the meaning and psychological functions of stimuli based on those relationships. Many species of animal are capable of respond-ing to stimuli based on their relations to other stimuli using formal properties such as shape, size, and location (e.g., Henderson, Hurly, & Healy, 2006). However, humans have the unique ability to relate stimuli not just on the basis of formal properties, but also on the basis of *arbitrary* properties. When Americans "pledge allegiance to the flag," for example, they are not actually pledging their allegiance to a brightly colored piece of cloth. They are pledging their allegiance to the United States of America, for which the flag is a symbol. In RFT parlance, the flag and the country are in a *frame of coordination* (i.e., a relation of *sameness*), and this relational responding is known as *relational framing*.

In addition to forming relations, humans have the ability to relationally respond to stimuli even if the relation was never directly trained. In other words, humans can *derive* relations between stimuli based on their relations with other stimuli (Dymond & Barnes, 1995). If a child learns in school that the flag is the *same as* the country, the child can also derive that the country is the *same as* the flag. The abilities to relate stimuli based on arbitrary properties and to derive relations that were never directly trained have been convincingly demonstrated only in humans (Hayes, 1989), begin to develop at a very early age (Lipkens, Hayes, & Hayes, 1993), and tend to correlate with verbal abilities and measures of intelligence (e.g., O'Hora et al., 2008). Taken together, they are referred to as *arbitrarily applicable derived relational responding* (AADRR) and form the basis of human language and cognition from an RFT perspective.

AADRR consists of three main processes: *mutual entailment, combinatorial entail-ment,* and *transformation of stimulus function.* An example of these within OCD might be a person with a contamination obsession who fears becoming ill due to germs and therefore avoids the use of public restrooms. Through language processes, the experience of illness is related to germs, germs are related to public restrooms, and the person avoids restrooms as he or she would avoid illness. More technically, germs are in a causal relation – or causal *frame* – with illness (i.e., germs *cause* illness) and a hierarchical relation with public restrooms (i.e., germs *are in* restrooms). Both of these relations may have, at one time or another, been directly trained. However, the individual now *derives* that public restrooms cause illness, a relation that was never directly trained between two stimuli that share no formal properties. The process through which the illness and the restroom become related is *combinatorial entailment*, because it involves three stimuli (see Figure 33.1). If the relation were only between two stimuli – such as illness and germs – this would be the process of *mutual entailment*. Because the restroom has acquired the same psychological functions for the person as illness, avoidance of the restroom is an example of the *transformation of stimulus function*. All of this takes place within a context and is determined by two contexts in particular – the relational context, which controls the relations derived, and the functional context, which controls the functions transferred (Steele & Hayes, 1991).

Rule-governed Behavior

Because humans have language, their behavior is capable of coming under the control of more than just direct environmental contingencies – it can also come under the control of *rules*. Rules are verbal statements that specify a contingency, or a cause and effect relationship (Skinner, 1966). "If you touch a hot stove, you will burn your hand," is an example of a rule. Through the transformation of stimulus function, rules can come to exert strong influence over behavior (Hayes, Brownstein, Zettle, Rosenfarb, & Korn, 1986). Often, rules and rule-governed behavior are quite helpful and adaptive because they allow learning to occur without the need to directly experience consequences. However, when rule-governed behavior is under the control of inaccurate rules or becomes rigid and inflexible, it can be harmful.

Using the previous example, a person with a contamination obsession may form the rule, "If I use a public restroom, I will get sick." Without ever having experienced sickness after using a public restroom, the person behaves in accordance with this rule

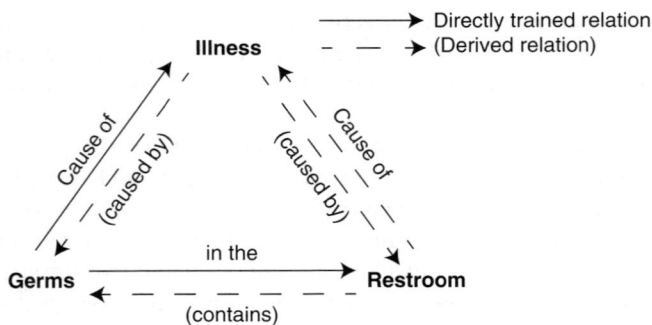

Figure 33.1   An example of combinatorial entailment

and avoids public restrooms. Because of this avoidance, he or she loses contact with the direct contingencies – how the world really works – and there is no longer an opportunity to learn from direct experience. Within ACT, it is this interaction of language with environmental contingencies that is considered a primary cause of psychopathology (Törneke, Luciano, & Salas, 2008). ACT therefore works to loosen the control of language on behavior for the sake of promoting contact with direct experience, which it is hoped will shape more functional behavior.

Importantly, ACT does not attempt to change the form of the cognitions, such as through challenging an inaccurate rule or attempting to alter an already established relation. Relational frames and networks are behaviors and, just as there is no "unlearning" of behavior (Bouton & Woods, 2008), there is no "unlearning" of verbal relations (Wilson & Hayes, 1996). Instead, ACT focuses on the *influence* those relations have on behavior through manipulating the environmental contexts in which verbal statements occur, particularly the context regulating which stimulus functions are transformed (i.e., the functional context). Thus, although the public restroom may always be in a causal frame with illness, the client learns to behave differently in its presence.

Processes of Change and Middle-Level Terms

The field of psychology often communicates its ideas with terms that are less technical than those of basic science, but more easily understood and disseminated, sometimes called *middle-level terms* (Hayes et al., 2012). One example of a middle-level term in ACT is *psychological flexibility*, the model of psychopathology/psychological health that underlies ACT, along with the six processes of change that compose it.

Psychological flexibility is the ability to connect with the present moment, in a particular context, in order to behave according to one's values (Hayes, Luoma, Bond, Masuda, & Lillis, 2006). Its opposite – *psychological inflexibility* – is the target mechanism of change in ACT. Specifically, the model aims to increase psychological flexibility by altering how one relates to internal experiences – thoughts, feelings, and physical sensations – in order to increase valued living. To do so, six processes are targeted: acceptance, cognitive defusion, self as context, present moment awareness, values, and committed action (see Figure 33.2). Each process is a middle-level term that is theoretically and empirically connected to basic behavioral principles and RFT – linking basic science to clinical contexts.

Acceptance means welcoming all internal experiences, whether pleasant or unpleasant, without attempts to affect their form or frequency. Acceptance is sometimes called *willingness*, because it does not require that a person like these experiences – it simply requires allowing the experiences to occur. When treating OCD from an ACT model, clients are encouraged to accept the presence of obsessions and the distress that results from them, without attempting to change these experiences through avoidance, compulsions, cognitive actions, or any other control strategy.

Cognitive defusion is a process in which the context that controls the functions of verbal relations (i.e., the functional context) is altered and, as a result, a new function of the verbal relation is established (Hayes et al., 2012). The goal of cognitive defusion is not to change the relations themselves but, rather, the way in which one relates

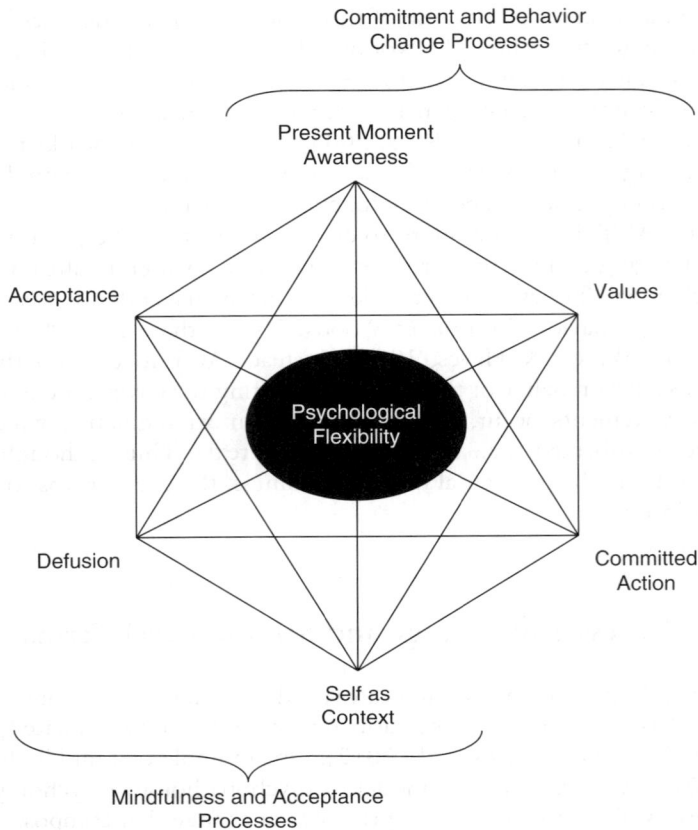

Figure 33.2 The ACT model: Psychological flexibility as six core processes of change

to them. Within the treatment of OCD, for example, clients are taught to view their obsessional thoughts as simply words or sounds, thus creating distance from the literal meaning of the thought and enabling greater flexibility with regard to that thought.

Self as context is the ability to view oneself from the "I/here/now" perspective (Twohig, 2012). That is, one experiences thoughts, feelings, and beliefs about oneself from the stance of an observer rather than being defined by those experiences. The individual takes the perspective of the context in which those experiences occur. Conversely, *the conceptualized self*, which is an evaluative perception of self, ultimately creates the rule that "this is who I am." The difference between these two perspectives is akin to that of a client who *experiences* anxiety versus one who *is* an anxious person.

Present moment awareness is the capacity to attend flexibly to all events, including thoughts, feelings, and emotions, in the here-and-now as opposed to the past or future. As described by Hayes and colleagues (2006), contact with the present moment is the world of direct experience, without the need to change that experience. By increasing present moment awareness, an individual becomes capable of contacting direct contingencies rather than getting caught up in verbally constructed rules or thoughts about previous or future experiences. In the treatment of OCD, the clinician encourages greater awareness of the current situation (e.g., during an exposure exercise) as well as distressing thoughts and fears that it may produce.

Values are verbal statements that identify meaningful areas of life. Although culture and family can influence them, values are personal and freely chosen. In ACT, behaviors are neither "right" nor "wrong"; they are only *workable* or *unworkable* within the context of the client's values. That is, behaviors either serve – or impede – an identified value. Clients are therefore assisted in constructing and clarifying values and using these as gauges for everyday choices. A client with OCD who has identified *spending time with family* as a value may find that excessive hand washing is interfering with this important area of life and, through transformation of stimulus function, hand washing becomes punishing and its frequency decreases.

Committed action consists of identifying and engaging in behavioral commitments – activities or experiences in which there is an opportunity to respond flexibly to the environment in a manner that is consistent with one's values. Over time, such commitments begin to build into larger patterns of valued living (Wilson, 2008). The techniques used to facilitate committed action follow basic behavioral principles and resemble traditional behavior therapy (Hayes et al., 2006). An exposure exercise is an example of a behavioral commitment that allows the client to engage in valued action while practicing acceptance, defusion, present moment awareness, and perspective-taking.

Data Supporting ACT and ACT Components

ACT as a Unified Model

Numerous randomized clinical trials have been conducted that support ACT as an effective treatment for a variety of psychological disorders. Recent meta-analyses have found that ACT had medium effect sizes across an array of disorders (Öst, 2008; Powers, Zum Vörde Sive Vörding, & Emmelkamp, 2009). Another meta-analysis examined mindfulness and acceptance based interventions (including ACT) for anxiety disorders (Vøllestad, Nielsen, & Nielsen, 2012), showing large effect sizes for anxiety symptoms pre- to posttreatment ($g = 1.08$) and between conditions ($g = 0.83$).

Processes of Change

Levin, Hildebrandt, Lillis, and Hayes (2012) conducted a meta-analysis that examined 66 laboratory-based component studies on the six core processes of ACT, along with other purported mechanisms of contextual behavior therapies. Specifically, the authors examined individual components of psychological flexibility (i.e., acceptance, defusion, self as context, present moment awareness, and values), comparing them with both inactive and active control conditions, on outcomes related to psychological flexibility. Results showed significant positive effect sizes for acceptance, defusion, present moment awareness, values, mixed mindfulness, and values plus mindfulness conditions compared to inactive conditions. Additionally, studies that included experiential exercises and metaphors had larger effect sizes than those with treatment rationales only.

Psychological Flexibility

Psychological flexibility has growing support as the mechanism of change within an ACT model (Hayes et al., 2006). In particular, studies have shown that increasing psychological flexibility has been related to changes in primary outcome measures of anxiety (e.g., Forman, Herbert, Moitra, Yeomans, & Geller, 2007). One randomized control trial compared ACT with CBT for the treatment of anxiety (Arch et al., 2012a). Although there were no significant differences between conditions at post, those in the ACT condition had lower clinical severity rating scores at 12-month follow-up, and those in the CBT condition had greater quality of life scores. Interestingly, participants in the ACT condition reported greater psychological flexibility from post to 12-month follow-up than those in the CBT condition (Arch et al., 2012a; Arch, Wolitzky-Taylor, Eifert, & Craske 2012b). Yet another study examined session-by-session data for 174 individuals randomized to receive ACT or CT for anxiety or depression (Forman et al., 2012). People in the CT condition applied cognitive change strategies more often than acceptance strategies, and people in the ACT condition employed acceptance strategies over change strategies. Furthermore, defusion and willingness were equivalent mediators across conditions.

Research on the role of psychological flexibility and OCD is mixed. Using clinical (Manos et al., 2010) and nonclinical samples (Abramowitz, Lackey, & Wheaton, 2009), researchers have found low correlations between psychological flexibility and measures of OCD and have also found that cognitive measures predict OCD better than measures of psychological flexibility. Other studies have found stronger correlations between measures of psychological flexibility and OCD (Briggs & Price, 2009; Gloster, Klotsche, Chaker, Hummel, & Hoyer, 2011; Wetterneck, Lee, Smith, & Hart, 2013). A recent meta-analysis on psychological flexibility and measures of OCD severity showed a significant medium correlation across all studies to date ($r = .36$) (Bluett, Homan, Morrison, Levin, & Twohig, 2014).

Data Supporting ACT for OCD

Although exposure exercises are a part of the ACT model (falling under the process of committed action), ACT without in-session exposure exercises has been tested in a handful of studies (Armstrong, Morrison, & Twohig, 2013; Dehlin, Morrison, & Twohig, 2013; Twohig, Hayes, & Masuda, 2006a; Twohig et al., 2010a). Across these studies, an 8–10 week, 1-hour per session protocol was tested. The largest and best controlled of these studies was a randomized clinical trial of ACT versus progressive relaxation training (PRT, an active control condition) for 79 adults diagnosed with OCD (Twohig et al., 2010a). This study utilized independent raters, therapists, and supervisors; sessions were scored and showed good treatment integrity. Using a full intent to treat analysis, results indicated that there was a significant difference in Y-BOCS scores between the ACT and PRT conditions at posttreatment ($p = .002$, effect size $= 0.77$) and 3-month follow-up ($p < .009$, effect size $= 0.62$). Most notably, clinical response rates supported ACT over the control condition – ACT showed response rates between 46–56% at post and 46–66% at follow-up versus 13–18% and 16–18% in the PRT condition (the range consists of completer vs. intent to treat data). Treatment refusal (2.4% in ACT and 7.8% in PRT) and dropout (9.8% in ACT and 13.2% in PRT) were low in both conditions. Secondary measures showed stronger effects for depression and quality of life in the ACT condition. Additionally, processes of change theoretically associated with ACT moved more in the ACT condition than the control condition.

A series of studies using multiple baseline across participants designs tested the same ACT protocol for adults with a variety of OCD presentations (Twohig et al., 2006a), adults with scrupulosity type OCD (Dehlin et al., 2013), and adolescents with OCD (Armstrong et al., 2013), with favorable results. In addition, a randomized controlled trial of ACT (including exposure exercises) was compared with a traditional CBT program for mixed anxiety disorders (Arch et al., 2012a). Results for the individuals with OCD ($n = 17$–12) were generally comparable on measures of clinical response and OCD severity. Finally, data also support ACT without exposure exercises (Twohig, Hayes, & Masuda, 2006b) and ACT in combination with habit reversal (Woods, Wetterneck, & Flessner, 2006) in the treatment of OCD spectrum disorders trichotillomania and skin picking disorder. This line of work, in addition to the general effectiveness (e.g., Strosahl, Hayes, Bergan, & Romano, 1999), efficacy, and component research on ACT suggests that it is a promising treatment for OCD.

The ACT Approach to Clinical Practice

The experience of anxiety and associated inner experiences are a large part of OCD. Paradoxically, avoidance of anxiety and obsessions increases the perception of threat and the future need to avoid such experiences. ACT therefore aims to decrease avoidance by changing the function of unwanted thoughts and feelings through directly targeting language and cognitive processes that maintain these functions (Hayes, Villatte, Levin, & Hildebrandt, 2011). Behavior is then directed toward the pursuit of meaningful life activities. In order to achieve this, the therapist targets the six core processes that constitute psychological flexibility through techniques intended to promote client contact with the here and now (Hayes et al., 2011).

Briefly, a context in which therapist and client are on equal ground is created; the therapist demonstrates present moment awareness as well as flexibility in responding. The therapist normalizes the client's struggle by highlighting the inevitability of human suffering and the paradoxical effects of attempting to avoid or reduce anxiety. Experiential exercises, metaphors, and discussions are woven into therapy in order to target processes of change. The therapist highlights the importance of moving towards one's values, with the aim of increasing quality of life rather than decreasing symptomatology.

ACT as a Treatment for OCD

A relatively brief description of the treatment is presented next. Please see Twohig (2009) for a description of ACT for OCD, as well as book-length treatments of ACT in general (Hayes, Strosahl, & Wilson, 2012) and ACT for anxiety disorders (Eifert & Forsyth, 2005). The short-term goal of ACT for OCD is to increase psychological flexibility; the long-term goal is to help the client live a life that is more consistent with his or her life goals and values. In most cases, notable avoidance behaviors and compulsions make doing this very difficult.

Initial Sessions: Setting Up Treatment

The initial hurdle that a therapist working from the ACT model faces is that, in some cases, the definition of successful therapy is at odds with what many clients entering treatment expect. Many clients enter treatment with a general rule such as, "If I experience less anxiety and obsessions, then I will be able to control my compulsions and life will be better." Written another way, clients often enter therapy believing that only after inner experiences are controlled can external actions be changed. It is only fair and ethical to explain to the client that anxiety reduction is not the goal in ACT and that therapy will take a different approach.

Therapy generally starts with a discussion of what the client wants out of treatment. Most clients will explain that they are struggling with their loved ones or with their work. There is often little fun in life, and many believe that only once OCD is gone will life be fun again. From the client's view, OCD is usually seen as an amalgam: obsessions and compulsions are tightly linked. Thus, clients want help managing both obsessions and compulsions. The ACT therapist will help the client to see that obsessions and compulsions are only related temporally – there is not a cause and effect relation between them (meaning one does not need to change in order for change to occur in the other).

A discussion occurs about the way most of the world, including advertisements, our friends, and our families, look at the relationship between inner experiences and actions. For most people, their loved ones work to make them feel happier when things go wrong, less nervous in fearful situations, or more confident when things are difficult. The comment, "Well, that is a scary situation, it is probably normal that you are feeling afraid," is rarely spoken. The ACT therapist helps the client to see that changing one's actions might be possible without changing one's inner experiences. The following might be said during this phase of therapy:

THERAPIST: What are you hoping for from therapy?
CLIENT: I am hoping to get rid of my OCD.
THERAPIST: What does OCD mean to you?
CLIENT: I would like to stop feeling so anxious, having such scary thoughts, and doing such odd things because of it all.
THERAPIST: Please tell me what the problem is with the anxiety, obsessions, and compulsions.
CLIENT: They are ruining my life! My husband can't stand me, I am driving my kids nuts, and I am only barely holding onto my job. Also, I have not done anything fun in so long because I spend all my time trying to keep germs away from me and my family.
THERAPIST: You want your life back.
CLIENT: Exactly.
THERAPIST: I want that for you too. What if there is a way to live the life you really want, only the best way to achieve it is not through the methods you came in here thinking? Most of society tells us that certain thoughts and feelings are "bad," and the "bad" ones cause us to do "bad" things. Therefore, we need to control these thoughts and feelings in order to control our actions. But what if thoughts, feelings, bodily sensations, and actions only occur together, without one causing the other? If that

were the case, then we could do whatever we wanted right now; it is just that our minds and bodies may disagree and yell at us while we do it.

CLIENT: This sounds odd to me.

THERAPIST: Okay, that is fine with me. I am okay with odd. But maybe there is a part that seems possible in here too. If trying to control obsessions and anxiety before getting back into life is not working, maybe your rule about the way the world works is wrong. That would actually be really cool. Then none of this is your fault. You have just been playing by poor rules. Would you be willing to work with me to find a new way out of this, even if it is a totally different route than the one you came in here with?

CLIENT: I'll try anything. Life is not good.

After a description such as this, the hope is that the client will be more willing to try something different with his or her OCD. The therapist would then go on to describe that the two of them will be working on getting life back, or simply living a life that is more consistent with the client's picture of how he or she wants life to be. The therapist could describe that:

THERAPIST: I too want to work on getting your life to be more like the one you want. But maybe we don't have to get all these thoughts and feelings under control first. I look at OCD this way: You have obsessions, anxiety, and compulsions, and these can affect your quality of life. Put all these together and you have OCD. Which is easier to control: your obsessions or your compulsions?

CLIENT: Compulsions.

THERAPIST: Sure. If I offered you a million dollars for no compulsions for a day or no obsessions for a day, we both know which one would be more possible. So maybe you have been asking yourself to do the impossible in controlling your obsessions and the anxiety that goes with them. Would you be willing to spend time in these sessions working on how to interact with your obsessions differently, while immediately changing what you do with your compulsions and how you live your life?

CLIENT: Yes, but it sounds scary.

This initial phase might involve exercises to help the client experience how difficult it is to control obsessions and how, in many cases, attempts to control them actually lower quality of life rather than improve it. A common exercise is to work with the client to create a list of ways in which he or she has tried to control obsessions (e.g., through compulsions, avoidance, self-talk, reassurance, exercising, even mindfulness) and to evaluate how successful these strategies have been in the short-term (immediately) and in the long term (weeks or months). It is almost always the case that these actions work well in the short term – they provide a break for a few minutes or even an hour – but they do not work in the long term; otherwise, the client would not be in need of services. Finally, the therapist helps the client to see that many of these strategies decrease quality of life and are poor answers to the problem of OCD.

Additional exercises aimed at helping the client experience the difficulty of controlling inner experiences are part of the initial phase of treatment. Generally, this is done is by asking the client (a) *not* to think of something, (b) *not* to feel an emotion,

(c) to feel an emotion on demand, and, finally, (d) *not* to do an action. If strong enough examples are used, almost all clients will experience how difficult it is to regulate an inner experience, but how easy it is to engage (or not engage) in an action. After this, the following might be said to the client:

THERAPIST: Isn't it interesting how you clearly found it difficult, if not impossible, not to think about the item I mentioned, not to get anxious if I asked you to sing in front of a crowd, or to hate the next person you see? But it was so easy not to touch that tissue box. And yet, you spend every day trying not to think about getting ill or getting your family ill, you fight against feelings of anxiety and fear, and you try to make yourself feel motivated. It was impossible for you to control the thoughts and feelings I gave you, and they were not even your own thoughts and feelings! I know you will still go home and try not to think about germs and try not to get anxious because it is hard to stop, but when you are doing these things, please pay attention to how well they are actually working, and think about whether this is how you want to spend your time.

Sessions 3–7: Acceptance, Defusion, Present Moment Awareness, Self as Context, and Committed Action

In an 8–10-session protocol, the middle sessions are spent teaching the ACT processes of acceptance, defusion, present moment awareness, self as context, and committed action. After the first two sessions, most clients will feel as though trying to control their anxiety and obsessions is a poor choice, but they will wonder what they should do with them instead. ACT's answer is to invite obsessions and anxiety in and to give them a place to live. Instead of fighting against them – radically accept them. Acceptance is more than toleration. Acceptance is not waiting for anxiety to eventually lessen; it is not presented as a means to an end. Acceptance is a way to live with big and strong emotions. The client becomes an expert at having what is there when it is there. When this is initially presented, it can be difficult for most clients. But after time and in combination with other processes, clients do well with it. Metaphors, such as "Tug-o-war with a Monster" (in which, instead of winning the fight, the client simply stops the fight) and "Two Scales" (in which the client is taught to look at the willingness "scale" rather than the anxiety and obsession "scale"), can help the client to understand these concepts experientially. It is never suggested that accepting anxiety will lessen it – acceptance will only allow anxiety to be there when the situation calls for it and to not be there when it does not. Acceptance gives anxiety the freedom to do what it needs to do. The benefit of acceptance is that the client may go on living, regardless of his or her level of anxiety. The conversation about acceptance may proceed as follows:

THERAPIST: It seems like there is not a good way to control these obsessions.
CLIENT: Nope.
THERAPIST: What do you think about that?
CLIENT: It is sort of frustrating. What am I supposed to do with them if I can't make them go away?

THERAPIST: Maybe we take all that effort you have been putting into controlling them and shift it over to doing things that matter to you while allowing the obsessions to come and go.

CLIENT: That sounds really hard.

THERAPIST: It does sound hard. I agree. But what if this is the way the world really works? What if, right now in life, obsessions are just going to come and go? They will likely be associated with fear and anxiety, and that is a fact, just like it is a fact that it rains sometimes. We could fight against the rain (or the sun) every day, or we could learn how to live the lives we want regardless of what occurs. After time, we may even get good at it. For example, I lived in Vancouver, BC for a year. It rained a little every day. It was odd at first, but after time, I learned how to function with it. That was the way it was going to be, and I learned how to bike and hike in the rain. Maybe we can find ways to live the life you really want with the cards you have been dealt.

The process of defusion supports the process of acceptance. It is much easier to accept a thought or feeling when the client can experience it as simply that – a thought or feeling. Being accepting is very difficult when the client's inner experience is regarded as a real thing. Defusion exercises, such as *Passengers on the Bus* (in which obsessions and anxious thoughts are treated like passengers on a bus that the client is driving) or labeling obsessions out loud as simply thoughts, help clients step back and see that the thoughts and feelings they are trying to accept are just thoughts and feelings, even if the content is disgusting or horrifying. The processes of acceptance and defusion are addressed at each session following session three. Because these are new skills for most clients, it will take practice to become proficient in them. Defusion might be described to the client as follows:

THERAPIST: Try to find anything in this room that you can't name.

CLIENT: I think I know what everything is.

THERAPIST: There is nothing odd in here?

CLIENT: There is that odd thing behind the door, but my guess is that it stops the door from hitting the wall.

THERAPIST: Okay, good. Notice how you could define everything in the room, even things you had not dealt with before. Now let me ask you, is that door-stopper "good" or "bad"?

CLIENT: I guess it is good because it saves the wall.

THERAPIST: Great. Now notice that your mind defines everything it sees and gives everything a value. Nothing just is. Everything has a definition and a function. Think about your day: I don't know about you, but my mind defines and evaluates everything it contacts.

CLIENT: Sure. My mind talks all the time. I can't stop it.

THERAPIST: Okay. So if your mind does that with little things like a door-stop, it will also do it with thoughts and feelings. It will judge this thought at "bad" and that one as "good." But what if they are just thoughts, and your mind adds definitions and functions to them?

CLIENT: Well, if they are just thoughts then I don't really have to do anything with them.

THERAPIST: Imagine that. If they were just words in your head, or feelings in your body, then you could just leave them alone. They could do what they are going to do, and you can do what you want to do. Are you willing to practice treating them like that?

Beginning at the end of session 3, after acceptance and defusion have been introduced, the therapist helps the client to engage in meaningful activities – committed actions – by making daily behavioral commitments. The final few minutes of each session are spent planning the behavioral commitments for the following week. Behavioral commitments serve two purposes: They are opportunities to (a) engage in meaningful activities that the client has been avoiding, and (b) practice psychological flexibility in situations where the client is usually inflexible. Therefore, the client and therapist agree to concrete behaviors that the client has been avoiding. Behavioral commitments should be clear actions, such as "using one public restroom per day," rather than vague actions, such as "using public restrooms more often." Behavioral commitments are generally small actions that contribute to larger meaningful activities with which OCD has been interfering. For example, a client may commit to touching a door handle once per day so that he or she can eventually go on a date. One key part of behavioral commitments is that the person practices the other ACT processes while engaging in the commitment. This creates opportunities for specific practice of acceptance and defusion that are tied to the client's values. Between sessions, behavioral exercises might be presented as follows:

THERAPIST: Between this session and the next one, are you willing to practice being open to your obsessions and seeing them for what they are?
CLIENT: Sure. What are you thinking?
THERAPIST: What is something that you like to do, but have generally given up because of OCD?
CLIENT: Going out with my wife.
THERAPIST: Okay, so this could be going somewhere with your wife that you have traditionally avoided. While you do this, I would like you to practice allowing your thoughts to show up and just watching them. I want you to be present with your wife and experience of being out with her, all while your mind screams at you. What might you do?
CLIENT: There is a coffee shop we used to go to. We could go get a coffee.
THERAPIST: Great idea, let's do that. On a particular day that we'll agree to, you and your wife will go to the coffee shop, order drinks, sit at a table for at least 30 minutes, and drink your whole drink. And while you do so, I want you to treat your thoughts like passengers on a bus who are yelling at you to leave. I want you to drive the bus to where you want to be – there with you wife.

As sessions continue, other processes are also taught to aid in developing psychological flexibility, namely, present moment awareness and self as context. Although acceptance and defusion are arguably the most common processes in ACT for OCD, there are times when being present and self as context are quite useful.

Self as context is especially useful for clients who have struggled with OCD for a long time or who see their OCD tendencies as part of "who they are." Exercises such as the

Chessboard (in which the client is guided to view the self as a chessboard and inner experiences as the pieces on the board) help to illustrate that he or she is not defined by self-evaluations or judgments but, rather, is the vessel in which those thoughts and feelings occur. The concept of self as context might be presented as follows:

THERAPIST: Are you an anxious person or a person who feels anxiety?
CLIENT: Given how long I have struggled with this I think I am an anxious person.
THERAPIST: What might be the benefit of being a person who feels anxiety?
CLIENT: I guess it would not define me.
THERAPIST: If thoughts and feelings are just thoughts and feelings, then wouldn't that even apply to one's anxiety? Maybe we should just act like you are a person who experiences anxious thoughts and feelings of anxiety.
CLIENT: It would have less control over me.

Exercises on present moment awareness are especially helpful for clients who get overly involved in fears about what might happen in the future or ruminate on events from the past. Both situations occur in certain presentations of OCD. Exercises such as watching one's thoughts as if they were leaves on a stream or mindfully watching one's breath can be good practice for staying in the present moment during difficult situations. The ability to detect when one is being mindful versus when one is caught up in a thought is also a useful skill. This can help when a client is engaging in a meaningful but difficult activity and is caught up in fears rather than being present. The following exercise is one that can be assigned to help practice being in the present moment:

THERAPIST: I am going to ask you to do something for about 10 minutes every day for the next week. The purpose is to help you see the difference between experiencing a thought and being caught up in a thought. I would like you to listen to music: you can be driving, exercising, or just hanging out. While listening, I want you to pay attention to one aspect of the music: the guitar, bass, drums, beat, or whatever. Pay close attention to that one part. At some point, you will realize that you are not listening to that part anymore, but thinking about something that happened in the past or something you need to do in the future. Once that happens, note that you are no longer in the present, but caught up in your mind. Let that thought go, and come back to the music. I just want you to see the difference between watching thoughts and being a thought. Just so you know, I only ever make it halfway through a song.

Session 8: Values and Larger Behavioral Commitments

As described earlier, the final sessions involve following one's values and engaging in larger and larger patterns of meaningful actions. The client has been working on engaging in valued activities between all sessions, and it has been a small topic of conversation at each session, but the final sessions are where big meaningful decisions are made. For many clients, they have been working so hard on controlling their OCD that they have given up on other parts of their lives. Some may know what is important to them, but for others it may be unclear. Values can help clients clarify the directions they want to go in life, and they can help motivate all clients to stay engaged in the future.

Values work generally focuses on helping the client become clear on what areas of life are important to them and how well they are doing in each of those areas. Everyone has their own values, and it is the therapist's job to help the client clarify his or her personal values. Once these are clear, the client is asked to stay in touch with these values and continue to work toward them no matter what internal experiences are occurring. The client is encouraged to continue to make daily commitments to work toward his or her values and to practice the other skills learned in therapy during these moments.

As clients get clearer about their long-term values, the therapist should discuss larger behavioral commitments that can be followed once therapy is over. Linking this back to rule-governed behavior, the hope is that the client engages in new patterns of action that are so rewarding that the natural contingencies keep them occurring without the praise of the therapist.

Exposure from an ACT Perspective

ACT for OCD has been successful without in-session exposures, but exposures are a traditional behavioral technique aimed to alter a behavioral pattern, and they are therefore a welcome component of a complete ACT protocol (e.g., Arch et al., 2012a; Meuret, Twohig, Rosenfield, Hayes, & Craske, 2012). ACT's approach to exposure is unique, however, in that it does not emphasize anxiety reduction; rather, ACT focuses on moving in valued directions with or without fear and anxiety. Encouraging the client to foster important life values has the potential to create meaningful exposures that encourage engagement in valued actions. For example, a client with contamination-related OCD might value being a stable, loving mother. This value could be used to develop ideas for exposures that would allow her to behave in ways that she identifies as consistent with being a loving mother.

Because of the focus on values, there is a particular approach to the process of building a client's exposure hierarchy. ACT exposures are chosen based on whether they would be meaningful in the context of the client's values. ACT treats exposures as opportunities to practice skills learned during therapy, such as acceptance and defusion, and to put those skills to use in the service of increasing the client's ability to engage in valued life activities. In a sense, exposures are highly structured behavioral commitments. The length of the exposure is not important – what is important is that the client practice whichever process is most needed at that time for that particular person. The therapist facilitates this by guiding the client through the exposure exercise, encouraging the use of the skill. The ACT approach places the initial focus on engaging in valued behaviors, however small they may be, allowing the client to contact naturally occurring reinforcement.

Conclusions

This chapter presents the ACT approach to the treatment of OCD. ACT is part of a larger program of psychological science known as contextual behavioral science; it is based on a functional contextual philosophy of science and a basic research program. The general ACT model has been further developed for the treatment of OCD as well as other disorders. Although there is a fair amount of research on ACT in general, research on ACT for OCD is still in its early stages. Aspects of the model and treatment components, such as acceptance and values, are beginning to make their way into empirically supported treatments for anxiety disorders. Nevertheless, the eventual position of ACT within the empirically supported treatment of OCD has yet to be seen.

References

Abramowitz, J. S., Lackey, G. R., & Wheaton, M. G. (2009). Obsessive-compulsive symptoms: The contribution of obsessional beliefs and experiential avoidance. *Journal of Anxiety Disorders*, 23(2), 160–166. doi: 10.1016/j.janxdis.2008.06.003.

Arch, J. J., Eifert, G. H., Davies, C., Vilardaga, J. C. P., Rose, R. D., & Craske, M. G. (2012). Randomized clinical trial of cognitive behavioral therapy (CBT) versus acceptance and commitment therapy (ACT) for mixed anxiety disorders. *Journal of Consulting and Clinical Psychology*, 80(5), 750–765. doi: 10.1037/a0028310.

Arch, J. J., Wolitzky-Taylor, K. B., Eifert, G. H., & Craske, M. G. (2012). Longitudinal treatment mediation of traditional cognitive behavioral therapy and acceptance and commitment therapy for anxiety disorders. *Behaviour Research and Therapy*, 50(7/8), 469–478. doi: 10.1016/j.brat.2012.04.007.

Armstrong, A. B., Morrison, K. L., & Twohig, M. P. (2013). A preliminary investigation of acceptance and commitment therapy for adolescent obsessive-compulsive disorder. *Journal of Cognitive Psychotherapy*, 27(2), 175–190. doi: 10.1891/0889-8391.27.2.175.

Bluett, E. J., Homan, K. J., Morrison, K. L., Levin, M. E., & Twohig, M. P. (2014). Acceptance and commitment therapy for anxiety and OCD spectrum disorders: An empirical review. *Journal of Anxiety Disorders*, 28(6), 612–624. doi: 10.1016/j.janxdis.2014.06.008.

Bouton, M. E., & Woods, A. M. (2008). Extinction: Behavioral mechanisms and their implications. *Learning and memory: A comprehensive reference*, 1, 151–171.

Briggs, E. S., & Price, I. R. (2009). The relationship between adverse childhood experience and obsessive-compulsive symptoms and beliefs: The role of anxiety, depression, and experiential avoidance. *Journal of Anxiety Disorders*, 23(8), 1037–1046. doi: 10.1016/j.janxdis.2009.07.004.

Dehlin, J. P., Morrison, K. L., & Twohig, M. P. (2013). Acceptance and commitment therapy as a treatment for scrupulosity in obsessive compulsive disorder. *Behavior Modification*, 37(3), 409–430. doi: 10.1177/0145445512475134.

Dymond, S., & Barnes, D. (1995). A transformation of self-discrimination response functions in accordance with the arbitrarily applicable relations of sameness, more than, and less than. *Journal of the Experimental Analysis of Behavior*, 64(2), 163–184. doi: 10.1901/jeab.1995.64-163.

Eifert, G. H., & Forsyth, J. P. (2005). *Acceptance and commitment therapy for anxiety disorders: A practitioner's treatment guide to using mindfulness, acceptance, and values-based behavior change strategies*. Oakland, CA: New Harbinger.

Forman, E. M., Chapman, J. E., Herbert, J. D., Goetter, E. M., Yuen, E. K., & Moitra, E. (2012). Using session-by-session measurement to compare mechanisms of action for acceptance and commitment therapy and cognitive therapy. *Behavior Therapy*, 43(2), 341–354. doi: 10.1016/j.beth.2011.07.004.

Forman, E. M., Herbert, J. D., Moitra, E., Yeomans, P. D., & Geller, P. A. (2007). A randomized controlled effectiveness trial of acceptance and commitment therapy and cognitive therapy for anxiety and depression. *Behavior Modification*, 31(6), 772–799. doi: 10.1177/0145445507302202.

Gloster, A. T., Klotsche, J., Chaker, S., Hummel, K. V., & Hoyer, J. (2011). Assessing psychological flexibility: What does it add above and beyond existing constructs? *Psychological Assessment*, *23*(4), 970. doi: 10.1037/a0024135.

Hayes, S. C. (1989). Nonhumans have not yet shown stimulus equivalence. *Journal of the Experimental Analysis of Behavior*, *51*(3), 385–392. doi: 10.1901/jeab.1989.51-385.

Hayes, S. C. (1993). Analytic goals and the varieties of scientific contextualism. In S. C. Hayes, L. J. Hayes, H. W. Reese, & T. R. Sarbin (Eds.), *Varieties of scientific contextualism* (pp. 11–27). Reno, NV: Context Press.

Hayes, S. C., Barnes-Holmes, D., & Roche, B. (2001). *Relational frame theory: A post-Skinnerian account of human language and cognition*. New York: Plenum.

Hayes, S. C., Barnes-Holmes, D., & Wilson, K. G. (2012). Contextual behavioral science: Creating a science more adequate to the challenge of the human condition. *Journal of Contextual Behavioral Science*, *1*(1/2), 1–16. doi: 10.1016/j.jcbs.2012.09.004.

Hayes, S. C., & Brownstein, A. J. (1986). Mentalism, behavior-behavior relations, and a behavior-analytic view of the purposes of science. *The Behavior Analyst*, *9*(2), 175–190.

Hayes, S. C., Brownstein, A. J., Zettle, R. D., Rosenfarb, I., & Korn, Z. (1986). Rule-governed behavior and sensitivity to changing consequences of responding. *Journal of the Experimental Analysis of Behavior*, *45*(3), 237–256. doi: 10.1901/jeab.1986.45-237.

Hayes, S. C., Levin, M. E., Plumb-Vilardaga, J., Villatte, J. L., & Pistorello, J. (2013). Acceptance and commitment therapy and contextual behavioral science: Examining the progress of a distinctive model of behavioral and cognitive therapy. *Behavior Therapy*, *44*(2), 180–198. doi: 10.1016/j.beth.2009.08.002.

Hayes, S. C., Luoma, J. B., Bond, F. W., Masuda, A., & Lillis, J. (2006). Acceptance and commitment therapy: Model, processes and outcomes. *Behaviour Research and Therapy*, *44*(1), 1–25. doi: 10.1016/j.brat.2005.06.006.

Hayes, S. C., Strosahl, K. D., & Wilson, K. G. (2012). *Acceptance and commitment therapy: The process and practice of mindful change* (2nd ed.). New York: Guilford Press.

Hayes, S. C., Villatte, M., Levin, M., & Hildebrandt, M. (2011). Open, aware, and active: Contextual approaches as an emerging trend in the behavioral and cognitive therapies. *Annual Review of Clinical Psychology*, *7*, 141–168. doi: 10.1146/annurev-clinpsy-032210-104449.

Henderson, J., Hurly, T. A., & Healy, S. D. (2006). Spatial relational learning in rufous hummingbirds (Selasphorus rufus). *Animal Cognition*, *9*, 201–205. doi: 10.1007/s10071-006-0021-z.

Herbert, J. D., & Forman, E. M. (2013). Caution: The differences between CT and ACT may be larger (and smaller) than they appear. *Behavior Therapy*, *44*(2), 218–223. doi: 10.1016/j.beth.2009.09.005.

Levin, M. E., Hildebrandt, M. J., Lillis, J., & Hayes, S. C. (2012). The impact of treatment components suggested by the psychological flexibility model: A meta-analysis of laboratory-based component studies. *Behavior Therapy*, *43*(4), 741–756. doi: 10.1016/j.beth.2012.05.003.

Lipkens, R., Hayes, S. C., & Hayes, L. J. (1993). Longitudinal study of the development of derived relations in an infant. *Journal of the Experimental Analysis of Behavior*, *56*, 201–239. doi: 10.1006/jecp.1993.1032.

Manos, R. C., Cahill, S. P., Wetterneck, C. T., Conelea, C. A., Ross, A. R., & Riemann, B. R. (2010). The impact of experiential avoidance and obsessive beliefs on obsessive-compulsive symptoms in a severe clinical sample. *Journal of Anxiety Disorders*, *24*(7), 700–708. doi: 10.1016/j.janxdis.2010.05.001.

Meuret, A. E., Twohig, M. P., Rosenfield, D., Hayes, S. C., & Craske, M. G. (2012). Brief acceptance and commitment therapy and exposure for panic disorder: A pilot study. *Cognitive and Behavioral Practice*, *19*(4), 606–618. doi: 10.1016/j.cbpra.2012.05.004.

O'Hora, D., Peláez, M., Barnes-Holmes, D., Rae, G., Robinson, K., & Chaudhary, T. (2008). Temporal relations and intelligence: Correlating relational performance with performance on the WAIS-III. *The Psychological Record*, *58*, 569–584.

Öst, L-G. (2008). Efficacy of the third wave of behavioral therapies: A systematic review and meta-analysis. *Behaviour Research and Therapy*, *46*(3), 296–321. doi: 10.1016/j.brat.2007.12.005.

Powers, M. B., Zum Vörde Sive Vörding, M. B., & Emmelkamp, P. M. G. (2009). Acceptance and commitment therapy: A meta-analytic review. *Psychotherapy and Psychosomatics*, *78*(2), 73–80. doi: 10.1159/000190790.

Skinner, B. F. (1966). What is the experimental analysis of behavior? *Journal of the Experimental Analysis of Behavior*, *9*(3), 213–218. doi: 10.1901/jeab.1966.9-213.

Steele, D., & Hayes, S. C. (1991). Stimulus equivalence and arbitrarily applicable relational responding. *Journal of the Experimental Analysis of Behavior*, *56*(3), 519–555. doi: 10.1901/jeab.1991.56-519.

Strosahl, K. D., Hayes, S. C., Bergan, J., & Romano, P. (1999). Assessing the field effectiveness of acceptance and commitment therapy: An example of the manipulated training research method. *Behavior Therapy*, *29*(1), 35–63. doi: 10.1016/S0005-7894(98)80017-8.

Törneke, N., Luciano, M. C., & Valdivia-Salas, S. (2008). Rule-governed behavior and psychological problems. *International Journal of Psychology and Psychological Therapy*, 8, 141–156.

Twohig, M. P. (2009). The application of acceptance and commitment therapy to obsessive-compulsive disorder. *Cognitive and Behavioral Practice*, *16*(1), 18–28. doi: 10.1016/j.cbpra.2008.02.008.

Twohig, M. P. (2012). Acceptance and commitment therapy: Introduction. *Cognitive and Behavioral Practice*, *19*(4), 499–507. doi: 10.1016/j.cbpra.2012.04.003.

Twohig, M. P., Hayes, S. C., & Masuda, A. (2006a). A preliminary investigation of acceptance and commitment therapy as a treatment for chronic skin picking. *Behaviour Research and Therapy*, *44*(10), 1513–1522. doi: 10.1016/j.brat.2005.10.002.

Twohig, M. P., Hayes, S. C., & Masuda, A. (2006b). Increasing willingness to experience obsessions: Acceptance and commitment therapy as a treatment for obsessive-compulsive disorder. *Behavior Therapy*, *37*(1), 3–13. doi: 10.1016/j.beth.2005.02.001.

Twohig, M. P., Hayes, S. C., Plumb, J. C., Pruitt, L. D., Collins, A. B., Hazlett-Stevens, H., & Woidneck, M. R. (2010a). A randomized clinical trial of acceptance and commitment therapy versus progressive relaxation training for obsessive-compulsive disorder. *Journal of Consulting and Clinical Psychology*, *78*(5), 705–716. doi: 10.1037/a0020508.

Twohig, M. P., Whittal, M. L., Cox, J. M., & Gunter, R. (2010b). An initial investigation into the processes of change in ACT, CT, and ERP for OCD. *International Journal of Behavioral Consultation and Therapy*, *6*(1), 67–83.

Twohig, M. P., Woidneck, M. R., & Crosby, J. M. (2013). Newer generations of CBT for anxiety disorders. In G. Simos, & S. G. Hofmann (Eds.), *CBT for anxiety disorders: A practitioner book* (pp. 225–250). Chichester: Wiley.

Vøllestad, J., Nielsen, M., & Nielsen, G. (2012). Mindfulness- and acceptance-based interventions for anxiety disorders: A systematic review and meta-analysis. *British Journal of Clinical Psychology*, *51*(3), 239–260. doi: 10.1111/j.2044-8260.2011.02024.x.

Wetterneck, C. T., Lee, E. B., Smith, A. H., & Hart, J. M. (2013). Courage, self-compassion, and values in obsessive-compulsive disorder. *Journal of Contextual Behavioral Science*, *2*(3), 68–73. doi: 10.1016/j.jcbs.2013.09.002.

Wilson, K. G. (2008). *Mindfulness for two*. Oakland, CA: New Harbinger.

Wilson, K. G., & Hayes, S. C. (1996). Resurgence of derived stimulus relations. *Journal of the Experimental Analysis of Behavior*, *66*(3), 267–281. doi: 10.1901/jeab.1996.66-267.

Woods, D. W., Wetterneck, C. T., & Flessner, C. A. (2006). A controlled evaluation of acceptance and commitment therapy plus habit reversal for trichotillomania. *Behaviour Research and Therapy*, *44*(5), 639–656. doi: 10.1016/j.brat.2005.05.006.

34

Family-Based Conceptualization and Treatment of Obsessive-Compulsive Disorder

Cynthia Turner, Georgina Krebs, and Jessie Destro

It is widely accepted that obsessive-compulsive disorder (OCD) is one of the most severe and disabling mental health disorders, and is associated with pervasive impairments in functioning in all life domains, including vocation, education, family and peer relationships, and personal development (see Chapters 1, 2, and 3). Childhood OCD is predictive of adult mental illness, and OCD across the lifespan is associated with high rates of burden, disability, and poor quality of life (Piacentini, Peris, Bergman, Chang, & Jaffer, 2007; Steketee, 1997). Cognitive-behavior therapy (CBT) is the recommended psychological treatment for mild to moderate OCD, and CBT plus a selective serotonin reuptake inhibitor (SSRI) medication is recommended for more severe or treatment resistant OCD (Geller & March, 2012; NICE, 2005). However, despite the effectiveness of these treatments, OCD persistence rates range from 40% to 70% (e.g. Micali et al., 2010). The persistence and chronicity of the disorder has resulted in ongoing research to better understand factors associated with poor treatment response, and family factors have emerged as one of the most compelling areas of inquiry (e.g., Ginsburg, Kingery, Drake, & Grados, 2008). OCD, perhaps more than any other disorder, draws family members in, and evidence shows that family members inadvertently play an integral role in maintaining the disorder.

This chapter will focus on the family factors associated with OCD. We will consider the impact that OCD has on family members, the nature and role of family accommodation, and other family factors associated with disorder persistence. In doing so, we will argue for the importance of a family-based conceptualization of OCD, for both children and adults given the role that family factors play across the lifespan. We will review current family-based treatment approaches for OCD, and highlight important future directions.

The Wiley Handbook of Obsessive Compulsive Disorders, Volume I, First Edition.
Edited by Jonathan S. Abramowitz, Dean McKay, and Eric A. Storch.
© 2017 John Wiley & Sons Ltd. Published 2017 by John Wiley & Sons Ltd.

The Impact of OCD on Family Members

Families of OCD sufferers report and exhibit high levels of distress. Depending on the nature and severity of symptoms, sufferers are sometimes unable to independently complete the most basic self-care tasks (e.g., toileting, showering, dressing, food preparation). In such circumstances, the burden of care can fall on family members, and usually on one caregiver in particular (Cooper, 1996). As a result, the lives of family members can be significantly altered by disruption to employment, leisure time, usual activities, interpersonal relationships, and even privacy. Conflict between family members, with regard to how best to manage a sufferer's symptoms, is common (Cooper, 1994). Extended family members can be critical, not only toward the OCD sufferer, but also toward caregivers, adding to the burden.

Even when symptoms are not so extreme, the impact of the disorder can be significant. Stengler-Wenzke, Kroll, Matschinger, and Angermeyer (2006) compared the quality of life of family members (29 parents, 33 spouses, 8 children, and 4 siblings) with the quality of life reported by the general (German) population. Family members' quality of life was significantly lower in the domains of physical and psychological well-being, and social relationships. Family members report that OCD causes them personal distress, particularly depression, rumination, anxiety and being unwittingly drawn into rituals (Amir, Freshman, & Foa, 2000).

Impact of OCD on Parents

Parents consistently report finding their child's OCD symptoms difficult to manage and distressing to watch, and they often face a dilemma about whether to give in to, or fight against, their loved one's obsessions and compulsions (Futh, Simonds, & Micali, 2012). Many parents become drawn into OCD symptoms in an effort to reduce their child's distress, as well as to alleviate their own emotional strain (Futh et al., 2012). Derisley, Libby, Clark, and Reynolds (2005) examined mental health and coping in parents of children with OCD and found that, compared with parents of healthy control children, parents of children with OCD reported significantly poorer mental health (higher levels of depression and anxiety), and a significantly greater reliance on maladaptive (avoidant) coping strategies. Storch and colleagues (2009) examined parental experiences of having a child with OCD and found that parents experienced poor adjustment (i.e., guilt, worry, unresolved sorrow and anger, and long-term uncertainty). There was an association between poor parental adjustment and high levels of child externalizing and internalizing behavior problems, parental distress and caregiver strain. Parental distress was also significantly positively associated with child OCD symptom severity and impairment.

Impact of OCD on Siblings

Not surprisingly, OCD also impacts upon siblings in a negative manner. Barrett, Rasmussen, and Healy (2001) found that siblings of children with OCD were frequently drawn into participating in OCD rituals (sometimes through bullying), and were distressed by the presence of OCD in their sibling. Internalizing symptoms were higher in siblings of children with OCD compared to siblings in a healthy control group, and quality of sibling relationships were poorer in OCD sibling dyads.

Several recent case studies have described poor sibling relationships and conflict, both sibling-to-sibling and sibling-to-parent conflict (e.g., Labouliere, Arnold, Storch, & Lewin, 2014; Lebowitz, 2013; Lehmkuhl et al., 2009). Siblings report that parents reprimand them for involvement in compulsions, resulting in their feeling forgotten, embarrassed, and resentful. Siblings also report restricted lifestyle, feeling as though their parents may favor the sibling with OCD and, "*walking on egg shells*" to keep their sibling with OCD happy (Lebowitz, 2013). In response to OCD, case reports illustrate that siblings can exhibit a wide range of responses, including participation in rituals, efforts to keep and make peace, antagonism, teasing and provoking rituals.

Difficult Child Behaviors Associated with OCD

Childhood OCD is a highly comorbid disorder (see Chapter 1); however, research has begun to document various internalizing and externalizing child behaviors that occur alongside childhood OCD, but which are not necessarily symptomatic of a comorbid psychological disorder. These include rage and aggression, coercive and disruptive behaviors, temper tantrums, and withdrawn or depressed mood. For example, rage attacks, defined as "recurrent episodes of explosive anger or aggression triggered by minor provocations," have been found to occur in more than half of pediatric OCD cases (Storch et al., 2012). Both verbal and physical rage attacks were common, typically directed at parents or other family members, and associated with multiple triggers (e.g., a change in routine or an OCD-related trigger). Rage attacks were found be associated with OCD symptom severity, higher family accommodation, and greater functional impairment, but there was no association with comorbid externalizing disorders. Similarly, Krebs and colleagues found than one-third of a large sample of young people with OCD displayed frequent temper tantrums (Krebs et al., 2013). Again, temper tantrums were not associated with other externalizing symptoms, but they were found to be related to depressed mood.

Parents of young people with OCD also frequently report high levels of coercive and disruptive behavior, defined as "attempts to impose rules on others such as forcing others to participate in rituals or demanding them to perform certain actions or behaviours" (Lebowitz, Omer, & Leckman, 2011). Moreover, in a survey study, the vast majority of health professionals specializing in childhood OCD reported encountering these behaviors in at least some of their clients (Lebowitz, Vitulano, & Omer, 2011; Lebowitz, Vitulano, Mataix-Cols, & Leckman, 2011). These experts viewed the coercive and disruptive behaviors as secondary to OCD (e.g., forbidding certain actions or activities of others, or forcing others to engage in certain rituals) rather than as symptoms of a comorbid disruptive behavior disorder.

Summary

There is considerable evidence for the highly negative impact that OCD can have on family members. All family members (spouses, parents, siblings, children, and extended family) exhibit poorer quality of life, higher rates of anxiety, depression, and emotional distress than community controls. The symptoms of OCD can, in themselves, cause this detrimental impact. However, OCD can also be associated with various other difficult behaviors, and recent evidence suggests that childhood OCD is associated with rage and aggression, tantrums, and coercive behaviors. These behaviors are thought to be secondary to OCD, and not fully explained by comorbid disorders. The negative impact of OCD can therefore be exacerbated by these other behaviors. Research shows that families of OCD sufferers struggle to cope well. The strain associated with managing OCD symptoms prompts a host of familial reactions, and Van Noppen and Steketee (2009) have proposed a continuum of family response patterns in which enmeshed, permissive, or accommodating strategies represent one endpoint and hostile, critical, or punitive responses reflect the other.

Family Accommodation

Family accommodation refers to the various ways in which family members can become drawn into OCD. It includes actions taken to assist with or participate in compulsions (e.g., straightening things until they are just right), to facilitate avoidance (e.g., opening doors so the patient can avoiding touching them), adapting family routines to minimize anxiety (e.g., walking out the back door rather than the front door), providing reassurance, respecting the rigid rules imposed by OCD on others (e.g., caregivers ensuring food on a plate is evenly spaced), or assisting a person with OCD to complete tasks of daily living.

Families of both adult (e.g. Amir et al., 2000; Calvocoressi et al., 1999) and child (e.g., Storch et al., 2007a; Peris, Benazon, Langley, Roblek, & Piacentini, 2008b) OCD sufferers provide high levels of accommodation, with studies demonstrating that between 60% and 96% of relatives assist in rituals or modify their behavior in some way (e.g., Stewart, Stack, & Wilhelm, 2008). Provision of reassurance, participation in rituals, and facilitation of avoidance of feared objects or situations are the three most commonly endorsed accommodating behaviors in caregivers of both adults and children with OCD (e.g., Albert et al., 2010; Peris et al., 2008a). As noted above, there is some evidence that patterns of response to OCD might vary between family members (Van Noppen & Steketee, 2009). However, examination of our own clinical data in relation to parental accommodation has shown that both mothers and fathers endorse accommodating their child's OCD on a daily basis.

Family accommodation in OCD is associated with more severe OCD symptoms (Albert et al., 2010; Caporino et al., 2012; Flessner et al., 2011), and may be more common in relatives of patients with contamination/cleaning symptoms (Albert et al., 2010; Flessner et al., 2011; Stewart et al., 2008). There are a number of reasons why family accommodation is an important construct. It may be a mechanism through which OCD negatively impacts on family members, and there is a documented relationship between higher levels of parental/caregiver distress and greater accommodation (e.g., Albert et al., 2010; Amir et al., 2000). Moreover, family accommodation has been shown to be related to treatment outcome in OCD. In adults with OCD, family accommodation is associated with treatment refractoriness (Ferrão et al., 2006). In childhood OCD, family accommodation predicts poorer treatment outcome (Garcia et al., 2010), and reductions in family accommodation over the course of treatment is associated with an improved treatment response (Merlo, Lehmkuhl, Geffken, & Storch, 2009).

Summary

Family accommodation of OCD symptoms is a maintaining factor for the disorder, and it occurs almost daily for many families. Its presence is associated with increased symptom severity and poorer treatment response. Better understanding of the clinical correlates and predictors of family accommodation of OCD symptoms is important because it can help to identify factors that may need to be targeted in treatment. It is also important for research to continue to examine other family factors that may play a role in OCD.

Additional Family Factors Implicated in OCD

It is well established that OCD is highly familial, tending to run in families (see Pauls, Abramovitch, Rauch, & Geller, 2014). The transmission of OCD within families is, at least in part, explained by genetic influences. Twin studies have shown that genetic factors explain 27–47% of the variance in OCD symptoms in adults, and 45–65% in children (van Grootheest, Cath, Beekman, & Boomsma, 2005). However, these twin studies have also highlighted the significant role of the nonshared environmental experience in the aetiology of OCD. Research has therefore focused on seeking to identify relevant environmental factors, and family factors have come to the fore in recent years, particularly parenting style and family environment.

Parenting Style

Parenting style can be defined as "a global set of parental attitudes, goals, and patterns of parenting practice" (Wood, McLeod, Sigman, Hwang, & Chu, 2003). While a range of parenting styles are likely to be relevant, the majority of research in this area has focused on the dimensions of criticism and overinvolvement. Parental criticism has been conceptualized as including criticism, negativity, and rejection at one end of a continuum, and warmth, approval, and acceptance at the other (e.g., Rapee, 1997; Wood et al., 2003). The dimension of overinvolvement includes overcontrol and overprotection at one end of a continuum, and autonomy-granting at the other (Wood et al., 2003).

Parenting Style and OCD

A number of studies have examined parenting style in adults with OCD, using both student and clinical populations. For example, Ehiobuche (1988) asked students with high OCD symptoms to report on parental child rearing characteristics, and their responses were compared with a comparison group of healthy students. Students with OCD symptoms rated their parents as more rejecting, overprotective, and less emotionally warm compared with control students, indicating higher perceived parental criticism and overinvolvement.

Similar patterns have emerged with adult patient samples. Turgeon, O'Connor, Marchand, and Freeston (2002) requested patients with OCD to recall their parental rearing, and found they reported parenting style as significantly more overprotective than controls. Lennertz and colleagues (2010) similarly found that patients with OCD reported their parents as being significantly more rejecting and controlling, and significantly less warm, than controls. While there are some studies that have failed to demonstrate the same differences as strongly (e.g., Alonso et al., 2004; Vogel, Stiles, & Nordahl, 1997), it seems the pattern of results supports a negative association with adult OCD symptoms. The flaw in such research is the retrospective nature of the reporting, and it is therefore compelling that research investigating parenting and OCD in childhood has documented similar findings, albeit with somewhat different methodology.

For example, Barrett, Shortt, and Healy (2002) compared the observed behaviors of parents and children with OCD with families whose children were diagnosed with other anxiety disorders, externalizing disorders and no clinical problems (Barrett et al., 2002). During family discussions, parent and child behaviors and affect were coded on behavioral dimensions of control, warmth, doubt, avoidance, confidence, positive problem-solving, and rewarding independence. Results revealed that parents of children with OCD could be differentiated from comparison families as they were less confident in their child's ability, less rewarding of independence, and less likely to use positive problem solving. Children with OCD showed less positive problem solving, less confidence in their ability, and less warmth in their interactions with their parents.

Expressed Emotion

The parenting constructs reviewed above are highly similar to the concept of expressed emotion (EE). EE is a construct that encompasses the affective quality of the family environment. If high in EE, a family environment is characterized by hostility, criticism, and/or emotional overinvolvement (Vaughn & Leff, 1976). Expressed emotion is measured on the basis of how relatives spontaneously talk about their family member with a psychiatric illness. A high level of criticism (CRIT) is indicated by judgmental or critical comments, dissatisfaction with the patient's behavior or characteristics, and/or the relationship is described in a negative manner. High emotional overinvolvement (EOI) is indicated when a relative describes extreme self-sacrificing behavior or overprotection, has a lack of objectivity, or becomes very emotional when talking about the patient.

Chambless and Steketee (1999) examined EE in relatives (mainly spouses) of adults with OCD compared with adults with panic and agoraphobia, and found high rates of EE (approximately 55%) in relatives of OCD patients. They also found that high EE predicted higher drop-out rates and poorer treatment outcome. Koujalgi, Nayak, Patil, and Chate (2014) found that adults diagnosed with OCD perceived significantly higher levels of EE (both CRIT and EOI) than age and gender matched healthy controls.

Hibbs and colleagues (1991) examined EE in childhood OCD. They found that 82% of their sample of children with OCD had either one or both parents classified as high EE, compared with 42% of healthy control children. There was also a high rate of parental psychopathology, with 72% of parents meeting criteria for one or more psychiatric diagnoses, compared with 29% of parents of control children. Parental psychopathology emerged as a strong predictor of EE. A number of other variables were related to high EE in parents of children with OCD, including family conflict, maternal hostility and maternal achievement orientation.

Expressed emotion has been found to impact upon treatment outcome for children with OCD. Leonard and colleagues (1993) followed the OCD sample from the Hibbs et al. (1991) study and found that high parental EE at baseline was predictive of poorer overall functioning 2–7 years after pharmacological treatment. Peris, Yadegar, Asarnow, and Piacentini (2012b) conducted a similar study, examining both correlates of maternal EE and the relation between EE and treatment outcome. They found a high level of maternal EE (55%) in a sample of 58 children with OCD. Within the sample of mothers with high EE, 69% were rated high CRIT, and 44% were rated as high EOI. There were relatively high rates of parental psychopathology (as measured by self-report), with 36% of mothers reporting OCD symptoms, 29% reporting clinically significant anxiety symptoms, and 33% depressive symptoms. The study did not provide a breakdown of the relative number of mothers who had clinically significant symptoms in one or more domains. High EE was not related to OCD symptoms at baseline; however, it was related to higher levels of child externalizing symptoms. Maternal criticism was not related to maternal psychopathology, however maternal EOI was. Finally, maternal EE was associated with poorer treatment response as measured by the CGI-I variable. It was not associated with OCD symptom severity at outcome as measured by the CY-BOCS.

Przeworski and colleagues (2012) also examined maternal EE in relation to children with OCD, and included a comparison with unaffected siblings. They found high EE was associated with severity of OCD symptoms at pretreatment, and that mothers were more critical of their child with OCD than they were toward their unaffected child. Comparative to other studies, they found relatively low rates of EE overall (only 16.1% of mothers rated as high EE). The study found that there was good concordance between child ratings of maternal EE and maternal ratings of child EE, indicating that both mothers and children were aware that their relationships was a negative one. They found that pretreatment EE was predictive of posttreatment OCD related functional impairment, although this finding was only true for school-related and social impairment. High EE at baseline was not found to be predictive of posttreatment OCD symptom severity, or family impairment. Clearly the relationship between familial EE and treatment outcome is a complex one, and requires further investigation, however it seems that EE is one aspect of a family environment that is important to consider, among others.

Family Environment

There are relatively few studies that have looked more widely at other aspects of the family environment, but those that have consistently indicate the importance of this area. For example, in a study focused on adolescents with OCD, Valleni-Basile and colleagues (1995) investigated family and psychosocial predictors of OCD and subclinical OCD in a community sample. Perceived family environment was measured using the Family Adaptability and Cohesion Evaluation Scale, a self-report questionnaire which comprises two subscales measuring family adaptability and cohesion. They found that family cohesion correlated significantly with OCD, reflecting a perception of less emotional warmth, support and closeness in the families of adolescents with OCD compared with controls.

Peris and colleagues (2008b) sought to examine the role of parent perceptions toward their child's OCD, as well as specific parental behaviors toward their child with OCD. They developed a measure specifically for this purpose, termed the Parental Attitudes and Behaviors Scale (PABS). They found that parental hostility and blame was associated with child OCD symptom severity, and particularly compulsive rituals, as these are observable and most likely to draw negative parental reactions. They also found that hostility and blame were associated with parental mental health symptoms, and that blame/hostility and accommodation were not mutually exclusive behaviors, validating the idea that behavioral responses toward OCD can change both within and between family members.

Peris and colleagues (2012a) investigated the effect of family conflict, cohesion and parental blame (i.e., believing that the child engages in OCD behaviors on purpose) on treatment outcomes for children and adolescents with OCD receiving family-focused CBT (FCBT). Measures were taken before and after treatment. Results showed that negative family environment variables (parental blame, conflict, and cohesion) tended to cluster together, with only 29% of families having an absence of any negative family environment characteristics, and 71% of families having one or more negative environment characteristics. Children of families with lower levels of parental blame and family conflict, and higher levels of family cohesion prior to treatment, were more likely to respond positively to family based CBT compared with families with higher levels of dysfunction. Conversely, only 10% of children in families with all three negative environment factors (poorer cohesion, greater conflict, and higher parental blame) were likely to respond. They also found that change in family cohesion from pre- to posttreatment significantly predicted treatment outcome. Changes in family conflict did not (although this may be attributable to statistical power). These findings are broadly consistent with Barrett, Farrell, Dadds, and Boulter (2005), who found that higher levels of family dysfunction at baseline, as measured by the McMaster Family Assessment Device, predicted poorer 18-month follow-up outcome for children with OCD.

Summary

Genetics plays a certain role in the familial aggregation of OCD, and it is one of the factors recognized to contribute to onset of the disorder. However, studies have shown that nonshared environmental factors are equally important. Parenting style, and particularly the parenting dimensions of (high) criticism and (high) overinvolvement have been found to be associated with OCD. These findings have led to further investigation into family climate, and EE has emerged as a relevant construct within this context. In studies with adult OCD sufferers, high EE has been indicated in approximately 55% of relatives (mainly spouses), and in children, rates of EE have been found to be as high as 82%. Parental psychopathology is associated with EE, and mothers have been found to display higher levels of EE in relation to their child with OCD as compared with an unaffected sibling. EE has been linked to poorer treatment outcome. Parental blame toward an OCD child for their symptoms, high levels of family conflict and low levels of family cohesion have all been shown to be relevant family environment factors, and families with more of these negative risk factors tend to respond less well to treatment than families without these characteristics.

The Importance of a Family-based Conceptualization

As outlined above, OCD can be a debilitating disorder, associated with a poor quality of life not just for the sufferer, but also for family members, and the negative impact of OCD on family members is widely recognized.

Conversely, however, the impact of the family on the onset and maintenance of the disorder is equally well documented. It is more likely than not that families of individuals with OCD will exhibit multiple indices of negative functioning. All of these negative family characteristics and environmental indices are associated with a poorer response to treatment, and research suggests that the greater the number of negative environmental risk factors, the poorer the response to treatment, and the greater the burden of disease for sufferers and family members.

From a scientific standpoint, there is clearly a limitation to much of the existing research documenting as association between OCD and family. While strong associations are clear, the direction of effect is less clear, and there are various possible pathways that could explain the links. It is most likely however that there is a bidirectional relationship between family factors and OCD, each negatively reinforcing the other and ultimately leading to an overly emotional and self-perpetuating set of circumstances. Regardless, however, each of the abovementioned family factors need to be carefully assessed and formulated into an individualized treatment plan that seeks to promote sustained recovery from OCD. Modifications to the usual CBT protocol may be required, depending on the nature of the associated factors assessed as relevant.

In the following section, we will outline the current guidelines on involving family members in the treatment of OCD. We will review the existing evidence for family-based CBT, examining possible benefits of involving family members. Finally, we will discuss emerging evidence for other family interventions, designed to be used as adjuncts to CBT for OCD in certain subgroups.

Family-based Treatment of OCD

Do Clinical Practice Guidelines Recommend Family Involvement in CBT?

Both UK and North American clinical practice guidelines for the treatment of OCD recommend family involvement (Geller & March, 2012; NICE, 2005). This recommendation applies to all children and adolescents with OCD. The recommendations with respect to adults are less absolute but nevertheless suggest that clinicians should attempt to work collaboratively with family members. Interestingly, both UK and North American guidelines emphasize the importance of assessing for family accommodation, presumably so that this can then be addressed in treatment. However, it is important to note that current guidelines do not cite empirical data to support their recommendation, and in fact most recommendations with regard to family involvement are based solely on expert clinical opinion. Furthermore, the details of how families should be involved and for what purpose are less clear. This ambiguity is a reflection of the limited research in the field.

How and Why are Families Involved in CBT?

Children and adolescents. Over 10 randomized controlled trials of CBT for pediatric OCD have been conducted to date and have consistently demonstrated the efficacy of CBT. The vast majority of trials have evaluated treatment protocols that include family involvement. Family-based CBT has been shown to be effective for young children (Freeman et al., 2008; Freeman et al., 2014; Lewin et al., 2014) and adolescents (e.g., Piacentini et al., 2011; Reynolds et al., 2013; Storch et al., 2007b; Storch et al., 2008b). This approach is effective when delivered in group and intensive formats (Barrett, Healy-Farrell, & March, 2004; Storch et al., 2008b). Furthermore, family-based CBT has been shown to be associated with superior outcomes relative to an alternative active psychological treatment (Piacentini et al., 2011).

Across trials, family involvement in CBT typically translates into including one or both parents in CBT sessions, rather than a wider family network. Many studies have included parents in all sessions (e.g., Freeman et al., 2014; Lewin et al., 2014; Storch et al., 2007b; Storch et al., 2011), while others involved parents in some sessions only (e.g., Bolton et al., 2011; Piacentini et al., 2011; POTS, 2004) and/or invited parents to participate in a "check-in" at the end of each session (e.g., Piacentini et al., 2011). Most recently, there is preliminary evidence for the efficacy of working solely with parents, when a child is reluctant to engage in treatment (Lebowitz, 2013).

Studies have involved parents in CBT with a variety of goals. First, is the provision of education about OCD and its treatment (Barrett et al., 2004; Bolton & Perrin, 2008; Lewin et al., 2014; Peris & Piacentini, 2013; Piacentini et al., 2011; POTS, 2004). This frequently includes discussion of causes of OCD, which can address parental blame or guilt about the origins of their child's disorder. It may involve the technique of externalizing OCD, whereby OCD is explicitly labeled as being separate to the child rather than an intrinsic part of their character, and may be framed as being like a bully which is to be fought in treatment. This can be motivating for the child, and can also help align parents and child and reduce parental blame and criticism toward a child's compulsive behaviors.

Second, parents can be trained to act as a co-therapist (Barrett et al., 2004; Bolton & Perrin, 2008; Lewin et al., 2014; Storch et al., 2008a; Storch et al., 2011). This may involve teaching parents about the principles of habituation (Lewin et al., 2014), upskilling them to set up exposure tasks (ERP) at home (Storch et al., 2008a; Storch et al., 2011), encouraging them to model exposure tasks (Lewin et al., 2014), and delivering rewards for their child's attempts to do ERP (Bolton & Perrin, 2008), which may promote the child's compliance with E/RP tasks at home. E/RP is considered to be the active component in treatment (Tolin, 2009).

Third, parents are included in CBT sessions in order to achieve reductions in parental accommodation (e.g., Freeman et al., 2014; Lewin et al., 2014; Peris & Piacentini, 2013; Piacentini et al., 2011; POTS, 2004; Storch et al., 2011). Encouragingly, greater decreases in parental accommodation during CBT are associated with a greater reduction in OCD symptoms, suggesting that effectively tackling family accommodation may improve outcomes (Storch et al., 2009). Ideally, reduction of accommodation is done in a graded and collaborative way (Storch et al., 2007b).

Fourth, a number of trials include parents in order to teach contingency management (Freeman et al., 2014; Lewin et al., 2014; Storch et al., 2008a; Storch et al., 2011). To some extent, this overlaps with encouraging parents to reward their child's attempts at E/RP and disengaging from rituals. However, some studies extend this to include broader and more systematic training in strategies such as differential attention. This may be motivating by removing external reinforcement of rituals (e.g., parental attention) and providing positive reinforcement for attempts to confront fears or resist ritual (e.g., praise). Furthermore, contingency management training may help parents to feel confident in managing temper outbursts, which are common in young people with OCD and often may occur when the young person's rituals are disrupted. These outbursts can be acute, and unless parents feel confident in managing them, they may respond by accommodating rituals.

Adults. Although RCTs of CBT for OCD in adults have typically involved working with the patient individually, a number of studies have evaluated family-based CBT protocols (e.g., Belotto-Silva et al., 2012; Emmelkamp & De Lange, 1983; Grunes, Neziroglu, & McKay, 2001; Mehta, 1990; Van Noppen, Steketee, McCorkle, & Pato, 1997). Some studies have specifically involved romantic partners (Emmelkamp & DeLange, 1983; Emmelkamp, de Haan, & Hoogduin, 1990), while others have adopted a broader approach and included any close or cohabiting relatives (Grunes et al., 2001; Van Noppen et al., 1997; Mehta, 1990). Similar to working with children and young people, common reasons for including family members in CBT are to provide education about OCD and treatment, to encourage families to act as a co-therapist, and to reduce accommodation of symptoms (Renshaw, Steketee, & Chambless, 2005).

Does Involving Families in CBT for OCD Enhance Outcomes?

While family-based CBT is widely advocated in the treatment of OCD, a key question which remains largely unanswered is *"what is the added benefit of involving family members?."* Only a handful of studies have systematically explored the question of whether involving family members in CBT improves outcomes.

Children and adolescents. In an early case series of four children, a multiple-baseline design was used to address the question of whether involving parents in CBT has a beneficial effect (Knox, Albano, & Barlow, 1996). In the first phase of treatment, patients received individual ERP-based CBT. In the second phase, parents were involved in CBT. They were provided with education about OCD and were coached in helping their child to conduct ERP. They were taught the principles of differential reinforcement, were encouraged to disengage from compulsions, and to praise and reward adaptive coping responses. None of the cases showed an improvement in OCD symptoms during the individual phase, but two of the four showed a notable decrease in compulsions after parents became involved in sessions. While these findings suggest that involving parents could be important, the lack of a control condition precludes firm conclusions.

More recently, Reynolds and colleagues conducted an RCT to compare outcomes of individual CBT for OCD versus parent-enhanced CBT (Reynolds et al., 2013). In the individual CBT condition, parents attended three sessions (at the beginning of treatment, at mid-treatment, and at end of treatment), whereas in the parent-enhanced CBT, one or both parents were involved in every session, and the formulation explicitly labeled parent and family maintaining factors. The study did not find evidence for enhanced outcomes in the high parental involvement group; the two treatment conditions were associated with equivalent improvements in OCD symptoms at both posttreatment and 6-month follow-up. This study suggests that CBT is effective, regardless of levels of parental involvement. However, it remains possible that parental involvement is more important for certain individuals or subgroups than for others. For example, it may be of added benefit to involve parents or family members in cases where there are particularly high levels of family accommodation, or when working with younger children.

Adults. A number of studies have examined the effect of involving family members in CBT for adult OCD with mixed findings. For example, Emmelkamp and colleagues randomly assigned 50 adults with OCD to individual ERP or partner-assisted ERP (Emmelkamp et al., 1990). The two groups displayed equal improvement with respect to OCD symptoms and a range of other outcomes, suggesting that involving partners did not augment treatment effects. However, this study used a particularly brief CBT protocol of only eight sessions, and it is possible that the lack of group difference reflected the modest improvements seen in both groups.

Mehta (1990) randomly assigned 30 adults with OCD to receive individual CBT or family-based CBT. Both groups received relaxation training and ERP, but in the family intervention, relatives were included in sessions and were coached as co-therapists and instructed in reducing their accommodation of rituals. Superior outcomes were obtained in the family-based condition at posttreatment and 1-month follow-up. Similar findings were obtained by Grunes and colleagues, in which adolescents and adults with treatment-resistant OCD were randomly assigned to receive either individual CBT or individual CBT plus a family intervention (Grunes et al., 2001). The family intervention consisted of eight weekly group sessions which included education about OCD and its treatment, guidance in being a co-therapist, explicit labelling of counterproductive accommodating behaviors, and guidance on graded reduction of accommodation. The study found that patients who received individual CBT plus the family intervention showed a greater reduction in OCD symptoms than the individual CBT only group. Furthermore, the family intervention group had superior outcomes on a number of other measures including depressive symptoms in the patient, and depression, anxiety, and EE in the family member. There was no group difference in the extent to which accommodation of OCD symptoms reduced over the course of treatment, suggesting that this variable did not mediate the positive effects of the family intervention. Nevertheless, taken together, these two studies suggest a possible beneficial effect of involving relatives in CBT for OCD.

Other Family-based Interventions for OCD

In recent years, a number of studies have moved beyond involving parents to examining broader family interventions. These are not intended as alternatives to CBT, but as an adjunct to CBT in an attempt to improve outcomes in difficult-to-treat groups. One example of such a treatment is illustrated by Peris and Piacentini (2013), who developed a Positive Family Interaction Therapy (PFIT), designed as an adjunct to adolescent treatment in families with high levels of dysfunction. This novel approach stemmed from two important observations. First, family conflict, blame and cohesion were found to be predictors of response to family-based CBT (Peris et al., 2012a). Second, although studies of family-based CBT have shown positive effects, most trials have failed to find significant improvements in indicators of family dysfunction. As well as involving education about OCD and reduction of family accommodation, PFIT also includes techniques specifically aimed at promoting family cohesion. For example, experiential exercises are used to promote problem-solving within the family, and enhance skills in negotiation of effective solutions, and emotion regulation. In an initial pilot study, families characterized by high conflict, high blame, and poor cohesion were randomly allocated to receive standard CBT, or standard CBT plus six PFIT sessions. The PFIT condition was associated with a 70% response rate, in contrast to a 40% response rate in the CBT condition, and gains were maintained through to a 3-month follow-up assessment. Although further research is needed, these findings highlight the potential value of targeting unhelpful family dynamics in order to improve OCD outcomes.

In another example, young people with comorbid disruptive behavior disorders (DBD) have been shown to respond less well to standard CBT (Garcia et al, 2010; Storch et al., 2008a). This is perhaps not surprising given that noncompliance is likely to interfere with ERP tasks within session and at home. Interest has therefore been raised in whether adjunctive parent management training could improve CBT outcomes in this group. In a preliminary study, Sukhodolsky, Gorman, Scahill, Findley, and McGuire (2013) examined the effect of PMT on outcome. Six participants, aged 9–14 years, with OCD and comorbid ODD were randomized to receive either six weekly sessions of PMT followed by 12 sessions of ERP, or to remain on a waitlist for 6 weeks and then receive 12 sessions of ERP. The PMT + ERP group displayed significantly greater reduction in OCD symptoms, compared with the E/RP only group, suggesting that PMT may successfully augment CBT in this patient group.

Summary

In summary, expert clinical opinion suggests that families should be involved in the treatment of OCD, especially for children. Family involvement strategies vary somewhat, and it is important to note that research to date has not attempted to dismantle the effects of individual strategies, therefore the extent to which any one of these strategies is necessary or beneficial remains unclear. Moreover, there is limited evidence that family involvement augments the effects of CBT. Failure of some studies to find effects for involving family members in treatment may in part reflect the fact that individual CBT is a highly effective treatment, and thus any incremental effects may be difficult to detect with modest samples. Of course, it remains possible, and even probable, that involving relatives in CBT is more important and valuable in some cases than others. Family involvement might be indicated in young children, cases presenting with high levels of family conflict/low cohesion, and with comorbid DBD. The clinical decision of whether to include relatives can be guided by individual formulation, including consideration of these factors, and by patient choice. Finally, there may be certain subgroups of patients who benefit from additional family interventions, beyond family-based CBT, but further research is needed to formally evaluate such approaches.

References

Albert, U., Bogetto, F., Maina, G., Saracco, P., Brunatto, C., & Mataix-Cols, D. (2010). Family accommodation in obsessive-compulsive disorder: Relation to symptom dimensions, clinical and family characteristics. *Psychiatry Research, 179*(2), 204–211.

Alonso, P., Menchón, J., Mataix-Cols, D., Pifarré, J., Urretavizcaya, M., Crespo, J. M. & Vallejo, J. (2004). Perceived parental rearing style in obsessive-compulsive disorder: Relation to symptom dimensions. *Psychiatry Research, 127*(3), 267–278.

Amir, N., Freshman, M., & Foa, E. B. (2000). Family distress and involvement in relatives of obsessive-compulsive disorder patients. *Journal of Anxiety Disorders, 14*(3), 209–217.

Barrett, P., Healy-Farrell, L., & March, J. S. (2004). Cognitive-behavioral family treatment of childhood obsessive-compulsive disorder: A controlled trial. *Journal of the American Academy of Child and Adolescent Psychiatry, 43*(1), 46–62.

Barrett, P. M., Rasmussen, P. J., & Healy, L., (2001). The effect of obsessive-compulsive disorder on sibling relationships in late childhood and early adolescence: Preliminary findings. *Australian Educational and Developmental Psychologist, 17*(2), 82–102.

Barrett, P. M., Shortt, A., & Healy, L. (2002). Do parent and child behaviours differentiate families whose children have obsessive-compulsive disorder from other clinic and non-clinic families? *Journal of Child Psychology and Psychiatry, 43*(5), 597–607.

Barrett, P., Farrell, L., Dadds, M., & Boulter, N. (2005). Cognitive-behavioral family treatment of childhood obsessive-compulsive disorder: Long-term follow-up and predictors of outcome. *Journal of the American Academy of Child and Adolescent Psychiatry, 44*(10), 1005–1014.

Belotto-Silva, C., Diniz, J. B., Malavazzi, D. M., Valério, C., Fossaluza, V., Borcato, S., Shavitt, R. (2012). Group cognitive-behavioral therapy versus selective serotonin reuptake inhibitors for obsessive-compulsive disorder: A practical clinical trial. *Journal of Anxiety Disorders, 26*(1), 25–31.

Bolton, D., & Perrin, S. (2008). Evaluation of exposure with response-prevention for obsessive compulsive disorder in childhood and adolescence. *Journal of Behavior Therapy and Experimental Psychiatry, 39*(1), 11–22.

Bolton, D., Williams, T., Perrin, S., Atkinson, L., Gallop, C., Waite, P., & Salkovskis, P. (2011). Randomized controlled trial of full and brief cognitive-behaviour therapy and wait-list for paediatric obsessive-compulsive disorder. *Journal of Child Psychology and Psychiatry, 52*(12), 1269–1278.

Calvocoressi, L., Mazure, C., Kasl, S. V., Skolnick, J., Fisk, D., Vegso, S. J., Van Noppen, B. L., & Price, L. H. (1999). Family accommodation of obsessive-compulsive symptoms: Instrument development and assessment of family behavior. *Journal of Nervous and Mental Disease, 187*, 636–642.

Caporino, N., Morgan, J., Beckstead, J., Phares, V., Murphy, T. K., & Storch, E. A. (2012). A structural equation analysis of family accommodation in pediatric obsessive-compulsive disorder. *Journal of Abnormal Child Psychology, 40*, 133–143.

Chambless, D. L., & Steketee, G. (1999). Expressed emotion and behavior therapy outcome: A prospective study with obsessive-compulsive and agoraphobic outpatients. *Journal of Consulting and Clinical Psychology, 67*(5), 658–665.

Cooper, M. (1994). A group for families of obsessive-compulsive persons. *Families in Society, 74*, 301–307

Cooper, M. (1996). Obsessive-compulsive disorder: Effects on family members. *American Journal of Orthopsychiatry, 66*(2), 296–304.

Derisley, J., Libby, S., Clark, S., & Reynolds, S. (2005). Mental health, coping and family-functioning in parents of young people with obsessive-compulsive disorder and with anxiety disorders. *British Journal of Clinical Psychology, 44*(3), 439–444.

Ehiobuche, I. (1988). Obsessive-compulsive neurosis in relation to parental child-rearing patterns amongst Greek, Italian, and Anglo-Australian subjects. *Acta Psychiatrica Scandinavica, 78*(Suppl. 344), 115–120.

Emmelkamp, P. M., de Haan, E., & Hoogduin, C. A. (1990). Marital adjustment and obsessive-compulsive disorder. *British Journal of Psychiatry, 156*, 55–60.

Emmelkamp, P. M. G., & De Lange, I. (1983). Spouse involvement in the treatment of obsessive-compulsive patients. *Behaviour Research and Therapy, 21*(4), 341–346.

Ferrão, Y. A., Shavitt, R. G., Bedin, N. R., De Mathis, M. E., Carlos Lopes, A., Fontenelle, L. F., & Miguel, E. C. (2006). Clinical features associated to refractory obsessive-compulsive disorder. *Journal of Affective Disorders, 94*(1), 199–209.

Flessner, C. A., Freeman, J. B., Sapyta, J., Garcia, A., Franklin, M. E., March, J. S., & Foa, E. (2011). Predictors of parental accommodation in pediatric obsessive-compulsive disorder: Findings from the pediatric obsessive-compulsive disorder treatment study (POTS) trial. *Journal of the American Academy of Child and Adolescent Psychiatry, 50*(7), 716–725.

Freeman, J. B., Garcia, A. M., Coyne, L., Ale, C., Przeworski, A., Himle, M., Compton, S., & Leonard, H. L. (2008). Early childhood OCD: Preliminary findings from a family-based cognitive-behavioral approach. *Journal of the American Academy of Child and Adolescent Psychiatry, 47*, 593–602.

Freeman, J., Sapyta, J., Garcia, A., Compton, S., Khanna, M., Flessner, C., ... Franklin, M. (2014). Family-based treatment of early childhood obsessive-compulsive disorder: The Pediatric Obsessive-Compulsive Disorder Treatment Study for Young Children (POTS Jr) – A Randomized Clinical Trial. *JAMA Psychiatry, 71*(6), 689–698.

Futh, A., Simonds, L., & Micali, N. (2012). Obsessive-compulsive disorder in children and adolescents: Parental understanding, accommodation, coping and distress. *Journal of Anxiety Disorders, 26*(5), 624–632.

Garcia, A. M., Sapyta, J. J., Moore, P. S., Freeman, J. B., Franklin, M. E., March, J. S., & Foa, E. B. (2010). Predictors and moderators of treatment outcome in the Pediatric Obsessive Compulsive Treatment Study (POTS I). *Journal of the American Academy of Child and Adolescent Psychiatry, 49*(10), 1024–1033.

Geller, D. A., & March, J. (2012). Practice parameter for the assessment and treatment of children and adolescents with obsessive-compulsive disorder. *FOCUS: Journal of Lifelong Learning in Psychiatry, 10*(3), 360–373.

Ginsburg, G. S., Kingery, J. N., Drake, K. L., & Grados, M. A. (2008). Predictors of treatment response in pediatric obsessive-compulsive disorder. *Journal of the American Academy of Child and Adolescent Psychiatry, 47*(8), 868–878.

Grunes, M. S., Neziroglu, F., & McKay, D. (2001). Family involvement in the behavioral treatment of obsessive-compulsive disorder: A preliminary investigation. *Behavior Therapy, 32*(4), 803–820.

Hibbs, E. D., Hamburger, S. D., Lenane, M., Rapoport, J. L., Kruesi, M. J., Keysor, C. S., & Goldstein, M. J. (1991). Determinants of expressed emotion in families of disturbed and normal children. *Journal of Child Psychology and Psychiatry, 32*(5), 757–770.

Knox, L. S., Albano, A. M., & Barlow, D. H. (1997). Parental involvement in the treatment of childhood obsessive compulsive disorder: A multiple-baseline examination incorporating parents. *Behavior Therapy, 27*(1), 93–114.

Koujalgi, S. R., Nayak, R. B., Patil, N. M., & Chate, S. S. (2014). Expressed emotions in patients with obsessive compulsive disorder: A case control study. *Indian Journal of Psychological Medicine, 36*(2), 138.

Krebs, G., Bolhuis, K., Heyman, I., Mataix-Cols, D., Turner, C., & Stringaris, A. (2013). Temper outbursts in paediatric obsessive-compulsive disorder and their association with depressed mood and treatment outcome. *Journal of Child Psychology and Psychiatry, 54*(3), 313–322.

Labouliere, C. D., Arnold, E. B., Storch, E. A., & Lewin, A. B. (2014). Family-based cognitive-behavioral treatment for a preschooler with obsessive-compulsive disorder. *Clinical Case Studies, 13*(1), 37–51.

Lebowitz E. R. (2013). Parent-based treatment for childhood and adolescent OCD. *Journal of Obsessive-Compulsive and Related Disorders, 2*(4), 425–431.

Lebowitz, E. R., Omer, H., & Leckman, J. F. (2011). Coercive and disruptive behaviors in pediatric obsessive–compulsive disorder. *Depression and Anxiety, 28*(10), 899–905.

Lebowitz, E. R., Vitulano, L. A., Mataix-Cols, D., & Leckman, J. F. (2011). Editorial perspective: When OCD takes over ... the family! Coercive and disruptive behaviours in paediatric obsessive compulsive disorder. *Journal of Child Psychology and Psychiatry, 52*(12), 1249–1250.

Lebowitz, E. R., Vitulano, L. A., & Omer, H. (2011). Coercive and disruptive behaviors in pediatric obsessive compulsive disorder: A qualitative analysis. *Psychiatry: Interpersonal & Biological Processes*, 74(4), 362–371.

Lehmkuhl, H. D., Storch, E. A., Rahman, O., Freeman, J., Geffken, G. R., & Murphy, T. K. (2009). Just say no: Sequential parent management training and cognitive-behavioral therapy for a child with comorbid disruptive behavior and obsessive compulsive disorder. *Clinical Case Studies*, 8(1), 48–58.

Lennertz, L., Grabe, H. J., Ruhrmann, S., Rampacher, F., Vogeley, A., Schulze-Rauschenbach, S., & Wagner, M. (2010). Perceived parental rearing in subjects with obsessive-compulsive disorder and their siblings. *Acta Psychiatrica Scandinavica*, 121(4), 280–288.

Leonard, H., Swedo, S. E., Lenane, M. C., Rettew, D. C., Hamburger, S. D., Bartko, J. J., & Rapoport, J. L. (1993). A 2- to 7-year follow-up study of 54 obsessive-compulsive children and adolescents. *Archives of General Psychiatry*, 50(6), 429–439.

Lewin, A., Park, J., Jones, A., Crawford, E., De Nadai, A., Menzel, J., & Storch, E. A. (2014). Family-based exposure and response prevention therapy for preschool-aged children with obsessive-compulsive disorder: A pilot randomized controlled trial. *Behaviour Research and Therapy*, 56C, 30–38.

Mehta, M. (1990). A comparative study of family-based and patient-based behavioural management in obsessive-compulsive disorder. *British Journal of Psychiatry*, 157(1), 133–135.

Merlo, L. J., Lehmkuhl, H. D., Geffken, G. R., & Storch, E. A. (2009). Decreased family accommodation associated with improved therapy outcome in pediatric obsessive-compulsive disorder. *Journal of Consulting and Clinical Psychology*, 77(2), 355–360.

Micali, N., Heyman, I., Perez, M., Hilton, K., Nakatani, E., Turner, C., & Mataix-Cols, D. (2010). Long-term outcomes of obsessive–compulsive disorder: Follow-up of 142 children and adolescents. *British Journal of Psychiatry*, 197, 128–134.

National Institute for Health and Clinical Excellence (NICE). (2005). *Core interventions in the treatment of obsessive-compulsive disorder (OCD) and body dysmorphic disorder (BDD)*. Stanley Hunt: London.

Pauls, D. L., Abramovitch, A., Rauch, S. L., & Geller, D. A. (2014). Obsessive-compulsive disorder: An integrative genetic and neurobiological perspective. *Nature Reviews Neuroscience*, 15(6), 410–424.

Peris, T. S., Bergman, R. L., Langley, A., Chang, S., McCracken, J. T., & Piacentini, J. (2008a). Correlates of accommodation of pediatric obsessive-compulsive disorder: Parent, child, and family characteristics. *Journal of the American Academy of Child and Adolescent Psychiatry*, 47(10), 1173–1181.

Peris, T. S., Benazon, N., Langley, A., Roblek, T., & Piacentini, J. (2008b). Parental attitudes, beliefs, and responses to childhood obsessive compulsive disorder: the parental attitudes and behaviors scale. *Child and Family Behavior Therapy*, 30(3), 199–214.

Peris, T. S., & Piacentini, J. (2013). Optimizing treatment for complex cases of childhood obsessive compulsive disorder: A preliminary trial. *Journal of Clinical Child and Adolescent Psychology*, 42(1), 1–8.

Peris, T. S., Sugar, C. A., Bergman, R. L., Chang, S., Langley, A., & Piacentini, J. (2012a). Family factors predict treatment outcome for pediatric obsessive-compulsive disorder. *Journal of Consulting and Clinical Psychology*, 80(2), 255–263.

Peris, T. S., Yadegar, M., Asarnow, J. R., & Piacentini, J. (2012b). Pediatric obsessive compulsive disorder: Family climate as a predictor of treatment outcome. *Journal of Obsessive-Compulsive and Related Disorders*, 1(4), 267–273.

Piacentini, J., Peris, T. S., Bergman, R. L., Chang, S., & Jaffer, M. (2007). Functional impairment in childhood OCD: Development and psychometrics properties of the child obsessive-compulsive impact scale-revised (COIS-R). *Journal of Clinical Child and Adolescent Psychology*, 36(4), 645–653.

Piacentini, J., Bergman, R. L., Chang, S., Langley, A., Peris, T., Wood, J. J., & McCracken, J. (2011). Controlled comparison of family cognitive behavioral therapy and psychoeducation/ relaxation training for child obsessive-compulsive disorder. *Journal of the American Academy of Child & Adolescent Psychiatry, 50*(11), 1149–1161.

POTS (2004). Cognitive-behavior therapy, sertraline, and their combination for children and adolescents with obsessive-compulsive disorder: The pediatric OCD treatment study (POTS) randomized controlled trial. *Journal of the American Medical Association, 292*(16), 1969–1976.

Przeworski, A., Zoellner, L. A., Franklin, M. E., Garcia, A., Freeman, J., March, J. S., & Foa, E. B. (2012). Maternal and child expressed emotion as predictors of treatment response in pediatric obsessive- compulsive disorder. *Child Psychiatry and Human Development, 43*(3), 337–353.

Rapee, R. M. (1997). Potential role of childrearing practices in the development of anxiety and depression. *Clinical Psychology Review, 17*(1), 47–67.

Renshaw, K. D., Steketee, G., & Chambless, D. L. (2005). Involving family members in the treatment of OCD. *Cognitive Behaviour Therapy, 34*(3), 164–175.

Reynolds, S. A., Clark, S., Smith, H., Langdon, P. E., Payne, R., Bowers, G., Norton, E., & McIlwham, H. (2013). Randomized controlled trial of parent-enhanced CBT compared with individual CBT for obsessive-compulsive disorder in young people. *Journal of Consulting and Clinical Psychology, 81*(6), 1021–1026.

Steketee, G. (1997). Disability and family burden in obsessive compulsive disorder. *Canadian Journal of Psychiatry, 42*, 919–928.

Stengler-Wenzke, K., Kroll, M., Matschinger, H., & Angermeyer, M. C. (2006). Quality of life of relatives of patients with obsessive-compulsive disorder. *Comprehensive Psychiatry, 47*(6), 523–527.

Stewart, S. E., Stack, D. E., & Wilhelm, S. (2008). Severe obsessive-compulsive disorder with and without body dysmorphic disorder: Clinical correlates and implications. *Annals of Clinical Psychiatry, 20*(1), 33–38.

Storch, E. A., Caporino, N. E., Morgan, J. R., Lewin, A. B., Rojas, A., Brauer, L., Larson, M. J., & Murphy, T. K. (2011). Preliminary investigation of web-camera delivered cognitive-behavioral therapy for youth with obsessive-compulsive disorder. *Psychiatry Research, 189*(3), 407–412.

Storch, E. A., Geffken, G. R., Merlo, L. J., Jacob, M. L., Murphy, T. K., Goodman, W. K., Larson, M. J., Fernandez, M., & Grabill, K. (2007a). Family accommodation in pediatric obsessive-compulsive disorder. *Journal of Clinical Child and Adolescent Psychology, 36*(2), 207–216.

Storch, E. A., Geffken, G. R., Merlo, L. J., Mann, G., Duke, D., Munson, M., Adkins, J., Grabill, K. M., Murphy, T. K., & Goodman, W. K. (2007b). Family-based cognitive-behavioral therapy for pediatric obsessive-compulsive disorder: Comparison of intensive and weekly approaches. *Journal of the American Academy of Child and Adolescent Psychiatry, 46*(4), 469–478.

Storch, E. A., Jones, A. M., Lack, C. W., Ale, C. M., Sulkowski, M. L., Lewin, A. B., & Murphy, T. K. (2012). Rage attacks in pediatric obsessive-compulsive disorder: Phenomenology and clinical correlates. *Journal of the American Academy of Child and Adolescent Psychiatry, 51*(6), 582–592.

Storch, E. A., Lehmkuhl, H., Pence, Jr., S. L., Geffken, G. R., Ricketts, E., Storch, J. F., & Murphy, T. K. (2009). Parental experiences of having a child with obsessive-compulsive disorder: Associations with clinical characteristics and caregiver adjustment. *Journal of Child and Family Studies, 18*(3), 249–258.

Storch, E. A., Merlo, L. J., Larson, M. J., Bloss, C. S., Geffken, G. R., Jacob, M. L., Murphy, T. K., & Goodman, W. K. (2008a). Symptom dimensions and cognitive-behavioural therapy outcome for pediatric obsessive-compulsive disorder. *Acta Psychiatrica Scandinavica, 117*(1), 67–75.

Storch, E. A., Merlo, L. J., Lehmkuhl, H., Geffken, G. R., Jacob, M., Ricketts, E., Murphy, T. K., & Goodman, W. K. (2008b). Cognitive-behavioral therapy for obsessive-compulsive disorder: A non-randomized comparison of intensive and weekly approaches. *Journal of Anxiety Disorders, 22*(7), 1146–1158.

Sukhodolsky, D. G., Gorman, B. S., Scahill, L., Findley, D., & McGuire, J. (2013). Exposure and response prevention with or without parent management training for children with obsessive-compulsive disorder complicated by disruptive behavior: A multiple-baseline across-responses design study. *Journal of Anxiety Disorders, 27*(3), 298–305.

Tolin, D. F. (2009). Alphabet soup: ERP, CT, and ACT for OCD. *Cognitive and Behavioral Practice, 16*(1), 40–48.

Turgeon, L., O'Connor, K. P., Marchand, A., & Freeston, M. H. (2002). Recollections of parent–child relationships in patients with obsessive-compulsive disorder and panic disorder with agoraphobia. *Acta Psychiatrica Scandinavica, 105*(4), 310–316.

Valleni-Basile, L. A., Garrison, C. Z., Jackson, K. L., Waller, J. L., McKeown, R. E., Addy, C. L., & Cuffe, S. P. (1995). Family and psychosocial predictors of obsessive compulsive disorder in a community sample of young adolescents. *Journal of Child and Family Studies, 4*(2), 193–206.

Van Grootheest, D. S., Cath, D. C., Beekman, A. T., & Boomsma, D. I. (2005). Twin studies on obsessive-compulsive disorder: A review. *Twin Research and Human Genetics, 8*(5), 450–458.

Van Noppen, B., & Steketee, G. (2009). Testing a conceptual model of patient and family predictors of obsessive compulsive disorder (OCD) symptoms. *Behaviour Research and Therapy, 47*(1), 18–25.

Van Noppen, B., Steketee, G., McCorkle, B. H., & Pato, M. (1997). Group and multifamily behavioral treatment for obsessive compulsive disorder: a pilot study. *Journal of Anxiety Disorders, 11*(4), 431–446.

Vaughn, C., & Leff, J. (1976). The measurement of expressed emotion in the families of psychiatric patients. *British Journal of Social and Clinical Psychology, 15*(2), 157–165.

Vogel, P. A., Stiles, T. C., & Nordahl, H. M. (1997). Recollections of parent–child relationships in OCD out-patients compared to depressed out-patients and healthy controls. *Acta Psychiatrica Scandinavica, 96*(6), 469–474.

Wood, J. J., McLeod, B. D., Sigman, M., Hwang, W. C., & Chu, B. C. (2003). Parenting and childhood anxiety: Theory, empirical findings, and future directions. *Journal of Child Psychology and Psychiatry, 44*(1), 134–151.

35

An Interpersonal Perspective on the Conceptualization and Treatment of OCD

Jonathan S. Abramowitz

Although there is considerable evidence for the effectiveness of treatment by exposure and response prevention (ERP) for individuals with obsessive-compulsive disorder (OCD), not all patients respond well, and some show relapse upon discontinuation (e.g., Abramowitz & Jacoby, 2014). For a number of reasons, involving a romantic partner or spouse might help improve the short- and long-term effects of ERP. Indeed, significant others often become involved in an individual's OCD symptoms (e.g., by helping with rituals and avoidance), creating an interpersonal dynamic that is in contrast to the aims of ERP; and this dynamic is associated with greater symptom severity, a more severe course, and poor global functioning; serving as a risk factor for long-term problems with OCD (Calvocoressi et al., 1999). Data also indicate that involving partners or spouses to serve as coaches for their OCD-affected partners during ERP improves the efficacy of this approach (Mehta, 1990). Yet partner-*assisted* ERP only partially addresses the role of the couple's relationship in the maintenance of OCD; and it does not identify and modify the stressful dynamics in couples' relationships which attenuate response to treatment and increase the risk of relapse. In this chapter we describe the nature and treatment of OCD focusing on these interpersonal dynamics, and outline a couple-based ERP program for individuals with OCD who are in long-term relationships. We employ case examples to illustrate the techniques used in our program.

The Nature of OCD

OCD from the Individual's Perspective

As discussed in other chapters in this volume, the individual's experience of OCD is characterized by *obsessions* and *compulsions* (American Psychiatric Association [APA], 2013). *Obsessions* are recurrent thoughts, ideas, images, or doubts that are experienced as senseless, unwanted, and distressing; for example, the persistent unwanted thought that one might have hit a pedestrian while driving. Although seemingly

---

The Wiley Handbook of Obsessive Compulsive Disorders, Volume I, First Edition.
Edited by Jonathan S. Abramowitz, Dean McKay, and Eric A. Storch.
© 2017 John Wiley & Sons Ltd. Published 2017 by John Wiley & Sons Ltd.

illogical or excessive, obsessions evoke anxiety, doubt, and avoidance behavior (e.g., of driving). In addition to harm, common themes of obsessions include violence, sex, blasphemy, contamination, and incompleteness/imperfection. The obsessional anxiety provokes urges to perform *compulsions* – behavioral or mental rituals that function to reduce anxiety. Examples include cleaning, checking, seeking reassurance, ordering and arranging, repeating routine activities, counting, and mental rituals.

For the individual with OCD, obsessions and compulsions are linked by an internally consistent "logic". For example, someone with obsessional thoughts that he or she is contaminated by "floor germs" might repeatedly wash his or her hands to reduce the fear of becoming ill. In a similar way, someone with obsessional doubts that he or she will be responsible for starting a house fire might spend hours checking and rechecking that appliances are unplugged and lights turned off. Short-term anxiety reduction usually follows the performance of rituals, which negatively reinforces these behaviors leading to their proliferation (e.g., Rachman & Hodgson, 1980). Yet compulsive rituals also prevent the natural extinction of obsessional fear, thus leading to the persistence of the obsessions. Avoidance behavior, which serves the same function as rituals, might be used when obsessional stimuli can be avoided.

Finally, there is variability in the degree of insight that patients have into the senselessness of their obsessions and rituals (APA, 2013). Whereas some individuals recognize that their fears are invalid, and rituals excessive, others believe more firmly that compulsive rituals are necessary to prevent obsessively feared outcomes. Research indicates that the less insight one has into his or her symptoms, the poorer the prognosis with exposure-based therapy (Foa, Abramowitz, Franklin, & Kozak, 1999).

OCD from an Interpersonal Perspective

OCD frequently has a negative impact on the sufferer's interpersonal relationships – such as with a romantic partner. In turn, dysfunctional relationship patterns can promote the maintenance of OCD symptoms so that a vicious cycle develops. One way this process might be manifested is when a partner or spouse inadvertently maintains symptoms by "helping" with compulsive rituals and avoidance behavior out of love for the OCD sufferer (aka, *symptom accommodation*). The second is when anxiety problems create relationship distress and conflict, which then exacerbates the anxiety. Third, the couple might struggle with general relationship distress that does not result from the OCD; in this instance, the chronic stress of a discordant relationship can exacerbate OCD symptoms for an individual who is vulnerable to the disorder. Frequently, all of these processes occur within the same couple.

Symptom accommodation. Accommodation occurs when a partner or spouse of someone with OCD participates in their loved one's rituals, facilitates avoidance strategies, assumes daily responsibilities for the sufferer, or helps to resolve problems that have resulted from the patient's obsessional fears and compulsive urges (Boeding et al., 2013). The accommodation might occur at the request (or *demand*) of the individual with OCD, who deliberately tries to involve loved ones to help with controlling his or her anxiety. In other instances, loved ones voluntarily accommodate because they feel the need to show care and concern for their suffering partner and do not wish to see them become highly anxious. The following example illustrates this phenomenon:

> Margaret was a 33-year-old woman with obsessional thoughts of being possessed by the devil. Finding these thoughts highly repugnant, she avoided stimuli that might trigger ideas of possession (e.g., words such as "demon," "devil," and "hell"). Margaret and her husband, Leo, also refrained from certain activities such as watching the news, viewing horror movies, and even using certain words. Leo agreed to watch only "wholesome" TV channels, such as HGTV, in order to avoid triggering Margaret's obsessions. Although he was frequently upset about what had become the status quo, he was willing to go along with his wife's wishes because he knew that anything different would lead to Margaret becoming very anxious and irritable. Leo reported that accommodating Margaret's OCD symptoms was one way he showed him how much he loved and cared for her.

Accommodation can be subtle or overt (and extreme) and is observed in couples who are both happy in their relationships as well as distressed couples. Leo, for example, boasted that he and Margaret rarely argued about OCD-related issues. But even if there is no obvious arguing, accommodation creates a relationship "system" that fits with the OCD symptoms to perpetuate the vicious cycle that maintains obsessional fears and compulsive urges. Table 35.1 shows examples of accommodation behaviors we have observed in our work with couples in which one partner has OCD.

Conceptually, since avoidance and compulsive rituals prevent the natural extinction of obsessional fear and ritualistic urges, accommodation to these symptoms by a spouse or partner also perpetuates OCD symptoms. For instance, consider a man with obsessional fears of acting on unwanted impulses to molest his newborn daughter. By accommodating her husband's avoidance of changing or bathing their newborn child (i.e., by doing it herself), his wife prevents him from learning that his distress over the senseless obsessions is manageable, temporary, and that he is unlikely to act on her unwanted obsessional thoughts.

Table 35.1 Examples of partner accommodation for different OCD symptoms

OCD symptom	Partner accommodation behaviors
Contamination and washing symptoms.	• Washing, cleaning, or changing clothes for the patient. • Avoiding contaminated stimuli. • Providing reassurance that items are safe to handle.
Obsessional doubting and compulsive checking.	• Checking for the patient. • Answering questions for reassurance. • Helping the patient avoid situations that might trigger doubts.
Violent, sexual, and religious obsessions.	• Providing reassurance. • Helping with avoidance of stimuli that trigger obsessional thoughts. • Helping with analyzing or interpreting Bible passages or religious doubts.
Ordering and symmetry ("not just right") obsessions and compulsions.	• Checking to make sure things are "in order" or arranged properly. • Repeating answers until they are "just right."

Accommodation has various additional negative consequences. First, it decreases an individual's motivation to participate in ERP since he or she might not recognize good reasons to change the status quo – especially given that ERP involves provoking distress through facing one's fears. For instance, a woman with fears of contamination from hospitals required that her husband shower and change his clothes immediately upon arriving home from work because he passed by a hospital on his route home. Although the patient regretted the impact of OCD on her (and her husband's) life, she struggled to engage in ERP partly because she did not view exposure as worthwhile: her husband's accommodation had diminished the consequences of having OCD to the point that obsessions and compulsions seemed tolerable relative to confronting her fears of hospitals.

Second, in some relationships, accommodation becomes the chief way in which the unaffected partner expresses warmth, caring, and compassion for his or her loved one. For example, one man prided himself on the fact that whenever his wife with OCD became worried about contracting a serious illness such as rabies, he would "come to the rescue" by traveling to wherever she was to calm her down, assess the situation, and reassure her that she was going to be fine. This became an important way of showing affection in their marriage. Not only does such accommodation maintain pathological fear and anxiety in the ways we have discussed previously, it also begets additional accommodation as the couple's relationship develops around this sort of "affectionate" behavior. Not surprisingly, accommodation is related to more severe OCD symptoms and poorer long-term treatment outcome (Calvocoressi et al., 1999; Merlo, Lehmkuhl, Geffken, & Storch, 2009).

Relationship conflict. Relationship stress and conflict also play a role in the maintenance of OCD. Couples in which one partner suffers with this and other similar conditions often report problems with interdependency, unassertiveness, and avoidant communication patterns that foster stress and conflict (Marcaurelle, Bélanger, Marchand, Katerelos, & Mainguy, 2005). In all likelihood, OCD symptoms and relationship distress influence each other, rather than one exclusively leading to the other. For example, a husband's contentious relationship with his wife might contribute to overall anxiety and uncertainty that develops into his obsessional doubting. His excessive checking, reassurance seeking, and overly cautious actions could also lead to frequent disagreements and relationship conflict.

Particular aspects of a relationship that might increase distress and contribute to OCD maintenance include poor problem solving skills, hostility, and criticism (Marcaurelle et al., 2005). Moreover, such communication problems are known to adversely affect the outcome of ERP. For instance, communication patterns characterized by criticism, hostility, and emotional overinvolvement are associated with premature treatment discontinuation and symptom relapse, whereas patterns characterized by empathy, hopefulness, and assertiveness are associated with improved outcomes with ERP (e.g., Chambless & Steketee, 1999).

Treatment of OCD from an Interpersonal Perspective

The bi-directional association described previously between OCD symptoms and relationship functioning suggests that for patients in close relationships, the effects of ERP would be enhanced by involving the partner in treatment and addressing the ways in which interpersonal factors maintain OCD. Only a few studies, however, have examined "partner assisted" ERP for OCD, and the results of these studies are mixed. Mehta (1990) found that including a partner (or other family member) as a coach during ERP was more effective than individual ERP without such a coach. In a similarly designed study, however, Emmelkamp, de Haan, and Hoogduin (1990) found no between-group differences. Finally, Emmelkamp and De Lange (1983) reported that partner-assisted ERP was more effective at posttest, but not at 1-month follow-up. It is difficult to draw strong conclusions from these studies as they suffered from various methodological limitations such as small sample sizes and suboptimal implementation of ERP (e.g., no therapist-supervised exposure), often resulting in substandard outcomes study-wide.

Another issue is that while partner-*assisted* ERP might facilitate cooperation between partners when it comes to completing specific exposure tasks, it does not directly address other couple interaction patterns (e.g., accommodation, hostile communication) that maintain OCD, attenuate treatment response, and increase the risk of relapse following treatment. Accordingly, it would be beneficial to also incorporate techniques to teach couples healthier ways of showing mutual care and concern that are not focused on OCD symptoms. Given the lack of interventions for OCD that target such relationship dynamics in combination with ERP, we developed a 16-session couple-based ERP program that involves: (a) psychoeducation; (b) partner-assisted ERP; (c) couple-based interventions focused on reducing OCD-specific accommodation behavior and increasing alternative strategies for couple engagement; and (d) general couple therapy focused on stressful aspects of the relationship not directly related to OCD (Abramowitz et al., 2013). Treatment sessions are 90–120 minutes; the first eight are conducted twice-weekly and the final eight, weekly. Finally, the couple attend all sessions together and work on out-of-office between sessions "homework practice." Table 35.2 provides an outline of the primary topics

Table 35.2   Components of couple-based exposure therapy for OCD

Session	Main components
1	Assessment of patient's history and OCD symptoms, psychoeducation about OCD and treatment rationale, introduce self-monitoring of rituals.
2	Review of treatment rationale and self-monitoring homework, assessment of couple's history with OCD, collaborative development of exposure list/hierarchy.
3	Finish developing the exposure hierarchy, review of treatment rationale, introduction of coping self-statements for managing with anxiety.
4	Emotional expressiveness training (EET), introduction and simulation of partner-assisted exposure, assign EET homework practice.
5–7	In-session partner-assisted exposure, response prevention, assignment of daily ERP homework.
8–9	Decision-making skills, partner-assisted ERP, daily ERP homework.
10–11	Accommodation, making decisions about how to reduce accommodation, ERP and decision-making homework practice.
12	Focus on applying EET and decision-making for areas of the relationship outside OCD, continued ERP and decision-making homework.
13–16	Continued ERP planning using decision-making and EET skills, focus on relationship both within and outside the context of OCD using EET and decision-making skills, continued ERP homework.

Table 35.3 Questions for assessing symptom–system fit within a couple with OCD (obtain responses from each partner)

When and how did the partner become aware of the patient's problem with OCD?

What effects have OCD symptoms (obsessional fear, avoidance, rituals) had on the relationship in terms of daily life?

If there are any patterns that seem to have developed because of the patient's OCD symptoms, what are they?

How does each partner think their relationship might be different if the patient did not have difficulties with OCD?

Is there anyone else (e.g., children) who is affected in any way by the patient having problems with OCD? (If so, explore who and how.)

What types of strategies has the couple used to try to cope with the patient's OCD?

When the patient is experiencing obsessional fear or performing rituals, does it ever lead to anger or arguments? What happens in these situations? Does the unaffected partner ever have a tendency to help the patient escape from the anxiety, avoid situations that cause obsessions, or assist with compulsive rituals to lower the anxiety?

How well has this worked?

Describe how the two of you communicate about the OCD problem.

covered in each session. In the next sections, we describe the main techniques used in this program, including an illustrative case example.

Assessment of Symptom–System Fit

An important focus of assessment concerns "symptom-system fit" – how the couple has structured their environment so as to accommodate OCD symptoms. As already discussed, accommodation may occur within seemingly "happy" relationships (i.e., "good" symptom–system fit), or within conflicted relationships in which the nonaffected partner refuses to accommodate to OCD symptoms, or overtly resents the negatively impact these symptoms have had (i.e., "poor" system–symptom fit). Table 35.3 provides a list of questions for assessing such symptom–system fit.

Although a goal of therapy is to help the healthy partner cease his or her accommodation of OCD symptoms, it is important that this is done in an agreeable way. Negative or sarcastic reactions increase relationship discord and maintain OCD symptoms. The healthy partner might initially try to resist accommodating, yet end up giving in after the patient makes repeated pleas or raises the stakes by making threats. For example, a 35-year-old woman repeatedly insisted that her husband clean all of the family's toilets in a certain ritualized way. At first, he refused to comply with the cleaning rituals, saying that he would not take part in such excessive behaviors. Yet after persistent nagging from his wife, he gave up and angrily washed the toilets in the ritualized fashion (and under his wife's careful observation).

We suggest an assessment of any partner who becomes involved in treatment for OCD for the purpose of noting whether this individual experiences any psychopathology of his or her own, and what factors might have contributed to the development of an interpersonal system in which the patient's OCD flourishes. For instance, a woman whose first husband died of a heart attack was especially sensitive to her current husband's obsessional anxiety for fear that it would also lead to a heart attack. She therefore willingly did everything she could to keep her husband from becoming even slightly anxious, thereby contributing to the maintenance of his OCD symptoms. This partner had to be educated about the short-term effects of anxiety, and how these are extremely unlikely to be dangerous.

Psychoeducation

Presenting the cognitive-behavioral conceptual model of OCD can help reduce a partner's expressions of resentment and criticism, normalize his or her experience, and begin to alleviate feelings of guilt and frustration. Similarly, learning about how exposure therapy works, and the evidence for its effectiveness, can increase hopefulness and reduce feelings of helplessness and of being overwhelmed. To illustrate, when a young man began to understand that his wife's resistance to spending time at his parents' home arose from her obsessional concerns about the possibility of asbestos in their home, rather than from dislike, he was less critical of her and her behavior. Knowing that she would be participating in treatment further increased his patience.

Without an explanation, many partners find the notion of ERP counterintuitive. Prior to psychoeducation, they might believe their role is to help their partner avoid or lower anxiety by staying away from anxiety-provoking situations or escaping whenever such encounters do occur. Therefore, it is helpful for them to understand their role in helping the patient confront and tolerate anxiety and obsessions rather than escaping from it. Without an understanding of ERP, many partners view the therapist's requests of the partner as confusing, unsupportive, or even sadistic toward the patient. Given the difficulty of complying with ERP, it is critical that both partners understand OCD, its treatment, and their relative roles in making treatment a success.

Partner-assisted Exposure

Once a significant other understands the principles underlying ERP, he or she can be taught how to assist with exposure exercises by serving as a coach. Partner-assisted exposure is optimally successful when both relationship conflict and partner accommodation are minimal to begin with. By learning how to play the role of "coach," the healthy partner begins to offer emotional support to the patient as he or she completes exposure practices within and outside of the session. The coach is taught to provide gentle, but firm reminders not to engage in avoidance or compulsive rituals. Most importantly, the coach is trained to help the patient correctly implement exposures by making sure the exercise matches what the patient fears, that the patient full engages, and that rituals are resisted (response prevention). The couple is introduced to four phases of confronting a stressor (described below), and how to communicate with each other at each phase. An emphasis is placed on helping the patient "get through" the obsessional anxiety, as opposed to the partner trying to immediately alleviate this distress.

An important aspect of this stage of treatment involves teaching couples two sets of communication skills to help them complete ERP practices effectively as a team. The first skill involves "sharing thoughts and feelings," or Emotional Expressiveness Training (EET) in which the couple is taught to discuss with one another *how they feel* (as opposed to offering solutions) during exposure; while also listening effectively to each other. The second skill involves learning how to make decisions as a couple around hierarchy building, implementing exposure tasks, and resisting rituals. The actual process of confronting the obsessional stimulus is broken down into four phases as follows:

1 Discussing the exposure task: initially, the therapist teaches the patient and coach to clarify the specifics of the exposure task. Both parties are encouraged to discuss how each is feeling about the exposure and to identify potential obstacles. The patient is helped to specify how he or she would like the coach to help out with the exercise.
2 Confronting the feared situation: the second component involves actually confronting the exposure item. The patient is encouraged to express his or her feelings to the partner, who listens carefully. If the patient becomes anxious, the partner acknowledges this and reinforces the patient's hard work with lots of praise (e.g., "You're doing such a great job. I'm really proud of you!"). The partner continues to compliment the patient on handling the situation throughout the exercise, and avoids making negative statements. The partner also resists the temptation to distract the patient or provide reassurance or any other anxiety reduction strategies.
3 Dealing with overwhelming anxiety: if the patient experiences extreme anxiety during the exposure, he or she is taught to communicate this to his or her partner. In turn, the partner is taught to acknowledge that the task is difficult but that the patient can manage the anxiety (which will eventually lessen). If the patient absolutely cannot continue with the exposure, a brief timeout can be taken during which the partner provides support in ways the patient would like (but *not* using reassurance, rituals, or accommodation behaviors). The two parties also discuss what went wrong and how they can approach resuming the exposure. Although the partner should remind the patient of the importance of resuming, the decision whether to do so is ultimately up to the patient.
4 Evaluation: the final component involves the couple evaluating how the exposure went. How did the patient feel about the experience and the partner's coaching? The partner should also let the patient know how he or she felt about the exposure and, when appropriate, provide copious praise for a job well done.

For many partners, helping a loved one confront situations the provoke fear/distress is a difficult process. In a sense, the partner is undergoing a form of ERP as well – seeing the patient in distress and allowing the distress to continue rather than reducing it by accommodating. Consequently, it is important to support the partner as well, both for being an effective coach and for tolerating the patient's distress.

Reducing Accommodation

When symptom accommodation is present, the therapist works with the couple to help them change interaction patterns that maintain OCD symptoms. In such interventions, the therapist begins by describing accommodation and its deleterious effects, noting that accommodation from the partner often is well intentioned (as discussed earlier). Then, the couple is helped to choose an activity which has become hampered by OCD symptoms, and the therapist facilitates a decision-making discussion regarding ways to handle this situation by promoting the idea of exposure, rather than relying on avoidance and rituals. In other words, without creating a specific hierarchy, the couple work on building ERP techniques into their everyday life and functioning as a couple. For example, a wife might resume leaving appliances such as the toaster or television plugged in when no one is home. A husband might stop checking doors and windows prior to coming to bed. The goal of these interventions is to work toward a life in which the couple confronts the situations and stimuli that patient has been avoiding, and remains in that situation (rather than using rituals) to gradually lower the anxiety.

When encouraging a partner not to accommodate to the patient's OCD symptoms, it is important to understand what function the accommodation plays in the couple's relationship and address these issues. For example, accommodation might have become a major way that a partner shows care, concern, and love for the patient. If the accommodation is removed from the couple's relationship, then the treatment might inadvertently have altered the couple's relationship such that they no longer feel as close to each other, or the patient does not feel as loved by the partner. Consequently, it is important to discuss with the couple what new ways they would want to show their love, care, and concern for each other instead of focusing their caring in terms of the OCD.

General Couple Therapy

Although the primary goal of couple-based ERP is to help the patient overcome OCD symptoms by employing the couple as a basis of intervention, some couples have broad relationship distress that needs to be addressed within the context of treatment for two reasons: first, relationship distress can be viewed as a chronic stressor on an individual that can exacerbate OCD and other psychological symptoms; and, second, the couple-based interventions discussed above are implemented most successfully when the two partners can work together as a team for this common goal. Asking a couple to work on an exposure task if they are angry and uncooperative with each other will result in less than optimal outcome. Whereas we prefer to focus initially on OCD before addressing relationship issues more broadly, at times with angry couples we begin intervention with some focus on improving overall relationship functioning so that they can implement the OCD treatment successfully. The case example that follows illustrates how the principles of this couple-based intervention can be individualized to provide assistance to a couple affected by OCD.

Case Examples

Lauren

Lauren, a 29-year-old stay-at-home mom, presented with OCD symptoms beginning in the postpartum. Immediately after bringing her first-born son home from the hospital, she began experiencing intrusive images of herself harming him, including distressing images of stabbing him with knives and car keys, putting him in the microwave, and suffocating him with a rope. Lauren experienced these thoughts as unwanted and extremely repugnant. She wondered why she was having them and feared they meant that she would actually harm her baby. Lauren tried to suppress the thoughts and she used mental rituals (i.e., repeating to herself "I would never hurt him") to reduce her distress. She also avoided holding her baby in certain situations (e.g., next to the microwave) and hid any stimuli that provoked obsessions (e.g., locking all knives away). Her OCD symptoms occupied hours per day and made it stressful for her to be around her son. She also feared that if she revealed to other people the extent of her intrusive thoughts, they would take the baby away.

On intake, Lauren's Yale–Brown Obsessive-Compulsive Scale (Y-BOCS) (Goodman et al., 1989) score was 29. Her husband, Dylan, had been unaware of the extent of her symptoms. Dylan reported knowing that Lauren harbored worries about becoming a mother, and she had told him that she sometimes had "bad thoughts"; but she had never revealed the specific content of her obsessions. The couple reported a generally good relationship, although they had occasional disagreements about household tasks.

For this couple, psychoeducation and assessment of Lauren's symptoms proved to be therapeutic. Over the first two sessions, the therapist assessed Lauren's intrusive thoughts, inquiring about (a) their content and triggers, (b) her interpretations of them, and (c) her responses to them. Dylan was surprised by the content of Lauren's obsessional thoughts, yet the therapist normalized these experiences by informing the couple that everyone has repugnant thought from time to time. This made sense to Dylan, who was even able to provide examples of his own unwanted thoughts. Lauren was relieved to see Dylan respond this way, instead of fearing that she would act on the thoughts or that he thought she was a dangerous person for thinking this way. Dylan, in fact, said that he was confident Lauren's obsessions were senseless since she was an extremely loving mother.

The therapist next introduced ERP as a way of learning that obsessional thoughts and anxiety are not dangerous, and indeed manageable even without needing to resort to rituals to reduce anxiety. Lauren and Dylan learned to use ERP techniques as a team. With the therapist's help, they constructed an exposure list that included actions such as Lauren tying a scarf around the baby's neck while imagining choking and suffocating him, and holding a sharp knife while the infant was in the room. Dylan coached Lauren through these exposures, offering emotional support but refraining from providing reassurance. Lauren found that when she did not fight her obsessions and anxiety – and instead allowed herself to have these experiences – these thoughts took on less meaning to her.

Later treatment sessions focused on reducing the couple's accommodation patterns, such as Lauren's refusal to use knives and the microwave, and her insistence that Dylan cook all meals and clean all of the knives. The couple used the decision-making skills they had been taught to take steps to reducing these behaviors (e.g., Dylan refusing to set the table and cut meat for Lauren).

Lauren and Dylan worked together planning and conducting exposures outside of the therapy office as well. After about 14 sessions, Lauren was able to enjoy spending time alone with her baby; and while she was still experiencing occasional unwanted intrusive thoughts, these no longer produced anxiety or the urge to perform rituals. Anna's Y-BOCS score had declined to 7 (in the mild range).

Conclusions

Most people with OCD are involved in interpersonal relationships of one form or another, and it is important to understand how the symptoms of OCD play out in such a social context. Partners are often drawn into helping the patient avoid anxiety-provoking situations, actually engaging in compulsive rituals with or instead of the patient, and providing frequent reassurance (which can be viewed as interpersonal checking). Whether out of concern for the patient or resulting from an attempt to avoid arguments about the OCD, such behaviors from partners serve to maintain obsessional fear and compulsive urges, although often unintended. Educating both partners about the nature and treatment of OCD, helping them understand the roles each can take to be of assistance, and teaching them to work together as a team provides opportunities to learn and practice ERP enhanced by an interpersonal component.

References

Abramowitz, J. S., Baucom, D. H., Boeding, S., Wheaton, M. G., Pukay-Martin, N. D., Fabricant, L. E., … Fischer, M. S. (2013). Treating obsessive-compulsive disorder in intimate relationships: A pilot study of couple-based cognitive-behavior therapy. *Behavior Therapy*, *44*(3), 395–407. doi: 10.1016/j.beth.2013.02.005.

Abramowitz, J. S., & Jacoby, R. J. (2014). *Obsessive-compulsive disorder in adults*. Boston, MA: Hogrefe.

American Psychiatric Association. (2013). *Diagnostic and statistical manual of mental disorders* (5th ed.). Arlington, VA: American Psychiatric Publishing.

Boeding, S. E., Paprocki, C. M., Baucom, D. H., Abramowitz, J. S., Wheaton, M. G., Fabricant, L. E., & Fischer, M. S. (2013). Let me check that for you: symptom accommodation in romantic partners of adults with Obsessive-Compulsive Disorder. *Behaviour Research and Therapy*, *51*(6), 316–322. doi: 10.1016/j.brat.2013.03.002.

Calvocoressi, L., Mazure, C. M., Kasl, S. V., Skolnick, J., Fisk, D., Vegso, S. J., … Price, L. H. (1999). Family accommodation of obsessive-compulsive symptoms: Instrument development and assessment of family behavior. *Journal of Nervous and Mental Disease*, *187*(10), 636–642.

Chambless, D. L., & Steketee, G. (1999). Expressed emotion and behavior therapy outcome: A prospective study with obsessive-compulsive and agoraphobic outpatients. *Journal of Consulting and Clinical Psychology*, *67*(5), 658–665.

Emmelkamp, P. M., de Haan, E., & Hoogduin, C. A. (1990). Marital adjustment and obsessive-compulsive disorder. *British Journal of Psychiatry*, *156*, 55–60.

Emmelkamp, P. M., & de Lange, I. (1983). Spouse involvement in the treatment of obsessive-compulsive patients. *Behaviour Research and Therapy*, *21*(4), 341–346.

Foa, E. B., Abramowitz, J. S., Franklin, M. E., & Kozak, M. J. (1999). Feared consequences, fixity of belief, and treatment outcome in patients with obsessive-compulsive disorder. *Behavior Therapy*, *30*(4), 717–724. doi: 10.1016/S0005-7894(99)80035-5.

Marcaurelle, R., Bélanger, C., Marchand, A., Katerelos, T. E., & Mainguy, N. (2005). Marital predictors of symptom severity in panic disorder with agoraphobia. *Journal of Anxiety Disorders*, *19*(2), 211–232. doi: 10.1016/j.janxdis.2004.01.005.

Mehta, M. (1990). A comparative study of family-based and patient-based behavioural management in obsessive-compulsive disorder. *British Journal of Psychiatry*, *157*, 133–135.

Merlo, L. J., Lehmkuhl, H. D., Geffken, G. R., & Storch, E. A. (2009). Decreased family accommodation associated with improved therapy outcome in pediatric obsessive-compulsive disorder. *Journal of Consulting and Clinical Psychology, 77*(2), 355–360. doi: 10.1037/a0012652.

Rachman, S. J., & Hodgson, R. J. (1980). *Obsessions and compulsions.* Englewood Cliffs, NJ: Prentice-Hall.

36

Metacognitive Model and Treatment of OCD

Adrian Wells, Samuel Myers, Michael Simons, and Peter Fisher

It is well known that obsessional thoughts are part of a family of intrusive cognitions that are normal and common cognitive experiences. Of course, obsessions do not inevitably lead to obsessive-compulsive disorder (OCD), so what is it that renders these common experiences problematic? According to the metacognitive model (Wells, 1997, 2009) three factors are important: (1) the significance that the individual assigns to such inner events; (2) the experiential perspective the person occupies in relation to them; and (3) the choice of strategies for self-regulation. Each of these factors has its origin in components of metacognition.

This chapter explains how these three factors are central to the model and treatment and can explain the transition from normal obsessions to clinical disorder.

The Metacognitive Model of OCD

An information-processing model that explains the development and maintenance of OCD and is based around the three factors mentioned above was proposed by Wells (1997). This is a *metacognitive* model as it assumes that beliefs about the power and importance of thinking cause individuals to assign high levels of personal significance to thoughts. Thus, when a person experiences an obsessional intrusion, such as an image of harming a child, metacognitive processing is activated which accesses knowledge or beliefs about the intrusion. Wells described three content domains of metacognitive beliefs that are typically involved, with one or more of these domains present in OCD cases: thought–event fusion beliefs (e.g., "Thinking of accidents can make them happen"); thought–action fusion (TAF) beliefs (e.g., "Thinking of doing something I don't want to do will make me do it"); and thought–object fusion beliefs (e.g., "Thoughts can contaminate objects"). Such beliefs lead the individual to negatively interpret the occurrence of the intrusion, leading to a sense of threat and concomitant anxiety, revulsion and shame (i.e., heightened negative affect). Such negative affect primes action modes of coping in which the individual is goal directed to process and escape from threat. Under these conditions there is a constrained ability to

The Wiley Handbook of Obsessive Compulsive Disorders, Volume I, First Edition.
Edited by Jonathan S. Abramowitz, Dean McKay, and Eric A. Storch.
© 2017 John Wiley & Sons Ltd. Published 2017 by John Wiley & Sons Ltd.

step back and distance oneself from the intrusion. The model also postulates a further domain of metacognitive knowledge for guiding coping strategies. This domain concerns beliefs about the usefulness of rituals for reducing threat associated with thinking (e.g., "Worrying about germs will help me avoid contamination").

Individuals who have beliefs about the importance of thinking may be inflexible in their ability to decenter and experience thoughts as simply events in the mind; instead thoughts become the source of threat and constantly dealing with them and worrying becomes the route to safety. The combination of believing that thinking can be harmful and that it can make a situation safe gives rise to conflict in self-regulation in which cognition becomes overimportant. To cope, the individual avoids triggers for obsessional thoughts or takes precautions so as not to act on them. For example, a person who experiences intrusive images of stabbing someone may insist all knives are locked away before entering a kitchen. The strategies used to reduce such worries have ironic effects in several ways. First, some strategies, such as suppression, are not particularly effective and increase attentional focus on target thoughts. Second, when they do work, they prevent the individual discovering that thoughts are not important. Third, strategies such as worrying maintain anxiety, and covert or overt washing and neutralizing create a network of associations between stimuli and thoughts such that the triggers for obsessions generalize.

A diagrammatic depiction of this model can be seen in Figure 36.1 and a case conceptualization derived from it is presented in Figure 36.2. As depicted in Figure 36.1, an intrusive thought, urge or impulse primes negative metacognitive beliefs about the intrusion. This leads to negative interpretation of the intrusion and distress. Subsequently or in parallel with this, positive metacognitive beliefs about neutralizing, worrying, or other coping/avoidance responses are activated. These metacognitions lead to a

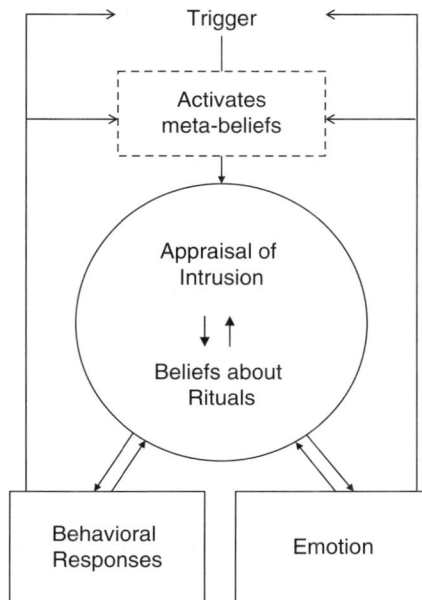

Figure 36.1 The metacognitive model of OCD. Source: Wells 1997. Reproduced with permission of Wiley

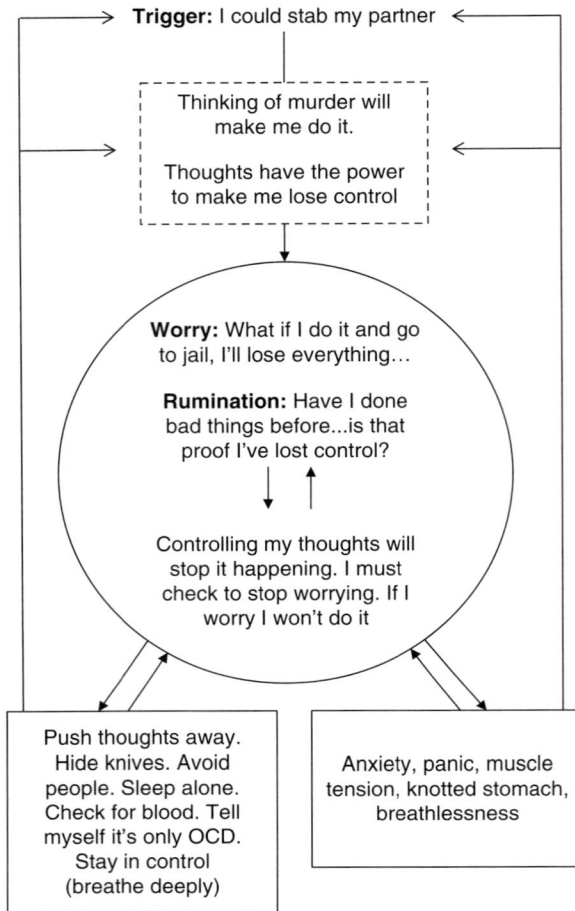

Figure 36.2 A metacognitive therapy case formulation

response style dominated by extended processing (worry/rumination) and other ironic behaviors, such as thought suppression or looking for signs of danger. This response style maintains or exacerbates distress and may be compounded further by other overt and covert rituals, such as washing, repeating, checking, counting, and using magical words or special imagery. The problem with these responses is that they maintain the person's *entanglement* with thoughts and prevent them from discovering that they are unimportant. In the model both anxious affect and coping responses increase awareness of intrusions such as doubts, urges, images and other mental events.

Metacognitive Therapy (MCT)

MCT for OCD is described in two treatment manuals (Wells, 1997, 2009) and is a time-limited approach based on an individual case formulation. The metacognitive model provides the basis for constructing the case formulation. Treatment is typically delivered in 10–12 sessions (1 × 1 hour sessions per week), although successful outcomes can be achieved in fewer sessions. In the first session, the therapist constructs the case formulation with the patient using a Socratic dialogue. To achieve this, a useful starting point is to ask about a recent distressing obsessional thought or episode of compulsive behavior. The therapist then follows with a series of questions aimed at determining a trigger thought, affect, and responses to trigger thoughts using repetitive negative thinking (worry/rumination), metacognitive beliefs, behaviors, and the beliefs about rituals/behaviors. The following example illustrates this sequence of questioning and provides an interview "template" in determining these factors:

THERAPIST: Can you describe a recent episode when you had an obsessional thought or doubt or found yourself engaging in your compulsive behaviors?

PATIENT: It happens every day; we could take last night as an example. I was getting ready for bed and the thought went through my mind – "I could murder my wife."

THERAPIST: When you had the thought how did you feel?

PATIENT: I panicked; I just felt it wasn't safe to go to bed.

THERAPIST: So you felt anxious and panicked. What kind of symptoms did you notice?

PATIENT: I felt a knot in my stomach, my muscles became tense and I just felt terrible.

THERAPIST: What did you go on to think after that thought?

PATIENT: I thought maybe I am a murderer and started to worry that I could do it. I then started to think about whether I had done anything like that in the past.

THERAPIST: How long did that thinking go on for?

PATIENT: At least a couple of hours. I couldn't go to bed until I'd got over the panic and I knew it was safe.

THERAPIST: Would it be possible for you to treat a thought about committing murder as irrelevant?

PATIENT: No. That would be difficult, because it's not normal to have thoughts like that.

THERAPIST: It sounds like you believe that thought means something important, what's the worst that could happen if you have it?

PATIENT: What I'm really afraid of is that if I keep thinking it I will do it.

THERAPIST: So it seems that one of your beliefs is that thinking a thought can lead to unwanted acts. How strongly do you believe that on a scale of 0 to 100?

PATIENT: If I don't control myself then I do believe it, 90 per cent.

THERAPIST: You mentioned controlling yourself. What strategies do you use to stop these bad things from happening or to deal with these thoughts?

PATIENT: I try to control my mind and stop violent thoughts; I also make sure there are no heavy objects around that I could use as a weapon. I sometimes don't sleep in the same room as my wife. Sometimes I go over my actions to make sure that I haven't harmed someone and then forgotten about it.

Through this or similar lines of metacognitive interviewing the therapist generates the information for the case formulation. The formulation is shared with the patient as it begins to "normalize" the experience of intrusions and sets the stage for an alternative and benign interpretation of thoughts. It helps in modifying metacognitive beliefs, as it begins to move the patient away from thinking thoughts are a sign of being bad or dangerous, toward an understanding that *OCD is a problem with worrying about thoughts*. The therapist uses hypothetical questions to illustrate this point. For example: "If you no longer worried about (e.g., contamination/having thoughts of harm) what would happen to your problem? Has neutralizing/washing been effective in stopping your worry and enabled you to overcome OCD? How easy is it to leave these thoughts alone as long as you continuously try to deal with them? Would it help if you discovered that you could leave these ideas alone?"

This line of questioning is called a *meta-level* Socratic dialogue (Wells, 2009) because it questions the *process* of worrying and the effects of behaviors on the *regulation* of thinking, rather than interrogating the content of cognition. By helping the patient see that the problem is with the regulation of worry and his or her reaction to thoughts, treatment shifts focus from dealing with cognitions concerning being responsible or unable to tolerate uncertainty, to working on the overimportance given to obsessional thoughts and worry.

In order to illustrate how some reactions to thoughts backfire and give them more importance, metaphors are used as part of the meta-level discourse and are often followed by a suppression experiment. For example, the following metaphors are commonly used:

> Intrusive thoughts are like fishhooks; they are sharp and can be uncomfortable. Let me ask you a question, if you were to get a fishhook in your mouth would it be a good idea to chew on it? Can you see how worrying, going over things, and reacting to your thoughts can make them more embedded and harder to get rid of?

> What would happen if you discovered these thoughts didn't mean anything? How can these thoughts become less important as long as you give them so much attention and arrange your behavior around them? For example, you try to stop them entering your mind, but let me ask you; is it possible to hold a door closed and walk away from it at the same time?"

Metaphors are followed by a thought suppression experiment in which the patient is asked to attempt not to think a target thought (e.g., an image of a yellow submarine) for a minute. The therapist then explores how this was not particularly easy or successful and is not a good long-term solution for dealing with negative thoughts that trigger worry and neutralizing. Hypothetical questioning is also used to socialize to the model by asking what would happen if metacognitive beliefs were found to be false. Some examples of these questions are given below:

- If you discovered that your thoughts of contamination were not important what would happen to your OCD?
- If you discovered that thoughts of harming someone did not have the power to make you act what would happen to your problem?
- If you gave your urges and feelings little importance, what would happen to your OCD?
- If you no longer believed that states of mind could contaminate objects how much of a problem would remain?
- If you no longer believed that doubts mean you have failed to complete an action properly what would happen to your distress?

This level of exploration also serves as a bridge to introduce the first change strategy in metacognitive therapy: *detached mindfulness* (DM) (Wells & Matthews, 1994), which is a specific way of relating to intrusive thoughts and disengaging from worry and rumination. Mindfulness refers to being aware of the intrusion and seeing it as separate from self and distinguishable from ones reactions (e.g., worry) to the intrusion. Detachment refers to disengaging from any kind of response. By practicing DM the patient begins to reduce maladaptive coping strategies and bring worry/rumination under control. Furthermore, the client can begin to have direct metacognitive experiences of control and choice over reactions to inner experiences. The therapist introduces the idea of DM in the following way:

> Would it be helpful if you could stand back from the thoughts that trigger your worry and let them go? There are useful ways of doing this that are better than suppressing, neutralizing or checking. One way is by applying *detached mindfulness*. You may not realize it but you can do this already. You had thousands of thoughts yesterday; did you react to all of them? Let's practice DM now; you can become familiar with it through a free-association task

The patient is then helped to practice this task in the session. The aim is to watch what happens in the mind whilst the therapist says a series of neutral words (e.g., "apple, bicycle, tree, friends, birthday, walking, seaside, elephant"). Through careful instructions and questioning the patient is guided towards allowing thoughts to occur spontaneously without interpreting or influencing them. For example the therapist provides the following rationale:

> When we try the free-association task, I want you to close your eyes and watch what happens in your mind when I say a series of words. All you need to do is passively watch what happens, you should not try to control your thoughts or try to think things; just be a passive observer. Maybe nothing will happen, that is fine, just go with that or whatever thoughts or images or memories you might experience. Okay let's start.

After applying this technique, it is crucial that the therapist engages the patient in a detailed meta-level exploration of his or her experiences. Specifically, it is necessary to determine if the patient had any thoughts/memoires, and if these occurred *spontaneously* or not. Furthermore, the therapist questions whether the patient tried to deal with thoughts in any way or questioned or analyzed them. These are examples of reacting to thoughts and are failures of applying DM. Spontaneous thought experiences that were not reacted to are singled out as examples of DM and of the type of nonreaction that should be applied to intrusions. As part of this dialogue the therapist also asks a powerful meta-level change question to conclude the experience: "What happened to the first thought by the time we reached the end? What does that tell you about the fate of thoughts if you leave them alone?"

In some cases the therapist must gradually work with the client to shape the correct experience of DM. If the therapist discovers that the patient was analyzing thoughts, trying to stop certain thoughts, or categorizing them, this is identified as an example of unhelpful control and the procedure is repeated until spontaneous *nonreactive experiences* are achieved. At this stage of treatment, homework is introduced which consists of applying detached mindfulness to obsessional thoughts that trigger worrying or neutralizing. In connection with this the patient may also be invited to try and postpone any neutralizing in response to intrusions until later in the day.

In the next session homework is reviewed and further socialization to the metacognitive model is undertaken. More practice of DM is introduced and, if appropriate, the therapist includes an idiosyncratic trigger word (e.g., germs, murder, poison) into the free-association task. The aim is for the patient to refrain from any response to it. For homework, the patient is asked to continue with DM in response to obsessional intrusions and to apply ritual postponement. Greater emphasis is placed on postponing rituals at this stage of treatment. For example, the client is instructed to delay neutralizing until a set time at the end of the day, at which time they are permitted to engage in neutralizing for 15 minutes only. This is framed as an experiment to discover what happens to thoughts, worries and feelings over time and it allows the therapist to question beliefs about the importance of thoughts and the need to deal with them.

In the third session, further practice of DM may be necessary; however, the therapist can also use *exposure and response commission* (ERC) (Wells, 2009). Unlike cognitive-behavior therapy where ritual prevention is vital to promote habituation, in MCT the mechanism of change is not considered to be habituation but metacognitive change. Therefore, it is not mandatory to remove all rituals to achieve recovery. The metacognitive model proposes that patients must become flexible and be able to disengage responses that have an ironic effect on mental control. Reactions to thoughts are linked to positive metacognitive beliefs that contain self-regulatory goals (e.g., "I must wash without thinking of germs"). Such goals can continue to give thoughts importance. ERC changes the rule system or goal, and in turn reduces the importance of thoughts. Patients can be instructed to use rituals with a different goal in mind. For example, the patient may be asked to hold an obsessional thought in mind while performing rituals. This technique (a) changes the relationship the client has with his or her thoughts, (b) begins to challenge the belief that thoughts are important, and (c) removes the ironic effect of suppression that occurs when rituals are aimed at removing thoughts.

Sessions 5–8 focus on the direct challenging of metacognitive beliefs in the domains of thought–event fusion, thought–action fusion, and thought–object fusion. The therapist uses verbal methods such as questioning the evidence supporting such beliefs, examining counterevidence, and generating alternative interpretations of the importance of thoughts. These strategies are supplemented with in-session behavioral experiments to directly test such beliefs. For example, to test the belief that thinking a thought can cause an event, the patient might be asked to think about (and *wish* that) the therapist will win the lottery or have an automobile break down. In the case of harming obsessions, the patient can be asked to hold a sharpened pencil and have thoughts of stabbing the therapist. The therapist uses such experiments to show how thoughts alone do not have the power to cause actions or events. Homework consists of additional behavioral experiments in real life situations, such as reversing avoidance and deliberately having thoughts in situations that constitute subjective risk for the client. For example, a patient who was concerned about abusing children was asked to think "dark thoughts" while driving past a school.

The remaining sessions include further work on fusion beliefs (as necessary) and a focus on beliefs about rituals; with exploration of the use of inappropriate stop signals for guiding behavior. The advantages and disadvantages of rituals are explored and the patient is asked to ban them. The patient might find it useful to explore and practice alternative criteria for knowing. For example, a patient with intrusive thoughts that he might have collided with a cyclist while driving his car would repeatedly review his memory of his most recent journey to determine if he could remember all of it, he then knew he could stop worrying. The therapist explored with him an alternative stop signal: if he could *not spontaneously remember* colliding with someone then there was no need to worry or go over his entire journey. In the last two sessions the therapist develops a blueprint to summarize what has been learned in treatment and provides a summary of strategies for dealing with intrusive thoughts in the future. The blueprint should use a metacognitive reframe that encapsulates new knowledge about thoughts and reflects a decentered perspective, for example: "Thoughts of harm are normal and unimportant."

Treatment is facilitated with measures, such as the Obsessive-Compulsive Disorder Scale (OCD-S) (Wells, 2009), to collect information that can be used in the case formulation and for monitoring session-by-session change in metacognitive beliefs, neutralizing, and distress. More comprehensive tools are also available including the Metacognitions Questionnaire (MCQ-30) (Wells & Cartwright-Hatton, 2004), Thought–Fusion Instrument (Wells, 2009, app. 3), as well as a case formulation interview schedule (Wells, 2009, app. 13). For a detailed manual of metacognitive treatment of adults with OCD, which includes a wide range of strategies for challenging metacognitions and promoting new relationships with cognition, the reader is referred to Wells (2009).

MCT for Children and Adolescents

There is growing evidence that metacognitive beliefs and dysfunctional thought control strategies play a vital role in the development and maintenance of anxiety disorders, including OCD, in children and adolescents (e.g., Crye, Laskey, & Cartwright-Hatton, 2010; Ellis & Hudson, 2011; Smith & Hudson, 2013; Wilson & Hall, 2012). One study compared MCT and CBT (i.e., exposure with ritual prevention) in a small sample of children and adolescents with OCD and found MCT to be feasible and acceptable (Simons, Schneider, & Herpertz-Dahlmann, 2006). In the next section we briefly present developmental adaptations of MCT for children and adolescents and metacognitive family oriented interventions.

Developmental Adaptations of MCT

We have found that most of the MCT techniques used with adults are appropriate for use with younger patients. In general, the younger the child, the more adaptations are needed to match the child's thinking style. It is generally recommended to conduct therapy in a practical and experience-oriented way instead of using a more verbal disputation style, especially when working with young children. Further, we recommend simplifying the basic concepts of MCT as needed, by making use of metaphors that match the child's experiences as exemplified in the following.

In the *case conceptualization*, the therapist would ask an adult for a fusion belief using questions such as: "What does it mean to have such a thought?" For a child this is often an overly abstract question. Instead, it is helpful for the therapist to guess the kind of underlying fusion belief and ask more concretely: "Do you fear that thinking this thought might make it happen?"; "Do you think this thought has the power to make you do things that you don't want to do?"; "Do you think this thought could be passed into an object?" If the child's answer does not refer to a fusion belief, it is wise to ask follow-up questions: "How important is this thought for you?" or "Do you treat this thought as important?"

The most useful question in *socialization* is: "If you no longer believed that these thoughts were important, how anxious would you feel?" To clarify the central role of negative metacognitive beliefs, it is often helpful to ask: "If you believed even more than you do now that these thoughts are important, how scared would you feel?" We have had positive outcomes by first conducting a simplified case formulation and socialization with the child alone. Afterwards, we bring the parent(s) into the session and ask the child to explain the case formulation to the parent(s).

As with adults, DM can be introduced using metaphors as illustrated here:

TELEPHONE METAPHOR:	"While we're sitting here, in the next moment my telephone could ring. Could we prevent this from happening?" "No." "So what should I do if the phone rings?" "Pick it up?" "You're right, I could do that. However, I could choose if I pick it up or just let it ring. In this special case I would decide to let it ring. And this reminds me of your thoughts. You cannot decide if you have them or not, but you can choose not to answer them. How would that be?"
MOSQUITO BITE:	"Thoughts can be unpleasant like a mosquito bite, but it's wise to leave it alone instead of scratching."
PARENT'S REQUEST:	"Have you ever found yourself ignoring your mother asking you to clean up your room? Could you do the same with your nasty thoughts?"

Therapy with children and adolescents should be fun, and ERC can be just that. One boy who repeatedly checked if he had left scrapes on parked cars he passed in the street was asked to walk along the street with the therapist and they both had to think aloud that they had damaged every car they walked past; "I've destroyed the car, look and see it's scratched and messy." After this exercise the therapist asked: "What has this taught you about your thoughts – do you still need to take them seriously?" Experiments aimed at testing fusion beliefs can also be conducted playfully. For example, a whole session was spent with a 7-year-old boy with thought–event fusion beliefs:

> "Let's have some fun testing the power of your thoughts. First, let's see if we can make the telephone fall off the desk by thinking about it. Now, let's try something scarier, let's try very hard to make the wall fall down. Can you think of another experiment? What would you like to test?" All the experiments failed and the therapist asked for the child's explanation. The child concluded that "these are just thoughts."

Family-oriented Interventions

Having a child with OCD can be very distressing for the whole family. In many cases, we find the parents involved in the child's rituals (family accommodation) (Storch et al., 2007). They may have to change their family routines, wait for the child to finish rituals before leaving the house, continually wash clothes, buy soap for excessive hand washing, and repeatedly give reassurance. As a rule of thumb, the younger the child, the more parents should be involved in treatment. In recent years there have been a number of CBT trials of family involvement (e.g., Lewin et al., 2014).

In MCT parents can be of great help in facilitating metacognitive change by reminding the child that the obsessive thoughts are just thoughts. Furthermore, parents can practice ERC while the child is performing rituals, such as by saying to the child as he or she repeatedly checks that a door is shut: "Yes, you can be sure: the door is really open." (Note that this should be done with a pre-agreement with the child and a shared rationale.) In some families we introduce therapeutic bets to help the child change their relationship with thoughts. When the parent hears the child asking if he or she really has shut the door, the parents say: "Would you bet that the door is open? How much money would you put on that? Or would you think this is just a thought?" In rare cases where the child really accepts the bet and loses it, the parents say: "How many bets will you need to lose until you know that doubts are just thoughts and not facts?"

Empirical Support for the Metacognitive Model of OCD

Evidence for the metacognitive model of OCD is available from a large number of studies, yet we will confine discussion to a brief overview of data that emerges from three of the research areas: (a) the relationship between general dysfunctional meta-cognitions, measured by the Metacognitions Questionnaire (MCQ) (Cartwright-Hatton & Wells, 1997) or its derivatives, and OCD and OC symptomology; (b) the role of thought–fusion beliefs; and (c) the centrality of metacognitive beliefs when compared with the beliefs (schemas) proposed by other theories of OCD.

The Metacognitions Questionnaire

The earliest studies examining metacognitive theory as applied to OCD used the Metacognitions Questionnaire (MCQ) (Cartwright-Hatton & Wells, 1997), which was developed to investigate several types of metacognition implicated by the Self-Regulatory Executive Function Model (S-REF model) (Wells & Matthews, 1994, 1996), a transdiagnostic model of psychological disorder on which the metacognitive model of OCD is based. Consistent with the model, studies using the MCQ and its derivatives have consistently demonstrated positive associations between metacognitive beliefs and OC symptom severity in nonpatient and patient samples (e.g., Irak & Tosun, 2008; Timpano, Rasmussen, Exner, Rief, & Wilhelm, 2014; Wells & Papageorgiou, 1998). These relationships remain significant when trait anxiety (Cartwright-Hatton & Wells, 1997), general worry (Wells & Papageorgiou, 1998; Yilmaz, Gencoz, & Wells, 2008), or non-metacognitive beliefs (e.g., Gwilliam, Wells, & Cartwright-Hatton, 2004; Myers & Wells, 2005) are controlled. Furthermore, changes in metacognitions measured by the total score of the short version of the MCQ-the MCQ-30, have been shown to be positively and significantly correlated with changes in OC symptoms following psychological treatment (Exposure and Response Prevention), and these relationships remain when changes in non-metacognitive schemas (e.g., responsibility) are controlled (Solem, Håland, Vogel, Hansen, & Wells, 2009).

The relationships between metacognition and OC symptoms are present in different cultures (Cho, Jang, & Chai, 2012; Yilmaz et al., 2008) and age groups (e.g., Cartwright-Hatton et al., 2004) suggesting metacognitive theory is applicable to OC symptomology in a broad range of populations. Cartwright-Hatton and Wells (1997) found that several types of metacognition were higher in OCD populations when compared with clinical and nonclinical controls. Several other studies have also found elevated scores on specific types of metacognition in OCD groups (e.g., Hermans, Martens, De Cort, Pieters, & Engelen, 2003; Hermans et al., 2008; Janeck, Calamari, Riemann, & Heffelfinger, 2003).

Experimental and prospective studies. Whereas studies showing a relationship between the metacognitions assessed by the MCQ, and OC symptoms are supportive of metacognitive theory, most studies are cross-sectional precluding conclusions about causation. Several additional studies have used methodologies that are indicative of causality. A prospective study by Sica, Steketee, Ghisi, Chiri, and Franceschini (2007) found that negative beliefs about the uncontrollability and danger of worry (a subscale of the MCQ-30) predicted OC symptoms in students over a 4-month period. The subscale explained 6% of the variance in symptoms after controlling for worry and OC symptoms at time. Additionally, experimental studies that have examined cognitive self-consciousness (the tendency to monitor thoughts) (Kikul, Vetter, Lincoln, & Exner, 2012) as well as beliefs about memory competence (Alcolado & Radomsky, 2011; Cuttler, Sirois-Delisle, Alcolado, Radomsky, & Taylor, 2013) are supportive of a causal role for these metacognitions in obsessive-compulsive symptomology.

Thought–Fusion Beliefs

While studies with the MCQ are indicative of the hypothesized relationships, more compelling evidence can be found in studies that have assessed the specific fusion beliefs that are central to the model. The earliest relevant cross-sectional studies explored an overlapping but distinct concept: thought–action fusion (TAF) as conceptualized by Rachman and colleagues (Rachman, 1993; Rachman, Thordrarson, Shafran, & Woody, 1995; Shafran, Thordarson, & Rachman, 1996). Studies using a measure of TAF, the Thought–Action Fusion Scale (TAFS) (Shafran et al., 1996), have found significant and positive associations between the TAFS, in particular its likelihood – TAF subscale, and obsessional symptoms in both clinical and nonclinical populations (see review in Shafran & Rachman, 2004). This supports the relevance of this concept to OCD.

Although studies using the TAFS are relevant to the metacognitive model, there are important differences between the constructs of thought-fusion in the metacognitive model and Rachman's conception of TAF (see Fisher, 2009; Solem, Myers, Fisher, Vogel, & Wells, 2010). For example, Purdon and Clark (1999) highlighted that although cognitive models involve metacognitive processing, as must be the case in all appraisal theories; metacognition was never an explicit feature of these models. Thought–action fusion (Rachman, 1993) was conceptualized as a cognitive bias and not as metacognitive beliefs about thoughts, even though it is most likely to be an index of such beliefs. Specific tests of the role of thought fusion as conceived in the metacognitive model required a measure of this concept. The thought–fusion instrument (TFI) (Wells, Gwilliam, & Cartwright-Hatton, in Wells, 2009) was designed to measure the three types of thought fusion implicated in the model, namely: thought–event, thought–action, and thought–object fusion. The expected positive relationship between the TFI and OC symptoms in cross-sectional studies is well established (Grøtte et al., 2015; Gwilliam et al., 2004; McNicol & Wells, 2012, Myers & Wells, 2005; Myers, Fisher, & Wells, 2009a; Solem et al., 2010). Correlations between the TFI total score and OC symptom measures in these studies ranged from .26 to .67 reflecting low-medium to high effect sizes. The relationship between the TFI and OC symptom measures remains when general worry and non-metacognitive beliefs (e.g., Inflated Responsibility schemas) linked to OCD by other theories are controlled for (Gwilliam et al., 2004; Myers & Wells, 2005; Myers et al., 2009a; Solem et al., 2010).

While most of these studies used nonclinical populations, Solem and colleagues (2010) and Grøtte and colleagues (2015), demonstrated significant relationships between the TFI and OC symptoms in OCD patients (range .26–.67). Solem et al. (2010) found significantly higher TFI scores in OCD patients when compared with a community control sample. In a test of the specificity of thought fusion beliefs, Myers (2010) compared TFI scores in OCD patients with that of a group with Generalized Anxiety Disorder and found that OCD patients had significantly higher scores. However, more studies comparing TFI scores in OCD patients with clinical and nonclinical controls are needed.

Prospective and experimental studies. Myers, Fisher, and Wells (2009b) examined the relative contribution of metacognitive and non-metacognitive beliefs as prospective predictors of OC symptoms in students over a 3-month period. Thought fusion, as measured by the TFI, emerged as the only independent prospective predictor. It predicted OC symptoms with worry, threat, and beliefs linked to OCD, namely responsibility and perfectionism controlled for. Additional analysis showed that OC symptoms did not prospectively predict thought fusion suggesting the relationship between thought fusion and OC symptoms was not bi-directional.

If thought fusion beliefs are causal in the development of OC symptoms, increasing or decreasing these experimentally should lead to concurrent changes in OC symptomology. A number of experimental studies using various paradigms have examined the effects of inducing thought fusion beliefs. Several studies have attempted to induce thought fusion related beliefs using the sentence-paradigm devised by Rachman, Shafran, Mitchell, Trant, and Teachman (1996). This consists of participants completing the sentence "I hope _____ is in a car accident," by putting a friend or relative's name in the blank. Participants are then asked to visualize the accident. Studies using the sentence paradigm have shown it induces OCD-like symptoms, that is, an urge to neutralize and anxiety (e.g., Bocci & Gordon, 2007; Rachman et al. 1996). These findings are supportive of the causal role of thought fusion in OC symptomology. However, some commentators question the effectiveness of the sentence paradigm in inducing thought fusion (van den Hout, Kindt, Weiland, & Peters, 2002), at least in people without pre-existing thought fusion beliefs (Shafran & Rachman, 2004).

Rassin, Merkelbach, Muris, and Spaan (1999) used a different paradigm to manip-ulate thought fusion experimentally. They gave students a fake EEG recording session and told them that if they had the thought "apple" this would be picked up by the machine. The experimental but not the control group was informed that having the thought "apple" would lead to an electrical shock being given to another participant, which they could interrupt by pressing a button. They found that the experimental group had more "apple" intrusions, discomfort and put more effort into avoiding the target thought.

As we described earlier whilst these studies are consistent with the metacognitive model they do not make metacognitive beliefs explicit and compound threatening events with thoughts. Adapting this paradigm as a specific test of the metacognitive model, Myers and Wells (2013) gave fake EEG recordings to students with high and low pre-existing obsessional symptoms. All participants were informed that the EEG could sense hypothalamus activity caused by having thoughts related to drinking. Participants in the experimental condition were told that if such thoughts were detected they may be exposed to an aversive noise. Those in the control condition were told that they may hear an aversive noise but this would be unrelated to the thoughts they had. Results showed a significant interaction effect between level of obsessional symptoms and belief induction. Analysis of this effect demonstrated that in the high obsession group, participants in the experimental condition had signifi-cantly more intrusions about drinking, time spent thinking about these intrusions and discomfort from them, than controls.

While most experimental studies manipulating thought fusion have examined the effects of increasing these beliefs, Fisher and Wells (2005a) examined the effects of decreasing thought fusion. They found that a short exposure and response prevention task when used as an experiment to challenge OCD patients' thought fusion beliefs led to greater reductions in anxiety and urge to neutralize than when the same task was used with a habituation rationale. This study provides further support for the causal role of thought fusion and suggests that reducing these beliefs may be an important focus of treatment.

Metacognitive versus Non-metacognitive Beliefs

A variety of dysfunctional beliefs have been linked to OCD in different models and theories of the disorder. Some models of OCD stress the role of beliefs such as inflated responsibility (Salkovskis, 1985), perfectionism (e.g., Frost & Steketee, 1997) and intolerance of uncertainty (Carr, 1974). The metacognitive model theorizes that although non-metacognitive beliefs and appraisals may be present in OCD, it is the metacognitive beliefs that are central and causal.If this is correct, we would expect to find metacognitive beliefs rather than non-metacognitive beliefs emerging as stronger and more consistent independent predictors of OC symptoms in studies testing their relative contribution.

Gwilliam and colleagues (2004) and Myers and Wells (2005) showed that while both responsibility and metacognitive beliefs were significantly related to OC symp-toms, only metacognitions were independent predictors when their interrelationship was controlled. Myers, Fisher, and Wells (2008) examined a wider range of beliefs using the Obsessive Beliefs Questionnaire (OCCWG, 2005), Four factors emerged: three non-metacognitive factors – (a) perfectionism and intolerance of uncertainty,

(b) responsibility, and (c) overestimation of threat; and one metacognitive factor – importance and control of thoughts. The metacognitive factor explained variance in OC symptoms beyond that explained by the schemas of responsibility or perfectionism. On the final step of the regression metacognitive beliefs, but not responsibility or perfectionism explained unique variance in OC symptoms.

Myers and colleagues (2009a) repeated the above analysis using measures directly drawn from the model, that is, the TFI, as well as the Beliefs About Rituals Inventory (BARI) (McNicol & Wells, 2012) and the Stop Signals Questionnaire (SSQ) (Myers et al., 2009a). Metacognition emerged as an independent predictor, but responsibility and perfectionism did not. A similar result was obtained by Solem and colleagues (2010), with metacognition emerging as an independent predictor of OC symptoms in two regressions after controlling for worry and non-metacognitive beliefs. However, in this study perfectionism – a non-metacognitive belief – also contributed in one regression model. While the above studies used nonclinical samples, Solem et al. (2009) examined the relative contribution of metacognitive and non-metacognitive beliefs using a sample of OCD patients. Their study examined predictors of change in OC symptoms following exposure and response prevention (ERP) treatment. They found that changes in metacognition (measured by the total score of the MCQ-30) predicted improvement in OC symptoms independently of non-metacognitive beliefs. However, changes in schemas such as responsibility beliefs did not explain improvement independently. A similar result was found by Grøtte et al. (2015) using metacognitive measures specifically designed for OCD (the TFI and BARI) in OCD patients who had received a multimodal treatment package. Changes in metacognition were independent predictors of improvements in OC symptoms in three out of the four analyses carried out but other, non-metacognitive belief domains did not emerge as independent predictors in any analysis. The specific and stronger relationship between metacognitive beliefs (compared with non-metacognitive schemas) and OC symptoms is present in prospective analyses (Myers et al., 2009b) supporting a causal role of metacognitions. Nonpatients completed measures at two time points, 3 months apart. When OC symptoms and worry measured at time 1 were controlled, only metacognitive beliefs and not non-metacognitive beliefs independently predicted later OC symptoms.

Evidence of Treatment Efficacy

Five small-scale studies have examined the efficacy of MCT for OCD with promising results. The first study (Fisher & Wells, 2008) demonstrated the potential of MCT in a case series of four patients with different subtypes of OCD. The patients received 12–14 1-hour weekly treatment sessions of MCT. Standardized Jacobson criteria for recovery on the Yale–Brown Obsessive Compulsive Scale (cut off point ≤ 14 and reliable change ≥ 10 points) as reported by Fisher and Wells (2005b) were applied. All four patients achieved recovery at posttreatment, which was maintained through to the 3-month follow-up. At the 6-month follow-up, data was only available for three patients; two maintained recovery status and one continued to have made reliable improvement.

The potential effectiveness of group metacognitive therapy for OCD has been evaluated in two open trials. Group MCT for OCD does not require a broad range of idiosyncratic formulations based on varying combinations of cognitive beliefs/appraisals or a variety of exposure hierarchies as metacognitive beliefs about intrusions and rituals are comparable across subtypes. The focus is on altering the patient's relationship with their thoughts as opposed to challenging the actual content of the thoughts In the first open trial, Rees and van Koesveld (2008) conducted a single group ($n=8$) of MCT. Three of the eight (38%) patients achieved recovery on the YBCOS at posttreatment, with very significant treatment gains made over the 3-month follow-up period, where seven of the eight (88%) treated patients were recovered.

In the second open trial, Fisher and Wells (2013) tested brief group implemented MCT across 19 patients in five small groups. Treatment was delivered by a single therapist and involved six 2-hour sessions conducted over nine weeks. The results of the study showed that all patients achieved large symptomatic gains at posttreatment, which were maintained through to the 6-month follow-up. The treatment was acceptable and feasible to deliver as 17 of 19 patients completed treatment and 65% of treatment completers were asymptomatic (score of 7 or less on the self-report Y-BOCS) at posttreatment. These encouraging data suggest that group MCT for OCD could prove to be an efficacious and cost effective psychological treatment.

Van der Heiden, van Rossen, Dekker, Damstra, and Deen (2016) examined the effectiveness of MCT in an open trial of 25 consecutively referred outpatients with OCD. The treatment was well tolerated with low drop-out rates (19 of 25 completers) and was associated with large and clinically significant reductions in all outcome measures. Levels of clinically significant change were encouraging with 74% of patients recovered at posttreatment and 80% at 3-month follow up (completer's sample).

A small controlled evaluation compared the effects of MCT in combination with CBT against ERP for children and adolescents (Simons et al., 2006). The results indicated that the combined treatment (MCT+CBT) was an effective intervention, although further studies are needed to partial the treatment effects from the combined intervention.

While the above studies examined the efficacy of MCT as a full treatment package, other studies have examined the effects of individual treatment techniques. Ludvik and Boschen (2005) gave 65 nonclinical students a repeated checking task which has been demonstrated experimentally to increase memory distrust (van den Hout & Kindt, 2003). Following this, participants were given a brief Detached Mindfulness intervention based on the metacognitive model, a brief cognitive restructuring (CR) intervention based on other models of OCD, or an unrelated task, which was given as a control condition. Participants were subsequently given the option of checking again on their last response in the checking task. Results showed that compared with the control group, significantly less participants in both the DM and CR groups took up the option to recheck. Additionally, DM led to significant increases in memory confidence and details of the memory about the task, a result not seen in either the CR or control groups. This study is supportive of the effects of DM on reducing checking symptomology but studies using clinical populations are needed to confirm the findings. Additionally, further studies are needed to examine the effects of DM on other types of OC symptoms. Fisher and Wells (2005b) tested the relative effects of one session of exposure and ritual prevention presented as a test of metacognitive beliefs against the same procedure administered with a traditional habituation rationale. The metacognitively delivered exposure produced significantly greater reductions in anxiety, urge to neutralize, and negative beliefs than the habituation condition.

Conclusion

The metacognitive model provides a framework for explaining distress across OCD subtypes. At the core of the approach are cognitive processes of repetitive negative thinking (e.g., worry, rumination) that are used to deal with intrusive internal experiences (i.e., thoughts, doubts and urges). As a result of metacognitive beliefs about the power and importance of thoughts to cause or signal negative events, the person vulnerable to OCD engages in sustained processing in reaction to intrusions. Sustained processing in the form of worrying, ruminating, and overt and covert neutralizing has a variety of negative consequences that impact on cognitive and emotional self-regulation. For instance, repeated checking in response to doubts leads to lowered confidence in memory, trying to suppress bad thoughts can maintain them, engaging in cleaning rituals increases monitoring for signs of contamination. As a result, the individual becomes entangled with thinking as both a source and solution to threat but is ultimately engaged in a cognitive-behavioral response pattern that strengthens the sense of danger.

Metacognitive therapy aims to formulate and reduce the process of extended thinking and to challenge metacognitive beliefs about thoughts, such as thought–event fusion. The model leads to new implications as it suggests that treatment strategies such as exposure and ritual prevention will be most useful when they change the nature of the relationship that individuals' have with their thoughts and their underlying metacognitive beliefs. For example, it implies that ritual prevention is best configured as an experiment to test beliefs that thoughts can cause negative events. In fact, the metacognitive approach implies that rituals may not be prevented at all in the service of promoting metacognitive change. In particular, the patient may be instructed to engage in a ritual, such as checking a door is locked, whilst continually and purposefully doubting their actions. This serves to change the nature of the relationship that the individual has with doubts, enabling them to discover that these are simply events in the mind that do not necessitate reparation. Techniques such as detached mindfulness and the postponement of worrying/ruminating provide powerful experiences that change the perspective an individual has in relation to their thinking, whilst direct verbal and behavioral challenges of fusion beliefs reduces the subjective threat presented by inner thoughts and feelings.

In this chapter we briefly reviewed research that provides support for the predicted role of metacognition in OCD. Whilst there are now many studies supporting the model there is clearly a need for more studies testing the causal role of central factors. There is an even greater need for larger scale treatment trials of the efficacy of metacognitive therapy in OCD to determine if the treatment is as successful in this disorder as it is proving to be elsewhere (e.g., Normann, Van Emerik, & Morina, 2014; Van der Heiden, Muris, & Van der Molen, 2010).

References

Alcolado, G. M., & Radomsky, A. S. (2011). Believe in yourself: Manipulating beliefs about memory causes checking. *Behaviour Research and Therapy, 49*, 42–49.

Bocci, L., & Gordon, P. K. (2007). Does magical thinking produce neutralising behaviour? An experimental investigation. *Behaviour Research and Therapy, 45*(8), 1823–1833.

Carr, A. T. (1974). Compulsive neurosis: A review of the literature. *Psychological Bulletin, 81*, 311–318.

Cartwright-Hatton, S., & Wells, A. (1997). Beliefs about worry and intrusions: The Meta-Cognitions Questionnaire and its correlates. *Journal of Anxiety Disorders, 11*, 279–296.

Cartwright-Hatton, S., Mather, A., Illingworth, V., Brocki, J., Harrington, R., & Wells, A. (2004). Development and preliminary validation of the Meta-cognitions Questionnaire – Adolescent version. *Journal of Anxiety Disorders, 18*, 411–422.

Cho, Y., Jang, S., & Chai, S. (2012). The factor structure and concurrent validity of the Korean version of the Metacognitions Questionnaire 30 (K-MCQ-30). *Journal of Clinical Psychology, 68*, 349–391.

Crye, J., Laskey, B., & Cartwright-Hatton, S. (2010). Non-clinical obsessions in a young adolescent population: Frequency and association with metacognitive variables. *Psychology and Psychotherapy: Theory, Research and Practice, 83*, 15–26.

Cuttler, C., Sirois-Delisle, V., Alcolado, G. M., Radomsky, A. S., & Taylor, S. (2013). Diminished confidence in prospective memory causes doubts and urges to check. *Journal of Behavior Therapy and Experimental Psychiatry, 44*, 329–334.

Ellis, D. M., & Hudson, J. L. (2011). Test of the metacognitive model of generalized anxiety disorder in anxiety-disordered adolescents. *Journal of Experimental Psychopathology, 2*, 28–43.

Fisher, P. L. (2009). Obsessive compulsive disorder: a comparison of CBT and the metacognitive approach. *International Journal of Cognitive Therapy, 2*, 107–122.

Fisher, P. L., & Wells, A. (2005a). Experimental modification of beliefs in obsessive-compulsive disorder: A test of the metacognitive model. *Behaviour Research and Therapy, 43*, 821–829.

Fisher, P. L., & Wells, A. (2005b). How effective are cognitive and behavioural treatments for obsessive-compulsive disorder? A clinical significance analysis. *Behaviour Research and Therapy, 43*(12), 1543–1558.

Fisher, P. L., & Wells, A. (2008). Metacognitive therapy for obsessive-compulsive disorder: A case series. *Journal of Behavior Therapy and Experimental Psychiatry, 39*, 117–132.

Fisher, P., & Wells. A. (2013). *Obsessive compulsive disorder and metacognition: What we think we know!* World Congress of Behavioral and Cognitive Therapies, Lima, Peru.

Frost, R. O., & Steketee, G. (1997). Perfectionism in obsessive-compulsive disorder patients. *Behaviour Research and Therapy, 35*, 291–296.

Grøtte, T., Solem, S., Vogel, P. A., Guzey, I. C., Hansen, B., & Myers, S. G. (2015). Metacognition, responsibility, and perfectionism in Obsessive-Compulsive Disorder. *Cognitive Therapy and Research, 39*, 41–50.

Gwilliam, P., Wells, A., & Cartwright-Hatton, S. (2004). Does meta-cognition or responsibility predict obsessive-compulsive symptoms: A test of the metacognitive model. *Clinical Psychology & Psychotherapy, 11*, 137–144.

Hermans, D., Engelen, U., Grouwels, L., Joos, E., Lemmons, J., & Pieters, E. (2008). Cognitive confidence in obsessive-compulsive disorder: Distrusting perception, attention and memory, *Behaviour Research and Therapy, 46*, 98–113.

Hermans, D., Martens, K., de Cort, K., Pieters, G., & Engelen, P. (2003). Reality monitoring and metacognitive beliefs related to cognitive confidence in obsessive-compulsive disorder. *Behaviour Research and Therapy, 41*, 383–401.

Irak, M., & Tosun, A. (2008). Exploring the role of metacognition in obsessive-compulsive and anxiety symptoms. *Journal of Anxiety Disorders, 22*, 1316–1325.

Janeck, A. S., Calamari, J. E., Riemann, B. C., & Heffelfinger, S. K. (2003). Too much thinking about thinking?: Metacognitive differences in obsessive-compulsive disorder. *Journal of Anxiety Disorders, 17*, 181–195.

Kikul, J., Vetter, J., Lincoln, T. M., & Exner, C. (2011). Effects of cognitive self-consciousness on visual memory in obsessive-compulsive disorder. *Journal of Anxiety Disorders, 25*(4), 490–497. doi: 10.1016/j.janxdis.2010.12.002.

Lewin, A. B., Park, J. M., Jones, A. M., Crawford, E. A., De Nadai, A. S., Menzel, J., ... Storch, E. A. (2014). Family-based exposure and response prevention therapy for preschool-aged children with obsessive-compulsive disorder: A pilot randomized controlled trial. *Behaviour Research and Therapy*, 56, 30–38.

Ludvik, D., & Boschen, M. J. (2015). Cognitive restructuring and detached mindfulness: Comparative impact on a compulsive checking task. *Journal of Obsessive-Compulsive and Related Disorders*, 5, 8–15.

McNicol, K., & Wells, A. (2012). Metacognition and obsessive-compulsive symptoms: The contribution of thought-fusion beliefs and beliefs about rituals. *International Journal of Cognitive Therapy*, 5, 330–340.

Myers, S. G. (2010). *Empirical tests of the metacognitive model of Obsessive-Compulsive Disorder*. Unpublished PhD thesis, University of Manchester, UK.

Myers, S. G., Fisher, P. L., & Wells, A. (2008). Belief domains of the Obsessive Beliefs Questionnaire-44 (OBQ-44) and their specific relationship with obsessive-compulsive symptoms. *Journal of Anxiety Disorders*, 22, 475–484.

Myers, S. G., Fisher, P. L., & Wells, A. (2009a). An empirical test of the metacognitive model of obsessive-compulsive symptoms: Fusion beliefs, beliefs about rituals, and stop signals. *Journal of Anxiety Disorders*, 23, 436–442.

Myers, S. G., Fisher, P. L., & Wells, A. (2009b). Metacognition and cognition as predictors of obsessive-compulsive symptoms: A prospective study. *International Journal of Cognitive Therapy*, 2, 107–122.

Myers, S. G., & Wells, A. (2005). Obsessive-compulsive symptoms: The contribution of meta-cognitions and responsibility. *Journal of Anxiety Disorders*, 19, 806–817.

Myers, S. G., & Wells, A. (2013). An experimental manipulation of metacognition: A test of the metacognitive model of obsessive-compulsive symptoms. *Behaviour Research and Therapy*, 51, 177–184.

Normann, N., Van Emmerik, A., & Morina, N. (2014). The efficacy of metacognitive thrapy for anxiety and depression: A meta-analytic review. *Depression and Anxiety*, 31, 402–411.

Obsessive Compulsive Cognitions Working Group (OCCWG). (2005). Psychometric validation of the Obsessive Beliefs Questionnaire and the Interpretation of Intrusions Inventory – Part 2: Factor analyses and testing of a brief version. *Behaviour Research and Therapy*, 43, 1527–1542.

Purdon, C., & Clark, D. A. (1999). Metacognition and obsessions. *Clinical Psychology and Psychotherapy*, 6, 102–110.

Rachman, S. (1993). Obsessions, responsibility and guilt. *Behaviour Research and Therapy*, 31, 149–154.

Rachman, S., Shafran, R., Mitchell, D., Trant, J., & Teachman, B. (1996). How to remain neutral: An experimental analysis of neutralization. *Behaviour Research and Therapy*, 34, 889–898.

Rachman, S., Thordarson, D. S., Shafran, R., & Woody, S. R. (1995). Perceived responsibility: Structure and significance. *Behaviour Research and Therapy*, 33, 779–784.

Rassin, E., Merckelbach, H., Muris, P., & Spaan, V. (1999). Thought–action fusion as a causal factor in the development of intrusions. *Behaviour Research and Therapy*, 37, 231–237.

Rees, C. S., & van Koesveld, K. E. (2008). An open trial of group metacognitive therapy for obsessive-compulsive disorder. *Journal of Behavior Therapy and Experimental Psychiatry*, 39, 451–458.

Salkovskis, P. M. (1985). Obsessional-compulsive problems: A cognitive-behavioural analysis. *Behaviour Research and Therapy*, 23, 571–583.

Shafran, R., Thordarson, D. S., & Rachman, S. (1996). Thought–action fusion in obsessive-compulsive disorder. *Journal of Anxiety Disorders*, 10, 379–391.

Shafran, R., & Rachman, S. (2004). Thought–action fusion: A review. *Journal of Behaviour Therapy and Experimental Psychiatry*, 35, 87–107.

Sica, C., Steketee, G., Ghisi, M., Chiri, L. R., & Franceschini, S. (2007). Metacognitive beliefs and strategies predict worry, obsessive-compulsive symptoms and coping styles: A preliminary prospective study on an Italian non-clinical sample. *Clinical Psychology & Psychotherapy, 14,* 258–268.

Smith, K. E., & Hudson, J. L. (2013). Metacognitive beliefs and processes in clinical anxiety in children. *Journal of Clinical Child and Adolescent Psychology, 42,* 590–602.

Simons, M., Schneider, S., & Herpertz-Dahlmann, B. (2006). Metacognitive therapy versus exposure and response prevention for pediatric obsessive-compulsive disorder: A case series with randomized allocation. *Psychotherapy and Psychosomatics, 75,* 257–264.

Solem, S., Håland, Å. T., Vogel, P. A., Hansen, B., & Wells, A. (2009). Change in metacognitions predicts outcome in obsessive-compulsive disorder patients undergoing treatment with exposure and response prevention. *Behaviour Research and Therapy, 47,* 301–307.

Solem, S., Myers, S. G., Fisher, P. L., Vogel, P. A., & Wells, A. (2010). An empirical test of the metacognitive model of obsessive-compulsive: Replication and extension. *Journal of Anxiety Disorders, 24,* 79–86.

Storch, E. A., Geffken, G. R., Merlo, L. J., Jacob, M. L., Murphy, T. K., Goodman, W. K., & Grabill, K. (2007). Family accommodation in pediatric obsessive-compulsive disorder. *Journal of Clinical Child and Adolescent Psychology, 36,* 207–216.

Timpano, K. R., Rasmussen, J. L., Exner, C., Rief, W., & Wilhelm, S. (2014). The association between metacognitions, the obsessive compulsive symptom dimensions and hoarding: A ocus on specificity. *Journal of Obsessive-Compulsive and Related Disorders, 3,* 188–194.

Van der Heiden, C., Muris, P., & van der Molen, H. T. (2012). Randomized controlled trial on the effectiveness of metacognitive therapy and intolerance-of-uncertainty therapy for generalized anxiety disorder. *Behaviour Research and Therapy, 50,* 100–109.

Van der Heiden, C., Van Rossen, K., Dekker, A., Daystar, M., & Den, M. (2016). Metacognitive therapy for obsessive-compulsive disorder: A pilot study. *Journal of Obsessive-Compulsive and Related Disorders, 9,* 24–29.

Van den Hout, M., & Kindt, M. (2003). Repeated checking causes memory distrust. *Behaviour Research and Therapy, 41,* 301–316.

Van den Hout, M., Kindt, M., Weiland, T., & Peters, M. (2002). Instructed neutralization, spontaneous neutralization and prevented neutralization after an obsession-like thought. *Journal of Behavior Therapy and Experimental Psychiatry, 33,* 177–189.

Wells, A. (1997). *Cognitive therapy of anxiety disorders: A practice manual and conceptual guide.* Chichester: Wiley.

Wells, A. (2009). *Metacognitive therapy for anxiety and depression.* New York: Guilford Press.

Wells, A. & Cartwright-Hatton, S. (2004). A short form of the metacognitions questionnaire: Properties of the MCQ-30. *Behaviour Research and Therapy, 42,* 385–396.

Wells, A., & Matthews, G. (1994). *Attention and emotion: A clinical perspective.* Hove: Erlbaum.

Wells, A., & Matthews, G. (1996). Modelling cognition in emotional disorder: The S-REF model. *Behaviour Research and Therapy, 32,* 867–870.

Wells, A., & Papageorgiou, C. (1998). Relationships between worry, obsessive-compulsive symptoms and meta-cognitive beliefs. *Behaviour Research and Therapy, 36,* 899–913.

Wilson, C., & Hall, M. (2012). Thought control strategies in adolescents: Links with OCD symptoms and meta-cognitive beliefs. *Behavioural and Cognitive Psychotherapy, 40,* 438–451.

Yilmaz, A. E., Gencoz, T., & Wells A. (2008). Psychometric characteristics of the Penn State Worry Questionnaire and Metacognitions Questionnaire-30 and metacognitive predictors of worry and obsessive-compulsive symptoms in a Turkish sample. *Clinical Psychology and Psychotherapy, 15,* 424–439.

37

Computer-Aided Interventions for Obsessive-Compulsive Spectrum Disorders

Erik Andersson, David Mataix-Cols, and Christian Rück

Despite the fact that cognitive behavior therapy (CBT) for obsessive-compulsive disorder (OCD) has been investigated in clinical trials for more than 40 years, consistently showing large effect sizes (Gava et al., 2007) and being recommended as first-line treatment for the disorder in various international guidelines (e.g., NICE, 2005), treatment accessibility is still very low. Epidemiological studies show that only a fraction of patients with OCD seek or receive help for their symptoms (Blanco et al., 2006; Fullana et al., 2009; Torres et al., 2007). For example, a British study by Torres and colleagues (2007) showed that only 5% of adults with OCD actually received CBT. In the United States, Blanco and colleagues (2006) found that 7.5% of OCD had received CBT. Furthermore, an Internet-survey by Marques et al. (2010) showed that, of those OCD patients who had received psychological treatments, the majority (67%) had actually received nonevidenced-based treatments (e.g., supportive counseling). Thus, despite a strong evidence base in terms of efficacy, most patients may still not be receiving the evidence-based treatment they need. Some possible barriers include the low numbers of properly trained CBT therapists within the health care system (Mataix-Cols & Marks, 2006; Shapiro, Cavanagh, & Lomas, 2003), financial and logistic (e.g., geographical) barriers to treatment seeking, as well as embarrassment due to symptoms (Griffiths, Lindenmeyer, Powell, Lowe, & Thorogood, 2006; Marques et al., 2010; Wootton, Titov, Dear, Spence, & Kemp, 2011b). For the OCD-related disorders, that is, body dysmorphic disorder (BDD), hoarding disorder (HD), trichotillomania (hair pulling disorder) and excoriation (skin picking) disorder, the evidence base for the efficacy if CBT is only beginning to accumulate and the availability of specialist treatment is severely limited to a handful of specialist centers worldwide.

This has prompted the development of multiple strategies to increase access to CBT for patients with OCD and, to a much smaller extent, patients with OCD-related disorders. These include bibliotherapy self-help, telephone-based interventions, and computer-aided interventions. For a recent review of bibliotherapy and

The Wiley Handbook of Obsessive Compulsive Disorders, Volume I, First Edition.
Edited by Jonathan S. Abramowitz, Dean McKay, and Eric A. Storch.
© 2017 John Wiley & Sons Ltd. Published 2017 by John Wiley & Sons Ltd.

telephone-based interventions for OCD, see Lovell and Bee (2011). This chapter focuses on both computer-based (CCBT) and Internet-based (ICBT) self-help interventions for OCD. We first offer some definitions of CCBT and ICBT, before reviewing the current evidence base for these treatment modalities. Future directions for research in this area are then discussed as are our experiences regarding the clinical implementation of such interventions in regular clinical practice.

What are CCBT and ICBT?

There is no universally accepted definition of CCBT, but it can best be described as a self-help treatment that adopts the same treatment components as a regular CBT, but that is conducted using a computer which makes at least some of the treatment decisions (Marks & Cavanagh, 2009). CCBT programs help the patient rather than the therapist make most of the decisions about how to devise, execute, and complete CBT, including appropriate homework and relapse prevention (Gega, Marks, & Mataix-Cols, 2004). CCBT programs should not be seen as therapist replacers but as therapist-extenders, in the sense that the routine aspects of treatment are delegated to the computer program, though the clinician still has an important role in this kind of treatment, for example, by reminding and motivating patients to comply with the treatment (Marks, Kenwright, McDonough, Whittaker, & Mataix-Cols, 2004; Marks et al., 2003).

Internet-based CBT (ICBT) is also a self-help treatment that is accessed through a web page (Andersson, 2009). In many respects, ICBT is a form of CCBT, as it is also a self-help treatment that is provided through a computer. One important difference is that in ICBT the clinical decision-making does not necessarily have to be replaced by a computer. Instead, the decision-making in ICBT is made by either the therapist or the patient or, most commonly, by them both (Andersson, 2009; Andersson, Cuijpers, Carlbring, & Lindefors, 2007). One characteristic that both CCBT and ICBT have in common is that they require only a fraction of therapist time, compared with standard CBT, thus potentially resulting in substantial cost savings.

ICBT programs differ regarding the degree of therapist involvement. Some ICBT programs are not supported by a therapist at all and can best be described as online bibliotherapy; the decision making is then entirely made by the patient. An important general finding in this field is that ICBT with therapist support is generally more effective than treatment without such support (Andersson, 2009; Andersson & Titov, 2014; Andersson et al., 2007). The therapist contact in ICBT can be provided in different ways; many protocols use email as means of communication, but in other treatments the therapist offers support via the telephone or videoconferencing. The amount of therapist contact can also differ in terms of duration (short or long emails), quality (contact on request or scheduled contact) and frequency (contact once or several times per week) (Andersson & Titov, 2014).

In this review, we do not consider videoconference-provided CBT as a form of ICBT. While the treatment is provided via the Internet, this form of remote treatment is identical to face-to-face CBT, with the difference that the patient and therapist meet behind a web camera instead at the therapist's office (Himle et al., 2006; Vogel et al., 2012). Like telephone-administered CBT, this form of remote treatment is convenient for patients and reduces travel time and expenses but it does not necessarily save therapist's time.

CCBT for ADULTS with OCD

OC-CHECK was developed in the late 1980s and was the first CCBT treatment for OCD (Baer, Minichiello, & Jenike, 1987; Mataix-Cols & Marks, 2006). This treatment consisted of a palmtop computer that asked the patient to resist the urge to check for at least 3 minutes and that provided the patients with reminders that nothing bad would happen during this time. The OC-CHECK program was tested on a single case with some temporary effects but that were not sustained at follow-up.

CAVE stands for "Computer-aided Vicarious Exposure" and was developed in the late 1990s by Kirby and colleagues (Clark, Kirkby, Daniels, & Marks, 1998). In this program, the patients were instructed to imagine they were the person shown on the computer screen and to practice ERP by moving the person on the screen to touch dirt and refrain from washing rituals. It also allowed patients to virtually turn off the light bulbs on a stove and refrain from checking rituals. CAVE was tested in a small open trial with 13 OCD subjects, but this study could not find any significant effects on the Yale–Brown Obsessive Compulsive Scale (Y-BOCS) (Goodman et al., 1989).

BT-STEPS is probably the most well-known form of CCBT (Bachofen et al., 1999b; Greist et al., 1998). In BT-STEPS, the patient worked with a self-help book and reported progress with the treatment using an automated phone interactive-voice-response (IVR) system. BT-STEPS consisted of nine steps on how to conduct self-administered ERP and also how to involve a friend or relative as support person in ERP. The program also contained a relapse prevention module.

BT-STEPS was first successfully tested in two open pilot studies (Bachofen et al., 1999b; Greist et al., 1998) and then in a large-scale multicenter randomized controlled trial, where 218 OCD subjects were allocated to either face-to-face CBT (but without any therapist-supported ERP), BT-STEPS or to audio guided systematic relaxation (Greist et al., 2002). Patients were assessed with the Y-BOCS at baseline, week 2, week 6, and at posttreatment (week 10). The mean Y-BOCS score at baseline was 25 and the patients had on average had OCD-symptoms for 22 years. Results showed that both face-to-face CBT and BT-STEPS were superior to the relaxation group, but patients randomized to face-to-face CBT improved more than BT-STEPS in the intention-to-treat analysis. However, when analyzing patients who commenced ERP and/or took part in at least two homework sessions, BT-STEPS had comparable effects to face-to-face CBT. There was also a dose–response relationship in both these groups compared with the relaxation, that is, patients who did more ERP-exercises had better response in the BT-STEPS and face-to-face CBT, but this was not true for the relaxation control patients. Thus, although patients seemed to be more motivated to do ERP in the face-to-face CBT group, patients who actually completed the BT-STEPS treatment had similar effects as those who completed the face-to-face CBT. Patients were in general more satisfied with the face-to-face CBT treatment and treatment satisfaction also correlated with better outcome in both groups. Thus, although BT-STEPS did not appear to be as effective as face-to-face CBT for the whole OCD patient population, it was still an effective treatment compared to relaxations and it was also equally effective for the highly motivated patients.

One study investigated how BT-STEPS worked in a naturalistic setting at a primary care clinic in London (Marks et al., 2003). In this study, 16 OCD patients were offered access to BT-STEPS. Although seven patients dropped out from treatment, large improvements were seen for the nine patients who completed treatment

(Cohen's $d = 1.2$). Given the relatively high drop-out rates observed with BT-STEPS, Kenwright, Marks, Graham, Franses, and Mataix-Cols (2005) subsequently investigated whether the treatment adherence and overall outcomes of BT-STEPS could be further improved by adding scheduled therapist phone calls to BT-STEPS. They randomized 44 OCD patients to either scheduled therapist support via telephone or to unscheduled calls on request from the patients. Patients randomized to the active telephone support were significantly more likely to stay in treatment and to benefit from the intervention. These results clearly suggested that therapist support of some kind is an important component in computer aided-interventions.

To the best of our knowledge, BT-STEPS is no longer available in its original IVR format, but an Internet-based version (renamed OCFIGHTER) is currently being tested in a large RCT (Gellatly et al., 2014).

Cost-effectiveness of CCBT for Adult OCD

The cost-effectiveness of BT-STEPS was analyzed using data from the randomized trial (McCrone et al., 2007). Results showed that although BT-STEPS was shown to be less efficacious than face-to-face CBT, the cost-effectiveness benefited CCBT due to lower treatment costs. However, as pointed out by the authors in this study, a major limitation was that societal costs were excluded from the analysis, for example, other medical costs, sick leave and work cut-back.

Predictors and Moderators of Treatment Response in CCBT

In their pilot BT-STEPS study, Bachofen and colleagues (1999a) found that patients who rated themselves as more motivated at baseline had better improvement and adherence rates. Furthermore, Mataix-Cols, Marks, Greist, Kobak, and Baer (2002) re-analyzed data from the BT-STEPS randomized trial, and found that overall higher OCD symptoms at baseline predicted less chance of being a responder, defined as at least 40% decrease on the Y-BOCS from baseline to posttreatment. Furthermore, both face-to-face CBT and BT-STEPS had lower responder rates in patients who had sexual/religious obsessions but BT-STEPS moderated a worse response, that is, although patients with sexual/religious obsessions did worse in general, it was higher chance of improvement for this patient group when receiving face-to-face CBT compared to BT-STEPS.

ICBT for Adults with OCD

Below follows a description of the three tested ICBT treatments available to date, henceforth referred to as the Swedish, the Australian and the German ICBT programs.

The Swedish ICBT program, developed by Andersson and colleagues, consists of an online self-help text (about 100 A4 pages) that can also be downloaded as an mp3-file, with homework assignments that are subsequently examined by a therapist. The patient gains gradual access to each chapter (module) and the treatment also uses some interactive features such that the treatment text adjusts itself based on the patient's primary symptom subtype (i.e., washing, checking, symmetry, violent thoughts) (Andersson et al., 2012). As therapist support has shown to be an important factor for both treatment efficacy and compliance in the treatment of OCD (Kenwright et al., 2005; Rosa-Alcazar, Sanchez-Meca, Gomez-Conesa, & Marin-Martinez, 2008), this treatment is supported by a high frequency proactive therapist support, that is, the therapist sends an email in the treatment platform if the patient has not logged in for 3 days and responds to the patient within 24 hours on weekdays. A text message is also sent to the patient's cell phone each time the therapist sends an email. Despite this relative high frequency communication, the duration of the contact is short and the total time spent for each participant is about 6–13 minutes per week (see below) (Andersson et al., 2012). The treatment content is summarized in Table 37.1.

The Australian ICBT program was developed by Wootton and colleagues, at the eCentreClinic at Macquarie University. As in the Swedish ICBT program, this treatment is provided on a secure website and each step is provided consecutively, that is, the therapist enables further access given that the patient have completed the homework assignments and shown that he or she understand the material. Content wise, this program is very much alike the Swedish ICBT treatment, that is, psychoeducation, cognitive restructuring, and ERP. The Australian ICBT treatment also incorporates additional treatment modules to address comorbid mood and anxiety problems. Another difference compared to the Swedish treatment is that the communication between therapist and patient takes place via the telephone (two scheduled phone calls per week).

The German ICBT treatment was developed by Herbst and colleagues at the University Medical Center Freiburg. The authors describe it as "Internet-based therapist-guided writing therapy" (Herbst et al., 2014). In this treatment, the patient and the therapist have two sessions per week, where they communicate in a treatment platform through text. There is no standardized self-help text, as in the Swedish and Australian ICBT protocols, but the complete treatment rationale is, as in face-to-face CBT, provided through the therapist. However, some text (e.g., the psychoeducation) was very similar for most patients and the therapists therefore reused and standardized some of their communication. The main intervention in this treatment is ERP.

Efficacy of ICBT in Adults with OCD

The Swedish ICBT program was first tested in an open pilot study where 23 adult OCD patients received 15 weeks of treatment (Andersson et al., 2011). Mean symptom duration was 13 years and most patients had received previous treatments for OCD. The majority of participants had education above high school level. The Y-BOCS was administered by a psychiatrist at pre- and posttreatment (there was no data loss), and a large within-group effect-size was observed ($d = 1.56$), with 61% responders (Jacobson and Truax criteria of clinical significant improvement) and 41% were in remission (i.e., not fulfilling the diagnostic criteria of OCD) at posttreatment. In a subsequent randomized trial (Andersson et al., 2012), 101 OCD subjects were randomized to either 10 weeks of ICBT or to control condition consisting of an online support therapy. Most patients were self-referred and blinded assessors conducted the Y-BOCS at posttreatment. Follow-up assessments were also conducted

Table 37.1   Content of the Swedish ICBT treatment manual for adults with OCD

Module 1 CBT and OCD explained	Treatment rationale is presented, including a description of OCD symptoms (obsessions and compulsions), prevalence, and main principles of conducting an online CBT treatment. Different fictional patient characters are introduced (each example represents a specific OCD symptom dimension). The participant has the opportunity to follow one or all four characters (washing, checking, symmetry, or violent thoughts). *Homework: Register OCD symptoms in the Internet platform diary.*
Module 2 Assessing OCD symptoms with the CBT model	The autonomic nervous system and its interaction with OCD symptoms is explained. Participants begin to link obsessions and compulsions to the OCD cycle and learn how to conduct a functional analysis of their OCD problems. Each OCD cycle is presented visually for each example character. *Homework: Continue OCD diary registrations and apply these to the OCD circle.*
Module 3 Cognitive restructuring	Common OCD metacognitions are explained, such as inflated responsibility, absolute need for certainty, thought-action fusion and exaggerated need to control. The focus is to register and discuss meta cognitions with the psychologist from a functional perspective. *Homework: Continue OCD diary registrations and use these registrations to analyze meta cognitions associated with obsessions.*
Module 4 Establish treatment goals and exposure hierarchy	Introduction to Exposure with response prevention (ERP). Different strategies for conducting ERP are explained and examples given of treatment goals and different ways of constructing exposure hierarchies for each example character. *Homework: Register treatment goals and then construct an exposure hierarchy with the information from these goals.*
Module 5 Exposure with response prevention (ERP)	Different aspects of ERP are highlighted, along with common obstacles associated with ERP and how to overcome them. The participant then chooses an ERP exercise at the bottom of the exposure hierarchy. *Homework: Start ERP and report to the psychologist after two days.*
Modules 6–9 ERP exercises	Each module focuses on certain ERP exercises with examples from each treatment character. The text for each module is short (1–2 pages), as the focus is reporting and planning the weekly exposures. *Homework: Conduct daily ERP and report to the psychologist at least once per week.*
Module 10 ERP exercises. Establishing valued directions for further improvements	The modules focus on daily ERP with further exercises added that are adopted from acceptance and commitment therapy. These include establishing valued based goals and how they are applied in daily exposure tasks. The treatment is summarized, and the participant learns the distinction between relapse and setback and further treatment strategies. The participant establishes a relapse prevention program based on his/her valued based goals. *Homework: Continue ERP. Establish valued based goals and applying them in daily exposure exercises. Summarize the treatment and establish a relapse prevention plan.*

4 months after treatment completion. The attrition rate was low (1%) and the average time spent on each patient was about 13 minutes per week. Results showed a significant difference with a large between-group effect size ($d=1.12$) favoring ICBT with 60% responders (Jacobson and Truax criteria of clinical significant improvement). Results were also sustained at the 4-month follow-up.

Similarly, the Australian ICBT program was first tested in an open trial (Wootton et al., 2011a) where 22 patients received 8 weeks of ICBT. As in the Swedish study, most participants (96%) had received previous treatment for OCD. Results showed significant and large effect sizes from pre- to posttreatment ($d=1.52$) and also sustained effects at the 3-month follow-up ($d=1.28$). Eighty-one % of the participants completed all treatment steps and the average total therapist time spent on each patient was 11 minutes per week. Following this, a randomized trial was conducted by the same research group where 56 OCD patients were allocated to either ICBT, bibliotherapy with therapist support (BCBT) or a waitlist control group (Wootton, Dear, Johnston, Terides, & Titov, 2013). Results showed that both the ICBT and BCBT groups made large within-group effect sizes at posttreatment (ICBT, $d=2.16$; bibliotherapy, $d=1.65$) and 3-month follow-up (ICBT, $d=1.28$; bibliotherapy, $d=1.29$), and both treatments were superior to the waiting list group, but no significant differences between ICBT and BCBT. The ICBT intervention required 11 minutes for the therapist per patient/week, on average, whereas the bibliotherapy program required 13 minutes per patient/week.

The German Internet-based therapist-guided writing therapy has been tested in a randomized trial where 34 OCD patients were allocated to either 8 weeks to active treatment or to a waiting list control group (Herbst et al., 2014). Results showed a significant effect favoring the ICBT group with large between group effect sizes ($d=0.83$) on the self-rated version on the Y-BOCS. The mean therapist time in this treatment was substantially higher than the other studies (66 minutes per week).

Long-term Efficacy OF ICBT and Additional Effects by Adding an Internet-based Booster

The Swedish ICBT trial included long-term follow-ups at 4, 7, 12, and 24 months (Andersson et al., 2014). Half of the sample was also, at the 4-month follow-up, randomized to receive a 3-week Internet-based booster in addition to ICBT. The booster treatment in this study followed the same procedure as in the previous studies (i.e., written self-help material, consecutively access, integrated therapist contact, etc.) but the treatment content differed from the original ICBT treatment with more focus on how to maintain treatment gains. More specifically, the treatment consists of three modules that are focused on that the patient would (a) make a retrospective analysis of how the treatment has worked so far, (b) involve a support person (e.g., friend or a relative) in the treatment that can coach and support the patient in continuing ERP, and (c) make a long-term plan and prospective prognosis how to maintain treatment gains. Results showed that all patients who had received ICBT had sustained treatment gains from posttreatment ($d=1.58$–2.09). Furthermore, the booster treatment group made larger improvements on the Y-BOCS than the control group (ICBT without booster) at 7 months but not at 12 or 24 months. The booster group had also better general functioning at 7, 12, and 24 months, with fewer relapses (five relapses in the booster group vs. 15 relapses in the control condition) and also a significantly slower relapse rate in the Kaplan-Mayer analysis. Thus, the effects of ICBT seem to be sustained up to 2 years after completed treatment and adding an Internet-based booster program seems to prevent relapse for some patients.

Cost-effectiveness of ICBT for Adults with OCD

The cost-effectiveness of ICBT was also analyzed using data from cost assessment questionnaires that were obtained in the Swedish wait-list controlled trial (Andersson et al., Submitted manuscript (a)). Results showed that, even when including all societal costs such as health care visits, time of work, medications, etc., ICBT produced one additional remission to a price under $1,300 compared with support therapy. When narrowing the perspective, only including the direct treatment costs of ICBT, the cost for one additional remission was even lower. Thus, it seems that ICBT is not only effective, but may also be a cost-effective treatment.

Predictors and Moderators of ICBT for Adults with OCD

A prediction study was also conducted on the data from the Swedish ICBT trial (Andersson et al., submitted manuscript (b)). Furthermore, as half of the sample received a booster treatment, potential moderators were also investigated. The only stable predictor of immediate positive treatment response was if the patient perceived the therapeutic alliance (measured using the working alliance inventory; Tracey & Kokotovic, 1989) to be good after three weeks of treatment. Patients who had worse outcome at post-treatment had higher baseline OCD symptoms and rated their primary emotions as disgust-related (i.e., not fear or anxiety related). At 24-months, higher levels of pretreatment OCD severity predicted both higher degree of change but also worse end state outcome. Level of education did not predict treatment response.

ICBT for Youths with OCD

The development of ICBT programs for child and adolescent psychiatric problems has lagged considerably behind, compared to the large and ever growing adult ICBT literature (Vigerland et al., 2013).

"BIP OCD" is an ICBT program for adolescents with OCD developed at Karolinska Institutet (Lenhard et al., 2014). In BIP OCD, the youth and his or her parents work through the treatment using a self-help manual provided through a secure Internet platform. The platform is especially designed with age-appropriate appearance, animations, and interactive scripts, and consists of texts to read, films and illustrations as well as different kinds of exercises for the parents to do on their own and together with the adolescent (Figure 37.1). Parents and adolescents have separate login accounts. The treatment is also supported by a therapist through emails, phone calls, and standardized forms within the program. Table 37.2 summarizes the various modules for both the adolescents and their parents.

The efficacy of BIP OCD has been initially tested in an open pilot study by Lenhard and colleagues (2014), where 21 adolescents with OCD (aged 12–17 years) and their

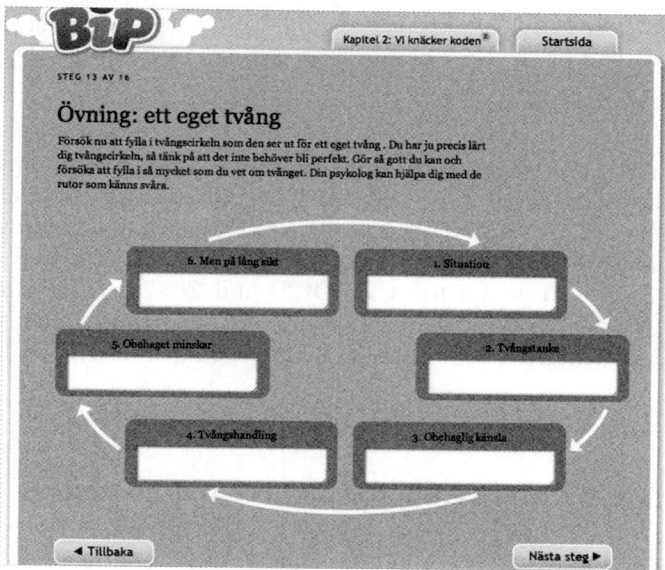

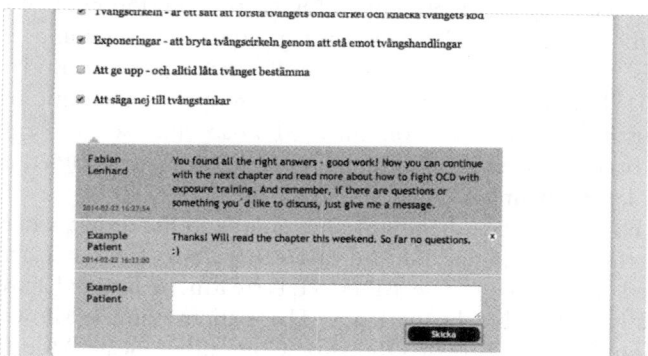

Figure 37.1 Screenshots of animated films and interactive screens in "BIP OCD," an ICBT program for adolescents with OCD

Table 37.2   An overview of "BIP OCD," an ICBT treatment protocol for adolescents with OCD

Treatment phase	Chapter	Parent chapters	Adolescent chapters
Psychoeducation	1	Introduction to ICBT	Introduction to ICBT
	2	About OCD	What is OCD?
	3		We are cracking the code: the OCD circle
	4	Exposure and response prevention	Building a hierarchy
Exposure with response prevention (ERP)	5		Testing exposure
	6	Being an exposure coach	Planning your ERP training
	7		New steps with ERP
	8	When the family has OCD	ERP: frequent problems and solutions
	9		More new steps with ERP
	10		Talking back to OCD: coping with obsessions
Relapse prevention	11		The final sprint
	12		Your treatment in the rear-view mirror

parents (typically the mother) were offered 12 weeks of therapist-supported ICBT. The acceptability of the program was high and the within-group effect sizes from pre- to posttreatment on the Children's Yale–Brown Obsessive-Compulsive Scale (CY-BOCS) (Scahill et al., 1997) were large ($d = 2.29$), with 71% were classified as responders (>35% decrease on the CY-BOCS) and 76% in remission (CY-BOCS score <12) at the 6-month follow-up. Average clinician support time was less than 20 minutes per patient per week. A wait-list controlled trial of BIP OCD is currently underway.

CCBT and ICBT for OC-related Disorders

Although several studies have shown that computer-aided treatments are effective and probably cost-effective in the treatment of OCD, the development of such clinician extenders for other OCD-related conditions lags considerably behind.

BDD-NET is an ICBT treatment specifically developed for Body Dysmorphic Disorder (BDD) (Enander et al., Submitted manuscript) by the same research group at Karolinska Institutet. Thus, the content is BDD-specific (see Table 37.3 for more details), but all other features (i.e., web page design, therapist contact, etc.) are identical to the ICBT treatment for OCD.

The BDD-NET has, to date, been tested in an open pilot study, where 23 patients were recruited through self-referral and assessed face-to-face at a clinic (Enander et al., Submitted manuscript). The BDD-NET treatment lasted 12 weeks and was deemed as highly acceptable by patients. The patient sample showed significant improvements on the Yale–Brown Obsessive Compulsive Scale Modified for BDD (BDD-YBOCS) (Phillips et al., 1997) with a large within-group effect size ($d = 2.01$)

Table 37.3 Description of consecutive treatment modules of "BDD-NET," an ICBT program for patients with BDD

Module	Contents
1	Psychoeducation: introduction the treatment and information about BDD, such as prevalence, known etiology, and common symptoms. Different fictional patient characters are introduced and used as examples to help clarify the treatment components throughout the treatment. Participants begin to register BDD-related behaviors and thoughts in an online diary.
2	A cognitive-behavior conceptualization: explanation of how self-defeating thoughts and BDD-related avoidance and safety behaviors maintain appearance concerns and fears. Participants learn how to conduct a functional analysis of how their own BDD symptoms are maintained.
3	Cognitive restructuring: a more in-depth rationale for how self-defeating thoughts and maladaptive thinking maintains BDD symptoms. Participants evaluate negative thoughts and engage in cognitive restructuring using online worksheets.
4	Exposure and response prevention (ERP): explanation of exposure and different strategies for conducting response prevention is presented. Participants set treatment goals and conduct their first in vivo ERP exercise. ERP continues during the remainder of treatment, and participants continuously assess outcome of ERP using an online worksheet.
5	More on ERP: different aspects of ERP are highlighted and a more in-depth explanation is given on how to work with ERP over time.
6	Values-based behavior change: participants identify values-based long-term goals within the domains of relationships, career, and leisure activities. An accepting stance toward negative thoughts and experiences is proposed as an alternative to attempts to control these experiences, while at the same time engaging in meaningful values-based activities.
7	Difficulties during treatment: commonly encountered difficulties during treatment, such as loss of motivation and problems integrating exercises into daily schedule, are presented and discussed, as well as common obstacles associated with ERP and how to overcome them.
8	Relapse prevention: how to handle relapses into avoidance behaviors and repetitive behavior. The participants also summarize the main lessons learned, what has been gained through the treatment and their future plans.

and 82% responders (defined as ≥30% improvement on the BBD-YBOCS) at post-treatment. These gains were maintained at the 3-month follow-up. Secondary outcome measures of depression, global functioning, and quality of life also showed significant improvements, with moderate to large effect sizes. On average, therapists spent 10 minutes per patient per week providing support. A randomized controlled trial of BDD-NET is currently underway.

DITCH is a private unlisted Yahoo group for people who self-report hoarding difficulties (Muroff, Steketee, Himle, & Frost, 2010). In this Internet group, the patient has electronic access to educational resources on hoarding, which is mainly based on established CBT methods developed by Steketee, Frost, Wincze, Greene, and Douglass (2000) and includes exposure exercises (discarding items) and cognitive restructuring. The users in DITCH are encouraged to read about these interventions and to post behavioral goals and progress at least once per month (e.g., how much sorting and discarding have you done this week?). The patient is coached by other hoarding sufferers who also routinely consult with professional advisors. The DITCH study analyzed self-rated outcomes from 105 active users compared with 155 users in a wait-list. Results showed that all members experienced significant reductions in clutter and hoarding symptoms over 15 months.

StopPulling.com is an Internet-provided interactive self-help program for trichotillomania (Mouton-Odum, Keuthen, Wagener, & Stanley, 2006). In this program, the patient reads about trichotillomania and how to treat it with established CBT techniques. The user is instructed to fill in a daily symptom diary and the program then suggests interventions to these registrations (e.g., how to deal with incompatible behaviors, stimulus control, etc.). This program is not supported by any therapist and costs about $30 per month. Data from the StopPulling.com treatment has also been analyzed from 265 users during the first year of public availability. Results showed significant improvement in symptoms, with about 32% being classified as responders on the self-rated outcome. StopPulling.com has also been tested in a randomized trial, where patients received the treatment for free in a stepped-care model (Rogers et al., 2014). Results showed small ($d = 0.21$) but significant improvements compared with a wait-list control on a clinician-administered outcome measure (Massachusetts General Hospital Hair Pulling Scale) (Keuthen et al., 2007), but not on self-rated measures.

StopPicking.com is an extension of StopPulling.com, but is tailored for patients suffering from skin picking disorder (Flessner, Mouton-Odum, Stocker, & Keuthen, 2007). As in the StopPulling.com treatment, a subscription without any therapist support costs about $30 per month and is based on standardized CBT methods, such as incompatible behavior interventions and stimulus control. Similar analysis was conducted on the StopPicking.com treatment with 372 users and results showed significant improvements with higher responder rates than for trichotillomania (63%). No controlled studies have been published to date.

Summary and Future Directions

Given the obvious shortage of CBT therapists and other barriers to access evidence-based treatment for many psychiatric disorders, there is a growing interest in the development of CCBT and ICBT for these problems. A recent review identified more than 100 RCTS conducted over the last decade (Hedman, Ljotsson, & Lindefors, 2012). OCD is no exception. A body of literature is beginning to emerge that suggests that CCBT and ICBT are highly acceptable to patients, are probably effective, and are cost-effective for adults with OCD. Research into pediatric samples and other OCD-related disorders is lagging considerably behind, but we expect it to grow substantially in the next decade. More definitive trials, using noninferiority or SMART designs, are warranted. Long-term follow-up studies of CCBT/ICBT are rare, and more of them will be needed to establish the maintenance of gains after such interventions. If these interventions survive strict scientific scrutiny, they have great potential to dramatically increase access to evidence-based treatment for these common and undertreated disorders.

CCBT/ICBT has the potential not only to increase access to CBT for those who want treatment but cannot access it, but also to reach people who would not otherwise seek treatment (e.g., due to stigma, practical circumstances, etc.). The literature shows that this represents a very large proportion of all sufferers in the community (Blanco et al., 2006; Griffiths et al., 2006; Marques et al., 2010; Shapiro et al., 2003; Torres et al., 2007; Wootton et al., 2011b).

Computer-aided interventions can help both clinicians and patients in a number of different ways. These interventions are much more accessible for patients and can help overcome logistic barriers, such as geographical distances, travel expenses, etc. Patients can conveniently access their treatment materials around the clock without needing to set up appointments to see their therapists. Many of the CCBT/ICBT programs reviewed in this chapter require considerably less therapist time compared with face-to-face CBT. Thus, CCBT/ICBT is probably a highly cost-effective treatment alternative; clinicians can potentially treat a much larger number of patients at the same time. CCBT/ICBT is also a highly structured treatment in terms of content and context of delivery, and this can minimize the risk of therapist drift (i.e., the therapist and the patient start to talk about other things irrelevant to the specific treatment).

Another promising feature with computer-based interventions is that they can serve as a platform for training therapists. For example, in the Andersson et al. (2012) trial, the therapists were psychology students in their final year of training. Our experience from this trial was that ICBT could provide a good basis for junior therapists to learn the basics of CBT for OCD. It is also easy for the supervisor to monitor the therapist feedback. This is an important issue as there is evidence that inexperienced therapists at Master's level can be as capable of treating OCD as experienced therapists are as long as proper supervision is provided (van Oppen et al., 2010). Thus, ICBT has the potential to serve as a secure and easily accessible education tool.

Does the therapist matter in CCBT/ICBT for OCD? The answer is yes. When comparing treatments that use therapist support compared with unguided treatments (e.g., Tolin et al., 2007) it seems that the therapist provides better treatment effects. However, this is probably not a linear relationship in the sense that more therapist support is always better. As seen in Figure 37.2, both the Australian and the Swedish ICBT trials yielded large effect sizes despite their very minimal therapist input (about 11–13 minutes per patient/week). The exact amount of therapist support needed to achieve the optimal balance between cost and effectiveness will be an important research question for the future.

For whom is CCBT/ICBT suitable? The answer is that we still do not know. Although there has been some research on predictors and moderators of both CCBT and ICBT, it is still to soon to give any definite answers. Our personal experience, from having treated many OCD patients with ICBT, is that it is important that the patients are motivated and have good insight into their difficulties. It is also important to note that most of the trials conducted to date have recruited their patients via advertisement, so it is plausible that patients seeking CCBT/ICBT are somewhat different compared with the patients that clinicians meet at a regular psychiatric clinic. Some research has shown that the source of patient referral may have a bearing on the type of patients seen and the degree of clinical improvement with CCBT/ICBT, with patients referred by mental health professionals having more comorbidity, being less

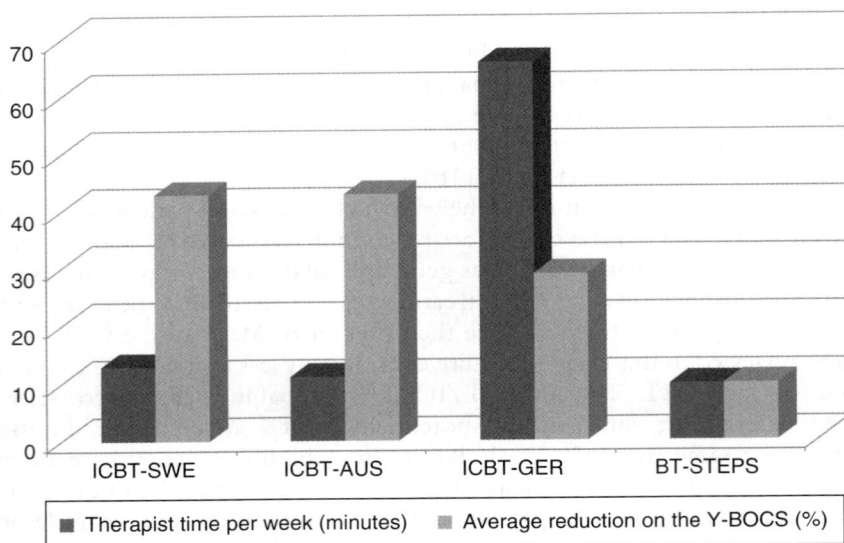

Figure 37.2   Relation between the amount of therapist support and magnitude of improvement in four CCBT/ICBT studies in adults with OCD

motivated for treatment, and achieving more modest outcomes compared with self-referrals or referrals from general practitioners (Mataix-Cols, Cameron, Gega, Kenwright, & Marks, 2006).

   Clearly, CCBT/ICBT should not replace standard care for OCD and related disorders. CCBT/ICBT will not be indicated for all patients and specialist input will be required for complex patients with very severe symptoms, complex comorbidities, absent insight, no motivation for change, or high suicide risk. In this regard, CCBT/ICBT may be particularly useful in the context of a stepped-care model, where moderately complex patients with low risk and high motivation for change are offered CCBT/ICBT in the first instance. Nonresponders or more complex and risky patients are then offered more intensive, clinic-based CBT alone or in combination with medication (Mataix-Cols et al., 2006).

Acknowledgements

We thank our colleagues Jesper Enander, Fabian Lenhard, and Eva Serlachius for kindly providing some of the content for this review.

References

Andersson, G. (2009). Using the Internet to provide cognitive behaviour therapy. *Behaviour Research and Therapy*, *47*(3), 175–180. doi: 10.1016/j.brat.2009.01.010.

Andersson, G., Cuijpers, P., Carlbring, P., & Lindefors, N. (2007). Effects of Internet-delivered cognitive behaviour therapy for anxiety and mood disorders. *Psychiatry*, *2*, 9–14.

Andersson, E., Enander, J., Andrén, P., Hedman, E., Ljótsson, B., Hursti, T., ... Rück, C. (2012). Internet-based cognitive behaviour therapy for obsessive-compulsive disorder: A randomized controlled trial. *Psychological Medicine, 42*(10), 2193–2203. doi: 10.1017/S0033291712000244.

Andersson, E., Hedman, E., Ljótsson, B., Wikström, M., Elveling, E., Lindefors, N., ... Rück, C. (submitted manuscript (a)). Cost-effectiveness of Internet-based cognitive behavior therapy for obsessive-compulsive disorder: Results from a randomized controlled trial.

Andersson, E., Ljótsson, B., Hedman, E., Enander, J., Kaldo, V., Andersson, G., ... Rück, C. (submitted manuscript (b)). Predictors and moderators of Internet-based cognitive behavior therapy for obsessive-compulsive disorder: Results from a randomized trial.

Andersson, E., Ljótsson, B., Hedman, E., Kaldo, V., Paxling, B., Andersson, G., ... Rück, C. (2011). *Internet-based cognitive behavior therapy for obsessive compulsive disorder: A pilot study. BMC Psychiatry, 11.* doi: 10.1186/1471-244X-11-125.

Andersson, E., Steneby, S., Karlsson, K., Ljótsson, B., Hedman, E., Enander, J., ... Rück, C. (2014). Long-term efficacy of Internet-based cognitive behavior therapy for obsessive-compulsive disorder with or without booster: A randomized controlled trial *Psychological Medicine*, 1–11. doi: 10.1017/S0033291714000543.

Andersson, G., & Titov, N. (2014). Advantages and limitations of Internet-based interventions for common mental disorders. *World Psychiatry, 13*(1), 4–11. doi: 10.1002/wps.20083.

Bachofen, M., Nakagawa, A., Marks, I. M., Park, J. M., Greist, J. H., Baer, L., ... Dottl, S. L. (1999a). Home self-assessment and self-treatment of obsessive-compulsive disorder using a manual and a computer-conducted telephone interview: Replication of a UK–US study. *Journal of Clinical Psychiatry, 60*(8), 545–549.

Bachofen, M., Nakagawa, A., Marks, I. M., Park, J. M., Greist, J. H., Baer, L., ... Dottl, S. L. (1999b). Home self-assessment and self-treatment of obsessive-compulsive disorder using a manual and a computer-conducted telephone interview: Replication of a UK–US study. *Journal of Clinical Psychiatry, 60*(8), 545–549.

Baer, L., Minichiello, W. E., & Jenike, M. A. (1987). Use of a portable-computer program in behavioral treatment of obsessive-compulsive disorder. *American Journal of Psychiatry, 144*(8), 1101.

Blanco, C., Olfson, M., Stein, D. J., Simpson, H. B., Gameroff, M. J., & Narrow, W. H. (2006). Treatment of obsessive-compulsive disorder by US psychiatrists. *Journal of Clinical Psychiatry, 67*(6), 946–951.

Clark, A., Kirkby, K. C., Daniels, B. A., & Marks, I. M. (1998). A pilot study of computer-aided vicarious exposure for obsessive-compulsive disorder. *Australian and New Zealand Journal of Psychiatry, 32*(2), 268–275.

Enander, J., Ivanov, Z. V., Andersson, E., Mataix-Cols, D., Ljótsson, B., & Rück, C. (Submitted manuscript). Therapist-guided Internet-based cognitive behavioral therapy for Body Dysmorphic Disorder (BDD-NET): A feasibility study.

Flessner, C. A., Mouton-Odum, S., Stocker, A. J., & Keuthen, N. J. (2007). StopPicking.com: Internet-based treatment for self-injurious skin picking. *Dermatology Online Journal, 13*(4).

Fullana, M. A., Mataix-Cols, D., Caspi, A., Harrington, H., Grisham, J. R., Moffitt, T. E., & Poulton, R. (2009). Obsessions and compulsions in the community: Prevalence, interference, help-seeking, developmental stability, and co-occurring psychiatric conditions. *American Journal of Psychiatry, 166*(3), 329–336. doi: 10.1176/appi.ajp.2008.08071006.

Gava, I., Barbui, C., Aguglia, E., Carlino, D., Churchill, R., De Vanna, M., & McGuire, H. F. (2007). Psychological treatments versus treatment as usual for obsessive compulsive disorder (OCD). *Cochrane Database Systematic Review* (2), CD005333. doi: 10.1002/14651858.CD005333.pub2.

Gega, L., Marks, I., & Mataix-Cols, D. (2004). Computer-aided CBT self-help for anxiety and depressive disorders: Experience of a London clinic and future directions. *Journal of Clinical Psychology, 60*(2), 147–157. doi: 10.1002/jclp.10241.

Gellatly, J., Bower, P., McMillan, D., Roberts, C., Byford, S., Bee, P., ... Lovell, K. (2014). Obsessive Compulsive Treatment Efficacy Trial (OCTET) comparing the clinical and cost effectiveness of self-managed therapies: Study protocol for a randomised controlled trial. *Trials, 15*, 278. doi: 10.1186/1745-6215-15-278.

Goodman, W. K., Price, L. H., Rasmussen, S. A., Mazure, C., Fleischmann, R. L., Hill, C. L., ... Charney, D. S. (1989). The Yale–Brown Obsessive Compulsive Scale – I: Development, use, and reliability. *Archives of General Psychiatry, 46*(11), 1006–1011.

Greist, J. H., Marks, I. M., Baer, L., Kobak, K. A., Wenzel, K. W., Hirsch, M. J., ... Clary, C. M. (2002). Behavior therapy for obsessive-compulsive disorder guided by a computer or by a clinician compared with relaxation as a control. *Journal of Clinical Psychiatry, 63*(2), 138–145.

Greist, J. H., Marks, I. M., Baer, L., Parkin, J. R., Manzo, P. A., Mantle, J. M., á Forman, L. (1998). Self-treatment for obsessive compulsive disorder using a manual and a computerized telephone interview: A US–UK study. *MD Computing, 15*(3), 149–157.

Griffiths, F., Lindenmeyer, A., Powell, J., Lowe, P., & Thorogood, M. (2006). Why are health care interventions delivered over the internet? A systematic review of the published literature. *Journal of Medical Internet Research, 8*(2), e10. doi: v8i2e10 [pii]10.2196/jmir.8.2.e10.

Hedman, E., Ljotsson, B., & Lindefors, N. (2012). Cognitive behavior therapy via the Internet: A systematic review of applications, clinical efficacy and cost-effectiveness. *Expert Review of Pharmacoeconomics & Outcomes Research, 12*(6), 745–764. doi: 10.1586/erp.12.67.

Herbst, N., Voderholzer, U., Thiel, N., Schaub, R., Knaevelsrud, C., Stracke, S., ... Kulz, A. K. (2014). No talking, just writing! Efficacy of an Internet-based cognitive behavioral therapy with exposure and response prevention in obsessive compulsive disorder. *Psychotherapy and Psychosomatics, 83*(3), 165–175. doi: 10.1159/000357570.

Himle, J. A., Fischer, D. J., Muroff, J. R., Van Etten, M. L., Lokers, L. M., Abelson, J. L., & Hanna, G. L. (2006). Videoconferencing-based cognitive-behavioral therapy for obsessive-compulsive disorder. *Behaviour Research and Therapy, 44*(12), 1821–1829. doi: 10.1016/j.brat.2005.12.010.

Kenwright, M., Marks, I., Graham, C., Franses, A., & Mataix-Cols, D. (2005). Brief scheduled phone support from a clinician to enhance computer-aided self-help for obsessive-compulsive disorder: Randomized controlled trial. *Journal of Clinical Psychology, 61*(12), 1499–1508. doi: 10.1002/jclp.20204.

Keuthen, N. J., Flessner, C. A., Woods, D. W., Franklin, M. E., Stein, D. J., Cashin, S. E., & Trichotillomania Learning Center Scientific Advisory Board. (2007). Factor analysis of the Massachusetts General Hospital Hairpulling Scale. *Journal of Psychosomatic Research, 62*(6), 707–709. doi: 10.1016/j.jpsychores.2006.12.003.

Lenhard, F., Vigerland, S., Andersson, E., Ruck, C., Mataix-Cols, D., Thulin, U., ... Serlachius, E. (2014). Internet-delivered cognitive behavior therapy for adolescents with obsessive-compulsive disorder: An open trial. *PLoS One, 9*(6), e100773. doi: 10.1371/journal.pone.0100773.

Lovell, K., & Bee, P. (2011). Optimising treatment resources for OCD: a review of the evidence base for technology-enhanced delivery. *Journal of Mental Health, 20*(6), 525–542. doi: 10.3109/09638237.2011.608745.

Marks, I., & Cavanagh, K. (2009). Computer-aided psychological treatments: Evolving issues. *Annual Review of Clinical Psychology, 5*, 121–141. doi: 10.1146/annurev.clinpsy.032408.153538.

Marks, I. M., Kenwright, M., McDonough, M., Whittaker, M., & Mataix-Cols, D. (2004). Saving clinicians' time by delegating routine aspects of therapy to a computer: A randomized controlled trial in phobia/panic disorder. *Psychological Medicine, 34*(1), 9–17.

Marks, I. M., Mataix-Cols, D., Kenwright, M., Cameron, R., Hirsch, S., & Gega, L. (2003). Pragmatic evaluation of computer-aided self-help for anxiety and depression. *British Journal of Psychiatry, 183*, 57–65.

Marques, L., LeBlanc, N. J., Weingarden, H. M., Timpano, K. R., Jenike, M., & Wilhelm, S. (2010). Barriers to treatment and service utilization in an internet sample of individuals with obsessive-compulsive symptoms. *Depression and Anxiety, 27*(5), 470–475. doi: 10.1002/da.20694.

Mataix-Cols, D., Cameron, R., Gega, L., Kenwright, M., & Marks, I. M. (2006). Effect of referral source on outcome with cognitive-behavior therapy self-help. *Comprehensive Psychiatry, 47*(4), 241–245. doi: 10.1016/j.comppsych.2005.11.007.

Mataix-Cols, D., & Marks, I. M. (2006). Self-help with minimal therapist contact for obsessive-compulsive disorder: A review. *European Psychiatry, 21*(2), 75–80. doi: 10.1016/j.eurpsy.2005.07.003.

Mataix-Cols, D., Marks, I. M., Greist, J. H., Kobak, K. A., & Baer, L. (2002). Obsessive-compulsive symptom dimensions as predictors of compliance with and response to behaviour therapy: Results from a controlled trial. *Psychotherapy and Psychosomatics, 71*(5), 255–262.

McCrone, P., Marks, I. M., Greist, J. H., Baer, L., Kobak, K. A., Wenzel, K. W., & Hirsch, M. J. (2007). Cost-effectiveness of computer-aided behaviour therapy for obsessive-compulsive disorder. *Psychotherapy and Psychosomatics, 76*(4), 249–250. doi: 10.1159/000101504.

Mouton-Odum, S., Keuthen, N. J., Wagener, P. D., & Stanley, M. A. (2006). StopPulling.com: An Interactive, self-help program for trichotillomania. *Cognitive and Behavioral Practice, 13*(3), 215–226. doi: 10.1016/j.cbpra.2005.05.004.

Muroff, J., Steketee, G., Himle, J., & Frost, R. (2010). Delivery of internet treatment for compulsive hoarding (D.I.T.C.H.). *Behaviour Research and Therapy, 48*(1), 79–85. doi: 10.1016/j.brat.2009.09.006.

National Institute for Clinical Excellence (NICE). (2005, November). Obsessive-compulsive disorder: Core interventions in the treatment of obsessive-compulsive disorder and body dysmorphic disorder. Retrieved from http://publications.nice.org.uk/obsessive-compulsive-disorder-cg31/guidance.

Phillips, K. A., Hollander, E., Rasmussen, S. A., Aronowitz, B. R., DeCaria, C., & Goodman, W. K. (1997). A severity rating scale for body dysmorphic disorder: Development, reliability, and validity of a modified version of the Yale–Brown Obsessive Compulsive Scale. *Psychopharmacology Bulletin, 33*(1), 17–22.

Rogers, K., Banis, M., Falkenstein, M. J., Malloy, E. J., McDonough, L., Nelson, S. O., … Haaga, D. A. (2014). Stepped care in the treatment of trichotillomania. *Journal of Consulting and Clinical Psychology, 82*(2), 361–367. doi: 10.1037/a0035744.

Rosa-Alcazar, A. I., Sanchez-Meca, J., Gomez-Conesa, A., & Marin-Martinez, F. (2008). Psychological treatment of obsessive-compulsive disorder: A meta-analysis. *Clinical Psychology Review, 28*(8), 1310–1325. doi: 10.1016/j.cpr.2008.07.001.

Scahill, L., Riddle, M. A., McSwiggin-Hardin, M., Ort, S. I., King, R. A., Goodman, W. K., … Leckman, J. F. (1997). Children's Yale–Brown Obsessive Compulsive Scale: Reliability and validity. *Journal of the American Academy of Child and Adolescent Psychiatry, 36*(6), 844–852. doi: 10.1097/00004583-199706000-00023.

Shapiro, D. A., Cavanagh, K., & Lomas, H. (2003). Geographic inequity in the availability of cognitive behavioural therapy in England and Wales. *Behavioural and Cognitive Psychotherapy, 31*(02), 185–192. doi: 10.1017/S1352465803002066.

Steketee, G., Frost, R. O., Wincze, J., Greene, K.., & Douglass, H. (2000). Group and individual treatment of compulsive hoarding: *A pilot study Behavioural and Cognitive Psychotherapy, 28*(3), 259–268.

Tolin, D. F., Hannan, S., Maltby, N., Diefenbach, G. J., Worhunsky, P., & Brady, R. E. (2007). A randomized controlled trial of self-directed versus therapist-directed cognitive-behavioral therapy for obsessive-compulsive disorder patients with prior medication trials. *Journal of Behavior Therapy, 38*(2), 179–191. doi: 10.1016/j.beth.2006.07.001.

Torres, A. R., Prince, M. J., Bebbington, P. E., Bhugra, D. K., Brugha, T. S., Farrell, M., … Singleton, N. (2007). Treatment seeking by individuals with obsessive-compulsive disorder from the British psychiatric morbidity survey of 2000. *Psychiatric Services, 58*(7), 977–982. doi: 58/7/977 [pii]10.1176/appi.ps.58.7.977.

Tracey, T. J., & Kokotovic, A. M. (1989). Factor structure of the Working Alliance Inventory. *Psychological Assessment, 1*(3), 207–210.

van Oppen, P., van Balkom, A. J., Smit, J. H., Schuurmans, J., van Dyck, R., & Emmelkamp, P. M. (2010). Does the therapy manual or the therapist matter most in treatment of obsessive-compulsive disorder? A randomized controlled trial of exposure with response or ritual prevention in 118 patients. *Journal of Clinical Psychiatry, 71*(9), 1158–1167. doi: 10.4088/JCP.08m04990blu.

Vigerland, S., Thulin, U., Ljotsson, B., Svirsky, L., Ost, L. G., Lindefors, N., ... Serlachius, E. (2013). Internet-delivered CBT for children with specific phobia: A pilot study. *Cognitive Behavior Therapy, 42*(4), 303–314. doi: 10.1080/16506073.2013.844201.

Vogel, P. A., Launes, G., Moen, E. M., Solem, S., Hansen, B., Haland, A. T., & Himle, J. A. (2012). Videoconference- and cell phone-based cognitive-behavioral therapy of obsessive-compulsive disorder: A case series. *Journal of Anxiety Disorders, 26*(1), 158–164. doi: 10.1016/j.janxdis.2011.10.009.

Wootton, B. M., Dear, B. F., Johnston, L., Terides, M. D., & Titov, N. (2013). Remote treatment of obsessive-compulsive disorder: A randomized controlled trial. *Journal of Obsessive-Compulsive and Related Disorders, 2*(4), 375–384. doi: 10.1016/j.jocrd.2013.07.002.

Wootton, B. M., Titov, N., Dear, B. F., Spence, J., Andrews, G., Johnston, L., & Solley, K. (2011a). An Internet administered treatment program for obsessive-compulsive disorder: A feasibility study. *Journal of Anxiety Disorders, 25*(8), 1102–1107. doi: 10.1016/j.janxdis.2011.07.009.

Wootton, B. M., Titov, N., Dear, B. F., Spence, J., & Kemp, A. (2011b). The acceptability of Internet-based treatment and characteristics of an adult sample with obsessive compulsive disorder: An Internet survey. *PLoS One, 6*(6), e20548. doi: 10.1371/journal.pone.0020548.

38

Neurosurgical Treatments for Obsessive Compulsive Disorder

Sarah M. Fayad and Herbert E. Ward

Neurosurgery for psychiatric disorders has a long, tenuous history, which has changed significantly in the past decade. Psychosurgery began in 1935 with prefrontal lobotomy for psychoses and the Nobel Prize for Physiology or Medicine awarded to Antonio Egas Moniz for his work in this (NobelPrize.org). This procedure was later adapted by Walter Freeman and became infamous (Diefenbach, Diefenbach, Baumeister, & West, 1999). It later lost favor due to lack of evidence about its efficacy, poorly defined clinical indications, and a multitude of severe side effects (Mashour, Walker, & Martuza, 2005). round the same time that Moniz won the Nobel Prize for the prefrontal lobotomy, psychosurgery was transitioning to a different era, with new procedures as well as a new name: *functional neurosurgery for psychiatric disease* (Mashour et al., 2005).

The excessive and often inappropriate use of prefrontal lobotomy that was popularized by Walter Freeman and later criticized and condemned made it difficult for functional neurosurgery for psychiatric disease to become successful.

In the late 1940s, stereotactic neurosurgical devices were developed (Spiegel, Wycis, Marks, & Lee, 1947). Figure 38.1 demonstrates a picture of a modern stereotactic neurosurgical device in use. These devices and stereotactic surgery allowed patients to have lesions much more precisely targeted and led to less morbidity and mortality (Mashour et al., 2005). The targeting for specific brain structures related to emotion were clarified through the work done by Papez (1937), which was further explored and confirmed by MacLean (1949). Despite these advances, society remained wary of surgery for psychiatric disease, and a prolonged ethical debate regarding the use of surgery for psychiatric indications ensued. The National Commission for the Protection of Human Subjects of Biomedical and Behavioral Research evaluated this, and later provided a report supporting the use of neurosurgery and providing guidelines for the appropriate use of functional neurosurgery for psychiatric conditions in 1977 (Culliton, 1976). This chapter will focus on the use of neurosurgical procedures for severe treatment refractory OCD. It is thought that up to 10% of patients with OCD will fit in this category despite numerous therapeutic trials of pharmacotherapy and intensive cognitive behavioral therapy (CBT) (Skoog & Skoog, 1999; Steketee, Frost, & Cohen, 1998).

The Wiley Handbook of Obsessive Compulsive Disorders, Volume I, First Edition.
Edited by Jonathan S. Abramowitz, Dean McKay, and Eric A. Storch.
© 2017 John Wiley & Sons Ltd. Published 2017 by John Wiley & Sons Ltd.

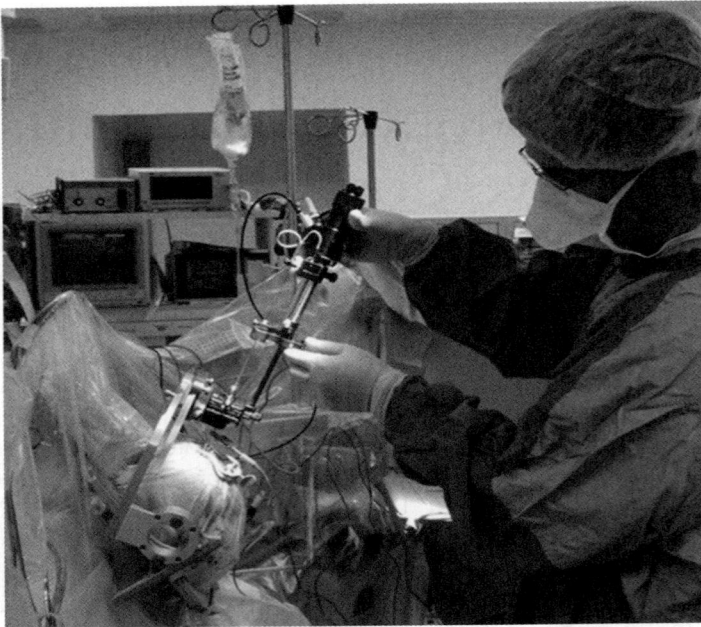

Figure 38.1   A stereotactic device in use in the operating room for placement of deep brain stimulation (DBS) electrodes

Neurocircuitry of Obsessive-Compulsive Disorder

It is important to have a general understanding of neuroanatomical models prior to consideration of the literature regarding functional neurosurgery for OCD. There has been a multitude of different hypotheses used to explain the pathophysiology of obsessive-compulsive disorder (OCD). These are generally based on phenomenology and include abnormalities in cognitive flexibility (Bradbury, Cassin, & Rector, 2011), reversal learning (Chamberlain et al., 2008), and reward processing and error recognition (Figee et al., 2011; Huey et al., 2008), emotion, and motivation (Aouizerate et al., 2004). There are, however, other theories that are based on neuroimaging and surgical experience. The most widely accepted of these theories involves the cortico-striato-thalmo-cortical circuit (CSTC). This was described by Alexander and colleagues, who detailed their hypothesis of thalamo-cortical loops with different functions (Alexander, Crutcher, & DeLong, 1990; Alexander, DeLong, & Strick, 1986). It has since been further expanded on by multiple investigators (Baxter, 2003; Insel, 1992; Modell, Mountz, Curtis, & Greden, 1989; Saxena, Brody, Schwartz, & Baxter, 1998). Brain structures thought to have the most significant role in the pathophysiology of OCD include the orbitofrontal cortex (OFC), thalamus, caudate nucleus and the anterior cingulate cortex. Others have postulated that the Papez circuit and basal ganglia circuits may have important roles (Kopell, Greenberg, & Rezai, 2004; Rauch, 2003; Saxena & Rauch, 2000).

Candidate Selection for Neurosurgery for OCD

Prior to being considered as a candidate for neurosurgery for OCD, several factors must be considered. The first consideration is confirmation of diagnosis and assessment of the severity of symptoms. Patients should be assessed using the Yale–Brown Obsessive-Compulsive Scale (YBOCS) (Goodman et al., 1989). Some posit that the YBOCS score should be a minimum of 28–30, indicating severe to extreme symptoms, in order to qualify for neurosurgery (Goodman et al., 1989). It is imperative that all candidates demonstrate treatment refractoriness to both pharmacotherapy and CBT (Ferrao et al., 2007; Giacobbe, Mayberg, & Lozano, 2009). Candidates should have been treated with an adequate dose of medication for a minimum of 10–12 weeks in order for a trial with a medication to be considered adequate (Koran, Hanna, Hollander, Nestadt, & Simpson, 2007). Many patients will require higher doses of serotonin reuptake inhibitors (SRIs) than are used to treat depression in order to achieve response, therefore, a thorough medication history should be obtained (Pallanti, Hollander, & Goodman, 2004). To be considered treatment refractory, a candidate should have failed at least two trials of SRIs for appropriate duration and at an appropriate dose with no response to treatment (Pallanti et al., 2004). In recent trials of deep brain stimulation (DBS) for OCD (Goodman et al., 2010), eligible candidates had to have failed an adequate trial (a minimum of 10 weeks of treatment at a maximally tolerated dose) of clomipramine and two selective serotonin reuptake inhibitors (SSRIs). Candidates must also have failed at least 25 hours of exposure and response prevention (ERP) by an expert therapist. In addition, augmentation with at least two agents in the following group led to no treatment response: clonazepam, haloperidol, risperidone, olanzapine, gabapentin. Treatment refractory symptoms must have been present for at least 5 years after the age of 18 and led to significant suffering as well as a marked decrease in functioning (Goodman et al., 2010).

Candidates for surgery should also be carefully screened for comorbidities that would predispose them to worse outcomes postoperatively (Bernal-Pacheco et al., 2013; Goodman et al., 2010; Okun et al., 2011). In one study (Goodman et al., 2010), exclusion criteria included a prior diagnosis of bipolar disorder or a psychotic disorder, substance use disorder in the previous 6 months, active suicidality, comorbid Axis II pathology from Clusters A or B, and brain pathology, including neurodegenerative disorders, strokes, tumors, or previous neurosurgical procedures.

Experts propose careful evaluation of potential candidates for DBS for OCD in an expert, multidisciplinary setting (Tierney, Abd-El-Barr, Stanford, Foote, & Okun, 2014) that is able to ensure thorough screening and follow up of this patient population. This will also allow for more structured pre-operative assessments and standardized outcomes. As neurosurgery for psychiatric disorders remains in its infancy, it is important that strict ethical standards are upheld and that those involved in the multidisciplinary evaluation use a standardized assessment with consistent rating scales.

At the current time, most patients will be implanted under a research protocol or Investigational Device Exemption (IDE). However, in 2009, the FDA approved a Humanitarian Device Exemption (HDE) for DBS for OCD. The HDE was established in the 1990s in an effort to foster device development for orphan conditions that might not attract industry attention. The HDE for DBS for OCD allows for implantation of DBS in the same patient population, however, the patient does not have to be part of a research protocol. However, the approval of the HDE for DBS OCD has drawn criticism (Fins et al., 2011). Fins and colleagues have posed several different concerns regarding this exemption, citing that it may be due to corporate motivations and could lead to inadequate research, as well as a therapeutic misconception. The term therapeutic misconception was coined originally by Applebaum and colleagues as a situation in which subjects are led to believe that investigational interventions are equivalent to established therapy (Appelbaum, Roth, & Lidz, 1982; Lidz, Appelbaum, Grisso, & Renaud, 2004).

Stereotactical Neurosurgery

The first subcortical stereotactic procedure was performed in the late 1940s by Wycis and Spiegel (Spiegel et al., 1947). This procedure was pioneering and led to the development of a model for neurosurgery for psychiatric disorders. Stereotactic surgery involves a specific coordinate system in which the brain is referenced in a three-dimensional Cartesian space (Lapidus, Kopell, Ben-Haim, Rezai, & Goodman, 2013). This is used to help surgeons accurately reach subcortical structures while minimizing destruction of brain tissue. There are four stereotactic procedures for severe, treatment refractory OCD. These are the anterior cingulotomy, anterior capsulotomy, subcaudate tractotomy, and limbic leucotomy (Mashour et al., 2005). The subcaudate tractotomy is no longer being used clinically (Lapidus et al., 2013).

Anterior Cingulotomy

The anterior cingulotomy was developed by Whitty and colleagues (Whitty, Duffield, Tov, & Cairns, 1952), and involved the bilateral removal of a small section of the anterior cingulate gyrus. Later, in the early 1960s, Ballantine introduced a modification of the procedure and instead used thermocoagulation (Ballantine, Bouckoms, Thomas, & Giriunas, 1987). The modern procedure involves the use of magnetic resonance imaging (MRI) guidance to aid in localization to make very small lesions in the anterior cingulate gyrus. This procedure is thought to work by interrupting neurocircuitry associated with the CSTC loop, and is the most widely performed neurosurgery for psychiatric conditions performed in Canada and the United States (Lapidus et al., 2013).

It has historically been quite difficult to assess in a scientifically rigorous fashion the efficacy of these procedures due to ethical concerns about using sham studies. However, a relatively large study involving more than 60 patients at Massachusetts General Hospital (Sheth et al., 2013), found that more than half of patients exhibited a full response to surgery. This was defined as a reduction in YBOCS of greater than or equal to 35% along with a clinical global improvement score of less than or equal to 2. A large percentage of patients who did not respond underwent additional neurosurgical procedures. Approximately 59% of these patients then achieved treatment response. Other studies have found similar rates of response (Greenberg et al., 2003; Kim et al., 2003). An important limitation of these open trial studies is that they do not control for factors such as the expectation of improvement and the passage of time (e.g., placebo effects). Thus, whether improvement is directly related to the surgical procedures themselves cannot be verified.

Importantly, there have been no deaths reported in a large cohort of more than 1,000 patients treated using these procedures at Massachusetts General Hospital (Sadock, Sadaock, & Ruiz, 2009). There was no increase in adverse events such as seizures or hydrocephalus when compared with other stereotactic procedures. In addition, unlike lobotomy, there have been no permanent cognitive or psychiatric deficits noted in patients undergoing cingulotomy for OCD (Greenberg et al., 2003).

Anterior Capsulotomy

This procedure began to be used for treatment refractory psychiatric conditions in the late 1940s (Lapidus et al., 2013). The lesion can be created by either radiofrequency or gamma radiation and lies around the level of the foramen of Monro in the anterior limb of the internal capsule. Its mechanism of action is hypothesized to be the interruption of ventral fibers that travel across the anterior internal capsule from the orbitofrontal cortex (OFC) and subgenual anterior cingulate cortex (ACC) to thalamic nuclei (Lapidus et al., 2013).

Response rates for capsulotomy range from approximately 48% to 78% (Greenberg et al., 2003) and is thought to be tolerated well. No deaths have been reported that were directly associated with the procedure (Lapidus et al., 2013). However, there were four patients who made their first attempt at suicide following this procedure and one completed suicide reported postoperatively (Ruck et al., 2008). In addition, many patients experience a weight gain in the first year postoperatively and others developed apathy, cognitive dysfunction, and even sexual disinhibition (Ruck et al., 2008).

Subcaudate Tractotomy

This procedure is no longer used as frequently due to the prevalence of the anterior cingulotomy and capsulotomy. It was performed for the first time in London in the early 1960s by Knight, who sought to interrupt fibers in the white matter fasciculus directly below the head of the caudate nucleus (Knight, 1965). It initially involved the placement of an isotope to produce the lesion, however, this has since been replaced by radiofrequency thermocoagulation (Malhi & Bartlett, 2000). This procedure is thought to relieve symptoms by interrupting the tracts connecting the OFC and subcortical structures such as the subgenual ACC, striatum, thalamus, and amygdala (Feldman, Alterman, & Goodrich, 2001). It was initially used in the treatment of major depression. Response rates for this procedure in patients with OCD were very similar to that of the anterior cingulotomy, nearing 50% (Greenberg et al., 2003). In addition, the majority of side effects were transient and low intensity. However, there have been reports of lasting personality changes and seizures in patients receiving this procedure (Greenberg et al., 2003). Personality changes were not confirmed in a subsequent study (Bridges et al., 1994).

Limbic Leukotomy

In 1973, Kelly and colleagues (Kelly, Richardson, & Mitchell-Heggs, 1973) developed this procedure in an effort to combine the effects of the anterior cingulotomy and subcaudate tractotomy. Given the fact that it does involve two separate areas, it involves a larger area of brain tissue that is lesioned when compared with the afore-mentioned procedures. This procedure is thought to be effective by interrupting fibers in the frontothalamic loop as well as in the Papez circuit (Lapidus et al., 2013). Efficacy is quite high with this procedure: Mitchell-Heggs, Kelly, and Richardson conducted a study of 66 patients and found that 73% were clinically improved at 6 weeks and 76% were improved at 16 months. At that time, they reported 89% of patients with obsessional neurosis showing improvement at 16 months (Mitchell-Heggs, Kelly, & Richardson, 1976). Another study found that 61% of patients with OCD were responders to the limbic leukotomy (Mindus, Rasmussen, & Lindquist, 1994). Again, caution is warranted in interpreting the results of these studies as they are not controlled trials. There have only rare occurrences of long-term side effects with this procedure; most side effects, such as headache, fatigue, perseveration are transient (Jenike, 1998). Some patients were noted to lose weight postoperatively.

Deep Brain Stimulation

Deep brain stimulation (DBS) has been established as an effective, safe treatment in movement disorders such as Parkinson's disease (PD) and Essential Tremor (ET) (Gross & Lozano, 2000). However, the use of this treatment in psychiatric disorders remains experimental. Nuttin and colleagues first described the use of DBS in patients with OCD (Nuttin, Cosyns, Demeulemeester, Gybels, & Meyerson, 1999). They targeted the anterior limb of the internal capsule based on results from bilateral anterior capsulotomy in four patients with treatment-resistant OCD. They found that three of these patients received at minimum, a partial benefit from the procedure (Nuttin et al., 1999). This pioneering procedure opened the door for additional investigation into this procedure which is both reversible and adjustable (Lapidus et al., 2013). Since that time, there have been four controlled studies examining the efficacy and safety of DBS in patients with treatment refractory OCD (Denys et al., 2010; Goodman et al., 2010; Huff et al., 2010; Mallet et al., 2008). The neuroanatomical targets for these procedures have varied and the procedure remains experimental, however, preliminary results have been promising. Table 38.1 shows the trials with more than one patient that have been conducted thus far, along with the neuroanatomical target and average change in Y-BOCS from baseline. We will further discuss efficacy and safety associated with the various DBS targets for treatment refractory OCD.

Anterior Limb of Internal Capsule and Ventral Capsule/Ventral Striatum

These two anatomical areas are relatively large (Morishita et al., 2014) and very close in location. This area was selected due to previous work in ablation of the anterior capsule. It is thought that this neuroanatomical region is helpful in ameliorating symptoms of OCD due to the placement of CSTC network fibers that course through the region. Greenberg and colleagues suggest that this region may be an easily accessible target for DBS modulation (Greenberg et al., 2010). It should be noted that with more recent studies, the exact target has migrated posteriorly due to observation of clinical results and lead placement.

Data taken from key multicenter studies have shown significant improvement in a treatment refractory population in symptoms of OCD. Recent data has shown close to

Table 38.1   Multi-patient studies of deep brain stimulation for OCD

Target	Author (Year)	N	Months follow up	Reduction in Y-BOCS to baseline (%)
ALIC	Abelson et al. (2005)	4	4–23	50% with no improvement. 25% with 36% reduction. 25% with 73% reduction.
VC/VS	Cosyns, Gabriels, and Nuttin (2003)	6	None	Average of 31.7%.
VC/VS	Greenberg et al. (2006)	10	36	34% overall. 40% of patients with more than 35% reduction.
VC/VS	Denys et al. (2010)	16	21	Average of 51.9%.
VC/VS	Greenberg et al. (2010)	26	3–36	Average of 61.5% of patients with more than 35% improvement.
VC/VS	Goodman et al. (2010)	6	12	Average of 46.7%.
Unilateral Nacc	Huff et al. (2010)	10	12	Average of 28%.
STN	Mallet et al. (2008)	16	3	Average of 32.1%.
STN	Chabardes et al. (2013)	4	6	Average of 64.5%.
ITP	Jimenez-Ponce et al. (2009)	5	12	Average of 49.1%.
ITP	Jimenez et al. (2013)*	6	36	Average of 62.9%.

Abbreviations: ALIC = anterior limb of internal capsule; VC/VS = ventral capsule/ventral striatum; Unilateral Nacc = unilateral nucleus accumbens; STN = subthalamic nucleus; ITP = inferior thalamic peduncle.
* In this study, three patients dropped out by the end of the study due to death by overdose on drugs, death by tuberculosis infection, and one who was lost to follow up.

an 80% response rate and an overall decrease of 60% in the YBOCS score (Lapidus et al., 2013). These studies have also shown improvement in depression and anxiety (Goodman et al., 2010; Greenberg et al., 2010). In addition, global functioning (GAF) improved significantly over time, with an average of an approximate 20-point increase in GAF.

Serious side effects included two small hemorrhages without permanent sequelae, a wound infection, hardware breakage, and a seizure. All these sequelae were managed with either medication or replacement hardware. There were also adverse effects on psychiatric symptoms in some patients, including reports of depression and suicidal ideation in patients with similar episodes prior to the procedure, stimulation-induced mania/hypomania, and possible worsening of OCD severity. It should be noted that one case of increased OCD severity coincided with the device's stimulation being turned off. Thorough scientific study of these results is difficult as many patients were in open-label studies without an adequate blind. Therefore, it is impossible to exclude a possible placebo effect in the reported results. It is, however, thought that the results seen are not the result of a microlesion effect, as patients whose devices are unexpectedly or unknowingly turned to an off stimulation state experience worsening of OCD symptoms which can be dramatic at times (Greenberg et al., 2010).

Unilateral Nucleus Accumbens

DBS for OCD in the region of the nucleus accumbens was first reported by Sturm and colleagues (Sturm et al., 2003). This study demonstrated the most benefit when the right nucleus accumbens was stimulated and noted no additional benefit with bilateral stimulation. It was later studied in a unilateral configuration based on these data (Huff et al., 2010). These investigators felt that this region of the brain was a promising target for DBS due to its role in modulating circuits thought to be associated with OCD pathology. They reported that due to the position of the electrode and trajectories used, it would also have action on the fibers of the internal capsule. This study found the procedure to have a similar efficacy to other DBS OCD studies with 50% of patients obtaining at least a 25% reduction in YBOCS score (Huff et al., 2010). In this study, there were similar adverse effects to stimulation of the ALIC and VC/VS with gustatory hallucinations and headaches noted. In addition, one patient experienced significant suicidal ideation. As in other studies, this group found that it may take many weeks to see benefit after DBS stimulation on OCD symptoms.

Subthalamic Nucleus

The *New England Journal of Medicine* published a study in 2008 that involved targeting the STN in DBS for OCD (Mallet et al., 2008). This group selected the target based on studies of DBS in patients with Parkinson's disease who were noted to have improvement following STN stimulation in reduction of repetitive behaviors, anxiety, and OCD (Ardouin et al., 2006; Fontaine et al., 2004; Houeto et al., 2006; Mallet et al., 2002). This study found significant efficacy, with YBOCS score noted to be significantly lower at the end of active stimulation than at the end of sham stimulation. Global functioning simultaneously increased. The investigators found that 75% of patients had a response as measured by the YBOCS at the end of 3 months of active stimulation. Serious adverse events were noted, with more than one-third related to surgery. One patient experienced a parenchymal brain hemorrhage with residual finger palsy. They also noted transient psychiatric and/or motor symptoms associated directly with stimulation that resolved with adjustment in settings.

Inferior Thalamic Peduncle

Jimenez and colleagues have studied the inferior thalamic peduncle (ITP) as a potential target in DBS for OCD (Jimenez-Ponce et al., 2009). This target was selected based on the hypothesis that the ITP is thought to be involved in neurocircuitry associated with OCD. Studies have shown significant improvements in YBOCS scores in 49–62% of patients receiving this treatment. However, one study included patients with comorbid substance abuse and had a high rate of dropout by the 36-month follow up. The 2013 study by Jimenez and colleagues had high rates of comorbidity with other disorders. The patient who had the best result had OCD exclusively without other comorbidities (Jimenez et al., 2013). This target is being further investigated with regard to safety and efficacy in a multicenter protocol and has set more stringent exclusion criteria.

DBS Programming

DBS programming can be difficult and requires careful consideration of the target and DBS lead placement. Clinicians should have expertise in the management of patients with both OCD and who have been implanted with DBS. There is a near infinite possibility of configurations with DBS due to the variables which can be adjusted. The lead configuration can be adjusted. In addition, one can change the pulse width, frequency, and voltage applied. See Figures 38.2 and 38.3 for diagrams of possible lead configurations and other programming variables.

Morishita and colleagues posit that optimal DBS programming should begin with lead localization to establish lead configuration, with consideration given to the DBS lead model used, as distances between contacts may vary depending on model (Morishita et al., 2014). The second step in programming is thought to be the identification of thresholds, which is defined by the voltage required to induce benefit or a side effect (Nuttin et al., 2003). This is systematically assessed at each of the contacts while frequency and pulse width remain constant. The contact configuration is then selected by choosing the contact with the lowest intensity for obtaining a positive effect without a side effect. This model has been used widely in programming DBS for movement disorders (Volkmann, Herzog, Kopper, & Deuschl, 2002), however, it is somewhat more difficult to use in patients who have received DBS for OCD as in acute stimulation, positive responses are usually not immediately encountered and may take weeks to develop.

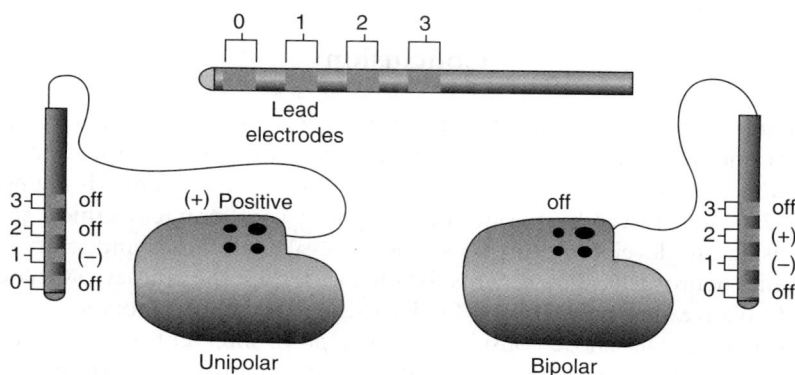

Figure 38.2 Diagram of DBS electrode contacts with possible monopolar and bipolar configurations

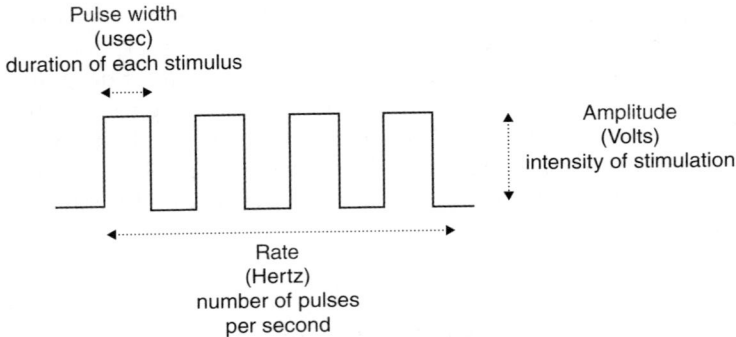

Figure 38.3 Programming variables in DBS

One interesting acute stimulation effect that has been observed during intraoperative testing while stimulating the ALIC is induction of mirthful laughter associated with an accompanying euphoric sensation. One group reported on this phenomenon and felt that it may represent a predictive factor of favorable outcomes in DBS for OCD (Haq et al., 2011). Other temporary stimulation induced effects may be uncomfortable and include dysarthria, olfactory and gustatory hallucinations, and transient mood changes such as fear, anxiety. and hypomania (Greenberg et al., 2006; Okun et al., 2004; Okun et al., 2007; Shapira et al., 2006)

Most cases will use high frequency DBS (100–145 Hz) (Morishita et al., 2014) with pulse widths less than 210 microseconds as higher pulse widths result in sensations such as nausea, fear, panic, and cold sensations (Okun et al., 2007). Of note, higher voltages than those used for movement disorders are typically required to manage OCD symptoms. DBS programming remains unstandardized at this time, although ongoing studies of the relationship between the DBS lead and associated neuroanatomy will aid researchers in improving DBS programming for the future. Morishita and colleagues recommend the development of a registry to track cases of OCD DBS to help monitor safety and improve outcomes while refining the art of DBS programming (Morishita et al., 2014).

Conclusion

Psychosurgery has had a checkered past over the past eight decades. There is promise in current methodologies and contemporary neurosurgery for the treatment of patients who otherwise do not respond to conventional treatments. It is imperative that clinicians and researchers continue to uphold very stringent ethical standards when considering developing further studies to evaluate efficacy and safety of these experimental neurosurgical treatments for OCD. Despite the efficacy associated with DBS and ablative neurosurgery for OCD, each of the contemporaneous surgeries remains experimental. Those considering this type of intervention for their patient should refer to an expert, multidisciplinary study with a record of stringent pre-operative screening and candidate selection along with the ability to readily and expertly manage any possible complications that could arise.

References

Abelson, J. L., Curtis, G. C., Sagher, O., Albucher, R. C., Harrigan, M., Taylor, S. F., … Giordani, B. (2005). Deep brain stimulation for refractory obsessive-compulsive disorder. *Biological Psychiatry, 57*(5), 510–516. doi: 10.1016/j.biopsych.2004.11.042.

Alexander, G. E., Crutcher, M. D., & DeLong, M. R. (1990). Basal ganglia-thalamocortical circuits: Parallel substrates for motor, oculomotor, "prefrontal" and "limbic" functions. *Progress in Brain Research, 85*, 119–146.

Alexander, G. E., DeLong, M. R., & Strick, P. L. (1986). Parallel organization of functionally segregated circuits linking basal ganglia and cortex. *Annual Review of Neuroscience, 9*, 357–381. doi: 10.1146/annurev.ne.09.030186.002041.

Aouizerate, B., Guehl, D., Cuny, E., Rougier, A., Bioulac, B., Tignol, J., & Burbaud, P. (2004). Pathophysiology of obsessive-compulsive disorder: A necessary link between phenomenology, neuropsychology, imagery and physiology. *Progress in Neurobiology, 72*(3), 195–221. doi: 10.1016/j.pneurobio.2004.02.004.

Appelbaum, P. S., Roth, L. H., & Lidz, C. (1982). The therapeutic misconception: Informed consent in psychiatric research. *International Journal of Law and Psychiatry, 5*(3/4), 319–329.

Ardouin, C., Voon, V., Worbe, Y., Abouazar, N., Czernecki, V., Hosseini, H., … Krack, P. (2006). Pathological gambling in Parkinson's disease improves on chronic subthalamic nucleus stimulation. *Movement Disorders, 21*(11), 1941–1946. doi: 10.1002/mds.21098.

Ballantine, H. T., Jr., Bouckoms, A. J., Thomas, E. K., & Giriunas, I. E. (1987). Treatment of psychiatric illness by stereotactic cingulotomy. *Biological Psychiatry, 22*(7), 807–819.

Baxter, L. R., Jr. (2003). Basal ganglia systems in ritualistic social displays: Reptiles and humans; function and illness. *Physiological Behavior, 79*(3), 451–460.

Bernal-Pacheco, O., Oyama, G., Foote, K. D., Dai, Y. E., Wu, S. S., Jacobson, C. E. T., … Okun, M. S. (2013). Taking a better history for behavioral issues pre- and post-deep brain stimulation: Issues missed by standardized scales. *Neuromodulation, 16*(1), 35–39; discussion 39–40. doi: 10.1111/j.1525-1403.2012.00477.x.

Bradbury, C., Cassin, S. E., & Rector, N. A. (2011). Obsessive beliefs and neurocognitive flexibility in obsessive-compulsive disorder. *Psychiatry Research, 187*(1/2), 160–165. doi: 10.1016/j.psychres.2010.11.008.

Bridges, P. K., Bartlett, J. R., Hale, A. S., Poynton, A. M., Malizia, A. L., & Hodgkiss, A. D. (1994). Psychosurgery: Stereotactic subcaudate tractomy. An indispensable treatment. *British Journal of Psychiatry, 165*(5), 599–611; discussion 612-593.

Chabardes, S., Polosan, M., Krack, P., Bastin, J., Krainik, A., David, O., … Benabid, A. L. (2013). Deep brain stimulation for obsessive-compulsive disorder: Subthalamic nucleus target. *World Neurosurgery, 80*(3/4), S31.e31-38. doi: 10.1016/j.wneu.2012.03.010.

Chamberlain, S. R., Menzies, L., Hampshire, A., Suckling, J., Fineberg, N. A., del Campo, N., … Sahakian, B. J. (2008). Orbitofrontal dysfunction in patients with obsessive-compulsive disorder and their unaffected relatives. *Science, 321*(5887), 421–422. doi: 10.1126/science.1154433.

Cosyns, P., Gabriels, L., & Nuttin, B. (2003). Deep brain stimulation in treatment refractory obsessive compulsive disorder. *Verh K Acad Geneeskd Belg, 65*(6), 385–399; discussion 399-400.

Culliton, B. J. (1976). Psychosurgery: National Commission issues surprisingly favorable report. *Science, 194*(4262), 299–301.

Denys, D., Mantione, M., Figee, M., van den Munckhof, P., Koerselman, F., Westenberg, H., … Schuurman, R. (2010). Deep brain stimulation of the nucleus accumbens for treatment-refractory obsessive-compulsive disorder. *Archives of General Psychiatry, 67*(10), 1061–1068. doi: 10.1001/archgenpsychiatry.2010.122.

Diefenbach, G. J., Diefenbach, D., Baumeister, A., & West, M. (1999). Portrayal of lobotomy in the popular press: 1935-1960. *Journal of the History of the Neurosciences, 8*(1), 60–69. doi: 10.1076/jhin.8.1.60.1766.

Feldman, R. P., Alterman, R. L., & Goodrich, J. T. (2001). Contemporary psychosurgery and a look to the future. *Journal of Neurosurgery, 95*(6), 944–956. doi: 10.3171/jns.2001.95.6.0944.

Ferrao, Y. A., Diniz, J. B., Lopes, A. C., Shavitt, R. G., Greenberg, B., & Miguel, E. (2007). Resistance and refractoriness in obsessive-compulsive disorder. *Revista Brasileira Psiquiatria, 29*(Supp. 2), S66–S76.

Figee, M., Vink, M., de Geus, F., Vulink, N., Veltman, D. J., Westenberg, H., & Denys, D. (2011). Dysfunctional reward circuitry in obsessive-compulsive disorder. *Biological Psychiatry, 69*(9), 867–874. doi: 10.1016/j.biopsych.2010.12.003.

Fins, J. J., Mayberg, H. S., Nuttin, B., Kubu, C. S., Galert, T., Sturm, V., ... Schlaepfer, T. E. (2011). Misuse of the FDA's humanitarian device exemption in deep brain stimulation for obsessive-compulsive disorder. *Health Affairs (Millwood), 30*(2), 302–311. doi: 10.1377/hlthaff.2010.0157.

Fontaine, D., Mattei, V., Borg, M., von Langsdorff, D., Magnie, M. N., Chanalet, S., ... Paquis, P. (2004). Effect of subthalamic nucleus stimulation on obsessive-compulsive disorder in a patient with Parkinson disease: Case report. *Journal of Neurosurgery, 100*(6), 1084–1086. doi: 10.3171/jns.2004.100.6.1084.

Giacobbe, P., Mayberg, H. S., & Lozano, A. M. (2009). Treatment resistant depression as a failure of brain homeostatic mechanisms: Implications for deep brain stimulation. *Experimental Neurology, 219*(1), 44–52. doi: 10.1016/j.expneurol.2009.04.028.

Goodman, W. K., Foote, K. D., Greenberg, B. D., Ricciuti, N., Bauer, R., Ward, H., ... Okun, M. S. (2010). Deep brain stimulation for intractable obsessive compulsive disorder: Pilot study using a blinded, staggered-onset design. *Biological Psychiatry, 67*(6), 535–542. doi: 10.1016/j.biopsych.2009.11.028.

Goodman, W. K., Price, L. H., Rasmussen, S. A., Mazure, C., Fleischmann, R. L., Hill, C. L., ... Charney, D. S. (1989). The Yale–Brown Obsessive Compulsive Scale – I: Development, use, and reliability. *Archives of General Psychiatry, 46*(11), 1006–1011.

Greenberg, B. D., Gabriels, L. A., Malone, D. A., Jr., Rezai, A. R., Friehs, G. M., Okun, M. S., ... Nuttin, B. J. (2010). Deep brain stimulation of the ventral internal capsule/ventral striatum for obsessive-compulsive disorder: Worldwide experience. *Molecular Psychiatry, 15*(1), 64–79. doi: 10.1038/mp.2008.55.

Greenberg, B. D., Malone, D. A., Friehs, G. M., Rezai, A. R., Kubu, C. S., Malloy, P. F., ... Rasmussen, S. A. (2006). Three-year outcomes in deep brain stimulation for highly resistant obsessive-compulsive disorder. *Neuropsychopharmacology, 31*(11), 2384–2393. doi: 10.1038/sj.npp.1301165.

Greenberg, B. D., Price, L. H., Rauch, S. L., Friehs, G., Noren, G., Malone, D., ... Rasmussen, S. A. (2003). Neurosurgery for intractable obsessive-compulsive disorder and depression: Critical issues. *Neurosurgery Clinics of North America, 14*(2), 199–212.

Gross, R. E., & Lozano, A. M. (2000). Advances in neurostimulation for movement disorders. *Neurological Research, 22*(3), 247–258.

Haq, I. U., Foote, K. D., Goodman, W. G., Wu, S. S., Sudhyadhom, A., Ricciuti, N., ... Okun, M. S. (2011). Smile and laughter induction and intraoperative predictors of response to deep brain stimulation for obsessive-compulsive disorder. *Neuroimage, 54*(Supp. 1), S247–S255. doi: 10.1016/j.neuroimage.2010.03.009.

Houeto, J. L., Mallet, L., Mesnage, V., Tezenas du Montcel, S., Behar, C., Gargiulo, M., ... Agid, Y. (2006). Subthalamic stimulation in Parkinson disease: Behavior and social adaptation. *Archives of Neurology, 63*(8), 1090–1095. doi: 10.1001/archneur.63.8.1090.

Huey, E. D., Zahn, R., Krueger, F., Moll, J., Kapogiannis, D., Wassermann, E. M., & Grafman, J. (2008). A psychological and neuroanatomical model of obsessive-compulsive disorder. *Journal of Neuropsychiatry & Clinical Neuroscience, 20*(4), 390–408. doi: 10.1176/appi.neuropsych.20.4.390.

Huff, W., Lenartz, D., Schormann, M., Lee, S. H., Kuhn, J., Koulousakis, A., ... Sturm, V. (2010). Unilateral deep brain stimulation of the nucleus accumbens in patients with treatment-resistant obsessive-compulsive disorder: Outcomes after one year. *Clinical Neurology and Neurosurgery, 112*(2), 137–143. doi: 10.1016/j.clineuro.2009.11.006.

Insel, T. R. (1992). Toward a neuroanatomy of obsessive-compulsive disorder. *Archives of General Psychiatry, 49*(9), 739–744.

Jenike, M. A. (1998). Neurosurgical treatment of obsessive-compulsive disorder. *British Journal of Psychiatry,35*(Supp.), 79–90.

Jimenez-Ponce, F., Velasco-Campos, F., Castro-Farfan, G., Nicolini, H., Velasco, A. L., Salin-Pascual, R., ... Criales, J. L. (2009). Preliminary study in patients with obsessive-compulsive disorder treated with electrical stimulation in the inferior thalamic peduncle. *Neurosurgery. 65*(6 Supp.), 203–209; discussion 209. doi: 10.1227/01. neu.0000345938.39199.90.

Jimenez, F., Nicolini, H., Lozano, A. M., Piedimonte, F., Salin, R., & Velasco, F. (2013). Electrical stimulation of the inferior thalamic peduncle in the treatment of major depression and obsessive compulsive disorders. *World Neurosurgery, 80*(3/4), S30.e17-25. doi: 10.1016/j.wneu.2012.07.010.

Kelly, D., Richardson, A., & Mitchell-Heggs, N. (1973). Stereotactic limbic leucotomy: Neurophysiological aspects and operative technique. *British Journal of Psychiatry, 123*(573), 133–140.

Kim, C. H., Chang, J. W., Koo, M. S., Kim, J. W., Suh, H. S., Park, I. H., & Lee, H. S. (2003). Anterior cingulotomy for refractory obsessive-compulsive disorder. *Acta Psychiatrica Scandinavica, 107*(4), 283–290.

Knight, G. (1965). Stereotactic tractotomy in the surgical treatment of mental illness. *Journal of Neurology, Neurosurgery, & Psychiatry, 28,* 304–310.

Kopell, B. H., Greenberg, B., & Rezai, A. R. (2004). Deep brain stimulation for psychiatric disorders. *Journal of Clinical Neurophysiology, 21*(1), 51–67.

Koran, L. M., Hanna, G. L., Hollander, E., Nestadt, G., & Simpson, H. B. (2007). Practice guideline for the treatment of patients with obsessive-compulsive disorder. *American Journal of Psychiatry, 164*(Supp. 7), 5–53.

Lapidus, K. A., Kopell, B. H., Ben-Haim, S., Rezai, A. R., & Goodman, W. K. (2013). History of psychosurgery: A psychiatrist's perspective. *World Neurosurgery, 80*(3/4), S27.e21-16. doi: 10.1016/j.wneu.2013.02.053.

Lidz, C. W., Appelbaum, P. S., Grisso, T., & Renaud, M. (2004). Therapeutic misconception and the appreciation of risks in clinical trials. *Social Science and Medicine, 58*(9), 1689–1697. doi: 10.1016/s0277-9536(03)00338-1.

Maclean, L. P. (1949). Psychosomatic disease and the visceral brain: Recent developments bearing on the Papez theory of emotion. *Psychosomatic Medicine, 11*(6), 338–353.

Malhi, G. S., & Bartlett, J. R. (2000). Depression: A role for neurosurgery? *British Journal of Neurosurgery, 14*(5), 415–422; discussion 423.

Mallet, L., Mesnage, V., Houeto, J. L., Pelissolo, A., Yelnik, J., Behar, C., ... Agid, Y. (2002). Compulsions, Parkinson's disease, and stimulation. *Lancet, 360*(9342), 1302–1304. doi: 10.1016/s0140-6736(02)11339-0.

Mallet, L., Polosan, M., Jaafari, N., Baup, N., Welter, M. L., Fontaine, D., ... Pelissolo, A. (2008). Subthalamic nucleus stimulation in severe obsessive-compulsive disorder. *New England Journal of Medicine, 359*(20), 2121–2134. doi: 10.1056/NEJMoa0708514.

Mashour, G. A., Walker, E. E., & Martuza, R. L. (2005). Psychosurgery: Past, present, and future. *Brain Research Review, 48*(3), 409–419. doi: 10.1016/j.brainresrev.2004. 09.002.

Mindus, P., Rasmussen, S. A., & Lindquist, C. (1994). Neurosurgical treatment for refractory obsessive-compulsive disorder: Implications for understanding frontal lobe function. *Journal of Neuropsychiatry & Clinical Neuroscience, 6*(4), 467–477.

Mitchell-Heggs, N., Kelly, D., & Richardson, A. (1976). Stereotactic limbic leucotomy: A follow-up at 16 months. *British Journal of Psychiatry, 128*, 226–240.

Modell, J. G., Mountz, J. M., Curtis, G. C., & Greden, J. F. (1989). Neurophysiologic dysfunction in basal ganglia/limbic striatal and thalamocortical circuits as a pathogenetic mechanism of obsessive-compulsive disorder. *Journal of Neuropsychiatry & Clinical Neuroscience, 1*(1), 27–36.

Morishita, T., Fayad, S. M., Goodman, W. K., Foote, K. D., Chen, D., Peace, D. A., … Okun, M. S. (2014). Surgical neuroanatomy and programming in deep brain stimulation for obsessive compulsive disorder. *Neuromodulation, 17*(4), 312–319. doi: 10.1111/ner.12141.

NobelPrize.org. 0000Retrieved from: http://www.nobelprize.org/nobel_prizes/medicine/laureates/1949/index.html.

Nuttin, B. J., Cosyns, P., Demeulemeester, H., Gybels, J., & Meyerson, B. (1999). Electrical stimulation in anterior limbs of internal capsules in patients with obsessive-compulsive disorder. *Lancet, 354*(9189), 1526. doi: 10.1016/s0140-6736(99)02376-4.

Nuttin, B. J., Gabriels, L. A., Cosyns, P. R., Meyerson, B. A., Andreewitch, S., Sunaert, S. G., … Demeulemeester, H. G. (2003). Long-term electrical capsular stimulation in patients with obsessive-compulsive disorder. *Neurosurgery, 52*(6), 1263–1272; discussion 1272–1264.

Okun, M. S., Bowers, D., Springer, U., Shapira, N. A., Malone, D., Rezai, A. R., … Goodman, W. K. (2004). What's in a "smile"? Intra-operative observations of contralateral smiles induced by deep brain stimulation. *Neurocase, 10*(4), 271–279. doi: 10.1080/13554790490507632.

Okun, M. S., Mann, G., Foote, K. D., Shapira, N. A., Bowers, D., Springer, U., … Goodman, W. K. (2007). Deep brain stimulation in the internal capsule and nucleus accumbens region: Responses observed during active and sham programming. *Journal of Neurology, Neurosurgery, & Psychiatry, 78*(3), 310–314. doi: 10.1136/jnnp.2006.095315.

Okun, M. S., Wu, S. S., Foote, K. D., Bowers, D., Gogna, S., Price, C., … Ward, H. (2011). Do stable patients with a premorbid depression history have a worse outcome after deep brain stimulation for Parkinson disease? *Neurosurgery, 69*(2), 357–360; discussion 360–351. doi: 10.1227/NEU.0b013e3182160456.

Pallanti, S., Hollander, E., & Goodman, W. K. (2004). A qualitative analysis of nonresponse: Management of treatment-refractory obsessive-compulsive disorder. *Journal of Clinical Psychiatry, 65*(Supp. 14), 6–10.

Papez, J. W. (1937). A proposed mechanism of emotion. *Archives of Neurology & Psychiatry, 38*(4), 725–743. doi: 10.1001/archneurpsyc.1937.02260220069003.

Rauch, S. L. (2003). Neuroimaging and neurocircuitry models pertaining to the neurosurgical treatment of psychiatric disorders. *Neurosurgery Clinics of North America, 14*(2), 213–223.

Ruck, C., Karlsson, A., Steele, J. D., Edman, G., Meyerson, B. A., Ericson, K., … Svanborg, P. (2008). Capsulotomy for obsessive-compulsive disorder: Long-term follow-up of 25 patients. *Archives of General Psychiatry, 65*(8), 914'921. doi: 10.1001/archpsyc.65.8.914.

Sadock, B. J., Sadock, V. A., & Ruiz, P.(2009). *Kaplan & Sadock's comprehensive textbook of psychiatry* (9th ed.). Philadelphia, PA: Wolters Kluwer Health/Lippincott Williams & Wilkins.

Saxena, S., Brody, A. L., Schwartz, J. M., & Baxter, L. R. (1998). Neuroimaging and frontal-subcortical circuitry in obsessive-compulsive disorder. *British Journal of Psychiatry, 35*(Supp.), 26–37.

Saxena, S., & Rauch, S. L. (2000). Functional neuroimaging and the neuroanatomy of obsessive-compulsive disorder. *Psychiatric Clinics of North America, 23*(3), 563–586.

Shapira, N. A., Okun, M. S., Wint, D., Foote, K. D., Byars, J. A., Bowers, D., ... Goodman, W. K. (2006). Panic and fear induced by deep brain stimulation. *Journal of Neurology, Neurosurgery, & Psychiatry, 77*(3), 410–412. doi: 10.1136/jnnp.2005.069906.

Sheth, S. A., Neal, J., Tangherlini, F., Mian, M. K., Gentil, A., Cosgrove, G. R., ... Dougherty, D. D. (2013). Limbic system surgery for treatment-refractory obsessive-compulsive disorder: A prospective long-term follow-up of 64 patients. *Journal of Neurosurgery, 118*(3), 491–497. doi: 10.3171/2012.11.jns12389.

Skoog, G., & Skoog, I. (1999). A 40-year follow-up of patients with obsessive-compulsive disorder. *Archives of General Psychiatry, 56*(2), 121–127.

Spiegel, E. A., Wycis, H. T., Marks, M., & Lee, A. J. (1947). Stereotaxic apparatus for operations on the human brain. *Science, 106*(2754), 349–350. doi: 10.1126/science.106.2754.349.

Steketee, G., Frost, R. O., & Cohen, I. (1998). Beliefs in obsessive-compulsive disorder. *Journal of Anxiety Disorders, 12*(6), 525–537.

Sturm, V., Lenartz, D., Koulousakis, A., Treuer, H., Herholz, K., Klein, J. C., & Klosterkotter, J. (2003). The nucleus accumbens: A target for deep brain stimulation in obsessive-compulsive and anxiety-disorders. *Journal of Chemical Neuroanatomy, 26*(4), 293–299.

Tierney, T. S., Abd-El-Barr, M. M., Stanford, A. D., Foote, K. D., & Okun, M. S. (2014). Deep brain stimulation and ablation for obsessive compulsive disorder: Evolution of contemporary indications, targets and techniques. *International Journal of Neuroscience, 124*(6), 394–402. doi: 10.3109/00207454.2013.852086.

Volkmann, J., Herzog, J., Kopper, F., & Deuschl, G. (2002). Introduction to the programming of deep brain stimulators. *Movement Disorders, 17*(Supp. 3), S181–S187.

Whitty, C. W., Duffield, J. E., Tov, P. M., & Cairns, H. (1952). Anterior cingulectomy in the treatment of mental disease. *Lancet, 1*(6706), 475–481.